CLASSICAL AND MEDIEVAL LITERATURE CRITICISM

Guide to Gale Literary Criticism Series

For criticism on	Consult these Gale series
Authors now living or who died after December 31, 1999	*CONTEMPORARY LITERARY CRITICISM (CLC)*
Authors who died between 1900 and 1999	*TWENTIETH-CENTURY LITERARY CRITICISM (TCLC)*
Authors who died between 1800 and 1899	*NINETEENTH-CENTURY LITERATURE CRITICISM (NCLC)*
Authors who died between 1400 and 1799	*LITERATURE CRITICISM FROM 1400 TO 1800 (LC)* *SHAKESPEAREAN CRITICISM (SC)*
Authors who died before 1400	*CLASSICAL AND MEDIEVAL LITERATURE CRITICISM (CMLC)*
Authors of books for children and young adults	*CHILDREN'S LITERATURE REVIEW (CLR)*
Dramatists	*DRAMA CRITICISM (DC)*
Poets	*POETRY CRITICISM (PC)*
Short story writers	*SHORT STORY CRITICISM (SSC)*
Literary topics and movements	*HARLEM RENAISSANCE: A GALE CRITICAL COMPANION (HR)* *THE BEAT GENERATION: A GALE CRITICAL COMPANION (BG)*
Asian American writers of the last two hundred years	*ASIAN AMERICAN LITERATURE (AAL)*
Black writers of the past two hundred years	*BLACK LITERATURE CRITICISM (BLC)* *BLACK LITERATURE CRITICISM SUPPLEMENT (BLCS)*
Hispanic writers of the late nineteenth and twentieth centuries	*HISPANIC LITERATURE CRITICISM (HLC)* *HISPANIC LITERATURE CRITICISM SUPPLEMENT (HLCS)*
Native North American writers and orators of the eighteenth, nineteenth, and twentieth centuries	*NATIVE NORTH AMERICAN LITERATURE (NNAL)*
Major authors from the Renaissance to the present	*WORLD LITERATURE CRITICISM, 1500 TO THE PRESENT (WLC)* *WORLD LITERATURE CRITICISM SUPPLEMENT (WLCS)*

ISSN 0896-0011

Volume 62

CLASSICAL AND MEDIEVAL LITERATURE CRITICISM

Criticism of the Works of World
Authors from Classical Antiquity through the
Fourteenth Century, from the First Appraisals
to Current Evaluations

Lynn M. Zott
Project Editor

Detroit • New York • San Diego • San Francisco • Cleveland • New Haven, Conn. • Waterville, Maine • London • Munich

Classical and Medieval Literature Criticism, Vol. 62

Project Editor
Lynn M. Zott

Editorial
Jessica Bomarito, Jenny Cromie, Kathy D. Darrow, Elisabeth Gellert, Edna M. Hedblad, Julie Keppen, Jelena O. Krstović, Michelle Lee, Thomas J. Schoenberg, Lawrence J. Trudeau, Russel Whitaker

Research
Nicodemus Ford, Sarah Genik, Tamara C. Nott, Tracie A. Richardson

Permissions
Margaret Chamberlain

Imaging and Multimedia
Robert Duncan, Lezlie Light, Kelly A. Quin

Composition and Electronic Capture
Carolyn Roney

Manufacturing
Stacy L. Melson

LIBRARY OF CONGRESS CATALOG CARD NUMBER 88-658021

ISBN 0-7876-6765-X
ISSN 0896-0011

Printed in the United States of America
10 9 8 7 6 5 4 3 2 1

Contents

Preface vii

Acknowledgments xi

Literary Criticism Series Advisory Board xiii

Preface

Since its inception in 1988, *Classical and Medieval Literature Criticism* (*CMLC*) has been a valuable resource for students and librarians seeking critical commentary on the works and authors of antiquity through the fourteenth century. The great poets, prose writers, dramatists, and philosophers of this period form the basis of most humanities curricula, so that virtually every student will encounter many of these works during the course of a high school and college education. Reviewers have found *CMLC* "useful" and "extremely convenient," noting that it "adds to our understanding of the rich legacy left by the ancient period and the Middle Ages," and praising its "general excellence in the presentation of an inherently interesting subject." No other single reference source has surveyed the critical reaction to classical and medieval literature as thoroughly as *CMLC*.

Scope of the Series

CMLC provides an introduction to classical and medieval authors, works, and topics that represent a variety of genres, time periods, and nationalities. By organizing and reprinting an enormous amount of critical commentary written on authors and works of this period in world history, *CMLC* helps students develop valuable insight into literary history, promotes a better understanding of the texts, and sparks ideas for papers and assignments.

Each entry in *CMLC* presents a comprehensive survey of an author's career, an individual work of literature, or a literary topic, and provides the user with a multiplicity of interpretations and assessments. Such variety allows students to pursue their own interests; furthermore, it fosters an awareness that literature is dynamic and responsive to many different opinions. Early commentary is offered to indicate initial responses, later selections document changes in literary reputations, and retrospective analyses provide the reader with modern views. The size of each author entry is a relative reflection of the scope of the criticism available in English.

An author may appear more than once in the series if his or her writings have been the subject of a substantial amount of criticism; in these instances, specific works or groups of works by the author will be covered in separate entries. For example, Homer will be represented by three entries, one devoted to the *Iliad,* one to the *Odyssey,* and one to the Homeric Hymns.

CMLC continues the survey of criticism of world literature begun by Gale's *Contemporary Literary Criticism* (*CLC*), *Twentieth-Century Literary Criticism* (*TCLC*), *Nineteenth-Century Literature Criticism* (*NCLC*), *Literature Criticism from 1400 to 1800* (*LC*), and *Shakespearean Criticism* (*SC*).

Organization of the Book

A *CMLC* entry consists of the following elements:

- The **Author Heading** cites the name under which the author most commonly wrote, followed by birth and death dates. Also located here are any name variations under which an author wrote, including transliterated forms for authors whose native languages use nonroman alphabets. If the author wrote consistently under a pseudonym, the pseudonym will be listed in the author heading and the author's actual name given in parenthesis on the first line of the biographical and critical information. Uncertain birth or death dates are indicated by question marks. Single-work entries are preceded by a heading that consists of the most common form of the title in English translation (if applicable) and the original date of composition.

- The **Introduction** contains background information that introduces the reader to the author, work, or topic that is the subject of the entry.

- A **Portrait of the Author** is included when available.

- The list of **Principal Works** is ordered chronologically by date of first publication and lists the most important works by the author. The genre and publication date of each work is given. In the case of foreign authors whose works have been translated into English, the list will focus primarily on twentieth-century translations, selecting those works most commonly considered the best by critics. Unless otherwise indicated, dramas are dated by first performance, not first publication. Lists of **Representative Works** by different authors appear with topic entries.

- Reprinted **Criticism** is arranged chronologically in each entry to provide a useful perspective on changes in critical evaluation over time. The critic's name and the date of composition or publication of the critical work are given at the beginning of each piece of criticism. Unsigned criticism is preceded by the title of the source in which it appeared. All titles by the author featured in the text are printed in boldface type. Footnotes are reprinted at the end of each essay or excerpt. In the case of excerpted criticism, only those footnotes that pertain to the excerpted texts are included. Criticism in topic entries is arranged chronologically under a variety of subheadings to facilitate the study of different aspects of the topic.

- A complete **Bibliographical Citation** of the original essay or book precedes each piece of criticism.

- Critical essays are prefaced by brief **Annotations** explicating each piece.

- An annotated bibliography of **Further Reading** appears at the end of each entry and suggests resources for additional study. In some cases, significant essays for which the editors could not obtain reprint rights are included here. Boxed material following the further reading list provides references to other biographical and critical sources on the author in series published by Gale.

Cumulative Indexes

A **Cumulative Author Index** lists all of the authors that appear in a wide variety of reference sources published by the Gale Group, including *CMLC*. A complete list of these sources is found facing the first page of the Author Index. The index also includes birth and death dates and cross references between pseudonyms and actual names.

Beginning with the second volume, a **Cumulative Nationality Index** lists all authors featured in *CMLC* by nationality, followed by the number of the *CMLC* volume in which their entry appears.

Beginning with the tenth volume, a **Cumulative Topic Index** lists the literary themes and topics treated in the series as well as in *Nineteenth-Century Literature Criticism, Twentieth-Century Literary Criticism,* and the *Contemporary Literary Criticism* Yearbook, which was discontinued in 1998.

A **Cumulative Title Index** lists in alphabetical order all of the works discussed in the series. Each title listing includes the corresponding volume and page numbers where criticism may be located. Foreign-language titles that have been translated into English are followed by the titles of the translation—for example, *Slovo o polku Igorove (The Song of Igor's Campaign)*. Page numbers following these translated titles refer to all pages on which any form of the titles, either foreign-language or translated, appear. Titles of novels, dramas, nonfiction books, and poetry, short story, or essay collections are printed in italics, while individual poems, short stories, and essays are printed in roman type within quotation marks.

Citing *Classical and Medieval Literature Criticism*

When citing criticism reprinted in the Literary Criticism Series, students should provide complete bibliographic information so that the cited essay can be located in the original print or electronic source. Students who quote directly from reprinted criticism may use any accepted bibliographic format, such as University of Chicago Press style or Modern Language Association style.

The examples below follow recommendations for preparing a bibliography set forth in *The Chicago Manual of Style,* 14th ed. (Chicago: The University of Chicago Press, 1993); the first example pertains to material drawn from periodicals, the second to material reprinted from books:

Sealey, R. J. "The Tetralogies Ascribed to Antiphon." *Transactions of the American Philological Association* 114, (1984): 71-85. Reprinted in *Classical and Medieval Literature Criticism.* Vol. 55, edited by Lynn M. Zott, 2-9. Detroit: Gale, 2003.

Bourne, Ella. "Classical Elements in *The Gesta Romanorum.*" In *Vassar Medieval Studies* edited by Christabel Forsyth Fiske, 345-76. New Haven: Yale University Press, 1923. Reprinted in *Classical and Medieval Literature Criticism.* Vol. 55, edited by Lynn M. Zott, 81-92. Detroit: Gale, 2003.

The examples below follow recommendations for preparing a works cited list set forth in the *MLA Handbook for Writers of Research Papers,* 5th ed. (New York: The Modern Language Association of America, 1999); the first example pertains to material drawn from periodicals, the second to material reprinted from books:

Sealey, R. J. "The Tetralogies Ascribed to Antiphon." *Transactions of the American Philological Association* 114. (1984): 71-85. Reprinted in *Classical and Medieval Literature Criticism.* Ed. Lynn M. Zott. Vol. 55. Detroit: Gale, 2003. 2-9.

Bourne, Ella. "Classical Elements in *The Gesta Romanorum.*" *Vassar Medieval Studies.* Ed. Christabel Forsyth Fiske. New Haven: Yale University Press, 1923. 345-76. Reprinted in *Classical and Medieval Literature Criticism.* Ed. Lynn M. Zott. Vol. 55. Detroit: Gale, 2003. 81-92.

Suggestions are Welcome

Readers who wish to suggest new features, topics, or authors to appear in future volumes, or who have other suggestions or comments are cordially invited to call, write, or fax the Project Editor:

Project Editor, Literary Criticism Series

The Gale Group

27500 Drake Road

Farmington Hills, MI 48331-3535

1-800-347-4253 (GALE)

Fax: 248-699-8054

Acknowledgments

The editors wish to thank the copyright holders of the criticism included in this volume and the permissions managers of many book and magazine publishing companies for assisting us in securing reproduction rights. We are also grateful to the staffs of the Detroit Public Library, the Library of Congress, the University of Detroit Mercy Library, Wayne State University Purdy/Kresge Library Complex, and the University of Michigan Libraries for making their resources available to us. Following is a list of the copyright holders who have granted us permission to reproduce material in this volume of *CMLC*. Every effort has been made to trace copyright, but if omissions have been made, please let us know.

COPYRIGHTED MATERIAL IN *CMLC*, VOLUME 62, WAS REPRODUCED FROM THE FOLLOWING BOOKS:

Beaumont, Daniel. From *Slave of Desire: Sex, Love, and Death in The 1001 Nights.* Associated University Presses, 2002. Copyright 2002 by Associated University Presses. All rights reserved. Reproduced by permission.—Benediktson, D. Thomas. From *Power, Literature, and Visual Arts in Ancient Greece and Rome.* University of Oklahoma Press, 2000. Copyright 2000 by University of Oklahoma Press. All rights reserved. Reproduced by permission.—Bowersock, G. W. From *Greek Sophists in the Roman Empire.* Oxford University Press, 1969. Copyright 1969 by Oxford University Press. All rights reserved. Reproduced by permission of Oxford University Press.—Conybeare, F. C. From *The Life of Apollonius of Tyana: The Epistles of Appollonius and the Treatise of Eusebius.* Harvard University Press, 1989. Copyright © 1989 by the President and Fellows of Harvard College. All rights reserved. Reproduced by permission Harvard University Press.—Flinterman, Jaap-Jan. From *Power, Paideia, & Pythagoreanism: Greek Identity, Conceptions of the Relationship between Philosophers and Monarchs and Political Ideas in Philostratus's Life of Apollonius.* J. C. Gieben, 1995. Copyright 1995 by J. J. Flinterman. All rights reserved. Reproduced by permission of the author.—Francis, James A. From *Subversive Virtue: Asceticism and Authority in the Second-Century Pagan World.* The Pennsylvania State University Press, 1995. Copyright 1995 by The Pennsylvania State University Press. Reproduced by permission.—Ghazoul, Ferial J. From *Nocturnal Poetics: The Arabian Nights in Comparative Context.* The American University in Cairo Press, 1996. Copyright 1996 by The American University in Cairo Press. All rights reserved. Reproduced by permission.—Jones, C. P. From "The Reliability of Philostratus," in *Approaches to the Second Sophistic: Papers Presented at the 105th Annual Meeting of the American Philological Association.* Edited by G. W. Bowerstock. The American Philological Association, 1974. Copyright 1974 by The American Philological Association. All rights reserved. Reproduced by permission.—Marrone, Steven P. From *William of Auvergne and Robert Grosseteste.* Princeton University Press, 1983. Copyright 1983 by Princeton University Press. All rights reserved. Reproduced by permission.—Naddaff, Sandra. From *Arabesque: Narrative Structure and the Aesthetics of Repetition in The 1001 Nights.* Northwestern University Press, 1991. Copyright 1991 by Northwestern University Press. All rights reserved. Reproduced by permission.—Pinault, David. From *Story-Telling Techniques in the Arabian Nights.* E. J. Brill, 1992. Copyright 1992 by E. J. Brill. All rights reserved. Reproduced by permission.—Sherwin-White, A. N. From *The Lives of the Sophists.* Oxford University Press, 1966. Copyright 1966 by Oxford University Press. All rights reserved. Reproduced by permission of Oxford University Press.—Southern, Richard William. From *Robert Grosseteste: The Growth of an English Mind in Medieval Europe.* Oxford at the Clarendon Press, 1986, 1992. Copyright 1986, 1992 by Oxford at the Clarendon Press. All rights reserved. Reproduced by permission.

COPYRIGHTED MATERIAL IN *CMLC*, VOLUME 62, WAS REPRODUCED FROM THE FOLLOWING PERIODICALS:

American Journal of Philology, v. 113, 1992; v. 116, 1995; v. 119, 1998. Copyright 1992, 1995, 1998 by The Johns Hopkins University Press. All reproduced by permission.—*Arethusa,* v. 31, winter, 1998. Copyright 1998 by The Johns Hopkins University Press. Reproduced by permission.—*Aufstieg und Niedergang der Romische Welt,* vol. II/16.2, 1978. Copyright 1978 by Walter De Gruyter, Inc. Reproduced by permission.—*Classical Antiquity,* v. 10, 1991 for "The Reliability of Philostratus's The Lives of the Sophists" by Simon Swain. Copyright 1991 by the Regents of the University of California. Reproduced by permission of the publisher and the author.—*The Classical Bulletin,* v. 58, April, 1982; v. 66, 1990. Copyright 1982, 1990 by *The Classical Bulletin.* Both reproduced by permission.—*Edebiyat,* v. 2, 1988. Copyright 1988 by Taylor & Francis Ltd. Reproduced by permission.—*The Emperor and the Giant in Classical Philology,* v. 95, October, 2000. Copyright 2000 by The University of Chicago. Reproduced by permission.—*Greece & Rome,* v. 16, April,

Gale Literature Product Advisory Board

The members of the Gale Group Literature Product Advisory Board—reference librarians from public and academic library systems—represent a cross-section of our customer base and offer a variety of informed perspectives on both the presentation and content of our literature products. Advisory board members assess and define such quality issues as the relevance, currency, and usefulness of the author coverage, critical content, and literary topics included in our series; evaluate the layout, presentation, and general quality of our printed volumes; provide feedback on the criteria used for selecting authors and topics covered in our series; provide suggestions for potential enhancements to our series; identify any gaps in our coverage of authors or literary topics, recommending authors or topics for inclusion; analyze the appropriateness of our content and presentation for various user audiences, such as high school students, undergraduates, graduate students, librarians, and educators; and offer feedback on any proposed changes/enhancements to our series. We wish to thank the following advisors for their advice throughout the year.

The Arabian Nights

(Also known as *Alf Layla wa-Layla, The Thousand and One Nights,* and *The Thousand Nights and One Night*) Arabic short story collection.

INTRODUCTION

The following entry presents criticism on *The Arabian Nights* from 1953 through 2002. For additional information on *The Arabian Nights,* see *CMLC,* Vol. 2.

The Arabian Nights is one of the world's best-known collections of stories. Although the tales, which were orally transmitted and composed over the course of several centuries, are mainly of Asian and Arabic origin, they have become an inextricable part of the Western cultural heritage as well. The stories of Princess Scheherazade, Aladdin, Sinbad the sailor, and Ali Baba, for example, are firmly established in the Western imagination. The original collection, comprised of legends, fairytales, romances, and anecdotes, stems from a number of folk traditions and contains motifs and fables from various geographical areas and historical periods. Since the eighteenth century, when it reached Western audiences, *The Arabian Nights* has been one of the most popular works of world literature, spawning numerous adaptations, imitations, and tributes from writers such as Johann Wolfang von Goethe, William Wordsworth, and Rainer Maria Rilke; drawings by Gustave Doré; musical works by Nikolai Rimski-Korsakov and Carl Maria von Weber; and even major Hollywood film adaptations. Since the twentieth century *The Arabian Nights* have also received serious critical attention and scholars have been almost unanimous in their praise of the way in which these tales transcend cultural and linguistic boundaries.

TEXTUAL HISTORY

Although they are traditionally associated with medieval Arabic culture, the tales of *The Arabian Nights* are rooted in several oral traditions, containing motifs from a variety of geographic areas and historical periods, including ancient Mesopotamia, India, early medieval Persia and Iraq, and Egypt of the Middle Ages. Scholars agree that the frame story is most likely of Indian origin. The first identifiable written version of *The Arabian Nights* is a book of Persian tales called *Hazar Afsanah* (*A Thousand Legends,* written between 225 and 250),

translated into Arabic around 850. Although the tenth-century Arab writer Al-Mas'oodi refers to this Arabic text, noting that it was known as *Alf Layla* (*A Thousand Nights*), it is now lost. The stories underwent considerable modification between the tenth and the sixteenth centuries, kept alive by professional storytellers, who would perform them in coffeehouses all over the Middle East. The title "Thousand and One Nights" was known in the twelfth century and likely originated from the Turkish expression *bin-bir* ("thousand and one"), which, like the Arabic *alf,* simply indicates a very large number. There is no definitive Arabic textual source of the work, but there are a number of surviving manuscripts containing many of the stories.

The first major European translation of *The Arabian Nights* was completed by the Frenchman Antoine Galland. The first part of his twelve-volume *Les mille et une nuits* (*The Thousand and One Nights*) appeared in 1704. The manuscript that he used to work from was acquired from Syria and dated from the fourteenth or fifteenth century. Galland's edition was quickly translated into English, with early editions of the so-called "Grub Street" version first appearing in 1708. Scholars then began searching for a complete original copy of *The Arabian Nights,* but were unsuccessful. However, in the early nineteenth century four important printed versions of the text—known as Calcutta I, Calcutta II, the Būlāq text, and the Breslau text—appeared. The Būlāq text, based on an Egyptian manuscript whose editor added many stories to make the total amount of material large enough to accommodate the full one thousand and one nights, is still considered one of the most important sources of the collection. Many European translations appeared based on the four nineteenth-century sources, including those by Dr. Jonathan Scott (1800), Edward Wortley Montague (1811), Henry Torrens (1838), Edward W. Lane (1838-41), John Payne (1882-84), Richard F. Burton (1885), Andrew Lang (1898), and J. C. Mardrus (1899-1904). Payne's is considered the first complete translation, and while it is meticulous and includes copious notes that remain valuable to this day, it was heavily expurgated, suppressing any fragment that the translator deemed offensive to Victorian sensibilities. Burton's translation, in contrast, emphasizes the exoticism and eroticism of the stories. There is still no definitive text of *The Arabian Nights,* but Muhsin Mahdi's *The 1001 Nights (Alf Layla wa-Layla) from the Earliest Known Sources*

(1984) and Husain Haddawy's selection of tales (1990) are two English translations that have been widely used by students and scholars since the late twentieth century.

PLOT AND MAJOR CHARACTERS

The frame story of *The Arabian Nights* describes the vindictive fury of King Shahryar who, upon executing his adulterous wife, vows to marry a different virgin every night, only to have her killed the following morning. Scheherazade, the daughter of the King's vizier, or principal officer of state, takes it upon herself to save the women of the kingdom from Shahryar's wrath, and offers herself as a bride to the King. The vizier, her father, tells Scheherazade two stories to try to convince her to change her mind—these are substories within the frame story—but she remains unconvinced and marries the King. With the help of her younger sister, Dunyazade, she obtains the King's permission to tell him a story just as their wedding night is about to end. This first tale is the story of the merchant and the demon—a traveling merchant stops to rest and eat, and tosses date pits onto the ground. An old demon appears and tells the merchant that he must kill him because the date pits the merchant tossed away struck the demon's son and killed him. The merchant pleads with the demon for his life. The parallels between this story and the fate of Scheherazade are obvious, as both the merchant and the young bride are to be killed despite being innocent of any crime. The story remains unfinished at daybreak, when the King must rise and attend to the affairs of state; his curiosity piqued, Shahryar resolves to postpone Scheherazade execution so he can hear the end of the story. But the following night only brings another tantalizing fragment, and the King postpones his wife's execution yet again.

What follows is a series of interlocking stories that cover a vast array of subjects. The tales have a deeply nested structure, with stories within stories within stories. They vary in length greatly, the shortest being around 700 words and the longest, the tale of Aladdin and his magical lamp, being nearly 40,000 words. The hundreds of fairytales, legends, romances, fables, anecdotes, and other fictions include, among other tales, the discovery of the unearthly City of Brass, Abu Hassan's waking dreams, the bizarre peregrinations of Sinbad the sailor, Ali Baba's dangerous and tempting encounter with the forty thieves, Aladdin's entry into the world of magic, the insomniac caliph Harun al-Rashid's wanderings throughout Baghdad, and many others. The stories and their connective narrative threads constitute an entire universe of human experience. The king eventually falls under the spell of Scheherazade storytelling magic and, fascinated by her seemingly inexhaustible fund of tales abounding in fantastic events and breathtaking denouements, willingly spares her life and accepts her as his queen.

MAJOR THEMES

Critics point out that the stories in *The Arabian Nights* deal with many fundamental questions about human life and experience. They address universal concerns such as love, death, happiness, fate, and immortality in a manner that transcends linguistic and cultural boundaries. They also cover spiritual matters, exploring questions about how to live in a world that contains both good and evil, with these opposites represented by various characters, such as tyrannical and kind rulers, magicians and witches, good and bad demons, and so on. In addition, the stories also address matters such as the relationship between the sexes, the inevitability of human desire, and the quest for spiritual perfection. The frame story of Scheherazade immediately introduces important themes of power, gender, justice, forgiveness, and the ability of art to transform beliefs and vanquish death. Many of these themes are also developed in subsequent tales.

Although *The Arabian Nights* covers a vast array of themes and subjects, the concept of power is particularly prominent throughout the tales. The depiction of the awesome might of rulers who hold absolute power, and the effects of such control are often highlighted. Another focus of the tales is the strength of women—many are represented in the tales as slaves and concubines who must obey the men who own them, and yet display incredible strength in overcoming adversity. Scheherazade is the most striking example of this type of figure. Notions of justice and forgiveness are also explored in many stories, with good eventually overcoming evil. Again, this theme is first developed in the frame story, as the king finally understands the true meaning of justice. The theme of the transforming power of art is also most obvious in the frame story as King Shahryar, entranced by his wife's tales, in the end understands forgiveness, justice, and humanity.

CRITICAL RECEPTION

The tales of *The Arabian Nights* have been an important part of Middle Eastern folk culture since medieval times. Their long history of transmission and development over the course of centuries are a testament to their enduring appeal. However, while the work has been an integral part of the cultural landscape of that region, it has not always enjoyed the status of high art. When the tales were first introduced to the Western world in the eighteenth century, they were regarded as little more than entertaining diversions with little literary merit. Arabic scholars also viewed the tales as mere popular fiction, unworthy of inclusion in the canon of classical Arabic literature. Early Western scholars also objected to what they perceived as the immoral beliefs and behavior of the Islamic characters in the tales. In contrast to the attitude of literary critics, the tales were well received by many Western poets, especially during the Romantic period. Writers such as Goethe, Wordsworth, Samuel Taylor Coleridge, and Edgar Allan Poe saw the collection as a work of unique imaginative power, and the tales were deeply influential on their thinking and work. They also gripped the popular European imagination, spawning a number of pseudo-Oriental works that depicted a highly extravagant, sensual, exotic East.

In the twentieth century the stories also began to receive serious and systematic critical attention. With the advent of interdisciplinary criticism, the tales of *The Arabian Nights* began to be studied by scholars from a variety of fields, including anthropology, linguistics, psychology, and literary theory. As a result, *The Arabian Nights* has been hailed not only as a brilliantly entertaining narrative, but also as a profound work of art. Modern scholars have extolled the ability of the tales to address, in accessible form, universal concerns ranging from love, death, and happiness to fate and immortality. It has been noted that the stories are of particular value for modern life because of the insights they provide into the individual's struggle with overpowering and frequently incomprehensible forces. A psychological analysis of the tales has pointed out that the stories speak to the unconscious and enable the individual to transform destructive impulses into harmless fantasies. Late-twentieth-century analyses of *The Arabian Nights* have focused more heavily on the manuscript history of the tales, their structure and narrative technique, the influence of classical European traditions on the stories, and their impact on Western literature and culture. Scholars continue to investigate the history and development of the work, regarding it as a complex text that is deserving of detailed textual and critical analysis. This commentary has taken a number of forms, including feminist, deconstructionist, and poststructuralist analysis. In terms of popular appeal, the stories of *The Arabian Nights* remain some of the most recognizable in all of literature. A number of stories from the collection have been adapted for the screen and collections of the stories continue to appeal to young and old audiences, having become part of the collective imagination not only of the cultures from which the stories originally emerged, but of people all over the world.

PRINCIPAL WORKS

Alf Layla wa-Layla [*A Thousand and One Nights*] (short stories) c. 9th century-10th century

Principal English Translations

The Thousand and One Nights, Commonly Called, in England, The Arabian Nights' Entertainments (translated by Edward William Lane) 1831-41

The Book of the Thousand Nights and One Night (translated by John Payne) 1882-84

The Book of the Thousand Nights and a Night: A Plain and Literal Translation of the Arabian Nights Entertainments (translated by Richard F. Burton) 1885

The Arabian Nights Entertainments (selected and edited by Andrew Lang) 1898

The 1001 Nights (Alf Layla wa-Layla) from the Earliest Known Sources (edited by Muhsin Mahdi) 1984

The Arabian Nights (edited by Hussain Haddawy) 1990

CRITICISM

Gustave E. von Grunebaum (essay date 1953)

SOURCE: von Grunebaum, Gustave E. "The Arabian Nights." *Midway: A Magazine of Discovery in the Arts and Sciences* 14 (spring 1963): 41-63.

[*In the following essay, originally published in* Medieval Islam *in 1953, von Grunebaum notes several influential elements from classical literature of the Hellenistic age in* The Arabian Nights, *contending that stories that center on sailors and related geographic details, as well as on tales of love, reflect narrative patterns of the Greek novel.*]

The classical contribution to the formation of Islamic civilization in general has been freely recognized, but the survival of classical traditions in Arabic literature is only now beginning to be traced and appraised in its true importance. The all too strict separation between oriental and classical studies is as responsible for the relative backwardness of our knowledge in this field as is the character of the Greco-Roman contribution itself. While, for example, the Indian or the Jewish influence manifest themselves primarily in the transmission of narrative plots or motives, the influence of the ancients makes itself felt for the most part in less easily traceable elements such as patterns of style, patterns of presentation, and emotional conventions. Perhaps even more elusive is the fact that the Arab's outlook on, and his expectations of, literature have been, to a remarkable degree, molded by the attitudes of the ancients as these developed from the Hellenistic period. The preference accorded by the Arab public to originality of presentation over originality of invention is a striking example; and the theoretical discussion of literature, so popular with Arab scholars and writers, frequently resumes classical problems and is conducted with the aid of a terminology that could never have been devised without the precedent set by the rhetoricians of later and latest antiquity.

What goes for Arabic literature in general applies pointedly to the *Arabian Nights* in particular. Here, too, individual motives or plots, patterns of presentation, and conventional shades of emotion have been assimilated by the narrators and redactors to add to the dazzling colorfulness of the corpus. Here, too, the changed cultural background, and especially the different religious atmosphere, necessitated adaptation of the survivals that tended to obscure their provenance. The mythological bywork of ancient story-telling had to be discarded. Arab realism forced oriental names and oriental habits on the foreign characters. Classical patterns of emotion were superimposed on Persian and Indian plots. Typical personages of later Greek literature such as the foolish schoolmaster reappear in the same light but in a new narrative frame. And, finally, the more obvious borrowings, such as the plot of an action or a major part of it, are far outnumbered by the more subtle imprints left by Hellenistic ideas of life and love on the responsive minds of the Arab public.

Of the many vestiges of classical literature in the *Arabian Nights,* three kinds stand out so as to deserve special attention. These are a small but significant number of plots which the Arabs inherited; a somewhat greater amount of ethnological and geographical detail that goes back to ancient geographers' accounts or sailors' yarns; and, most important of all, the narrative pattern of the Greek novel and its concept of love are mirrored in many of the *Nights'* stories. The influence of the peculiar touch with which the Hellenistic age and its heirs treated love and the lover has been a major factor in the development of Arab ideas about love as shown in poetry and prose both within and outside of the *Arabian Nights.*

Pyrgopolynices, the braggart soldier of Plautus' *Miles Gloriosus,* has kidnaped Philocomasium, the lady-love of Pleusicles, a young Athenian gentleman. When Pleusicles discovers her whereabouts, he settles down in the house next to that of the soldier, and a tunnel dug secretly through the separating walls enables the lovers to meet at their pleasure. When a servant of the soldier sees the girl in the neighbor's house, he is told that her twin sister has arrived and that it is she and not Philocomasium whom he has watched in the arms of the young stranger. By hurrying back and forth through the tunnel, Philocomasium succeeds in making this story plausible. A further ruse rouses the soldier's desire to exchange Philocomasium for another woman, and he is

persuaded to send her off and to bribe her with magnificent gifts that include her favorite slave (and helper in the intrigue) into leaving him quietly. Before his eyes and with his blessing the disguised Pleusicles takes her away.

The resemblance to the *Arabian Nights* story of "Qamar az-zamân and the Jeweler's Wife" is unmistakable. After Qamar az-zamân has won the affection of Halîma, he rents the house next door to the jeweler's, a passageway is broken between the two houses, and Halîma proceeds to transport her husband's riches into the home of her lover, who in the meantime has made friends with the luckless jeweler. On one occasion the jeweler notices a precious dagger of his in the hands of his new friend; on another he discovers his watch in Qamar az-zamân's apartment. In both cases his suspicions are allayed when, upon returning to his own house, he finds the objects in their customary place. A little later Halîma, disguised as a slave-girl, is introduced to her husband in Qamar az-zamân's house. She is called by her true name, and the jeweler is asked to suggest a fitting sales price for her. Again his doubts are put to rest when he finds his wife waiting for him on his return. Finally, the lovers prepare their escape. The pair who have tucked away the jeweler's valuables bid him farewell in a moving scene. At the last moment Halîma succeeds in obtaining for herself her favorite slave girl, and the elopers reach safely the Egyptian border.

The similarities are striking and go far beyond the identity of the outline of the plot: the farewell scene, the plundering of the victim, the assistance rendered the eloping lovers by their dupe, and the final gift of a slave—all these traits bespeak some relationship between the Roman play, or rather its Greek model or models, and the Cairene story. It is undeniable that the Arabic story excels the Plautine comedy in consistency. To mention only two details, "In the *Miles* the passage through the wall does not in any way serve to ensure the escape of Philocomasium; in the story it serves the manoeuvres of the lovers and helps in the mystification of the husband to the very end," as Ph. E. Legrand has pointed out in *The New Greek Comedy.* In the *Miles,* again, it is not the soldier whose suspicion is roused and allayed but a menial who never tells his master of his curious experience, whereas in the *Nights* it is the husband himself who allows the evidence of his own eyes to be discredited.

These and other circumstances make it evident that "Qamar az-zamân" does not directly reproduce or imitate the *Miles* but that both go back to a common source, which in all likelihood was an Ionic love story which either Plautus or the author of the Greek prototype of the *Miles* combined with episodes of a different origin, whereas the redactor of the Arabic novel stuck more closely to his model.

Some recensions of the *Nights* contain another, though more remote, parallel to the *Miles* in the story of the "Butcher, His Wife, and the Soldier," in which once more a secret passage between two houses serves to dupe the husband. One day the husband is made drunk, his hair and beard are shorn, and he is given Turkish clothes and carried off to a remote district. When he awakes, he convinces himself of his changed identity as a Turk and makes off to Isfahan, leaving his wife and her lover undisturbed.

Reminiscences of old travel tales and of fabulous ethnographical lore can be traced in many of the stories of the *Arabian Nights.* Nowhere are they as numerous as in the reports of Sindbad the Sailor on his seven perilous voyages. Although the Sindbad tales do not belong to the original core of the *Arabian Nights,* they must have been in existence as an independent work no later than *ca.* A.D. 900. It is hardly an exaggeration to say that every single enthological or frankly legendary trait used by the unknown author or redactor can be amply paralleled from both Eastern and Western literatures. Geographical lore seems to lend itself particularly well to being borrowed and reborrowed, and this fact reduces considerably the number of cases where we are able to assign a definite origin to a motive. The following instances, however, culled from the first four Voyages of the adventurous mariner, can with certainty be assigned a Western, that is, a Greek source, at the very least in the sense that the motives, whatever the region of their invention, made their literary debut in Greek and were taken up and developed by the oriental narrator from the form they had been given by the classical author.

In the third book of his *Life of Alexander,* the Pseudo-Callisthenes inserts a letter alleged to have been written by the great king to his teacher Aristotle in order to keep him informed about the remarkable happenings on his Indian campaign. And there we read, right at the beginning of this curious collection of *mirabilia,* this sad incident.

> ". . . (Some barbarians at the coast of the Indian Ocean) showed us an island which we all could see in the middle of the sea. They said it was the tomb of an ancient king in which much gold had been dedicated. (When we wished to sail to the island) the barbarians had disappeared leaving us twelve of their little boats. Pheidon, my closest friend, Hephaistion, Krateros and the other friends of mine did not suffer me to cross over (to the tomb in person). Pheidon said: Let me go first so that if anything should go wrong I would face the danger rather than you. If everything is alright I shall send the boat back for you. For if I, Pheidon, should perish, you will find other friends, but should you, Alexander, perish, the whole world would be steeped in grief. Convinced by his plea I gave them leave to cross over. But when they had gone ashore on

what they thought was an island, after no more than an hour the animal suddenly dived down into the deep. We cried out loud while the animal disappeared and the men including my dearest friend came to a horrible end. Embittered I made a search for the barbarians but could not find them."

In this account the unexplained disappearance of some of Alexander's men near an ill-omened island as reported by Nearchos from his voyage in the Indian Ocean and the legend of the tomb of King Erythres, the *heros eponymos* of the Erythrean Sea, supposed to be another island of the same ocean, are combined with the fable of the *aspidochelidone,* the giant tortoise, whose carapace the sailors mistake for an isle. This intriguing animal reappears in St. Basil's *Seventh Homily on the Hexaemeron* and, with some additional detail about its melodious voice with which it lures small fish to their death, in St. Eustathius' (a contemporary of Basil) *Commentary* on the same biblical text.

In the ninth century this giant tortoise, probably an outgrowth of the imagination of the Persian Gulf population but introduced into literature by the Greeks, appears in an Arabic work on animals. Al-Jâhiz (d. 869), with creditable skepticism, sets out to destroy the belief in certain sea monsters and winds up his harangue by observing: "Of course, if we were to believe all that sailors tell. . . . For they claim that on occasion they have landed on certain islands having woods and valleys and fissures and have lit a great fire; and when the monster felt the fire on its back, it began to glide away with them and all the plants growing on it, so that only such as managed to flee were saved. This tale outdoes the most fabulous and preposterous of stories."

The tone of al-Jâhiz' note makes it plain that the motive was a familiar one in his time. So it was from an established tradition that the author of Sindbad's confabulations borrowed when he made his hero tell this episode of his first voyage.

> "We continued our voyage until we arrived at an island like one of the gardens of Paradise, and at that island the master of the ship brought her to anchor with us. He cast the anchor, and put forth the landing-plank, and all who were in the ship landed upon that island. They had prepared for themselves fire-pots, and they lighted fires in them; and their occupations were various: some cooked; others washed, and others amused themselves. I was among those who were amusing themselves upon the shores of the island, and the passengers were assembled to eat and drink and play and sport.

> "But while we were thus engaged, lo, the master of the ship, standing upon its side, called out with his loudest voice, O ye passengers, whom may God preserve! come up quickly into the ship, hasten to embark, and leave your merchandise, and flee with your lives, and save

yourselves from destruction; for this apparent island, upon which ye are, is not really an island, but it is a great fish that hath become stationary in the midst of the sea, and the sand hath accumulated upon it, so that it hath become like an island, and trees have grown upon it since times of old; and when ye lighted upon it the fire, it felt the heat, and put itself in motion, and now it will descend with you into the sea, and ye will all be drowned: then seek for yourselves escape before destruction, and leave the merchandise!—The passengers, therefore, hearing the words of the master of the ship, hastened to go up into the vessel, leaving the merchandise, and their other goods, and their copper cooking-pots, and their fire-pots; and some reached the ship, and others reached it not. The island had moved, and descended to the bottom of the sea, with all that were upon it, and the roaring sea, agitated with waves, closed over it."

Nothing could illustrate more strikingly the decline of critical scholarship in the following centuries than the readiness with which the learned al-Qazwînî (*ca.* 1203-83) accepts this piece of sailors' yarn in his *Cosmography.* Quoting "a merchant" as his authority, he tells succinctly what Sindbad had reported at such comfortable length. Nothing is missing, neither the luscious vegetation on the animal's back nor the fire lighted by the visitors which causes it to move off into the depth. The only deviation consists in al-Qazwînî's replacing the fish of the Sindbad story by the tortoise of the older sources.

On his second voyage Sindbad is left behind on a deserted island. When he explores the place, he perceives a white object which upon his approach turns out to be "a huge white dome, of great height and circumference." He walks around it—the circumference measures no less than fifty paces—finds its walls extremely smooth, but fails to discover an entrance. All of a sudden the sky becomes dark, and he imagines a cloud to have covered the sun, but he soon realizes that the darkness is due to a huge bird. He recalls stories told him by "travelers and voyagers" about a bird of enormous size, called the *ruh,* and even before the bird alights on it he reaches the conclusion that the large white object he had been scrutinizing was its egg. This motive had accrued to the narrator's arsenal from Lucian's *True History,* where the hero "ran aground on an enormous kingfisher's (*alkyon*) nest, really, it was sixty furlongs (*stadia*) in circumference." He then "cut open one of the eggs with axes and took from the shell a featherless chick fatter than twenty vultures."

As soon as the *ruh* had fallen asleep on the egg, Sindbad tied himself to its leg with his turban, and next morning the bird rose with him to the highest region of the sky and finally landed in some remote country, where Sindbad loosed his turban and continued his wanderings.

In this story the author has made good use of an adventure ascribed to Alexander the Great in some manuscripts of Pseudo-Callisthenes. Here the king has himself carried up into the highest dome of the sky by four hungry eagles that are tied to a chest in which Alexander has taken his seat and that are vainly attempting to reach a piece of horse liver fixed to the end of the pole to which they are harnessed.

This picturesque scene also affected Persian legend. The *Book of the Kings* ascribes the same procedure to King Kâ'ûs when this monarch, succumbing to the devil's tempting, tries to ascend to heaven. Originally, the Persians had the king bid the demons build him a city floating between heaven and earth; but the impact of the Alexander saga effected the change.

Here again, Sindbad's tall tale was accepted into respectable scientific literature. Al-Quazwînî opens the pages of his *Cosmagraphy* to an amplified version of the strange event.

The central episode of Sindbad's third voyage is a fairly exact replica of Odysseus' adventure with Polyphemus. The Arabic version, replete with lurid detail, omits the captured hero's ruse in claiming "No Man" to be his name, nor does he have any need to hide his companions and himself tied to the belly of thick-fleeced sheep to make good his escape from the monster's cave. On the other hand, the blinded giant's aim is luckier than Polyphemus': assisted by a female giant—an addition of the Arab narrator—he kills all but two of Sindbad's companions by throwing rocks at the small rafts in which they are struggling to reach the open sea. It is rather strange that the Sindbad story eliminated what would seem to us the most striking feature of the man-eating monster, viz., his one-eyedness. In all but one of the manuscripts the cannibal has two eyes, which, accordingly, Sindbad has to put out with two red-hot iron spits.

This same change occurs in a doublet of the story, the account of Sa'îd's adventures in the tale of "Saif al-mulûk and Badî'at az-zamân." In one version of this account the murderous giant is called "Eli-Fanioun," an obvious echo of "Polyphemus." But the survival of the Cyclops' name did not entail the survival of the Greek idea of the one-eyed Cyclopes. Thus, the Arab rendering of this Greek motive is a telling symptom of that adaptation of the foreign subject matter to the thinking habits of the borrowing society which so frequently obscures the origin of a literary trait.

Although it is not necessary to cast about for a channel through which the Polyphemus story could have reached the Arabs, it may in this connection be recalled that educated Eastern circles kept up a certain interest in the

Homeric poems to a relatively late date. Theophilus of Edessa (d. 785), a favorite of the caliph al-Mahdî (775-85) and a celebrated astrologer, translated "the two Books of Homer" into Syriac. This translation was, in all probability, not a complete version of the *Iliad* and *Odyssey,* but in addition there exist quotations from Homer in various other and later Syriac authors. The influence of the Syriac writers and translators on Arab thought down to the middle of the tenth century is too well known to need more than a passing mention.

Before the ghûl slaughters his prisoners in the "Saif al-mulûk" story he gives them a drink of milk which immediately blinds them. A similar device is practiced by the demon-ruled people into whose power Sindbad falls on his fourth voyage. They hand every new arrival to their town a drink of coconut oil and some unspecified food "in consequence of which his body becomes expanded, in order that he might eat largely, and his mind is stupefied, his faculty of reflection is destroyed, and he becomes like an idiot. Then they give him to eat and drink in abundance of that food and oil, until he becomes fat and stout, when they slaughter him and roast him, and serve him as meat to their king. But as to the companions of the king, they eat the flesh of men without roasting or otherwise cooking it." Al-Qazwînî preserves another form of this motive in which the cannibals are represented as the dog-faced inhabitants of an island in the sea near Zanzibar.

These stories remind one of the beginning of the *Acts of Andrew and Matthew,* where we read: "At that time all the apostles were gathered together and divided the countries among themselves, casting lots. And it fell to Matthew to go to the land of the anthropophagi. Now the men of that city ate no bread nor drank wine, but ate the flesh and drank the blood of men; and every stranger who landed there they took and put out his eyes, and gave him a magic drink which took away his understanding." Nobody can fail to recall the draught which Circe uses to transform Odysseus' companions into pigs. Circe's magic technique is duplicated by Queen Lâb and her adversary in the story of "King Badr Bâsim," although it is not pigs but birds and a mule that result from their craftily employed foods and drinks.

The combination of travel adventures with a love action is held in common by certain of the *Arabian Nights* stories with the Greek novel. This Greek novel, traceable from *ca.* 100 B.C. to A.D. 300 with a curious revival in Byzantine Literature in the twelfth century, builds its intricate plot around the basic scheme of accompanying a pair of beautiful and chaste lovers who are separated and tossed about by the whims of fate on their perilous wanderings until they are finally reunited in blissful happiness. One of the late Byzantine imitators, Nicetas

Eugenianus, prefaced his work with a short *argumentum* that sums up aptly the content not only of his but of all Greek romance.

> Here read Drusilla's fate and Charicles'—
> Flight, wandering, capture, rescues, roaring seas,
> Robbers and prisons, pirates, hunger's grip,
> Dungeons so deep that never sun could dip
> His rays at noon-day to their dark recess,
> Chained hands and feet; and greater heaviness,
> Pitiful partings. Last the story tells
> Marriage, though late, and ends with wedding bells.

The purpose of the trials to which the lovers are exposed is not the development of their characters. As a rule, the lovers remain what they started out to be. What is more, the heroes resemble each other pretty much. The women usually are somewhat more elaborately drawn; they are more alive and better capable of taking the initiative when beset by difficulties. But it is clear that the public was interested in action and that any incident however improbable was welcome. Many of the lovers' troubles are brought on by their irresistable beauty and are again overcome by their passionate chastity.

In contemplating the transfer of the pattern from the Hellenistic to the Muslim milieu, we have to take into account the inevitable recrudescence of the popular character of the romances when they passed from the hands of the professional writer-rhetorician into those of the professional story-teller. The artistic level is bound to drop. The background of religion, so important in the novels, becomes meaningless. The Arab was not accustomed to that historical narrative in which some of the romances excel, and he had, on the whole, no experience in inventing and carrying through a complicated action, with many secondary actions to boot, stretching over hundreds of pages. These differences in literary tradition make for a loss of refinement, greater simplicity, or, perhaps, obviousness of the Arabic tales, but they leave the borrowed pattern unaltered.

A detail that survives in the **Arabian Nights,** the attempted but frustrated suicide of the easily discouraged hero, is particularly significant of the strength of the ancient pattern. For Islam condemns self-destruction. This attitude reduces but does not eliminate the suicide motive from the Arab love stories. In every Greek novel with the exception of Longus' *Daphnis and Chloe* one or both of the heroes at least plan to take their lives if they do not actually attempt to; but nowhere do they succeed. When overtaken by shipwreck while voyaging in quest of his beloved, Saif al-mulûk is ready at once to drown himself, but his servants forcibly prevent him from throwing away his life. In another tale the young squanderer who is compelled to sell his beloved slave girl throws himself into the Tigris but is saved by the bystanders. The close connection in the lovers' minds of love and death is the supreme expression of that peculiar type of emotion with which both the Greek and the Arab authors animate their protagonists.

This emotion is extremely sentimental and self-indulging, emotion for emotion's sake. It even seems somewhat impersonal in its indiscriminate ecstasies. He who falls prey to this passion very nearly loses his individuality; he becomes a lover, thus entering the ranks of what could almost be called a profession. The public takes an interest in his doings and expects certain actions and reactions of him as it would *mutatis mutandis* of a king, a priest, or a soldier. In this capacity the lover enjoys great liberties; he is forgiven everything except disloyalty. His mood vacillates between delirious joy and deadening dejection. On the whole, suffering outweighs pleasure. He is given to weeping, he cannot find rest or sleep, he becomes emaciated, he will fall ill, and he may die when hopelessness overtakes him. Both in happiness and in despair he is likely to swoon; before he acts he has to pass through a stage of protracted moaning. And with all his impetuous passion and despite the predominantly sensual coloring of his feelings, his love is chaste—so much so at times in the Arab tales that the reader cannot help wondering whether the self-conscious lover is enamored of his alleged beloved or of his own luxuriant sensibility.

In Chariton's *Chaereas and Callirhoe,* Dionysius, one of the more interesting and engaging characters of the Greek novel, "disappointed in his love for Callirhoe, and no longer able to carry on, had determined to starve himself to death and was writing his last will with directions for his burial. In the document he begged Callirhoe to visit him even after he was dead." In this moment he receives the news that the girl had changed her mind and agreed to marry him. "At this unexpected announcement Dionysius suffered a great shock. A dark cloud settled down over his eyes and in his weakened condition he collapsed and presented the appearance of a dead man."

The Arab author is less discreet in picturing Hasan of Basra's state when he has lost his lady-love. "Hasan . . . despaired . . . and he desired to rise and descend from his place, but he could not rise. His tears ran down upon his cheek, and his desire became violent, and he recited these verses:

> May Allah deny me the accomplishment of my vow,
> 　if after your absence I know pleasant sleep,
> And may my eyes not be closed after your separation,
> 　nor rest delight me after your departure!
> It would seem to me as though I saw you in sleep:
> 　and would that the visions of sleep might be real!
> I love sleep, though without requiring it; for perhaps a
> 　sight of you might be granted in a dream. . . ."

Finally, Hasan dragged himself to his chamber, "and he lay upon his side, sick, neither eating nor drinking . . . he wept violently, till he fainted, and fell prostrate upon the ground. . . . The night had come and the whole world was strait unto him, and he ceased not to weep and lament for himself all the night until the morning came and the sun rose over the hills and the lowlands. He ate not nor drank nor slept, nor had he any rest: during the day he was perplexed, and during the night sleepless, confounded, intoxicated by his solicitude, expressing the violence of his desire in some verses of a distracted poet."

Literary recognition—which, however, does not imply moral approval—to this turbulent and unrestrained type of emotion was first extended by Plato, who, in the *Symposium,* has Pausanias discourse on the peculiar attitude the world takes toward a lover. "Consider, too, how great is the encouragement which all the world gives to the lover; . . . and in the pursuit of his love the custom of mankind allows him to do many strange things, which philosophy would bitterly censure if they were done from any motive of interest, or wish for office or power. He may pray, and entreat, and supplicate, and swear, and be a servant of servants, and lie on a mat at the door (of his beloved). . . . The actions of a lover have a grace which ennobles them; and custom has decided that they are highly commendable."

All of the pattern's significant topics can be traced backward from the *Arabian Nights,* whose poetical parts mostly stem from poets living between A.D. 850 and 1350, through earlier Arabic poetry to Hellenistic verse. And even before the Hellenistic age popular poetry seems to have moved in this direction. Aristophanes inserts in his *Ecclesiazusae* (first performance in 392 or 389 B.C.) a love song of unmistakably popular hue in which the swain implores the lass in these words:

> Hither, O hither, my love,
> This way, this way!
> Run, run down from above,
> Open the wicket, I pray:
> Else I shall swoon, I shall die!

Theocritus elevated the phrase to full literary dignity in his *Third Idyll.* His (probably spurious) *Twenty-third Idyll* makes the spurned lover who prepares to hang himself at her door ask his beloved to write upon his grave: "This man love slew. . . ." The poet Yazîd b. aṭ-Ṭaṭriyya (d. *ca.* 744) narrowly escaped the same fate when separated from his beloved Wahshiyya. But the lovers are reunited in time, and Yazîd recovers. It remains for a pedestrian critic like the Sayyid Murtaḍà (d. 1044) to explain that the phrase, "somebody was killed by his love for someone else," was nothing but poetical hyperbole.

An occasional protest of this kind did not, however, affect the popularity of this stylized sentimentality among those who boasted a polite education. In laying down the requirements of such education, al-Washshâ' (d. 936) defines in detail and with complete seriousness the symptoms of love à la mode.

> "Know that the first signs of love in the man of polite behavior (*dû adab*) are the emaciation of his body, long sickness, the paling of his color, and sleeplessness. His eyes are cast down, he worries unceasingly, his tears are quick to flow. He carries himself with humility, moans a great deal, and shows openly his yearning. There is no end to his shedding of tears and his heaving of deep sighs. A lover will not remain hidden even if he conceal himself, nor will his passion remain secret even if he control himself. His claim to have joined the ranks of the addicts to love and passion cannot but become public knowledge, for the signs of passion are glowing and the symptoms of the claim are manifest."

This love is conducted by the fashionable in obeisance to an established code exacting different behavior from men and women. Dress, perfume, gifts, food, and drinks of the elegant lover are, so to speak, standardized. Any infringement on this polite convention removes the impetuous from the circle of the cultured. It is obvious, and al-Washshâ' states it expressly, that this type of love is a matter for the well-to-do. It took copious resources to defray the obligation of flooding the beloved with exquisite presents. To love in style you had to live in style, too.

The elaborate mannerisms of polite passion provoked gentle satire. "The Caliph Mutawakkil (847-861) said to Abû'l-'Anbas: 'Tell me about your ass and his death and the poetry which he recited to you in a dream.' 'Yes, O Prince of the Faithful: my ass had more sense than all the *qâdîs* together; 'twas not in him to run away or stumble. Suddenly he fell ill and died. Afterwards I saw him in a dream and said to him, "O my ass, did not I make thy water cool and thy barley clean, and show thee the utmost kindness? Why didst thou die so suddenly? What was the matter with thee?" "True," he answered, "but the day you stopped to converse with so-and-so the perfumer about such-and-such an affair, a beautiful she-ass passed by: I saw her and lost my heart and loved so passionately that I died of grief, pining for her." "O my ass," said I, "didst thou make a poem on the subject?" "Yes," he said; then he chanted:

> I was frenzied by a she-ass at the door of a perfumer.
> She enthralled me, smiling coyly, showing me her lovely side-teeth,
> Charmed me with a pair of soft cheeks colored like the shaiqurânî.
> For her sake I died; and had I lived, then great were my dishonor!

I said: "O my ass, what is the *shaiqurânî?*" "This," he replied, "is one of the strange and uncommon words in the language of the asses.'" Mutawakkil was delighted and ordered the minstrels to set the poem of the ass to music and sing it on that day. No one had ever seen him so gay and joyous before. He redoubled his marks of favor to Abû'l-'Anbas and loaded him with gifts."

The influence on Arabic civilization exerted by Greek literature and thought during the ninth and tenth centuries is well recognized. It is less widely realized, however, that even the earliest Arabic poetry shows definite traces of Hellenistic tradition. As early as ca. A.D. 500 the poet al-Muraqqish the Elder died of love. Before his demise he addressed his beloved cousin Asmâ' in these words:

> And whenever thou hearest, whereso it reaches thee,
> of a lover who's dead of love or is dying,
> Know that that wretch is I without doubt, and weep
> for one whom Love chained and slew with none to avenge.

By the middle of the sixth century al-Muraqqish's story had become a common theme. Tarafa (d. *ca.* 565) illustrates his own passion for Salmà by a reference to the older poet's fate and expressly states that al-Muraqqish met his death through love. Not much later, al-A'shà (*ca.* 565-629) calls his beloved "a slayer of men."

This same poet introduced another Hellenistic motive to Arabic literature. In his *Fifth Fragment* Moschos (*ca.* 150 B.C.) thus draws the picture of an exasperating tangle of emotions: "Pan loved his neighbor Echo; Echo loved a frisking Satyr; and Satyr, he was head over ears for Lyde. As Echo was Pan's flame, so was Satyr Echo's, and Lyde master Satyr's. 'Twas love reciprocal; for by just course, even as each of those hearts did scorn its lover, so was it also scorned being such a lover itself."

Horace's imitation of the passage is familiar. In al-A'shà's verse the mythological names are, of course, discarded.

> I fell in love accidentally, but she was attached to another man who in turn was in love with another girl.
> This man again was loved by a young lady who was unapproachable for a kinsman, who was dying from longing, delirious about her, a madman.
> But I myself was loved by a little woman who did not suit me—so with all of us love was odious in each case.
> Each of us yearned deliriously for his companion in suffering, remote and close at the same time, entangled and entangling.

No sooner had the Arabs set foot on and conquered territories formerly held by the Eastern Empire and Greek civilization than a second wave of Hellenistic influence swept into love poetry.

While in pre-Islamic days sentimental love of the kind described above is met with on comparatively rare occasions, it becomes the accepted emotional pattern during the second part of the seventh century, and, with it, the love-death topic comes to be employed by every poet of rank. Famous are the lines of Jamîl al-'Udrî (d. 701) in which he awakens his sleeping comrades in the dead of night to ask them, "Does love kill a man?" "Yes," they replied, "it breaks his bones, leaves him perplexed, chased out of his wits."

The real contribution of this age to the love-death concept is, however, the idea that the chaste lover who dies of his love is a martyr and thus as sure of Paradise as the martyr of the Holy War. The Prophet Mohammed himself is represented as pronouncing this verdict and thereby conferring "official" standing on this type of lover.

The suggestion may be ventured that the concept of the martyr of love constitutes an original contribution of Arabic poetry. In it are fused two earlier developments: the originally Greek notion of the victim of love and that other Greek idea of the lover as fighter or soldier. It is well known that Christian martyrology made extensive use of erotic phraseology, and there is no doubt that the Arabs had, by that time, become familiar with Christian martyrology. The transfer of the fighter-martyr concept to the battles of love appears as a rather bold and perhaps somewhat frivolous, at any rate, a highly original, innovation of the later seventh century. The trend of the times toward using religious topics in love poetry and love phraseology in religious verse strongly supports this assumption.

Either Jamîl or his contemporary, Ibn Qais ar-Ruqayyât, was the first to call love madness, *junûn*—another testimony to the increasing effectiveness of Greek ideas. Perhaps a hundred years later, when a theoretical interest in the nature of love began to show, the Platonic definition of love as a sort of divine madness is brought forward by one of the disputants of that famous conference on love held by the learned circle of the Barmakid vizier, Yahyà b. Hâlid (disgraced in 803). Plato's definition recurs many times.

There is no need to trace the models of every major *topos* of this "Medinese" love poetry (as easily could be done), nor is it necessary to follow any further the fascinating development of Arabic love poetry destined to reach a new peak in the lyrics of al- Abbâs b. al-Ahnaf in order to understand the spiritual kinship of the lyrical passages of the *Arabian Nights* with Hellenistic poetry. At least one section of the Arab public and the

Arab littérateurs took over the erotic conventions of the Hellenistic epoch; for the most part, we will have to assume, without realizing the true source of outlook or phraseology.

How perfectly the Arabic poet entered into the spirit of his predecessors will be perceived through an analysis of these verses culled again from the larmoyant story of Hasan of Baṣra.

> You made a covenant with me that you would remain
>   faithful; but when you had gained possession of my
>   heart you deceived me.
> I conjure you by Allah, if I die, that you write upon
>   my tombstone, This was a slave of love:
> That perchance some mourner who hath felt the same
>   flame may pass by the lover's grave and pity him.

Nearly every conceit employed in these lines could be matched from Meleager of Gadara (first century B.C.):

> We swore, he to love me, and I never to leave him;
>   but now he says that such vows are in running water.
> When I am dead, I pray thee lay me under earth and
>   write above, Love's gift to Death.
> I will leave letters uttering this voice, Look, stranger,
>   on Love's murdered man.
> Even myself I carry the wounds of Love and shed
>   tears over thy tears.

Thus fully has the Arab lover and poet responded to the tune of the love-lorn Greek.

Indian and Persian, Jewish and Greek, Babylonian and Egyptian, together with genuinely Arabian elements, have been welded into one by the unknown masters responsible for the overwhelming richness of the corpus of the *Arabian Nights.* Outwardly, the Arabic language, inwardly, the spirit of Islam unite those manifold threads into one dazzling tapestry. In this synthesis of the disparate the *Arabian Nights* present a likeness on a small scale of Islamic civilization as a whole.

With a certain shift in emphasis, away from the Indian, Babylonian, and Egyptian, and toward the Persian, the Greek, and the Judeo-Christian, and, of course, with much greater stress on the genuinely Arabic, the structure of Islamic civilization repeats the structure of the *Nights.* Islamic civilization is thoroughly syncretistic, and it proves its vitality by coating each and every borrowing with its own inimitable patina.

Mia I. Gerhardt (essay date 1963)

SOURCE: Gerhardt, Mia I. "Structure." In *The Art of Story-Telling: A Literary Study of the Thousand and One Nights*, pp. 377-416. Leiden, Netherlands: E. J. Brill, 1963.

[*In the following essay, Gerhardt studies the motifs, character descriptions, use of dialogue, and structure of*

The Arabian Nights, *noting that it is difficult for a non-Arabist to easily understand the structural nuances of this work.*]

If we define structure, in the largest sense, as the manner in which the material is arranged and presented, it follows at once that not all structural aspects of the *1001 Nights* lend themselves to being adequately studied by anyone who is not an Arabist. The basic material of story-telling is words; the choice and arrangement of words, which is what we call, strictly, style, can be duly appreciated only in the original language of a literary work and by one thoroughly familiar with that language. Consequently, even such relatively unsubtle stylistic devices as the use of stock descriptions and of standing formulas in the *1001 Nights* will not come into consideration here. It would, no doubt, be rewarding to examine exactly how a given description is applied, adapted and, if necessary, varied in each case; a still more intriguing subject for study of detail would be the manner in which the opening and closing formulas are chosen and worded. But these and all other stylistic matters must necessarily be left to the Arabic scholar.

The non-Arabist literary student can grasp, and legitimately assess, such structural aspects as regard the arranging and presenting of the narrative material: incidents and motifs, characters and plots; in other words, the compositional features of the stories. An exhaustive examination of all such features would, of course, far exceed the scope of this work. On frequent and infrequent motifs, on the number of characters generally involved in an incident, on the means used—and not used—to describe characters and their reactions, on the story-tellers' comments, on the function and nature of the dialogue, on the various denouement devices and on the very patterns of the stories, nearly everything is still to be investigated[1], and much could be elucidated and explained by critical study. In order to fix the limits of the present chapter, however, a restrictive choice had to be made, and one particular subject singled out to the exclusion of many others that would be equally interesting to go into.

For our purposes, the most appropriate subject to choose for closer study seemed to be the telling of stories within the *1001 Nights,* in its various modes and functions. For the book is not only a story-book, but also, in many respects, a book about story-telling. One way to sum it up is to say that it contains the stories told by a young woman who, by telling them, tries to save her life. And in its individual pieces, long and brief, sundry forms of narrating and relating and reporting loom surprisingly large. This is what I propose to examine more closely here.

The subject necessitates a preliminary reference to the conceptions prevailing in medieval Arabic literature. The flourishing period of Arabic letters (roughly speaking, the 8th-11th centuries) created and settled, with regard to the relating of events, a peculiar convention, of which a notable characteristic is the well-known "witnessing system". This was evolved, originally, to preserve and to authenticate the sayings of Mohammed on all sorts of points not exhaustively treated in the Koran[2]. Such a saying could become a well-established "tradition" only if and when it was accompanied by an unbroken chain of witnesses, historical persons who transmitted it the one to the other, beginning with the contemporary who heard it from the Prophet himself, and ending with the trustworthy man who finally committed the saying and its whole witness-chain to writing for definitive preservation. We need not go here into the problems which the gradually increasing number of Traditions of the Prophet and the attendant witnessing system could not fail to create. Essential to our subject is that the same principles were extended also to profane matters such as biography, historiography and anecdote; even, to a certain degree, legend. In all branches of letters, a high regard for authenticity, of which the only adequate guarantee was the witness-chain, went hand in hand with an increasing depreciation of free invention, and consequently, of all unauthenticated fiction[3]. Thus, Arabic narrative literature, in the widest sense, came to range between two extremes: on the one hand, the anonymous non-erudite fictitious story that begins with some equivalent of our "Once upon a time, there was . . .”; on the other hand, the account fit to be taken seriously among the learned, which is characterized as historical by beginning with a string of duly-attested names: "A told, on the authority of B who had it from C . . . , that . . .”

To the modern observer, perhaps the most striking thing about the witnessing system with its rules and its usage, is the strong awareness of and regard for the individual which it implies. Surely such a system could only develop within a small community, of which each member knew, personally or by report, the other members or anyway their families, and where each man knew his own genealogy and that of the members of his tribe in all particulars. Such was, indeed, the state of affairs among the Arabs immediately before, and for a short while after the rise of Islam. Soon, though, when spectacular conquests had immensely increased the Moslem territories, and the great cities of the Islamic world began to develop, the small-community situation was bound to change. And yet, just as the witnessing system had become an indispensable element of Arabic learning, the trend towards recognizing and particularizing the individual continues to stand out in Arabic writing[4]. The man of note, be it a poet, a traveller, a scholar, a mystic or simply a man of high culture, is remembered by name, and his sayings and doings are remembered in connexion with him, not just for their general validity.

Something of the same trend is recognizable even in popular story-telling. In fact, a distinctive quality of the Arabic story is precisely its sure way of singling out the man from the crowd, of setting the hero apart, unique, neatly outlined, not to be confused with any other. In the Baghdad of the *1001 Nights,* a merchant is not merely a member of his estimable class, but always a well-known merchant named so-and-so, son of an equally well-known father. It seems characteristic that the story-tellers hardly ever leave a principal character unnamed. Only when several characters function *ex aequo* can they be designated by no more than a general appellation: three sheiks, three ladies, three mendicants, seven demon princesses, and in **"The Hunchback,"** the amusing series of professions. Even in the Egyptian stories, where attention to the individual becomes a shade less marked and in which the anonymous bustling crowd not unfrequently plays a part, the heroes always have their name, and their fame "in the neighbourhood", in the city-quarter that is the city to them and which, according to the stories, sometimes takes them for an eponym[5]. The intentional namelessness of the tales, with their pensive and pious whisperings about "a man", stands out by contrast as an almost sacrificial discretion in honour of the ascetic's and the saint's self-effacement.

Seen against the background briefly sketched here, the *1001 Nights* is found to represent both the contrasting conceptions indicated above: it offers not only anonymous stories of free invention, but also, thanks to the activity of the compilers, duly witnessed reports.

Several anecdotes and anecdotic short stories, and some tales as well (all in all, about a quarter of the brief pieces), are presented on the authority of a witness named at the beginning; which, historically speaking, is a sure sign that they have been taken from erudite works. Comparison with such works may show that the witness mentioned in the *1001 Nights* is merely the first one of the whole chain that originally went with the story[6]. But even the one remaining name is sufficient to set the little piece apart and to confer upon it something of the prestige inherent to the witnessing system. This is especially true if the name is that of a famous ascetic or scholar: *Mâlik ibn Dinâr related:* . . . (III, 715); *Abu el-Abbâs el-Mubarrad related:* . . . (III, 560). However legendary or romantic the related event may be, the well-known name lends to it a semblance of authenticity, and an additional impressiveness. The reverse, for that matter, also applies: if a fine little piece is introduced by *Abu Suwaid related:* . . . (III, 590), it makes us feel that this Abu Suwaid, on whom no information can be found[7], must have been a

remarkable man and that recollections of his were rightly held to be worth while preserving. And when the story tells of an eminently personal experience, the naming of the central character himself as the witness is particularly apt: the anxieties and final rescue of the debt-ridden judge Abu Hassân ez-Ziyâdi[8] gain in poignancy because the anecdote is headed: *Abu Hassân ez-Ziyâdi used to tell:* . . . (III, 331) and ends: *I told them the story from beginning to end; and it spread among the people.* (III, 335).

An anonymous witness—they are, naturally, comparatively rare—is qualified by social standing or personal merit: *One of the Descendants of the Prophet related:* . . . (III, 712); *I pious man related:* . . . (III, 749); *One of the men of polite education related:* . . . (III, 579); and in each case, the story is well adapted to the outlook of the witness thus described. The effect becomes more curious, in the perspective of the '1001 Nights', when one of the favourite characters of the Harûn cycle is given the witness's part: *Abu Ishâk Ibrahîm el-Mausili related:* . . . (IV, 645; IV, 678); *Ishâk ibn Ibrahîm el-Mausili related:* . . . (III, 115; III, 550; IV, 674). But, although to the reader they appear in the first place as story characters, Ibrahîm and Ishâk were historical figures, and great celebrities[9]; there is nothing improbable in the supposition that their reminiscences, as told in several short stories of the *1001 Nights,* were first taken down from their own mouths. In any case, the personal presentation makes the stories all the more vivid. That the anecdotes about that other celebrity, Abu Nuwâs, are not thus presented, has a good artistic reason: they turn on the witty quips and astounding improvisations of the poet[10], the appeal of which would be somewhat spoiled if he reported them himself. In one instance, it is Harûn's black sword-bearer who gets a witness's part: *Masrûr the eunuch related:* . . . (IV, 650); here the interlocking of history, which attests that Masrûr existed[11], and fiction, to which he owes his fame, gives an unintentional surprise effect that is very pleasant.

Quite apart from the historicity and renown of the persons named, the scholarly witnessing device furnishes, in the *1001 Nights,* a most attractive manner of presenting such little pieces as anecdotes, tales, and anecdotic short stories; it pins them down, gives them weight, and sometimes adds just the personal touch they would otherwise lack.

The full-length stories on the contrary, that were not taken from erudite works by the compilers, but made up by story-telling artists, and which belong properly to the essentially popular collection of the *1001 Nights,* are presented in an entirely different fashion. Without any regard for authenticity, historicity or foundation in fact, they ask us all at once to accept on faith the hero and his status: "In Baghdad (or: In Cairo) there lived a merchant . . .". Sometimes it is added that he lived long ago, "in times of yore, in bygone days that are no more", for a story is apt to be more appealing in so far as it is more remote and detached from present-day worries; and occasionally, the Egyptian story-tellers reinforce the distance in time by distance in space, pretending that it all happened "in China" (without, for that matter, making China appear at all different from Egypt). After this plain and unpretentious opening, it is up to the story-teller to interest us in the personalities of the merchant and his offspring, and he will not fail to do so. Not fortuitously, such stories are almost exclusively given to the use of the third person: the freely inventing, all-knowing, allmighty story-teller is the "I" who remains hidden off-stage, and the hero is the "he" whose adventures he imagines and narrates[12]. Sometimes only, under the stress of a particularly captivating occurrence, the roles may temporarily be changed, and the central character is made to take up the thread of the narration, saying "So I went . . ." "I did . . ." and himself recounting what befell him. But the shifting remains incidental, and it always is the story-teller who concludes the account of the hero's career and assures us, at the end, that he lived on in happiness and prosperity until the inevitable hour of death. This is the, we may well say classical, straight narrative, the most common presentation in story-telling all over the world, and the standard procedure for the popular stories of the *1001 Nights.*

However, it must not be supposed for a moment that the *1001 Nights* modes of presentation are exhausted with the extremes of erudite witness-story and popular straight narrative. On the contrary: long or brief, the pieces of the collection abound in remarkable and sometimes highly ingenious devices to introduce, to justify, to authenticate the telling of a story, to set it off, to make it serve a purpose. Stories are fitted one into the other like Chinese boxes; characters become witnesses or story-tellers in their turn; kings and caliphs are given, as their most important function, the listener's part, and even fierce demons can be tamed by telling them what happened to people.

Broadly speaking, three structural proceedings can be distinguished throughout the book. A character in a story may assume the function of a witness, relating adventures or repeating accounts of others and thus lending them an apparent guarantee of authenticity; this oblique presentation, as it might be called, is especially frequent in the short pieces of the collection. In the full-length stories, the characters may interrupt the action to tell an incident from their lives or a story, to illustrate a point or just to pass the time: then a small inserted story lies imbedded in the, longer, main story like a nut in a cake. Or also, and frequently, a character is

introduced with no other purpose than to make him tell a story: this gives the whole which we call a frame-story, consisting of a, most often relatively slight, framework surrounding one or more framed stories. The three techniques, of increasing literary consequence, will be examined in that order in the following pages.

OBLIQUE PRESENTATION

In the *1001 Nights,* it is the brief pieces that display the greatest variety in presentation. The simple act of telling a little story is performed in all sorts of ways, ranging from straight narrative via reporting and framing devices to the witness story proper. As one example among many, the minute series of schoolmaster stories uses, in its three pieces, three different techniques. The first one (96) is a witness story: *An eminent man related: Once I passed by a school where a schoolmaster was teaching the children.* (III, 533). He proceeds to tell how he made the schoolmaster's acquaintance and was favourable impressed by his learning; but after some time, when paying him a visit, he found him obsessed by a silly fancy[13]. *And so I was convinced that he really was a stupid fellow, and I left him and went my way.* (III, 535). The second (97) incorporates the witness into the story as a secondary character, but robs him of the reporting part: *Once there was a schoolmaster; to him came an eminent man, who sat down with him and tested his learning.* (III, 536). The occurrences are then related in the third person, but from the viewpoint of the eminent man: he finds the schoolmaster well-read and accepts an invitation to be his guess only to see him commit an extremely foolish act. *The guest left him and said to himself: "He was right who said that a schoolmaster who teaches children never has much common sense, however learned he may be."* (III, 537). The last of the three (98) has neither witness nor secondary character and takes to straight narrating: *Among those who frequented the academy there was a fellow who could neither read nor write [. . .]. One day he got it into his head to open a school and teach the children; [. . .] To one child he said "Write!" and to another: "Read!" and in that way they taught each other.* (III, 537). The straight presentation of this last piece and the witness's account of the first are both perfectly logical. But there is something slightly unfocussed about the second one, where the character of the eminent man is, strictly speaking, superfluous, since he does not act as a witness. To give him a function, the story ought to have been reported by him; as perhaps it was in a former redaction.

Even the witness stories proper display various possibilities of presentation, similar to those found in the other brief pieces, and determined by the position of the witness in relation to the facts of his story. He may remain entirely outside the event; after the mention of his name at the beginning, his report follows in the third person, just like any other story, save that it now goes on the authority of a definite individual. *The sherif Husain ibn Raiyân related: One day the Commander of the Faithful Omar ibn el-Khattâb sat in his chair of justice . . .* (III, 512). On the other hand, he may give a purely autobiographical report, naturally in the first person, like Abu Hâssan ez-Ziyâdi, already mentioned[14], or Abu el-Hasan ed-Darrâj in the tale that bears his name (135). And frequently, the witness reports events in which he played a part, but only a small one, while other people are the protagonists. *Abdallâh ibn Ma'mar el-Kaisi related: One year I made the pilgrimage to the holy House of Allah . . .* (IV, 616); there he met a young man whom he helped to win his bride, and whom he later saw treacherously slain[15].

Now there are a considerable number of brief pieces—mostly short stories—where a secondary character has exactly this same function: he assists at the occurrence, plays a small part in it, and afterwards reports it. Only the express mention of his name at the beginning, rudiment of a scholarly witness-chain, is lacking. Strictly speaking, therefore, such pieces are not witness stories, although it would seem that sometimes the omission is simply a matter of redaction. Their technique, however, is essentially a witnessing technique. The facts of the narration are not presented straight, but obliquely, through one of the characters, who tells them in the first person, while playing but a subordinate part in the story. No doubt, the deep-rooted preference for having memorable sayings reported by someone who heard them at first hand, and events by someone who saw them with his own eyes, explains this characteristic oblique presentation, which enhances the charm of several short stories in the *1001 Nights.*

Let us take as an example **"The Lovers from the Tribe of Udhra,"** an early Arabic lovers' tale incorporated in the Harûn cycle by means of the framework. Harûn has the poet Jamîl ibn Ma'mar brought in[16] and asks him to tell a curious happening, preferably one at which he was present himself. Jamîl then relates with much personal detail how in the desert he met a cousin of his, who camped there to be near the girl he loved; she was married by her parents to another. She visits him secretly every night, and Jamîl sees them sitting together, lamenting their lot[17]. He is still there when, a few nights later, the girl is killed by a lion and his cousin consequently dies of grief. He buries them in a common grave.—Now in this story, the very plot makes the presence and the report of a witness a plain necessity. If the lovers had died in the desert all alone, their secret love and their sad end would, logically speaking, have remained unknown; a story about them in straight narrative would therefore be clearly marked as an invention. Only by means of a surviving secondary character

could it be presented as something that really and indubitably happened. To the modern reader, if decidedly not to the Arabs, the distinction is inessential in itself; but the oblique presentation makes a literary difference that vitally affects the story. The adventure becomes more interesting by being seen through the eyes of Jamîl and coloured by his reactions: curiosity, emotion, pity and sorrow. The fate of the lovers becomes something else as well: a personal experience of the poet.

Although rather often, it is not always the logical need for a survivor that determines this presentation. In **"Jubair Ibn Umair and Budûr,"** for instance, a bystander to report the lovers' emotional crisis is not strictly indispensable: they live to tell about it themselves. Yet the presence of the nice old gentleman who becomes their confident, tries to mend their quarrel, and finally sees them happily married is an asset to the story, and it is fitting that he is the one who tells it. It is better seen from the outside than through the eyes of the interested parties themselves, who are too deeply engaged in it; let us note in passing that Jubair's own explanation of his sudden reversal of feeling hardly makes sense, except, of course, to himself[18]. The outsider, at once sympathetic and detached, is the proper person to describe the strange behaviour of the temperamental and headstrong lovers.

Occasionally, the various devices which the *1001 Nights* employs in order to have stories told entail a certain implausibility, in supposing a strength of memory and a gift for talking far beyond the ordinary person's capacities. In **"The Man from Yemen"** the caliph asks one of his table-companions, Mohammed el-Basri, to tell something interesting; the latter obliges by reproducing a whole debate held by the Yemenite's six accomplished slave-girls[19], thus repeating from memory a tremendous lot of quotations, proverbs, verse, rhyming prose and other such verbal fireworks. Still, however improbable, the presentation is not absurd: we need only suppose that Mohammed el-Basri was endowed with an excellent memory and was willing to give a stunt performance[20]. Such high-quality entertainment as provided by the six girls assuredly deserved to be recorded, and may well have been unforgettable to a listener who knew how to appreciate it. So, charmingly, he repays a debt of gratitude to the girls and their master by his faithful report.

The full-length stories of the *1001 Nights* are generally presented in straight narrative, occasionally set off by a framework of some kind; the subtler technique of oblique presentation is hardly ever employed here. Still, it does occur: rather unaccountably in **"Alî Ibn Bakkâr**

and Shams En-Nahâr," and with all the marks of a deliberate artistic choice in **"The Hunchback."** Both cases are interesting enough to warrant a brief discussion.

The badly transmitted story of **"Alî Ibn Bakkâr"**[21] presents, successively, two secondary characters in the familiar role of helper to the lovers: first the distinguished merchant Abu el-Hasan ibn Taher, and later his friend, the jeweller. In the first episodes of the story, Abu el-Hasan assists at the events, but except for a few brief passages he does not report them; the narrative proceeds in the third person as customary. Later, though, when he has taken flight and has been succeeded by the jeweller, the latter is given, at first incidentally and towards the end consistently, a reporting function: he tells, in the first person, what happened, and concludes the story in his own name.—The whole set-up raises several intriguing questions, which the present version does not permit to answer. Why should Abu el-Hasan, who is very emphatically introduced at the beginning (in terms that would seem to make him fit a witnessing part) be replaced half-way by the less eminent jeweller? Why does the jeweller, an important secondary character, remain nameless? And above all, why does the latter half of the story take to presenting the events through him? Probably all these puzzling features came about in the course of transmission; but it would be mere guesswork to try and reconstitute a previous, more coherent version, let alone the original. Still, it does not seem improbable that from the very beginning there was a secondary character with a reporting function: for **"Alî Ibn Bakkâr"** is a story about amorous martyrs, who must love in secret and are united only in death. Such a plot, which in its whole conception is strongly reminiscent of the early Arabic love-stories, traditionally called for a surviving friend to tell about the fate of the lovers. However that may be—to refrain from further speculation—we are confronted here with an unusual presentation of an in more than one respect exceptional full-length story.

A consistent, even pointed use of oblique presentation is one of the many remarkable traits of **"The Hunchback."** One of the collection's finest specimens of the frame-story, it will presently be examined as such; at this point, attention must be drawn to the fact that all its stories but one report adventures of third persons, which gives a most peculiar cascade effect. Each of the four men who successively are compelled to tell a story reports how he met some other man who related an incident from his life: the broker tells about a merchant; the steward, about another merchant; the doctor, about a young man from Mosul; finally, the tailor, about a young man from Baghdad, who had an unlucky encounter with a barber. The said barber—as the tailor proceeds to report—first told a "story of himself" and then six

stories about his six brothers, whom we thus get to know through the double intermediary of the barber and the tailor. In this way the framework is filled by two sets of, differently presented, biographical stories, separated by an autobiographical one; a very distinctive pattern, doubtless entirely intentional, and flawlessly executed. The result is that **"The Hunchback"** appears marvellously rich, crowded with people and their adventures, while yet it contains only four characters— the broker, the steward, the doctor and the tailor—who have a major speaking part. (As an additional stunt, the hunchback about whom all the fuss is and who rightly gives the story its title, does not utter a single word.) If ever, the literary possibilities of that very trivial phenomenon, people telling about people, have been fully realized here.

INSERTED STORIES

The structural difference between inserted stories and framed stories is one of relative proportions and weight. The inserted story is not only much shorter than the main story in which it is inserted, but also of lesser consequence; it never is the centre of gravity of the whole. The framed story on the contrary is longer and, particularly, more important than the framing story that surrounds it; in the whole called frame-story, the framework is always subordinate to the story or stories it serves to frame. Now it is a curious fact that, while frame-stories occur with great frequency all through the *1001 Nights,* the insertion technique is employed only in the first part of the book. Inserted stories are found repeatedly until no. 21 inclusively, and thereafter not any more, except in one piece that is a curiosity in all respects, and in two that do not belong to ZER [Zotenberg's Egyptian Recension]. Already in the framing story of the collection, Shehrezâd's father tells her a moral tale (0a); **"The Fisherman and the Demon"** has a triple insertion (2a, 2aa, 2ab), and **"The Three Ladies,"** in one of its framed stories, has one (3ba). **"Ghânim"** contains the two eunuch stories (7a, 7b), **"Omar Ibn En-Nu'mân"** is enlivened with a double love-story (8a, 8aa), and two other, brief, pieces (8b, 8c). Next, the series of fables and moral tales presents no less than six insertions (13a, 16a, 16b, 16c, 17a, 18a). Lastly, a love-story (21a) is inserted in the third part of **"Kamar Ez-Zamân."** As far as ZER is concerned, the technique then suddenly goes out of favour; it only crops up once more in **"The Serpent Queen"** (136aa). Moreover, two of the asterisk pieces of our title-list present inserted stories: there is one (79a) in **"The Awakened Sleeper,"** and one (173a) in the orphan story of **"Khudadâd."**

This uneven distribution, in ZER, seems to a large extent accounted for by a historical factor. The Indian influences that, through Persian models, came to bear on material and structure of the *1001 Nights,* have left the most perceptible traces on the old core of the book, which also in ZER stands mainly at the beginning. Although recent research tends somewhat to diminish the importance which older scholars accorded to Indian elements in the *1001 Nights,* there is no doubt that Indian story-telling furnished one particular insertion device that haunts some of the older stories. This device, which we may well call the instructive insertion, consists in making one of the characters in the main story tell a tale or a little story to convey a moral lesson. As Littmann, among others, points out[22], Indian literature abounds in examples of the typical manner in which such insertions are presented. A character says, for instance: "Don't do this or that, or else the same will happen to you as happened to . . ." The other asks: "What was that?" whereupon the warning story is told. In framed collections, the framed stories may be given the same instructive function, as we shall see later on.

The instructive insertion occurs in several stories for which Persian models containing Indian elements may be presumed. The most illustrative case is **"The Fisherman and the Demon"**[23]. When the fisherman has tricked the bloodthirsty demon back into the bottle, he refuses to liberate him again, despite his supplications and promises: *"You lie, wretch",* exclaimed the fisherman; *"you and I are to each other as the vizir of king Yunân and the sage Dubân." "How was that about the vizir of king Yunân and the sage Dubân? What is their story?"* asked the demon; and the fisherman began . . . (I, 56). The story tells how the sage Dubân healed king Yunân from leprosy, so that he came to high favour; but the king's vizir, envious, slanders him. *The king said: "O vizir, you are filled with envy for this sage, and you want him to be put to death; but I should repent of it afterwards, just as king Sindibâd repented of having killed his falcon." And the vizir said: "By your leave, o greatest king of our time, how was that?" So the king began* . . . (I, 62). In the secondary tale, king Sindibâd gets angry when his falcon keeps him from drinking, and kills it; too late, he perceives that the drink was poison, and that the falcon saved his life. The vizir of king Yunân, however, is not convinced, and maintains that he has spoken the truth about the sage: *"You might perish, like the vizir perished who was disloyal towards his king." So king Yunân asked: "How was that?"* and *the vizir began* . . . (I, 65). Follows another secondary tale, somewhat inadequately told and not quite to the point: a vizir lets the son of his king go hunting alone, so that he barely escapes being eaten by a ghoul; the vizir is executed. This is a punishment for neglect of duty, and does not apply to the situation of king Yunân. Galland (or the ms. G) saves the parallel by making the vizir say: *"S'il [mon avis] est faux, je mérite qu'on me punisse de la même manière qu'on punit autrefois un*

vizir." (1, p. 50)[24]. However, king Yunân lets himself be persuaded by the arguments of his vizir, and prepares ungratefully to kill the sage who healed him, just as the demon, once out of the bottle, prepared to kill the fisherman who set him free; the dominant parallel of the fisherman's story is effective throughout.

At this point, the device crops up in a singular variant, which leaves only the introductory dialogue and suppresses the insertion. The sage Dubân, standing with blindfolded eyes waiting to be beheaded, says to the king: *"This reward you intend to pay me is the reward of the crocodile." The king asked: "What is the story about the crocodile?" But the sage answered: "I cannot possibly tell it in this plight; I entreat you by Allah, spare me . . ."* (I, 69-70). The king, though, refuses, and the crocodile story is not told[25]. We may well ask if the omission is intentional and part of the story-pattern, or simply an accident of transmission. Surely the sage's excuse is understandable enough, and it can even be supposed that he tries to make a play for the king's curiosity and thereby at least to gain time. But the attempt has so little success that he might as well have told the story.—Later on, when the inserted story told by the fisherman has been brought to a conclusion, relating the sage's posthumous revenge on king Yunân, the variant occurs once more in the main story. The demon, still in his bottle, pleads: *"Spare me and forgive me! if I did evil, so do you good, for in the proverbs of the people it is said: O renderer of good for evil, unto the criminal sufficeth his crime. And don't do to me as Umâma did to Atika." The fisherman asked: "What did Umâma do to Atika?" But the demon answered: "This is not the time to tell it, while I am here imprisoned. Let me out, and I will tell you."* (I,73). Here the promise of a story is evidently used as bait, which the fisherman, however, refrains from taking. It is only later, and on other conditions, that he liberates the demon, who rewards him by doing him a good turn; but the story of Umâma and Atika which has been missed is never told.

The instructive insertion is, in **"The Fisherman and the Demon,"** employed with a fair amount of skill; this permits to assess its intrinsic literary qualities. It certainly is an excellent way to give the inserted story a function within the whole, and the grouping of parallel situations all around the knot of the main story permits a varied and at the same time coherent display of story-material. On the other hand, the predominance of the stories' moral purpose soon makes for a certain dreariness. The device is essentially ungratuitous, and thereby something of an exception in the *1001 Nights,* where most of the story-telling indulged in by the characters is done for its own sake, simply for the listener's and the speaker's pleasure.

That the series of fables and moral tales, where an abundant if not very interesting use is made of instructive insertions, occurs also at the beginning of the book, is probably an effect of chance; it seems as good as certain that the series was added by the Egyptian compilers, and that they placed it at random[26]. On the contrary, the **"Ass and Bull"** story in the Shehrezâd framework, and the **"Envier and Envied"** story of the Second Mendicant in **"The Three Ladies,"** both instructive insertions too, belong to the old core. They all contribute to the curiously intricate Chinese-boxes pattern that characterizes the whole first part of the *1001 Nights.*

If the majority of the inserted stories in the book are thus presented by way of moral advice proffered by the characters in the main story, a small number are given for other reasons or even, apparently, for hardly any reason at all. The somewhat dogmatic pertinence of the Indian device contrasts sharply with the varied and mostly rather offhand proceedings we meet in stories which are less old. But just because of this greater liberty, the degree of craftsmanship and skill in using the insertion technique can be all the more clearly distinguished.

Thus for instance, a completely purposeless, non-functional and, moreover, clumsily presented insertion is found in the feeble third part of **"Kamar Ez-Zamân"**[27], with the story of **"Ni'ma and Nu'm."** The cruel Magian Bahrâm, the villain of the plot, is on the point of being beheaded, but escapes execution by accepting Islam. To the two princes, who lament their sad experiences, he then says: *"Noble lords, do not weep! In the end you will be reunited with your family, just as Ni'ma and Nu'm were reunited." And as they asked: "what happened to Ni'ma and Nu'm?" Bahrâm related* . . . (II, 530). The old opening move works, but that is about all. The inserted love-story does in no conceivable manner apply to the situation of the princes, who, for that matter, can hardly be imagined as yearning for reunion with their family, since their father ordered their death and their mothers misconducted themselves and slandered them. The Magian for his part, although now a Moslem, has not been made sufficiently likable for the position of entertainer to the whole company. And lastly, the Ommayad court intrigue of **"Ni'ma and Nu'm,"** thus placed within the remote **"Kamar Ez-Zamân"** story, which moves vaguely through far-away countries and olden times, constitutes an anachronism that is glaring even for the *1001 Nights.* All this does not mean to say that the presence of the love-story is unfortunate. On the contrary, since it is as charming as the main story is tedious at this point, it provides a most welcome diversion. But this, unintentional, relieving effect does not in itself justify the thoughtless inserting, which only accentuates the incompetence of the creator or narrator who made up the third part of **"Kamar Ez-Zamân."**

On the other hand, a convincing use of insertions meets us in **Omar Ibn En-Nu'mân.** This novel, much worked over by, apparently, Egyptian narrators, carries several inserted stories, which vary with the different manuscripts[28]. One might suspect that later story-tellers found the main plot, on the whole, a little stern, and thought fit to brighten it up with contrasting material. Moreover, the unwieldy length of the novel may well have acted as an inducement to make it still longer. However that may be, the Calcutta II version displays some clever as well as pleasant insertions, showing that the old and in later times somewhat disused technique still had, on occasion, its artisans.

In the last part of **Omar Ibn En-Nu'mân,** two little stories are neatly made to serve a purpose. The jest of the **"Hashish-Eater"** is told by a murderess to her prospective victim, in order to put him at ease and make him forget caution. We see him fall into the trap: *When Kânmâ-kân had heard this story from the slave-girl, he laughed till he fell over backwards. And he said to Bakûn: "Nurse, that's an excellent story; I never heard the like of it. Do you know another?" "Yes, to be sure",* she said. *And now the slave-girl Bakûn continued to tell Kân-mâ-kân marvellous happenings and memorable merry events, till sleep came over him.* (II, 195-196). When tension has thus been carefully built up, Kân-mâ-kân's life is saved just in the nick of time.—Further on, the story of the **"Bedouin Hammâd"** makes for a surprise effect. The Bedouin, a robber, has been captured and is about to pay his misdeeds with his life; but he begs to be spared, promising to tell extraordinary adventures. Kân-mâ-kân intercedes for him, *and the kings ordered: "Well then, tell us a story!" "O greatest kings of our time",* he asked, *"if I tell you a wonderfully fine story, will you let me off?" This was granted by the kings, and the Bedouin began to tell the most interesting of his experiences.* (II, 210-211). This gambit—a good story for a life—is not unusual, as we shall see later on; but here the point is that the Bedouin candidly proceeds to tell about one of his own villainous crimes. He murdered a noble Arab warrior, who gave him hospitality in the desert, because he coveted the young man's sister; she killed herself out of grief. To the Bedouin, who lacks all moral sense, this is merely a curious occurrence[29]; but the listeners are naturally moved to indignation and execute him on the spot. Instead of ransoming his life with his story, he has brought upon himself the punishment he fully deserved.

In the middle of the **Omar** novel, and considerably increasing its bulk, occurs the insertion of the full-length **"Tâj El-Mulûk,"** in which **"Azîz and Azîza"** is inserted in its turn as an autobiographical secondary story[30]. It is placed, aptly, at a moment when the war-like action has come to a temporary standstill. The

Mural depicting the winged ebony horse from The Arabian Nights *(Aladdin Resort, Las Vegas).*

heroic king Sharkân has been murdered in his sleep by an enemy agent; his young half-brother Dau el-Makân and the faithful vizir have set up siege before Constantinople, intending to conquer it and to revenge Sharkân's death, but it can already be foreseen that they will not achieve their aim. They deliberate day and night about matters of strategy, *but Dau el-Makân continued to be depressed by mournful sorrow, and finally he said: "I long to hear stories about people, adventures of kings and stories of the slaves of love; perhaps Allah then will take from my heart this sorrow deep, so that I may cease to lament and weep." And the vizir said: "If your sorrow can be cast out only by hearing notable stories and adventures of kings and tales about the slaves of love from olden times and suchlike things, the matter is easy; for when your late father lived I had nothing to do but to tell stories and to recite verse to him. This very night I will tell you the story of a lover and his beloved, so that your breast will not be constricted any more."* (I, 765).

Dau el-Makân looks forward greatly to the entertainment; a few emirs are invited too, and they settle down comfortably by lamplight, *with everything they needed*

in the way of food, drink and perfumes. (I, 765). Still, it is hardly to be supposed that the vizir finished his double love-story that same night, as it runs to a hundred and thirty pages. The point is not cleared up, perhaps intentionally, for the long insertion represents, as it were, the time spent on the unsuccessful siege: *All this happened while they were besieging Constantinople. But after four years had passed, they began to long for their country; the troops murmured [. . .]. And the vizir said to the king: "Know, o greatest king of our time, our staying here has been to no avail. Therefore I think we should depart now and return to our native land, and remain there for a few years on end. Then we will again march out valiantly, and wage war against idolatry." "That is excellent advice", said the king.* (II, 134-135). Thus sped along by the insertion, which distracts attention from the failure and creates, indeed, the illusion that something "happened", the main story nimbly moves away from where it had got bogged down.—The Egyptian compilers, when they put in the **Omar** novel, did not choose the most appropriate place for it; but, by design or by chance, it furnishes a fine contribution to the display of inserted stories in the first part of the book.

As we have seen, the story-tellers of the Baghdadian and of the Egyptian period forsook the instructive insertion along with the foreign models that imported it; this particular device, which does not quite agree with the spirit of Arabic story-telling, was never assimilated. As far as they still employ inserted stories, they present them without any moralizing or didactic intention, in a free and easy manner, variously adapted to the situations arising in the main story. In a few cases, the insertion serves a purely artistic purpose: thus in **"The Awakened Sleeper,"** where the little **"The Tramp and the Cook"** amusingly mirrors the theme of the main story[31], and in **"Ghânim,"** where the two eunuch stories provide suspense and contrast[32]. The autobiographical insertion acquaints us with the past life and adventures of the characters in the main story: thus **"The Princess of Daryabâr"** in **"Khudadâd,"** and the proportionally too long story of **"Janshâh,"** which satisfies the curiosity of Bulûkiya in **"The Serpent Queen."**

Practised in this way, insertion is an unpretentious but quite satisfactory technique. It brings about a sudden shifting of the interest that is refreshing, and it may achieve all sorts of pleasant effects, by providing a foil to the main story, a surprise, a transition, or just an ornament. All in all, it seems so well suited to the ways of the *1001 Nights* that one wonders why it is so sparingly employed. My impression is that, from early times on, the prevailing tendency was to make the surrounding story subservient to the one that is placed inside it; in other words, that frame-story technique was preferred to the inserting of stories. Their essential difference is that, while the latter creates merely a narrative diversion, the former is determined by and centred upon the act of narrating. To put it strongly: the subject of the frame-story is story-telling. So it seems very appropriate that this pattern should be the prevailing one in the *1001 Nights*.

FRAME-STORIES

A frame-story[33] may be defined as a narrative whole composed of two distinct but connected parts: a story, or stories, told by a character or several characters in another story of lesser dimensions and subordinate interest, which thus encloses the former as a frame encloses a picture. The *1001 Nights* presents three basic types of the pattern, determined by the function of the framed story in relation to the plot of the framework: we may call them the entertaining frame, the time-gaining frame and the ransom frame. They will be discussed here in this order, which corresponds to an increasing importance of the issue involved in the telling of the framed story.

ENTERTAINING FRAME

The simplest type is the entertaining frame; it merely presents a character (or several in turn) telling a story for the pleasure of one or more listeners. It mostly dispenses with elaborate stage-setting, except in those Harûn stories that begin by making the disguised caliph assist at some intriguing scene. The interest concentrates on the framed story, which is told for its own sake and serves merely to provide entertainment, or occasionally, to satisfy curiosity. Harûn er-Rashîd needs stories to allay his restlessness and prepare him for sleep; and other caliphs too, thought not endowed with the distinctive feature of insomnia, often ask one of their familiars to relate a memorable experience, by way of pastime. Even the mamluk sultan Baibars, the story says, *had a liking for all that is told among the folk, and all that men choose to believe; and he always wanted to assist in person and to listen when there was talk about such things* (IV, 776); so he had the captains of his watch assembled to hear about the strange events they met with in the course of their careers. (If this is authentic, it might be a case of "life imitating art": Baibars modelling himself upon the caliphs as presented in fiction.) Normally, the entertainer is of a humbler condition than the listener who is being entertained; there are no examples, in the *1001 Nights,* of a caliph telling a story himself. Only in **"Sindbad the Sailor,"** the customary roles are reversed, and the distinguished, wealthy man's entertaining—in every sense of the word—the poor man gives added point to the frame.

In this type, structural interference between the frame and the related story is comparatively rare. Most often, the listening caliph simply dismisses the teller with a few words of comment, and a reward. Occasionally, he orders that the persons about whom he has just heard be brought before him, to make their acquaintance and bestow benefits upon them: thus, el-Mamûn wants to see the six well-spoken slave-girls (46), and the generous merchant (103). However, already here there is sometimes a striving to connect frame and story more closely, making each of them dependent on the other for its point. The stories of the Ladies of Baghdad account for their strange behaviour, as described in the framework; in **"Nocturnal Adventures,"** too, the autobiographical stories of the three protagonists explain the puzzling things that were first related about them. A less spectacular, but extremely skilful connexion is made in **"Abu El-Hasan from Khorasân,"** where a veritable little mystery is set up in the frame, to be solved in the story. The caliph's amazement and displeasure at noticing valuable property marked with the name of his grandfather el-Mutawakkil in the house of an unknown businessman, are dispelled when he is told how this came about through his grandfather's magnanimity. Still, the only case where the entertaining frame is an integral part of the whole, not only completely motivated, but functional in bringing out the story's intention, is, again, **"Sindbad the Sailor"**[34].

To this first, simple type belongs also the very elaborate and historically interesting frame of "Saif El-Mulûk," which even has a title of its own, **"Story of King Mohammed Ibn Sabaïk and the Merchant Hasan."** It shows how high a value was set, at the time, upon a good story, and it certainly has some foundation in fact, for all the romantic embellishment of the circumstances. The figure of the dignified sheik, who gives permission to copy the **"Saif El-Mulûk"** story, but strictly specifies the kinds of public worthy or unworthy of hearing it, may in a certain measure correspond to the reality of a good story-telling period[35]. It also seems authentic that the story is copied from a book, and carefully checked, whereas the king, every time he wants to hear it again, has it read out aloud to him.—Artistically, however, this unique frame is a misfit, because, as Lane already remarked[36], the story it serves to frame does not live up to it. After having been made to expect something incomparable, the reader is disappointed by an unoriginal and mediocre piece, remarkable chiefly for its length.

The entertaining frame, which prepares the telling of the story and surrounds it with a definite atmosphere, certainly adds to the appeal of the whole; from a technical point of view, though, it most often remains relatively ingenuous. The frame-story offers other, less obvious possibilities.

TIME-GAINING FRAME

The time-gaining frame, a more complicated type than the one just discussed, serves notably to string together large collections of stories, whose function within the frame is to help put off an execution or another calamitous event. This pattern, apparently of Indian origin[37], is not indigenous in the *1001 Nights;* it is found only in a few stories that were adapted from the Persian. Nevertheless it occupies a place of unique importance, as it furnished the framework for the collection itself: Shehrezâd temporizes by making one story follow another, until at last she has gained her victory.

The Shehrezâd story, though made up from bits and pieces[38] and having an indefinable air of foreignness and oddity about it, is all that a framing story should be. The story-teller who patched it together is a little long in coming to the point, but he struggles valiantly along with a firm purpose in mind[39]. First, the misconduct of the two queens shows that women can be very depraved, then the demon episode illustrates their appalling boldness and resourcefulness in depravity, and finally, in striking contrast to this black picture of womanhood, Shehrezâd appears on the scene, self-sacrificing, chaste, learned; she, too, is bold and resourceful, but she uses her gifts nobly, not viciously. She is going to play for time, to save herself and many

other girls fated to die, just by telling stories. It is no wonder that this plot had a world-wide success: it works up a quite unexpectedly charming and simple suspense situation, to which the story-book itself will finally furnish the denouement.

Notwithstanding this excellent start, though, as a framed collection the *1001 Nights* has no firm structure: the working-out falls short of the idea. As soon as the telling of the stories begins, the framework seems gradually to fade away. King Shehriyâr rarely comments on what he has heard[40]; only in the little series of fables in the first part of the book, a compiler put in some grateful remarks and requests: *"O Shehrezâd, you have given me still more wise warnings and lessons by what you have told. Do you also know any stories about the animals of the field?"* (II, 248)[41]. The last of such remarks occurs, as an afterthought, at the end of 22; from then on, there is no more comment between the stories[42], which follow each other without transition or with a simple "Furthermore it is told . . .". The failure to keep the framework functioning throughout the collection is illustrated by the fact that its conclusion varies in the different texts, and sometimes is lacking altogether.—All this must partly be put down to the plot itself, which, involving only one reciter and one listener (two if we count Dinazâd in), is not solid enough, as it were, to carry the weight of so many stories. A very large framed collection is more convincingly presented when the roles are distributed among a little company, every member of it telling a story in his turn while the others listen. A larger cast also favours the exchange of comment, which lends variety and depth to the whole; and above all, it offers an opportunity for creating a relation between the personality and circumstances of each character, and the stories he tells[43].

Such a relation between the framed stories and the frame is lacking in the *1001 Nights.* To be sure, it would have been difficult to keep up in so vast a collection, and necessarily would have limited its scope. Yet, especially in the beginning it is somewhat surprising when Shehrezâd's stories seem so ill-adapted to the dangerous situation she had put herself in. The first one, **"The Merchant and the Demon,"** already presents two wicked wives, and in the second one, **"The Fisherman and the Demon,"** the last part seems a particularly tactless choice under the circumstances: the queen's morbid infatuation with the negro slave can scarcely have been a pleasant topic to king Shehriyâr. In the fourth one, **"The Three Apples,"** the plot turns again upon a negro slave supposed to have won his mistress's favours, although the suspicion turns out to be unfounded. All in all, in the first few stories, if we try to connect them with the frame, Shehrezâd appears to be rubbing in the king's conjugal misfortune, rather than helping him to get over it; unless we interpret her choice as destined to show the king that he is not the only one to suffer, but nothing bears out this interpretation[44].

The obvious explanation is that the compilers did not consider the point; they did not strive to interrelate stories and frame, nor to keep alive the interest in the framing story itself. Consequently, just as they did, we gradually forget Shehrezâd and her plight, and concentrate all our attention upon the stories she tells. There remains only the rhythmical division into Nights, with its standing transition formulas, to remind us in passing of the clever woman who is still playing for time.

Apart from the Shehrezâd story, the time-gaining frame is something of a rarity in the *1001 Nights.* A doubtful case is **"The Serpent Queen,"** where it does not become quite clear whether the long framed story with its oversized insertion[45] is told for its own sake, or to put off the young hero's return to the upper world, which will cause the Serpent Queen's death. At first she refuses to let him go, and keeps him occupied with the story of Bulûkiya; later, when he has obtained permission to return, he voluntarily stays on for a while to hear the story of Janshâh. I confess that I should need more data on the framework of **"The Serpent Queen"**[46]—which looks like a batch of old material in a mediocre Egyptian version—to grasp its implications.

The framed collection of **"The Seven Vizirs"**[47] on the contrary, an adaptation from the Persian that was incorporated in the *1001 Nights* by later compilers, is carefully arranged in an elegant time-gaining frame. The telling of the stories is doubly functional here, as it serves a double purpose: to persuade, as well as to gain time. A king's favourite has treacherously accused the prince, his son, of trying to seduce her, and the king proposes to put his son to death. His vizirs are trying to save the prince, not only by the delaying action of the stories, but also by making them furnish arguments against the deed: they try to exemplify the dangers of rashness and the malice of women, while the spiteful favourite retaliates by telling about unreliable vizirs and the wickedness of men. The advantages of the pattern are evident: a captivating interrelation of framework and stories, and, in the series of stories itself, a debate effect that makes for variety and surprise. The result might have been a structural masterpiece, if only the stories were to the purpose; but, oddly enough, most of them are not[48]. The first vizir, already, opens the series with a tale in which a woman, tactfully defending her virtue, has the *beau rôle*. The first tale of the second vizir is, at best, a warning against stinginess, and in that of the fourth vizir, the husband is really more immoral than the wife (139a, e, k). The favourite, in her turn, misses the mark with her fourth story (139m), about a man who invents an unusual stratagem to conquer his

beloved, but without meaning or doing any harm at all[49]. And so on: even the gem of the series as it stands in the *1001 Nights,* the memorable **"Woman with Five Suitors,"** is too ambiguous to make the point required by the framing story. Told by the sixth vizir, it certainly sets forth an uncommonly fine example of the malice of women, but it is the men who are dissolute and abuse their power; the woman merely takes advantage of their illicit pursuits to further her own, relatively legitimate aim—freeing her lover from prison—and shames them quite deservedly. All these inconsistencies detract from the effect of the pattern; they may, however, be due not to carelessness on the part of the original creator, but to the transformations which the story underwent in the course of transmission.

Thus, the *1001 Nights* offers no examples of a particularly skilful use of the time-gaining frame. And yet, the two are inseparable in every reader's memory. Beyond all technical cavilling, the compelling plot of the Shehrezâd story remains one of the most remarkable artistic achievements of the book.

RANSOM FRAME

Lastly, there is the ransom frame, which must be examined here with particular care, as it is represented in the *1001 Nights* by some very interesting pieces, more or less connected with and dependent upon each other, as I hope to show. In this type, the telling of stories has a paramount function: it serves to redeem a human life. The frame is set up to show how somebody came to be threatened with imminent execution; the story or stories told, either by the condemned man himself or by people intervening in his favour, may, if found good enough, redeem him. A very important issue depends, therefore, on their quality, and on the taste of the listener who holds the decision in his hands.

The very first story of the *1001 Nights* in all known recensions, **"The Merchant and the Demon"**[50], shows the pattern in its simplest form. A merchant travelling in the desert is menaced by a demon; three sheiks save his life by telling a story each. Now it has often been remarked upon, and every reader can see for himself, that Shehrezâd is given a surprisingly insignificant piece for a beginning. Indeed, its shortcomings are only too apparent. The arrival of the three sheiks with their animals at the right time and place is in no way motivated; the demon, after each story, willingly renounces a third of the merchant's blood, so that there is no uncertainty as to the final success; and worst of all, the three narrations rather monotonously develop the same motif, the transformation of human beings into animals. Almost any story in the collection might have made a better opening than this one.

Macdonald[51] has attempted to offer, for this anomaly, a historical explanation, which seems very plausible; it is connected with an anecdote apropos of the Arabic word *khurâfa,* meaning "a (pleasant) fictitious story". A 13th-century author states, giving the chain of witnesses, that Mohammed once told Aïsha a story about a man named Khurâfa, who was captured by three demons, and redeemed by three passers-by who each told an amazing incident (one of these involving a transformation). Our **"The Merchant and the Demon"** is so like the Khurâfa story as to appear just another, somewhat more elaborate version of it. Macdonald therefore surmises that it is a left-over, taken along with the Shehrezâd frame, of an older form of the *1001 Nights,* composed throughout of simple, relatively short, and purely Arabic stories such as this one.

If the Khurâfa story really goes back to Mohammed's time, the ransom frame would be quite an old pattern indeed. If, on the other hand, it was made up later, as an attempt to provide the word *khurâfa* with an etymology[52], it may have been modelled upon **"The Merchant and the Demon,"** though on internal criteria this latter seems the younger one. Yet even in that case, the place of honour assigned to **"The Merchant and the Demon"** is still well explained by its being assuredly one of the oldest stories in the book, "of a pronounced desert and Arabic type"[53], as Macdonald says.

From a literary point of view, the question is how we are to understand the peculiar ransom frame here displayed, and what assured the lasting success of this pattern. Its two essential features seem to be: the value of good stories, rated so high that they balance the scales against a human life; and the fact that the bargain is made—in this oldest form, represented also by the Khurâfa story—not with another human being, but with a demon, of the species called Jinni (plural Jinn).

The lively appreciation of a good story may perhaps be explained, to a certain extent, by the conditions of life in pre-Islamic and early Islamic times. In a society where entertainments were few and reading not within everybody's reach, the resources of human intercourse were of great importance: they not only provided diversion, but ranked among man's principal means of asserting himself as a civilized being. Stories, as much as poetry, could be perpetuated by oral tradition, and there is ample proof that they were. Later, when a more refined urban culture prevailed over desert life, the particular form of pastime offered by story-telling found its professionals; this development affirms its lasting popularity, of which the *1001 Nights* in all its aspects offers such interesting proof.

Stranger, at first sight, seems the role of the demons. In the Khurâfa story, they take the man prisoner for no reason at all, and then deliberate among themselves what they shall do: kill him, enslave him, or let him off.

"The Merchant and the Demon" gives a motivation: the merchant has accidently killed the Jinni's son, and the father has a right to revenge. But in both cases, the stories told by the human intercessors apparently afford such gratification to the Jinn that they willingly consent to let their captive go free. As the *1001 Nights*-story has it: *when the third sheik had told his story, even more wonderful than the first two, the demon was all amazement; he wriggled with pleasure, and exclaimed: "Lo, I acquit you of the rest of the merchant's debt, and I grant his freedom unto you all."* (I, 48).

There is an odd naïveté, at the same time endearing and puzzling, in this gratitude of an other-world being for stories from this world. But no doubt it seems stranger to us than it did to the Arabs, who lived on a footing of relative familiarity with Jinn and regarded them as different, certainly, from humans, but not basically or incommensurably so[54]. (They are not immortal, and may be killed by men; most of them accepted Islam.) The implication of the stories under discussion seems to be, if we put it in modern terms, that Jinn are subject to boredom and want entertainment, just as humans do[55]. Their wanton capturing of Khurâfa and then not quite knowing what to do with him is well in keeping with this interpretation. And we might even remember, in this context, the Koran's telling how the Jinn try to ascend to the lowest spheres of heaven because they want to overhear the angels, who chase them away by hurling meteors at them[56]. Fundamentally, the ransom frame as presented here affirms human superiority: Jinn may be stronger than men and often redoubtable, but men's words charm them, men's lives are more interesting than theirs.

Let us now turn to a general survey of the beginning of the *1001 Nights.* In the chief mss. of the Oriental family as well as in ZER, the first five pieces are the following:

(1) "The Merchant and the Demon."

(2) "The Fisherman and the Demon," + "The Petrified Prince."

(3) "The Three Ladies."

(4) "The Three Apples" + "Nûr Ed-Dîn and Shems Ed-Dîn."

(5) "The Hunchback."

Of these five stories, four display the ransom frame in one form or another; and, curiously enough, thereafter it is not found any more in the whole of the *1001 Nights*[57]. Oestrup did remark that the first stories of the collection are characterized by an "Einschachtelungsmethode"[58], which, however, he did not analyse in detail, nor try to explain. To find out the possible reasons for this recurrence of the same pattern in just one place of the book, we must closely examine the first five stories, and compare them from a structural point of view.

After (1) **"The Merchant and the Demon,"** already discussed, follows (2) **"The Fisherman and the Demon,"** which treats the same theme: when the fisherman has unintentionally liberated the menacing demon (a Mârid this time) who is resolved to kill him, he says to himself: *"This is a demon, and I am a human being, Allah has given me intelligence; so by my astuteness and intelligence I will undo him, even as he meant to undo me in his treacherous wickedness."* (I, 54). And he defeats the demon by his superior human wit. This piece is the only one of the five that is not a frame-story; its first part employs the kindred insertion technique[59], its sequel, **"The Petrified Prince,"** is half-appended, half-inserted in a somewhat puzzling manner[60], probably due either to an unskilful narrator or to damage in transmission. In the next story, the Baghdadian (3) **"The Three Ladies,"** the ransom device crops up in an unsatisfactory form, as we shall presently see. To (4) **"The Three Apples,"** a short and well-constructed Harûn story of the Baghdad period, was joined later the much longer, Egyptian, **"Nûr Ed-Dîn and Shems Ed-Dîn,"** in such a way that the latter functions as a ransom for the culprit of the former. And lastly, there is **"The Hunchback,"** a ransom-frame story throughout, and a highly complicated one, displaying no less than eleven stories within its frame.—In the last three pieces, the old frame-pattern is, as it were, secularized: instead of a Jinni, it is a caliph or a king, or a wealthy lady, who threatens people's lives and listens to the ransom stories[61]. It will be necessary now to discuss these last three pieces one by one, with special reference to the way in which the ransom frame is employed in each of them, in order to establish their relation to the opening story and to each other.

First of all, an analysis of the problematical **"The Three Ladies"**[62], which will require an exact outline of the plot.

Three ladies admit into their house a porter who has carried the provisions bought by the lady housekeeper. They are passing a merry evening with him, when three one-eyed mendicants knock at the door, and are admitted. A little later Harûn er-Rashîd arrives with Ja'far and Masrûr, disguised as foreign merchants, saying they have lost their way in the city. To all these seven men, the ladies give warning that they must not ask questions about what does not concern them. After some more drinking and amusement follows the intriguing episode where the eldest lady whips two bitches, and the lady doorkeeper faints three times upon hearing a sad song, thereby revealing scars of a beating. Harûn forces Ja'far to ask questions; the eldest lady, indignant, summons

seven negro slaves, who make ready to behead the guests. The caliph, frightened, wants to give up his incognito, but the lady is already questioning the mendicants, who state that they are all sons of kings. Thereupon the eldest lady invites them, and by implication the other guests also, to tell their stories, after which she will let them go free; but it is not expressly stipulated that the stories are to serve as a ransom. First the porter, by way of a joke, describes the shopping tour he made with the lady housekeeper, saying: "This is my story"; the eldest lady laughs, and lets him off. But he prefers to stay and hear the others: it has already become clear that the lady's anger has spent itself, and that the guests are no longer in great danger. Then the three mendicants successively tell the stories of their lives and adventures, which for each of them involve notably the explanation of how they came to be blinded in the left eye. There is a marked climax in the series: each story is longer and more complicated than the preceding one. In the **"First Mendicant"**'s there is no relation between his cousin's crime and subsequent death, and his own misfortunes; the whole thing is rather indifferently put together. The **"Second Mendicant"** reports his adventure with a dangerous demon (an Ifrît) who nearly killed him, and to whom he tells the tale of **"The Envier and the Envied"** by way of a moral lesson[63]. The Ifrît relents in so far that he merely changes the prince into a monkey; it takes a frightful transformation combat to restore him to human shape. The **"Third Mendicant"**'s story is extremely long: it stresses the ineluctability of fate, makes an abundant use of the number 40, and in its last part exploits the well-known marvellous motif of the forbidden door[64].—The caliph and his company, finally, are not required to tell anything; they simply repeat that they are foreign merchants. The eldest lady forgives all the guests, saying: *"I grant you each other's lives"* (I, 185), which we apparently must take to mean that the mendicants, by telling their stories, have redeemed the rest.

The next day, the caliph has them all brought before him, and now it is the ladies' turn to tell their stories. The **"Eldest Lady"**'s is an elaborate version of the story of the Second Sheik in **"The Merchant and the Demon"**: the two bitches are her wicked sisters, transformed by a demoness whose life she saved[65]. The **"Lady Doorkeeper"**'s is a purely Baghdadian short story of married life, involving as a husband Harûn's own son el-Amîn. The Lady Housekeeper does not tell a story. Harûn puts things right: the demoness is summoned and takes the spell off the two sisters, while el-Amîn is reconciled with his repudiated wife. The eldest lady and the two sisters who just returned to human shape are given in marriage to the mendicants, who are granted posts and incomes, and the lady housekeeper takes a place among Harûn's wives. All the stories are put down in the annals of the realm.

As this outline shows, the structure of the whole seems more than a little out of joint in several places. The mendicants' stories are too long, particularly the last one. What is unusual, though, in the *1001 Nights,* is not their length, but their being misplaced: they hold the story up with a minor issue when a major one has just been raised. Coming immediately after the ladies' strange behaviour, which arouses a much stronger curiosity than do the persons of the mendicants, they cause an unwelcome delay in the explanation of the mysteries of the household. Then, when we finally come back to the ladies and their stories, it is strange and somewhat disappointing that the lady housekeeper, who was introduced first and seems the most attractive person of the three, has nothing to tell. Even symmetry would demand that she, too, should have had a misfortune which caused her to live with her sisters, instead of being a married woman.

But above all, the telling of the mendicants' stories is not sufficiently motivated. There can be distinguished an attempt to employ the ransom device: the eldest lady's anger at the indiscretion of Ja'far, and the menacing display of seven negro slaves—one for each guest— with drawn swords, are clearly meant to prepare for it. The attempt, however, does not come off: the conditions are not clearly stated and the anger is soon forgotten. Now the reason why the device fails to work lies in the plot itself: the characters are miscast. The role belonging to a demon (or a king) falls to a mere Baghdadian lady, which causes an improbability not easily glossed over; and what is worse, the caliph, who would have fitted the part much better, is among the threatened guests. This fact alone would thwart the setting-up of a ransom frame: it is impossible to believe that Harûn could ever be in serious danger of being beheaded in a private house. One hint at his identity would be enough to change the whole course of events. As a matter of fact, the story wavers at the point where Harûn wants to protect himself by telling who he is, but does not get a chance, because the lady has already turned to the mendicants.

This particular passage most clearly demonstrates the clash between the two different patterns that can be distinguished throughout in the story. On the one hand, there is the well-known plot that turns on the presence of Harûn incognito; on the other hand, the ransom device that is intended to motivate the telling of the mendicants' stories. The two are incompatible, and the result is that neither of them really takes shape. Evidently, a simpler but much more satisfactory plot would emerge if the story were not encumbered by the mendicants. Its obvious, and traditional, outline would be the following:

(1) The porter introduced into the house of the three ladies; drinking and singing.

(2) Arrival of Harûn and his company, attracted by the noise; whipping of the bitches, fainting of the lady doorkeeper.

Either the guests leave without asking questions, or Harûn asks questions, but justifies himself by revealing his identity.

(3) The next day, the three sisters are brought before him, and tell:
    a. the story of the Eldest Lady and the two bitches;
    b the story of the Lady Doorkeeper and el-Amîn;
    [c. the story of the Lady Housekeeper].

(4) Harûn arranges things for all three of them.

The stories of the ladies would be quite sufficient to justify the framework—evidently of the entertaining frame-type—presenting Harûn as an unknown visitor. With the mendicants' stories the abortive ransom frame disappears, together with the improbability it entails. In this hypothetical form, **"The Three Ladies"** would be strikingly similar to another Harûn story, **"Nocturnal Adventures."** Here, too, we have a common entertaining frame for three stories of personal experience (one of them, again, an elaborate version of one of the sheiks' stories from **"The Merchant and the Demon"**). But seeing that **"Nocturnal Adventures,"** one of the orphan stories, probably owes its present structure to Galland[66], it does not afford conclusive proof of the existence of this very pattern in the *1001 Nights.*

The foregoing literary analysis raises a historical question: whether the mendicants' stories are a later addition. The fact that they are of no great artistic merit and dislocate the whole is not in itself a sufficient reason to consider them as such. It would be different if they were manifestly younger than the rest of the story; but that is not the case. They present many elements that point to old, presumably Persian, sources[67], and may well belong to the Persian layer of the collection. Thus there are no chronological grounds to consider the mendicants episode as alien to the original of the story.

We are left, therefore, with two equally valid suppositions as to the origin of **"The Three Ladies."** Either, the story was first created in the simple form tentatively outlined above; thereafter a narrator, wishing to extend and to enrich it, worked it over to fit in the mendicants' stories, failing, however, to bring off their ransom frame, because it clashed with the already existing pattern. Or, alternatively, it was the original creator of the story who made an ambitious effort to set up a sort of double frame, but, having attempted too much, did not quite succeed.—As to the Lady Housekeeper's story, perhaps it was never there; perhaps it was lost in transmission; or just possibly it may have been struck out, if and when the mendicants' stories were worked in by a second hand, for reasons we can only guess at: did it by any chance contain the incest motif now figuring, somewhat disconnectedly, in the **"First Mendicant"**'s story? Unless an Arabic text is found that can throw new light on these historical problems and alternatives, we must needs leave them as they are.

As we saw, **"The Merchant and the Demon"** undoubtedly influenced **"The Three Ladies"**: it furnished the tentative ransom frame of the mendicants' episode as well as the plot of the **"Eldest Lady"**'s story. Returning to our examination of the first five pieces of the collection we may now conclude that the first three, in any case, are connected in more than one respect. It seems a reasonable surmise that the early compilers realized this connexion, and that it determined the placing together of these stories in the order still extant. The old relic, **"The Merchant and the Demon,"** traditionally came first; then follows **"The Fisherman and the Demon"** as another demonstration of man's superiority, and then **"The Three Ladies"** as an elaborate offspring of the opening story.

This surmise gains in plausibility because it can be demonstrated that in the Egyptian period, the impact of the pattern set by the opening story was still felt, and continued to shape the beginning of the book. It determined the Egyptian narrator who prolonged **"The Three Apples"** by **"Nûr Ed-Dîn and Shems Ed-Dîn,"** to link up the two by means of the ransom device: Ja'far tells the story to Harûn in order that his guilty negro slave shall be spared, and Harûn consents, on condition that the story be more amazing than the case of the three apples. It must be said, however, that the device is out of place here just as it is in **"The Three Ladies,"** although to a lesser degree: it does not harm the whole, but it lacks motivation. The plot of **"The Three Apples"** does not ask for the slave's life to be spared: on the contrary, it would be more satisfactory to see him punished for the wanton harm he has done[68]. And why should Ja'far take such pains to save just one slave, among the many he had? The Egyptian narrator, wanting to place the delightful **"Nûr Ed-Dîn"** story, must have given it a ransom frame, deliberately, although not very judiciously, in order to follow the prevailing pattern of the preceding stories.

Lastly, there can be no doubt that this same awareness of the pattern provoked the crowning of the first batch with **"The Hunchback,"** which is a kind of virtuoso's performance among ransom frame-stories. The device is given here exactly the same turn as in the framing of **"Nûr Ed-Dîn and Shems Ed-Dîn"**: the king promises grace on condition that the stories told to him be more amazing than what he has just heard. The similarity is probably due to influence of the one on the other, but it is impossible to establish priority on chronological grounds[69]. Now in **"The Hunchback,"** at last, every-

thing functions to perfection; if the story had been expressly contrived for the purpose of rounding off the "ransom frame series", it could not have been more satisfactory. To complete the present survey, therefore, particular attention must be paid to this last and best example of the pattern in question.

"The Hunchback"[70] derives its amazing pleasantness mainly from the expert framing, as the eleven stories fitted into it, though mostly good, are none of them outstanding. It almost seems as if the creator—or possibly, the narrator who achieved the present version—realized that he was working with somewhat commonplace and heterogeneous material, and, in order to make something new and surprising out of it, concentrated upon the framework. He certainly was familiar with the ransom device from the older stories to which his is a follow-up, and he well understood its possibilities and its requirements. He realized, as the man who added the sequel to **"The Three Apples"** did not, that the life or lives to be redeemed with stories must be those of innocent people; and also, as the creator or narrator of **"The Three Ladies"** did not, that the Jinni of the original form can be adequately replaced only by someone who wields absolute power: a king, and the more wilful and arbitrary a king, the better. And his is, too, the only story of the four where it remains captivatingly doubtful till the very end as to whether the ransom will be accepted or not.

The first episode, which sets up the frame for all that is to follow, exploits the well-known comic effects of repetition. A tailor and his wife invite an amusing little hunchback to supper; but unfortunately he chokes on a bite of fish, and dies. They quickly invent a pretext to carry him into the house of a Jewish doctor, who falls over the corpse on the stairs and thinks he killed it. So he puts the corpse in the yard of his neighbour, a steward, who in the dark mistakes it for a thief and deals it a heavy blow. Believing himself to be the killer, he hastily drags the corpse away and leaves it in a dark street, where a Christian broker, who is blind drunk, falls to fighting with it; caught beating the dead man, he is taken for a murderer, brought before the prefect of police, and sentenced to the gallows. The various misfortunes of the four men become more amusing every time they are repeated, unaccountably, as if the dead hunchback was accident-prone. The same applies to their reactions, each of them in his turn deciding to get rid of the corpse no matter how. When the last one in the chain, the Christian broker, is about to be hanged, the repetition is reversed: one after the other, the self-supposed hunchback-killers come forward, conscience-stricken, and confess, so that the hangman gets fed up with taking them off the rope in turn. This ludicrously repetitive pattern gives (as do similar devices on the stage) an odd impression of something mechanical and quite unlike real life, which fits in very well with the preposterousness of the whole affair.

At the end of the first episode, the frame is ready for the stories to begin. Brought before the king, who very much resents the death of the hunchback, his favourite jester, the four men are going to tell, each in his turn, the most memorable story they ever heard. It soon becomes clear, although it is not expressly stated at once, that by doing so they are going to fight for their lives; for the required ransom is not just any story, but a story still more amazing than the hunchback's posthumous adventures. And the king, unlike the Jinni of old, is not easily satisfied. After each of the first three stories—the Christian broker's, the Moslem steward's, and the Jewish doctor's—he declares: *"This story is not more amazing than the story of the hunchback. And so you shall have to hang, all of you."* (I, 318, 330, 343). The judgment is fair enough: the three stories are indeed less surprising than what has just been told about the hunchback. But the inference is, again, preposterous; and here the effect of the repetition is sinister as well as comic, a kind of "humour noir".

The first series of four stories is knit together by several analogies, among with the repetition of the mutilation motif is prominent. Each of the four men reports, not a personal experience, but an extraordinary adventure told by someone else[71], some man he met in the course of his day's work or at a social function; and every time the account of this adventure serves to explain a bodily defect. Two of the stories' heroes had their right hands cut off, having been taken for thieves; one is deprived of his thumbs and great toes, to remind him of having offended a woman; and the last one is lame from an unfortunate accident. The motif might be due to a reminiscence of the three one-eyed mendicants from **"The Three Ladies"**; but in this homely form it appears less far-fetched and artificial than it does there. Another improvement is the fact that the mutilation is attributed to a third person, which puts the man who reports about it in the same position as the reader: intrigued at first, and subsequently pleased when his curiosity is satisfied by the mutilated man's account.

But, as we saw, after three of these stories the victims are still under the menace of death. So everything comes to depend on the fourth one, the Moslem tailor's; which is only right and proper, for the tailor was the initial cause of the whole chain of accidents. The king, with grim joviality, puts the responsibility plainly before him: *"Why, there still is the tailor, who made this sad mess."* And he added: *"Tailor, my little fellow, if you can tell something that is more amazing than the story of the hunchback, I'll forgive every man of you."* (I, 343). So the tailor comes forward and embarks upon

what to all appearances is going to be the fourth mutilation story. But he knows well enough that merely another specimen like the foregoing will not save their necks: a special effort is called for. Therefore he presently makes it clear that the real hero of his story is not the lame young man from Baghdad, but a character that at first seemed only episodical: the barber. And as soon as the barber is in the limelight, the whole situation changes. For wherever stories are traded, the barber would spoil the market: he gives more than anyone ever bargained for.

The tailor has not set himself an easy task. First he gives the story told by the lame young man, who repeated for the benefit of his fellow-guests (among whom he found, to his dismay, the barber) the unbearable chatter by which the barber made him late for a rendezvous. Then he proceeds to tell how the barber tried to justify himself before the guests by relating an occasion where, brought before the caliph el-Mustansir-billâh[72], he discreetly held his tongue—though just then it would have been simpler to speak up. But that is not all: in order to illustrate his superior wisdom and discretion, the barber forced upon the caliph the life-stories of his six brothers, which he now tells once more to the guests. (These brothers are all of them deformed or mutilated too: the motif of physical disgrace continues to run through the framed stories, incessantly reminding us of the hunchback whose death they are to atone for.) The tailor draws upon the astonishing verbal memory that reporting characters in the *1001 Nights* occasionally display, and repeats all this before the king.

The effect of this wildly complicated, but at the same time perfectly clear pattern is, as it were, stratified: the reader enjoys the impact of the barber's torrent of talk on several planes of the story at once. First we have the caliph el-Mustansir-billâh, who for all his authority does not succeed in dismissing the barber, and must submit helplessly to hearing the stories of the man's six disgusting brothers till the very end. (Then he merely exiles him, a leniency that may be attributed as well to sheer fatigue as to a sense of humour.) Secondly, there are the guests at the banquet, who get all of it too, with the caliph's reactions added; and among them is the luckless young man from Baghdad, submitted once more to the word-flow of his former torturer, whom he wished never to see any more in his life. Thirdly there is the tailor, feverishly concentrating upon reproducing it all without skipping a word; for he hopes, thanks to the barber, to win the day by exhaustion tactics. Finally, the whole build-up ends with the "king of China", who has, in a way, asked for it, and who now is nearly as helpless as el-Mustansir-billâh was. The difference is that he gets it all at second hand, from the tailor; but just because of that, the barber becomes almost a mythical figure, a sort of god of loquacity who speaks through the tailor's mouth and cannot be silenced. It gradually becomes hard to believe that he exists at all. But the cumulative epic that involves him and his six brothers and the caliph and the young man from Baghdad and the tailor, has the success it was calculated to have. When the tailor has rounded off his performance by reporting briefly how the guests put the barber under lock and key (indeed the only efficacious way of dealing with him) and how he himself, coming home from the banquet, ran into his misadventure with the hunchback, the king confesses defeat. *When the king of China had heard the tailor's story, he shook his head in a pleased manner, manifested amazement, and said: "This story about the young man and the garrulous barber is indeed better and funnier than the story of the hunchbacked fool."* (I, 403). And then, striving to get back his hold upon reality after such a debauch of words, he orders the barber to be brought before him, which is a wise and sober decision.

Thereupon begins the brief final episode of the story, which is as fine as what went before. At last, then, the barber is there in the flesh, and the Egyptian feeling for detail asserts itself in a description: *he was a very old man of over ninety, with a dark complexion, white beard and eyebrows, small ears, a long nose, and a silly and conceited expression on his face.* (I, 404). And now, as it is hardly possible to cumulate still more, the whole construction is swiftly and expertly broken up. When the king jokingly invites him to tell a story, the barber asks instead for the stories of those he sees present; for, he huffily says, he is a discreet man and not for nothing is he dubbed "the Silent". So, it is briefly stated, they give him the story of the hunchback and all that has just been told by the broker, the steward, the doctor and the tailor, thus paying him back in his own coin[73]. Thereupon the barber, unruffled, and still extremely taciturn, examines the hunchback's corpse, pulls a fishbone out of his throat, and restores him to life.

It is extremely satisfying and right, not only that the tabor-playing little hunchback should still be alive, but that so much ado, such preposterous happenings and such heroic exploits with words should turn out to be, after all, about nothing. Because the hunchback was killed, there has been all this telling of stories, and stories within stories; but now that all the bags of words have been deflated and no one is talking any more, not even the barber, there is time at last to find out that nobody killed the hunchback at all. The pattern has been undone even to the basic knot; the story is finished indeed.

In the foregoing pages only one structural aspect of the *1001 Nights* has been investigated: the presenting of the stories, either independent or placed within other stories. As we have seen, the book displays many samples of remarkable craftsmanship in this matter. There is a careful appropriateness in the oblique presentation of witness pieces and short stories, a deft touch in many of the insertions, while frame-story technique is carried to perfection: Sindbad's Voyages and the narrations of **"The Hunchback"** are like precious (or, in the latter case, semi-precious) stones of which the value is enhanced by a superb setting. Evidently the story-tellers—I use the word here in the widest sense—were not content with just telling something; they show a particular regard for the narrative performance in its own right, and so does the listening public evoked in many of the stories.

The contents of the *1001 Nights* represent, by and large, a highly developed art of story-telling; the manner in which these contents are presented testifies to an intelligent feeling and liking for story-telling as a pastime. Yet, prose-fiction in Arabic never attained an acknowledged literary standing; while on the other hand its nobler competitors, epic poetry and drama, are conspicuously lacking. This state of affairs, within a literature so obviously endowed with narrative and descriptive gifts, puzzles the historian of literature and culture[74]. The "popular"[75] art of story-telling, though, doubtless profited greatly by its modest condition; it remained untrammelled by formalizing conventions, such as for centuries continued to govern the Kasîda. Its direct and easy way of being, combining effective artistry with freedom from period-bound literary rules, largely accounts for its lasting appeal to readers of any time and civilisation.

Notes

1. Some of these aspects are treated incidentally in other chapters [of this book], apropos of the stories examined: story patterns, Chap. IV, Part I, pp. 154-8, Part III, pp. 253-7, Chap. VI, pp. 437-8: a curious denouement device, Chap. VI, pp. 447-9; tripartition, Chap. IV, Part II, pp. 184-90, Part IV, pp. 285-95; types of Harûn stories, Chap. VI. [Chapter and page references throughout this essay are to *The Art of Story-Telling*.]

2. For the matters touched upon in this paragraph, an extremely clear summary is that of Mac Guckin de Slane in the *Introduction* to his translation of Ibn Khallikân's invaluable *Biographical Dictionary*, I, pp. XVII-XXXV.

3. For a recent aperçu, see Weisweiler, *Arabesken*, introduction, pp. 1-2.

4. In exploring, as far as I could, the literature of the Arabic Middle Ages, this has struck me as one of its most remarkable characteristics. It has not escaped me that G. von Grunebaum 1956, pp. 275-287, records and illustrates an almost opposite

impression. The reason of the divergence seems to lie in the different points of comparison: Von Grunebaum's, Greek literature, and mine, medieval European.

5. Thus for Jaudar (140), Wardân (60), also Abu Kîr (169).

6. See for instance Paret, *Liebesgeschichten.*

7. Not in Ibn Khallikân; not in *E.I.*.

8. See Chap. VI, p. 463.

9. See Chap. VI, pp. 454-6.

10. See Chap. VI, pp. 456-60.

11. Mas'udi [Abul Hasan Ali Ibn Husain Ibn Ali Al-Masu'di, 10th century chronicler and author of *Muruj adh-Dhahab (Meadows of Gold)*], *Golden Meadows, transl. cit.,* VI, p. 333; Ibn Khallikân, *transl. cit.,* I, p. 310.

12. The only notable exception is the seven Voyages of Sindbad the Sailor, which he naturally relates himself, within the surrounding framework that presents him and his listener in the third person.

13. See Chap. IV, Part I, p. 125.

14. Above [in this book], p. 381.

15. For the subtle use of oblique presentation in the tale of "The Nile-Ferryman and the Saint," see Chap. IV, Part V, pp. 371-2.

16. Which is a story-teller's anachronism, since this famous Udhrite poet (see Ibn Khallikân, *transl. cit.,* I, pp. 331-337) died in 701.

17. See Chap. IV, Part I, p. 126.

18. See Chap. IV, Part I, pp. 132-3.

19. See Chap. IV, Part V, pp. 345-6.

20. It is well known that medieval Moslem scholars possessed prodigious memories; they thought nothing of learning whole books by heart. But the extraordinary thing here is the memorizing and reproducing of something only once heard: cf. the story about the stingy king, in Lane 1, p. 107.

21. See Chap. IV, Part I, pp. 147, 158-65.

22. Littmann VI, pp. 680, 684. Cf., notably, the *Pantshatantra* and the *Parrot Book.*

23. I follow the Calcutta II version in Littmann's translation. Galland, as also Calcutta I and Breslau, has a, better, parrot tale (duplicated in 139b) instead of the king's falcon tale, and in Bulak the sage is called Ruyân, not Dubân; for the rest, they are similar to each other and to Calcutta II.

24. The same turn in Lane's Bulak translation. It would seem that Calcutta II slipped up here.

25. Lane gives it from another source, 1, pp. 114-115 note; it is, as might be expected, a fable of the type *Ungrateful serpent* (S. Thompson, Types, no. 155).

26. See Chap. I, p. 30; also Chap. IV, Part V, pp. 352-3.

27. See Chap. IV, Part IV, pp. 293-4.

28. Paret 1927.

29. On Bedouin robbers in "Omar Ibn En-Nu'mân," see also Chap. IV, Part II, p. 176.

30. The link-up of "Azîz and Azîza" with "Tâj El-Mulûk" has been discussed Chap. IV, Part I, pp. 134-5.

31. See Chap. VI, pp. 444-5.

32. See Chap. II, p. 49, and Chap. IV, Part I, pp. 154-5.

33. The following pages were published, in French translation and somewhat less developed, in *Arabica* 8 = 1961, pp. 137-157.

34. See Chap. IV, Part III, pp. 253-63.

35. Horovitz 1903.

36. Lane 3, p. 343; he therefore put the framing story in a note.

37. There seems little doubt that the time-gaining frame, like other framing and inserting devices, is an Indian invention. It is displayed to advantage in the *Parrot Book,* which we possess i.a. in a 14th-century Persian adaptation; the original Sanskrit text, "Seventy tales of a Parrot", of which a mention occurs in the 12th century, but which may have been considerably older, is lost. See, however, also for the Shehrezâd story, Perry 1960 on the "Seven Vizirs."

38. On this point, see notably Cosquin 1922. There is much to be said for the view, held by several scholars, that the version found in the *101 Nights* is rather firmer and more coherent.

39. As Dyroff 1908, p. 280, so well puts it: ". . . kein bedeutender Künstler; er benützt unbedenklich fremde Lappen und stückt ohne besonderen eigenen Aufwand ein neues Gebilde daraus zusammen; aber wir müssen doch anerkennen, dass er mit Energie auf sein Ziel lossteuert."

40. Except in the "translation" of Mardrus, who made up little comic dialogues between the king and Shehrezâd.

41. After no. 12; also before 9 and after 11, 14, 16, 17 and 19.

42. In one single instance, Shehrezâd is made to point out the moral of a tale she has just told, "The Just King Anusharwân"; see Chap. IV, Part V, pp. 360-1.

43. Boccaccio and Chaucer, and in some measure also Marguerite de Navarre, made expert use of the possibilities of this pattern. The Persian poet Nizami (12th century), in *The Seven Princesses,* connects the seven narrations with each other and with the framework by a subtle use of symbols and moral implications; the result is enchanting, but from a story-telling point of view almost over-refined.

44. An attempt to trace the developing of a long moral lesson throughout the whole of the '1001 Nights' has been made by A. Gelber 1917, but his constructions are the opposite of convincing. The same applies to M. Lahy-Hollebecque 1927, who bases his demonstration on Mardrus.

45. The "Janshâh" story, forcibly inserted in "Bulûkiya," is doubtless a random addition; the narrator did not even trouble to put it in the first person.

46. There is some information on the framed stories, especially "Bulûkiya": see Chap. IV, Part IV, p. 282 and note 2; on the framework, I have found none at all.

47. Studies about the *Book of Sindbad* in its numerous versions—Persian, Arabic, Syriac, Hebrew, Greek, Latin, Romance languages—are countless; I include only a few specimens in my Bibliography. The version that came to be incorporated, apparently at a late date, in the '1001 Nights', derives from an Arabic prose version which was adapted from the Persian, probably in the 8th century, and gave rise to many imitations, among which seems to count *Jali'âd and Wird Khân.* It has long been unanimously supposed that the Persian version, in its turn, was adapted from an Indian original, of which, however, no trace has ever been found. Perry 1960, clearly dissatisfied with the old "India theory" as a whole, defends fresh views: Persian origin, possibly a 2nd-century Greek prototype, *Jali'âd and Wird Khân* the model (also Persian) rather than an imitation.

48. [Th.] Nöldeke 1879, pp. 522-523, aptly established that originally, the vizirs' stories formed two parallel series, the first one devoted to the theme of rashness and the second one to that of women's malice. This arrangement, which can never have been very efficacious, to judge by what is still left

of it, has got broken up and obfuscated in the '1001 Nights'-version, especially towards the end.

49. See Chap. IV, Part I, pp. 122-3.

50. On the framed stories of "The Merchant and the Demon," see Chap. IV, Part IV, pp. 307-10. I follow the Calcutta II version in Littmann's translation, for reasons explained there.

51. Macdonald 1924, pp. 372-379.

52. This is quite possible, and all the more probable as there is still another, similar anecdote extant to explain the word: Dyroff 1908, pp. 253-254.

53. Macdonald 1924, p. 376.

54. On Jinn, see especially the fine article of Macdonald 1919.

55. On this point, see also Chap. IV, Part IV, p. 288.

56. *Koran,* Sura 72; transl. Arberry, II, pp. 305-307.

57. The ransom device is merely hinted at in introducing one of the little inserted stories in "Omar Ibn En-Nu'mân": see above, p. 393.

58. Oestrup 1925, p. 48. The same remark already in Dyroff 1908, pp. 263-264, with some, mostly excellent, comment.

59. See above, pp. 389-91.

60. Notably, the intriguing motif of the fishes who recite verse in the frying-pan when an apparition comes out of the wall, remains, in what follows, completely blind.

61. In the Indian Vetāla stories (written down by Somadeva in the 11th century) the pattern appears reversed: the demon tells *casus*-stories, and the king has to furnish answers to save his life, although by speaking he frustrates his enterprise.

62. I keep to Calcutta II in Littmann's translation. Galland has the same version, minus the bath scene (see Chap. III, p. 72) and plus proper names for the three ladies—Zobéide, Safie and Amine—which are perhaps of his own invention; the mendicants are blind in the right eye, not in the left.—Lane emended the Bulak text by some judicious corrections and additions; notably he completed the "Third Mendicant"'s story, of which Bulak gives only the beginning, with the aid of Calcutta I. As a result, his translation runs parallel to Littmann's.

63. See above, p. 391.

64. See W. H. Roscher 1909, and W. F. Kirby 1887.

65. See Chap. IV, Part IV, pp. 310-12.

66. See Chap. VI, pp. 431-2.

67. Littmann VI, p. 703, points out ancient Egyptian, Persian, and Indian traits; the latter part of the "Third Mendicant's" story is a duplicate of "The Man Who Never Laughed Any More," from the "Seven Vizirs," and used also by Nizami.

68. See Chap. IV, Part II, p. 170. Burton 1, p. 19, remarks: "it is supposed that slaves cannot help telling these fatal lies. Moreover it is held unworthy of a freeborn man to take over-notice of these servile villanies; hence the scoundrel in the story escapes unpunished."

69. Since both stories originated approximately in the same period. On the date of "Nûr Ed-Dîn and Shems Ed-Dîn," see Chap. IV, Part IV, p. 295, note 1; on that of "The Hunchback," below, note 70.

70. Calcutta II, Bulak and Galland have the same version; I keep to Littmann's translation.—On the story's date, see particularly Macdonald 1924, pp. 383-390: he puts the composition of the present version in the 14th century.—On the hunchback episode, Suchier 1922; cf. also S. Thompson, *Types,* no. 1537.—On the framed stories, I have collected the following data. De Goeje 1886 shows that the story of the "Steward" occurs in a chronicle of Ibn el-Jauzi (d. 1200), and that the '1001 Nights'-version is rather garbled and overelaborate, in comparison with the anecdote as given there; cf. also Amedroz 1904. Burton 1, p. 317, notes, after Lane 2, p. 452, that the "Barber's Story of Himself" goes back to a historical anecdote related by Ibn Abd Rabbihi of Córdoba (d. 940); and also, for that matter, by Mas'udi, *Golden Meadows, transl. cit.,* VII, pp. 12-16. The trick played in the "Barber's Second Brother" also occurs in Ibn Abd Rabbihi: see Weisweiler, *Arabesken,* no. 74. "The Barber's Fifth Brother" uses, in its first part, the old "Air-castles" motif (S. Thompson, *Motif-Index,* nos. J 2060 and 2061), occurring also in 168b, while the second part recalls a "Baibars" story (157h).

71. On this point, see above, pp. 387-8.

72. Who reigned 1226-1242; Bulak gives el-Muntasir-billâh, who reigned 861. Both names create chronological difficulties, which have been commented upon by Lane and others. It need hardly be pointed out that the matter is not really relevant: the story cheerfully mixes a history, and a geography, of its own.

73. Thus in Calcutta II and Bulak; in Galland, they tell him merely what befell the hunchback.

74. See for instance G. von Grunebaum 1956, pp. 287 ff.

75. In the sense as defined earlier, Chap. II, pp. 42-3.

Works Cited

Section I: On the 1001 Nights

A. Translations

[A.] Galland, *Les Mille et Une Nuit, contes arabes;* trad. en françois; nouv. éd. corrigée. Paris, 1726, 12 livres en 6 vols.

[A.] Galland, *Les Mille et Une Nuits, contes arabes;* nouv. éd. revue et préfacée par G. Picard. Paris, 1955, 3 vols. (*Classiques Garnier.*) Quotations are from this edition.

E. W. Lane, *The Thousand and One Nights,* commonly called, in England, *The Arabian Nights' Entertainments;* a new transl. from the Arabic, with copious notes; new ed. [. . .] by E. Stanley Poole. London, 1877, 3 vols. Quotations are from this edition, which reproduces the standard ed. of 1859.

R. F. Burton, A plain and literal translation of the *Arabian Nights' Entertainments,* now entituled *The Book of the Thousand Nights and a Night;* with intr., explanatory notes [. . .] and a Terminal Essay [. . .]. Benares [= Stoke Newington], 1885, 10 vols. Quotations are from this edition.

E. Littmann, *Die Erzählungen aus den Tausendundein Nächten;* zum ersten Mal nach dem arabischen Urtext der Calcuttaer Ausgabe aus dem Jahre 1839 übertragen; [2. Neudruck]. Wiesbaden, Insel-Verlag, 1954, 6 vols. Quotations are from this edition.

B. Studies

a. On the collection as a whole

M. J. de Goeje, *De Arabische Nachtvertellingen.* In: *De Gids,* 50 = 1886, pp. 385-413.

W. F. Kirby, *The forbidden doors of the 1001 Nights.* In: *Folklore Journal,* 5 = 1887, pp. 112-124.

K. Dyroff, *Zur Entstehung und Geschichte des arabischen Buches 1001 Nacht.* In: F. P. Greve, *Die Erzählungen aus den 1001 Nächten;* vollst. Deutsche Ausg. auf Grund der Burton'schen Engl. Ausg.; Bd. 12, pp. 229-307. Leipzig, 1908.

D. B. Macdonald, *From the Arabian Nights to Spirit.* In: *The Moslem World,* 9 = 1919, pp. 336-348.

D. B. Macdonald, *The earlier history of the Arabian Nights.* In: *J.R.A.S.* [*Journal of the Royal Asiatic Society*], 1924, pp. 353-397.

J. Oestrup, *Studien über 1001 Nacht; aus dem Dänischen (nebst einigen Zusätzen) übers. von O. Rescher.* Stuttgart, 1925.

W. H. Roscher, *Die Zahl 40 im Glauben, Brauch und Schrifttum der Semiten; ein Beitrag zur vergleichenden Religionswissenschaft, Volkskunde und Zahlenmystik.* B.G. Teubner. Leipzig, , 1909

b. On individual stories

HUNCHBACK

W. Suchier, *Der Schwank von der viermal getöteten Leiche in der Literatur des Abend- und Morgenlandes.* Halle (Saale), 1922.

SAIF EL-MULÛK

J. Horovitz, *Saif al-Mulûk.* In: *Mittheilungen des Seminars für Or. Sprachen zu Berlin,* 6 = 1903, 2. Abt., pp. 52-56.

SEVEN VIZIRS

Th. Nöldeke, *Sindban oder die sieben weisen Meister.* [. . .]. In: *Z.D.M.G.* [Zeitschrift der deutschen morgenländischen Gesellschaft], 33 = 1879, pp. 515-536.

B. E. Perry, *The origin of the Book of Sindbad.* In: *Fabula,* 3 = 1960, pp. 1-94.

SHEHREZÂD STORY

E. Cosquin, *Le prologue-cadre des 1001 Nuits.* In his *Etudes folkloriques;* pp. 265-347. Paris, 1922.

G. E. von Grunebaum, *Medieval Islam; a study in cultural orientation;* 3ᵈ impr.. Chicago, 1956.

SECTION II: GENERAL DOCUMENTATION

B. LITERARY STUDY; ON STORY-TELLING.

S. Thompson, *The types of the folk-tale; a classification and bibliography.* Helsinki, 1928. (*Folklore Fellows Comm.,* 74.) Quoted as: S. Thompson, *Types.*

S. Thompson, *Motif-index of folk-literature;* rev. and enl. ed.. Copenhagen, 1955-'58, 6 vols. Quoted as: S. Thompson, *Motif-index.*

C. "MÄRCHENDEUTUNG"

A. Gelber, *1001 Nacht; der Sinn der Erzählungen der Scheherezade.* Wien/Leipzig, 1917.

M. Lahy-Hollebecque, *Le féminisme de Schéhérazade; la révélation des 1001 Nuits.* Paris, 1927.

SECTION III: BACKGROUND READING

A. COLLECTIONS OF STORIES, STORY-BOOKS, ETC.

a. Oriental

M. Weisweiler, *Arabesken der Liebe;* früharabische Geschichten von Liebe und Frauen, ges. und übers. Leiden, 1954.

R. Paret, *Früharabische Liebesgeschichten.* Bern, 1927.

B. HISTORY, GEOGRAPHY AND MISCELLANEA

a. Arabic

The Koran; interpreted [= transl.] by A. J. Arberry. London, 1955, 2 vols.

Ibn Khallikân, *Biographical Dictionary;* transl. from the Arabic by BⁿMac Guckin de Slane. Paris, 1842-'71, 4 vols.

C. Knipp (essay date 1974)

SOURCE: Knipp, C. "The *The Arabian Nights* in England: Galland's Translation and Its Successors." *Journal of Arabic Literature* 5 (1974): 44-54.

[*In the following essay, Knipp offers a reevaluation of Antoine Galland's early-eighteenth-century translation of* The Arabian Nights, *arguing that despite its limitations, the work should be regarded as the preeminent translation, a creative work, and a version that is as faithful to the original source as could have been rendered.*]

The story of the translations of the **Arabian Nights** is a colorful and even lurid one. In this story's English segment, very close to center stage, gesticulating wildly, is Sir Richard Burton—explorer, adventurer, polemicist, orientalist, scribbler, and enemy of Victorian morality. We might as well begin with him, since the curtain will not go down anyway until he has done his turn. Here is how Burton, already waving both sock and buskin, begins the *Foreword* of his edition of the **Arabian Nights:** "This work," he says,

> laborious as it may appear, has been to me a labour of love, an unfailing source of solace and satisfaction. During my long years of official banishment to the luxuriant and deadly deserts of Western Africa, and to the dull and dreary half-clearings of South America, it proved itself a charm, a talisman against ennui and despondency. Impossible even to open the pages without a vision starting into view; without drawing a picture from the pinacothek of the brain; without reviving a host of memories and reminiscences which are not the common property of travellers, however widely they may have travelled. From my dull and commonplace and "respectable" surroundings, the Jinn bore me at once to the land of my predilection, Arabia, a region so familiar to my mind that even at first sight, it seemed a reminiscence of some by-gone metempsychic life in the distant Past. Again I stood under the diaphanous skies, in air glorious as aether, whose every breath raises men's spirits like sparkling wine. Once more I saw the evening star hanging like a solitaire from the pure front of the western firmament; and the after-glow transfiguring and transforming, as by magic,

the homely and rugged features of the scene into a fairy-land lit with a light that never shines on other soils or seas . . .[1]

And so on, and so on: Burton continues in this vein for some time, becoming purpler and purpler, rising to the bathetic pinnacle of the English pseudo-oriental style.

And English and pseudo-oriental it certainly is, for Burton was laying the groundwork of a deception. The "long years of official banishment", as he self-pityingly calls them, spent in such "dull and commonplace and 'respectable' surroundings" as South America and the deserts of West Africa, were never spent laboring on a translation of the *Arabian Nights.* Burton did not work on this text for twenty-five years, as his mendacious dedication to Steinhauser implies, and he did not graciously hold back its publication for four years merely to give John Payne "precedence and possession of the field", as his *Foreword* rather disingenuously asserts. He waited in order to crib. He based his translation, which is therefore hardly a translation at all, on John Payne's version (1882-84);[2] he did it in only two years, toward the end copying Payne verbatim for whole pages at a stretch; he did it to make money, and he sold it as he had planned in advance to the 1,500 subscribers left over from Payne's limited edition of 500.

This story was told by Thomas Wright in 1906 and 1919 and repeated by the two eminent authorities on the *Alf Layla,* Duncan B. Macdonald (1929; 1938) and Enno Littmann (1956).[3] But Burton's most recent biographers, as Mia Gerhardt points out,[4] have not been aware of the extent of Burton's debt to Payne.[5] Burton did his publicizing well, and its boom drowns out the quiet voice of scholarship. As Jorge Luis Borges (himself characteristically unaware of Payne) has written, the romantic legend of Burton the explorer gives him a prestige that no other English Arabist can compete with. He was a far more colorful figure than Payne. The Burton legend gives his version the attraction of the forbidden, an attraction on which the fame of Burton's *Arabian Nights* still rests.[6] The result is another confusion: just as westerners mistakenly consider the *Arabian Nights* a "classic" of Arabic literature, whereas it is obscure to, and largely despised by, the Arabs themselves, so English readers for the most part erroneously think that Sir Richard Burton is the pre-eminent translator of the *Arabian Nights,* whereas the chief distinction his version can claim is to be the most recent lengthy one in English, and, despite its undeniable interest as an element in the Burton legend, the most nearly unreadable one in our language. Burton's edition is certainly fascinating as a personal document; but a translation that is to this extent a personal document is at cross-purposes with itself. The famous sexological *Terminal Essay* (the title itself borrowed from Payne) is an interesting piece of Victorian pornography; I myself doubted the authenticity of the strange and supposedly first-hand observations of eastern sexual practices when I first read them some ten years ago, and subsequent studies strengthen the suspicion that many of them are Burton's own fantasies and extrapolations. This feeling is shared by Mia Gerhardt,[7] whose excellent chapter on the major European versions, wider in scope than this paper, should be read by anyone who wants an informed, thorough, and critical discussion of the subject.

The East as seen by westerners has always contained a strong element of legend. Burton deserves credit for recognizing this fact and capitalizing upon it to increase English sympathies toward the Islamic world, and thus help to change ignorance and suspicion to curiosity and sympathetic interest. In this cause, Sir Richard performed an invaluable service. But it must be admitted that his methods were not highly scrupulous. Just as many minor and half-forgotten works have a secondary, parasitical kind of existence, so Burton's famous translation depends for its existence on the much-neglected John Payne. It was Payne, not Burton, who gave the English-speaking world its first lengthy and unbowdlerized version of the *Arabian Nights* translated directly from the original; and yet this parasite has survived to engulf its host.[8]

So, too, have the subsequent versions engulfed Antoine Galland's original one. The scene has greatly expanded since 1703-1713, when Galland's twelve handy duo-decimo volumes first appeared and were brought across the Channel, where they were immediately both read in French and translated into English by a "Grub-street" unknown.[9] In England and America, there are two basic kinds of *Arabian Nights* to contend with in the nineteenth and twentieth centuries: the children's, which exists in many forms, always short and always derivative, though sometimes very different from the base translation; and the adults', usually long and heavily annotated, putatively scholarly, and "unexpurgated"—though the latter claim is mainly post-Victorian advertising and perhaps designed to counteract the tedium produced by the repetitious length. There is not so much to "expurgate" unless one possesses the Victorians' inexhaustible ability to create prurience where there is none; there is merely more repetitious length than any children and most adults have time for—so that it is now the children's versions that chiefly matter to our culture. Galland, from the beginning, was both: suitable for young listeners, worthy of adult readers. The division and diffusion of interest and scope came later.

My purpose now is to re-evaluate Galland's translation of the Arabic *Alf Layla wa-Layla* and present it in just relation to other versions available in English since. So many pretentious new translations, so many popular editions, so many children's condensations have come along since Galland, that even students of Arabic literature find the scene confusing. Translators, though not all by any means as unscrupulous as Sir Richard Burton, must be good publicists: to sell their version, they are obliged to provide a strong hint for the critic by including a preface debunking or undercutting the work of their predecessors. The inevitable result is that though still nodded to respectfully by all—he is, by now, at a safe distance—Galland has lost his place of pre-eminence. He deserves to have it back.

To begin with, we need to be told (or reminded) that any acquaintance with the *Arabian Nights,* whether limited or extensive, is due to Galland. The book was *discovered* by him in a larger sense than is generally known. Arabists perhaps need not be told, but western readers at large are almost wholly unaware, that Galland discovered the *Arabian Nights* for the literate Arab of today, and for us, as well as for the eighteenth-century European readers who first encountered his *Mille et une Nuit.* Only recently, with Suhayr al-Qalamāwī's book-length study in Arabic (1966), has there been solid evidence that the medieval collection of tales is beginning to be taken seriously in the Arab World as well as in the West.[10] As Suhayr al-Qalamāwī makes clear, it is the *Alf Layla's* familiarity in the West that has led to this belated interest on the part of Arab scholars and men of letters such as Ṭaha Ḥusayn.[11] Thus the obscurity and humble status of the work are such, that if Galland had not come upon the story manuscripts he acquired and translated, the *Arabian Nights* not only might never have become well known to westerners, but also would remain despised, little known, and unread in the Arab countries. Galland's moment was special. The European public was eager for just the sort of stories he supplied in just the form in which he was able to supply them. There is no certainty that translated oriental tales would have caught on, and hence ultimately become the "classic" they are now said to be, had they made their first appearance at some time and place other than France in the early eighteenth century. Burton would certainly never have discovered them; and no fame would have echoed back from the West to the point of origin. For all of us, then, for orientalists and common readers, for easterners and westerners alike, Galland is the discoverer and source of the *Arabian Nights.*

All this might be true, of course, and yet Galland's translation might remain dated and inadequate. In fact this is not the case: Burton's is far more dated, and the question of what is "adequate" is a complicated one with many special but no universal answers. Naturally Galland was "handicapped" by the lack of all the paraphernalia of modern scholarship, and by the lack of all that specialized knowledge of the *Alf Layla wa-*

Layla which he could not have, because his pioneering work alone was to lead to its acquisition. But Galland's knowledge was the most advanced possible in his time, and it enabled him to produce that rare thing among scholars, an entertaining, readable, gracefully written book which at the same time only a man of very special learning could have done.

No; speaking as one who has compared various Arabic texts of the *Arabian Nights* with as many English and European versions as were available to me, and speaking also as one who, though biased a little in favor of the literature of the eighteenth century, at least has no new translation to sell, I am compelled to say that I prefer Galland's French, and the Grub-street Englishing of Galland, to any other version and even to the original, which, in its more authentic written forms—after all, it is essentially an oral work—is poor and uninteresting Arabic. In its chief printed manuscript versions,[12] as distinguished from the bowdlerized and grammatically "corrected" modern Arabic editions, the Arabic *Alf Layla wa-Layla* is a bastardized mixture of literary language and colloquial dialect which in the context of Arabic literature as a whole must seem ungraceful.

Mia Gerhardt rather begs the question in her interesting book on the *Arabian Nights* when she argues that her ignorance of Arabic need not hamper her from judging the translations reliably, because in the case of stories the precise wording is not important.[13] Words do matter. "Style" is not easily separated from "content." Each translation ought to be judged finally on its own merits as a collection of stories, but can be judged *as a translation* only by comparison with the principal manuscripts. Ideally a translation will pass both tests, and it competes successfully with all other translations of the work only if it does. The question of the special requirements of particular readers apart, Galland is most successful in achieving the delicate compromises translation requires. His free-flowing version captures the simplicity of the original, but the genius of the French language allowed him to do this without being (as the Arabic tales are) inelegant.

I have said that Burton's translation is "far more dated" than Galland's, and that Burton's only real distinctions are that his version of John Payne's version of the *Nights* is the lengthiest and the most unreadable. Perhaps the most telling remark on this subject is that of the distinguished Italian Arabist and the editor of the Italian *Arabian Nights* translation, Francesco Gabrieli, to the effect that to understand Burton's translation he often has to refer to the Arabic text:[14] this is very nearly true even for a native English speaker. The other "adult" versions of the *Nights* in English suffer from similar stylistic defects, which have been best described by the late A. J. Arberry in the *Introduction* to his *Sche-*

herezade (a pleasant, but fragmentary and, like some of its predecessors, subtly prudish entry into the field of *Alf Layla* translation). "Earlier translators of the *Arabian Nights*", Arberry remarks, referring to his own countrymen,

> have almost without exception been so mesmerized by the stylistic peculiarities of Arabic that they have not hesitated to imitate them slavishly in their versions, a thing they would probably have scorned to do, and been soundly schooled to avoid, were their task Homer or Herodotus or Horace or Livy. Not content with inventing a strange Eurasian sort of English, that was the more readily accepted because it seemed profanely to echo the Old Testament in the Authorized Version— and for a good reason, the Semitic original of those Scriptures—they went farther than they needed to have done and, being caught up in the eddies of the Gothic Revival, imported into their diction all the bogus flummery of Ye Olde Englysshe.[15]

As Arberry says later on in his discussion, the Arabic of the *Alf Layla wa-Layla* is "colloquial or half-colloquial", is consequently close to the conversational in its flavor, and in fact "differs surprisingly little from the Arabic of conversation today".[16] In substance surely Arberry is speaking with wisdom here. Certain Arabic works, the *Maqāmāt* for example, could perhaps best be translated into some kind of *Kunstprose;* but the simplicity and naturalness of the *Alf Layla* unmistakably call for more direct language. Yet the "adult" English versions of the *Arabian Nights* are not at all conversational or contemporary. Lane's is overly literal: instead of finding equivalents of idioms, we get things like "he almost flew with delight" . . . ; but Lane's biblical style is not the *mere* result of this literalness: a phrase like "rejoiced with exceeding joy" is not *merely* "literal", but reflects its author's conscious efforts to echo biblical style. Lane's translation is further marred by excessive prudery and is incomplete. For the seeker of an "adult" *Arabian Nights,* it is of no use; contrarily, Lane has been frequently used as the basis of modern "children's" versions. Payne's translation suffers from a greater degree of overwroughtness (a pity, since his is the only complete and genuine translation from Arabic into English): he adds archaic verb and pronoun forms, a more recherché vocabulary than Lane's, and a more involuted sentence structure. To Payne's style, which Burton had found not "plain"—that is, vulgar—enough, the latter adds stronger words ("rascal" becoming "pimp", "impudent woman" "strumpet", "vile woman" "whore", and so on); odd hyphenated words, often of his own coinage and occasionally barbarous; still more archaisms, usually with an added pseudo-Elizabethan flavor; and still greater misplaced faithfulness to "literal" meaning. "Literal" seems to be one of those words—like "reality"—which should rarely be used without quotation marks; it is obvious that one man's "literalness" is another's grotesque and artificial clumsi-

ness. The pseudo-medieval approach to the *Arabian Nights,* culminating in Burton's cribbed and crabbed Elizabethan-Gothic style, is seriously inappropriate, since the language of the original is as simple as it could be, and Arabic has changed relatively much less than English since the Middle Ages; it is probably best, at any rate, for a translator to stay close to the idiom he is most familiar with and therefore most able to handle with ease—the idiom of his own time and country. Arberry's clear, lively, accurate translations of Arabic prose (his sparkling version of the *Ṭawq al-Ḥamama* of Ibn Ḥazm is an outstanding example) show that, in most respects at least, he was a man for the job; it is a pity that the lengthier project he evidently had in mind[17] was never continued beyond the "Aladdin" and "Judar" stories published in 1960.

Although he meant his bowdlerized selection of the *Nights* for a general audience, Lane made the accompanying notes so lengthy and elaborate that his nephew (and champion against the inroads of Payne and Burton) was later able to publish them as a separate volume complete unto itself.[18] As Mia Gerhardt concludes,[19] this imbalance suggests a certain confusion in the overall planning of the project; and the failure to meet more than *some* of the demands of such a project is characteristic of English translations of the *Arabian Nights.* The producers of the many English and American children's editions have chiefly, perforce, used Scott (1811) or Lane as their basis. Since Scott's edition is a translation of Galland (with a few dubious additions at the end),[20] and since the children's editions far outnumber the adults', and Lane's version did not come along until the 1880's, it is still true that the Grub-street Galland, or some abridged, amended version of it, is the form in which most English-speaking readers have been encountering the *Arabian Nights* over the past two hundred and fifty years. Macdonald (1932) was not able to identify the author of the original English translation, whose exact date of first publication (no complete set being extant)[21] is unknown (1706? 1708?), but certainly close to that of the French. Re-translators of Galland (e.g., Frederick Gilbert: London, 1868), predictably enough, have remarked on the Grub-street version's "errors" and "inelegancies". In fact, as befits a piece of hack work far less pretentious than Burton's, the Grub-street Galland departs little from its source; one finds few actual cuts or alterations. The following example is illustrative:

Galland's French	Grub-street version
Il s'entretint avec cet ambassadeur	[He] discoursed with that ambassador
jusqu'à minuit. Alors, voulant encore	till midnight. But willing once more

Galland's French	Grub-street version
une fois embrasser la reine,	to embrace the queen,
qu'il aimoit beaucoup,	whom he loved entirely,
il retourna seul à son palais.	he returned alone to his palace, and
Il alla droit à l'appartement	went straight to her majesty's
de cette Princesse,	apartment;
qui ne s'attendant pas à le revoir,	who not expecting his return,
avoit reçu dans son lit un des	had taken one of the meanest officers
derniers Officiers de sa Maison.	of the household to her bed,
Il y avoit déjà long temps qu'ils	where they both lay fast asleep,
étoient couchez, & ils dormoient	having been there a considerable time.[22]
tous deux d'un profond sommeil.	

One notes the carelessly awkward "who", and the alteration of the pace and flow of Galland's last sentence ("Il y avoit déjà long temps"), with the suspenseful story-teller's pause it creates, to the flat dependent clause ("where they both lay") with a prosaic ending ("a considerable time") in disappointing contrast to the fairy-tale magic effect of "ils dormoient tous deux d'un profond sommeil". But if one agrees to admire Galland's translation, a few small betrayals are preferable to total abandonment.

Using slightly different Arabic texts, here is how Mardrus (1899-1904) and Khawan (1965-67) in French, and Lane, Payne, and Burton in English, have rendered the passage; and following these I give . . . my translation of that text:

Mardrus:

> Mais, vers le milieu de la nuit, il se rappela une chose oubliée au palais, et revint et entra dans le palais. Et il trouva son épouse étendue sur sa couche et accolée par un esclave noir d'entre les e sclaves. À cette vue, le monde noirçit sur son visage.
>
> (I, 4-1918)

Khawan:

> Lorsqu'il pénétra dans la chambre de celle-ci, il la trouva endormie à côté de l'un des adolescents préposés au service des cuisines. Ils dormaient enlacés l'un à l'autre.
>
> (I, 32)

Lane:

> At midnight, however, he remembered that he had left in his palace an article which he should have brought with him; and having returned to the palace to fetch it,

he there beheld his wife sleeping in his bed, and attended by a male negro slave, who had fallen asleep by her side. On beholding this scene, the world became black before his eyes . . .

Payne:

> In the middle of the night, it chanced that he bethought him of somewhat he had forgotten in his palace; so he returned thither privily and entered his apartments, where he found his wife asleep in his own bed, in the arms of one of his black slaves. When he saw this, the world grew black in his sight . . .

Burton:

> But when the night was half spent he bethought him that he had forgotten in his palace somewhat which he should have brought with him, so he returned privily and entered his apartments, where he found the Queen, his wife, asleep on his own carpet-bed, embracing with both arms a black cook of loathsome aspect and foul with kitchen grease and grime. When he saw this the world waxed black before his sight . . .

Calcutta II:

> . . . When it was the middle of the night he remembered something he had forgotten in his castle, so he went back, entered his castle, and found his wife lying in his bed embracing one of the black slaves. When he saw this he became enraged.

Of course the unadorned (and unpunctuated) Arabic narrative requires a little padding to give it a more natural flow in English or French. . . . More subordination is natural in French or English: hence Lane's "*having* returned . . . he *then* beheld". But one remains unconvinced of the need for Lane's bowdlerization (the slave *attending* instead of *embracing*) or for Burton's (typical) exaggeration of the loathsomeness of the black slave—who certainly moves around freely on the social (and professional) scale as one goes from one translation to another.

In the larger context such comparisons as these provide, we can see Galland's virtues and limitations fairly clearly. One of course notices the seventeenth-century Frenchman's decorum, the restraint and poise of his tone, and comparing that with the grotesqueries of Payne-Burton or even the relatively simple style but still heavy movement of Lane, at first one is inclined to feel that Galland may have watered down his source. After consulting the Arabic texts, however, one realizes that simplicity, even spareness of diction to the point of crudeness, is quite appropriate here. Mardrus and Khawan aim at capturing this crudeness in repetitions that are probably deliberately somewhat awkward ("palais . . . palais"; "endormis . . . dormaient"). Galland's chief unfaithfulness consists in adding polish. But he adds nothing else irrelevant. As Muhammed Abdel-Halim shows in his authoritative *Antoine Galland: sa vie, son œuvre* (1970), Galland was so imbued with the spirit and schooled in the method of Arabic story-telling that, faithful though he was, he was capable of creating an Arabic story himself out of a slender outline, had in effect himself become an Arabic story-teller—a feat not, in practical terms, ever duplicated by translators of the **Alf Layla wa-Layla** since the French scholar's historic discovery.

Galland's story-telling skill is not only unusual in a scholar but perhaps also represents a deeper affinity with the Arabic tales than other redactors have shown, the kind of affinity without which any translation is likely to be cold and mechanical, no matter how well-meaning the translator may be. The reader who goes back to Antoine Galland's **Les Mille et une Nuit** is truly returning to the source. It is difficult to find a more happy, creative, and successful translation in the West. One could only wish that this good fortune had befallen some greater work of the literature of the Islamic and Arabic worlds, which contains so many treasures still unknown among us.

Notes

1. Richard F. Burton, *A Plain and Literal Translation of the Arabian Nights' Entertainments,* Burton Club "Baghdad Edition" (printed in England), 10 vols. (London, 1885-86), I, vii.

2. *The Book of the Thousand Nights and One Night,* 9 vols., "For Subscribers Only" (London, 1884). Since Payne was over-subscribed for the ultimately small printing (500 copies), Burton determined to gather up the remaining 1,500 ready customers, the other subscribers to Payne's translation.

3. Wright, *The Life of Sir Richard Burton* (London, 1906) and *The Life of John Payne* (London, 1919); Macdonald, "Thousand and One Nights", in *Encyclopaedia Britannica,* 14th ed. ff., 1929, and "Alf Laila wa-Laila", in *Enzyklopeidie des Islam* (Ergänzungsband, 1938); Littmann, "Alf Layla wa-Layla", in *Encyclopaedia of Islam,* new ed. (Leiden, 1956).

4. Mia Irene Gerhardt, *The Art of Story-Telling: A Literary Study of the Thousand and One Nights* (Leiden, 1963), p. 78.

5. The most recent biography of Burton, Seton Dearden, *The Arabian Knight* (1936; rev. London, 1953), Ch. XII, presents Burton's highly fictionalized version of his translation work without reservations.

6. Jorge Luis Borges, "Los traductores de las *1001 Noches*" (1935), in *Historia de la eternidad* (Buenos Aires, 1953), pp. 101-111.

7. Gerhardt, pp. 91-93.

8. It has proliferated in America through the omnipresent Modern Library abridgement (New York, 1932; many reprintings), among whose few selections is included an apocryphal story invented by Burton, "How Abu Hasan Brake Wind".

9. For the most complete description of early editions and translations of Galland, see Duncan B. Macdonald, "A Bibliographical and Literary Study of the First Appearance of the *Arabian Nights* in Europe", *Library Quarterly,* II (1932), 387-420.

10. Suhayr al-Qalamāwī, *Alf Layla wa-Layla* (Cairo, 1966).

11. The late Tawfiq Sayegh, a writer and teacher with an exceptional range of knowledge of both Arabic and English literatures, once told me how he read the tales first in English, and then only later, at Harvard, was eventually moved by contact with western orientalists to shut himself in his rooms and devour the Arabic original.

12. See the entry "Alf Layla wa-Layla" (by Littmann) in *The Encyclopedia of Islam* (Leiden, 1960) for summary of data on the principal recensions and reprints of MSS.

13. Gerhardt, *Introduction,* pp. 1 ff.

14. "Nel Burton, l'orientalista non inglese per capire certi passi trova piu spiccio ricorrere al testo arabo!" "Le Mille e una notte nella cultura europea", in *Storia e civiltà musulmana* (Naples, 1947), p. 103.

15. Arberry, *Scheherezade* (London, 1960), pp. 9-10.

16. *Ibid.,* p. 15.

17. *Ibid.,* pp. 9, 17.

18. Stanley Lane-Poole, ed., *Arabian Society in the Middle Ages* (London, 1883; rpt. 1971).

19. Gerhardt, p. 77.

20. Gerhardt, p. 68.

21. See Macdonald (1932; *op. cit.*), pp. 405-406, and "Notes on Sales: Oriental Tales", *The Times Literary Supplement,* April 10, 1930, p. 324.

22. Opening sequence.

Peter D. Molan (essay date July-September 1978)

SOURCE: Molan, Peter D. "Sinbad the Sailor: A Commentary on the Ethics of Violence." *Journal of the American Oriental Society* 98, no. 3 (July-September 1978): 237-47.

[In the following essay, Molan comments on the ironic disparity between Sinbad's actions versus his professed

moral stance, characterizing the tale as a parable that is meant to instruct King Shahriyar about ideas of self-deception and justice.]

Sinbad the Sailor has become, for his modern audience, a Romantic hero. Jabra Ibrahim Jabra, the Palestinian poet and critic, says of him:

> So human in wishes, in reactions, in dreams, and yet, because of his endurance and invention no death or destruction can get at him. His vision is all men's dream: his ship is wrecked, his fellow-travelers drown, death and horror overtake the world, but Sindbad battles on and survives. The original land-dream was so powerful that the sea has to be conquered, and so have the lands beyond the sea, the islands, the valleys of serpents and jewels.[1]

This view, however, is one based on a popular, children's abstraction of the medieval folkloric figure of Sinbad. Even Jabra confesses that his view of Sinbad was formed by the children's stories which he first heard in his own youth and which he, in turn, read to his own children, carefully expurgating the more potent tales of "death and horror."[2] Our view of Sinbad is not based on the reading of the medieval tales of *Dolopathos, Syntipas,* or **The Thousand and One Nights**.[3] Instead, our view is formed by the Sinbad the Sailor as portrayed by Douglas Fairbanks Jr., who battled Walter Slezak and Anthony Quinn for the island of gold and the favors of Maureen O'Hara in the RKO-Radio film. As Bosley Crowther has pointed out, the screenplay writers, no Shahrazads at telling an engaging tale, spurred [Fairbanks] to elegant bravado, set him to vaulting oriental walls, and generally playing the bold hero in this gaudy fable.[4] But, it is a spurious fable which Fairbanks' Sinbad undertakes, not one of the so significant *seven* voyages of the traditional tale.[5]

So firmly fixed has this romantic view of Sinbad become that even his most recent and most sophisticated critic, who does examine the **1001 Nights** tales, concludes that:

> Sindbad is, before all else, a man of action and it is in his actions that his characteristic qualities are revealed. In all the terrible situations from which he must extract himself, he, time after time, makes use of [both] boldness and discretion.[6]

And that:

> Regarded from this angle, the *Voyages of Sindbad the Sailor* become a veritable glorification of navigation and maritime commerce; and Sindbad, as a model set up for the admiration of a sympathetic public, is the proper symbol of the sailor's profession such as it could appear in that privileged moment in its long history.[7]

In the following pages, we shall present a different analysis of the Sinbad tales, as they occur in the **1001 Nights**.[8] It will reveal a very different appreciation of the character of Sinbad and of the significance of the voyages which, we hope to demonstrate convincingly, is more in keeping with the structure of the medieval tales not only in their Arabic, but also in their Greek and Latin versions.[9]

There are two versions of the Sinbad tales. The best known is that of the editions of Bulaq (1835), of Calcutta (1839-42 [MacNaghten ed.]), and of the later Arab versions in general. The second version is that of the first Calcutta edition (1818) and that of the manuscripts, now lost, upon which Galland based his translation of the entire **1001 Nights** and upon which L. Langles based his *Les voyages de Sind-Bād le Marin et La Ruse des Femmes* (Paris, 1814). The two versions differ in two ways. The second is generally shorter and sparer in its narrative treatment of the various themes. Of considerably more importance, however, is the fact that the end of voyage VI and voyage VII is entirely different in the two versions. It has been the view of most of the translators of the **1001 Nights** that, while the more fully articulated first version is "better" for the bulk of the stories, the conclusion of the second version is more satisfactory to a properly formed tale. Thus Lane follows the first version until the ending of voyage VI. He then shifts to the second version for the translation of the end of voyages VI and VII. Burton simply combines the two as does Mardrus in his French edition of the **Nights** (Paris, 1900-1904). E. Littmann, in his German version (Wiesbaden, 1953), follows the first version to its conclusion and then adds the ending of the second version as an "important variant."[10]

Littmann's is the appropriate procedure, for the significance of the two versions is precisely that they form two *equally valid* versions of the tale. They offer a marvelous example of the way in which an oral tale may be altered in its presentation and yet remain unaltered as to its significance, its "message," and its "structure." For, though markedly different in narrative detail, the two versions are structurally identical and thus fulfill the same function in the development of the tale. The analysis that follows, then, will be based on MacNaghten's 1839 Calcutta edition of the **Nights** but will include reference to the second version of voyage VII for the sake of interest only. Either of the other versions could have been equally well used.

As is so common in the tales of the **1001 Nights**, the fundamental structural element in the Sinbad stories is a "framing" technique. The stories of the seven voyages made by Sinbad, "the merchant of Baghdad," are first framed within the story of the relationship between that Sinbad, *al-Sindibād al-Baḥarī*, and the poor porter, *al-Sindibād al-Ḥammāl*. This story, in turn, is framed within the continuing story of Shahrazad and the cruel

King Shahriyar. This point is essential, for we must always keep in mind that Sinbad the Sailor is only the "putatative" narrator of the stories of the voyages. In fact, the "real" narrator, as we are constantly reminded, is Shahrazad. Despite the fact that the bulk of the story is made up of Sinbad's *first person* narrative, the figure of Shahrazad narrates the opening and closing of the tales and intrudes some thirty times, never more than three pages apart, reestablishing her role as the narrator by the familiar, formulaic device and once more putting the words in Sinbad's mouth:

> And morning came upon Shahrazad and she fell silent from [this] lawful discourse. Then when it was fully the sixtieth night after the five hundredth, she said, "It has come to my attention, oh happy king, that Sinbad the Sailor, when he had prepared his shipment, stowed it in the ship at the city of Basra, and embarked, said: 'We went on traveling from place to place and from city to city, selling and buying and taking a look at the countries of [various] people.'"[11]

Thus there is inherently an ironic disparity between the point of view of the protagonist, Sinbad, and that of the "narrator," Shahrazad (along with her audience). The knowledge and values of the protagonist are almost inevitably different from those of the narrator; for she, and we, know the characters as they could not possibly know themselves.[12]

Shahrazad then, hoping once more to beguile the King with yet another story (and so stay by yet another day her execution),[13] assures him that the story she has just completed is "not nearly so wonderful as the story of **'Sinbad'**." The King replies, "How's that?" and the familiar tale begins.[14] Shahrazad tells that on a burning hot Baghdad afternoon, a poor and lowly porter comes upon the magnificent palace of a rich merchant. Though nominally recognizing God's justice, his true distress at his situation relative to that of the merchant is clear as he recites a short song:

> How many wretched persons are destitute of ease! and how many are in luxury, reposing in the shade!
>
> I find myself afflicted by trouble beyond measure; and strange is my condition, and heavy is my load!
>
> Others are in prosperity, and from wretchedness are free, and never for a single day have borne a load like mine;
>
> Incessantly and amply blest, throughout the course of life, with happiness and grandeur, as well as drink and meat.
>
> All men whom God hath made are in origin alike; and I resemble this man and he resembleth me;
>
> But otherwise, between us is a difference as great as the difference that we find between wine and vinegar.

> Yet in saying this, I utter no falsehood against Thee, [Oh my Lord;] for Thou art wise, and with justice Thou hast judged.[15]

His feelings are clear to the owner of the palace too, for he calls the porter in, tells him the story of each of seven adventurous voyages and concludes that the porter has been wrong:

> These pleasures are a compensation for the toil and humiliation that I have experienced.[16]

The porter is convinced and agrees; but are we, the audience to whom Shahrazad tells the tale, convinced? Let us have a closer look at the tales themselves.

Though at first view simply adventure stories, the tales of the seven voyages of Sinbad are in fact subtly structured in a very sophisticated way to bring home a moral through irony. I do not mean to imply by this that the Sinbad tales are a didactic morality play in disguise. The *1001 Nights* are not the conveyance for a moral message. In that sense, they are "amoral," as the term that has so frequently been applied to them would have it. That does not imply, however, the lack of an ethical framework or point of view; and, even more to the point, it in no way precludes an acute and often cynical perception of the relationship to ethical principles of such human foibles and weaknesses as self-righteousness, self-delusion, greed and hypocrisy. Indeed, these are the fundamental perceptions of the *Nights.*

It may do here, too, to mention that the Sinbad tales find their origin in a universal, oral folk tradition which has analogues everywhere from China to the British Isles.[17] The attempts to trace the "origins" of the *1001 Nights,* as opposed to its "analogues," (through a chain of translations) to Persian and Indian texts is thus dubious at best. The *1001 Nights* Sinbad, however, has been completely Islamicized and Arabized. A Muslim teller of traditional tales reciting before a Muslim audience will inevitably, even if unconsciously, infuse his tale with a Muslim ethical structure—however the characters, events, and story line may have entered his tradition. Thus, Sinbad's constant evocation of Allah and his performance of Islamic ritual is not mere window dressing, but reflects the thorough-going infusion of Islamic ideals in the story. The impact of the story is the fact that, in spite of his apparent and self-avowed Muslim piety and righteousness, Sinbad finally contravenes Islamic ideals in the most astounding way during his adventures.

It is the relative number and nature of the adventures and catastrophes which befall Sinbad on his voyages which make up the major structural elements of the tales. These may be schematized here as follows:[18]

Voyage	I	II	III	IV	V	VI	VII¹	VII²
	C	C	C	C	C	C	C	M
	Ab	A	Ap	Ap	Ap	A	A	C
		A	Ap	Ab	Ab	Ab		A
			Ap					
	M	M	M		M	M		
	R	R	R	R	R	R		R

C = Catastrophe
A = Adventure (b = benign; p = perilous)
M = Marvels
R = Return

As may be seen at a glance, in each of his voyages, Sinbad suffers a catastrophe, usually a shipwreck or desertion upon the high seas. He then experiences a series of adventures which ebb and flow as the tales proceed. Not only does the number of adventures rise and then symmetrically fall off again, however; so, too, do the violence and horror which characterize the adventures.

In the first story, Sinbad is lost at sea when, having landed on an island, the island sinks! The "island" is, in fact, a huge fish which has been dozing on the surface so long that trees and bushes have sprouted on its back. Upon feeling the cooking fires of the landing party, it dives into the ocean. Sinbad's ship has pulled off to save itself, and Sinbad must save himself by paddling to land in a large wooden bowl. He is taken in by the King of the Sea Horses, becomes the latter's minister, and finally returns home rich.

In the second story, Sinbad is abandoned on a desert island. He manages to escape by tying himself to the leg of the Rukh, which flies him off of the island but deposits him in the valley of snakes and diamonds. He again escapes, this time loaded with diamonds, and finally returns home rich.

In the third story, catastrophe overtakes Sinbad when apes attack his ship. He and his companions are cast ashore, where they encounter a huge but man-like monster who eats many of the castaways. They collaborate to put out the monster's eyes; and, though he kills several more of the company by hurling stones at them as they escape in a boat they have made, some finally make good their escape.[19] They fall foul of a man-eating snake, however, and only Sinbad escapes by building a cage in which to hide from the snake. He is soon rescued by a passing ship, fortuitously the very ship from which he had been lost in the preceding voyage, retrieves his goods, and again returns home wealthy.

The fourth story is the keystone of the entire piece. Driven ashore by a storm, the crew and passengers of Sinbad's ship fall into the hands of ghouls who fatten them up and eat them. Sinbad escapes, and happily settles among a nearby people. He becomes rich, initially by introducing the people (especially their King) to saddlery. He marries, but then falls foul of a bizarre custom of the people in which the spouse of a deceased person is buried alive with the corpse in a huge communal tomb. So buried, Sinbad stays alive by killing the newly interred and taking the meager supplies that are initially sent down with each new victim. Sinbad finds a way out of the tomb but returns, amasses the golden jewelry of the corpses, and continues to live by killing those who are sent down until he has enough.[20] He then hails a passing ship and returns home, rich.

In the fifth tale, Rukhs attack Sinbad's ship. He is captured by the Old Man o' the Sea, whom he manages to trick into getting drunk, but then kills him. With the aid of residents of a nearby city, he overcomes imprisonment by apes and makes a fortune out of coconuts which he induces the apes to throw at him by throwing stones at them. Again he returns home rich.

The sixth voyage finds Sinbad battling only the elements and circumstances. Cast ashore on a desert island, his companions die of disease and starvation. Sinbad must raft through an underground river to reach safety, but he does so; and the King of the people whom he finds commissions him as ambassador to the Khalifah Haroun. He makes his way home to wealth and honor.

In the seventh voyage of the fuller version, Sinbad's ship is blown off course and into a distant sea where it is attacked by huge fish and destroyed. Sinbad once again manages to save himself by rafting away from the desert shore upon which he is thrown, through an underground river and to salvation. Salvation comes in the form of an encounter with a wealthy merchant who takes Sinbad in and eventually makes Sinbad his son-in-law and heir. Sinbad relates his encounters with marvels more in the manner of his description of adventures than has been the case in the previous voyages. Usually the marvels are simply enumerated. Here, the descriptions of flying men and heavenly beings are more fully articulated. Nonetheless, the scenes appear in the proper relative position and bear no more upon the development of the structure of the tales than do the listed marvels of the previous voyages. Sinbad returns again to Baghdad, wealthy.

The format of the shorter version of the seventh voyage differs materially in its narrative detail, but only marginally in its structure as may be seen from the tabulation of topoi. It carries out the theme of Sinbad's entrance into politics. The impetus for this version of the seventh voyage is the Caliph Haroun al-Rashid's desire to have Sinbad head a return embassy to the king with whom Sinbad had stayed in the previous voyage. Nonetheless,

Sinbad suffers the usual catastrophe, this time at the hands of "devil-like" pirates. He then has the one expected fearsome adventure with elephants which leads him to the elephants' graveyard, and makes his fortune yet once more.

Having briefly summarized the catastrophes and adventures which befall Sinbad, let us again tabulate these structural elements of the narrative—but this time, from another point of view: according to the nature of the beings involved in the encounters.

Voyage	Catastrophe	Adventure	Adventure	Adventure
I	Fish	Sea-horse King	X	X
II	(Desertion)	Rukh	Snakes	X
III	Apes	Cyclopsian monster	Snakes	X
IV	(Storm)	Ghouls	Men bury him	Men are murdered & robbed by him
V	Rukhs	Old Man o' the Sea	Apes	X
VI	(Lost at Sea)	Disease	Underground river	X
VII¹	Fish	Underground river	X	X
VII²	Devil-like pirates	Elephants	X	X

It can thus be seen that there is, in addition to the rise, climax, and fall of the *number* of adventures, a concurrent rise, climax and fall in the "sensibility," or say even "humanity," of the beings whom Sinbad encounters in his adventures. Though not quite as rigidly symmetrical in these terms as in terms of the abstractions, "catastrophe" and "adventure," the same curve of rise and fall operates here. As the tales progress, the nature of those whom Sinbad encounters rises and falls along an almost evolutionary scale: I. sea-animals; II. non-mammalian land animals; III. animals (snakes, apes, cyclops); IV. man; V. animals (Rukhs, sea-man, apes); VI. anomalous; VII. sea-animals.

Let us tabulate Sinbad's adventures from yet one more point of view: the violence involved in his encounters.

Voyage	Catastrophe	Adventure	Adventure	Adventure
I	None (Fish)	None (Sea-horse King)	X	X
II	None (Desertion)	Minor (Rukh flight)	Minor (Snake threat & dangerous rescue)	X
III	Major (Ape attack)	Horrible** (Cyclopsian murders; blinding of Cyclops)	Horrible (Snake attack; defensive cage)	X
IV	Minor (Threat of storm)	Horrible (Threat of Ghouls)	Horrible (Buried alive)	Horrible** (Killing of innocents)
V	Major (Rukh attack)	Horrible** (Old Man o' the Sea killed)	Major (Apes imprison him)	X
VI	None (Ship lost)	Minor (Disease kills)	Minor (Threat of underground river)	X
VII¹	Minor (Fish attack ship)	Minor (Threat of underground river)	X	X
VII²	Minor/ Major (Capture by pirates)	Minor (Carried off by elephants)	X	X

** Sinbad himself commits violent acts in these strategically located instances.

An interesting echo of the basic rise and fall structure of the stories is to be found, too, in Sinbad the Porter's reactions to each of the stories:

Voyage	Sinbad the Porter's Reaction
I	"Thinks" about what befalls people.
II	Is "astounded" at what befell the sailor; prays for him.
III	Is "astounded."
IV	Is "astounded" and spends the night in the utmost contentment and pleasure.
V	Is "astounded."
VI	(No reaction recorded.)
VII	(No reaction recorded.)

But why, while the audience reacts with shock and horror, should the porter respond to the most chilling of the tales with "contentment and pleasure?" Perhaps because Sinbad only begins his stories after he has lavishly plied his guests, the nameless and faceless "companions" and the porter, with the finest of food and drink:

> When morning dawned, lit [things] up with its light and appeared, Sinbad the porter arose, prayed the morning prayer and came to the house of Sinbad the sailor as [the latter] had ordered him. He entered and said good morning to him. [The sailor] welcomed him and sat with him until the rest of his companions, his group, had arrived and they had eaten, drunk, enjoyed themselves, been pleasured and relaxed. Then Sinbad the sailor began to speak and said: . . .[21]

Perhaps also because the sailor closes each tale with a lavish gift to the porter. He gives a fabulous dinner and then loads the porter with one hundred *mithqāls* of gold.

In the final tale, Sinbad the porter takes up permanent residence with the sailor and they live out a happy and contented life:

> They remained in friendship and love with increasing joy and relaxation until [that] destroyer of pleasures, that divider of companions, that destroyer of indolence, that filler of graves—the cup of death—came to them. So praise be to the Living One who does not die.[22]

Sinbad the Sailor, then, tells his tales as an apology. He has been challenged by the porter's song and feels the need to justify his life and actions. But whom is he trying to convince, and how does he proceed to do so? Perhaps he needs to justify his actions to everyone who passes his door. Sinbad the porter receives an impression of the sailor's "companions" at the outset:

> He saw, in that abode, a number of noble gentlemen and great lords.[23]

But, this is all we know of them. Thereafter, they are merely Sinbad's companions who arrive each day to hear the tales of the sailor's adventures. Perhaps they are fellow merchants whose perceptions and rationalizations are akin to those of Sinbad the sailor himself. Or, perhaps they too are men who have doubted the justness of Sinbad's wealth and have been rewarded for their acquiescence to his self-justification just as the porter has been rewarded. In any case, the significance of the identity of names between Sinbad the sailor and Sinbad the porter is clear. It can hardly be fortuitous. Sinbad the porter is the sailor's alter-ego, the Sinbad who questions the distribution of wealth and the ways in which it has been gained. Finally, the questioning Sinbad is satisfied; but how? If Sinbad's self-justification stands on its own merits, why the need for the lavish presents of gold at the end of each story? Why the need to keep the porter's bought acceptance close at hand for the rest of their lives?

The answers are clear: Sinbad's actions are not finally justifiable. The crescendo and decrescendo of terror and violence that characterize the stories lead the audience from an attitude of readiness to believe, to questioning, doubt and downright rejection at the climax of the fourth tale. We then trail off into a knowing and cynical skepticism as the stories wind to a close.

Sinbad is plunged into horrible situations to be sure; but they are in large measure of his own making. The fundamental reason for his voyages is greed and his actions are often more violent than those of his antagonists. He himself notes at one point:

> I said to myself: 'I deserve all that has happened to me. All this is fated for me by God Most High so that I might turn from the greed by which I am [consumed]. All that I suffer is from my greed.'[24]

Sinbad's wealth and position are, then, a material reward for a vicious determination to "get on" in the world of commercial wheeling and dealing at the expense of anyone who happens to be in the way. They are clearly no heavenly reward for patience, forbearance and charity.

The cyclopsian monster's actions are horrible to be sure; but not apparently malicious. His act is not a moral one, but simply feeding behavior. Sinbad's plot to kill the monster and his blinding of it are, however, gratuitous; for the monster's castle is always open and Sinbad is free to build and provision a boat for his escape. Only after doing so does he return and blind the monster.[25]

> So, we carried the wood out of the castle and we built a raft. We tied it at the sea shore and brought a bit of food down to it. Then we returned to the castle.

Such is the situation with the Old Man o' the Sea. The Old Man has used Sinbad harshly to be sure by forcing Sinbad to carry him around under threat of severe punishment.[26]

> If I crossed him, he would beat me with his feet more harshly than with a whip.

Having gotten him drunk and having escaped, however, Sinbad's murder of the Old Man, regardless of how subhuman and sinister he might have been, is again a gratuitous act of violence.

It is not suggested that either the modern or the medieval audience could not justify Sinbad's actions in the third and fifth stories. Indeed, the shock value of the Old Man of the Sea story arises from the brusque shift from the comical scene of Sinbad making wine in a gourd, arousing the Old Man's curiosity, and getting him drunk, to crushing his skull with a rock. Rather, these two stories serve to raise and then slow the tempo of violence and horror. They shock the audience into an awareness of Sinbad's potential for murder which culminates horribly in the killing of innocent people in the tomb of the fourth story.

This latter situation is perhaps ambiguous in Muslim law for the action clearly takes place outside the Dār al-Islām. Thus, the case could never be brought before a *shari'ah* court. Furthermore, the victims are not even *dhimmi*.[27] Murder of the innocent, however, is abhorrent to Islamic morality under any circumstances: "Hast thou slain an innocent person not guilty of slaying another? Thou hast indeed done a horrible thing!"[28] Whatever justification might have been felt to be attached to Sinbad's being trapped in the tomb is obviated by the fact that he continues to murder after having found his way out of the tomb and to rob the corpses to make his fortune.[29]

> Whomever they buried, I would take his food and water and kill him whether man or woman. Then I would go out of the hole and sit on the sea shore.

Thus, while the first two stories find the audience in sympathy with Sinbad and ready to accept the view which he puts forward, our sensibilities begin to be seriously disturbed in the third and we are utterly repulsed by Sinbad's behavior in the fourth tale despite the fact that he has been presented to us as a grave and dignified figure of benign authority:

> In the midst of that company was a great, respectable man. Gray had touched his temples and he was fine of stature and handsome of face. He had dignity, sobriety, power and pride.[30]

Three more topoi which occur and reoccur concurrently with the major structural elements of the tale suggest that even Sinbad himself is aware of the indefensibility of the actions for which he is apologizing.[31] In the beginning and ending stories, Sinbad tells the tale of his adventures to all and sundry. But in the middle tales, he does so less and less until, in the fourth—the keystone tale—he not only does not tell his tale but consciously conceals the story of what has befallen him and what he had done. The captain and crew of the ship which picks him up do ask for his story, but he tells them only of a shipwreck and adds:

> I did not inform them of what had happened to me in the city or in the tomb fearing that there might be someone from the city with them aboard the ship.[32]

In his own mind, Sinbad represses the memory of his actions. At the end of each story, he tells us that he would forget the hardships of his voyages. But in the middle stories, he increasingly treats the events as if they "had been a dream." In psychological terms, his repression of guilt is clear.

Finally, Sinbad's conscience obviously bothers him, for in the middle stories he returns home not only to enjoy his wealth as he has in the first stories, but to give alms and to clothe the widows and orphans. A tabulation of these topoi will make their significance immediately apparent, inversely corresponding as they do to the rise and fall pattern of the story as a whole.

Thus, the structure of the relevant topoi of the story reveals a discrepancy between Sinbad's apology and the ethical principles of his, and the audience's, world. By it, we are led back to the outer frame story of Shahrazad and the king, for the stories are parallel. As Sinbad justifies his unjustifiable murders, so does the king justify the unjustifiable murder of his wives by their potential infidelity. But, as Shahrazad hopes to delay her own murder until the king may see the injustice of his own actions, she spins him a tale of self-justification which can only be had by buying off the conscience. The moral is not stated and the story is not didactic in any overt sense. It is merely one more example of the cunning cleverness of women which is such a common theme of the *1001 Nights.* That cunning is not necessarily condemned, merely noted and here once again it works for Shahrazad who does finally have her way. As with the king, so for the audience. Not overcome by greed for more material wealth, the audience sees the ironic disparity of an external view of Sinbad's actions and his own unconvincing apology which provides the ethical impact of the story. To be sure, many in any given audience might accept Sinbad's apology. Those who are caught up in the same greed for surplus wealth might need to justify similar actions and so find justification in Sinbad himself. It is that greed that speeds Sinbad on his voyages for, as he points out in introducing each of his tales, he undertakes his voyages not out of need but for the desire for adventure which is subsumed under and intimately related to the desire to buy and sell: the desire for profitable commercial ventures-greed.

Voyage	Telling the Tale	Reaction	Charity
I	To horse herder	Forgets	—
	To herder's friends		
	To the king		
	To ship's captain		
II	To merchant	Forgets	Gives alms and presents
	To merchant's friends		
III	(To sailors—mentioned)	All seems a dream	Gives alms, presents;
	To ship's captain	Forgets	Clothes widows & orphans
IV	(To pepper gatherers and their king—mentioned)	Forgets	Gives alms, presents;
		All seems a dream	
			Clothes widows & orphans
		As though his mind is lost	
	REFUSES TO TELL HIS TALE TO SHIP'S COMPANY		
V	To ship's company	Forgets	Gives alms, presents;
	To man from city		
	(To man from city—mentioned)		Clothes widows & orphans
VI	To Indians and Ethiopians	Forgets	Gives alms, presents

Voyage	Telling the Tale	Reaction	Charity
	To their king		
	(To the Caliph—mentioned)		
	To the Caliph		
VII	(To his family—mentioned)	—	—

Seen in this light, the Sinbad story becomes more coherent in its internal structure and fits nicely into its external frame, the Shahrazad/Shahriyar story. It also comes to tally more closely with its Greek and Latin analogues for in those stories the protagonist is of questionable moral character at the outset: he is a thief.[33]

The irony is most subtle; it is never stated. Only the audience's own reaction to Sinbad's stories affords an entrance to the teller's ironic intent. Indeed, the second version points out one more irony of the business world. Commercial acuity, however rapacious, piratical, even murderous, can also lead to political preference and power. In the sixth story, the King of Ceylon, impressed by Sinbad's stories of his adventures and by his commercial successes, commissions Sinbad as his Ambassador to Haroun al-Rashid. In the second version of the seventh voyage, Haroun takes Sinbad into the court and, in turn, entrusts him with the return mission to Ceylon. Thus, Sinbad has attained political power and success as well as commercial success and material wealth. But the story has become, not "a veritable glorification of navigation and maritime commerce," but a critique of the disparity between ethics and action. For, the audience, including Shahrazad's king, is aware of the cost of Sinbad's successes: the suppression of the merchant's ethical sensibility in his pursuit of material gain.

AN INDEX OF THE TOPOI OF THE SINBAD STORIES

(Numbers refer to pagination of MacNaghten edition)

	VOYAGE						
	I	II	III	IV	V	VI	VII
Reason for Voyage*	8	18	27	39	53	64	73
Catastrophe	9-10	18-19	27-28	39	54-55	64	73
Reaction to Catastrophe*	—	19;21	—	—	—	67;69	74-75
Adventure I	10	19-21	28-32	40	56-58	65	76-80
Adventure II	—	21-23	32-34	43	59-62	67	—
Adventure III	—	—	—	46-51	—	—	—
Telling the Tale	11;13 13;15	24;24	34; (36)	(43) 52	59;(59) 60	70;70; 70;72; 72	82
				(Refuses)			
Marvels Seen*	14	24-25	37	—	62-63	65-68	80-81
Recognition*	15-16	—	37	—	—	—	—
Return	17	26	38	52	62	71	82
Reaction to	19	26	34;	43;45;	62	72	—

	VOYAGE						
	I	II	III	IV	V	VI	VII
Return			(38)	50;52			
Charity	—	(26)	35	52	62	(72)	—
Porter's Payment	17	26	38	53	62	72	—
Porter's Reaction	17	26	38	53	—	—	(83)

* Typical topoi not directly relevant to the narrative.

Notes

1. J. I. Jabra, *Art Dream and Action,* Unpub. paper presented at UC Berkeley, 26 May, 1976, p. 7.

2. Private communication, 26 May, 1976.

3. Cf. Bibliography in note 32.

4. NY Times, 23 January, 1947, 31:2.

5. So also the more recent *Seventh Voyage of Sinbad,* which bears little or no resemblance to the *1001 Nights* tale. Cf. A. H. Weiler's review, *New York Times,* 24 December, 1958.

6. Gerhardt, Mia I., *Les Voyages de Sindbad le Marin,* Utrecht, 1957, p. 33.

7. Ibid., p. 39.

8. My thanks to all the students of Intermediate Literary Arabic at UC Berkeley, 1975-76, with whom I read the Sinbad stories and whose perceptive comments and questions have done much to make my own views more clear and concise.

9. Gerhardt ignores one fundamental, and several minor, structural elements in the *1001 Nights* tales which, with a predisposition to see Sinbad as a Romantic hero, leads to problems.

10. For a fuller analysis of the variations in the Arabic textual tradition, cf. Gerhardt, pp. 17-27.

11. *Alf Layla wa-Layla,* Calcutta, 1839, MacNaghten ed., Vol. III, p. 64. (Hereafter MacN.).

    It is interesting to note that not only does the Sinbad tale contain this first person narrative in biographical form, but that the frame story and episodes form a continuous and integrated whole, no part of which is expendable. Most Western literary historians consider the anonymous, Sixteenth Century *Lazarillo de Tormes* and *Don Quixote* as the "progenitors" of the novel precisely because of these features, which distinguish them from the "romance." That they occur here, in an obviously older tale deriving (at least) from an oral tradition, is of rather great significance for our understanding of the narrative art.

12. Cf. Scholes and Kellog, *The Nature of Narrative,* Oxford, 1975, pp. 52-53, for a discussion of this ironic disparity as a constant in fiction. We would

suggest a caveat on the Scholes-Kellog point of view, however. They make a sharp distinction between "traditional," i.e., oral, narrative and "written" narrative and confine the sort of irony described above to the written. We would argue that the irony exists in the *1001 Nights.* The *Nights,* however, even in their written form, must represent a transitional stage between oral and written narrative in which elements of the two modes cross fertilize each other. The terms "narrator" and "protagonist" are, therefore, used to distinguish between the two levels of perception represented by Shahrazad and Sinbad. The potential third level, that of the "narrator" of Shahrazad's story, seems not to be structurally or literally relevant.

13. We will return to this point at some length in our conclusions, but it should be noted here that Gerhardt ignores entirely the relationship of the Shahrazad element in her analysis and thus skews her entire perception of the tale.

14. MacNaghten, Vol. III, p. 4.

15. Ibid., p. 6. The translation is from Lane, v. VI, p. 327.

16. From Lane, p. 429. MacN.'s text is less precise: "So, look Oh Sinbad, Oh landsman, at what has befallen me, at what has happened to me, and at what my circumstance has been. Then Sinbad the landsman said to Sinbad the sailor, 'By God, you must forgive me for what I felt about your just rewards." p. 82. Sinbad's view of his riches is prefigured when he first meets the porter, too: "For verily I have not attained this happiness and this position save after harsh fatigue, great toil and many terrors. How I suffered, at first, from fatigue and hardship'." MacN., pp. 7-8. Here, though, the notion of heavenly reward is lacking.

17. I use the term, "analogue" as in Wm. F. Bryan ed., *Sources and Analogues of Chaucer's Canterbury Tales,* Humanities Press, New York, 1958. Analogues are tales having close similarities in plot, characterization and structure which are not demonstrably derived the one from the other or do not demonstrably form parts of a chain of direct transmission. While a common ancestor may exist for "analogue" tales, said ancestor exists too far removed in time and space to be established by any other means than the comparative method established for the reconstruction of proto-typical linguistic forms. Should said reconstruction be made, it must be treated as are such linguistic reconstructions—with a certain circumspection. Furthermore, until a full family tree is made of all of the analogues, great care must be taken about

applying the term, "source" to any given tale in its relationship to another. While not wanting to exclude the possibility of a direct Greek influence on the Sinbad tales, and particularly the third story which is an obvious analogue to the Ulysses and Polyphemus story, I find that G. E. von Grunebaum's conclusion as to the Greek origins of much of the Arabian Nights is overly positive in its statement [Cf. *Medieval Islam,* Chapter Nine, Creative Borrowing: Greece in the Arabian Nights, esp. III, pp. 298-305 on Sinbad]. As von Grunebaum himself points out, there are discrepancies between the Homeric and Arabian Nights versions. These, however, should not be put down merely to corruption by the Arab tellers, for there are discrepancies too between the Greek and the proto-typical story as it occurs in so many different versions of the story. To cite but one instance, neither Sinbad nor Ulysses makes reference to the magic ring that figures so prominently in the analogous stories, British and Turkish, to mention but two.

The relationship between the Ulysses and Polyphemus stories and all of their analogues, such as Sinbad's third voyage, is dealt with at length in appendix xiii to *Apollodorus: The Library,* Loeb Classical Library, New York, 1921, translated by Jas. G. Frazer.

18. This point is apparently missed by all the translators and commentators until Gerhardt. Burton, for instance, feels, "In one point, this world famous tale is badly ordered. The most exciting adventures are the earliest, and the falling off of interest has a somewhat depressing effect. The Rukh, the Ogre and the Old Man o' the Sea should come last." v. VI, p. 77, n. Gerhardt, however, has developed a very good analysis of these major structural elements; and we can do no better than to use her categorization. The chart is based on Gerhardt's, p. 30.

19. Cf. Note 17 above.

20. It is interesting to note that the theme of premature burial, salvation from the tomb and pirating of funerary treasures is a common one in Greek romances. Cf. Moses Hadas, *A History of Greek Literature,* Columbia U. Press, 1950, pp. 293-4.

21. This particular version of the scene introduces the third voyage. Cf. MacN. op. cit. p. 27. The topos does not precede the seventh tale.

22. MacN. op. cit. p. 83. The suggestion that they actually lived together comes from Lane, p. 429.

23. MacN. op. cit. p. 6.

24. MacN. op. cit. p. 75.

25. Ibid., pp. 28-32.

26. Ibid., pp. 56-58.

27. Ambiguous is perhaps the wrong term, for the situation is one in contention in Muslim law. Cf., for instance, Muhammad Ibn al-Ḥasan al-Shaybānī, *Kitāb al-Siyar* (The Islamic Law of Nations), translator Majid Khadduri, Baltimore, 1966. Esp. "The Application of Ḥudūd Penalties," pp. 171-74. Shaybānī holds that any *ḥadd* crime committed by a Muslim in the *Dār al-Ḥarb* would be null and void, as "they were committed [in a territory] where Muslim rulings are not applicable to them." pp. 171-2. Awzā'ī and Shāfi'ī, however, hold the opposing view. Cf. n. 49, p. 172. In any case, Shaybānī would apparently agree that the Muslim would be subject to the local law on such matters. Cf. pp. 173-4.

28. *Al-Qur'an al-Karīm,* "Sūrat al-Kahf", verse 74.

29. MacN. op. cit. pp. 49-50.

30. Ibid., p. 6.

31. It is interesting to note the topoi used in the development of Sinbad the sailor which are *not* structurally relevant to the whole of the tale. They occur and reoccur, not regularly as do the themes with which we have been dealing here, but sporadically even where not called for. They suggest another level or element of structure in the technique of oral composition. Oral composition has been well defined for poetry, but not so well defined for the prose tale. Nonetheless, many of the same techniques are found in oral prose tales as in poetry. The "formula" as defined by Parry and Lord is readily apparent in the prose tale, as are the "themes." What we have labeled "topos" seem to be intermediate features. Larger than the formula, though akin to it in form, they are not yet definable as themes. They appear to serve as building blocks for the tale teller. Each may be formed by a bundle of formulas and be recognizable as a mini-theme. They are, in turn, bundled together to form the major themes of the tale. Whereas, given themes become structurally significant in the tale individual topoi, unlike Propp's *functions,* may be, without affecting the tale, left out, added or interspersed between themes simply to flesh out the story in a familiar way.

We will attempt to pursue this observation in subsequent work.

32. MacN. op. cit. p. 52.

33. We will make no attempt to make a detailed analysis of the Medieval Greek and Latin analogues, but merely make one or two points which may have been obscured in our article and give some bibliography to the materials besides n. 17 above. It should be noted that Syntipas and Dolopathos are not analogues to Sinbad the Sailor in their entirety, but rather analogues to the Arabian Nights tale of the seven wise viziers. In this story, also known as the Seven Sages of Rome in other European versions, a young prince is falsely accused by one of his father's (the king's) wives of attempted rape. The details already provide an analogue to the Biblical and Quranic stories of Joseph. Being under a one week vow of silence, the prince cannot answer the charges; and the king determines to execute him. The boy's tutor calls in a series of wise men, each of whom spins a tale showing that hasty judgments are dangerous and that women are perfidious. Each time the king relents in his judgment, only to have the favorite again incite him against the prince. Much to the distress of the favorite, however, they do manage to get through the week, the prince is able to defend himself, she is discomfited and king and prince live happily ever after. One of the stories told by one of the wise men is of a famous thief who, when called to recite the stories of his most famous exploits, tells of being captured by a cyclops and of how he managed to escape. This particular tale provides the analogue to the third voyage, in particular, of Sinbad the sailor. For these tales, Cf. the following:

> *Essai sur les fables indiennes,* L. Deslongchamps, Paris, 1838. Which deals with the origin and transmission of many of the analogues and a prose version of the Seven Sages of Rome (in Old French) as well as an analysis of the Old French version (13th century) of Dolopathos.

> *Dolopathos sive de rege et septem sapientibus,* H. Oesterley, ed. London, 1873. Edition of the Latin version of Dolopathos.

> *Li romans de Dolopathos,* after Herbers, 13th century poet, ed. C. Brunet and A. Montaiglon, Paris, 1846.

> *Researches Respecting The Book of Sindibād,* D. Comparetti, London, 1882, Publications of the Folk Lore Society, X.

> "Syntipas" in *Fabulae Romanenses Graecae Conscriptae ex recensione et cum adnotationibus Alfred Eberhardi,* Lipsiae (Teubner), 1872.

Muhsin Mahdi (essay date 1983)

SOURCE: Mahdi, Muhsin. "Exemplary Tales in the *1001 Nights*." *Mundus Arabicus* 3 (1983): 1-24.

[*In the following essay, Mahdi discusses the stylistic origins of the tales in* The Arabian Nights*, arguing that* *they comprise a complete and unified text that reworks earlier stories, particularly the 'exemplary tales,' to create the effect of linguistic unity.*]

Literary criticism of **1001 Nights** must begin with the following question: Is the **1001 Nights** a collection, or a number of independent collections, of stories that follow one another with no connection between them other than the fact that they happen to be placed in this or that order in the edition or translation we chanced to be reading? If the critic's answer to the question is in the affirmative, he should refrain from speaking about the **1001 Nights** as a whole, as a literary work that has a beginning and an end and parts that show a recognizable relation among themselves, or even as a "book" in the generally understood sense of this word. He should look instead at each one of the stories contained in the **1001 Nights** and analyze it critically, but not attempt to relate it to the following story or to speak of all of them as a totality, at least not more than he would have done had each story been found between the covers of a separate book and the series had a general title such as "The 101 Books." If, on the other hand, his answer to the question is in the negative, he must ask yet another question: What is the connection between all these stories that exist today in the well-known editions of the book, such as the first Būlāq edition (2 vols., 1251 A.H./1835 A.D.; reprinted by al-Muthannā Library: Baghdad, n.d.)? Is it the result of the labor of the eighteenth-century Cairene scribe who, in order to please and profit from the European tourist who requested a "complete" version of the book that must include "all" the 1001 Nights, not more or less? For the fact of the matter is that whoever examines this edition with care and reads it from beginning to end finds no connection between all the stories in it other than the brittle thread woven by Shahrazad who narrates them, her sister Dinarzad who requests them, King Shahriyar who listens to them, and the Nights that follow one another numbered from 1 to 1001. As for the view that the connection between all of these stories is to be seen in Shahrazad's scheme to avoid being beheaded the next morning through arousing King Shahriyar's desire to hear the rest of each story or other stories and that this went on for 1001 Nights—that view is of little account, especially when one remembers the fact that the first Būlāq edition declares in the 148th Night (1:307), that is, long before the completion of the first quarter of the 1001 Nights, that King Shahriyar said to Shahrazad: "O Shahrazad, you have spoiled my pleasure in my kingdom and made me regret my misdeed of killing the women and my young wives." How then can one explain the stories that follow this passage, now that Shahrazad is no longer in danger of being beheaded? And the view that Shahrazad narrates her stories for the love of telling them, that the book is a compendium of stories, or that the book means to bring together every

type or kind of story—all that is another way of confessing that one has failed to find a connection between these stories beyond the obvious fact that they are stories; and the truth is that so far no literary critic has been able to find a connection between these stories that is any closer than this.

The literary critic who continues to think or feel, or who is driven by his initial reading of the book to imagine that there is a connection between the stories in it, should ask a third question: Is it possible that a connection exists, not between all of these stories, but between a portion or a particular collection of them, and which portion or collection is it? And since the various editions of the **1001 Nights** do not all include the same stories or collections of stories, he should ask yet a fourth question: Is there a portion or collection of stories present in all the editions and arranged in all of them in the same way? To have a measure of success, careful literary criticism in this case must be based on a reliable text of some sort; and it is well known among scholars who have examined the editions of the **1001 Nights** that the more pretentious of these are trumped up or pieced together from various known (and some unknown) manuscript sources, and that none of them— this holds true for the ones published in the West as well as ones published in the East—presents a critical text. Therefore the literary critic must ask a fifth question: Is there a portion or collection of these stories that is contained in all, or in the earlier and more reliable, manuscripts of the book? This is a question that can be answered in the affirmative. The oldest manuscript of the book belongs to a group that forms what we shall call the "Syrian branch" (the manuscripts preserved and copied in Syria). All manuscripts of this group contain the stories with which all the other manuscripts begin and they break off after giving a good portion of the story of Qamar al-Zamān. They agree with the manuscripts that form what we shall call the "Egyptian branch" (the manuscripts preserved and copied in Egypt) in the arrangement of the stories up to the story of the hunchback; this is then followed by the story of 'Alī the son of Bakkār, the story of Anīs al-Jalīs, the story of Jullanār of the sea, and finally the story of Qamar al-Zamān, in this order. All these stories exist in the "Egyptian branch," but their arrangement and position there, as will be explained later, is not the same. The stories contained in the manuscripts that belong to the "Syrian branch" are the oldest as well as the most artful and complex stories of the **1001 Nights** as we know this book today. If there is collection of stories in the **1001 Nights** that deserves the attention of the literary critic who wishes to ascertain whether there is any connection between them, it is this one; and if he fails to find any connection, even between the stories in this collection, then he must lose all hope; for we know of no other collection of stories that deserves to be called the *1001 Nights.* We must therefore ask a sixth question: Is there a connection between the stories in this collection, and how is one to go about trying to find it?

It is perhaps useful to clarify at the outset what is meant here by "connection." When we look at a book, we normally expect it to have an author with his own style of writing who has organized the book in a way that indicates its beginning and end and the parts in between; selected from his sources what he wanted to select and left out what he did not approve of, did not suit his purpose, or did not believe it to be true or correct; and indicated what he approved or disapproved of explicitly, implicitly, or by way of silence—that is, we usually think that the book's author has a point of view presented explicitly or implicitly in the book's content and organization. And we do not normally refuse to consider that the author has written a book simply on the ground that he did not invent everything in it but derived or gathered some or most or even all of its content from existing written or oral sources, or because the book did not come down to us from its author through written transmission but was transmitted orally over a short or long period of time, as long as the book has a particular form and expresses the purposes of its author or authors. The *1001 Nights* is a book the name and identity of whose author (or authors) is not known to us. But to ignore the name and identity of a book's author or authors does not mean that it is "a book without an author," as some scholars are in the habit of describing the *1001 Nights.* For though we may ignore the name and identity of a book's author of authors, we can still ask: Is this an "authored" or "composed" book—that is, does it have a characteristic form, language, style, or point of view, and do these indicate a particular time or place of composition? These are matters that can be found out, pinpointed, and used as indications on the basis of the "composition" itself, even if we ignore the name of the author and the time and place of the composition. There is nothing then to prevent us from asking: Is the collection of stories preserved in the manuscripts of the Syrian branch of the book we are dealing with (and the content of these manuscripts is what we will from now on call the *1001 Nights* in this paper unless reference is made to some other version) "authored" or "composed" in this sense?

I must confess that I do not find in the hundreds of books and articles dedicated to the investigation of the Indian and Iranian sources of the book and their translation into Arabic, or in the handful of reports in the Arabic sources about a book called "A Thousand and One Nights" or "A Thousand Nights" during the centuries that precede the oldest manuscript of the Syrian branch, anything that militates against raising this question; indeed, they make one more eager to raise and pursue it. I am not referring now to the fact that

most of the secondary literature makes use of one unknown source to prove the existence of another unknown source; speaks of Indian sources and prototypes of which we find only meager and scattered fragments today, and suggests that they were transmitted through many centuries and countries without anyone having a clear idea as to how they were transmitted or retold by untold generations of reporters or storytellers none of whom can be identified; or how they were assembled or pieced together to form longer, more complex stories of the type we find in the *1001 Nights.* For all this belongs to the history of mythology and is itself quasi-mythological in character. What I mean is rather this. There are a few stories in Arabic that can be shown to have been textually adapted and incorporated in some of the stories of the *1001 Nights;* these should teach us something about how the process of "transmission" took place. After examining these prototypes and comparing them with their counterparts in the *1001 Nights,* I could find no instance in which a story was incorporated in its original form. They were all changed, rewritten, dismembered, and recombined with other stories in such a way that their style, content, or point of view was fully transformed, leaving no doubt that we are not in the presence of a hand that merely copied, but a storyteller who deliberately selected elements and aspects of the story before him and rejected or changed others. Thus the sources of which we know play in the *1001 Nights* a role similar to the role played by sources used in the production of the vast majority of fictional compositions, which draw their material from earlier models but transform it in various ways. Similarly, what is said about oral transmission does not militate against raising the last question or the way it was formulated. Orally composed and transmitted stories do not necessarily lack order, structure, connection, or unity of purpose. If the stories of the *1001 Nights* were transmitted orally rather than recited from a written text—and I no longer believe that the manuscripts of the book, even after taking into account their variety and different branches and versions, require or justify the adoption of the view that they were transmitted orally—the storytellers must have memorized the stories, and their memories must not have been less accurate than the copyists' hands. A book may be composed by an anonymous author, composed from unknown sources, composed by more than one author, and transmitted orally: none of these things prevents it from being "authored" or "composed" in the sense indicated earlier.

There is no doubt that the *1001 Nights* adapted most of its stories from written sources. Some of these have survived and are known, while the rest have not survived or have not been identified and therefore we know next to nothing about them apart from the version perserved in the *1001 Nights.* But there is no doubt also that the *1001 Nights* represents a reworking of the earlier stories by way of additions and omissions and stylistic changes that resulted in a new form recognizable in the book's general linguistic and stylistic unity. In addition, there are many indications that the storyteller who reworked the earlier stories was acquainted with at least the general characteristic elements—narrative style, form, and complexity—of the different kinds of stories. Each of these elements deserves a separate study. All I can do here is present the reader with an example by examining the style of a single type, the exemplary tale, by which I mean stories that interpret proverbs or wise sayings, make use of similes, and offer examples or parables of events that have taken or will take place and as proofs or lessons with which the narrator means to urge the addressee to do or abstain from doing something. The exemplary tale is normally a short story; it occurs very rarely in the *1001 Nights;* and it is never a main story but always embedded in a main story or in a story in turn embedded in a main story. I will present these tales in some detail and comment on each in order to show that, although they occur in widely separate locations in the book, they all agree in their form, structure, purpose, and impact on the progress of the story in which they are embedded. (The text of these tales quoted here is throughout that of the oldest manuscript of the Syrian branch. Should it become necessary to refer to the first Būlāq edition, this fact will be indicated by inserting the volume and page numbers of this edition in parentheses after the quotation.)

The first exemplary tale in the *1001 Nights* is the tale of the merchant, the donkey, and the ox, embedded in the general framestory, that of the two kings, Shahzaman and Shahriyar. King Shahriyar has been engaged in his customary practice for some time: every night taking a young woman as wife only to have her beheaded the next morning, until there are hardly any eligible young women left and the city is in mourning. The following dialogue takes place between Shahrazad and her father, the vizier whose function it is to find the young women for the king and take charge of beheading them the next morning. "O father, I will let you in on my secret." "Oh! What is it?" "I desire that you give me in marriage to King Shahriyar; I will either succeed in delivering the people, or else die and perish like the rest." Her father (who thinks she must be stupid, for he cannot understand why she is courting certain death) tries to dissuade her, but she is firm. "Listen father! You must present me to him. That is all there is to it. I have made up my mind." He is understandably angry with her and tries to make her change her mind by citing three proverbs ("Whoever does not know how to handle things meets with misfortune"; "Fortune does not befriend those who do not think of the consequences of their actions"; "I was stretching out in comfort but my curiosity would not let me be") followed by the

introduction of the tale, which consists of a comparison, a question about the thing to which the comparison is made, and an expression that announces the tale's beginning. "I am afraid that you will end up in the same situation as the donkey and the ox and the husbandman." "And what did the husbandman do to the donkey and the ox?" "Know that there was. . . ." The husbandman worked for a merchant who owned a farm. The merchant was acquainted with the languages spoken by animals. He happened to hear the donkey advise the ox to feign sickness as a clever device to avoid working as hard as he did. When the ox followed the donkey's advice, the merchant told his husbandman to get the donkey to do the ox's work. The donkey spent a miserable day at hard labor, began to blame himself for the advice he gave, and thought of a ruse to get the ox back to work.

At this point the vizier interrupts the tale in the hope that the parable was enough to dissuade his daughter from insisting on going forward with what she had decided to do, and the following dialogue takes place. "You too, my daughter, will perish because of your ill-conceived plan. So do sit down, be quiet, and not court danger. Heed my advice and tender solicitation." "Father! I must go to this king. You simply must present me to him." "Do not do this." "It must be done." "Unless you sit down I will deal with you the way the merchant dealt with his wife." "And how did he deal with his wife, father?" The vizier continues the tale, "Know that. . . ." It appears from this that the vizier believed that the portion of the tale he had just narrated in which he compared Shahrazad to the donkey might be sufficient to restrain her from what she had decided to embark on. But he realizes that he has overestimated his proficiency as storyteller and his trust in the efficacy of his short parable, and that he must go on and offer a more telling tale. So he tells the rest of the tale. The donkey's stratagem was to frighten the ox by telling him that he had heard the merchant order the husbandman that, if the ox did not go back to work the next day, he is to take him to the butcher to slaughter him. When the ox heard the donkey's story, he got up screaming and decided to go back to work. The merchant, who was sitting nearby with his wife and children, heard all this and started to laugh. His wife thought he was ridiculing her and demanded an explanation. But he could not explain. His knowledge of animal languages was a secret not to be divulged to others, for divulging it meant his death. His wife was not convinced by this explanation and demanded that he divulge the secret anyway, even if it meant his death. The merchant was now getting ready to divulge his secret and making preparations for his death. He heard a dialogue between a dog and a cock who was powerful enough to please fifty hens. The cock was telling the dog that the merchant must be a fool who could not manage a single woman; were he to push her into a closet, close the door, and beat her hard with a stick, she would no doubt give up asking him to do what will lead to his death. The merchant followed the cock's advice. His wife entreated him to stop and was no longer interested in the secret. The tale completed, the following dialogue takes place between the vizier and his daughter. "Are you too not going to give up this affair until I deal with you as the merchant dealt with his wife?" "No, by God, I will not give up. These are not the kind of tales that can hold me back from what I am after. If you like I can tell you many such tales. And to make a long story short, if you do not present me to King Shahriyar of your own free will, I will go to him behind your back and say you did not permit a girl in my station to marry him because you thought I was too good for your master." "Would you really do this?" "O yes I would."

The formal characteristics of the exemplary tale can be observed in these introductory, central, and concluding passages. The vizier begins with reminding his daughter of three proverbial sayings and then claims that Shahrazad is like the donkey that got itself in trouble. When he finds that this parable makes no impression on Shahrazad, he claims she is like the merchant's wife who was about to cause her husband's death and he is like the merchant whose secret knowledge enabled him to find the solution to his difficulty and beat his wife until she gave up what she was after. It is also clear that the purpose for which this exemplary tale is told—that Shahrazad renounce her plan—fails twice and that Shahrazad derides this kind of tales, does not find them persuasive at all, and sees nothing in them to lead her to renounce her plan. Again, because Shahrazad does not believe that tales of this kind are useful or effective, she does not try to convince her father by narrating an exemplary tale (although, she says, she could tell him many such tales); she responds to the threat implicit in her father's tale, not with a threat implicit in an exemplary tale of her own, but with something she will do, which will enable her to marry the king, make him angry with her father, and may even lead to his death. Unlike the threat implicit in her father's tale, this threat achieves its purpose: the vizier goes to King Shahriyar and gives him Shahrazad in marriage.

If we now compare the exemplary tale with the general framestory in which it is embedded and ask why it is that the framestory moves on without being in any way influenced by the presence of the exemplary tale, we notice that what gives rise to all the actions in the general framestory is direct observation and experience. Thus initially we become aware that an important turn has taken place in the normal course of events, disturbing the lives of the two kings, Shahriyar and his younger brother Shahzaman, when we are presented first with what King Shahzaman observed as he went back to his bedchamber—his wife sleeping with the cook—just before he was to leave and visit his older brother. Seeing this with his own eyes is what caused his suffering and sickness. What gives rise to his recovery is again something he observed as he was looking out of the window of his brother's guest house while his brother was away hunting—his brother's wife with the black man Mas'ūd in the palace garden. When his brother King Shahriyar asks him what brought about his sickness, King Shahzaman relates to him what he saw in his own bedchamber just before his departure. King Shahriyar is amazed and wonders about the cunning of women, and threatens that he would have done all sorts of things if what happened to his brother had happened to him, but he does not do anything beyond consoling his younger brother, telling him all is well now that he has recovered. When King Shahzaman relates to King Shahriyar what he had observed in the palace garden during the latter's absence, King Shahriyar is extremely angry; yet, because he had not seen the thing with his own eyes, he does not believe his brother. So King Shahzaman says to him, "If you want to see your misfortune with your own eyes in order to believe me . . . let us both enter secretly . . . to your palace and you will then see with your own eyes." King Shahriyar does not decide to do anything about what he has heard from his younger brother except after he sees his misfortune with his own eyes. Finally, when the two kings leave the city and wander about, their purpose is not to hear tales, but to find someone whose misfortune is greater than theirs. They find the demon and his wife (the young girl he had stolen on her wedding night and placed inside a box at the bottom of the ocean in order to protect her virtue); she forces both of them to sleep with her while the demon is asleep; and it turns out that she has been engaged in this practice for a long time. Again, it is what the two kings see and experience that leads King Shahriyar to decide to kill his wife and the female and male servants and form the notion that he could protect the virtue of his wives if he married one for a night and had her beheaded the next morning. The general framestory does not cease emphasizing the central importance of seeing with one's own eyes and of direct experience. What the two kings see with their own eyes and what they experience is the cunning of women. It is their observation and experience that convince them of the truth of the statement of the demon's wife, "if a woman wants something, no one can restrain her."

Shahrazad is a woman who wants something. Her father the vizier tries to restrain her with an exemplary tale about things he had not himself observed or experienced. She is also a woman who "is knowledgeable, intelligent, and educated; she had read a lot and learned a lot." She has decided to deliver her people through stories meant to restrain the king from killing his wives.

She is not like the donkey who cannot stand hard labor nor like the merchant's wife who is ignorant of the language of animals. The first exemplary tale in the ***1001 Nights*** fails because the vizier who tells it knows nothing about the cunning of his daughter, does not know her real worth, and does not appreciate her learning, especially her knowledge of stories, their many types, and the impact of each type. The fact that the general framestory proceeds without this exemplary tale leaving the slightest trace in its means that there is no difference between the presence or absence of this exemplary tale in the general framestory in which it is embedded. This may explain why two manuscripts of the Egyptian branch (Oxford, Bodleian, No. 550 Or.; Paris, National Library, No. 3615 Ar.) neglect to require it and therefore omitted it, without noticing, however, that it was placed there in order to make the reader aware of the difference between the general framestory and the exemplary tale embedded in it, and the reason for the success of the former and the failure of the latter.

It is true that the general framestory and all the stories that will be narrated by Shahrazad are invented examples. But we are now dealing with what takes place inside these stories, its impact on the course of the story and on what the characters of the story say or do, and the reason why the characters of the story are persuaded or not persuaded by what they see or hear. The purpose of the general framestory and of most of the stories narrated by Shahrazad is to make the hearer or the reader imagine that the characters in these stories speak about and act upon existing, not invented, things. The characters of the general framestory do not act on the basis of what they are told in a tale; they are not persuaded by a tale that claims it is about things that have existed in the past. Beyond this, the exemplary tale narrated by the vizier for the benefit of his daughter Shahrazad offers a comparison that does not fit the character of his daughter. Unlike the merchant's donkey, Shahrazad was not stretching out doing nothing, but working hard at reading and learning about human nature and human wisdom; for though still young, she had "read many books and assorted compilations, books dealing with wisdom and medical matters, and memorized poems, looked into historical reports, and got to know the sayings of the common people and the words of the wise and of kings." Nor is she an ignorant, weak woman lacking in self-assurance like the merchant's wife who at first insists on causing her husband's death because she does not know that there are languages other than her own and believes in her ignorance that her husband is mocking her, and then allows him to beat her with a stick and is unable to stand much beating before she surrenders. The vizier's exemplary tale differs then from the general framestory in which it is embedded, not only in its form, but in its content as

well—that is, its examples are incompatible with the character it aims to exemplify and lack a meaningful point of comparison. This is why Shahrazad mocks and rejects it.

No exemplary tale is embedded in the story of the merchant and the demon (the first story narrated by Shahrazad to King Shahriyar), perhaps because Shahrazad's life is in danger and she must narrate a persuasive story the first Night if she is to survive. She has not had the opportunity to test the king's intelligence; he may have as low an opinion of exemplary tales as she; and if he fails to understand the point of telling an unpersuasive tale, he may very well have Shahrazad beheaded the next morning, in which case she would have failed in her design to deliver her people and ended as yet another victim of the king's passion. The three stories embedded in the story of the merchant and the demon are narrated by three old men, each of whom tells his own life story or an important event that was a turning point in his life. And each one produces for the demon a proof with which he demonstrates that his story is not something he had heard or imagined: as they narrate their stories to the demon, each of them points to his proof, the first to his wife the enchanted gazelle, the second to his two brothers the enchanted dogs, and the third to his wife the enchanted she-mule. The next story, that of the fisherman and the demon, begins in the eighth Night. Seven nights have by now passed and the king has not beheaded her. It appears that his desire to hear Shahrazad's stories has overcome his intention to behead his wives. In the story of the fisherman and the demon Shahrazad inserts an exemplary tale that is more complex than her father's, for there are two further exemplary tales embedded in hers. The exemplary tale occurs near the beginning of the story, after the fisherman had figured out a stratagem to return the demon (who was about to kill him) to his bottle, sealed it, and was threatening to throw him back into the ocean and arrange for him to stay there until doomsday.

At this point the exemplary tale is introduced in the form of a dialogue betwen the demon and the fisherman. "O fisherman, open the bottle so that I can do you a favor and make you rich." "You are lying. You are lying. You and I are like King Yūnān and the sage Dūbān." "And what is their story?" This is the story of the sage Dūbān who became the king's favorite courtier after treating and curing his leprosy and the king's envious vizier ("And no man is free of envy") who reminded the king of the proverb "Fate does not befriend the man who does not consider the consequence" and claimed that the sage Dūbān was an enemy of the king who had come to seek the destruction of his dominion. Here begins the first embedded exemplary tale, introduced by a dialogue between the king and his vizier. "I believe you are doing this because you envy him, as in the tale told of the vizier of King Sindbād when the king was about to kill his son." "Excuse me, O king of the time, what was it that the vizier of King Sindbād said when the king was about to kill his son?" "Know that King Sindbād was about to kill his son because an envious person had maligned him to his father, but his vizier told him, 'Do not do something you will regret later on, for I have heard it told that . . .'." King Yūnān narrates to the vizier the tale told by King Sindbād's vizier to King Sindbād. It is the tale of the husband who bought a parrot and kept it in his house to watch over his wife. When he returned from his voyage, the parrot told him about his wife's affair with her friend, so he went and beat his wife. The wife learned that it was the parrot that disclosed her affair to her husband and worked out a stratagem to deceive the parrot and make it tell the husband that something took place which he knew had not occurred. He now thought the parrot must have lied about his wife and killed it. Then, after learning from the neighbors that the parrot had told him the truth after all, he ended by regretting having killed it. This is followed by the conclusion of the first embedded exemplary tale. First, the king addresses the vizier as follows, "I am in a similar situation, O vizier. . . . And you, O vizier, have become envious of this sage and want me to kill him and then regret as the parrot's owner regretted after killing it." Thus King Yūnān compares in his tale the sage Dūbān to the parrot that was truthful but could be deceived to tell something that led to its death, and compares himself to the husband whose wife was faithless and yet hoodwinked him and made him kill the parrot and regret his deed. This comparison, as we shall see, is not completely incongruous, although it does not predict what the vizier will do or the way the king will meet his end.

As for the cunning vizier, he begins with a critical evaluation of the king's exemplary tale which compared him to the scheming wife, claiming that he himself has not been harmed by the sage Dūbān (as the wife had harmed the husband) and that he is only solicitous for the king's welfare and afraid lest he lose his dominion and die—that is, he compares the king to the poor parrot and compares the sage Dūbān to the scheming wife, which means that he compares himself to the husband who unjustly killed the poor parrot, a comparison that predicts the king's end but that escapes the king. Then the vizier defends himself. "If you do not find out that this is the case, destroy me like the vizier who was destroyed after having schemed against a king's son." "And how was that?" This is the introduction of the second embedded exemplary tale, which is told by the vizier. It is the tale of the vizier who accompanied a king's son on a hunt and drove him to follow a wild beast. The king's son followed the wild beast and lost its trace. He then came across the same wild beast transformed into a girl who claimed she was the

daughter of an Indian king, but who later transformed herself into an ogre and wanted to feed him to her children. The king's son was frightened, prayed to God for aid, was saved, and returned to his father and told him about what the vizier had done. The king called in the vizier and had him killed. This is followed by the conclusion of the vizier's exemplary tale. "Similarly you, O king, if at any time you should trust this sage, favor him, and make him your close companion, he will work to destroy and kill you." In addition, the vizier accuses the sage Dūbān of being a spy who had come to kill the king, using as evidence Dūbān's ability to cure the king's leprosy by an external process and without making him drink any medicine. The king believes this accusation, is convinced that his vizier is giving the right counsel, and starts to consult him on what he ought to do. The vizier counsels him to behead the sage Dūbān and the king consents.

It is clear from the fact that King Yūnān was persuaded by the tale told by his vizier and took his advice on what he ought to do next that the king lacked the capacity to examine the vizier's tale. He does not ask him, for example, when and how, once he had beheaded the sage, he will be able to ascertain the truth of the vizier's claim that he is a spy who had come seeking his destruction, or when and how he will get to know that his vizier was giving him sincere advice rather than planning to remove the sage Dūbān from the scene out of jealousy or other ulterior motives. Further, the comparison in the vizier's tale begins as if the vizier is planning to compare himself to the vizier in his own tale who had planned to destroy the king's son; for he begins his tale by asking King Yūnān to destroy him in case the king does not confirm his claim that the sage Dūbān had come to work for the king's destruction. But the tale he tells does not explain what motivated the vizier in the tale to destroy the king's son or why the vizier in the tale was sure that the king's son was in fact destroyed and could not save himself and return to his father and inform him about what the vizier had done; nor is the tale clear as to what the king's son and the ogre stand for or who it is they are meant to represent. Then at the end of the tale the vizier changes the comparison: it is now the sage Dūbān, not himself as he claimed at the beginning of the tale, who corresponds to the vizier in the tale. King Yūnān's vizier, who engaged in the criticism of the king's tale, is taking advantage of the king's ignorance and uncritical attitude and narrates to him a tale that is flimsy in structure, lacking in points of correspondence, and having no purpose other than to confuse the king. Beyond this, the vizier does not depend on the impression that his tale makes on the king, but arouses his doubts, instills in him the fear of death, and makes him afraid of the sage Dūbān for nothing that he had done but merely because he may be able to destroy the king, and the king begins to think that "he who cured me by means of something I held in my hand is also able to kill me by giving me something to smell," though he knows of nothing to justify his doubts concerning the sage's fidelity and attachment to him. It is thus that the vizier succeeds in driving the king to do what he wants him to do, not by means of the tale he had narrated, but by what he tells him afterwards and the manner in which he arouses in him the passions of fear and uncertainty about his survival.

Having finished with the two embedded exemplary tales, the fisherman proceeds with the main tale and narrates to the demon how the sage Dūbān came to know that he had been the object of the courtiers' jealousy and that they had lied about him before the king, but also "that the king is ignorant, indecisive, and not fully in charge." He regrets having healed the king and entreats him to spare his life. (At this point the fisherman interrupts the tale and addresses the demon, comparing himself to the sage Dūbān and the demon to King Yūnān: "Just as I repeatedly asked you to spare my life, O demon, and you insist on killing me.") The sage Dūbān then reproaches the king for treating him so badly after having cured him and compares himself to the crocodile and the evil repayment it received for its good deed. When the ignorant king asks, "And what is the tale of the crocodile?" the sage Dūbān thinks it is pointless to tell the tale and answers him, "I cannot tell it now in the condition I am in." And when he finds out that he cannot escape death, he asks the king to allow him to go back to his own residence to arrange for his will and take care of his affairs, including the donation of his books to those who "deserve them," especially a book called the *Arcane of the Arcane* he intends to present to the king. This book has many virtues, "but the first secret contained in it is that when you, O king, behead me and open the sixth page and read three lines from the page on your left and speak to me, my head will speak and answer whatever question you ask of it."

The sage succeeds in arousing the ignorant king's curiosity, and he is now eager to experience the strange affair and converse with the decapitated sage, who might enlighten him about such questions as the truth of the statement of his scheming vizier. By beheading the sage Dūbān, he could have thought, he would avoid the danger of being destroyed by him, learn the truth about his vizier's plans, and satisfy a passing whim, "to see how your head talks to me." The book entitled the *Arcane of the Arcane,* however, contains no writing, only empty pages soaked in poison; when the king tries to open the pages, he is forced to moisten his finger by putting it in his mouth and dies along with the sage Dūbān. The fisherman concludes his tale by comparing himself to the sage Dūbān and the demon to King Yūnān: "Had King Yūnān spared the sage Dūbān, he

would have survived and God would have saved him. But he insisted on killing him, so God on high caused his death. And you, O demon, had you spared my life to begin with, I would have now spared yours. But you insisted on killing me, so I will kill you by imprisoning you in this bottle and throwing you into the bottom of this ocean." The demon begins to scream and asks the fisherman to free him, reminding him of the proverb "O you who was kind to him who had done you harm," and compares himself to 'Ātika and the fisherman to Imāma, but when the fisherman asks him, "And what did Imāma do to 'Ātika," he excuses himself from telling their tale, "This is not the time to tell tales, confined in this narrow prison as I am. Not until you set me free"—the demon compares himself to the sage Dūbān who refused to tell the tale of the crocodile.

The exemplary tale told by the fisherman fails at the end; the fisherman does not throw the demon into the ocean as his tale would require him to do. His exemplary tale is similar to that of King Yūnān's vizier in that it does not correspond to what it is meant to exemplify and in that it changes its point of view as it proceeds. The fisherman is not a sage who knows how to cure kings of their sickness and possesses no secret book; it is in fact the demon who possesses secret knowledge with which he can enrich the fisherman. The story begins with comparing the fisherman to the sage Dūbān and the demon to King Yūnān. But this comparison, faulty as it is, loses its sense after the king orders that the sage Dūbān be beheaded and he himself dies of poison. Therefore the fisherman retracts this comparison and begins to speak of the unknown—what would have happened had the king spared the sage's life and what would have happened had the demon not tried to kill him—matters quite extraneous to his exemplary tale. The demon is not persuaded by the fisherman's exemplary tale, does not argue with him about the correctness of his comparison, and does not find it useful to tell the exemplary tale of Imāma and 'Ātika. Instead, he takes a pledge that he will not try to harm him and also that he will make him rich. What leads the fisherman to open the bottle is not the impact of his exemplary tale on the demon, but rather the fact that he himself is now persuaded that the demon will not harm him because of the pledge, which the demon took swearing by the Great Name, and also because he is persuaded that the demon is able to make him rich. The fisherman opens the bottle because of his newly-won feeling of security and his desire for riches. Neither the demon nor the fisherman are persuaded by an exemplary tale; and the demon finally persuades the fisherman, not by means of an exemplary tale, but by swearing by the Great Name and arousing his passion for wealth.

This then is the exemplary tale embedded in the story of the fisherman and the demon. Each one of the three exemplary tales—the tale of the sage Dūbān and King Yūnān and the two tales embedded in it—fails to achieve its purpose and leaves no trace in the course of the affairs it is meant to influence. Neither the fisherman throws the bottle into the ocean as he would have done had he been truly persuaded by his own tale and the comparison he makes, nor does King Yūnān refuse to kill the sage Dūbān as he would have had to do had he been truly persuaded by his own tale and the comparison he makes; and the vizier tells a tale knowing full well that the comparison made in it does not correspnd to his relation to the king, that the ignorant king does not comprehend the point of the tale, and that he was not about to drive the king to kill the sage by means of an exemplary tale, so he concludes by persuading him in a more direct manner by playing on his fear of violent death.

It is of interest to point here to an external clue that indicates that narrators of the *1001 Nights* were not unaware of the formal structure, content, purpose, or impact of the exemplary tale. The two exemplary tales inserted in the tale the fisherman narrates to the demon are adapted from a well-known book translated into Arabic in the early 'Abbāside period called the "Story of Sindbād" or the "Story of the King's Son and the Seven Viziers." This was originally an independent book, not part of the books known at that time as "Hezār Afsāne" and "A Thousand Nights," and was incorporated in the *101 Nights* and *1001 Nights* at a much later time (in the case of the *1001 Nights* this may have taken place as late as the twelfth century A.H./ eighteenth century A.D., that is, after having survived as an independent book for a millennium). The fact that these two exemplary tales were inserted in the story of the fisherman and the demon and that the name Sindbād was given to the king (in the "Story of Sindbād" it was the name of the sage in charge of the king's son's education, not the king's name) indicates also that the "Story of Sindbād" was not part of the *1001 Nights* when the story of the fisherman and the demon in the form we have it was narrated as part of the latter book. The original story of Sindbād is an exemplary tale that is quite complicated in form and structure. It is the story of the king's son and his tutor, the sage Sindbād, who one day looks into his pupil's horoscope and finds that if the young man speaks a single word during the next seven days he will meet an evil end, and the story of the king's concubine who tries to seduce the young prince. The prince refuses her advances and tells her that, at the end of the seven-day period, he plans to inform the king of what she did and have him kill her. The concubine goes to the king and accuses his son of trying to seduce her and then kill her because she had refused to submit to him. The king is angry and is about to have his son killed. But the viziers are apprehensive lest the king kill his son, regret what he has done, and

blame them for not restraining him. So each day one of the viziers narrates to the king one or more exemplary tales about the cunning of women meant to hold him back from killing his son, and, after each vizier ends his tale or tales, the concubine narrates one or more exemplary tales about the cunning of viziers or the sons of kings meant to drive the king to kill his son before the end of the seven-day period when the prince would be able to speak and disclose the truth of the affair. For seven days the concubine fails, while the viziers succeed in restraining the king from killing his son, after which the prince is free to speak and inform the king of the concubine's guilt.

The different versions of the "Story of Sindbād" that have come down to us do not agree on the number of the embedded exemplary tales or on their form, and thus do not permit a satisfactory account of that book's structure. But most of the embedded tales begin with citing a proverb or a saying that functions like a proverb, and every one of them is a tale related by a narrator who has "heard" it or to whom it was "transmitted," but who has not himself observed or experienced the events told in it. The tale of the parrot, which is told in the *1001 Nights* by King Yūnān, is told in the "Story of Sindbād" by the king's concubine during the third day. By adapting the two exemplary tales from a well-known collection of such tales, the author or narrator of the *1001 Nights* reminds the reader of the existence and popularity of these tales; and by introducing them with expressions in the form of similes he draws the reader's attention to the fact that they are exemplary tales. But the interesting point is that he reverses the impact of the two tales he adapts from the "Story of Sindbād." In the "Story of Sindbād" the tale of the parrot succeeds in prevailing upon the king not to kill his son at the end of the first day, and the tale of the king's son and the ogre succeeds in making him angry and commanding that his son be killed early in the third day, after which he is dissuaded by two tales told by his vizier that same day. In the *1001 Nights,* in contrast, the tale of the parrot fails to save the sage's life and the tale of the king's son and the ogre fails to lead to his death, although at the end he is decapitated due to the king's fear of death. It is as if Shahrazad—or the author or narrator of the *1001 Nights*—is pointing out to the reader that the exemplary tales that fill the "Story of Sindbād" and similar storybooks are paltry, insignificant, and insipid stories that fail to achieve their purpose and that, in any case, they do not play a positive role in the stories of the *1001 Nights* in which they are embedded.

The lesson did not escape the author of the odd version of the exemplary tale narrated by the fisherman to the demon in the first Būlāq edition of the *1001 Nights.* The exemplar of the manuscript from which the first Būlāq edition was printed must have mentioned that

King Yūnān narrated a tale to his vizier (it probably mentioned also the title of that tale, "the owner of the parrot's regret for having killed it," as we find it in MS, Paris, National Library, No. 3612 Ar., fol. 11r), but not the tale itself (just as we do not find the tale in the Paris manuscript just mentioned), so it replaced it with another tale, "King Sindbād's regret for killing the falcon" (1:14-15), not found in the earlier manuscripts of the *1001 Nights,* which is the tale of the king who killed his falcon because it prevented him from drinking from a cup containing poison and not water, as he had imagined, and then found out that the falcon had saved his life and regretted killing it. This indifferent story, as Edward William Lane characterizes it in the notes to his translation, was thought by the scribe an adequate substitute for the tale of the parrot, since it predicted the end of King Yūnān who will die of poison. But what interests us in this substitution is that the scribe knew that the actions and characters of these exemplary tales are not organically related to the actions and characters of the story in which they are embedded and therefore did not trouble himself to search for the tale of the parrot in other manuscripts; instead, he simply substituted another exemplary tale for it, went on copying the rest of his exemplar, and produced the confused state of affairs in the manuscript from which the first Būlāq edition was printed.

The third exemplary tale in the *1001 Nights* is the tale of the envier and the envied narrated by the second kalandar in the story of the porter and the three ladies, which follows the story of the fisherman and the demon. This is the last exemplary tale in the manuscripts of the Syrian branch. The second kalandar is a king's son fated to become a wood gatherer. One day he comes upon a trap door leading to an underground apartment where he finds a demon's wife, spends the night with her, and is discovered by the demon who kills her because, he says, he is certain that she has betrayed him and, according to the prescriptions of the legal system he follows, is no longer lawfully his wife. Since he is not certain that the prince is the guilty person, however, he decides to transform him into whichever animal form the prince wishes to assume. Here begins the introduction of the exemplary tale. "I said, having entertained the desire that he may pardon me, 'O demon, it is more fitting that you pardon me, so pardon me as the envied pardoned the envier.' The demon said, 'And how did that happen?' I said, 'It is claimed, oh demon. . . .'" This is the tale of the envied who pardoned the person who envied him and did not scold him for spoiling his pleasure in life or for trying to end it by throwing him into a well. The prince concludes the tale by addressing the demon again. "So consider, O demon, how the envied pardoned the envier, how the latter had envied him, harmed him, and pursued him until he threw him in the well and meant to kill him, while the envied did

not counter by harming him but rather forgave and pardoned him." This too is an exemplary tale in which the example does not correspond to what is being exemplified. The prince did not envy the demon or try to destroy him, and the tale contains nothing that may be compared to the demon's wife who betrayed her husband. Further, the envier in the tale had no doubt about the identity of the envier or that it was the envier who threw him into the well and meant to destroy him. So the tale is rather pointless. There is no reason for its presence in this place, unless the author or narrator wanted to present the reader with yet a third example of a tale that fails to address the issue at hand and leaves no trace in the story in which it is embedded. The demon pays no attention to the tale, proceeds to do exactly what he had meant to do before hearing it, and transforms the prince into a monkey. Whether this was the reason for which the scribe who copied the exemplar from which all the manuscripts of the Egyptian branch are derived decided to omit this tale, we will never know. But we find no trace of it in any of these manuscripts or in the first Būlāq edition.

Before concluding the account of exemplary tales in the *1001 Nights* we ought perhaps to mention a story that imitates but is not in fact an exemplary tale. This is the story of Ni'ma and Nu'm narrated by the magian Bahrām after his conversion to Islam at the hand of Qamar al-Zamān's sons al-Amjad and al-As'ad in the story of Qamar al-Zamān. The early part of the story of Qamar al-Zamān is found in the manuscripts of the Syrian branch, but the story is incomplete. The complete story is found, however, in a manuscript of the Egyptian branch copied in 1177 A.H./1763-4 A.D. (Oxford, Bodleian, No. 551 Or.) and in the more recent manuscripts of that branch, which contain a version similar to that of the first Būlāq edition with its numerous additions of material of a sexual nature, on the one hand, and omissions that disfigure the logic of the story, on the other (1:343-416; the story of Ni'ma and Nu'm is in 1:403-414; the quotations below are from the Bodleian manuscript). Bahrām suggests that al-Amjad and al-As'ad prepare to journey with him to the city of their father Qamar al-Zamān where he will reconcile them with their father who had ordered their execution because of unfounded accusations against them made by their mothers-in-law. At this point the story is introduced as follows. When they heard their father's name, they began to weep. Bahrām said to them, "Do not weep, my brothers, for in the end you will meet your father as Ni'ma and Nu'm met." "And what happened to Ni'ma and Nu'm?" "The story of Ni'ma and Nu'm is an amazing and strange affair." "For God's sake, do tell us what happened to Ni'ma and Nu'm. Who knows, it may lighten our burden and make us forget our troubles." "Very well then. It has reached me, and God knows best, that there was. . . ." Bahrām narrates to them the story of the young lovers, Ni'ma the son of al-Rabī'of Kufa and his girl Nu'm, how they were separated by al-Hajjāj the governor of Kufa who arranged for the girl to be abducted and sold to the caliph 'Abd al-Malik the son of Marwān, and what happened to them until they met again in the caliph's palace in Damascus. After hearing the story, al-Amjad and al-As'ad say to Bahrām, "By God, what happened to these two *is* more amazing and strange. You have indeed made us forget our troubles, O Bahrām." The story, which begins as though it would take the form of an exemplary tale, does not exemplify what happened to al-Amjad and al-As'ad except remotely in that it speaks of the ultimate reunion of the two lovers. Neither the separation of al-Amjad and al-As'ad from their father corresponds in any way to the separation of Ni'ma and Nu'm, nor was their separation caused by someone who corresponds to al-Hajjāj, nor do their adventures after their separation from their father correspond to anything that happened to the two lovers. This is a story of the-type known as "amazing and strange stories" meant to amuse the hearer and make him forget his troubles because it happens to be more amazing and strange than what had happened to him (as pointed out by what the narrator says at the beginning and the way the hearers react at the end), and in this respect it is similar to what King Shahzaman saw in the garden of King Shahriyar's palace, which helped him overcome his sorrow. It is perhaps meant to indicate that Bahrām foretells the meeting between al-Amjad and al-As'ad and their father, which takes place sooner than he had thought. For he does not travel with them to their father's city and does nothing to help them to meet him or to reconcile them as he plans to do at the beginning of the story; were this the point of his story, it would have been pointless, since immediately after Bahrām concludes the story of Ni'ma and Nu'm, the story in which it is embedded gathers momentum and reaches a speedy conclusion: all the sons and fathers whom fate had separated meet again but they meet in the city where Bahrām narrated the story of Ni'ma and Nu'm. This then is a story whose beginning reminds us of the exemplary tales we have been discussing earlier. But the fact of the matter is that it is not an exemplary tale.

Having reached this point in our exposition, we need to explain how we can distinguish between the exemplary tale and other forms of embedded stories. As their name indicates, all embedded stories occur within the longer stories in which they are embedded. (As far as I know the longer stories do not have a common name indicating their function as stories that contain embedded stories.) But before we do so, we need to distinguish between two forms of embedded stories, the "inserted" stories and the "framed" stories. (The longer stories in the latter case are known, with a view to this function, as "framestories," but, since this name is sometimes ap-

plied to both the story that is the frame and the story that is framed by it, it is perhaps better to call the longer stories "framing stories.") Now something like this classification has been known to students of narrative forms, but the distinction between the two types of embedded stories has not been clearly drawn in connection with the stories of the *1001 Nights*. For it is said that "inserted" stories in the *1001 Nights* are much shorter, less significant, and have less weight than the stories in which they are embedded, while "framed" stories are longer, more significant, and weightier than the "framing stories." This is generally true in the *1001 Nights* of "framed" stories and of that sub-group of the inserted stories which we have been discussing here, the exemplary tales, but not of inserted stories in general. Thus the story of the two viziers Nūr al-Dīn and Shams al-Dīn, which is narrated by Ja'far the Barmakide to Harūn al-Rashīd and embedded in the story of the three apples, is an "inserted" story, yet much longer and by far more significant than the story in which it is embedded. It is not useful then to concentrate on the story's length and importance and use these as measures for distinguishing "inserted" from "framed" stories. What is needed is a measure that holds true for all "inserted" stories and distinguishes them from all "framed" stories in a way that leaves no room for hesitation or doubt.

Since framed stories are the most common in the *1001 Nights,* let us begin with these. My own observation has led me to the view that in the *1001 Nights* the framed story is characterized by the fact that its narrator had either himself observed the characters and experienced the actions in the story he narrates, or else heard the story from someone who in turn had observed the characters and experienced the actions in the story he narrates, and so on—that is, the framed story is always or in the end a story about personal experience. When it is transmitted on the authority of an earlier narrator, it is not characterized by the fact of the transmission as such, but by the fact that the chain of transmission terminates in a narrator who personally observed the characters and experienced the actions in the story he narrates. The inserted story, on the other hand, is characterized and distinguished from the framed story by the fact that the narrator had not observed the characters or experienced the actions he narrates, had not heard it from someone who observed the characters and experienced the actions he narrates, and so forth— that is, the inserted story is always or in the end an invented story or a story about invented things that have not been observed or experienced. These, it seems to me, are the marks that distinguish the framed story from the inserted story in the *1001 Nights.*

As for the exemplary tale, that which marks it off from the inserted story in general is that it is the type of inserted story in which the narrator declares at the beginning (and sometimes also in the course of the tale and/or at the end) that his purpose is to present an example, using one or more expressions in the form of similes in which he mentions the characters or actions in the story in which the tale is being embedded and the characters or actions with which the former are to be compared, and connects them through expressions ("as," "like," etc.) that show explicitly that he intends to show a similarity. Comparison, correspondence, or similarity as such are not the distinguishing marks of the exemplary tale. It is not these as such that distinguish the exemplary tale from the inserted story in general or even from the framed story, for they are common to all inserted and framed stories. What distinguishes the exemplary tale is the narrator's declared intention of making a comparison and his use of a particular device, the simile. Thus the difference between the exemplary tale and the inserted story in general is the difference between the use of what rhetoricians call "simile," on the one hand, and "metaphor," on the other. In addition, we have pointed out that the exemplary tale in the *1001 Nights* is usually brief. We can add further that they all make comparisons with animate beings other than man and contain at least one such character (the donkey and the ox, the dog and the cock, the parrot, the ogre), or such things as a decapitated man who speaks or demons that speak a human language; in this respect they are mythical and can be called fables ("fables" and "parables" are terms that King Shahriyar applies to the exemplary tales crammed into the *1001 Nights* by the copyists of the more recent manuscripts; see the first Būlāq edition, 1:318 [line 10], 319 [line 10]), but with the understanding that inserted stories in general as well as framed stories may contain fabulous characters also.

After presenting, describing, and characterizing the exemplary tales in the *1001 Nights,* we need to consider briefly their place in the vastly expanded late version of which the first Būlāq edition is a fair representative, for this is the version that has been studied by most of those who classified the book's stories. Mia I. Gerhardt, author of the *Art of Story-telling: A Literary Study of the Thousand and One Nights* (Leiden, 1963, 388), pointed out that what she called inserted stories do not occur in this version after the story of Qamar al-Zamān except in the story of Jānshāh, which is embedded in the story of the serpent queen (1:657-710; the story of Jānshāh is in 1:673-702). The story of Jānshāh, however, is not an inserted story but a framed story in which Jānshāh narrates the amazing and strange things he himself observed and experienced. After Jānshāh hears the story of Bulūqiyā he tells him, "Poor man! You have not seen much in your life, have you? You should know, O Bulūqiyā, that I saw the prophet Solomon during his lifetime and saw innumerable other things. I have an amazing story and a strange tale to tell, and I want you to stay with me so that I can tell

you my story and inform you of the reason for which I have been staying here." He starts to tell his story, then interrupts it to say, "And here I am, I Jānshāh, the one who saw all this, O brother Bulūqiyā." Bulūqiyā is amazed by what Jānshāh has told him and asks him why he is sitting in that particular place, and Jānshāh proceeds with the rest of his story. "When Bulūqiyā heard this account by Jānshāh, he was amazed . . . and said, 'By God, I thought I had journeyed all over and covered the entire world. By God, hearing your story made me forget all I had seen.'" There is nothing in the form or content of Jānshāh's story to distinguish it from other framed stories. Let us turn then to the inserted stories contained in this version before the story of Qamar al-Zamān.

The manuscripts of which the first Būlāq edition is a fair representative changed the order of the stories in the manuscripts of the Syrian branch after the story of the hunchback. Thus instead of the earlier order described at the beginning of this paper, in these manuscripts the story of the hunchback is followed by the story of Anīs al-Jalīs, then the story of 'Umar the son of al-Nu'mān, then a collection of animal fables and other exemplary tales, then the story of 'Alī the son of Bakkār, and then the story of Qamar al-Zamān, while the story of Jullanār of the sea is postponed to the fourth quarter (*Nights* 738-756; 2:242-63). Thus when Mia I. Gerhardt speaks of the inserted stories in the *1001 Nights* she means the three stories we have presented as found in the manuscripts of the Syrian branch and the stories crammed in the late Egyptian branch between the story of Anīs al-Jalīs and the story of Qamar al-Zamān. Let us then consider the so-called inserted stories in this portion of the first Būlāq edition. To begin with, she says that the story of the slaves Bakhīt and Kāfūr embedded in the story of Ghānim the son of Ayyūb (1:127-30) are inserted stories, when the fact of the matter is that the two slaves tell their life stories and how they came to be castrated (the third castrated slave, whose name is Sawāb, does not tell his life story because "my own story is too long and this is not the right time to tell it" [1:130]; compare the story of the third old man framed in the story of the merchant and the demon, which was not told in the manuscripts of the Syrian branch and in most of the manuscripts of the Egyptian branch) and are therefore framed rather than inserted stories. As for the story of 'Umar the son of al-Nu'mān (a long epic tale that must have been an independent book and belongs to the art of epic story-telling rather than the art of storytelling encountered in the *1001 Nights*), it contains the long inserted story of Tāj al-Mulūk and Princess Dunyā (1:228-71) narrated by the vizier Dandān to King Daw' al-Makān ("all this while they were besieging Constantinople"); in this inserted story is embedded in turn the story of 'Azīz and 'Azīza [1:235-55] in which 'Azīz tells the story of his affair with his cousin 'Azīza (it is a framed story); the story of the hashish addict (1:290-91) narrated by the girl Bākūn to Kān Makān, which is an inserted story; and finally the two stories narrated by the Bedouin Ḥammād the son of al-Fazārī (1:295-99) to the three kings about the most amazing things he has seen or that have happened to him, which are framed stories. So far then we find only two inserted stories neither of which is an exemplary tale.

As for the collection of stories that follow the story of 'Umar the son of al-Nu'mān (no student of the *1001 Nights* entertains any doubt that they are foreign to the book in their language, style, and structuring, or that they have been placed in the book for no clear reason), they are a series of animal stories and short parables (1:301-20); the content of all of them indicates that they are exemplary tales adapted from the work of the Brethren of Purity, earlier collections of animal stories, and elsewhere. They include six inserted exemplary tales: the tale of the falcon and the partridge, the tale of the flea and the mouse, the tale of the hawk and the birds of prey, the tale of the sparrow and the eagle, the tale of the merchant and the two men who duped him, and the tale of the foolish weaver (1:311, 316-19), not to mention the numerous short proverbial sayings. All of these begin with similes or expressions that declare the narrator's intention to present an example, such as "I consider you to be like" so and so, "I have a tale that deals" with this or that, "so that I can repay you for your good deed as it happened" to so and so, "what you did for me is not unlike" so and so, "I am afraid that you will encounter what happened to" so and so, "you will be like the husbandman who," "so that you do not meet the end of" so and so, or "he was in the same situation as" so and so. Some of these exemplary tales succeed in achieving their purpose, others fail, and still others have no purpose beyond narrating the tale. Their style indicates that the copyist who crammed them in the *1001 Nights* was aware of the fact that they are not of the same type as the book's other stories and therefore tried hard to emphasize that they do form part of it. Thus he began by making King Shahriyar demand that Shahrazad narrate such tales in particular, making him say to her, "I desire that you narrate to me some bird tales," and he follows this up by making King Shahriyar confess that these tales are making a deep impression on him by having him repeat to her: "O Shahrazad, you have spoiled my pleasure in my kingdom and made me regret my misdeed of killing the women and my young wives. Do you have some tales about birds?"; "O Shahrazad, you have provided me with many more exhortations and lessons. Do you have some tales about wild beasts?"; "O Shahrazad, by God this is a fine tale. Do you have an account dealing with good friendship and its preservation in hard times so as to save one's friend from death?"; "O Shahrazad, your

tales are beautiful indeed. Do you know of similar fables?"; "O Shahrazad, you reminded me of something of which I have been heedless. Will you not narrate more examples of this sort?"; "O Shahrazad, narrate more tales of this sort" (1:301, 307, 308, 315, 318, 319, 320; and in so doing he places the king in a position that is even less commanding than the crow who, when told by the fox, "I have tales concerning good friendship; if you want me to tell them to you I will do so," answers haughtily, "I permit you to narrate them" [1:316]). All of this is a confession on the part of the copyist that these tales are out of place here, that the original narrators of *1001 Nights* disdained narrating tales of this sort, and that their insertion in the book needed to be justified by praising them, exaggerating King Shahriyar's desire to hear them, and bragging about the impression they made on him.

This is true also of the other exemplary tale dragged into the *1001 Nights* after the story of Qamar al-Zamān. Thus the exemplary tales inserted in the story of Sindbād or the king's son and the seven viziers (2:52-86) are not framed stories (as Mia I. Gerhardt thought in her book [400-401]), though they and similar tales may have their own structures; they are all inserted exemplary tales, as explained earlier. The copyists who dragged in the collection of animal stories discussed above, the story of the king's son and the seven viziers, and the rest of the exemplary tales found in the manuscripts of the late Egyptian branch did not read the *1001 Nights* that reached them in its earlier form with any measure of care and did not consider the reason for the rare occurrence of such tales in the book they had before them, why only a few exemplary tales were inserted in it, or the point of view of its author or narrator concerning exemplary tales in general.

The author or narrator of the *1001 Nights* was neither a literary critic nor a man engaged in the classification of stories. He was a storyteller who expressed his point of view concerning exemplary tales in the way he narrated them and the way he inserted them in his other stories. Subsequent authors or narrators who understood his purpose followed in his footsteps. Copyists who missed what he was after and thought that the book was like a hole in the ground in which one could dump one story after another regardless of their styles, structures, or contradictory aims, disfigured the book and produced the confusing text we find in the first Būlāq edition. The author or narrator of the *1001 Nights* preserved in the manuscripts of the Syrian branch makes it plain at the very beginning that Shahrazad was perfectly capable of narrating a large number of exemplary tales. Nevertheless, after the general framestory in which her father narrates for her benefit the first exemplary tale, she herself narrates no more than two exemplary tales. All three exemplary tales, whether told to Shahrazad by her father or told by Shahrazad herself, agree in their structure, style, and failure to have any effect on the course of the stories in which they are inserted. Each of them begins with declaring explicitly and at length its purpose in a way that leaves no doubt in the mind of the reader that the author or narrator intended to draw his attention to the fact that what will follow is an exemplary tale: it is as if the author or narrator meant to fatten the cow before slaughtering and opening it up to show the reader that there is nothing there but skin and bones—like the first old man's concubine in the story of the merchant and the demon, who had been transformed into a cow by the jealous wife, after she was sacrificed by her husband during the Great Feast. Then he narrates the tale, only to show that it is inept, inappropriate, proceeds at random, strays from what is being exemplified, and fails to make its point. Finally, he criticizes it through the character to whom it is narrated, who makes fun of it, pays no attention to it, and does not perform the action the exemplary tale is meant to make him perform or performs the action it is meant to prevent him from performing.

Heinz Grotzfeld (essay date 1985)

SOURCE: Grotzfeld, Heinz. "Neglected Conclusions of the *Arabian Nights*." *Journal of Arabic Literature* 16 (1985): 73-87.

[*In the following essay, Grotzfeld asserts that a careful study of noncanonical materials associated with* The Arabian Nights *can shed important light on the history of the collection.*]

Certainly no other work of Arabic literature has become so universally known in the West as the *Stories of Thousand and One Nights,* more commonly called *The Arabian Nights' Entertainments* or simply *The Arabian Nights.* Since their first appearance in Europe (Galland's French translation 1704 sqq.; English and German translations of Galland only a few years later), the *Nights* met with lively interest from a large public. In the latter part of the 18th century, this interest generated something like a run on manuscripts of the *Nights,* especially in the English world, as is documented by the relatively large number of Arabic MSS of the *Nights* that were purchased by British residents or travellers in the East and are now to be found in British libraries. Even the I Calcutta edition of the *Nights* of 1814 and 1818 as well as the II Calcutta edition of 1839-1842 are due to British activities, since they are both based on MSS brought from Syria or Egypt to India by Englishmen.[1] On the continent, too, one library or another contains MSS of the *Nights,* most of them, however, purchased after 1800 and representing the same recen-

sion as the Bulaq edition; a considerable number of older MSS of the *Nights* are to be found only in the Bibliothèque Nationale de Paris.

The interest in MSS of the *Nights,* which is to be observed in the 18th century, diminished at the beginning of the 19th century. Arabists, anyway, did not make the most of the MSS treasured in European libraries. They were satisfied with picking out stories which had not been translated at that time and, in their own translations or expansions of Galland, simply added them to the repertoire of *Nights* stories already existing. There are two exceptions. One is Joseph von Hammer, whose French translation, made in Constantinople from 1804 to 1806 on the basis of a complete Egyptian MS and sent to Silvestre de Sacy for publication, came out only in 1823, not in its original form, but in a stylistically rather unsatisfactory German version for which his publisher Cotta was responsible. The important information given by Hammer in his introduction about the *Nights,* the complete list of the stories, their order and segmentation into nights, as well as his view of the history of the work, had been published earlier in the *Fundgruben* and the *Journal Asiatique.* The other exception is Maximilian Habicht, "who, through close intercourse with Orientals during his long residence in Paris, had come to embrace entirely the irresponsible Oriental attitude towards MSS and editing" (Macdonald 1909, p. 687) and made out of fragments of the *Nights* and other material a compilation of his own, which he published in the years 1825-1839 (vols. I-VIII of the Breslau edition; the remaining four vols. were published after Habicht's death by H. L. Fleischer, 1842-1843).

The Bulaq edition of 1835, which was widely circulated both in the Arab world and in Europe, and the II Calcutta edition, which is of the same recension, superseded almost completely all other texts and formed the general notion of the *Arabian Nights.* For more than half a century it was neither questioned nor contested that the text of the Bulaq and II Calcutta editions was the true and authentic text. This opinion did not change even when in 1887 H. Zotenberg in his *Notice sur quelques manuscrits des Mille et Une Nuits et la traduction de Galland* showed that the text of the Bulaq and II Calcutta editions represented only one recension of the work[2] and that other recensions of the *Nights* were attested by manuscript evidence much older than any evidence for ZER.[3] It is not that the results of Zotenberg's research were disregarded. But a process not uncommon in the history of texts made it possible to preserve the generally accepted notion of the *Nights* more or less unaffected by them: ZER was given, by tacit convention, the status of a *canonical* text, whereas other recensions were degraded to the rank of *apocrypha.* Still another group of texts was classified as *pseudepigrapha,* e.g. the Breslau edition, which was revealed by Macdonald to be a compilation made by its editor Habicht.[4] Even texts which since Galland had been considered to be integral parts of the *Nights,* e.g. Aladdin or Ali Baba, became classified as spurious.[5] Disregarding "apocryphal" or "pseudepigraphical" material may frequently be of little or no consequence. But focusing the view on ZER rather blocked philological research concerning the text. It is one of the purposes of this paper to show that a careful study of "apocryphal" materials can throw new light on the history of the *Nights.*

The original conclusion of the *Nights* seems to be lost. Galland never had a text for the conclusion he gave to his *Mille et Une Nuits,* and he was considered—wrongly, see below, n. 21—to have invented this end himself. Thus it was not before the early 19th century, when copies of ZER came into the hands of Europeans, that an Arabic text of the end of the *Nights* became known in Europe. Hammer boasted of being the first European to have discovered the unexpected conclusion of the *Nights* (for his *unexpected* conclusion, see below). The conclusion of the *Nights* as it stands in the Bulaq and II Calcutta editions is no doubt a very simple piece of literature.[6] Nevertheless, it reflects the conclusion outlined in the latter half of the 10th century in the following famous passage of the *Fihrist:*

> ". . . until she had passed a thousand nights, while he at the same time was having intercourse with her as his wife, until she was given a child by him, which she showed to him, informing him of the stratagem she had used with him. Then he admired her undertaking and inclined to her and preserved her alive. And the king had a qahramāna who was called Dīnārzād, and she assisted her in that."[7]

The central idea of the conclusion in ZER, thus, is obviously the same as that of a *Nights*-recension which circulated in Bagdad 800 years earlier, though more obscured than at that time.

We do not know what the conclusion was in the Indian archetype nor in *Hazār Afsānah,* the Persian recension. Reflexes of the frame story in the popular literatures of India and its neighbouring countries compel us to assume that in the original form of the frame story, Shahrazād continues to tell her stories, in the well-known manner, thus postponing her execution from one day to the other, until she has given birth to a child[8] and therefore feels safe enough to reveal her stratagem to the king, whereupon the king preserves her alive and definitely makes her his queen. The new title the work was given in the Arabic world, **alf layla,**[9] in which the number was taken literally, suggests that Shahrazād has to survive a fixed number of nights by the telling of stories, not the period until she has reached the status of mother, which then safeguards her against execution.

The connection between Shahrazād's reaching this status and her ending the story-telling became obscured. That seems to be the case already in the conclusion summarized in the *Fihrist.* The wording of the *Fihrist,* however, does not exclude, even if it does not suggest, that Shahrazād needed exactly 1000 nights to become a mother. Compared with that conclusion, ZER presents a slight but not unimportant change: during the 1001 nights, Shahrazād has borne the king three children. It is difficult to decide whether Shahrazād now has three children because naive tradition could not imagine the king and Shahrazād enjoying the delight of communion 1001 nights successively without the number of children Shahrazād is plausibly to have in that time, and therefore amended the number, or whether she has them because three children were thought to touch the king's heart more effectively than only one child. The latter does not seem to be wholly incompatible with ZER, since here changed numbers occur in two other places in the frame-story as well. In the well-known orgy observed by Shāhzamān, the queen enters the garden together with twenty slave girls and twenty male slaves; in G (see n. 30) and other earlier texts, the queen is escorted only by twenty slave girls, ten of whom, however, are disguised male slaves, which becomes clear to Shāhzamān only some time later, when they strip off their clothes. In ZER, the trophies of the young woman held captive in the chest are five hundred and seventy seal-rings; in G and most of the other texts, the number is ninety-eight. The change in both instances is no doubt due to a defective or somewhat illegible text.[10] Nevertheless, it shows the predilection of the redactor of ZER, or more likely of one of his predecessors, for strengthening essential elements of the narration by quantitative arguments.

By linking the end of Shahrazād's story-telling with the thousand and first night, the internal logic of the conclusion is lost: when Shahrazād on the 1001th night requests the king to grant her a wish, namely to exempt her from slaughter for the sake of her three children whom she presents to him, her step has not been prepared in the narrative. Nor has any reason been given—except through the title—that she should do so this very night, since the period of story-telling has nowhere previously been limited, unlike the period of seven days in the *Book of the Seven Sages,* where the span to be bridged by telling stories is set in advance by the horoscope of the hero. One or other among the copyists or compilers of *Nights*-recensions also realized this lack. Hammer owned (and translated) a ZER-MS containing a revised ZER-version. Its conclusion says that on the 1001th night, after the story of Ma'rūf the Cobbler, king Shahriyār was bored by Shahrazād's story-telling and ordered her to be excuted the following morning, whereupon Shahrazād sent for her three children and asked for mercy, which was granted her, in the same way as in the other ZER-versions. This surprising turn, which could have been borrowed from a parody of the frame-story, fully explains why Shahrazād must proceed to act as well as why she finishes telling stories to the king.[11]

Even the author of the poor conclusion which ends the recension contained in the so-called Ṣabbāgh-MS[12] conceived such a double motivation, though one which perfectly fits the poorness of the composition: Shahrazād has related to the king all she knew (*hādā mā ʿindī min tawārīḫ as-sālifīn wan-nās al-awwalīn*), "and when king Shahriyār had heard all the tales of Shahrazād, and since God had blessed him by her (sc. with children) during the time he had been occupied by listening to her tales, he said to himself: 'By God, this wife is intelligent, erudite, reasonable, experienced, so I must not slay her, specially since God has blessed me by her with two children.' And he continued that night admiring her wisdom, and his love for her increased in his heart. In the following morning, he rose and went to the cabinet, bestowed a robe of honour and all kinds of favour upon her father the wazīr, and lived together with her in happiness and delight until the angel of Death came to them and made them dwell in the grave" (MS arabe 4679, fol. 401b). In these artless, simple or poor conclusions[13] we meet the same deterioration that is often to be observed in stories transmitted by long oral tradition: the elements as such of the stories are still preserved, but the original connection between them has become distorted or totally lost. So it is reasonable to assume that the conclusions of ZER and the Ṣabbāgh-MS reproduce what was known about the end of the *Nights* from oral tradition in a more or less skilful arrangement by the respective compiler.

There exists, however, an elaborate skilful conclusion, entirely different from that of ZER. It is attested by some manuscript sources considerably older than ZER, and one printed one, namely Habicht's edition. But since this edition, following Macdonald's article in *JRAS* [*Journal of the Royal Asiatic Society*] 1909, was discredited in its entirety, though parts of it reproduce "authentic" *Nights*-material, particularly fragments of *Nights*-recensions prior to ZER, its conclusion was no longer paid any attention.

So far, I know of four sources for this conclusion:

H: Habicht's edition or compilation of the *Nights;* the end of his compilation, nights 885-end, is based upon the transcript made by Ibn an-Najjār (Habicht's Tunisian friend) of a fragment of a *Nights*-recension transcribed in 1123/1711 (see Macdonald 1909, p. 696).

K: MS Edebiyât 38 in Kayseri, Raşid Efendi kütüphane; this MS is described by H. Ritter in *Oriens* 2, 1949, pp. 287-289; on the basis of its script Ritter gives the 16th or the 17th century as the date of its transcription ("frühestens 10.jh.H."). The text is divided into nights, but the nights are not numbered, the space for the numbers, which probably were to have been rubricated, not having been filled.

B: MS We.662 in Berlin, Stiftung Preussischer Kulturbesitz-Staatsbibliothek (formerly Royal Library), Nr. 9104 in Ahlwardt's catalogue; the transcription of the part concerning us is from 1173/1759. The night-formulae and the numbering have been crossed out (see below p. 87).

P: MS arabe 3619 in Paris, Bibliothèque Nationale; the MS. was formerly marked "Supplément arabe 1721 II" (so in Zotenberg 1887, p. 214); "d'origine égyptienne écrit au XVIIᵉ siècle ou au commencement du XVIIIᵉ siècle".

The conclusion of these sources differs from the conclusion attested by the *Fihrist* and narrated in ZER, in that Shahrazād does not implore the king's mercy by referring to her status as mother of his child or children, but "converts" the king by telling stories which make him reflect on his own situation so that he begins to doubt whether it was right to execute his wives after the bridal night. No sooner is Shahrazād sure that her stories have taken effect than she begins to tell the prologue/frame-story of the *Nights* themselves, somewhat condensed and slightly alienated in that the characters have no names, but are labelled "the king", "the wazīr", "the wazīr's daughter" and "her sister", and the scene is simply "a town":[14]

> It has reached me, o auspicious King, that someone said: People pretend that a man once declared to his mates: I will set forth to you a means of security against annoy. A friend of mine once related to me and said: We attained to security against annoy, and the origin of it was other than this; that is, it was the following: I over-travelled whilome lands and climes and towns and visited the cities of high renown . . . Towards the last of my life, I entered a city,[15] wherein was a king of the Chosroës and the Tobbas and the Caesars. Now that city had been peopled with its inhabitants by means of justice and equity; but its then king was a tyrant dire who despoiled lives and souls at his desire; in fine, there was no warming oneself at his fire, for that indeed he oppressed the believing band and wasted the land. Now he had a younger brother, who was king in Samarcand of the Persians, and the two kings sojourned a while of time, each in his own city and stead, till they yearned unto each other and the elder king despatched his Wazir to fetch his younger brother . . .

(Burton XII, pp. 192-193; I shall skip the rest of the story, which ends as follows)

> . . . on the fifth night she told him anecdotes of Kings and Wazirs and Notables. Brief, she ceased not to entertain him many days and nights, while the king still

said to himself, 'Whenas I shall have heard the end of the tale, I will do her die,' and the people redoubled their marvel and admiration. Also the folk of the circuits and cities heard of this thing, to wit, that the king had turned from his custom and from that which he had imposed upon himself and had renounced his heresy, wherefor they rejoiced and the lieges returned to the capital and took up their abode therein, after they had departed thence; and they were in constant prayer to Allah Almighty that He would stablish the king in his present stead. And this said Shahrazad is the end of that which my friend[16] related to me." Quoth Shahriyar, "O Shahrazad, finish for us the tale thy friend told thee, inasmuch as it resembleth the story of a King whom I knew; but fain would I hear that which betided the people of this city and what they said of the affair of the king, so I may return from the case wherein I was."[17] Shahrazad replies that, "when the folk heard how the king had put away from him his malpractice and returned from his unrighteous wont, they rejoiced in this with joy exceeding and offered up prayers for him. Then they talked one with other of the cause of the slaughter of the maidens and they told this story and it became obvious for them, that only women had caused all that [18] and the wise said, 'Women are not all alike, nor are the fingers of the hand alike.'"

(Burton XII, p. 197).

The king comes to himself and awakens from his drunkenness; he acknowledges that the story was his own and that he has deserved God's wrath and punishment, and he thanks God for having sent him Shahrazād to guide him back on the right way. Shahrazād, then, lectures on the interrelation between ruler and army, between ruler and subjects, on the indispensability of a good wazīr (which is all somewhat inappropriate in this context), argues by reference to sūra 33:35 that there are also chaste women,[19] and by relating the Story of the Concubine and the Caliph (Burton XII, pp. 199-201; Chauvin's Nr. 178) and the Story of the Concubine of al-Maamun[20] (Burton XII, pp. 202-206; Chauvin's Nr. 179) she demonstrates for Shahriyār that his case is not as unique as he thought, because "that which hath befallen thee, verily, it hath befallen many kings before thee . . . all they were more majestical of puissance than thou, mightier of kingship and had troops more manifold" (Burton XII, p. 199). The king is now fully convinced that he was wrong and that Shahrazād has no equal. He arranges his marriage with her, and marries Dīnāzād to his brother Shāhzamān, who in Samarcand behaved the same way as he had done until Shahrazād entered the scene. Dīnāzād, however, stipulates that the two kings and the two sisters should live together for ever. So the wazīr is sent to Samarcand as their governor. The king orders the stories told by Shahrazād to be recorded by the annalists; they fill thirty volumes. There is no mention in these texts of a child, much less three children, as an argument for granting mercy to Shahrazād.[21]

The texts of the four sources mentioned above are essentially identical, the variants in number and nature being within the usual confines. But though derived from one and the same version, they constitute the end of two different recensions of the *Nights*. In H, this conclusion follows the "Tale of the King and his Son and his Wife and the seven Wazirs" (i.e. the Arabic version of the *Book of Sindibād* or *Book of the Seven Sages*); the transition from this tale to the conclusion is seamless and logical:

> King Shahriban (i.e. Shahriyār's name in the Breslau edition) marvelled at this history and said, 'By Allah, verily, injustice slayeth its folk!'[22] And he was edified[23] by that, wherewith Shahrazad bespoke him, and sought help of Allah the Most High. Then he said to her, 'Tell me another of thy tales, O Shahrazad; supply me with a pleasant story and this shall be the completion of the story-telling.' Shahrazad replied, 'With love and gladness! It has reached me, O auspicious King, that a man once declared . . .'

(Burton XII, p. 192; see above p. 79).

In the three other texts, this conclusion is interwoven with the "Tale of Baibars and the Sixteen Captains of Police"[24] as follows: the 16th Captain tells to King Baibars the prologue-story as if related to himself by a friend. The stories told in the Breslau edition by the 14th, 15th, 16th Captain (*n, o, p* in Burton's translation) in this recension of the Baibars-cycle are told by the 13th, 14th and 15th respectively (this shift is already prepared in the first half of the cycle: the 5th Captain relates two stories, his "own" and that of the 6th Captain). The stories of the Clever Thief and of the Old Sharper (Burton's *na* and *nb*) remain in their place in the order of tales between *n* and *o*. The 15th Captain thus tells, in the first person singular, the story of the traveller who was threatened by a robber sitting on his breast with a knife drawn in his hand, but is delivered by a crocodile which came

> 'forth of the river and snatching him up from off my breast plunged into the water, with him still hending knife in hand, even within the jaws of the beast which was in the river. And I praised God for having escaped from the one who wanted to slay me.' The king[25] marvelled and said: 'Injustice harms[26] its folk.' Then he was alarmed[27] in his heart and said: 'By God, I was in foolishness before these exhortations, and the coming of this maiden is nothing but (a sign of God's) mercy.' Then he said: 'I conjure thee, O Shahrazad, supply me with another one of these pleasant tales and exhortations, and this shall be the completion of the Story of King aẓ-Ẓāhir and the sixteen Captains.' And she said: 'Well, then came forward another Captain, and he was the sixteenth of the Captains, and said: 'I will set forth to you a means of security against annoy. One of my friends once related to me . . .'
>
> (B, fol. 113a; I have borrowed from Burton XII, p. 44 and 192 the translations of the corresponding parts in the Breslau edition = H).

The text of the story told by the 16th Captain (see [above]) is somewhat fuller in B than in H, which is, for its part, close to the text of K. B and K coincide, however, in minor details both internal (e.g. even the first wives of the two brother-kings are sisters) and external (e.g. the 16th Captain's story has night-divisions at the same places), so there is no doubt that B and K derive from the same version, the fuller text of B being due to a more recent polishing. In P, a considerable portion of the text is missing here: the "Tale of the two Kings" which is told by the Captain, breaks off after the words characterizing the elder kind ('. . . and wasted the land'); then follows immediately the "Tale of the Concubine of the Caliph" (fol. 163b, lines 5-6). The lacuna is superficially dissimulated by the interpolation of *fa-ta'aġġab al-malik aẓ-Ẓāhir min hādihi l-umūr, fa-lā ta'aġġab ayyuhā l-malik Šahriyār* at the end of the second Concubine-tale (fol. 170a). Even the division into nights continues; the numbering, however, runs thus: fol. 163a: 908; fol. 165b: 909; fol. 168a: 1000 (!). Shahrazād finishes telling her stories in that night.

Incorporating the prologue-story into the Baibars-cycle involved a threefold oblique narration, which necessitated some adjustments in the text to be transcribed. The redactor mastered this task well, but eventually, certainly because of failing attention, made a mistake, which then was copied by over-scrupulous scribes. In K, as in B (P: lacuna), the Baibars-cycle ends as follows (somewhat less abruptly than in the Breslau edition, vol. 11, p. 399):

> '. . . and this is the end of what my friend related to me, O King aẓ-Ẓāhir.' Those who were attending and King aẓ-Ẓāhir marvelled, then they dispersed. And this is said Shahrazad what reached me from their invitation. Then King Shahriyar said: 'This is indeed marvellous, but O Shahrazad, this story which the Captain related *to me (aḥkā lī)*, resembles the story of a king whom I know . . .'

He then asks what the reaction of the subjects was, "so I may return from the case wherein I was." (K, fol. 122b). Shahrazād replies by using nearly the same words as in H (see above), though on the basis of the premises of this composition she cannot have any further information. In the text of B, the inappropriate *to me* has been eliminated. The story then continues and ends in the same way as in H.

The literary ambition and the skill of this composition—at least of parts of it—are clearly discernible in spite of the somewhat degenerated versions in which it is accessible to us. Redactional mistakes as the aforementioned one indicate that this conclusion was not originally composed for these versions, but is a "recycled" fragment.[28] Since the recensions into which this conclusion has been inserted were in all probability compiled as early as the 16th century,[29] the recensions to which this conclusion originally belonged must be considerably older.

Such an early date of origin is suggested by some characteristic details in which the Story of the Two Kings and the Wazīr's Daughter, i.e. the prologue-story, agrees with the prologue in Galland's MS, the earliest extant MS of the *Nights*.[30] As in G, the story immediately begins with two kings who are brothers (ZER begins with a king who divides his kingdom and assigns it to either of his two sons); the younger brother returns to his castle, as in G, to take leave of his wife (in ZER he returns because he forgot *ḥāǧa* 'something' or *ḥaraza* 'a pearl') and, as in G, he perceives in the garden the wife of his brother together with ten white slave girls and ten male negro slaves (in ZER the number is twenty for each group). The lover of the younger brother's wife is "a man" (*raǧul*, K and B) or "a strange man" (*raǧul aǧnabī*, H), which fits in better with the "man from the kitchen-boys" (*raǧl min ṣubyān al-maṭbah*) in G than with the "negro slave" in ZER. Last not least, the epithets *ǧabbār—lā yuṣṭalā lahū bin-nār* ("a tyrant dire—there was no warming oneself at his fire", see above) which characterize the elder brother occur even in G among the epithets of Shahriyār (they are not found in ZER nor in any other MS which is independent of the G-group).[31] This congruence does not necessarily imply that this conclusion ever constituted the end of that recension of which G is an initial fragment, since the prologue in G, too, is most probably a literary spolium;[32] it implies, however, that a prologue like that of G and a conclusion like that of H and K, B, P once formed the beginning and the end of a recension of the *Nights* considerably earlier than G.

Though the conclusion incontestably bears an Islamic stamp and at first sight hardly has anything in common with the conclusion summarized by Ibn an-Nadīm, we have to ask ourselves, considering the great age of the composition, whether it is a totally new creation achieved without any knowledge of other conclusions of the *Nights*—or at least without any regard to them—, or whether the author of this composition has perhaps also inserted, besides comparatively young elements such as the two concubine tales,[33] fragments of older recensions. I think we have good reasons to assume that this composition includes an element which was part not only of a very old recension of the *Nights,* but also, most probably, of the Indian archetype. Ibn an-Nadīm's words concerning the end of the *Nights,* "until she was given a child by him, which she showed to him, informing him of the stratagem she had used with him", imply, no doubt, the device by which in this composition the king is informed of the matter. For, how did Shahrazād instruct the king? It is hardly conceivable that the structural element par excellence of the (older parts of the) *Nights,* namely telling a story for the most varied purposes (to obtain ransom, to gain time, to entertain, to instruct), should not be employed here: for Shahrazād nothing is better suited to reveal her stratagem to the king than to relate to him the story in its alienated form in which Shahriyār recognizes himself and his own fate as in a mirror. I have no doubt that in the recension of the *Nights* which the author of the *Fihrist* had before his eyes the conclusion was introduced by this revelation story, but I consider it also very likely that this was the case already in the Indian archetype of the *Nights.*

Since the king is converted from his hatred for women to an indulgent attitude towards them, and does not simply show mercy, as he does in the *Fihrist/*ZER-conclusion, there is no need for Shahrazād to produce a child, or three children respectively, as an argument to obtain pardon. Children would even mar the picture of the sumptuous wedding by which this composition is closed. Therefore I assume that the author of this conclusion dropped the children-motif on purpose.

A third version of the end is found in the recension represented by the so-called MS Reinhardt.[34] After the tale of Hārūn ar-Rashīd and Abū Ḥasan, The Merchant of Oman, which is the last tale of this recension (nights 946-952 in ZER), Shahrazād immediately begins the Tale of the Two Kings and the Wazīr's Daughters, without any preparatory transition except for the usual *wa-ḥukiya,* "one relates". The first part of this tale repeats almost verbatim, without any abridgement, the prologue of this recension,[35] the two kings and their father, for instance, being given their names. Only the latter part of the tale is more condensed (the two daughters of the wazīr remain nameless here):

> (Shahrazād is still talking:) '. . . and she occupied him with tales and stories until she got pregnant and gave birth to a boy, got pregnant once again with a girl, and for a third time got pregnant with a boy. They bought white and black slave girls and populated the palace anew, as it had been before, the king not being aware of any of this.' The king turned his face to her (i.e. he pricked his ears) and asked: 'Where are *my* children?'— She replied: 'They are here.' Then he said: 'So that is the way to let me know! By God, if you had not acted in this manner and caught me with your stories, you would not have remained alive until now. Well done!' Shahrazād replied: 'A woman is worth only as much as her intelligence and her faith. Women are very different form one another.' And she ordered (*amarat*) her sister Dunyazad to bring the children. . . .

(4281, fol. 477 b—478a)

The king rejoices at his children and tells Shahrazād that he loves her still more. Complying with her request, he brings back servants and domestics to the palace;[36]

he writes a letter to his brother relating to him this happy ending; the brother sends his congratulations and gifts for all of them, "and King Shah Baz and the wazir's daughter abode in all solace of life and its delight until there came the Destroyer of delights and the Sunderer of societies" (the translation of this frequent end-clausula is borrowed from Burton).

I have evidence that the Reinhardt MS is the original copy of this recension or compilation;[37] so the date of transcription, 1247/1832, is at the same time that of the compilation. In view of this recent date one is not inclined to assume that the end of this recension is a proof of another ancient conclusion of the *Nights.* Nevertheless, it cannot be contested that this conclusion comes closest to that summarized by Ibn an-Nadīm: There are children involved;[38] Shahrazād reveals her stratagem to the king; the king admires her intelligence, he inclines towards her and preserves her alive. Shahrazād's sister has, in this conclusion, the same function as Shahrazād's accomplice in the *Fihrist*-version: she is only a nurse (thus, there is no need to marry her to the king's brother); there is no trace of a "conversion" or "listening to reason". These congruences are not accidental; there must be a connection between the end of the recension known to Ibn an-Nadīm and the conclusion of the Reinhardt MS. It is not likely that the compiler of this recension knew a version of the conclusions discussed above. It is true that he did not hesitate to recast stories radically, as is shown by the prologue, but if he had rewritten the end, there should be some traces left from the former text. As to Shahrazād's device of informing the king of her stratagem, namely relating his own story to him, there is no model for it in the finale of ZER (which was certainly known to the compiler), nor does it follow immediately from what the *Fihrist* (which the compiler can hardly have known) says about the end. On the other hand, it is obvious that the stories are gathered from very shifting traditions; even such tales as occur under the same title in ZER are not all taken from ZER-fragments; the tale of Tawaddud, for instance, is from a tradition which can be traced back to the 16th century,[39] quite independently of ZER. Thus, we cannot but deduce that the compiler of the Reinhardt MS knew a model stemming from a separate tradition, and we must for the present accept the curious fact that the latest recension of the *Nights* obviously presents the very conclusion which is closest to its original form.[40]

Since ZER was regarded as canonical not only in Europe but also in the Arabic World, other recensions were less appreciated even there. The *Nights*-fragment B, then, less than a hundred years after its transcription was considered to be trash and was rehashed; by means of a rather superficial revision it was turned into a "new" work: *Kitāb samarīyāt wa-qiṣaṣ 'ibarīyāt.* The redactor's work, however, consisted chiefly in crossing out the Night-formulae and numbers and in adding a few excerpts from other books as well as a new title page (cf. Ahlwardt Nr. 9103 and 9104). We should not let ourselves be deluded by this procedure, any more than that unknown Arabic reader of the "new" work who wrote the following beneath its new title: *hāda kitāb min sīrat alf layla ilā intihā' as-sīra* ("this is a part of the Story of the Thousand Nights right to the end of the story").

Notes

1. Cf. Macdonald, D. B., *A preliminary classification of some MSS of the Arabian Nights.* In: *A Volume of Oriental Studies, presented to E. G. Browne;* ed. by T. W. Arnold and R. A. Nicholson, Cambridge 1922, pp. 313 and 305. The "Egyptian MS brought to India by the late Major Turner Macan", from which II Calcutta was printed, is lost. I rather doubt if this MS was a *complete* ZER-copy. Bulaq and II Calcutta differ chiefly in the first quarter, Calcutta presenting in its prose passages an unrevised "middle Arabic" like any other MS of ZER. In the three remaining quarters, the text of Bulaq and II Calcutta is almost identical, Calcutta presenting here the same "polished" Arabic as Bulaq, which is somewhat strange. But this can easily be explained by the—heretical—assumption that these parts of II Calcutta were printed directly or indirectly from the *printed* Bulaq text.

2. Zotenberg called this recension "la rédaction moderne d'Égypte", Macdonald introduced the abbreviation ZER = Zotenberg's Egyptian Recension.

3. All known manuscript evidences for ZER were transcribed shortly before or after 1800; in all probability, the compilation of ZER itself had been carried out only a few years earlier. Mardrus's affirmation that he owned the very MS "de la fin du XVII⁽ᵉ⁾ siècle" from which the Bulaq edition was printed (cf. Chauvin IV, p. 109) is a lie.

4. Macdonald, D. B., *Maximilian Habicht and his recension of the Thousand and One Nights,* JRAS 1909, p. 685-704.

5. It was out of reverence for their first translator that Mia Gerhardt, *The Art of Story-Telling,* Leiden 1963, p. 15, did not call them so, but euphemistically spoke of "Galland's orphan stories".

6. Burton expanded it with passages taken from the Breslau edition. Lane translated the end as he had found it in his Bulaq copy.

7. Ibn an-Nadīm, *Kitāb al-Fihrist, maqāla* 8, *fann* 1; I quote the translation of Macdonald, D. B., *The earlier history of the Arabian Nights,* JRAS 1924, pp. 353-397; p. 365.

8. Or until she was pregnant, as in the frame-story of the *Hundred and One Nights,* which corresponds much better to our feeling of plausibility. It is quite unreasonable of ZER to demand the audience or the reader to believe that Shahrazād managed to hide her three pregnancies from the king.

9. The oldest documentary evidence for the actual title *alf layla wa-layla* is from the 12th century and comes from the Cairo Geniza; see S. D. Goitein in JAOS [*Journal of the American Oriental Society*] 78, 1958, pp. 301-302.

10. The number 570 is obviously a *tashīf* of 98, the *rasm* of a carelessly written *amāniya wa-tis'īn* being very close to that of *amsimi'a wa-sab'īn;* it is to be found already in the Paris MS 3612, which is prior to the compilation of ZER. The twenty male slaves have been added in order to make plausible a text in which the passage relating the disguise had been dropped, obviously by a copyist who was unable to guess how the story could have run.

11. Burton missed the point of this modification or interpolation. Though he knew that this reading was to be found in some MSS, he accused Trébutien, the French translator of Hammer-Zinserling, that he "cannot deny himself the pleasure of a French touch" (X, p. 54, n. 2).

12. Paris, Bibliothèque Nationale, MS arabe 4678-4679, formerly marked "Supplément arabe 2522-2523", transcribed at the beginning of the 19th century in Paris by Michel Ṣabbāġ from an unknown MS which had been transcribed in 1115/1703 in Bagdad, according to its colophon copied literally by Ṣabbāġ; cf. Zotenberg p. 202.

13. Burton says that the Wortley Montague MS in the Bodleian Library "has no especial conclusion relating the marriage of the two brother kings with the two sisters" (XV, p. 351). Does this mean that the MS has a poor conclusion, like that in ZER, or no conclusion at all?

14. This is certainly what was originally intended. The beginning of H and B is still in accord with this intention. In the sequel, names have slipped into the narration: the younger brother lives in Samarcand, the elder in Ṣīn. In K, the alleged friend who relates the story came to "a town in Ṣīn".

15. Burton has added here "of the cities of China" and explained in note 6 that this "is taken from the sequence of the prologue where the elder brother's kingdom is placed in China". He missed the point that in this tale, which he qualifies as "a rechauffé of the Introduction" (note 4), persons and places must remain nameless. *Fīāhir al-'umr*

(H = the text translated by Burton; B) is no doubt a corruption of *fī āhir al-'umrān* (K); the best reading is to be found in P: *dahaltu madīna fī āhir al-'umrān* 'I came to a town at the end of the civilized world' (fol. 163b).

16. This short-cut *isnād* is in contradiction with the longer *isnād* in the introductory passage, but it is no doubt that of the older version.

17. The words *hādihi l-ḥikāya tušbih li-ḥikāyat malik anā a'rif-hu* are certainly an integral part of this revelation scene; so is the king's request to hear about the reaction of the subjects *urīd an asma'mā ǧarā li-ahl hādihi l-madīna wa-mā qālū min amr al-malik*. But the subsequent final clause *li-arǧi''am-mā kuntu fīhi* is not quite logical. An emendation *lammā raǧa''am-mā kān fīhi* 'when he returned from the case wherein he was', which, regarding the *rasm,* seems to suggest itself, would make the text reasonable.

18. This passage has been dropped from H, but the following statement of the wise presupposes at least *sabab hādā an-nisā;* the addition is from B, fol. 114b; nearly the same text is to be found in K, fol. 124b.

19. Women qualified as *muslimāt, mu'mināt, qānitāt, ṣādiqāt . . . ḥāfiẓāt* (sc. *furūǧahunna*) must exist in reality, as they are mentioned in this *āya*.

20. The name of the Caliph in this story is al-Ma'mūn al-Ḥākim bi-amrillāh. The *ism* of the historical caliph al-Ḥākim (who reigned from 996 to 1021) was al-Manṣūr. The scene of the story is Cairo.

21. The spread of this conclusion in the 17th century is attested indirectly by Galland. He had tried in vain to get a complete copy of the *Nights,* nor had he ever had at his disposal an Arabic text of an end-fragment. The ending of his translation therefore has been suspected, until quite recently, to be of Galland's own invention. But from oral information he knew at least the basic concept of this conclusion: as early as August 1702, two years before he published the first volume of his translation, he outlined in a letter "le dessein de ce grand ouvrage: (. . .) De nuit en nuit la nouvelle sultane le mesne [Schahriar] jusques à mille et une et l'oblige, en la laissant vivre, de se défaire de *la prévention où il étoit généralement contre toutes les femmes*". The words in italics are to be found in the conclusion of Galland's translation, in which Shahrazād does not present children, but is granted mercy because the king's "esprit étoit adouci" and the king is convinced of Shahrazād's chastity. (The quotation from Galland's letter in M. Abdel-Halim, *Galland, sa vie et son œuvre,* Paris 1964, pp. 286-287).

22. Text: *al-baġyu yaqtulu ahlahū.* This looks like a proverb, a variant of the one recorded by al-Maydānī, *Maǧma'al-amāl,* Cairo 1953, nr. 555 = Freytag, Proverbia Maidanii, cap. II, nr. 129: *al-baġyu āhiru muddati l-qawmi, ya'nī anna ẓ-ẓulma idā mtadda madāhu, ādana bi-nqirāḍi muddati-him.*

23. Text: *itta'aẓa;* but see the parallel texts, note 27.

24. Translated by Burton from the Breslau edition, XII, pp. 2-44.

25. In K, the king is nameless; P: *al-malik aẓ-Ẓāhir;* in B, his name is Šahribāz.

26. B: *yaḍurru;* P: *yuhliku;* K: *yusri'u* (=?).

27. B: *irtā'a fī nafsihī;* K: *irtada'a,* obviously a *taṣḥīf* instead of *irtā'a.* This passage is not in P, nor is the following dialogue between the king and Shahrazād.

28. In most cases fragments of older recensions were inserted into the new compilation without extensive revision. So quite often it is not difficult to detect such *spolia* by inconsistent distribution of the roles (speaker, hearer etc.), stylistic peculiarities and the like. The ZER-text however, specially the printed one, has undergone a careful revision.

29. The corruptions found in the text of K, the oldest of the four MSS and carefully calligraphed, show that already that text had been transmitted within a long written tradition.

30. Paris, Bibliothèque Nationale, arabe 3609-3611 (formerly marked "ancien fonds 1508, 1507, 1506"). This MS, commonly designated as G, was transcribed after 1425, the year in which the *ašrafī-*dinar (mentioned in 3610, fol. 43b) was introduced, and before 943/1535, the earliest date of a reader's expression of thanks at the end of 3610.

31. *lā yuṣṭalā lahū bin-nār* is among the epithets of 'Umar ibn an-Nu'mān at the beginning of the 'Umar-Romance.

32. It does not come up to the same stylistic and narrative level as the tales inserted into the frame, which are, by the way, far better in the version of G than in ZER. Shahrazād's first tale however, that of the Merchant and the Jinnī, is as poor as in the printed texts, which proves that even it was part of the initial fragment left from preceding recensions.

33. The tale of the Concubine of al-Ḥākim can have taken its actual shape only after the eccentric person of the historical al-Ḥākim had been transfigured by time, so that he could become a nucleus of popular story or romance. The Zuwayla-Gate mentioned in all the texts was built in 1092; as a *terminus ante quem non,* such an early date is

rather insignificant.—Also six of the seven poems describing the bride's seven dresses in the Tale of Nūr al-Dīn and his Son (Burton I, pp. 217-219) are used (again?) here for the same pupose.

34. Strasbourg, Bibliothèque Nationale et Universitaire, MS 4278-4281. Date of transcription 1247/1831-2. As for the date of the compilation, see note 37. Table of contents in Chauvin, *Bibliographie* IV, pp. 210-212.

35. The prologue has been considerably remodelled in its details: the seats of the two kings have been exchanged; the younger brother is deceived by his chief concubine, the elder by his wife; the number of slave girls and male slaves who accompany the queen into the garden has been raised to eighty; Shahrazād is the younger of the two daughters of the wazīr.

36. The untrue slaves had all been executed, so the palace, at least the *ḥaramlik,* had been totally depopulated.

37. The text has been divided into nights by relatively long formulae with separate spaces left for the numbers of the nights. The night-formulae always fill half a page; the nights themselves measure two and a half pages, the formulae not included. The scribe has evidently inserted the night-formula rather automatically, on every third or fourth page, into the text he was copying. But he has made a mistake, for there is one too many: after the formula used for the 1001st night, there is yet another, which was crossed out later. If the MS was a transcription from a compilation already lying before the copyist's eyes, the lines that were crossed out and the free space for the night-number would not have been copied.

38. The composition does not say how many children Shahrazād herself is supposed to have. The number of the heroine's children in Shahrazād's revelation-story is no doubt borrowed from ZER.

39. The version of Tawaddud is very different from that in ZER, but close to freely circulating versions of the story, e.g. that of MS We.702 in Berlin (Ahlwardt Nr. 9179), transcribed in 1055/1645.

40. "A quite modern MS may carry a more complete tradition than one centuries older" (Macdonald 1922, p. 321).

Peter D. Molan (essay date 1988)

SOURCE: Molan, Peter D. "The *Arabian Nights:* The Oral Connection." *Edebiyat: The Journal of Middle Eastern Literatures* 2, no. 1-2 (1988): 191-204.

[*In the following essay, Molan argues that the stories of* The Arabian Nights *are grounded in folk tradition and attempts to trace changes in the various manuscript adaptations and translations, concentrating especially on a number of anomalous words and phrases that appear in a European translation but are not found in early Arabic versions.*]

In attempting to establish an "operational definition" of folk literature,

Francis Lee Utley has noted that:

> In the Middle East we have vast repositories (of tales), like the *Arabian Nights* and the *Midrash Rabbah,* which certainly have some connection with folklore, but which bear always the marks of artistic handling.[1]

Utley's statement raises certain obvious questions which have not been quite precisely posed in the scholarly literature on the *Arabian Nights.* What is the connection of the *Nights* to folklore? Are they popular literature which Richard Dorson has characterized as ". . . sophisticated compositions written for and responsive to a popular audience, but nevertheless literary products . . ."?[2] Are they popular literature containing folkloric elements? Or are they, fundamentally, folk tales drawn from an oral tradition and polished up by their redactors upon being written down?

I would suggest that a good deal of early scholarly work indicates clearly, though not intentionally, that the latter is the case. We may cite, for example, Charles Huet's 1918 article, "Les origines du conte de Aladdin et la lampe merveilleuse."[3] Huet fails to demonstrate the origins of the story but does provide an extensive catalogue of analogues to the Aladdin story which includes the *Arabian Nights* tale of **"Ma'rūf the Cobbler"** (we must remind ourselves that the Aladdin tale itself is not, generally considered, an *Arabian Nights* tale) and a number of demonstrably oral folk tales from both the Arab world and beyond.

Similarly, James G. Frazer, in his translation of Apollodorus' writings, gives an extensive appendix of analogues to the Homeric story of Ulysses and Polyphemus.[4] It properly includes the *Arabian Nights* tale of **"The Third Voyage of Sinbad"** as well as, again, a large number of demonstrably oral folk tales in a geographic dispersion stretching from Mongolia to the British Isles. We might add here mention of the Cyclops tale among the Palestinian Arabic folk tales collected by Paul Kahle.[5] Finally, we may also note Joseph Campbell's use of the *Arabian Nights* story of **"Qamar al-Zamān"** in *The Hero with a Thousand Faces,* which juxtaposes that story with mythic lore from around the world.[6]

It may thus be seen that one of the major criteria for identifying folklore in a written document, i.e., the discovery of variant forms of the tale in question known to be of oral provenance, has been fulfilled, at least for the *Arabian Nights* stories of **"The Third Voyage of Sinbad," "Ma'rūf the Cobbler,"** and **"Qamar al-Zamān."**[7]

The foundation for further work of this sort has also been laid by Elisseeff's important work, *Thémes et motifs des 1001 nuits*[8] and by Mia Gerhardt's *The Art of Story-Telling*.[9] A comparison of the themes, motives, and story outlines given by Elisseeff and Gerhardt with the standard catalogues of folk tale types, such as that of Nowak's,[10] finally allows us to determine the extent to which the *Arabian Nights* tales are analogues of authentic oral tales.

Gerhardt's work also represents the beginning of an interest in the application of broadly formalist techniques to the analysis of individual *Arabian Nights* tales, and even to the whole body of stories.[11] As with the work of Huet, such studies do not have as their aim an identification of the folkloric connections of the *Arabian Nights,* but much that is found in them seems relevant to the question.

Gerhardt, for instance, observes that the arrangement of the Sinbad tales is structurally significant[12] and not, as Richard Burton had asserted, "bad ordering."[13] But neither Gerhardt nor I, in our assessments of the symmetrically rising and falling number of adventures in Sinbad's seven voyages, connected the "lozenge" shaped order of the tales with the techniques of oral composition. Let me defend Ms. Gerhardt and myself by saying that it was not our immediate purpose to make that connection, but I will try to do so here.

Axel Olrik, the distinguished Danish folklorist, at the beginning of this century attempted to determine "laws" governing the composition of folk narrative.[14] His analysis must still, today, be considered basic. Among Olrik's "laws" of folk narrative are "the laws of opening and closing." Let me quote Olrik at some length:

> The *Sage* [Olrik's inclusive term for all types of folk narrative] begins by moving from calm to excitement, and after the concluding event . . . the *Sage* ends by moving from excitement to calm. For example, the epos cannot end with the last breath of Roland. Before ending, it needs to relax the clenched fist of the sword-hand; it needs the burial of the hero, the revenge, the death through grief of the beloved, and the execution of the traitor. A longer narrative needs only one. Hundreds of folk songs end, not with the death of the lovers, but with the interweaving of the branches of the two roses which grow out of their graves . . . The constant reappearance of this element of terminal calm shows that it is based, not just on a manifestation of the inclination of an individual narrator, but on the formal constraint of an epic law.[15]

When Sinbad has one additional adventure, each being more perilous than the last, in each of his first three

voyages; when he has yet another adventure culminating in being sealed in a tomb and then murdering innocent men and women after finding an escape from the tomb in the fourth voyage, and when his adventures decrease in number and perilousness in the fifth, sixth and seventh voyages, we see neither Burton's "bad ordering" nor merely Gerhardt's and Molan's "beautiful structuring," but rather the exact operation of Olrik's "epic laws of opening and closing" in oral narrative.

Olrik goes on to note that ". . . if there are not other possibilities for continuation, then the storyteller always adds a long jesting closing formula in order to quiet the mood."[16] Here again we recognize the closing formula of the *Arabian Nights* tales which, if not quite jesting, is certainly ubiquitous. By way of example, we need cite only their version which occurs in the story of Ma'rūf. The climax of the story comes when Ma'rūf's son kills Ma'rūf's evil first wife. But the story goes on further and then closes with the familiar *Arabian Nights* formula:

> After this, King Ma'rūf sent for the farmer whose guest he had been when he was a fugitive, and made him his Prime Minister and Chief Counselor. Then learning that he had a daughter of unsurpassed beauty and loveliness, of qualities enobled at birth by nature, of exalted worth, he took her to wife. In due time he married his son. So, they abode a while in all solace of life and its delight and their days were serene and their joys untroubled until there came to them that destroyer of delights, that sunderer of societies, that depopulator of populous places, the orphaner of sons and daughters. So, glory be to the Living One who does not die and whose hands are the keys of the seen and the unseen.[17]

Many more stories from the *Arabian Nights* must be analyzed in terms of the catalogues of folk tale types and in the light of folklore studies such as Olrik's or Lord Raglan's[18] before concluding finally that the whole body of *Arabian Nights* tales are drawn from an oral tradition and not popular literary compositions. When we recall Archer Taylor's observations on the ". . . curious unawareness of the commonplaces of folklore style"[19] among most literate authors attempting to imitate folklore, however, we may conclude that it seems likely that the rest of the stories of the *Arabian Nights* will prove to be as fully grounded on a folk tradition as the stories of Sinbad and Ma'rūf have proven to be.

To the extent that this is true, we must turn to the problem of trying to identify the nature and extent of "artistic handling" to which Arab folktales have been subjected in being brought into the written versions of the *Arabian Nights* that we know today. It is to one aspect of this question that I would like to devote the remainder of this paper.

In rereading portions of the *Arabian Nights,* my attention has been drawn back to a number of apparently anomalous words and phrases which occur in the MacNaghten edition of the work but which do not appear in the Būlāq edition. For example, when King Shahriyār's brother informs him that his wife is being unfaithful, Shahriyār demands to see this with his own eyes. They secret themselves to watch, and it is true. The wife, her handmaids and the household slaves hold a day-long orgy lasting, as the two texts say, respectively,

> *MacNaghten:* . . . ilā adhāni al-'asri qāla fa-lammā ra'ā al-malik
>
> *Bulaq:* . . . ilā al-'asri fa-lammā ra'ā al-malik[20]
>
> . . . till (the call to prayer of) the afternoon. (He said,) when the king saw . . .

The use of the otherwise totally anomalous *qāla,* 'he said,' in the MacNaghten text suggests to me the phrase *wa-qāla al-rāwī,* 'and the reciter said,' of so many Arabic texts which we know to derive from oral sources. The phrase *wa-qāla al-rāwī* does actually occur in one instance known to me in the MacNaghten edition.[21] I would argue, therefore, that its use here implies that the MacNaghten text has been taken down from an oral reciter with the scribe inserting the common phrase and reminding us of the tale's oral provenance.

The suppression of the anomalous verb *qāla* in the Būlāq text, on the other hand, seems to suggest exactly that artistic handling to which Francis Utley referred. The same is probably also true of the suppression in the Būlāq text of the term *adhān,* 'call to prayer.' For the Muslim teller of tales, the phrase *ilā adhān al-'asr,* 'until the afternoon call to prayer,' is probably no more than the extremely common and perfectly usual cliche to express 'late afternoon.' For the literate and history-bound philologist who, I assume, edited the Būlāq text, it is a clear anachronism as the story is about pre-Islamic, Persian kings.

There are, in the first seventy-five pages of the MacNaghten text, thirteen similar examples of this verb *qāla.* They are grammatically anomalous unless recognized as interpolations signaling the oral origins of the text. All but one, which seems to have escaped him, are omitted by the editor of the Būlāq text. It might be argued, of course, that the phrase *wa-qāla al-rāwī* is inserted by a literate author or editor to give the tale a folkloric air. The use of the verb *qāla* alone, however (which is, at first reading, merely confusing), and the particular relationship of occurrence and nonoccurrence in the two editions seems clearly to militate against such an assertion.

Included in the texts immediately surrounding the verbs in question are several other examples of emendations of the type noted above in the use of the word *adhān.*

For example, Shahriyār, having disposed of his unfaithful wife, still finds no solace. His shame is so great that only finding someone who is more powerful than he who has suffered yet greater pain will console him. If he fails to do so, the two texts continue respectively,

> *MacNaghten:* . . . mawtu-nā khayrun min hayāti-nā.
>
> *Būlāq:* . . . fa-yakūnu mawtu-nā khayrun min hayāti-nā.
>
> . . . (then) our dying (will) be better than our living.
>
> *MacNaghten:* qāla thumma inna-humā kharajā.
>
> *Būlāq:* fa-ajāba li-dhālika thumma inna-humā kharajā.[22]
>
> (So he agreed to that.) (He said,) then the two went out.

Besides the use of the *qāla,* we also notice the insertion of the phrase 'so he [that is, the king's brother] agreed to that.' Logically, the insertion is useful, for the king's brother, it may be remembered, had been suffering the same sense of shame, having also been deceived by his wife. His grief, however, had been abated precisely because he learned that such a thing could happen even to his own, more powerful brother. Technically, he has no further need to relieve his already allayed misery. Such an addition does not, of course, demonstrate a literate emendation on a point glossed over in a necessarily oral work. Taken as one or more element in an assemblage of stylistic details, however, it may be instructive.

Considerably more interesting is another item to be found in the "Story of the Three Apples." Hārūn al-Rashīd has discovered the murder of a beautiful young woman. Outraged that such an occurrence could happen in his realm, he orders his Prime Minister, Ja'far the Barmakī, to find the killer or die in his place. Ja'far fails, and the Caliph's men erect the gibbet to hang him (or "crucify" him in Būlāq). A crowd gathers and, the two texts continue respectively,

> *MacNaghten:* sārū yantaẓirūna al-idhna min al-khalīfa.
>
> *Būlāq:* sārū yantaẓirūna al-idhna min al-khalīfa.
>
> They began awaiting permission from the Caliph.
>
> *MacNaghten:* wa-kanāt al-ishāra hākadhā. wa-sāra al-khalqu
>
> *Būlāq:* wa-sāra al-khalqu
>
> (And the signal was thus.) And the crowd began
>
> *MacNaghten:* yatabakawna 'alā Ja'far.
>
> *Būlāq:* yatabakawna 'alā Ja'far.[23]
>
> crying over Ja'far.

As may readily be seen, the MacNaghten text includes, and the Būlāq text suppresses, the phrase "and the signal was thus." It seems inescapable that the statement must have been accompanied by the gesture of an oral performer. This is hardly surprising. As D. B. Mac-Donald points out in his *Encyclopedia of Islam* discussion of the term *hikāya,* "the oriental storyteller always acts out his story."[24] MacDonald goes on to relate the term *hikāya* directly to mime.

Yet another item seems to bear on a number of points relating to oral performance. In the story of the "Merchant and the Jinni," each of three shaykhs comes by the merchant who is waiting to keep his appointment with the *jinnī.* Each is astounded to find the merchant sitting and waiting in such an inauspicious place as a *ma'wā,* 'a place where the *jinn* howl.' Each demands an explanation and after the third shaykh is told the story "from its beginning to its end," the Mac-Naghten and Būlāq texts read respectively,

> *MacNaghten:* laysa fī al-i'ādati ifādatun yā sādah.
>
> *Būlāq:* laysa fī al-i'ādati ifādatun.[25]
>
> There is no benefit in repetition (O sirs).

The phrase 'O sirs,' which occurs in the MacNaghten text but not in the Būlāq, again seems to imply the presence of an audience, but what of the phrase 'there is no benefit in repetition?'

One of the recurring themes of the oral literature conference of which this article was a part is that repetition is a particularly characteristic trait of oral literature. This is hardly a new discovery to folklorists nor was it unobserved in earlier eras. Muhammad ibn Daniyāl, the 13th-century Egyptian author, notes of the folkloric shadow plays to which he attempts to give a literary polish:

> You state that oral reports have spit out [news of] the shadow theater, but that natural good taste has shunned it because of its repetitiveness.[26]

One might suppose that a denial of the utility of repetition ought not to occur in a type of literature which is characterized by repetition. Interestingly enough, this is not the case. As B. Connelly points out in her work on the three Egyptian *Rabāb* poets whom she recorded, the singer whose performance depends most particularly on repetition states on several occasions:

> wa-lli a'āūl-uh ma a'īd-uh
>
> 'That which I say I will not repeat'[27]

Connelly's work also bears on another aspect of difference between the MacNaghten and Būlāq editions of the *Arabian Nights.* As may be seen, from an examination of the texts cited above and in the appendix, the MacNaghten and Būlāq editions, despite the differences which do occur, seem at first glance to be really quite close to each other. Nonetheless, substantial differences do occur, and one of the most common, I suspect, is the replacement or paraphrase of poetic texts of the Mac-Naghten edition by prose texts in the Būlāq edition. One of the texts which exhibits the anomalous use of the verb *qāla* also exhibits this phenomenon.

When the porter in the story of the "Three Ladies of Baghdad" first sees the *bawwāba,* the lady doorkeeper of the mansion, he goes, in the MacNaghten text, into poetic raptures over her beauty. The poem which describes the lady's charms, however, has been replaced, in the Būlāq edition, with a prose description. The texts then come together again after the appearance (in MacNaghten) and suppression (in Būlāq) of the verb *qāla.*

> *MacNaghten:* (poem) qāla fa-lammā nazara al-hammāl ilāy-ha
>
> *Būlāq:* (prose) fa-lammā nazara al-hammāl ilāy-ha[28]
>
> (He said,) then when the porter looked at her

Many other examples of poetry in MacNaghten being replaced by prose in Būlāq may be readily observed. This phenomenon is strikingly similar to a parallel feature found by Connelly in the development of the *Sirat Bani Hilāl* where, she observes, each subsequent printing of the text further reduces the oral bard's poetry and music into prose narrative.[29]

On the basis of the evidence presented here, then, we may hypothesize that the MacNaghten edition of the *Arabian Nights* (and the Egyptian manuscript upon which it is based) stand in fairly close relationship to an authentically oral tradition. Conversely, the Būlāq edition (and the manuscript tradition upon which it is based), by suppressing elements which are only relevant in the setting of oral performance, by polishing up certain logical and chronological details, and in general by reducing the poetic passages in favor of prose, exhibits the kind of literate handling of folklore to which Francis Utley refers.

On the basis of this hypothesis, we may proceed to a heretofore unattempted stylistic analysis of the various *Arabian Nights* texts. In conjunction with a continuing effort in structural or formal analyses, we may achieve a much fuller appreciation of this collection of Arabian tales to which we have been instinctively drawn for so long.

APPENDIX

I. ANOMALOUS USES OF THE VERB QALA IN MACNAGHTEN, SUPPRESSED IN BULAQ (M=MACNAGHTEN; B=BULAQ)

1. M (p. 4): ilā adhāni al-'asri qāla fa-lammā ra'ā al-malik

B (p. 3): ilā al-'asri fa-lammā ra'ā al-malik

till (the call to prayer of) the afternoon. (He said) Then, when the king saw. . . .

2. M (p. 4): mawtu-nā khayrun min hayāti-na fa-ajāba li-dhālika qāla thumma inna-humā kharajā

B (p. 3): mawtu-nā khayrun min hayāti-na fa-ajāba li-dhālika thumma inna-humā kharajā

Our death (will) be better than our life. (So, he agreed to that.) (He said) Then, the two of them went out.

3. M (p. 6): khā'ifun 'alā nafsi-hi min al-maliki qāla wa-kāna al-wazīru

B (p. 4): khā'ifun 'alā nafsi-hi min al-maliki wa-kāna al-wazīru

. . . fearing for himself because of the king. (He said) and the minister had . . .

4. M (p. 7): tastarīhu min al-ta'bi wa-al-jahdi qāla wa-kāna al-tājiru

B (p. 5): tastarīhu min al-ta'bi wa-al-jahdi wa-kāna al-tājiru

. . . you will rest from fatigue and effort. (He said) And the merchant . . .

5. M (p. 8): al-yawma kulla-hu qāla fa-lammā raja'a

B (p. 5): al-yawma kulla-hu fa-lammā raja'a

. . . all day. (He said) Then, when he returned . . .

6. M (p. 8): nasahtu-ka wa-al-salām qāla fa-lammā sami'a al-thawru

B (p. 5): nasahtu-ka wa-al-salām fa-lammā sami'a al-thawru

I have advised you and so peace. (He said) Then, when the bull heard . . .

7. M (p. 9): ilā al-mamāti qāla fa-lammā sami'at ibnat-al-wazīri

B (p. 6): ilā al-mamāti fa-lammā sami'at ibnat-al-wazīri

. . . until death. (He said) then, when the minister's daughter heard . . .

8. M (p. 23): fī hādhā al-qimqimi qāla fa-lammā sami'a al-māridu

B (p. 11): fī hādhā al-qimqimi fa-lammā sami'a al-māridu

. . . in this bottle. (He said) Then, when the jinnī heard . . .

9. M (p. 37): [poem] qāla fa-lammā farigha ra's al-hakīmu kalāma-hu

B (p. 18): [poem] fa-lammā farigha rūyān al-hakīmu kalāma-hu

(He said) Then, when ra's/rūyān) al-hakim finished his say . . .

10. M (p. 40): lil-jāriyati al-tabbākhati qāla wa-kānat hādhihi al-jāriyatu

B (p. 19): lil-jāriyati al-tabbākhati wa-kānat hādhihi al-jāriyatu

. . . to the slave girl cook. (He said) And when this slave girl . . .

11. M (p. 58): [poem] qāla fa-nahadat al-sabiyyatu al-thālithatu

B (p. 25): [poem] fa-nahadat al-sabiyyatu al-thālithatu

(He said) Then, the third maiden arose . . .

12. M (p. 58): [poem] qāla fa-lammā nazara al-hammālu ilay-hā

B (p. 25): [prose] fa-lammā nazara al-hammālu ilay-hā

(He said) Then, when the porter looked at her . . .

13. M (p. 74): li-man i'tabara qāla wa-sa'alat al-thāniya wa-al-thālitha

B (p.): li-man i'tabara wa-sa'alat al-thāniya wa-al-thālitha

. . . for he who has taken a lesson. (He said) she asked the second and third . . .

II. ANOMALOUS USE OF THE VERB QALA IN MACNAGHTEN, RETAINED IN BULAQ

1. M (p. 9): lā ta'ūd tas'alu-hu 'an shay'in qāla fa-lammā sami'a

B (p. 6): lā ta'ūd tas'alu-hu 'an shay'in qāla fa-lammā sami'a

Ask him no more about anything. He said Then, when he heard . . .

III. OTHER DEICTIC ELEMENTS

1. M (p. 143): al-idhnu min al-khalīfati wa-kānat al-ishāratu hākadhā wa-sāra al-khalqu

B (p. 52): al-idhnu min al-khalīfati wa-sāra al-khalqu

. . . permission from the caliph. (And the signal was thus) And the people began . . .

2. M (p. 12): laysa fī al-i'dati ifādatun ya sādah fa-jalasa 'inda-hum wa-idhā bi-ghabaratin qad aqbalat. . . .

B (p. 7): laysa fī al-i'dah ifādah wa-idhā bi-ghabarah qad hājat

There is no benefit in repetition (O sirs. Then he sat with them) and all of a sudden a dust cloud came along . . .

Notes

1. Francis Lee Utley, "Folk Literature: An Operational Definition," *Journal of American Folklore* 74 (1961): 193-206 [pp. 7-24 in *The Study of Folklore,* ed. Alan Dundes (Englewood Cliffs, N.J., 1965)].

2. Richard M. Dorson, "The Identification of Folklore in American Literature," in "Folklore in Literature: A Symposium," *Journal of American Folklore,* 70 (1957): 1-24.

3. C. Huet, "Les origines du conte de Aladdin et la lampe merveilleuse," *Revue de l'histoire des religions* 77 (1918): 1-50.

4. Apollodorus, *The Library,* 2 vols., trans. J. G. Frazer, Loeb Classical Library (New York, 1921), 2: 751ff.

5. Paul Kahle, *Bauernerzählungen aus Palestina* [*Volkserzählungen aus Palästina**], ed. H. Schmidt and P. Kahle (Göttingen, 1918).

6. Joseph Campbell, *The Hero with a Thousand Faces* (Princeton, 1968).

7. Dorson, op. cit., esp. p. 4.

8. N. Elisseeff, *Thèmes et motifs des 1001 nuits: essai de classification* (Beirut, 1949).

9. Mia I. Gerhardt, *The Art of Story-Telling: A Literary Study of the Thousand and One Nights* (Leiden, 1963).

10. Ursula Nowak, *Beiträge zur Typologie des arabischen Volksmärchens* (Freiburg, 1969).

11. See Gerhardt, op. cit.; Andras Hamori, *On the Art of Medieval Arabic Literature* (Princeton, 1974), pp. 145-180; Peter D. Molan, "Sinbad the Sailor: A Commentary on the Ethics of Violence," *JAOS* [*Journal of the American Oriental Society*] 98/3 (1978): 237-247; idem., "Ma'rūf the Cobbler: The Mythic Structure of an *Arabian Nights* Tale," *Edebiyat,* III/2 (1978): 121-136; and Ferial Ghazoul, "Nocturnal Dialectics: A Structural Study of the 1001 Nights" (Ph.D. thesis, Columbia U., 1978).

12. Gerhardt, op. cit., pp. 236-263.

13. Richard F. Burton, *A Plain and Literal Translation of the Arabian Nights Entertainments* (New York, n.d.) vol. 6, p. 77, n. 2.

14. The following discussion of Olrik is based on Axel Olrik, "Epic Laws of Folk Narrative" in *The Study of Folklore,* pp. 129-141.

15. Ibid., p. 132.

16. Ibid.

17. Burton, op. cit., p. 53.

18. Lord Raglan, "The Hero of Tradition," *Folklore* 45 (1934): 212-231 [*The Study of Folklore,* pp. 142-157].

19. Archer Taylor, "Folklore and the Student of Literature," *Pacific Spectator* 2 (1948): 216-223 [*The Study of Folklore,* pp. 32-42, esp. p. 42].

20. W. H. MacNaghten ed., *Alf Lailā wa-Lailā* (Calcutta, 1839), vol. I, p. 4; *Alf Lailā wa-Lailā* (Būlāq, 1252 A.H.), vol. I, p. 3.

21. MacNaghten, op. cit., p. 29.

22. MacNaghten, op. cit., p. 4; Būlāq, p. 3

23. MacNaghten, op. cit., p. 143; Būlāq, p. 52.

24. D. B. MacDonald, "Hikaya," EI[1].

25. MacNaghten, op. cit., p. 12; Būlāq, p. 7.

26. Escorial Ms. 469, folio I verso.

27. Private communication.

28. MacNaghten, op. cit., p. 58; Būlāq, p. 25.

29. Private communication.

Fatma Moussa-Mahmoud (essay date 1988)

SOURCE: Moussa-Mahmoud, Fatma. "English Travellers and the *Arabian Nights.*" In *The* Arabian Nights *in English Literature,* edited by Peter L. Caracciolo, pp. 95-110. London, England: Macmillan, 1988.

[*In the following essay, Moussa-Mahmoud presents a brief survey of English travel literature influenced by the tales of* The Arabian Nights.]

In the opening years of the eighteenth century the strange distant East was brought vividly and imaginatively before the eyes of French and English readers with Antoine Galland's translation of the *Nights* into French (1704-17). The French version was immediately translated into English and the tales were so popular that they started a literary fashion on both sides of the Channel, the 'oriental tale' of the eighteenth century.[1] There were so many preposterous imitations of the *Nights* that some genuine translations such as the *Persian Tales* (1710) and the *New Arabian Nights* (1792) were long taken for forgeries. As travelling to the East was difficult and relatively infrequent, readers were very curious about the customs and religion of the infidel inhabitants of those far-off lands. Galland's translation was from the first advertised as a book where 'the customs of Orientals and the ceremonies of their religion were better traced than in the tales of the travellers. . . . All Orientals, Persians, Tartars and Indians . . . appear just as they are from sovereigns to people of the lowest condition. Thus the reader will have the pleasure of seeing them and hearing them without taking the trouble of travelling to seek them in their own countries'. The rich imaginative power of the *Nights* and the dazzling splendour of its descriptions, together with the realistic, homely atmosphere of some of the tales have kept their hold on European imagination to this day.

It soon became part of the task of the travellers to verify the authenticity of the *Nights* and relate them to what they saw. Lady Mary Wortley Montagu was the first English lady to visit Turkey and reside in Constantinople, as the wife of the British Ambassador to the Porte (1716-18). In her letters she gave lively descriptions of Turkish houses, mosques and public baths. She had the chance to penetrate into the harems of the great officials of the Ottoman Court. She wrote in one of her letters, 'This is but too like (says you) the Arabian tales; these embroider'd Napkins and a jewel as large as a Turkey's egg! You forget dear Sister, those very tales were writ by an Author of this Country and (excepting the Enchantments) are a real representation of the manners here.'[2] Lady Mary's letters were widely circulated during her lifetime and some of the details of Turkish life were regarded as being as fabulous as the *Nights.* 'We travellers', she complained, 'are in very hard circumstances if we say nothing but what has been said before us, we are dull. . . . If we tell anything new, we are laugh'd at as fabulous and Romantic' (p. 385).

In 1756 Alexander Russell, resident physician to the English factory in Aleppo, described how oriental men of fashion were lulled to sleep with 'stories told out of the *Arabian Nights Entertainments* . . . which their women were taught to repeat for this purpose'.[3] Patrick Russell's enlarged edition of *Aleppo* (1794) provided more interesting information on the *Nights,* together with more detailed description of the life of the inhabitants among whom he spent many years as his brother's successor. He added a chapter on Arabic literature, and in a note on the *Nights* he testified to their authenticity:

> The Arabic title of our Arabian Nights is Hakayat Elf Leily wa Leily a Thousand and one Nights. It is a scarce book at Aleppo. After much inquiry, I found only two volumes, containing two hundred and eighty nights, and with difficulty obtained liberty to have a copy taken. I was shown more than one complete copy in the Vatican Library; and one at Paris in the King's Library said also to be complete.[4]

He added that he had collected a number of separate tales which he later found in the first and third volumes of the 'Continuation of the Arabian Nights published at Edinburgh in 1792'. His note was quoted by the *Oriental Collections* (Caddell and Davies, 1797, I, 246-7). The editor announced that Jonathan Scott, a retired servant of the East India Company, had acquired a complete manuscript of the *Nights* in five volumes, brought by Edward Wortley Montagu from the East, which he intended to translate.[5] Queries appeared in the *Gentleman's Magazine* as to the two manuscripts and the authenticity of Galland's version. Dr Russell in reply gave a description of his manuscript and again testified to the authenticity of Galland's translation.[6]

In an account of entertainments at coffee houses, Russell's *Aleppo* gives a description of the manner of narration by professional story-tellers that was widely quoted by other travellers and by students of the *Nights:*

> The recitation of Eastern fables and tales partakes somewhat of a dramatic performance. It is not merely a simple narrative; the story is animated by the manner, and action of the speaker. A variety of other story books, besides the Arabian Nights Entertainment (which under that title, are little known at Aleppo) furnish material for the story teller, who by combining the incidents of different tales, and varying the catastrophe of such as he has related before, gives them an air of novelty. . . . He recites walking to and fro, in the middle of the coffee room, stopping only now and then when the expression requires some emphatical attitude. He is commonly heard with great attention, and, not infrequently, in the midst of some interesting adventure, when the expectation of his audience is raised to the highest pitch, he breaks off abruptly, and makes his escape from the room, leaving both his heroine and his audience, in the utmost embarrassment . . . and the auditors, suspending their curiosity, are induced to return at the same hour next day to hear the sequel. He no sooner has made his exit, than the company in separate parties, fall a disputing about the characters of the drama, or the event of the unfinished adventure. The controversy by degrees becomes serious, and opposite opinions are maintained with no less warmth, than if the fate of the city depended on the decision.
>
> (I, 148-50)

An increasing number of travellers sought scenes from the *Nights* in the crowded bazaars and narrow streets of oriental cities, and their testimonies and experiences were quoted in new editions of the *Nights.* Edward Forster in 1802 quotes Dallaway's book on Constantinople:

> Much of the romantic air which pervades the domestic habits of the persons described in the Arabian Nights, particularly in inferior life, will be observed in passing through the streets of Constantinople. And we receive, with additional pleasure, a remembrance of the delight, with which we at first perused them, in finding them authentic portraits of every Oriental nation.

James Capper's *Observations on the Passage to India through Egypt* (1783) is cited as recommending the *Nights* as a necessary piece of equipment for a traveller in the East: 'they are in the same estimation all over Asia, that the adventures of Don Quixote are in Spain, and it is presumed no man of genius or taste would think of making the tour of that country without previously reading the works of Cervantes'.[7]

The establishment of the British Empire in India by the end of the eighteenth century, the French Expedition to Egypt (1797-1801) and the continued rivalry between Britain and France for influence with oriental rulers, whose territory lay on the short routes to India, resulted in an unprecedented increase in the number of British travellers to the East. The traveller, whether soldier, diplomat or antiquarian, took notes, preparatory to producing the heavy volumes of travel consumed by a reading public eager for any new information on the East. James Justinian Morier (1780-1849) made two journeys to Persia in 1808 and 1810, as secretary of two successive ambassadors, and, after the signing of a treaty with the Shah to counteract French influence, he resided for some time in Teheran. He published two travel books,[8] but some writers think that his third and most famous book, the *Adventures of Hajji Baba of Ispahan* (1824), is actually a travel book in disguise:

> it is proper to regard [*Hajji Baba*] both as a novel and a book of travel, since in its episodes and characters it follows closely the author's actual experiences as recorded in his *Journeys,* and was intended by him to present facts in a dramatic form that would create a vivid impression on readers completely ignorant of the customs of a Mohammedan Community.[9]

Morier was partly influenced by Thomas Hope's *Anastasius,* an oriental picaresque tale which met great success in 1819, but he only confessed to the influence of Le Sage and the *Nights.* His choice of a barber for his rogue hero is indicative. In the Introductory Epistle, Morier states that for 'delineation of Asiatic manners . . . the *Arabian Nights' Entertainments* give the truest picture of the Orientals . . . because it is the work of one of their own community'. He adds, however,

that 'few would be likely to understand them thoroughly who have not lived some time in the East'. He summarises a story from the *Nights,* an episode of the Three Calenders, where Amina buys wine from the house of a white-bearded Christian without their exchanging a word. He assumes that the explanation would be only understood by someone who had lived in the East. His intention was to write a kind of supplement to the *Nights* that would illustrate the manners and customs of an oriental nation. The reference to the *Nights* was taken up by the *Quarterly Review:*

> We have subjected these little volumes, as far as regards the measure of their agreement to the test of a severe examination . . . we turned over the pages of several of the tales in the Arabian Nights Entertainments . . . it is really curious to observe how exactly . . . [he] has identified the current of the hero's fortunes, the character of his adventures and associates; the customs, feelings and opinions of his country, with the example of everyday Eastern life which may be gathered from those singular chronicles of Asiatic manners.[10]

The triumph of *Hajji Baba* lay in Morier's clever imitation of Eastern style and imagery. The narrative, which is supposed to be in Hajji's own words, keeps up the illusion of the narrator's nationality. When the author wishes to introduce episodes or descriptions of places the hero could not have seen, the tale-within-a-tale is a handy device. As he has no chance of seeing the inside of a grandee's harem or observing how it is run, the fair Zeenab, his sweetheart and the slave of his master the doctor, gives us the details in a most natural way. She takes him on a tour of her mistress's apartment, in the absence of that lady, and the description could have come from the pages of the *Nights.* There were numerous editions of *Hajji Baba* before the end of the century and the book has remained a classic. It was translated into French, German and even Persian. The Persians were understandably furious at the picture of them given in the book, for Hajji Baba, like other picarós, is shown as a mean liar, a coward and a thief; moreover, he was taken by European readers as a typical Persian and a typical oriental. Morier later devoted himself to a literary career. He wrote 'oriental tales' but he never repeated the triumphant success of *Hajji Baba.* In *The Mirza* (1841) he tried to give an imitation of the *Nights,* a series of tales narrated by the court poet (the Mirza), strings of anecdotes and tales within tales he composed for the entertainment of the Shah. The author keeps the outward trappings of the 'oriental tale' and tries to give a picture of manners and customs in three volumes, but the collection is far inferior to *Hajji Baba* and has deservedly sunk into oblivion.

Nineteenth-century interest in the manners and customs of orientals was still fed by publications of various degrees of impartiality or downright bigotry. Missionaries in India provided horrific accounts of the lives and practices of benighted Hindu heathens, but descriptions of the Muslim Near East were much more sympathetic. The popularity of the *Nights* and the 'oriental tale' together with the growing bulk of travel literature explain the difference in attitude. Impartial objectivity in portraying Arab Muslim manners and customs was brought to a peak with E. W. Lane's *Modern Egyptians* (1836). Lane (1801-76) also became famous for producing the first direct translation into English of the *Nights*. He first arrived in Egypt as a young engraver, who had studied Arabic for a year before leaving England. He followed the routine of former travellers who sailed up the Nile to Luxor. He joined a group of artists who were making detailed drawings of Ancient Egyptian monuments. He spent some time in Egypt taking notes on the life of contemporary Egyptians. Though he could not find a publisher for the long account of his travels, the section on contemporary life was accepted by the Society for the Diffusion of Useful Knowledge. He returned for a year and a half in 1833-4 to prepare that section for publication. His *Modern Egyptians* has never been superseded. Lane was fully equipped for his task. On his second visit he assumed Arab dress and lived away from the Frank colony in Cairo. He had native informants and he was steeped in oriental literature, not least the *Nights*. In a note to the Preface to his book he pointed out the importance of the *Nights* as a guide to the customs of the Arabs:

> There is one work, however, which presents most admirable pictures of the manners and customs of the Arabs, and particularly those of the Egyptians; it is 'The Thousand and One Nights; or, Arabian Nights' Entertainments'. If the English reader had possessed a close translation of it with sufficient illustrative notes, I might almost have spared myself the labour of the present undertaking.[11]

His partiality for the *Nights* was obviously no impediment to absolute objectivity. He told his readers in the same Preface, 'I am not conscious of having endeavoured to render interesting any matter that I have related by the slightest sacrifice of truth.'

Lane had two models which he reluctantly admitted in the Preface, Russell's *Aleppo* and Chabrol's 'Essai sur les moeurs des habitants modernes de l'Egypte', published in one of the volumes of the French Institute's *Description de l'Egypte* (1822). Actually Lane modelled the organisation of his material on Chabrol's example, but he had more information to offer than the French writer. Lane, the translator of the *Nights* could give a more comprehensive picture of the life of Muslim Arabs. He could always bring in an incident from the *Nights* to illustrate a custom or an opinion held by the people he so closely observed. When discussing the women's reputation for licentiousness he reminds his readers, 'Some of the stories of the intrigues of women in **"The Thousand and One Nights"** present faithful pictures of occurrences not infrequent in the modern metropolis of Egypt' (p. 304). On the other hand, his impartiality induces him to translate a note which a sheikh, one of his friends, wrote commenting on a passage on this subject in the *Nights*. The sheikh testifies that many women do not marry a second time after they are widowed or divorced, thus defending his countrywomen against the imputations in the *Nights* (p. 304). In an earlier chapter, describing the customs at mealtime, he is naturally reminded of the constant feasting and drinking in the *Nights* and tries to correct the impression it gives:

> Though we read, in some of the delightful tales of 'The Thousand and One Nights', of removing 'the table of viands' and bringing 'the table of wine', this prohibited beverage is not often introduced in general society . . . by the Muslims of Egypt in the present day. Many of them, however, habitually indulge in drinking wine with select parties of their acquaintance.
>
> (p. 154)

A chapter entitled 'Language, Literature and Science' is immediately followed by a chapter on superstition, 'a knowledge of which is necessary to enable [the reader] to understand their character'. The first elements of superstition are of course the 'Ginn', who naturally bring in the *Nights*. Precautions against offending the 'Ginn' are best understood through certain incidents in the *Nights* (p. 229). When he is told of a wali's head speaking after it was cut off, it brings in the story of the Sage Dooban (p. 241 n. 1). Three chapters are devoted to 'Public Recitations of Romances', including the *Nights*. The manner of recitation, which had excited the curiosity of Russell's readers about forty years before, is again described accompanied by a good engraving (p. 399). Lane finds it necessary to give a summary of a number of the romances recited in the coffee shops, but he expects his readers to be familiar with the *Nights*. He admits, however, that recitations from the *Nights* have become rare, for 'when a complete copy of **"The Thousand and One Nights"** is found, the price demanded for it is too great for a reciter to have it in his power to pay' (p. 420). One would guess that foreign demand for copies of the *Nights* must have raised the price, for it was the ambition of every European traveller to acquire a copy of the famous tales. In a note to a later edition he cites that the *Nights* and other important books were printed at the government press at Boulak (p. 227 n. 1). It was actually this printed edition that Lane used for his translation of the *Nights*.

When he brought out the third edition of *Modern Egyptians* in 1842, Lane had already published his translation of the *Nights*. He added some notes on songs and anecdotes mentioned in the *Nights.* The story of the ignorant 'fikee' (schoolmaster) on p. 63 is related to a similar anecdote in his translation. He concludes, 'either my informant's account is not strictly true, or the man alluded to by him was, in the main, an imitator; the latter is not improbable, as I have been credibly informed of several similar imitations, one of which I know to be a fact' (p. 63n.). So some of the Egyptians he describes actually imitate the *Nights*! In his account of public festivals, he gives a full translation of a song sung in a 'zikr' (a fervently devotional performance) then adds in a note, 'since the above was written, I have found the last six of the lines here translated with some slight alterations, inserted as a common love song in a portion of the Thousand and One Nights' (p. 454n.).

Lane's translation of the *Nights* (1839-41) was one of the first attempts at a direct translation from Arabic into English. He used the Boulak edition, which supported his view that the tales were originally Egyptian. He dispensed with the division into nights and divided his narrative into chapters. The translation proved a great commercial success, for the text was expurgated to suit family reading. It was elucidated with copious notes written by Lane for the purpose. The tales lost much of their charm under the heavy hand of the scholarly orientalist. In spite of its faults, Galland's version had been powerfully imaginative and had consequently fascinated its readers. Lane's translation had a pronounced biblical tone which did not suit the homely atmosphere of some of the tales or the romantic exaggerations in others. The notes, however, were illuminating. They were later published separately as *Arabian Society in the Middle Ages* (1883). In the Preface to his own unexpurgated translation of the *Nights* (1885), Richard Burton, though contemptuous of Lane's version of the *Nights,* greatly appreciated the notes: 'The student who adds the notes of Lane ('Arabian Society', etc . . .) to mine will know as much of the Moslem East and more than many Europeans who have spent half their lives in Orient lands.'[12]

Another traveller who toured the Near East at the time of Lane's second visit to Egypt (1833-4) produced a classic of travel literature the opposite of Lane's scholarly *Modern Egyptians:* A. W. Kinglake (1809-91) rewrote the text of *Eothen* (1844) three times. The final version was an intimate account of his personal experience of travelling in the area, addressed to his friend Eliot Warburton, who intended to make the same tour. His excuse for dwelling only on 'matters that happened to interest [him]' was that these countries had 'been thoroughly and ably described and even artistically illustrated by others'. Kinglake was devoted to the *Nights;* he carried a copy in his luggage which he sometimes read in his lodgings in Cairo. He classed it with Homer's *Iliad* as a book dear to him from childhood. While crossing from Smyrna to Cyprus on a Greek ship, he heard a folktale narrated to the mariners in Greek and 'recognised with some alterations an old friend of the Arabian Nights'. Further reading of the *Nights* produced a theory:

> I became strongly impressed with a notion that they must have sprung from the brain of a Greek. It seems to me that these stories, whilst they disclose a complete and habitual *knowledge* of things Asiatic, have about them so much of freshness and life, so much of the stirring and volatile European character, that they cannot have owed their conception to a mere Oriental, who for creative purposes is a thing dead and dry—a mental mummy . . .[13]

As Kinglake's intention, expressed in his Preface, was to steer free from 'all display of "sound learning"' or 'antiquarian research', the problem of the 'European dress' of the translation of the *Nights* he read, still based on Galland, is not mentioned, nor is the subject of frequent borrowings in folk literature.

He sought the *Nights* in the streets of Cairo, though the city was ravaged by the plague. His interests were mainly erotic and supernatural. He visited the open slave market and was not satisfied with the sight of fifty girls, all black. The slave agent promised to show him a Circassian girl as 'fair as the full moon'. This too proved a disappointment, for she was too fat for his taste. She gave him the impression 'of having been got up for sale, of having been fattened or whitened by medicines or by some peculiar diet' (pp. 199-200). Later, he 'thought it worth while to see something of the magicians'. The old man hired by his servants failed to satisfy the inquisitive traveller. However, he bargained to 'raise the devil for two pounds ten, play or pay—no devil, no piastres' (p. 203). The magician did not keep his part of the bargain, for he was carried off by the plague.

Kinglake's fresh, individualistic approach to his subject matter secured him lasting fame as a man of letters. No oriental, however, can easily like *Eothen,* for the Englishman who had come to test his mettle against the hardships of Eastern travel proves his superiority to things Arabic and Islamic at every turn. This attitude was regularly adopted by later travellers, starting with his friend Warburton's *The Crescent and the Cross* (1843).

Richard Burton (1821-90) is most remembered for his translation of the *Nights* (1885-8). It was the crowning work of a long career as soldier, linguist and explorer. It was the outcome, after more than thirty years, of his first visit to the Arab East, his pilgrimage to Makka and Madina in 1853. Burton taught himself Arabic at Oxford and continued studying the language in India, where he served as officer in the army of the East India Company (1842-9). He acquired other oriental languages, both classical and vernacular, learned parts of the Koran by heart and studied Sufism. Burton was familiar with the *Nights* from an early age. His colleagues in India, when engaged on intelligence work, were content with getting information from paid native agents. Burton assumed disguises reminiscent of Harun al-Rashid and his minister in the *Nights.* He pretended to be a rich merchant, half Arab and half Persian, and set up shop in the market as Mirza Abdalla, a name he kept to the end of his life. It is decoratively painted on the first page of his translation of the *Nights.* He was sent home in 1849, ostensibly on sick leave, because his superiors were shocked at the detailed information on male brothels in his reports. The information was later used in his chapter on pederasty in the Terminal Essay in volume x of his translation of the *Nights.*[14] Like Sindbad the Sailor, he could not rest quietly at home, and he obtained financial support from the Royal Geographical Society to explore what he could of Arabia. He intended to make the pilgrimage in disguise as Mirza Abdalla, a Persian. He landed in Alexandria in April 1953 and was advised to change his supposed nationality to Afghan. He travelled to Cairo by steamboat on the Nile and set up in a 'wekallah' or inn, practising as a 'hakim' or physician, which opened many houses before him, giving him the chance to make valuable observations. In his description of Cairo in the first volume of his *Personal Narrative of a Pilgrimage to al Madinah and Meccah* (1855), he cites and corrects Lane on almost every page. Burton stayed in Cairo for some weeks perfecting his pronunciation of Arabic and his knowledge of Muslim customs before joining the pilgrim caravan to Suez. He undertook the strict Ramadan fast in spite of the long days of scorching heat in June. The realities of the traveller's experience and his detailed observations are vividly described (and annotated) without the least attempt at glossing or romanticising. The *Nights,* however, is part of the furniture of his mind. When describing a fellow pilgrim, who at the age of twenty-eight had not yet acquired a wife, the example of Kamer al-Zaman is cited, and he expects his readers to recognise its relevance: 'His parents have urged him to marry, he like Kamer al-Zaman, has informed his father that he is "a person of great age, but little sense".'[15] The caliph Harun al-Rashid is mentioned a number of times in his account of the Hijaz, but it is not the mythical figure of Tennyson's 'good Haroun Al Raschid' in his 'golden prime', but the Abbasid monarch who had many wells sunk on the pilgrim road from Baghdad to Makka (*Personal Narrative,* II, 70, 134).

Burton's great achievement in 1853 was his visit to Makka and Madina and his detailed description of the ceremonies of Haj and Umra, though he was not the first European to do either. His account of the itinerary, together with the crowning visit to the two holy cities of Islam, is full of absorbing details, livened by the sense of danger hanging over 'the pilgrim from the north'. He shows good knowledge of Arab history and literature and of the work of previous travellers, chastising some of them for their erroneous sense of superiority towards customs and literature they did not understand. Harriet Martineau's attack on Muslim harims brings out a defence of marriage customs in the East, which he was later to repeat in the notes of his translation of the *Nights:* 'In quality of doctor I have seen a little and heard much of the harim. It often resembles a European home composed of a man, his wife and his mother. And I have seen in the West many a "happy fireside" fitter to make Miss Martineau's heart ache than any harim in Grand Cairo' (*Personal Narrative,* II, 91). He proceeds to give examples of the importance of love in Arabia, taken from Arabic poetry. Burton retained the same curiosity for marriage customs and sexual practices of different nations that had horrified his compatriots in India. He included some such information in the notes to his travel book, but the publisher suppressed it all as 'garbage'. Burton later used it in the notes to his translation of the *Nights.* Burton was in Aden in 1854, preparing for his second journey of exploration to an Islamic stronghold, the city of Harar in Somaliland, when he conceived the idea of producing a 'full complete unvarnished, uncastrated copy' of the *Nights.*[16] He had a copy of the tales with him when he crossed from Aden to Zayla on the East coast of Africa in October 1854. He had assumed his Arab disguise and from Zayla he travelled inland with a party of nine. It was presumably during this march that 'the wildlings of Somaliland' enjoyed his recitations from the *Nights,* as mentioned in his Translator's Foreword. Two cookmaids who accompanied the party were 'buxom dames about thirty years old, who presently secured the classical nicknames of Shehrazade and Deenarzade'.[17] Another member of the party, 'one-eyed Musa', was dubbed the 'Kalendar'. To his report of the expedition (1856), Burton added an appendix on the sexual customs of the Somalis and an account of the practice of female circumcision (written in Latin). It was torn out by the publisher before the copies were bound, but Burton later used some of the material in a long note in the fifth volume of his *Nights.*

In 1869, after a long career of exploration in Africa and South America, he was finally appointed Consul in Damascus. To him it was again the land of the *Arabian Nights,* 'the land of [his] predilection'. Burton and his wife were very happy in Damascus, and he thought he would spend the rest of his life there. He assumed Arab dress and rode in the Syrian desert. According to his wife, he recited the *Nights* to the bedouins, some of whom 'rolled with pleasure' at some exciting points of the recitation.[18] He vividly describes the scene in his

Foreword to the *Nights.* 'The Shaykks and "white-beards" of the tribe take their places sitting with outspread skirts . . . round the campfire. . . . The women and children stand motionless as silhouettes with attention' (p. viii). In Syria Burton took up archaeology, one of the typical traveller's interests he had never indulged before. He went on trips to Baalbek and Palmyra and made a visit to Palestine. Burton was unpopular with the Turkish wali (the provincial governor), with his superior the British Consul General in Beirut, and with the British Ambassador in Constantinople, because of his unconventional and sympathetic relations with the Arab population. His position was undermined by the proselytising zeal of his Roman Catholic wife and by the intrigues of money-lenders, who had functioned under the protection of his predecessors, but whose applications for help in extorting debts from poor inhabitants he angrily spurned. He was recalled in 1871 'at the age of fifty, without a month's notice or wages or character'. Burton made two short visits to Egypt and the Eastern coast of Arabia in 1877 and 1878. He had written to the bankrupt Khedive Ismail of Egypt about the possibility of prospecting for gold in Midian in the north-west of Arabia, because of a story he had heard more than twenty years before from Haj Wali, a man he had met in Cairo in 1853. The two expeditions were a failure, Burton lost a lot of money but he produced two volumes with detailed accounts of his travels.[19] He did not realise at the time that he did not need to prospect for gold on desert shores, for he had a goldmine in hand, his translation of the *Nights.* He was working on it when in 1881 he read of John Payne's intention of publishing a complete translation of the *Nights.* Burton wrote to the *Athenaeum* welcoming Payne's project and announcing his own intention of publishing an unexpurgated translation. In the correspondence between him and Payne which followed, he urged the poet to be as literal as possible, but Payne resisted Burton's urging as his intention was basically aesthetic rather than anthropological. When Payne's nine volumes of the *Nights* started appearing in 1882 (dedicated to Richard Burton), the latter saw that there was still a need for *his* translation.

Burton's *Plain and Literal Translation of the Arabian Nights* was privately printed, allegedly for the Kamashastra Society in Benares, a society he invented. It was limited to 1,000 copies for subscribers only, and he made a profit on it of 10,000 guineas. The work is monumental, ten volumes of the original tales with six volumes of *Supplemental Nights* from the Wortley-Montagu manuscript in the Bodleian Library. The 'Terminal Essay' in volume x gives a scholarly study and bibliography of the *Nights,* together with a chance for Burton to hit back at his critics with more anthropological data 'to shock Mrs Grundy' to the utmost. The notes to the tales carry details of varied information he collected in his extensive travels. His main point was that previous translations had degraded 'a chef d'oeuvre of the highest anthropological and ethnographical interest and importance to a mere fairy-book, a nice present for little boys'.

Burton's devotion to the *Nights,* which were 'an unfailing source of solace and satisfaction' during his travels, is in great contrast to the attitude of the next traveller of importance in Arabia. Charles M. Doughty spent twenty months in the country, starting from Damascus with the pilgrim caravan in 1876, but he had no use for disguise, for Islam or for the *Arabian Nights.* He was a scientist interested in noting the land formation in the regions he crossed as well as the customs of the bedouins with whom he travelled. He saw parts of Arabia that had not been visited by any European before him, and, when he published his travel book nine years later,[20] he warned his readers 'that nothing be looked for in this book but the seeing of a hungry man and the telling of a most weary man'. His intention in writing was mainly literary 'to redeem English from the slough into which it had fallen since the days of Elizabeth'. The hardships of desert life came over in language suited to Bedouin austerity. The translation of Arabic sentences into biblical or Shakespearian idiom, the Arabic words transliterated into English and the numerous newly coined Anglo-Arabic words all add to the beauty and literary value of the work.

It must be confessed that travellers such as Doughty who had to cope with genuine desert life in the Arabian peninsula at the latter end of the nineteenth century had little occasion or use for the *Nights.* T. E. Lawrence, whose name is associated with Arabia more than any Englishman before him, does not mention the *Nights* in *Seven Pillars of Wisdom* except to show the romantic element in the Arab Revolt:

> A second buttress of a polity of Arab motive was the dim glory of the early Khalifat whose memory endured among the people through centuries of Turkish misgovernment. The accident that these traditions savoured rather of the Arabian Nights than of sheer history maintained the Arab rank and file in their conviction that their past was more splendid than the present of the Ottoman Turk. Yet we knew that these were dreams.[21]

Lawrence was right, for he best knew what lay in wait for the Arab Revolt, but the dream persisted with both Arabs and Europeans. Travellers continued to flock into the cities of the Near East changed by the advent of steam and later of the aeroplane. They still looked for the *Nights,* for the flourishing tourist industry adopted them for its own. From Aladdin nightclubs to Harun al-Rashid restaurants, chartered groups are regaled with oriental experience packaged and ready-made. Only the perceptive traveller armed with real knowledge of the *Nights* may suddenly light on an old house with latticed windows and a marble hall of which the fountain is dry, or a row of little old shops in a side street in Cairo, Damascus or Baghdad, and see the scene come alive peopled with the familiar characters of the tales.

Notes

Books published in London unless otherwise stated.

1. Martha Pike Conant, *The Oriental Tale in England in the Eighteenth Century* (New York: Columbia University Press, 1908).

2. Lady Mary Wortley-Montagu, *The Complete Letters,* I: *1708-1720,* ed. Robert Halsband (Oxford: Clarendon Press, 1965) pp. 385.

3. Alexander Russell, *The Natural History of Aleppo* . . . (A. Millar, 1[7]56; p. 90.

4. *The Natural History of Aleppo,* 2nd edn, rev. and illustrated by Patrick Russell (G. G. and J. Robinson, 1794) I, 385-6.

5. For details of this manuscript, see my 'A MS Translation of the *Arabian Nights* in the Beckford Papers', *Journal of Arabic Literature* (Leiden) VII, (1976) 7-23.

6. *Gentleman's Magazine,* Apr 1798, pp. 304-5, and Feb 1799, pp. 91-2.

7. *The Arabian Nights,* in 5 vols, tr. Edward Forster (William Miller, 1802) I, xli, xliii.

8. *A Journey through Persia, Armenia and Asia Minor* . . . (1812); *A Second Journey through Persia* . . . (1818).

9. *The Adventures of Hajji Baba* . . . , intro. by C.W. Stewart, The World's Classics (Oxford University Press, 1923).

10. *Quarterly Review,* xxx (1824) 200-1.

11. E. W. Lane, *The Manners and Customs of Modern Egyptians,* Everyman edn (Dent, 1908) p. xxi n.

12. Richard Burton, *A Plain and Literal Translation of the Arabian Nights* . . . (Kamashastra Society, Benares, 1885) I. Translator's Foreword.

13. A. W. Kinglake, *Eothen* (Macmillan, 1960) p. 64.

14. Fawn M. Brodie, *The Devil Drives: A Life of Sir Richard Burton* (Eyre and Spottiswoode, 1967) p. 66.

15. Richard Burton, *Personal Narrative of a Pilgrimage* . . . Memorial Edition (New York: Dover) I, 161.

16. In the Foreword to his translation of the *Nights,* Burton erroneously gives the date of the inception of the plan for the translation as 1852. In 1852 he was in Europe, and the visit to Aden after the pilgrimage took place in 1854.

17. Richard Burton, *First Footsteps in East Africa,* Everyman's Library (Dent, 1910) p. 101.

18. Isabel Burton, *Inner Life of Syria, Palestine and the Holy Land,* 2 vols (H. S. King, 1875) I, 128, 353; see Brodie, *The Devil Drives,* p. 254.

19. Richard Burton, *The Gold-Mines of Midian* . . . (1878), and *The Land of Midian (Revisited),* 2 vols (1879).

20. Charles M. Doughty, *Travels to Arabia Deserta* (Cambridge: Cambridge University Press, 1888). See I, 263 for his adverse comments on the *Nights.*

21. T. E. Lawrence, *Seven Pillars of Wisdom,* Penguin Modern Classics (Harmondsworth: Penguin, 1962) p. 344.

Sandra Naddaff (essay date 1991)

SOURCE: Naddaff, Sandra. "Magic Time: The Movement and Meaning of Narrative Repetition." In *Arabesque: Narrative Structure and the Aesthetics of Repetition in the* 1001 Nights, pp. 89-108. Evanston, Ill.: Northwestern University Press, 1991.

[*In the following essay, Naddaff argues that* The Arabian Nights *uses repetition to structure narrative discourse, thus exploring and emphasizing the relation between time, repetition, and narrative; she goes on to examine how these structural devices are used to comment on power and gender in the tales.*]

I

We come finally to the crucial connection between repetition and time, a connection that, although of particular interest vis-à-vis the repetitive mode, is of course maintained with all types of narrative discourse. For all narrative must take first root in the temporal realm. Indeed, not only must narrative move within the various confines of its own temporal boundaries, but we as readers can participate in narrative only by following the temporal continuum of our own universe, by establishing a time of reading. What is the relation between these two temporal spheres? How does one clock narrative time so that the reader's sense of time remains mains intact? How can one move forward or backward in narrative time without destroying the limits of temporality? The answers differ according to individual narrative genre and effect. Epic, romance, realist novel: each genre requires a different temporal perspective specific to its narrative structure. But regardless of generic constraints, each must engage on some level with Proust's "jeu formidable . . . avec le Temps."

In the cycle of **"The Porter and the Three Ladies,"** it is primarily the repeated recurrence of certain patterned structures of story and discourse which undeniably and somewhat ironically signals the movement of the cycle in time and the correlative unfolding of the narrative. One must again remember that exact identity between repeated events of whatever nature is, strictly speaking, impossible; that the linear constraints of the temporal realm must necessarily prevent the exact repetition of events no matter how similar, simply because any repeated event occurs at a time later than that of the instigating event. At best, narrative can know only near repetition, the replaying of the same events, the same verbal components at a different time.[1] The very fact that the same phrase exists at one or more points in a text points to the necessary temporal movement of the narrative, its incapacity to maintain a static position. In the third dervish's description of the opening of the forbidden doors, for example, the repetition of both story and discourse underscores not only the significance of the act of discovery but both the temporal movement that accompanies the act and the narrative that describes it. The repeated interruption at the end of each night serves much the same function—only in this case the act being described is that of narration itself. In short, given the insistent foregrounding of repetition as a means of structuring narrative discourse, the *1001 Nights* seems to be telling us something significant about the relation between time, repetition, and narrative.

That repetition within narrative is essentially a temporal phenomenon cannot be disputed, since without the context of advancing linear time, repetition has no frame of reference and therefore no meaning. A narrative structured by repetition consequently relies upon and often silently points to its temporal framework. Not surprisingly, then, time is of the essence, both structurally and thematically, in the three ladies cycle. Everyone is trying to beat the clock in both narrative and performative terms, and time's passage accordingly assumes critical importance. Repetition appropriately underscores this temporal movement.

I will return to this crucial relationship shortly, but let me digress briefly here to note that other levels of narrative time are operative within the cycle as a whole. While the repetition of structures of story and discourse is sustained primarily on the horizontal plot axis of the narrative and accordingly manipulates the temporal movement within the individual narratives, there is a corresponding vertical axis along which the temporal

movement of the act of narration itself moves. This temporal movement can be designated as narrational time, that time specific to a given act of narration. Given the basic repetition of the narrative act within the cycle, as discussed earlier, the corresponding temporal movement is clearly significant.

We must again go back to the beginning. The first level of time specific to the narrative act—and there is here an equivalence between narrative time and narrative voice—is that in which the storyteller tells his story about Shahrazad telling her stories. This level of primary narration remains largely implicit and substantially unvoiced. It is, in fact, brought to the fore only in the interruption that occurs at the end of each night— "But morning overtook Shahrazad, and she lapsed into silence"—and in the occasional voice markers, "said Shahrazad," which necessarily follow this interruption. The second level of narrational time and voice is appropriately that of Shahrazad herself. This level is only slightly more pronounced than that of the primary narrator; indeed, since both share the third-person past tense, it is easy to mistake the one for the other. The only time Shahrazad's voice comes through clearly is at the beginning of each night when she refers to herself in the first person and directly addresses the king: "I heard, O happy King." But it should be emphasized that within the primary narrative of the storyteller, the time and voice of Shahrazad are themselves primary; they repeat the function of the time and voice within which they are embedded. It is within their limits that the most substantial narratives of the cycle unfold.

The Chinese box syndrome continues. The third level of narrational time belongs to the story being told by Shahrazad. This is the realm which is initially indicated by the indeterminate equivalent of the implicit "once upon a time" that opens the three ladies cycle, but which is later specified by Shahrazad as the time of Harun al-Rashid. It is in this time that the characters of the tale exist and tell their own stories. In the case of the three ladies cycle, this level is established initially in the frame story and subsequently reasserted in the intervals that separate the individual tales. It is at this point that the story is evaluated and its narrator summarily dismissed. At the end of the first tale, for example, the dervish concludes: "But God drove us to your house, and you were kind and generous enough to let us in and help me forget the loss of my eye and the shaving off of my beard"; and the narrative continues: "The girl said to him, 'Stroke your head and go.' He replied, 'By God, I will not go until I hear the tales of the others.' . . . It is related, O happy King, that those who were present marveled at the tale of the first dervish. The caliph said to Ja'far, 'In all my life I have never heard a stranger tale.' Then the second dervish came forward and said: . . ." (91-92). Again, the third-person past tense prevails. The voice is ostensibly Shahrazad's, but the tone of the narrative bears a strong resemblance to that of an unspecified, omniscient narrator. It would seem that the further back in narrational time we go, the fainter the original narrative voice becomes.

The loss of the primary narrative voice—be it that of the storyteller or of Shahrazad—is finalized in the fourth level of narrational time. This is that time in which the narrative-men and -women speak, a time that is necessarily antecedent to that of the act of narration. These stories are also told in the past tense, but there is here a switch in the narrative voice from the third person to the first person: "Then the first dervish came forward and said: 'My lady, the cause of *my* eye being torn out and *my* beard being shaved off was as follows. *My* father was a king . . .'" (emphasis added) (86). A complete narrative transition involving the transference of the authoritative narrative voice and a corresponding shift in the level of narrational time has been made.

With the exception of the narrative night markers, nowhere else in the cycle is the passing of time noted with such care as it is in this final narrational realm. Each dervish makes a deliberate point of marking the amount of time spent in any given place. The first dervish spends four days looking for his cousin. The second dervish spends one year chopping wood. The beautiful woman has spent twenty-five years in her underground prison; the demon comes to stay with her once every ten days; and she rather calculatingly informs her new-found companion: "He has been away for four days, so there remain only six days before he comes again. Would you like to spend five days with me and leave on the day before he arrives?" (96). The third dervish in his turn sails at sea for forty days before the storm; he spends forty days with the boy whom he eventually kills, and one year minus forty days with the women in the palace. Clearly, time's passage has a peculiar significance within these tales, as if the careful marking of time were to compensate for the narrative and corresponding temporal distance that has been traveled between the primary narrative and those at the furthest narrational remove. Yet no matter how deep into the past we travel with the dervishes, and no matter how long they stay there, we and they all end up in the same place in and at the same time. In the end, we all rejoin the narrative present.

What results is a fundamental disturbance and confusion of temporal levels within the work as a whole and the cycle in particular. In addition to the standard horizontal range of the temporal spectrum within which narrative can move from left to right at ease, the three ladies cycle offers as well vertical levels of time whose only connection is that the one contains the other. If within each level a certain horizontal progression (or regression as is often the case) occurs, it is eventually confounded by the narrative constraints restricting each level. In short, a simple diachronic, linear connection in time cannot be made among the individual tales within the cycle. As the story unfolds, one must move up and down within the various levels of narrational time as well as back and forth in narrative time. A fundamental jarring of temporal perspective occurs.

Ultimately, one of the main reasons it is so difficult to maintain a distinction among the separate stories of the cycle, to remember what the *1001 Nights* narrative of **"The Porter and the Three Ladies"** is all about—a difficulty I suspect every reader encounters—is because the line against which the narrative unfolds is so deviant. It is a difficulty that the use of repetition as a mode of narrative discourse largely maintains and essentially instigates; indeed, the vertical movement of narrational times and voices is itself little more than the echoing, the verbal mirroring of one time and voice by another. That narrative repetition has no significance without a linear temporal base, indeed derives its essence from its temporal affiliation, is clear. What is not so clear, perhaps, is that by its very nature repetition is an attempt to destroy its own essence, to kill the natural movement of linear time, to turn time back upon itself, to make time repeat itself, reflect itself, do anything but continue its unimpeded advance. That such an attempt is ultimately fruitless is the necessary result of the condition that all narrative must somehow move from one point to another, from beginning to end by way of the middle, if it is to maintain its status not only as narrative but as a linguistic construct. The fact remains, however, that every effort has been made to slow this movement, indeed to subvert this movement, to alter the inevitable march of narrative time without altering the fundamental nature of narrative.

One of the prerogatives of any narrative is to play with time, to create its own time. If the *1001 Nights* is a narrative telling about the making and telling of other narratives, it is also necessarily a work about the relation between narratives, or specific types of narrative, and their temporal foundation. The motivating force behind Shahrazad's telling of the *1001 Nights* is, as it is for her counterparts in Baghdad, a desire to forestall death, to impede time's natural flow, to ward off the sense of an ending. At the behest of their audience, these tellers of tales must kill time, or be killed themselves. It is ironic but essential that in order to kill time, and thereby to avoid the inevitable end of time, the narrators must make time, create narrative time. Not surprisingly, they narratively manifest this irony by developing their tales according to repetitive structures of story and discourse which counteract the forward movement of time and in so doing undercut the fundamental impulse of narrative.

II

It stands to reason that this effort to forestall the inevitable human end of time, the physical sense of an ending, affects the narrative sense of an ending as well. Given that narrative repetition is essentially a kind of recurrent textual return, a backward narrative movement that seeks to reunite, realign a later textual moment with its original preceding one, it is not surprising that the ending of a work structured according to various patterns of repetition is significantly different from that of a work that progresses more or less straightforwardly from beginning to end. Peter Brooks notes that in the grammar of plot, "repetition, taking us back again over the same ground, could have to do with the choice of ends."[2] The pertinent suggestion is that the ending of a repetitive narrative functions differently in relation to the preceding whole. The particular intent of this difference is focused on the narrative beginning.

If one accepts Todorov's premise that the ideal narrative consists in its broadest outlines of a fundamentally stable situation (the beginning), which is subsequently disturbed (the middle), and finally resolved (the end)—that is, that any narrative moves between two equilibriums that are related but not identical (the same but different)—one looks to the ending of a traditional narrative as a resolution marked by its necessarily later difference from the beginning.[3] In short, the movement inherent in any narrative structure requires a distance between beginning and end along which the narrative can unfold, and this distance in turn requires a difference between the two limiting points of the narrative. The absence of this distance of difference would seemingly lead to a kind of narrative collapse, an inability on the part of narrative to pursue its necessary course. A repetitive narrative, however, a narrative whose structural impulse is always to look backward, to turn back upon itself, necessarily subverts this sense of an ending as something in the distant and different future.

The cycle of **"The Porter and the Three Ladies"** drives the point home. When the second woman has finished her tale and the caliph has ordered that it be entered as a recorded history and placed in the treasury, the closing frame of the story as told by Shahrazad to the king follows. This last section of the tale, structurally separated from the preceding section of the narrative by a night break, fulfills much the same function as an epilogue. Not only are the primary characters of all five embedded tales gathered together at one time and in one place, but the future of each one is irrevocably determined by the political and narrative authorities in question, with some assistance from a dea ex machina in the guise of a Muslim ifrit. In sum, the ultimate conclusion of the narrative, the final weaving together of assorted narrative strands, is achieved.

What happens at the end of the three ladies cycle is not unlike what happens at the happy end of a nineteenth-century novel: people are married; losses are compensated; futures are ensured. The ifrit is instrumental in this activity. In gestures that remind us that at a certain point it is potentially the women in this tale who wield the power (especially the narrative power), she helps to bring the cycle to its close by releasing the two sisters of the eldest lady from their inhuman captivity as black bitches and by informing the caliph of the true identity of the second woman's jealous husband, who, conveniently, is both geographically and genetically close at hand. Harun al-Rashid then takes over and asserts his secular authority. He expediently marries the three sisters of the first woman's story to the three dervishes, whom he subsequently enlists as his chamberlains; he reunites the second woman with his son, her estranged husband; and he obligingly offers himself as a spouse to the third woman, the shopper, who curiously is richly rewarded for having no story to tell. A fearful, perhaps because unearthly, symmetry results. It is no wonder that at the close of the entire narrative, the caliph orders that all the preceding stories be recorded and thereby preserved for posterity.

What has happened at the end of this cycle is remarkable for reasons other than its patterned design. Instead of progressing toward a future state, a condition distantly different because later than the beginning, the narrative has moved backward, has restored its characters to a time and a state predating that of the cycle's opening. The narrative has been markedly conservative, even retrograde in its driving impulse. When the ifrit, muttering words that no one can understand, releases the two women from bestial captivity, she expresses in summary form the basic thrust of the cycle's ending. The women return to their original state; the three dervishes reacquire their royal status (the narrative interestingly reminds us of this, as if to underline the socially conservative nature of the caliph's act: "He married the first girl and her sisters who had been cast under a spell to the three dervishes, who were the sons of kings" [150]). And finally, the doorkeeper is returned to her former husband. The happy end of the cycle has not provided a new and different because importantly later equilibrium on which the narrative can rest. It has, on the contrary, done little more than return the narrative to an earlier state, one prior to that of its beginning. The status quo has been reestablished. Time has not doggedly marched onward and taken its inevitable toll; it has, in fact, moved backward and ultimately been frozen through narrative at a still and stable moment.

III

I would like now to move from this discussion about the conservative power of repetition to examine the way in which this narrative pattern relates to issues centering on the female body and questions of gender raised earlier in this study. Such generic issues of narrative time are not, I would suggest, unrelated to the way that gender (the etymological connection between genre and gender is here significant) means in a given narrative context. And they are particularly connected to the kinds of power struggles that gender, almost by definition, elicits.

Such struggles are at the very center of *Alf Laylah.* Indeed, one might argue that the text itself is instigated by the unanticipated appropriation of power by women. It is worth digressing to reexamine the familiar though crucial first scene. Shahzaman, Shahrayar's brother, has returned to his palace to find his wife in bed with a cook. Shahzaman responds to this scene by cutting his wife and her lover in two, only to discover some time later his brother's wife in a similar situation. This time, however, the treachery is magnified. Twenty concubines initially accompany the queen into the garden, ten of whom quickly reveal themselves to be men, specifically black slaves. Shahrayar's wife then allies herself with another black slave, who descends from a tree in response to her call. The scene is repeated a second time for the voyeuristic and legalistic benefit of Shahrayar, following which the two brothers go forth to seek comfort in the possibility of similar wrongdoing.

In an article entitled "Infidelity and Fiction," Judith Grossman has examined this scene with an eye to the question of women's subjectivity in the *1001 Nights* and has argued that what Shahzaman and Shahrayar are encountering here is "the problem which the recognition of female subjectivity has set for male-dominated cultures";[4] that the two brothers are confronting the fact that women have autonomous desires and, perhaps more frightening, the capacity to satisfy these desires at the expense of the "normal" boundaries of patriarchal society and culture. What is particularly interesting, though, is that it is not simply the women in whom these subversive desires are embodied. Shahzaman's wife, one recalls, was found with a cook, a representative of the domestic realm; while Shahrayar's wife, whose garden party suggests the way such subversive gestures are fruitful and multiply, has her male cohorts assume female guise, further intensifying this association between the feminine and the subversive. That her lover is himself black and a marginal figure (suggested by his tree-house location) suggests that such subversive behavior is distributed among all those who are not part of the dominant hierarchy. Clearly, speaking about gender is a constant reminder of the other categories of difference, such as race and class, that structure culture.

The response of the two kings to the potential for social revolution within their realm is to eradicate the threat in an effort to maintain the status quo. Both destroy the actual bodies that have sinned against authority, though it is interesting that while Shahzaman wreaks his own vengeance, Shahrayar delegates the punitive action to his wazir, Shahrazad's father, perhaps thereby formally asserting his unqualified resumption of power. Since it is precisely the declaration of unrestrained sexuality and desire that inaugurates this potential revolution, it makes perfect sense within the logic of the situation to mutilate the body that is the locus of such threatening actions.

It is not for nothing, I would argue, that as the interlude in **"The Porter and the Three Ladies"** has suggested, the *1001 Nights* is haunted by bodies. Bodies scarred, transported, naked, metamorphosed, bodies that seem incapable of maintaining a secure, stable, respectable position in society are, in a sense, the signature of *Alf Laylah.*[5] There are three groups of these specifically female bodies both in the frame tale and again in **"The Porter and the Three Ladies of Baghdad"** that are worth examining in order to explore the ways in which sex and text, male and female, come to grips with each other in this work, and to suggest thereby one kind of power struggle generated both in and by the *Nights* as well as the way the narrative, as suggested above, resolves it.

As Grossman notes, the presence that immediately counters the precipitating actions of those first female bodies, those of the kings' wives, is, surprisingly, not Shahrazad, but the woman possessed by the demon. Having discovered the betrayal of Shahrayar's wife, Shahzaman and his brother have responded by going forth to compare their fate with that of other men. Soon after their departure from the city they encounter a woman whose body, if not spirit, is quite literally possessed by a demon who contains her in a glass box with four padlocks. (The fact that the chest is glass is interesting because it gives the illusion of free will and movement.) It is this woman who forces the two brothers to have intercourse with her, as she has done with many hundreds of men before them, and it is, consequently, this woman who convinces them of the essential depravity and subversive nature of the feminine. It is after encountering her that Shahrayar returns home and implements his plan of daily execution. Grossman remarks that what is particularly noteworthy here is that the authority commanded by the woman is not her own. In clear bondage to her demon husband, she is only able to manipulate her situation within the terms of power established by the one who possesses her body. She can only compel Shahzaman and Shahrayar to do her bidding by invoking the power of her husband. Three times she threatens the two brothers with the wrath and ensuing violence of the ifrit if they deny her satisfaction; and although she brings her encounter with Shahzaman and Shahrayar to a close by pronouncing,

"When a woman desires something, no one can stop her" (10), what neither she nor the kings realize is that she is doing so according to the conditions established by a society that legislates the possession of the female body. She is not acting subversively; she is simply appropriating the power that belongs to her husband.

The woman who is eventually summoned by this encounter is Shahrazad. But I would like to return for the moment to those three Baghdadian women, who mirror not only Shahrazad in their commanding narrative presence and power but also—in their ultimate narrative objectification and confinement—those women she sets out to redeem. I argued earlier in this study that what the three ladies are doing in the frame story of their cycle is establishing a specific kind of discourse, a discourse that focuses on the female body and on the relation of this body to metaphoric language. These are, apparently, the first fully self-possessed, seemingly integral and unmarked female bodies that the reader encounters in the *Nights* (though this cycle is immediately followed by **"The Story of the Three Apples,"** a story ostentatiously generated by the discovery of a mutilated female body). These are women who, apparently, not only control their own bodies and celebrate their own sexuality but also determine their own language and their own narrative rules. When the women demand further on in the frame tale that the men who have joined them for the evening either tell their tales or be permanently silenced, they are asserting their prerogative as the essential lawmakers in this particular realm.

It would seem that these three women are establishing an alternative society with radically different customs and laws that they themselves have determined. The specifically feminine space that they inhabit and that separates them from medieval Baghdad, the autonomous control they have over their own bodies, their legislative powers, which are backed by both oral and written authority and unquestioningly asserted, all suggest that within the confines of the frame tale at least, the actions and aims of these women are driven by anything but a desire to maintain the status quo of the society from which they have divorced themselves.

Indeed it seems that the three ladies are anxious to throw into question the values of those men who enter their privileged realm. But the facts of the extended narrative tell otherwise. The women's power turns out to be short-lived and confined to the initiating frame. It takes only the simple assertion of the real, historical, and political power of Harun al-Rashid, the embodiment of the dominant, established culture, to override the women's voices. Ja'far states: "You are in the presence of the seventh of the sons of 'Abbas, al-Rashid, son of al-Mahdi son of al-Hadi and brother of al-Saffah

son of Mansur. Take courage, be frank, and tell the truth and nothing but the truth, and do not lie, for 'you should be truthful even if truth sends you to burning Hell'" (134). And once commanded by this authority, the three ladies revoke the essential rule of their realm, Speak not of what concerns you not, lest you hear what pleases you not, and obey the caliph's commands that they tell their own story—the truth and nothing but the truth.

The result of this all-too-ready abdication of power on the part of the three women leads to the reestablishment, or, since it has never really been threatened, the reassertion, of historical authority and the status quo it embodies. Again, the closing frame of the cycle as told by Shahrazad to Shahrayar drives the point home. The potential for a state of change and difference, a state in which the linguistic and social order suggested by the three ladies might be enacted, has been abolished. The interlude initiated by the three ladies has proved to be just that—a playful, insignificant moment prior to real action whose suggestions for rewriting the social and linguistic codes have been appropriated by the proper authorities. In this light it seems important to note that the bodies these three women so proudly reveal in the opening frame are not as whole and unmarked as they initially appear. The back of the doorkeeper bears the tell-tale traces of a previous whipping, and it is these signs that initially excite the caliph's curiosity. Significantly, the caliph himself, by association, is responsible for these bodily etchings since, ironically, it is his son who has engraved them on the woman's back.

There is one more encounter with a dis-rupted body in this cycle that warrants examination. Physical metamorphosis—the transformation of a person from one bodily state to another—occurs almost as frequently in the *Nights* as physical mutilation. Both men and women are subject to metamorphic transformation, though women seem more likely to lose their human aspect than men. The great example of metamorphosis in the three ladies cycle is, of course, that of the king's daughter, who through her powers of autometamorphosis releases the second dervish from bestial captivity.

The incident is interesting in part because of the way it plays off of earlier moments of physical enclosure or transformation. The dervish whom the princess redeems has been transformed as a result of his encounter with the woman in the underground cave. This woman, held there against her will by an ifrit, is, in essence, a duplicate of that other woman in captivity, discussed earlier, who instigates Shahrayar's revenge. The underground woman is content to entertain her unexpected, and indeed uninvited, visitor until she needs to fulfill her obligations to the ifrit in much the same way that her double economically uses the short measure of the demon's sleep to assert her own desires. Their fates, however, are radically different. The demon husband responds to the woman's infraction of justice by engaging in nothing less than physical torture and mutilation. (The dervish reports first, "Then he [the demon] seized her, stripped her naked and, binding her hands and feet to four stakes, proceeded to torture her"; and later, "I saw the girl stripped naked, her limbs tied, and her sides bleeding"; and finally, "Then he took the sword and struck the girl, severing her arm from her shoulder and sending it flying. Then he struck again and severed the other arm and sent it flying" (98-101).

For his part in the deception, the dervish is transformed into an ape, but an ape who, critically, can still write though not speak. In order to release him, the king's daughter herself willingly undergoes a series of stunning metamorphoses during which she engages in combat with the ifrit, who counters with his own transformations. What is unusual about this encounter is that the princess alone controls what happens to her body. Her intellectual and corresponding metamorphic powers have been transmitted to her by an old woman (emphasizing, perhaps, the connection between such powers and the feminine) and are unbeknownst even to her father, who values her over a hundred sons. In her capacity for autonomy and self-determination, she counters the previous images of contained and possessed women with the image of a female body so supple and unbounded that it can change shape at will. Indeed, in her metamorphic powers, she recalls the three ladies and their metaphoric powers—both united in their potential to alter the given structure of reality. The affiliation, unfortunately, extends further, for like these other women, the princess's power is only temporary and, indeed, self-destructive. In working to release the second dervish from his bestial form, the princess effects not only the death of the ifrit but her own annihilation as well. Her final transformation into a heap of ashes suggests the ultimate ineffectualness of her power. In order to reestablish the "natural" order of things, in order to reassert the "normal" boundaries that structure society—the division between human and animal, between higher and lower, between male and female—the princess must extinguish her own "unnatural" powers precisely because they threaten such order. It is striking in this context that the dervish, who is both the instigator of all this trouble and one of the primary beholders of this scene, escapes almost wholly intact. The lost eye, the only mark he bears of this encounter, is the price he must pay for having borne witness, for having seen what should not be seen or even allowed to become visible. What the king's daughter has done is to stave off the breakdown of all "normal," established boundaries and limits, a breakdown that would force a reorganization of reality in the same way that the metaphoric language of the three

ladies would. In sum, what she has indicated through her metamorphosis and consequent death, and what the three ladies themselves ultimately acknowledge, is the necessity, perhaps even the desirability, of returning society to its earlier patriarchal state.

IV

I would argue that the use of repetition in this narrative is the structural device that has worked its will in this reestablishment, in this conservative movement back to an earlier, more stable moment before narrative became necessary. For the most part, in any case. But what of the stories of the two women, which bring the embedded portion of the cycle to an asymmetric close? Why the growing attenuation of repetitive patterns of story and discourse precisely at that point closest to the final return, the final inversion of beginning and end, achieved by the frame's close? The answer lies in the very nature of the narrative movement associated with repetitive structures. If, as discussed earlier, such a narrative does move in a fashion contrary to that of a more horizontal, linear narrative; if repetition as a mode of narrative discourse structurally urges a narrative to return to its origins, ever to antecede its narrative beginnings, the narrative must, in practical storytelling terms, never end, for it must always and eternally repeat itself at the very point of its real narrative beginning. No matter how hard a narrative might try to counteract the sense of an ending as a future moment, then, it must inevitably concede at some point to the basic dictates of the narrative movement it is subverting. A practical end point must be located, since the potential of and for repetition is infinite. The endlessly repeating is, in fact, the interminable; there is theoretically no way to halt a narrative that has embarked on a fundamentally repetitive course. Just as metaphor must have metonymy in order to achieve its final metaphoric state, so must a repetitive narrative engage in a forward movement not only to assert the very fact of its repetition but also to bring the narrative at some arbitrary point to its practical close.

I would suggest that the final two tales of this cycle gradually provide a counter to this overriding movement of repetition; that in unwinding the ever more complicated structures of the preceding tales, they help to ease this potentially endless narrative to its rest. And I would further suggest that it is important that these are the stories of two of those ladies who sought to overturn the dominant culture in which they, as narrative-women, are embedded, for it is yet another concession to the literary, social, and political norms embodied in Harun al-Rashid.

The way in which the actual story of each of the five major tales is handled in the closing frame is significant. The three dervishes' narratives receive barely passing notice. No steps are taken to counteract their action; no attempt is made to right any of the physical wrongs committed in their course. The response to the two ladies' tales, however, is quite different. Not only is the ifrit necessary literally to undo the damage cited by the two women, but the narrative takes great pains to track this reversal in some detail. The story of the ifrit is repeated by the ifrit herself before she returns the dogs to their former human state, in much the same way that she reminds the caliph of his son's action before al-Amin can confirm it himself. Fortunately, the repeated narratives are relatively brief. The ifrit waxes fairly eloquent about her own personal history but repeats only in shortened form the story of the second lady and her jealous husband. The same narrative attitude is maintained with al-Amin: "Then the caliph, O King, summoned his son al-Amin and questioned him to confirm the truth of the story" (150). The closing frame of the cycle employs in relatively concentrated fashion many of the repetitive patterns discussed in relation to the three dervishes' tales; but what the ifrit's retelling of the ladies' stories suggests is that since the structural underpinnings of the stories are themselves of little use in returning the ladies to an earlier state, since the ladies have apparently lost their metaphoric power, the story and discourse of the closing frame must compensate.

Regardless of the means, we finally arrive at the cycle's end, which predates, in a sense, its beginning, at the point at which all of the characters (with the exception of the luckless porter, who has long disappeared from narrative sight) are restored to their former condition and forever removed from further narrative influence. I have suggested throughout this discussion that the kind of narrative movement that instigates such an ending is intimately linked to an effort to contradict and counteract the forward-moving march of time, which necessitates the kind of change and potential for revolution that the *1001 Nights* is apparently arguing against.

But this forward temporal movement also brings us all, characters and readers alike, to our natural end. One might argue that the drive of such a repetitively structured narrative is to achieve the status of the timeless, the eternal, the ultimate conservative state, and to move beyond the boundaries of beginning and end. It is a status achieved on a minimal level by every narrative in its capacity to be reread, reexperienced, repeated, at any time and place. It is, nonetheless, particularly significant in a narrative created according to the structures and restrictions of a repetitive mode. Shahrazad's own narrative is intensely aware of such time-breaking narrative potential. Not only is it structured according to the fundamental repetitive act of narration, which provides the foundation upon which the *1001 Nights* is built; but its very title accentuates the narrative drive that actualizes such potential. As Ferial

Ghazoul notes, in Arabic the number one thousand (1000) connotes a number beyond count; one thousand and one (1001) suggests that final move into eternity, into the realm where the mere passing of days and nights has no significance.[6] Shahrazad tells stories for one thousand and one nights in order to move beyond time, to reassert certain deeply embedded cultural norms and patterns of literary and social behavior that are being subject against their will to alteration and reconsideration. The three ladies and their companions in Baghdad do the same.

Notes

1. See Kawin, *Telling It Again and Again,* p. 7.

2. Brooks, "Freud's Masterplot," p. 286.

3. See Todorov's discussion of this issue in "La grammaire du récit."

4. Grossman, "Infidelity and Fiction," p. 114. I have found Grossman's article particularly suggestive for the terms in which she discusses the problem of women's selfhood and subjectivity in the *Nights.*

5. The two meanings of the word *corpus* again intersect. Richard Burton most demonstrably suggests this etymological conjunction when in the "Translator's Foreword" to his *Thousand Nights and a Night* he remarks, "Before parting we [a colleague and himself] agreed to 'collaborate' and produce a full, complete, unvarnished, *uncastrated* copy of the great original" (emphasis mine).

6. I have benefited greatly from the fascinating discussion of the significance of numbers in the *1001 Nights* in Ghazoul, *The Arabian Nights,* pp. 62-65. She addresses the issue of the number 1001 on p. 65.

Bibliography

Brooks, Peter. "Freud's Masterplot." *Yale French Studies* 55-56 (1977): 280-300.

Kawin, Bruce. *Telling It Again and Again.* Ithaca, N.Y., 1972.

Burton, Richard, trans. *The Book of the Thousand Nights and a Night.* 16 vols. N.d.

Ghazoul, Ferial. *The Arabian Nights: A Structural Analysis.* Cairo, 1980.

Grossman, Judith. "Infidelity and Fiction." *Georgia Review* 34, no. 1 (Spring 1980): 113-26.

Todorov, Tzvetan. "La grammaire du récit." *Langages* 12 (1968): 94-102.

David Pinault (essay date 1992)

SOURCE: Pinault, David. "An Introduction to the Arabian Nights." In *Story-Telling Techniques in the Arabian Nights*, pp. 16-30. Leiden, Netherlands: E. J. Brill, 1992.

[*In the following excerpt, Pinault introduces some of the narrative devices used in* The Arabian Nights, *including repetitive designation,* Leitmotifstil, *or, lead-word style, and patterns of theme and form.*]

C. A DESCRIPTION OF SELECTED STORYTELLING TECHNIQUES FROM THE NIGHTS

In [what follows] I describe narrative devices used by redactors in numerous stories found in the *Alf lay-lah*. . . .

I. REPETITIVE DESIGNATION

Under this heading I group repeated references to some character or object which appears insignificant when first mentioned but which reappears later to intrude suddenly on the narrative. At the moment of the initial designation the given object seems unimportant and the reference casual and incidental. Later in the story, however, the object is brought forward once more and proves to play a significant role.

A good example of this technique can be found in one of the early episodes in the frame-story of King Shāhrayār and Scheherazade as presented in the Leiden edition of the G manuscript [a certain fourteenth-century text of the *Alf laylah* know as Bibliothèque Nationale 3609-3611].[1] Shāhrayār's brother Shāhzamān arrives for a visit, and the G redactor offers a detailed description of the guest-quarters where Shāhzamān is housed: a palace overlooking an enclosed garden and facing a second house containing the women's quarters. Furthermore, it is carefully explained that his chambers have windows overlooking the garden. Finally, we are told that the nobleman repeatedly sighs and laments, "No one has ever had happen to him what happened to me!," a reference to the adulterous betrayal by his wife which opened the story. These references seem incidental enough at first, but in fact the redactor has made mention of all these details—the women's quarters, the garden, the guest-chamber windows which happen to overlook the garden, Shāhzamān's lament—by way of foreshadowing and preparation for the next development in the plot. One day King Shāhrayār departs to go hunting, and Shāhzamān, the redactor tells us, chances to look out his window at the garden which is visible below. Suddenly he sees his brother's wife, followed by an entourage of men and women, emerge from the harem opposite and enter the garden. From his window-perch he sees them all join lustily in sexual congress.

Shāhzamān then realizes that his repeated lament is untrue, for his brother too has had happen to him what happened to Shāzamān.

Another instance of repetitive designation emerges in the Leiden version of *The Merchant and the Genie.*[2] The tale opens with a description of the protagonist putting loaves of bread and dates in his saddlebag as provisions for a journey he is about to undertake. Trivial enough data this seems at first, a description of the food a man takes on a business trip. But to the contrary: in the next scene the merchant pauses in his journey for lunch and eats his dates, flinging away the date-stones at random. Shortly thereafter a wrathful genie appears, which informs the man that his life is now forfeit: the date-stones he flung away so thoughtlessly at lunch struck and killied the genie's invisible son; in turn the genie must now kill him. The hapless merchant pleads for mercy, a plea which will ultimately trigger the stories-told-for-ransom which comprise the bulk of this narrative-cycle.

Thus in the two examples cited above the initial reference establishes an object (e.g., a garden-window or a saddlebag full of dates) in the background of a scene and readies it for its appearance at the proper moment. Repetitive designation creates thereby an effect of apparently casual foreshadowing and allows the audience the pleasure of recognition at that later moment when the object reappears and proves significant.

II. LEITWORTSTIL

In his work *The Art of Biblical Literature* Robert Alter explains that the term *Leitwortstil* ("leading-word style") was coined by Martin Buber and Franz Rosenzweig and applied to the field of Biblical textual studies. Alter states that the term designates the "purposeful repetition of words" in a given literary piece. The individual *Leitwort* or "leading word" usually expresses a motif or theme important to the given story; the repetition of this *Leitwort* ensures that the theme will gradually force itself on the reader's attention.[3]

In the preface to his German Bible translation Buber discusses the triliteral root system in Hebrew and the opportunities it offers for verbal repetition. He labels this technique of repetition as a *Leitwortstil* and defines the term as follows:

> A *Leitwort* is a word or a word-root that recurs significantly in a text, in a continuum of texts, or in a configuration of texts: by following these repetitions, one is able to decipher or grasp a meaning of the text . . . . The repetition, as we have said, need not be merely of the word itself but also of the word-root; in fact, the very difference of words can often intensify the dynamic action of the repetition. I call it "dynamic"

because between combinations of sounds related to one another in this manner a kind of movement takes place: if one imagines the entire text deployed before him one can sense waves moving back and forth between the words.[4]

What is true for Hebrew triliteral roots and the Bible holds good, I believe, for Arabic and the *Arabic Nights.* *Leitwortstil* can be discerned at work in the MN version of **The Magian City,** a minor narrative enframed within **The Tale of the First Lady** (which in turn belongs to the story-cycle known as **The Porter and the Three Ladies of Baghdad**).[5]

Three sisters leave Baghdad to undertake a business trip by sea. Their ship goes off course, and for several days the vessel drifts without direction. Neither captain nor crew has any idea where they are; but after a number of days an unknown shore is sighted. The lookout cries, "Good news! . . . I see what looks like a city"; and the ship is brought to harbor. The captain goes ashore to investigate:

> He was gone for some time; then he came to us and said, "Come, go up to the city and marvel at what God has done to His creatures, and seek refuge from His wrath! (*wa-ista'īdhū min sukhṭihi*). And so we went up to the city.
>
> Then when I came to the gate I saw people with staves in their hands at the gate of the city. So I drew near to them, and behold!: they had been metamorphosed and had become stone (*wa-idhā hum maskhūṭīn wa-qad ṣārū aḥjāran*). Then we entered the city and found everyone in it metamorphosed into black stone (*maskhūṭan aḥjāran sūdan*). And in it [i.e., in the city] there were neither houses with inhabitants nor people to tend the hearths. We marveled at that and then traversed the markets.[6]

A note by Edward Lane from his translation of the *Nights* suggests the significance of the verbal root *s-kh-ṭ* which occurs three times in the above passage:

> The term "maskhoot," employed to signify "a human being converted by the wrath of God into stone," is commonly applied in Egypt to an ancient statue. Hence the Arabs have become familiar with the idea of cities whose inhabitants are petrified, such as that described in "The Story of the First of the Three Ladies of Baghdad."[7]

In his *Arabic-English Lexicon* Lane also notes that the primary sense of the passive participle *maskhūṭ* is "transformed, or metamorphosed . . . in consequence of having incurred the wrath of God." In addition, Lane records the gerund *sukhṭ*, which he defines as "dislike, displeasure, disapprobation, or discontent."[8]

The term *maskhūṭ* may of course be understood in a very general sense simply to mean "transformed" or "metamorphosed." Burton's commentary on this tale

notes that *maskhūṭ* is "mostly applied to change of shape as man enchanted to monkey, and in vulgar parlance applied to a statue (of stone, etc.)"; elsewhere in his edition of the *Nights* he offers the gloss "transformed (mostly in something hideous), a statue."[9] But the connotations enumerated by Lane are brought forward in the MN edition by the captain's exclamation at the beginning of the Magian City episode: *ta'ajjabū min ṣan'Allāh fī khalqihi wa-ista'īdhū min sukhṭihi* ("Marvel at what God has done to His creatures, and seek refuge from His wrath!"). The redactor uses this sentence to achieve a resonance of meanings between *sukhṭ* ("divine wrath") and *maskhūṭ* ("metamorphosed"), words derived from the same verbal root, *s-kh-ṭ.* The presence of the noun *sukhṭ* gives *maskhūṭ* a religious connotation; and the implication that arises from this juxtaposition of words is that the city's inhabitants were transformed specifically as a punishment for having aroused God's anger.

Of interest to our discussion is a remark by 'Abd al-Qāhir al-Jurjānī (d. AD 1078) on the subject of context and meaning in his work *Dalā'il al-i'jāz* ("Demonstrations of Qur'anic Inimitability"):

> It becomes clear then, with a clarity that leaves no place for doubt, that verbal expressions are not remarkable for their excellence insofar as they are mere abstracted utterances, nor insofar as they are isolated words. Rather the worth or lack of worth of a given expression depends on the harmony established between the meaning of a given expression and the meaning [of the word or phrase] which follows that expression.[10]

As G. J. H. van Gelder notes in his analysis of al-Jurjānī's work: "The qualities do not depend on the single words but on the 'wonderful harmony' (*ittisāq 'ajīb*) in the passage."[11] Al-Jurjānī's insight can be applied to the 'harmony of meanings' found in a story such as *The Magian City.* By placing the phrase *ista'īdhū min sukhṭihi* immediately before the sentences describing the lost city and its metamorphosed populace, the MN redactor reminds the reader of the root-meaning of *maskhūṭ,* with its original denotation of God's wrath against the impious. The words *sukhṭ* and *maskhūṭ* will recur throughout this narrative-frame as related *Leitwörter* highlighting the tale's moralistic concerns.

The story continues with a description of how passengers and crew disembark and then wander the lifeless city. The protagonist ventures on her own into a palace where she discovers the preserved corpses of a king and queen, each of which has been transformed into black stone (and each described with the term *maskhūṭ*). Finally she encounters a young man who alone has survived the fate of all the other inhabitants. He tells her the story of this city, explaining that all its people were Magians and devoted to the worship of fire. He himself, however, was secretly Muslim. Year after year divine warnings visited the city to the effect that the infidel inhabitants must abandon their fire-worship and turn to the true God; to no avail. And so, the young man explains:

> They never ceased with their adherence to the way they were, until there descended upon them hatred and divine wrath (*al-maqt wa-al sukht*) from heaven, one morning at dawn. And so they were transformed into black stone (*fa-sukhiṭū ahjāran sūdan*), and their riding beasts and cattle as well.[12]

The Magian City frame ends when the protagonist rejoins her companions and conveys to them the story she has just heard:

> I reported to them what I had seen, and I told them the tale of the young man and the reason for the metamorphosis of this city (*wa-sabab sukhṭ hādhihi al-madīnah*) and what had happened to them; and they marveled at that.[13]

Thus in this story the condition of the city's inhabitants (*maskhūṭ, sukhiṭū*) is explained as a consequence of divine wrath (*al-sukhṭ*), with the two states described in terms of the single root *s-kh-ṭ*. Not only does this motif-word accent relationships among events within *The Magian City;* it also demarcates this enframed minor narrative at both beginning and end and distinguishes the tale from the surrounding major narrative.

In other *Alf laylah* stories one notes the operation of what may be termed (as an extension of Buber's model) *Leitsätze* ("leading-sentences"): entire clauses or sentences which are repeated at salient points throughout a narrative and encapsulate its theme. In chapter 2 we will see how the *Leitsatz* "Spare me and God will spare you" is used to link minor narratives to the overarching tale of *The Fisherman and the Genie.* The sentence "This is a warning to whoso would be warned" is a familiar moralistic utterance encountered frequently throughout the *Nights;* in *The City of Brass,* however . . . , the redactor repeatedly introduces variants of this conventional admonition (all built around the *Leitwörter 'ibrah*—"warning"—and *i'tabara*—"to take warning") so as to draw attention to the thematic concerns which unite the various episodes in the tale.

III. THEMATIC PATTERNING AND FORMAL PATTERNING

In those stories from the *Alf laylah* (as with works of fiction in general) which are especially well crafted, the structure is disposed so as to draw the audience's attention to certain narrative elements over others. Recurrent vocabulary, repeated gestures, accumulations of descriptive phrases around selected objects: such patterns guide the audience in picking out particular actions as important in the flow of narrative. And once the audience has had its attention drawn to the patterns which give shape to a story, it experiences the pleasure of recognition: so *this* is the revelation toward which the storyteller is guiding us; *this* must be the object which constitutes the story's focus. The reader attempting to discern such patterns in a story, however, should beware of examining too narrowly any one given incident from the tale, for an individual dialogue or isolated event, taken alone, may not have enough context to let the observer establish its significance for the story at hand. The observer's emphasis, rather, should be on the particular event as it exists in relation to the rest of the narrative and the way in which the events and other narrative elements in a story join to form a structural pattern.

In my study of individual tales I have noted two kinds of structural patterning, thematic and formal. By thematic patterning I mean the distribution of recurrent concepts and moralistic motifs among the various incidents and frames of a story. In a skilfully crafted tale, thematic patterning may be arranged so as to emphasize the unifying argument or salient idea which disparate events and disparate narrative frames have in common.

Thematic patterning binds the tales contained within *The Fisherman and the Genie.* The argument of this narrative-cycle may be baldly stated as: violence against one's benefactors or intimate companions, whether triggered by mistrust, envy, or jealous rage, leads inevitably to regret and repentance. This concept is illustrated both in the major narrative of the *Fisherman* and in its enframed minor narratives such as *Yunan and Duban* and *The Jealous Husband and the Parrot.* . . . Of course all these stories are also linked thematically to the outermost narrative frame, where Scheherazade is quite literally trying to talk her way out of violent death at the hands of a husband who himself is dominated by mistrust and jealous rage.

Another example of thematic patterning can be found in *The City of Brass,* a story which at first glance may appear to have little structural unity. The primary action, in which a party of travellers crosses the North African desert in search of ancient brass bottles, is continually interrupted by subsidiary narratives: the tale recorded on inscriptions in the lost palace of Kūsh ibn Shaddād; the imprisoned 'ifrīt's account of Solomon's war with the jinn; and the encounter with Queen Tadmur and the automata which guard her corpse. But each of these minor narratives introduces a character who confesses that he once proudly enjoyed worldly prosperity: subsequently, we learn, the given character has been brought low by God and forced to acknowledge Him as greater than all worldly pomp. These minor tales ultimately reinforce the theme of the major narrative: riches and pomp tempt one away from God; asceticism is the way to salvation. Thus a clearly discernible thematic pattern of pride—punishment from God—submission to the Divine Will unifies the otherwise divergent stories which are gathered into this tale.

By formal patterning I mean the organization of the events, actions and gestures which constitute a narrative and give shape to a story; when done well, formal patterning allows the audience the pleasure of discerning and anticipating the structure of the plot as it unfolds. An example can be found in *The Tale of the Three Shaykhs,* where three old men come upon a merchant in the desert about to be slain by a demon which has a claim of blood-vengeance against him (we have encountered the earlier part of this tale already, in my analysis of incidents from *The Merchant and the Genie*). First the redactor takes care to note that each shaykh has with him some object of interest: the first, a chained gazelle; the second, a pair of black hunting dogs; the third, a mule. Then the first shaykh approaches the genie and pleads with it for the merchant's life: if you grant me one-third of the blood-claim due you from this man, he states, I will recite for you a wondrous tale concerning this chained gazelle. The demon accepts, and the audience can already recognize the symmetries of the formal patterning at work in this story-cycle: each of the three shaykhs in turn will advance to tell a wondrous tale concerning his animal and claim one-third of the blood-punishment. And such in fact is what happens: the merchant is saved by the recitation of the three tales.[14]

A more elaborate instance of formal patterning is at work in a story-cycle entitled **The Tale of the Hunchback.**[15] Four characters, a Christian broker, a steward, a Jewish doctor, and a tailor, are summoned before a sultan and each must tell a satisfyingly amazing anecdote in order to have his life spared. This story-as-ransom motif obviously connects the entire cycle with the Scheherazade frame, where the heroine also recites tales to avert death. But there is more. Each of the four characters in **The Hunchback** tells a story in which he describes an encounter with a young man who has been mysteriously maimed or crippled. In each encounter the narrator asks the young man how he suffered his hurt, and the latter's explanation constitutes the tale offered to the sultan as ransom. The last of the four reciters, the tailor, tells how at a marriage-feast he met a young man who had been lamed. The youth recounts the misfortunes whereby he came to be crippled; and it turns out that the person responsible for this injury, an insufferably garrulous barber, is seated at the same table as the tailor. No sooner does the youth conclude his tale than the barber insists on offering the tailor and his friends a succession of stories, first one about himself, then a

good half-dozen anecdotes about his six unfortunate brothers. The tales narrated by the barber are not demanded as any kind of ransom by the tailor, in contrast to the four tales required by the sultan in the overarching *Hunchback* cycle. Nor do the barber's stories seem controlled by a common thematic concern or moral argument. All six brothers suffer harm, but some deserve punishment for their foolishness or lust, while others (especially the third and fourth brothers) are clearly innocent victims of malicious sharpsters. But common to the vignettes in this series is that each tells how one of the brothers was blinded, castrated or somehow deprived of lips and ears.[16] This structural pattern of mutilation links the six tales formally to one another and in turn unites the *Barber* cycle as a whole with *The Hunchback,* where each of the four enframed tales also displays a formal patterning of mutilation/crippling. Thus the stories contained in *The Barber's Six Brothers* constitute an example of a narrative cycle where the unity lacking at the thematic level is compensated for by a consistent formal patterning.

IV. DRAMATIC VISUALIZATION

I define dramatic visualization as the representing of an object or character with an abundance of descriptive detail, or the mimetic rendering of gestures and dialogue in such a way as to make the given scene 'visual' or imaginatively present to an audience. I contrast 'dramatic visualization' with 'summary presentation,' where an author informs his audience of an object or event in abbreviated fashion without dramatizing the scene or encouraging the audience to form a visual picture of it. In *The Rhetoric of Fiction* Wayne Booth analyzes the modern novel by making analogous distinctions between what he calls "showing" and "telling": when an author "shows" his audience something he renders it dramatically so as to give the "intensity of realistic illusion"; when he "tells" his audience about a thing he is using his authorial powers to summarize an event or render judgment on a character's behavior, without, however, using descriptive detail to make the given event or character imaginatively present.[17]

To understand how these techniques function let us compare the wording of analogous scenes in two different **Alf laylah** stories. Both portray exemplary punishment in the form of amputation which is to be inflicted on the protagonist. The first scene is from *The Lover Who Pretended to be a Thief.* Khālid, governor of Basrah, is confronted with the men of a family who have caught a handsome young man breaking into their home. They accuse the boy of theft, and the prisoner confesses freely. To Khālid the youth seems too well-spoken and of too noble a bearing to be a thief; yet given the boy's insistence on his own guilt, the governor has no choice but to order the legally mandated punishment. Suspecting nevertheless that the prisoner is for some reason concealing the truth, Khālid counsels him privately to "state that which may ward off from you the punishment of amputation" the next morning when he is to be interrogated one last time by the judge before the sentence is executed (not till the end of the story do we learn that the youth is a lover who had entered the home for a tryst with the daughter of the house, and that he has allowed himself to be labeled a thief so as to protect her honor). The punishment-scene reads as follows:

> When morning dawned the people assembled to see the youth's hand cut off; and there was not a single person in Basrah, neither man nor woman, who failed to be present so as to see the punishment of this young man. Khālid came riding up, and with him were prominent dignitaries and others from among the people of Basrah. Then he summoned the judges and called for the young man to be brought. And so he approached, stumbling in his chains; and not one of the people saw him without weeping for him. And the voices of the women rose up in lamentation.
>
> The judge thereupon ordered the women to be silenced; and then he said to him, "These persons contend that you entered their home and stole their possessions. Perhaps you stole less than the amount which makes this a crime legally necessitating such punishment?"
>
> "On the contrary," he replied. "I stole precisely an amount which necessitates such punishment."
>
> He said, "Perhaps you were co-owner with these persons in some of those possessions."
>
> "On the contrary," he replied. "Those things belong entirely to them. I have no legal claim to those things."
>
> At this point Khālid grew angry. He himself stood up, went over to him and struck him in the face with his whip, quoting aloud this verse:
>
> > Man wishes to be given his desire
> > But God refuses all save what *He* desires.
>
> Thereupon he called for the butcher so that the latter might cut off his hand. And so he came, and he took out the knife. Then he stretched out the boy's hand and placed upon it the knife.
>
> But suddenly there rushed forward a young woman from the midst of the women, clad in soiled and tattered clothes. She screamed and threw herself upon him. She drew back her veil, to reveal a face like the moon for beauty. And there rose up from the people a great outcry.[18]

The beloved has appeared: she will sacrifice her reputation and their love-secret so as to save the boy from punishment.

We will return to the lovers in a moment, but let us look first at our second amputation-scene, this one from *The Reward of Charity.* A capricious king has ordered that henceforth no one in his realm is to offer alms or bestow charity under any circumstances; all those caught violating this command will have their hands chopped off. In what follows a starving beggar approaches a woman who proves to be the protagonist:

> The beggar said to the woman, "Give me something in the way of charity!"
>
> She replied, "How can I give you alms when the king is cutting off the hand of everyone who gives alms?"
>
> He said, "I beg you in God's name, give me something in the way of alms!"
>
> So when he asked her in God's name she felt pity for him and gave him two loaves of bread as an act of charity.
>
> Thereafter report of this reached the king and he ordered that she be brought to him. Then when she appeared he cut off her hands and she returned to her home.[19]

Brief, brutal, and to the point.

But the two passages, juxtaposed as they are here, trigger a question: why is dramatic visualization employed in the amputation-scene from *The Lover,* while the redactor contents himself with the technique of summary presentation in an analogous episode from *The Reward of Charity*? The answer I believe is related to the fact that the punishment-scene in *The Lover* is the climax of the entire story. Throughout the **Alf laylah** dramatic visualization is reserved especially for scenes which form the heart of a given narrative. Such is the case here. What *follows* the girl's appearance in the public square is narrated succinctly: the boy's punishment is averted, the couple's love is made known, and Khālid prevails on the girl's father to allow them to marry. But the redactor lingers over the spectacle of punishment: the wailing crowds, the pathetic glimpse of the youth stumbling in his chains, the extended dialogue between judge and prisoner, and the sketch of the frustrated Khālid giving up all attempt to save the boy and lashing out with his whip. The effect of all this visualized detail is to slow the pace of narration; and we are not permitted any resolution till the last possible moment, when the heroine is introduced just as the butcher is about to apply his knife. Thus the technique of dramatic visualization enables the storyteller to heighten the tension in a scene and increase his audience's experience of pleasurable suspense.

By way of contrast the amputation in *The Reward of Charity* is not the narrative focus of the story at all. The punishment is presented in summary fashion because it is only a prelude to the true climax: the scene where the woman's generous impulse is vindicated. Mutilated as she is and subsequently expelled to the desert with her infant son clinging to her, she wanders until she comes upon a stream:

She knelt down to drink, because of the extreme thirst which had overtaken her from her walking and her fatigue and her sorrow. But when she bent over, the boy fell into the water. She sat weeping greatly for her child.

And while she was crying, behold!: two men passed by; and they said to her, "What is making you weep?"

She answered them, "I had a boy who was holding me about the neck, and he fell into the water."

They said to her, "Would you like us to bring him forth for you?"

She replied, "Yes," and so they called on God most high. Thereupon the child came forth to her unharmed; nothing ill had befallen him.

Then they said to her, "Would you like God to restore your hands to you as they had been?"

She replied, "Yes," and so they called on God—all praise and glory to Him!—and her hands were restored to her, more beautiful than they ever had been before.

Then they said to her, "Do you know who we are?"

She replied, "Only God knows!"

They said, "We are your two loaves of bread, which you bestowed in charity on the beggar."[20]

The redactor has reserved dramatic visualization for the scene which most merits it, that episode illustrating the moralistic theme which drives the whole narrative.

Notes

1. Leiden edition, vol. 1, pp. 57-59.

2. Leiden edition, vol. 1, pp. 72-73.

3. Robert Alter, *The Art of Biblical Narrative* (New York: Basic Books, 1981), p. 92.

4. Quoted and translated by Alter, op. cit., p. 93.

5. The MacNaghten (MN) version of *The Magian City* is found in vol. 1, pp. 123-128. Būlāq (B) (vol. 1, pp. 44-46) and Leiden (vol. 1, pp. 203-207) lack MN's pattern of *Leitwörter*. The three versions are compared in D. Pinault, "Stylistic Features in Selected Tales from *The Thousand and One Nights*" (Ph.D. diss., University of Pennsylvania, 1986), pp. 172-194.

6. MN vol. 1, p. 123.

7. Edward William Lane, *The Arabian Nights' Entertainments* (New York: Tudor Publishing Co., 1927), p. 1209, n. 1.

8. Edward William Lane, *An Arabic-English Lexicon* (Beirut: Librairie du Liban, 1968), vol. 4, p. 1325.

9. Richard Burton, *Book of the Thousand Nights and a Night* (London: Burton Club for Private Subscribers, "Bagdad Edition," n.d.), vol. 1, p. 165, n. 1, and vol. 10, p. 362.

10. 'Abd al-Qāhir al-Jurjānī, *Dalā'il al-i'jāz,* ed. Muḥammad 'Abd al-Mun'im Khafājī (Cairo: Maktabat al-Qāhirah, 1969), p. 90.

11. G. J. H. van Gelder, *Beyond the Line: Classical Arabic Literary Critics on the Coherence and Unity of the Poem* (Leiden: E. J. Brill, 1982), p. 131.

12. MN vol. 1, p. 127.

13. MN vol. 1, p. 128.

14. Such at least is the structure of this story-cycle as found in B [Būlāq edition] (vol. 1, pp. 7-10) and MN [MacNaghten edition] (vol. 1, pp. 12-20); but it is of interest to note that, from the point of view of formal patterning, G (as found in the Leiden ed., vol. 1, pp. 78-86) is markedly deficient. As in the two Egyptian texts, in G the first of three shaykhs advances to claim one-third of the blood-punishment, and the audience is prepared for a pattern of three stories. The first two shaykhs bring forward their beasts and recite wondrous tales concerning them, as in B and MN. But when it comes the third shaykh's turn, he is not described in G's version as having with him any animal; hence he quite literally has no tale worth speaking of. And G in fact at this juncture (Leiden, p. 86) contains no more than the bald statement:

> The third shaykh told the genie a tale more wondrous and stranger than the other two tales. Then the genie marvelled greatly and shook with pleasure and said, "I grant you one-third of the blood-claim."

Thus in G we are told only that the shaykh recited his story, but we are not permitted to hear the story itself, in contrast to the pattern followed with the full recitals given by the first two shaykhs. The audience is denied hearing the third tale which it had been led to expect by the narrative's structure. The passage quoted above shows that G acknowledges the structure dictated by the formal patterning of the three shaykhs and the blood-punishment divided into thirds; but G disposes of this structure at the end in very perfunctory fashion.

15. The story is found in Leiden, vol. 1, pp. 280-379; B vol. 1, pp. 73-106; and MN vol. 1, pp. 199-278.

16. Some of these mutilations are central to the given story, others incidental. One significant variant among the three editions occurs in the account of *The Barber's Fifth Brother.* The Egyptian texts (MN, vol. 1, p. 271 and B, vol. 1, p. 103) conclude this story by having thieves fall upon the barber's fifth brother and cut off his ears, an incident not

found in the Leiden version. This act is not essential to the story proper of the fifth brother, but it does link the tale to its larger frame by bringing forward the motif of maiming/mutilation which characterizes all the stories of the *Hunchback* cycle. As such the Egyptian versions of *The Barber's Fifth Brother* offer a more consistent example than does the Syrian text of the use of formal patterning as a means of achieving structural unity for a series of otherwise unrelated tales.

17. Wayne Booth, *The Rhetoric of Fiction* (Chicago: University of Chicago Press, 1961), pp. 3-9, 40.

18. B vol. 1 (Night 298), p. 471.

19. B vol. 1 (Night 348), p. 527.

20. Ibid., p. 527.

PUBLISHED EDITIONS OF THE ALF LAYLAH
WA-LAYLAH AND THE MI'AT LAYLAH
WA-LAYLAH

Habicht, Maximilian, and Fleischer, M. H. L., eds. *Tausend und Eine Nacht, Arabisch. Nach einer Handschrift aus Tunis herausgegeben.* 12 vols. Breslau: Josef Max & Co., 1825-1843.

MacNaghten, W.H. ed. *The Alif Laila or Book of the Thousand Nights and One Night . . .* 4 vols. Calcutta: W. Thacker & Co., 1839-1842.

Mahdi, Muhsin, ed. *The Thousand and One Nights (Alf layla wa-layla) from the Earliest Known Sources.* 2 vols. to date. Leiden: E. J. Brill, 1984.

OTHER SOURCES

Alter, Robert. *The Art of Biblical Narrative.* New York: Basic Books, 1981.

Booth, Wayne C. *The Rhetoric of Fiction.* Chicago: University of Chicago Press, 1961.

Burton, Richard. *The Book of a Thousand Nights and a Night.* 10 vols. [London]: Burton Club for Private Subscribers, "Bagdad Edition," n.d.

al-Jurjānī, 'Abd al-Qāhir. *Dalā'il al-i'jāz.* Edited by Muḥammad 'Abd al-Mun'im Khafājī. Cairo: Maktabat al-Qāhirah, 1969.

Lane, Edward William. *The Arabian Nights' Entertainments.* New York: Tudor Publishing Co., 1927.

Lane, Edward William. *An Arabic-English Lexicon.* 8 vols. Beirut: Librairie du Liban, 1968.

Pinault, David. "Stylistic Features in Selected Tales from *The Thousand and One Nights.*" Ph.D. dissertation, University of Pennsylvania, 1986.

van Gelder, G. J. H. *Beyond the Line: Classical Arabic Literary Critics on the Coherence and Unity of the Poem.* Leiden: E.J. Brill, 1982.

Ferial J. Ghazoul (essay date 1996)

SOURCE: Ghazoul, Ferial J. "Narrative Dialectics." In *Nocturnal Poetics:* The Arabian Nights *in Comparative Context*, pp. 17-28. Cairo, Egypt: The American University in Cairo Press, 1996.

[*In the following essay, Ghazoul argues that the operational structure of* The Arabian Nights *consists of four major blocks: the story of Shahrayar as king, Shahrayar as a traveler seeking knowledge, the story of Shaharazad, and the frame story as narrated by the vizier.*]

SEGMENTATION

Roman Jakobson defined literature as a message centered on its mode of expression. Every literary text poses two questions to the specialist: *how* is the text generated and *what* is its final outcome? The answer to the first question, on how the text flows from its beginning to its end, throws light on the message that the text enunciates. The first step, therefore, is to try to understand the essential course of the text.

The Arabian Nights is a narrative discourse, but the narrative component does not cover the entire discourse. There are certain parts in the story which can be discarded without damaging the narrative line. This is evident enough since we know that there are many ways of telling the same story. Vladimir Propp has shown that the functions in a tale are the crucial points in the unfolding of narrative—these help us to see the story as a series of functional transformations connected in a causal relationship.[1] Tzvetan Todorov went further by demonstrating the hierarchical nature of these functions, and that some of them are more essential to the narrative line than others, thus condensing the narrative to its essential identity.[2] The analysis of ***The Arabian Nights*** in this chapter will follow the operations undertaken by Propp and Todorov, to observe the phenomenal changes in their essential role, and then to retain the principal transformations which will lead to the significance of the fiction.

The overall structure of ***The Arabian Nights*** is that of a principal preposition enclosing other prepositions connected by conjunctions, and so on. The fundamental preposition in ***The Arabian Nights,*** at the basic level, is the story of a king who, having found himself betrayed by his wife, vows to marry a virgin every night and behead her in the morning. After a succession of such wives, one of them—Shahrazad—manages to postpone her verdict and eventually waive it by narrating stories which captivate the king. This is the indispensable part of the narrative; it covers but a few pages at the beginning and the end. This is called the frame story. The stories related by Shahrazad (as well as one related to her by her father to dissuade her from marrying the king) can be omitted from the discourse without infringing on the narrative thread. On the other hand, if the frame story were omitted, the result would simply be unconnected stories. In the first case, we have a necklace without beads; in the latter, beads without a necklace.

The narrative line can be retold in more abstract terms as that of a rupture leading to a curse and its ultimate undoing. This invariably carries with it overtones of Semitic sacred narratives of Creation where an initial order and equilibrium are lost. In this sense, *The Arabian Nights* is essentially a demotic version of paradise lost and recovered. The bliss of the original couple was ruptured when they ate the fruits of the forbidden tree, that is, by tasting the fruits of knowledge. Similarly, taboo and knowledge are keys to the unfolding of *The Arabian Nights.* Sin and death go hand in hand in both. The sacred narrative in Genesis underlines the loss. *The Arabian Nights* points to recovery and redemption. Shahrazad's story echoes and develops the myth of Origin.

Apart from the power of *The Arabian Nights* to evoke dormant mythological texts, its structure offers a model of symbolic economy. The essence of narrative is a chronological transformation, a series of changes along a diachronic axis. Succession is as vital to narrative as seriality—that is, paradigmatic repetition—is to poetry. The narrative is the temporal discourse *par excellence.* There is an element of poetic justice in Shahrazad's struggle against deadline (and it is literally a dead line) armed with narrative: she fights time with time. In the *Odyssey,* Penelope's struggle to gain time is based on a simple device of doing and undoing; she unravels at night what she weaves in the daytime. Penelope marks time in order to delay temporal events, but Shahrazad's art lies in annulling the very limits of time. Penelope's struggle is against given time, while Shahrazad's is against the notion of time itself. *The Arabian Nights* deals with one of the most excruciatingly difficult philosophical concepts, that of abstract time.

Technically, *The Arabian Nights* offers an example of a struggle that has been used frequently in more modern literary works, such as *Tristram Shandy* and *Through the Looking Glass,* where the initial binary opposition of thesis and antithesis is not resolved by a mediating synthesis, but by the triumph of parentheses and digressions. The frame story can be broken down into four narrative blocks. In other words, the frame story combines four narratives which could stand independently, one from the other, although in this case they are artfully linked together.³ The four blocks are the story of Shahrayar as a king, the story of Shahrayar as

a traveler seeking knowledge, the story of Shahrazad, and the story narrated by her father.

The Story of Shahrayar

The beginning narrative block relates the story of two brothers who are monarchs; the older is called Shahrayar and the younger Shahzaman. After twenty years of happy rule, Shahrayar misses his brother and sends his vizier to fetch him. Shahzaman sets out to visit his brother. At midnight, he remembers something he had forgotten and goes back to his palace. There he finds his wife in bed with a black slave. He kills them both and goes on to visit his brother. Although Shahrayar had ordered a proper welcome for his brother upon his arrival, Shahzaman remains sullen. Sharayar assumes that his brother is homesick and Shahzaman will only refer enigmatically to an internal wound that is bothering him. One day, there is a royal hunting expedition but Shahzaman refuses to join the group and stays home. As Shahzaman is looking into the garden of his brother's palace, twenty slave girls, twenty slave men, and his sister-in-law come strolling along. They all undress and Shahrayar's wife copulates with a black slave, while the other girls do likewise. Shahzaman feels somewhat better after witnessing this orgy as it proves that his calamity is no worse than his brother's, and he soon regains his gaiety. On returning, Shahrayar is surprised by the sudden change in his brother, and he questions him about it. But Shahzaman only explains the reason for his grief by relating how his wife betrayed him, and will not explain how he got over it. Upon the insistence of his brother, Shahzaman gives in and explains how the betrayal of his sister-in-law had lessened his grief. Shahrayar then wants to check the story for himself and he arranges another royal hunting expedition, but secretly comes home and watches his wife's orgy with his own eyes.

The narrative line of this story is interrupted by introducing another narrative block, but it will be continued later.

The Voyage

Shahrayar decides with his brother to travel in order to find out if theirs is a singular case. They walk until they come to a spring next to the sea and they sit down to rest. After a while, a black column appears from the sea, and the two brothers become frightened and climb up a tree. It turns out to be a giant demon carrying a chest on top of his head. He comes and sits underneath their tree. The demon then proceeds to open the chest, from which he removes a beautiful young maiden. He puts his head in her lap and goes to sleep. The girl looks up, sees the two brothers, and asks them to come down. They protest, to no avail, and in the end they have to come down for fear that she will turn the demon against them. She orders them to copulate with her and they obey. When this is over, she takes out a bag with five hundred and seventy rings, which she has gotten from previous lovers who made love to her while the demon slept, and she asks them for a ring each.[4] They do as she requests. She relates to them how she had been kidnapped on her wedding night by the demon, put into a box, placed in a trunk with seven locks, and then put at the bottom of the sea so as to assure her chastity. The two brothers are amazed at what has befallen such a mighty demon and are somewhat consoled.

Here the line of the first narrative block is resumed. The two brothers go back to Shahrayar's kingdom, and there Shahrayar puts his wife and her slaves to death.

THE STORY OF SHAHRAZAD

For three years, Shahrayar marries a virgin every night and has her killed the next morning. It becomes increasingly difficult to find brides for him. The vizier, having failed to do so, goes home worried. The vizier has two daughters, Shahrazad the elder, who is well read, and Dinazad the younger. When the vizier is questioned by his elder daughter, he tells her all that has happened. Shahrazad offers to marry the king with the hope of delivering her fellow women. Her father warns her that she might have to face what befell the ass and the bull with the farmer. She inquires about that, and her father starts relating the story.

The story line of this narrative block is interrupted here and resumed later.

THE FABLE

There was a farmer who knew the language of animals. He owned an ass and a bull. The bull found out that the ass was much better off and told him how much he envied his leisurely life, as he was only occasionally used for his master's transport. The ass advised the bull to pretend to be sick, to lie down and not to eat, and by so doing avoid hard work. The bull did so accordingly, but since the farmer had overheard the conversation, he gave instructions that the ass be used to replace the bull in drawing the plough. The ass regretted his advice and tried to get out of the new situation by telling the bull that he had better return to work soon, as the owner intended to have him slaughtered if he continued to be sick. The next day, the bull did his best to display appetite when eating and energy at work. The farmer, who had overheard these conversations, roared with laughter. Although he knew the language of animals, he was required not to divulge what he knew, otherwise he would surely die. His wife asked him why he was laugh-

ing and he told her that it was a secret which, if revealed, would entail his death. But she insisted on knowing, even at the cost of her husband's life. The husband did not know what to do, since he loved his wife dearly. He called his relatives and neighbors and told them about his predicament. Everyone entreated the wife to abandon the matter, to no avail. So the man resigned himself to her wish and went to perform his last ablutions before telling the secret. He then overheard his dog cursing the cock and accusing him of lightheartedness when his master was about to die. The cock inquired how that had come about and the dog told him the story of their master and his wife. The cock accused his master of stupidity on the grounds that he could not manage even one wife when the cock succeeded in satisfying fifty of them, and wondered why his master did not give his wife a good beating. The farmer, having overheard this, decided to take up the cock's suggestion. He hid some branches in the closet and invited his wife in, pretending he was about to reveal the secret to her. When she came in, she got a beating and consequently asked to be pardoned.

Then the narrative takes up the story of Shahrazad, which eventually fuses with the story of Shahrayar. The vizier says to his daughter Shahrazad that her fate might very well be that of the farmer's wife. But Shahrazad insists on going ahead with her plan. Shahrazad has instructed her sister that she will ask for her on the wedding night, and that Dinazad is to ask for tales to pass the night. The vizier takes Shahrazad to Shahrayar and she requests that her sister be with her. Dinazad comes and sits under the bed. After the deflowering of Shahrazad, Dinazad asks her to relate some stories to pass the time. Shahrazad agrees to do so, if the king will permit it. He does, and is delighted with her discourse. Shahrazad continues to tell her story all night but stops at daybreak. Shahrayar, anxious to hear more, postpones her sentence night after night until one thousand nights have passed. On the thousand and first night, after finishing a story, Shahrazad asks to be granted a wish. She brings her three sons and asks Shahrayar to free her from beheading for the sake of the children. Shaharyar embraces his children and assures her that he has pardoned her. She is delighted and joy overwhelms the people. Then, Shahrayar summons his vizier and thanks him for arranging his marriage with his daughter, who has begotten him three sons. He also orders festivities for thirty days and charitable acts for the people. They live happily ever after until death separates them.

BINARISM

CHARACTERS

These narrative blocks exhibit a rigorous organizational system in terms of major characters. The first block presents the reader with the most striking impulse in *The Arabian Nights,* that of binarism. The two brothers present to us in full dimension the question of duplication. They are both knights and kings and rule happily. Shahzaman's experience foreshadows Shahrayar's and is almost identical to it. He kills his wife instantly when he finds her in bed with a black slave, while Shahrayar's death order is delayed and undertaken only after his searching voyage. The striking similarity of Shahzaman's and Shahrayar's stories makes them sound like a voice and an echo. Here the text provides us with the first variant of binarism: pairing. This form of male pairing is symmetrically balanced by female pairing, represented in Shahrazad's and Dinazad's relationship in the third narrative block. However, there is a subtle difference in these two pairs. The male pair (Shahrayar and Shahzaman)—as in Flaubert's *Bouvard et Pécuchet*—is two parties in two performances of the same drama. Each reinforces the other but is completely independent in his actions. With the female pair, there is an explicit complicity between the two sisters. Dinazad is a shadow or a negative of Shahrazad, who accompanies her all along. Shahzaman is more than a negative; he is a double and a copy of Shahrayar.

The names of the dramatis personae also carry with them a phonetic duplication. Shahrazad and Dinazad share an end rhyme, Shahrayar and Shahzaman an initial rhyme. The sonorous repetition in the system of names manifests itself in the characters of the enframed stories, such as Sindbad the Porter and Sindbad the Sailor, Abdallah the Hunter and Abdallah the Mariner, and in the story of the two brothers 'Ajib and Gharib. It is a common feature of legends and mythological narratives to have two parallel characters with rhyming names, such as the two giants Gog and Magog who were believed to have been imprisoned by a great wall during the reign of Alexander the Great. Another example is that of Harut and Marut, the fallen angels who were hung by their feet in a well in Babylon, yet another is that of Qahtan and 'Adnan, the mythical ancestors of the Arabs. This phonetic parallelism in *The Arabian Nights,* a phenomenon that can be observed on the surface of the text, confirms and accentuates parallelism on the semiotic level. The significance of the correspondence between these two levels lies in the reinforcement of the impact on the reader and consequently prepares the reader for a deeper assimilation of the text and its patterns.

The protagonists in *The Arabian Nights* are Shahrayar and Shahrazad. They are the backbone of the narrative. While Shahzaman and Dinazad can be removed from the narrative, it is impossible to remove Shahrayar or Shahrazad without damaging the story. The relationship between Shahrayar and Shahrazad presents the second variant of binarism: coupling. This is how their at-

tributes contrast:

Shahrayar	*Shahrazad*
husband	wife
sultan	subject
listener	narrator

This royal couple offers opposed and complementary polarity. The terms "husband," "sultan," and "listener" connote antinomically "wife," "subject," and "narrator" because they are parts of a split union. A husband cannot be comprehended as a term without its complementary contrast—a wife. Similarly, a king or sultan without subjects is such an incongruity that Antoine de Saint-Exupéry played on its absurdity in *Le petit prince.* In the same vein, a listener, by definition, conjures up a speaker, a narrator, or at least a voice. Shahrazad's attributes are, thus, mirror reflections of Shahrayar's, and vice versa. The interlocking of these two poles produces a totality and generates a process. They are a model of a structural couple: opposed and complementary like the yin-yang principles in Chinese cosmology. This coupling is realized on the phonetic level as well; Shahrazad and Shahrayar share both an initial and a medial "rhyme."

There is yet a third variant of binarism—ambivalence—which is presented in the character of Shahrazad on the one hand and Shahrayar on the other. On the surface, Shahrayar is a paradigm of power: an Oriental despot and virile male who consumes a woman every night, while Shahrazad embodies the very principle of female vulnerability. She is at the total mercy of Shahrayar's monstrous appetite. However, she does not try to strike at him as in the wonder tales of giants and monsters, as in "Jack and the Beanstalk" or the Biblical story of David and Goliath. She tries to appease his appetite, to tame him, as it were, and replaces his steady diet of women with tales of women. Shahrazad's genius lies in turning women from objects of sex to objects of sexual fantasy. This entry into the symbolic is the most critical step undertaken by Shahrazad. It is a crucial transformation that parallels the substitution of ritual enactment for the concrete offering of a sacrifice in religion. Once the signifier replaces the signified, language becomes possible—and once language is installed, unlimited discourses become possible.

By obtaining the privilege of narrating, Shahrazad has inverted her relationship with her master. As the narrator, she has the upper hand. Shahrazad has become a "dictator" in the etymological sense of the word—derived from the verb *dicere* (to say). The listener, by definition, is the passive party in the act of narration. Shahrazad's position is the reversal of the conventional one, where discourse is the prerogative of the sovereign. Shahrazad's narrative gift and gigantic knowledge are stressed in *The Arabian Nights:*

> The former [Shahrazad] had read various books of
> histories, and the lives of preceding kings, and stories
> of past generations: it is asserted that she had collected
> together a thousand books of histories, relating to
> preceding generations and kings, and works of the
> poets.[5]

Shahrazad is, therefore, an exceptional person in her
own right. She is potentially powerful though technically helpless. Her status is ambivalent and so is her
condition. She is—to borrow the paradox of Kierkegaard—put to death but kept alive.[6] Shahrayar, by being
completely entangled in her fictional web, mesmerized
by her narration, evokes the image of an enslaved titan.
Both hero and heroine dramatize a case of ambivalence
and are examples of *coincidentia oppositorum.*

The relationship between Shahrazad and Shahrayar
becomes consequently more complex, or at least more
subtle, since their opposition is further complicated by
internal contradictions. Neither is a pure type. There is
something of the empowerment associated with Shahrayar in Shahrazad, and something of her helplessness in
him. Their struggle is not a clear-cut one of forces of
light versus forces of darkness. It is by no means a
Manichean struggle, but something of an unblocking of
dormant potentials in the weak partner and exposing the
underlying limits of the strong partner. At bottom, both
Shahrayar and Shahrazad are complex and ambiguous
types, combining strength with weakness.

Throughout, the text persistently displays binarism and
uses the principle of duality in three logically possible
ways: duplication, opposition, and ambiguity. It is
perhaps worth pointing out that these three variants of
binarism correspond faithfully to three orders in
semantics: synonymy, antinomy, and heteronomy.

ACTIONS

The binary scale which governs the relationships
between the principal characters permeates the thematic
contents of the story as well. The major themes of the
narrative are the principal actions that occur. In the
frame story these are unequivocally those of love and
death. The relationship between these fundamental acts
in the unfolding of the story falls under three dialectics—repetition, inversion, and fusion—which parallel
the relationship of pairing, opposition, and ambivalence.
In analyzing these three dialectics within the text, it is
often important to note how stylistic craftsmanship
superbly coordinates the move from love to death and
from death to love.

The first dramatic incident occurs when Shahzaman
finds his wife in bed with a black slave. This erotic
motif recurs when Shahzaman sees his sister-in-law
copulating with a black slave, and it is seen once again

by Shahrayar himself. This tripling of the one single
incident amplifies it. The accompanying twenty slave
girls and twenty slave men copulating in the royal
garden further intensify the image. The death motif is
equally insistent—participants in the orgy are slain—so
the first narrative block presents us with the binarism of
Eros and Thanatos.

The second narrative block displays the principle of
inversion, where one act changes syntactic position and
becomes reversed. The force seems to change direction
while maintaining its full thrust. In the voyage undertaken by the two monarchs in the second narrative
block, both Shahrayar and Shahzaman have experiences
which constitute a drastic change from their earlier ones
in the first narrative block. The two kings have sexual
intercourse with a young woman kidnapped on her wedding night and kept under many locks. Earlier, their
wives had managed to have lovers despite the fenced
protection of a royal palace. Shahrayar's love-making
with the young woman parallels that of the black slave
with his wife. The analogy is evident:

> Slave: Shahrayar = Shahrayar: Demon

This neat criss-crossing process also occurs within the
story related by the vizier, Shahrazad's father, about the
ass and the bull. The ass who has advised the bull to
feign sickness in order to have an easy life ends up
replacing the bull at hard work, while the bull indulges
himself in the pleasures formerly enjoyed by the ass.

The difference between the inverted dialectic of Shahrayar and the bull is that the bull's inversion represents a
complete transposition in the two elements given,
something akin to the rhetorical figure of antimetabole,
while the inversion of Shahrayar is something of a chi-
asmus. Both inversions—Shahrayar's and the bull's—
are crucial in the narrative context. Shahrayar learns a
lesson from his experience, acknowledges that this is
not a singular case, and goes back to his throne. The
ass, too, realizes that he is paying dearly for his advice
and sets out to regain his former prestige.

The third dialectic in the narrative text is that of fusion,
where two seemingly contradictory motifs are soldered
together. Both the powerful notions of blackness and
defloration carry with their use in the text what Arab
grammarians have called the principle of *addad,* or the
fusion of two opposing meanings in one term.

The episode of Shahzaman's return to his palace shows
amply the clever use the text makes of blackness:

> [He] set out towards his brother's domains. At midnight,
> however, he remembered that he had left in his Palace
> an article which he should have brought with him, and
> having returned to the palace to fetch it, he there beheld

his wife sleeping in his bed, and attended by [in the arms of] a male negro slave. On beholding this scene, *the world became black before his eyes,* and he said within himself, if this is the case when I have not departed from the city, what will be the conduct of this vile woman while I am sojourning with my brother? He then drew his sword, and slew them both in bed.[7]

The text alone plays to the utmost on the semantic fields and associations of blackness, linking this opening and crucial incident to the stuff of the book—nocturnal narration. The text specifies that Shahzaman remembers the article he forgot in his palace at night, indeed, at the very peak of night. Night evokes darkness and midnight evokes the heart of darkness. Shahzaman, then, finds his wife in bed with a *black* slave. Blackness seems to crown this darkness. And when Shahzaman sees all this, "the world became *black* before his eyes." The final blackening of death completes the somber process. One pigment has been sufficient to describe the timing, the adulterer, and the reaction. The swift movement from one situation to the other is unified by the color scheme.[8]

The concentration on one color is a clear example of textual economy where one term functions as a conceptual transformer of the night, from being read as equivalent to erotic time to a reading of it as murder time. The darkness of the night works as a cover and is associated both with sexual love and illicit actions. In Arabic literature, the night of lovers has been glorified in the most celebrated lines in Arabic poetry (though occasionally lovers were portrayed as meeting at other times of day, such as dawn). Both Imru' al-Qays, the pre-Islamic paragon poet, and 'Umar ibn abi Rabi'a, the early Islamic playful poet, set the mode and the model. The love scene set at night builds simply on a literary cliché, but the text moves from presenting the night as a protective veil into the night as absence of vision, where it infuriates Shahzaman to the point where he kills both his wife and her lover instantly. Here, night evokes darkness and blindness. Both opposed semantic poles of the night are used in this short passage.

What turns this discourse into a text is precisely this stylistic compactness. Thematically and logically, the sequence of events in the above passage is banal enough. A man finds his wife in bed with another and commits a *crime de passion* killing both of them. It sounds rather journalistic and of only passing interest. However, the style enhancing the sequence of events turns the report of such an occurrence into a literary text. In this case, the leitmotif of blackness shows how repetitions of one vehicle can produce highly differentiated and somewhat opposing tenors, to use the terms of I. A. Richards. The fusion here can be called duality in unity.

The text offers, furthermore, a fusion in which different vehicles are united by one overriding tenor, displaying the principle of divergence in convergence. The text specifies the kind of women Shahrayar wanted every night:

> and henceforth he made it his regular custom, every time he took a virgin to his bed, to kill her at the expiration of the night. This he continued to do during a period of three years.[9]

It is clear that Shahrayar suffers from a wound and is trying to avenge himself, but what he is after is not women qua women but virginity. His own innocence, i.e., his mental "virginity," has been wounded and he is making up for it by inflicting wounds. Defloration, a symbol of the erotic act and the procreative drive, is juxtaposed and simultaneously contrasted with beheading. The antithetical nature of the defloration, which is both a synecdoche for life while being literally a bloody rupture, renders the development of the paradox possible. Shahrayar, by the very act of rendering a female procreative and life-producing by inseminating her, is condemning her to death. On the other hand, Shahrayar is doing unto his brides the same act twice over: a metaphoric death followed by a literal death. Eros and Thanatos are fused together. Deflowering and killing, opposite rites, turn out to be facets of one act, namely laceration.

Thus, the binary impulse in *The Arabian Nights* manifests itself both in characters and themes, in the nouns and in the verbs of this great preposition which constitutes the text. Binarism is used in three distinct ways which I shall call—borrowing terms from medieval Arabic rhetoric—(1) correlation (*mumathala*) which covers pairing and repetition, (2) confrontation (*muqabala*), which includes opposition and inversion, and (3) antithetical meaning (*addad*), which delineates internal contradictions in characters and cleavage in actions. The effect is invariably that of amplification and hyperbole in the first place (*mumathala*), revolution and upside-down transformations in the second place (*muqabala*), and paradox and reversibility in the third place (*addad*).

A dyadic organizational system such as that of *The Arabian Nights,* which cannot build a third term, is invariably committed to radical changes but not to growth. A paradox may split apart, and a force may change its position in the syntactic order, but the constituent units remain essentially the same.

If we were to think of *The Arabian Nights* as *parole,* an enunciation, then the organizational system outlined above would constitute its language (*langue*). There is something disturbingly inorganic about this *langue*. It works through sedimentation, mutation, and explosions. The metaphors describing this text should perhaps be drawn from geology rather than biology. The mode of expression, as Jakobson points out, is profoundly linked to the message. *The Arabian Nights,* in using a binary structure, falls inevitably into repetition rather than growth.

Notes

1. Vladimir Propp, *The Morphology of the Folktale,* second edition, ed. L. A. Wagner (Austin and London: University of Texas Press, 1968).

2. Tzvetan Todorov, "The Two Principles of Narrative," *Diacritics* I: 1 (Fall 1971): 37-44.

3. A narrative block is a textual unit. It constitutes a segment of the story that can (potentially) make narrative sense autonomously.

4. The number of rings varies in the different manuscripts/editions of *The Arabian Nights*. In Mahdi's edition, there are ninety-eight. But the exact number of rings in itself and in this specific context is not important. What is significant is the indication of an enormous quantity (be it ninety-eight or five hundred and seventy) of lovers.

5. Lane, *The Thousand and One Nights,* I:10.

6. Søren Kierkegaard, *Repetition: An Essay in Experimental Psychology,* trans. W. Lowrie (Princeton: Princeton University Press, 1946), 152.

7. Lane, *The Thousand and One Nights,* I:4. Emphasis mine.

8. At the end of *The Thousand and One Nights,* when the happy ending is announced and Shahrayar pardons Shahrazad, the color of the night is said to have been "whiter than the face of the day." Lane, III:672.

9. Ibid., I:10.

Works Cited

Lane, E. W., trans. *The Thousand and One Nights.* 3 vols. London: Chatto and Windos, 1912.

Mahdi, Muhsin. "Mazahir al-riwaya wa-l-mushafaha fi usul alf layla wa layla." In *Revue de l'Institut des Manuscrits Arabes* 20 (May 1974): 125-44.

Daniel Beaumont (essay date 2002)

SOURCE: Beaumont, Daniel. "*Alf Laylah wa Laylah* or *The Thousand and One Nights.*" In *Slave of Desire: Sex, Love, and Death in* The 1001 Nights, pp. 15-31. Cranbury, N.J.: Associated University Presses, 2002.

[*In the following excerpt, Beaumont traces the literary history of* The Arabian Nights, *offering an overview of European translations that he contends have influenced modern versions of the tales, examining the original sources of the stories, and discussing the research and criticism generated a "multiple text" that he considers not at all representative of medieval Arabic literature.*]

> By the night when she hides with her veil,
> By the day when he reveals,
> By that which created male and female—
> Truly your paths are varied
>
> —Qur'ān, Surah "Night" (92: 1-3)

Like one of the Jinn who suddenly materialize and vanish in its pages, *Alf laylah wa laylah* or *The Thousand and One Nights* is a book that is in many ways difficult to pin down. Indeed, exactly what texts and what stories constitute the *Nights* has always been the subject of some disagreement, and so whoever would write about *The Thousand and One Nights* must say exactly what entity he means by that title. I have relied for the most part on the Arabic edition printed in Calcutta in the 1830s and known as Macnaghten's Second Calcutta edition, but I would certainly not claim that the Second Calcutta is the definitive *Nights.* I have used two other important nineteenth-century Arabic editions, the Bulaq and the Breslau editions, and I have also consulted some of the major European translations such as Burton and Lane. But the only way to respond to the question of what I mean by *The Thousand and One Nights* is to give some account of the history of the book. That account will also refer to the European editions, not only because I have made use of some of them but, more importantly, because it can be argued that these translations influenced modern Arabic versions of the *Nights,* such as the Second Calcutta edition.

THE MEDIEVAL ARABIC NIGHTS

The first thing to be said is that *The Thousand and One Nights* is a rather exceptional work in the context of medieval Arabic literature. It happens sometimes that a person takes up the study of a language because of his love for a single work, but if someone were tempted to begin the task of learning Arabic because of his love of *The Thousand and One Nights,* he should be forewarned that the book is sui generis. He will really find nothing else like it in the literature, one reason being that the *Nights* seems to have absorbed a number of once independent medieval Arabic fictions; the story of "Sindbad" is probably the most famous example. The borders of this text were not, it seems, ever very well defined. Hence the size of the *Nights.* Unfortunately, in the case of the *Nights* its marginality in this respect has also worked to veil its history in a good deal of obscurity. Indeed, in recounting its history in the medieval period, there is no need to summarize; a fairly complete account will read like a summary, since most of its medieval history is unknown and is likely to remain unknown. To retell the story, let us think of it for the moment as a piece of architecture—a palace, as Borges calls it. "To erect the palace of *The Thousand and One Nights,* it took generations of men, and those men are our benefactors, as we have inherited this inexhaustible book, this book capable of so much metamorphosis," Borges said of one of his favorite books.[1]

The "palace" of the *Nights,* in the form in which we now know and enjoy it—which is to say the nineteenth-century Arabic editions printed in Egypt, India, and Germany that have served as the basis for all but one of the translations since Galland—that structure with its spacious pavilions, its charming recesses, its secret chambers and mysterious passages must have been the work of many literary hands, and it must have been the result of a development in Arabic alone that lasted seven or eight centuries. Evidence about the development of the book may be divided into two categories: testimony by medieval writers and what in a legal hearing would be called "material evidence"—here, textual evidence—those stories in *The Thousand and One Nights* that show some relation to other works in medieval Arabic literature and to works in other literatures.

Earliest mention of a text with a clearly antecedent relation to the contemporary work is found in a papyrus dating from the ninth century A.D. The papyrus mentions two characters, Dînâzâd and Shîrâzâd—later to become Dunyâzâd and Shahrazâd—and has a few lines of narrative in which the former asks the latter to tell a story.[2] There is also mention of a title that anticipates the title we now know: "The Book of Stories from the Thousand Nights."

About a century later two writers in Baghdad, al-Mas'ûdî and Ibn al-Nadîm, mention the same work. In his book *Meadows of Gold* (*Murûj al-dhahab*), the historian Mas'udi (d. 956) states that among the translations made in Baghdad of stories from Persian, Indian, and Greek sources was a book called "A Thousand Tales" (*Alf khurâfah*), also known as **"A Thousand Nights"** (*Alf laylah*).[3] Mas'udi says that it is the story of a king, his vizier, the vizier's daughter and her slave, and that the last two are called Shirazad and Dinazad. They are not yet sisters, as they will be later. In his bibliographic work *The Catalogue* (*Al-Fihrist*), Ibn al-Nadim (d. circa 995) mentions a work translated from Persian called "The Thousand Stories." He also gives a summary of the frame story, but he criticizes it as "a coarse book, without warmth in the telling."[4]

For the next seven centuries, there are only two even briefer references to its existence. In the twelfth century, a loan record for a Jewish bookseller in Cairo mentions the title **"The Thousand and One Nights"**—the earli-est mention of its present title: "Majd ibn al-'Azîzî has *The One Thousand and One Nights.*"[5] And in the early fifteenth century the Egyptian historian al-Maqrîzî (d. 1442) cites authors who indicate the work was in circulation in Cairo in the late eleventh century.[6] These brief references separated by long periods when the book all but vanishes from view suggest an analogy with an unconscious thought that only infrequently and briefly makes its presence known in conscious thought and then quickly vanishes again beneath the force of repression—and repression is not mere metaphor here, as we shall see.

On the basis of these facts, we know that there are three main layers to the book: a translation of a group of Persian stories (which themselves incorporated Indian stories), a Baghdad layer, and a Cairo layer. D. B. Macdonald, in an important article published in 1924, "The Earlier History of the Arabian Nights,"[7] further divided its development into five stages: a Persian core "The Thousand Stories" (*Hazâr Afsânah*); an Arabic version of this; the frame story of "The Thousand Stories" with new Arabic stories added to it; a late Fatimid version (twelfth century); and the Syrian recension whose sixteenth-century manuscript was the basis of the first European translation, that of Galland. Stages two and three correspond to the Baghdad layer, while four and five are part of the later Egyptian layer. To this we may add a sixth and final stage, suggested by Nabia Abbott, a stage that extends into the sixteenth century and introduces the materials from popular epics.

The infrequency of the medieval references to the work cited above, their brevity, and their tone all point to the insignificance of the work in the eyes of recognized practitioners of medieval Arabic literature. Yet it seems to have been a popular work—the work has not completely shed this paradoxical reputation in Arab countries even today.

In addition to these testimonies, there is also the textual evidence: stories in the *Nights* that bear unmistakable links to other works in medieval Arabic literature and to works in other literatures. Here it will be useful to distinguish between three categories.

The first category would contain stories that reveal its links with a few specific works in medieval Arabic literature. For example, "The Story of the Steward," told within the longer story of **"The Hunchback,"** is roughly the same story recounted as fact by the tenth-century author al-Tanûkhî (d. 994) in his book *Happiness after Hardship* (*Al-Faraj ba'd al-shiddah*). It is the story of a husband who offends the delicate sensibility of his wife on their wedding night by forgetting to wash his hands after having eaten a certain spicy stew called *zîrbâjah*.[8] Years later, the same dish is served at a banquet and the other diners demand that he eat some of it; the unfortunate man washes his hands one hundred and twenty times, then tells the story of his disastrous wedding night.

Another story narrated within **"The Hunchback," "The Story of the Lame Young Man,"** also shares its plot with stories and anecdotes found elsewhere in the literature. In the other versions this plot makes use of a certain stew called *maḍîrah,* which similarly provokes the recounting of a painful story. However, in **"The Story of the Lame Young Man,"** as regards its plot function, the dish of stew is transformed and split into two human characters: a judge and his daughter.[9] A purportedly factual *madirah* anecdote which focuses on a clash between guest and host over the provocative dish is fairly widespread in medieval anecdotal literature. An example can be found in the anecdotal work *The Misers (Al-Bukhalâ')* by the eleventh century writer al-Khatîb al-Baghdâdî (d. 1071).[10] Interestingly, the anecdote there is attributed to the same author, Tanukhi, who has the analogue of the previous story, "The Story of the Steward," in one of his books. The story "The Madirah Maqamah," found in a late tenth or early eleventh-century work *Al-Maqâmât* by al-Hamadhânî (d. 1008), makes use of the same *madirah* plot.[11] The eleventh-century physician Ibn Butlân (d. 1066) also makes use of this plot in his comic work *The Physicians' Banquet (Da'wat al-aṭibbâ').* And, finally, it is also found in an anonymous thirteenth-century work *Wonderful Stories (al-Ḥikâyât al-'ajîbah).*

Finally, more such textual links are found in the story "The Sleeper Awakened," a story that Galland translates, but which is not found in two of the major nineteenth-century Arabic editions, the Bulaq or the Second Calcutta editions. The story is comprised of two parts. In the first part, the main character, Abû'l-Ḥasan, is drugged by the caliph Hârûn al-Rashîd and tricked into believing that he is the caliph. In the second part, Abu'l-Hasan tricks Harun into thinking that he and his wife have died. The first part of the story is also found in a work by a seventeenth-century Egyptian author al-Ishâqî (d. 1651). Ishaqi writes when Egypt is a province in the Ottoman Empire, and in his work *Accounts of Previous Rulers of Egypt,* he gives the first half of the story as fact in the section devoted to Harun al-Rashid. The second half of the story seems to be an elaboration of an anecdote told of the Abbasid poet/buffoon Abû Dulâmah that is found in the famous work of Abû'l-Faraj al-Iṣfahânî (d. 967), *The Songs (Al-Aghânî).*[12] The relative lateness of Ishaqi makes the occurrence there more interesting from the perspective of literary history, for with him we are within a few decades of Galland's discovery of the manuscript of the *Nights* in Istanbul. Another brief passage in Ishaqi is also of interest in this context. In an account of a visit to a graveyard by an anonymous narrator said only to be one of the "people of refinement," the narrator states that the purpose of his visit is "to visit the dead and reflect on the lessons of what has passed . . . and to remember the destroyer of delights, the separator of societies, he who makes orphans of son and daughters."[13] The phrase "the destroyer of delights" (*hâdim al-ladhdhât*) is found at the end of numerous stories in *The Thousand and One Nights,* and indeed the version here with mention of the "maker of orphans" (*muyattim al-banîn wa'l-banât*) is, word for word, the same as the version of this sentence that comes at the end of the last story Shahrazad tells, the story of **"Ma'rûf the Cobbler."**[14] The nature of Ishaqi's work is also telling; much of it is patent fiction passed off as historical and edifying anecdote. These things suggest that Ishaqi knew the *Nights* in a version very much like the one we know, and we are only a few decades removed from the date when Antoine Galland, the first European translator of the *Nights,* purchases his Syrian manuscript in Istanbul.

The second category of textual evidence contains stories in *The Thousand and One Nights* that make use of and revise the plots of extremely well-known stories in Islamic culture; stories about figures like Abraham, Joseph, and Solomon are examples.

Finally, in the third category are the stories that make use of plots which are even more widely spread, the "Cinderella" plot, the "Phaedra" plot, and so on.

What do these textual links suggest about the development of the text of *The Thousand and One Nights* at any particular stage in the Middle Ages? Unfortunately, not very much more than I have already said. The latter two categories of material tell us nothing at all since the material is pervasive throughout the period. With regard to the first, more specific, category, the safest assumption would seem to be that the storytellers involved in the creation of the *Nights* sometimes made use of "factual" anecdotal collections for plots, revising them freely to suit their purposes. But even this modest conclusion must carry a caveat.

The earliest manuscripts of *The Thousand and One Nights* date from the fourteenth century, and most of the works cited above for containing analogues are earlier. Yet as we have seen, on the basis of the testimony of earlier authors we know that some sort of collection with a title *The Thousand Nights* existed centuries prior to the fourteenth century. So lacking any knowledge of what the book contained in, say, the tenth and eleventh centuries, it is not absolutely certain that material moved only in one direction, out of established writers and works and into the *Nights.* For, a priori, it is not impossible that an author like Tanukhi and a *One Thousand and One Nights* storyteller drew upon a common store of material. Or a third possibility: it is not out of the question that some material might have moved in the other direction, out of the *Nights* and into the "factual" works of a writer like Tanukhi. After all, writers do lie sometimes. In fact, in some instances in Tanukhi's *Happiness after Hardship* I think this third possibility is the most likely one—that it is Tanukhi who is borrowing from some version of *The Thousand and One Nights.* For example, in the first chapter Tanukhi tells as fact a brief story about a traveler who is shipwrecked. The story has two parts. In the first, a voice from the sky shouts at the man and his fellow travelers that they should throw their money overboard in order to gain a piece of knowledge that will be of spiritual benefit to them. But only the one man does so. Then, when a storm destroys the ship, he is saved while all the others drown. In the second part, the saved man washes ashore on a desert island and finds a subterranean chamber that contains a treasure and a beautiful girl (also shipwrecked).[15] While these elements are found in various combinations in many stories in *The Thousand and One Nights,* this story is basically that of **"The Story of the Second Qalandâr"** told in **"The Porter and the Three Ladies of Baghdad."** In this case, since the story is an obvious fiction for which he gives no sources, it seems likely that Tanukhi has borrowed the second part from one of two places, either from some version of the *Nights* or from a store of narratives (perhaps as yet unwritten) that the *Nights* also uses; this he joined to a Sufi conversion tale. In view of its similarity to **"The Story of the Second Qalandâr,"** it is tempting to say that the first case is what happened, and that, therefore, **"The Story of the Second Qalandâr"** must have existed in the tenth century. But given the ubiquity of these plots and motifs, given the instability of the texts, especially in a manuscript culture, and given the question of oral and written versions and their possible interaction—given all these factors, who can say for certain what happened in any particular case?

Thus, while the textual evidence—its demonstrated links with other works—may tell us something about the sorts of literature that furnished the raw materials for the storytellers of *The Thousand and One Nights* and how they reworked it, that evidence does not, in my opinion, tell us much about the specific content and shape of the text at any particular stage prior to the fourteenth century, roughly the date of the earliest Arabic manuscript.

THE EUROPEAN NIGHTS

The first appearance of *The Thousand and One Nights* in Europe in 1704 was not unlike the uncanny appearance of the jinni in the first story Shahrazad tells. The jinni is a paradoxical being, now tiny and now enor-

mous; he towers over the merchant and yet his son is so small that the merchant's date pit has killed him. A similar sort of paradox attached to Antoine Galland's French translation of an Arabic manuscript. The book immediately enjoyed huge popular success, yet, as Georges May points out, it drew scarcely any critical or scholarly attention.[16] The disparity between popular success and critical attention, which recalls its status in medieval Arabic literature, has waxed and waned over the course of almost three centuries but has never entirely disappeared—a fact all the more problematic when one considers that the publication of Galland's translation is an early landmark in what Raymond Schwab was to call "The Oriental Renaissance." And there are other complications and paradoxes, for ever since Galland's translation the book has led an unusual double life in Europe and the Arab world. Indeed, to speak of "doubles" here merely hints at the complicated relations between various European translations and Arabic editions.

In 1704 Antoine Galland began to publish his translation of a manuscript he had purchased in Istanbul while serving there as an assistant to the French ambassador to the Ottoman Empire. The first six volumes of Galland's translation contained 234 Nights, after which he abandoned the divisions of Nights in the last six volumes. Given the title however, some of his readers may well have wondered when the rest of the *Nights* would appear. And at this point things get a little complicated.

There are basically two opposed explanations of what happened next. The first and simplest is that Europeans seeking the rest of the book more or less found it, either in manuscript form or in the form of persons—Arabs—who knew more stories that had made their way into the work by this time. The result was the "complete editions" published in the nineteenth century, the Arabic editions of Bulaq and Second Calcutta and Breslau—the latter two we should note were the work of Europeans. According to this version of its history, the late medieval *Nights* looked much like the texts of Bulaq and the First and Second Calcutta and Breslau. This version has its contemporary defenders who have made some important arguments (and revisions) to support it.

Those adherents must deal in one way or another with a "revisionist" version put forth recently by Muhsin Mahdi that opposes the first explanation on almost all the important points. Mahdi devoted years to the study of Galland's manuscript sources, some of which are now lost, and to the reconstruction of a prototype manuscript for *The Thousand and One Nights.* The results of those labors were a reconstructed Arabic text faithful, in Mahdi's view, to the presumed antecedent of Galland's manuscript, a fourteenth-century Syrian manuscript, and a book detailing his views on the history of the *Nights*.[17] His conclusions as to which stories belong in *The Thousand and One Nights* are based on this research. Mahdi argues that European demand for a "complete version" of the work distorted the Mamluk-era original.[18] Europeans wanted a book with literally one thousand and one nights of stories, which the work, in Mahdi's view, did not have through most of its existence. The result was the creation of Arabic manuscripts in the eighteenth and nineteenth centuries that delivered more nights and more stories, and, as Mahdi puts it, the book came to be a "catch all" for popular narratives to meet European demand. In his view, the medieval *Nights* was a much smaller and more coherent work, perhaps one-quarter the length of the nineteenth-century editions. In this view, the number "one thousand and one" for much of its history simply meant "a lot," in accordance with the rather free use of numbers in medieval Arabic literature. But after Galland the number proved fateful, and, if Mahdi is right, the subsequent history of *The Thousand and One Nights* followed "the path of the signifier," so to speak. From that point on, the work's dual versions in European translations and in Arabic manuscripts became intertwined in a very complicated relation, with its popularity in Europe creating a demand for a "complete version." Mahdi's comparison of his presumed "original" with the Bulaq edition and Macnaghten's Second Calcutta, which are based on later Egyptian manuscripts, leads him to conclude that a huge number of the stories in modern versions of *The Thousand and One Nights* do not "belong" in it. Thus, Mahdi's version of the *Nights* and a nineteenth-century Arabic edition like the Second Calcutta confront each other as uncanny doubles with a claim to the same name. It is rather like the Amphitryon-like moment in "The False Caliph" when Harun al-Rashid is confronted with his double in the form of the false caliph.

Mahdi's investigations have done much to clarify the modern history of the text. It seems clear that European demand influenced, to some degree, the shape and content of subsequent Arabic editions. He has also produced an Arabic text that is probably closer in style to the medieval work than any of the nineteenth-century editions.[19] But recent criticism of his "revisionist" version raises some important objections to it. Robert Irwin argues that Mahdi's conclusions proceed from mistaken assumptions about what sort of book *The Thousand and One Nights* was in the medieval period. Mahdi's work on the transmission of the manuscripts is based on theories about manuscript transmission developed from the study of texts by known and esteemed classical authors; but, as Irwin says, the *Nights* never was accorded the sort of respect that such texts enjoyed, hence we cannot assume that its manuscripts were copied and transmitted with anything like the same

sort of care.[20] Moreover, there is manuscript evidence for medieval versions of the *Nights* with many more nights than Mahdi would allow. In her recent book, Eva Sallis points out that there are manuscripts predating Galland with many more nights. Moreover, these manuscripts contain stories—"'Umar ibn Nu'mân," for example—that must be regarded as relatively late additions. Hence, she argues that the "expansion" beyond Mahdi's "core" of stories "was a feature of *Nights* compilation earlier than the eighteenth century."[21] In other words, well before the "European demand" created by Galland's work, Middle Eastern writers had already created a text much longer than Mahdi's "original" Mamluk-era text.

Although Mahdi's argument does not bear directly on the analyses that follow, my position on it is largely that of Irwin and Sallis. Even were Mahdi right about what constituted the real medieval *Nights,* only the logic of the specialist could impel someone to reach the conclusion that such stories as "The Seven Voyages of Sindbad" or "Aladdin and His Lamp" do not "belong" in *The Thousand and One Nights.* At this point in its history, this seems rather like mounting a campaign to change the name of the West Indies to rectify Columbus's error. The most recent English translation of the work, which is based on Mahdi's Arabic text, illustrates my point.

In 1990 Husain Haddawy published a translation called *The Arabian Nights* based on Mahdi's reconstructed Arabic text. In his introduction, Haddawy naturally enough subscribes to Mahdi's position; he writes of the Egyptian manuscript tradition that it "produced an abundance of poisonous fruits that almost proved fatal to the original."[22] "Aladdin and His Lamp," he tells us, must be regarded as a "forgery" (xiii). Five years later, however, Haddawy brought out a second volume, *The Arabian Nights II* containing—yes, the "forgeries" and "poisonous fruits."[23]

For my part, the diversity of stories in the later manuscripts does not bother me, and I think, in any case, there is rather more unity to be found in the nineteenth-century Arabic editions than Mahdi is ready to allow—a point I will argue in chapter 8. Even later stories like "Jûdar and His Brothers" show features that relate them stylistically and thematically to earlier stories. But more importantly, given the general aversion of the medieval Arabic literary elite for outright fictions, we should be happy if the book did act as a kind of "catch-all" for stories. For, setting aside the popular *sîrahs* like "'Antar" and his literary kin (which admittedly are not to my taste), if a story did not find its way into *The Thousand and One Nights,* it likely did not survive.[24] Beginning probably from a core of translated and reworked stories, the book must have grown by process of accretion—the Ottoman royal palace Topkapi may furnish an architectural image for the process; what were originally independent structures are gradually joined together. And what we know of the later history does not seem to depart from this pattern. Insofar as the later additions preserve more stories, I think they are welcome additions to the palace. After all, in such a vast structure, if one does not care for a certain passage, one can move along.

For the reader who is interested in a more detailed history of the text, there is a fairly extensive literature. Unfortunately, much of it is printed in old and obscure journals. Besides Mahdi's work, a few of the more important works in English and French may be mentioned here. The article in the new edition of *The Encyclopedia of Islam* under its Arabic title **Alf laylah wa laylah** is a good place to start. Irwin and Sallis offer the best and most recent "anti-revisionist" accounts. Irwin devotes a chapter in *The Arabian Nights: A Companion* to both the development of the Arabic work and its European editions. I would recommend Irwin's whole book without hesitation; it is an excellent work. The second chapter of Sallis's book offers a very readable and current account of the history of the Arabic text with a good discussion of various manuscripts. The first chapter by André Miquel in the work *Les mille et un contes de la nuit* speculates in a very interesting way on the reasons for the "eclipse" of the work in Arabic in the Middle Ages. Mia Gerhardt's book, *The Art of Storytelling,* published in 1963, also discusses the history of the work, though her account is superseded in some degree by recent work. Lastly I will mention a book by David Pinault, *Story-telling Techniques in The Arabian Nights,* which tries to show us how the storyteller worked; Pinault's analysis is based on a detailed examination of differences between manuscripts.

In my view, despite the antiquity of many of the plots in **The Thousand and One Nights,** the stories as we have them now seem to wear the garb of the late medieval period in the Arab-Islamic world; that is, the eras of the Mamluks and the Ottomans. Thus, stories about the Abbasid caliph Harun al-Rashid, who ruled about five centuries before the Mamluks established their power, may reflect popular notions about how a Mamluk sultan lived in the fourteenth century rather more than they reflect such images of the way Harun lived five hundred years earlier. Not that ornate palaces, gardens, wine drinking, cup bearers, and slave consorts were not features of the Abbasid court, but as found here these features often seem like those of the Mamluks or the Ottomans. An obvious example comes in the frame story, in the scene in which King Shahriyâr's wife commits adultery in the garden with a black slave; the lover and the enclosed garden are stock elements in

any Ottoman Turkish *gazel* or love poem. On the general question of the work's historical context, I might finally remark that the Ottoman period is viewed in the Arab world now as one of cultural decadence, a view propounded by Arab nationalism. However, the very existence of this book is testimony, I think, to cultural vitality in that period.

On the basis of the preceding discussion of the various versions of the **Nights,** my reader may well wonder at this point which Arabic text or texts (and which translations) are in my view the "real" **Nights.** My answer is simple: all of them. **The Thousand and One Nights** is a multiple text, and I see no reason to exclude any standard Arabic edition or any of the translations based on it, no matter how controversial they may be. I have for the most part relied on Macnaghten's Second Calcutta edition, an edition based, it seems, on the Bulaq edition and a now-lost manuscript probably copied sometime shortly after 1830. The manuscript belonged to the late Egyptian recension on which the Bulaq edition was also based. Those manuscripts are now known as Zotenburg's Egyptian Recension (ZER) after the scholar who studied them. But I have made free use of other editions (and of various translations) as it suited my purposes and in accordance with my "maximalist" position.

So much for literary history. Much more important for this study are the reasons *why* the book had such a shadowy existence in the pre-modern Arabic literature. That is to say, the historical problems posed by the book's orphan-like existence in Arabic literary culture are of less importance for what follows than the characteristics of the book that made it an orphan. These call for some discussion here because, as I have said, my readers should know that **The Thousand and One Nights** is an exceptional, even aberrant work with respect to some of the most important conventions of medieval Arabic literature.[25] Hence, that the stories say the things I contend they do stems in many ways from the fact that this work is the "repressed" of the literature. The factors that contribute to this status may be discussed under three headings: its genre, its linguistic style, and its content. Foremost is genre, and this raises the question of the place of narrative in medieval Arabic literature.

Narrative in Medieval Arabic Literature

The early development of medieval Arabic literature was part and parcel with the development of Islam. While there existed a rich poetic tradition in pre-Islamic Arabia and a body of narratives that accompanied it and purported to provide the factual background of the poetry, this material seems to have been preserved in oral form until it began to be written down in the late eighth and early ninth centuries—that is, at the same time that, with one exception, the other early texts of Arabic literature are being written. The one exception, of course, is the Qur'an.

The death of Muhammad in 632 A.D. furnishes a reference point. The Qur'an is the only major text that we know to have existed in some *written* form in the century after his death. It is, we should note, a work that contains little narrative as compared to the Bible.

After the Qur'an, the next major work we possess is *The Life of the Prophet* (*Sîrat al-nabî*), composed in the first half of the eighth century by Ibn Isḥâq (d.767), but available to us in the recension of Ibn Hishâm (d. 828 or 833), who made his own cuts and additions. Close on its heels comes a book by al-Wâqidî (d. 823) called *The Raids* (*Al-Maghâzî*) describing the raids Muhammad and his followers made on the pagan tribes of western Arabia.

Because of their priority and the importance of their subject matter, these works established precedents for the use of narrative that would have lasting effects throughout the Islamic Middle Ages. They are made up of the earliest narratives in Arabic, traditions about what Muhammad and his followers said and did in the course of conquering western Arabia. These narratives are known as *akhbâr; al-akhbar* in modern vernacular simply means "the news." The singular *khabar* means a piece of information recounted for someone—the same term is used in Arabic grammar to mean the predicate of a sentence. In the early literature a *khabar* is a short narrative, usually a half page or less in length, and hence confined to the pithy recounting of a single incident. Because of its religious significance and to buttress its factual claims, each *khabar*-narrative came to be preceded by a feature known as the *isnâd* or "chain," a series of names representing a kind of bucket brigade of tradents who, it is claimed, have passed the narrative along to the writer from an eyewitness to the original event. Both with respect to narrative form and the *uses* to which narrative may be put, these traditions exerted enormous influence on subsequent narrative literature. Thus, in its beginning, narrative literature in Arabic purports to confine itself to fact, to the recounting of real events by eyewitnesses, real people. If one accepts everything at face value in works such as Ibn Ishaq's *Life of the Prophet* and Waqidi's *Raids,* then Ibn Ishaq and Waqidi, the "authors," have composed very little of their books' texts, having simply copied verbatim the "accounts" from other people and other written sources.

For various historical and ideological reasons, it proved very difficult for narrative literature to free itself of these conventions.[26] The theoretical and practical problems these conventions pose for the development of fictional narrative should not be underestimated. First of all, narratives are always about "real events."[27] Within the literature proper, a generic space for fiction never really opened up. That which never happened is simply a lie. Curiously, *The Thousand and One Nights* is in agreement with this attitude—it has "internalized" the prejudice, so to speak. Shahrazad does not make up stories. As Abdelfattah Kilito writes: "It sometimes happens that characters in the *Nights* make up a story, that is to say, they affirm that they know it to be false. Invention is then synonymous with lying."[28]

Secondly, the device of the *isnad* poses a formal obstacle for beginning a fiction. It bars the way to the space where a fiction unfolds. This can be seen in some of the few fictional narratives composed by recognized authors. Thus Ibn Butlan, deferring to the need for an *isnad,* begins his *The Physicians' Banquet,* "One of them said. . . ." One of whom? We can imagine a novel beginning with those words, but we would expect shortly to be given at least a hint as to the identity of "one of them" within the fiction. That never happens in Ibn Butlan's work. We never learn anything about "one of them," for this "one of them" exists in some extra-textual place. The French Symbolist Paul Valéry remarks somewhere that he could not write fiction because he could never bring himself to write a sentence like, "The marquise went out at five." Being so used to the conventions of fiction, we may underestimate the amount of literary development that prepares the way for someone to begin with a sentence like that.

The *isnad* can also pose a problem with respect to the length of a narrative if one must represent a fiction as fact. Here I might remark that speculation about length per se as a factor that distinguishes *The Thousand and One Nights* narrative from the anecdotal works of *adab* like those of Tanukhi misses the larger point. It is not a question of length in and of itself, but of length as an index of fictionality.[29] A second glance at a work like Tanukhi's *Happiness after Hardship*—which, as we have seen, contains some analogues with stories found in *The Thousand and One Nights*—shows this. The stories in Tanukhi are almost entirely anecdotal, by which I mean most are a page or less in length. They rarely have the scope or the detail found in the full-blown fictions of *The Thousand and One Nights.* The very length of a narrative would pose a problem vis à vis the assertion of fact staked out by the *isnad.* To focus on only one aspect, any *khabar* is likely to contain direct speech, but if such an account extends for many pages, one must grant the original eyewitness/reporter extraordinary powers of recollection to think that the reported speeches are the verbatim words of the various persons involved. The question must inevitably arise, "How could he (and all of the other persons in the *isnad*) have remembered all of this exactly as it was said?"

Other conventions pose other sorts of difficulties for the development of fictional narrative. Being supposedly a literature of hard fact, in a *khabar*-narrative no one would presume to make a statement about what someone else was thinking or feeling, for how would he know such a thing? Thus, only the grossest sorts of emotions are registered—"He was very angry"—and thought, unless it is spoken, remains absent. The continuing influence of these features will be seen in *The Thousand and One Nights.*

There may also have been ideological constraints. M. Arkoun has written: "The theological and philosophical tradition imposed an ontological weakness on the imagination. The Koran contributed to this weakening with its attacks against 'the poets whom the erring follow, who wander in every valley and who say what they do not do' (26:224-226)."[30] And a well-known episode in the *sirah* and *maghazi* literature shows Muhammad's anger with a storyteller who claimed his stories were "better" than Muhammad's. Naḍr ibn al-Ḥārith so vexed Muhammad that the latter ordered him killed.[31]

In time, to be sure, some obvious fictions came to exist within the literary canon; *Kalîlah wa Dimnah,* the fables translated by Ibn al-Muqaffaʻ(d. 756), and the *Maqamat* or "Seances" of al-Hamadhani (mentioned above) and al-Ḥarîrî (d. 1122) are the most notable examples. But such works are also exceptional. *Kalilah wa Dimnah* is a translation of a Persian work based on the *Panchatantra,* and Hariri was attacked for having made up his stories by Ibn al-Khashshâb (d. 1172).

As a result of all of these developments, in the general view of the literate minority inventing stories was not distinguishable from simply telling lies. And on all these accounts, *The Thousand and One Nights* just goes too far. Its excessively fictional character in this respect can be seen in the way the *Nights'* version of "The Sleeper Awakened" adds a second part to the story that Ishaqi has. Thus its genre, its clearly fictional nature, is the first major reason why *The Thousand and One Nights* is an exceptional work; there is no generic space in the medieval literary canon for it.

Another important factor has to do with its style; the sort of Arabic found in *The Thousand and One Nights* also counted against it. As far back as linguists can determine, Arabic seems to have been characterized by a considerable divergence between the written and spoken forms, a divergence in both vocabulary and grammar. The difference is perhaps most visible in the

case endings that are preserved in the written language, but almost completely ignored in spoken dialects. With such a divergence, literacy is a rather more difficult and elusive goal to attain—something that remains the case today in the Arab world. In the Middle Ages, the spoken dialects were not even considered real languages by the literate minority. The power of that minority rested in their grasp of *al-ʻarabîyah,* the classical written language in which the official discourse of the culture was carried on, while the illiterate were excluded from speech, in their view, since they had no language proper. They were, in a sense, "unspeakable"—one could say "repressed" in the strict sense that they were denied the words to express themselves.

In such a vast work as *The Thousand and One Nights* there are many registers of language, but apart from perhaps conscious stylistic variations, the different manuscripts of *The Thousand and One Nights* all are salted with significant amounts of colloquial usages. These usages have led various scholars to speak of it as being written in "Middle Arabic," but that term, coined by a modern Western scholar, had no status at all among the authors who wrote "Middle Arabic"; those men were attempting to adhere to the classical grammar— they simply no longer mastered it. In the case of the *Nights* the writers may simply not have thought enough of it to go to the bother of adhering to *al-ʻarabiyah* with the result being "Middle Arabic." It may also have been in part the result, as Sallis suggests, of "the accretions of a random textual history."[32] In any case, the language of *The Thousand and One Nights* works against it. The influence of popular tongues, Syrian and Egyptian, is heard in it, and those sounds were, no doubt, repellent to the ears of the litterateurs who wrote in the "pure language" of *al-ʻarabiyah.*

Finally, there is the subject matter. Illicit sex and wine stain the pages. Hashish is used frequently. Despite the way the book is used as a stock reference for certain sorts of events ("It was like something out of *The Arabian Nights*"), many people are surprised by the real contents of the book. There is a widespread assumption that it is something like children's literature, but it is not.

On the other hand, whether the book is "a faithful mirror of medieval Islam," as one edition touts it, is difficult to say. In such a view, one of the reasons the *Nights* is so valuable is that it depicts many things that are not often treated in the literature proper. That literature, as I have said, was the product of an elite who seldom wrote about such homely subjects. But since the *Nights* is in many ways a unique source, the argument threatens to become circular if one claims it is a faithful picture of medieval Muslim society. Moreover, the book is a "catch-all" or *omnium gath-*

erum—to use Irwin's phrase—and as Irwin says, "one can use its texts, through selective quotation from stories, to support the argument that homosexuality was widely approved of, or to argue that it was indifferently accepted, or to argue that it was absolutely abominated."[33] In other words, one would have to take a Hegelian stance—("the truth is the whole")—to make it a "faithful mirror." It is some sort of reflection no doubt, but some literary refraction and distortion must be involved. The fantastic elements that abound also seem to pose some problems for this view of the book: jinn fly back and forth between China and the Near East in the course of a single night; humans are transformed into animals and back into humans; islands turn out to be whales; mountains pull the nails from ships' hulls by means of mysterious, magnetic powers. So, even while one "feels" the truth of its stories, as a source for social history *The Thousand and One Nights* must be used carefully. Yet this much is clear: its subject matter could be an affront to the pious writers who always made up a considerable portion of the literary elite, men who wrote books with titles like *The Condemnation of Fun* (*Dhamm al-lahû*).

For all of these reasons *The Thousand and One Nights* was a marginalized work in medieval Arabic literature, and that is one reason why it is so valuable. It escaped the self-censorship of more typical narrative works, and from the outset its pages are filled with desires and ideas that are rarely articulated elsewhere in the literature. . . .

Notes

1. Jorge Luis Borges, *Seven Nights,* trans. Eliot Weinberger (New York: New Directions, 1980), p. 54.

2. First described by Nabia Abbott in her article "A Ninth-Century Fragment of the Thousand Nights: New Light on the Early History of the Arabian Nights," *Journal of Near Eastern Studies* 8 (1949), pp. 129-64.

3. Al-Mas'ûdî, *Murûj al-dhahab,* ed. and trans. C. Barbier de Meynard and Pavet de Courteille, as *Les prairies d'or* (Paris: Imprimerie imperiale, 1861-1877), vol. 4, pp. 89-90.

4. Ibn al-Nadîm, *The Fihrist of Ibn al-Nadim,* trans. Bayard Dodge (New York: Columbia University Press, 1970), vol. 2, p. 714.

5. Samuel Goitein, "The Oldest Documentary Evidence for the title *Alf layla wa layla*," *Journal of the American Oriental Society* 78 (1958), p. 301.

6. Al-Maqrîzî, *Al-Khiṭaṭ* (Cairo: Bulaq, 1854), vol. 1, p. 484.

7. D. B. Macdonald, "The Earlier History of the Arabian Nights," *Journal of the Royal Asiatic Society* (July 1924), pt. 3, pp. 353 ff.

8. The similarities were first noted and discussed by H. F. Amedroz in his article "A Tale of the Arabian Nights Told as History in the 'Muntazam' of Ibn al-Jawzî," in *Journal of the Royal Asiatic Society* (1904), pp. 273-93. Muhsin Mahdi has recently discussed them in his book *The Thousand and One Nights* (Leiden: E. J. Brill, 1995), in appendix 3, "From History to Fiction," pp. 164-80.

9. This and other transformations of the *madirah* plot tell us something of the plasticity of the material in the hands of the medieval storyteller, matters I discuss in an article called "A Mighty and Never Ending Affair," *Journal of Arabic Literature* 24, pt. 2 (July 1993), pp. 139-59. One finds other echoes in the *Maqamat* of al-Hamadhani: in "The Hunchback" the barber brings the apparently dead hunchback back to life, and in al-Hamadhani's "The *Maqamah* of Mosul," the trickster Abu'l-Fath comes upon a corpse and also tells an astonished crowd, "This man is not dead!" He promises to raise him within two days, but he fails—the man is dead after all.

10. Al-Khatîb al-Baghdâdî, *Al-Bukhalâ'* (Baghdad: Al-Majma' al-'Ilmî al-'Iraqî, 1964), p. 148.

11. The *Maqâmât* are written in a style of rhymed prose peculiar to Arabic known as *saj'*, and are rich in word play and rhetorical tricks. Al-Hamadhani's eleventh century work *Al-Maqâmât* (Beirut: Dâr al-Mashriq, 1986) is the first example.

12. The story in al-Isḥâqî's *Accounts of . . . Egypt* (*Akhbâr al-uwal fî man taṣarrafa fî Miṣra min arbâb al-duwal*) (Cairo: Al-Maṭba'ât al-Fakhrah, 1859) begins on p. 129. The anecdote in al-Iṣfahânî's *Al-Aghânî* (Cairo: Bulaq, 1868-69) is in vol. 9, p. 131.

13. Al-Isḥâqî, *Akhbâr al-uwal fî man tasarrafa fî Misra min arbâb al-duwal,* p. 91.

14. *Book of the Thousand and One Nights Commonly Known as "The Arabian Nights Entertainments" Now for the First Time Published Complete in the Original Arabic,* ed. W. H. Macnaghten (Calcutta: Thacker, 1839-1842), vol. 4, p. 730. Unless otherwise noted, all references to an Arabic text will be to this edition, the so-called Second Calcutta, giving volume and page numbers in the text.

15. In *Al-Faraj ba'd al-shiddah* (Cairo: Khanji, 1956), pp. 23-24. I discuss this and other examples in "In the Second Degree: Fictional Technique in Tanukhi's *Al-Faraj ba'd ash-shiddah*," *Journal of Arabic and Middle Eastern Literatures* 1, no. 2 (July 1998), pp. 125-39.

16. Georges May, *Les Mille et une nuits d'Antoine Galland* (Paris: Presses universitaire de France, 1986), pp. 8-23.

17. *Kitâb alf layla wa layla,* ed. Muhsin Mahdi (Leiden: E. J. Brill, 1984), and *The Thousand and One Nights,* (Leiden: Brill 1995).

18. The Mamluk dynasty ruled Egypt from 1258 to 1517.

19. Robert Irwin, *The Arabian Nights: A Companion* (New York: Penguin, 1995), pp. 55-56.

20. Ibid., pp. 57-62.

21. Eva Sallis, *Sheherazade through the Looking Glass* (London: Curzon, 1999), p. 34. Sallis even speculates that by the close of the twelfth century that work "incorporated most probably literally one thousand and one nights . . . and around two hundred tales" (p. 27). It is certainly possible, but then again—who knows?

22. Hussain Haddawy, *The Arabian Nights* (New York: Norton, 1990), p. xii.

23. Hussain Haddawy, *The Arabian Nights II* (New York: Norton, 1995).

24. They are called "popular" *sirahs* to distinguish them generically from works like the first biography of Muhammad, also a called a *sirah*. They are long fictions of chivalry, relating the adventures of a hero/knight; *'Antar* and *Sultan Baybars* are notable examples of which at least parts are now available in English and French. In my view, these works do not have the formal brilliance of *The Thousand and One Nights,* and while individual episodes may be entertaining enough, in the aggregate, they take on a monotonous character.

25. Even measured against other works of a hitherto denigrated "popular literature," *The Thousand and One Nights* is a rather singular work. More typical representatives of that literature are the "popular *sîrahs*" mentioned above.

26. S. A. Bonebakker considers the problematic status of fiction in his essay "*Nihil obstat* in Storytelling?" found in the recent volume *The Thousand and One Nights in Arabic Literature and Society,* ed. Richard C. Hovannisian and Georges Sabagh (New York and Cambridge: Cambridge University Press, 1997), pp. 56-77. But he seems to think the question is an open one. I think I have shown that something does tend to obstruct it in my articles on parody and lying, on Tanukhi, and on early Muslim historical traditions. I am more or less going over the same ground here.

27. This, despite the fact that the greater portion of "legal" traditions or *ḥadîths* and much of the "historical" ones are now known to be "fictions."

28. Abdelfattah Kilito, *L'oeil et l'aiguille* (Paris: Éditons la Découverte, 1992), p. 14.

29. The same can be said of attempts to distinguish between different forms of the fantastic that would act as criteria. It is not a question of forms of the fantastic per se, but of forms that would be unmistakable indices of fictionality. Joseph Sadan's review, in *Journal of Arabic Literature* 25 (March 1994), pp. 81-83, of a book by Wiebke Walther discusses some of these questions.

30. Cited by Mohammed Arkoun in *L'Islam, morale et politique* (Paris: Desclée de Brouwer, 1986), p. 12.

31. Ibn Isḥâq, *Sîrat an-nabî,* trans. Alfred Guillaume, *The Life of Muhammad* (London: Oxford University Press, 1955), pp. 135-36, p. 308.

32. Eva Sallis, *Sheherazade through the Looking Glass,* p. 40.

33. Irwin, *The Arabian Nights: A Companion,* p. 169.

FURTHER READING

Criticism

Beaumont, Daniel. "'Peut-on . . .': Intertextual Relations in *The Arabian Nights* and Gensis." *Comparative Literature* 50, no. 2 (spring 1998): 120-35.

Uses postmodern methods to understand how "The Story of the First Sheikh" takes up and revises the story of Abraham in Genesis 1 and how "The Merchant and the Jinn" is connected to the story of Tamar, Er, Onan, and Judah in Genesis 38.

Cannon, Garland, "'The Lady of Shalot' and 'The Arabian Nights' Tales.'" *Victorian Poetry* 8, no. 4 (winter 1970): 344-46.

Argues that one of the tales in the *The Arabian Nights* provided Alfred Lord Tennyson with devices he used in his poem "The Lady of Shalott."

Caracciolo, Peter L., ed. The Arabian Nights *in English Literature: Studies in the Reception of* The Thousand and One Nights *into British Culture,* London:: Macmillan Press, 1988, 320 p.

Collection of essays focusing on the use of *The Arabian Nights* in English literature, including popular works, nursery rhymes, and writings by authors such as Samuel Taylor Coleridge, Charles Dickens, William Makepeace Thackeray, Elizabeth Gaskell, and others.

Carroll, Alicia. "'Arabian Nights': Make Believe, Exoticism, and Desire in *Daniel Deronda*." *Journal of English and Germanic Philology* 98, no. 2 (April 1999): 120-35.

Remarks on the use of *The Arabian Nights* in George Eliot's *Daniel Deronda* to underscore the presence of exoticism, sexual pleasure and danger, fantasy and nightmare.

Furtato, Antonio L. "*The Arabian Nights:* Yet Another Source of the Grail Stories?" *Quondam et Futurus: A Journal of Arturian Interpretations* 1, no. 3 (fall 1991): 25-40.

Claims that the "The Fisherman and the Jinni" from *The Arabian Nights* is a possible source for an important episode in Chrétien de Troyes's*Perceval.*

Haddawy, Husain. Introduction to *The Arabian Nights,* translated by Husain Haddawy, pp. ix-xxix. New York: W. W. Norton & Company, 1990.

Offers a general introduction to *The Arabian Nights* and discusses the stories' origin, their adaptations to manuscript form, the various translations of the tales, and his own method of translation.

Irwin, Robert. *The Arabian Nights: A Companion*, 344 p. New York: Penguin Press, 1994.

Detailed history and "anti-revisionist" analysis of *The Arabian Nights.*

Moussa-Mahmoud, Fatma. "A Manuscript Translation of *The Arabian Nights* in the Beckford Papers." *Journal of Arabic Literature* 7 (1976): 73-87.

Urges that a manuscript edition of *The Arabian Nights* in the Bodleian Library not be dismissed as unimportant by critics and scholars.

Plotz, Judith. "In the Footsteps of Aladdin: De Quincey's *Arabian Nights*." *Wordsworth Circle* 29, no. 2 (spring 1998): 120-26.

Discusses Thomas de Quincey's version of the Aladdin tale.

Trapnell, William H. "Destiny in Voltaire's *Zadig* and *The Arabian Nights*." *Studies in Voltaire and the Eighteenth Century* 278 (1990): 147-71.

Compares the use of the theme of destiny between *The Arabian Nights* and Voltaire's *Zadig.*

Additional coverage of *The Arabian Nights* is contained in the following source published by the Gale Group: *Classical and Medieval Literature Criticism,* Vol. 2.

Robert Grosseteste
c. 1160-1253

English theologian, philosopher, scientific writer, and translator.

INTRODUCTION

A prolific writer, gifted administrator, and respected teacher, Grosseteste was a leader of the English church in the thirteenth century. Considered one of the most learned men of the Middle Ages, he was a chancellor at Oxford University and also served as Bishop of Lincoln for eighteen years. During both terms he instituted significant reforms at these institutions while continuing wit his own studies. Grosseteste composed over three hundred works, including essays on theological subjects as well as original works addressing scientific and philosophical questions. Notable among his publications are the scientific treatise *De Luce* (1939; *On Light*); a commentary on Genesis, the *Hexaëmeron* (1982; *Hexaëmeron*); the philosophical essay *De Veritate* (*On Truth,* 1214-35); translations of *The Testaments of the Twelve Patriarchs* and Aristotle's *Nichomachean Ethics* (both published between 1235 and 1253); and a commentary on Aristotle's *Posterior Analytics* (1214-35). The ideas expressed in Grosseteste's writing had a significant impact on the philosophy and theology of the Middle Ages and he is credited with bringing the thought of ancient Greece, particularly Aristotle, to Christian Europe. His influence can also be seen in the works of John Wyclif, Albert the Great, and Thomas Aquinas. In his own day, Grosseteste was regarded as a pioneer of a new literary and scientific movement and as the first mathematician and physicist of his age. Although specialists continue to consider Grosseteste one of the central figures of the thirteenth century, because of the technical nature and subject matter of his works, he is largely unknown to a general audience. Scholars continue to investigate his writings and discuss the importance of his contributions in the areas of early experimental science, philosophy and theology.

BIOGRAPHICAL INFORMATION

Grosseteste was born around 1160 into a humble family from Stowe, Suffolk. Details about the early years of his life are obscure, but it is likely that he completed the first stages of his education at a cathedral school, perhaps in Hereford; he is recorded as being a member of the household of Bishop William de Vere at Hereford in 1190. He studied law, medicine, and the natural sciences at Oxford, and sometime after 1198 he began teaching there. From then until 1225, there is no historical record of his life, although there is evidence that he acted as judge-delegate in Hereford sometime between 1213 and 1216. Some scholars speculate that during 1209 and 1214, when the university ceased to exist because of a murder case, Grosseteste went to Paris to study theology. An early thirteenth-century charter from Paris names a Robert Grosseteste residing at a house in Paris, but since it concerns the property claims of his children, some historians believe that it refers to another Robert Grosseteste. It was during these "missing" years that Grosseteste produced many of his most important scientific writings. Sometime around 1214 Grosseteste returned to teach at Oxford and by 1225 he was chancellor there. The next mention of Grosseteste in any historical document is in the Episcopal register of Hugh of Lincoln, which notes that he was given a benefice with pastoral responsibilities in the diocese of Lincoln, also mentioning his position at Oxford. Grosseteste left the university in 1229 and devoted his time to teaching the young Franciscan friars at Oxford, a practice that led to the humanities becoming a major part in the education of the friars, enabling them to read and interpret sacred Scripture in a critical manner. During these years Grosseteste continued to write prolifically on a variety of subjects, although he began to move away from scientific and philosophical treatises focusing his energies increasingly on works on theology.

In 1235 Grosseteste was elected Bishop of Lincoln, the largest diocese in England. Soon after he was consecrated Bishop, he launched into a vigorous reformation campaign, organizing a team of translators to produce clear and precise translations of Greek and Hebrew works. During his eighteen years as Bishop he also produced his own translations, gaining a reputation as a brilliant but highly demanding church leader. He insisted that all his clergy be literate and receive some training in theology. He also became involved in a number of disputes in various parts of his dioceses, and his treatise on his concept of church leadership, included with his collected letters (not published until 1861), is regarded as one of the most comprehensive discussions of ministry and authority in the medieval church. Grosseteste also clashed with the papacy on several occasions, pointing out major problems of the contemporary church. This led some scholars, particularly those writing after the Reformation, to view him as a protoprotestant, but most modern historians now reject this characterization. Grosseteste died in October 1253 while serving as Bishop of Lincoln.

MAJOR WORKS

Due to the uncertainty surrounding the details of his early life, and because of his busy and varied career in later years, it is difficult to date many of Grosseteste's writings. The sheer volume of his output also makes it difficult for scholars to organize his works. He likely began his writing career after he began teaching at Oxford, at first producing texts on the liberal arts, particularly astronomy and cosmology. Many of his scientific and philosophical treatises are believed to have been written between 1214 and 1235, although at least one scholar claims that he did not write down any of his ideas until after 1225. Grosseteste's most famous scientific work is his *On Light,* in which he argues that light is the basis of all matter, combining Christian creation doctrine with Aristotle's system of the universe. Grosseteste also wrote important essays on meteorology, color, and optics as well as on mathematics; he was one of the first western thinkers to argue that natural phenomena can be described mathematically. Among Grosseteste's original philosophical contributions are an attempt to classify the various forms of knowledge in *On Truth.* Grosseteste also wrote a number of short theological treatises between 1214 and 1235, covering subjects such as free will, causes emanating from God, and the knowledge of God. These writings also engaged his scientific and philosophical interests; critics note that Grosseteste's writings, whether on scientific, philosophical, or theological subjects, emphasized a synthesis of ideas across disciplines.

Although science was important to Grosseteste, he devoted most of his intellectual energies in later life to questions of theological import. Of particular interest to biblical scholars are his translations and works of pastoral care written between 1235 and 1253. He also produced a new translation of the works of the Byzantine theologian John Damascene as well as the *Testament of the Twelve Patriarchs,* a text that he considered further proof that Jesus was the promised Messiah. His *Hexaëmeron,* or commentary on the Book of Genesis, which emphasized the eternity of the world, was particularly influential on other thirteenth-century authors.

Grosseteste also played a pivotal role in the introduction of Aristotle to scholastic thought, producing commentaries on a number of the ancient philosopher's works. His translation of the *Nicomachean Ethics* made this important work available to the West in its entirety for the first time. Grosseteste's translation was used, for example, by Albert the Great and Thomas Aquinas, opening up a whole new area of moral discussion in the Middle Ages.

CRITICAL RECEPTION

Scholars concede that it is difficult to define Grosseteste's position in the history of thirteenth-century thought. Today he is virtually unknown outside a small scholarly circle of medievalists, yet his impact on the development of learning in the Middle Ages is immeasurable. He was one of the pioneers of scholasticism, although his interests lay in moral questions rather than in logic or metaphysics. He laid great emphasis on clear thinking and intellectual pursuits, yet he also stressed the importance of the study of scripture. During his own time Grosseteste was known for his scientific learning; the writer Roger Bacon, who was also a critic of Grosseteste, declared that "No one really knew the sciences, except the Lord Robert, Bishop of Lincoln, by reason of his length of life and experience, as well as of his studiousness and zeal." Bacon also admired Grosseteste's broad knowledge of mathematics, philosophy, language, and the Bible, noting, "he knew mathematics and perspective, and there was nothing which he was unable to know, and at the same time he was sufficiently acquainted with languages to be able to understand the saints and the philosophers and the wise men of antiquity." His translations of Aristotle from the Greek and theological works from the Hebrew were invaluable to medieval thinkers after him, including Aquinas, Albert the Great, and Wyclif. Critics have asserted that perhaps Grosseteste's greatest achievement was in producing a synthesis of thought in science, philosophy, and theology that was to become central in the intellectual development of the Middle Ages, paving the way for the synthesis of reason and faith that was Aquinas's great contribution.

Because of its technical nature, much of Grosseteste's work remains unedited. Most modern scholars have concentrated on his scientific writings, although there has been some discussion about his contributions to the development of the intellectual history of the thirteenth century. Critics have also been impressed by Grosseteste's care and accuracy in translating Aristotle's works, with his wide range of intellectual interests and his concern with more practical matters, and by his sensitive discussion of detailed theological issues. They have also remarked on the evolution in Grosseteste's thought from his time in Oxford to his days as Bishop. All in all, Grosseteste is an admired figure among specialists in medieval philosophy and theology for his vast learning and contributions to the intellectual development of his age.

PRINCIPAL WORKS

De artibus liberalibus (philosophical-scientific-theological treatise) 1214-35

De Calore Solis [*On the Heat of the Sun*] (scientific treatise) c. 1214-35

De Colore [*On Colors*] (scientific treatise) c. 1214-35

De Cessatione Legalium [*On Setting aside the Law*] (theological treatise) c. 1214-35

Le Chasteau d'Amour [*The Castle of Love*] (romance) c. 1214-35

Commentarium in VIII Libros Physicorum [*Commentary on the Eight Books of* [*Aristotle's*] *Physics*] (commentary) c. 1214-35

Commentarius in Posterium Analyticorum Libros [*Commentary on* [*Aristotle's*] *Posterior Analytics*] (commentary) c. 1214-35

De Cometis [*On Comets*] (scientific treatise) c. 1214-35

De Computo [*On Computation*] (scientific-mathematical treatise) c. 1214-35

Confessioun [*Confession*] (theological treatise) c. 1214-35

De Decem Mandatis [*On the Ten Commandments*] (theological commentary) c. 1214-35

De Differentiis Localibus [*On the Differences of Places*] (scientific treatise) c. 1214-35

De Finitate Motus et Temporis [*On the Finitude of Motion and Time*] (scientific treatise) c. 1214-35

De Generatione Sonorum [*On the Generation of Sounds*] (scientific treatise) c. 1214-35

De Generatione Stellarum [*On the Generation of the Stars*] (scientific treatise) c. 1214-35

Hexaëmeron [*Commentary on Genesis*] (commentary) c. 1214-35

De Impressione Aeris [*On Atmospheric Impressions*] (scientific treatise) c. 1214-35

De Impressionibus Elementorum [*On the Impressions of the Elements*] (scientific treatise) c. 1214-35

De Intelligentiis [*On the Intelligences*] (scientific-philosophical treatise) c. 1214-35

De Iride [*On the Rainbow*] (scientific treatise) c. 1214-35

De Libero Arbitrio [*On the Freedom of the Will*] (scientific-theological treatise) c. 1214-35

De Lineis, Angulis et Figuris [*On Lines, Angles, and Figures*] (scientific treatise) c. 1214-35

De Motu Corporali [*On the Movement of Bodies*] (scientific treatise) c. 1214-35

De Motu Super-caelestium [*On Supracelestial Movement*] (scientific treatise) c. 1214-35

De Natura Locorum [*On the Nature of Places*] (scientific treatise) c. 1214-35

De Ordine Emanandi Causatorum a Deo [*On the Order of Causes Emanating from God*] (theological treatise) c. 1214-35

De Poenetencia [*On Penitence*] (theological treatise) c. 1214-35

De Potentia et Actu [*On Potency and Act*] (scientific-philosophical treatise) c. 1214-35

Quod Homo Sit Minor Mundus [*That the Human Being is a Microcosm*] (scientific treatise) c. 1214-35

Questio de Fluxu et Refluxu Maris [*On the Tides*] (scientific treatise) c. 1214-35

De Scientia Dei [*On the Knowledge of God*] (theological treatise) c. 1214-35

De Sphaera [*On the Sphere*] (scientific treatise) c. 1214-35

De Statu Causarum [*On the Status of Causes*] (scientific-philosophical treatise) c. 1214-35

De Unica Forma Omnium [*On the Unity of All Forms*] (scientific-philosophical treatise) c. 1214-35

De Utilitate Artium [*On the Usefulness of the Arts*] (essay) c. 1214-35

De Veritate [*On Truth*] (scientific-philosophical treatise) c. 1214-35

De Veritate Propositionis [*On the Truth of Propositions*] (scientific-theological treatise) c. 1214-35

De Luce [*On Light*] (scientific treatise) 1225-41

De operationibus solis (scientific treatise) 1230-35

Aristotle, *De Caelo et Mundo* [*On the Heavens and the Earth*] (translation) 1235-53

Aristotle, *Ethica Nicomachea* [*Nichomachean Ethics*] (translation) 1235-53

John Damascene, *Dialectica* [*Dialectic*] (translation) 1235-53

John Damascene, *Disputatio Christiani et Saraceni* [*Dispute between a Christian and a Saracen*] (translation) 1235-53

John Damascene, *De Hymno Trisagio* [*On the Hymn of Threefold Wisdom*] (translation) 1235-53

John Damascene, *Introductio Dogmatum Elementaris* [*Introduction to Elementary Doctrine*] (translation) 1235-53

Testamentum XII Patriarcharum [*Testament of the Twelve Patriarchs*] (translation) 1235-53

Divine Names Commentary (theological commentary) 1239-43

Expositio in Epistolam ad Galatas (theological commentary) date unknown

Roberti Grosseteste episcopi quondam Lincolniensis Epistolae (letters) 1861

Principal English Translations

The Testament of the twelve patriarchs, the sons of Jacob. *Translated out of Greek into Latin, by Robert Grosthead . . . and out of his copy into French and Dutch by others, and now Englished . . .* (translated by Anthony Gilby) 1706

The castle of love, a poem, (translated by J. O. Halliwell Phillipps) 1849

On light, or the incoming of forms (translated by Charles Glenn Wallis) 1939

Robert Grosseteste 'On light' (De luce) (translated by Clare C. Riedl) 1942

Dicta I-L of Robert Grosseteste, Bishop of Lincoln, 1235-1253 (translated by Edwin Jergen Westermann) 1942

The Greek commentaries of the Nicomachean ethics *of Aristotle / In the Latin translation of Robert Grosseteste, Bishop of Lincoln (1253)* (translated by Henri Mercken) 1973

Hexaëmeron: *Robert Grosseteste* (translated by Richard C. Dales and Servus Gieben) 1982

On the Six Days of Creation, *by Robert Grosseteste* (translated by C. F. J. Martin) 1996

CRITICISM

Francis Seymour Stevenson (essay date 1899)

SOURCE: Stevenson, Francis Seymour. "Chapter X: 1239-1244." In *Robert Grosseteste, Bishop of Lincoln: A Contribution to the Religious, Political, and Intellectual History of the Thirteenth Century,* pp. 223-40. New York: Macmillan and Co. Limited, 1899.

[*In the following essay, Stevenson discusses Grosseteste's literary and academic activities between 1239 and 1244, including his efforts in promoting the revival of learning, his translations of* The Testament of the Twelve Patriarchs, *and other writings.*]

It might have been thought that Grosseteste's time, during the period which elapsed between 1239 and 1244, would have been so fully occupied with the reorganisation of religious work within his diocese, with the numerous disputes in which he was engaged, and with the active part he took in public affairs, that he would have found no opportunity either for literary occupations or for sustained interest in the fortunes of the University with which his career had been so closely interwoven. Such, however, was not the case. To the period in question must be assigned (1) his renewed effort to promote the revival of Greek studies; (2) his translation from Greek into Latin of the work known as the *Testament of the Twelve Patriarchs,* as well as of a treatise ascribed to Dionysius the Areopagite, and other writings;[1] (3) his contributions to the literature of rural and domestic economy; and (4) the action he took to obtain for the Chancellor and University of Oxford a royal privilege defining the extent of their jurisdiction.

Roger Bacon's assertion[2] that Grosseteste was not sufficiently acquainted with Greek to be able to translate out of that language until the latter portion of his life, taken in conjunction with other passages, merely means that he did not carry out actual and continuous translations until that period of his career, and that even then he required a certain amount of assistance. He had commenced the study of that language, as has been seen, whilst he was at the University, and had doubtless used, or at any rate consulted, the original text, in his lectures and commentaries on the *Posterior Analytics* and other writings of Aristotle. The importance, however, of his work as a pioneer of the study of Greek, lies rather in the impulse he gave to the efforts of others, than in the results he achieved himself. It was with that object that he summoned Greeks to England, and arranged for Greek manuscripts to be brought from Athens, Constantinople, and elsewhere.[3] Some of the Greek teachers thus invited by Grosseteste still remained in this country at the time when Roger Bacon wrote his *Compendium Studii Philosophiae* in 1271.[4] In the same work Bacon maintains that for seventy years no one but Grosseteste had enriched the Church by translations, as he had done in the case of Dionysius the Areopagite, St. John of Damascus, and some other sacred teachers.[5] Trivet mentions in terms of special commendation, in addition to his *Testament of the Twelve Patriarchs,* his *Commentary on the Books of Dionysius,* which he had "caused to be translated." It is to Grosseteste and his assistants that must also be attributed the Latin version of the letters of St. Ignatius, brought to light by Bishop Ussher in 1646, and of which the late Bishop Lightfoot has given a luminous account.[6] It is possible, too, that the renderings from the Lexicon of Suidas ascribed to Grosseteste by Boston of Bury also belong to this period of his life.[7]

The difference between the translations which he effected, when unaided, and those which he carried out with the assistance of others, may, perhaps, be inferred from a comparison of the description he gives of his method of translating the Greek work on the monastic state which he sent to the Abbot and convent of Peterborough,[8] with the account given by various writers of the later versions connected with his name. In the former instance he says that he extracted as best he could the meaning of the words, and added what was necessary to elucidate their meaning. His later translations, such as those which belong to the greater part of the period now under review, which he effected with the aid of others working under him, are, on the other hand, extremely literal. Matthew Paris notes that the *Testament of the Twelve Patriarchs* was rendered "verbo ad verbum,"[9] and Bishop Lightfoot has given several instances of Grosseteste's close adherence to the original wording and even to the construction of the

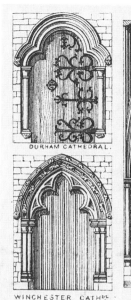

Early English

1189 то 1272.

The Arch lancet shaped, or equilateral. The Doorways still deeply recessed, & the jaumbs filled with light shafts with foliaged capitals. The arch mouldings very numerous & of bold character, & often filled with rich foliage, and the dog tooth ornament. Large Doorways often divided into two by single or clustered shafts. The Windows usually long & narrow, & of one light with lancet head, but often arranged in triplets. Late in the style the Window is divided by mullions into two or three lights, with circles in the head.

Examples of architectural arches from various English cathedrals of Grosseteste's era.

sentences.[10] For the efforts thus made he is deserving of the highest praise, and the difficulties and the defects inseparable from the initial stages of the study of a language are in themselves a tribute to the novelty as well as to the importance of the undertaking.

It was in 1242, according to Matthew Paris and most chroniclers,[11] that Grosseteste, assisted by Nicholas the Greek, translated the *Testament of the Twelve Patriarchs* into Latin. Nicholas, after being clerk to the Abbot of St. Albans, had become an inmate of the Bishop of Lincoln's household. It is probable, that Grosseteste had been acquainted with him during his university career at Oxford, and possibly at Paris. He appears to have resided at Oxford in 1238, as his name is to be found in the list of those who were bailed out by the Bishop after the attack on the Legate at Osney, and in the following year he had been presented to the living of Datchet by the Abbot and convent of St. Albans.[12] In view of the large number of Italians who held livings in England, though unacquainted with the English language, it is not remarkable that a Greek who had studied at Oxford, and spent apparently most of his life in this country, should have been made a rector; and it must be borne in mind that the Latin Empire existing at that time at Constantinople formed an additional link between East and West, and rendered intercourse more easy.[13] Even Armenians came to England during that period: an Armenian archbishop, for example, visited St. Albans, one of their bishops died at St. Ives, others of that race travelled all the way to this country in 1250 to pay their respects at his tomb, and some found their way to St. Albans two years later, and related many

things concerning Mount Ararat and the ark, as well as respecting the persecutions inflicted upon them by the Tartars.[14]

Grosseteste's principal English collaborator was his own Archdeacon of Leicester, John de Basingstoke, who is described as "a man of great experience in the 'trivium' and the 'quadrivium,' and fully educated in Greek and Latin literature."[15] He had studied at Athens, and it was through him that Grosseteste obtained a copy of the Greek original of the *Testament of the Twelve Patriarchs* for the purpose of translation. John de Basingstoke also introduced, according to Matthew Paris, Greek numerals into England, and instructed his intimate friends in their use and significance,[16] and composed a grammar called the *Greek Donatus,* based on a work written in that language. He was instrumental in bringing to England many valuable manuscripts.

Matthew Paris relates the following curious story which John de Basingstoke told to a friend of his with reference to his sojourn at Athens: "There was a certain damsel, daughter of the Archbishop of Athens,[17] Constantina by name, hardly twenty years of age, endowed with every virtue and well acquainted with the difficulties of the 'trivium' and 'quadrivium'; for which reason, on account of her eminence in knowledge, the said Master John used in jest to call her another Catherine. She it was who was the teacher of Master John, and all the good he acquired in the way of science, as he often asserted, he had obtained from her, although he had studied and read for a long time in Paris. This damsel was able to foretell, with unfailing foresight, pestilence, thunderstorms, eclipses, and, what was more remarkable, earthquakes."

Grosseteste's translation of the **Testament of the Twelve Patriarchs,** the sons of Jacob, produced a great sensation at the time, as is shown by the references in almost all the chronicles, and was frequently printed in later ages.[18] Of the English versions of his work, which subsequently appeared, nearly thirty editions are enumerated in Hazlitt's bibliographical collections. It is, perhaps, a matter for regret that he should have devoted so much care to what was unquestionably a spurious, though an early and highly interesting, work.[19] The Greek original purported to be a version of one of the books of the Hebrew Scriptures, which had been suppressed or secreted by the Jews on account of its prophetic references to Christianity, and that is why Matthew Paris says that Grosseteste's desire was to confute the Jews, thus bringing his purpose into harmony with that of his **De Cessatione Legalium.**[20] Grosseteste was certainly misled, in common with many others, into a belief in the authenticity of the work he was translating; and in a letter to Henry the Third,[21] who had addressed to him the inquiry, What does anointing add to the royal dignity? he quotes as authoritative, in the course of his reply, a passage from the **Testament of the Twelve Patriarchs** on the superiority of the priesthood to the kingly office. However, as Dr. Pauli well remarks,[22] the revival of learning in the thirteenth century commenced, like that of the fifteenth, with what was least valuable and least profitable. It was, in fact, the impetus given to intellectual progress by the opening up of an access to new modes of thought and sources of information, which constituted the great step in advance, apart from the particular materials which were in the first instance brought into requisition.

Of a lighter but not less useful character were the attempts made by the Bishop during that period to spread sound notions respecting the management of landed estates and of domestic households. His interest in agriculture had doubtless been acquired in his early days at Stradbroke, and had never completely died out. Walter of Henley's *Treatise on Husbandry,* written at some time during the first half of the thirteenth century, was translated from French into English either by him or under his auspices.[23] The need for a translation shows that some of those for whose use the work was intended, whether lords or bailiffs, were unacquainted with, or at any rate imperfectly versed in the former language; though, perhaps, the object was to familiarise a wider circle with the contents. Nothing is known definitely with regard to the personality of Walter of Henley beyond the fact, which he mentions, that he had served the office of bailiff; but the title of one of the manuscripts of his treatise states that he became a friar

preacher.[24] If it were not for that reference, it might be permissible to conjecture that he was identical with the W. de Hemingburgh, or Hemingberga, who was one of Grosseteste's clerks, and a correspondent of Adam Marsh, in view of his connection with the Bishop of Lincoln, and also seeing that Henley in Oxfordshire was sometimes called Henneburgh, or some other name of similar sound. Adam Marsh's letter to him,[25] recommending the messenger of the Archbishop of Canterbury to his good offices, implies, however, that he was a Franciscan and not a Dominican; and the hypothesis must therefore be abandoned, unless it be assumed that on the above-mentioned title-page the words "Friar Preacher" were inserted by mistake for "Friar Minor." In any case, Walter of Henley's work, whoever the author may have been, was one of real importance, and was regarded for several centuries as being of considerable utility. Numerous manuscripts of it are still extant; it was translated into Welsh and Latin, and the English version was printed by Wynkyn de Worde. The authority for the statement that the latter was due to the Bishop of Lincoln, is not the mere *ipse dixit* of Bale, in his *Scriptores Britanniae:* the title of a fifteenth-century manuscript[26] distinctly states that the work was written in French, and translated into English by Robert Grosseteste, and other manuscripts contain the same account of its origin.[27]

With greater certainty, however, can the Rules, written in French, which bear the name of **Les Reules Seynt Roberd** be ascribed to him. They are described in the title as "The Rules that the good Bishop of Lincoln, Saint Robert Grosseteste, made for the Countess of Lincoln to guard and govern her Lands and Hostel: whoever will keep these Rules well, will be able to live on his means, and keep himself and those belonging to him." The Countess of Lincoln in question was Margaret, widow of John de Lacy, Earl of Lincoln, who died on the 22nd of June 1240.[28] Various manors were assigned by the King for her maintenance until her dowry out of her husband's lands should be set forth.[29] She afterwards married, in 1242, Walter Marshall, seventh Earl of Pembroke, the same who two years later served with Grosseteste on the famous Committee of twelve. If, therefore, the Bishop's rules were written for her guidance during her widowhood, as is most in accordance with probability, they must have been composed between 1240 and 1242. Pegge points out[30] that Grosseteste's acquaintance with the de Lacys may have commenced at the time when he was Archdeacon, and John de Lacy, Constable of Chester. The Countess' mother was also connected with Chester, as she was the sister of Ranulf, seventh earl of that name, with whom Grosseteste may possibly, too, have come in contact during his tenure of the archdeaconry of Leicester, as

Ranulf held for several years the Montfort property in that district through a grant made by King John,[31] and is recorded to have kept Christmas of 1223 in the town of Leicester.[32]

Walter of Henley's Treatise and Grosseteste's Rules cover different ground. The former deals with the two-field and the three-field system, and the practical details connected with the general management of an estate, on the supposition, as Professor Cunningham points out, that the lord or the bailiff would look into everything himself. The Rules, on the other hand, were intended for the personal use of the Countess of Lincoln, who could not look into everything with her own eyes; and they deal not only with production, but with the consumption of products in the household, and explain the methods by which a large number of retainers can be directed to the best purpose. Both treatises, however, have this in common, that they are concerned with a condition of things in which comparatively little was bought or sold, as the difficulties of communication rendered the interchange of heavy commodities expensive and often impossible, so that the object was to work the estate, as far as was feasible, on self-supporting principles. At the same time a change was gradually coming over the management of estates. The great Benedictine monasteries were setting the example of improvements in tillage, the Cistercians were producing wool in large quantities for purposes of export, and the commercial activity encouraged by the Crusades was gradually affecting the methods of rural economy. Under the old state of things the villain worked, say, three days a week on the domain land, besides extra days at harvest-time, and performed sundry incidental duties, in return for which he had the benefit of his holding of about thirty acres, stocked with a yoke of oxen and half-a-dozen sheep.[33] Under the new order of things, the custom, on the part of the villains, of discharging their obligations in money, in lieu of labour or produce, was gradually spreading. The twofold effect of the change was to allow them more time to look after their own holdings, and to introduce the necessity for the use of hired labour on the home farm or domain land, not, indeed, to such an extent as to supersede altogether the services of the villains, but in such a way as to diminish their importance, to concentrate the attention of the lord upon the requirements of the home farm, and to necessitate the keeping of accounts. Walter of Henley and Grosseteste wrote during the transitional period, and their works must accordingly have been of the utmost practical value. The obligations of the villains were generally stated in terms of money: they might, however, be discharged wholly in service or in kind, or else be commuted in their entirety for a cash payment; or, again, a middle course might be adopted, according as the special needs of the district or the will of the lord might direct.

Grosseteste's Rules show how a lord or lady shall know in each manor the rents, customs, usages, services, franchises, fees, and tenements, and tell the live and dead stock; they indicate the best way of dealing with seneschals and bailiffs; the method of making the various estates self-sufficing, leaving a certain surplus for sale; when the granges should be shut and opened, and how the accounts should be examined. Grosseteste then deals, in a number of brief maxims, with the subject of household economy and the management of servants, hospitality, alms-giving, dress, and the service at table. In one rule he refers to the practice prevailing in his own palace, where "each quarter of wheat makes nine score loaves of white and brown bread, together of the weight of five marks each, and the hostel at meat is served with two meats, large and full, to increase the alms, and with two lighter dishes also full for all the freemen, and at supper with one dish not so substantial, and also light dishes followed by cheese; and if strangers come to supper they shall be served with more according as they have need." After some further injunctions of that kind he reverts to the subject of agriculture, and touches upon the mode of threshing and selling corn, and the importance of keeping plenty of cows and sheep: the wool of a thousand sheep in good pasture ought, he says, to yield at least fifty marks a year, in scant pasture forty, and in coarse and poor pasture thirty; and he observes that the return from cows and sheep in the way of cheese is in itself worth a considerable sum, without counting calves and lambs, and apart from the manure, all of which help the growth of corn and fruit. The minuteness with which he enters into questions likely to be of assistance to the Countess may be inferred from the fact that he even advises her when and where to make her purchases. "I recommend," he says, "that at two seasons of the year you make your principal purchases, that is to say, your wines and your wax and your wardrobe at the fair of St. Botolph what you shall use in Lindsey and in Norfolk, in the vale of Belvoir, in the country of Caversham, in that of Southampton for Winchester, and in that of Somerset at Bristol; your robes purchase at St. Ive's." Grosseteste's Rules, being intended for private use, did not attain to the wide circulation enjoyed by the translation of Walter of Henley's Treatise with which he is credited. They were also translated at a later date into English, and a portion of them is printed in the *Monumenta Franciscana*.[34] The translator was, however, under the impression that they were intended by the Bishop for the management of his own household and estates, whereas they were really addressed to the Countess of Lincoln, or Nicole, as the city was called in Norman French; though it is possible, as Professor Cunningham points out,[35] that he composed separate sets of Rules, similar in character, for his own household and for her guidance. Apart from the light they throw on the condition of agriculture and of estate management at that time, and on Grosseteste's sustained interest in those questions, they reflect credit on the painstaking good nature with which he placed his experience at the disposal of those who had most need of it.

It has been seen how Grosseteste's thoughtfulness for the welfare of the University of Oxford continued unabated after his promotion to the See of Lincoln. In 1238 he defended its liberties, and allayed the differences which had arisen in consequence of the attack upon Cardinal Otho at Osney. In 1240, owing to a "town and gown" disturbance, a good many scholars migrated to Cambridge.[36] In 1244 he was called upon to take a step which may not, perhaps, have appeared of much importance at the time, but which produced a lasting effect on the constitution and the jurisdiction of the University. In that year a serious riot occurred, probably in connection with some question of usury. The clerks invaded the Jewry, broke into the houses, and sacked the contents, with the consequence that forty-five of them were sent to prison. They were, however, released by the king at the instance of Grosseteste, as no direct evidence could be brought against them showing that they had been guilty of felony.[37] A few weeks later a royal charter was procured, doubtless through Grosseteste's efforts, by which the Jews of Oxford were forbidden to take more than twopence in the pound per week as interest from the scholars, and a definite jurisdiction was granted to the Chancellor in all actions concerning debts, rents, and prices, transactions relating to horses, clothing, and provisions, and all other "contracts of movables" in which one party was a clerk.[38] The charter involved the local recognition of a principle for which Grosseteste had often contended on wide and general grounds. Although it did not include—as was the case with the charter of 1255, issued two years after Grosseteste's death—criminal jurisdiction over laymen for breach of the peace, its immediate effect was to confer upon the Chancellor a civil jurisdiction in addition to the spiritual jurisdiction which he already possessed by virtue of the ordinary ecclesiastical law as the Bishop's representative.[39] Its indirect effect was that, in course of time, the Chancellor became less and less of a Bishop's officer, and more and more a president of the University. His authority was strengthened, and the self-governing power of the educational organisation correspondingly increased. In Grosseteste's time matters constantly came before the Bishop of Lincoln, which in later years were left to the University authorities on the spot; and, although the explanation is to be found partly in his commanding eminence as a man, and partly in the special character of his previous connection with Oxford, it must also be ascribed in some measure to the fact that the Chancellor's powers were merely delegated to him by the Bishop.

Thus it was that, on the occasion of some disputes which occurred seven years later in 1251, when Henry the Third and his Queen were on a visit to Oxford, two clerks happened to have been imprisoned for certain offences, whereupon the "whole body of scholars"[40] requested that all clerks, whatever might be the offence of which they were accused, should be surrendered out of the royal prison into the hands of the Chancellor; "for," writes Adam Marsh to Grosseteste, "the King has granted to them that it should be done in the case of offences which the Chancellor, as the Bishop's delegate, is able to visit with condign punishment; but in the case of serious crimes, requiring either deposition or degradation, the King has only consented that incarcerated clerks should be handed over to the Bishop, or his official, or a vicar specially appointed for the purpose. . . . The King has in this instance released the two clerks aforesaid unconditionally at the request of the scholars. The masters, however, had ceased their lectures for several days, and they have not yet resumed them." Mr. Rashdall notes that "so long as the See of Lincoln was filled by Robert Grosseteste, the most distinguished son that the University has yet produced, almost unbroken harmony prevailed between the University and the Diocesan," and that it was not until the accession of his successor, Henry de Lexington, that the first disagreements of any consequence broke out. Doubtless, as he also points out, the distance of Lincoln from Oxford tended to render the University gradually and at last wholly independent of episcopal control, and differentiated it in that respect from many of the mediæval universities of continental Europe.

Grosseteste's correspondence with Adam Marsh shows the continuous interest he felt in the organisation of the Oxford curriculum, and the management of the affairs of the University. He was frequently asked to help individual scholars by letters of recommendation or by pecuniary assistance, and appeals to his generosity were never made in vain. Memorials forwarded by the masters and scholars were often transmitted to the Bishop through Adam Marsh, and it was through him that Grosseteste communicated to them his wishes with respect to certain articles which they were to draw up for the government of the University.[41] It was on that occasion, in all likelihood, that a committee of seven was appointed to frame what is known as the first statute of the University, enacted in 1252 or 1253, which provided that no one should be admitted to inception or theology who had not previously been a regent in arts, and read one book of the Canon or the Sentences, and preached publicly in the University.[42] Questions relating to the use of a University seal were also transmitted to Grosseteste: Ralph de Sempingham, for instance, the Chancellor, "to whom he had committed the duty of governing the congregation of the scholars of Oxford," is rebuked by him for making use of that symbol.[43] In

1248 Grosseteste writes to Robert Marsh, his official,[44] with reference to the murder of a scholar who was passing by St. Martin's Church, Oxford, and orders the murderers to be excommunicated, and to be punished in accordance with the agreement which had been made between the University and the town, under the auspices of Nicholas of Tusculum, the Papal legate, in 1214.[45]

Of greater interest is the fact that Grosseteste was the first who instituted the loan chests, which were the nearest approach presented at that time to the scholarships and exhibitions of a later date. It was by an ordinance of his that the annual fine imposed upon the town of Oxford by the Legate Nicholas in 1214,[46] and which in 1219 had been transferred by arrangement to the Abbot and convent of Eynsham,[47] was applied in 1240 to the establishment of a University chest at St. Frideswyde's, where Christ Church now stands.[48] The immediate object was to enable poor scholars to borrow without interest for a reasonable period of time, and to keep them from falling into the hands of the Jewish and other usurers. The plan was that would-be borrowers should deposit some pledge, such as an article of clothing, or a cup, or a book, exceeding in value the amount of the loan, and liable to be sold by auction if the pledge was not redeemed within the year. The strictness of the rule appears to have been relaxed in specially deserving cases. The idea gained ground rapidly, and not only was the St. Frideswyde's chest increased by private donations and bequests, but numerous other chests were founded at Oxford in subsequent years. It is to the University chest thus established that Adam Marsh refers in the letter[49] in which he asks R. de St. Agatha, who was Chancellor in 1256, to allow a certain Symon de Valentinis to borrow forty pounds from the funds of the University of Oxford, deposited through the benefaction of Master William of Durham. As that scholar and patron of learning had died in 1249, the reference shows that, within nine years of Grosseteste's institution of the University chest, it had already begun to be augmented by bequests, which may, perhaps, in certain cases have been earmarked for special purposes.

It was Grosseteste, again, who obtained from Innocent IV., in May 1246, a bull to prevent any of the scholars at Oxford from teaching in any Faculty unless they had been examined as at Paris, and approved by the Bishop or his deputies.[50] In the same year, in all likelihood,[51] he wrote his celebrated letter[52] to the Regents of Theology at Oxford, exhibiting at one and the same time the deep interest he took in the course of studies, and the predominant importance he attached to a thorough knowledge of the Scriptures. In that letter he holds up to them as an example worthy of imitation the system of teaching adopted at Paris, and insists upon the need for ensuring that the foundation-stones of learning should be truly such, and not merely called by that name, and that non-fundamentals should not be mistaken for fundamentals. Hence he argues that, as the Scriptures must be the basis of all their teaching, and as they can best be inculcated at the morning hour, presumably because the mind is then freshest and most receptive, the subjects of all their lectures at that time should be taken from the New Testament or from the Old, in order, he says, that, "like the scribe who is instructed into the kingdom of heaven, you may be like unto a man that is an householder, which bringeth forth out of his treasure things new and old." For other matters, such as aids to Biblical study, and the study of the Fathers, other opportunities should be selected. Grosseteste here emphasises the importance of Biblical study above other departments of theology, and takes his stand, as on other occasions, on the 'auctoritas irrefragabilis Scripturæ.' Although the letter, however, relates mainly to the order and relative importance of the studies, and must be interpreted, not as an attempt to eliminate any branches of knowledge, but merely as an effect to subordinate them to what he deemed the primary object to be pursued, it appears at the same time to differentiate Grosseteste's attitude from that of the new scholasticism which endeavoured to combine theology with philosophy. When Roger Bacon wrote in 1267, that new scholasticism had completely captured the Paris theological schools, the methods of which Grosseteste had approved some twenty-one, or it may be some twenty-seven years earlier. In Grosseteste's estimation, as in that of the Fathers of the Western Church, and of the pre-scholastic writers, the two streams of theology and of philosophy flowed in separate channels, and were not to be intermingled. It is true that, in his teaching, he finds himself unable to adhere rigidly to that doctrine, and his influence is to be discerned in the writings of the schoolmen, as well as in those of the men whose methods are most akin to his own; and it must be borne in mind that both Albertus Magnus and Thomas Aquinas eliminate the essential mysteries of Christian dogma from the domain of metaphysical discussion, assigning to them the province of faith. In the main, Grosseteste may be said to represent a conservative force in theology, whilst in other departments of thought and learning, as well as in the political sphere, he represents a progressive force. In the former case he acknowledges the reason of authority, in the latter he bows to the authority of reason.[53]

Notes

1. Grosseteste's translation of the *Mystical Theology,* with a commentary, is the only one of his works relating to the author known as Dionysius the Areopagite which has been printed. The commentary is in the *Opera Dionysii Areopagitae,* Argent., 1503, pp. 264*b*-271*b*. He translated other works of

that writer, and commented on them.—Tanner's *Bibliotheca;* Wharton's *Anglia Sacra,* ii. p. 347; Felten, p. 75.

2. *Opus Tertium,* ed. Brewer, p. 91. See p. 23.

3. R. Bacon, *ibid.*

4. *Ibid.* p. 434.

5. *Ibid.* p. 474. Trivet, p. 243, etc.

6. Lightfoot's *Apostolic Fathers,* part ii. vol. i. pp. 76 *sqq.* It is what is known as the Latin version of the Middle Recension of St. Ignatius' Epistles. Lightfoot thinks that the circulation of Grosseteste's translation was probably confined to the Franciscan convent at Oxford, to which he bequeathed his books. John Tyssington and William Woodford, both of whom quote the Latin version of those Epistles, belonged to that convent in the thirteenth century. A MS. in the library at Tours, mentioned in Dorange's *Catalogue des Manuscrits de la Bibliothèque de Tours,* and examined by Canon Armitage Robinson on behalf of Bishop Lightfoot, distinctly ascribes the translation to Grosseteste, pp. 77, 274.

7. The author of the above-named version of the Epistles of St. Ignatius shows acquaintance with Suidas. Lightfoot, *ibid.* p. 85.

8. "Extractum pro modulo meo verborum sensum, adjectis alicubi paucis ad dilucidationem in hanc paginam redigens, vobis destinare curavi."

9. *Hist. Maj.* iv. 232.

10. *Apostolic Fathers,* l.c. Cp. Felten, p. 86.

11. *Hist. Maj.* iv. 232; R. Bacon, p. 474; Trivet, p. 243; Salimbene, *Chronicle of Parma* (Parma, 1856), p. 99; *Joh. de Oxenedes,* ed. Ellis, p. 171, etc. Matthew Paris with his own hand transcribed a copy of the work for the use of the Benedictine monks at St. Albans. It is in the Royal MS. 4 D. vii. British Museum, together with a "tractatus quem episcopus Lincolniensis Robertus transtulit de Graeco in Latinum, de probatione virginitatis Beatae Mariae et sacerdotio Jesu." The colophon says: "Hoc quoque scriptum adquisivit frater Matthaeus Parisiensis ab episcopo memorato et ad usus claustralium manu sua scripsit; cujus anima in pace requiescat. Amen." See Sir T. Duffus Hardy's *Descriptive Catalogue,* iii. p. 57, and plate 9 of the facsimiles at the commencement of the volume.

12. For the evidence see Pegge, pp. 163, 164.

13. It lasted from 1203 to 1261.

14. *Hist. Maj.* iii. 163, 164; v. 116, 340, 341. Dean Stanley (*Eastern Church,* p. 8) states that the *Testament of the Twelve Patriarchs* forms part of the canon of the Armenian Church. If so, Grosseteste's belief in its authenticity may have been confirmed by one of the Armenian visitors to this country. Malan, however, in his *Philosophy of Truth,* pp. 176 *sqq.,* disputes the statement. See note on p. 240 of the present work.

15. *Hist. Maj.* v. 284 *sqq.*

16. See Pegge's Appendix 11. The symbols are drawn by Matthew Paris, *Hist. Maj.* v. 285.

17. Michael Acominatus.—Finlay's *History of Greece,* ed. Tozer, iv. 134. Luard also refers to the *Oriens Christianus,* ii. 174.

18. *E.g.* at Haguenau in 1532 and Paris in 1539, and in Galland's *Bibliotheca Patrum,* i. 193 *sqq.* An edition without printer's name, place, or date, black letter, was probably printed about 1520. Fabricius (ed. Mansi, Padua) mentions an edition printed at Vienna in 1483.

19. On the *Testament of the Twelve Patriarchs,* see the works of the Rev. R. Sinker, D.D., who published the text in 1869, with notes, etc., an English translation in 1872, and a valuable appendix in 1879. He regards it as one of the earliest monuments of Christian literature, written not later than the middle of the second century, and perhaps before the end of the first, and holds that it can hardly have had a Hebrew original, though intended primarily for Hebrew readers. The Greek MS. which Grosseteste actually used, and which was sent to him at his request by John de Basingstoke from Athens, is probably the one in the Library of the University of Cambridge, to which it was left by Archbishop Parker, numbered Ff. i. 24.

20. *Hist. Maj.* iv. 232, 233; v. 285.

21. Letter 124. See Selden's *Titles of Honour,* part i. ch. 8. Arthur Taylor's *Treatise of the Anointing and Crowning of the Kings and Queens of England.* Besides the Holy Roman Emperor, only four Kings received unction in addition to coronation: the Kings of Jerusalem, France, England, and Sicily. Dean Stanley suggests (*Memorials of Westminster*) that Henry the Third's recollection of his twofold coronation may have prompted the question he addressed by the "young king" to Grosseteste. Letter 124 must, however, have been written after 1245, when at least twenty-nine years had elapsed since the King's accession.

22. Page 41.

23. "Walter of Henley, etc.," ed. for the Royal Historical Society by Miss Lamond, with introduction by Prof. Cunningham (London, 1890), contains

Walter of Henley's *Husbandry,* the English translation of that work attributed to Grosseteste, an anonymous *Husbandry,* a *Seneschaucie,* and Grosseteste's *Rules* (*Les Reules Seynt Roberd*).

24. Prof. Cunningham's Introduction, p. 21.

25. *Mon. Francisc.* p. 255.

26. Sloane MSS. 686, f. 1; Cunningham, Introd. p. 31.

27. Cunningham, Introduction, pp. 37, 39, 41. A copy of Wynkyn de Worde's extremely rare edition is in the Cambridge Library.

28. *Hist. Maj.* iv. 34.

29. Dugdale's *Baronage,* quoted by Pegge, p. 95.

30. Page 95.

31. Bémont, *Simon de Montfort,* p. 3, and the authorities there quoted.

32. *Hist. Maj.* iii. 83.

33. Cunningham, Introduction, p. 10.

34. *Mon. Francisc.* p. 582.

35. Introduction, p. 43.

36. *Hist. Maj.* iv. 7.

37. The *Chronicle of Osney* (*Ann. Monast.* i. 91) says: "Ad instantiam Sancti Roberti Lincolniensis episcopi jussu regis fuerunt liberati, eo quod nullus impeteret eos de pace regis fracta vel alio crimine." T. Wykes' *Chronicle,* on the same page, says: "Per dominum Robertum Lincolniensem episcopum liberatisunt omnes, quia nullus apparuit qui eos directe posset impetere de crimine feloniae." See also the *Chron. of Abingdon,* ed. Halliwell (Reading, 1844), p. 5.

38. *Patent Rolls,* 28 Henry III. m. 6, a. 7; Rashdall, vol. ii. pp. 393, 394. The deed of acknowledgment was executed at Reading, and signed and sealed on behalf of the University by the Prior of the Friars Preachers, the Minister of the Friars Minors, the Chancellor of the University, the Archdeacons of Lincoln and Cornwall, and Friar Robert Bacon.—Little's *Grey Friars in Oxford,* p. 8.

39. Rashdall, *l.c.*

40. "Universitas scholarium," *Mon. Francisc.* p. 115.

41. *Mon. Francisc.* pp. 99, 346.

42. *Ibid.* p. 346; Anstey's *Munimenta Academica,* p. 25. Most writers have assigned the discussions to 1251, and the statute to 1252; but Mr. Little (*Grey Friars at Oxford,* p. 38, note) gives strong reasons for preferring 1252 as the date of the former, and 1253 as the date of the latter.

43. *Mon. Francisc.* p. 100.

44. Letter 129.

45. *Munimenta Academica,* pp. 1 *sqq.*

46. *Munimenta Academica,* p. 1.

47. *Ibid.* p. 4. Cp. *Lincoln Cathedral Statutes,* ed. Bradshaw and Wordsworth, part ii. introduction p. 67.

48. *Munimenta Academica,* p. 8; Rashdall, ii. p. 350.

49. *Mon. Francisc.* p. 257.

50. Bliss, *Calendar of the Papal Registers,* i. p. 225; Wood (i. p. 236) was under the impression that the bull only applied to degrees in arts.

51. Luard, Introd. to the *Letters,* p. 129. Wood attributes the letter to 1240.

52. Letter 123.

53. Since the present chapter has been in the press, the Rev. Dr. Sukius Baronian, whom I have consulted with regard to the hypothesis suggested in note 4, has informed me that Mr. Malan's view that the *Testament of the Twelve Patriarchs* never formed part of the canon of the Armenian Church, is correct. This is shown (1) by the statement of Moses of Khorene in the fifth century (*Hist. of Armenia,* iii. 53) that the number of books of the Old Testament then translated into Armenian amounted to twenty-two, the same as now, a figure which does not admit of the inclusion of the work in question, and (2) by the fact that it has never been authorised to be read at the services of the Church, and has not been made the subject of a commentary. At the same time Dean Stanley's view was undoubtedly based upon the occurrence of the *Testament of the Twelve Patriarchs* in some Armenian copies of the Scriptures of comparatively late date, and it is quite possible that some of the Armenian visitors to England in the thirteenth century may have been guided by those copies.

Jean Dunbabin (essay date 1972)

SOURCE: Dunbabin, Jean. "Robert Grosseteste as Translator, Transmitter, and Commentator: The *Nichomachean Ethics.*" *Traditio: Studies in Ancient and Medieval History, Thought, and Religion* 28 (1972): 460-72.

[*In the following essay, Dunbabin examines Grosseteste's translation of the* Nichomachean Ethics, *commenting on its accuracy, range of scholarship, clarity, logical precision, and philosophical skill, and lauding it as an example of the foundation Grosseteste laid for future commentators on Aristotle's work.*]

Because Robert Grosseteste's translation of Aristotle's *Nicomachean Ethics* is now seen as having provided the framework for a dynamic study of Aristotle's moral philosophy, more significance must be attached to what itself became the standard translation in the Middle Ages. That Grosseteste was responsible both for the full translation of Aristotle's text and for the translation of the Greek commentaries which accompany the *Ethics* in twenty-one known manuscripts[1] modern scholars are now in agreement.[2] Grosseteste's work on the *Nicomachean Ethics* has been dated confidently to the 1240s, arguably to 1246-47,[3] and scholars have tended to stress the rapidity with which the Aristotelian ethics were assimilated in the thirteenth century,[4] in contrast, for example, with the slow progress recorded by John of Salisbury on the *Posterior Analytics* in the twelfth.[5] These results of recent research seem, it should be noted in passing, strangely at odds with the verdict of Roger Bacon, that there was comparatively little work on the *Ethics* in his period. He, Grosseteste's most ardent admirer, appears not to have known that this master translated the text and comments: 'Tardius communicata est Ethica Aristotelis et nuper lecta a magistris et raro.'[6]

Grosseteste's work is interesting not only for the insight it offers into one of the outstanding minds of the thirteenth century, but also for the direction it gave to future studies. Not all the seeds that he sowed in the course of his ethical labours bore fruit later. But it is surely safe to say that, without his translations and annotations, it would have taken far longer for thirteenth-century scholars to have reached the sophistication found in, for example, Albertus Magnus' two commentaries on the *Nicomachean Ethics*. I hope, in the course of this article, to show what kind of foundations the bishop had laid for them to build on.

Robert Grosseteste's ability to contribute to scholarship while at the same time running the largest episcopal see in England has always excited admiration. It is interesting that it is to these busy years, rather than to the comparatively tranquil period of his Oxford studies, that his great works of translation belong. Bacon explains this by saying that it was only towards the end of his life that he got the help he needed from southern Italy, where many people still spoke Greek, and where Greek texts were to be found.[7] Grosseteste's chosen texts for translation cover a wide range, theological, philosophical, and glossarial; probably his best-known and most used were the Pseudo-Dionysian works. But in the philosophical sphere, the *Nicomachean Ethics* was by far his most ambitious and important project.

As it stands, Grosseteste's work on the *Ethics* consists firstly of a full Latin translation of Aristotle's text, books I - X. This is preceded in many manuscripts by the ***Summa in Ethica Nicomachea,*** a neat index which Grosseteste provided to the whole work. After each section of the text there follows a commentary by a Greek author. In addition, there are notes interspersed into the text of the Greek commentaries by a thirteenth-century Latin author. And there are marginal notes, several of which are definitely ascribed to Grosseteste in some manuscripts. Finally, in Peterhouse 116, one of the oldest manuscripts, all this is rounded off by translations of two more brief works, the *De passionibus* of Pseudo-Andronicus, and the *De virtutibus et vitiis,* generally ascribed to Aristotle in the thirteenth century. These were probably originally intended to be part of what Fr. Callus has described as 'a corpus of Aristotelian ethics.'[8]

I. THE TRANSLATION

The labor involved in all this translating must have been immense. So large was the work that few medieval scribes could copy out the whole text, and no complete version of the marginal notes is known. In his task Grosseteste almost certainly received help from his *familia,* probably from Magister Robertus Graecus, Magister Nicolaus Graecus, and John of Basingstoke. But modern scholars have tended to stress that these men played a very subsidiary role.[9] Perhaps more important, Grosseteste could and did draw on a number of existing partial translations of the *Ethics*. Since the end of the twelfth century books II - III had been known to the Western world in a translation called *Ethica vetus* and book I in a translation known as *Ethica nova*.[10] Parts of books VII and VIII, fragments known as *Ethica Borghesiana,* had been used shortly before the appearance of Grosseteste's work by Albertus Magnus.[11] All these parts seem to have belonged to a full translation, additional fragments of which are to be found interspersed in the later text in Cambridge (Mass.) Bibl. Hoferiana typ. 233 H.[12] So the bishop was not ploughing entirely virgin ground. He also had more than one manuscript available to him. Eton 122 fols. 26[r], 195[v], and 219[v] refer to variant readings.

But even where he was following a previous translator, Grosseteste's meticulous attitude towards his task caused him to alter extensively. Perhaps he, like his younger disciple Roger Bacon,[13] was afraid that most translations of Aristotle were doing harm because they were so carelessly rendered. Professor Franceschini in an important article[14] has made plain Grosseteste's aim: he hoped to translate *de verbo ad verbum* in such a way that not one jot or tittle of the original meaning should be lost. Inevitably, this was a frustrating task.

> Sciendum quoque quod in translatione latina . . . in quantum occurrit transferenti facultas, necesse est plu-

ries esse multa ambigue et multipliciter dicta, que in greco ydiomate non possunt esse multiplicia.[15]

Where possible, he kept Greek constructions, and at the places where he felt the result was confusing, he inserted a marginal note to assist the reader. So, against 'non expectandum autem neque causam in omnibus similiter' (Mercken 110), he notes that in Greek two negatives do not cancel out, but rather strengthen each other (Eton College 122 fol. 16[r]). And against 'omni autem passioni et omni actui sequitur delectatio' (Mercken 181), he points out that since the Greek word for 'follow' always takes a dative, he has kept the construction in Latin (Eton 122 fol. 35[r]).

Such pedantry leads to a disjointed piece of ugly-sounding prose which demands constant effort on the part of the reader. Every letter of the original may be there, but the true meaning is often elusive. This said, it must be conceded that Grosseteste's translation was a great improvement on its precursors and that it had lasting value. The subsequent recension (of William of Moerbeke?) changed the text only slightly; and the Renaissance scholar Leonardo Bruni Aretino used it as the basis of his translation, even while denouncing it in violent terms.[16]

At last, then, by about 1247, the schoolmen had available to them a full translation of a major ethical work, the presuppositions of which were entirely alien to them, and yet which was couched in a convincingly rational form. The stage was set for an intriguing display of intellectual gymnastics as scholars tried to cope.

II. THE TRANSLATION OF THE GREEK COMMENTATORS

But it is doubtful whether serious work could have begun so soon—Albertus Magnus' first *quaestiones* belong to the period 1250-52[17]—if Grosseteste had not done his fellow-scholars a further service. Not only did he provide them with the **Summa in Ethica,** which helped them to find their way around in the text, but also, and much more importantly, he translated the Greek commentaries on the *Ethics* which had been put together and edited in Byzantium in the late-twelfth or possibly the early-thirteenth century.

These commentaries have long been valued by Byzantine historians for the light which they shed on the standards of classical scholarship in that period, and for the continuity of the classical tradition. In the form in which Grosseteste found them, they consist of: Eustratius of Nicaea on book I; an early Anonymous, tentatively placed in the sixth century, on books II - V; a second commentary, by Michael of Ephesus amplifying that of the Anonymous, on book V; Eustratius of

Nicaea on book VI; a later Anonymous, perhaps a twelfth-century figure, on book VII; the second-century Peripatetic Aspasius on book VIII; Michael of Ephesus, precursor of Psellos and Italos in the eleventh-century Byzantine revival, on books IX and X. Eustratius of Nicaea also produced an introduction to the whole work.[18]

All the commentaries are literal, having as their object the elucidation of the text sentence by sentence. But as they differ in date, so they differ in standpoint. Aspasius shows some Stoic influence (the text of book VIII in the Latin is longer and fuller than any surviving Greek one, so it is possible that Aspasius was not responsible for all that is found in Grosseteste's work). The early Anonymous shows no Christian influence, and has a very wide knowledge of Greek literature. Eustratius' contributions are very heavily imbued with Christian Neoplatonism. Those of Michael of Ephesus are truer to Peripatetic tradition.

But in the Latin West, all this went unmarked. Very little attention was paid to the commentaries as works of philosophy in their own right. Even so, their contribution to the task of assimilation was considerable, particularly initially. Put at its lowest, a reader who found Aristotle's meaning elusive in the stilted Latin rendering could refer to the explanation below, which would usually be in different words. Often the examples used by Aristotle to illustrate his point were more fully explained in the commentary (e.g. Mercken 75 and 191). Furthermore, all the Greek authors provided the West with good models for future literal commentaries, being solid, workmanlike, and untainted by possibly dangerous Arab influences. Eustratius in his introduction with its strongly Neoplatonic overtones may have played his part in lulling the fears of early Western readers by stressing that enquiry into human goodwill necessarily shed light on the supreme good:

> Ad imaginem enim Dei plasmati sumus et similitudinem, et necesse est nosmet ipsos abdolare ad archetypum (id est principalem formam vel principale exemplar), omne quod praeter naturam est repurificantes et materialem irrationabilitatem excutientes et eam quae ad mortale corpus habitudinem persequentes et propriam nobis ipsis bonam vitam coinducentes, siquidem cura est nobis incausatae causae copulari
>
> (Mercken 8).

After the pioneer work of Grosseteste and Albertus Magnus, the importance of the Greek commentaries almost certainly declined in the West. Fr. Gauthier has shown that St. Thomas Aquinas used his memory of Albertus' lectures rather than referring back to the Greeks in his *Sententia super Ethicam,*[19] and lesser men probably followed suit. Nevertheless, several important points raised by the commentators found their way into the standard Scholastic treatment of the *Ethics*. For example, when Eustratius of Nicaea amplifies Aristotle's argument on whether happiness comes immediately from God or not, he adds that the answer to this problem relates to the value of prayer (Mercken 127). Fr. Gauthier has shown that the stress on human effort in the acquisition of happiness, which is found in all thirteenth-century commentators in the West, is sometimes accompanied by statements which come perilously near to undermining the value of prayer, particularly among those commentators who cite Eustratius' argument.[20] And, as we shall see, the Anonymous commentator's treatment of expediency in book III contributes a very important element to Grosseteste's own interpretation of the *Ethics*. So, even when readily-available Latin commentaries made the Greek ones redundant for the purpose of understanding the text, they continued to have a certain amount of influence indirectly on the questions which scholars raised.

III. The Insertions

In his work on the Latin version of the Greek commentaries in 1871, Valentin Rose pointed to passages which have no Greek source.[21] Professor Harrison Thomson discovered many more such insertions, studied them, and came to the conclusion that

> There is no apparent divergence, among the manuscripts, as to these insertions. We have but a simple tradition, and it reaches back to the lifetime of Grosseteste.[22]

Most of the insertions deal with technicalities of translation, or add further information to the brief explanations of the text. Often such information comes from the Suda,[23] extracts of which Grosseteste himself translated. Therefore there seems to be very little doubt that the bishop was the author of the insertions.

At this point, the breadth of Grosseteste's aims as a transmitter becomes visible. It was not enough for him simply to provide accurate translations; he also hoped to rouse his reader's interest in Greek studies in their own right. As an example, the following passage serves well:

> Quando autem Graeci auctores enumerant quattuor virtutes principales, scilicet fortitudinem, temperantiam, iustitiam et prudentiam, semper ponunt in significationem temperantiae hoc nomen sophrosine. Quod nomen et nos hic transtulimus in nomen sobrietatis, ut qui epistolas beati Pauli transtulerunt, et librum Sapientiae, in quo scriptum est: Sobrietatem enim et sapientiam docet, et iustitiam et virtutem
>
> (Balliol 116 fol. 68[ra]).

Here we see Grosseteste, in his painstaking way, facing the fact that no Latin word exactly fits *sophrosine*, explaining that he picked the one which he believes to

be the best, and showing, in passages which would be immediately familiar to his readers, how the word is elsewhere used. In fact, this is only one of the many passages in which it seems that he is deliberately trying to enrich the philosophical vocabulary of the Latin West with common Greek terms. Perhaps the frustrations of searching for Latin equivalents had convinced him that this was the best long-term solution. In any case, he habitually keeps Greek abstract nouns in their original form, following them with a Latin explanation; for example, *philantropiam, id est amorem hominum* (Balliol 116 fol. 267[va]) and *theophilestaton, id est deo amatissimum* (Balliol 116 fol. 262[vb]).

Then, relying largely on the Suda, he imparts a wealth of Greek history. He gives an extensive biography of Sardanapalus, far more than is needed to understand Aristotle's fleeting reference (Mercken 53). And when Speusippus is mentioned, he produces every detail he knows about him:

> Erat autem Speusippus Eurymedontis filius fratruelis Platonis philosophi a Potona ipsius sorore, auditor ipsius Platonis et successor effectus Akademiae in centesima octava olympiade. Hic autem conscripsit plurima et maxime philosophica. Austerus secundum aspectum et ad summum velocis irae
>
> (Mercken 76).

This seems to be going beyond strict editorial needs in order to enlarge his readers' horizons.

Most of the insertions are linguistic or historical. But there is one which is the comment of a thirteenth-century bishop. Where the Anonymous commentator on book III says:

> Mentiri autem turpe, sed si pro utilitate non turpe. Et miscere aliene mulieri, sed si pro tyranni ablatione non turpe
>
> (Balliol 116 fol. 52[vb]).

Grosseteste expresses vehement dissent:

> Christiana autem religio fatetur et tenet non esse peccandum alicuius utilitatis consequendae vel alicuius incommodi vitandi gratia. Unde cum mentiri et aliene uxori miscere utrumque sit peccare, neutrum est aliquo modo faciendum. Unde superior doctrina non doctrina, sed error est in exemplis propositis. Non enim sunt facienda mala peccati ut eveniant bona
>
> (Balliol 116 fol. 52[vb]).

It may well be that he chose to insert this passage into the text, rather than writing a marginal note on it, because he attached special importance to it.

IV. The Marginal Notes

The insertions were meant to be incorporated into the text in all manuscripts, and in fact are so. They are almost never confused with the marginal notes.[24] This does suggest that to the author and to his early scribes there was a distinction in purpose between insertions and notes; but if so, it is not clearly discernible. Admittedly there are far more marginal notes than insertions which offer comment on the text, but equally there are many marginal notes which are philological and historical.

The marginal notes have not survived in their entirety in any known manuscript. Eton 122 (fol. 106ᵛ) refers to the *Liber episcopi*,[25] presumably the original text, but this has not been found. The number of manuscripts which carry any notes at all is fairly small—Harrison Thomson found eight—and in the three which I have used, there are considerable variations. The neat synopses of Aristotle's meaning in diagram form to be found in All Souls 84 do not appear elsewhere, while Paris Arsenal 698 reports more fully than the other two Grosseteste's arguments on the question of virtue. Eton 122 is on the whole closer to Arsenal 698 than All Souls 84, but there are still many differences. All Souls 84 also contains notes by another scholar, and therefore there is a possibility of confusion.

Many of the marginal notes reflect the same scrupulous treatment of Greek words seen in the insertions, though it is perhaps fair to say that in the notes, Grosseteste feels freer to deal with full derivations. So he analyses and traces to their origin *urbanitas* (All Souls 84 fol. 10ᵛᵇ, relating to Mercken 3), *synesis* (All Souls 84 fol. 140ᵛ, Eton 122 fol. 124ᵛ, Arsenal 698 fol. 88ᵛ) and *epeiekeia* (Arsenal 698 fol. 8ᵛ). Then he sorts out *philodoni, philopluti, philotimi,* and *philodoxi* (Eton 122 fol. 8ᵛ, relating to Mercken 43). He points out that what the Greek commentator says of the derivation of temperance is not true in Latin (Eton 122 fol. 53ʳ, Arsenal 698 fol. 40ᵛ). He defends his own translation:

> In graeco, omnis ars et omnis methodus; nos autem pro hoc nomine methodus posuimus hoc nomen doctrina, quia alii ante nos sic transtulerunt
>
> (Eton 122 fol. 2ᵛ, relating to Mercken 18).

A fair number of notes are purely explanatory. One calls attention to the Peripatetic habit of using letters of the alphabet to show the order of books in a work (Eton 122 fol. 194ʳ, Arsenal 698 fol. 136ᵛ). Another produces information about Homer and Hesiod, using a florilegium for quotations (Eton 122 fol. 46ʳ).[26] A third appears to be misleading. Where Phalaris is mentioned, Grosseteste recounts the story usually told of Procrustes, that he had a bed to which he fitted his victims, cutting off the legs of the long and stretching the short (Arsenal 698 fol. 100ᵛᵇ, Eton 122 fol. 141ᵛ).

All these notes reflect most accurately Grosseteste the scholar, trying to convey as broad a base as possible of Greek grammar, syntax, history, myth, and custom to his relatively ignorant readers. Few editors of texts have seized the opportunity for transmission so wholeheartedly.

Then there are the marginal notes which simply clarify Aristotle's argument, using the familiar vocabulary of the schools. One of the best, and the most quoted,[27] puts together the teaching of book I and book X on the nature of happiness:

> Felicitas est animae operatio secundum virtutem perfectam cum delectatione (vel non sine delectatione) in vita perfecta, optimum, perfectum, pulcherrimum, delectabilissimum, et a deo datum, possessum per virtutem et disciplinam, et studium et exercitationem, et est communissimum, et non laudabile quia supra laudem, sed honorabile et beneficabile
>
> (All Souls 84 fol. 34 *N*, Eton 122 fol. 25ʳ, Arsenal 698 fol. 18ᵛ).

The same function is served by the notes in diagram form, to be found only in the All Souls manuscript. One is particularly interesting because it introduces the distinction between *aspectus mentis* and *affectus mentis* which Grosseteste himself developed:[28]

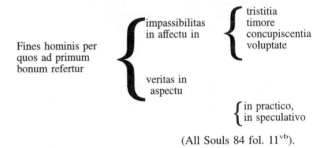

(All Souls 84 fol. 11ᵛᵇ).

Clarification of Aristotle's meaning is particularly necessary where Grosseteste feels that the Greek commentator might mislead his readers. Eustratius of Nicaea, understandably enough in a Neoplatonist, takes issue with Aristotle on the origin of ideas, regarding his treatment of the *summum bonum* as self-contradictory (Mercken 68). Grosseteste comments:

> Notandum quod Aristoteles non intendit improbare opinionem Platonis quoad hoc quod ponebat unum bonum separatum a quo dependent omnia bona. Nam et ipse Aristoteles in 12 *Metaphysicae* ponit quoddam bonum separatum a toto universo ad quod universum ordinatur, sicut exercitus ad bonum ducis. Improbat autem eam in hoc quod ponebat idem bonum separatum esse quandam idealem rationem omnium bonorum
>
> (All Souls 84 fol. 21ʳᵇ).

The same motive, to clear up possible confusion, lies behind Grosseteste's extensive treatment of voluntary and involuntary actions. This had been a problem on which earlier commentators on the *Ethica vetus* had expatiated. And, as Dom Odo Lottin has shown,[29] some of them saw a conflict here between Aristotle's teaching and the traditional Augustinian doctrines of the Church. So it is hardly surprising that the bishop should seek to make Aristotle's meaning as clear as possible by stressing the logic which lay behind it:

> Quaecumque operationes quae sunt circa consiliabilia voluntariae sunt. Virtutum autem operationes sunt circa consiliabilia; ergo virtutum operationes sunt voluntariae. Hanc autem conclusionem subiecit Aristoteles more suo, ex qua sequitur quod virtus est voluntaria et eorum quae est in nobis. Cum enim ex operationibus sint virtutes, et operationes sint voluntariae, erunt virtutes voluntariae, et a simili et malitia voluntaria, et in nobis. Quod probat sic: Quaecumque in nobis est operari, in nobis est et non operari illa; et e converso, quae in nobis est non operari, in nobis est et operari illa. Et hanc universalem propositionem insinuat per haec verba

> (All Souls 84 fol. 59ᵛ, Arsenal 698 fol. 34ᵛ).

And:

> Et quia in nobis est esse studiosos et pravos, dicere quod nullus volens est malus, mendacium; et dicere quod nullus nolens beatus, verum est. Unde sententia dicentium hoc partim est mendax, partim verax, quia verum est nullum nolentem esse beatum, et verum est malitiam esse voluntariam, quia et ipsius oppositum falsum

> (Arsenal 698 fol. 34ᵛ).

And on the next page, he again rams home Aristotle's belief in the moral responsibility of individuals, who cannot be excused for sin:

> Unde falsum supponunt opinantes peccata involuntaria, decepti per hoc quod [ipsi] non distinguunt inter necessitatem determinatam et necessitatem simpliciter, nec inter praedicationem quae per se est et praedicationem quae per accidens

> (All Souls 84 fol. 60ᵛ, Arsenal 698 fol. 35ʳ).

Here the now-familiar logical distinctions of the *Analytics* are used to sum up the teaching of the *Ethics*. Grosseteste had added nothing to Aristotle's argument, but has phrased it in a way to which it would be hard to take exception.

Another point which Grosseteste treats at length is whether good actions make good habits, or good habits come first. Again, this is a problem which had much exercised the earlier commentators on the *Ethica vetus*, particularly the anonymous author of Paris B. N. lat. 3894 A, who had seen a clash here between Aristotle's acquired virtues and Augustine's infused virtues.[30] Grosseteste simply crystalizes Aristotle's conclusion, making it quite plain that the relationship between habit and action is a reciprocal one, even in philosophical terms:

> Ostendit quod non solum ex operationibus et ab operationibus generentur et amittantur habitus, et ex operationibus deficientibus et superabundantibus corrumpantur, sed quod e converso, operationes ab habitibus fiant et sint in habitibus sicut in causis. Quod manifestatur satis evidenter a similitudine et inductione

> (All Souls 84 fol. 44ᵛ).

He then goes on to examine the objective and subjective aspects of a virtuous act, using a much tighter syllogistic form than is found in the *Ethics:*

> Res enim operatae in se consideratae dicuntur iustae et temperatae, quando in se ipsis sunt tales, quales operabitur ille qui iustus et temperatus. Nec sequitur quod qui tales operatur iam sit in se ipso talis, sicut patet ex praedictis. Non sequitur autem quod licet res operatae sint tales in se ipsis, ideo sint iuste vel temperate operatae. Et ideo non secundum perfectam significationem iuste temperate operatae. Et ideo non secundum perfectam significationem iusti et temperati iustae et temperatae sunt. Perfectum enim non solum ab esse, sed a bene esse est. Secundum perfectam igitur significationem iusti et temperati, comprehendentem in se tam esse, quam bene esse, sequitur quod qui facit iusta et temperata iam iustus et temperatus est. Secundum vero alterum modum, non sequitur

> (All Souls 84 fol. 46ʳ, Arsenal 698 fol. 26ʳ).

These two points, the freedom of human actions and the relationship between virtue and action, are treated more fully than any others in the book. That Grosseteste should have been interested in them is hardly surprising, in view of the contemporary absorption with such topics. What is remarkable about these notes is the absence of Christian influence, and the systematically logical approach. Here Grosseteste is at his most Aristotelian.

But there are two or three places where a slight Christian bias may be detectable in the notes. For example, in a note specifically ascribed to him in the All Souls manuscript, but which appears to be out of place, he says:

> Non orat quis de virtutibus et operationibus ipsius in quantum sunt in nostra potestate, sed tamen est de his oratio in quantum sunt a Deo data

> (All Souls 84 fol. 83ᵛ).

If this is authentic, its purpose seems to be to preserve a sphere for prayer in human life. Then there are two notes in which he stresses the positive contribution to human happiness which suffering can make, where Aristotle only shows that suffering cannot destroy happiness.

> Semper igitur existet felix homo et felix vir studiosus, qui ab operando secundum virtutem non desistit, et in summis adversitatibus non etiam per has impeditur ab

operari secundum virtutem. Decidet tamen per magnas adversitates a felicitate politica, quae est operatio secundum virtutes politicas. Non tamen decidet ab ipsis virtutibus politicis, cum sint habitus animi. A virtutibus autem speculativis et earum operationibus non cogunt decidere adversitates, quapropter neque a felicitate simpliciter, sed magis occasionem praestant et velut quandam compulsionem ad maiorem felicitatem

(Arsenal 698 fol. 20ᵛ).

This point is also illustrated by reference to the story of Job:

Job . . . Priamicis seu maioribus incidit infortuniis, in medio quorum summe philosophabatur. Et felicitate speculativa quae ex sola speculatione constituitur non impeditus, sed magis adiutus tribulationibus iocundabatur

(All Souls 84 fol. 170ʳ, Eton 122 fol. 151ᵛ, Arsenal 698 fol. 108ʳ).

This extension of Aristotle's words is of the same kind as another note on friendship. Where Aristotle says that a man wishes all good things for his friend, except the one supreme good, that he should become a god (Stinissen 43), because friendship between man and god cannot survive, Grosseteste adds a note which specifically separates love from friendship, making it possible for love to survive:

Non adhuc remanet amicitia, non quin Deus amet hominem et homo Deum, sed quia tam superexcellens est distantia, ut non possit omnino salvari aequalitas secundum quantitatem vel analogiam quae significatur per naturam amicitiae

(All Souls 84 fol. 180ᵛ, Eton 122 fol. 160ʳ, Arsenal 698 fol. 114ᵛ).

In this small and unimportant group of notes, then, Grosseteste's comments seem to be coloured by his religious interests; he seems to be bridging the gap between Aristotle and Christianity. Yet there are other places where those same religious interests lead the bishop sharply to take issue with the text. He returns again to the argument that circumstances may make wrongful acts less wrong, and to the Anonymous commentator's examples of lying and adultery. He declares 'secundum perfectionem vitae Christianae nullo modo mentiendum' (All Souls 84 fol. 50ᵛ, Arsenal 698 fol. 29ʳ). He then modifies this slightly, by referring to the example of Abraham who passed Sarah off as his sister, and explains that it is acceptable to hide the truth if necessary. Awareness of the Christian position does not prevent him from following Aristotle in book IV; he agrees that lying by overstatement is a worse offence than lying by understatement, though neither should happen:

Quid veretur mendacium non solum eo quod turpe, sed secundum seipsum eo quod est mendacium, laudabilis est. Talis enim non mentietur nisi alicuius evidentis

utilitatis gratia, ut scilicet propter alicuius salutem. Et cum sic mentitur, magis et libentius declinat a vero in minus, hoc est in eironeam, quam in maius, hoc est in iactantiam. Prudentius enim est in hoc declinare ad minus, eo quod superabundantiae in hac parte sunt onerosiores et peiores defectionibus. Sicut enim ipse dixit superius, ambo mendaces, scilicet eiron et iactator, sunt vituperabiles, magis autem iactator

(All Souls 84 fol. 80ʳ, Eton 122 fol. 62ᵛ, Arsenal 698 fol. 48ᵛ).

But it is characteristic that he should immediately add:

Sicut autem in superioribus diximus, secundum perfectionem Christianae religionis, nec pro salute alicuius est mentiendum

(All Souls 84 fol. 80ʳ, Eton 122 fol. 62ᵛ, Arsenal 698 fol. 48ᵛ).

Lying is the point at which Grosseteste most clearly sees the conflict between Christianity and Aristotelianism. Still, the connection between lying and adultery made by the Anonymous commentator, quoted above, rests at the back of his mind, and against Aristotle's treatment of incontinence, he puts a firmly episcopal note:

Venerea agere necessarium esse coniugato et non alio, nec illi nisi aut uxore petenti debitum aut spe prolis procreandae ad Dei servitium. Et hoc solum est commensurate venerea agere

(All Souls 84 fol. 171ʳ, Eton 122 fol. 152ʳ, Arsenal 698 fol. 108ʳ).

Christian ethics cannot be stretched to accommodate circumstances in the same way as pagan ethics.

On courage, the conflict is not so fundamental; Grosseteste takes issue not so much with the doctrine as with the examples cited. Homer's heroes are not in the fullest sense brave because they fight for love of honour or to avoid shame (Arsenal 698 fol. 37ʳ). He then makes a sweeping condemnation of other motives for death mentioned in classical literature, and contrasts the pagan suicides with those who chose to die in order to achieve some good more worthwhile than life itself—surely the Christian martyrs:

Quidam semet interficiunt ne patiantur inopiam, magis eligentes mori quam inopiae miseriam sustinere. Et quidam propter cupidinem, id est propter amorem qui dicitur eros, se interficiunt. Sicut leguntur in poetis quaedam mulieres fecisse, magis volentes mori quam talis amoris angustias et afflictiones sustinere. Quemadmodum legitur apud Vergilium in 4 Aeneidos de Didone. Sed non est fortitudo mortem eligere et assumere, ut altera transitoria quaecumque poena vitetur, sed fortitudinis est mortem assumere, ut bonum melius quam sit hac vita transitoria ex morte perveniat

(All Souls 84 fol. 62ᵛ, Eton 122 fol. 49ᵛ, Arsenal 698 fol. 37ʳ).

These notes, then, reflect the spontaneous reaction of a thirteenth-century theologian to something recognizably un-Christian. It is interesting that it is only on the doctrine of expediency and its ramifications that Grosseteste is drawn to make very positive statements. Other parts of the text which bothered later commentators, as for instance the nature of magnanimity and the apparent discounting of immortality, draw no notes at all. And elsewhere Grosseteste is at pains, as we have seen, to stress the convincing nature of Aristotle's argument and even at times to give it a slightly 'benign' interpretation.

The mere form of a marginal note leaves Grosseteste freer to express his own opinion than would the form of a commentary *per modum quaestionis*. He has no need to justify his views at length, nor to be too precise over whether he is speaking *secundum theologum or secundum philosophum*. The result is that the notes offer an illuminating glimpse into the mixed reactions inspired by the brilliant but alien Aristotelian ethics in the mind of the only Latin commentator who knew them in the original.

. . . . .

As a whole, Grosseteste's corpus of Aristotelian ethics bears witness to the breadth of his aims in producing the work. Accuracy in translating, broad scholarship in editing, logical skill in clarifying, and a combination of philosophical and theological knowledge in commenting, all play their part. And through it all there is great sensitivity to the needs of his readers. In fact, the annotations enable us to picture a typical reader, trying to cope with complex philosophical concepts in a language insufficiently flexible to convey their full meaning, bothered by strange syntax, overwhelmed by passing references to unknown figures, and unable to see in the Philosopher's subtle thought-patterns the strict lines of logic which he had expected of him. Grosseteste not only coped with the reader's problems, but also by his comments stimulated and on occasion warned him. Here was a flying start to the study of the whole of the *Ethics* in the schools. The fact that Albertus Magnus was able to produce his *quaestiones*—the model for almost all future study—within three or four years of Grosseteste's work's appearance, is in itself a tribute to the bishop's achievement.

Notes

1. Lists of the manuscripts and editions of Grosseteste's works on the Aristotelian *Ethics* are provided by S. Harrison Thomson, *The Writings of Robert Grosseteste, Bishop of Lincoln 1235-1253* (Cambridge 1940) 65f. (*Ethica*), 68-70 (Greek comms.), 85f. (*Notulae*), 88 (*Summa*). Books I-II of the translation of the *Ethics* have been edited by H. P. F. Mercken, *Aristoteles over de menselijke Volkomenheid* (Brussels 1964), Books VIII-IX by W. Stinissen, *Aristoteles over de Vriendschap* (Brussels 1963). For citations of the text of these books these editions have been used; elsewhere I have used Oxford Balliol College MS 116, a late-thirteenth or early-fourteenth-century MS, in which the text of Grosseteste's work fills fols. 1^r-266^v. For the text of Grosseteste's *Notulae* I have used the following MSS: Eton College 122 (s. XIII) fols. 1^r-221^v; Oxford All Souls College 84 (s. XIII) fols. 10^r-240^v; Paris Bibliothèque de l'Arsenal 698 (s. XIII) fols. 3^r-155^v.

2. A. Jourdain, *Recherches critiques sur l'âge et l'origine des traductions latines d'Aristote* (nouv. éd.; Paris 1843) 59-63; V. Rose, 'Über die griechischen Commentare zur Ethik des Aristoteles,' *Hermes* 5 (1871) 61-113; C. Marchesi, *L'Etica Nicomachea nella tradizione latina medievale* (Messina 1904) 57f, 62-7; L. Baur, *Die philosophischen Werke des Robert Grosseteste* (Münster i. W. 1912) 24*-29*; M. Grabmann, *Forschungen über die lateinischen Aristotelesübersetzungen des XIII. Jahrhunderts* (Münster i. W. 1916) 220-37, 251-6; P. Minges, 'Robert Grosseteste Übersetzer der Ethica Nicomachea,' *Philosophisches Jahrbuch* 32 (1919) 230-43; A. Pelzer, 'Les Versions latines des ouvrages de morale conservés sous le nom d'Aristote en usage au XIIIe siècle,' *Revue Néo-Scolastique de Philosophie* 23 (1921) 316-41, 378-400 (repr. in his: *Études d'histoire littéraire sur la scolastique médiévale* [Louvain-Paris 1964] 121-87); F. M. Powicke, 'Robert Grosseteste and the Nicomachean Ethics,' *Proceedings of the British Academy* 16 (1930) 22p.; E. Franceschini, 'Roberto Grossatesta, vescovo di Lincoln, e la sua traduzioni latine,' *Atti del Reale Istituto Veneto di scienze, lettere et arti* 93, II (1933-34) 1-138; S. H. Thomson, 'The "Notule" of Grosseteste on the "Nicomachean Ethics,"' *Proceedings of the British Academy* 19 (1934); E. Franceschini, 'Una nuova testimonianza su Roberto Grossatesta traduttore dell'Etica a Nicomaco,' *Aevum* 27 (1953) 370-1.

3. D. A. Callus, 'The Date of Grosseteste's Translations and Commentaries on Pseudo-Dionysius and the Nicomachean Ethics,' *Recherches de théologie ancienne et médiévale* 14 (1947) 186-210. A convenient summary of all this research may be found in D. A. Callus, 'Robert Grosseteste as Scholar,' *Robert Grosseteste, Scholar and Bishop* (ed. Callus; Oxford 1955) 62-5.

4. M. Grabmann, 'Das Studium der aristotelischen Ethik an der Artistenfakultät der Universität Paris

in der ersten Hälfte des 13. Jahrhunderts,' in his: *Mittelalterliches Geistesleben* III (Munich 1956) 128-41; O. Lottin, 'Saint Albert le Grand et l'Éthique à Nicomaque,' *Aus der Geisteswelt des Mittelalters: Festschrift Grabmann* (Münster i. W. 1935) 611-26; M. Grabmann, 'Der lateinische Averroismus des 13. Jahrhunderts und seine Stellung zur christlichen Weltanschauung: Mitteilungen aus ungedruckten Ethikkommentaren,' *Sb. Akad. Munich* (1931) Heft 2; R.-A. Gauthier, 'Trois commentaires "averroïstes" sur l'Éthique à Nicomaque,' *AHDLMA* [*Archives d'Histoire Doctrinale et Litteraire du Moyen–Age*] 16 (1947-48) 187-336 at 244f, 203f. Cf. D. A. Callus, 'Introduction of Aristotelian Learning to Oxford,' *Proceedings of the British Academy* 29 (1943) 229-81 at 252-5; R.-A. Gauthier and J. Y. Jolif, *L'Éthique à Nicomaque: Introduction, Traduction et Commentaire* (3 vols.; Louvain-Paris 1958-59) I 78*-85*.

5. *Metalogicon* IV 6 (ed. C. C. J. Webb [Oxford 1929] 170f.).

6. *Compendium studii theologiae* (ed. H. Rashdall [Aberdeen 1911] 37). Cf. S. D. Wingate, *The Mediaeval Latin Versions of the Aristotelian Scientific Corpus* (London 1931) 112-17.

7. *Opus tertium* 25 (ed. J. S. Brewer, *Opera quaedam hactenus inedita* I [London 1859] 91). Cf. Franceschini, 'Roberto Grossatesta' 10f.

8. Callus, 'Robert Grosseteste' 65.

9. *Ibid.* 43.

10. These texts have been edited by C. Marchesi, *L'Etica Nicomachea* Appendice l-xxvi (*Ethica vetus*), xxvii-xl (*Ethica nova*). Cf. *Aristoteles latinus Codices* I (Rome 1939) 67-71; II (Cambridge 1955) 788; *Supplementa altera* (Bruges-Paris 1961) 21.

11. Pelzer, 'Les Versions latines' 329-35.

12. *Aristoteles latinus Supplementa altera* 21.

13. *Opus maius* III 5 (ed. J. H. Bridges, *The Opus maius of Roger Bacon* I [Oxford 1897] 67-9; revd. ed. [Oxford 1900] 82). Cf. Franceschini, 'Roberto Grossatesta' 10.

14. Franceschini, 'Roberto Grossatesta.'

15. *Ibid.* 75.

16. R.-A. Gauthier and J. Y. Jolif, *L'Éthique à Nicomaque: Introduction, Traduction et Commentaire* (3 vols.; Louvain-Paris 1958-59) I 77*-81*, 85*. Cf. also the literature cited by C. H. Lohr, 'Medieval Latin Aristotle Commentaires, Authors: Johannes de Kanthi—Myngodus,' *Traditio* 27 (1971) 251-351 at 316f. s. v. Leonardus Brunus.

17. W. Kübel, 'Prolegomena,' in: *Alberti Magni Opera omnia*: XIV, 1 *Super Ethica* (Münster i. W. 1968) vi.

18. Rose, 'Über die griechischen Commentare.'

19. R.-A. Gauthier, 'Praefatio,' in: *Sancti Thomae de Aquino Opera omnia* XLVII, 1 *Sententia libri Ethicorum* (Rome 1969) 254*.

20. Gauthier, 'Trois commentaries' 277.

21. Rose, 'Über die griechischen Commentare' 109-113.

22. Thomson, 'The "Notule"' 204f.

23. Franceschini, 'Roberto Grossatesta' 63-7.

24. Thomson, 'The "Notule"' 214.

25. *Ibid.* 204.

26. On the Florilegium see Franceschini, 'Roberto Grossatesta' 67 note 2.

27. E.g. Albertus Magnus, *In I Ethicorum* tr. VII cap. 8 (ed. Borgnet VII 118f.).

28. Callus, 'Robert Grosseteste' 21.

29. O. Lottin, *Psychologie et morale aux XIIe et XIIIe siècles* I (2. éd.; Gembloux 1957) 515-19.

30. *Ibid.* 521f.

Kevin M. Purday (essay date October 1976)

SOURCE: Purday, Kevin M. "The *Diffinicio Eucariste* of Robert Grosseteste." *Journal of Theological Studies* 27, no. 2 (October 1976): 381-90.

[*In the following essay, Purday discusses the theological issues described in the* Diffinicio Eucaristie, *arguing that the work, whose authorship has been under dispute, should be attributed to Grosseteste.*]

The philosophical and scientific works of Robert Grosseteste, first chancellor of Oxford University and Bishop of Lincoln from 1235 until his death in 1253, have in recent decades received considerable attention.[1] His theological works, however, have been somewhat neglected. Edward Brown published some of the sermons and **Dicta** in 1690,[2] a few of the sermons have been individually published,[3] and there has been a recent publication of sixteen **Dicta** in translation.[4] These, together with a few other individual pieces, represent the sum total of the printed theological works of Grosseteste. Of all his theological writings, his treatise on the Eucharist is particularly interesting since it provides an insight into the state of Eucharistic theology well after the Berengarian controversy but before the full impact of Aristotelianism was felt.

As far as is known, Robert Grosseteste's treatise on the Eucharist is to be found in only one place in the manuscript collections. Professor Harrison Thomson, who made an extensive survey of all the manuscripts known to contain works of Grosseteste,[5] found that this treatise exists only in MS. B. 15. 20 of Trinity College, Cambridge, although, as he stated, it may still turn up elsewhere in an as yet unrecorded manuscript.

MS. B. 15. 20 is made up of two distinct collections of his works. They are written on vellum measuring $11\frac{3}{8}$ × $8\frac{1}{8}$ inches. At least two scribes were involved in the work and the script would point to a date somewhere in the second half of the fourteenth century. The numbering of the manuscript is by columns, two to a page, until column 742 after which the numbering is by folia with the exception of the single page immediately following column 742 which is numbered 743. The section numbered by columns contains the first collection of Grosseteste's works: the 147 *Dicta,* misnumbered 148; sixteen Sermons including the *De Confessione* and *Templum Domini.* These are all written by one hand whom we may call scribe A. Scribe B then took over and he wrote the *De Confessione,* this time as a separate treatise; the *Diffinicio Eucaristie;* and *Epistola* 128. Whereas scribe B took over from Scribe A with no gap, after letter 128, half of column 522 and the whole of columns 523 to 526 are blank. Scribe A then resumes on a new sheet of vellum on which he starts at column 527 the *De Cessacione Legalium* which is followed by the *De Decem Mandatis.* This last item in the first collection is incomplete. The second collection starts on what is marked as page 743 with twelve sermons followed by the 147 *Dicta, Excerpta Notabilia* from letters 2 to 89, and lastly a fragment of the *De Regimine Principum* not by Grosseteste at all but by Egidius Romanus.[6]

When we turn to the history of this manuscript, we are faced with an even more confusing picture although it does provide some internal evidence. The binding, which is not modern, is uninformative especially as it was re-backed, probably in the 1930s. Tracing its history in reverse chronological order, we know that it was in Trinity College Library by 1697 since it is listed as no. 284 in Bernard's catalogue of that year.[7] Edward Brown, whose notes are on the manuscript, saw it in the Library in 1688,[8] and by following up an old cataloguing number on the front paste-down, it can be ascertained that it was in the Library as C 3 29 in 1667 from the Library catalogue of that year.[9] Between that date and its previous known owner there is an unfortunate lacuna. James, when he described the manuscript,[10] was unable to trace the donor and there certainly appears to be no trace of the manuscript in the College's *Memoriale.*[11] From internal evidence the next known fact is that the manuscript was at some time in the possession of Henry, Earl of Northampton since we find his 'H. Northampton' on folio 1. This pinpoints his ownership as being between 1606, when he was created Earl, and 1614, the time of his death. James suggests that it may have been he who gave the manuscript to Trinity College,[12] but with the lack of evidence this can only be treated as a possibility. The next owner back in time was Henry Savile of Banke and the manuscript can be identified as no. 16 in his catalogue.[13] We know little about his ownership except that it must have been some time before 1614 when the subsequent owner, the Earl of Northampton, died. Henry Savile probably obtained the manuscript from Dr. John Dee whose '44' marks are on folio 1 and whose hand occurs *passim.* His ownership must date from 1583 at the latest since the manuscript is probably the one entered as no. 63 in his catalogue of that year[14] although this is by no means certain since the *De Oculo Morali* mentioned in the description is no longer in the manuscript.[15] Dr. Dee wrote in his diary that he first came to know a Mr. Savile on 3 February 1582[16] and there are further references to him in the entries for 14 June, 15 June, and 5 July 1596.[17] If, as seems highly probable, the 'Mr. Harry Savill, the antiquary'[18] is the same man who later owned the manuscript,[19] it would indicate that it came into his possession in all probability some time after the start of their acquaintance in 1582 but not earlier than 1583.

The last clue we have for the history of the manuscript is supplied by the antiquary Thomas Talbot. He saw the manuscript about the year 1580 and described it in his notebook as item 46.[20] There are two interesting but tentative conclusions that can be drawn from this. The first is that it seems likely from his description of the manuscript that the whole of Egidius' *De Regimine Principum* was still present. It is possible, therefore, that this same work was wrongly described as the *De Oculo Morali* in Dee's catalogue which does contain discrepancies. This, of course, cannot be substantiated. The more profitable, although still tentative, conclusion is that the manuscript originally came from a monastery in Yorkshire. We lack the final clue that would clinch the exact provenance, but we do know that all the manuscripts seen by Talbot were northern and that he saw them in or around York.[21] If we link this with the fact that some of Dee's manuscripts and a great number of Savile's are known to have come from Yorkshire and other northern monasteries, there is a strong likelihood that the manuscript of Grosseteste's works has the same pedigree.[22]

There must be some doubt as to Grosseteste's authorship of the treatise on the Eucharist in view of its solitary appearance in the manuscript collections and the relatively late date of the manuscript containing it. It is certainly strange that it is known to exist in only the one manuscript, but it would not be the first time that a work has been preserved in one copy and, as said before, it may still turn up elsewhere. The late date of the manuscript, at least a hundred years after Grosseteste's death, certainly casts doubt on the veracity of the ascription. Apart, however, from the fragment of the *De Regimine Principum* of Egidius Romanus which is to be found right at the end of the manuscript, all the other works are ascribed to Grosseteste and are accepted as his. The position of the treatise on the Eucharist in the middle of the first collection of works and the explicit ascription to Grosseteste both support his authorship.

Internal evidence from the treatise itself also adds weight to this view. The simple use of Greek in the opening lines to explain the meaning of *Eucharistia* not only points to Grosseteste as author, but also, if we accept his authorship, goes some way to pinpointing the dates between which the treatise was probably written, and the analogy with the sun in column 519, line 19 is reminiscent of certain passages from the *De Luce*. Accepting that Grosseteste is likely to be the author, we can ascertain from the one elementary use of Greek that this treatise must predate the time when he seriously set about learning the language, which we can place as about 1231 to 1235.[23] Such a use of Greek to explain a simple etymology bears comparison with his notes on Psalms i-lxxxix which he made before 1231.[24] At the same time it is unlikely that Grosseteste would have written the treatise prior to his return to Oxford about 1214 after his studies in Paris.[25] It seems likely, therefore, that it was written some time during the period 1214 to 1231.

The treatise may well be notes for a sermon or lecture. The ideas it expresses are frequently disjointed with the result that it often reads like a series of headings or shorthand jottings. Despite its awkwardness, however, the work is of great value. Grosseteste was familiar with several of Aristotle's works and was indeed responsible for translations and commentaries which were written either by himself or under his direction.[26] He was therefore more acquainted with the philosopher than were most people at the time. The result of his contact with Aristotle was a willingness to employ the philosopher's terms and ideas when he found them useful, while remaining firmly rooted in the school of thought which is loosely called Augustinian. The effect is an unusual mingling which at first can be confusing.

Probably the most interesting theological issue dealt with in the treatise is the manner of Christ's presence in the Eucharist and it is precisely in this area that we come across a striking use of Aristotelian terminology. Grosseteste employs the terms *substantia* and *substantialis* on six occasions[27] but their connotation is very different to that attached to them in, for example, the oath presented to Berengar at the Council of Rome in 1079.[28] The term *transsubstantiatus* is to be found in a decree promulgated by the Fourth Lateran Council in November 1215[29] and again its meaning there is quite different to that attached to its cognates by Grosseteste at about the same time. Certainly by 1273, when Thomas Aquinas was writing the *Tertia Pars* of the *Summa,* it was the common practice to assert that although some people had stated that the substances of bread and wine remained after the consecration, this position was to be avoided as heretical.[30]

Grosseteste was not always on the best of terms with the papacy thanks to his denunciations of what he considered to be various abuses of power. Despite this his reputation as a theologian remained untarnished so it is likely that his use of the term *substantia* was sufficiently orthodox in England at that time. Indeed he identifies sacramental with substantial change[31] but then goes on to say that the change takes place without affecting the substance of the bread.[32] He is well aware of the opinion held by some that the substance of the bread is changed, but he prefers to compare the Body of Christ in the Eucharist with oil in a jar: 'Just as the jar is seen and not the oil, so the bread is seen and not the body of Christ.'[33]

It is interesting that such a view could be put forward during the first quarter of the thirteenth century and not provoke any reaction. It seems likely, however, that although transubstantiation became the only orthodox method of describing the Eucharistic change on the Continent, thanks very largely to the Aristotelian influence of Paris University, English theology, dominated by the more Augustinian outlook first of Oxford and then of Cambridge as well, remained outside the mainstream of Aristotelianism and retained a more eclectic approach. Such an approach showed itself, for example, during the following century in the Eucharistic theology of Wyclif who knew and made use of the writings of both St. Augustine and Grosseteste.[34] The debt of Grosseteste himself to Augustine is considerable. Although only quoting him explicitly once in the treatise on the Eucharist, there are many passages which contain echoes of his thought which give a distinctly Augustinian tone to the whole work.

Unfortunately the text of the treatise in the manuscript is roughly written. The scribe has not been consistent with his contractions and would appear to have made some mistakes while copying. Until such time as another copy of the **Diffinicio Eucaristie** is found and a textual comparison made, the present text cannot be accepted as anything but an interim measure. With regard to the text, the following procedure has been adopted. All letters which have been omitted by means of suspension or contraction are shown in italics. Where there has been any special doubt as to the correct reading, there is a footnote to that effect. The punctuation, unsatisfactory as it often is, has been left largely in the form it is found in the manuscript. The work is made up of eighty-two lines of text preceded by two lines of heading and followed by four lines containing four hexameters. The first eight lines of column 519 are taken up by the end of the *De Confessione* and after the finish of the treatise on the Eucharist the remaining lines of column 520 are occupied by the start of *Epistola* 128.

Col. 519

line 9. *DIFFINICIO EUCARISTIE* SECUNDUM SANC-

10. TUM ROBERTUM EPISCOPUM LINCOL*NIENSEM*[35]

11. Eucaristia d*icitur* ab eu q*uod* est bonu*m et* ca-

12. ris[36] q*uod* est gr*acia* id *est* bona gracia. Unde

13. eucaristia est panis angelor*um* vel

14. contractus[37] minist*er*io angelor*um*. Panis enim

15. d*icitur* q*uia* panis est in apparencia h*oc* est ex*tra*. Caro

16. intra in existencia. Non *enim* potest vid*er*i car-

17. nalibus oculis corpus Ch*risti* glorificatu*m*. *S*ed p*otest*

18. vid*er*i q*uas*i latent*er et* non aperte in rota panis.

19. Sic*ut* sol videt*ur* nube int*er*posita in rota.[38] Item

20. sacramentu*m* eucaristie maius *est* cet*er*is sacra-

21. mentis *et* non potest p*ro*spici carnalibus o-

22. culis. Recte[39] d*icitur* sacr*amentum* q*uia* sacrat mentem

23. h*abet* ita*que* formam qua*m* sp*iritua*lit*er*[40] videm*us* signum

24. p*er* q*uod* corpus esse credimus q*uia* in ea s*ubstantia*[41] in q*ua*

25. d*ebet esse* videm*us* q*uod* no*n* possunt h*oc* sustin*er*e oculi

26. carnales. *S*ed que*ritur* a quibusdam q*uando* h*oc* sacra-

27. mentu*m* datum fuit. *R*espondetur q*uod* p*ri*die q*u*am pater-
etu*r*.[42]

28. *S*ed que*ritur* si h*ab*uit duo corp*ora* q*uando* elevatis oculis[43]

29. post agnu*m* misticu*m* panem b*e*nedicens ait h*oc*

30. est corpus meu*m*[44] cu*m* ipse Ch*ristus et* corpus Ch*risti* adhuc

31. passibile *et* corruptibile erat q*uod* tenebat. *R*espondetur

32. q*uod* Christus non h*ab*uit duo corp*ora* s*ed* de seipso dixit h*oc*

33. est corpus meu*m*. De pane vero sic intellige*ndum*

34. est h*oc* est corpus meum id *est* quociens in meam

35. co*m*memoracione*m* facietis[45] h*ab*ebitis p*ro* meo corp*ore*

36. hunc panem. It*em* eucaristia tria sunt, forma

37. panis, sacramentu*m et* res sacramenti; forma panis

38. q*uod* apparet ext*er*ius, sacr*amentum* est misticu*m* corp*us*

39. Ch*risti et* d*icitur* p*er* similitudi*n*em. Quia sic*ut* ex multis

40. granis unus panis *et* ex multis ramis effi-

41. cit*ur* vitis ita ex multis fidelib*us* constituitur

42. corpus Ch*risti*.[46] Ipse *enim* est capud *et* fideles sunt mem-

43. bra, un*de* versus: Christus *et* eterna duo sunt sed

44. carne sub una. Hic capud hoc corpus. Nos

45. quo*que* membra sum*us*. Duplex est caro Ch*risti*, mis-

46. tica *et* vera quia est sup*er*nis vera q*uia* assu*m*psit

47. in virgine maria que glorificata est sp*iritu*alis

48. res *et* sacr*amentum est vera* caro Ch*risti* qua*m* quidam come—

49. dunt sp*iritu*alit*er*. Un*de* Aug*ustinus*, ut quid paras den-

50. tem *et* ventrem. Crede *et* manducasti.[47] Et q*uo*-

51. modo p*er* verba sacrata effic*itur* corpus Ch*risti*. *R*espondetur di-

52. cim*us* q*uod* deus dedit potestatem tribus reb*us*

53. *scilicet* verbis *et* herbis *et* lapidibus pr*e*tiosis. V*er*bis

54. q*uia* quidam incantatores sunt p*er* verba. In

55. cena effic*itur* corpus d*omi*nicu*m* in cantacio*n*ibus

56. *et* verbis. It*em* oppo*n*it*ur* de h*oc* q*uod* deus dixit in

57. cena an*te* passionem discipulis, h*oc* est corpus

58. meu*m*, demo*n*strans panem *igitur* h*ab*uit duo corp*ora*

59. unu*m* q*uod* traxit de virgine alt*er*um q*uod* erat in

Col. 520

line 1. pane. *R*espondetur q*uod* ita[48] est intelligendu*m*. Dominus dixit

2. h*oc* est corpus meu*m* set dixit accipite *et* comedite

3. hoc erit pro corpore meo demonstrans seipsum non panem.

4. Item queritur quando mutatur sine substantia panis ille in corpus.

5. Respondetur quod multiplex est mutacio, scilicet artificialis, mater—

6. ialis, naturalis, accidentalis, moralis, substantialis sive sacra-

7. mentalis. Artificialis est que fit mediante

8. hominis artificio ut de feno vel felice fit nitrum

9. et ex lacte fit caseus. Materialis quando ex una materia

10. fit alia vel procreatur unde de materia ovi fit pullus

11. unde ovum materia est carnis propter quod quidam non co-

12. medunt ova videlicet fratres et maius confirmatum

13. est quam caseus. Naturalis sicut ex putrefectione grani nas-

14. citur seges unde nisi granum frumenti cadens in terram mortuum fuerit ipsum solum manet.[49]

15. Aliter quia nisi prius putrificeret non possit parere.

16. Accidentalis quando de alba re fit nigra. Moralis quando

17. aliquid prius bonus postea fit malus et rapax

18. unde Licaon[50] mutatus in lupum et remus et[51] romul-

19. us nutriti a lupa id est a meretrice quia malos homines

20. dicimus esse lupos. Substantialis sive sacramentalis est

21. miraculosa qui fit in corpore Christi in substantia panis

22. non mutata. Super hoc multiplex est oppinio; quidam

23. dicunt quod substantia panis mutatur. Sed ibi latet corpus

24. Christi sicut unguentum in vase. Vas enim videtur; un-

25. guentum non. Ita panis videtur; corpus Christi non. Notandum

26. quod de pane remanet sapor odor et forma ut

27. magis invitetur sensus hominis accipiendum. Item

28. videtur quod habet diversa corpora quia est in ista et in illa et

29. totus hic et totus ibi. Respondetur quod totus hic et totus

30. ibi. Corpus Christi informe intelligitur, illud scilicet quod in celis re-

31. sidet et quod in terra ambulat et quod in sepulcro re-

32. mansit. In omni creatura deus est per presenciam per

33. potenciam per essenciam.[52] VERSUS DE CORPORE DO-

34. MINI NOSTRI JESU CHRISTI. Panis mutatur specie

35. remanente priore. Et non est talis qualis sen-

36. titur in ore. Res occultatur qualiter quia si videretur ffor-

37. sitan horreres et manducare timeres.

Notes

1. See Servus Gieben, *Bibliographia Universa Roberti Grosseteste ab an. 1473 ad an. 1969,* in *Collectanea Franciscana,* 39 (1969), entries 127-44, 296-312, etc.

2. Edward Brown, *Fasciculus rerum expetendarum et fugiendarum* (London, 1690), ii, pp. 250-415.

3. e.g. Servus Gieben has edited the sermon *Tota Pulchra Es* in *Collectanea Franciscana,* 28 (1958), pp. 221-7; and the sermon *Ex rerum initiarum* in *Collectanea Franciscana,* 37 (1967), pp. 120-41. He has also edited the *Dictum, Omnis creatura speculum est* in *Franciscan Studies,* 24 (1964), pp. 153-8.

4. Gordon Jackson, *Dicta Lincolniensis, a selection of the Dicta Theologica of Robert Grosseteste* (Lincoln, 1972).

5. S. Harrison Thomson, *The Writings of Robert Grosseteste* (Cambridge, 1940).

6. Egidius Romanus, Giles of Rome, was the most outstanding thinker in the Order of St. Augustine's Hermits during the second half of the thirteenth century. See F. Copleston, *A History of Philosophy* (London, 1950), ii, pp. 460-5.

7. Edward Bernard, *Catalogi Librorum Manuscriptorum Angliae et Hiberniae* (Oxford, 1697), Tom. I, Part iii, p. 96, no. 284: 'Opera quaedam Rob. Grosthead Lincolniensis'.

8. There is a signed note by him in the margin of column 520. It is dated 5 April 1688.

9. *Catalogus Librorum in Bibliotheca SS. et Individuae Trinitatis Collegii Cantabrig., Anno Domini 1667* (Add. MS. a. 101), p. 10, col. 1, 'Grosthead Ep(iscop)us Lincolniensis'. There were some additions made to this catalogue on 19 October 1674 but the two lots of entries are easily distinguishable by the ink.

10. Montague Rhodes James, *The Western Manuscripts in the Library of Trinity College, Cambridge* (Cambridge, 1900), i, entry 356, pp. 483-5.

11. The *Memoriale Collegii Trinitatis* (MS. R. 17. 8) is a list of donors with some details of their gifts. It dates back to about 1614.

12. Montague Rhodes James, op. cit., p. xxii.

13. There are in fact two versions of the catalogue; British Museum MSS. Add. 35213, ff. 5-32 and Harley 1879, ff. 1-10. J. P. Gilson used the first for his edition, *The Library of Henry Savile of Banke,* Transactions of the Bibliographical Society, ix (Oct. 1906-March 1908). For entry 16, see pp. 148-9. See also A. G. Watson, *The MSS of Henry Savile of Banke* (no. 16) (Bibliographical Society, 1969), p. 20.

14. Published in *Lists of Manuscripts formerly owned by Dr. John Dee* by M. R. James, Supplement to the Bibliographical Society's Transactions no. 1, 1921. Catalogue entry 63, p. 22: 'Roberti Groshed Lincolniensis episcopi Dicta quorum initium est "Spiritus sanctus per os Salomonis" etc. Eiusd. tract. de oculo morali una cum aliis variis.' The entry is also to be found in James Orchard Halliwell, *The Private Diary of Dr. John Dee and the Catalogue of his Library and Manuscripts* (London, 1842), p. 73.

15. The *De Oculo Morali* was written by Pierre de Limoges, Petrus Lacepiera.

16. James Orchard Halliwell, op. cit., p. 18, 'Feb. 3rd. Mr. Savile, Mr. Powil the yonger, travaylors, Mr. Ottomeen his sonne, cam to be acquaynted with me'.

17. James Orchard Halliwell, op. cit., pp. 55 and 56.

18. Ibid., p. 55.

19. A. G. Watson, op. cit., p. 5, says of these references to a Henry Savile in Dr. Dee's diary that they may refer to the elder Savile, the father of the man in question. This is possible but seems the less likely of the alternatives.

20. Thomas Talbot's notebook (British Museum MS. Cotton Vespasian D. XVII) is published as an appendix in A. G. Watson's *The MSS of Henry Savile of Banke.* Item 46 of the notebook: 'Dicta Roberti Grostead Lincolniensis episcopi, notabilia ex epistolis eiusdem. Sermones eiusdem. Idem de confessione. de decem preceptis. Egidius de regimine principum'. A. G. Watson, p. 82.

21. See A. G. Watson, op. cit., Appendix II.

22. M. R. James, *Lists of Manuscripts formerly owned by Dr. John Dee,* gives the provenance of Dee's MSS. where known. For Savile's MSS., see A. G. Watson, op. cit., p. 9.

23. See Daniel A. Callus, 'Robert Grosseteste as Scholar' in *Robert Grosseteste Scholar and Bishop,* ed. D. A. Callus (Oxford, 1969), p. 37.

24. D. A. Callus, op. cit., pp. 37-8.

25. Ibid., pp. 5-7.

26. See F. Copleston, op. cit., ii, p. 228.

27. Col. 519, line 24; Col. 520, lines 4, 6, 20, 21, and 23.

28. The oath is to be found in J. P. Migne, *Patrologiae Cursus Completus, Series Latina,* CL, 411, and Denzinger-Schönmetzer, *Enchiridion Symbolorum,* Rome, 1965, no. 700. The importance of their use in the oath lies in the fact that they were inserted precisely as a touchstone of orthodoxy.

29. Denzinger 802.

30. Thomas Aquinas, *Summa Theologica,* iii. 75. 2. '. . . quidam posuerunt post consecrationem substantiam panis et vini in hoc sacramento remanere . . . haec positio vitanda est tanquam haeretica'.

31. Col. 520, lines 6 and 20.

32. Col. 520, line 21.

33. Col. 520, lines 24-5. 'Vas enim videtur; unguentum non. Ita panis videtur; corpus Christi non.'

34. See John Stacey, *Wyclif and Reform* (London, 1964), pp. 94-121.

35. I am very grateful to the Master and Fellows of Trinity College, Cambridge, for their permission to publish this treatise. I am also indebted to the Librarians of Trinity College Library for their kind help during my various searches and Mr. T. A. M. Bishop of St. John's College, Cambridge, for his valuable advice on the text.

36. The *c* of *caris* more closely resembles a *t*. The meaning, however, demands the reading given.

37. The word *contractus* is badly pinched by the decorated majuscule *E* of Eucaristia in line 11. *Contractus* seems the most likely reading.

38. *Cf.* Grosseteste, *De Luce:* 'Lux enim per se in omnem partem se ipsam diffundit, ita ut a puncto lucis sphaera lucis quamvis magna subito generetur, nisi obsistat umbrosum.' L. Baur, *Die philosophischen Werke des Robert Grosseteste, Bischofs von Lincoln* (Munich, 1912), p. 51.

39. The *R* of *Recte* here closely resembles a majuscule *S.*

40. Alternative reading: *specialiter.*

41. The scribe occasionally uses an *s* very similar to a Greek sigma. In this treatise such an *s* is to be found only twice: the *s* in the contraction of *substantia* here and in column 520, line 21. Other

examples of such an *s* written by the same scribe are to be found in the *De Confessione* (*sint;* MS. B. 15. 20, col. 507, line 44) and *Epistola* 128 (*supremo;* MS. B. 15. 20, col. 521, last line).

42. *Cf.* the prayer *Qui pridie* in the Western canons of the Mass. See A. Fortescue, *The Mass* (London, 1937), pp. 99 and 335.

43. The phrase *elevatis oculis* is a traditional part of the prayer *Qui pridie.* See A. Fortescue, op. cit., p. 335.

44. Mt. xxvi, 26; Mk. xiv, 22; Lk. xxii, 19; I Cor. xi, 24.

45. Cf. I Cor. xi, 25.

46. A common analogy started by St. Paul (I Cor. x, 17) and developed by St. Cyprian (*Epistola 62/63, De Sacramento domini calicis*) onwards.

47. St. Augustine, *In Iohannis Evangelium Tractatus,* xxv, 12. However, *dentes* and not *dentem* is the accepted reading. Cf. *Corpus Christianoru* (Turnbolt, 1954), xxxvi, p. 254.

48. Alternative reading: *intra.*

49. Jn. xii, 24.

50. An interesting allusion to Lycaon, King of Arcadia who, according to mythologists, either offered human sacrifice to the gods or served human flesh at his table. Tradition has it that he was turned into a wolf by Jupiter as a punishment for his impiety. He is mentioned, for example, by Ovid, *Metamorphoses* 1. v. 198.

51. The scribe has written not *et* but *in.* The twin nominatives and the general meaning, however, seem to require the amended reading.

52. It is possible that the treatise as such finishes here. The four hexameters which follow would therefore form a separate section.

G. R. Evans (essay date December 1983)

SOURCE: Evans, G. R. "The 'Conclusiones' of Robert Grosseteste's Commentary on the *Posterior Analytics.*" *Studi Medievali* 24, no. 2 (December 1983): 729-34.

[*In the following essay, Evans remarks on the clarity of the demonstrative style used by Grosseteste in his commentary on Aristotle's* Posterior Analytics, *noting that Grosseteste points out the* conclusiones, *or principles of demonstrative science, as they emerge from the philosopher's work.*]

In the middle of the twelfth century Thierry of Chartres made a collection of all the textbooks of the seven liberal arts of which he was able to obtain copies. He was able to include all the works of Aristotle's *Organon* except the *Posterior Analytics*[1]. A decade later John of Salisbury wrote an abrasive account of the work of the schools as he had known them twenty years earlier when he was a student at Paris, with, no doubt, additional matter which he had heard about since. He knew of the *Posterior Analytics* but he has little to say in its favour. It is a *subtilis scientia* which is incomprehensible to all but a few (*paucis ingeniis pervia*)[2]. He knows that it deals with the *ars demonstrandi,* which he considers to be the most difficult of all the techniques of formal reasoning (*prae ceteris rationibus disserendi ardua*)[3]. Hardly anyone studies it because it is useful only to mathematicians (*usus apud solos mathematicos est*), and even among mathematicians only geometers really find it helpful[4]. The only serious students of geometry John of Salisbury knows are the astronomers of Africa and Spain[5]. He does not find it difficult to account for this neglect of the *Posterior Analytics;* it seems to him a confused book, its examples not its own but borrowed from other disciplines; some say it has not been accurately translated, so difficult and full of errors and obstacles does it appear to be[6].

It is likely that John of Salisbury was able to read the *Posterior Analytics* only in James of Venice's translation[7]. By the late twelfth century Gerard of Cremona's translation from the Arabic was in circulation and the *Posterior Analytics* was beginning to be available in more than one version in England[8]. Among the scholars there whose own command of Greek[9] made it possible for him to make intelligent use of the text was Robert Grosseteste, future bishop of Lincoln, who commented on the *Posterior Analytics* about 1230[10].

Grosseteste's interest in the *Posterior Analytics* is not in itself remarkable. There was a good deal of enthusiasm for the new Aristotle in contemporary Oxford[11], and he himself commented on several scientific as well as logical works[12]. But it is notable in two ways. First, Grosseteste's impression of the *Posterior Analytics* was quite the reverse of John of Salisbury's. He finds it far from obscure. Indeed he takes a sharp pleasure in Aristotle's exposition where he finds it especially elegant. *Ecce quam elegans ordo*[1] he exchaims[13]. At each stage, with a clarity of mind which is characteristic of him, Grosseteste takes stock. He states what has been established so far and what is to be covered in the section to come. He brings out for his readers anything he thinks may not be fully apparent to them, so that they will be able to enjoy the unfolding of the argument with him: «Once these principles are grasped, the whole meaning is clear up to this point» (*His intellectis, tota littera plana est usque . . .*)[14].

In this directness of appreciation, the sheer intellectual satisfaction he finds in the work, Grosseteste is perhaps unique among his contemporaries. He descends to the level of workaday commentary from time to time, where the text requires it. When Aristotle says something less than explicitly, Grosseteste suggests a word or phrase which may be supplied, or he paraphrases, as any other commentator might do[15]. He refers to other commentaries[16]. But this detailed examination of the text is never an end in itself. He clears up a difficulty in order to stand back and consider the import of the argument as a whole. «This chapter is connected (*coniunctum*) with the second chapter in the order of the science treated here, and Aristotle demonstrates at the beginning of this chapter the fifth conclusion of this book, which immediately follows on the above-mentioned four conclusions»[17]. A comparison with Aquinas' commentary makes the difference apparent at once. Aquinas is clear, but he is methodical in the extreme in his progression through the text. He takes a portion of the text, for example Aristotle's statement that first principles ought to be known better than the conclusions which follow from them, and considers its technical implications. First principles bear the same relation to conclusions in demonstrative arguments as active causes do to their effects in the natural world. A parallel is adduced from the *Physics,* and the mode of preexisting by *actus* or by *virtus* is analysed. The result is the addition of useful cross-references and explanations, but it is an addition which takes the form of baggage[18]. Grosseteste's commentary leaves the structure of Aristotle's text bare and standing proud of the surface. Aquinas's commentary buries it in flesh.

It is this distinctive quality of Grosseteste's clarity which points to the second feature of his commentary. Grosseteste saw it, as John of Salisbury does, as a book with much that is geometrical about it. Aristotle himself suggests as much, not only in his use of a number of geometrical examples but in his systematic study of the principles of geometrical method. Grosseteste cannot have known that Euclid's *Elements* constituted the first systematic attempt in the ancient world to frame the laws of geometry. But he tries to superimpose Euclid upon Aristotle as a means of tidying and ordering what Aristotle is saying in his earlier attempt to explore some of those laws. He demonstrates the truths of the science of demonstration, following the sequence of Aristotle's argument but maintaining his own progression from *conclusio* to *conclusio.*

The demonstrative method had its admirers in the thirteenth and fourteenth century. But in the particular emphasis he places upon *conclu-* upon *conclusiones,* Grosseteste was perhaps drawing upon a fashion of the late twelfth century as well as directly upon Euclid. Sometimes self-evident principles were collected[19];

sometimes an attempt was made to derive one from another and construct something corresponding to Euclid's geometrical system for theology or some other subject[20]. Grosseteste was certainly greatly interested in the notion that such principles existed[21], to an extent which Aquinas does not match in his discussion of related topics[22].

The essence of Euclid's method is the demonstrable dependence of all more advanced principles upon those earlier shown to be either self-evident or to be themselves dependent upon self-evident first principles. Alan of Lille attempted a more or less linear progression of rules in his *Regulae Theologicae,* Nicholas of Amiens something closer to Euclid in his *De Articulis Catholicae Fidei,* in which he talks of axioms, postulates and definitions and calls his rules «theorems»[23]. Grosseteste explores the *Posterior Analytics* in search of a series of principles which he calls *conclusiones* and which he shows to follow from one another and ultimately from definitions, from self-evident truths and «suppositions» or postulates in a way which is clearly intended to be Euclidean in spirit.

«Aristotle begins to teach the science with which he deals in this book by first setting out (*ponens*) two definitions and one 'supposition', from which he concludes (*consequenter concludit*) the first conclusion of this science»[24]. The first definition is the definition of what it is to know (*quod est scire*)[25]. The supposition is that everything which is known is known by demonstration[26]. Grosseteste is able to show that this sequence possesses the elegance and inevitability which ought to characterise demonstration.

Scire, to know, is the purpose of this science, and therefore it is necessary to set it before us at the beginning, because it is proper to adapt everything that is said to the requirements of the end or purpose (*quia secundum exigentiam finis convenit omnia cetera moderari*)[27]. It is possible to define *scire* in three ways (which correspond to the three kinds of knowledge in Boethius' *De Trinitate*)[28]. Properly (*proprie*) it means the grasp of the truth (*comprehensio veritatis*) of those things which are always or most often so, contingent truths, which can in a common usage of the term, be said to be «demonstrated» (*quorum est demonstratio communiter dicta*)[29]. «More properly» (*magis proprie*) it can be defined as the grasp of the truth of those things which are always so, such as mathematical principles and conclusions[30]. «Most properly» (*maxime proprie*) it is said to be the grasp of that which is immutably so by grasping that from which it has its immutability[31]. «This is simply and most properly "to know"»[32].

Thus we come irresistibly to the supposition that everything which is known (as «to know» has now been defined), is known by demonstration. This is derived partly from the *Prior Analytics,* where Aristotle demonstrates that syllogisms bring doubtful matters to the point where they are known, says Grosseteste, and partly from grasping (*in cognoscendo*) what is meant by the term *demonstratio*. In order to grasp the point we must have a definition: «Demonstration » is a syllogism which brings about knowledge: *demonstratio est sillogismus faciens scire*[33].

At each stage Grosseteste is careful to point to the connection: *consequenter; propter explanationem precedentis et propter sequentia subiungit Aristoteles hanc diffinitionem; subnectitur hec conclusio*[34]. Following this sequence of entailment he comes to his first *conclusio;* the demonstrative science, as Aristotle says, proceeds from principles which are true, primary, immediate, prior to, better known than and causative of the conclusion[35].

Conclusion II follows directly upon Aristotle's definition of the terms «true», «primary», «immediate» and so on, and it is that we know the premisses in a demonstrative syllogism better than we know the conclusions[36]. The third conclusion again follows hard on (*hec sequitur immediate ex proxima*)[37]: no one can know the conclusion better than the premisses (*principia*) of the conclusion[38]. Grosseteste's fourth conclusion is that nothing is known more surely than those first principles: in his discussion of the point he considers the idea of necessity[39]. This brings him to his fifth *conclusio:* every demonstration is a syllogism derived from necessary principles (*omnis demonstratio est sillogismus ex necessariis*)[40]. He notes with satisfaction that it follows closely upon the four previous ones[41]. As he goes on he points out carefully for each conclusion how it follows either upon the one before or upon one or more earlier conclusions. The sequence goes on throughout Book I, with an interruption at Chapter 14, where nine conclusions are arrived at as a more or less self-contained sequence within a single chapter[42]. A fresh sequence begins in Book II and runs through to the end.

What are these *conclusiones*? Grosseteste regularly calls them: *conclusiones huius scientie,* or: *conclusiones de his que sunt de substantia huius scientie*[43]. They are the principles—the derived principles, for they are conclusions not *principia*–of the science of demonstration. There is a strong probability that Grosseteste is the author of an analysis of the *Prior Analytics* into *Regulae*[44] which suggests that even in this work which yields *principia* and *conclusiones* far less readily, Grosseteste was looking for those fundamentals which he found so intellectually satisfying in the *Posterior Analytics*. The commentary on the *Physics* was written soon after the one on the *Posterior Analytics*[45] and Grosseteste refers to his earlier work from time to time[46]. He was still thinking about the first principles proper to particular

sciences. His opening reflections—among the parts of the *Physics* commentary most often cited by later mediaeval scholars and containing thoughts on the matter which are entirely Grosseteste's own[47]—tell us that: «Since to know and to understand is arrived at from first principles, the first principles of natural things must first be determined so that they may be known and understood»[48]. There follows a consideration of the fitness of natural science to be studied in this way. In the *Posterior Analytics* commentary Grosseteste had placed the things of the natural world in Boethian manner below mathematical truths and theological truths in his hierarchy of things which can be known (*proprie, magis proprie* and *maxime proprie*)[49]. The *Physics* commentary must have seemed a natural sequel to the commentary on the *Posterior Analytics,* posing special and interesting difficulties in establishing the first principles of the science.

Grosseteste, attracted by the ideas about such principles and their relationships which he found in the *Posterior Analytics,* appears to have set out to discover the principles of the demonstrative science as they emerge from the book, and these are the *conclusiones* he gives us in his two books. Some of them, but by no means all, are stated by Aristotle. For the most part, close though he keeps to Aristotle's text, Grosseteste has to frame them for himself. He does not always succeed completely in achieving the elegance and economy he seeks. But in making the attempt he was doing something new in the history of mediaeval commentary. He was standing away from the discussion of first principles and asking himself what were the principles of those principles. The *Posterior Analytics* was intelligible to him—indeed luminously clear—as it had not been to John of Salisbury. But unlike the common run of commentators he did not stop at clarification in his exposition. He saw the science of demonstration as a whole and in its interrelated parts. With all its limitations the *Posterior Analytics* commentary is a work which approaches the *Posterior Analytics* itself in its pioneering spirit and in its originality of conception. It can be set beside Grosseteste's other great perception: that the realities of the natural world are there to be learned from, that not all knowledge worth having is intuitive, the shift of emphasis which makes him one or the founders of mediaeval science[50]. The problem of the nature of certainty lies at the heart of Grosseteste's commentary, and it is in this area of the problem of knowledge that these two great insights come together in his thought.

Notes

1. On THIERRY OF CHARTRES' *Heptateuch* see E. JEAUNEAU, *Prologus in Eptateuchon,* in *Medieaeval Studies,* XVI (1954), pp. 171-175.

2. JOHN OF SALISBURY, *Metalogicon,* ed. C. C. J. WEBB, Oxford, 1929, IV. 6, p. 170.30-31.

3. Ibid., p. 172.1-2.

4. Ibid., p. 172.3-5.

5. C. HASKINS, *Studies in the History of Mediaeval Science,* Cambridge, Mass., 1927, p. 4 ff., cfr. PETER THE VENERABLE, *Epistola De Translatione Alcorani,* P. L., CLXXXIX, col. 650.

6. WEBB., ed. cit., p. 172-9-19. Compare Alexander Neckam's comments for a more friendly view of the *Posterior Analytics. De Naturis Rerum,* ed. T. WRIGHT, London, 1863, pp. 37 and 293.

7. See L. MINIO-PALUELLO, *Jacobus Veneticus Graecus, Canonist and Translator of Aristotle* in *Traditio,* VIII (1952), pp. 265-304 (also in the same author's *Opuscula: the Latin Aristotle,* Amsterdam, 1972, p. 191 ff.).

8. See ROBERT GROSSETESTE, *Commentarius in Posteriorum Analyticorum libros,* ed. P. ROSSI, Florence, 1981, pp. 12-15 for a bibliography and discussion on the verses circulating and available in England up to the early thirteenth century. The commentaries are edited by L. MINIO-PALUELLO and B. G. DOD in *Aristoteles Latinus,* IV.1-4, Bruges/Paris, 1968). Grosseteste seems to have worked from the James of Venice version, *ibid.,* p. xvii. John of Salisbury himself mentions a *nova translatio, Metalogicon,* ed. cit., II.20, p. 111.

9. On Grosseteste's life and works see *Robert Grosseteste: Essays in Commemoration of the Seventh Centery of his Death,* ed. P. A. CALLUS, Oxford, 1955, especially pp. 33-37 on Grosseteste's study of Greek, and see, too, D. A. CALLUS, *The Introduction of Arabic Learning to Oxford,* in *Proceedings of the British Academy,* XXIX (1943), pp. 229-281; R. C. DALES, *Robert Grosseteste's Scientific Works* in *Isis,* LII (1961), pp. 381-402, and for a full bibliography, S. GIEBEN, *Bibliographia Universa Roberti Grosseteste,* in *Colictanea Franciscana,* XXXIX (1969), pp. 362-418.

10. On the dating of the *Posterior Analytics* commentary in relation to the *Physics especially,* see R. C. DALES' edition of the *Commentarius in VIII Libros Physicorum Aristotelis,* Colorado, 1963, p. XV.

11. CALLUS, *The Introduction* cit., pp. 229-281.

12. On the chronology of Grosseteste's works, see R. C. DALES, *Grosseteste's, Scientific Worlds* cit., pp. 381-402.

13. Ed. cit., p. 110.31, on 73^e 21.

14. Ed. cit., p. 116.163.

15. Ed. cit., p. 112.79, on 73^e 35.

16. Ed. cit., p. 114.111 on 73 ^{e} 5.

17. Ed. cit., p. 109.1.

18. AQUINAS, *In Posteriorum Analyticorum Expositio,* ed. R. SPIAZZI, Rome, 1955, p. 156 (Lectio III.22, 1).

19. C. Baeumker edits one of these in *Das pseudo-hermetische «Buch der vierundzwanzig Meister»,* in *Beiträge zur Geschichte der Philosophie des Mittelalters,* XXV (1927), pp. 194-214.

20. See my article, *Boethian and Euclidean Axiomatic Method in the Teleology of the Later Twelfth Century,* in *Archives internationales d'histoire des sciences,* CV (1980), pp. 36-52. Grosseteste himself refers explicitly to Euclid, e.g., ed. cit., pp. 163-4.

21. See for example, ed. cit., I. 14, pp. 212.27-213.218 ff., on the knowledge of universals and particulars in the divine mind and in human minds.

22. Cfr. Aquinas on a key passage in BOETHIUS *De Trinitate, Expositio super Librum Boethii De Trinitate,* ed. B. DECKER, Leiden, 1959, p. 173-901, Q.V., aII-IV, where there are no references to the *Posterior analytics.*

23. Art. cit. supra, note 20.

24. Ed. cit., p. 99.2 ff.

25. Ed. cit., p. 99.5.

26. Ed. cit., p. 100.38-39.

27. Ed. cit., p. 99.7-8.

28. BOETHIUS *De Trinitate,* in *Theological Tractates,* ed. E. STEWARL, E. K. RAND, S. J. TESTER, London, 1973, reprint), p. 8.

29. Ed. cit., p. 99.11 ff.

30. Ed. cit., p. 99.14 ff.

31. Ed. cit., p. 99.19-20.

32. Ed. cit., p. 99-23-24.

33. Ed. cit., p. 100.38-39.

34. Ed. cit., p. 100.29-30.

35. Ed. cit., p. 100.40-2, 51^{e}23-5.

36. Ed. cit., p. 102.67.

37. Ed. cit., p. 102.78.

38. Ed. cit., p. 102.77.

39. Ed. cit., p. 103.103 ff., 72ᵉ-1-2.

40. Ed. cit., p. 109.4-5: *omnis demonstratio est syllo-gismus ex necessariis.*

41. Ed. cit., p. 109.3-4.

42. Ed. cit., p. 210.163-211.194.

43. E. g., ed. cit., p. 231.48; p. 234.117, *Conclusiones* XIX and XX of Book II.

44. S. H. THOMSON, *The Writings of Robert Gros-seteste,* Cambridge, 1940, p. 87.

45. DALES, *Commentarius in VIII libros Physicorum* cit., p. xv.

46. Ibid., p. xiv.

47. Ibid., p. xxiv-xxv.

48. Ibid., p. 1: «cum scire et intelligere adquirantur ex principiis, ut sciantur et intelligantur naturalia, primo determinanda sunt naturalium principia».

49. See supra, note 29.

50. For a study, see A. CROMBIE, *Robert Grosseteste and the Origins of Experimental Science,* Oxford, 1953.

Steven P. Marrone (essay date 1983)

SOURCE: Marrone, Steven P. "Truth in Simple Knowledge according to Grosseteste's Early Works." In *William of Auvergne and Robert Grosseteste*, pp. 144-56. Princeton, N. J.: Princeton University Press, 1983.

[*In the following essay, Marrone examines Grosseteste's early theological treatises, arguing that they offer insights into Grosseteste's later views, particularly regarding his ideas about truth as a simple quality, and the scientific ideal of knowledge as it evolved in his work.*]

The theological treaties of Grosseteste's early years represented a less elaborate and complete investigation of the problem of truth than was to be found in his commentaries on Aristotle, but more important than this, they struck a philosophical tone quite different from that of his later works. It should hardly be surprising that this was the case, since as much as fifteen years may have intervened between the composition of the two sets of works, and they were years of great intellectual ferment both at Oxford and at the University of Paris. Nevertheless, the shift in Grosseteste's views has been virtually overlooked in modern expositions of his thought.[1] Its importance for a study of this sort cannot be stressed too much.

The key to the difference between the two sets of works is that only in the latter did Grosseteste come to espouse the scientific ideal of knowledge and to take an interest in formulating an explicit set of criteria upon which to establish it. His earlier writings were free of these concerns, and in them he could speculate about truth without any of the constraints they imposed. Among other things this meant that in his theological treatises he could pass over the whole question of the truth of complex knowledge—knowledge that lay at the heart of science—with only a comment. For Grosseteste's views on the nature of complex truth it is necessary to turn to his later works, where he indeed devoted most of his attention to that aspect of the problem. The case of truth in simple cognition was a different matter, and Grosseteste gave a full account of his ideas on this aspect of the problem of truth in both his early and his later writings. An examination of these accounts reveals that in the years between the composition of the two sets of works, Grosseteste radically altered his vision of the nature of simple truth and man's knowledge of it. In order to understand him it is necessary to keep these two accounts separate and to realize that for all the points of comparison between them, they represent the two poles of a development that was of critical importance in his thought.

Grosseteste, like William of Auvergne, followed Aristotle in holding that of the two types of knowledge, simple and complex, only the latter could be qualified by the notions of truth and falsehood. He maintained that the truth of knowledge was a measure of the value of a proposition or statement and not of a simple idea.[2] Indeed, it made no sense to talk of the truth of a simple concept or to speak of a true idea. Every concept or idea referred to something, whether that thing itself truly existed or not, and so each concept or idea had its own validity outside of any judgmental considerations. This was not to say that the problem of truth had nothing to do with the problem of simple cognition, and Grosseteste, again like William of Auvergne, made a large place for the idea of truth on that cognitive level. The kind of truth that entered into simple knowledge did not attach to the knowledge itself but rather to the object understood; it belonged in the extramental world as something toward which the intellect was directed.

For his primary definition of simple truth in the early treatise **De veritate,** Grosseteste went back to Anselm, who in his own *De veritate* had maintained that truth was first and foremost a rightness (*rectitudo*).[3] The adoption of such a definition shows how traditional Grosseteste's thought still was when he wrote his theological treatises and contrasts sharply with the identification of simple truth and being that would appear later in William of Auvergne's *Magisterium divinale* or in Grosseteste's own mature speculation on truth. Grosseteste glossed Anselm's definition by explaining that being right involved conforming to a rule that revealed what ought to be.[4] In the case of simple truth the rule was the divine word itself, and so the truth of things could be defined quite plainly as their conformity to God's eternal word.[5] In more precise terms, this meant conforming to an idea (*ratio*) in the mind of God, for the divine ideas were the exemplars or standards by which His word created all things in the universe.[6]

By casting his definition the way he did Grosseteste made it clear that simple truth was an attribute of created things. Defined as a relation attached to real objects in the world, it was involved in human cognition only as it became known. Thus, while it made no sense to speak of the truth of simple knowledge, it was perfectly reasonable to talk about knowledge of the simple truth, and so to explain the place of truth in simple cognition was not so much a matter of the logical analysis of the form of thought or expression as a question of noetics. It was necessary to describe the process of simple cognition by which simple truth was perceived.

Grosseteste realized this and devoted a section of his *De veritate* to a discussion of just such noetic concerns. It is, however, difficult to make an absolutely unambiguous analysis of this work. Although Grosseteste spoke as if he were giving a perfectly straightforward exposition of a single epistemological procedure, in fact he offered two different descriptions of the way the mind came to know simple truth, each one dependent on a model not fully compatible with the other.

The terms of the formal definition of simple truth in *De veritate* made it necessary to explain human knowledge of such truth as dependent on some sort of Godly intervention, and it was only natural that Grosseteste should have turned to the traditional way of explaining such a process, the notion of divine illumination. As he said at the beginning of his discussion: "Since the truth of each thing is its conformity to its exemplar (*ratio*) in the eternal Word, it is clear that every created truth is perceived only in the light of the Highest Truth."[7] Yet even though Grosseteste introduced his subject by referring to God's role in terms of light, he cast his first account of knowledge of simple truth in language that did not make use of this image. Instead, he built this account on a model derived directly from the formal definition, by which truth was the conformity of thing to idea. He maintained that one could perceive the conformity of one thing to another only if one could see that other thing to which the first object should conform. Likewise, one could not know a thing as right (*rectificata*) or know its rightness (*rectitudo*) unless one knew the rule or standard (*regula*) by which it was judged to be so. In the case of simple truth, of course, the rule or idea lay in God Himself, so that knowledge

of the truth depended on seeing the true object and at the same time having a mental vision of the divine idea that made it true. By comparing one to the other the mind came to perceive truth itself.[8]

Immediately after this first description Grosseteste offered a second one. It was not, however, completely congruent with what he had just said. In this second account he returned to the image of light.[9] As he characterized things, there were three elements, besides the mind, that had to do with the process he was examining: they were the light of divine Truth (*lux summae veritatis*), created truth (*creata veritas*), and *id, quod est*. The light of divine Truth needs no explanation. The created truth Grosseteste had in mind was the simple truth in the world he had been speaking of all along, that special relationship between a created thing and its divine exemplar. This is evident from the fact that he substituted for the term "created truth" the term "truth of the thing" (*veritas rei*), which he later defined as a conformity along exactly the same lines as his formal definition of simple truth.[10] *Id, quod est* was, as has been shown above, a term principally associated with a much-debated text from the works of Boethius. As Boethius had used it, the term referred to the complete substance of a real thing, and Grosseteste held to essentially the same definition, alternating the term with an equivalent form, "the true thing" (*res vera*).[11]

The way these three elements cooperated in knowledge of the simple truth was relatively uncomplicated. Drawing on a phrase of Augustine's, Grosseteste maintained that created truth revealed the substance of a thing (*id, quod est*), which was to say the existing substance (*res vera*).[12] It could not, however, do this on its own, without relying on the Highest Truth, God Himself. Grosseteste compared the workings of the three basic elements in the process to that of light, color, and body in sensory vision. Just as color indicated the colored body, but only in the presence of light, so created truth revealed an existing substance, but only in the light of the First Truth.[13] Another way Grosseteste described the process was to say that the divine Truth illuminated created truth, which then showed the mind the true thing.[14] In any case primary efficacy in revealing existing substance lay with God, the First Truth; created truth was the secondary and more immediate cause. In Grosseteste's words: "The light of the Highest Truth alone reveals substance (*id, quod est*) first and completely on its own, just as light alone reveals bodies. Yet through this light the truth of a thing (*veritas rei*) also reveals substance (*id, quod est*), just as color reveals bodies through the light of the sun."[15]

From this simple exposition alone it is clear how different Grosseteste's two descriptions appear when subjected to close analysis. He not only employed a different model in each case, he even changed the basic nature of the process he was trying to explain. In the first of the two cases, the true thing along with the Highest Truth made it possible for the mind to see simple truth in the world. In the second, it was created simple truth, along with the Highest Truth, that revealed the true thing. The role of instrument and final object had been reversed.

Yet surely Grosseteste intended his two accounts to be compatible, and he had no reason to believe they would be read in any other way. The whole tradition surrounding the notion of divine illumination, going back at least as far as Augustine, had contained a similar imprecision concerning the exact role of the divinity, providing an umbrella wide enough to cover both of the descriptions Grosseteste gave. In fact, Augustine's language about truth and human knowledge of it would never have survived the kind of critical scrutiny being applied here. His ideas had not been intended to meet the scientific standards that began to be demanded in the schools of the West over the course of the thirteenth century. But the ambivalent theoretical model Grosseteste used not only had a long history, it also had strengths, ones deriving in large part from the ambivalence itself. The body of images associated with divine illumination, because of its two-faced nature, could serve two somewhat different functions at the same time. On the one hand, those elements emphasizing a comparison of exemplars explained how the formal definition of truth as a rectitude could be applied to the objects of human intellection. On the other hand, the literal image of a divine light shining over the intellective process, in some way generating it, made more plausible the role of divine intervention in the business of understanding, although at the expense of some formal clarity. The fact that each specific explanation had its own drawbacks makes it easier to understand why no one was in any hurry to settle the difference between the two for the sake of consistency alone. Grosseteste's language did, therefore, purchase a certain philosophical advantage, if at the cost of imprecision and ambivalence. So long as he was not concerned with close analysis, he could use this language without hesitation.

The way Grosseteste drew on the strengths and skirted the weaknesses is clear enough. His first description of the knowledge of simple truth focused in the nature of the objects of that knowledge—that is, on the exact referential conditions that had to obtain. According to his formal definition, simple truth in the world was the conformity of a real thing to its divine exemplar. In order for the mind to recognize this truth, therefore, it had to make a comparison between the two elements, and this implied that it had to be able in some way to see them both. The first description translated this

requirement literally into the terms of cognitive object. In effect, it stipulated that there were two referents in human knowledge of the simple truth, one a created thing and the other a divine idea.

Yet there was a problem with Grosseteste's first description of knowledge of simple truth, and it stemmed from the very fact that he stuck so literally to the terms of his formal definition. By insisting that there was a divine object as well as a created one in human knowledge of the truth, Grosseteste implied that knowing the truth involved in some way knowing or seeing God in the literal sense of having some vision of the ideas in His mind.[16] Common sense alone seemed to require as much, since if one were going to compare a standard with the object it was designed to measure, then one had to see the standard in itself. Any less straightforward access to the standard, in this case to the divine essence, would have appeared to make a mockery of the formal definition of simple truth. The problem was that on every other occasion throughout his early works, Grosseteste maintained that in the world the mind could not have any direct intellectual vision of the divine essence or the exemplary forms inhering in it.[17] To say differently would come dangerously close to bringing the beatific vision down to earth.

It was probably Grosseteste's appreciation of this shortcoming of his first model that prompted him to give it so little attention and to turn instead to his second model, which offered an escape from his dilemma. In lieu of analyzing the exact makeup of the object of knowledge of the simple truth, this model focused more on the process by which such knowledge was attained. The key lay in drawing an analogy between sensory sight and intellectual vision. The eyes were capable of seeing only in an atmosphere of light, and the same was true, on a more spiritual level, when it came to the sight of the mind. The point was that for most cases of vision, whether sensible or intellectual, there were two sorts of agent, one proximate and the other primary and fundamental. In sensory vision both color and light were necessary for the eyes to see an object. On the level of the intellect these two agents were replaced by simple truth in the world and the light of God's Truth, and both were necessary for human knowledge. Although truth in the world might be the proximate cause of knowledge of true things, it could work only if aided by the Highest Truth.

This second description avoided the difficulties of the first. God retained a fundamental role in the process of knowing the truth, but since this role was to act as a light in which perception of the true object took place, it was possible to say that man could know the truth without having any direct knowledge of God or the exemplars in His mind. Grosseteste explained how this was so by following out his analogy with sensory vision:

> Just as the weak eyes of the body cannot see colored bodies except as they are enveloped in the light of the sun, and nevertheless they do not see the light of the sun in itself but only as it envelops colored bodies, so the weak eyes of the mind do not perceive true things except in the light of the Highest Truth, even though they are not able to perceive this Highest Truth in itself but only in a kind of conjunction with those true things it envelops.[18]

The crucial distinction lay between seeing the First Truth in itself and seeing other things in its light. Since it was only in the latter way that the mind perceived true objects and hence the truth, knowing the simple truth did not imply directly and consciously knowing God's Truth itself. Nevertheless, Grosseteste insisted that the terms of this process, even if they allowed knowledge of the truth without a direct vision of God, did show that whoever recognized the truth, whether he was the worst of sinners, in some meager way made contact with God.[19] The fact that few men realized this was no argument that it was not so. Just as someone who spent his time looking only at colored things in the world would not know of the sun until he raised his eyes to see it or was told about it by someone else, so the mind might spend its worldly days discovering truths without ever knowing it was depending on God's light.[20] Since only the blessed could see God in Himself, and only the wise understood the process of divine illumination, most men never had any occasion to know that their perception of the truth in some way participated in the Highest Truth. In short, Grossseteste's second model allowed him in his early works to maintain God's role in the everyday cognition of simple truth without sacrificing the uniqueness of the blessed vision.

Yet there were problems with the second model, too. While the first model risked attributing a power to the human mind that might be theologically embarrassing, the second obscured the formal nature of truth itself. To a great extent the difficulty rested on an ambiguity. The second account was based, after all, on an analogy drawn with sensible cognition. Unfortunately, the analogy did not exactly fit the terms to which it was meant to apply. It was easy enough to compare the sun's light with God's Truth, given the traditions of Neoplatonic thought, and a corporeal substance with a true object; but it was practically impossible to see how color had anything in common with the created truth. Comparing the latter two elements did, to be sure, drive home the lesson that created truth was the secondary agent in knowledge of true things, but it only made it harder to

understand what created truth actually was. Up to this point in *De veritate*, Grosseteste had consistently described created truth as a relation, but if it were to be comparable to color, it would have to be described as something like a simple quality of the object to which it adhered. Whatever this colorlike truth was, it could hardly have come very close to the formal definition Grosseteste gave in this work. What sense would it have made to say that God's light had to shine on truth, which in turn revealed the real object, if that truth were in fact the relation between God and thing? Of course, the visual analogy could have been read as a loose metaphor for the process explained by means of the first model as a comparing of exemplars, but that would have then denuded it of its value and contradicted Grosseteste's explicit statement that it was because God was involved in human cognition as a light, and not as a direct object, that the mind could be said to have some access to Him in the world.

In short, the terms of Grosseteste's second description threatened to undermine his formal definition of simple truth as a conformity, implying instead that it was a simple objective quality that revealed existing things to the mind. It is interesting to note that on a few occasions in *De veritate* Grosseteste actually described the truth of things as something simple. It was, so he maintained, the same as the being (*esse*) or *id, quod est* of a thing—that is to say, its existing reality as an object in the world.[21] In this way he conflated the last two elements of his second description: created truth and the true thing. The logical manifestation of this simple truth was the thing's definition, and in fact it was even possible to say, although only in a manner of speaking, that the truth of a thing was the definition itself.[22] Whichever way one described it, truth according to this new and secondary notion was something complete in itself and did not formally involve a comparison between thing and divine idea. To this extent Grosseteste anticipated the position that William of Auvergne would take in his *Magisterium divinale* and that he himself would fully adopt in his *Commentary on the Posterior Analytics.*

The view of truth as a simple quality or substance was, however, an exception to the rule in Grosseteste's early works. For the most part he adhered to his original formal definition, whereby simple truth consisted in the conformity of a thing to its divine exemplar. And he continued to see this definition as a perfectly logical part of the traditional notion of divine illumination. The ambiguities of this tradition—so interesting to the modern historian concerned with the development of the notion of truth in general and of God's role in human cognition in particular—although in some way already apparent in his struggles to explain how the process worked, did not yet bother him sufficiently to drive him to look for a new solution. This alone shows how much he still held to a traditional, uncritical view of the problem and how far he was from the scientific aspirations of his later years. Grosseteste's allegiance in his early works lay firmly with a definition of simple truth that explicitly implicated God and with an explanation of the process by which this truth was known that gave the divine Truth a fundamental role. The central theme around which all his discussions of truth in the theological treatises turned was that God was instrumental to man's knowledge of simple truth.

Notes

1. The major works on Grosseteste's philosophy are Ludwig Baur, *Die Philosophie des Robert Grosseteste, Bischofs von Lincoln,* Beiträge XVIII, 4-6 (Münster, 1917); Crombie, *Robert Grosseteste;* and Callus, "Robert Grosseteste as Scholar." (An interesting critique of Crombie can be found in Alexandre Koyré, "The Origins of Modern Science: A New Interpretation," *Diogenes* 16 [1956], 1-22.) Three more recent publications of considerable importance for the subject of the present study are Bruce S. Eastwood, "Medieval Empiricism: The Case of Grosseteste's Optics," *Speculum* 43 (1968), 306-21; William A. Wallace, *Causality and Scientific Explanation,* I: Medieval and Early Classical Science (Ann Arbor, 1972); and Eileen F. Serene, "Robert Grosseteste on Induction and Demonstrative Science," *Synthese* 40 (1979), 97-115. On Grosseteste's thought in general, see also Ludwig Baur, "Das Licht in der Naturphilosophie des Robert Grosseteste," in *Festgabe zum 70. Geburtstag Georg Freiherrn von Hertling* (Freiburg im Br., 1931), pp. 41-55; Dorothea E. Sharp, *Franciscan Philosophy at Oxford in the Thirteenth Century* (Oxford, 1930), pp. 7-46; Alistair C. Crombie, "Robert Grosseteste on the Logic of Science," *Actes du XIᵉ Congrès International de Philosophie,* Brussels, 22-26 August 1953 (Amsterdam, 1953), XII, 171-73; and "Grosseteste's Position in the History of Science," in *Robert Grosseteste, Scholar and Bishop,* pp. 98-120; and Rossi, "Un contributo." Other studies of Grosseteste's thought, in particular his epistemology, are Johannes Beumer, "Robert Grosseteste von Lincoln der angebliche Begründer der Franziskanerschule," *Franziskanische Studien* 57 (1975), 183-95; Lawrence E. Lynch, "The Doctrine of Divine Ideas and Illumination in Robert Grosseteste, Bishop of Lindoln," *Mediaeval Studies* 3 (1941), 161-73; V. Miano, "La teoria della conoscenza in Roberto Grossatesta," *Giornale di Metafisica* 9 (1954), 60-88; and Robert J. Palma, "Robert Grosseteste's Understanding of Truth," *The Irish Theological Quarterly* 42 (1975), 300-306; and "Grosseteste's Ordering of *Scien-*

tia," *The New Scholasticism* 50 (1976), 447-63. An interesting recent work that interprets Grosseteste differently from the present study, particularly on the issue of divine illumination, is James McEvoy, "La connaissance intellectuelle selon Robert Grosseteste," *Revue Philosophique de Louvain* 75 (1977), 5-48.

2. *De veritate (Die philosophischen Werke des Robert Grosseteste Grosseteste, Bischof von Lincoln Ed Ludwig Baur. Beiträge IX. Münster 1912, p. 134.)* Grosseteste's language here echoes that of Anselm in *De veritate,* 2 (Schmitt, ed., Anselm, *Opera Omnia,* I, 1–87, Edinburgh, 1946, p. 177).

3. "Possumus igitur, nisi fallor, definire quia veritas est rectitudo mente sola perceptibilis." Anselm, *De veritate,* 11 (Schmitt, ed., *Opera omnia,* I, 191). Grosseteste quoted this passage in his *De veritate (Phil. Werke,* p. 135).

4. *De veritate (Phil. Werke,* pp. 134-35).

5. *De veritate (Phil. Werke,* p. 135). Grosseteste's account was consonant with the ideas Anselm himself propounded in *De veritate,* 7.

6. See *De veritate (Phil Werke,* pp. 137 and 139).

7. *De veritate (Phil. Werke,* p. 137).

8. Ibid.

9. Ibid.

10. The term *"veritas rei"* appears as an equivalent for *"creata veritas"* in *De veritate (Phil. Werke,* p. 138). In *De veritate (Phil. Werke,* p. 139), Grosseteste defined *veritas rei* as the conformity of a thing to divine idea. It is essentially the same as the *veritas essentiae rerum* or *veritas rerum* Anselm spoke of in his *De veritate,* 7. See above, Chapter II, n. 14.

11. Grosseteste cited several occasions where Augustine had spoken of *id, quod est.* (See below, nn. 12 and 21.) Augustine's meaning was, however, perfectly compatible with the way the term was later used by Boethius.

12. "Veritas igitur etiam creata ostendit id, quod est. . . ." *De veritate (Phil. Werke,* p. 137). Grosseteste attributed this formula to Augustine (see *De veritate [Phil. Werke,* p. 132]). It came from *De vera religione,* 36.

13. *De veritate (Phil. Werke,* pp. 137 and 138).

14. *De veritate (Phil. Werke,* p. 137).

15. *De veritate (Phil. Werke,* pp. 137-38).

16. When describing knowledge of the truth in this first way, Grosseteste was explicit about the need to see the exemplar itself: "Aut qualiter cognosce-

tur, quod res est, ut esse debet, nisi videatur ratio, secundum quam sic esse debet?" *De veritate* (*Phil. Werke*, p. 137). It was a commonplace of medieval thought that the divine ideas were one with the divine essence, so that seeing the ideas inevitably implied seeing at least some aspect of God's essence.

17. At the end of *De veritate*, Grosseteste stated that the mind's eye, when it was healthy, had the power to see God in Himself, and in Him all the things he had created (*De veritate* [*Phil. Werke*, p. 142]). This was the same sort of vision or knowledge which, in his *Quaestiones theologicae*, Grosseteste had reserved for God alone (see Callus, "Summa theologiae," p. 195). The only way to reconcile these two passages is to assume, as must surely be the case, that when in *De veritate* Grosseteste spoke of the healthy mind's eye he was referring to the intellect before the Fall or after the Resurrection, so that when in the *Quaestiones* he limited knowledge of the divine exemplars to God alone he was simply contrasting God's powers with those man could exercise here on earth.

18. *De veritate* (*Phil. Werke*, p. 138). Note how close Grosseteste's metaphor was to Augustine's in the *Soliloquia*, I, 6, 16, quoted above in the general Introduction, n. 14.

19. *De veritate* (*Phil. Werke*, p. 138).

20. Ibid.

21. *De veritate* (*Phil. Werke*, p. 141). Compare *De veritate* (*Phil. Werke*, p. 135). As an authority for his identification of truth and *id, quod est,* Grosseteste cited Augustine. In his *Soliloquia*, II, 5, 8 (PL, 32, 889), Augustine did define truth as *id, quod est,* although he offered other, incompatible definitions for truth in the same work. He was, however, not interested in the definitions as such but rather hoped that while juggling several different notions of truth at the same time he could ultimately make the point that truth was inextinguishable and that therefore the soul, the seat of truth, was immortal.

Another medieval source that defined truth similarly—as *quod est res*—was the Latin translation of Isaac Israeli's *Book of Definitions* (J. T. Muckle, ed., "Isaac Israeli: *Liber de definicionibus,*" *Archives d'Histoire Doctrinale et Littéraire du Moyen Age*, 12-13 [1937-38], 322). See also the discussion in Altmann and Stern, *Isaac Israeli*, pp. 58-59.

By identifying truth (*veritas*) with *id, quod est,* Grosseteste broke down the distinction he otherwise maintained in *De veritate* between *veritas rei*

and *id, quod est* or *res vera*. He thereby momentarily abandoned Anselm's definition of simple truth. What is more, when he made *esse* equivalent to *id, quod est,* he forsook the meaning Boethius had given to these two terms, much in the way William of Auvergne would do. Grosseteste's language was, however, more explicit than William's, who never went so far as to declare in so many words that *esse* and *id, quod est* could be seen as the same thing.

22. *De veritate* (*Phil. Werke*, p. 142).

M. de Jonge (essay date April 1991)

SOURCE: De Jonge, M. "Robert Grosseteste and the *Testaments of the Twelve Patriarchs*." *Journal of Theological Studies* 42, Part I (April 1991): 115-25.

[*In the following essay, de Jonge explores the reasons for Grosseteste's interest in the* Testament of the Twelve Patriarchs, *also speculating on why the text was considered so significant by his contemporaries.*]

I. INTRODUCTION

This article is devoted to the introduction of the *Testaments of the Twelve Patriarchs* in the West by Robert Grosseteste, who had it brought from Greece to England and translated it into Latin in 1242.

Modern scholars number the *Testaments of the Twelve Patriarchs* among the pseudepigrapha of the Old Testament, and generally regard them as a Jewish writing with substantial Christian interpolations. In his dissertation and in subsequent writings, the present author has argued that much more than interpolation is involved.[1] In 1953 he treated the *Testaments* as a Christian writing, but since then he has adopted a more cautious attitude.[2] At the least this is a case of thoroughgoing redaction, and it is impossible to reconstruct the original Jewish Testaments (if they existed at all) by means of literary criticism. The text as we have it is a Christian text, probably dating from the end of the second century CE.

In the course of a succession of years I have, in cooperation with H. J. de Jonge, Th. Korteweg, and H. W. Hollander, worked on a critical edition of the Testaments which was completed in 1978.[3] Three years earlier, a volume appeared with preliminary studies and other contributions by the collaborators in the critical edition.[4] Both this edition and the earlier volume demonstrate the difficulty, if not the impossibility, of establishing the text which the first readers had before them. From the early Church we have only two references to the *Testaments* (no verbatim quotations, unfortunately): by Origen (preserved only in Latin) and Jerome. The oldest Greek manuscript we have is Cambridge Univ. Library Ff 1. 24, fos. 203^r-261^v, dating from the end of the tenth century—the one brought to the West at the instigation of Robert Grosseteste, for which reason we shall return to it later. By far the most important among the ancient translations is the Armenian, of which no less than fifty-one manuscripts are known. Until recently, the oldest manuscripts we knew dated from 1269 and 1282-3, but recently M. E. Stone of Jerusalem, a specialist in the field of Armenian pseudepigrapha, has published the text of fragments of the Armenian Testaments found on fos. 251^r-252^v of Erevan Matenadaran MS 2679, going back to 981.[5] Dr Stone is of the opinion that the new find proves that the Armenian translation must have been made in the beginning of the ninth century at the latest. Personally, he thinks it stems from the eighth century, leaving open the possibility of an even earlier date in view of the nature of the Armenian used.

The question of the dating of the Armenian translation is of importance because its Greek *Vorlage* belongs to the collection of manuscripts called 'family II' which is clearly distinct from 'family I' consisting of only two manuscripts (*b* = Cambridge Univ. Libr. Ff 1. 24 and *k* = Venice, Bibl. Marc. Codex Gr. Z 494 (= 331), fos. 263^r-264^v from the thirteenth century, containing excerpts only). H. J. de Jonge,[6] in an important study of the variants between these two families, has demonstrated that in thirteen cases we very probably have to do with a different transliteration of Greek majuscules. This, in his opinion, means that when in the ninth century Greek texts written in uncials were copied in minuscule script, the *Testaments* were transcribed twice. In other words, the extant text-tradition does not go back to *one* ninth- or tenth-century minuscule codex copied from an uncial codex lost since then, but to two uncial codices which will have been copied from one common archetype at an earlier date. This archetype in any case goes back beyond the ninth century; it is obviously impossible to establish the date of origin more precisely. In theory, anything may have happened between the second and, say, the eighth centuries, but that eludes our observation for want of reliable older data.

Before engaging in literary and historical criticism of the *Testaments,* one has first to pay due attention to textual criticism; and textual criticism presupposes a thorough study of the textual history which, in its turn, leads to the study of the history of the codices in which the Testaments have been transmitted. Indeed H. J. de Jonge, in the volume of studies of 1975, has devoted two articles to the history of *b* and *k* and one to the marginal annotations in MS. *d* = Cod. Vatic. Gr. 1238,

fos. 350^r-379^v, dating from the end of the twelfth century.[7] In the following the present author gratefully falls back on these studies, as well as on his contribution 'Die Patriarchentestamente von Roger Bacon bis Richard Simon'.[8]

II. ROBERT GROSSETESTE'S INVOLVEMENT WITH THE *TESTAMENTS*

Very little is known about the first part of Robert Grosseteste's life. He was born around 1170 in a place near Bury St Edmunds in Suffolk. He was of humble descent, and it is not clear where he spent his school-days. R. W. Southern, author of the most recent biography of Grosseteste,[9] considers it probable that he received his entire education in England. In any case he developed into an independent and universal scholar; he was an influential teacher at Oxford from 1225 until 1235, and a forceful and conscientious bishop of the very extensive diocese of Lincoln from 1235 until 1253.

On his arrival at Oxford Grosseteste, after long years of scientific study, applied himself to theology. In the years that followed he taught and wrote about the Bible (writing, for example, a commentary on the first hundred Psalms) and studied the Fathers. Being deeply interested in the original Greek sources, he applied himself to the study of Greek.[10] It is quite possible that he was taught Greek by John of Basingstoke, who in his youth had lived in Athens for a considerable period, and who in time to come was to play an important part in the acquisition of the Greek codex of the *Testaments of the Twelve Patriarchs* by Robert Grosseteste which is now preserved at Cambridge. Grosseteste knew him well and had great confidence in him; indeed only a few months after his accession to office as bishop of Lincoln he made John archdeacon of Leicester (an office Grosseteste himself had held from 1229 until 1232).

Matthew Paris, in his Chronicle,[11] tells us that John of Basingstoke informed Robert, the bishop of Lincoln, that during his student days in Athens he had heard from Greek experts about all sorts of writings unknown to Latin readers, among them the *Testaments of the Twelve Patriarchs*. The bishop, says Matthew Paris, thereupon sent messengers to Athens to locate and secure these *Testaments;* on acquiring them he translated them from Greek into Latin. Earlier in his chronicle it is said that this happened in or around the year 1242, and that Grosseteste was assisted in this work by magister Nicholaus Graecus, a priest attached to the abbey of St Albans.[12] We find much the same information in the colophon that already at a very early date is found in manuscripts of the Latin translation of the *Testaments*.[13] It does not mention John of Basingstoke, though we do read how the bishop sent 'diligentissimos exploratores' to Greece, and urged them to get hold of this writing at any cost. This colophon also mentions the year 1242 and the co-operation of Nicholas the Greek.

The information to be gained from Matthew Paris and the contents of the colophon are closely connected. Matthew Paris, a monk of St Albans, reports on matters he has personally witnessed: he must have known Nicholas the Greek. In view of the date of the oldest manuscript containing the colophon, this must have been added at a very early date—possibly by Nicholas himself.[14] How important a part he played in the realization of the translation is not clear. Matthew Paris and the colophon speak about *coadiuvare* and *iuvare* respectively. Both sources also emphasize that the translation was done thoroughly and meticulously ('plene et evidenter' and 'evidenter et fideliter' respectively, and 'de verbo in verbum'). It has often been remarked that the translation of the *Testaments* is less literal and easier to read than other translations for which Grosseteste was responsbile. D. A. Callus ascribed this to a considerable contribution by Nicholas,[15] but C. A. Dionisotti has given a more convincing explanation: the other translations were intended for scholars and therefore were profusely provided with footnotes and comments. Not so the *Testaments:*

> It seems to me significant that this translation has no glosses or notes, no learned apparatus. It was not meant to be studied by scholars, but to be read as widely as possible. And it succeeded: seventy-nine copies survive today; no doubt there were many more. Are we really entitled to assume that Grosseteste himself could not adapt his skills to different purposes?[16]

The number of manuscripts of Grosseteste's translation is indeed remarkably great. In the list in S. H. Thomson's *The Writings of Robert Grosseteste* we find no less than eight manuscripts from the middle of the thirteenth century and six from the second half of that century. H. J. de Jonge, in a supplementary list of manuscripts, mentions yet another thirteenth-century manuscript.[17] Obviously Grosseteste's initiative found considerable response. This is also evidenced by a number of other facts. Vincent of Beauvais, in his *Speculum Historiale* which appeared in 1253, incorporated excerpts from the *Testaments* because of the extremely clear and superbly beautiful prophecies concerning Christ, 'quas nuper transtulit magister robertus grossum caput, lincolniensis episcopus de greco in latinum'.[18] Bonaventura, in his commentary on the *Sententiae* of Petrus Lombardus written *ca.* 1250-1252, in a particular passage refers to Gen. 28: 1-5 with the words: 'et illud [viz. the annihilation of the seed of Canaan in the land] clare insinuatur in textu et clarius in quodam libello, qui dicitur Testamentum Patriarcharum'.[19] Finally, there are two references to the *Testaments* in Roger Bacon's *Opus Maius,* written *ca.* 1266-1268.[20]

Why was Robert Grosseteste at such great pains to acquire the *Testaments* from Greece and then to translate them? And why the overwhelming response?

III. *The Testaments of the Twelve Patriarchs in the View of Robert Grosseteste and His Contemporaries*

In his article 'La bibliothèque de Michel Choniatès' H. J. de Jonge considers it possible that Grosseteste's translation of the *Testaments* should be connected with plans to convert English Jews.[21] In 'Die Patriarchentestamente von Roger Bacon bis Richard Simon' he is more positive:

> Die lateinische Übersetzung der Testamente hatte also apologetische und missionarische Ziele, und stand im Dienst einer Campagne zur Bekehrung der Juden in England. Den Grund dafür ersehen wir aus den Ausführungen von Roger Bacon.[22]

In the article first mentioned reference is made to L. M. Friedman, *Robert Grosseteste and the Jews.*[23] This author adduces three arguments. First, he quotes Matthew Paris's statement that Grosseteste translated the *Testaments* 'ad majorem Judaeorum confusionem' (iv. 233) and infers from this that the bishop wrote it 'as a missionary tract for the Jews' (p. 8). This is a misrepresentation. Grosseteste followed an apologetic course, and wanted to demonstrate conclusively that the Jews held wrong views. In the passage mentioned Matthew Paris speaks about 'illum gloriosum tractatum' and says that the translation was made 'ad robur fidei Christianae et ad majorem Judaeorum confusionem'.[24]

Friedman's second argument concerns the construction of a 'domus conversorum', a house for converted Jews, in Oxford in 1231, in the period in which Grosseteste taught at Oxford. In the same year Grosseteste wrote a letter to Margaret de Quincy, the widow of the Earl of Winchester, who wanted to admit Jews who had been driven away from Leicester, where Grosseteste was archdeacon (pp. 11-12).[25]

Friedman's third argument is that in the same period Grosseteste started on his writing *De cessatione legalium* which he (along with earlier authors) considered as a writing that could be used in disputations with the Jews with a view to converting them to Christianity (p. 21).

Friedman's last two arguments also cannot be accepted. In the introduction to the new edition of *De cessatione legalium*[26] R. C. Dales and E. B. King remark that this writing is characteristically intended for scholars and stands in a scholarly tradition: 'Grosseteste's interest in this subject was undoubtedly stimulated by the extensive debate on the Mosaic law current in the schools of late twelfth- and early thirteenth-century Europe' (p. xii).[27] Dales and King further quote Matthew Paris's information about two houses founded by King Henry III in London and Oxford for converted Jews[28] and draw the conclusion that it was a matter of protecting those who were converted in order to preclude their reverting to their old belief rather than a matter of missionary activity. It seems, moreover, that in that period it was not unusual for Christians to become Jews.

There remains the letter Grosseteste wrote to the Countess of Winchester. This should obviously be read within the context of contemporary views, but even so R. W. Southern is right in remarking 'it does not show Grosseteste in an attractive light'.[29] Any effort to convert the Jews is out of the question: not until the end of time will the Jewish people be converted to Christ (Rom. 11: 25, 26), and only then will the nation's exile come to an end. In the meantime Christian princes will have to follow a strict course: on the one hand they have to prevent Jews from being killed, on the other they have to see to it that the Jews with their usurious practices will not oppress others. Let them earn their meagre wages with hard physical labour! Princes should not show favours to Jews and in no way profit from their usurious practices. Just as Abel is a prefiguration of Christ, Cain is a prototype of the Jew: he is damned but nobody is free to kill him; he has to work hard and will be a vagrant and fugitive on earth. Grosseteste concludes: 'Secundum hanc itaque Domini praelocutionem maledictus est populus ille dum perstat in infidelitate et blasphemia.'

It is interesting, however, that he infers the prohibition to kill Jews from Ps. 58: 12 (in the Vulgate),[30] quoting St Augustine's interpretation.[31] This author has stated that the Jews are not to be killed because they 'portant codices nostros, de quibus prophetatus et promissus est nobis Christus'. Grosseteste continues: 'Ac per hoc sunt testes fidei Christianae contra infidelitatem Paganorum.'

This last passage is of interest because it fits in with what we read in the colophon to Grosseteste's translation of the *Testaments* and in Matthew Paris. These texts repeatedly emphasize the many and unambiguous prophecies concerning Christ found in the *Testaments.* Thus, for instance, we read at the end of the colophon (already partly quoted above) that thanks to Grosseteste's translation 'sic luculentae prophetiae, quae in hoc scripto, luce clarius, coruscant, in majorem confusionem Judaeorum et omnium haereticorum et inimicorum Ecclesiae gloriosius prorumpant'.[32] Matthew Paris also speaks about the 'manifestas, quae in eisdem patent de Christo prophetias'.[33] In the same connection he says of the *Testaments:* 'quae constant esse de substantia Bibliothecae.' In the Middle Ages, the term 'bibliotheca' is often used to denote the Bible.[34] Mat-

thew Paris, then, wants to make clear that it was an established fact that the *Testaments* contained genuine biblical material. Of course they did not belong to the canonical books, but as to their substance they were on a par with these writings. Really very old witnesses were speaking in the *Testaments,* and consequently their testimony concerning Christ was reliable and convincing.

But how was it that these important witnesses had remained unknown for so long a time? The Jews kept them hidden for the very reason that they spoke in such unequivocally clear terms about Christ. In this connection Matthew Paris and the colophon mention the 'invidia Judaeorum' and the machinations of the 'Judaeorum antiquorum malitia'. That is the reason why many wise and learned men of the Church never quote the *Testaments.* We owe it to the Greeks, 'omnium scriptorum diligentissimi investigatores',[35] that this writing was translated from Hebrew into Greek[36] and preserved over a long period, so that now, thanks to Robert Grosseteste, it could shed its glorious light.

Robert Grosseteste as well as his contemporaries (as is evidenced by their response) clearly considered the *Testaments of the Twelve Patriarchs* to be of utmost importance. The patriarchs' testimony to Christ ranked with that in the writings of the Old Testament. Everybody reading the *Testaments* could read in unmistakable terms that the Jews were wrong in rejecting Christ. Their efforts to suppress these prophecies had proved vain in the end; their very own ancestors now turned out to have been witnesses of Christ. On the basis of the remarks in the colophon and Matthew Paris's chronicle we have no choice but to say that the Testaments were not used for missionary purposes but to make clear, once and for all, to Jews (and probably also to those sympathizing with Judaism) as well as to all who opposed orthodoxy, that salvation can only be expected from Christ and the true Church which obeys Holy Scripture.

For Vincent of Beauvais, whose *Speculum historiale* appeared immediately following the translation of the *Testaments,* it was specifically the prophecies concerning Christ that occasioned him to incorporate a number of suitable fragments from the *Testaments* in his book. In a number of manuscripts of the *Testaments* we find written in the margin *peri tou christou,* put there by anonymous readers. They are especially plentiful in *d* (*inter alia* Latin ones borrowed from the *Speculum historiale*). *Peri tou christou* was added close on thirty times by the writer of the manuscript written in Calabria in 1195.[37] It is also obvious that the excerpts in *k* were selected primarily because of their Christological interest.

In conclusion, we have to discuss at greater length Roger Bacon's view of the *Testaments* on which, as remarked above, H. J. de Jonge's 'Die Patriarchentestamente von Roger Bacon bis Richard Simon' offers some highly interesting observations. Bacon speaks about the *Testaments* in two places. In Pars II, cap. XVI he emphasizes that the philosophers are dependent on the patriarchs and the prophets, whose books are recorded in Holy Scripture. These patriarchs and prophets have also written other books which are not incorporated in the canon but which nevertheless 'sancti et sapientes Graeci et Latini usi sunt a principio ecclesiae'. Indeed did not Judas in his letter (VV. 14-15) already acknowledge the authority of Enoch, later followed by St Augustine in his *De Civitate Dei*? In this connection also the *Testaments of the Twelve Patriarchs* are brought up:

> Nam praeter caeteros libros liber de testamentis patriarcharum [. . .] quae de Christo adimpleta sunt. Quilibet enim patriarcha in [Illegible Text] praedicavit filiis suis et tribui suae, et praedixit eis ea quae de Christo tenenda sunt, sicut manifestum ex libro illo.[38]

Here, again, the emphasis is on the prophecies concerning Christ; they are reliable because they originated with the patriarchs. True, these words had not been incorporated in the canonical books, but their authority had been acknowledged of old by holy and wise men.

In Pars VII, pars IV Bacon returns to this subject:

> Item in libro duodecim Patriarcharum docetur manifestissime de Christo. Nam quilibet Patriarcha docebat tribum suam certificationem de Christo, sacut adimpletum est.[39]

If one would object that those writings are apocryphal, in other words that their authorship is not established, one should bear in mind: 'hoc non tollit veritatem quia libri hi recipiuntur a Graecis, Latinis et Judaeis.'

This does not only apply to the *Testaments* but also to a great many other writings. Lack of authenticity does not preclude authority; we may safely rely on the *Testaments of the Twelve Patriarchs* and other writings because their authority has been acknowledged by wise and reliable men.

All this has been lucidly expounded in H. J. de Jonge's article. We may now add that Bacon in the two passages mentioned works out what Matthew Paris indicates with the words 'quae constant esse de substantia Bibliothecae'. Whoever exactly may have been the author of the *Testaments,* the words of the sons of Jacob they contain are as true and reliable as the testimonies of Christ contained in Holy Scripture.

Notes

1. See *The Testaments of the Twelve Patriarchs. A Study of their Text, Composition and Origin* (Assen, 1953).

2. See, e.g., H. W. Hollander and M. de Jonge, *The Testaments of the Twelve Patriarchs. A Commentary,* SVTP 8 (Leiden, 1985), 82-5 and 'The Testaments of the Twelve Patriarchs: Christian and Jewish', *NTT* 39 (1985), 265-75.

3. *The Testaments of the Twelve Patriarchs. A Critical Edition of the Greek text,* PVTG i. 2 (Leiden, 1978). This 'editio maior' followed on the 'editio minima' *Testamenta XII Patriarcharum edited according to Cambridge University Library MS Ff 1.24, Fol 203a-216b,* PVTG i (Leiden, 1964, 2nd edn. 1970).

4. M. de Jonge (ed.), *Studies on the Testaments of the Twelve Patriarchs. Text and Interpretation,* SVTP 3 (Leiden 1975).

5. 'The *Epitome* of the Testaments of the Twelve Patriarchs', *Revue des Études Arméniennes, NS* 20 (1986-7), 69-107.

6. See his 'The earliest traceable stage of the textual tradition of the Testaments of the Twelve Patriarchs', in M. de Jonge (ed.), *Studies,* 63-86.

7. See, resp., 'La bibliothèque de Michel Choniatès et la tradition occidentale des Testaments des XII Patriarches', in *Studies,* 97-106; 'Additional notes on the history of MSS. Venice Bibl. Marc. Gr. 494 (*k*) and Cambridge Univ. Libr. Ff. 1.24 (*b*)', 107-15 and 'Les fragments marginaux dans le MS. *d* des Testaments des XII Patriarches', 87-95.

8. In *Studies,* 3-42. I have been so fortunate as to be able to profit from the written as well as from the oral tradition in writing this article: H. J. de Jonge kindly discussed some problems in connection with this article with me.

9. R. W. Southern, *Robert Grosseteste* (Oxford 1986, 2nd edn. 1988). The book carries the programmatic subtitle 'The Growth of an English Mind in Medieval Europe'.

10. See on this R. W. Southern, *Robert Grosseteste,* 181-6 and A. C. Dionisotti, 'On the Greek Studies of Robert Grosseteste' in A. C. Dionisotti, Anthony Grafton and Jill Kraye (eds.), *The Uses of Greek and Latin. Historical Essays,* Warburg Institute Surveys and Texts 16 (London, 1988), 19-39.

11. H. R. Luard (ed.), *Matthaei Parisiensis, Monachi Sancti Albani, Chronica Majora,* 7 vols. (London 1872-83), esp. vol. v, p. 285. On his time in Athens see vol. v, pp. 286-7. Both passages are discussed in detail in H. J. de Jonge, 'La bibliothèque de Michel Choniatès'. He argues that the manuscript of Grosseteste was in the library of Michel Choniatès until 1204.

12. *Chronica Majora* iv. 232-3. Among the events in 1242 he mentions: 'Ipsis quoque temporibus, epis-

copus Lincolniensis Robertus, vir in Latino et Graeco peritissimus, Testamenta duodecim Patriarcharum de Graeco fideli interpretatione transtulit in Latinum.'

13. Already in London B. M. Royal 4.D.VII, fos. 232ᶜ-246ᶜ, 248ᶜ-249ᵃ; see S. H. Thomson, *The Writings of Robert Grosseteste Bishop of Lincoln 1235-1253* (Cambridge, 1940), 42-4 (esp. 43). The text is to be found in, for instance, the printed edition Hagenau 1532.

14. H. J. de Jonge assumes that M. Paris was dependent on the text of the colophon (see 'Die Patriarchentestamente von Roger Bacon bis Richard Simon', cq. n. 7; 'Les fragments marginaux dans le MS *d*, 93 n. 1).

15. See his 'Robert Grosseteste as Scholar' in D. A. Callus (ed.), *Robert Grosseteste. Scholar and Bishop* (Oxford, 1955), 1-69, esp. 55-6.

16. 'On the Greek Studies of Robert Grosseteste', 29.

17. 'Les fragments marginaux dans le MS *d*', 91 n. 1. In the two lists mentioned we find eighty-two manuscripts.

18. See on this H. J. de Jonge, 'Les fragments marginaux dans le MS *d*', *passim*. For the introduction to the fragments see p. 93 n. 1. For the dating see D. A. Callus, 'Robert Grosseteste as Scholar', 61.

19. See *Commentaria in Quattuor Libros Sententiarum* IV = Opera Omnia IV (ed. Quaracchi, 1899). Dist. XXIX, Qu. III, p. 703. For the dating see E. W. Platzeck, 'Bonaventura', *L. Th.K.* 2, 582-4.

20. On Bacon see in more detail H. J. de Jonge, 'Die Patriarchentestamente von Roger Bacon bis Richard Simon', esp. 4-10.

21. Pp. 100–01.

22. Pp. 9-10.

23. Cambridge (Mass.), 1934.

24. See in the colophon: 'ad robur fidei christianae' and: 'in maiorem confusionem Judaeorum et omnium haereticorum et inimicorum Ecclesiae.' See also D. A. Callus, 'Robert Grosseteste as Scholar', 61: 'a powerful apologia in favour of the Christian religion against the Jews.'

25. H. R. Luard (ed.), *Roberti Grosseteste Episcopi quondam Lincolniensis Epistolae* (London, 1861), Epistola V (33-8). English translation in Friedman, pp. 12-18.

26. Robert Grosseteste, *De Cessatione Legalium,* ed. R. C. Dales and E. B. King (London 1986) (= Auctores Britannici Medii Aevi VII), see esp. pp. ix-xv.

27. In this, Dales and King follow Beryl Smalley, 'The Biblical Scholar' in D. A. Callus (ed.), *Robert Grosseteste, Scholar and Bishop,* 70-97, esp. 81: 'Grosseteste wrote for the student rather than the missionary.'

28. *Chronica Majora,* iii, 262-3 (see p. x).

29. *Robert Grosseteste,* 245. See the entire section 'The Jews of Leicester', 244-9. Cf. also Letter CVII, probably written in 1244 to the archdeacons of his diocese (ed. Luard, 317-18), in which Grosseteste categorically enjoins: 'et cohabitationem Christianorum cum Judaeis quantum vobis possibile est, impedire curetis.' In passing it may be pointed out that Grosseteste, in Epistola cxxiv to Henry III (ed. Luard, 348-51; probably from 1245), dealing with the relationship between royal and priestly power, very appositely quotes T. Jud. 21: 2-4. See also R. W. Southern, *Robert Grosseteste,* 268-9.

30. 'Deus ostendit mihi super inimicos meos, ne occidas eos, ne quando obliviscantur populi mei. Disperge eos in virtute tua, et depone eos, protector meus, Domine.' In the argumentation the emphasis is on 'ne occidas' as well as on 'depone' (Grosseteste stresses that the text does definitely not say 'exalta').

31. S. Aurelii Augustini, *Enarrationes in Psalmos,* vol. 2 (CCL 39; *Aurelii Augustini Opera* 10. 2) (Turnhout 1956), Sermo 1. 22 (p. 744): 'Ipsi habent codices de quibus prophetatus est Christus, et nos tenemus Christum. Et si quando forte aliquis paganus dubitaverit, cum ei dixerimus prophetias de Christo, quarum evidentiam obstupescit, et admirans putaverit a nobis esse conscriptas, de codicibus Iudaeorum probamus quia hoc tanto ante praedictum est.'

32. Cf. also in the beginning 'propter evidentissimas et manifestissimas, ac crebras de Christo prophetias, quae in illis scribuntur', and further on: '. . . ut memoriam lucidissimarum prophetiarum, ad robur fidei Christianae perpetuaret.'

33. *Chronica Majora* v. 285. Cf. in iv. 232: 'Propter manifestas prophetias de Salvator in eis contentas.'

34. See the dictionaries of Du Cange, J. F. Niermeyer, and A. Blaise, and the *Mittellateinisches Wörterbuch* s.v.; see also R. E. Latham, *Dictionary of Medieval Latin from British Sources* i (London, 1975), 196c.

35. So Matthew Paris, iv. 232. The colophon here speaks of 'veterum scripturanum exploratores diligentissimi'.

36. This is an inevitable assumption if one considers this writing a collection of the words of the sons

of Jacob. It does not necessarily mean that people were aware of the existence of Hebrew Testaments.

37. See H. J. de Jonge, 'Les fragments marginaux dans le MS *d*', 88.

38. J. H. Bridges (ed.), *The 'Opus Majus' of Roger Bacon,* suppl. vol. (London, 1900), 71-2.

39. Ed. J. H. Bridges, vol. ii (Oxford, 1897), 391.

James McEvoy (essay date January-December 1991)

SOURCE: McEvoy, James. "Robert Grosseteste on the Ten Commandments." *Recherches de Theologie Ancienne et Medievale* 58 (January-December 1991): 167-205.

[*In the following essay, McEvoy argues that Grosseteste's popular treatise on the decalogue was written for a well-educated clerical public; that its most notable doctrinal theme is Christian love; and that it comments favorably on the structure of feudal society while also pointing out and castigating abuses within that system.*]

The treatise of Grosseteste on the decalogue bore in medieval times a number of titles: *de decem preceptis; de mandatis; summa de decem mandatis; de dileccione et decem mandatis; libellus de decem preceptis decalogi*[1]. No such doubt, however, or variation of opinion affected its authenticity, and no scribe attributed the treatise to any but *Lincolniensis*. Such connoisseurs of Grosseteste as Gascoigne and Wyclif were quite certain of its attribution, about which indeed no doubt has ever been entertained: the bibliographers, beginning with Boston of Bury, all knew it as a writing of Grosseteste.

If we are to judge by the surviving witnesses to the text and by their owners, the treatise on the decalogue was read less in the century of its composition than in the subsequent period up to c.1500; almost all of the manuscripts date from the fourteenth and fifteenth centuries, and of the known references made to it the earliest is that of Boston of Bury (early fourteenth century). No less than twenty-four surviving manuscripts attest the popularity of the work, but it is significant for the shape of Grosseteste's theological influence that all the owners and readers who can be identified were Englishmen: Master John Malberthorpe; Nicolas Kempston; M. Medekoke; Thomas Gascoigne (who owned a surviving copy, viz Oxford *ms.Lincoln College lat.105*); Robert Flemmyng, Bishop of Lincoln (who inherited Gascoigne's copy); John, Lord Lumley; William Gray; Simon Greene; William Horman; Henry Howard, Earl

of Northampton; Thomas Nevile, and William and Gregory Webb[2]. Wyclif quoted from it in his *De Mandatis Divinis* and his *Opus Evangelicum.* Only two of the manuscripts are held in continental libraries, and one of these, the Douai *ms B.M.451,* belonged to William Hyde, who was professor at the English College there c.1650, while the other, *Vat.lat.4367,* was copied in England. As in the case of *De Cessatione Legalium,* all the evidence suggests that some of the most important theological and pastoral writings of Grosseteste reached an English readership only[3].

The first printed edition of *DXM* has been published by the editors who have so recently given us the *DCL* (*De Cessatione Legalium*), Professors Dales and King. It will be warmly welcomed by all students of Grosseteste and of his age. The importance of this edition as a contribution to the study of Grosseteste warrants a close examination of the purpose and achievement of the treatise itself[4].

DATE OF COMPOSITION AND RELATIONSHIP TO
OTHER WRITINGS

Thomson was prepared to place the composition of *DXM* [*De Decem Mandatis*] firmly between 1225 and 1230, but if he is right (which is by no means clear) then he is so entirely for the wrong reasons[5]. The editors plump for 1230 or shortly after then. They argue that the pastoral purpose of the book fits well with Grosseteste's period of pastoral experience after his priestly ordination, which presumably took place in 1225 that in *DXM* themes later to be developed in *DCL* and *Hexaëmeron* appear in a preliminary draft; and that Grosseteste's knowledge of Greek is in its early stages only, so that the work was written not much later than 1230, 'the date of the beginning of his interest in the Greek language' (p. vii).

Now it appears to me that *DXM* allows us no grounds at all for judging Grosseteste's knowledge of the Greek language. The single quotation from Chrysostom (p. 2) is taken from a work, the *Homilies on Matthew,* which was known and widely used in the Latin translation of Anianus from late patristic times onwards; it is too short to allow us to say whether Grosseteste was correcting Anianus from a manuscript. The brief reference to Aristotle is to the *De Generatione Animalium,* but this is not of much help since the translation cannot be pinpointed in time; it survives in only one manuscript and is anonymous[6]. The single reference to the LXX ('*in greca autem translacione*', p. 84) may well have been taken from a Latin source such as Jerome, who frequently refers to it in his exegetical writings. Does this negative evidence allow us to conclude that Grosseteste 'had certainly not made much progress in his Greek studies at the time he wrote' (p. vii)? I do not think so. For one thing, some students of Grosseteste will certainly feel that this argument assumes too much about our knowledge of the stages of his acquisition of Greek, a subject on which the traditional position (as represented especially by Thomson) is currently undergoing revision[7]; and for another (to take a parallel case), Grosseteste revealed comparatively little use of Greek even in *DCL* (after 1230; I am inclined to place its composition towards the end of his teaching career, or even at the beginning of his episcopate, c.1235)[8], even though he had already shown considerable and refined knowledge of the language when writing what he called his *exposicio parvula* on Galatians, a work which was certainly composed prior to the *DCL,* as two back-references in the latter clearly attest[9].

DXM is silent concerning its own place in Grosseteste's output; as a general rule he was extremely sparing of cross-references. I cannot find any external evidence, such as the use of recently-translated sources, which would help to place it in time. However, there is the theme of the work itself, which fits in with a major preoccupation of his mature theological teaching, namely, the interrelationship of the two testaments and the originality of the New Testament teaching. If we view the treatise in this light we can relate it quite directly to two other important works, the *Expositio in Epistolam ad Galatas* and the *De Cessatione Legalium,* and we can regard the three as a sort of trilogy, despite the differences of genre manifested internally as among them.

I have long been convinced that the project which took the form of *De Cessatione Legalium* grew out of Grosseteste's commentary on St. Paul and above all out of his reading of Galatians. In the letter to Galatians Paul vigorously attacks the counter movement of certain Jewish members of the Church of Galatia, who wished to re-impose the Old Testament legislation upon all who believed in Christ, both gentiles and former Jews, and who had seized upon the rite of circumcision as their test case for the continuity of the covenant, which they regarded as one and indivisible. As against these, Paul argues that there have been two covenants and two Israels, and that in the second covenant and the true Israel of God there is no place for ethnicity, nor for the traditional practices with which the Mosaic covenant was surrounded. For Paul, the Torah has served its pedagogical function in bringing the human child to the school of Christ. In his commentary Grosseteste developed the themes of Galatians in depth and at considerable extent, and even used the words *cessatio legalium*[10].

The treatise on the ending of the Torah grows naturally out of Grosseteste's preoccupations with the Pauline writing, and indeed refers back to the *expositio* for a

crucial point (viz, the question, debated with some heat between Augustine and Jerome, as to when precisely the old law ceased to have effect)[11].

Beginning from his reconstruction of the judaïzing movement within the primitive Church, Grosseteste studies the interrelationship of the Old and New Testaments. He shows how the prophecies, especially those of Isaiah, are fulfilled in the paschal events. He finds abiding value in the moral precepts of the Mosaic code (as distinct from its ritual and ceremonial law), since none of these is abolished but rather subsumed, and manifested as an expression of true, redeemed love. He extends his reflections magnificently to the unity and harmony of the entire divine plan of redemption, attempting to show that providence could not be frustrated by the fall of Adam but worked truly in and through the long preparation of the covenanted people towards the Incarnation, an event which, he argues, would have taken place even if man had not sinned[12].

Now as it happens, one of the titles of *DXM* (or at least of its prologue), preserved in *ms British Library Royal 11 B III* is '*de dileccione et x mandatis*'; nothing more apt could be found to express the theme of the work[13]. The commandments, after all, do remain in force within Christianity where, furthermore, they are surrounded by thickets of laws and regulations; how is this multiplicity to be understood and lived in a unity, in the light of the *mandatum novum* of love which is Christianity's unique precept? This is, clearly, the perspective of the treatise and the way in which its central problem is addressed, from the very first lines of the prologue right through to its concluding paragraphs.

If the perspective I have advocated is correct, and if we should regard the three works mentioned as a sort of trilogy carried by a broadly unitary project in the mind of Grosseteste, does that help to date *DXM*? Not with the accuracy one might desire, I think, save that it places it in quite close thematic connection with a project of the mature Grosseteste. The *Expositio in Galatas* cannot, unfortunately, be dated with precision either. It was certainly based upon Grosseteste's lecturing activity as a theologian, as several school references make clear; it was re-written and is sometimes quite literary in form and finish; but its origins in teaching notes is not in doubt. It betrays a developed knowledge of Greek, but other criteria (independently of the *Expositio [Expositio in Galatas]* itself) would have to be found if the actual stage of Grosseteste's Greek learning in it were to be used for dating the *Expositio;* but there is not much that is hard and fast in this line before the episcopal period. The 'trilogy' may have occupied a good deal of Grosseteste's time off and on during his final decade of teaching (c.1225-1235), but beyond that I do not see grounds for any further precision of dating, not at least at the present time.

The relationship between *DXM* and the *Expositio* is extremely close and will merit detailed study when the edition of the latter is published. In the meantime, a few illustrative details may be given concerning the nature of an interrelationship which strikes the reader of both works already in the opening lines of the prologue to *DXM*. After quoting from Rm 13.10, Grosseteste passes at once to a thought of St Augustine, one of which he likewise makes use in the *Expositio:* 'who possesses charity in act has both what is latent and what is patent in the words of God'[14]. Now the Augustinian theme of charity in practice as being the sole valid interpreter of the senses of Scripture (for the quotation really makes reference to the literal and spiritual senses) runs throughout both works of Grosseteste like a dominant theme, accompanied by the doctrine of *amor ordinatus* and the reduction of the commandments to one, which is inseparably the love of God and of neighbour—the Johannine theme so beloved of Augustine. The hallowing of the Day of the Lord as the prophesied fulfilment of the Old Testament Sabbath is developed in closely parallel terms in the two works, and indeed in *De Cessatione Legalium* also[15]. I Tim.5.8 (on the care of members of the household as a criterion of faith), is invoked in the discussion of the Fourth Commandment, and also in the exegesis of Gal.6.2: 'Bear ye one another's burdens and so fulfil the Law of Christ'[16]. The only direct reference to the Philosopher in the *DXM* is one of only two found in the *Expositio*[17]. When Grosseteste argues that the Sixth Commandment prohibits not only adultery but also fornication and the unnatural acts of homosexuality, he quotes from Ephes.5.5 and Gal.5.19-21, and continues: 'the act of unnatural sexual indulgence is in this context called uncleanness, as the expositors say'[18]. This cryptic reference to the commentators on Scripture is illuminated by his discussion of the same Galatians passage in the *Expositio,* where, distinguishing within the Pauline list of vices of the flesh between fornication and adultery, on the one hand, and *immunditia* 'and what is called in Greek *aselgeia*', on the other, he states that a Greek expositor has called the latter two 'unclean modes of union which should not even be named' (cf Ephes.5.3)[19].

I have referred to this sample of detailed interrelations between the two works to suggest how close they are to one another; the reader who comes to one of them finds many significant words and phrases already familiar from the other. He will discover no differences even in nuances of doctrine, nor any hint of development of thought as between the two writings. I can find no clear evidence to establish relative priority as between the two, but I think it is fairly likely that both were written around the same time, and that when Grosseteste came to write on the commandments he had already made his serious study of Galatians and its commentators. Now the *Expositio in Galatas* is certainly a work of his

mature years in the schools, it arises directly from his teaching and it manifests a good reading knowledge of Greek, including extensive and independent access to what was apparently a new exegetical work in the Latin world, viz Chrysostom's commentary on Galatians; Grosseteste used it in a way and to an extent that suggests he may have possessed a full copy rather than simply extracts in a catena, and it is entirely possible that he read it in Greek, since no trace of any medieval Latin version has been found.

If *DXM* and the *Expositio* are roughly contemporary in origin, why then does the *Expositio* throw so much light on Grossesteste's study of Greek whereas *DXM* might as well have been written by an author who knew nothing of the language? I am inclined to think that the answer must lie in the different readership Grosseteste had in mind for the two writings. The Galatians commentary was intended for the use of scholars, that relatively restricted group of masters in theology, whereas the *DXM* seems to have been aimed at the growing number of learned priests whose ministry and general influence Grosseteste was ever anxious to support: in his eyes there never were and never could be enough of them. Hence the treatise *DXM* is quite learned without being at all pedantic or self-indulgent in a scholarly sense. In the Prologue and in many places scattered throughout, Grosseteste addresses his reader with the familiar 'tu'; such familiarity is absent from the *Expositio,* where it would have been quite out of place. Moreover, the hypothesis of the difference in intended readership is in a way borne out by the very different pattern of circulation of the two writings: the *Expositio* survives in a single manuscript (of the early fifteenth century) once in the possession of Gascoigne, and it was read by Wyclif and used by Alexander Carpenter[20]; but of any readership beyond those two no trace has hitherto come to light. *DXM,* on the other hand, was copied and read throughout the fourteenth and fifteenth centuries in England, and the large number of surviving manuscripts attests to a very respectable number of readers[21]. Indeed, one fifteenth-century student of the work throws light on its readership by bequeathing his copy to preachers, to be handed on but never sold 'by one priest, learned in the law of the Lord for the preaching of the Word of God, to another, and so on for as long as this book lasts'[22].

In general, Grosseteste's intended readership provides an important clue to his employment or otherwise of Greek in a given work. This hypothesis receives support from a comparison between the *Expositio* and *De Cessatione Legalium.* In the latter work, which was written with a wider readership in mind and which (rather like *DXM*) attained an influential dissemination within England, there is little of Greek learning exhibited, save for frequent references to the LXX—

and it is always possible that some of these were derived from his reading of Jerome. Greek authors are quoted in existing Latin versions, including the Ps-Dionysius and Damascene, both of whom Grosseteste was later to render in the form of *correctae translationes*. If we were to regard the use of Greek in a given work as a firm criterion for relative dating we would have to place the composition of the ***Expositio in Galatas*** a good deal later than that of ***De Cessatione Legalium;*** but in fact, the precedence of the Galatians commentary is affirmed by two very explicit back-references to it in ***De Cessatione Legalium.*** Grosseteste's knowledge of Greek was greater by far than he was prepared (taking his intended readership into consideration) to show while composing ***De Cessatione Legalium;*** the same may very well have been true in the case of ***DXM.***

There is one other writing of Grosseteste to which ***DXM*** can be related, and a dateable one at that. In a letter (printed as Epistle 2) addressed to his sister, Grosseteste says the following:

> '"Man", when taken without qualification, means the interior man, with the result that a man remains one and the same even when parts of the exterior man have been cut off. For if my hands and feet were to be cut off and my eyes torn out, I still could truly affirm—or at least think, if my tongue were cut out—that I am Robert and that I am *I*, and that this 'I', formerly whole, has suffered truncation'[23].

Now in the richly reflective prologue to ***DXM*** we find the following close parallel, given in answer to the question as to how a man can love himself if he hates the better part of himself, that is to say his soul:

> 'For if my hand has been cut off, I still remain 'I' without qualification. In the same way, even after individual members are cut off I remain 'I' and can truly say that *I* have been cut, *I* suffer, *I* live, *I* am dying'[24].

Part of the interest of these two passages is that they reveal Grosseteste as the avid reader he was of the *De Anima* of Avicenna[25]. For Grosseteste, self-consciousness is immediate and belongs to the soul, it does not depend upon the body; for the interiority of the soul, the immediate access it has to itself without the mediation of images (through which external things and even the body's members are communicated to it) constitutes the subject or *ego* as such. Grosseteste's thoughts on these matters were those framed by St Augustine in *De Trinitate X* under the heading *cognosce te ipsum:* the soul does not need to seek to know itself, as though it were originally unknown to itself: it simply has to distinguish itself from all that it knows as other than itself. To know what I am I have only to leave aside all the knowledge that comes to me from without by the media-

tion of the senses, and to consider myself; for every soul knows itself with a certitude that is only further revealed and reaffirmed by doubt (*si fallor, sum*). What is most truly the self is the inner self, or *homo interior*[26].

In the two passages in question, however, Grosseteste is drawing less immediately upon Augustine than upon Avicenna. It is admittedly difficult to distinguish between the two sources, so much do they agree that the experience of the self is immediately given[27]. In a famous passage, which occurs twice in the *De Anima* and is also found closely paralleled in the same author's *Book of Directives and Remarks,* the philosopher Avicenna argues that the presence of the mind to itself is spontaneous and immediate, and is not dependent upon sensible experience[28]. Let us suppose, he argues, that a man were created in the adult state, but in a void such that no sensible reality affected his senses and he had no impressions from without, his members being spread out so that they did not touch: *tamen sciret se esse*—the 'flying man' would know that he existed, even though he would not be conscious of his limbs. Avicenna uses this ingenious illustration to double effect, arguing (against the Peripatetic view) that not every intellectual act of knowledge reposes upon sensible experience, the vital exception being the immediate affirmation of self-conscious existence; and that the limbs and other members are not constitutive of the human being but are like clothing in which the self is dressed, but which, because they cannot be taken off like clothes, run the risk of being confused with the self, granted their continual state of adherence. '*Sciendum quod esse animae aliud est quam esse corporis; immo non eget corpore ad hoc ut sciat animam et percipiat eam*'. G. Verbeke concludes his exposé of Avicenna's doctrine with the well-chosen words: "Le moi est donc conçu comme le centre spirituel de la personne humaine qui est immédiatement présente à elle-même"[29].

Grosseteste's argument may seem to diverge from that of Avicenna, since it goes at the business in another way, imagining the hand or the tongue cut off in order to affirm that the 'I' remains the 'I', even in loss or under torture. I suggest, however, that the inspiration of Grosseteste's 'tortured man' remains the 'flying man', and that Grosseteste, struck by a detail in Avicenna's argument, pursued and developed it to create his own illustration of the superiority of self-consciousness to the body. In Avicenna we read the following:

> Si autem, in illa hora, possibile esset ei imaginari manum aut aliud membrum, non tamen imagineretur illud esse partem sui nec necessarium suae essentiae . . . Et quoniam essentia quam affirmat esse est propria illi, eo quod illa est ipsemet, et est praeter corpus eius et membra eius quae non affirmat, ideo expergefactus habet viam evigilandi ad sciendum quod esse animae aliud est quam esse corporis.

The 'flying man', in brief, affirms that he is; but what he affirms is over and beyond his body and his members, which he does not affirm; for if he could represent to himself his hand or any other member (which, of course, *ex hypothesi* he cannot), he would not represent it as necessary to the very essence of what he is.

Grosseteste extended the thought and made it more graphic, not to say imaginatively traumatic: if my hands were cut off, and my feet, and my tongue torn out, I remain to the end I; I affirm as long as I live, and even as I expire, that 'I am I'. He argues that to anyone who looks carefully further within his makeup (*interius perscrutanti*), it becomes apparent that if he hates his own soul by loving iniquity, then it is himself that he hates; but if he hates himself, how can he love another? The evil are incapable of true love or friendship; in order to love, we must first love ourselves and our own true good, in order to discover that the true good is the absolute common good, God himself, who is neither mine nor yours, but ours.

Grosseteste's argument differs somewhat, then, from Avicenna's. He would, of course, agree with Avicenna on both points of the latter's argument, i.e., the substantiality of the soul and its immediate self-awareness. His is, however, more of a spiritual exercise, an invitation to true interiority, than an abstract argument. What am I in truth? For one accustomed from his youth to the pratice of the interior life, the answer is that *verus homo homo est interior:* yes, my hand is *my* hand and my foot is *my* foot; but I, Robert, am a knowing and a free self, constitued by love in relationship to myself and others, and above all to God. In *DXM,* as in the *Expositio in Galatas,* the emphasis on relational freedom is striking: no created power can overcome my interior freedom, neither by force not by torture or seduction, provided only that my freedom stands in true relationship to God and to his Spirit, the giver of that inner fruit in which truest liberty consists. Love grounded upon truth and ordered by Being is invincible[30].

The reader does well to bear in mind that the Sermon on the Mount has come between the 'flying man' and the man contemplating his mutilation, for the latter is at the task of convincing himself that if the right hand is a stumbling block then it is to be cut off, if the alternative would be the loss of his soul. Or if the right eye, then pluck it out, for the same eternal stakes[31].

I have tried to relate the prologue of *DXM* to the second letter, which is dated c.1232. This relationship lends some support to the other strands of evidence suggesting that *DXM* was written somewhere in the final decade of Grosseteste's teaching career.

The Decalogue up to the Time of Grosseteste

In undertaking his study of the Decalogue, Grosseteste was contributing in his own way and in his rather unique voice to a need that evidently was widely felt in his time. The series of Lateran Councils had served to focus the minds of two or three generations of ecclesiastics upon the renewal of the Church and the intensification of its spiritual life at every level. In the face of heresy the faith was to be defined and defended; superstition was to be countered by the active instruction of the people; parish priests were to be formed with a new consciousness of their vital local role and were to be given the means of instructing the peole in simple and memorable terms; and the practice of the faith was to be attached more and more to participation in the sacraments of the Church. Fr. Leonard Boyle is inclined to trace the sudden and unprecedented appearance, between 1179 and 1215, of penitential *summae* and other pastoral manuals of diverse genera to three principal causes: the parish clergy became aware of its collective identity and tasks in a new way, as *presbyteri parochiales;* the teaching developed in the schools was available for wide diffusion; and the literary forms of *summae, distinctiones* etc. were to hand, or were created. Among these pastoral genres Boyle ranges above all, of course, the *summae penitentiales* and *summae de casibus;* and side by side with these, treatises on the virtues and vices, the articles of faith, the Ten Commandments, the paternoster and the sacraments. All of these were aimed above all at the academic or practical formation of priests with the cure of souls[32].

The impact of the Fourth Council of the Lateran upon the life of Robert Grosseteste has been for too long underestimated. The year 1215 marked the culmination of the activity and influence of the most impressive, attractive and innovative Pope since Gregory VII. The Council he convened carried his message of pastoral renewal, of ecclesiastical liberty of action, and of administrative centralisation, to every corner of the Latin Patriarchate. Grosseteste's pastoral writings and his activity as bishop (including the statutes he instituted for the Diocese of Lincoln, which were to be widely imitated in England for the remainder of the century), all bear the stamp of the great reforming council[33]. We may legitimately see even in his expression of disappointment with the council in which he himself had participated, at Lyons in 1245, a continued effect of the deep impression left upon his mind by 1215; for the council of Innocent IV, proclaimed as a reforming council, inevitably invited comparison with the model of the genre, and that comparison could only have an unfavourable outcome[34].

Thanks to a number of recent editions we are afforded a much better insight into Grosseteste's pastoral mind than was possible even a decade ago, and we can furthermore attempt to place the series of pastoral writings within the rest of Grosseteste's work, to the extent that it is known[35].

DXM can be placed broadly within the genre of *pastoralia,* as a work of *haute vulgarisation,* rather than of simple *vulgarisation* in the style of *Templum Dei;* it occupies as it were a place on the highest shelf of popular writings. It is not the equivalent of a school treatise, such as that incorporated into the *Sentences* of Peter Lombard, and hence mirrored in the commentaries on that work up to the close of the Middle Ages; nor is it destined, on the other hand, for the use of simple parish priests, who were better served by more easily memorizable material—such as the *Templum* itself. *DXM* was, I feel, intended for the more learned higher clergy, who combined developed reading tastes with correlatively higher pastoral responsibilities.

The newer literature on the Ten Commandments, whether taking the form of simple manuals, of a treatise like that of Grosseteste himself, or of groups of questions incorporated into properly scholastic syntheses of theology, all goes back fairly directly to St Augustine, who may be considered as in a way its progenitor, at least as regards content.

The Decalogue appears to have had an uneven history within early Christianity[36]. Though the variations between its two biblical forms (Exod.20.2-17 and Deut.5.6-18) are minor, the numbering of the Ten Commandments betrays a variation which is of Jewish origin. According to the Talmud, Philo and the Fathers of the Church before Augustine (e.g., Gregory of Nazianzen and Jerome), the verses are to be divided up as follows:

1. adoration of the one God—Exod.20.v.3;

2. prohibition of idols—v.4-6;

3. do not take the name of the Lord in vain—v.7;

4. work on six days but rest on the sabbath, a rest for Jahweh—v.8-11;

5. honour father and mother—v.12;

6. do not kill—v.13;

7. do not commit adultery—v.14;

8. do not steal—v.15;

9. do not bear false witness—v.16;

10. do not covet the wife or goods of another—v.17.

Now Augustine was to exercise a lasting influence by linking 1 and 2 of the old enumeration, thus assimilating polytheism to idolatry under a single prohibition, and in making the final commandment double, thus according due respect to the status of woman. In doing so he opened the way to a new bipartite classification of the Decalogue. In the enumeration which preceded him, the First Table of five elements prescribed the proper religious attitude to the God who gives life and to the parents who transmit it, in a way that no doubt reflects an Israelite mentality. The re-division of the two tablets into three commands relative to God and seven relative to the neighbour, Augustinian in origin[37], was to become part of the common wisdom of Latin Christendom (and eventually to be retained by Lutherans also); it is faithfully reflected by Grosseteste in the prologue and in the concluding lines of *DXM* (p. 91).

Augustine was also responsible for a theology of the Decalogue which was in its own way to become part of the patrimony of medieval Christianity and to exercise an influence which continued up to and even beyond the Council of Trent. His originality emerges by way of contrast with the treatment of the commandments in the primitive Church and up to his own time. The earliest Church was conscious above all that the Lord himself had presented the New Law as the perfection and completion of the Old, not its abolition (Mt.5.17-20; 19.17; Mk.10.19; Lk.18.20); hence the Old Testament was indeed to be read and studied within the Church. Perhaps it was the effort of the Post-apostolic Church to detach itself from the Synagogue that led to an emphasis upon originality and difference, so that the Sermon on the Mount appeared almost in the light of a rejoinder to the Mosaic Decalogue together with its entire accompanying context of Torah and rabbinical commentary. The *Didache* accords no place to the Decalogue in its catechetical and moral instruction. The early writers (Justin, Clement of Alexandria and Irenaeus, for example) regarded the Decalogue as a summary of the natural law, but placed no particular stress upon it; Ambrose remained within their tradition. It is with Augustine that the commandments enter the instruction of both catechumens and the faithful in general, and find a place in the articulation of Catholic doctrine. Perhaps it was his opposition to Manichaeanism which more than anything else inspired his upgrading of the Decalogue, for the Manichaeans shunned the Old Testament as the work of the evil creator. Augustine displays the Decalogue in his sermons and elsewhere as the natural law written in the heart of man and expressly repeated by God to his chosen people. This legislation is taken up again, purified and completed, in the New Law which, adding to it a higher ideal as well as further precepts, proposes it as the foundation of practical morality.

The theological study of the Decalogue, begun by the Fathers, held a prominent place in the renewal of theology in the course of the twelfth and thirteenth centuries. Hugh of St Victor included a treatise on the commandments in *De Sacramentis*[38]. The School of Abelard explained the Decalogue within the comprehensive framework of salvation history, applying the great categories of promise, sacrament and commandment. Peter Lombard gave later commentators on his work the opportunity to extend his own quotations, references and reflections, which went largely in the same sense as those of the Victorines and Abelardians. Extensive and independent scholastic treatises appeared on the Decalogue and the New Law, for instance the *De Legibus* of William of Auvergne and the *De Legibus et Praeceptis* of Jean de la Rochelle and Alexander of Hales[39]. Bonaventure and Aquinas discussed the commandments and the new dispensation when commenting the *Sentences,* and Aquinas returned to the theme in the *Summa*[40]. Following Augustine unanimously regarding the enumeration of the commandments and the divisions of the tablets, the Scholastics accepted his theology also: the commandments are the expression of the natural law written in the hearts of men; only the third contains a determination of positive divine law, prescribing in the Old Testament the observation of the Sabbath and in the New that of the *dies dominica*. Within the Church the theological virtues are to give life to the commandments, and the Christian ideal is to be their crown. In this way the *lex Moysi* was understood as having been ordered to the *lex evangelii* and promulgated in a movement of salvation history towards the freedom and grace of love.

It may be of interest to outline the structure of the *distinctiones* accorded by Peter Lombard to the Decalogue[41].

The Lombard reproduced faithfully the Augustinian division of the two tables: Table I, Commandments 1-3, is discussed in the first three chapters of *Distinctio XXXVII;* Table II, including Commandments 4-10, is treated from chapter 4 to the close of the discussion in *Dist.XL.* Regarding the First Commandment, Lombard (drawing on the *Glossa Ordinaria*) reports that for Origen it is two commandments, whereas for Augustine it is only one. The second and third are discussed in a few lines, but with a distinction made each time between the literal and allegorical senses. In the wake of Isidore (quoted to this effect in the *Glossa*)[42] the first three commandments are interpreted as referring successively to the Father, the Son and the Holy Spirit (ch.3). The first three of the Second Tablet are dealt with summarily in a few lines, but once more with reference to literal and spiritual senses. The fourth (the prohibition of stealing) allows the Lombard to comment on sacrilege, rapine, usury and the spoliation of the Egyptians. The fifth, on false

testimony, is a series of extracts from Augustine (including *De Mendacio,* which Grosseteste will quote extensively) on a subject on which that Father held a firm and unshakeably severe view. *Dist.XXXIX* explores the permutations of *periurium. Dist.XL* spends little time on the Sixth and Seventh Precepts of the Second Tablet, but rather more on the distinction between *lex* and *evangelium,* or inner and outer adherence. The Lombard concludes with a resounding quotation from St Augustine on the difference between the Law and the Gospel. Thus the transition is prepared between the third book of the *Sentences* and the fourth, on the sacraments.

LITERARY FORM

Thomson listed **DXM,** aptly enough, under 'Pastoral and Devotional Works'. In the manuscripts it takes the form of a prologue followed by nine sections: Grosseteste discusses the Ninth and Tenth Commandments together in one section. This may seem strange for one who unreservedly accepts the division by three and seven proposed by Augustine, with the First Tablet of three concerning the love of God, and the Second, of seven, that of the neighbour. Augustine, it will be recalled, separated the commandments of Exodus 20.1-17 into two, which became the ninth and the tenth, the ninth referring to the neighbour's wife and the tenth to his possessions. Grosseteste is not retrograde by comparison with Augustine nor is he less affected by the dignity of woman, but he has worked out his own approach to the ninth and tenth and sets it out lucidly at the beginning of his discussion of both[43].

In Exodus 20.17, he remarks, the prohibition of coveting the neighbour's wife is not placed first and given priority over the prohibition of coveting his goods, but is placed in the middle of the commandment which prohibits both. In the Greek translation, however (which he quotes, in Latin), reference is made in the first place to the neighbour's wife. Following the LXX order, it is clear that the Ninth Commandment prohibits coveting the neighbour's wife; the sixth and seventh prohibit respectively acts of sexual wrongdoing and taking what is another's; while it is reserved to the ninth and tenth to prohibit illicit desire to do the things prohibited by the sixth and seventh. True to his conviction of the value of the LXX, Grosseteste devotes his final chapter to the twofold concupiscence distinguished by Paul in Galatians 5.17[44], i.e., of the flesh and of the spirit, to which he opposes *amor ordinatus* or *caritas,* which renews the soul and reforms it in the image of the Creator, who is supreme Beauty. Grosseteste then discusses Commandments Nine and Ten as one because, even though he is indeed sensitive to the dignity of woman, he has decided that both are sins of the will, and that being the case he has the opportunity to analyse the very root of evil, which is disordered desire and wilful abandonment of the true order of love.

The structure of the work is given by Exodus 20.1-17, in so far as Grosseteste comments each phrase and each word, even of the longer commandments. Thus the literary form of **DXM** is that of an exegetical study. Though aimed at a wider audience than his more academic commentaries, such as the **Hexaëmeron** and those on Ecclesiasticus 43 and Galatians, certain of its stylistic features are commonly met with in the writings mentioned. The longer commandments are broken down into lemmata, and the sections of comment connected by *sequitur;* where several explanations are possible he lists them (*vel . . . vel . . . vel forte*) and adds *quasi diceret,* or *potest sic intelligi,* or *et est sensus sermonis quasi diceret*[45]. He draws freely upon the *expositores* for help, above all on Augustine and Jerome. He may be said to avoid points of detail in exegesis in favour of the broad picture and to give himself great freedom to quote parallel scriptural passages and authors, just as he does in **De Cessatione Legalium.** And there are certainly more exempla in **DXM** than in the exegetical writings properly speaking—destined no doubt for preachers to retain and adapt. Despite all that, the differences that separate **DXM** from the more academic scriptural commentaries should be regarded as being of degree rather than kind.

DXM manifests Grosseteste's usual attentiveness to the spiritual sense of the Bible, and in particular of the Old Testament. Of course, not every commandment is susceptible of a mystical interpretation according to the rules expounded in **De Cessatione Legalium;** for there is no need to attend to a mystical sense unless the literal or historical sense either gives no instruction in faith or charity or else invites the passage to a higher understanding[46]. The prohibitions on stealing, lying and coveting simply are what they are and say what they say, whereas on the other hand the prohibition of graven images and of idols (*'non facies sculptile' DXM* I,17-18, p. 15) does, Grosseteste thinks, contain a spiritual sense, for any creature at will can be distorted by elevation to the rightful place of God. The keeping holy of the Sunday is already a spritualisation of the Sabbath Commandment; beyond that, the Sabbath/Sunday has the mystical sense of rest and peace in God through faith, and of the everlasting resurrected life which Sunday in a special way prefigures[47]. Commandments 2, 4, 5, 6, 7, 8, 9 and 10 are not, it seems, susceptible of mystical interpretations—not as Grosseteste sees it, at any rate.

One other stylistic feature is worth adverting to, viz the lengthy question raised about Exodus 20.5 ('visiting the sins of the fathers upon the children'), for *quaestiones* are very rare in Grosseteste's writings. This question has a loose and unscholastic allure. Grosseteste finds an apparent contradiction between Cicero, who opposes the justice of punishing children for parental misdeeds[48], and the text of Scripture, and suggests 'various solutions' which he explores by means of a distinction (temporal punishment—eternal punishment) destined to defend the perfect justice of God. In a passage reminiscent of portions of **De Cessatione Legalium** he expresses his conviction that in the great republic of creation no-one is made to suffer any penalty unjustly, despite the wrong introduced by the abuse of freedom; suffering is in fact always the providential restoration of true order after its disturbance by wrong action. His question is aimed at reconciling his authorities.

THE PROLOGUE

Grosseteste prefaces his study of the commandments with an introduction that stands among the finest pages in the entire corpus of his writings. Destined to set the theological framework in which the Ten Commandments are to be understood and lived by the Christian believer, it opens with Rom.13.10: *Plenitudo legis est dilectio . . .* The sources of moral precepts are multiple: written (Scripture and its *expositores*—but also the *mundane philosophie expositores* or *ethnici*) and unwritten (for deeds can be a rule of life as well). Thus, unobtrusively, Grosseteste announces the place that Cicero (*De Natura Deorum*) and Seneca (*De Beneficiis* and *Epistulae*) will occupy in the book[49].

The wisdom of God has subsumed the multiplicity of precepts into one mandate, indeed into one word: *ama!* This word must, he insists, be understood dialectically, as ordered love: love nothing that must not be loved; do not fail to love anything that must be loved, but love each thing as much as it ought to be loved by you and in the way it ought to be loved. If you find that as a pilgrim on the way you are unable to do this, then at least retain the invincible love of this love, and love your loving each single thing, as and as much as it should loved by you. For if you love that love, then in a way you have that love as it were in its very root, though not as yet unfolded into the branches of the tree. This tone of patience with oneself and others on the way or pilgrimage of life towards perfection is a notable and pleasing feature of the book. It comes back again in the discussion of desire, for desire cannot be wholly overcome in this life, and the Ninth and Tenth Commandments point us in the direction of a process which ressembles the building of a house: a man may be commanded to build, but he cannot be commanded to build in a day; the finished job takes as long as it takes . . . (pp. 88-89). The Golden Rule, which follows (quoted from Mt. 7.12), is also a theme of the book.

Grosseteste embarks upon an allegory of the Tree of Love. Its purpose is to show how from a unique root there comes a bifurcation (the twofold commandment of love), and from these two shoots there ramify ten branches, three from one shoot and seven from the other; like twigs from branches are the almost innumerable[50] moral precepts of scripture. Chrysostom is quoted on the twofold law of love, but in fact it is Augustine's Johannine theology of the indissoluble unity of the love of God and of neighbour that is expressed in the prologue. Unless we love ourselves we cannot love others: Grosseteste finds the old theme of Aristotle included in the evangelical precept of love. Once again, this love of ourselves must be conceived in dialectical terms, for there is a yawning gulf between base and vicious self-regard (the evil are incapable of loving either themselves or others—a reminiscence of Aristotle, perhaps, as well as of Psalm 10.6), and love of the *verum bonum* which is the *summum bonum*[51]. The study of the commandments in their organic relationship to their unique root and double shoots is to command all our attention, for that is the scripture in a privileged sense, written by the Spirit of God for our salvation[52].

Non-Biblical Sources

The number of quotations in *DXM* is very great in proportion to the relatively short work, and practically all the explicit quotations have been identified by the patience of the editors. Grosseteste, however, does not attach a name to certain ideas and expressions he uses; life is short but pedantry long. Still, a few notes on words and expressions that betray some part of his reading that has found its way through his pen may be of some interest, without pretending to be exhaustive.

A glance at the *Index Auctorum* reveals many writers and books that were perennial favourites with Grosseteste (Augustine, Jerome, Ambrose, Gregory, Anselm, Bernard, Isidore and Bede)[53]. Philosophers are incomparably less present, but I detect a brief reminiscence of Aristotle in the discussion of the Second Commandment: *Quicquid enim minus est quam Deus, aut creatura est aut artificium aut ymaginacionis figmentum aut corrupcio aliqua aut privacio (si tamen et has aliquomodo inter encia numerare velimus), quia et hec esse dicuntur, cum tamen vere nihil sint.* These things, which are scarcely to be called being, are in *Metaphysics* Γ2 privations and negations of being, which, though nothing in themselves, still derive their meaning from being, which is expressed in many ways. The Aristotelean notion of science as *habitus adquisitus per experientiam,* which Grosseteste develops in his commentary on the *Posterior Analytics,* makes a brief appearance (p. 56.34) but is not developed for its own sake. A further philosophical note is struck with the deservedly famous definition of justice: *ut sic observata iustitia reddatur unicuique quod suum est;* Cicero has this at *De Finibus* V.23,65 and it went into Justinian's *Instituta* (I,i) as a sort of headline for the entire codification.

There is a discreet but detectable presence of the *Glossa Ordinaria.* Much of Grosseteste's discussion of the Second Commandment is structured by the repeated association of the commandment with—rather perplexingly, for it looks at first sight like sheer literary artifice—Rom.8.20: *creatura vanitati subiecta est.* It is puzzling, as I say, until one looks at the Gloss on Exodus and finds there the source of the association: taking the name of the Lord *in vain* includes thinking of the Son of God as a creature, and hence as subject to the *vanitas* of every creature[54].

'God will not leave unpunished the man who has taken his name in vain' (Exod.20.7); yet God cannot possibly be harmed by the words of man. To this difficulty Grosseteste replies that although neither God nor man is harmed, and men, who judge 'by the face', may not punish the blasphemer, the judgment of God is not external and legal but of the heart, will and intention. Now the phrase *quorum legibus manus, non animus, cohibetur* ('the laws of man restrain the hand but not the mind') appears a number of times, both in *DXM* and in the *Expositio in Galatas.* The Lombard also has it in his Gloss, but he applies it to the contrast between the Old Law and the New; though he limits the force of the opposition in the *Sentences* by referring it to the *caeremonialia,* not the *moralia.* The Lombard's source in turn is the Gloss at Psalm 18.8: *lex Domini immaculata convertens animas,* to which the Gloss adds 'Voluntates, non modo manus, ut vetus.' The Lombard comments in his own Gloss (which Grosseteste employed frequently when commenting upon Galatians), that the Old Law '*manum maxime, non animum cohibebat*'[55].

Use of Concordance

The reader of *DXM* cannot fail to be struck by the regularity with which Grosseteste quotes from both scriptural and non-scriptural (patristic, early medieval and philosophical) sources on themes which he considered of special importance. He seems to be able to summon up parallel or related texts almost at will, and to develop their sense by apt quotations from his favourite authorities one after another, interlocked sometimes by little more than connecting words and phrases. To quote is part of his method for handing on the tradition he has received, for he is not in search of any personal originality—even though he is quite capable of it[56].

The concordance of scripture and ecclesiastical authorities which Grosseteste compiled gives the clue to his remarkable facility for quotation and offers an insight into his working method[57]. Just for interest I decided to compare the *DXM* with the concordance, selecting two topics which seemed *a priori* to depend upon a ready-made string of entries.

The First Commandment prohibits and outlaws superstition, and Grosseteste gives examples of the sort of sins he has in mind when expounding it, such as new moon rites which have survived from pagan times with only a thin veneer of Christianity. He passes from that to the frequentation of the games, circus and amphitheatre, which was forbidden by the Fathers under the First Commandment because of the paganism and the hint of demonic worship they sensed there[58]. He quotes from Isidore (*Etymologies* bk 18), Rabanus (*De Universo* bk 20.27), Jerome (*Ad Furiam Viduam*) and Augustine ('*in primo libro de civitate dei*'), to show the offensive nature of the games.

Now if we turn to fol.28[r] of the concordance we find, under the heading *De prohibitione spectaculorum,* the following list of references[59]:

> ys.5 / aug.ep.43. De ci dei l. 1.2.4.8. de 10 cordis.de vera relig.ser.10. om.7.100. de concordia evangeliorum./ iero.ep.88. contra iovin.c.23. / basilius exa.4.6.8.10 / isid.etym.l.27 c.5.15.c.6.10.c.7.8./rabanus de natura rerum 1.20.c.15.25.33.36./ cris.super mt.om.6.7.

Grosseteste did not use all his references but selected among them; one would only discover on what basis he made his selection by looking up all the references he gives, but I have not done that. Isidore bk 18 is present in *DXM,* though the chapter numbers do not correspond to those of the modern edition; Rabanus *De Natura Rerum* bk XX is in both; Jerome also, but with a different letter-number; and Augustine, *De Civitate Dei* bk I, again with a chapter reference that differs from the modern edition.

The second probe took the exposition of the Fourth Commandment, which has a strikingly large number of quotations, for purposes of comparison with the entry *De honorando patrem et matrem* in the concordance. This time the entry is double, the first level containing scriptural references, the second ecclesiastical authors. In the margin, separated from the Biblical references, appears *seneca de benef.*1.3./ *aristoteles de animalibus* 8. The list reads as follows:

> tob.4.11 / ec.3.7.23 / exo.20.21./ deuter.21./ iere.2./ leviticus 2./ ephes.6./ hebreos.12. aug.ep.40.112 / de c.dei.1.22. ser.10. / om.100.19./ de vera relig. / gregor.mor.1.7. ambo.exa.1.5.c.33./ is.c.13./ iero. ep.86.88.118./ basilius exa.9.

The comparison is more positive this time. Though Grosseteste does not follow the order of the entry, it does indeed contain substantially the references and authorities he quotes.

I list these as follows, in the order of his use of them in *DXM* (omitting doubles):

> Exod.20.12; Ephes.6.1; Ecclus 3.8-9; Matt.25.31-46; Augustine, *Epist.*243.12; I Tim.5.8; Jerome, *Epist.*54.3; Ps.26.13; Ecclus 3.9-10; Ecclus 3.11; Prov.9.1; Jerome,

> *Epist.* 117.2; Tob.4.3-4; Jerome, *Epist.* 117.4; Ecclus.7.29-30; Seneca, *De Beneficiis* 3,35.1-3 and 3,28.2-3; Ioan.19.26-27; Augustine, *Tract.in Ioan.* 119.2; Reg.2.19; Ambrose, *Hexaëm.*5; Levit.20.9; Deut.21.18-21; Exod.21.15-17.

Exodus chs.20 and 21, Deut. ch.21, Eccles. chs.3 and 7, Tobias ch.4, Ephesians ch.6, and Hebrews ch.12 are found in both lists (Leviticus 2. in the concordance might just be a mistake for 20); Ambrose, *Hexaëmeron* 5, is in both; the references to letters of Augustine and Jerome differ, but that might remain a topic of further study concerning the numbering of their letters in medieval collections[60]. Seneca, *De Beneficiis* bk 3 is common to both lists.

The evidence strongly suggests that Grosseteste drew on his concordance, making a methodical choice among the entries, using the concordantial sign prefacing the entry in order to refer to his library, and turned up the passages marked within, say, bk I of *De Civitate Dei* with the sign for 'honouring father and mother'. In composing *DXM* he had added references over and beyond those entered in the concordance, something which indicates that the concordance as we have it represents only a stage on the way of his study of the Scriptures and the ecclesiastical authors.

The limited sounding made here cannot throw much light upon the general nature of the compilation and its employment in other works, for that will of necessity have to be a piecemeal undertaking; it can scarcely be said even to have begun as yet. Nevertheless, it is sufficient to give us an idea as to how he went about things and just how he managed to pack his treatise with such an anthology of biblical and ecclesiastical references.

DOCTRINE

Grosseteste wrote on the Ten Commandments to disseminate solid doctrine among the clergy of his country; he did not seek originality. None the less, some doctrinal points in his book deserve a word of comment, either because they do in fact attain to an originality not aimed at, or because they are particularly representative of his approach in theology.

The opening page on the First Commandment belongs decidedly in the former category (*DXM* I, paragr.1,2, pp. 6-7). I translate it as follows:

> From the love of God, then, there grows like a first branch the First Commandment of the Decalogue: *Thou shalt not have strange gods before me.* For he who loves God above all clings lovingly to him as the supreme good and believes that he alone is the supreme good. For if he believed something other to be a good equal to or greater than that which he loves supremely, then that thing loved supremely would not be God,

since God is that greater than which cannot be thought, and is indeed greater than can be thought. Therefore, since faith is nothing other than thinking with assent (as Augustine says), if he believed in, and thus thought, a good equal to or greater than that which he loves supremely, then that thing loved supremely would not be God, and so he would not love God.

Furthermore, he who loves God incomparably above all does not accord to another the reverence and worship due to God alone, for by giving to another what he believes to be due to God alone he knowingly insults God and does not turn upon him a loving affection incomparable above all. It follows, therefore, that if he loves God supremely he clings lovingly to him alone as the supreme good, he believes him alone to be the supreme good, and he renders to him alone the reverence and worship which are due to him alone; and thus neither does he believe something other than God to be the supreme good, nor does he cling lovingly to something else as the supreme good or offer to something else the reverence and worship due to him alone; in other words, he has no strange God. To have a strange God is to believe something other than God to be the supreme good, or to love it maximally as the supreme good, or to give to something other than God the reverence and worship due to God alone—or to do all three, viz to believe something other than him to be the supreme good and to love it maximally as the supreme good, and to give to that other reality the worship due to God alone.

For since God is by definition the supreme good, what the supreme good is for each man, in his belief or his love or his worship or his reverence—in all of these at once, or in several of them—*is* God. We are forbidden by the First Commandment to believe anything other than the true supreme good to be the supreme good, or to love it as such, or to adore it with the reverence and worship due to the supreme good alone. Thus the First Commandment opposes both the impiety of idolatry and the declension of love from the supreme good to lower things.

We can safely say that not many expositors of the First Commandment in medieval times—or modern for that matter—would have been capable of giving it such a dialectically metaphysical turn as we find it accorded here; I can think of only one other theologian who interweaves the argument of St Anselm with the First Commandment: even allowing for all the contextual differences that separate their thought, there is an analogy (if I may be permitted to use the word!) between Robert Grosseteste and Karl Barth[61]. The dialectical element is for the most part muted in Grosseteste, but it may never be neglected by his reader, for it is a feature intrinsic to a mind which frequented over many years authors who were themselves imbued with Neoplatonism, such as Augustine, Boethius, Anselm and (especially after 1235 or so) the Pseudo-Dionysius.

The idea of 'strange gods *before* me' (i.e., before the face of Jahweh), evokes at once in Grosseteste's reflective mind the metaphysical absurdity of any reality's

being placed higher than God, who is Being itself and the source of all 'other' beings, supreme good and creator of all goods or values. Since God is not the first being in a merely hierarchical sense, like the summit of a pyramid which, though placed at the top of the structure, is nevertheless related to its lower levels and dependent upon them for its crowning place, but is on the contrary first and supreme in the sense of incomparable to any (for if God had not created, the fulness of all that there could be would none the less be present in Him, and indeed not only present but also reflected and expressed in the *Verbum),* it follows that anything *aliud,* or other than God, cannot ontologically speaking be his rival; and if our love is to mould itself upon the order of being, rather than attaching itself to its own self-generated fantasies and arbitrary whims (and that is the whole sense of the Augustinian *ama et fac quod vis*— the *amor ordinatus* of the prologue to *DXM*), then to posit as an object of unrestricted and exclusive love something other than the *summum bonum* is every bit as much a contradiction, as to try to take as the object of thought a reality equal to or greater than 'that than which no greater can be thought'[62].

St Anselm himself would have admired this page and recognized in it a legitimate and genial extension of his *unum argumentum* to the order of the will. Anselm, who was surprisingly little read in the twelfth century, was being revived in Grosseteste's time, and no-one was more responsible for the new interest being taken in his thought than Grosseteste himself. Alexander of Hales, Jean de la Rochelle and St Bonaventure were to be the promoters of a similar revival at Paris within a few years[63].

By the way, it would be difficult to convince me that this page was written with barely-lettered parish priests in mind.

If we may generalize for a moment, we might say that Grosseteste's theology is trinitarian, Christocentric and biblical in character, its biblicism being of that mystical-allegorical and spiritual character that goes right back to Origen (whom Grosseteste knew, in part at least through the sometimes lengthy extracts quoted or reported by Jerome), and which Ambrose and Augustine developed with particular conviction within the Latin Church. Grosseteste remains within the patristic trinitarian outlook, which finds the tri-personality of God revealed and manifested in creation and in both Testaments, as distinct from the more Aristotelean-inspired theological approach which was just beginning to show itself at Paris during his old age. This new theology saw the Creator and provident Lord revealed in different ways in nature and in the Old Covenant and it regarded the existence of God as provable by arguments taken from creation, but considered that the mystery of the Trinity was revealed in the New Testament exclusively.

In **DXM,** trinitarian theology is a vein of reflection that runs right through the exposition: every occasion is welcomed that allows the writer to relate the living of Christianity to the Trinity. The dialectical reconciliation of the unity of nature and the trinity of persons in God is pursued in a way that recalls the **Hexaëmeron,** where it is a major theme of discussion[64]. The reference to the triad of *magnitudo, species* and *ordo,* present in even the least of creatures, recalls the **Dictum** devoted to the same theme[65]. And Grosseteste adopts Augustine's view that the Commandments of the First Tablet relate distributively to the Father, the Son and the Holy Spirit[66].

Christology is represented in a sense throughout **DXM,** since the whole law and the prophets, including the commandments and the ceremonial law of the Old dispensation, have their place in salvation history in virtue of the promise which is fulfilled by the coming of the Messias. The paschal event puts a definitive end to the rituals, and the enactment of the *mandatum novum* of love subsumes into itself the moral precepts. This perspective is shared fully with **De Cessatione Legalium** where, however, it is incomparably more developed.

Grosseteste's theology is biblical, and heavily textual at that, devoting a large proportion of space and of effort to the meaning of words. At Exod.20.5, for instance ('*Ego sum Dominus Deus tuus, fortis, zelotes*') each word is analyzed, and a biblical conjugation is made with Exod.3.14 ('*Ego sum qui sum*')[67]. Augustine's rationale of the application of the allegorical method is adopted with approval[68]. Particular attention is given to the justification of divine providence in nature and history, something quite typical of Grosseteste, who explores the concept of providence both biblically and theologically; biblically, through research into the truth of the literal sense of God's rewarding and punishing (Exod.20.5)[69]; and theologically, by developing the theme of the finality of nature[70]. Since nature is the product of the divine ideas and not of chance, it is shot through with intelligibility, there is nothing in that is vacuous or purposeless, and man can learn the setting of the moral order and the true nature of his own dignity by studying the behaviour of the animals, their care for their young and spirited defence of them, their provision for the aged of their species. Grosseteste has recourse to Ambrose for these themes, for Ambrose was an attentive and receptive student of the Stoic nature-piety[71].

Grosseteste's ecclesiology may be said to centre upon the Augustinian vision of the Head and body of the Church as one: *caput et corpus unus est Christus, totus Christus caput et corpus est.*[72]. By a sort of extension of the Mystical Body doctrine he regards humanity itself as an organic body, with the result that he can view certain sins in the light of the damage inflicted by one member of the body of humanity upon another. Oppressors guilty of rapine are like deformed members of that body, who act in contradiction to the health and well-being of the organic whole. *Raptores,* who seize and appropriate to themselves the life-requisites of others, act like a member of the human body which tried to consume the nutriment of the other members and stock it in an immense pile, while the others became emaciated[73]. He draws upon the Prophetic and Wisdom Literature of the Old Testament[74], including the ringing condemnation of Ecclesiasticus 34.25: 'The bread of the needy is the life of the poor man; he who defrauds him is a man of blood'[75].

To the Mystical Body belong the souls of the dead. Honour to one's parents should continue after their death; their children are not to forget those who may suffer the pains of purgatory, but are to assist them by the giving of alms, by their own devout prayers and through the prayers of the Church[76].

Finally, we may pick out the theme of the dignity of man, a recurrent and deeply-meditated motif of Grosseteste's philosophical theology. He conjugates the biblical theme, of man made in the image and likeness of God, with the philosophical idea that man is the microcosm of the universe, in order to underline the uniqueness of man among creatures: not even the angel is superior to him. Under the Seventh Commandment, he views the crime of homicide as the destruction of the representative product of the entire handiwork of the Creator, an assault as it were upon the finality of the entire universe:

> Since the rest of the universe was made with man in mind, he who attempts to bring death to man, who is placed over the remainder of creation (Gen.1.28), does violence to the other creatures, made as they are on account of man. For he does his very best to wrest from them the purpose of their existence, if he takes a man from the centre of creation and kills him: he does his best to deprive them of their well-being, since a reality is in a good state when it has attained to the end for which it was made. And since man possesses something of every creature (whence he is called the microcosm, and even the voice of Truth itself refers to him as 'every creature', when it says 'Preach the Gospel to every creature'), he who deprives a man of his existence by that very act mutilates the being of every creature, in some part of itself[77].

FEUDALISM

'Who deceives a judge and corrupts his judgment disrupts the bonds of peace, so far as in him lies. Since, moreover, judges are the throne of God, sitting on which the Lord decrees his judgment by their mouths, what does the false witness do in deceiving the judge, but to do his utmost to withdraw the support of truth and to unsettle the seat of God?'[78]. The reader who ponders these lines on the Eighth Commandment (which prohibits false testimony), may be tempted to view them as a thread which, when pulled gently, might begin to unravel a considerable part of the woven garment, that part, namely, which can be headed 'feudal'; for the bonds of peace of which Grosseteste writes so earnestly he calls not *vincula,* but *foedera;* and those *oaths* of loyalty which made the always-threatened unity and peace of medieval society—whether in the Empire or in the kingdoms—depended entirely upon truth, fidelity and the sense of honour. It is not to be wondered at if medieval discussions of the commandments, and Grosseteste's among them, accorded an important place to lying, the swearing of oaths and perjury in the judicial setting, in proportion as all of these represented incomparably more than merely individual aberrations: they were social sins right from the start, since they threatened the very fabric of peace.

Now the medieval theologian found in patristic texts a thoroughly social view of language, of truth and lying, he did not have to invent it for his own contemporary purposes. In the nature of things, his purpose coincided largely with that of Jerome and Augustine, namely, to inculcate the virtues of truth-telling and of faithfulness to one's given word, and to the Lord who had instructed his disciples to let their yes be yes and their no, no (Mt.5.37).

Between the Fathers and the medieval theorists, however, the dimension of feudalism had intervened, to render all the more urgent the task of ensuring in so far as possible the public peace and order that depended upon fealty and loyalty, both of which reposed in their turn upon the sense of honour. Liars, pronounces Grosseteste, have no honour[79]. Liars bring it about that even those who tell the truth are not believed, Jerome had complained—and Grosseteste prolongs the thought to the social consequences of this vice: their evil practice has brought mistrust into the affairs of men; from mistrust there has ensued the requirement of oath-taking, and thence the evil of perjury. Only truth can reconcile the inner with the outer, the heart with the tongue, and prevent their alienation from one another. Grosseteste resorts to the fairground for an analogy, in a few vivid, though excoriating, lines:

> Men who lie are like illusionists (*prestigiatores*), for as these make white appear black to the bodily eye, or a dead thing seem alive, or a motionless object appear moved, liars make the false appear true to the eye of the mind, even though the truth is no less far removed from falsehood than white from black, and the grasp of

truth is more precious than the sight of white or black—and the deception of the interior sense worse by far than illusionism[80].

The trouble in medieval times was that oaths abounded where documents were lacking, as the means of filing and retaining them were only being discovered, above all at the Roman Curia following the accession of Innocent III, through practices which administrations throughout Europe sought, in fairly amateurish ways for the most part, to imitate. You had no document to prove what you asserted—but you could always offer to raise your right hand and invoke the name of God, swearing that you had indeed fulfilled the requirements for the examinations at another (suitably inaccessible) place; that you were of legitimate birth; that you would not remove books from the library of the college . . . No wonder that Grosseteste inveighs against the multiplication of oaths (which offends against the Second Commandment) and invokes the Sermon on the Mount; however, it would have required more than literary and theological fulminations to rid society of a bad habit to which there appeared to be no ready alternative. Perjury makes God, the invited witness to a lie, into a liar; Grosseteste gives a current formula for oaths: the taker of the oath looks upon holy objects and swears: '*hoc est verum, sic adiuvet me Deus et hec sacrosancta*'—and if they perjure themselves then they have turned their backs upon God's help, they have invited illness and the plague and evil and everything that is fearful[81].

Grosseteste does not hesitate to sacralize the judicial power, as we have seen, assimilating judges through a reminiscence of Psalm 9 to the throne of God's judgment: '*Sedisti super thronum, qui iudices iustitiam . . . Et Dominus in aeternum permanet . . . Paravit in iudicio thronum suum*'. The judge who under just laws condemns the guilty to death, the judge's servant who carries out the sentence *ex officio,* the soldier defending his country against an unjust invader, do not sin against the Fifth Commandment; but at this point Grosseteste is merely repeating the teaching of Augustine[82]. He adds, however, the severest condemnation of the abuse of legal or military power for gain or vengeance, just as he condemns public authority which turns that chaste matron, justice, into a whore by the oppression of subjects whom by right it is there to protect[83].

Grosseteste's book is rich in brief *exempla* relating some aspect of the commandments to the society in which he lived. It is possible that they are not all his own; but that is of little account, for they are so embedded in his work as to be an integral part of it and they contribute quite disproportionately to its savour. They have a feudal setting, they are memorable and they are not overdrawn. I paraphrase a sample of them.

(The Fourth Commandment). Let us imagine an earthly king seated upon the throne of the kingdom and a servant of his expelling him from the throne and heaping ordure from the streets and the squares upon the throne, as an insult: that such a deed merits the most severe punishment is patent to all. But how much more severely will they be punished who place something before God in their love—before the high king, the high priest and the high judge! Is not the faithful soul his city and his temple, and is not the heights of faithful love like the soil of the kingdom, and the throne and the priestly seat and the judge's tribunal? Those who expel God from the most inward reach of their love, and who pile up in that high and inward place the filth of gluttony or of luxury or any other evil desires, there to be the object of their highest love—how they insult him, and what great punishment they merit it would be difficult to say[84].

(The Ninth and Tenth Commandments). The concupiscence of the flesh is like an enemy who is part of the family household, fighting in our own castle, simulating friendship but in truth acting out of enmity. Against such a one we need greater prudence and livelier fortitude and more measured temperance and sterner justice, and in a word, resistance that never tires[85].

(The Sixth Commandment). The marriage of husband and wife is the sacrament of the spiritual union (*copula*) of the Word of God and the faithful soul which adheres to God, and which is one spirit through union with the Word. Therefore, to violate so sacred a thing and the manifest sign of so sacred a thing by adultery, is a heinous sin. If someone were to take the royal standard, or some such object that signifies the king's person, and trample it in the mud, he would do no little dishonour to the king and the insult would be no small one. Worse still if he of his own will were in the midst of battle to throw the royal standard down in the mud, for in that case he would be adjudged worthy of death. But how much greater dishonour is done to Christ and the Church by the one who in the dirt of indulgence tramples the diginity of wedlock and soils it, especially since that which matrimony signifies is incomparably more excellent than all royal dignity, and the filth of indulgence incomparably more sordid than any mud of the field[86].

Personal

There never was a writer but was greater than his book. Grosseteste's style is unhurried, purposeful and objective; but despite his objectivity the man himself, though on only a very few occasions, slips unselfconsciously through, and we catch him in a moment of uncommonly good common sense, or even in a vein of humour—just sufficiently so to make us aware of his massive intellectual and spiritual presence, as he dictated his thoughts

to an *amanuensis* or an *adiutor*—or perhaps to both at once, the one to write and the other to fetch and carry the many volumes of reference as they were in turn required.

Grosseteste is a scholar, and as such is distinctly aware of the engrossing nature of studies and the way they can wholly possess the person who feels their attraction; not that there are not higher things than philosophy and scholarship, though, as he reflects at the close of his prologue:

> The emergence of the Ten Commandments from the twin love (of God and neighbour) is put before us for our consideration. We should concentrate upon that emergence with all our power and effort, because these Ten Commandments are referred to as the Writing of God in a altogether privileged way. Now if the discoveries in some domain of human enquiry and writings produced by human toil frequently arouse our total interest and involvement, how much more should we rise with all our powers of concentration to meet what is written down by the eternal and ineffable all-knowing Wisdom of God for the salvation of our race, and by the finger of God; which is to say, by his own work, or by His Spirit![87]

Christians are to pass the entire Sunday in good works: before breaking fast, in praise and prayer, in listening to the Word of God or teaching it, or in reading and meditation; while eating (with moderation, of course), they should engage in edifying conversation with one another on the things of eternal life, or on historical or other stories. And they must take care to see that the holiness of morning and midday should not become something else entirely in the afternoon, because the afternoon is, after all, closer to our death than was the morning—and as the Philosopher says, the nearer you come to the goal the more you must increase the good you do!

One can imagine Grosseteste's smile, as he thought of readers who might take this lugubrious warning seriously, lent apparent weight and pseudo-solemnity as it was by what he himself knew to be a wholly forced quotation from Aristotle, on animals![88]

Grosseteste's exhortations to parents concerning the education of their children are based upon Scripture and the common sense of the ages, and have much of the 'spare the rod and spoil the child' about them. Education, he insists, must begin early:

> Fatherly discipline must begin from the tender years of childhood, for just as wax receives impressions more easily and truly when it is soft than when it is hard, so a young and tender age can be formed more easily to moral teaching than when it has grown tougher with the passage of time. A young reed takes easily the bent given it by the shaping hand, but when it has grown

strong it usually is more easily broken than bent. Horses and even wild animals, while still young and tender, take the discipline of their trainers, but if they grow old undisciplined and untamed it is a waste of time even to try to tame them. That is why the holy Tobias did well to 'teach his son from infancy to fear the Lord' (Tob.1.9-10). And the wise author of Ecclesiasticus warns, 'You have children? Instruct and shape them from their very childhood '(Ecclus.7.25); for if you did not mould them when you could you may not complain that you cannot mould them when you would, but instead find them rebelling, whom you indulged to your own harm and were unwilling to subject to stern discipline[89].

At the close of his discussion of the Ninth and Tenth Commandments Grosseteste turns from the theme of the double concupiscence back again to that of love, in lines warmly replete with overtones of St Augustine, the *Doctor amoris.*

> As against these, well-ordered love, which is virtue and charity, is to be sought with all one's might. For it is what is best in creatures, and the rational creature is called good, and is good, from none other than the order of love. That is why the order of love is the very good itself of the rational creature, and love is more exalted than knowledge, just as the angelic order called the Seraphin, which means 'burning' or 'burnt', is more exalted than the order of the Cherubin, whose name means 'fulness of knowledge'. Furthermore, ordered love is what renews the soul and reforms it to the image and likeness of its creator, that is to say, of the supreme beauty. This is the 'fire that consumes' (Deut.4.24) the scarlet of vices, that separates the alien, lower things that cling basely to the soul by cupidity, and that collects the soul together again, from dispersal and unlikeness into wholeness and harmonious likeness. This love is the sweetest thing, because things cannot be sweetened save by it, whereas lacking it everything is bitter. Through it the most difficult things become easy and the most burdensome things light; for it is the sweet yoke of the Lord and his light burden (Mt.11.30); and if it cannot while we live here below be entirely pure, then it can at least be upright through repentance[90].

Notes

1. Robert Grosseteste, *De Decem Mandatis,* ed. Richard C. DALES and Edward B. KING (Oxford 1987), *Auctores Britannici Medii Aevi X,* pp.xix-107; see pp. 1 and 92.

   The treatise will hereafter be referred to as *DXM.*

2. ibid., pp.xviii-xix.

3. For an assessment of Grosseteste's medieval reading public see Beryl SMALLEY, 'The Biblical Scholar', in *Robert Grosseteste, Scholar and Bishop,* ed. D. CALLUS (Oxford 1955), pp. 70-79.

4. For a study of the biblical allusions and other related matters, see the writer's review-article, in

this issue of *Recherches de Théologie ancienne et médiévale* 58, 1991.

5. S. H. THOMSON, *The Writings of Robert Grosseteste, Bishop of Lincoln 1235-1253* (Cambridge Mass., 1940), p. 131.

6. See *The Cambridge History of Later Medieval Philosophy,* p. 77. Grosseteste had access to a copy of *De Animalibus* while compiling his concordance (see p. 190 ff.).

7. See the fresh and comprehensive survey of Grosseteste's Greek learning by A. C. DIONISOTTI, 'On the Greek Studies of Robert Grosseteste', in *The Use of Greek and Latin. Historical Essays,* ed. A.C. DIONISOTTI and J. KRAYE (London, The Warburg Inst. 1988), pp. 19-39.

8. Arguments in favour of this dating may be found in the present writer's *The Philosophy of Robert Grosseteste* (Oxford 1982), pp. 489-490.

9. Robert Grosseteste, *De Cessatione Legalium,* ed. Richard C. DALES and Edward B. KING (Oxford 1986), *Auctores Britannici Medii Aevi vii;* see pp. 68 and 179.

10. For example, when commenting on Gal.5.18 Grosseteste remarks: 'Iusto igitur solummodo lex caerimonialis est posita, sed non lex mandatorum moralium. Legitur quoque et hoc secundum consequentiam doctrinae apostolicae de cessatione legalium, et est sensus: *si ducimini spiritu,* hoc est, spirituali intelligentia legis scriptae, *non estis sub lege'.*

   The commentary has been edited by the present writer and is being prepared for publication in the British Academy series of medieval authors, where it will appear accompanied by the edition (by R. C. Dales) of the extracts made by Thomas Gascoigne from Grosseteste's lost Pauline glosses.

   DXM, by the way, uses the following interesting words when introducing the Third Commandment: 'Nunc autem, exhibita et patefacta nostre redempcionis gratia, cessat hec legalis observancia, sicut in multis locis veteris testamenti est predicta cessatura'. That is an excellent summary of *De Cessatione Legalium!*

11. See n. 9.

12. See the present writer's article 'The absolute predestination of Christ in the Theology of Robert Grosseteste', in *Sapientiae Doctrina. Mélanges de théologie et de littérature médiévales offerts à Dom Hildebrand Bascour O.S.B.* (Louvain 1980), pp. 212-230.

13. *DXM,* p. 1.

14. *DXM, Prologus,* p. 1. The reference is given to St Augustine, *Sermo* 350, 2, but see also *qu.* 73 of the *Quaestiones ad Simplicianum,* which is in turn quoted in the *Glossa Ordinaria* on Exodus ch.20 (*P.L.,*113, col.255).

15. *DXM* pp. 30-31; *De Cessatione Legalium* I.2, pp. 7-9.

16. *DXM* 42.1-3. On both occasions Grosseteste is inspired by Augustine's reflections on I Tim.5.8 in *De Civitate Dei* XIX, 14.

17. ' . . . iuxta sententiam philosophi dicentis, quanto appropinquas fini plus bonum cum augmento operare', *DXM* iii, 2, p. 31; the ed. refers to Aristotle, *De Generatione Animalium* III,5, 756a, but this does not seem to correspond.

18. *DXM* vi.1, p. 65.9.

19. I reproduce the entire relevant passage (*Ms Magdalen College 57,* fol.26ʳ):

Dividitur autem vitium in fornicationem simplicem et immunditiam quae fit contra naturam, et impudicitiam, quae est specialiter contra legem matrimonii, scilicet adulterium.

Luxuriam forte nominat expletionem libidinis caeterorum carnalium sensuum exterius agentium, utpote libidinem videndi, audiendi, olfaciendi, et toto exteriori corpore mollia et temperata tangendi. *Fornicationem* et *impudicitiam* vocat, ut dictum est, fornicationem simplicem et adulterium, ubi non est turpis modus mixtionis contra naturam; immunditiam vero et luxuriam vocat modos turpes mixtionum, quos non necesse est nominare. Sic enim habet codex graecus: *Manifesta autem sunt opera carnis, quae sunt fornicatio, adulterium et immunditia,* et quod dicitur graece *aselgeia,* quae duo ultima dicit graecus expositor modos turpes mixtionum, quos non necesse est nominare.

20. *In Destructorium Viciorum;* noted by B.Smalley, *The Biblical Scholar,* p. 83 n.

21. *DXM* was copied four times with *De Cessatione Legalium,* and quite frequently with pastoral works by (or attributed to) Grosseteste: sermons; *De Confessione;* or the spurious *De Lingua, De Venenis* and *De Oculo Morali.* See *DXM* Introduction, pp. x-xv.

22. *DCM,* p. xviii, n. 6.

23. 'Homo namque simpliciter est homo interior, unde et exterioris hominis partibus detruncatis, non minus remanet unus et idem homo. Manibus enim et pedibus abscissis, oculisque erutis, adhuc vere dicere, et lingua praescisa vere cogitare possum,

quod sum Robertus, et quod sum ego, et quod ille ego sum truncatus, qui prius fui integer'. *Robert Grosseteste Epistolae,* ed. H. Luard (Rerum Brit.Medii Aevi Scriptores), London 1861, p. 19.

24. *DXM, prol.* p. 3.

25. For an account of the influence of Avicenna on Grosseteste's theory of the relationship between soul and body, see McEvoy, *The Philosophy of Robert Grosseteste,* pp. 257-258.

26. St Augustine, *De Trinitate X.12-16.*

27. It has been suggested that Avicenna somehow knew and used Augustine for the inspiration of the 'flying man' argument; but in fact the ressemblances between the psychology of Avicenna and of Augustine are sufficiently accounted for by their common dependence upon Greek Neoplatonic sources, as Gerard Verbeke has remarked; see his doctrinal introduction to the *De Anima* in the edition of S. Van Riet, *Liber de Anima IV-V,* Louvain-Leiden 1968, p. 37* n. 127.

28. *De Anima* I.1.49-68; V.7.51-64; also the commentary of Verbeke (with additional references to works of Avicenna), vol. I, pp. 36*-37*.

29. Ibid. p. 37*.

30. This very theme of the invincibility of spiritual freedom by any created reality is developed vigorously in the lines following the example under discussion.

31. Mt.5.29: 'Quod si oculus tuus dexter scandalizat te, erue eum' (cf Grosseteste, oculis *erutis*) . . . Et si dextera manus tua scandalizat te, abscinde eam' (cf Grosseteste, manibus *abscissis*).

32. L. E. Boyle, O. P., 'The Inter-conciliar Period 1179-1215 and the Beginnings of Pastoral Manuals', in F. Liotta, ed. *Miscellanea Rolando Bandinelli, Papa Alessandro III,* Sienna 1986, pp. 43-56. See also the same author's *Summae Confessorum,* in *Les genres littéraires dans les sources théologiques et philosophiques médiévales. Définition, critique et exploitation* (Louvain-la-Neuve 1982), pp. 227-237.

33. C. R. Cheney, *English Synodalia of the Thirteenth Century,* Oxford 1968, ch.v: 'The Statutes of Robert Grosseteste . . . and Related Texts', pp. 110-139.

34. Hans Wolter & Henri Holstein, *Lyon I et Lyon II,* Paris, Ed. Orante 1966, p. 122.

35. These editions are the work of that remarkable 'double act', J. Goering and F.A.C. Mantello, beginning with *Templum Dei. Edited from Ms.27*

of Emmanuel College, Cambridge (PIMS Toronto 1984) (cf BTAM 1985, n° 1844); 'The *Meditaciones* of Robert Grosseteste', in *Journal of Theol. Stud.* NS 36,1985, pp. 118-128 (cf *BTAM* 1987, n° 729); The '*Perambulavit Iudas ('Speculum confessionis')* attributed to Robert Grosseteste, in *Rev. Bénéd.* 46, 1986, pp. 125-168 (cf *BTAM* 1987, n° 726); 'The early penitential writings of Robert Grosseteste', in *Rech.Théol.anc.méd.* 54, 1987, pp. 52-112 (see *BTAM* 1987, n° 732); *Notus in Iudea Deus:* Robert Grosseteste's Confessional Formula in *Lambeth Palace Ms 499,* in *Viator* 18, 1987, pp. 253-273 (cf *BTAM* 1989, n° 732).

BTAM carries annually reviews of books and notices of articles relating to Grosseteste.

36. See the articles 'Décalogue' in *Catholicisme,* vol.III, cols 500-505 (R. Brouillard) and in *Dictionnaire de Théologique Catholique,* vol.IV, cols.164-176; 'Dekalog', in *Lexikon des Mittelalters,* Bd.3, cols.649-651 (L. Hödl).

Aside from studies of individual thinkers, there is no historical-theological synthesis of the discussions of the Decalogue in the medieval schools.

37. Augustine, *De Decem Chordis* (= *Sermo 9, P.L.* 38,79; *CCL* 41, 117-122): 'Habet enim decalogus decem praecepta, quae sunt decachordum psalterium. Quae sic sunt distributa, ut tria quae sunt in prima tabula pertineant ad Deum, scilicet ad cognitionem et dilectionem Trinitatis; septem quae sunt in secunda tabula ad dilectionem proximi'. Cf *Epist.55,* 11-13, quoted by Grosseteste in *DXM,* on p. 36.

38. I,12,5-8, *P.L.* 176, 352A-360B.

39. *Summa Halensis* III, pars 2.

40. *Summa Theologiae* Ia-IIae qu 100,a.4 ff.

41. *Mag.P.Lombardi Sententiae,* t.II, l.III et IV, ed. 3a, Grottaferrata (Romae) 1981, see Dist. XXXVII-XL (pp. 206-229).

42. *Glossa Ordinaria, P.L.* 113, col. 250.

43. p. 84.26 ff.

44. By a slip of the pen, which apparently remained uncorrected, he actually wrote *ad Ephesios.*

45. e.g., p. 18

46. *De Cessatione Legalium* I.6-8 (pp. 50-51).

47. *DXM* III, 13-18 (pp. 35-38) studies these meanings, largely by means of quotations from Augustine, *Ad Inquisitiones Ianuarii* (= *Epist.* 55), *CSEL* 31/2, pp. 190-195

48. Cicero, *De Natura Deorum* 3,38,90.

49. The study of the Stoic influence on Grosseteste would be worthwhile. The first to draw attention to Grosseste's use of the *De Beneficiis* of Seneca was Thomson, 'Un unnoticed Autograph of Grosseteste', in *Mediaevalia et Humanistica* 14, 1962, pp. 55-60. In *DXM,* aside from the quotations from Cicero and Seneca, the themes of self-preservation (p. 61.28) and of finality (p. 25) reveal Stoic influence.

50. Reading *numerabilia* at 4.18, for sense.

51. The passage on the true love of self (or love of the *true* self) has been discussed already; see pp. 175-178.

52. The kernel of scripture, consisting of the commandments in their organic relationship to love, was written '*digito Dei*'; Grosseteste finds a spiritual sense here of Exod.8.19 ('*digitus Dei est hic*'): the finger of God is the Spirit; cf Ambrose, *In Lucam* 7.93, and the *digitus paternae dexterae* of the hymn *Veni creator Spiritus.*

53. The unidentified paraphrase of Augustine at 6.9 refers to *De Praedestinatione Sanctorum* 2.5 (*P.L.,* 44,962): 'ipsum credere nihil aliud est, quam cum assensione cogitare'.

54. *P.L.,* 113, col.250: '*Non assumes nomen Domini Dei tui in vanum,* id est, non putes creaturam esse Christum Dei Filium, quia *omnis creatura vanitati subiecta est,* sed aequalem Patri, Deum de Deo, lumen de lumine'. Grosseteste takes up this theme at p. 24.6.

55. *P.L.,* 191, col. 210.

56. *DXM* p. 69, lines 9-12 depend upon *Etymol* XIII.19.3, 'De lacis et stagnis', but the following lines (12-15) do not appear to come from this source.

57. Thomson identified the concordance in the Lyons *Ms B.M. 414:* 'Grosseteste's Topical Concordance of the Bible and the Fathers', in *Mediaevalia et Humanistica* 9, 1955, pp. 39-53. The surviving codices containing indexing symbols of Grosseteste related to the concordance were studied to remarkable effect by R.W. Hunt, 'Manuscripts containing the indexing symbols of Robert Grosseteste', in *Bodleian Library Record* 4, 1952-3, pp. 241-255. Fr. Servus Gieben has made original use of the concordance to tell us what authorites Grosseteste would have drawn on, had he written on the meaning of 'philosophy': 'Das Abkürzungszeichen Φ des Roberts Grosseteste: Quom do philosophia accipienda sit a nobis', in *Die Metaphysik im Mittelalter* (Misc.Mediaev.2), Berlin 1963, pp. 522-534. More recently, R. H.

Rouse has found a different, perhaps later, form of the Concordance in *Paris, B.N.n.a.l. 540* (which I have not seen). Finally, R. Southern has added to our knowledge of Grosseteste's employment of the concordance in conjunction with his own indexed books, but thinks it likely that he failed to keep it up to date after c.1230; see R. SOUTHERN, *Robert Grosseteste*, pp. 188-193.

58. *DXM* I,9 (pp. 10-11). It should not be forgotten that as Bishop of Lincoln Grosseteste included in his diocesan Statutes a ruling forbidding the Feats of Fools to take place in churches or churchyards; however, when discussing the patristic opposition to the ancient games he makes no contemporary application, and in fact his reasons for introducing the ban had little or nothing to do with those given by the Fathers for prohibiting attendance at the amphitheatres. See Glynne X. G. WICKHAM, 'Robert Grosseteste and the Feast of Fools', in *Sewanee Mediaeval Colloquium Occasional Papers*, n. 2, 1985, pp. 81-99.

59. The hand is small and some of the numbers I find difficult to read; I may have mistranscribed certain of them.

60. According to HUNT, 'The Library of Robert Grosseteste', in *Robert Grosseteste, Scholar and Bishop* (ed. Callus), the *Epistolae* of Augustine are numbered in the Lyons *Tabula* up to 124, and those of Jerome to 119; see p. 142.

61. K. BARTH, *Anselm: 'Fides Quaerens Intellectum'*, transl. I. W. Robertson (London, SCM Press 1960). Barth interprets Anselm's premise as a prohibition which commands us not to try to think of anything greater or better than God: 'It does not say that God is, nor what he is, but rather, in the form of a prohibition that man can understand who he is' (p. 75).

62. An echo of the *Proslogion* is found in the discussion of the Second Commandment: 'intelligamus eum non hoc vel illud verum, sed ipsum verum verum; non hoc vel illud bonum, sed ipsum bonum bonum. Intelligamus eum quo nichil est superius, nichil est melius: non solum optimum quod excogitari potest, sed et melius quam excogitari potest'. *DXM* II,5 (p. 24). Anselm clearly has become in Grosseteste's eyes the theologian of the transcendence of God and of his incomparability with creation.

63. Fr. Michael ROBSON, O.F.M.Conv., author of a Cambridge Ph.D. on Anselm and the Franciscan theologians (1988), presented a paper entitled 'St Anselm, Robert Grosseteste and the Franciscan Tradition', to the Warburg Colloquium on Robert Grosseteste (May 1987); it will appear in the acts of the colloquium.

64. *Hexaëmeron*, VIII, chs.I-V.

65. S. GIEBEN, 'Traces of God in Nature According to Robert Grosseteste. With the Text of the Dictum, "Omnis creatura speculum est"', in *Franc. Stud.* 24, 1964, pp. 144-158.

66. *DXM* III, paragr. 15 (p. 36), including a quotation from Augustine, *Ad Inquisitiones Ianuarii* (= *Epist.* 55).

67. *DXM* I, paragr.19-23 (pp. 16-18).

68. *DXM* III, paragr.16 (pp. 36-37).

69. *DXM* I, paragr.24-33 (pp. 18-22).

70. *DXM* II, paragr.7,8 (pp. 25-26).

71. Under the Fourth Commandment Grosseteste writes: 'Habemus quoque exemplum pietatis prolis in parentes etiam ab ipsis irracionabilibus'. He quotes Ambrose, *Hexaëmeron* V,16,55, who gives examples of animals which by instinct (*nata lex*) succour their parents.

72. This is a ubiquitous theme in Augustine: see, for example *Ennar.2 in Ps.* 90.1 (*P.L.* 37, 1159): *En.3 in Ps.* 36.4 (*P.L.* 36, 385); *In Ioan.Evang.tr.108.5* (*P.L.* 35, 1916). Grostesteste developed this doctrine and even proposed it as the unifying context for the study of theology, in the Prologue to the *Hexaëmeron*. Robert of Melun before him, and the Dominican Roland of Cremona, his contemporary, likewise took the *subiectum* of theology to be *Christus integer.*

73. *DXM* VII, paragr.3 (p. 76).

74. Amos 5.11; Ecclus 21.9; 34.21; 24-25; Prov.11.24; Exech.19.3; Mic.3.24; Amos 3.9-11.

75. *DXM* IV, paragr.8 (p. 62), which takes up the same quotation.

76. *DXM* V, paragr.24 (p. 48). Purgatory also features in the commentary on Galatians.

77. *DXM* V, paragr.4 (p. 61).

78. *DXM* VIII, paragr.1 (p. 80).

79. *DXM* VIII, paragr.9 (p. 83).

80. *DXM* VIII, paragr.7 (p. 82). The word Grosseteste used for 'illusionist' is *prestigiator.* It is an uncommon word, but is attested in later Latin: Souter (*Glossary of Later Latin*) refers to the Ps.-Ausconius and Prudentius for the meaning 'imposter', 'deceiver', and *praestigio* is attested in the 5th century with the meaning 'to do conjuring

tricks'. In Latham's dictionary, *prestigium,* c.731, has the meaning of 'wonderful work'; *prestigiatura,* c.1114, that of deceit, illusion; and *prestigiatrix,* 1513, a witch. The *Petit Robert* notes '*prestige*' (1518) in the senses of *illusion: artifice séducteur (vieilli ou littéraire); magie.* '*Prestidigitateur*' is a later and literary word (1823). The modern meaning of 'prestige' dates from the 18th century: that which produces an impression of artifice or magic.

81. *DXM* II, paragr.11 (p. 28).

82. Augustine, *De Civitate Dei* I.21.

83. *DXM* V, paragr.11 (p. 64).

84. *DXM* I, paragr. 6 (p. 8).

85. *DXM* IX and X, paragr. 5 (p. 6).

86. *DXM* VI, paragr. 5 (p. 66).

87. *DXM,* prol. (p. 4).

88. *DXM* III, paragr. 2 (pp. 30-31).

89. *DXM* IV, paragr. 27 (p. 49). At 44.34 read *quos* instead of *quod.*

90. *DXM* IX and X, paragr. 11 (p. 90).

Richard William Southern (essay date 1992)

SOURCE: Southern, Richard William. "The Grosseteste Problem." In *Robert Grosseteste: The Growth of an English Mind in Medieval Europe,* pp. 3-25. Oxford: Clarendon Press, 1986.

[*In the following essay, Southern examines contrasting interpretations of Grosseteste's ideas, demonstrating how commentators perceive Grosseteste as both a moderate figure representative of papal reform and an eccentric extremist.*]

I. DIVERGENT VIEWS

The thoughts and actions of all notable historical characters offer grounds for wide differences of interpretation. But Robert Grosseteste offers more grounds, and has been the subject of more widely contrasting interpretations, than most. Observers in his own day, and interpreters ever since, have tended to portray him either as an extremist, in varying ways original, eccentric, discordant; or as an essentially moderate and representative figure in the central stream of European scholastic and scientific thought, and of papally directed ecclesiastical reform and pastoral care. The second of these views has won an increasing measure of support in recent scholarship, but his

contemporaries and their medieval successors were more evenly divided. Two of the main reporters of the thirteenth century, Matthew Paris and Roger Bacon, emphasize (for blame or praise) his eccentricity and his violent—or at least prolonged and determined—opposition to some of the main tendencies of his day. This view was later taken up and developed by Wycliffe and the Lollards, who saw him as their main medieval precursor. On the other hand, we have good contemporary evidence of his urbanity and large hospitality, and several later writers—conspicuous among them the Oxford theologian Thomas Gascoigne—insisted, against the Lollard enthusiasts, on the learned centrality of his thought.

Which of these views is right?

As a preliminary to the enquiry, we must briefly put him in his setting. He was born of humble parentage in the county of Suffolk, probably in the village of Stow Langtoft not far from Bury St Edmunds, at a date which cannot be later or much earlier than 1170. The evidence for the first fifty-five years of his life is meagre in the extreme. Then, quite suddenly, a change sets in. From 1225 we can be quite sure that he was lecturing on theology in Oxford, at first in the secular schools of the university, and from about 1230 in the recently established community of Franciscans just outside the city walls. Then in 1235, quite unexpectedly, he was elected bishop of Lincoln. The next eighteen years are as notable for the abundance of documentation as the earlier years are notable for its absence. When he died on 9 October 1253, he was one of the best known and least understood men in England.

His life, therefore, covered the central period in the consolidation of institutions, habits of thought and religious practices of medieval Europe: the development of papal government from Alexander III to Innocent IV, and of scholastic thought from the first users of Peter Lombard's *Sentences* to the maturity of Albert the Great and Thomas Aquinas; the growth of Canon Law from the first commentators on Gratian's *Decretum* to the first users of Gregory IX's *Decretals;* the translation and penetration into the schools of the whole body of Aristotle's scientific works with their Arabic commentators; the great series of General Councils of 1179, 1215 and 1245; the short-lived Latin Empire of Constantinople from 1204 to 1260. This whole body of events expressed and defined the expansion and unification of the Western world in Grosseteste's life-time. It is against this background that the question of where Grosseteste stood in relation to his contemporaries must be answered.

But no one lives only in the context of great events. Grosseteste must long have struggled with the brutal problem of mere survival. In order to understand him it is necessary above all to explore the almost impenetrable silence of the first fifty-five years of his life. The first requirement for this task is an open mind. This is not easy, perhaps not possible, to achieve. It is inevitable that—at least as a first approximation—he should be fitted into one or other of the recognizable patterns of his day. This has generally meant the pattern which the historian finds most abundantly documented. Grosseteste has shown himself in this respect remarkably adaptable. To recent scholars, the most plausible pattern of his early life and training has been that of other successful scholar-bishops of his time, and there is an inherent probability in this pattern. Nearly all the great scholar-bishops of the period had come up the same ladder of training in the great schools of Paris or Bologna and had acquired a normality of outlook which fitted them for the highest positions in the Church. The position at which Grosseteste belatedly arrived in 1235 seems to require the normality which we find in other men in similar positions. He became a bishop at a time when the procedure for making a bishop was very complicated and required a wide variety of assents. No one could become bishop of the largest diocese in England unless he was acceptable to the pope and king, as well as to the canons of the cathedral. As a body, the bishops of his time were the most important group of administrators and upholders of order and orthodoxy in the country. There were not many among them who had risen from poverty, unless they belonged to a great religious Order or had the support of a great patron. Grosseteste was a friend of the Franciscans, but he belonged to no Order; so far as we know he had no patron; his origins were extremely humble. He had a unique combination of disadvantages. To rise despite these drawbacks would seem to argue not only great abilities, but also an easily recognizable normality of beliefs, social attitudes, and intellectual background. The great schools of Europe provided the best training grounds for these qualities; proficiency in their methods of thought was the best guarantee of doctrinal consistency. The more we know of government in the thirteenth century, the more important a background of international scholastic training appears to be. It seems self-evident that, in order to rise as he did, Grosseteste must have shared this background with the other learned bishops of his day. Yet the contemporary observers who described him most fully say nothing about it. Their emphasis is on his oddity rather than his conformity to contemporary standards of thought and action. This is the first problem with which we are faced.

II. CONTEMPORARY WITNESSES

We may take as our starting-point the accounts of him given by two contemporary, or near contemporary, writers who saw him from very different points of view. The first observed him at fairly close quarters, and wrote down his impressions from year to year during the last eighteen years of Grosseteste's life. The second may never have seen him, but he knew well some of his closest collaborators and he had access to his literary remains. What he learnt from these sources made him feel that he was the heir to Grosseteste's thought, and perhaps the only man who could carry it forward. The first of these writers was Matthew Paris; the second Roger Bacon. Neither of them has a very good reputation among modern scholars for judgement, accuracy or veracity. But with this warning we may turn to what they say. And first to Matthew Paris.

MATTHEW PARIS

Matthew Paris, whatever his demerits may prove to be, had one great advantage over all other observers: at St Albans he was a monk of the greatest monastery in Grosseteste's diocese of Lincoln. Moreover, at the moment when Grosseteste became bishop, Matthew Paris was in the process of taking over from his predecessor, Roger Wendover, the duty of historiographer in the monastery.[1] The historian and the bishop who was to play a central role in his history for the next eighteen years both emerged from obscurity in the same year, and both made their mark at once. The historian announced the new management of the Chronicle by sharpening its tone. Having at first written that the new bishop was 'a worthy and religious man, competently learned in ecclesiastical law', he scratched this out and substituted a phrase of similar length but very different emphasis. The new bishop, he wrote, was 'a man of too much learning, having been brought up in the schools from his early years'.[2] So here, right at the beginning of his independent history, we have an indication of what to expect: a sharp reporter, who does not hesitate to strike out a complacent meaningless phrase and substitute a pointed and abrasive one. It may not be right, and it is certainly not based on deep knowledge or long consideration, but it records a vivid first impression. It is not likely that Matthew Paris knew much about Grosseteste's early years, but he knew that he came straight from the schools of Oxford, and immediately from the school of the Franciscans—a body of men whose influence he distrusted. All this inclined him to think that Grosseteste had too much book-learning and knew too little of the world.

This first impression was not contradicted by the experience of the next few years. Almost at once he saw the bishop engaged in an endless, expensive, acrimonious and—so far as he could judge—stupidly pointless disagreement with the canons of Lincoln over his right to examine and correct their behaviour and the conduct of their affairs. And he saw this as only one example of Grosseteste's insistence on his personal responsibility for the spiritual welfare of every single soul in his diocese, except those formally excluded from his responsibility by an earlier papal privilege. Civilized behaviour, custom, established usages, the common way of life, seemed to mean nothing to this strange bishop. He acted with brutal truculence, and all, so Matthew Paris was inclined to think, for nothing: his actions were a vast waste of energy and resources, a breach of all charity, an implacable effort to insist on changes which could do little good at best, and at worst caused pointless ill-feeling.[3]

From Matthew Paris's point of view, this unfeeling violence was especially odious in the bishop's treatment of the monasteries in his diocese. His own monastery had almost nothing to fear from the bishop's pastoral care. A hundred, no less, papal privileges of recent date and unparalleled particularity protected St Albans and all its dependent churches from any interest that the bishop might take in their welfare. But St Albans had been lucky in having a pope, Hadrian IV, who was almost a son of their church. He had showered privileges on them with a liberal hand, and his successors had followed his example.[4] Other monasteries were less securely guarded. They had to rely on the goodwill of bishops who respected established rights and found in them an essential support for the peace and serenity of the whole fabric of the Church. But Grosseteste came from the great mass of the underdogs of the world. Unlike most bishops he had not learnt from childhood to respect ancient rights and possessions, because he had never enjoyed them. What others saw as rights, he saw as attempts to evade the rigours of religious observance and the pastoral care of the bishop of their souls.

Matthew Paris saw things differently. The civilized life and religious amenity of a great abbey provided the inspiration for all his work. Inevitably, his first suspicions about Grosseteste were hardened into hostility when he found him an unrelenting, persistent, unreasonable and violent enemy, not only to the rights of the canons of Lincoln, but also to the rights of the religious communities in his diocese. Strangely enough, Matthew Paris did not mention, as the Dunstable annalist did, that in his very first episcopal visitation, within a year of his election, Grosseteste deposed no less than eleven heads of religious houses for irregularities of one kind or another.[5] But he saw plenty of other examples of similar wholesale and, as he thought, disproportionate severity towards members of religious communities: 'If all the tyrannies which he practised in his visitations were recorded, he would be reckoned not just a severe man, but a heartless and inhuman one.'[6] Such was Matthew Paris's considered verdict on this side of Grosseteste's activity. The two men were incompatible in their outlook. Matthew Paris, by his upbringing, tastes, and the traditions of his Order, was a humane man. Grosseteste was not. He drove everything to extremes; and, in his pursuit of even good ends, he behaved with a violence which was at least as objectionable as the disorders he sought to eradicate. This was Matthew Paris's view, and he provided abundant detail to support it in his chronicle.

But, in addition to the vivacity and immediacy of his impressions, Matthew Paris had another quality which made him a first-rate journalist: his eyes were open to events of many different kinds, and he gradually became aware of other sides of Grosseteste's character. His first distinctly favourable impression was recorded in 1242, when he reported that the bishop had been responsible for getting hold of, and translating from Greek, a hitherto unknown Old Testament text, which the Jews were alleged to have suppressed because of its testimony to the coming of Christ.[7] This was the work known as the *Testaments of the Twelve Patriarchs,* and Grosseteste's enterprise in making it available to Latin Christendom aroused the chronicler's enthusiasm: it was 'a glorious treatise for strengthening the Christian faith and confounding the hatred of the Jews'. And it appealed to the chronicler's local patriotism, for Grosseteste translated it with the help of Nicholas the Greek, who was connected with the Abbey of St Albans. For the first time, he could express a warmth of admiration for the bishop.

After this date, Matthew Paris found other points to admire. He began to see that the rough violence which was so intolerable when directed against monks, nuns, clergy and common people, could be exhilarating when directed at other targets. He observed that, whenever there were discussions among bishops or at meetings of bishops and lay magnates, it was always Grosseteste who sharpened their resistance to royal encroachments, rallied their wavering pusillanimity and pressed for the excommunication of the enemies of Magna Carta. Also, and increasingly, he saw and applauded his implacable resistance to papal financial demands. On this point, Grosseteste stood out as a friend of local liberties, and Matthew Paris was careful to preserve the proofs in a remarkable collection of documents.[8]

As these varied symptoms of a large and ruggedly independent personality and spiritual presence gradually displayed themselves to his observation, Matthew Paris warmed in his appreciation. In his final summing up he paid him a magnificent tribute in which he tried to do justice to a very complex character. Grosseteste, he wrote, was 'an open reprover of pope and king, a critic of prelates, a corrector of monks, a director of priests, a preacher to the people, a sustainer of scholars, a diligent student of Scripture, a hammer and despiser of the Romans; hospitable, liberal, urbane, cheerful, affable in his hall; devout, tearful, contrite in church; diligent, grave, untiring in his episcopal duties'.[9]

These words must have been written immediately after Grosseteste's death.[10] Then came reports of miracles at his tomb, and Matthew Paris entertained the thought that, besides being a riveting personality, Grosseteste might even be a saint. He contemplated this possibility with sympathy, but with some scruples. What was he then to make of all the excesses he had reported in the course of his Chronicle? This is how he dealt with them:

> Let no one be disturbed by the violent acts which he did in his life-time, as recorded in this book—his treatment of his canons whom he excommunicated and harassed, his savage attacks on monks, and even more savage against nuns . . . They arose from zeal, though perhaps 'not according to knowledge'. And I confidently assert that his virtues pleased God, though his excesses displeased him. It was like this too with David and St Peter. In David, I admire his mildness while reprehending his betrayal of Uriah; in Peter, I admire his constancy while reprehending his thrice-repeated denial.[11]

Then more miracles followed, and Matthew Paris, who was making an abbreviated version of his Chronicle, edged a little further towards complete conviction by altering the assessment of the above paragraph to a 'confident assertion that his virtues pleased God *more* than his excesses displeased Him'.[12] In the same revision, he took the opportunity to revise his initial impression of Grosseteste's election. He recalled facts which he had not thought worth reporting in 1235: the acute divisions and long altercations among the canons of Lincoln during the election, and the totally unexpected unanimous decision in the end to elect Grosseteste, whom no one had supported except the Franciscans. Matthew Paris did not know, or did not report, from whom the initiative which brought this decision had come, but he took the chance to strike out his earlier estimate of the man and to give a new account based on his later experiences: Grosseteste, he wrote, was 'born from the very humblest stock, a man of refined learning in both trivium and quadrivium, unconventional in his manner of life, following his own will and relying on his own judgement, as the narrative which follows will make plain'.[13] These words, written in his own hand, survive to give Matthew Paris's final judgement on the man he had observed over a period of eighteen years.

These small touches have a greater significance than might at first appear, for two reasons. First, because in this revision of his work Matthew Paris was engaged in a drastic reduction in length to about one-eighth of the original narrative. So any *additions* which he makes had some special importance for him. Generally, they indicate his growing interest in the intellectual and scientific movements of his time; and his growing appreciation of Grosseteste is to be seen in this context. Then, they show that Matthew Paris was a more reflec-

tive and conscientious observer than is often realized. Too often he is portrayed as a slap-dash writer who used his Chronicle as a medium for his own prejudices without much regard for truth. But a closer attention to his changes shows that he was a laborious reviser of first impressions, a conscientious collector of evidence, and one with wide views and some refined scruples. This does not mean that he can be accepted without question; but it does mean that he should not be dismissed lightly.

This remark is especially relevant when we come to the longest and most dramatic scene in his whole account of Grosseteste—his death-bed. Matthew Paris was fully aware of the importance of death-bed scenes in winding up accounts of both saints and sinners. This was the moment when eternity impinged on this world in prophecies, visions, premonitions, unusual natural phenomena and miraculous events. It was the time for special revelations about the future course of events; the time too when the dying person might be expected to sum up the experience of a life-time in pregnant phrases, to leave a last message for his disciples, to pass a final judgement on hostile powers, and to give an example of the art of dying. Matthew Paris worked most of those themes into his account of the last days of Grosseteste. The dying man is represented as speaking with force and indignation about all the griefs of his later years—the general neglect of pastoral care, the universal presence of heresy and unbelief in the Western Church, the cause of these evils in the worldliness of the papal curia, which amounted to nothing less than apostasy and foreshadowed the coming of Antichrist. His words blaze with hostility to Innocent IV and the Roman curia as the source of the manifold evils of Christendom. In the light of these evils, the dying man believed that a general disaster was imminent.[14]

Matthew Paris's account of those conversations has not been well received by modern scholars, and we shall have later to examine the grounds for this distrust. All that needs to be said at present is that, if the account turns out to be unreliable, the cause cannot be found in Matthew Paris's blindly one-sided picture of Grosseteste, for we have seen some evidence of his thoughtful and even delicate assessment of the varied strands in Grosseteste. Nor can it be due to indifference to the current ideal of a holy death, for he had recently written a full account of a model death in his biography of Archbishop Edmund of Canterbury.[15] Matthew Paris certainly knew how the elements of contrition, confession, supreme unction and Holy Communion should contribute to such a scene. He gave them a large place at the death-bed of Archbishop Edmund; but he ignored them all in his account of Grosseteste's last days. Despite this, he was willing to believe that Grosseteste too was a saint. Certainly not a conventional one: a seer rather; a man whose heartless persecution of sinners was governed by a deep concern for souls, and whose violence of speech hid a man who in daily life was affable, courteous, hospitable and openhanded. He had long wrestled with the complexities of Grosseteste's character and outlook; and, if he left him mysterious and perplexing in the end, this may be a tribute to the honesty of his reporting. We shall see.

Roger Bacon

We turn now to our other important contemporary witness, Roger Bacon. In every way, both in what he says about Grosseteste and what he himself was, he forms a striking contrast to Matthew Paris. The chronicler had seen Grosseteste in action over a period of nearly twenty years: as a monk in his diocese he had observed and experienced his activity; he had disapproved of much, been puzzled by more, and had felt the appeal of an intense earnestness and power in all that Grosseteste did, without understanding the connecting links which held it all together. Roger Bacon had seen nothing of all this. Indeed, it is not even quite certain that he had ever set eyes on Grosseteste in person: he may have known him only from the reports of his friends and associates, and more especially from Grosseteste's chief friend and disciple, Adam Marsh.[16] But also, after he became a Franciscan in about 1257, he had access to the literary remains which Grosseteste left to the community at Oxford. It was from these sources that Bacon got a picture of Grosseteste which was clear, consistent and inspiring, entirely lacking in the dark corners and contradictory features of Matthew Paris's portrait. The contrast points to an essential difference between the two observers. Matthew Paris saw Grosseteste as a contemporary in his everyday world. Bacon saw him as a man of an earlier age, a forerunner.

So far as we can judge, Grosseteste left no mark on Bacon's early studies nor on any of his writings before he joined the Franciscans. But from 1267 onwards, he wrote a series of works inspired by a new vision of scientific, linguistic, and biblical study designed to save Christendom from its internal and external enemies. The key document in this second phase of his life is a letter, now lost, written to Pope Clement IV in 1265/6 giving a brief account of his ideas and the obstacles under which he laboured. The pope replied on 22 June 1266 asking him to send a full account of his ideas as soon as possible, in secret and without regard to the orders of his superiors. Bacon replied in 1267 by sending his *Opus Minus* as an introduction to his new programme, and his *Opus Maius* which gave a full account of his whole plan. He also set about preparing an intermediate work, his *Opus Tertium*. This was going ahead in 1267.

Clement IV died in 1268 and it is doubtful whether the *Opus Tertium* was ever finished, but Bacon went on expounding his programme in several forms until 1292.[17] His plan became an obsession, and the works in which he developed it are extraordinarily detailed, complicated, and repetitive. They are frequently bizarre and always idiosyncratic. They have the grandeur and impracticability of passionate conviction and unremitting zeal. In all of them he mentions Grosseteste with extravagant praise as his precursor in every main branch of his proposals: it is this that gives his programme a special interest to us here.

What Bacon urged was that Western Christendom should change the direction of its studies: first, that it should master the philosophical and scientific resources of its enemies with a view to meeting them on their own ground; and, secondly, that it should clarify its own position by discarding harmful accretions and concentrating on the central documents of its tradition. For the first of these aims, it was necessary that the Latins should learn the languages—especially Greek—in which scientific knowledge, hitherto available only in debased translations, was to be found most fully expounded. Having done this, it would then be possible to master the sciences to which these writings were no more than the introduction. For the second aim, a deeper understanding of the Bible was the primary requirement. To achieve this, a knowledge of Greek and Hebrew, and a much greater familiarity with the writings of Greek theologians and commentators than the West had hitherto possessed, were essential. Add to these studies the use of science to clarify the symbolism of the Bible; cut out the distractions of Peter Lombard's *Sentences* and the obsessive interest of the West in Roman Law; and the West would be on the road to recovery and able to meet the Muslims both in the field of action and in debate.

In support of this programme in all its branches Bacon invoked the name of Robert Grosseteste. In his view, Grosseteste had pioneered every one of the developments which he advocated. Bacon had gone further—much further—but it was Grosseteste who had shown the way. That is how Bacon saw the situation, and his point of view explains several oddities in his account of his predecessor. In the first place, it accounts for his very extravagant praise of Grosseteste and his associates. Then also, despite the praise, it accounts for his constant tendency to criticize Grosseteste and to follow him very rarely in detail. And it explains why he always and only saw Grosseteste as a proto-Bacon. We can see all these tendencies at work as we go through his references to Grosseteste one by one.

The most extravagantly laudatory passage is one in which he described the heroic Grosseteste brushing aside the wholly inadequate translations of Aristotle and going straight to the sciences. Bacon was very eloquent on the subject of the uselessness of the earlier translations: they were so useless, he said, that the more they were read, the less they brought understanding of the subject. Grosseteste alone had had the courage to ignore them:

> Robert, formerly bishop of Lincoln of blessed memory, neglected the books of Aristotle and their arguments and, by using his own experience and other authors and other means of learning, he worked his way into the wisdom of Aristotle and came to know and write about the subjects of Aristotle's works a hundred thousand times better than those who used only the perverted translations of these works. You can see this in his treatises on Rainbows, on Comets, and other works which he wrote.[18]

This passage has often been quoted, and as a factual statement it is absurd. Grosseteste did not neglect Aristotle; and he was not unduly bothered by the shortcomings of the existing translations. And yet, if we can imagine Bacon as a Franciscan in Oxford reading Grosseteste's little scientific treatises for the first time, noticing their freshness of approach, their arguments from the phenomena themselves, their interest in the geometry of celestial movements, and their independence with regard to Aristotle; and if we further imagine Bacon meeting the men whom Grosseteste had inspired to undertake the greatest cooperative work of translating Greek sources ever attempted in the West; and if we make allowances for the highly charged, superlative-laden, style of writing to which the Franciscans (not least Adam Marsh, and even Grosseteste himself) were addicted, then Bacon's reconstruction of Grosseteste's achievement is understandable. So also are his criticisms. If the lack of adequate translations had forced Grosseteste to plunge into the sciences without a reliable guide, this explained why his methods were sometimes clumsy and his conclusions wrong. He had the great merit of seeing the fundamental role of mathematics in science, but his mathematical methods were crude and old-fashioned.[19] A similar critical note is struck when Bacon refers to Grosseteste's work on the calendar—the only subject on which Bacon wrote a rival work, perhaps intended to replace Grosseteste's. He criticized Grosseteste for retaining the common distinctions of spring, summer, autumn, winter, instead of following the philosopher Abu Ma'shar in dividing the seasons, in a manner consistent both with nature and reason, into three periods of growth, equilibrium, decline.[20] Yet, despite this weakness, which we may be inclined to see as a preference for common sense over highfalutin theory, he saw Grosseteste as the only modern man who had understood the sciences: 'Only Boethius, the first of all the translators, understood the

power of languages; only Robert Grosseteste knew the sciences. The other translators were defective both in languages and in sciences.'[21]

Bacon revered Grosseteste also as a pioneer in the study of languages, but he had started too late, for—so Bacon tells us—it was only towards the end of his life that he was sufficiently competent to translate Greek without help.[22] Modern scholars have thought that Bacon was here, as elsewhere, too severe; but he was not far from the mark, and if he unduly depreciated Grosseteste's linguistic ability, he did full justice to his energy and foresight in collecting Greek books and gathering together a group of translators. Bacon mentions their names: Adam Marsh, Robert Marsh, Thomas Wallensis, William Lupus, and William of Sherwood. Strangely enough, he does not mention the earliest and most notable of them, John of Basingstoke, who had died the year before Grosseteste in 1252, and this is another indication that Bacon knew about Grosseteste's life only from those who survived him.

His mention of Grosseteste's work as a translator brought Bacon to another of his favourite themes: the need to enlist the help of the old Greek theologians in understanding the Bible. His list of neglected authors in need of study and further translation runs thus: Origen, Basil, Gregory of Nyssa, John of Damascus, Denys, Chrysostom. Grosseteste had been responsible for bringing all of them except Origen to wider notice in the West. So here too Bacon could claim Grosseteste as the originator of the programme which he advocated.[23]

Then, last and most important of all, he claimed Grosseteste and his friend Adam Marsh as the chief men of his own day in maintaining the primacy of the Bible over all other texts for the study of theology.[24]

Brief though these notices are, they form a magnificent eulogy of Grosseteste as the initiator in all parts of Bacon's ambitious programme—in the study of science and Greek, in organizing translations, in the primacy of the Bible, against the main scholastic tendencies of the period before about 1220. No doubt Bacon pressed Grosseteste too firmly into his own mould. They were men of very different temper. Bacon was a grandiose and systematic planner of an ideal scheme of studies designed to lead to effective action against the enemies of Christendom. Everything that he wrote in his later years, for which he claimed Grosseteste as his exemplar, was directed to this end. But there is not the slightest reason to think that Grosseteste was interested in grand plans of scholastic reform. We shall find him going from one activity to another as circumstances and the inspiration of the moment led him. Bacon was altogether more aggressive, systematic, polemical, and scholastic in outlook. Grosseteste could indeed on occasion be both polemical and aggressive, but only under the impact of immediate events. In his scientific and theological writings, in his Greek studies and his translations, he took up subjects as they presented themselves to his notice, and it is very unlikely that he would have approved the framework in which Bacon placed him. Yet Bacon correctly identified the four areas of his essential originality. This perception entitles him to a high place among the interpreters of Grosseteste's achievement: he was the first to pick out the things which are most worthy of attention.

A MEMBER OF GROSSETESTE'S HOUSEHOLD: FR. HUBERT

A different aspect of Grosseteste's complexity is revealed in the lavish hospitality and urbanity which (as Matthew Paris saw) presented a vivid contrast to his harshness in action. This sunny side of Grosseteste's character was beautifully portrayed in a brief biography, or rather lament, written shortly after his death by an unknown friar Hubert.[25] Biographically, this effusion tells us no single fact about him which was not already known. The writer seems to have known nothing about Grosseteste's early life, except that he was born in Suffolk. His words would have been no more than a general eulogy if they had not provided a serene and convincing picture of Grosseteste in the circle of his *familia,* to which the writer evidently belonged. The portrait is both moving and life-like. We should not have guessed that such a man lay behind the details which occupy so many pages of Matthew Paris or formed the subject of Roger Bacon's observations. Here we see him as a courteous and lavish host, a great spender of his revenues, intensely interested in the education of the noble children in his household, amenable, encouraging, talkative to all around him, sombre yet lighthearted, perpetually active, deeply contemplative, dedicated to prayer and worship; the protector of the poor, the critic of kings and popes, the patron of both orders of friars. This was the man as his intimates knew him, as contrasted with the man whom others knew either as a disturber of worldly peace or as an intellectual innovator.

III. LATER HISTORICAL RECONSTRUCTIONS

Grosseteste presented several different views of his aims and activities to his contemporaries. All of them responded to him in ways which reflected their own circumstances and interests; and later scholars and chroniclers down to the present day have continued to make similarly weighted responses. The first important new alignment of the Grosseteste material is to be found in the various recensions of Ranulf Higden's Chronicle during the fifty years after 1327.[26] It was Higden who first drew the outlines of a national hero suffering for his resistance to the papacy. And it is interesting that he did not draw the material for this portrait, as he might have done, from Matthew Paris: rather, it would seem, he drew from the experiences of the canons of Lincoln, whose long-continued efforts to obtain Grosseteste's canonization had been finally repelled by the papal curia shortly before 1330.[27]

On an objective view, the curia had good reasons for their refusal. But this was not how it seemed to his local advocates, and Higden adopted their point of view. Brief though his account is, it contains several elements which were to endear Grosseteste to the Lollards fifty years later: Grosseteste's opposition to papal exactions, his excommunication, his posthumous judgement on Innocent IV, followed by the refusal of the curia to canonize him despite the miracles at his tomb. Later, in the 1340s, Higden added more details, including an imperfectly understood reference to Grosseteste's speech to the pope and cardinals in 1250, which does not seem to have been noticed by any earlier chronicler. So here we see that in the mid-fourteenth century the picture of the uncanonized saint and heroic anti-papal figure, in whom Wycliffe and the Lollards were later to see their great exemplar, was already being built up.

Wycliffe and the Lollards perfected this picture of the persecuted saint and religious teacher who suffered for his denunciation of the worldly papacy and its curialist minions. Two centuries later, the 'Protestant Grosseteste' received his final consummation in Foxe's *Book of Martyrs.* Foxe took some care in constructing his portrait of Grosseteste. He made full use of Matthew Paris, and he examined Grosseteste's literary remains 'in the Queen's Majesty's Library at Westminster'.[28] His book continued for another two hundred years to keep the Wycliffite Grosseteste alive in many remote parish churches. But Foxe's account was the last gasp of Grosseteste the religious agitator. A few years after the publication of the *Book of Martyrs,* an equally eccentric but less significant figure was given a wide circulation in Holinshed's Chronicle. Holinshed ignored the anti-papal bishop, but extracted from Matthew Paris a portrait of a sour martinet. He chose details which portrayed a busybody bishop, who excommunicated sinners and negligent officials with a hasty hand; a prurient investigator of monastic sins, who in his visitations of monasteries 'entered into the chambers of the monks and searched their beds, and, coming to the houses of the nuns, went so near as to cause their breasts to be tried that he might understand their chaste livings', and so on.[29] All these details are indeed to be found in Matthew Paris, and it is by no means clear that Grosseteste was incapable of these actions. But they had lost their interest, and Grosseteste was effectively dismissed from the pages of national, still more international, history for three hundred years.

What brought him once more to a central position in the history of his time was the constitutional theme as developed by William Stubbs. The few pages which Stubbs devoted to him marked a decisive new beginning in Grosseteste studies. For the first time, serious historical scholarship was brought to the interpretation of Grosseteste, not as an eccentric extremist or lonely figure in a hostile age, but as an essentially moderate and central influence in the greatest of the medieval centuries. To Stubbs he was as great a hero as he had been to Wycliffe and Foxe, but in a different mould: 'the most learned, the most acute, the most holy man of his time, the most devoted to his spiritual work, the most trusted leader and confidant of princes, at the same time a most faithful servant of the Roman Church.' 'The great mauler of the Romans' of Foxe has become a farsighted statesman whose 'attitude to the papacy was not one of unintelligent submission'. In Stubbs's pages Grosseteste emerged at last as a central figure in a great age of construction: 'the prophet and harbinger of better times coming', 'the friend and adviser of the constitutional opposition', 'more than once the spokesman of the constitutional party in parliament; the patron of the friars who represented learning and piety as well as the doctrines of civil independence in the universities and country at large'.[30] Stubbs wrote about Grosseteste with a quite unaccustomed warmth. He was the first scholar to see Grosseteste as a representative of all that was best in the thirteenth century, a great man in a great age displaying all the normality of a superior mind.

A hundred years have now passed since Stubbs wrote, and an ever growing number of studies have been published which have concentrated attention on scientific and theological works which Stubbs scarcely knew. These studies have largely undermined Stubbs's picture of Grosseteste as a great figure in the constitutional development of England, and they have increasingly placed him in the setting of European scholastic thought. But they have all preserved one essential feature of Stubbs's portrait: Grosseteste's centrality. As the constitutional theme has withered, Grosseteste has emerged as a central exponent of the scientific and theological developments of the early thirteenth century.

The first, and still in its general outlines the best, expression of this new normality is to be found in the collection of studies edited by Fr. Daniel Callus to commemorate the seventh centenary of Grosseteste's death in 1953.[31] I linger over it, for it is one of the most distinctive products of the school of history associated with Sir Maurice Powicke, to which I have had the honour to belong.

To understand its emphasis it is necessary to recall the circumstances of its publication and the aims of what may broadly be called the Powicke school of history. It had always been the special aim of this school to assert the normative role of the twelfth and thirteenth centuries in the development of European civilization, and to emphasize the importance of European influences in English history. Grosseteste seemed to offer an ideal illustration of these two principles: he could be seen as an Englishman fully immersed in the European tradition, reflecting all that was latest and best in the scholastic tradition of Paris and Oxford, exemplifying this tradition in his own writings, and giving effect to the recent legislation of the Fourth Lateran Council of 1215 in his work as a bishop.

This was the general picture; and the moment was peculiarly propitious for giving it a new expression. Its guiding principles had been fashioned in the inter-war years, under the growing threat of a war which seemed likely to destroy everything of most importance in European history. The threat had risen to its climax, and had (as it seemed) finally receded. A subject which revived the hopes of earlier years was, therefore, approached with a certain sense of euphoria. At last it was possible to take a long and peaceful look at Grosseteste in the light of the great advances which had been made in the study of European scholastic thought during the previous generation. He could be portrayed as Oxford's, and perhaps as England's, greatest exponent of the all-embracing European normality created by the joint influences of the great schools, the papacy, and the new religious orders—as a link connecting these European themes with the university of Oxford and with the legislation of the English church.

All these aspects of the subject were brought together in Powicke's introduction to the volume. Then the tale was taken up by Father Callus, certainly the most profound and sympathetic Grosseteste scholar of the time. He saw Grosseteste as a joint product of the schools of Paris and Oxford, exhibiting the fine polish of a highly developed scholastic training, following (or even leading) the fashion of writing a *Summa Theologiae* on the model of Peter Lombard's *Sentences,* contributing to the growth of ideas in almost every branch of contemporary study:

> one of the greatest glories of the university of Oxford, her first chancellor in the crucial years of her formation . . . he gave a powerful impetus in every department of intellectual activity in which he himself excelled, and left behind him a tradition of learning which was destined to grow, increase, and deepen throughout the centuries.[32]

These two contributions set the tone for the whole volume. Even when it came to a consideration of Grosseteste's diatribes against the papal curia, the note of moderation which separated him—despite all superficial resemblances—from Wycliffe was strongly maintained:

'Grosseteste, I think (wrote Dr Pantin), envisaged an unlawful command as a temporary aberration, which deprives the superior's command of validity *pro hac vice,* but does not permanently destroy the superior's authority or the office that he holds . . . Wycliffe on the other hand, at least in his final stage, seems to regard reprobate popes and prelates as permanently lacking authority. Even the epithet 'Antichrist', which Grosseteste used more than once of the pope and papal curia, despite its 'ominous sound to modern ears', was given an interpretation which brought it well within the bounds of normality: 'what he (Grosseteste) has in mind is a moral, not a doctrinal failure, and he does not envisage the possibility of the papacy or the Church erring in doctrine.'[33]

Fr. Callus's volume is so full of wise and balanced words, so impregnated with civilized sentiments, and has so strong a hold on the minds of those who have lived with it, that it is hard to call in question the attitude it expresses. Yet one must ask whether it does not drain the life out of a tempestuous character and flatten the contours of a strongly independent and unconventional thinker. Have not the jagged edges, the violence of feeling, the extremist tendencies in thought and expression, been smoothed away? Have not the actual circumstances of his life, and the influences which they brought to bear on him, been forgotten?

Notes

1. For details of the change of authorship, see Richard Vaughan, *Matthew Paris,* Cambridge, 1958, 28-30, and Richard Kay, 'Wendover's last annal', *EHR* [*English Historical Review*] lxxxiv, 1969, 779-85, where it is shown that Roger of Wendover wrote his last annal in spring 1234. From this point Matthew Paris was the sole author, at first retaining the general style and attitude of his predecessor, but rapidly developing his own personal style and point of view.

2. He omitted both descriptions when he enlarged the passage in his final revision (see below, p. 11 [in Richard William Southern, *Robert Grosseteste: The Growth of an English Mind in Medieval Europe*]).

3. For Paris's opinion of this quarrel, see *Chron. Maj.* iii. 528-9, 638-9; iv. 497.

4. For Hadrian's privileges granted to St Albans, see Holtzmann, *Papsturkunden in England,* Abh. der Akademie der Wissenschaften in Göttingen, 1952, iii. 100-13, 117-19; those of his successors, *passim.*

5. *Annales de Dunstaplia,* 1235 (*Ann. Mon.* iii. 143-4).

6. *Chron. Maj.* v. 226.

7. Ibid. iv. 232-3.

8. The first occasion on which Paris reported with approval a speech of Grosseteste was in October 1244 when he stiffened the resistance of the bishops against a papal demand for their consent to a subsidy to the king (*Chron. Maj.* iv. 366: for the date and circumstances, see F. M. Powicke, *Henry III and the Lord Edward,* Oxford, 1947, i. 298-30). See also *Chron. Maj.* v. 325-6, for Grosseteste's intervention in October 1252 to prevent the payment of a papally supported subsidy to the king for the Crusade; v. 377-8, 395-400, for his excommunication of breakers of Magna Charta; and v. 355 for his calculation that the 'present Pope Innocent IV' had impoverished the church more than all his predecessors put together. All these incidents were recorded with favourable or neutral intention. For the main documents relating to Grosseteste preserved by Paris among his *Additamenta,* see *Chron. Maj.* vi. 134-44, 148-50, 152, 186-7, 200-1, 213-17, 229-31.

9. *Chron. Maj.* v. 407.

10. Matthew Paris originally intended to bring his Chronicle to a close in 1250 and he wrote an elaborate ending at this point (*Chron. Maj.* v. 198). But after an interval of a year or two he resumed it and brought it down to the end of 1253 (v. 420). The final entries of this year give the impression of being written at the same time as the events they describe: for instance, the first summing up of Grosseteste's character quoted above appears immediately after his death. But then came reports of daily miracles at his tomb, and Paris wrote a new summing up, repeating some examples of Grosseteste's violence, but expressing confidence in his sanctity (v. 419, as quoted below). Then, a little later, *c.*1255, Paris made his abbreviation of the annals for these years, and he curtailed the examples of Grosseteste's violence (probably erasing one of them in *Chron. Maj.* as noted by the editor) and strengthened the confident note of the final sentence.

11. *Chron. Maj.* v. 419.

12. *Hist. Angl.* iii. 148-9.

13. Ibid. ii. 376. The printed text is unintelligible at this point, so I give a corrected version of the essential sentence from BL MS Royal 14 C vii f. 123[r]: 'Ipse autem Robertus ex humillima stirpe procreatus, eleganter tam in trivio quam quadrivio eruditus, sui ipsius consilio non alieno regi volens, singularis erat conversationis et propriae sectator voluntatis, suae innitens prudentiae, quod perspicue postea manifestavit, sicut sequens narratio

manifestavit.' The erasures and alterations in the manuscript bear witness to the care with which the whole passage was composed. A slightly later corrector was responsible for a misunderstanding of the phrase 'sui ipsius consilio non alieno regi volens', which has got into the printed edition: he read 'volens' as 'nolens', wrongly understood 'regi' as meaning 'to the king', and added 'praesentari' in the margin in a desperate attempt to make sense. It is in this corrupt form that it is generally quoted.

14. *Chron. Maj.* v. 400-7; abbreviated in *Hist. Angl.* iii. 145-6.

15. Printed in C. H. Lawrence, *St Edmund of Abingdon: A Study in Hagiography and History,* 1960, pp. 264-71.

16. Roger Bacon seems to have been born in about 1219. His career is at all points extremely elusive, but his early writings on the liberal arts appear to be connected with Paris. In 1267 (in his *Opus Tertium,* p. 59) he says that he has been buying scientific books and instruments for twenty years, but there is no firm evidence for his presence in Oxford or knowledge of Grosseteste before he entered the Franciscan Order, perhaps in 1257 and probably in Oxford. For Bacon's early career, see S. C. Easton, *Roger Bacon and his Search for a Universal Science,* Oxford, 1952. Also A. C. Crombie and J. N. North in the *Dictionary of Scientific Biography,* ed. C. C. Gillespie, i, 1970, 377-83.

17. The best survey of Bacon's works is still A. G. Little's account in *Roger Bacon Commemoration Essays,* Oxford, 1914, pp. 373-419. For our present purpose it will suffice to mention the *Opus Tertium* and the *Opus Minus* printed in *Rogeri Bacon Opera hactenus inedita,* ed. J. S. Brewer, RS, 1859; a supplementary fragment of *Opus Minus* printed by Cardinal Gasquet, *EHR* xii, 1897, 494-517; and a supplementary part of the *Opus Tertium,* ed. A. G. Little, *Brit. Soc. of Franciscan Studies, iv, 1912; the Opus Maius,* ed. J. H. Bridges, 3 vols. 1897-1900, with supplements ed. by E. Massa, *Rogeri Baconis Moralis Philosophia,* Padua, 1953, and by K. M. Fredborg, Lauge Nielsen, and Jan Pinborg, 'An Unedited Part of Roger Bacon's *Opus Maius: De Signis*', in *Traditio,* xxiv, 1978, 75-136. Later works of Bacon on related themes are his *Compendium studii philosophiae* (1271) in Brewer, op. cit., pp. 393-519; and *Compendium studii theologiae* (1292) ed. H. Rashdall, *Brit. Soc. of Franciscan Studies,* iii, 1911.

18. *Compendium studii philosophiae,* ed. Brewer, p. 469.

19. For Grosseteste's understanding of the fundamental importance of mathematics, see *Opus Maius,* i. 108; and for his technical shortcomings, *Communia mathematica,* ed. R. Steele, *Opera hactenus inedita Rogeri Baconi,* fasc. 16, 1940, pp. 117-18.

20. Roger Bacon, *Compotus,* ed. R. Steele, 1926, p. 40.

21. *Opus Maius,* i. 67; cf. *Opus Tertium,* p. 33, and *Compendium studii philosophiae,* p. 472. Also *Opus Minus,* p. 317, for a probable reference to Grosseteste on rainbows and similar phenomena: 'Certus sum quod nullus apud Latinos praeter unum qui est sapientissimus Latinorum poterit satisfacere in hac parte.'

22. For Bacon's assessment of Grosseteste as a Greek scholar with the names of other translators (chiefly Grosseteste's helpers), see *Opus Maius,* i. 73.

23. Roger Bacon's words on this subject deserve to be quoted because they put Grosseteste's translations in their correct theological context and emphasize their scale. Bacon has been speaking of the need for new translations of Greek scientific works, and he continues: 'Innumerabiles etiam libri expositorum Hebraeorum et Graecorum desunt Latinis, ut Origenis, Basilii, Gregorii, Nazianzeni, Damasceni, Dionysii, Chrysostomi, et aliorum doctorum nobilissimorum tam in Hebraico quam in Greco. Dormit igitur ecclesia quae nihil facit in hac parte, nec aliquid a septuaginta annis fecit, nisi quod dominus Robertus, episcopus Lincolniensis sanctae memoriae, tradidit Latinis de libris beati Dionysii, et Damasceni, et aliquibus aliis doctoribus consecratis. Mirum est de negligentia ecclesiae, quia a tempore Damasi papae non fuit aliquis summus pontifex nec aliquis alius inferior, qui solicitus fuit de promotione ecclesiae per translationes, nisi dominus praefatus episcopus gloriosus.' (*Compendium studii philosophiae,* ed. Brewer, p. 474; cf. also *Opus Maius,* i. 70, on the same theme). For the justice of Bacon's estimate of Grosseteste's importance in this field, see below, chapter 8.

24. *Opus Minus,* ed. Brewer, p. 329. Bacon marks the generation gap between himself and these *maximi viri* by referring to them as *sapientes antiqui,* some of whom he had nevertheless seen with his own eyes.

25. This lament was discovered and printed by R. W. Hunt, 'Verses on the Life of Grosseteste', *Medievalia et Humanistica,* NS i, 1970, 241-51. There is a full and sympathetic account of it in McEvoy, 1982, 40-2. McEvoy's 'Portrait of Grosseteste', ibid., pp. 3-48, deserves to be studied as a whole,

and I have not thought it necessary to go over again the ground which he covers.

26. See *Polychronicon Ranulphi Higden,* ed. J. R. Lumby, RS, 9 vols., 1865-86, viii. 240-3. The growth of the text at this point can be made out with the help of the analysis of the recensions of Higden's Chronicle in John Taylor, *The Universal Chronicle of Ranulph Higden,* Oxford, 1966. It was Higden who gave currency to the story, beloved by the Lollards, that Grosseteste had been excommunicated by Innocent IV. In Matthew Paris's account the cardinals persuaded the pope not to proceed to extreme measures, and it is likely that he was simply suspended from some or all of his episcopal duties. Nevertheless, the generally well-informed Lanercost Chronicle (p. 43) preserved an earlier Franciscan tradition that he died excommunicate.

27. For the attempts at canonization, see E. W. Kemp in Callus, 1955, 241-6.

28. John Foxe, *Actes and Monuments of thynges passed in every kynges tym in this realm* (generally known as the *Book of Martyrs*), edition of 1570, pp. 404-10. Among other works of Grosseteste, Foxe saw 'one sermon writen and exhibited in four sondry skroles, to the pope and other four Cardinals beginning "Dominus noster Jesus Christus"'. This was the speech distributed to the pope and four cardinals and read to the curia in 1250 (see below, p. 276), almost certainly the copy in BL MS Royal 7 F ii.

29. R. Holinshed, *Chronicles of England, Scotland and Ireland,* edition of 1585, pp. 242, 244, 246, 249, quoting Matthew Paris, *Chron. Maj.* v. 226-7, 256.

30. W. Stubbs, *Constitutional History of England,* ii, 3rd edn. 1887, pp. 74, 313-15.

31. *Robert Grosseteste, Scholar and Bishop,* ed. D. A. Callus, Oxford, 1955.

32. Ibid., p. 69.

33. Ibid., pp. 191-2.

Abbreviations

AHDLMA: *Archives d'histoire doctrinale et littéraire du Moyen Âge*

BGPMA: *Beiträge zur Geschichte der Philosophie des Mittelalters,* 1891–

BL: British Library, London

BLR: *Bodleian Library Record*

BRUO: A. B. Emden, *Biographical Register of the University of Oxford,* 3 vols, Oxford 1957-9

MGH: Monumenta Germaniae Historica

Coll. Franc.: *Collectanea Franciscana*

CPR: *Calendar of Entries in the Papal Registers relating to Great Britain and Ireland,* ed. W. H. Bliss, vol. i, 1893, London

EHR: *English Historical Review*

Ep.: Roberti Grosseteste *Epistolae* (referred to by number)

Franc. Stud.: *Franciscan Studies*

HUO: *History of the University of Oxford,* i. *The Early Oxford Schools,* ed. J. I. Catto, Oxford, 1984

JTS: *Journal of Theological Studies*

MARS: *Mediaeval and Renaissance Studies,* London

Med. Hum.: *.Medievalia et Humanistica*

PG: Migne, *Patrologia Graeca*

PL: Migne, *Patrologia Latina*

RTAM: *Recherches de théologie ancienne et médiévale*

RS: Chronicles and Memorials of Great Britain and Ireland published under the direction of the Master of the Rolls, London, 1858-96

SB: *Sitzungsberichte*

TRHS: *Transactions of the Royal Historical Society,* London

FURTHER READING

Criticism

Callus, Daniel A. "Robert Grosseteste as Scholar." In *Robert Grosseteste, Scholar and Bishop: Essays in Commemoration of the Seventh Centenary of His Death,* edited by D. A. Callus, pp. 1-69. Oxford: Clarendon Press, 1955.

    Collection of essays by notable medievalists on the 700th anniversary of the death of Grosseteste, covering topics such as his status as a scholar, his position in the history of science, his library, his administration of the diocese of Lincoln, his relations with the papacy and crown, and the attempt to canonize him.

Crombie, A. C. "Grosseteste's Writings on the Theory of Science." In *Robert Grosseteste and the Origins of Experimental Science 1100-1700,* pp. 44-60. Oxford: Clarendon Press, 1953.

Speculates on the dates of Grosseteste's writings on the theory of science and offers a detailed examination of the foundations of his position.

Dales, Richard C. "The Influence of Grosseteste's *Hexameron* on the *Sentences* Commentaries of Richard Fishacre, O. P. and Richard Rufus of Cornwall, O. F. M.." *Viator: Medieval and Renaissance Studies* (1971): 271-300.

Charts the nature and extent of the influence of Grosseteste's *Hexaëmeron* on some thirteenth-century authors.

————. "Robert Grosseteste's Place in Medieval Discussions of the Eternity of the World." *Speculum: A Journal of Medieval Studies* 61, no. 3 (July 1986): 544–63.

Explores Grosseteste's views on the eternity of the world, noting that he was an influential if conservative figure in the long-running debate on this central point of disagreement between Christian and sectarian philosophers.

Friedman, Lee M. *Robert Grosseteste and the Jews.* Cambridge: Harvard University Press, 1934, 34p.

Claims that Grosseteste's writings contain the earliest extant expression of sympathetic understanding of the difficult position of medieval Jews.

Goering, Joseph F. A. C. Mantello. "Robert Grosseteste's Confessional Formula in Lambeth Palace Palace MS 499." *Viator* 18 (1987): 253-73.

Reproduces for the first time, in a modern edition, Grosseteste's brief confessional formulary, *Notus in Iudea Deus.*

Laird, Edgar S. "Robert Grosseteste, Albumasar, and Medieval Tidal Theory." *Isis* 81, no. 4 (December 1990): 684-94.

Points out the influence of the Arabic astrologer Albumasar on Grosseteste's short treatise on tides, *Questio De Fluxu et Refluxu Maris..*

Laird, W. R. "Robert Grosseteste on the Subalternate Sciences." *Traditio: Studies in Ancient and Medieval History, Thought, and Religion* 43 (1987): 147-69.

Claims that Grosseteste's approach to the subalternate sciences, as seen in his commentary on the *Posterior Analytics,* was fundamentally Aristotelian.

McEvoy, James. *The Philosophy of Robert Grosseteste.* Oxford: Clarendon Press, 1982, 560p.

Study of Grosseteste's life and works, covering his influences and early works, theological writings, and philosophical and scientific treatises.

————. "The Chronology of Robert Grosseteste's Writings on Nature and Natural Philosophy." *Speculum: A Journal of Medieval Studies* 58, no. 3 (July 1983): 614-55.

Reconstructs the chronology of Grosseteste's scientific writings.

————. "The Text and Source of the Treatise *De Decem Mandatis* of Robert Grosseteste." *Recherches de Theologie Ancienne et Medievale* 58 (January-December 1991): 206-12.

Comments on the modern edition of Grosseteste's *De Decem Mandatis* and identifies the biblical quotations and allusions contained in the text.

————. "Grosseteste on the Soul's Care for the Body: A New Text and New Sources for the Idea." In *Aspectus et Affectus: Essays and Editions in Grosseteste and Medieval Intellectual Life in Honor of Richard C. Dales,* edited by Gunard Freibergs, pp.37-56. New York: AMS Press, 1993.

Presents an extract from an unedited sermon by Grosseteste that explores the nature of Christ's redemptive suffering.

————. "Contribution to Philosophy." In *Robert Grosseteste,* pp. 76–95. New York: Oxford University Press, 2000.

Comments on Grosseteste's philosophical interests, including his contributions to the liberal arts, his knowledge of Aristotle, and his ideas on the metaphysics of light.

Schulman, N. M. "Husband, Father, Bishop? Grosseteste in Paris." *Speculum: A Journal of Medieval Studies* 72, no. 2 (April 1997).

Speculates on the details of Grosseteste's activities from 1198 to 1225.

Townsend, David. "Robert Grosseteste and Walter of Wimborne." *Medium Aevum* 55 (1986): 113-17.

Explores the connection between Grosseteste and the Franciscan poet Walter of Wimborne.

Additional coverage of Grosseteste's life and career is contained in the following source published by the Gale Group: *Dictionary of Literary Biography,* **Vol. 115.**

Flavius Philostratus
c. 179 (?)-c. 244-49

(Full name Lucius Flavius Philostratus) Greek philosopher and biographer.

INTRODUCTION

Known as one of the leading sophists, or popular philosopher-orators, of his time, Philostratus was an important member of the Roman imperial court. He is best remembered as the author of two works, a collection of biographies titled *Vitae Sophistarum* (1921; *The Lives of the Sophists*) and *Vita Apollonii* (1809; *Life of Apollonius of Tyana*), the life of a charismatic miracle worker. Although neither work is well regarded among classicists, most scholars agree that Philostratus's texts offer important information about the history of ancient rhetoric, and that his biography of Apollonius is one of the best historical sources available about the first-century sage. Not much is known about Philostratus's other writings, mostly because his father, son-in-law, and grandson—all named Philostratus as well—were also well-known authors, making it difficult to say precisely which Philostratus was responsible for what work. While authorship of several works remains disputed, other texts most likely written by Philostratus include *Gymnasticus,* an essay on sport (written after 220), the *Heroikos,* a dialogue on the heroes of the Trojan War (date unknown), *Imagines* [1931; *Imagines*], a description of thirty-four paintings on mythological themes (date unknown), and several collections of letters.

BIOGRAPHICAL INFORMATION

Not much is known about Philostratus's life—most of the information available has been culled from his own writings, but because the authorship of most of these texts continues to be disputed, the details of his life are difficult to confirm. Philostratus was probably born around the year 179 on the Greek island of Lemnos and spent at least part of his youth there. His father, also a sophist, sent him to Athens as a young man to study rhetoric under Proclus of Naucratis. His other teachers included Damianus of Ephesus and Antipater of Hierapolis. Philostratus began his career as a sophist after completing his education and when, between 203 and

208, he was introduced by Antipater into the court of the Emperor Septimius Severus. The Emperor's wife, Julia Domna, was Philostratus's patron until 217.

When Septimius Severus went to Britain to fight against the Picts, Philostratus accompanied the royal family and he remained at the court even after the Emperor died during the war. He continued to travel with the royal family, and at one point visited Tyana (in modern Turkey), where a temple was dedicated to the charismatic teacher Apollonius. Scholars speculate that it was during this trip that Julia Domna commissioned the *Life of Apollonius*. Philostratus also spent some time in Antioch, although it is unknown when, where he met the future Emperor Gordian. *Lives of the Sophists* is dedicated to him. Little information is available about Philostratus in the years immediately following Julia Domna's death in 217. He may have spent some time in the Phoenician city of Tyre and then returned to Athens, where he was associated with the leading cultural and political circles of Greece. He published his two major works at this time. A statue was erected in his honor in Olympia before his death, which probably occurred between 244 and 249.

MAJOR WORKS

Although several works have been attributed to Philostratus, *Life of Apollonius of Tyana* and *Lives of the Sophists* are the only two texts that were unquestionably composed by him. Critical commentary in English has therefore concentrated on these two works, although there has been some discussion of the *Heroikos* by scholars who view the treatise as his. In addition to being a biography of the first-century teacher, *Life of Apollonius* is also a travel romance and novel that highlights the divine powers of the sage. In the work Philostratus quotes Apollonius's disciple Damis. While there is some discussion among scholars about the existence of the notebooks of Damis, most classicists agree that "Damis" is a fictional figure, a literary device used by Philostratus to lend authenticity to his account. Philostratus's other major work, *Lives of the Sophists,* is a collection of essays on famous sophists of the second and third centuries. In these biographies, Philostratus expostulates on the technical capacities of his subjects and includes personal anecdotes from their lives. Philostratus distinguishes two ages of the art of speaking, the "first sophistic," founded in the fifth century by Gorgias, and the "second sophistic," founded by Aeschines in the fourth century While classical scholars do not regard these sketches as works of high literary merit, they are considered an invaluable source of information about the state of rhetorical speaking at a time when it was a high art and when its practitioners, the sophists, were some of the most popular, wealthy, and influential men in Greece. The *Heroikos,* a text that is sometimes ascribed to Philostratus, is a dialogue about the cult of the mythical hero Protesilaos. In this work a Phoenician merchant and a vine-grower discuss the reality of heroes and giants before talking about Protesilaos himself, whom the vine-grower believes is real. The work has been discussed by several scholars in relation to ancient attitudes toward heroes.

CRITICAL RECEPTION

The importance of *Apollonius of Tyana* and *Lives of the Sophists* as historical sources have preserved continuing interest in Philostratus since ancient times. Although much of the debate surrounding these texts is focused on issues of authorship, modern critics writing about Philostratus have tended to examine the authenticity of *Apollonius of Tyana* as a biography, examining the extent to which the work can be considered fictional or historical. Other areas of critical interest include study of the attitude toward magic and heroes as displayed in the work. Discussions of the *Lives of the Sophists* have concentrated on the differences between Philostratus's depictions of the sophists and those of other ancients; the accuracy of the biographies; the sources used by Philostratus; the author's attitudes toward politics and philosophy; and the idea of the "sophistic" used in the work. Although questions of accuracy are central to most discussions of Philostratus's work, it continues to be regarded as the best source of historical information available on his subjects.

PRINCIPAL WORKS

Vita Apollonii [*Life of Apollonius of Tyana*] (biography) c. 217

Vitae Sophistarum [*Lives of the Sophists*] (biographies) c. 231-37

Erotic Epistles (fictional letters) date unknown

Gymnasticus (essay) date unknown

Heroikos [*Heroicus, On the Heroes*] (dialogue) date unknown

Imagines. 2 vols. (art criticism) date unknown

On Nature and Law (essay) date unknown

Principal English Translations

The Life of Apollonius of Tyana (translated by Edward Berwick) 1809

Philostratus and Eunapinius; Lives of the Sophists (translated by Wilmer Cave Wright) 1921

Imagines (translated by Arthur Fairbanks) 1931

CRITICISM

F. C. Conybeare (essay date 1912)

SOURCE: Conybeare, F. C. "Introduction." In *The Life of Apollonius of Tyana: The Epistles of Apollonius and the Treatise of Eusebius*, by Philostratus, translated by F. C. Conybeare, pp. vii-xvii. Cambridge, Mass.: Harvard University Press, 1912.

[*In the following essay, an introduction to his translation of Philostratus's* Life of Apollonius of Tyana, *Conybeare summarizes the work and evaluates the veracity of Philostratus's account.*]

The *Life of Apollonius of Tyana* has only been once translated in its entirety into English, as long ago as the year 1811, by an Irish clergyman of the name of E. Berwick. It is to be hoped therefore that the present translation will be acceptable to the English reading public; for there is in it much that is very good reading, and it is lightly written. Of its author, Philostratus, we do not know much apart from his own works, from which we may gather that he was born in the island of Lemnos about the year 172 of our era, that he went to Athens as a young man to study rhetoric, and later on to Rome. Here he acquired a reputation as a sophist, and was drawn into what we may call the *salon* of the literary and philosophic Empress Julia Domna, the wife of Septimius Severus. She put into his hands certain memoirs of Apollonius, the sage of Tyana, who had died in extreme old age nearly 100 years before during the reign of the Emperor Nerva, and she begged him to use them for the composition of a literary life of the sage in question. These memoirs had been composed by a disciple and companion of Apollonius named Damis, a native of the city of Nineveh, whose style, Philostratus says, like that of most Syrian Greeks, was heavy and wanting in polish. Besides these memoirs Philostratus used for his work a history of the career of Apollonius at Aegae, written by an admirer of the name of Maximus. He also used the many letters of Apollonius which were in circulation. His collection of these agreed partly, but not wholly, with those which are preserved

Emperor Septimus Severus, whose wife, Julia Domna, was Philostratus's patron.

mouth of the sage, on the authority of Damis, conversations and ideas which, as they recur in the *Lives of the Sophists of Philostratus,* can hardly have been reported by Damis. But because he resorted to this literary trick, it by no means follows that all the episodes which he reports on the authority of Damis are fictitious, for many of them possess great verisimilitude and can hardly have been invented as late as the year 217, when the life was completed and given to the literary world. It is rather to be supposed that Damis himself was not altogether a credible writer, but one who, like the so-called *aretalogi* of that age, set himself to embellish the life of his master, to exaggerate his wisdom and his supernatural powers; if so, more than one of the striking stories told by Philostratus may have already stood in the pages of Damis.

However this be, the evident aim of Philostratus is to rehabilitate the reputation of Apollonius, and defend him from the charge of having been a charlatan or wizard addicted to evil magical practices. This accusation had been levelled against the sage during his lifetime by a rival sophist Euphrates, and not long after his death by the author already mentioned, Moeragenes. Unfortunately the orations of Euphrates have perished, and we know little of the work of Moeragenes. Origen, the Christian father, in his work against Celsus, written about the year 240, informs us that he had read it, and that it attacked Apollonius as a magician addicted to sinister practices. It is certain also that the accusations of Euphrates were of similar tendency, and we only need to read a very few pages of this work of Philostratus to see that his chief interest is to prove to the world that these accusations were ill-founded, and that Apollonius was a divinely-inspired sage and prophet, and a reformer along Pythagorean lines of the Pagan religion. It is possible that some of the stories told by Byzantine writers of Apollonius, notably by John Tzetzes, derive from Moeragenes.

The story of the life of Apollonius as narrated by Philostratus is briefly as follows. He was born towards the beginning of the Christian era at Tyana, in Cappadocia, and his birth was attended according to popular tradition with miracles and portents. At the age of sixteen he set himself to observe in the most rigid fashion the almost monastic rule ascribed to Pythagoras, renouncing wine, rejecting the married estate, refusing to eat any sort of flesh, and in particular condemning the sacrifice of animals to the gods, which in the ancient world furnished the occasion, at any rate for the poor people, of eating meat. For we must not forget that in antiquity hardly any meat was eaten which had not previously been consecrated by sacrifice to a god, and that consequently the priest was the butcher of a village and the butcher the priest. Like other votaries of the Neo-Pythagorean philosophy or discipline, Apollonius

to us and translated below. He tells us further that the Emperor Hadrian had a collection of these letters in his villa at Antium. Philostratus also possessed various treatises of Apollonius which have not come down to us. Beside making use of the written sources here enumerated Philostratus had travelled about, not only to Tyana, where there was a temple specially dedicated to the cult of Apollonius, but to other cities where the sage's memory was held in honour, in order to collect such traditions of the sage as he found still current. From these sources then the work before us was drawn, for although Philostratus also knew the four books of a certain Moeragenes upon Apollonius, he tells us he paid no attention to them, because they displayed an ignorance of many things which concerned the sage. The learned Empress seems never to have lived to read the work of Philostratus, for it is not dedicated to her and cannot have been published before the year 217.

It has been argued that the work of Damis never really existed, and that he was a mere man of straw invented by Philostratus. This view was adopted as recently as the year 1910 by Professor Bigg, in his history of the origins of Christianity. But it seems unnecessarily sceptical. It is quite true that Philostratus puts into the went without shoes or only wore shoes of bark, he allowed his hair to grow long, and never let a razor touch his chin, and he took care to wear on his person nothing but linen, for it was accounted by him, as by Brahmans, an impurity to allow any dress made of the skin of dead animals to touch the person. Before long he set himself up as a reformer, and betaking himself to the town of Aegae, he took up his abode in the temple of Aesculapius, where he rapidly acquired such a reputation for sanctity that sick people flocked to him asking him to heal them. On attaining his majority, at the death of his father and mother, he gave up the greater part of his patrimony to his elder brother, and what was left to his poor relations. He then set himself to spend five years in complete silence, traversing, it would seem, Asia Minor, in all directions, but never opening his lips. The more than Trappist vow of silence which he thus enforced upon himself seems to have further enhanced his reputation for holiness, and his mere appearance on the scene was enough to hush the noise of warring factions in the cities of Cilicia and Pamphylia. If we may believe his biographer he professed to know all languages without ever having learned them, to know the inmost thoughts of men, to understand the language of birds and animals, and to have the power of predicting the future. He also remembered his former incarnation, for he shared the Pythagorean belief of the migrations of human souls from body to body, both of animals and of human beings. He preached a rigid asceticism, and condemned all dancing and other diversions of the kind; he would carry no money on his person and recommended others to spend their money in the relief of the poorer classes. He visited Persia and India, where he consorted with the Brahmans; he subsequently visited Egypt, and went up the Nile in order to acquaint himself with those precursors of the monks of the Thebaid called in those days the Gymnosophists or naked philosophers. He visited the cataracts of the Nile, and returning to Alexandria held long conversations with Vespasian and Titus soon after the siege and capture of Jerusalem by the latter. He had a few years before, in the course of a visit to Rome, incurred the wrath of Nero, whose minister Tigellinus however was so intimidated by him as to set him at liberty. After the death of Titus he was again arrested, this time by the Emperor Domitian, as a fomenter of sedition, but was apparently acquitted. He died at an advanced age in the reign of Nerva, who befriended him; and according to popular tradition he ascended bodily to heaven, appearing after death to certain persons who entertained doubts about a future life.

Towards the end of the third century when the struggle between Christianity and decadent Paganism had reached its last and bitterest stage, it occurred to some of the enemies of the new religion to set up Apollonius, to whom temples and shrines had been erected in various parts of Asia Minor, as a rival to the founder of Christianity. The many miracles which were recorded of Apollonius, and in particular his eminent power over evil spirits or demons, made him a formidable rival in the minds of Pagans to Jesus Christ. And a certain Hierocles, who was a provincial governor under the Emperor Diocletian, wrote a book to show that Apollonius had been as great a sage, as remarkable a worker of miracles, and as potent an exorcist as Jesus Christ. His work gave great offence to the missionaries of the Christian religion, and Eusebius the Christian historian wrote a treatise in answer, in which he alleges that Apollonius was a mere charlatan, and if a magician at all, then one of very inferior powers; he also argues that if he did achieve any remarkable results, it was thanks to the evil spirits with whom he was in league. Eusebius is careful, however, to point out that before Hierocles, no anti-Christian writer had thought of putting forward Apollonius as the rival and equal of Jesus of Nazareth. It is possible of course that Hierocles took his cue from the Emperor Alexander Severus (A.D. 205-235), who instead of setting up images of the gods in his private shrine, established therein, as objects of his veneration, statues of Alexander the Great, Orpheus, Apollonius of Tyana, Abraham, and Christ. This story however in no way contradicts the statement of Eusebius, and it is a pity that this significant caution of the latter has been disregarded by Christian writers of the last three centuries, who have almost unanimously adopted a view that is utterly unwarrantable, namely, that Philostratus intended his life of Apollonius as a counterblast to that of the Christian gospel. The best scholars of the present generation are opposed to this view, for they realise that demoniac possession was a common feature in the ancient landscape, and that the exorcist driving demons out of afflicted human beings by use of threats and invocations of mysterious names was as familiar a figure in old Pagan society as he was in the early church.

We read that wherever Apollonius travelled, he visited the temples, and undertook to reform the cults which he there found in vogue. His reform seems to have consisted in this, that he denounced as derogatory to the gods the practice of sacrificing to them animal victims and tried to persuade the priests to abandon it. In this respect he prepared the ground for Christianity and was working along the same lines as many of the Christian missionaries. In the third century Porphyry the philosopher and enemy of Christianity was as zealous in his condemnation of blood-offerings, as Apollonius had been in the first. Unquestionably the neo-Pythagorean propaganda did much to discredit ancient paganism, and Apollonius and its other missionaries were all unwittingly working for that ideal of bloodless sacrifice which, after the destruction of the Jewish Temple, by an inexorable logic imposed itself on the Christian Church.

It is well to conclude this all too brief notice of Apollonius with a passage cited by Eusebius[1] from his lost work concerning sacrifice. There is no good reason for doubting its authenticity, and it is an apt summary of his religious belief:—

> "In no other manner, I believe, can one exhibit a fitting respect for the divine being, beyond any other men make sure of being singled out as an object of his favour and good-will, than by refusing to offer to God whom we termed First, who is One and separate from all, as subordinate to whom we must recognise all the rest, any victim at all; to Him we must not kindle fire or make promise unto him of any sensible object whatsoever. For He needs nothing even from beings higher than ourselves. Nor is there any plant or animal which earth sends up or nourishes, to which some pollution is not incident. We should make use in relation to him solely of the higher speech, I mean of that which issues not by the lips; and from the noblest of beings we must ask for blessings by the noblest faculty we possess, and that faculty is intelligence, which needs no organ. On these principles then we ought not on any account to sacrifice victims to the mighty and supreme God."

Notes

1. Eusebius, *On the Preparation for the Gospel,* Bk. iv. Ch. 13.

Wilmer Cave Wright (essay date 1921)

SOURCE: Wright, Wilmer Cave. "Introduction." In *The Lives of the Sophists*, by Philostratus and Eunapius, translated by Wilmer Cave Wright, pp. ix-xli. Cambridge, Mass.: Harvard University Press, 1952.

[*In the following essay, originally published in 1921, Wright offers an overview of Philostratus's* Lives of the Sophists, *discussing the date of composition, its style and content, as well as including summaries on several sophists who were overlooked by Philostratus in his treatise.*]

The island Lemnos was the ancestral home of the Philostrati, a family in which the profession of sophist was hereditary in the second and third Christian centuries. Of the works that make up the Philostratean corpus the greater part belong to the author of these *Lives.* But he almost certainly did not write the *Nero,* a dialogue attributed by Suidas the lexicographer to an earlier Philostratus; the first series of the *Imagines* and the *Heroicus* are generally assigned to a younger Philostratus whose premature death is implied by our author who survived him and was probably his father-in-law; and the second series of the *Imagines* was by a Philostratus who flourished in the third century, the last of this literary family.

There are extant, by our Philostratus, the *Gymnasticus,* the *Life of Apollonius of Tyana,* the *Lives of the Sophists,* the *Erotic Epistles,* and a brief discourse (διάλεξις) *On Nature and Law,* a favourite commonplace of sophistic. In the *Lives* he quotes the *Life of Apollonius* as his own work, so that his authorship of the two most important works in the corpus is undisputed.

Flavius Philostratus was born about 170, perhaps in Lemnos, and studied at Athens with Proclus, Hippodromus, and Antipater, and at Ephesus with the aged Damianus from whom he learned much of the gossip that he retails about the second-century sophists. Philostratus wrote the *Lives* of his teachers. Some time after 202, perhaps through the influence of the Syrian sophist Antipater, who was a court favourite, he entered the circle of the philosophic Syrian Empress, Julia Domna. Julia spent much of her time in travelling about the Empire, and Philostratus may have gone with her and the Emperor Septimius Severus to Britain[1] in 208, and to Gaul in 212; and we may picture him at Pergamon, Nicomedia, and especially at Antioch,[2] where Julia preferred to reside. All three towns were centres of sophistic activity. The husband of Julia, the Emperor Septimius Severus, was himself a generous patron of letters, and, as Philostratus says, loved to gather about him the talented from all parts. But it was Julia who, first as his consort, and later as virtual regent in the reign of her son Caracalla, gave the court that intellectual or pseudo-intellectual tone which has reminded all the commentators of the princely Italian courts of the Renaissance. I say pseudo-intellectual, because, when Philostratus speaks of her circle of mathematicians and philosophers, it must be remembered that the former were certainly astrologers—the Syrian Empress was deeply dyed with Oriental superstition—and that the latter were nearly all sophists. However, to converse with sophists on equal terms, as Julia did, she must have been well read in the Greek classics, and so we find Philostratus, in his extant letter[3] to her, reminding her of a discussion they had had on Aeschines, and defending Gorgias of Leontini from his detractors. We do not meet with such another court of literary men until, in the fourth century, the Emperor Julian hastily collected about him the sophists and philosophers who were so soon to be dispersed on his death. Cassius Dio[4] tells us that Julia was driven by the brutality of her husband to seek the society of sophists. However that may be, it was during her son's reign that she showed especial favour to Philostratus. After her downfall and death he left Antioch and went to Tyre, where he published the work called generally the *Life of Apollonius,* though the more precise translation of its title would be *In Honour of Apollonius.* His wife, as we learn from an inscription[5] from Erythrae, was named Aurelia Melitine. From the same source we may conclude that the family had senatorial rank, which was no doubt bestowed on Philostratus during his connexion with the court. We have no detailed knowledge of the latter part of his life, but he evidently settled at Athens, where he wrote the *Lives of the Sophists.* He survived as late as the reign of Philip the Arab.[6] Like other Lemnians he had the privilege of Athenian citizenship, and he is variously called in antiquity "Tyrian," from his stay in Tyre, "Lemnian," and "Athenian." That he himself preferred the last of these epithets may be gathered from the fact that he calls the younger Philostratus "the Lemnian," evidently to avoid confusion with himself.

Philostratus dedicates the *Lives* to Gordian, and on this we depend for the approximate date of their composition. Gordian was consul for the second time in 229-230, and, since Philostratus suddenly changes his form of address, first calling him consul and then proconsul, he seems to have written the dedication when Gordian was proconsul of Africa, immediately after his consulship. Gordian at the age of eighty assumed the purple in 238, and shortly after committed suicide. The *Lives* were therefore ready to publish between the years 230 and 238, but there is no certain evidence for a more precise date.

Philostratus in writing the *Lives* evidently avoided the conventional style and alphabetical sequence used by grammarians for biographies; for he had no desire to be classed with grammarians. He wrote like a well-bred sophist who wished to preserve for all time a picture of the triumphs of his tribe, when sophists were at the height of their glory. His *Lives,* therefore, are not in the strict sense biographies. They are not continuous or orderly in any respect, but rather a collection of anecdotes and personal characteristics. He seldom gives a list of the works of a sophist, and when he does, it is incomplete, so far as we are able to check it, as we can for Dio or Aristeides. He was, like all his class, deeply interested in questions of style and the various types in vogue, but he must not be supposed to be writing a handbook, and hence his discussions of style are capricious and superficial. He had collected a mass of information as to the personal appearance, manners and dress, temperament and fortune of the more successful sophists, and the great occasions when they triumphantly met some public test, and he shows us only the *splendeurs,* not the *misères* of the profession. He has no pity for the failures, or for those who lost their power to hold an audience, like Hermogenes, who "moulted" too early, and from a youthful prodigy fell into such insignificance that his boyish successes were forgotten. But to those who attained a ripe old age and made great fortunes Philostratus applies every possible superlative. They are the darlings of the gods, they have the power of Orpheus to charm, they make the reputation of their native towns, or of those in which they condescend to

dwell. In fact, he did not observe that he made out nearly every one of these gifted beings to be the greatest and most eloquent of them all. Polemo and Herodes are his favourites, and for them he gives most details, while for Favorinus he is unusually consecutive. But no two *Lives* show the same method of treatment, a variety that may have been designed. He succeeded in founding a type of sophistic biography, and in the fourth century, in Eunapius, we have a direct imitation of the exasperating manner and method of Philostratus. To pronounce a moral judgement was alien to this type of biography. Philostratus does so occasionally and notably in the *Life* of Critias, whom he weighs in the balance. This is, perhaps, because, as a tyrant, Critias was often the theme of historical declamations, and Philostratus takes the occasion to use some of the commonplaces of the accusation and defence.

After his hurried and perfunctory review of the philosophers who were so eloquent that they were entitled to a place among the sophists, of whom the most important are Dio Chrysostom and Favorinus, he treats of the genuine sophists; first, the older type from Gorgias to Isocrates; then, with Aeschines, he makes the transition to the New Sophistic. Next comes a gap of four centuries, and he dismisses this period with the bare mention of three insignificant names which have no interest for him or for us, and passes on to Nicetes of Smyrna in the first century A.D. This break in the continuity of the *Lives* is variously explained. Kayser thinks that there is a lacuna in the MSS., and that Philostratus could not have omitted all mention of Demetrius of Phaleron, Charisius, Hegesias, who is regarded as having founded Asianism, not long after the death of Alexander the Great; or of Fronto, the "archaist," that is to say Atticist, the friend and correspondent of Herodes Atticus, not to speak of others. In ignoring the sophistic works of Lucian in the second century, Philostratus observes the sophistic convention of silence as to one who so excelled and satirized them all. He was a renegade not to be named. In accounting for the other omissions, a theory at least as likely as Kayser's is that there lay before Philostratus other biographies of these men, and that he had nothing picturesque to add to them. Hesychius evidently used some such source, and Philostratus seems to refer to it when he remarks with complete vagueness that on this or that question, usually the place of birth or the death of a sophist, "some say" this and "others" that. In the *Life* of Herodes he says that he has given some details that were unknown "to others"; these were probably other biographers. Thus he arrives at what is his real aim, to celebrate the apotheosis of the New Sophistic in the persons of such men as Polemo, Scopelian, and, above all, Herodes Atticus, with whom he begins his Second Book.

Without Philostratus we should have a very incomplete idea of the predominant influence of Sophistic in the educational, social, and political life of the Empire in the second and third Christian centuries. For the only time in history professors were generally acknowledged as social leaders, went on important embassies, made large fortunes, had their marriages arranged and their quarrels settled by Emperors, held Imperial Secretaryships, were Food Controllers,[7] and high priests; and swayed the fate of whole cities by gaining for them immunities and grants of money and visits from the Emperor, by expending their own wealth in restoring Greek cities that were falling into decay, and not least by attracting thither crowds of students from the remotest parts of the Empire. No other type of intellectual could compete with them in popularity, no creative artists existed to challenge their prestige at the courts of phil-Hellenic Emperors, and though the sophists often show jealousy of the philosophers, philosophy without eloquence was nowhere. But besides all this, they kept alive an interest in the Greek classics, the ἀρχαῖοι or standard authors; and a thorough knowledge of the Greek poets, orators, and historians such as we should hardly find equalled among professors of Greek to-day was taken for granted in Syrian, Egyptian, Arab, and Bithynian humanists, who must be able to illustrate their lectures with echoes of Homer, Plato, Thucydides, and Demosthenes. In their declamations historical allusions drawn from the classics played much the same part and were as essential as the heroic myths had been to the *Odes* of Pindar or Bacchylides. Not only were they well read, but their technical training in rhetoric was severe, and they would have thought any claim of ours to understand the art of rhetoric, or to teach it, superficial and amateurish. We do not even know the rules of the game. Moreover, they had audiences who did know those rules, and could appreciate every artistic device. But to be thus equipped was not enough. A successful sophist must have the nerve and equipment of a great actor, since he must act character parts, and the terminology of the actor's as well as the singer's art is frequently used for the sophistic profession; he must have unusual charm of appearance, manner, and voice, and a ready wit to retort on his rivals. All his training leads up to that highest achievement of the sophist, improvisation on some theme which was an echo of the past, stereotyped, but to be handled with some pretence to novelty. The theme was voted by the audience or propounded by some distinguished visitor, often because it was known to be in the declaimer's *répertoire*. He must have a good memory, since he must never repeat himself except by special request, and then he must do so with perfect accuracy, and, if called on, must reverse all his arguments and take the other side. These themes were often not only fictitiously but falsely conceived, as when Demosthenes is represented pleading for Ae-

schines in exile, a heart-breaking waste of ingenuity and learning; or paradoxical, such as an encomium on the house-fly. Lucian from his point of view ridiculed the sophists, as Plato had satirized their intellectual and moral weakness in his day, but the former could not undermine their popularity, and the latter might well have despaired if he could have foreseen the recurring triumphs of the most sensational and theatrical forms of rhetoric in the second, third, and fourth Christian centuries. For now not only the middle-class parent, like Strepsiades in the *Clouds,* encourages his son to enter the sophistic profession; noble families are proud to claim kinship with a celebrated sophist; sophists preside at the Games and religious festivals, and, when a brilliant sophist dies, cities compete for the honour of burying him in the finest of their temples.

The official salaries were a small part of their earnings. Vespasian founded a chair of rhetoric at Rome,[8] and Hadrian and Antoninus endowed Regius Professorships of rhetoric and philosophy in several provincial cities. At Athens and, later, Constantinople, there were salaried imperial chairs for which the normal pay was equivalent to about £350, and professors enjoyed certain immunities and exemptions that were later to be reserved for the clergy. The profession was definitely organized by Marcus Aurelius, who assigned an official chair to rhetoric and another to political oratory, and as a rule himself made the appointment from a list of candidates. Many municipalities maintained salaried professors. But, once appointed, a professor must rely on his powers of attraction; there was complete liberty in education; anyone who wished could open a school of rhetoric; and sometimes a free lance would empty the lecture theatre of the Regius Professor, as Libanius did in the fourth century. Nor did the Christian Emperors before Julian interfere with the freedom of speech of famous sophists, though these were usually pagans without disguise who ignored Christianity. In order to reserve for pagan sophists the teaching of the classics Julian tampered with this freedom and, as is described in the *Lives* of Eunapius, extended the powers of the crown over such appointments.

Political oratory, which was a relatively severe type and must avoid emotional effects and poetical allusions, was reduced to school exercises and the arguing of historical or pseudo-historical themes, and was not so fashionable or so sought after by sophists as the chair of pure rhetoric. Though officially distinct in the second century, the "political" chair was gradually absorbed by its more brilliant rival, and in the third and fourth centuries no talented sophist would have been content to be merely a professor of political oratory, a πολιτικός. The study of law and forensic oratory was on a still lower plane and is referred to with some contempt by Philostratus. The writing of history was an inferior branch of literature. In short every form of literary composition was subservient to rhetoric, and the sophists whom Plato perhaps hoped to discountenance with a definition were now the representatives of Hellenic culture. "Hellene" had become a technical term for a student of rhetoric in the schools.

Philostratus had no foreboding that this supremacy was doomed. For him, as for Herodes, Sophistic was a national movement. The sophist was to revive the antique purer form of religion and to encourage the cults of the heroes and Homeric gods. This was their theoretical aim, but in fact they followed after newer cults—Aristeides for instance is devoted to the cult of Asclepius whose priest he was, and there were probably few like Herodes Atticus, that ideal sophist, who was an apostle of a more genuinely Hellenic culture and religion. By the time of Eunapius the futility of Philostratus' dream of a revival of Greek religion and culture is apparent, Sophistic is giving way to the study of Roman law at such famous schools as that of Berytus, and the best a sophist can hope for is, like the sober Libanius, to make a living from his pupils and not to become obnoxious to the all-powerful prefects and proconsuls of the Christian Emperors who now bestow their favours on bishops.

There are two rival tendencies in the oratory of the second and third centuries, Asianism and Atticism. The Asianic style is flowery, bombastic, full of startling metaphors, too metrical, too dependent on the tricks of rhetoric, too emotional. In short, the Asianic declaimer aims at but never achieves the grand style. The Atticist usually imitates some classical author, aims at simplicity of style, and is a purist, carefully avoiding any allusion or word that does not occur in a writer of the classical period. In Aristeides, we have the works of an Atticist, and we know that he had not the knack of "improvisation" and was unpopular as a teacher. He was thought to be arid, that is, not enough of an Asianist to please an audience that was ready to go into ecstasies over a display of "bombast and importunate epigram." Philostratus never uses the word Asianism, but he criticizes the "Ionian" and "Ephesian" type of rhetoric, and it was this type which then represented the "theatrical shamelessness" that in the first century Dionysius of Halicarnassus deplored.

Philostratus was one of those who desired to achieve simplicity of style, ἀφέλεια, but when a sophist attempts this the result is always a spurious naïveté such as is seen at its worst in the *Imagines,* the work of his kinsman. Above all the classical writers he admires for his style Critias, who was the ideal of Herodes Atticus also, and the fluent eloquence of Aeschines. He was an Atticist, but not of the stricter type, for he held that it was tasteless and barbarous to overdo one's Atticism.

He writes the reminiscence Greek of the cultured sophist, full of echoes of the poets, Herodotus, Plato, and Xenophon. His sentences are short and co-ordinated, his allusions are often so brief that he is obscure, and in general he displays the carelessness of the gentlemanly sophist, condescending to write narrative. If we may judge from his scornful dismissal of Varus as one who abused rhythmical effects in declamation, he himself avoided such excess in his sophistic exercises, μελέται, which are no longer extant. He was a devoted admirer of Gorgias, and in one passage[9] at least he imitates the careful distinction of synonyms that was characteristic of Prodicus. In fact he regarded the Atticizing sophists of his day as the true descendants of the Platonic sophists, and scolds Plutarch[10] for having attacked, in a work that has perished, the stylistic mannerisms of Gorgias. Like all his Greek contemporaries he lacked a sense of proportion, so that his literary criticisms are for the most part worthless, and the quotations that he asks us to admire are puerile. He longed for a revival of the glories of Hellenism, but it was to be a literary, not a political revival, and he shows no bitterness at the political insignificance of Greece. The Hellenes must impress their Roman masters with a sense of the inferiority of Roman culture and he will then have nothing to complain of. In the opinion of the public, improvisation was the highest achievement of Sophistic, and so thought Philostratus. He believed that the scorn of Aristeides for this fashionable form of display, ἐπίδειξις, masked chagrin at his failure, and dismisses with contempt[11] the later career of Hermogenes the technical writer; whereas Norden[12] praises Hermogenes for giving up declamation and devoting himself to more sober and scientific studies. Philostratus has preserved the renown of a number of these improvisators who, but for him, would have perished as completely as have the actors and dancers of those centuries. More than half the sophists described by him are ignored even by Suidas. Yet they were names to conjure with in the schools of rhetoric all through the Roman world, until the Christian Fathers and the rhetoric of the pulpit took the place of the declaimers. Christianity was fatal to Sophistic, which seems to wither, like a Garden of Adonis, never deeply rooted in the lives of the common people. But sophists for centuries had educated Christians and pagans alike, and it was from their hands, unintelligent and sterile as they often were in their devotion to Hellenic culture, that the Church received, though without acknowledgement, the learning of which she boasted, and which she in her turn preserved for us.

The following notices of the sophists of whom we know more than is to be found in Philostratus are intended to supplement him with dates and facts that he ignored, or to correct his errors. They are in the order of the *Lives.*

Eudoxus of Cnidus (408-352 B.C.), famous for his researches in geometry, astronomy, and physics, was for a short time a pupil of Plato. He went to Magna Graecia to study with Archytas the Pythagorean, and to Egypt in the reign of Nectanebus. Strabo[13] describes his observatories at Heliopolis and Cnidus. He opened a school at Cyzicus and made laws for Cnidus.[14] Plutarch[15] praises the elegance of his style.

Leon of Byzantium was a rhetorician and historian about whom we have confused and contradictory accounts in Suidas and Hesychius, especially as to the precise part that he played when Philip of Macedon tried to take Byzantium in 340 B.C. The story is partly told by Plutarch, *Phocion* 14, where Leon probably played the part there assigned to one Cleon.

Dias may be, as Natorp suggests, a mistake for Delios. Others read Bias. Delios of Ephesus is mentioned by Plutarch as a contemporary of Alexander the Great. In any case we know nothing more of this philosopher than is related here.

Carneades (213-129 B.C.) is reckoned as an Athenian, though he was born at Cyrene. He founded the New Academy at Athens, and in 155 was sent to Rome on an embassy for the Athenians. He is so celebrated as a philosopher that Philostratus, whose interest is in the genuine sophists, can dismiss him in a sentence, but no doubt Cato, who disapproved of his influence at Rome, would have called him a sophist.

Philostratus the Egyptian was not connected with the Lemnian family. But for the facts of his life something may be added to the scant notice by his biographer. In his *Life of Antony* 80 Plutarch relates that after the defeat of Antony by Octavian, the latter pardoned the members of Cleopatra's circle, among them Areius[16] the Stoic, who was then in Alexandria. "Areius craved pardon for himself and many others, and especially for Philostratus the most eloquent man of all the sophists and of orators of his time for present and sudden speech; howbeit he falsely named himself an Academic philosopher. Therefore Caesar, who hated his nature and conditions, would not hear his suit. Thereupon Philostratus let his grey beard grow long, and followed Areius step by step in a long mourning gown, still buzzing in his ears this Greek verse:

> A wise man if that he be wise indeed
> May by a wise man have the better speed.

Caesar understanding this, not for the desire he had to deliver Philostratus of his fear, as to rid Areius of malice and envy that might have fallen out against him, pardoned him." We have also an epigram by Crinagoras of Mytilene, a contemporary, a lament over the downfall of this favourite of princes:—"O Philostratus, unhappy for all thy wealth, where are those sceptres and constant intercourse with princes? . . . Foreigners have shared among them the fruit of thy toils, and thy corpse shall lie in sandy Ostrakine."[17]

Dio Chrysostom, the "golden-mouthed," was born in Bithynia about A.D. 40. Exiled for fourteen years by his fear of Domitian, he acquired the peculiar knowledge of the coast towns of the Black Sea and of the savage Getae that is shown in his writings. We have eighty of his speeches, or rather essays; they are partly moral lectures or sermons delivered both during and after his exile, which ended in 96 with the accession of his friend Nerva. He denounces the "god-forsaken" sophists, but for part at least of his life he was a professed sophist, and many of his essays are purely sophistic. Dio labelled himself a philosopher, and he was one of Plutarch's type, borrowing the best from all the schools. He wrote the "plain" style and Xenophon and Plato were his favourite models. Next to Lucian he is the most successful and the most agreeable to read of all the Atticizing writers with sophistic tendencies.

Favorinus (A.D. 80-150) was a Gaul who came to Rome to study Greek and Latin letters in the second Christian century; he spent much of his professional life in Asia Minor. He became the intimate friend of Plutarch, Fronto, and other distinguished men, and had a powerful patron in the Emperor Hadrian. He wrote Greek treatises on history, philosophy, and geography. A statue of him was set up in the public library of Corinth to encourage the youth of Corinth to imitate his eloquence. He was regarded as a sort of encyclopaedia, and his learning is praised by Cassius Dio, Galen, and Aulus Gellius. He belonged to the Academic school of philosophy, but composed numerous sophistic speeches including paradoxical panegyrics, *e.g.* an *Encomium of Quartan Fever.* Lucian[18] speaks of him disparagingly as "a certain eunuch of the school of the Academy who came from Gaul and became famous in Greece a little before my time." He was an Asianist in his use of broken and excessive rhythms. We can judge of his style from his *Corinthian Oration,* which survives among the *Orations* of Dio Chrysostom. It is the longest extant piece of Asianic prose of the early second century.[19] The *Universal History* of Favorinus was probably the chief source used by Athenaeus for his *Deipnosophists,* and was freely borrowed from by Diogenes Laertius.

Gorgias of Leontini in Sicily came to Athens in 427 B.C., at the age of about fifty-five, on an embassy from Leontini, and that date marks a turning-point in the history of prose-writing. The love of parallelism and antithesis was innate in the Greeks, and the so-called "Gorgianic" figures, antithesis, similar endings (homoioteleuta), and symmetrical, carefully balanced clauses were in use long before the time of Gorgias. They are to be found in Heracleitus and Empedocles, and in the plays of Euripides that appeared before 427. But by his exaggerated use of these figures and his deliberate adoption for prose of effects that had been held to be the property of poetry, Gorgias set a fashion that was never quite discarded in Greek prose, though it was often condemned as frigid and precious. He is the founder of epideictic oratory, and his influence lasted to the end. But the surer taste of Athenian prose writers rejected the worst of his exaggerations, and later, when Aristotle or Cicero or Longinus points out the dangers of making one's prose "metrical" by abuse of rhythms, or condemns short and jerky clauses, *minuta et versiculorum similia* (Cicero, *Orator* 39), they cite the mannerisms of Gorgias. A fragment of his *Funeral Oration* survives, and, though scholars are not agreed as to the genuineness of the *Helen* and the *Palamedes* which have come down under his name, these are useful as showing the characteristic features of his style. We have the inscription that was composed for the statue of Gorgias dedicated at Olympia by his grand-nephew Eumolpus; in it he defends Gorgias from the charge of ostentation in having in his lifetime dedicated a gold statue of himself at Delphi.

Protagoras of Abdera in Thrace was born about 480 B.C. and came to Athens about 450. His agnostic utterances about the gods led to his prosecution for impiety by the Athenians who would not tolerate a professed sceptic. He may be called the founder of grammar, since he is said to have been the first to distinguish the three genders by name, and he divided the form of the verb into categories which were the foundation of our moods. In speech he was a purist. His philosophy was Heracleitean, and to him is ascribed the famous phrase "Man is the measure of all things." His aim was to train statesmen in civic virtue, by which he meant an expert knowledge how to get the better of an opponent in any sort of debate. We have no writings that are certainly his, but can judge of his style by Plato's imitation in the *Protagoras*. A treatise on medicine called *On the Art,* which has come down to us among the works of Hippocrates, has been assigned by some to Protagoras. For his *Life* Philostratus used Diogenes Laertius.

Hippias of Elis was the most many-sided of the early sophists, the polymath or encyclopaedist. He professed to have made all that he wore, taught astronomy and geography, and was a politician rather than a professed teacher of rhetoric. In the two Platonic dialogues that bear his name he appears as a vain and theatrical improvisator. In the *Protagoras* his preference for teaching scientific subjects is ridiculed, in passing, by Protagoras. Philostratus derives his account of Hippias

from Plato, *Hippias Maior* 282-286, where Socrates draws out Hippias and encourages him to boast of his versatility and success in making money.

Prodicus of Ceos was a slightly younger contemporary of Protagoras. He was famous for his study of synonyms and their precise use, and may be regarded as the father of the art of using the inevitable word, *le mot juste*. Plato speaks of him with a mixture of scorn and respect, but perhaps Prodicus showed him the way to his own nice distinction of terms. "Cleverer than Prodicus" became a proverbial phrase.

Polus of Sicily, "colt by name and colt by nature," is the respondent to Socrates in the second part of Plato's *Gorgias,* and on that dialogue and the *Phaedrus* we rely mainly for our knowledge of this young and ardent disciple of Gorgias. He had composed an *Art of Rhetoric* which Socrates had just read, and he provokes Socrates to attack rhetoric as the counterfeit of an art, like cookery. In the *Phaedrus* 267 B, he is ridiculed as a Euphuist who had invented a number of technical rhetorical terms and cared chiefly for fine writing; but he is far inferior, we are told, to his teacher Gorgias, and exaggerates his faults.

Thrasymachus of Chalcedon is said to have been the first to develop periodic prose, and hence he may be said to have founded rhythmic prose. In the *Phaedrus* 267 C, D Plato parodies his excessive use of rhythm and poetical words. In the First Book of the *Republic* Plato makes him play the part of a violent and sophistic interlocutor whom Socrates easily disconcerts with his dialectic. He wrote handbooks of rhetoric, and according to the *Phaedrus* he was a master of the art of composing pathetic commonplaces (τάποι), *miserationes,* "piteous whinings," as Plato calls them. Like Polus, his name, "hot-headed fighter," indicates the temperament of the man.

Antiphon of the Attic deme Rhamnus was born soon after 480 B.C., and was a celebrated teacher of rhetoric at Athens. He was deeply influenced by Sicilian rhetoric. Thucydides says that no man of his time was superior to Antiphon in conceiving and expressing an argument and in training a man to speak in the courts or the assembly. He was an extreme oligarch, and was deeply implicated in the plot that placed the Four Hundred in power in 411. When they fell he was condemned to death and drank hemlock, his fortune was confiscated, and his house pulled down. We have his *Tetralogies,* fifteen speeches all dealing with murder cases; twelve of these are in groups of four, hence the name, and give two speeches each for the plaintiff and the defendant in fictitious cases. He uses the commonplaces of the sophists, but his style is severe and archaic. The only other authority for the generally discredited statement of

Philostratus that he increased the Athenian navy is pseudo-Plutarch, *Lives of the Ten Orators.* Recently there have been found in Egypt four fragments of his *Apology,* that defence which Thucydides[20] called "the most beautiful apologetic discourse ever given." Antiphon tries to prove that his motives in bringing the oligarchs into power were unselfish. He reminds the judges of his family, whom he did not want to abandon, and without whom he could easily have made his escape. I assume that Antiphon was both orator and sophist, though some maintain that throughout the *Life* Philostratus has confused two separate Antiphons.

Critias, "the handsome," son of Callaeschrus, is remembered chiefly for his political career as a leader of the oligarchy, a pro-Spartan, and one of the Thirty Tyrants. He was exiled from Athens in 407 B.C., and returned in 405. It was Xenophon who said[21] that he degenerated during his stay in Thessaly. He was killed fighting against Thrasybulus and the democrats a year later. Critias was a pupil of Socrates and also of the sophists. He wrote tragedies, elegies, and prose works, of which not enough has survived for any sure estimate to be made of his talent. He was greatly admired by the later sophists, especially by Herodes Atticus.

Isocrates (436-338) was trained by the sophists, by Prodicus certainly, and perhaps Protagoras, for a public career, but a weak voice and an incurable diffidence barred him from this, and after studying in Thessaly with Gorgias he became a professional rhetorician at Athens, where he opened his school about 393. In that school, which Cicero calls an "oratorical laboratory," were trained the most distinguished men of the fourth century at Athens. It was his fixed idea that the Greeks must forget their quarrels and unite against Persia, and towards the end of his life he believed that Philip of Macedon might reconcile the Greek states and lead them to this great enterprise. The tradition that, when Philip triumphed over Greece at Chaeronea, Isocrates, disillusioned, refused to survive, has been made popular by Milton's sonnet, *To the Lady Margaret Ley.* Isocrates did in fact die in 338, but he was ninety-eight, and it is not certain that he would have despaired at the success of Philip. He was a master of epideictic prose, and brought the period to perfection in long and lucid sentences. Since Cicero's style is based on Isocrates, the latter may be said to have influenced, through Cicero, the prose of modern Europe.

Aeschines was born in 389 B.C. of an obscure family, and after being an actor and then a minor clerk, raised himself to the position of leading politician, ambassador, and rival of Demosthenes. He supported Philip of Macedon, and in 343 defended himself successfully in his speech *On the False Embassy,* from an attack by Demosthenes, whom he attacked in turn without suc-

cess in the speech *Against Ctesiphon* in 330; to this Demosthenes retorted with his speech *On the Crown.* After this failure, Aeschines withdrew to Rhodes, where he spent the rest of his life in teaching, and it is because he taught rhetoric that Philostratus includes him here and calls him a sophist.

Nicetes flourished in the latter half of the first Christian century under the Emperors Vespasian, Domitian, and Nerva. After the *Life* of Aeschines Philostratus skips four centuries and passes to a very different type of orator. He is the first important representative of Asianic oratory in the *Lives.* Philostratus calls this the Ionian type, and it was especially associated with the coast towns of Asia Minor, and above all Smyrna and Ephesus. Nicetes is mentioned in passing by Tacitus,[22] as having travelled far from the style of Aeschines and Demosthenes; Pliny the Younger says[23] that he heard him lecture. Nothing of his is extant. There was another sophist of the same name whom Seneca quotes, but he lived earlier and flourished under Tiberius.

Isaeus will always be remembered, but he does not owe his immortality to Philostratus, but rather to the fact that Pliny[24] praised his eloquence in a letter to Trajan, and Juvenal,[25] in his scathing description of the hungry Greekling at Rome, said that not even Isaeus could pour forth such a torrent of words. He came to Rome about A.D. 97 and made a great sensation there.

Scopelian of Clazomenae lived under Domitian, Nerva, and Trajan. His eloquence was of the Asianic type, as was natural in a pupil of Nicetes. In the letter addressed to him by Apollonius of Tyana,[26] Scopelian is apparently warned not to imitate even the best, but to develop a style of his own; this was shockingly heterodox advice. For Philostratus, his popularity with the crowd was the measure of his ability.

Dionysius of Miletus is mentioned in passing by Cassius Dio lxix. 789, who says that he offended the Emperor Hadrian. Nothing of his survives, for he almost certainly did not write the treatise *On the Sublime* which has been attributed to him, as to other writers of the same name, though on the very slightest grounds. He was inclined to Asianism, if we may trust the anecdote of his rebuke by Isaeus; see p. 513.

Lollianus of Ephesus, who lived under Hadrian and Antoninus, is ridiculed by Lucian, *Epigram* 26, for his volubility, and his diction is often criticized by Phrynichus. He wrote handbooks on rhetoric which have perished. From the quotations of Philostratus it is evident that he was an Asianist. He made the New Sophistic popular in Athens. He was *curator annonae,* an office which in Greek is represented by στρατοπεδάρχης or στρατηγὸς ἐπὶ τῶν ὅπλων; the title had lost its military significance.[27] We have the inscription[28] composed for the statue of Lollianus in the agora at Athens; it celebrates his ability in the lawcourts and as a declaimer, but in a brief phrase, while the rest of the inscription aims at securing the immortal renown of the "well-born pupils" who dedicated the statue.

Polemo of Laodicea was born about A.D. 85 and lived under Trajan, Hadrian, and Antoninus. There have survived two of his declamations in which two fathers of Marathon heroes dispute the honour of pronouncing the funeral oration on those who fell at Marathon. We can judge from them of the Asianic manner of the time, with its exaggerated tropes, tasteless similes, short and antithetic clauses, and, in general, its obvious straining after effect and lack of coherent development of ideas. Polemo makes an attempt at Attic diction, but is full of solecisms and late constructions. These compositions seem to us to lack charm and force, but his improvisations may have been very different. Even as late as the fourth century he was admired and imitated, *e.g.* by Gregory Nazianzen.

Herodes Atticus, the most celebrated sophist of the second century, was born about A.D. 100 at Marathon, and died about 179; he was consul in 143. With him begins an important development of Sophistic, for he and his followers at least strove to be thorough Atticists and were diligent students of the writers of the classical period. They set up a standard of education that makes them respectable, and we may say of them, as of some of the sophists of the fourth Christian century, that never has there been shown a more ardent appreciation of the glorious past of Greece, never a more devoted study of the classical authors, to whatever sterile ends. But it is evident that Herodes, who threw all his great influence on the side of a less theatrical and more scholarly rhetoric than Scopelian's, failed to win any such popularity as his. For the main facts of his life we rely on Philostratus. Of all his many-sided literary activities only one declamation remains, in which a young Theban oligarch urges his fellow-citizens to make war on Archelaus of Macedonia. But its authenticity is disputed, and it shows us only one side of his rhetoric. Its rather frigid correctness is certainly not typical of the New Sophistic, nor has it the pathos for which he was famed. There are many admiring references to Herodes in Lucian, Aulus Gellius, and Plutarch. In the *Lives* that follow his it will be seen how deeply he influenced his numerous pupils, and, through them, the trend of the New Sophistic.[29] The notice of Herodes in Suidas is independent of Philostratus. If we accept the theory of Rudolph, Athenaeus in his *Deipnosophists* (*Banquet of the Learned*), has given us a characterization of Herodes as the host, disguised under the name Larensius.

There are extant two long Greek inscriptions[30] found at Rome, composed for Regilla, the wife of Herodes, one for her heroum or shrine on the Appian Way, the other for her statue in the temple of Minerva and Nemesis. Her brother Braduas was consul in 160. The inscription for the Appian Way must have been composed before 171, the date of the encounter at Sirmium of Herodes and Marcus Aurelius related by Philostratus, since in it Elpinice his daughter is named as still alive; it was partly grief for her death that made Herodes indifferent to his fate at Sirmium.

Aristocles, the pupil of Herodes, wrote philosophical treatises and rhetorical handbooks which have all perished. He was evidently a thorough Atticist. His conversion from philosophy to sophistic and his personal habits are described by Synesius, *Dio* 35 D. Synesius says that, whereas Dio was converted from sophistic to philosophy, Aristocles in his old age became a dissipated sophist and competed with his declamations in the theatres of Italy and Asia.

Alexander the Cilician probably derived his love of philosophy from his teacher Favorinus, but his nickname "Clay Plato" implies that his pretensions were not taken seriously. However sound may have been the studies of these more scholarly sophists of the type of Herodes, they evidently resorted to the trivial devices and excessive rhythms that the crowd had been taught by the Asianists to expect from a declaimer. If Alexander really declaimed more soberly than Scopelian, as Herodes said, the quotations from him in Philostratus do not show any real difference of style. Alexander was, however, something more than a mere expert in the etiquette of Sophistic.

Hermogenes of Tarsus is the most famous technical writer on rhetoric in the second century, though one would not infer this from Philostratus. His career as a declaimer was brief, but it is improbable that, as Suidas says, his mind became deranged at twenty-four. He was a youthful prodigy, a boy orator, who turned to the composition of treatises when his knack of declamation forsook him in early manhood. We have his *Preparatory Exercises*, Προγυμνάσματα, his treatise, *On the Constitution of Cases*, Περὶ τῶν στάσεων, *On Invention*, Περὶ εὑρέσεως, and, best known of all, *On the Types of Style*, Περὶ ἰδεῶν. For him Demosthenes is the perfect orator who displays all the seventeen qualities of good oratory, such as clearness, beauty, the grand manner, and the rest. Hermogenes defines and classifies them, together with the formal elements of a speech. His categories are quoted by all the technical rhetoricians who succeed him. All his work was intended to lead to the scientific imitation of the classical writers, though he admired also a few later authors, especially the Atticist Aristeides, the strictest of the archaists.

Philostratus, who can admire only the declaimer, says nothing of his success as a technical writer.

Aelius Aristeides, surnamed Theodorus, was born in Mysia, in 117. According to Suidas, he studied under Polemo, but no doubt he owed more to the teaching of Herodes. He is the chief representative of the religious and literary activity of the sophists and their revival of Atticism in the second century, and we must judge of that revival mainly from his works which are in great part extant. We have fifty-five *Orations* of various kinds, and two treatises on rhetoric in which he shows himself inferior in method and thoroughness to Hermogenes. He was proverbially unpopular as a teacher of rhetoric, and though the epigram on *the seven pupils of Aristeides, four walls and three benches,* which is quoted in the anonymous argument to his *Panathenaic Oration,* is there said to have been composed for a later rhetorician of the same name, it somehow clung to his memory, and a denial was felt to be necessary. His six *Sacred Discourses,* in which he discusses the treatment by Asclepius of a long illness of thirteen years with which he was afflicted, are one of the curiosities of literature. They mark the close association of Sophistic and religion in the second century, and it is to be observed that Polemo, Antiochus, and Hermocrates also frequented the temple of Asclepius. The sophists constantly opposed the irreligion of the contemporary philosophers, but it is hard to believe that an educated man of that time could seriously describe his interviews with Asclepius and the god's fulsome praises of his oratory. It is less surprising when Eunapius, in the fourth century, reports, apparently in good faith, the conversations of his contemporaries with Asclepius at Pergamon, for superstition, fanned by the theurgists, had by that time made great headway.

For the later sophists described by Eunapius, Aristeides ranks with Demosthenes as a model of Greek prose, and he was even more diligently read; it was the highest praise to say that one of them resembled "the divine Aristeides." For them he was the ideal sophist, and he did indeed defend Sophistic with all his energy against the philosophers, whom he despised. He even carried on a polemic against Plato, and made a formal defence of Gorgias whom Plato had attacked in the *Gorgias.* In spite of his lack of success as a declaimer, he was an epideictic orator. He rebuked his fellow sophists for their theatrical methods, and his Oration *Against the Dancing Sophists* is the bitterest invective against Asianic emotional eloquence that we possess. But he was no less emotional than they, when there was a chance for pathos. When Smyrna was destroyed by an earthquake in 178 he wrote a *Monody on Smyrna* which has all the faults of Asianism. There is little real feeling in this speech over which Marcus Aurelius shed conventional tears. Yet he was in the main an Atticist, who

dreamed of reproducing the many-sided eloquence of Demosthenes and pursued this ideal at the cost of popularity with the crowd. He had his reward in being for centuries rated higher than Demosthenes by the critics and writers on rhetoric. Libanius, in the fourth century, was his devout imitator, though he himself practised a more flexible style of oratory. Aristeides died in the reign of Commodus, about A.D. 187.

Adrian, the Phoenician pupil of Herodes, is hardly known except through Philostratus. He can scarcely have been as old as eighty when he died, for, as Commodus himself died in 190, that is the latest year in which he can have sent an appointment to the dying Adrian, as Philostratus relates. Now Herodes had died about 180 at the age of seventy, and Philostratus makes it clear that Adrian was a much younger man. This is of small importance in itself, but it illustrates the carelessness of Philostratus as a chronicler.

Julius Pollux of Naucratis came to Rome in the reign of Antoninus or Marcus Aurelius, and taught rhetoric to the young Commodus to whom he dedicated his *Onomasticon.* His speeches, which even Philostratus found it impossible to praise, are lost, but we have the *Onomasticon,* a valuable thesaurus of Greek words and synonyms, and especially of technical terms of rhetoric. It was designed as a guide to rhetoric for Commodus, but Pollux was to be more useful than he knew. He is bitterly satirized by Lucian in his *Rhetorician's Guide,* where he is made to describe with the most shameless effrontery the ease with which a declaimer may gull his audience and win a reputation. How far this satire was justified we cannot tell, but we may assume that Pollux had made pretensions to shine as a declaimer, and Lucian, always hostile to that type, chose to satirize one who illustrated the weaknesses rather than the brilliance of that profession. Nevertheless the passage quoted from a declamation of Pollux by Philostratus is not inferior to other such extracts in the **Lives**.

Pausanias the sophist is assumed by some scholars to be the famous archaeologist and traveller. But the latter was not a native of Lycia, and though he speaks of Herodes, he nowhere says that he had studied with him. Nor does Suidas in his list of the sophist's works mention the famous *Description of Greece.* The Pausanias of Philostratus is perhaps the author of the *Attic Lexicon* praised by Photius. We have some fragments of this work.

Antipater the Syrian was one of the teachers of Philostratus. At the court of Septimius Severus he had great influence, perhaps due in part to his Syrian birth, for the compatriots of the Empress Julia were under her special patronage. At Athens he had been the pupil of Adrian, Pollux, and a certain Zeno, a writer on rhetoric whom Philostratus does not include in the **Lives.** He educated the Emperor's sons, Caracalla and Geta, received the consulship, and was for a short time Governor of Bithynia. Galen, the court physician, praises Severus for the favour shown to Antipater. He starved himself to death after Caracalla's favour was withdrawn. This was about 212. We may therefore place his birth about 144. Philostratus studied with him before he became an official. Antipater's marriage with the plain daughter of Hermocrates took place when the court was in the East, but whether Philostratus in his account of this event means the first or the second Eastern expedition of Severus he does not say, so that we cannot precisely date Antipater's appointment as Imperial Secretary; it occurred about 194 or 197; Kayser prefers the later date. We learn from Suidas that Antipater was attacked by Philostratus the First in an essay, *On the Name,* or *On the Noun.* This statement is useful as fixing the date of the father of our Philostratus. The Antipater of the **Lives** must not be confused with an earlier sophist of the same name mentioned by Dio Chrysostom.

Claudius Aelian, the "honey-tongued," as Suidas tells us he was called, is the most important of the learned sophists of the third century. He was born at Praeneste towards the close of the second century, and was a Hellenized Roman who, like Marcus Aurelius, preferred to write Greek. He was an industrious collector of curious facts and strange tales, but, in spite of the statement of Philostratus as to the purity of his dialect, he hardly deserves to rank as a writer of Greek prose. Though he claims to write for "educated ears," his language is a strange mixture of Homeric, tragic, and Ionic Greek, with the "common" dialect as a basis. He is erudite in order to interest his readers and with no purpose of preserving a literary tradition; and in his extant works he observes none of the rules of rhetorical composition as they were handed down by the sophists. He aims at simplicity, ἀφέλεια, but is intolerably artificial. We have his treatise in seventeen books, *On Animals,* a curious medley of facts and anecdotes designed to prove that animals display the virtues and vices of human beings; and the less well preserved *Varied History,* a collection of anecdotes about famous persons set down without any attempt at orderly sequence or connexion. Two religious treatises survive in fragments. In choosing to be a mere writer rather than an epideictic orator he really forfeited the high privilege of being called a sophist.

Notes

1. This is Münscher's conclusion from a remark in the *Life of Apollonius* v. 2, where Philostratus says that he has himself observed the ebb and flow of the Atlantic tides in "the country of the Celts." But this may have been Gaul, not Britain.

2. In the dedication to Gordian Philostratus refers to their intercourse at Antioch.

3. *Letter* 63.

4. lxxv. 15.

5. Dittenberger, *Sylloge* i. 413.

6. A.D. 244-249; the Emperor Philip was elected by the army after the murder of Gordian III.

7. Lollianus in the second, and Prohaeresius in the fourth century, were appointed to the office of στρατοπεδάρχης, for which Food Controller is the nearest equivalent.

8. A.D. 67-79.

9. *Life of Adrian,* p. 589, where he carefully distinguishes between δωρεαί and δῶρα.

10. *Letter* 63.

11. See p. 577 for Hermogenes.

12. *Antike Kunst-Prosa* i. 382.

13. xvii. 806.

14. Diogenes Laertius viii. 88.

15. *Marcellus* 4.

16. See Julian, *The Caesars* 326 B; Cassius Dio lvi. 43.

17. *Palatine Anthology* vii. 645. The "foreigners" are Romans, and Ostrakine is a desert village between Egypt and Palestine.

18. *Eunuch* 7; *cf. Demonax* 12.

19. Norden, *Kunst-Prosa,* p. 422.

20. viii. 68

21. *Memorabilia* i. 3. 24.

22. *Dialogus* 15.

23. *Epistles* vi. 6.

24. *Epistles* ii. 3.

25. *Satire* iii. 24.

26. *Letter* 19.

27. See for this office the *Lives* of Eunapius, especially the *Life* of Prohaeresius.

28. Kaibel, *Epigrammata Graeca* 877.

29. See Schmid, *Atticismus* 201.

30. Kaibel, *Epigrammata Graeca* 1046, gives a useful commentary on the dates in the life of Herodes.

Bibliography

Manuscripts.

There are a number of mss. of the *Lives,* of which the following are the most important: *Vaticanus* 99, eleventh century; *Vaticanus* 64, fourteenth century; *Vaticanus*

140, fifteenth or sixteenth century (contains also the *Lives* of Eunapius); *Laurentianus* 59, twelfth century; *Marcianus,* 391, fifteenth century. Cobet's emendations are in *Mnemosyne,* 1873, Jahn's notes and emendations in his *Symbolae ad Philostrati librum de vitis sophistarum,* Berne, 1837.

EDITIONS.

Aldine, 1502. Juntine, 1517, 1535. Morell, 1608. Olearius, Leipzig, 1709. Westermann, Didot, Paris, 1822, reprinted 1849 and 1878 (with a Latin version, often incorrect). Heyne and Jacobs, 1797. Kayser, Heidelberg, 1838, with notes. Kayser, Zürich, 1842-1846, 1853. Kayser, Teubner, Leipzig, 1871. [The text of the present edition is that of Kayser, revised. The paging is that of Olearius.] Bendorf, Leipzig, 1893.

POLEMO: Hinck, Leipzig, 1873. HERODES ATTICUS: In *Oratores Attici,* Paris, 1868. Hass, *De H. A. oratione* περὶ πολιτείας, Kiel, 1880. ARISTEIDES: Dindorf, Leipzig, 1829. Kiel, Berlin, 1897.

LITERATURE.

Fertig, *De Philostrati sophistis,* Bamberg, 1894. Schmid, *Atticismus,* vol. iv. Stuttgart, 1896, on the style of Philostratus; vol. i. on the style of Aristeides, 1887. Baumgart, *Aelius Aristeides,* Leipzig, 1874. Jüttner, *De Polemone,* Breslau, 1898. Rohde, *Der griechische Roman,* Leipzig. 1876, 1900. Norden, *Antike Kunst-Prosa,* Leipzig, 1898. Leo, *Griechisch-römische Biographie,* Leipzig, 1901. Bruns, *Die atticistischen Bestrebungen,* Kiel, 1896. Volkmann, *Die Rhetorik der Griechen und Römer,* 2nd edition, Leipzig, 1885. Kohl, *De scholasticarum declamationum argumentis ex historia petitis,* Paderborn, 1915. Rohde in *Rheinisches Museum,* xli. Kaibel in *Hermes,* xx. Radermacher in *Rheinisches Museum,* lii., liv. (the last three articles are discussions of the historical development of the New Sophistic). Münscher, "Die Philostrate" in *Philologus,* Supplement 10, 1907 (this is the best discussion of the identity and the ascription of the works of the Philostrati), Wilamowitz in *Hermes* xxxv. (on Atticism and Asianism). Stock, *De prolaliarum usu rhetorico,* Königsberg, 1911. Burgess, *Epideictic Literature,* Chicago, 1902. *Philologische Abhandlungen,* Breslau, 1901, *Quaestiones rhetoricae* (articles on the lives and works or second and fourth century rhetoricians).

G. W. Bowersock (essay date 1969)

SOURCE: Bowersock, G. W. "The Biographer of the Sophists." In *Greek Sophists in the Roman Empire,* pp. 1-16. Oxford: Oxford University Press, 1969.

[*In the following essay, Bowersock discusses Philostratus's notion of the "sophistic," characterizing his writing as a "reliable evocation of a grand baroque age."*]

Literature, illuminating the society of an age through acquiescence or dissent, must always have its place in history as a reflection of attitudes and taste. The relation of literature to politics, however, has not been uniform throughout the ages; from time to time there have developed close alliances between literature and politics,—in England, for example, in the early eighteenth century. Similarly, in the second century of the present era, literary men helped to determine the destiny of the Roman empire and never enjoyed more public renown. Their social and political eminence was not necessarily matched by superior literary attainments. The quality of the second-century works we possess (and they are many) is not high:[1] they are often over-elaborated productions on unreal, unimportant, or traditional themes. Such works were rhetorical showpieces, whose authors, highly trained in oral presentation, were showmen. Yet this fact does not preclude composition for important persons and occasions. The authors were themselves important men.

These were the sophists, still better known (where they are known at all) to philologists than to historians. They are crucial for the history of the second century A.D., which would look far different without them. Their enormous popularity and influence is characteristic of that exquisitely refined epoch; and their extensive travels, with numerous friends in diverse cities, illustrate a coherence of the Roman empire that had been long in the making and was not to exist again. Authors like Lucian and Aelius Aristides brilliantly mirror the world in which the sophists flourished.

From the writings of the second century alone it would have been possible to construct an adequate account of the sophists. In addition, the plentiful evidence of inscriptions and papyri reveals a staggering abundance of practitioners of the sophistic arts. From all this material alone favourite subjects of discourse and standard treatments of them can be adequately established; so can certain details of the sophists' petty quarrels. But, by some good fortune, Flavius Philostratus, a sophist born in the second century and dying in the third, composed the lives of many of his distinguished predecessors and near-contemporaries; his work has survived and provides a convenient basis and limit for historical studies of the movement which he himself designated the Second Sophistic (to detach it from the age of Gorgias). Inasmuch as Philostratus exemplifies what he is writing about and is at the same time so important a source, discussion of the man and the whole notion of a 'sophistic' is inevitable.

The family of Philostratus is a notorious snare. A late Greek lexicon registers three sophists with the name Philostratus,[2] and the confusion generated by these items has long frustrated scholarly certitude.[3] The first man to be listed belongs second chronologically: he is manifestly the biographer of the sophists. The **Lives of the Sophists** and the romantic biography of Apollonius of Tyana are numbered among his works. The conjunction is supported by a reference in the **Lives** back to the account of Apollonius, which is automatically established as the earlier of the two works.[4]

While it is agreeable to recognize one of the Philostrati in the lexicographer's trio, the pleasure is spoiled by obscurities in the two other items. The biographer is said to have flourished under Septimius Severus and to have survived until the reign of Philip the Arab. Those chronological indications are approximately correct.[5] Yet this Philostratus is credited with an eminent father who practised the sophistic arts under Nero.[6] Something has gone wrong; hence an inclination on the part of scholars to see pure fiction in the report of the biographer's famous father. However, there may be truth in it up to a point. The man is said to have composed a work entitled *Nero;* whatever that work may have been, it is just the sort of thing that would induce a lexicographer like this one to lodge the author in Nero's reign. The biographer's father ought to have flourished under the Antonines. Three of the writings attributed to the father can be assigned precisely to that period: a letter to the sophist Antipater, a *Proteus,* and the *Nero* itself. Antipater was one of the biographer's teachers and would plausibly have belonged to his father's generation.[7] Proteus was a name of the notorious Cynic of whom Lucian composed a satiric biography—Peregrinus Proteus, who immolated himself at Olympia in 165.[8] No less a theme for a Philostratus than for a Lucian.[9] Finally, the *Nero* calls swiftly to mind the dialogue now extant in the corpus of Lucian, *Nero or Digging Through the Isthmus of Corinth.* Whether this work, associated falsely with Lucian, is or is not the Philostratean *Nero,* it directs attention to Nero's great scheme to put through a canal from the Corinthian to the Saronic Gulf.[10] That was a matter of relevance in the Antonine age, for the sophist Herodes Atticus contemplated the same plan but was deterred by the ominous example of the emperor Nero.[11] It seems best to allow a historical existence to the eldest Philostratus and to leave him with the works assigned to him. All the chronological indications cohere, apart from one that is wholly impossible (but easily explicable). There is insufficient warrant to remove the man altogether and to ascribe his writings to his son.[12]

The case of the third Philostratus is hopeless. The lexicon blandly states that he was a grand-nephew and a son-in-law of the biographer.[13] He is said to have composed a set of word pictures, and indeed the biographer is also credited with a similar production. Curiously there survive under the name of a Philostratus one set of *imagines* and under the name of 'Philostratus the Younger' another set. But if the latter *imagines* are associated with the third Philostratus in the lexicon, that man emerges (from an avowal in the opening paragraph of the set) as a grandson of the biographer.[14] This is too much to believe, in addition to everything else. It is more judicious to create a fourth Philostratus, author of the second set of *imagines;* it is probably best to remain baffled.

The biographer Philostratus, it seems, came from Lemnos.[15] If his father was a sophist, it should not be surprising, since often in the high empire the profession descended within a family.[16] There were years of study at Athens.[17] In the course of the **Lives** Philostratus mentions several men as his teachers, including Proclus of Naucratis and Hippodromus of Larissa, both themselves taught by pupils of the great Herodes Atticus.[18] Philostratus also names among his teachers the celebrated Damian of Ephesus and Antipater from Phrygian Hierapolis (to whom his father may have addressed a letter).[19] The last of these was instructor of the sons of Septimius Severus. It cannot be said whether Philostratus studied with Antipater at Rome or elsewhere;[20] since, however, Philostratus belonged to the circle of the Syrian empress, Julia Domna, he may well have been introduced to it by Antipater himself.[21] From early in the third century, in all probability, Philostratus mingled with the luminaries of the empress and travelled with them in the great lady's entourage. The opening of the **Lives of the Sophists** records a conversation conducted with a certain Gordian, perhaps a member of the group, in a suburb of Syrian Antioch. It was in Antioch precisely that Julia Domna received word in 217 of Caracalla's death and thereupon took her own life.[22]

Philostratus was at the time engaged in the composition of his Apollonius novel, undertaken at the behest of Julia Domna but completed, or at any rate published, only after her death.[23] It is impossible to say how long it was after her suicide before the work appeared: perhaps not too long, or the reference to Julia's influence might have been less interesting. In any case, Philostratus' allusion to the Apollonius novel in the **Lives** establishes that they at least were written after it.

A juxtaposition of several items compels an inference that the sophists' biographies were done in Athens. A lexicographical entry concerned with one Fronto of Emesa records that Philostratus was teaching in Athens at the same time as Apsines of Gadara, and we happen to know from the biographer himself that Apsines was a younger contemporary and friend of his.[24] Therefore, Philostratus will have found himself in Athens with Apsines in the later years of his career and formed then the association which he attests at the end of the **Lives.** Furthermore, an inscription at Olympia alludes clearly to the biographer Flavius Philostratus and calls him

Athenian.[25] In view of Philostratus' presence at the court for many years, there seems little doubt that the residence in Athens implied by these items followed Julia Domna's suicide.

A text from Erythrae must not be forgotten here: it displays senatorial descendants of Flavius Philostratus 'the sophist', and his wife, a certain Aurelia Melitine.[26] The progression from sophist to senator in successive generations was not uncommon in this age. Examples abound from the second and third centuries.[27]

The dedication of the *Lives of the Sophists* has a peculiar interest. The recipient is Antonius Gordianus ὁ λαμπρότατος ὕπατος; at the end of the dedicatory preface he is addressed as ἄριστε ἀνθυπάτων. Who is this Gordian, and what is the date of the dedication? Standard and accessible works declare that the forms of address indicate that this is Gordian I, at the time proconsul of Africa,[28]—a post he was definitely holding when he became in 238 the first emperor of that name.[29] In the Augustan History Gordian I is said to have held two consulates, the second with Severus Alexander: allegedly in 229.[30] On this uncertain evidence a date of 229/30 has long been considered the *terminus post* for the *Lives,* with Gordian's elevation to the Purple as the *terminus ante*.[31] These *termini* presuppose a possibility which is altogether inadmissible: that Gordian could have gone to the proconsulate of Africa directly after his consulate and stayed there until he became emperor.

Objections can and have been raised against such an assumption. There is no warrant for believing in a second consulate for Gordian or that he held the African proconsulate for longer than a year. Moreover, Philostratus will have addressed Gordian at the outset by his highest and most recent office, while at the same time acknowledging him to have been an excellent proconsul of a province not specified. The consulate was thus Gordian's most recent office (Philostratus' ὕπατος need mean no more than ὑπατικός);[32] the proconsulate was praetorian, not consular. This conclusion furnishes an explanation for the absence of a province's name in connection with the proconsulate: it was the praetorian proconsulate of Achaea, the province in which Philostratus was living.[33] Accordingly, the old chronological *termini* for the *Lives of the Sophists* vanish. The work was composed some time after the year of Gordian's only consulate, a year regrettably unknown.

There is, however, another possibility, recently propounded.[34] Perhaps Gordian II, not I, is the recipient of Philostratus' work. In his preface Philostratus states that his Gordian was descended from Herodes Atticus,[35]—on any hypothesis an exceedingly difficult detail to elucidate. One is reluctant to doubt the connection with Herodes; Philostratus' account of that sophist is

certainly the longest of any and prominently placed at the opening of the second book of the *Lives*. The second Gordian is more easily traced back to Herodes than the first,[36] but in neither case is the evidence sufficient. Credibility does not permit belief that Gordian I was the author of an epic poem in thirty books on the exploits of Pius and Marcus, as the Augustan History avers;[37] but it is not impossible that he was a man of literary tastes whom Philostratus may have known in the salon of Julia Domna. Until more evidence or argument accrues, Gordian I has a slightly superior claim as the honorand of Philostratus.

The Gordiani probably came from Asia Minor.[38] It is an instructive spectacle to see the sophist Philostratus presenting a work on sophists to an East Greek, soon to be emperor, whom he may have known at an earlier time in the Roman salon of a Syrian empress and whom he had encountered more recently as governor of the Greeks in Achaea. This is a fitting illustration of the historical significance of the so-called Second Sophistic.

Philostratus himself insisted upon the term 'Second Sophistic' for the efflorescence of sophists under the Roman empire. One ought not, he said, to call it the 'New Sophistic' (which evokes a suspicion that someone had), since it was old.[39] It began, according to Philostratus, with Aeschines, the great rival of Demosthenes.[40] Gorgias is credited with an older type of sophistic which concerned itself with philosophical themes, such as justice and the universe, treated rhetorically; it was 'philosophic rhetoric'.[41] The second form of the sophistic art, rightly or wrongly traced to Aeschines, is characterized by historical themes or at any rate types of persons who figure in history (princes, dynasts, the rich, the poor). Philostratus' rather arbitrary distinction would disqualify the prose hymns of Aristides; but, after all, these were quite self-consciously new contributions to sophistic literature.[42] The definition of Philostratus is serviceable enough; as for the antiquity claimed for the movement by allusion to Aeschines, even Philostratus is hard put to think of any other representatives after Aeschines before the reign of Nero.[43] He mentions exactly three names from that vast intervening period and dismisses them immediately with a reference to the paucity of noble sophists in those times.[44] The plain fact is that the Second Sophistic, whether it might have derived from Aeschines or not, was a distinctive growth of the high empire, and it would not have been a senseless man who called it new.

It was, however, a growth, and there were certainly sophists before Nicetes of Smyrna, whose biography follows directly upon that of Aeschines in Philostratus. Cicero and Strabo leave no doubt of the activity of sophists and rhetors in the late republic and early empire; the reminiscences of the elder Seneca convey a similar impression.[45] Moreover, these earlier figures often had careers in politics and diplomacy: so, for example, Hybreas of Mylasa and the Augustan Polemo.[46] And as Polemo's family makes clear in subsequent generations,[47] there are palpable links between these earlier cultivated men and the true representatives of the Second Sophistic. There is continuity and development throughout, so much so that the Second Sophistic would not have occurred, had the way not been prepared. The Second (or New) Sophistic is a culmination, not a sudden burst or fad. This is true of the sophists' style as much as it is of their role in Roman history.

In the late nineteenth century the question of style in the Second Sophistic was hotly debated by the scholarly giants of the day. In retrospect the whole argument has an air of absurdity. It began when Erwin Rohde devoted a division of his thick book on the Greek novel to detailing the spread of Asianic rhetoric so as to demonstrate that the second century saw nothing more than a perpetuation of the Asianic style of Cicero's era.[48] Kaibel denied this, and he summoned as witnesses the Atticists among the sophists;[49] Rohde replied.[50] Norden observed sanely that the Second Sophistic had both Atticist *and* Asianic manifestations.[51] Wilamowitz finally closed the case by synthesizing everyone's views in a long and important article.[52]

Continuity, one has always to realize, does not require sameness; and an opposite reaction can nevertheless belong to a single line of development. The Second Sophistic is distinguishable and new not because it introduced a new type of person into literature and history, but rather because in the second century a type, long in existence, became so widely diffused and enjoyed such unprecedented authority. An access of inscriptions and papyri, enlarging our knowledge of social and political history, has authoritatively vindicated Philostratus' recognition of a great sophistic movement. The notion, once fashionable among scholars, that the Second Sophistic was a pure invention of its chronicler has to be banished.[53] Philostratus was not a scholar himself and his work is often superficial, but his subject was a real one.

In the work presented to Gordian Philostratus claimed to be writing biographies not only of true sophists (τοὺς οὕτω κυρίως προσρηθέντας σοφιστάς) but also of philosophers who could be regarded as sophists (τοὺς φιλοσοφήσαντας ἐν δόξῃ τοῦ σοφιστεῦσαι).[54] A little later Philostratus alludes to those philosophers who are not actually sophists but seem to be, and they are therefore so denominated; such philosophers are said to attain the rank of sophist by virtue of fluency.[55] It is fortunate that Philostratus provides guidance in

these matters of professional titles, for in the second century they were sometimes important.

Of a genuine rivalry between philosophers and rhetors there can be no doubt (let sophists, for the moment, be subsumed in the general category of rhetors), for philosophy and rhetoric constituted the two principal parts of higher education.[56] Their practitioners competed with each other for the allegiance of the young. Because of the nature of their work rhetors were, of course, more eloquent in denouncing philosophers than were philosophers in denouncing rhetors. Among the most powerful assaults on the philosophers is the latter part of Aelius Aristides' Oration on the Four: philosophers, we are told, do not speak or write λόγοι, adorn festival assemblies, honour the gods, advise cities, comfort the distressed, settle civil discord, or educate the young.[57] This remarkable passage is nothing less than a catalogue of the work of a sophist, for it is in the various points enumerated by Aristides that sophists are superior to philosophers. Aristides' antipathy to philosophers was strong, and his strictures were not altogether just. Philosophers had been known to advise cities, comfort the distressed, settle civil discord, and educate the young.

It was, in fact, possible for the professions of philosopher and rhetor to be conflated and confused. They had many tasks in common, and both were obliged to use the spoken and written word. Accordingly, as Philostratus recognized, eloquent philosophers might be numbered among the sophists. As such, Favorinus of Arelate and Dio of Prusa figure in the *Lives of the Sophists*. The two professions are similarly conjoined on inscriptions, confuting Aristides and lending credibility to Philostratus. For example, the poet T. Flavius Glaucus appears on an honorific text as rhetor and philosopher;[58] on an epigram from Athens a man is declared to be a rhetor in his speaking and a philosopher in his thinking.[59] Another man appears as a sophist and philosopher,[60] and examples could be multiplied. There is a notable text in Alexandria in which Aelius Demetrius the rhetor is honoured by a group of philosophers (presumably those of the Museum).[61] Cassius Dio, a contemporary of Philostratus, wrote of Julia Domna that because of the prefect Plautianus' hostility she began to study philosophy and associate with sophists.[62] Philostratus, therefore, accurately reflects the relations of philosophers and sophists in the intellectual milieu of the second century.

In the elucidation of professional titles the distinction between rhetor and sophist poses a far more difficult problem than that of philosopher and rhetor (or sophist). It is clear from sundry texts that there was some kind of distinction felt between the titles ὁ ῥήτωρ and ὁ σοφιστής. Philostratus, on occasion, deliberately eschewed the word 'sophist' in alluding to certain persons,[63] and Galen once wrote of the sophist Hadrian that in his earlier years he was a rhetor but not yet a sophist.[64] However, often on inscriptions the terms 'rhetor' and 'sophist' coexist without discomfort: Dionysius of Miletus, the celebrated Hadrianic sophist, appears in an Ephesian text, for instance, as ῥήτορα καὰ σοφιστήν.[65] Also in a letter to the Koinon of Asia Antoninus Pius can be seen using the word sophist and rhetor interchangeably.[66]

Scholars have put forward various explanations of the terms 'sophist' and 'rhetor'. For some ancient authors anyhow, it has been claimed, a rhetor was exclusively a forensic speaker and a sophist a professor or school teacher.[67] Strabo's phrase σοφιστεύειν τὰ ῥητορικά can be invoked in support of this view; but Strabo also uses the verb ῥητορεύειν for the same idea.[68] Certainly for the second century such an interpretation is quite unacceptable in view of the fact that Aristides, an undoubted sophist, rarely taught anyone and was opposed to the idea of teaching for pay.[69]

On another interpretation the designation of sophist is purely honorific and ranks higher than that of rhetor.[70] Yet this notion is hard to reconcile with certain epigraphical evidence or the letter of Pius, or—for that matter—with Galen's phrase. To say, as Galen does, that a man was not yet a sophist would have to be likened to calling a man a εὐεργέτης but not yet a κτίστης. Furthermore, Philostratus admits among his sophists a man like Varus of Laodicea for whom he has the lowest possible opinion.[71] More to the point, it seems, is Dessau's conjecture that a rhetor practises his art in a less polished and more dilettantish fashion than a sophist.[72] Philostratus can be cited in support of his view: he asserts that earlier generations called sophists not only those rhetors who were fluent and distinguished but also certain philosophers.[73] The implication is that sophists represent a category within the general group of rhetors, which will have been the broader term. The sense of sophist can perhaps best be had from the modern notion of professionalism. The sophist was a virtuoso rhetor with a big public reputation. So when Galen said of Hadrian the Sophist, ὁ ῥήτωρ οὔπω σοφιστεύων, he probably meant that Hadrian had not yet embarked upon his professional, public career as a performing rhetor.

It appears, then, that rhetors and sophists are the same, except that not all rhetors will have been sophists. In Pius' letter to the Koinon the emperor refers to the two groups, γραμματικοί and ῥήτορες / σοφισταί, by the collective phrase οἱπαιδεύοντες ἑκατέραν παιδείαν.[74] He has only teachers in mind, and for that reason he sees no difference between rhetors and sophists, since both might or might not be teachers. He was occupied with the distinction between teachers and non-teachers, and a distinction between professionals and non-professionals was of no concern to him. It was, however, of concern to Sextus Empiricus, who provides a particularly striking support for the interpretation preferred here: sophists, he declares, have reached the peak of rhetorical skill.[75]

It has been necessary to dilate on these titles because much confusion exists, and these things clearly meant something to the sophists themselves. Pride in petty titles looms large in the second century, for cities—as everyone knows—as well as for individual men.[76]

It has sometimes been claimed in support of the view of 'sophist' as a purely honorific term that the careers of Athenaeus' sophists at dinner were not exclusively rhetorical. The diners included philosophers, grammarians, a doctor, a musician, and (possibly) a famous lawyer.[77] The musician is somewhat surprising as a sophist; the others are not. In so far as rhetoric can be a relevant province of various professional persons, the title of sophist is open to them. The case of philosophers has already been examined. It is obvious that lawyers could have been adjudged sophists through forensic rhetoric of a polished kind; and whether or not Athenaeus really included a lawyer among his diners, there is no reason why he should not have done so. A doctor's claim to being a sophist can derive . . . from an interest in philosophy and fluent exposition of his subject. Presumably a musician could be entitled to sophistic rank in much the same way.

Both in his career and in his ideas Philostratus was a representative specimen of the sophistic movement he chronicled. His information came to him directly, either from his own teachers or from others who had known the great sophists of the second century. He was not attempting scholarly or authoritative biography. He was attracted by anecdotes and fond of quoting from the sophists' works (a feature of the *Lives* which may, on occasion, induce tedium). But he could hardly have been better placed to write about the sophistic movement. This is reporting at first hand.

Like many of his subjects, Philostratus had a career closely bound up with the imperial court and with certain leading Romans. The intimate relation between sophists and the masters of the empire must not, however, deceive. The men of whom Philostratus wrote were Greeks, in the broad sense—from Greece, Asia Minor, Syria, Egypt. Favorinus from Gaul was a special case (in this and in other respects too),[78] but his culture was indubitably Hellenic. These men were not oblivious of their tradition, and when they became so integral a part of the Roman world it was not because they turned upon their inheritance. On the contrary, their preoccupation with the glorious past of their ancient predecessors became more conspicuous. It is everywhere apparent, in their teaching, their examples, the very topics of their discourse. This is not because the sophists were eaten up by nostalgia for the old times, nor were they affirming the independent greatness of the Greeks against the Romans. They bore no grudge for belonging to the Roman empire; they did not object to the word 'Ρωμαῖοι, a collective and non-prejudicial term.[79] In fact, if there was any submergence of one nationality in another, it was at times the Roman which gave way to the Greek. The emperor Hadrian was, after all, a thoroughgoing philhellene; and Marcus Aurelius wrote his meditations like a Greek and in Greek. But there had been Roman philhellenes for centuries, not however—apart from Nero—conspicuously on the throne of the Caesars. It was possible for a proud Greek to be a Roman without any loss of national pride or abnegation of cultural tradition. Aelius Aristides' panegyric of Rome can *only* be understood when read in conjunction with his other speeches in praise of cities, the panegyrics of Cyzicus, Corinth, Athens, Rhodes, Smyrna.[80] These were all cities of the same world, Rome included in it.[81]

Within that great and hitherto unparalleled οἰκουμένη Greeks and Romans dwelt together, sharing in friendship and government without sacrifice of national integrity. The age had common tastes which worked themselves out in different ways according to different traditions. This proves the point. It is no secret that the second century shows a predilection for antiquity and archaism, and this predilection extended from East to West, dominating the literary activity of Greeks and Romans. But the Greeks looked back to Athens of the fifth century and to Attic purity, whereas the Romans turned to the Punic Wars, studying the old Cato and exploring archaic Latin vocabulary. The mood was shared in common; its expression was appropriately diverse. To see a serious nationalistic split in (at any rate) the cultivated classes of the Roman empire in the second century would be to miss perhaps the most striking feature of the age and something quite unique in ancient history. The equilibrium was far from perfect, and there was doubtless dissatisfaction in lower strata of society; moreover, personal ambition and chaotic rule can make any imperial coherence transitory, and did. But Philostratus and his sophists, with all the attendant witnesses of inscriptions and papyri, are a reliable evocation of a grand baroque age before its dissolution, an age in which Herodes Atticus and Cornelius Fronto could be consuls at Rome in the same year.[82]

Notes

1. B. A. van Groningen, 'General Literary Tendencies in the Second Century A.D.', *Mnemosyne* 18 (1965), 41 ff.

2. Suid., s.v. Φιλόστρατος, nos. 421-3 (Adler).

3. Cf. the survey in F. Solmsen, 'Philostratus', *P-W* 20. 1. 125 ff. and Solmsen, 'Some Works of Philostratus the Elder', *TAPA* [*Transactions of the American Philological Association*] 71 (1940), 556 ff.

4. Philostratus, *Vitae Sophistarum* (VS) p. 570: εἴρηται σαφῶς ἐν τοῖς ἐς 'Απολλώνιον.

5. Suid., s.v. Φιλόστρατος, no. 421 (Adler): ἐπὶ σευήρου τοῦ βασιλέως καὶ ???ως Φιλίππου. The Severus is Septimius (cf. Rohde, *Rh. Mus* 33 [1878], 638-9). For the accuracy of this rough chronology, see the discussion of Philostratus' career later in the present chapter.

6. Suid., s.v. Φιλόστρατος, no. 422 (Adler).

7. See below [in this text] pp. 55-6.

8. Lucian, *Peregrinus:* the immolation is described in ch. 36 (cf. *VS*, p. 563, Amm. Marc. 29. 1. 39). On the date of the event: K. von Fritz, *P-W* 19. 1. 657 and G. Bagnani, *Historia* 4 (1955), 108.

9. Suidas also ascribes to this Philostratus a work entitled τὰ ἐν 'Ολυμπία ἐπιτελούμενα. Perhaps including an account of Peregrinus' immolation?

10. On Nero's plan, see Dio 62. 16. 1-2.

11. *VS,* pp. 551-2.

12. It is true that Philostratus does not mention his father at all (cf. F. Grosso, *Acme* 7 [1954], 376 n. 23). Should he? Plutarch says relatively little, in all his vast writings, about his father. As a sophist, the biographer's father may have had no importance.

13. Suid., s.v. Φιλόστρατος, no. 423 (Adler).

14. On all this, see Solmsen, *Transactions of the American Philological Association* (*TAPA*) 71 (1940), 556 ff.

15. Eunapius, *Vit. Phil. et Soph.,* p. 454 (ὁ Λήμνιος, of the biographer of sophists); Synesius, *Dio* 1; Suid., s.v. Apollonius Tyaneus and s.v. Crates Cynicus. Cf. Schmid, *Philol.* 57 (1898), 503. Note Philostratus' reference to Lemnos in *Vit. Apoll.* 6. 27 and his allusion to a younger contemporary (and, presumably, relative), Philostratus of Lemnos, at *VS*, p. 617. Cf. Philostr. *Epist.* 70.

16. Observe, e.g., the Licinii Firmi of Athens (*IG* ii/iii². 3563, cf. *Anth. Plan.* 322), the Flavii Menandri of Ephesus (*Forsch. Ephesos* 3. 145, no. 62), the Claudii Aurelii of Aphrodisias (L. Robert, *Ant. Class.* 35 [1966], 396-7), the Flavii Alexander, Phylax, and Phoenix of Thessaly (*PIR*², F 199; cf. J. Pouilloux, *REG* 80 [1967], 379 ff.).

17. Suid., s.v. Φιλόστρατος, no. 421 (Adler). Eusebius and Hierocles called him an Athenian (*PIR*², F 332). Philostratus will have heard Proclus and Hippodromus in Athens. See next note.

18. *VS*, pp. 602 (Proclus), 618 (Hippodromus).

19. *VS*, pp. 605-6 (Damian), 607 (Antipater). On the letter to Antipater, see the foregoing discussion in this [essay].

20. In *P-W* 20. 1. 136, Solmsen objected rightly to a *terminus ante* of 193 for Philostratus' study with Antipater: this *terminus* was postulated by K. Münscher in *Philol.* Supp. 10 (1905-7), 475-6, on the unsupported assumption that Philostratus heard Antipater at Athens. *VS*, p. 607 tells how Philostratus used to praise Antipater's lectures *at Rome*.

21. On Philostratus' membership in Julia's circle, *Vit. Apoll.* 1. 3: μετέχοντι δέ μοι τοῦ περὶ αὐτὴν κύκλου.

22. *VS*, p. 480 (the conversation outside Antioch). On the suicide of Julia: Dio 79. 23-4.

23. The work is not dedicated to Julia, although Philostratus states explicitly that he wrote it at her instigation (*Vit. Apoll.* 1. 3).

24. Suid., s.v. Φρόντων Ἐμισηνός: the biographer is called, in this entry, ὁ πρῶτος (cf. W. Schmid, *Der Atticismus* [1896], p. 6 with n. 6). See also *VS*, p. 628. An Athenian inscription now provides the nomen Valerius for Apsines and links him with an important family of Athens, the Claudii of Melite: *Hesperia* 10 (1941), 261.

25. *SIG*³ [W. Dittenberger, *Sylloge Inscriptionum Graecarum* (Third Edition)] 878: Φλ. Φιλόστρατον Ἀθηναῖον τὸν σοφιστήν.

26. *SIG*³ 879 = *IGR* 4. 1544.

27. Many illustrations of this progression will be found in the pages that follow.

28. e.g. Münscher, op. cit. (p. 5, n. 1), p. 471, or Solmsen, *P-W* 20. 1. 138 and 170.

29. *HA* Tres Gordiani 2. 4, 5. 1, 7. 2, 18. 6. Cf. B. E. Thomasson, *Die Statthalter der römischen Provinzen Nordafrikas von Augustus bis Diokletianus* (1960), pp. 120-1.

30. *HA* Tres Gordiani 2. 4, 4. 1. Alexander Severus was *consul ordinarius* III in 229 with Cassius Dio, *cos. ord.* II; it would have to be assumed that a suffect replaced Dio while the emperor remained in office. Alexander was also *cos. ord.* in 222 and 226.

31. Cf. *PIR*², A 833.

32. For Philostratus' usage, observe the following instances where ὕπατος means 'consular' (ὑπατικός): p. 512 (ἀνὴρ ὕπατος), p. 536 (τοῦ ὕπατός τε καὶ ἐξ ὑπάτων δοκεῖν), p. 555 (ἐν ὑπάτοις), p. 567 (ἐς ὑπάτους), p. 576 (Κοδρατίων ὁ ὕπατος), p. 588 (ἀνδρὸς ὑπάτου), p. 609 (ἀνὴρ ὕπατος). Scholars have attended insufficiently to this usage in Philostratus. It is not unlike the word *consul* on a cursus inscription well after a man has ceased actually being consul.

33. Cf. E. Groag, *Die römischen Reichsbeamten von Achaia von Augustus bis auf Diokletian* (1939), 87-8. Philostratus was writing after 222: *VS*, pp. 624-5.

34. A. R. Birley, *Britain and Rome: Essays pres. to E. Birley* (1966), pp. 58-9. For a full discussion of this possibility: T. D. Barnes, 'Philostratus and Gordian', *Latomus* 27 (1968), 581 ff.

35. *VS*, p. 479: γένος ἐστί σοι πρὸς τὴν τέχνην ἐς Ἡρώδην τὸν σοφιστὴν ἀναφέροντι. For the view that Philostratus errs here, cf. J. H. Oliver, *AJP* 89 (1968), 346.

36. Since Gordian I was about eighty years old when he became emperor in 238 (Herodian 7. 5. 2; *HA* Tres Gord. 9. 1), he was born *c.* 159. Of Herodes' two daughters it is hard to see which could have been Gordian's mother, although Elpinice, dying after Athenaïs and without recorded husband, is possible (cf. *PIR*², C 802). However, Claudia Regilla, wife of M. Antonius Antius Lupus, might be exploited as mother of Gordian II in a previous marriage (she predeceased Lupus, cf. *ILS* 1127). The name Claudia Regilla proclaims some connection with Herodes and his wife Regilla.

37. *HA* Tres Gordiani 3. 3.

38. A. R. Birley, op. cit. (p. 7. n. 3), pp. 59-60, and the opinion of H.-G. Pflaum cited by Birley.

39. *VS*, p. 481.

40. Ibid., p. 507.

41. Ibid., p. 480: ῥητορικὴ φιλοσοφοῦσα.

42. Cf. Aristid. 45. 4-14 Keil (Hymn to Serapis) on the writing of prose hymns.

43. *VS*, p. 511, Nicetes of Smyrna. He has to be dated to the reign of Nero: the emperor on p. 512 is not Nerva but Nero (cf. A. Boulanger, *Aelius Aristide* [1923], p. 84, n. 1).

44. The three (all unknown) are Ariobarzanes of Cilicia, Xenophron of Sicily, and Peithagoras of Cyrene (*VS*, p. 511).

45. U. von Wilamowitz, *Litteris* 2 (1925), 127. Cf. Bowersock, *Augustus and the Greek World* (1965), ch. 1. For Strabo, there is the very useful book of

E. Stemplinger, *Strabons literarhistorische Notizen* (1894); for Seneca some of the persons in H. Bornecque's register are relevant: *Les déclamations et les déclamateurs d'après Sénèque le père* (1902).

46. Bowersock, op. cit., pp. 5-6.

47. Ibid., pp. 143-4.

48. E. Rohde, *Der griechische Roman* (1914), pp. 310-87. This material appeared in the first edition of 1876.

49. G. Kaibel, 'Dionysios von Halikarnassos und die Sophistik', *Hermes* 20 (1885), 497 ff.

50. E. Rohde, 'Die asianische Rhetorik und die zweite Sophistik', *Rh. Mus.* 41 (1886), 170 ff. = *Kl. Schr.* (1901) 2. 75 ff.

51. E. Norden, *Die antike Kunstprosa* (1915), pp. 351-92, which appeared in the first edition of 1898.

52. U. von Wilamowitz, 'Asianismus und Attizismus', *Hermes* 35 (1900), 1 ff. Cf. the very sensible remarks on this controversy by A. E. Douglas in *CQ* N.S. 5 (1955), 241-7, and in his commentary on Cicero's *Brutus* (1966), p. xiii.

53. Cf. U. von Wilamowitz, rebuking A. Boulanger in a review of his *Aelius Aristide*: 'Von der schlechthin unbrauchbaren Erfindung des Philostratos, der zweiten Sophistik, hat er sich nicht losgemacht' (*Litteris* 2 [1925], 126).

54. *VS*, p. 479.

55. Ibid., p. 484: τῶν φιλοσόφων τοὺς ξὺν εὐροίᾳ ἑρμηνεύοντας.

56. H. I. Marrou, *Histoire de l'éducation dans l'antiquité* (1960), pp. 288 ff. Cf. also M. D. Brock, *Studies in Fronto and his Age* (1911), ch. 8.

57. Aristid. 46, p. 404 Dindorf.

58. *Hesperia*, Suppl. 8 (1949), 246 ff.

59. Kaibel, *Epigrammata Graeca*, no. 106 = Peek, *Griechische Versinschriften* 588: ῥήτωρ μὲν εἰπεῖν, φιλόσοφος δ' ἃ χρὴ νοεῖν.

60. Suid., s.v. Hippias of Elis.

61. E. Breccia, *Cat. général, musée d'Alexandrie, Iscrizioni greche e latine,* no. 146 (an improved text of *OGIS* 712). See C. P. Jones, *CQ* 17 (1967), 311 ff.

62. Dio 76. 15. 7: φιλοσοφεῖν . . . ἤρξατο καὶ σοφισταῖς συνημερεύειν. Note also Plut. *Quaest. Conv.* 710 B: βαθυπώγων σοφιστὴς ἀπὸ τῆς στοᾶς.

63. Observe *VS*, p. 605, where a group of men are designated ἀθύρματα of the Greeks rather than σοφισταὶ λόγου ἄξιοι. However, one of this group, Soterus, is attested on inscriptions at Ephesus and Delphi, indicating that not everyone was of Philostratus' opinion: *JÖAI* 40 (1953), 15-18, and *Fouilles de Delphes* iii. 4 (1954), no. 265, p. 290 (plate 35, 4). Similarly Phylax, attested at Olympia and Delphi: *REG* 80 (1967), 379 ff.

64. Galen 14. 627 Kühn: ὁ ῥήτωρ οὔπω σοφιστεύων.

65. *JÖAI* 40 (1953), 6.

66. *Dig.* 27. 1. 6. 2. See below, pp. 33-4.

67. This was the view of R. Jeuckens, *Plutarch und die Rhetorik* (1907), pp. 47-54 ('Der Begriff des σοφιστός'). Cf. C. Brandstätter, 'De notionum πολιτικής et σοφιστής usu rhetorico', *Leipzig. Stud. z. class. Phil.* 15 (1894), 129-274. The definition of the late rhetorical theorist, Victorinus, is not relevant here: Vict. *Rhet. Lat. Min.* 156. 21 Halm.

68. Strabo, p. 614 (σοφιστεύειν τὰ ῥητορικά), p. 650 (ἐρρητόρευε).

69. The word 'sophist' is claimed as a term of abuse in Aristides: E. Mensching, *Mnemosyne* 18 (1965), 62, n. 3; C. A. Behr, *Aelius Aristides and the Sacred Tales* (1968), p. 106, n. 39. But cf. Aristid. 50. 100 Keil, which Behr emends.

70. This is the view of K. Gerth in his article 'Zweite Sophistik' (unreliable), *P-W* Suppl. 8. 723. Note the comment of W. Spoerri on Gerth's article: 'une mine inépuisable d'inexactitudes et d'erreurs' (*Rev. de Philol.* 41 [1967], 118, n. 1).

71. *VS*, p. 620.

72. *Hermes* 25 (1890), 160, n. 1.

73. *VS*, p. 484.

74. See p. 12, n. 8 above.

75. Sextus Empiricus, *adv. math.* 2. 18: οἱ σοφιστεύοντες ἐπ' ἄκρον μὲν τὴν ῥητορικὴν ἐξήσκησαν τεχνολογίαν.

76. On cities' squabbling for titles like μητρόπολις or πρώτη πόλις see D. Magie, *Roman Rule in Asia Minor* (1950), i. 635-7, ii. 1496, n. 17.

77. The Ulpian at dinner may or may not be the lawyer: cf. W. Dittenberger, 'Athenäus und sein Werk', *Apophoreton* (1903), 1 ff., and W. Kunkel, *Herkunft und soziale Stellung der römischen Juristen* (1952), pp. 245-54.

78. He was a hermaphrodite (*VS*, p. 489).

79. Cf. J. Palm, *Rom, Römertum, und Imperium in der griechischen Literatur der Kaiserzeit* (1959), and G. W. Bowersock, *JRS* 58 (1968), 261 f.

80. D. Nörr, *Imperium und Polis in der hohen Prinzipatszeit* (1966), pp. 83 ff. makes much use of the εἰς 'Ρώμην but is largely ignorant of Aristides' other panegyrics. The attempt of J. Bleicken to extract what is original in the εἰς 'Ρώμην is more substantial: *NGA* 1966, 7, pp. 225-77. Cf. H. Bengtson, *Gymnasium* 71 (1964), 150 ff.

81. It is worth observing that at Greek games encomia of members of the imperial house were among the fields of competition: cf., e.g., *SEG* 3. 334; *Corinth*, VIII. 3. 153 (on which *REG* 79 [1966], 743).

82. Namely A.D. 143.

Bibliography

VON ARNIM, J., *Leben und Werke des Dio von Prusa* (1898).

ATKINSON, K. M. T., 'The Third Cyrene Edict of Augustus', *Ancient society and institutions: studies pres. to V. Ehrenberg* (1966), 21 ff.

BABELON, E., 'Le Faux-Prophète, Alexandre d'Abonuteichos', *Rev. Num.* 4 (1900), 1 ff.

BACKMANN, P., 'Galens Abhandlung darüber, dass der vorzügliche Arzt Philosoph sein muss', *NGA* 1965, no. 1.

BAGNANI, G., 'Peregrinus Proteus and the Christians', *Historia* 4 (1955), 107 ff.

BALSDON, J. P. V. D., *Roman Women* (1962).

BARIGAZZI, A., *Opere: Favorino di Arelate* (1966).

BARNES, T. D., 'A Note on Polycarp', *JTS* 18 (1967), 433 ff.

———'Pre-Decian *Acta Martyrum*', *JTS* 19 (1968), 509 ff.

———'Philostratus and Gordian', *Latomus* 27 (1968), 581 ff.

BARROW, R. H., *Plutarch and his Times* (1967).

BEHR, C. A., *Aelius Aristides and the Sacred Tales* (1968).

BENGTSON, H., 'Das Imperium Romanum in griechischer Sicht', *Gymnasium* 71 (1964), 150 ff.

BIRLEY, A. R., 'The Origin of Gordian I', *Britain and Rome: essays pres. to Eric Birley* (1966), 56 ff.

———*Marcus Aurelius* (1966).

BLEICKEN, J., 'Der Preis des Aelius Aristides auf das römische Weltreich', *NGA* 1966, no. 7.

BLOCH, H., *I Bolli laterizi e la Storia edilizia romana* (1938-9).

BOMPAIRE, J., *Lucien écrivain* (1958).

BORNECQUE, H., *Les Déclamations et les déclamateurs d'après Sénèque le père* (1902).

BOSWINKEL, E., 'La Médecine et les médecins dans les papyrus grecs', *Eos* 48, i (1956; Symbolae Taubenschlag, i), 181ff.

BOULANGER, A., *Aelius Aristide* (1923).

BOWERSOCK, G. W., *Augustus and the Greek World* (1965).

———'A New Inscription of Arrian', *GRBS* 8 (1967), 279 f.

———'The Proconsulate of Albus', *HSCP* 72 (1968), 289 ff.

———Review of D. Nörr, *Imperium und Polis, JRS* 58 (1968), 261 f.

BRANDSTÄTTER, C., 'De notionum πολιτικός et σοφιστής usu rhetorico' *Leipzig. Stud. z. class. Phil.* 15 (1894), 129 ff.

BROCK, M. D., *Studies in Fronto and his Age* (1911).

BUCKLER, W. H., 'T. Statilius Crito, Traiani Augusti medicus', *JÖAI* 30 (1937), Beibl. 5 ff.

CASTER, M., *Études sur Alexandre ou le Faux-Prophète de Lucien* (1938).

CICHORIUS, C., *Rom und Mytilene* (1888).

———*Römische Studien* (1922).

COHN-HAFT, L., *The public physicians of Ancient Greece* (1956).

DAY, J., *An economic history of Athens under Roman domination* (1942).

DESSAU, H., 'C. Sallius Aristaenetus', *Hermes* 25 (1890), 158 ff.

DITTENBERGER, W., 'Athenäus und sein Werk', *Apophoreton* (1903), 1 ff.

DODDS, E. R., *Pagan and Christian in an Age of Anxiety* (1965).

DURUY, V., *Histoire de Rome,* vol. vi (1879).

EDELSTEIN, E. J. and L., *Asclepius* (1945), 2 vols.

FITZ, J., 'Ummidio Quadrato, governatore della Moesia inferiore', *Epigraphica* 26 (1964), 45 ff.

FLACELIÈRE, R., 'Inscriptions de Delphes de l'époque impériale', *BCH* 73 (1949), 464 ff.

FREND, W. H. C. 'The Date of Polycarp's Martyrdom', *Oikoumene* (1964), 499 ff.

GEAGAN, D. J., *The Athenian Constitution after Sulla, Hesperia,* Suppl. 12 (1967).

GRAINDOR, P., *Un Milliardaire antique: Hérode Atticus et sa famille* (1930).

GROAG, E., 'Cn. Claudius Severus und der Sophist Hadrian', *Wiener Studien* 24 (1902), 261 ff.

————*Die römischen Reichsbeamten von Achaia von Augustus bis auf Diokletian* (1939).

GRONINGEN, B. A. VAN, 'General Literary Tendencies in the Second Century A.D.', *Mnemosyne* 18 (1965), 41 ff.

GROSSO, F., 'La Vita di Apollonio di Tiana come fonte storica', *Acme* 7 (1954), 333 ff.

HANSLIK, R., 'Fronto und Herodes', *Opus. Phil. kath. Phil.* (Vienna) 6 (1934), 29 ff.

HEPDING, H., '"Ρουφίνιον ἄλσος"', *Philologus* 88 (1933), 90 ff., 241 ff.

HERZOG, R., 'Urkunden zur Hochschulpolitik der römischen Kaiser' *Sitzungsberichte d. preuss. Akad.* 1935, 967 ff.

HÜTTL, W., *Antoninus Pius* i (1936), ii (1933).

ISNARDI, M., 'Techne', *Parola del Passato* 16 (1961), 257 ff.

JAMESON, S., 'Cornutus Tertullus and the Plancii of Perge', *JRS* 55 (1965), 54 ff.

JEUCKENS, R., *Plutarch von Chaeronea und die Rhetorik* (1907).

JONES, A. H. M., *The Greek City* (1939).

————'The Greeks under the Roman Empire', *Dumbarton Oaks Papers* 17 (1963), 3 ff.

JONES, C. P., 'Towards a Chronology of Plutarch's Works', *JRS* 56 (1966), 61 ff.

————'The Teacher of Plutarch', *HSCP* 71 (1967), 205 ff.

————'A Friend of Galen', *CQ* 17 (1967), 311 f.

JÜTTNER, H., *De Polemonis Rhetoris Vita Operibus Arte* (1898).

KAIBEL, G., 'Dionysios von Halikarnassos und die Sophistik', *Hermes* 20 (1885), 497 ff.

KAPETANOPOULOS, E. A., '"Ἀναθηματικὴ ἐπιγραφὴ ἐξ Ἐλευσῖνος"', Ἀρχ. Ἐφ. 1964, publ. 1967, 120 ff.

KEIL, J., 'Vertreter der zweiten Sophistik in Ephesos', *JÖAI* 40 (1953), 5 ff.

KORNEMANN, E., *Grosse Frauen des Altertums* (1942).

KUNKEL, W., *Herkunft und soziale Stellung der römischen Juristen* (1952).

DE LACY, P., 'Galen and the Greek Poets', *GRBS* 7 (1966), 259 ff.

DE LEEUW, C. A., *Aelius Aristides als Bron voor de Kennis van zijn Tijd* (1939).

MAGIE, D., *Roman rule in Asia Minor* (1950), 2 vols.

MARROU, H. I., *Histoire de l'éducation dans l'antiquité* (1960).

MENSCHING, E., *Favorin von Arelate* (1963).

————'Zu Aelius Aristides' 33. Rede', *Mnemosyne* 18 (1965), 57 ff.

MEYER, Th., *Geschichte des römischen Arztestandes* (1952).

MILLAR, F., *A study of Cassius Dio* (1964).

————'Emperors at Work', *JRS* 57 (1967), 9 ff.

MOMIGLIANO, A., Review of Peretti, *Luciano,* in *Rivista Storica Italiana* 60 (1948), 430 ff.

MOMMSEN, Th., 'Die Chronologie der Briefe Frontos', *Hermes* 8 (1874), 198 ff. = *Ges. Schr.* 4. 469 ff.

MÜNSCHER, K., 'Die Philostrate', *Philologus,* Suppl. 10 (1905/7), 469 ff.

NEUGEBAUER, O., and VAN HOESEN, H. B., *Greek Horoscopes* (1959).

NOCK, A. D., 'Alexander of Abonuteichos', *CQ* 22 (1928), 160 ff.

NORDEN, E., *Die antike Kunstprosa* (1915).

NÖRR, D., *Imperium und Polis in der hohen Prinzipatszeit* (1966).

OLIVER, J. H., 'Two Athenian Poets', *Hesperia,* Supp. 8 (1949), 243 ff.

————*The Athenian expounders of the sacred and ancestral law* (1950).

————*The ruling power* (1953).

————'The Sacred Gerousia and the Emperor's Consilium', *Hesperia* 36 (1967), 329 ff.

————*The civilizing power* (1968).

————'The Ancestry of Gordian I', *AJP* 89 (1968), 345 ff.

PACK, R., 'Two Sophists and Two Emperors', *CP* 42 (1947), 17 ff.

PALM, J., *Rom, Römertum, und Imperium in der griechischen Literatur der Kaiserzeit* (1959).

PERETTI, A., *Luciano: Un intellettuale greco contro Roma* (1946).

PERRY, B. E., *Secundus the silent philosopher* (1964).

PETERSEN, L., 'Iulius Iulianus, Statthalter von Arabien', *Klio* 48 (1967), 159 ff.

PFLAUM, H.-G., *Les Procurateurs équestres sous le Haut-Empire romain* (1950).

———'Lucien de Samosate, *Archistator praefecti Aegypti*', *Mélanges de l'École française de Rome* 71 (1959), 281 ff.

———*Les Carrières procuratoriennes équestres* (1960-1), 4 vols.

———'Les Correspondants de l'orateur M. Cornelius Fronto de Cirta', *Hommages Bayet* (1964), 544 ff.

———'Le Règlement successoral d'Hadrien', *Historia-Augusta Colloquium Bonn 1963* (1964), 91 ff.

PLATNAUER, M., *The life and reign of the Emperor Lucius Septimius Severus* (1918).

POHL, R., *De graecorum medicis publicis* (1905).

POUILLOUX, J., 'Une famille de sophistes thessaliens à Delphes au IIᵉ s. ap. J.-C.', *REG* 80 (1967), 379 ff.

VON PREMERSTEIN, A., *Das Attentat der Konsulare auf Hadrian, Klio,* Beiheft 8 (1908).

REIDINGER, W., *Die Statthalter des ungeteilten Pannonien und Oberpannoniens* (1956).

REINMUTH, O., 'A working list of the Prefects of Egypt 30 B.C.-A.D. 299', *Bulletin of the American Society of Papyrologists* 4 (1967), 75 ff.

RÉVILLE, J., *La Religion à Rome sous les Sévères* (1885).

ROBERT, L., *Les Gladiateurs dans l'orient grec* (1940).

———*La Carie* ii (1954).

———'Inscriptions d'Aphrodisias', *Ant. Class.* 35 (1966), 377 ff.

ROHDE, E., 'Γέγονε in den Biographica des Suidas', *Rh. Mus.* 33 (1878), 161 ff., 638 ff.

———'Die asianische Rhetorik und die zweite Sophistik', *Rh. Mus.* 41 (1886), 170 ff. = *Kl. Schr.* 2 (1901), 75 ff.

———*Der griechische Roman* (1914).

SARIKAKIS, Th., *The hoplite general in Athens* (1951).

———"Αἱ ἐπὶ τοῦ ἐπισιτισμοῦ τῶν Ἀθηνῶν ἁρμοδιότητες τοῦ στρατηγοῦ ἐπὶ τὰ ὅπλα", *Platon* 9 (1957), 121 ff.

SARTON, G., *Galen of Pergamum* (1954).

SCHISSEL, O., 'Lollianos aus Ephesos', *Philologus* 82 (1927), 181 ff.

———'Die Familie des Minukianos', *Klio* 21 (1926), 361 ff.

SCHMID, W., *Der Atticismus* iv (1896).

SCHWARTZ, J., *Biographie de Lucien de Samosate* (1965).

SHERWIN-WHITE, A. N., *The Letters of Pliny: A social and historical commentary* (1966).

SOLMSEN, F., 'Some Works of Philostratus the Elder', *TAPA* 71 (1940), 556 ff.

STEIN, A., 'Zu Lukians Alexandros', *Strena Buliciana* (1924), 257 ff.

———'Zur sozialen Stellung der provinzialen Oberpriester', *Epitymbion Swoboda* (1927), 300 ff.

———*Die Präfekten von Aegypten* (1950).

STEMPLINGER, E., *Strabons literarhistorische Notizen* (1894).

SYME, R., 'Antonine Relatives: Ceionii and Vettuleni', *Athenaeum* 35 (1957), 306 ff.

———*Tacitus* (1958), 2 vols.

———'Hadrian the Intellectual', *Les Empereurs romains d'Espagne* (1965), 243 ff.

———'The Ummidii', *Historia* 17 (1968), 72 ff.

———*Ammianus and the Historia Augusta* (1968).

THOMASSON, B., *Die Statthalter der römischen Provinzen Nordafrikas von Augustus bis Diokletianus* (1960), 2 vols.

THOMPSON, H. A., 'The Odeion in the Athenian Agora', *Hesperia* 19 (1950), 31 ff.

TOD, M. N., 'Sidelights on Greek Philosophers', *JHS* 77 (1957), 132 ff.

TOWNEND, G. B., 'The Post *Ab Epistulis* in the Second Century', *Historia* 10 (1961), 375 ff.

WADDINGTON, W. H., *Mémoire sur la chronologie de la vie du rhéteur Aelius Aristide* (1867).

WALDEN, J., *The universities of ancient Greece* (1912).

WELLES, C. B., 'The Romanization of the Greek East', *Bulletin of the American Society of Papyrologists* 2 (1965), 75 ff.

WILAMOWITZ-MOELLENDORFF, U. VON, 'Asianismus und Atticismus', *Hermes* 35 (1900), 1 ff.

———Review of Boulanger, *Aristide,* in *Litteris* 2 (1925), 125 ff.

————'Der Rhetor Aristides', *Sitzungsberichte Akad. Berlin* 1925, 333 ff.

————'Marcellus von Side', *Sitzungsberichte Akad. Berlin* 1928, 3 ff.

WIRTH, G., "'Ἀρριανὸς ὁ φιλόσοφος", *Klio* 41 (1963), 221 ff.

————'Helikonios der Sophist', *Historia* 13 (1964), 506 ff.

WOOD, J. T., *Discoveries at Ephesus* (1877).

WOODHEAD, A. G., 'The State Health Service in Ancient Greece', *Cambridge Historical Journal* 10 (1952), 235 ff.

ZWIKKER, W., *Studien zur Markussäule* (1941).

ABBREVIATIONS

AE L'Année épigraphique

AJA American Journal of Archaeology

AJP American Journal of Philology

Ant. Class. L'Antiquité classique

Ath. Mitt. Mitteilungen des deutschen archäologischen Instituts, Athenische Abteilung

BCH Bulletin de correspondance hellénique

CIG Corpus Inscriptionum Graecarum

CIL Corpus Inscriptionum Latinarum

CP Classical Philology

CQ Classical Quarterly

CR Classical Review

FGH F. Jacoby, *Die Fragmente der griechischen Historiker*

GRBS Greek, Roman, and Byzantine Studies

HA Historia Augusta

HSCP Harvard Studies in Classical Philology

IG Inscriptiones Graecae

IGR Inscriptiones Graecae ad Res Romanas Pertinentes

ILS H. Dessau, *Inscriptiones Latinae Selectae*

JHS Journal of Hellenic Studies

JÖAI Jahreshefte des österreichischen archäologischen Instituts

JRS Journal of Roman Studies

JTS Journal of Theological Studies

MAMA Monumenta Asiae Minoris Antiqua

NGA Nachrichten der Akademie der Wissenschaften in Göttingen, Phil.-Hist. Klasse

OGIS Orientis Graeci Inscriptiones Selectae

PIR Prosopographia Imperii Romani (*PIR*^{2} referring to available volumes of the Second Edition)

P-W Pauly-Wissowa-Kroll, *Real-Encyclopädie*

REA Revue des études anciennes

REG Revue des études grecques

REL Revue des études latines

Rh. Mus. Rheinisches Museum

SEG Supplementum Epigraphicum Graecum

SIG^3 W. Dittenberger, *Sylloge Inscriptionum Graecarum* (Third Edition)

TAPA Transactions of the American Philological Association

VS Philostratus, *Vitae Sophistarum* (with reference to the Olearius pagination)

All other abbreviations should be clear enough without further expansion.

C. P. Jones (essay date 1974)

SOURCE: Jones, C. P. "The Reliability of Philostratus." In *Approaches to the Second Sophistic: Papers Presented at the 105th Annual Meeting of the American Philological Association*, edited by G. W. Bowersock, pp. 11-16. University Park, Pa.: The American Philological Association, 1974.

[*In the following essay, Jones examines the reliability of Philostratus's account of the second sophistic, comparing it to other sources from the time, and contends that the value of Philostratus's text lies in the individual details preserved by the sophist, rather than the manner in which he presents them.*]

Philostratus' **Lives of the Sophists** are the principal source for the phenomenon which we know by the name he gave it, the Second Sophistic. We have indeed an abundance of other material: inscriptions, coins, allusions in such writers as Galen and Lucian, and in a few cases the works of the sophists themselves. But for our knowledge of the general history of the Second Sophistic and of many of its details, we rely on Philostratus. It therefore becomes a matter of considerable importance to know how much we can depend on him where our other sources fail, and it is to this question that the following paper is addressed.

It will help to judge Philostratus' achievement if we can tell what he was trying to do. Something that he was *not* trying to do, it seems clear, is to write biographies of the sophists in any real sense. Although he sometimes notices their family background, parents, education, and the principal events of their lives down to their deaths, many of these items that would seem indispensable for true biography are left out: the closest that Philostratus comes to such a thing is in his account of Herodes Atticus. A parallel in Latin literature is Suetonius' *De grammaticis et rhetoribus,* in which, like Philostratus, he begins with a general account of the early history of his subject, and then gives brief notices of its main representatives in chronological order. Like Suetonius, I suspect, Philostratus did not in fact call his work "The Lives of the Sophists," but perhaps just "The Sophists" or "On the Sophists." All he says to Gordian in his preface is, "I have written up for you (*anegrapsa soi*) the philosophers . . . and the sophists";[1] and so far as I can see he never talks in the course of the work as if he were writing the life of any of his subjects, but merely, for instance, "Let us not forget Secundus," "About Herodes the following is worth knowing."[2] It is true that "The Lives of the Sophists" was the title already in use in the early fifth century;[3] and it is also true that Philostratus' account of Apollonius of Tyana, which we should certainly call a biography, is not so entitled by the author. Even so, it is perhaps worth considering whether "The Lives of the Sophists" was the title given by Philostratus, rather than a later title which he might well have repudiated.

More important than the title, however, is the general scheme of the work, and this is an item for which Philostratus must take the responsibility. Not so very long ago, it was fashionable to call in question the very notion of a sophistic movement beginning, as Philostratus begins, in the first century A.D.: Wilamowitz regretted that Boulanger had not freed himself from Philostratus' "useless invention of a Second Sophistic."[4] On this point, however, Philostratus needs now no vindication: it suffices to point to Professor Bowersock's demonstration of the reality of the Second Sophistic as a historical phenomenon.[5] Philostratus' working out of this scheme, however, is another matter, and deserves a longer scrutiny.

As is well known, he divides his "sophists" into two classes, "those who were philosophers but were thought to be sophists" and "sophists properly so called."[6] In the first class he begins with Eudoxus of Cnidus in the fourth century and ends near his own time with Dio of Prusa and Favorinus. In the second class, he includes as "sophists properly so called" the ancient sophists from Gorgias to Critias, then Isocrates and Aeschines, and thence skips several centuries to his first modern sophist, Nicetes of Smyrna. This scheme immediately raises questions of definition. What is a philosopher? What is a sophist? Moreover, what is a rhetor (since Philostratus occasionally characterizes men as rhetors in a way that shows him to consider them different from sophists)?[7] His notion of "philosopher" does not seem to be unconventional: thus he calls Sextus of Chaeronea, as we should, a philosopher.[8] The term "sophist," by contrast, is notoriously elusive. Bowersock has, I think, successfully shown that Philostratus means by it a virtuoso speaker, particularly concerned with declamation, and that this sense was a widely accepted one.[9] But of course it is by no means the only one, and we may well wonder whether all of Philostratus' readers would have been satisfied with it. The term "sophist" had originally connoted an "expert," in a sense almost indistinguishable from "philosopher";[10] it is in this sense that Protagoras and his like were called "sophists" and not, surely, as Philostratus implies, because they were the spiritual ancestors of such men as Polemo or Herodes Atticus. More important, long before Philostratus' day the term "sophist" had acquired a strong pejorative coloring, which he chose simply to ignore. Primarily it is used of "inferior" or "false philosophers": it is instructive that Plutarch considers it a mark of Herodotus' malice to call certain of the Seven Wise Men "sophists."[11] It could also be used of inferior or false rhetors: thus Aristides brands his rivals as "sophists."[12] Similarly, Philostratus seems to consider a "rhetor" a speaker who does not declaim, but uses all his art for practical ends, principally politics and law: sophists are "those rhetors who spoke with unusual art and brilliance."[13] This, clearly, is why Demosthenes does not receive a notice, though there is no doubt that Philostratus shared the general veneration of him. Here again Philostratus was not alone in his definition: the term "rhetor" in later Greek often means simply "lawyer."[14] Yet his definition of "rhetor" is again not universal: it can, I think, be shown that even certain of his "sophists properly so called" shunned a title that had such a taint of charlatanry, and called themselves "rhetors," or even "philosophers."

An example is Isocrates, whom Philostratus treats as a sophist. Isocrates himself, as is well known, claimed to teach "philosophy," and called his rivals "sophists":[15] other authors who call Isocrates a "sophist" clearly use the term slightingly.[16] Nearer to Philostratus' own day, his sophist Secundus of Athens has been argued by Bowersock to be the Silent Philosopher of the same name and time;[17] similarly, Habicht has proposed that Hermocrates of Phocaea, again a "sophist" in Philostratus, is the same man as we find called a "philosopher" in an inscription of Pergamon.[18] Conversely, it seems hard to believe that Dio of Prusa or Favorinus were called "sophists" except by those who wished to belittle them: Dio's works are full of contemptuous references to "sophists,"[19] and an inscription recently found, again at Pergamon, calls him what he no doubt wished to be called himself, a philosopher.[20]

Yet other of Philostratus' sophists may have preferred to be called "rhetors." An almost certain example is Aristides: his speeches *On behalf of Rhetoric* and *On behalf of the Four,* in which he answers Plato's attacks in the *Gorgias,* clearly imply that he considers himself a rhetor. Thus he says in the *Defence of Rhetoric,* "I have valued this faculty (that of speaking) from the start, and considered it more precious than any profit or material thing, not in order to flatter the mob or to aim at the majority or for money: anyone who has his eyes on that and is at the mercy of those who give, such a man I call a hireling, not an orator (*rhêtora*)."[21] We must be careful before inferring from these two speeches that Aristides must always have called himself a rhetor: after all, he could not have repulsed Plato's attacks in the name of sophistry. Père Festugière has recently, and rightly, criticized the view of Behr that "sophist" is always a term of abuse in Aristides, and collected many passages in which he uses the word neutrally.[22] But Festugière goes further than the evidence when he claims that "Aristides could not despise his own calling of 'sophist': the whole immunity affair proves that, since he claimed his privilege as a sophist."[23] Aristides' claim to immunity rested on his being an eminent speaker, not specifically a sophist; and, as Bowersock has shown, the rescript of Pius on which Aristides based his claim is studiously vague on the question of whether such speakers are to be called "rhetors" or "sophists," presumably because of the very confusion of usage that is in question here.[24] The evidence, therefore, while not conclusive, strongly suggests that Aristides shunned the title of "sophist" and preferred to be called "rhetor"; it may be surmised that he was influenced both by Plato's attacks on sophists and also by one of his chief literary models, Isocrates, who as we have seen similarly abhorred the title.

Another of Philostratus' "sophists" who would have repudiated the term and called himself a rhetor is, I suspect, none other than his prime exhibit, Herodes Atticus. As far as I can see, the sixty-odd inscriptions referring to Herodes never call him either a sophist or a rhetor. Philostratus, of course, in his notice of Herodes calls him a sophist, and he makes Alexander the Clay-Plato say to him, "Herodes, all we sophists are mere slices of you"; in another work, however, he calls him a rhetor, and even in his notice of him he says that Herodes was called by his admirers "One of the Ten," that is, equal to the classical Ten Rhetors.[25] It is true that, again according to Philostratus, some of Herodes' enemies called him the "stuffed rhetor,"[26] which might imply that he preferred the other title; but the insult may be in the adjective and not the noun, or alternatively these people may have considered that they were insult-

ing Herodes by calling him a rhetor, simply because most of his peers liked to call themselves sophists. Herodes' motive for avoiding the title of "sophist," if he did, may like Aristides' have been partly due to the influence of Plato; we know that he had two Platonists among his teachers, Favorinus and Taurus, and his interest in philosophy is shown by Marcus' choosing him to appoint the heads of the four philosophic schools in Athens, including the Academy.[27] Professor De Lacy has shown how high the authority of Plato was in the second century, among the sophists as well as the philosophers; it may be that he was powerful enough to dissuade some of the sophists from using the name at all.

The case of Dionysius of Miletus is similar, though even more uncertain. Though Philostratus calls him a sophist, we now have two inscriptions referring to him, one of which calls him a rhetor and sophist, while the other, on his sarcophagus, calls him simply a rhetor.[28] This variation may be due merely to uncertainty of usage, though the cause could be that Dionysius' distinguished public career led him to prefer an appellation that connoted forensic rather than scholarly activity.

The sum of all this, I submit, is that Philostratus has taken these three terms, "philosopher," "sophist," and "rhetor," in senses that were widely though not universally accepted, and has imposed them upon his subject with confusing and undue rigidity. The reason for his high valuation of the name of "sophist," and for his refusal to admit any taint on its meaning, is no doubt to be ascribed to the fact that he himself and other members of his family were professed and practising sophists.[29] And we must admit that if Philostratus had not been so rigid as he is in his classification, the result might have been hopelessly confusing for his readers: his schematism at least makes for clarity.

Another area in which Philostratus sometimes inspires misgiving is that of historical truth. Here there are two separate questions, that of honesty (*alêtheia*) and that of accuracy (*akribeia*). To begin with the first, Philostratus shares with other biographers of antiquity a protective attitude towards his subjects: he is inclined either not to relate facts that discredit them or, if the facts are too well known to be suppressed, to present them in as innocuous a light as possible. Of his not relating discreditable facts, we may note as an example his statement that Favorinus "quarrelled with the emperor Hadrian and did not suffer for it": we know now, thanks to a papyrus published in 1931, that Favorinus was in fact exiled by Hadrian.[30] So also when Philostratus says that Dio of Prusa's travels "should not be called exile, since he was not ordered into exile, nor yet a mere journey, since he retired from the public eye," he is convicted out of Dio himself, who several times refers to his "exile," as Philostratus must have known.[31] In both instances, exile clearly seems a disgrace to Philostratus, and so he does his best to conceal it. On the other side, there is his denial that Herodes Atticus went into exile after his great quarrel with the Athenians in the 170's.[32] Here again Philostratus contends that this was only a self-imposed retirement, but this time he appears to be correct: the new inscription from Athens recently published by Professor Oliver, which reveals so much about this affair, certainly gives the impression that Herodes retained the emperor's favor.[33]

As an example of Philostratus' presenting unfavorable facts as innocuously as possible, there is the story about Herodes and his wife Regilla. Herodes is supposed to have had her beaten by a freedman when she was eight months pregnant, and thus to have caused her death, for which he was accused of manslaughter by his brother-in-law Bradua; one is reminded of how Nero is supposed to have caused the death of Poppaea.[34] Though Philostratus recounts this affair, he asserts that the charge was false, and makes Bradua out to be a conceited fool: his main answer to the charge is the excess of Herodes' grief for Regilla. The naiveté of that defence was already apparent to contemporaries,[35] however, and again we think of Nero's extravagant mourning for Poppaea.

As for Philostratus' accuracy, he is as liable to small slips as any writer is, even a Tacitus. Thus he says that Dionysius of Miletus was buried in the agora of Ephesus when we now know that it was elsewhere in the city;[36] he makes Aristides' birthplace Hadriani and not Hadrianutherae.[37] When he calls Herodes' daughter Panathenais, however, and not Athenais, that may not be a slip.[38] On the whole, evidence outside Philostratus tends to corroborate his statements of detail even in minute particulars. For example, he names three men, Demostratus, Praxagoras, and Mamertinus, as particular enemies of Herodes in his quarrel with the Athenians and in the suit heard by Marcus at Sirmium; the new inscription from Athens reveals these three among several others as plaintiffs against Herodes, and the emperor mentions precisely that he is occupied with "military activities."[39]

For the historian at least, the difficulties caused by Philostratus lie not so much in the small details but in the relation between them: in other words, he often overlooks, and sometimes seems even to be ignorant of, the larger background. To revert to the quarrel of Herodes with other leading Athenians and the subsequent hearing before Marcus, there would perhaps not have been so much confusion about the chronology of this affair, and the role of the Quintilii *fratres* in it, if Philostratus had been less vague about their official position, and had not merely said that "they were both

governing Greece." On the other hand, we must allow that his account did enable Edmund Groag, followed by Bowersock, to infer what their official status was even before the inference was confirmed by the new text.[40] A case in which Philostratus' account has proved seriously misleading is, I think, that of Dio of Prusa: his version of Dio's exile, decked out with tales of Dio's going in disguise and earning his keep by manual labour, does not at all agree with that of Dio himself.[41] However, this is not the universal view, and Philostratus' account is substantially accepted, for example, in von Arnim's standard work on Dio.

To sum up, we may say that on the whole Philostratus' value for the historian lies in the individual details that he has preserved, rather than in the way in which he has arranged them: here, as we have seen, he is arbitrary in his categories and sometimes confusing in providing background. We are suitably impressed by the exotic objects he presses to our attention; but we feel as if we were in a pawnbroker's shop, rather than a museum.

Notes

1. Philostratus, *Vitae Sophistarum* (henceforth "*VS*"), pref. p. 479.

2. *VS* 1.26 p. 544, 2.1.1 p. 545.

3. Eunap. *Vitae Philosophorum* pref., p. 346 Wright = p. 2.21 Giangrande; Synes. *Dion* 35ᴀ, p. 313.37 von Arnim = p. 233.4 Terzaghi.

4. *Kleine Schriften* 3 (1969) 421.

5. G. W. Bowersock, *Greek Sophists in the Roman Empire* (1969) (henceforth "Bowersock").

6. *VS* pref. p. 479; cf. 1.8.4 p. 492.

7. Thus *VS* 2.11.1 p. 591.

8. *VS* 2.1.9 p. 557.

9. Bowersock 13.

10. Cf. Aristides, vol. 2, p. 407 Dindorf; Barrett on Eur. *Hipp.* 921.

11. Plut. *De Herod. mal.* 857ꜰ.

12. Examples collected by A.-J. Festugière, *REG* [*Revue des études grecques*] 82 (1969) 148.

13. *VS* pref. p. 484.

14. Averil and Alan Cameron, *JHS* [*JHS Journal of Hellenic Studies*] 86 (1966) 10, 15-16.

15. Isocr. 13.1, 11; 15.270-71.

16. Thus anon. *De subl.* 4.2.

17. Bowersock 118-19.

18. Chr. Habicht, *Altertümer von Pergamon VIII 3: Die Inschriften des Asklepieions* (1969) 76-79, no. 34.

19. Thus *Or.* 4.28, 6.21, 8.9 etc.

20. *Archäologischer Anzeiger* 81 (1966) 473; cf. Habicht (above, note 18) 162.

21. *Huper rhētorikēs* 431 Behr (Loeb Aristides, vol. 1, 1973).

22. A.-J. Festugière, *REG* 82 (1969) 148-49.

23. *REG* 82 (1969) 149.

24. Bowersock 12, 33-34, 39.

25. Alexander: *VS* 2.5.3 p. 574; Rhetor: *Dialexeis* 1; the Ten: *VS* 2.1.14 p. 564.

26. *VS* 2.1.14 p. 565.

27. Favorinus: *VS* 1.8.3 p. 490, 2.1.14 p. 564; Taurus: 2.1.14 p. 564; heads: *VS* 2.2 p. 566.

28. *JÖAI* [*Jahreshefte des österreichischen archäologischen Instituts*] 40 (1953) 6; *AE* [*AE L'Année épigraphique*] 1969/1970, no. 597.

29. Bowersock 2-6; J. S. Traill, *Hesperia* 40 (1971) 324-25.

30. *VS* 1.8.2 p. 489. M. Norsa and G. Vitelli, *Il papiro vaticano greco 11 = Studi e Testi* 53 (1931). Cf. Bowersock 36.

31. *VS* 1.7.2 p. 488; Dio Prus. 13.1, 36.1, 45.1, etc.

32. *VS* 2.1.12 p. 562.

33. James H. Oliver, *Marcus Aurelius: Aspects of Civic and Cultural Policy in the East = Hesperia* Supplement 13 (1970) 3-9.

34. *VS* 2.1.8 p. 555; Tac. *Ann.* 16.6.1.

35. *VS* 2.1.8 p. 556.

36. *VS* 1.22.4 p. 526; F. Eichler, *Anz. Wien* 106 (1969) 136-37 (J. and L. Robert, *Bull. épigr.* 1971, 574).

37. *VS* 2.9.1 p. 581; on his birthplace, L. Robert, *Études anatoliennes* (1937) 207-22; in favor of Hadriani, C. A. Behr, *Aelius Aristides* (1968) 3, note 3.

38. *VS* 2.1.10 p. 557; cf. T. D. Barnes, *Phoenix* 26 (1972) 148.

39. *VS* 2.1.11 pp. 559-60; Oliver (above, n. 33), lines E 1 (Praxagoras, Demostratus), 9 (Mamertinus), 26 (activities).

40. *VS* 2.1.11 p. 559; Bowersock 100.

41. See especially Dio, *Or.* 13.10-12.

Ewen Lyall Bowie (essay date 1978)

SOURCE: Bowie, Ewen Lyall. "Apollonius of Tyana: Tradition and Reality." *Aufstieg und Niedergang der Romischen Welt* 2, no. 16, 2 (1978): 1652-71.

[*In the following excerpt, Bowie asserts that although Philostratus's work is a primary source of information on Apollonius of Tyana, the writer altered and amplified the subject of his biography, and therefore, the information contained in this text must be studied with discrimination.*]

Modern accounts of Apollonius of Tyana are necessarily dominated by the biographic work of Philostratus[1]. Earlier independent testimony is exiguous, and much of the later tradition in antiquity betrays the influence of his work. But it is clear that the sophist Philostratus has greatly altered and amplified the picture of a Cappadocian magician such as must have been presented to him by part at least of his material: investigators of Apollonius must try to determine how much belongs to the first century character and how much is attributable to elaborations in the second century and to Philostratus himself, while a student of Philostratus will wish to concentrate on the latter part of the enquiry and add the question how far and with what intent Philostratus was perpetrating a work of fiction. This paper does not concern itself with the tradition after Philostratus except where it is pertinent to an assessment of the questions outlined above: recent work has made some progress in the later tradition[2]. However advances in our understanding of Philostratus' rôle and materials have been vestigial since the fundamental work of EDUARD MEYER published in 1917: some will judge the analogy ominous, but in my view MEYER did for Philostratus' work on Apollonius what DESSAU did 30 years earlier for the 'Scriptores Historiae Augustae'[3]. Accordingly I offer no apology for taking MEYER's position as a starting point for the following discussion, some of which aims to do no more than to refine or correct it in details while taking account of subsequent adversaria.

I. THE DAMIS QUESTION

1. INTRODUCTION

Meyer saw Philostratus' work as a '*Reiseroman*' offering a mixture of fantasy and education. Apollonius' travels to the orient and Egypt were a fiction in whose construction Philostratus drew on Herodotus, Ctesias, Xenophon and the historians of Alexander: the discourses of Apollonius treat themes of general sophistic interest, sometimes peculiarly Philostratean. These elements discounted, little remains for the scribe and disciple Damis whom Philostratus parades as his source: Damis is an invention of Philostratus, who will not have expected his readers to take him seriously[4].

So bold a contention could not win universal support: in 1919 MESK reiterated arguments for Damis' existence in some form, and further points in his favour were made by HEMPEL in 1920[5]. But an extended rehabilitation of Damis was only put forward by GROSSO in 1954. GROSSO mounted a close comparison of the historical information on the first century A.D. in Philostratus with our other evidence for the period and tried to show both that Philostratus' account of historical events is accurate and that the part given to Apollonius therein is coherent. From this, and from the distribution of praise and blame between Domitian and the circle of Nerva, GROSSO concluded that the picture was composed in the reign of Nerva and that the composer was, as Philostratus claims, a pupil of Apollonius called Damis[6].

GROSSO's arguments have been either accepted or ignored by scholars dealing with Apollonius[7] and must be assessed before investigation of Damis can proceed further. It should first be pointed out that GROSSO's method has no formal validity. The coherence of Philostratus' picture only requires him to know the history of the period well enough to insert the activities of Apollonius without contradictions of the existing tradition. It does not of itself demonstrate that the part given to Apollonius is historical. Since Philostratus must have had at his disposal a wider range of literary sources than are available to us we should not be surprised if he avoids contradicting our tradition.

Here, however, the further difficulty arises that in many details Philostratus does contradict what is either recorded explicitly or inherently probable in the light of other testimony. The contention that Philostratus cannot be refuted "*sul terreno documentato*" cannot be upheld; and little is achieved by the argument that the most improbable assertions must be factual or Philostratus would not have made them![8] The following paragraphs analyse some passages where there is conflict with other evidence and also offer some suggestions about the origins of Philostratus' version.

2. THE VARDANES EPISODE

Vardanes appears to have acceded to the throne of Parthia in 42 A.D. and to have died in 45 A.D. In Philostratus' narrative[9] Apollonius arrives in his kingdom two years and two months after his accession and leaves him in good health after one year and eight months: moreover he is still king on Apollonius' return from India some considerable if unspecified time later. This crux has driven most scholars to the view that Philostratus is working in ignorance of the length of Vardanes' reign. There is little that is convincing in GROSSO's attempt to save him on the hypothesis that he calculated the beginning of Vardanes' reign from a different year and that the 'sources' on Apollonius' return

from India referred to him simply as ὁ βασιλεύς, then interpreted by Philostratus as referring to Vardanes.

3. MUSONIUS RUFUS

The tradition concerning Musonius Rufus preserved in Tacitus and Cassius Dio conflicts with that of Philostratus in one important point. The historians record that Musonius was banished in the year 65: the sophist has him imprisoned and divulges an exchange of letters with Apollonius in which, as GROSSO remarks, he emerges as a man of lesser stature than Musonius. This GROSSO tried to adduce as evidence that 'Damis' cannot be the source of the incident. The conclusion may be correct (it will not disturb the unbeliever) but it does not follow that we are thereby disqualified from using this passage to discredit the existence of such a source as 'Damis' at all. The more often we find Philostratus purveying material which cannot derive from a pupil of Apollonius writing in the reign of Nerva the less plausibility remains for such an hypothesis[10].

As GROSSO remarks, Philostratus was attracted by the character of Musonius and picked up some of the traditions which circulated uncontrolled (for Musonius himself allegedly committed nothing to writing). These included the story of his hard labour on the Isthmus and his exile on Gyara until Nero's death. The latter very probably has a factual basis, albeit somewhat embroidered by legend, but the former is hard to credit. It is the sort of detail we might expect to appear in the Neronian life of Suetonius, but it is not there, nor in any other reliable source: no corroboration is offered by its exploitation in the pseudo-Lucianic 'Nero', usually attributed to one of the Philostrati[11].

The exchange between Musonius and Apollonius is equally hard to accept. We know the former as a Stoic who opposed Demetrius the Cynic in a prosecution and had for his followers Euphrates and Dio[12]. It could be argued, of course, that Apollonius' quarrel with Euphrates, a major theme in Philostratus, had not yet developed in 65, but the suspicion remains that Philostratus has infiltrated his sage into a circle of Stoic philosophers where he has no proper place. The traditional connection with Euphrates, albeit one which portrayed the men as enemies, might have suggested the adaptation of the story, and Philostratus will have gained on two counts. He wanted, we are told, to tone down the bitterness of the quarrel, and we can also infer that he sought a coherent backcloth to his presentation of Apollonius as a constructive philosopher offering positive advice to cities and individuals[13]. It is most embarrassing that Apollonius does not elsewhere appear in the extensive catalogue of Musonius' friends[14]. In this situation it is only safe to remain sceptical about the alleged connection. The possible relevance of

Philostratus' use of a tradition on Musonius to his characterisation of Apollonius will be considered further in due course[15]. Here it suffices to establish the divergence of Philostratus' account from our other evidence.

4. DEMETRIUS THE CYNIC

It is frequently observed that the tales offered by Philostratus are almost unrecognisable as an account of the philosopher Demetrius we have in other sources[16]. In the year 66, the consulate of Telesinus, Philostratus' Demetrius inveighs against the dedication of a new gymnasium in Rome and is expelled from the city by Tigellinus. The gymnasium is indeed attested elsewhere, but for the year 61 or 60: the expulsion appears nowhere. Indeed the testimony on Demetrius, obscure and incomplete though it is, affords hints that he might not have been uncomfortable under Neronian rule. In 70 A.D. he is found defending P. Egnatius Celer against the prosecution of Musonius Rufus, *ambitiosius quam honestius*. Celer had turned against his friend Barea Soranus in 66, allegedly bearing false witness. It is strange to find Demetrius defending a man responsible for a persecution of which he himself, if expelled in 66, must have been a victim[17]. Tantalisingly, the last chapters of the 'Annales' have been so mutilated as to rob us of Tacitus' full story of the relationship between Demetrius and Thrasea Paetus: we are left with the cynic in attendance at Thrasea's death bed[18]. This in itself is not enough to show that Demetrius displayed active opposition to Nero or was likely to have been exiled in 66: the scene could well have been narrated as a foil to Demetrius' own readiness to compromise and have given openings for vicious and exposing Tacitean comment[19]. The balance of Tacitus' evidence is against the likelihood of an expulsion in 66, but is too fragmentary to permit certainty.

GROSSO postulates a brief or imperfectly observed expulsion order in 62 which Philostratus amalgamated with another in 66, eschewed because it would involve Philostratus in discussion of Thrasea Paetus' circle[20]. The expulsion invented for 62 not only lacks foundation but does not in fact help GROSSO's case. If 'Damis' synchronises Demetrius' castigation of the practice of bathing on the dedication of a gymnasium in 60/61 A.D. with Apollonius' arrival in Rome in 66 A.D. then he is not narrating fact, and any support this passage might give to the 'Damis' hypothesis crumbles. Alternatively, if Philostratus is distorting the narrative of 'Damis', then this distortion amounts to more than an *"inesattezza del retore"* which *"non deve sorprendere"*, and attempts to establish Damis' credibility from what is passed on by Philostratus are destined for ruin. We may reasonably doubt if Philostratus had any evidence at all for a meeting of Demetrius and Apollonius. GROSSO gives the false impression that he adduces

the testimony of Favorinus: but this is claimed only for the character of Demetrius, whereas the meeting purports to be part of the Damis narrative[21].

Demetrius' relations with the Flavians are equally disturbing. Apolonius commends him to Titus: yet all traditions attest implacable hostility of Cynics to the régime, and Demetrius' banishment is recorded for the very year in which Apollonius is made to introduce him to Titus[22]. The motive for distortion is patent. The philosopher is shown to be in favour with good rulers and hostile to tyrants: thus under Domitian Demetrius is presented as living defiantly near Rome. His exile by Vespasian is never hinted, and we may suspect that it has been transferred to the door of Nero. It might be that this is not Philostratus' perpetration, since it is less easy to see a motive for him than for a Demetrian biographer chronicling the opposition of great men to Nero (cf. n. 20). What is certain is that a 'Damis' of GROSSO's specification would have little incentive to distort, for men alive in 96-98 A.D. could expose the fiction and discredit his story of Apollonius in Neronian Rome[23].

5. THE CONSECRATION AT ALEXANDRIA

Apollonius' encounter with Vespasian at Alexandria is integral to his presentation as a politically active philosopher. The rumoured summons of the new autocrat, his arrival and request to be made *basileus* by Apollonius, the debate of Euphrates, Dio and Apollonius culminating in a decisive symbouleutic speech by the last—all these combine to elevate the Greek intellectual world and reveal the Italian as an executive in the hands of policy-making Greeks. Behind the incident lies the truth that Vespasian's power derived from the East. Many details fit 69 A.D., such as enthusiasm in Alexandria and widespread anti-Semitism, and on the constitutional level the emphasis on Vespasian's sons as a guarantee of dynastic stability.

These elements of historical accuracy cannot prove the historicity of Apollonius' part. It can be challenged on a general and on a particular level. Both Tacitus and Suetonius have a surprisingly full account of Vespasian's confirmation as emperor in Alexandria, but in neither are the philosophers mentioned, and nothing emerges from our other testimonia on Dio or Euphrates. Worse still, the career of Vespasian betrays only limited sympathy for the intellectual life of the Greek world, and the elevation of a Greek to a privileged role as imperial friend and adviser seems an anachronism in the first century and evokes the status alleged by Philostratus in his ***Lives of the Sophists*** for Dio, Polemo or Herodes[24].

It is hard to dismiss the suspicion that Philostratus is inventing. Apart from a brief notice in Josephus, who had reasons to be silent[25], Vespasian's arrival figures in a papyrus and in the narratives of Tacitus, Suetonius and Philostratus[26]. The papyrus merely attests enthusiasm for Vespasian and offers some support for a visit to the Serapeum. It is the relationship between the others that bears on the veracity of Philostratus.

In Tacitus one Basilides, *e primoribus Aegyptiorum,* appears to Vespasian in a vision in the Serapeum after Vespasian has already enhanced his own authority by the performing of miracles. The name Basilides is taken as confirmation of his destined principate. But nothing is said or done by Basilides, who is later proved to have been eighty miles distant at the time.

In Suetonius a *libertus* Basilides appears to Vespasian in the same circumstances and offers him ritual gifts associable with Egyptian insignia of kingship[27]: he is proved to have been ill and far distant at the time. Miracles by Vespasian follow the incident, and, as it were in confirmation, letters arrive from Rome *statim* announcing the Flavian victory.

In Philostratus' account Apollonius is waiting in the temple (unspecified, but for Alexandria most obviously the Serapeum): in reply to Vespasian's request ποίησόν με βασιλέα Apollonius says he has already made him king, and after an uplifting exchange on imperial virtues concludes with a reference to the burning of the Capitolium at Rome which has been communicated to him in a vision.

The conflicting traditions have been analysed by DERCHAIN and HUBAUX with corrections and modifications by HENRICHS[28]. DERCHAIN and HUBAUX give no precise pattern of development for the traditions, and it is hard to accept their hypothesis that an original version involved 'bilocation' in the form offered by Philostratus, as they use the same term 'bilocation' to connote both Apollonius' vision of events in Rome (while he is in Alexandria) and the appearance of Basilides to Vespasian simultaneously with his presence in reality elsewhere. It may also be doubted whether an Alexandrian version included the connection with events in Rome that is common to Suetonius and Philostratus. DERCHAIN and HUBAUX rightly detect a depreciation of Alexandria's king-making rôle in both Tacitus and Suetonius. Accordingly it cannot be, as they suggest[29], that the confirmation of news from Rome is an original element retained by Suetonius. This would date the incidents some time after 21st December, 69 A.D., whereas the original version, to have point as Alexandrian propaganda, must have located the confirmation of Vespasian's principate in Alexandria before the decision in Rome. This indeed is implied by Philostratus' narration, setting the king-making at Vespasian's arrival in Alexandria, well before 21st December[30]: at the same time his chronology is complicated by a different dating, to 21st December, given by Apollonius' vision. The contradictions show that at least two versions lie behind Philostratus and the Roman writers:

(A) Alexandrian propaganda, reflected in the papyrus, in which he is confirmed emperor in the Serapeum by Egyptian ritual and performs miracles demonstrating the power and favour of Serapis. This happens immediately on his arrival and before victory in Italy.

(B) A version with Roman bias. The coronation of Vespasian is made more symbolic and mysterious, partly to obscure the presumptuous act of formal investiture, and is robbed of its primacy among the confirmations of his principate by being itself confirmed and post-dated by association with the arrival of news from Rome. However, embedded elements, the context of his arrival in Alexandria and his miracles, are retained despite inconsistency with the remodelled account.

It is (B) that was available both to the Latin historians and to Philostratus. Speculation on its precise origin would be unproductive[31]. Its exploitation by Philostratus is easier to conjecture. He found a tradition in which some Alexandrian dignitary gave mystical confirmation of Vespasian's principate. This suggests to him a similar role for Apollonius: instead of corroboration by letters from Rome he has a vision of events there that looks suspiciously like a doublet of Apollonius' vision in Ephesus of Domitian's assassination in Rome (the only event in Apollonius' career noticed by Cassius Dio[32]). Vespasian's miracles are omitted because all divinity must pass through the sage Apollonius.

If such an hypothesis is near the truth then we need not be surprised at contemporary themes and atmosphere in Philostratus' account. His source would be a Flavian historian with contemporary documents at his disposal. He is no doubt responsible for the anti-Semitism which emerges only in the context of Apollonius' oriental meetings with Flavian princes. The astounding assertion that Egypt's decline was arrested by Vespasian may also be from this source, arguably a supporter and encomiast of the régime[33]. Nowhere is there room for an eye-witness account of 'Damis': the chronological confusions would be unexplained, whereas the political background is treated in too competent a manner for the naïve scribe and disciple introduced by Philostratus. This objection is common to all the above passages: 'Damis' presents a historical background too sophisticated for his station while the palpable inexactitudes come precisely where he ought to be best informed, at Apollonius' entrances on stage. If 'Damis' was not what Philostratus asserts, what was he?

5. THE INVENTION OF DAMIS

Many scholars are prepared to admit that 'Damis' was not what he is said to be by Philostratus yet shrink from dismissing him as mere invention. The reference to Julia Domna's receipt of Damis' 'Deltoi' and request to Philostratus to rewrite the narrative with suitable attention to style has played a central part in the debate[34]. Philostratus, it is urged, could not have abused the name of his patron, so he must in truth have received a book from her purporting to be a memoir of Damis. The most recent proponent of this view, W. SPEYER, suggests that it was a forgery of neo-Pythagorean admirers of Apollonius, stimulated by the analogous diary which appears in the introduction of Dictys of Crete. Dictys claims to have been taken to Troy by Idomeneus and Meriones especially to set down a narrative of the war. When he died in Crete his work was buried beside him on wooden tablets and discovered when the grave was opened in the 13th year of the emperor Nero: Nero had it translated from the Phoenician in which it was written and put in his library, and it was then translated into Latin by one L. Septimius[35]. The recognition that Damis is in the same category is of fundamental importance[36]. It is extraordinary, however, that once SPEYER saw the connection, and even pointed out that the Dictys fabrication was almost certainly known to Philostratus (he might have added that our evidence for this, the **Heroicus,** betrays Philostratus using roughly the same technique in inventing his ghostseeing vintner![37]) he failed to proceed to one easy and obvious hypothesis: that Philostratus (and not neo-Pythagorean friends of Julia Domna) could himself be responsible for the invention of Damis in conscious evocation of a novelistic tone and setting. No abuse of Julia Domna's name is involved if the technique and its implications were as patent to every Greek reader as is suggested by consideration of the motif's ramifications in novelistic productions.

For Dictys is not alone. The Τὰ ὑπὲρ Θούλην ἄπιστα of Antonius Diogenes (published by the time Lucian wrote his 'Verae historiae') claimed to have been written on cypress-wood tablets and buried beside the grave of one of the characters, there to be discovered by historical figures at the sack of Tyre in 332 B.C.[38] One of the two versions of the 'Historia Apollonii regis Tyrii' concludes: *casus suos suorumque ipse descripsit et duo volumina fecit: unum Dianae in templo Ephesiorum, aliud in bibliotheca sua exposuit*[39]. An analogous frame is alleged by Xenophon for his 'Ephesiaca', although here the form of the record is not written but pictorial: a dedicatory painting set up in the temple of Artemis at Ephesus. A similar sort of picture is alleged as the source of his narrative by Longus and stimulates the romance of Achilles Tatius[40]. Iamblichus follows a different technique: he learned his story from a Babylonian τροφεύς whose authenticity he purports to guarantee by referring to his capture in Trajan's Parthian wars[41].

That Philostratus' work on Apollonius must have been approached by ancient readers as « *presque un roman* »[42] can be established by further considerations of form and content. In the latter category the travels are the most obvious element. They link the work on Apollonius with the 'Historia Alexandri Magni' and with those romances where travel plays a greater part than love, most obviously those of Antonius Diogenes and Heliodorus. Ninos, the home town of Damis (which MEYER argues to be Hierapolis-Bambyke rather than ancient Nineveh) and Babylon, where the travellers find a Persian monarch whom history would have located in Parthian Ctesiphon, are names evocative of romance with its Near Eastern locations[43]. A particular link with Iamblichus' 'Babyloniaca' might be suggested by other shared themes. One factor which marks Philostratus' work off from the rest of the novelistic genre (if there was such) is the absence of a love interest (necessarily, given the ascetic limitations of its central figure!) but as if to redress the balance the author introduces a spectacular tale of incest and both discussion and example of eunuchs' sexuality in the first book[44]. The theme of the eunuch in love seems to have been prominent in Iamblichus' 'Babyloniaca'[45]. So too the dead maiden shown to be alive by the sage at the very time of her funeral—in Iamblichus a Χαλδαῖος γέρων, in Philostratus Apollonius: the motif also appears in the 'Historia Apollonii regis Tyrii' and is widespread in various forms in the novels[46]. It is also of interest that Iamblichus' aged Chaldean makes a prophecy of kingship to the hero: the same prophecy appears in the 'Historia Apollonii regis Tyrii' and its variant in Vespasian's interview with Apollonius should not require us to see that episode as serious biographical history in the manner of Josephus[47].

The form and structure support this interpretation. The title Τὰ ἐς τὸν Τυανέα Ἀπολλώνιον is not of the normal biographic form τοῦ δεῖνος βίος but rather suggests the novelistic formula Τὰ περὶ / κατὰ Λευκίππην καὶ Κλειτοφῶντα etc.[48] The work's division into eight books would be unparalleled for a biography: but this is precisely the form of Achilles Tatius' and Chariton's novels, and is the rough scale of several others[49]. Moreover the structure whereby hero or heroes are persecuted by some hostile power appears in several novels. In Antonius Diogenes the power of evil is chiefly represented by the wicked wizard Paapis, although at times he appears as minister of persecution to the tyrant Aenesidemos, rather as is Euphrates to Domitian. In Iamblichus the bad king Garmos persecutes hero and heroine, and a similar rôle is given in the 'Historia Apollonii regis Tyrii' to king Antiochus. Apollonius of Tyana's persecution by Nero and Domitian, although it has respectable parallels in historiography and *acta martyrum,* is quite at home in a novelistic narrative[50].

The foregoing arguments are offered to support the view that 'Damis' was most probably an invention of Philostratus himself, and, in that his readers would be expected to recognise the novelistic topos, the connection with Julia Domna cannot be used to warrant his authenticity. I would question the distinction that SPEYER draws between Dictys and Damis when he classes the former as *"nur eine literarische Erfindung"*whereas the latter's fabrication had *"außerliterarische Absichten"*[51]. That would be true if Damis had indeed been a creation of neo-Pythagorean associates of Julia Domna. But if Philostratus is entirely responsible then his aim was most plausibly that of a professional writer, to produce a well-rounded and entertaining piece of literature, rather than to further a propagandist interpretation of Apollonius as a Pythagorean sage. SPEYER justly remarks that Philostratus' other writings give no hint of enthusiasm for neo-Pythagoreans or Apollonius. This leaves open the possibilities (to which I shall later return) that Apollonius had indeed Pythagorean tendencies or that these were foisted on him at some stage in the tradition before the Severan period: a neo-Pythagorean côterie of Julia Domna is not the only explanation.

Other considerations reinforce the arguments against a non-Philostratean 'Damis'. Just what was in it? SPEYER suggests: *"Die Erinnerungen des Damis werden die Geschichte von der wunderbaren Geburt des Apollonius enthalten haben, ferner Berichte über seine Wundertaten, Hinweise auf seine Reisen, Aussprüche und Prophezeiungen, seinen Bekennermut und wunderbares Ende*[52].*"* One of these can be excluded forthwith: Philostratus states explicitly that Damis' narrative said nothing about Apollonius' end, and it is clear that several oral or written traditions were available[53]. The novelistic links of travels, miracles and prophecies have already been adumbrated above: but of course miracles and prophecies, even if represented in a sinister light, will have featured in Moiragenes' work on Apollonius which Philostratus attacks and which we know from Origen to have presented Apollonius partly in the guise he is given by Cassius Dio, γόης καὶ μάγος. SPEYER later suggests that Moiragenes did narrate Indian and Ethiopian travels, but his only evidence is a passage of Basil of Thecla which could stem exclusively from a hostile reading of Philostratus' account, and I would be hesitant firmly to accept the attribution to Moiragenes[54]. If accepted, of course, it should surely deny their invention to Damis!

The remaining element is the story of the miraculous birth. Again Philostratus does not attribute this to Damis but says λέγεται and οἱ δὲ ἐγχώριοί φασιν. The latter phrase introduces a miraculous thunderbolt: it is disturbing that a thunderbolt also intervenes in Philostratus' account of the sophist Scopelianus' birth, this time killing his concumbent twin and slaying or injuring many bystanders[55]!

7. PHILOSTRATUS' PICTURE OF APOLLONIUS: SOME INFLUENCES AND MODELS

The birth is not the only affinity with Philostratus' Scopelianus. A similar generous and disinterested administration of his inherited property is asserted for Apollonius as for Scopelianus, even to the adaptation of the same *gnome* of Anaxagoras[56]. Scopelianus is indeed brought into personal contact with Apollonius both in the *Lives* and in the work on Apollonius: the former passage asserts Apollonius' high opinion of Scopelianus, the latter quotes a letter in which "he urges the sophist to take pity on the Eretrians and prays him, in case he should ever compose a discourse about them, not to deprecate even the shedding of tears over their fate"[57]. The fiction of this attribution of sophistic friendship and interests to the Cappadocian *magus* is patent. Why did Philostratus choose Scopelianus as Apollonius' only sophistic friend (allowing Dio his philosophic claims)? Chronology must be the chief limitation: Scopelianus' successor in the series of the *Lives,* Dionysius of Miletus, was still active under Hadrian. Thus only Nicetes, Isaeus and Scopelianus were in question. Nicetes was stained by Neronian favour, Isaeus had a dissolute youth: by contrast Scopelianus successfully opposed Domitian's vine edict[58]. It is no surprise that Apollonius turns out to know about the vine edict and delivers a conceit worthy of a sophist's lecture hall on Domitian's legislation: in this context Philostratus is silent about Scopelianus—understandably, for readers might suspect that both attitude and apophthegm had been stolen from Scopelianus[59]. Even the link with the Eretrians is illuminated by the sophist's biography: Scopelianus was especially admired for his treatment of themes involving Dareius and Xerxes[60].

These points raise two related questions. How far does Apollonius' range of intellectual interests and conversations overlap with the sophists of the *Lives* and the known predilections of the author? Secondly, how many traits in Apollonius' public activity can be related to sophists or philosophers described by or known to Philostratus?

The first question need not detain us long. The overlap has long been recognised and documentation is readily available: as early as GÖTTSCHING it has been seen that much credited by Philostratus to Damis smacks of his own sophistic tastes[61].

The second issue has not been so fully exploited. The sophist's role as imperial adviser is a recurrent theme in the *Lives:* most memorably Dio, but Polemo, Herodes and Aristides are also given a part as σύμβουλος[62]. In

Apollonius' advice to Vespasian, Titus and Nerva, another model also suggests himself, the very Musonius Rufus with whom Philostratus fabricates an association. The Greek tradition knew Musonius as an adviser of Titus and an authority on the philosophy of kingship[63].

A related sophistic function is intervention to quell or avert city strife. Several speeches of Dio and two of Aristides have this aim, and the part is attested for Marcus of Byzantium and Polemo of Laodicea. Moreover Tacitus gives a caustic description of Musonius' attempt to exercise *intempestivam sapientiam* in this way in the Roman civil disturbances[64].

More telling is the exploitation by the Philostraten Apollonius of themes developed in Dio or ascribed to Musonius. We are told by Dio that a distinguished Roman philosopher rebuked the Athenians for watching gladiatorial shows in the theatre of Dionysus: that philosopher is now generally agreed to have been Musonius. However Apollonius is made to deliver a similar homily, sophistic in its allusion to classical antiquities and tragedy[65]. It follows a still more florid condemnation of dancing which has close links with a passage in Dio's speech to the Alexandrians[66]. It must be admitted to be a common enough theme in the literature of the period, but there are some close parallels. Dio asks ἀρά γε μὴ Λακεδαιμονίους μιμεῖσθε[67]; which Philostratus adapts to εἰ μὲν γὰρ Λακωνικὴ ταῦτα ὄρχησις, εὖ γε οἱ στρατιῶται, γυμνάζεσθε γὰρ πολέμῳ καὶ ξυνορχήσομαι. Dio alludes to Bacchae, so Philostratus actually furnishes the allusion with a quotation[68].

The same Alexandrian speech of Dio seems to be used to build up Apollonius' address to the Alexandrians castigating their fondness for horse-racing, and one or two other echoes can be detected.

It should be no surprise to discover sophistic and philosophic models for Apollonius, but it raises a further question of chronology. How deeply was Philostratus involved in the *Lives of the Sophists* when he wrote the work on Apollonius? A reference to the latter in the life of Alexander Peloplaton is normally taken to establish the simple priority of the work on Apollonius[69]. But all that follows is that the work on Apollonius was published by the time the passage was written: preparation of both works could have been proceeding concurrently for some time. A date before 238 A.D. seems mandatory for the *Lives*. There is no firm terminus post quem for the work on Apollonius other than Julia Domna's death in 217 A.D., and it would be naïve to insist on a date as soon after that as possible. The attested admiration of Severus Alexander for Apollonius and the possibility that elements of the Philostratean picture of monarchs' dealings with Apollonius are aimed at the

young Alexander would suggest a date between 222 and 235 A.D.[70] The probability of an overlap in preparation is high.

8. WHY DAMIS?

A conjectural elucidation of the Damis figure may now be hazarded before that theme is finally abandoned. If Damis is a fiction, Philostratus may have meant the story of a descendent approaching Julia Domna to be discounted as part of the novelistic topos. But there might be a hint for the discerning reader. A descendant of one Damis who had been in favour with Vespasian and Titus would predictably be styled Flavius Damianus: such was the name of one of the richest of the late second century sophists at Ephesus, greatly admired in Philostratus' *Life* and offered as a source for Philostratus' information on Aristeides and Hadrianus. Damianus showed loyalty to the Severan house (for which the advancement of his sons to senatorial rank was doubtless a due reward) and granted Philostratus three interviews in his old age[71]. They may have been devoted to sophistic discussion. But it is notable how much that is arguably genuine tradition on Apollonius comes from western Asia Minor and in particular from Ephesus (as does the only story outside Philostratus before Byzantine legends, viz. the vision of Domitian's death in Cassius Dio). Philostratus' own family has no obvious connections with Ephesus, and I would suggest (no more than tentatively) that Philostratus' information on Apollonius in Ephesus came partly from the philoseveran sophist Damianus, and that in his introduction of a novelistic 'witness' to his version Philostratus incorporated a complimentary allusion to the now deceased Damianus[72].

Notes

1. Philostratus' Τὰ ἐς τὸν Τυανέα Ἀπολλώνιον is cited from C. L. KAYSER, Flavii Philostrati Opera, vol. I (Leipzig, 1870) and will throughout be abbreviated as VA (although the work is not properly a Vita); likewise Ἀπολλωνίου τοῦ Τυανέως ἐπιστολαί (abbreviated as Epist. Ap.). His Βίοι σοφιστῶν are cited from C. L. KAYSER, Flavii Philostrati Opera, vol. II (Leipzig, 1871) with the addition of the OLEARIUS (ed. Leipzig, 1709) pagination, and will be abbreviated Vit. Soph. Likewise the *Heroicus*.

2. W. L. DULIÈRE, Protection permanente contre des animaux nuisibles assurée par Apollonius de Tyane dans Byzance et Antioch. Evolution de son mythe, Byz. Zeits. 63 (1970), 247-277; W. SPEYER, Zum Bild des Apollonius von Tyana bei Heiden und Christen, Jahrb. f. Ant. u. Christentum 17 (1974), 47-63 (hereafter simply cited as SPEYER). The most recent extensive discussion of all stages

of the tradition on Apollonius is by G. PETZKE. Die Traditionen über Apollonius von Tyana und das neue Testament (Leiden, 1970): for reservations cf. W. SPEYER, Jahrb. f. Ant. u. Christentum 16 (1973), 133-135. PETZKE treats most problems raised in this paper but I cite him only where his arguments are of particular relevance.

3. E. MEYER, Apollonios von Tyana und die Biographie des Philostratos, Hermes 52 (1917), 371-424, repr. in: ID., Kleine Schriften 2 (Halle, 1924), 131-191, hereafter cited as MEYER with the original pagination. The analogy of the 'Historia Augusta', not seen by MEYER himself, is pertinently drawn by B. F. HARRIS, Apollonius of Tyana: Fact and Fiction, Journ. Relig. Hist. 5 (1969), 189-199, at p. 192, n. 16, in relation to the authentication techniques of the historical romancer, and invoked to parallel mixture of real and bogus sources by G. W. BOWERSOCK in his introduction to C. P. JONES' translation of Philostratus' 'Apollonius' (Harmondsworth, 1970), 17.

4. MEYER, esp. 371-382, and 421f. He was not working in a vacuum. Notable landmarks had been C. L. NIELSEN, Apollonius fra Tyana (Copenhagen, 1879); J. GÖTTSCHING, Apollonius von Tyana (Leipzig, 1889); J. MILLER, Die Beziehungen der Vita Apollonii des Philostratus zur Pythagorassage, Philologus 51 (1892), 137-145; ID., Zur Frage nach der Persönlichkeit des Apollonius von Tyana, ibid. 51 (1892), 581-584; ID., Apollonius von Tyana, in: PAULY-WISSOWA, RE [*Real-Encyclopädie der Klassischen Altertumswissenshaft*] 2.1 (Stuttgart, 1895), col. 146-148; ID., Die Damispapiere in Philostratos Apolloniosbiographie, Philologus 66 (1907), 511-525; R. REITZENSTEIN, Hellenistische Wundererzählungen (Leipzig, 1906), 40-54 (hereafter cited as REITZENSTEIN). On the novelistic form E. SCHWARTZ, Fünf Vorträge über den griechischen Roman (Berlin, 1896).

5. J. MESK, Die Damisquelle des Philostratos in der Biographie des Apollonios von Tyana, Wiener Studien 41 (1919), 121-138; J. HEMPEL, Untersuchungen zur Überlieferung von Apollonios von Tyana (Stockholm, 1920), esp. 26-32 (hereafter cited as HEMPEL); ID., Zu Apollonius von Tyana, ZKG [*Zeitschrift für Kirchengeschichte*] 40 (1922), 130f.

6. F. GROSSO, La 'vita di Apollonio di Tiana' come fonte storico, Acme 7 (1954), 333-533. (This work was unfortunately unknown to PETZKE). An earlier attempt to vindicate the Indian travels of Apollonius had been made by J. CHARPENTIER, The Indian Travels of Apollonius (Uppsala, 1934). A more sceptical view was taken by T. HOPFNER, Apollo-

nios von Tyana und Philostratos, Studien des Seminarium Kondakovianum (Prague, 1931), 135-164 and again in: Die Brachmanen Indiens und die Gymnosophisten Aegyptens in der Apolloniosbiographie des Philostratos, Archiv Orientální 6 (1934), 58-67. Pertinent to the Damis problem are also the remarks of E. NORDEN, Agnostos Theos, 2nd. ed. (Leipzig/Berlin, 1923), esp. 37, n. 1.

7. GROSSO is not cited by PETZKE or SPEYER, nor by J. PALM, Rom, Römertum und Imperium in der griechischen Literatur der Kaiserzeit (Lund, 1959). B. P. REARDON, Courants littéraires grecs des IIe et IIIe siècles après J.-C. (Paris, 1971), 189 cites GROSSO but maintains a sceptical position. GROSSO is accepted by B. FORTE, Rome and the Romans as the Greeks Saw Them, Pap. & Monogr. Amer. Acad. Rome 24 (1972), 232, nn. 138-139, and the VA continued to be used as if it provided valuable documentary evidence for the 90s by G. S. KNABE, Philostratus' Life of Apollonius of Tyana and Cornelius Tacitus (Russian, with an English Summary), Vestnik Drevnej Istorii 121 (1972), 30-73 as it was by A. VASSILEIOU, Sur la date des thermes de Néron, Rev. Ét. Anc. 74 (1972), 93-106 for the 60s (cf. below n. 17). The need to reach a firm and clear decision on the problem (properly emphasised by BOWERSOCK, op. cit. [n. 3], 17 who silently rejects GROSSO's conclusions) is underlined by the approach of R. MACMULLEN, Enemies of the Roman Order (Cambridge, Mass., 1967): at 311, n. 28 he is critical of GROSSO, but he clings to a belief in Damis and the trial scene before Domitian, so that in his text (p. 71) Apollonius' anti-Domitianic exploitation of Harmodius and Aristogeiton is presented as a fact about the 90s whereas his note (310, n. 24) adds "whether or not historically". G. M. LEE, Had Apollonius of Tyana read St. Mark?, Symbolae Osloenses 48 (1973), 115-116 even tried to use the presumed date of the Damis narrative to give a terminus ante quem for the composition of St. Mark's gospel.

8. So GROSSO, 511f.; and, with particular reference to Apollonius' commendation of Demetrius to Titus, 383f.

9. VA 1.28; 1.39; 3.58 (GROSSO dates this return to the year 61). Most scholars concede a problem (e.g. GÖTTSCHING, op. cit. 47f., countering GUTSCHMID; MEYER, op. cit. 374-375 dismisses Philostratus' details as worthless). GROSSO's case is not supported by his other wise interesting connection of VA 1.37 with Tac. ann. 11.10.1.

10. Banishment Tac. ann. 15.71; Cassius Dio 62.27.4: imprisonment VA 4.35 and 46. GROSSO 373f. There is a problem in the designation of Musonius as ὁ

Βαβυλώνιος in 4.35 whereas in 7.16 he is τὸν Τυρρηνόν. The *eques Romanus* of Tacitus is *Tusci generis* (ann. 14.59 cf. ILS 2944) and it is out of the question that Philostratus refers to two homonymous foes of Nero (nor need we postulate two Musonii to explain the fragments and traditions, as von Fritz, Musonius, in: Pauly-Wissowa RE XVI.1 [Stuttgart, 1933], 893-897). Nieuwland's conjecture ὁ Βουλσίνιος is tempting. But given the context of μαντική in which Musonius is introduced it should be considered whether ὁ Βαβυλώνιος might here indicate the practice of astrology: this is a common enough use of *Babylonius* in Latin, but none is cited by LSJ for Greek: note however Teucros of Cyzicus, arguably the same as Teucros ὁ Βαβυλώνιος, who wrote περὶ τῶν παρανατελλόντων (W. Schmid-O. Stählin, Geschichte der griechischen Literatur, 2.1. [Munich, ⁶1959], 416 and 448). That Philostratus believed Musonius to have dabbled in astrology could not be taken as evidence that he did, but the charge may well have been made in material available to Philostratus.

11. The relationship with the 'Nero' is sensibly discussed by Meyer, 416f. The dialogue 'Nero' was first attributed to Philostratus II (the biographer) by Kayser: it was assigned to Philostratus I, the father of the biographer, by K. Münscher, Die Philostrate, Philologus Suppl. 10 (1905/07), 469ff. G. W. Bowersock, Greek sophists in the Roman empire (Oxford, 1969), 3, assigns a 'Nero' to the father of the biographer but leaves open its identification with the surviving work. The remark in VA 5.19 is frequently brought into this discussion: καὶ ἐάσθω τὰ Μουσωνίου πλείω ὄντα καὶ θαυμασιώτερα, ὡς μὴ δοκοίην θρασύνεσθαι πρὸς τὸν ἀμελῶς αὐτὰ εἰπόντα. A reading of the Lucianic 'Nero' should suffice to show that it cannot be the work in question: there nothing but Gyara, the Isthmus excavations and criticisms of Nero are involved, i. e. no more than mentioned by VA, certainly not πλείω . . . καὶ θαυμασιώτερα. Nor can ἀμελῶς stand: how can one θρασύνεσθαι against something admittedly inferior? Olearius' conjecture ἐμμελῶς is attractive, but if accepted excludes reference to a work by the biographer himself, even once allowances have been made for sophistic self-importance, while θρασύνεσθαι seems to me to exclude reference to a work of his father as being too strong a term for emulation within the family circle. Therefore if Philostratus the biographer did write the 'Nero' it must have been after VA (so, on other grounds, F. Solmsen, Some Works of Philostratus the Elder, TAPA [*Transactions of the American Philological Association*] 71 [1940], 556ff.) and

not before (as Meyer 416f.). This may be the best solution for the Lucianic 'Nero', since little weight can be given to the distribution of works among the Philostrati by the Suda, giving a 'Nero' to Philostratus I, or to circumstantial arguments about the Antonine topicality of cutting the Isthmus as advanced by Bowersock. There remains a problem at VA 5.19, which should probably be seen as a reference to a full biography (this was seen by Schmid-Stählin⁶, 357, n. 4, hazarding an allusion to Pollio: the Lucius of VS 556-57, there much admired by Philostratus and described as Μουσωνίῳ δὲ τῷ Τυρίῳ [? leg. Τυρρηνῷ] προσφιλοσοφήσας might also be considered, if one is prepared to identify him with Lucius the collector and editor of Musonius' works and admit προσφιλοσοφήσας as a description of posthumous study). ἀφελῶς might be what Philostratus wrote: ἀφέλεια was a quality admired by Philostratus (W. Schmid, Der Atticismus in seinen Hauptvertretern [Stuttgart, 1887-96], IV. 1-11) and would fit philosophic *apomnemoneumata*.

For a list of references to Musonius' banishment see O. Hense, C. Musonii Rufi Reliquiae, (Leipzig, 1905), XXVf., to which should now be added Favorinus, Περὶ φυγῆς, ed. M. Norsa and G. Vitelli, Studi e testi 53 (Roma, 1931), 21,1.35.

12. Tac. hist. 4.40 (cf. 4.10); followers: Fronto 2.50 (Haines) = 133.9-10 (van den Hout).

13. VA 5.39.

14. See Hense, op. cit. XXIIf., XXVII.

15. [See in this article] p. 1668.

16. Most recently Bowersock, op. cit. (n. 3), 17-18.

17. For testimonia on Demetrius see Pros. Imp. Rom.² D 39 (Stein). A. Vassileiou, op. cit. (n. 7), 93-106, attempts to vindicate the date of 66 A.D. for the dedication of *thermae Neronianae* which he wishes to distinguish from the *gymnasium* of Tac. ann. 14.47: neither his attempt to distinguish the Greek γυμνάσιον (applicable to baths) from the Latin *gymnasium* (allegedly not so extended) nor his analysis of Suet. Nero 12.7-8 (where the *atque* of *dedicatis thermis atque gymnasio* excludes their separation) carry conviction, and the postulate that the baths' dedication figured in the lost chapters of Annales 16 raises a problem (seen but inadequately explained) in the silence of Dio. If the chronographers' dates of 63 (Jerome) and 64 (Cassiodorus) are not simply errors for 61 (Tacitus) then they may refer to the rebuilding of the complex or parts of it burned down in 62: they are no support for Philostratus' date of 66.

18. Tac. ann. 16.34-35.

19. It might be objected that the frequent allusions of Seneca show the character of Demetrius as incapable of evil. But the career and earlier rank of Seneca himself should suffice to show how far he could allow a philosopher's conduct to diverge from his professed ideals. It is clear that Tacitus' judgement on Demetrius was less favourable, and the anecdote in Lucian, de salt. 63 suggests that Demetrius knew when to abandon cynic *convicia* for praise of what Nero liked. Not much reliance can be placed on the Juvenal scholiast (ad sat. 1.33) who offers a Demetrius *causidicum cui multos Nero detulit*. If the reference is to our Demetrius (doubted by STEIN loc. cit.) it is hardly good evidence for extensive delation but only for an unfavourable tradition about him which may have well derived from and generalised his role in 66 and 70: if there had been good evidence for *multos . . . detulit* Tacitus would hardly have characterised his defence of Celer with the mild *ambitiosius quam honestius*.

20. GROSSO had to abandon Philostratus' synchronisation with the opening of the gymnasium (60-61 A.D.) since Tigellinus had not yet come to power, and tried to link the anecdote with its conflagration in 62 *ictu fulminis* (Tac. ann. 15.22) by which time Tigellinus (pace BOWERSOCK, loc. cit.) was *praefectus praetorio*. The fire he tries to connect with the ground of Tigellinus' accusation VA 4.42 ὡς τὸ βαλανεῖον κατασκάψαντα, οἷς εἶπε . . . : but this is simply a grandiloquent sophistic metaphor to point up the injustice of Tigellinus' jurisdiction-a verbal dismantling of the baths counted as a real one; and there is no hint that Philostratus knew of their destruction unless it is his exploitation of the *fulmen* in a different context in 4.43. Even if he did, his narration of the whole matter as an event of 66 does not suggest he was closely following a reliable source (? a laudatory life of Demetrius which moved the invective to 66 precisely to distract from his dubious loyalty to Paetus in that year: it might be that Lucian, de salt. 63, derives from the same source as VA 4.42 since each highlights Nero's artistic penchant).

GROSSO's explanation for Philostratus' 'distortion' is odd: avoidance of the Stoic circle of Paetus as part of a purely Roman world from which Apollonius is always excluded. But elsewhere Philostratus repeatedly attempts to equip Apollonius with Roman connections! It should be emphasised that the only explicit date (presumably that to which Philostratus wants readers to attach the incident) is 66 A.D., the consulate of Telesinus (VA 4.40) and not, as GROSSO's argument would require, ca. 62 A.D.

21. GROSSO, 379; VA 4.25.

22. VA 6.31-33; the friendship of Musonius with Titus does not help to show (as GROSSO wishes) that Titus might have philosopher friends who were not liked by Vespasian, for Musonius was also exempted from Vespasian's banishment decree (Cassius Dio 66.13.2).

23. For such biographers of Neronian martyrs cf. Plin. ep. 5.5 (C. Fannius); 8.12 (Titinius Capito). Were such a biography of Demetrius published by the reign of Nerva it would be formally possible that 'Damis' (rather than Philostratus) used it for the Neronian deeds of Apollonius. But why should 'Damis' have to use such a source? To suggest (as GROSSO, 52) that 'Damis' did not have much material on Apollonius under Nero gives the lie to the claim of a Damis who accompanied Apollonius from the start of his travels, and effectively to the whole Damis story.

24. Ti. Iulius Alexander is of course in a different category, as are others who enter equestrian or senatorial service. Informal power as an *amicus* of the *princeps* (a matter of concern in Rome at the time: Tac. hist. 4.7) can be documented for some Greeks in the reign of Augustus, e. g. Areius of Alexandria, as characterised in Themistius Or. 13.173a, 248.19 (DOWNEY), or Athenodorus of Tarsus: cf. PIR^2 1035 and 1288 and G. W. BOWERSOCK, Augustus and the Greek World (Oxford, 1965): but this can be seen as a direct consequence of the conflict of Octavian with Antonius, and in the settled period of the Julio-Claudians the importance of the Greek world was much reduced.

25. Bell. Iud. 4.603-606 and 616-618. Cf. A. BRIESSMAN, Tacitus und das flavische Geschichtsbild (Wiesbaden, 1955), 12f.; A. HENRICHS, Vespasian's Visit to Alexandria, Zeits. f. Pap. u. Epig. 3 (1968), 76f.

26. Tac. hist. 4.81-82; Suet. div. Vesp. 7; VA 5.27 ff. The papyrus is P. Fouad I.8, cf. HENRICHS, op. cit. 59, n. 24 for bibliography. I do not accept the view that P. Vind. Gr. 25 787 (= SB 9528) relates to Vespasian as argued by its publisher H. GERSTINGER, Anz. d. Oester. Akad. d. Wiss. 15 (1958), 192f., but this cannot be argued here. Cf. HENRICHS, 54, n. 11.

27. P. DERCHAIN, J. HUBAUX, Vespasien au Sérapéum, Latomus 12 (1953), 38-52; cf. HENRICHS, op. cit., 61.

28. Opp. citt. (nn. 25 and 27).

29. Op. cit., 49.

30. A date in November or very early December seems most probable: cf. Tac. hist. 3.48.

31. The problem of its relation to the confirmation of Vespasian by a Jewish priest Basilides on Mount Carmel (Tac. hist. 2.78) cannot be discussed in detail here: cf. DERCHAIN and HUBAUX, op. cit.; K. SCOTT, The Rôle of Basilides in the Events of A.D. 69, Journ. Rom. Stud. 24 (1934), 138f.; L. HERMANN, Basilides, Latomus 12 (1953), 312f.

32. 67.18.

33. For anti-Semitism cf. VA 5.27; 33; 34 and 6.29. The aggressive dismissal of the view that Vespasian developed imperial ambitions while blockading Jerusalem (VA 5.27) looks like a thrust at Josephus' version where he is (reluctantly) proclaimed in Judaea before Alexandria (cf. HENRICHS, 76f.). The arrest of Egypt's decline (VA 5.29 init.) is incompatible with Suet. Vesp. 19.5; Cassius Dio 66.8.2-4: cf. M. ROSTOVTZEFF, The Social and Economic History of the Roman Empire² (Oxford, 1957), 294-295 with notes p. 674.

34. Since at least GÖTTSCHING, op. cit., 71: most recently SPEYER, 49 with n. 17. For a distribution of other scholars between outright and modified scepticism, ib. n. 16. . . .

35. Dictys, ed. W. EISENHUT² (Leipzig, 1958, 1973), prol. 2-3 and 5.17.119. Cf. SPEYER, 51 with nn. 29-34.

36. SPEYER's *"noch nicht angestellt worden"* (51) is true of material in print. Not to assert priority, but simply to indicate independent observation and similar conclusions, I should note that I propounded the views argued in the text in lectures in Oxford in 1964/65.

37. SPEYER, 50, n. 28: add perhaps the interview of Apollonius with Achilles in VA 4.12f. where he obtains new information on the Troian war (Palamedes' grave).

38. Photius Biblioth. cod. 166, 111 a 20 f. (II.146 HENRY).

39. Version β c. 51. Note also the fraudulent tablets of Lucian, Alex. 10.

40. Xen. Ephes. 5.15.2; Longus, praef. 1-2; Achilles Tatius 1.1-2.

41. Photius Biblioth. cod. 94 (II.40 n. 1 HENRY) = Iamblichi Babyloniacorum reliquiae, ed. HABRICH (Leipzig, 1960), 2.

42. The correct assessment of REARDON, 189.

43. MEYER, 376f. discusses dependence on Alexander histories. REARDON, 189 adduces the parallel of Heliodorus: since, however, Heliodorus may well be under the influence of Philostratus (as REARDON suggests) and his date is still in dispute (cf. B. E. PERRY, The Ancient Romances [Berkeley/Los Angeles, 1967], 349, n. 13) I do not wish to pursue parallels in this context. Ninos the Assyrian prince notoriously figures in our earliest dated novelistic fragment: the choice of Ninos/Nineveh for Damis' *origo* is hardly accidental, and although geography suggests Philostratus must be thinking of Hierapolis-Bambyke (so MEYER 373/74) on the Roman side of the Euphrates the name evocative of Assyrian antiquity is more important to him than facts of topography. Babylon, VA 1.25f.

44. The absence of *erotica* is seen as crucial by REARDON, 189 and PERRY, op. cit., 85. Incest VA 1.10; eunuchs VA 1.33,36. For other *erotica* cf. 3.38; 4.16, 25.

45. ed. HABRICH, 3; 64; 72 (fr. 96).

46. ib. 20; VA 4.45; hist. Apoll. reg. Tyr. 26. Similarly Luke 7.11f., cf. PETZKE, 129, who ignores the novelistic flavour. The *Scheintod* is a repeated motif in Achilles Tatius and is fundamental to Chariton's plot.

47. Iamblichus, ed. HABRICH 6; hist. Apoll. reg. Tyr. 8.

48. A. HENRICHS, Lollianus, Phoinikika, Zeits. f. Pap. u. Epig. 4 (1969), 205f. argues that this form of title is a Byzantine invention, the Greco-Roman convention being 'Ephesiaka', etc. This might only be true of those novels which pretended (without attempting deception) to be local histories: Τὰ ὑπὲρ Θούλην ἄπιστα evades harmonisation to this stereotype as do the Alexander histories.

49. Heliodorus and (according to the Suda) Xenophon divided their novels into 10 books (as Curtius Rufus his Alexander history). It is relevant that Xenophon's 'Cyropaedeia' has eight books: it falls on the same frontier between biography and novel.

50. Perhaps the culmination in a trial scene should be added: so Achilles Tatius and Heliodorus. A court scene also figured in Chariton and Iamblichus. But this may well be a feature deriving from other genres (especially as manipulated by declamatory sophists) and in the case of VA the biography of Pythagoras could be the chief influence (cf. MEYER, 383f.; 414f.).

51. op. cit., 52.

52. ibid.

53. VA 8. 29-30.

54. op. cit. 59-60: Basil. Pat. Gr. 85, 540 C (cf. SPEYER, n. 80) asserts that Apollonius παρὰ τῶν ἐν Αἰθίοψι καὶ ᾽ινδοῖς γυμνοσοφιστῶν μήτε ὑποδεχθῆναι σπουδαίως, ἀλλὰ γὰρ θᾶττον ἀποπεμφθῆναι, ὡς οὐκ εὐαγὴς οὐδὲ ὅσιος ἄνθρωπος, οὐδὲ φιλόσοφος ἀληθῶς, πολὺ δὲ τοῦ κατὰ τὴν γοητείαν μιάσματος ἔχων. This is certainly not what Philostratus says, but in his account Apollonius does depart from the Indian and Ethiopian gymnosophists after a relatively short visit rather than becoming a long-term member of their community, and a hostile witness could distort this into θᾶττον ἀποπεμφθῆναι, adding his own explanation with ὡς on the basis of allegations against Apollonius known from elsewhere in Philostratus. On the travels and Moiragenes see further below p. 1675 with n. 89.

55. VA 1.5; Vit. Soph. 1.21 (515). Again there are links with the Pythagoras legend, MEYER 414f.

56. Vit. Soph. 1.21 (517-518); VA 1.13.

57. VA 1.23, transl. F. C. CONYBEARE, vol. 1 (Loeb, London/New York, 1912), 69.

58. Nicetes, Vit. Soph. 1.19 (512): of the MSS readings Νέρωνα suits Philostratus' chronology better than Νερούαν: cf. BOWERSOCK, Greek Sophists . . . , 9, n. 1. Isaeus, Vit. Soph. 1.20 (513). Scopelianus and vines ib. 1.21 (520).

59. VA 6.42: the conceit cannot be Scopelianus' as it stands, for he was no eunuch, but Favorinus may have been exploited by Philostratus too.

60. Vit. Soph. 1.21 (519/20). Cf. now R. T. PENELLA, Scopelianus and the Eretrians in Cissia, Athenaeum 52 (1974), 295-300.

61. GÖTTSCHING, 61f. Cf. MEYER, 376f.

62. Dio, Vit. Soph. 1.7 (488); Polemo, ib. 1.25 (534); Herodes, ib. 2.1 (562); Aristides, ib. 2.9 (583).

63. Musonius advises Titus, Themistius Or. 13.173a, 248.19 (DOWNEY); discusses kingship HENSE, 32f., cf. VA 5.27f.

64. Dio Orr. 33-34; 38-41; Aristides Orr. 23-24 (KEIL); Polemo, Vit. Soph. 1.25 (531); Marcus, ib. 1.24 (529); Musonius, Tac. hist. 3.81. Of course nonsophistic holy men might also intervene in city affairs, cf. below p. 1690 with n. 149.

65. Dio Or. 31. 122; VA 4.22. On Musonius as Dio's reference, H. VON ARNIM, Leben und Werke des Dio von Prusa (Berlin, 1898), 216. A similar condemnation of Athens is put into the mouth of Demonax by Lucian, Dem. Vit. 57: here too the Corinthians are mentioned. The form of Lucian's work is such that Dio's reference is more likely to be factual and transferred by the satirist to his 'hero' than vice versa, although it is conceivable that both are historical. On the Demonax cf. K. FUNK, Untersuchungen über Lukians Vita Demonactis, Philol. Suppl. 10 (1907), 561f. (on this passage 652). One further link with Apollonius should be registered: Apollonius' silent appearance quelled a bread riot at Aspendus (VA 1.15), precisely the effect of Demonax's appearance at a riot in Athens (Lucian, Dem. Vit. 64): this may be a philosopher's topos (Philostratus, Vit. Soph. 1.23 [526] has a similar story of Pancrates the cynic at Athens, but Pancrates actually utters), but it would not be surprising if he looked to the 'Demonax' or its models for material. Cf. [in this article] p. 1681 with nn. 110-111, 149. The link between Philostratus' image of Apollonius and Dio was already seen by SCHWARTZ, op. cit. (n. 4), 129.

66. VA 4.21; Dio Or. 32. 58f.

67. Dio Or. 32.60.

68. γυναικομίμε δώ μορφάματι, κατὸ τὸν Εὐριπίδην, αἰσχρῶς διαπρέπον, quoting the Antiope (Eur. fr. 185 NAUCK) γυναικομίμῳ διαπρέπεις μορφώματι (already exploited by Plato, Gorgias 485 E). . . .

69. Vit. Soph. 2.5 (570). If this is a reference to a specific refutation of a story that Apollonius was in love with Alexander's mother then no such refutation appears in the work on Apollonius and the suspicion must arise that the term εἴρηται is prospective (as might be argued for some of the cross-references in Plutarch's Lives): hence no priority for the work on Apollonius. But the reference may simply be to the unswerving asceticism attributed to Apollonius in the work.

70. On the date of the Lives see BOWERSOCK, Greek Sophists . . . , 7 with bibliography: add V. NUTTON, Herodes and Gordian, Latomus 29 (1970), 719f. The work on Apollonius is normally dated after Julia Domna's death on the grounds that Philostratus would have dedicated it to her, its inspiration, had she been alive. This supposition might also be questioned: if the work required a dedication, then it should have one, to another if not to Julia Domna. That it has no dedication merely assimilates it to other novelistic literature and should not, perhaps, be used as a dating argument. There is, however, some plausibility in GÖTTSCHING's arguments, 74-87, that descriptions of good and bad rulers in the work on Apollonius are intended to criticise the reigns of Caracalla and Elagabalus and inspire the young Severus Al-

exander, though they cannot be taken so far as GÖTTSCHING wishes: and Alexander's admiration for Apollonius attested by the Historia Augusta, Alex. Sev. 29.2 (if reliable: dismissed by R. SYME, Ammianus and the Historia Augusta [Oxford, 1968], 61 and 138; for a less sceptical interpretation, S. SETTIS, Severo Alessandro e i suoi lari, Athenaeum 50 [1972], 237f.) might offer slender support. (I am not persuaded by A. CALDERINI's arguments for a first redaction ca. 202-205 in: Teoria e pratica politica nella 'Vita di Apollonio di Tiana', Rendic. dell. Ist. Lomb. 74 [1940/41], 213.)

71. Vit. Soph. 2.23 (606).

72. VA 4.4,10 on the plague at Ephesus fit the popular tradition of the miracle worker and provider of talismans. For Domitian's death, Cassius Dio 67.18.

I. TEXTS AND TRANSLATIONS

E. BALTZER, Apollonius von Tyana, übersetzt und erläutert (Rudolstadt, 1883).

F. BOLL, Βίβλος σοφίας καὶ συνέσεως ἀποτελεσμάτων Ἀπολλωνίου τοῦ Τυανέως, in: Catalogus Codicum Astrologorum Graecorum VII (Bruxelles, 1908), 175f.

F. C. CONYBEARE, Philostratus, The Life of Apollonius of Tyana (London/New York, 1912), 2 vols.

R. HERCHER, Epistolographi Graeci (Paris, 1973), 110f.

C. L. KAYSER, Flavii Philostrati Opera (Zürich, 1844).

C. L. KAYSER, Flavii Philostrati Opera, vol. I (Leipzig, 1870), vol. II (Leipzig, 1871).

F. NAU, Βίβλος σοφίας καὶ συνέσεως ἀποτελεσμάτων Ἀπολλωνίου τοῦ Τυανέως, in: Patrologia Syriaca I.2 (Paris, 1907), 1363f.

G. OLEARIUS, Philostratorum quae supersunt omnia (Leipzig, 1709).

R. J. PENELLA, An Unpublished Letter of Apollonius to the Sardians, Harv. Stud. Class. Phil. 79 (1975), 305-311.

R. J. PENELLA, The Letters of Apollonius of Tyana: Introd., transl. and selective commentary (Diss. Harvard 1971: microfilm).

J. S. PHILLIMORE, Philostratus in Honour of Apollonius of Tyana (Oxford, 1912).

W. C. WRIGHT, Philostratus and Eunapius, Lives of the Sophists (Loeb, London/Cambridge, Mass., 1921).

Note: an abridged translation by C. P. JONES with an introduction by G. W. BOWERSOCK has been published by Penguin with the title 'Philostratus, Life of Apollonius' (Harmondsworth, 1970).

II. SECONDARY LITERATURE

G. ANDERSON, Lucian: Theme and Variation in the Second Sophistic, Mnemosyne Suppl. 41 (Leiden, 1976).

G. ANDERSON, Studies in Lucian's Comic Fiction, Mnemosyne Suppl. 43 (Leiden, 1976).

J. ANNEQUIN, Recherches sur l'action magique et ses représentations, Ann. litt. de l'Univ. de Besançon 146, Centre de Rech. d'hist. ancienne 8 (Paris, 1973).

H. VON ARNIM, Damis, in: PAULY-WISSOWA, RE [*Real-Encyclopädie der Klassischen Altertumswissenshaft*] 4 (Stuttgart, 1901), 2056-2057.

F. C. BAUR, Drei Abhandlungen zur Geschichte der alten Philosophie und ihres Verhältnisses zum Christentum, ed. E. ZELLER (Leipzig, 1876).

N. A. BEES, Darstellungen altheidnischer Denker und Autoren in der Kirchenmalerei der Griechen, Byzant.-neugriechische Jahrb. 4 (Berlin, 1923), 107-128.

O. BÉLIARD, Un saint païen, Apollonius de Tyana, Les Annales 53 (1936), 584-586.

TH. BERGK, Fünf Abhandlungen zur Geschichte der griechischen Philosophie und Astronomie (Leipzig, 1883).

G. BERTERMANN, De Iamblichi vitae Pythagoricae fontibus (Königsberg, 1913).

H. D. BETZ, Lukian von Samosata und das Neue Testament (Diss. Mainz 1957) (Berlin, 1961).

L. BIELER, ΘΕΙΟσ ΑΝΗΡ, Das Bild des 'göttlichen Menschen' in Spätantike und Frühchristentum, vol. I (Wien, 1935), vol. II (Wien, 1936).

A. BIGELMAIR, Apollonius von Tyana, in: Lex. Theol. Kirch., 2nd ed., vol. I (Freiburg, 1957), 718-720.

E. BIRMELIN, Die Kunsttheoretischen Gedanken in Philostrats Apollonius, Philol. 88 (1933), 149-180, 392-414.

F. BOLL, Die Erforschung der antiken Astrologie, Neue Jahrb. f. d. klass. Altertum 21 (1908), 103-126.

G. W. BOWERSOCK, Greek Sophists in the Roman Empire (Oxford, 1969).

E. L. BOWIE, Greeks and their Past in the Second Sophistic, Past and Present 46 (1970), 3-41, repr. in: Studies in Ancient Society, ed. M. I. FINLEY (London, 1974), 166-209.

M. BOWMAN, A Lost Work of Apollonius of Tyana, Trans. Glasgow Univ. Oriental Soc. 14 (1950-1952), 1-10.

M. BRAUN, Griechischer Roman und hellenistische Geschichtsschreibung (Frankfurt, 1934).

M. BRAUN, History and Romance in Graeco-Oriental Literature (Oxford, 1938).

A. BRINKMANN, Ein Denkmal des Neupythagoreismus, Rhein. Mus. 66 (1911), 616-625.

P. BROWN, The Rise and Function of the Holy Man in Late Antiquity, Journ. Rom. Stud. 61 (1971), 80-101.

K. BURESCH, Klaros. Untersuchungen zum Orakelwesen des späteren Altertums (Leipzig, 1889).

W. BURKERT, Hellenistische Pseudopythagorica, Philologus 105 (1961), 16-42 and 226-246.

W. BURKERT, ΓΟΗσ. Zum Griechischen 'Schamanismus', Rhein. Mus. 150 (1962), 36-55.

W. BURKERT, Weisheit und Wissenschaft. Studien zu Pythagoras, Philolaos und Platon, Erlanger Beiträge z. Sprach- u. Kunstwiss. 10 (Nürnberg, 1962), transl. as: Lore and Science in Ancient Pythagoreanism (Cambridge, Mass., 1972).

W. BURKERT, Zur geistesgeschichtlichen Einordnung einiger Pseudopythagorica, in: Entretiens Hardt 18: Pseudepigrapha I (Vandoeuvres, 1971), 25-55.

A. CALDERINI, Teoria e pratica politica nella 'Vita di Apollonio di Tiana', Rend. Ist. Lomb. di scienze e lettere 74 (1940-1941), 213-241.

F. W. G. CAMPBELL, Apollonius of Tyana. A Study of His Life and Times (London, 1908).

M. CANNEY, Apollonius of Tyana, in: Encycl. of Relig. and Ethics, 3rd ed. 1 (Edinburgh, 1955), 609-611.

W. CAPELLE, Altgriechische Askese, Neue Jahrb. f. d. klass. Altertum 25 (1910), 681-708.

F. J. CARMODY, Arabic Astronomical and Astrological Sciences in Latin Translation, a Critical Bibliography (Berkeley, 1956).

H. CHADWICK, The Sentences of Sextus (Cambridge, 1959).

J. CHARPENTIER, The Indian Travels of Apollonius of Tyana, in: Skrifter utgivna av. K. Humanistika Vetenkaps-Samfundet i Uppsala 29.3 (1934), 1-66.

W. V. CHRIST-W. SCHMID-O. STÄHLIN, Geschichte der griechischen Literatur, 6th. ed., Handb. d. Altertumswiss. VII, II.1 (München, 1920), II.2 (München, 1924).

P. CORSSEN, Der Abaris des Heraklides Ponticus. Ein Beitrag zur Geschichte der Pythagoraslegende, Rhein. Mus. 67 (1912), 20-47.

P. CORSSEN, Der Altar des unbekannten Gottes, Zeits. f. Neut. Wiss. 14 (1913), 309-323.

F. CUMONT, Les religions orientales dans le paganisme romain, 4th ed. (Paris, 1929).

L. W. DALY and W. SUCHIER, The 'Altercatio Hadriani Augusti et Epicteti philosophi' and the Question and Answer Dialogue, Illinois Studies in Language and Literature 24 (1939), no. 1-2.

A. DEISSMANN, Licht vom Osten (Tübingen, 1908).

K. DEISSNER, Das Idealbild des stoischen Weisen (Greifswald, 1930).

P. DERCHAIN and J. HUBAUX, Vespasien au Sérapéum, Latomus 12 (1953), 38-52.

E. DIEHL, Maximos (36), in: PAULY-WISSOWA, RE 14.2 (Stuttgart, 1930), 2555-2556.

H. DIELS, Hippokratische Forschungen V, Hermes 53 (1918), 77, n. 1.

A. DIHLE, Studien zur griechischen Biographie, Abh. Ak. Göttingen, phil.-hist. Kl. 3.37 (Göttingen, 1956).

A. DIHLE, The Conception of India in Hellenistic and Roman Literature, Proc. Camb. Phil. Soc. 10 (1964), 15-23.

E. R. DODDS, Pagan and Christian in an Age of Anxiety. Some Aspects of Religious Experience from Marcus Aurelius to Constantine (Cambridge, 1965).

H. DÖRRIE, Apollonios (3), in: Der Kleine Pauly 1 (Stuttgart, 1964), 452-453.

D. R. DUDLEY, A History of Cynicism from Diogenes to the 6th century A.D. (London, 1937).

W. L. DULIÈRE, Protection permanente contre des animaux nuisibles assurée par Apollonius de Tyane dans Byzance et Antioch. Évolution de son mythe, Byz. Zeits. 63 (1970), 247 to 277.

J. FERTIG, De Philostrati sophistis (Bamberg, 1894).

A.-J. FESTUGIÈRE, Sur une nouvelle édition du 'De Vita Pythagorica' de Jamblique, Rev. Ét. Gr. 50 (1937), 470-484.

A.-J. FESTUGIÈRE, Trois rencontres entre la Grèce et l'Inde, Rev. Hist. Rel. 125 (1942-1943), 35-57.

A.-J. FESTUGIÈRE, La révélation d'Hermès Trismégiste, I. L'astrologie et les sciences occultes, (Paris, 1944).

B. FORTE, Rome and the Romans as the Greeks saw them, Papers and Monographs of the American Academy in Rome 24 (Rome, 1972).

K. VON FRITZ, Musonius (1)-(3), in: PAULY-WISSOWA, RE 16.1 (Stuttgart, 1933), 893-897.

H. FUCHS, Der geistige Widerstand gegen Rom in der antiken Welt (Berlin, 1938, repr. ibid. 1964).

H. GÄRTNER, Philostratos (3)-(6), in: Der Kleine Pauly 4 (Stuttgart, 1972), 780-784.

J. GEFFCKEN, Die christlichen Martyrien, Hermes 45 (1910), 481-505.

J. GEFFCKEN, Der Ausgang des griechisch-römischen Heidentums, Religionswiss. Bibl. 6 (Heidelberg, 1920, repr. Darmstadt 1963).

J. GEFFCKEN, Religiöse Strömungen im ersten Jahrhundert nach Christus (Gütersloh, 1922)

J. GÖTTSCHING, Apollonius von Tyana (Leipzig, 1889).

B. A. VAN GRONINGEN, Apollonius de Tyane, Bull. de la Fac. des Lettres de Strasbourg 30 (1951), 107-116.

P. GRIMAL, Deux figures de la correspondance de Pline: le philosophe Euphratès et le rhéteur Isée, Latomus 14 (1955), 370-389.

F. GROSSO, La vita di Apollonio Tianeo come fonte storica, Acme 7 (1954), 333-552.

K. GROSS, Apollonius, in: Reallexikon für Antike und Christentum 1 (Stuttgart, 1950), 529 to 532.

A. VON GUTSCHMID, Kleine Schriften V. Schriften zur römischen und mittelalterlichen Geschichte und Literatur, hrsg. v. F. RÜHL (Leipzig, 1894).

E. H. HAIGHT, More Essays on the Greek Romances (New York, 1945).

W. R. HALLIDAY, Damis of Nineveh and Walter of Oxford, Ann. Brit. Sch. Athens 18 (1911 to 1912), 234-238, repr. in: ID., Folklore Studies (Oxford, 1924).

B. F. HARRIS, Apollonius of Tyana: Fact or Fiction?, Journ. Rel. Hist. 5 (1969), 189-199.

E. B. HARRISON, The Athenian Agora. Results of Excavations conducted by the American School of Class. Studies at Athens, vol. 1. Portrait Sculpture (Princeton, 1953).

R. HELM, Der antike Roman, Handb. d. griech. u. lat. Philol. I,1 (Berlin, 1948).

J. HEMPEL, Untersuchungen zur Überlieferung von Apollonius von Tyana (Leipzig, 1920).

J. HEMPEL, Zu Apollonius von Tyana, Zeits. f. Kirchengeschichte 40 (1922), 130-131.

J. HEMPEL, Apollonius, in: Die Religion in Geschichte und Gegenwart, 2nd ed., I (Tübingen, 1927), 410f.

A. HENRICHS, Vespasian's visit to Alexandria, Zeits. f. Papyrologie u. Epigraphik 3 (1968), 51-80.

L. HERRMANN, Basilides, Latomus 12 (1953), 312-315.

G. HERZOG-HAUSER, Die Tendenzen der Apollonius-Biographie, in: Jahrb. d. österreichischen Leo-Gesellschaft (Wien, 1930), 177-200.

G. HOFMANN, Über Apollonius von Tyana und zwei in seinem Leben berichtete Erscheinungen am Himmel, Programm des k.k. Gymnasiums in Triest, 21 (1871), 1-29.

R. HÖISTAD, Cynic Hero and Cynic King (Uppsala, 1948).

K. HOLL, Die schriftstellerische Form des griechischen Heiligenlebens, Neue Jahrb. f. d. klass. Altertum 29 (1912), 406-427.

T. HOPFNER, Apollonios von Tyana und Philostratos, in: Studien des Seminarium Kondakovianum 4 (Prag, 1931), 135-164.

T. HOPFNER, Die Brahmanen Indiens und die Gymnosophisten Ägyptens in der Apollonios-biographie des Philostratos, Archiv Orientální 6 (1934), 58-67.

F. HUHN and E. BETHE, Philostratos Heroikos und Diktys, Hermes 52 (1917), 614-624.

H. JAEGER, Die Quellen des Porphyrios in seiner Pythagoras-Biographie (Diss. Zürich, 1919).

W. JAEGER, Early Christianity and Greek Paideia (Cambridge, Mass., 1961).

J. JESSEN, Apollonius von Tyana und sein Biograph Philostratus (Hamburg, 1885).

C. P. JONES, The Reliability of Philostratus, in: Approaches to the Second Sophistic, ed. G. W. BOWERSOCK (Pennsylvania, 1974), 11-16.

J. JÜTHNER, Hellenen und Barbaren (Leipzig, 1923).

K. KERÉNYI, Die griechisch-orientalische Romanliteratur in religionsgeschichtlicher Beleuchtung, 2nd ed. (Darmstadt, 1962).

C. KIESEWETTER, Apollonius von Tyana, Sphinx 2 (1887), 245-252 and 374-380.

G. S. KNABE, Philostratus' Life of Apollonius of Tyana and Cornelius Tacitus, Vestnik Drevnej Istorii 121 (1972), 30-63 (Russian, Eng. summary).

W. JACKSON KNIGHT, Apollonius of Tyana, Psychic News (London, 1962), May 26, June 2 and June 9.

P. KRAUS, Jābir Ibn Ḥayyān. Contribution à l'histoire des idées scientifiques dans l'Islam, vol. 2, Mém. prés. à l'Inst. d'Égypte 45 (Cairo, 1946).

P. DE LABRIOLLE, La réaction paienne. Étude sur la polémique antichrétienne du Ier au VIe siècle (Paris, 1934).

M. J. LAGRANGE, Les légendes pythagoriennes et l'évangile, Rev. Bibl. 46 (1937), 13-28.

K. LATTE, Römische Religionsgeschichte, Handb. d. Altertumswiss. V 4 (München, 1960).

B. LATZARUS, Un pythagoricien thaumaturge: Apollonius de Tyane, Rév. des cours et conférences 40.2 (1939), 33-47; 240-252; 516-525 and 41.1 (1940), 51-64; 267-280; 420-434.

M. L. Leclerc, De l'identité de Balinas et d'Apollonius de Tyane, Journ. Asiat. 6e. sér. 14 (1869), 111-131.

G. M. Lee, Had Apollonius of Tyana read St. Mark?, Symb. Oslo. 48 (1973), 115-116.

F. Leo, Die griechisch-römische Biographie nach ihrer litterarischen Form (Leipzig, 1901).

A. Lesky, Geschichte der griechischen Literatur, 2nd. ed. (Bern, 1963) (Eng. trans. London, 1965).

G. Levi della Vida, Something more about Artefius and his Clavis Sapientiae, Speculum 13 (1938), 80-85.

G. Levi della Vida, La dottrina e i dodici legati di Stomathalassa, Atti dell'Accad. Naz. dei Lincei, Classe Sc. Mor. Stor. Filol., 8.3 (1951), 477-542.

I. Levy, Recherches sur les sources de la légende de Pythagore (Paris, 1926).

L. Lo Cascio, La forma letteraria della Vita di Apollonio Tianeo, Quad. dell. ist. di filol. grec. dell. Univ. di Palermo 6 (Palermo, 1974).

R. MacMullen, Enemies of the Roman Order (Cambridge, Mass., 1966).

D. Magie, Roman rule in Asia Minor, 2 vols. (Princeton, 1950).

G. R. S. Mead, Apollonius of Tyana (London/Benares, 1901).

R. Merkelbach, Roman und Mysterium in der Antike. Eine Untersuchung zur antiken Religion (München, 1962).

J. Mesk, Ein unedierter Tractat περὶ λίθων, Wien. Stud. 20 (1898), 309-321.

J. Mesk, Die Damisquelle des Philostratos in der Biographie des Apollonios von Tyana, Wien. Stud. 41 (1919), 121-138.

M. Meunier, Apollonius de Tyane ou le séjour d'un dieu parmi les hommes (Paris, 1936).

E. Meyer, Apollonius von Tyana und die Biographie des Philostratos, Hermes 52 (1917), 371-424, repr. in: Id., Kleine Schriften 2 (Halle, 1924), 131-191.

R. Meyer-Krämer, Apollonius von Tyana, der Magus aus Osten, Monatsh. d. Comeniusgesellschaft 15 (1906), 1-41.

F. Millar, A Study of Cassius Dio (Oxford, 1964).

J. Miller, Die Beziehungen der Vita Apollonii des Philostratos zur Pythagorassage, Philol. 51 (1892), 137-145.

J. Miller, Zur Frage nach der Persönlichkeit des Apollonius von Tyana, Philol. 51 (1892), 581-584.

J. Miller, Apollonius (98), in: Pauly-Wissowa, RE 2 (Stuttgart, 1895), 146-148.

J. Miller, Die Damispapiere in Philostratos Apolloniosbiographie, Philol. 66 (1907), 511-525.

C. Mönckeberg, Apollonius von Tyana (Hamburg, 1877).

K. Münscher, Die Philostrate, Philolog. Suppl. 10 (1907), 496-558.

F. Nau, Une ancienne traduction latine du Bélinous arabe, Rev. de l'orient chrét. 12 (1907), 99-106.

W. Nestle, Griechische Religiosität von Alexander dem Großen bis auf Proklos (Berlin, 1934).

C. L. Nielsen, Apollonios fra Tyana og Filostrats Beskrivelse af hans Levnet (Copenhagen, 1879).

M. P. Nilsson, Die Religion in den griechischen Zauberpapyri, in: Id., Opuscula selecta 3 (Lund, 1960), 129-166.

M. P. Nilsson, Geschichte der griechischen Religion, 2nd ed., vol. II, Handb. d. Altertumswiss. V 2, 2 (München, 1961).

A. D. Nock, Oracles théologiques, Rev. Ét. Anc. 30 (1928), 280-290, repr. in: Id., Essays on Religion and the Ancient World, I (Oxford, 1972), 160-168.

A. D. Nock, Conversion (Oxford, 1933).

A. D. Nock, Orphism or popular philosophy?, Harv. Theol. Rev. 33 (1940), 301-315, repr. in: Id., Essays on Religion and the Ancient World, I (Oxford, 1972), 503-515.

A. D. Nock, A Cult Ordinance in Verse, Harv. Stud. Class. Phil. 63 (1968), 415-421, repr. in: Id., Essays on Religion and the Ancient World, II (Oxford, 1972), 847-852.

E. Norden, Agnostos Theos, 2nd ed. (Leipzig-Berlin, 1923).

J. Palm, Rom, Römertum und Imperium in der griechischen Literatur der Kaiserzeit, Acta Soc. hum. Litt. Lundensis 57 (Lund, 1959).

E. Pélagaud, Un conservateur du second siècle (Laon, 1878).

R. J. Penella, Scopelianus and the Eretrians in Cissia, Athenaeum 52 (1974), 295-300.

B. E. Perry, Secundus the Silent Philosopher, Philol. Monogr. publ. by the Amer. Philol. Assoc. 22 (Ithaca, 1964).

B. E. Perry, The Ancient Romances. A literary-historical account of their origines, Sather Class. Lect. 37 (Berkeley/Los Angeles, 1967).

G. Petzke, Die Traditionen über Apollonius von Tyana und das Neue Testament, Studia ad Corp. Hellenist. N.T. 1 (Leiden, 1970).

M. Plessner, Neue Materialien zur Geschichte der Tabula Smaragdina, Der Islam 16 (1927), 77-113.

M. Plessner, Beiträge zur islamischen Literaturge-schichte, Islamica 4 (1929-1931), 551f.

M. Plessner, Hermes Trismegistos and Arab Science, in: Studia Islamica 2 (Paris, 1954), 45-59.

M. Plessner, Balinus, in: Encyclopaedia of Islam, 2nd ed., I (Paris, 1960), 1024-1026.

T. Plüss, Apollonius von Tyana auf dem Nil und der unbekannte Gott zu Athen, in: Festgabe f. H. Blümmer (Zürich, 1914), 36-48.

K. Preisendanz, Papyri graecae magicae, II (Leipzig, 1931).

O. de B. Priaulx, The Indian Travels of Apollonius of Tyana, Journ. Roy. As. Soc. 17 (1860), 70-105.

A. Priessnig, Die literarische Form der spätantiken Philosophenromane, Byz. Zeits. 30 (1929), 23-30.

A. Priessnig, Die biographische Form der Plotinvita des Porphyrios und des Antonioslebens des Athanasios, Byz. Zeits. 64 (1971), 1-5.

K. Prümm, Religionsgeschichtliches Handbuch für den Raum der altchristlichen Umwelt (Rome, 1954).

L. Radermacher, Zur Sacherklärung des Heroikos, Sitzungsb. d. Wiener Akad. 182 (1916), 18-23, 108-111.

B. P. Reardon, The Greek Novel, Phoenix 23 (1969), 55-73.

B. P. Reardon, Courants littéraires grecs des IIe et IIIe siècles après J.-C., Annales litt. Univ. de Nantes 3 (Paris, 1971).

B. P. Reardon, The Second Sophistic and the Novel, Approaches to the Second Sophistic, ed. G. W. Bowersock (Pennsylvania, 1974), 23-29.

R. Reitzenstein, Hellenistische Wundererzählungen (Leipzig, 1908).

R. Reitzenstein, Die Areopagrede des Apostels Paulus, Neue Jahrb. f. d. klass. Altertum 31 (1913), 393-422.

R. Reitzenstein, Die hellenistischen Mysterienreligionen, 3rd. ed. (Leipzig, 1927).

K. Reyhl, Antonius Diogenes (Diss. Tübingen, 1969).

H. Ritter and M. Plessner, Picatrix. Das Ziel des Weisen von Pseudo-Maǧriti (London, 1962).

E. Rohde, Die Quellen des Jamblichus in seiner Biographie des Pythagoras, Rhein. Mus. 26 (1871), 554-576 and 27 (1872), 23-61, repr. in: Id., Kleine Schriften, II (Tübingen-Leipzig, 1901), 102f.

E. Rohde, Besprechung von Th. Bergk, Fünf Abhandlungen, in: Id., Kleine Schriften, I (Tübingen-Leipzig, 1901), 338-344.

E. Rohde, Besprechung von E. Schwartz, Fünf Vorträge, in: Id., Kleine Schriften, I (Tübingen-Leipzig, 1901), 5-9.

E. Rohde, Der griechische Roman und seine Vorläufer, 4th ed. (Darmstadt, 1960).

H. Rommel, Die naturwissenschaftlich-paradoxographischen Exkurse bei Philostratos, Heliodoros und Achilleus Tatios (Stuttgart, 1923).

V. Rose, Damigeron, De lapidibus, Hermes 9 (1874), 471-491.

F. Rosenthal, Das Fortleben der Antike im Islam (Zürich, 1965).

J. Ruska, Tabula Smaragdina. Ein Beitrag zur Geschichte der Hermetischen Literatur, Arbeiten aus dem Inst. f. Gesch. d. Naturwiss. 16 (Heidelberg, 1926).

N. Sacerdoti, A proposito delle fonti di un passo di Porfirio (vita Pyth. 14-17), in: In memoriam A. Beltrami (Genova, 1954), 213-219.

W. Schmid, Der Atticismus in seinen Hauptvertretern von Dionysius von Halikarnaß bis auf den zweiten Philostratus, vol. IV (Stuttgart, 1896).

G. Schnayder, De infenso alienigenarum in Romanos animo, Eos 30 (1927), 113-149.

G. Schnayder, Quibus conviciis alienigenae Romanos carpserint (Cracow, 1928).

H. J. Schütz, Beiträge zur Formgeschichte synoptischer Wundererzählungen, dargestellt an der Vita Apollonii des Philostratus (Diss. Jena, 1953).

E. Schwartz, Fünf Vorträge über den griechischen Roman (Berlin, 1896).

S. Settis, Severo Alessandro e i suoi lari, Athenaeum 50 (1972), 237-251.

V. A. Smith, The Indian Travels of Apollonius of Tyana, Zeits. d. Deutsch. Morgenl. Gesellsch. 68 (1914), 329-344.

R. Söder, Die apokryphen Apostolgeschichten und die romanhafte Literatur der Antike, Würzburger Studien z. Altertumswiss. 3 (Stuttgart, 1932).

F. Solmsen, Some Works of Philostratus the Elder, Trans. Amer. Philol. Soc. 71 (1940), 556-572.

F. Solmsen, Philostratus (9-12), in: Pauly-Wissowa, RE 20.1 (Stuttgart, 1941), 124-177.

W. Speyer, Besprechung von G. Petzke, Die Traditionen von Apollonius von Tyana und das neue Testament, Jahrb. f. Ant. u. Christentum 16 (1973), 133-135.

W. Speyer, Zum Bild des Apollonius von Tyana bei Heiden und Christen, Jahrb. f. Ant. u. Christentum 17 (1974), 47-63.

E. Strazzeri, Apollonio di Tiana e la cronologia dei suoi viaggi (Terranova, 1901).

R. Syme, Ammianus and the Historia Augusta (Oxford, 1968).

M. Steinschneider, Apollonius von Tyana (oder Balinas) bei den Arabern, Zeits. d. Deutsch. Morgenl. Gesellsch. 45 (1891), 439-446.

D. M. Tredwell, A Sketch of the Life of Apollonius of Tyana (New York, 1886).

A. Treloar, Ethiopians, Prudentia 4 (1972), 42-50.

A. Vassileiou, Sur la date des thermes de Néron, Rev. Ét. Anc. 74 (1972), 93-106.

B. Carra de Vaux, Balinus, in: Encyclopaedia of Islam, 1st ed., I (Leiden/Leipzig, 1913), 645.

W. Weinberger, Zur Philostrat-Frage, Philol. 57 (1898), 335-337.

O. Weinreich, Antike Heilungswunder, Religionsgeschichtl. Versuche und Vorarbeiten 8 (Gießen, 1909).

O. Weinreich, Alexander der Lügenprophet und seine Stellung in der Religiosität des zweiten Jahrhunderts nach Christus, Neue Jahrb. f. d. klass. Altertum 47 (1921), 129-151.

O. Weinreich, Antikes Gottmenschentum, Neue Jahrb. f. Wissenschaft u. Jugendbildung 2 (1926), 633-651.

O. Weinreich, Gebet und Wunder, in: Genethliakon W. Schmid zum 70. Geb. (Stuttgart, 1929), 169-464.

M. Wellmann, Die Georgika des Demokritos, Abh. Preuss. Ak. Wiss., phil.-hist. Kl. (Berlin, 1921, Nr. 4).

M. Wellmann, Die ΦΥσIKA des Bolos Demokritos und der Magier Anaxilaos aus Larissa, 1, Abh. Preuß. Ak. Wiss., phil.-hist. Kl. (Berlin, 1928, Nr. 7).

P. Wendland, Antike Geister- und Gespenstergeschichten, Festschrift zur Jahrhundertfeier der Universität Breslau, ed. T. Siebs (Breslau, 1911), 33-55.

P. Wendland, Die hellenistisch-römische Kultur, 3rd ed. (Tübingen, 1912).

T. Whittaker, Apollonius of Tyana and Other Essays (London, 1906).

U. von Wilamowitz-Moellendorff, Der Glaube der Hellenen, ii, 2nd. ed. (Basel, 1956).

U. von Wilamowitz-Moellendorff, Lesefrüchte 198(a), Hermes 60 (1925), 307-313, repr. in: Id., Kleine Schriften, IV (Berlin, 1962), 394-401.

F. A. Wright, A History of Later Greek Literature (London, 1932).

M. Wundt, Apollonius von Tyana: Prophetie und Mythenbildung, Zeits. Wiss. Theol. 49 (1906), 309-366.

E. Zeller, Die Philosophie der Griechen in ihrer geschichtlichen Entwicklung, 2nd. ed., III.2 (Leipzig, 1923).

Simon Swain (essay date 1991)

SOURCE: Swain, Simon. "The Reliability of Philostratus's *The Lives of the Sophists*." *Classical Antiquity* 1, no. 2 (1991): 148-63.

[*In the following essay, Swain provides a summary of the sources Philostratus used in compiling his* Lives of the Sophists, *and how he interpreted and presented the information available to him.*]

For those interested in investigating the Greek society and culture of the first three centuries A.D. Philostratus's record of sophistic activity in the *Lives of the Sophists* (*VS*) is unavoidable. There have been a number of important treatments of the *Lives*, including most recently a useful commentary on those of the sophists who held an official chair of rhetoric at Athens or Rome.[1] The question of the reliability of Philostratus's testimony is still open. In particular, his relationship with his sources, which are so far as we can tell oral, has not been properly explored. In what follows here I wish to consider the material that was available to Philostratus, and how it is packaged by him. The value we place on Philostratus's sources is closely connected with the value he places on them himself. If the *Lives* are intended to be read primarily as a species of literary creation, mention of sources will be seen as part of a standard *Beglaubigungsapparat*. Clearly, the *Lives* can be read in this way. In Reardon's *Courants Littéraires,* the fundamental discussion of the Greek literature of the period, they are naturally categorized as "une série de petites esquisses littéraires, élaborée à partir d'une matière donnée et de façons variées."[2] This judgment is influenced by a comparison with another Philostratean work, the *Imagines,* where Philostratus goes far beyond simple exposition of his imaginary pictures and interprets the narratives with the help of rich allusion to classical myth and literature. But the *Lives of the Sophists* are more than mannered vignettes designed to display Philostratus's command of myth and literature. They can be of real value to us in forming an idea of the social and cultural background of the age known to us from Philostratus as the Second Sophistic, so long as we are aware of Philostratus's own terms of reference.

Philostratus applied the term Second Sophistic to the rhetorical movement that "handled the standard types of the poor men and the rich men and the war heroes and the tyrants and the named subjects that history provides" (*VS* 481). This sort of rhetoric began formally with Aeschines (481, 507), but really with Nicetes of Smyrna in the time of Nero (511). Philostratus's conception was derided by Wilamowitz.[3] Right in terms of the history of rhetoric, Wilamowitz was wrong in that rhetoric is not the principal interest of the *Lives*. When Philostratus says he is to discuss those who are "properly called sophists," as he puts it (479, 492), he is not thinking simply of exponents of a certain type of oratory, but of a group that shared a distinctive set of cultural, social, and political values. Many of the biographies, indeed, have nothing on teaching or rhetorical production and offer no *flosculi* for imitation. The longest biography, that of Herodes Atticus, is a perfect example of this. "It is felicitous," says Philostratus in his preface to the *Lives,* "to know the virtues and vices of a man, where he succeeded or failed, and whether by fortune or judgment" (480). The narrative makes it plain that this statement (which could have come from one of Plutarch's preambles) refers not simply to cultural attainments, but rather to the social, economic, and political criteria that are presented as underpinning and complementing the sophists' *paideia*. It is the economic upturn distinguishing the Greek world of the Principate from that of the Republic that entitles us to apply the term Second Sophistic to this period in terms of Greek history. Economic power brings leisure power, and Philostratus is charting a leisure industry. The sophists discussed by him are shown combining wealth, culture, and power in a way that is especially characteristic of this age, as we know from other literary and lapidary sources.[4]

The diffusion of Second Sophistic culture has been made clear during this century by the unearthing of the epigraphical record, which attests the enormous and widespread popularity of the rhetors and their counterparts in other performance industries, such as theater and pantomime, in terms of their agonistic triumphs, membership on councils, and honorary statues. The ability to travel and the availability of money made the sophists of the Principate. As a practicing sophist himself Philostratus was well placed to capture all this. On the other hand his work on the sage Apollonius of Tyana treats another real figure of this age in a manner that is obviously not biographical, but is rather part encomium, part novel, and is extraordinarily difficult to use as historical testimony.[5] How do we know the *Lives of the Sophists* are any different? The difference between the *Apollonius* and the *Lives* was evident in antiquity. *Apollonius* was viewed as encomium. That is shown by the title it was given (by Philostratus or others), Τὰ ἐς τὸν Τυανέα Ἀπολλώνιον, which Reardon renders correctly as *En l'Honneur d'Apollonios de Tyane*.[6] The title has clear analogues in the Greek novels, where besides those that allude to locality, such as Lollian's *Phoinikika* or Xenophon's *Ephesiaka*, we have Chariton's Τὰ περί Χαιρέαν καὶ Καλιρρόην and Achilles Tatius's Τὰ κατὰ/περὶ Λευκίππην καὶ Κλειτοφῶντα. Consideration of structure and content of *Apollonius* leads us in the same direction. It is in eight books, like the works of Chariton and Tatius. Other characteristics of the novels, travel and adventure, loom large in it. Philostratus's story of the origin of the work, ostensibly an assertion of the fidelity of his source, is in fact a novelistic topos. Philostratus says the work was written up first by a contemporary of Apollonius, Damis, who hailed from Nineveh. The tablets on which Damis wrote his narrative were brought to light by a descendant, and Philostratus claims to be merely restyling the ὑπομνήματα he found.[7] Bowie is almost certainly right to take this story as a compliment to the great sophist Flavius Damianus, whom Philostratus used as an important source for the *Lives of the Sophists* (see below).

What of the *Lives*? Philostratus does not call his work βίοι. He refers only to his λόγος. In her recent commentary Rothe argues that the *Lives* really belong to the genre of λαλιαί, the introductory speeches to declamations, often called διαλέξεις from their conversational tone, which sometimes constituted complete performances.[8] But although Philostratus's relaxed style is suitable for these preambles, and his allusions to οἱ ἐλλόγιμοι—the classical greats—are characteristic of them, the *Lives* differ significantly in lacking the customary appeal to the audience to favor the speaker and to receive his message. This appeal may be seen, for example, in short pieces of Lucian, such as the *Amber,* or *Heracles*.[9] Eunapius was right to refer to Philostratus's work as βίους (454 B. = 2.1.2 G.). The *Lives* are not of course biography in the sense that Suetonius offers it in the *Caesars* or Plutarch in the *Parallels* (but cf. *VS* 480, quoted above). They are rather a sort of cross between biography and the blend of biography and doxography offered by Seneca (*Controversiae*), Suetonius (*De Grammaticis et Rhetoribus*), Favorinus (*Apomnemoneumata*), and Diogenes Laertius. This is an important realization, since, while inference or conjecture is always employed by ancient authors to some extent, the typology here does indicate a commitment to truth.

One concern about the credibility of the biographies focuses on their uneven lengths and varying content. Leo, indeed, was quite affronted by Philostratus's inattention to his own belief in "die fortlaufende Erzählung," a sort of narrative by numbers that he had identified in ancient biography.[10] At the outset Philostratus is awkward. He says that he is not especially interested in listing his subjects' parentage (479-80), which is normally a prerequisite of biographical technique. As a rhetorical commentator Philostratus again behaves improperly. Some of the *Lives,* for example that of Julius Pollux (592-93) or Onomarchus (598-99), do concentrate on rhetorical production, but many more are concerned with the pretense and prestige of the sophists, who fascinate our biographer as much as they fascinate us. One of the least satisfactory aspects of the *Lives* in the view of the older generation of moderns is their failure to record Greek rhetoric between Aeschines in the fourth century B.C. and Nicetes in the first century A.D. Kayser had no hesitation in postulating a lacuna.[11] Wilamowitz's insistence on the continuity of Greek rhetoric from the classical to the imperial age was aimed partly at exposing Philostratus's impercipience.[12] He did not understand Philostratus's approach. There are perhaps three reasons for the omission, all of which must be considered. One has to do with Philostratus's desire of producing a work that reflected the spirit of his age. In this sense it is hardly surprising that he draws the majority of his subjects from the time of Nero and beyond. A second reason, which Philostratus gives implicitly, is connected with his own tastes in rhetoric. Philostratus does in fact allow the continuity of rhetoric at the service of philosophy, and begins the *Lives* with eight philosopher-sophists stretching from the fourth-century Eudoxus of Cnidus to the second-century Favorinus of Arles.[13] However, purely sophistic rhetoric had, he thought, declined to "desperate straits" (but not vanished) before the epiphany of Nicetes (511). Clearly, by placing the biography of Nicetes immediately after that of Aeschines, Philostratus is out to suggest that Nicetes was directly picking up the ancient tradition. The oratory practiced by those "properly called sophists" is characterized by fictional declamation, sometimes on themes offered by history. As has been said, Philostratus believed that Aeschines had initiated this type of speaking (481, 507). A similar opinion was held by Quintilian.[14] Philostratus cannot have been ignorant of those rhetors who intervened between Aeschines and Nicetes. The fame of Hegesias, for example, from the third century was such that stories about him must have circulated in the schools. Or again, Hybreas from the first century was a powerful, charismatic man, who plays a memorable (if brief) role in Plutarch's *Antony* and features in the literary reminiscences of Seneca. Philostratus judged them deficient in talent. His bad opinions of them, perhaps on the grounds of Asianism, and of others who are passed over in silence for whatever reason, must be allowed him, whether they are agreeable to us or not. None of this is to deny that lack of information is another reason for omitting the Hellenistic rhetors. Indeed, given the fact that Philostratus depends greatly on oral sources, it may well be that Nicetes, who lived about 170 years before the *Lives* were published, might represent an upper limit for recollection.

How far can we trust Philostratus's use and understanding of his sources? The answer to this question is not supplied by old-fashioned *Quellenforschung.* There were, of course, other written traditions about the sophists, which were perhaps transmitted through the schools. Hesychius drew on them for his Ὀνοματολόγος and handed them down to the *Suda.* Comparative inquiry with Philostratus's *Lives* appealed to Leo.[15] We do not know what these sources really were. To be sure, Philostratus's account of the sophists of the first to third centuries is unique as far as extant literary texts go. But in using him we are not presented with the problems facing, for example, the historian who uses Cassius Dio's solitary account of Augustus.[16] Naturally, Philostratus like Dio packages and plots his information. But in attempting to define the reliability of the *Lives* from their sources two considerations keep us from *aporia.* First, Philostratus's assessment can be checked against the extensive epigraphic record now available, which confirms the general picture he gives of cash, power, and culture. The importance of this cannot be overstated. Second, consider Philostratus's background. He was a member of the political and economic elite. His wife, Aurelia Melitine, came from a senatorial family, and at least one of his sons was a senator (*I Erythrai* I.63). He knew Julia Domna well, and was friendly with one of the Gordians, to whom the *Lives* are dedicated (479).[17] To distort the substance of the information received from his teachers and friends—members of the same cultural and economic class—would involve Philostratus in a disrespect of which he shows no sign (cf. for example the elaborate compliment in the *Apollonius* mentioned above to the sophist Damianus, who is a major source for the *Lives*). The huge variation in the scope of different biographies suggests in fact that Philostratus did keep closely to what these sources said, and did not treat them in a cavalier fashion by "filling out" when they ran dry.

The *Lives of the Sophists* "were done in Athens." So Bowersock, unimpeachably.[18] What Athenian sources can be traced? First, there is Philostratus himself. He was *de facto* an Athenian.[19] His student days were spent in the city. One of his teachers was the sophist Proclus of Naucratis. Philostratus's statement that he "knew the man well" (602) is borne out by details of Proclus's methods of instruction. Hippodromus of Larissa also features in Philostratus's student memories (617) and those of his son-in-law, Philostratus of Lemnos (617).[20] Information from Hippodromus about his relative Philiscus the Thessalian (621), who held the imperial chair of rhetoric at Athens (622-23), might have supplemented what Philostratus knew of the man from the court of Julia Domna (622).[21] From his "elders," as he calls them, Philostratus heard of Philagrus of Cilicia's unhappy performance in Athens (579-80), when the Cilician sophist was exposed as a fraud.[22] Finally, Philostratus attests to the existence of two statues of the sophist Lollianus (527), one of which is known to us from epigraphy.[23]

The chief beneficiary of Philostratus's access to Athenian sources is the plutocrat Herodes Atticus.[24] Philostratus claims originality to a degree. He tells us that his biography of Herodes was made up "partly of oral information, partly of things unknown to others" (566). Herodes' influence on the sophistic is sometimes decried, and the number of his pupils unkindly scrutinized.[25] He was not simply a rhetor, of course, and Philostratus brings out his leading political and cultural role very well. Memories of Herodes and his family would have survived to attract our biographer. Philostratus "heard" details of the extravaganza of Herodes' Panathenaic festival in 140 (550).[26] Less widely known—perhaps one of the ἠγνοημένα ἑτέροις—may be Herodes' secret desire to slice the Isthmus, which he revealed to one Ctesidemus, who regaled Philostratus with the story in turn (552).[27] Philostratus knew Ctesidemus well enough to send him a note on the propriety of erotic letters (*Ep.* 68, 255 K.²). As an epistolographer himself Philostratus thought highly of Herodes' epistolary style (*Dial.* 1, 258 K.²). Use of his letters is clear.[28] One to the rebel Avidius Cassius was proof of τὰ τῆς γνώμης ὅπλα: "Herodes to Cassius. You were mad" (*VS* 563).

Another letter of Herodes, written to Barbarus,[29] gives details of declamations held by the sophist Polemon over a three-day period at Smyrna (537-38).[30] The letter raises a problem of chronology. The occasion mentioned seems to be identical to that described immediately before (536-37), where Herodes is said to have come to Smyrna τὸν Πολέμωνα δὲ οὔπω γιγνώσκων in order to study with him (ἐπὶ ξυνουσίᾳ). Philostratus asserts that this meeting took place at the time when Herodes was *diorthōtēs* of the free cities, an office that can be dated by his traffic accident in the Troad with the future Antoninus Pius during his proconsulship of Asia in 134-35/135-36 (554-55).[31] It is thus implied that Herodes had not heard Polemon's speech at the inauguration of the Olympieion in Athens at the end of 131 or the beginning of 132,[32] something that seems unlikely (despite Herodes' tribunate at Rome during 131).[33] If there is an error, the cause may lie in the fact that the information Herodes gives to Barbarus on Polemon seems to postdate Barbarus's consulship in 157.[34] Herodes is looking back over twenty years, and it is possible that Philostratus has become confused about the time of the meeting sketched in the epistle. Moreover, there is an element of suspense in the late meeting of such great men, which improves the tale.[35] It is, however, easier and more plausible to accept Philostratus's account. Herodes may well have been in Rome from his quaestorship in 129 to his practorship in 133.[36]

By the time he met Polemon he was plainly advanced in both his political and his rhetorical careers.[37] At the meeting Herodes believes initially that Polemon will hesitate "to run a risk before such a man as himself" (537). In fact Polemon straightaway delivers "a long and appropriate encomium" on Herodes' political and oratorical achievements (537, λόγων τε καὶ ἔργων). Finally, after three days of declamatory prowess, which costs Herodes 250,000 dr., it is Herodes who hesitates and "conceded to Polemon not to come against him in an oratorical display nor to declaim after him, but to leave Smyrna by night lest he should be compelled (for he thought that even to be compelled [to speak against Polemon] would seem bold)" (538-39).[38] The theme of Herodes' modesty before the maestro is continued ("he kept on . . . praising Polemon and saying how wonderful he was"), and Herodes tells his correspondent Barbarus that "I had such and such a teacher when I was being taught, but Polemon when I was already teaching" (539), a statement that again suggests an established reputation for Herodes in rhetoric and adds weight to the contention that he did not meet Polemon until the mid-130s.

The letter to Barbarus is a precious document for its description of Polemon's stage technique (σκηνή). Apart from the lengthy narrative of Herodes and Agathion (the wild man cultivated by Herodes for the purity of his Attic [552-54]), which is related from "one of the letters to Julian,"[39] the letter to Barbarus is the only occasion in the *Lives* when Philostratus avers that he is making extensive use of a written source.[40] That is worth stressing. In the introduction to his *Lives of the Philosophers and Sophists* Eunapius suggests that Philostratus "spat out his *Lives* in a cursory, glib manner" (454 B. = 2.1.2 G.). The disparagement has not gone unnoticed.[41] The basis of Eunapius's scorn is that, while he uses oral information like Philostratus, he also claims membership of an elite written tradition of biography (453-55 B. = 1.1.5-2.2.8 G.). Eunapius does not in fact justify his claim to have used "precise commentaries," whose mistakes he solicitously disavows. By contrast Philostratus seems more revealing about his own oral sources. For example, the meeting between Dionysius of Miletus and Polemon of Sardis "I heard of from Aristaeus, who was the oldest of the Hellenes [i.e., πεπαιδευμένοι] in my time and knew most about sophists" (*VS* 524-25). Again, Megistias of Smyrna, a preeminent physiognomist and no doubt rhetor besides, told Philostratus of the visit to his school and to Smyrna by Hippodromus of Larissa (618-19). Aristaeus and Megistias might well have provided further information; they are only cited for particular incidents. Of much higher importance is the sophist Damianus of Ephesus (605-6).[42] Philostratus met Damianus thrice in Damianus's old age (606). It is a good indication of his unevenness in reporting the sophists' interests that there is much on Damianus's wealth and building activities, but only a brief and superficial verdict on his output as a speaker (cf. Herodes). Damianus's value to Philostratus lay in his study with Aristides at Smyrna and Hadrian at Ephesus. "Whatever I have recorded about these men I stated on the authority of Damianus, who knew both well" (605). The *Life* of Hadrian in fact makes no mention of Ephesus. It begins with information about Hadrian's student days under Herodes Atticus, which Philostratus heard of "from my own teachers" (585-86)—meaning perhaps Antipater of Hierapolis, a pupil of Hadrian (606-7)—[43] then develops to Hadrian's imperial chair at Athens (586-89), his chair at Rome (589), and finally his belated appointment as *ab ep. gr.* (590). Much of this, but not what came "from my own teachers,"[44] will have originated from Damianus. That Philostratus passes over Hadrian's period of residence at Ephesus, where he is attested in the 160s honoring M. Aurelius's son-in-law, Cn. Claudius Severus, may be attributed to his own Athenocentricity rather than to a lack of sophistic activity on Hadrian's part before he assumed the Athenian chair in 176 (586-87, 588-89).[45]

The *Life* of Aristides precedes that of Hadrian. Damianus is cited for the first meeting between the sophist and M. Aurelius at Smyrna (582-83). But Philostratus did not rely only on him: "I have not given the theme of the declamation [before Marcus], since people report it differently" (583; Megistias may be meant). Damianus is then credited again in a note on Aristides' attitude to improvisation. Philostratus notes variants concerning Aristides' death, including perhaps written accounts (585, γράφουσιν). As with Hadrian it is difficult to gauge the degree of dependence on Damianus. Aristides' own works are important—more so than for any other of the sophists except Polemon—and Philostratus spends a quarter of the *Life* quoting from them. His source for these works is the doxographical/school tradition, as is shown by the quotation of extracts and titles that show Aristides' merits and demerits. Damianus may also have helped out. It was pointed out by von Arnim that such stylistic examples in the **Lives** come mainly from declamations and are quite likely to have been circulated by versions taken down shorthand during delivery, perhaps by unauthorized copyists.[46] Clearly, though, Philostratus had access to fully published material also. In the case of Aristides he seems to assume the availability of the speeches whose titles are cited in support of the sophist, and indeed one of these, "The Speakers' Deliberations Concerning Affairs in Sicily" (584), represents orations 5 and 6 in the surviving corpus. One thing is sure: the selection offered for Aristides, of objectionable and of commendable passages, is typically Philostratean in its preference for historical themes.[47] Damianus's anecdote about the meeting between Aristides and Marcus stands out from

this material, and elaboration by Damianus or by Philostratus (and probably by both) should not be denied; complete fiction should never have been suggested.[48] On one point only may Damianus as reported by Philostratus be wrong: his claim to have paid Aristides 10,000 dr. (605) for tuition is contradicted by Aristides' boast that he never charged (*Or.* 3.99 L.-B., 28.127 K., 33.19 K.), unless of course the money was offered and taken *ex gratia*.

As one would expect, then, Philostratus uses other sources in addition to Damianus, even for Aristides and Hadrian. That does not disallow Damianus prominence among his oral sources. Information on some of the other sophists must have come from him. Dionysius of Miletus taught first at Lesbos (526), then established himself at Ephesus (568, κατέχοντος), where he died greatly honored with burial in the agora (526).[49] Through Damianus Philostratus may have gained information about those who studied with his teacher Hadrian, like Apollonius of Naucratis (600), and Apollonius of Athens (601).[50] Lollianus of Ephesus is an obvious candidate for Damianus's local knowledge. Damianus may also be responsible in part for the list of worthless sophists dismissed at the beginning of his *Life* (605), though the scorn is as likely to come from Philostratus himself. It is interesting that among the condemned is Soterus, who is honored by the Ephesians in two inscriptions of Antonine/Severan date, one at Delphi, the other at Ephesus.[51] The Ephesian text hails Soterus for his move to the city from Athens, secured at the second attempt by the lure of 10,000 dr. (equivalent to the salary of the imperial chair at Athens). The denigration of Soterus at least is likely to reflect enmity between him and Damianus.[52] One of the other ridiculed sophists, Phylax, is more probably contemned by Philostratus, since he is almost certainly the brother of Philostratus's previous subject, Phoenix of Thessaly, who is damned with the faintest of praise (604).[53]

Most of the activity of the sophists was, of course, in the East; some information was available to Philostratus about those who worked in the West. Heliodorus "the Arab" was observed by our biographer on the make before Caracalla among the Gauls (625-26), and "is growing old at Rome, neither admired nor neglected." Since Philostratus lived at Rome for a number of years, information about sophists in Rome, for example, Hadrian's deathbed appointment as imperial secretary, or Euodianus's final injunction to his friends (597), doubtless stems from oral sources in the capital. Philostratus must have met Aelian there (cf. 625, ἔφασκε). Aspasius of Ravenna "was teaching in Rome, having grown quite old, when these things were being written by me" (628). Other Western information is provided by Philostratus of Lemnos. Philostratus's son-in-law quarreled with Aspasius in Rome and Ionia (627-28).

The Lemnian's disdain for Aelian is also noted (625), and either he or Philostratus himself may have been at Rome to see Philiscus of Thessaly lose his immunity before Caracalla (622-23).[54]

Philostratus's data can often be checked, and he is mostly found to be correct: for example, Aristides' statue at Smyrna from the citizens of the Delta (582), Dionysius's appointment as "satrap" (i.e., procurator; 524), Damianus's building program at Ephesus (605), Herodes' stadium at Delphi (551), the curse inscriptions on statues of Herodes' foster sons (558-59), and so on.[55] Some errors are simple slips. Herodes' daughter is called Panathenais in the *Lives* (557), but is known from epigraphy only as Athenais.[56] The birthplace of Aelius Aristides is almost certainly Hadrianeutherae rather than Hadriani (581).[57] A more serious mistake concerns Philostratus's statement that Herodes ἐτέλει μὲν ἐκ πατέρων ἐς τοὺς δισυπάτους (545; cf. 536, *Suda* H 544), since there is no evidence that Atticus was consul twice (and indeed no certain *cos. suff. II* is known after 104).[58] A similar mistake is probably made about Aristocles (ἐτέλει μὲν γὰρ ἐς ὑπάτους, 567), for whom no consular ancestors are known.[59] However, other errors, omissions, or areas of confusion are located where none exist (e.g., the arbitrary change of "Barbarus" to "Varus," Herodes' Athenian chair of rhetoric, Favorinus's claim for immunity).[60] The temptation to do this stems from the anecdotal nature of much of the material Philostratus purveys. Our prejudice is at fault, not his reporting.

A particular charge of unreliability is made against Philostratus on the basis of his omission of certain sophists. The charge is unfair. The title "sophist" is slippery. It is not uncommon in inscriptions, and many who held it or claimed it will not have been worthy exponents. The word itself should be scrutinized. Does Philostratus use it correctly? Interpretation of "sophist" turns upon Galen's allusion to Ἀδριανὸς ὁ ῥήτωρ, οὔπω σοφιστεύων ἀλλ' ἔτι συνὼν τῷ Βοηθῷ (in 163; see *supra*, n. 45). For Philostratus Hadrian had a marked sophistic bent from the beginning ("the displayed a great natural talent for sophistic, and it was quite clear that he would go a long way," 585), whereas Galen seems to imply that Hadrian did not become a sophist until many years after his training. The Galenic passage has been taken as a starting point for uncovering the meaning of the word. Bowersock has correctly observed that "sophist" appears to be contained within the term "rhetor," and designates someone who was "a virtuoso rhetor with a big public reputation." Bowie has rightly stressed that the employment of the verb σοφιστεύων is significant, pointing to the "pursuit of a career" involving public performances as the hallmark of a sophist.[61]

One aspect of the pursuit of a sophistic career was the requirement to travel widely, making oneself known to as large an audience as possible. Galen's remark could be read in conformity to this—Hadrian was still a rhetor, not one of those who traveled around as professionals, and was residing at Rome in the house of his friend and countryman, the peripatetic philosopher and consul Flavius Boethus.[62] However, the accepted distinction between rhetor and sophist may ironically not be that intended in the *De Praecognitione* passage. The facts of Hadrian's career suggest that Galen has something more particular in mind. No one will believe that Hadrian, who was at least fifty at the time Galen is recalling (163), had never yet given public declamations.[63] Further, there is evidence that suggests he had in fact embarked on a career as a sophist before 163. Certainly Hadrian was no ordinary rhetor, if we may judge him by his pupils from the 150s or earlier. Philostratus says of Damianus that "when Aristides and Hadrian were in control respectively of Smyrna and of Ephesus, he attended the lectures of both at a cost of 10,000 dr." (605).[64] Damianus must have been born about 135,[65] and is therefore likely to have been a pupil of Hadrian during the 150s. That cannot be proved. However, there are other pupils of Hadrian (Apollonius of Naucratis, Apollonius of Athens, Proclus of Naucratis), who come before Damianus in the *Lives*. Everything supports the thought that Philostratus orders his subjects in a roughly chronological series. One of these pupils, Proclus, lived to be ninety (604). His biography is separated from that of Damianus by that of Phoenix. We may assume that Proclus was born before Damianus (say 120-25) and died after (say 210-15). When he was a νέος (i.e., up to 30) at Athens, Proclus "attended the school of Hadrian ['Ἀδριανῷ ἐφοίτα]" (603). Hadrian, then, was teaching at Athens in the 150s or even 140s distinguished pupils who graduated as sophists.

Lucian's *Pseudologista*, in which Hadrian is maliciously arraigned, reveals a sophistic career for Hadrian himself. The main dispute between Lucian and Hadrian seems to have occurred at Ephesus in 163 or 164,[66] but the seeds had been sown at an Olympic Games some time before, when Lucian had laughed at Hadrian for feigning the extempore speech "Pythagoras Is Excluded from Initiation at Eleusis Because He Is a Barbarian" (*Pseud.* 5). Hadrian is there called a "sophist" (cf. 25). The games of 165, when Lucian was present (Hieronymus, *Chron.* 204.24-26 H.[2]; Lucian, *Peregr.* 35), are clearly too late. Those of 161, 157, or 153, when Lucian was also present (*Peregr.* 35), come into account. The fake improvisation had been "written up long before [πρὸ πολλοῦ συγγεγραμμένον]" it was delivered at Olympia. Philagrus of Cilicia's similar attempt to pass off an old piece as an extempore production at Athens (*VS* 579) makes it quite clear that Hadrian is here engaging in sophistic activity.[67] This activity can be placed many years before Galen would appear to allow. The title "sophist" is applied to Hadrian by Lucian also at the time of the Ephesian quarrel (8; 9, ἀοίδιμος; cf. *VS* 589). In 19 Hadrian is ῥήτωρ καὶ σοφιστής. We know from other sources that Hadrian was at Athens, Ephesus, and Rome. Lucian lists these and a number of other cities and countries as the scene of Hadrian's unprofessional conduct (5, 10, 20, 21, 22, 27). We may assume professional activity in these places too. And in the end it is Hadrian's traveling between famous centers like Alexandria and Antioch (cf. Libanius, *Or.* 64 *Pro Salt.* 41) that certainly marks him out as a sophist.

There are no good grounds for maintaining that Hadrian was not a sophist at the time when Galen calls him as a rhetor. What, then, does Galen mean? The *De Praecognitione* was written in 178.[68] Might it not be that Galen's οὔπω σοφιστεύων is pointing to Hadrian's official position at Athens, or even Rome, after 176 ("not yet [in 163] holding a professorship [as he is now in 178], but living [or studying?] with Boethus")? If that is correct, it does not undermine the general sense of the term "sophist" as it is now understood (partly from *De Praecogn.*). Rather, Galen is seen to be in a very particular train of thought, alluding momentarily to Hadrian's current official position in 178.[69] What, after all, was Hadrian doing in Rome in the early 160s? Even if M. Aurelius did not hear him till 176 in Athens (*VS* 588-89), it is difficult to imagine that he gave no display of his talents at Rome, but simply taught quietly in a school. In sum, Philostratus is probably correct in his contention that when Hadrian arrived at Herodes' school he was already a sophist in the making.

It has been suggested by Jones that Philostratus uses the terms "philosopher," "sophist," and "rhetor" with "confusing and undue rigidity."[70] But as Jones noted himself Herodes Atticus (for example) is called "rhetor" by Philostratus in *Dialexeis* (258 K.[2]), and in the *Lives* "sophist" by Alexander Clay-Plato (574), "one of the Ten [rhetors]" by his supporters, "the stuffed rhetor" by his critics (564-65). On the definition of Bowersock and Bowie "sophist" is included within the term "rhetor"— one does not cease to be a rhetor when one becomes a sophist. This is reflected in Philostratus. In the case of Herodes, indeed, different contexts produce the different labels. In *Dialexeis* 1 Philostratus is talking of Herodes' skill at composing letters, not declamation (hence rhetor); Alexander's remark comes immediately after a virtuoso performance by Herodes; Herodes' supporters could hardly have called him "one of the Ten Sophists," "the Ten" being, of course, the Attic canon; similarly, Herodes' detractors could not (on the pages of Philostratus; contrast Lucian, above) have dignified him with the title "sophist." Philostratus is not especially rigid in applying the term "sophist," nor ignorant of its applica-

tion. The list of six bogus sophists given at *Lives* 605 is a case in point. They clearly claimed to be sophists— that is why Philostratus remarks that they should rather be called ἀθύρματα. We can say that Damianus misled Philostratus about one of these men, Soterus, while another, Phylax, is probably belittled (justly or not) by Philostratus himself (see above); but we may ask whether the other four should really have been included if the *Lives* were to be any sense selective. Again, if Attalus, the son of Polemon, is omitted as a sophist,[71] Philostratus clearly felt he had good reason to do so (cf. 544, "the qualities of Polemon went no further than Polemon," etc.). Attalus is in fact mentioned *en passant* at 609, as are two other sophists, Nicomedes and Diodotus, who are attested epigraphically.[72] Again, if the *Suda* refers to Hadrian's secretary Julius Vestinus as a sophist (O 835), it also makes it plain that his oeuvre was primarily scholarly, as does his career, so that Philostratus's silence is justifiable.[73] Philostratus would probably have justified what looks like a serious omission—the complete absence of Alexandrian sophists—in some similar way. Only in the case of Lesbonax of Mytilene is it possible (that is all) that personal enmity on the part of our biographer lies behind his exclusion.[74]

Lies, lapses, the license of memory—these were traps for Philostratus as for anyone dependent on oral sources. They should not be held against him. Philostratus was no doubt capable of supplying τὰ δέοντα: for example, the calumniation of Scopelian by Cytherus, his father's cook (517). However, note that these words (at any rate) are introduced as τοιαυτὶ λέγων—Philostratus makes no claim for their veracity. Other snatches of converse may also reasonably be suspected. But, as has been indicated, the Philostratus of the *Lives* is not the same as the Philostratus of the *Apollonius,* where (for example) Apollonius's (undelivered) apologia before Domitian (8.7) is a remarkably sustained piece of fiction, accorded fake realism by an introductory analysis of style (8.6). In the *Lives of the Sophists* the conversation between Herodes and Ctesidemus, for which Ctesidemus is the avowed source (cf. above), should never have been impugned, at least as far as Philostratus is concerned (Ctesidemus's truthfulness and memory are another matter).[75] Philostratus could only report what he was told. That is of course most often the cause of his limitations for us. He himself is gullible on certain points (Herodes' defense for murder: τἀληθὲς ἴσχυεν, 556;[76] M. Aurelius's suspicions of L. Verus, 560-61[77]). He can be unclear (the poor distinction between the municipal and imperial chairs of rhetoric;[78] Herodes' δευτέραν κλήρωσιν τῆς ὑπάτου ἀρχῆς, 556[79]). On the other hand, he is not afraid of confessing uncertainty (the origin of the quarrel with the Quintilii, 559; the burial places of many of the sophists); this is not simply a literary ploy. Taking everything together, it seems that, unless we can be sure that Philostratus's information is muddled or mistaken, we should be inclined to believe it.

Notes

1. C. L. Kayser, *Philostrati Opera*^{2} (Leipzig, 1871) iii-x; U. von Wilamowitz, *Hermes* 35 (1900) 9-14 = *Kl. Schr.* III (Berlin, 1969) 231-36; F. Leo, *Die griechische-römische Biographie nach ihrer literarischen Form* (Leipzig, 1901) 254-59; K. Münscher, *Philologus* Suppl. X.4 (1907) 469ff., esp. 491-96; F. Solmsen, *RE* [*Real-Encyclopädie der Klassischen Altertumswissenshaft*] XX.1 (1941) 171-73; G. W. Bowersock, *Greek Sophists in the Roman Empire* (Oxford, 1969), esp. ch. 1; B. P. Reardon, *Courants littéraires grecs des IIe et IIIe siècles après J.-C.* (Paris, 1971), 115-19, 188-89; C. P. Jones, in G. W. Bowersock, ed., *Approaches to the Second Sophistic* (University Park, Pa., 1974) 11-16; G. W. Bowersock, in P. E. Easterling and B. M. W. Knox, eds., *Cambridge History of Classical Literature* 1 (Cambridge, 1985) 655-58; A. Brancacci, *Rhetorike philosophousa: Dione Crisostomo nella cultura antica e bizantina* (Naples, 1985) 82-110; G. Anderson, *Philostratus* (New York, 1986), esp. chs. 2-6; S. Rothe, *Kommentar zu ausgewählten Sophistenviten des Philostratos* (Heidelberg, 1989), esp. 1-36.

These works are referred to by author's name (N. B. "Bowersock" means *Greek Sophists*), as also are W. Ameling, *Herodes Atticus* I-II (Hildesheim, 1983); and H. Halfmann, *Die Senatoren aus dem östlichen Teil des Imperium Romanum bis zum Ende des zweiten Jahrhunderts n. Chr.* (Göttingen, 1979).

2. Reardon, 188.

3. Wilamowitz 13-14 = 235.

4. Cf. Münscher 494: "Wir spüren in Phil.s Buche den Pulsschlag seiner Zeit-das ist und bleibt sein Verdienst".

5. See E. L. Bowie, *ANRW* [*Aufstieg und Niedergang der Römischen Welt*] II.16.2 (1978) 1652-99.

6. Reardon 189. This use of ἐς/εἰς is often found in the lemmata of the *Anth. Pal.* with a like meaning. On what follows, note esp. Bowie (*supra*, n. 5) 1663-65, 1670-71.

7. There are close parallels for the origin of the *Apollonius* in the alleged origin of Antonius Diogenes' *Incredible Tales Beyond Thule* (Photius, *Bibl.* 166, 111b), of Dictys Cretensis's *Diary of the Trojan War* (prologue = 2-3 Eisenhut^2; 5.17 = 119

Eisenhut^2), both probably earlier than Philostratus, and in one of the versions of *The History of Apollonius King of Tyre* (β 51 = 411 Kortekaas).

8. Rothe 35-36.

9. Cf. D. A. Russell, *Greek Declamation* (Cambridge, 1983) 77-79.

10. Leo 256.

11. Kayser ix.

12. Wilamowitz 9-10, 12-14 = 231-32, 234-35.

13. See Brancacci 89-90.

14. Quintilian *Inst. Or.* 2.41; cf. Russell (*supra*, n. 9) 19.

15. Leo 256ff.

16. Cf. J. W. Rich, in A. Cameron, ed., *History as Text* (London, 1989), 87-110.

17. Julia Domna: Bowersock 101-9. Gordian: Ameling II.21-22; Rothe 5-6.

18. Bowersock 5-6.

19. Cf. *SIG*^{3} 878, Φλ. Φιλόστρατον Ἀθηναῖον (Olympia).

20. On the problems of the precise relationship between these Philostrati, see most recently Anderson 293.

21. Hippodromus: H. Müller, *ZPE* [*Zeitschrift für Papyrologie und Epigraphik*] 3 (1968) 207-9. Philiscus: R. Flacelière, *FD* [*Fouilles de Delphes*] III.4 (1954) no. 273.

22. On the incident, note A. J. Papalas, *RCCM* [*Rivista di Cultura Classica e Medioevale*] 21-22 (1979-80) 93-104; see also *infra*, n. 67.

23. *IG* [*Inscriptiones Graecae*] II/III^2 4211; see J. Keil, *JÖAI* [*Jahreshefte des österreichischen archäologischen Instituts*] 40 (1953) 8-9.

24. On his career, see P. Graindor, *Un milliardaire antique: Hérode Atticus et sa famille* (Cairo, 1930); Halfmann no. 68; Ameling. Apart from oral sources there were available to Philostratus ἐπιστολαὶ δὲ πλεῖσται Ἡρώδου καὶ διαλέξεις καὶ ἐφημερίδες ἐγχειρίδιά τε καὶ καίρια τὴν ἀρχαίαν πολυμάθειαν ἐν βραχεῖ ἀπηνθισμένα (*VS* 565). Given all this material, uncorroborated statements found in the literary sources may be discounted (e.g., the report of Aristides' *Prolegomena* that Herodes in the 150s was ὁ τὸν θρόνον ἐπέχων τὸν σοφιστικόν [114 L. = 739 D.]; cf. I. Avotins, *HSCP* [*Harvard Studies in Classical Philology*] 79 [1975] 315-16, 319; note that acceptance is urged by Ameling I.126 n. 53).

25. Graindor (*supra*, n. 24) 155-56 (cf. Anderson 85: "too sweeping").

26. Note M. L. Clarke (*CP* [*Classical Philology*] 68 [1973] 120) for the suggestion that *Ciris* 21-35 reflects the festival of that year. On the date, cf. Ameling II.14.

27. Cf. Bowerstock 3; B. Baldwin (*Studies in Lucian* [Toronto, 1973] 28) on the relation between Herodes' plan and ps.-Lucian, *Nero*, which is probably to be identified with the *Nero* attributed to Philostratus's father.

28. They were "vielleicht nur sinngemäss zitiert" (Ameling 1.119).

29. M. Vettulenus Civica Barbarus, *cos. ord.* 157, uncle of L. Verus (Eck, *RE* Suppl. XIV [1974] 845-46; G. Alföldy, *Konsulat und Senatorenstand unter den Antoninen* [Bonn, 1977] 328, further in index s.v.; Halfmann 209). For Herodes' friendship, see Ameling II, no. 188. N.B. some earlier editions of the *Lives* arbitrarily changed the MSS. lection at 537 and 539 to *Varus;* see Graindor (*supra*, n. 24) 157-58; I. and M. Avotins, *An Index to the Lives of the Sophists of Philostratus* (Hildesheim, 1978) 52.

30. Cf. M. Aurelius in Fronto, *ad M. Caes.* 2.7.1 v.d.H. 29: "Polemona ante hoc triduum declamantem audivimus" (Naples, 143).

31. On the date, see Ameling II.2 n. 9 (with literature); add W. Eck, *Chiron* 13 (1983) 178 (135-36).

32. Date: H. Halfmann, *Itinera Principum* (Stuttgart, 1986) 208-9.

33. Amelling I.51, II.4 n. 23, 105 no. 76.

34. Barbarus is "consul" the second time he is mentioned (539). On ὕπατος in Philostratus, see *infra*, n. 79.

35. Cf. perhaps Polemon and Dionysius of Miletus (524, ἐγήρασκε μὲν ὁ Διονύσιος ἐν δόξῃ λαμπρᾷ, παρῄει δ᾽ ἐς ἀκμὴν [aged ca. 35] ὁ Πολέμων οὔπω γιγνωσκόμενος τῷ Διονυσίῳ). There is no real cause to suspect M. Aurelius's delayed meeting with the sophists Aelius Aristides (582-83) and Hadrian of Tyre (588) in 176.

36. Ameling I.51 ("vermutlich"), II.4 n. 23.

37. Political career: Ameling I.48ff., II.1ff. Rhetorical career: cf. *VS* 567 (Ti. Claudius) Aristocles of Pergamum ἐς τοὺς τοφιστὰς μετερρύη θαμίζων ἐν τῇ ῾Ρώμῃ τῷ ῾Ηρώδῃ διατιθεμένῳ σχεδίους λόγους. This must belong to the period 129-33, for Aristocles seems to have been a teacher himself by the later 130s, taking Aelius Aristides

(at Pergamum, 581), who was born 26 Nov. 117 (C. A. Behr, *AJP* [*American Journal of Philology*] 90 [1969] 77), and Herodes was not again in Rome till 140/1 (Ameling I.71). Aristedes himself studied at Athens κατὰ τὴν ῾Ηρώδου ἀκμήν (*VS* 581), which the *Suda* (A 3902) reasonably interprets as ἠκροάσατο δὲ ῾Ηρώδου κατὰ τὰς ᾿Αθήνας. This will have been in the later 130s after Herodes' office as corrector; but Herodes did teach in Athens earlier, in the 120s, since Hadrian of Tyre, born 105-10 (C. P. Jones, *GRBS* [*Greek, Roman, and Byzantine Studies*] 13 [1972] 480-85; my note to appear in *CP* 85 [1990]), became his student about the age of 18 (*VS* 585), when Herodes himself (b. 101-3) was not more than 25.

38. To translate this passage taking Polemon as the subject of the infinitives (e.g., Wright in the Loeb) is plainly wrong; cf. Ameling I.59 n. 65.

39. Ti. Claudius Julianus, *cos. suff.* 154-56; see Bowersock 78-79; Halfmann no. 94; Ameling II.180.

40. Note other short examples from Herodes' correspondence to Favorinus (490); from Polemon (543); to and from M. Aurelius (562-63).

41. A. Brancacci, *Elenchos* 6 (1985) 396-400.

42. For his well-connected family, see the stemmata at *Forsch. in Eph.* III (1923) 166-68 (Keil); *PIR²* [*Prosopographia Imperii Romani*, second edition] [III.178 (Groag); *IEphesos* VII.1, p. 90.

43. Note that Antipater, Severus's *ab epist. gr.,* was known also to Philostratus's father: *Suda* Φ 422 (Bowersock 3-4).

44. Münscher (476) and Solmsen (136) wrongly include Damianus as a teacher of Philostratus.

45. On Hadrian's activity as a sophist before 176, see below. Claudius Severus (Halfmann no. 101): *IEphesos* V.1539; this is securely dated before 168-69 (R. Syme, *Historia* 17 [1968] 102 = *Roman Papers* II [Oxford, 1979] 690) and after 163, when Hadrian was staying with Flavius Boethus (Halfmann no. 95) at Rome in the first summer of Galen's first visit (Galen, *De Praecogn.* 14.627 K. = 96 Nutton, ᾿Αδριανὸς ὁ ῥήτωρ, οὔπω σοφιστεύων ἀλλ᾽ ἔτι συνών τῷ Βοηθῷ; on the date, see V. Nutton, *CQ* [*Classical Quarterly*] 23 [1973] 158ff.); see also E. L. Bowie, *ANRW* II.33.1 (1989) 247. Hadrian's residence in Ephesus during the early 160s is suggested also by the sure identification of Hadrian with Lucian's enemy in *Pseudologista*, a work that probably dates to that decade (see Jones [*supra*, n. 37] 478-86; *id.*, *Culture and Society in Lucian* [Cambridge, Mass., 1986] 110-15). For Hadrian's assumption of the Athenian chair, see Avotins (*supra*, n. 24) 320; Ameling I.159.

46. H. von Arnim, *Leben und Werke des Dion von Prusa* (Berlin, 1898) 172-79; cf. Münscher 494 n. 57.

47. Of the 87 titles that may safely be attributed to Aristides (incl. fragments) Philostratus cites 9 (36%) of the 25 historical themes and 9 (14.5%) of the 62 other works. Similar distortion is found with other subjects in the *Lives*.

48. U. von Wilamowitz, *Sitzungsberichte der Preussischen Akademie der Wissenschaften*, Phil.-hist. Kl., (1925) 345. Cf. C. A. Behr, *Aelius Aristides and the Sacred Tales* (Amsterdam, 1968) 142. Note also the fancies about Aristides, Herodes, and the meeting of Aristides with Marcus at Smyrna, in A. J. Papalas, *Aevum* 53 (1979) 88-93.

49. *IEphesos* II.426 (Τ[ίτος] Κλαύδιος Φλαουιανὸς Διονύσιος ῥήτωρ). Dionysius was in fact buried just outside the tetragonal agora, under the ramp leading from the Street of Marble to the small piazza immediately behind the south gate of the agora and before the Library of Celsus (cf. C. P. Jones, *GRBS* 21 [1980] 374; E. Atalay, *JÖAI* 52 Beiblatt [1978-80] 53-58); Philostratus is not completely accurate (cf. *Bull.* 1971 no. 574), but to say that "we now know that [the burial] was elsewhere in the city" (Jones 15) is essentially misleading.

50. Antipater, also a pupil of Hadrian and teacher of Philostratus, will have been the major source.

51. Flacelière (*supra*, n. 21) no. 265; *IEphesos* V.1546; discussion in Keil (*supra*, n. 23) 15-18; see also Bowie (*supra*, n. 45) 248.

52. Cf. Keil (*supra*, n. 23) 23 (= *IEphesos* III.826) for another Ephesian sophist unknown from Philostratus; two other sophists suggested by Keil (23-24) are doubtful (cf. *IEphesos* III.825, V.1789).

53. "Phoenix of Thessaly deserves neither admiration nor yet complete contempt" (cf. the disparagement of Pollux, 592); see C. P. Jones, *BCH* [*Bulletin de correspondance hellénique*] 96 (1972) 265-67.

54. Cf. Münscher 480, Solmsen 137.

55. Statue of Aristides at Smyrna: cf. that erected by the residents of the Delta at Alexandria, *OGIS* [*Orientis Graeci Inscriptiones Selectae*] 709. Dionysius as procurator: *IEphesos* VII.1.3047. Damianus's building program: D. Knibbe, *ANRW* II.7.2 (1980) 790-91. Herodes' Delphic stadium: P. Aupert, *FD* II (1979) 174. Curse inscriptions: Ameling II. 23ff.

56. Ameling II.18 n. 21; cf. also T. D. Barnes, *Phoenix* 26 (1972) 148.

57. W. M. Ramsay, *The Historical Geography of Asia Minor* (London, 1890) 157 with addenda 437, looks conclusive (so L. Robert, *Études anatoliennes* [Paris, 1937] 207 n. 1); Philostratus is supported by Behr (*supra*, n. 48) 3 n. 3.

58. Ameling I.27.

59. Cf. *PIR*² C 789; Halfmann no. 121.

60. Barbarus/Varus: *supra*, n. 29. Herodes' chair of rhetoric: *supra*, n. 24. Favorinus: Philostratus's account is impugned by A. Barigazzi, *Favorino di Arelate: Opere* (Florence, 1966) 7-9; see my paper in *ZPE* 79 (1989) 150-58.

61. Bowersock 12-14; E. L. Bowie, in M. I. Finley, ed., *Studies in Antiquity* (London, 1974) 169 (cf. *YCLS* [*Yale Classical Studies*] 27 [1982] 39); cf. also G. R. Stanton, *AJP* 94 (1973) 350-64.

62. On Boethus cf. *supra*, n. 45.

63. Galen's phrase cannot apply to Hadrian "in his earlier years" (Bowersock 12).

64. For κατειληφότοιν, τοῦ μὲν τὴν Σμύρναν, τοῦ δὲ τὴν ʼʼΕφεσον, cf. 568, κατέχοντος [Dionysius] ἤδη τὴν Ἐφεσίων.

65. Cf. my note to appear in *JHS* [*Journal of Hellenic Studies*] 111 (1991).

66. 163; Jones (*supra*, n. 37) 484-85 (Jones [*supra*, n. 45] 115 is more cautious). 164: V. Nutton, ed., *Galeni De Praecognitione*, CMG [*Corpus Medicorum Graecorum*] V.8.1 (1979), 190 n. 4. The essay was probably composed at the same time in Ephesus.

67. Von Arnim (*supra*, n. 46: 177) suggests the two cases are different because Philagrus's piece had probably been published without his knowledge; however, Philostratus makes it clear that Philagrus regularly passed off "stale pieces" as improvisations and had, indeed, learned the piece in question by heart (μνήμην ξυνελέξατο; on this translation, see Rothe 76).

68. Nutton (*supra*, n. 66) 50.

69. *Contra* Nutton (*supra*, n. 66) 190: "The phrase οὔπω σοφιστεύων cannot be pressed to indicate that [Hadrian] was already the holder of the . . . chair at Athens when 'On Prognosis' was written . . . it merely denotes the difference between the small town rhetor and the virtuosi professionals"; but (a) by Nutton's (correct) dating of *De Praecogn.* (178) Hadrian had been chairholder at Athens for two years; (b) Hadrian was never a small-town rhetor.

For a similarly strict interpretation of the word "sophist" as depending on an official position, cf. Eunapius 487 B. (10.3.8-3.11 G.), where inferior men elected to chairs at Athens after the death of Julian the Cappadocian acquire the name of sophist by virtue of their posts, but did not deserve it (οἱ μὲν εὐτελέστεροι Sopolis and Parnasius] τὸ ὄνομα εἶχον, καί μέχρι τῶν σανίδων ἦν τὸ κράτος καὶ τοῦ βήματος ἐφ' ὃ παρῆεσαν, εἰς δὲ τοὺς δυνατωτέρους [Prohaeresius, Epiphanius, Diophantus] ἡ πόλις εὐθὺς διῄρητο); cf. L. Cracco-Ruggini, *Athenaeum* 49 (1971) 416.

70. Jones 12-14.

71. Cf. Anderson 94 n. 50. On Attalus, see Jones (*supra*, n. 49) 374-77.

72. C. Habicht, *Alt. v. Perg.* VIII.3 (1969) no. 31, Ti. Claudius Nicomedes (*VS* 591, ῥήτωρ εὐδόκιμος); no. 35, Marcius Acilius Diodotus (*VS* 617, died young φύσιν μὲν παρεσχημένῳ μελέτῃ ἐπιτηδείαν).

73. E. L. Bowie, *YCLS* [*Yale Classical Studies*] 27 (1982) 40; cf. Anderson 94 n. 50. Philostratus is similarly justified (in his own terms) in leaving out Zenobius, another "sophist" under Hadrian (*Suda* Z 73), since none of the sophists in the *Lives* would care to have been known for translating Latin literature (Sallust's *Histories* and "so-called *Wars*") into Greek.

74. Σ. Lucian, *De. Salt.* 69 (189 Rabe): Lesbonax's μελέται ῥητορικαὶ φέρονται θαυμάσιαι καὶ ἐνάμιλλοι Νικοστράτου [T. Aurelianus Nicostratus, *IGR* [*Inscriptiones Graecae ad Res Romanas Pertinentes*] IV.1134] καὶ Φιλοστράτου. On the disputed identity of Lesbonax, see *RE* XII [1925] 2103-6 (Aulitzky); R. Hodot, *EAC* [*Entretiens sur l'Antiquite Classique*]5 (1976) 27-28; R. Penella, *The Letters of Apollonius of Tyana* (Leiden, 1979) 103 on *Ep.* 22; Jones (*supra*, n. 45) 73 n. 23. Any suggestion that Nicostratus (a friend of Philostratus: *VS* 624; Menander, *Peri Epideikt.* 3.390 Sp.) and Philostratus were rivals of Lesbonax is unsustainable if Lesbonax is a pupil of Timocrates of Heraclea Pontica (*Lucian, De Salt.* 69), teacher of Polemon ca. 110-15 (*VS* 536, 541) and Demonax (Lucian, *Demonax* 3; cf. Jones 92-93). Aulitzky's "ἐνάμιλλοι vielleicht kein Recht gibt, L. in ein engeres zeitliches Verhältnis zu Nikostratos und Philostratos zu setzen" is clearly correct. Nevertheless the scholiast's report-unless inferred from the omission-may reveal some envy over reputations.

75. Münscher (*RE* VIII [1913] 933) suggested fiction because the theme of canalizing the Isthmus was used in the schools; cf. Aemling I.87 n. 19 "ich ihm aber nicht folgen kann." N. B. Müncher (949) rightly rejected the contention that Herodes' letter to Julianus (see *supra*, n. 39) was an invention of Philostratus.

76. Cf. Jones 15; but Philostratus was right not to repeat Fronto's allegations about another murder charge concerning Herodes' behavior after his father's will (*ad M. Caes.* 3.3.2 v.d.H. 38, "carnifex quidam Herodes," etc.).

77. Cf. P. A. Brunt, *JRS* [*Journal of Roman Studies*]64 (1974) 6 n. 28; weak support for the credibility of Philostratus (and *HA*) is given by A. J. Papalas, *Athenaeum* 51 (1978) 182-85.

78. Avotins (*supra*, n. 24) 315-19.

79. "Sortition for a proconsulship" or "sortition for a second consulate" (cf. Ameling II.7-9, in support of the former). On ὕπατος = ὑπατικός in Philostratus (and others), see Bowersock 7 n.1; H. J. Mason, *Greek Terms for Roman Institutions: A Lexicon and Analysis* (Toronto, 1974) 167.

Jaap-Jan Flinterman (essay date 1995)

SOURCE: Flinterman, Jaap-Jan. "The Writer." In *Power, Paideia & Pythagoreanism: Greek Identity, Conceptions of the Relationship between Philosophers and Monarchs and Political Ideas in Philostratus's* Life of Apollonius, pp. 29-51. Amsterdam, Netherlands: J. C. Gieben, 1995.

[In the following excerpt, Flinterman summarizes the preface and introduction to Philostratus's The Lives of the Sophists, *discussing the author's attitude toward the sophists and various Greek literary and political issues, and finally, challenges scholarly analyses that claim Philostratus did not identify with his fellow sophists.]*

The *Suda* (Φ 421) calls the author of the *VA* (*Apollonius of Tyana*) and the *VS* (*The Lives of the Sophists*) a sophist,[1] and the mere fact that Philostratus is also referred to as such in inscriptions honouring himself and his son is enough to show that he was attached to this title. Attempts to formulate a comprehensive definition of the phenomenon of the *sophistēs* as it is known from the imperial age usually run up against the problem of individual cases to which (some) contemporaries considered the title applicable, but which evade part of the definition. It is clear at all events that the term was primarily used for individuals who earned recognition from a broad public as exceptionally gifted orators; that this reputation was due in the first place to improvised declamations on historical or imaginary themes (*meletai*); and that they generally combined demonstrations of their ability as a form of public entertainment with the provision of lessons in rhetoric.[2] Show speakers of this kind occupy a central position in the *VS,* a collection of biographical sketches, in which Philostratus deals with his own cultural milieu and that of his predecessors since the second half of the first century, as well as trying to establish a link between the sophists of the imperial age, on the one hand, and sophists and orators from the classical period, on the other. In other words, the *VS* is about the cultural and social phenomenon to which Philostratus himself belonged and which he labelled as the 'Second Sophistic'. It is in the *VS* more than in his other extant writings that we should expect to find a record of his views, ideas, norms and values in a relatively pure state, uncontaminated by the ideas and conceptions which other themes inevitably entailed. The discussion in this section is thus based on the assumption that Philostratus identified to a large extent with his fellow sophists of the imperial period whose vicissitudes, successes and failures take up most of the *VS*.

Although the latter point may appear platitudinous to readers of the *VS,* the identification of the author with his subject matter has been called into question in recent publications. In a study of the reception of Dio of Prusa in antiquity and in the Byzantine period, the Italian scholar A. Brancacci has tried to use the preface and introduction of the *VS* as a source for the formation of theory associated with the concepts of philosophy, rhetoric and sophistic in the imperial philosophical schools and literary circles;[3] his conclusions with regard to Philostratus' cultural ideal are as astonishing as they are unconvincing. Since Brancacci's treatment of the author of the *VS* has met with a warm reception from authoritative quarters,[4] it is worthwhile to combine the presentation of my own view of Philostratus' cultural ideal with a refutation of the views of the Italian scholar on this point. For a proper grasp of the differences of interpretation, I shall first present a summary paraphrase of the preface and introduction to the *VS*.

In the dedicatory preface to Gordian, Philostratus mentions two categories of intellectuals that he has dealt with in his work: persons who concerned themselves with philosophy but had the reputation of sophists; and sophists in the real sense of the word (*VS* 479; cf. *VS* 492). At the conclusion of the introduction he explains that certain philosophers earned the title of sophist by virtue of the verbal virtuosity which they displayed in bringing their views to the notice of the public (*VS* 484). This passage is preceded by descriptions of the ancient sophistic and of what Philostratus refers to as the 'Second Sophistic'. The ancient sophistic is defined as eloquence on philosophical issues (ῥητορικὴ φιλοσοφοῦσα) of an ethical, theological or cosmological nature. He distinguishes the ancient sophistic from philosophy through the way in which epistemological premises are suggested by the manner of presentation: while philosophers follow Socratic dialectic, the ancient sophists speak as if they are in possession of knowledge. In this respect—the form of presentation of discourse—

Philostratus compares philosophy with human divination i.e. astrology, while sophistic is compared with the divinely inspired divination of prophets and oracles. He regards Gorgias as the founder of ancient sophistic. The Second Sophistic, in his view, differs from ancient sophistic in its object and manner of treatment: elaborate discussions of philosophical themes are replaced by a literary (κατὰ τέχνην) characterisation of social types, such as the poor, the rich, war heroes and tyrants, and the treatment of specific themes furnished by history. Philostratus regards Aeschines as the founder of the Second Sophistic, which thus has its roots in the classical period. It should be noted in passing that the author of the *VS* ascribes the founding of the Second Sophistic to Aeschines after the conclusion of the latter's political career in Athens (*VS* 480f.).

After the introduction, Philostratus discusses the 'philosophers with the reputation of sophists' (*VS* 484-492), from Eudoxus of Cnidus (first half of the fourth century B.C.) to Favorinus of Arelate (*floruit* under the emperor Hadrian). The only ones to be given something of a biographical sketch are Favorinus and Dio of Prusa; the other six 'philosophers with the reputation of sophists' are dealt with in brief characterisations. The author of the *VS* then proceeds to tackle those whom he considers to represent ancient sophistic, from Gorgias to Isocrates (*VS* 492-506). This review is followed by a treatment of the Second Sophistic, beginning with Aeschines (*VS* 507-510). The next representative of the Second Sophistic whom Philostratus deems worthy of consideration after Aeschines is Nicetes of Smyrna (second half of the first century). He characterises the intervening period as one in which there was a lack of respectable sophists (*VS* 511: ἀπορία γενναίων σοφιστῶν): sophistic was in an impasse (ἐς στενὸν ἀπειλημμένη) until Nicetes restored it to new vigour. The rest of the *VS,* which accounts for most of the work (*VS* 511-628), is devoted to the imperial sophists.

According to Brancacci, Philostratus presents himself in the introduction to the *VS* and in his treatment of the life of Dio of Prusa as a spokesman for a cultural ideal in which eloquence, philosophy and politico-didactic activity form a harmonious whole under the name of sophistic. To this end, Brancacci argues, the author of the *VS* constructs an absolute continuity between the ancient and the Second Sophistic, and defines sophistic as a 'philosophical rhetoric' (ῥητορικὴ φιλοσοφοῦσα). Closely related to this is the category of the 'philosopher-sophist' that he creates. In this way, the Italian scholar argues, Philostratus is out to underline the legitimacy of the intellectual claims of rhetoric and to enhance the prestige of the sophistic of his own day, while at the same time carefully detaching a number of important intellectuals 'dai declamatori che popolano le pagine più numerose delle *Vite dei sofisti,* e con i quali Filostrato stesso non desiderava essere confuso'.[5]

I consider Brancacci's view of Philostratus' cultural ideal to be fundamentally misguided. No one who has read more of the *VS* than just the introduction and the life of Dio can accuse the author of wanting to distance himself from the 'declamatori che popolano le pagine più numerose' of his work. There is a simple explanation for the fact that they occupy the lion's share of the *VS:* the author felt an affinity with these show speakers in every fibre of his cultural being. Brancacci himself notes the existence of an actual gap between the type of the philosopher-sophist—whom he seems to regard as the embodiment of Philostratus' cultural ideal—on the one hand, and the 'sophists in the real sense of the word', the 'declamatori', on the other hand. He thus concludes that, in spite of Philostratus' theoretical efforts, the writer's construction is incomplete and inconsistent. However, if Brancacci's interpretation of Philostratus' discussion in the introduction to the *VS* is correct, there is more at stake: in that case, the position adopted by the author in the introduction would be in flagrant contradiction with the value judgements expressed in the rest of the work. Even though one always has to take into account the possibility of inconsistencies in Philostratus' writings, in the present case the problems seem to lie in Brancacci's interpretation rather than in the introduction to the *VS* itself.

First, the Italian scholar is wrong in suggesting that Philostratus attributes the superiority of the manner of discourse of the ancient sophists, as against the method of the philosophers, to the idea that the former had a firmer grip on reality.[6] What Philostratus actually says is that the manner of discourse of the ancient sophists *suggests* a superiority of this kind: he is not interested in the relative epistemological merits of ancient sophistic and philosophy, but in their different effects on the audience, which result from a difference in the manner of presentation, i.e. style.[7] Second, now and then Brancacci seems to forget that Philostratus does not use the term 'philosophical rhetoric' to characterise sophistic in general, but as a definition of ancient sophistic which is not applicable to the Second Sophistic.[8] As a result—and this is the third objection to his theory—he presents the type of the 'philosopher-sophist' as the embodiment *par excellence* of Philostratus' cultural ideal,[9] ignoring the fact that the author of the *VS* is primarily interested in this category of intellectuals because of their verbal skills. Philostratus introduces the category of 'philosophers with the reputation of sophists' not to distinguish an important group of intellectuals from the representatives of the Second Sophistic, but in order to give a number of important intellectuals—especially Dio and Favorinus—a legiti-

mate place in the history of sophistic. This tendency to annexation has nothing to do with any reservations *vis-à-vis* show rhetoric, but is connected with the author's fixation on rhetorical performances and stylistic qualities.[10] This is confirmed by the way in which these criteria recur time and again in his explanations of what was responsible for the reputation of each of the 'philosopher-sophists' singled out for discussion.[11]

The fact that Philostratus primarily evaluates philosophers in terms of their literary and/or rhetorical merits can also be seen from his letter to Julia Domna (*ep.* 73), in which he defends Gorgias against Plutarch's criticisms by referring to the enormous influence of the sophist's style, not least on Plato. As in the introduction to the *VS,* stylistic quality functions here as the element of coherence in an indivisible Greek literary culture.[12] The letter is indicative of a literary way of reading philosophical texts which irritated philosophers.[13] The embodiment of Philostratus' cultural ideal is not the philosopher-sophist but the virtuoso rhetor; the appreciation of the latter's skills is of an artistic kind which discounts the epistemological and ethical aspects of the discourse.[14]

A comparison of Philostratus' letter to Julia Domna with Aristides' defence of rhetoric against Plato is conventional and illustrative.[15] According to Philostratus, Plato is indebted for his verbal skills to Gorgias, Hippias and Protagoras; the Antonine rhetorician adds eloquence to Plato's skills and even calls the philosopher 'father and teacher of the orators'.[16] However, the differences are at least as significant as the correspondences. The deadly seriousness with which Aristides defends eloquence as an essential condition of the functioning of human society[17] and as a comprehensive intellectual activity[18] is lacking in Philostratus' text. This is not due to the boundaries of the themes discussed in the letter to Julia Domna,[19] but it is typical of the limitations of the cultural ideal of the author of the *VS.*

The content of the introduction to the *VS,* as we have seen, is by no means at odds with the author's identification with the imperial sophists as expressed in the work as a whole. Of course, this does not tell us anything about the cultural historiographical merits of the scheme introduced by Philostratus. It is curious that the writer ascribes the foundation of the Second Sophistic to Aeschines, while he is unwilling or unable to name a successive representative of the phenomenon before the second half of the first century. The introduction of Aeschines as founder of the Second Sophistic is clearly an expression of an attempt to connect the flowering of show rhetoric in the imperial age with the classical past.[20] But why does Philostratus delay the revival of the Second Sophistic until Nicetes of Smyrna?

In a study of Dionysius of Halicarnassus, K. Goudriaan has argued that a break in the professional practice of rhetoric did actually occur in the Hellenistic period—in part of the third and the beginning of the second centuries B.C.[21] However, this break is considerably smaller than the abyss which Philostratus sets between Aeschines and Nicetes; the latter does not reflect the actual development of Greek rhetoric between the fourth century B.C. and the early imperial age, but the range of interests and value judgements of the author of the *VS*. As Goudriaan has demonstrated, the literary sources from the first century B.C. refer to sophists whose style of performance, didactic activities and choice of stylistic examples and themes are very similar to the representatives of Philostratus' Second Sophistic.[22]

One factor of importance is undoubtedly the central place which Philostratus accords to Herodes Atticus in Greek rhetoric of the imperial age.[23] As a young man, the Athenian sophist had received tuition from Scopelian of Clazomenae (*VS* 521), who was a former pupil of Nicetes (*VS* 516). The most important sophist among Herodes' contemporaries was also a former pupil of Scopelian: Polemo of Laodicea, who had followed in his master's footsteps as the most prominent representative of the sophistic in Smyrna (*VS* 521 and 536). Philostratus therefore connects the revival of the Second Sophistic with a sophist who was associated with Herodes Atticus and his most important contemporary through Scopelian, the teacher of the Athenian sophist and of Polemo. In itself the key position assigned by Philostratus to Herodes would be enough to explain the fact that he sets Nicetes at the head of the cultural current to which he himself belonged. However, there may be another factor involved as well. Although the author of the *VS* repeatedly emphasises that rhetorical performance is more important than provenance (*VS* 480 and 522), he suggests that the imperial sophists who feature in his work were virtually without exception members of the curial order or higher.[24] His own predilections and antipathies are by no means exempt from class snobbism: in one and the same breath he can claim that background is of lesser importance, while, in providing information on the background of the sophists, limiting his remarks to those who could boast illustrious parentage (*VS* 480).[25] As we have seen, he notes a 'lack of respectable sophists' (*VS* 511: ἀπορία γενναίων σοφιστῶν) in the period before Nicetes; he mentions Nicetes' contribution to sophistic together with the visible results of the latter's activities as a benefactor (*euergetēs*) of his native city: "This Nicetes found sophistic in an impasse, but he furnished her with access roads which were far more splendid than those which he had built for Smyrna to connect the city with the Ephesian gate—works which equalled his words in compass."[26] It is not inconceivable that Nicetes is not only the embodiment of the revival of the practice of

rhetoric in Philostratus' eyes, but that his career was one of the first to be characterised by what the author of the *VS* recognised as an exemplary combination of the practice of sophistic with high social prestige. As Goudriaan has shown, it is probably no coincidence that the title 'sophist' first appears in honourary and funerary inscriptions in the same period to which Philostratus dates the revival of the Second Sophistic; the explanation for this phenomenon is probably to be found in the fact that from the second half of the first century the practice of show rhetoric was held in much higher esteem among the urban elites of the eastern half of the empire than previously.[27]

It is clear at any rate that the imperial sophists dealt with in the *VS* often shared the author's social rank. They participated in the administration of the Greek cities and leagues, acted as benefactors of their fellow citizens by funding public works, religious festivals, cultural events and the distribution of grain and other vital necessities, represented the same fellow citizens in delegations to the emperor, and took part in the gradual integration of parts of the urban aristocracies from the eastern half of the empire in the imperial aristocracy of knights and senators. Various of Philostratus' sophists held positions within those careers that were reserved for these orders, especially as *ab epistulis graecis* and *advocatus fisci*, both equestrian functions. In his classic *Greek Sophists in the Roman Empire*, Bowersock placed great emphasis on the importance of the Second Sophistic as a socio-political phenomenon and suggested a causal connection between the professional status of the sophists and their political role. He summarises his own view as follows: "It could be argued without apology that the Second Sophistic has more importance in Roman History than it has in Greek Literature."[28]

Bowersock's interpretive framework was challenged in 1982 by E. L. Bowie. He argued that the main explanation for the role of sophists as administrators and benefactors in Greek cities and as participants in delegations to the imperial court lay not in their professional prestige and rhetorical qualities, but in the fact that they came from families that belonged to the leading social and political circles of the population in the eastern half of the empire. Since parts of this Greek elite were integrated in the imperial aristocracy from the Flavian era, it is hardly surprising that sophists are occasionally found in positions which were confined to the senatorial or equestrian orders. The demands made by a career as a sophist, however, were difficult to reconcile with a career as an *eques* or senator, Bowie claimed; hence if an urban aristocrat from the eastern half of the empire went in for sophistic, this implied a certain preference for an intellectual career to a political one. Bowie recognises that Greek intellectuals were particularly well qualified for the position of *ab epistulis graecis,* but he tries to explain the fact that a number of *sophists* are attested in this post from the second half of the second century as a combination of two factors: the rise of Greek aristocrats, especially from Asia Minor and Athens, in the imperial aristocracy; and the penchant for sophistic among these urban elites. Moreover, Bowie claims that in general the post did not open up career opportunities for sophists in the equestrian or senatorial orders; the relatively large number of sophists who functioned as *ab epistulis graecis,* in his view, cannot be used as evidence for the political significance of the Second Sophistic.[29]

The great service rendered by Bowie's article is to have posed the decisive question of the character of the relation between the two roles played by representatives of the Second Sophistic: as virtuoso orators, on the one hand, and as members of a socio-political elite, on the other. Without denying that eloquence could be very important in a political context,[30] he points out that rhetorical skills were fairly well distributed among the members of the urban aristocracies, and that one may harbour reservations as to the political relevance and effectiveness of the type of show rhetoric that was practised by the sophists. Since Philostratus identifies completely with these show orators, as we have seen, seeing in them the perfect embodiment of his cultural ideal, it is important to investigate what view is encapsulated in the *VS* of the relation between the practice of sophistic, social status and political activity. The present focus is thus not on the prosopographical data which can be distilled from the *VS* and other sources (which can be found in Bowersock's *Greek Sophists in the Roman Empire*), but on the implicit and explicit value judgements which can be found in the *VS* on such matters as the desirability for sophists of political activity, the holding of public offices and acting as benefactors, as well as Philostratus' views on the social function of sophistic and on the relation between this show rhetoric and other forms of eloquence. I shall deal with the activities of Philostratus' sophists in cities in the eastern half of the empire, and their contacts with representatives of the imperial aristocracy and the emperor.

Only a few sophists are explicitly reported by Philostratus to have given speeches in public meetings and advised their fellow citizens. Scopelian, who preferred Smyrna as his sphere of operations above his native Clazomenae, used to discuss public affairs with the magistrates of his city and put in regular appearances at the assembly, where his cheery eloquence enabled him to keep things calm (*VS* 518f.). Smyrna later benefitted from the presence of Polemo, whose words of admonition convinced the citizens to abandon their squabbles and to live in harmony; although Philostratus does not

state explicitly where these speeches were delivered, it is natural to suppose that they were addressed to the assembly or to the council (*VS* 531). The author of the *VS* (529) records that Marcus of Byzantium managed to get the citizens of Megara to resolve a dispute with Athens, and Dio of Prusa is said to have regularly reprimanded cities, an activity which is amply documented in the extant speeches of Dio (*VS* 487).[31] The *VS* also mentions a large number of sophists who occupied important positions at city or federal level. Scopelian was high priest of Asia (*VS* 515), Lollianus of Ephesus served Athens as hoplite general (*VS* 526f.), Herodes Atticus held the office of eponymous archon in his native city (*VS* 549), and Theodotus held an unspecified Athenian magistracy (*VS* 566). Euodianus of Smyrna was hoplite general in his native city and high priest of Asia (*VS* 596). Apollonius of Athens held the positions of eponymous archon and hoplite general (*VS* 600).

What significance does the author of the *VS* attribute to these political activities on the part of the sophists under discussion, and what connection does he make between their professional and their political activities? The impression given by the *VS* is that holding political functions and practising as a sophist are two different ways of acquiring prestige, but that there is no direct link between them. Euodianus of Smyrna, Philostratus tells us, was honoured with the high priesthood of Asia and the office of hoplite general in his native city; he obtained the Roman chair for his eloquence (*VS* 596). In Philostratus' characterisation of the two parallel careers, there is a close affinity between the class consciousness of the urban aristocrat and the mentality of the sophist, both marked by an ambitious and competitive attitude. However, keeping one's distance from urban politics in no way detracts from the reputation of the sophist as such in the eyes of the author of the *VS*. Besides sophists who take an active part in the political life of their native city, place of residence or elsewhere, the *VS* also contains cases of sophists who are explicitly reported to have abstained from such activities. Both Nicetes of Smyrna and Antiochus of Aegae were reluctant to appear in assemblies (*VS* 511 and 568); Philostratus remarks that his own teacher Proclus preferred the calm of Athens to the turbulence of his native city (*VS* 602f.).[32] Philostratus records the aloofness of Nicetes, Antiochus and Proclus from political activity, but without any word of reproof.

All the same, Philostratus expects his heroes to act as aristocrats in some way and to refrain from activities which do not accord with that status. He seems to regard *euergesia* in the public or private sphere as the most laudable method for sophists to confirm their social status: a man of quality knows how to use his wealth appropriately by assisting friends in need or by making civic contributions, thereby increasing his reputation (*VS* 603 and 610).[33] Nicetes and Antiochus, who abstained from direct political participation, enhanced their native cities (Smyrna and Aegae respectively) with public works; Antiochus also paid for grain distributions to the citizens when there was a shortage (*VS* 511 and 568). Proclus managed to save an Athenian acquaintance from losing his house, which he had mortgaged for a loan (*VS* 603). Damianus of Ephesus assisted his needy fellow citizens, had public buildings restored, and financed the construction of a colonnade linking the city with the temple of Artemis and of a dining room in the temple itself (*VS* 605). However, Philostratus notes, no one made better use of his wealth than Herodes, whose *euergesia* benefitted not only friends and cities, but entire provinces (*VS* 547). He provided Athens with a stadium of white marble and the well-known odeum, and elsewhere in the province of Achaea—Corinth, Delphi, Thermopylae, Euboea, the Peloponnese and Boeotia—he paid for the construction of buildings and works of art (*VS* 550f.). In the great importance that Philostratus attaches to this display of wealth and generosity, the author of the *VS* appears as a typical representative of the social elite in the eastern half of the empire. His pattern of expectation with regard to sophists includes both a professional component—he attaches particular importance to improvisation[34]—and a social component, ensuing from his class consciousness; an essential ingredient of this social component is the 'proper use of wealth' in the form of *euergesia,* in contrast to direct political activity at the level of the city, which may well make a signal contribution to the prestige of the urban aristocrat, but is not a sine qua non for a sophist.[35]

Philostratus' comments on the fee (*misthos*) which sophists usually requested for their lessons and on the practice of courtroom oratory both confirm and supplement this pattern of expectation. The author of the *VS* justifies the demand for a fee with an argument which is completely in line with the importance that he attaches to the 'right use of wealth'. By demanding payment for his lessons, the sophist enables his pupils to show that they make the right priorities: the pattern of spending is a reflection of the pattern of values.[36] For example, as a young man Damianus attended the declamations of Aristides and Hadrian and paid each of them ten thousand drachmae; he preferred to spend his money on this hobby rather than on male or female beauties.[37] Herodes was already a celebrated sophist when he spent three successive days in Smyrna as a member of Polemo's audience. He sent him the sum of 150,000 drachmae as *misthos*. Polemo refused to accept it. It was only when Herodes raised the sum to 250,000 drachmae that Polemo was prepared to accept it, and he did so with the attitude of one who is only receiving his deserts (*VS* 537f.). In the case of these two giants, the

scale by which the pattern of spending is reflected in the pattern of values assumes gigantic proportions as well. On the other hand, Philostratus is appreciative when sophists moderate their demands with an eye to the spending power of their students.[38] The desire for material gain alone is a sign of a poor character in his opinion. . . . Philostratus takes pains to clear his teacher Proclus of this charge in connection with his commercial activities on the side. Of course, banausic activities in general do not receive his approval (*VS* 506), nor does accepting a position as a domestic teacher with a family whose social position is below that of the sophist in question (*VS* 599f.).

The same type of norms in connection with the desire for material gain also makes its appearance when the author of the *VS* deals with the activities of the sophists in the field of courtroom rhetoric. We can begin by noting that Philostratus regards courtroom orators (*agoraioi*) as forming a distinct category from sophists *pur sang*: sophists are primarily occupied with education in rhetoric and show performances, and they therefore lack the courage and daring which are the first requirements of a forensic orator.[39] Nevertheless, he does mention various sophists who put up a fight in the courts, and in such cases too he attaches great importance to a display of altruism. Damianus, who tailored his *misthos* to the pockets of his students, offered his legal services free of charge to people in financial difficulties.[40] Quirinus of Nicomedia, who was appointed *advocatus fisci,* showed himself to be mild and uninterested in making a profit in the exercise of his profession (*VS* 621). Of course, not everyone was equally altruistic: Polemo, whose superior arrogance is described by Philostratus in a mixture of disapproval, indulgence and admiration, received the sum of two talents for appearing in court on behalf of his client.[41] In general, Philostratus' remarks on the legal activities of the sophists dealt with in the *VS* confirm the picture of his norms and values that emerged earlier: aristocratic generosity and the absence of a thirst for gain are the cornerstones of the social component of the pattern of expectation which sophists are expected to meet, both in their professional activity (with regard to the *misthos*) and elsewhere (in forensic rhetoric). The clear distinction that he makes between sophistic and courtroom rhetoric also confirms the fact that he regards sophistic as a cultural phenomenon with a significance of its own, independent of the practical application of eloquence in assemblies, in council meetings or in court.

A number of the most entertaining and informative anecdotes in the *VS* concern the contacts of sophists with leading Romans, primarily emperors. As we shall see, these anecdotes also confirm the view that Philostratus did not consider sophistic as rhetoric for utilitarian ends, although this does not prevent him from quoting instances of the successes of sophists in representing the interests of their native city, place of residence or province.[42] Scopelian went to Rome as a representative of Asia and managed to get Domitian to withdraw the prohibition on viniculture in the province.[43] Polemo persuaded Hadrian to build a grain market, gymnasium and temple for Smyrna (*VS* 531); a posthumous speech by the same sophist earned Smyrna a victory in a hearing before Antoninus Pius (*VS* 539f.). Marcus Aurelius, who had heard a declamation by Aristides during a visit to Smyrna, was later brought to tears by a monody on the destruction of the city by an earthquake sent to him by the sophist, and agreed to pay for the rebuilding of the city. Philostratus characterises this case as an instance of the influence of good counsel and eloquence on genuinely royal, divine natures, thereby complimenting both the sophist and the emperor.[44] At the same time, he was aware that the show element which generally characterised the sophists' performances could be counterproductive in connection with a delegation to the emperor.[45] His view of the relation between sophists and political authorities, especially emperors, is more complex than one might be tempted to suppose on the evidence of the success stories of Scopelian, Polemo and Aristides.

The pattern of norms and values underlying the anecdotes in the *VS* on the contacts between sophists and emperors can be understood if one realises that the context in which these contacts took place can change, and that the roles of the two parties and the corresponding patterns of expectation with regard to their actions can change with it. As long as a sophist does not act as such—i.e., in virtually all situations except his declamations—his relationship with the emperor is that of a subject to his master. This also applies when a sophist is defending his own interests or those of his fellow citizens in connection with a delegation or a hearing before the emperor. Typical in this respect is Philostratus' comment on the action of Herodes when the latter came to argue his case before Marcus Aurelius in Sirmium against his opponents in Athens. The sophist had to appear before the emperor soon after the death of two daughters of one of his freedmen, to whom he was deeply attached. At the time he was frenzied with grief and levelled direct accusations against Marcus without making any attempt to cloak them in allusions and ambiguities.[46] It is clear that Philostratus regards the behaviour of his favourite sophist with disapproval in this case; the fact that the trial did not take a fatal turn for Herodes, he believes, was entirely due to the philosophical attitude of the emperor.[47] Not all autocrats possess such laudable characteristics as Marcus Aurelius; sophists may even be confronted with tyrants. In such cases, Philostratus claims, they should still observe correct behaviour and refrain from provocative remarks which might arouse the wrath of the tyrant;[48] he makes it clear

that those who stray from this code of behaviour have only themselves to blame for the consequences. This applies, for instance, to Antipater, who sent Caracalla an accusatory letter after the murder of Geta. Philostratus' comments on the behaviour of his colleague amount to saying that Antipater should have realised that he was bound to arouse the anger of the emperor by casting doubt on the justification for the murder—an alleged conspiracy by Geta.[49] Philosophical bravery and courage in voicing criticism (*parrhēsia*) is the last thing the author of the *VS* expects a sophist to display.[50]

Philostratus' years of experience as a sophist in the Severan court no doubt lie behind his explicit warnings not to abandon the correct mode of behaviour in one's dealings with emperors.[51] At the same time, this attitude is closely connected with his view of sophistic as an autonomous cultural phenomenon. This can be seen if we consider his pattern of expectation with regard to the behaviour of emperors towards sophists. While the sophist is expected to respect the position of the emperor as sovereign, the emperor is expected to respect the sophist as a representative of *paideia*, Greek literary culture. This aspect of Philostratus' view of the relation between emperors and sophists can be seen most clearly in his account of the relations between Aristides and Marcus Aurelius (*VS* 582f.). The emperor had already been in Smyrna for three days without the sophist's coming to welcome him. When Marcus finally summoned him and asked why he had not been to see him, Aristides replied that he was totally engrossed in his studies and could not tolerate any distraction. Philostratus relates that the emperor was pleased to hear of Aristides' dedication to his scholarly duties. He asked the sophist to declaim for him; at Aristides' request the declamation was postponed to the following day and the sophist received permission to bring his students with him. When Aristides asked the emperor whether they were allowed to applaud their teacher, Marcus replied with a smile that it was up to him. The typical feature of this case—besides the emperor's desire to meet the sophist—is his unconditional acceptance of Aristides' excuse for the delay in making an appearance: the emperor accepts the sophist's breach of the code of behaviour out of respect for his role as a representative of *paideia*.[52] He then proceeds to turn his court temporarily into a sophists' school by allowing Aristides to bring his students with him; and he emphasises the fact that he lays aside his role as sovereign for the duration of the declamation and accepts that of an admiring member of the audience, by stating that only Aristides himself is in a position to elicit tokens of appreciation from his students.[53]

Even when the emperor complied with this aspect of the pattern of expectations and changed roles, his position remained ambivalent: he could make or break the sophist. This ambivalence is well illustrated by an anecdote on Hadrian and Favorinus in the *Historia Augusta.* When Favorinus was attacked by the emperor for using a word which Hadrian did not consider to be pure Attic, the philosopher-sophist immediately acknowledged his mistake. When friends pointed out to him that the word was attested by canonical authors, Favorinus replied that the learning of someone who had thirty legions at his disposal was beyond any doubt.[54] There was always a tension between the role of the emperor as devotee of the arts and his political power, as sophists repeatedly found out. Although Philostratus does not voice this tension as explicitly as the author of the *Historia Augusta,* it is possible to distil the beginnings of a view of the relation between *paideia* and political power in the *VS.* This requires a scrutiny of the theme of imperial favours and honours which recurs in the biographical sketches of the sophists.[55]

Philostratus certainly expects an emperor to express his appreciation of the skills of sophists in favours and honours; these can be roughly broken down into three categories. First, there is the appointment of sophists to positions for which their rhetorical and literary qualities stood them in good stead (*ab epistulis graecis* or *advocatus fisci*). The two sophists dealt with by Philostratus who held the position of *advocatus fisci,* Quirinus of Nicomedia and Heliodorus, owed their positions, according to the author of the *VS,* primarily to their skill in courtroom speaking, a branch of eloquence which, as we have seen, he clearly distinguishes from sophistic itself; it is the latter which attracts his interest and appreciation.[56] Mutatis mutandis, the same applies to the sophists who obtained a position in the imperial bureaucracy as *ab epistulis graecis;*[57] letter-writing and sophistic are hardly synonyms. A capable *ab epistulis* like Celer is still no sophist,[58] and Antipater, according to Philostratus, was a brilliant imperial secretary but a mediocre declaimer.[59] Philostratus is more interested in letter-writing than in courtroom rhetoric, as can be seen from the comments on the stylistic merits of the letters of Antipater and Aspasius. This is hardly surprising in view of his own exercises in letter-writing, even though in a completely different branch of this genre. However, in Philostratus' opinion, the positions of both *advocatus fisci* and *ab epistulis graecis* do not call for the same talent for the holding of *meletai* which is the preeminent qualification of a sophist.

A secondary category of imperial honours which features in the *VS* consists of appointments to one of the other posts which formed part of those careers confined to members of the equestrian and senatorial orders. Nowhere does Philostratus make a direct connection between these appointments and the professional qualities of the sophists in question. The cases mentioned in the *VS* are very rare indeed;[60] probably

such a connection was not at issue, and these appointments were only what was to be expected in view of the status achieved by the families of the sophists in question in previous generations or of their upward social mobility.[61] As noted earlier, Bowie has pointed out that many sophists came from families that already belonged to the imperial aristocracy. Their decision to become sophists was more or less tantamount to declining a career in the imperial administration: "A man from such a family who chose to be a sophist was in some measure preferring the intellectual to the practical life."[62] It is interesting that the author of the *VS* explicitly formulates the pattern of values which must have underlay such choices. He relates that Herodes attached more importance to his successes as a sophist than to his consular status and origin.[63] Elsewhere he enjoys describing how Chrestus of Byzantium rebukes a haughty student who thought of nothing but a career in the service of the emperor.[64] For Philostratus, the prestige that one can obtain as a sophist is different but certainly not inferior to the prominence associated with the holding of public positions in the urban or imperial administration.

Most of the favours conveyed on sophists by emperors that are related in the *VS* belong to a third category: gifts or purely ceremonial honours as tokens of the recognition of the artistic merits of their recipients, and appointment to the imperial chair in Athens or the chair of Greek rhetoric in Rome. The pretext for the conferral of such favours is often a declamation in the presence of the emperor. Polemo and Dionysius of Miletus were appointed members of the Museum in Alexandria by Hadrian; and Polemo was overwhelmed by material privileges by Trajan, and especially by Hadrian.[65] During a visit to Athens in 176, Marcus Aurelius had Hadrian of Tyre perform for him; the emperor had already appointed him to the imperial chair, but the suitability of Hadrian for the post had been called into question. Hadrian's declamation put an end to the criticisms and the emperor rewarded him richly with honours and gifts.[66] Commodus was so enchanted by the declamations of Pollux that he appointed him to the imperial chair (*VS* 593). Apollonius of Athens (*VS* 601) and Hermocrates of Phocaea (*VS* 611) received rewards for declamations from Septimius Severus, and Philostratus of Lemnos was granted exemption from public office and civic contributions by Caracalla for a declamation (*VS* 623). However, what an emperor could grant he could also withdraw. Heraclides lost a declamation contest against Apollonius of Athens in the presence of Septimius Severus; his defeat cost him his exemption from public office and civic contributions (*VS* 601). The protection of Julia Domna resulted in an appointment to the imperial chair for Philiscus of Thessaly, but this did not stop Caracalla from depriving him of the related *ateleia* (*VS* 622f.). An emperor could also express his admiration for a sophist by granting material favours to his favourite city. According to Philostratus, Aristides' success with a declamation for Marcus Aurelius paved the way for the emperor's later decision to restore Smyrna after it had been heavily hit by an earthquake (*VS* 582f.); the author of the *VS* supposed a similar connection to exist between Polemo's popularity with Hadrian and the material favours bestowed on Smyrna by the emperor (*VS* 531; cf. *VS* 533). Of course, in such cases part of the prestige connected with the imperial *euergesia* reflected on the sophist as well; in connection with Aristides' successful intervention with Marcus Aurelius, Philostratus calls him 'founder of Smyrna' (οἰκιστὴς τῆς σμύρνης).[67]

Leaving Marcus Aurelius aside, Hadrian is the favourite emperor of the author of the *VS;* of all the past emperors, according to Philostratus, he was the one who was most inclined to foster talent.[68] This is hardly surprising in view of Hadrian's legendary love of things Greek. However, it worth considering Philostratus' comments on this emperor in more detail, since they are illustrative of his views of the relation between *paideia* and political power, and enable us to define his pattern of expectations with regard to the behaviour of emperors *vis-à-vis* sophists. Philostratus' characterisation of Hadrian as the emperor most prepared to encourage talent is prompted by the report of the admiration that the emperor displayed for Marcus of Byzantium when the latter visited the emperor as a delegate of his native city (*VS* 529f.). This admiration no doubt concerned Marcus' artistic abilities. Elsewhere Philostratus makes it clear that, in his opinion, Hadrian's interest in Greek culture, especially sophistic and philosophy, was not essential to his view of himself as emperor, but that it was a form of diversion from imperial concerns—a regal leisure activity (*VS* 490). The author of the *VS* certainly does not disdain such a view of sophistic and philosophy; on the contrary, in the introduction to the *VS* he expresses the hope that his work will serve precisely this entertainment function for Gordian (*VS* 480). His view of sophistic as an autonomous cultural phenomenon, as an art form, implies that he harbours no illusions on the direct relevance of this type of eloquence in social and political life. What he expects from emperors and members of the imperial aristocracy is an appreciation of sophistic as art. The artistic appreciation on the part of political authorities is of great importance in the eyes of the writer of the *VS:* it makes an irreplaceable contribution to the prestige of sophists and underlines that a sophist's career is equivalent to, if not better than, an active political career as a method of obtaining prestige. Competition between sophists therefore assumes more serious forms in the presence of political authorities. Thus the dispute between Favorinus and Polemo in Ionia, where the two fighting cocks were the respective favourites of Ephesus and

Smyrna blazed up during their stay in Rome, where the appreciation of consulares and their sons fanned the flames of ambition and mutual rivalry (*VS* 490f.).

It is remarkable that Hadrian's non-committal attitude toward *paideia,* according to Philostratus, applied to philosophy as well as sophistic. His view of the intellectual activities of this emperor recalls Tacitus' account of the philosophers who entertained Nero after dinner with doctrinal debates (*Ann.* 14.16.2). Of course, philosophers themselves generally tended to cast themselves in a different role in their relation to political authorities than that of entertainer, preferring to be seen as confidants and personal advisors.[69] In the *VS,* where Philostratus expresses his views on the practice of the relation between Greek intellectuals and Roman emperors, he has no time for such pretensions; but he adopts an entirely different attitude in the *VA,* where idealised views of the relation between philosophers and political authorities affect his portrayal of Apollonius.

Philostratus was certainly not the only sophist to attribute such importance to imperial honours. Aristides, whom we may include as a member of the Second Sophistic without too many scruples—he disliked the title 'sophist' and preferred to call himself 'rhetor'[70]—frequently dreamed of meetings with emperors, as can be seen from his *Hieroi Logoi.* One of the most striking cases of this type of dream concerns a stay in the court of Marcus Aurelius and Lucius Verus:

> "On the nineteenth I dreamed that I was staying in the palace. The attention paid me by the emperors and the honour they showed me in everything they did were wondrous and unsurpassable: I alone received all of what is not even in small measure granted to another."[71]

This dream is not only a confirmation of the great importance of imperial recognition for sophist's self-esteem; it also illustrates how well Philostratus hit the nail on the head in a moment of honesty in characterising sophistic as 'a profession for narcissistic boasters'.[72]

To sum up the previous remarks, we may state that *paideia* and political power are autonomous terrains for Philostratus. In his view, sophistic is an art form and must be distinguished as such from utilitarian rhetoric. As for the relation between sophists and political authorities, he believes that it should be characterised by mutual respect for the sovereignty of each party on its own ground. In practice, the boundary between culture and politics was naturally a vague one, and phenomena which transgressed the dividing line were common enough. Two main factors were involved. First, the prestige attaching to achievements in the field of culture was so great that it could lie at the root of conflicts of a partly political nature. Second, there was a measure of interchange between sophistic and utilitarian rhetoric; indeed, to a certain extent it was unavoidable, as members of the urban aristocracies attended the schools of the sophists in their youth and regularly attended declamations by sophists in their adult life. This could lead to politically inappropriate or undesirable remarks in meetings of the council or the assembly. In order to understand Philostratus' view of sophistic and its implications, it is important to discuss the two types of 'mixed' phenomena briefly.

As for the first type, the reputation of athletes, actors, sophists and other intellectuals contributed substantially to the prestige of their place of birth or of the city where they lived. One form of expression of mutual competition between cities in a province was in the admiration of rival idols. We have already seen how the dispute between Polemo and Favorinus at first followed the traditional rivalry between Smyrna and Ephesus (*VS* 490).[73] This phenomenon is of the same kind as the disputes between cities claiming to be the 'first city' of a province.[74] Examples of conflicts of this kind that raged in the imperial age are the dispute between the Bithynian cities of Nicaea and Nicomedia, and that between the three leading cities of Asia, Smyrna, Ephesus and Pergamum. The dispute in Bithynia was the occasion for a speech by Dio of Prusa in Nicomedia, while Aristides lectured the cities of Asia on the blessings of mutual concord.[75] Dio and Aristides did not fail to remind their audiences of the pointlessness of such conflicts. Only one city was the first, and that was Rome; quarrels concerning titles were merely a question of 'the shadow of a donkey', as Dio so plastically puts it in his second speech in Tarsus, a city which also had its share of quarrels with its neighbours.[76] However, since disputes of this kind were one of the few safety valves for interurban rivalry under the Pax Romana, the parties involved saw no point in devoting a lot of energy to the fight for titles.[77] Under normal conditions, this Greek penchant was a source of amusement to the Roman authorities and served as an opportunity to implement the adage 'divide and rule'; at least, that is how Dio of Prusa saw it (*or.* 38.36-38). However, in exceptional circumstances such conflicts could escalate. Thus Nicomedia sided with Septimius Severus during the civil war of 193/4, while Nicaea supported Pescennius Niger.[78]

The same civil war was the pretext for an incident reported in the *VS* involving a dilution of the boundary between politics and culture. At the beginning of Severus' campaign Byzantium served as a base for Niger, and after the definitive defeat and death of the pretender the city still resisted a siege by the victorious troops for a long time.[79] During this siege, the Byzantine actor Clemens put on brilliant displays during tragic performances, but the juries were understandably reluctant to accord him the laurels of victory. According to Philostratus, they wanted to avoid proclaiming as victor, in the person of one man, a city which had revolted against Rome.[80] The same problem occurred during the Pythian games until the president, Hippodromus of Larissa, intervened; he appealed to his obligations as a member of the jury and accorded Clemens the victory that was his due. The sophist thus refused to be influenced by the political implications of the case. When a rival of Clemens appealed against the decision to the emperor, Severus sanctioned Hippodromus' intervention (*VS* 616). The incident is illustrative of how fragile the line dividing culture from politics was, but at the same time it shows that the norm in such cases was that the autonomy of each of the two areas should be respected. Hippodromus restored this norm, which had been disregarded by the juries, and the emperor confirmed its validity. The sensitiveness of juries at Panhellenic events to political pressure was a sore point. In his Rhodian speech dating from the early years of the reign of Vespasian, Dio of Prusa refers to Roman attempts to influence arbitration in the Olympian games (*or.* 31.110f.). In claiming that the judges leave letters of recommendation for athletes unopened until after the contest, he reflects the same norm that is found in the *VS,* even though actual practice will not always have been the same.

Sophistic does not bear comparison with athletic or dramatic contests in every way, of course, but they do have certain points in common. Although in many cases it is the emperor himself who acts as arbitrator for the sophists described by Philostratus and who rewards their performances with such bounties as gifts, honours and academic chairs, in the case of a declamation, as we have seen, the roles of sophist and emperor are changed: the emperor abdicates his role as sovereign for the duration of the speech and assumes the role of an appreciative listener. It may be supposed that, while this was theoretically the case, in practice the granting of imperial favours to the sophists was often dependent on other factors than the appreciation of purely professional merits. All the same, the norm which can be distilled from the *VS* is that in such cases the emperor proceeds on the basis of artistic appreciation. The fragile line dividing culture from politics is thus retained to a certain extent. A few sophists certainly displayed a striking indifference to imperial favours. When the Athenians wanted to propose Chrestus of Byzantium for the imperial chair in their city, he declined with a deprecatory comment on the value of such academic chairs: "The ten thousand drachmae do not make a man."[81] Most of his colleagues were milder in their judgement: besides the material aspect, imperial favours and honours formed a substantial contribution to their prestige and self-esteem.

As mentioned above, interaction between sophistic and utilitarian rhetoric was more or less inevitable, but it could be problematical. The themes which the sophists chose for their declamations or which were proposed by their audience were imaginary or historical. The vast majority of historical declamations dealt with themes from the classical period, and sophists enjoyed expatiating on the greatness of Greece in the past. Plutarch's *Political Precepts* for a local politician from Sardis, a text dating from the late first or early second century, warns against presenting the people with historical examples which are not in line with the existing conditions, i.e. Roman domination. In his opinion, eulogies of Marathon, Plataeae and the Eurymedon belong to the sophists' schools and not to the assembly, although it may be appropriate for a local politician to allude to examples of a different kind from the Greek past, such as the amnesty in Athens after the fall of the thirty tyrants.[82]

The caution advocated by Plutarch in tackling historical exempla within a political context can be seen in some of the speeches of Dio of Prusa. For instance, after recalling the greatness of Thebes under Epaminondas in a speech before the assembly of his native city, Dio immediately adds that the times have changed and that in the present situation the development of a power like that of Thebes in the past is no longer possible. Patriotism is still a virtue and a possibility, but the consequences of devotion to one's native country are now less far-reaching (*or.* 43.4). In another speech Dio tells the citizens of Prusa that Athens and Sparta owed their ancestral greatness and fame to orderly behaviour in civic matters (τὸ κοσμίως πολιτεύεσθαι). These are also worthy and profitable objectives in the present situation, according to Dio: good government is more beneficial to a city than privileges like the status of 'free city' granted by the Roman authorities (*or.* 44.11f.). The same attitude can be detected in Aristides' speech before the cities of Asia in which he reminds his audience of the benefits of the concord between Athens and Sparta during the Persian wars: the times have changed and present conditions are not comparable, but the need for a good mutual understanding remains the same (*or.* 23.41f. Keil). Both Dio and Aristides adopt a somewhat defensive attitude in presenting historical examples in a political context. They seem to anticipate a combination of irritation and amusement on the part of their audience when they parade classical exempla, and they try to anticipate such a reaction by appealing to a certain Greek chauvinism which they assume to be shared by their audience. Apparently the latter also felt that the standard repertoire of the sophists' schools was out of place in a political context, not so much—as Plutarch claimed—because it obfuscated reality and could lead to political adventurism, but because it was utterly irrelevant.[83]

We do not know to what extent Philostratus displayed his rhetorical talents and made use of historical exempla in council meetings and assemblies, for example during the holding of public offices in Athens. However, there is at least one case in the *VS* in which he explicitly connects a political lesson with an anecdote over a representative of ancient sophistic. Overstepping the boundary of historical accuracy, he relates that Antiphon provoked Dionysius of Syracuse and paid for it with his life. The author considers the sophist to have been in the wrong in provoking the tyrant and criticising his tragedies; literary activities make a tyrant less tyrannical and render his regime easier for his subjects to bear (*VS* 499f.). In drawing a lesson from history, then, Philostratus is acting entirely in accordance with his view of the relation between sophists and those holding political power; it is tailored to suit the status quo and is by no means subversive.[84]

There can be no doubt that Philostratus himself exercised the activity which was most typical for sophists: delivering improvised speeches on historical or imaginary themes. Unfortunately, none of the *meletai* ascribed to him in the *Suda* (Φ 421) has survived. Roughly two-thirds of the declamations by colleagues that he mentions in the *VS* are concerned with historical themes, the most popular being situations from the Persian wars, the Peloponnesian war, and the Athenian struggle under Demosthenes against Macedonian expansion.[85] This pattern corresponds reasonably to the data on the choice of themes by Greek declaimers collected by D. Russell,[86] and there is no good reason to suppose that Philostratus' choice of themes for his own declamations was significantly different from that of his colleagues. The image of prominent Greeks from the imperial age who assume the role of Demosthenes in advising the Athenians to take to their triremes at the approach of Philip (*VS* 543),[87] who lament Chaeronea (*VS* 522), who dwell at such length on Marathon that the battle becomes a nickname for them (*VS* 595), who advise the Lacedaemonians not to accept those who had surrendered at Sphacteria as citizens any longer (*VS* 528), or who follow the Athenian wounded at Syracuse in begging their comrades to kill them with their own hands (*VS* 574), immediately raises questions on the relation of the sophists and the social elite of the eastern half of the empire from which they originated and which appreciated their performances, on the one hand, and the Imperium Romanum, on the other. The fact that there was a tension between acceptance of this reality and the evocation of the greatness of the Greek past can be seen from Plutarch's recommendations (discussed above), the politico-rhetorical practice of Dio and Aristides, and from the combination of irritation and amusement which they expected their audiences to display whenever the familiar exempla were paraded before them. It is equally clear that the sophists combined a fixation on the classical past, associated with a negation of the Hellenistic period and of the more recent past, with an attitude which could range from unproblematical acceptance to positive appreciation and far-reaching identification with Roman rule, and which never assumed the form of a fundamental rejection of the status quo. The fixation on the classical past was a cultural phenomenon which cannot be interpreted as an expression of resistance to Roman rule. The question that remains is why a socio-political elite whose position was consolidated by the power of Rome and which became increasingly involved in the imperial administration saw its cultural self-awareness to a large extent reflected in a literary genre which continually reproduced situations in which Rome was conspicuously absent and in which autonomous Greek *poleis* sparred with the Persians, the Macedonians or one another.

In a controversial article, Bowie has tried to explain this phenomenon in terms of the political situation of the Greek aristocracies; though their leading position was guaranteed by Rome within the cities in the eastern half of the empire, their room for manoeuvre, both internally and in their relations with other cities, was at the same time reduced to a minimum. Bowie argues that the contrast between the material prosperity and cultural affluence of the cities in Asia Minor in particular, on the one hand, and the actual political insignificance of these elites, on the other, led Greek aristocrats increasingly to turn to the political glories of the past in their major forms of cultural expression. The integration of sectors of these aristocracies from the eastern half of the empire in the imperial aristocracy mitigated this contrast without eliminating it entirely, and Greek cultural superiority, which was also recognised by the Romans, was insufficient compensation for the lack of real political power. The corollary of acquiescence in Roman rule was a fixation on the Greek past: "By recreating the situations of the past the contrast between the immense prosperity and the distressing dependence of the contemporary Greek world was dulled."[88] Bowie sees this historical background as going at least some way to explaining the fact that sophistic came into fashion among the urban elites of the eastern half of the empire.[89]

Bowie's attempt to connect the widespread archaizing tendencies in Greek cultural life of the imperial period with the political insignificance of the urban elites has met with considerable opposition, some of which is the result of misunderstandings with regard to the precise content of his explanation. Thus C. P. Jones associates Bowie with those scholars who see the very pronounced cultural self-awareness of Greek aristocrats in the imperial period and their fixation on the classical past as an expression of a *rejection* of the Roman present[90]—a position which one will search for in vain in Bowie's

article. It may be conceded that Bowie's formulations are sometimes responsible for such misunderstandings,[91] and that he tends to typify the attitude of Greek intellectuals *vis-à-vis* Rome exclusively in terms in resignation, while he virtually ignores the by no means sparse testimonia which evidence a more positive appreciation of Roman rule by literary representatives of the Greek elite. All the same, his argument is sound in so far as it allows for recognition of the fact that it was precisely the constant harking back to the past of Greece by members of the social elite in the eastern half of the empire which created the conditions within which they could accept Roman rule and could function with unswerving loyalty within that system, as members of urban aristocracies or—more and more—as members of the imperial aristocracy, without giving up their identity and the self-respect which depended on it.[92] The readiness of the Roman emperors to heed the wishes of the Greek elite in this respect and to take them seriously was naturally of great importance. In particular, by founding the *Panhellēnion,* Hadrian created a framework which facilitated the combination of devotion to the greatness of the Greek past with positive appreciation of the Roman present.[93]

For its practitioners and their audience, sophistic was the medium *par excellence* for the continual reaffirmation of their Greek identity: Philostratus uses terms like *hoi Hellēnes* and *to Hellēnikon* to refer to the students of the major sophists.[94] The show rhetoric linked the participants—the sophist and his audience—to the classical past, which had a normative significance, but which was matched by contemporary achievements in this field. When Herodes was praised as 'one of the ten', he remarked modestly that he was no lesser a light than Andocides (*VS* 564f.), and the Smyrneans found that Hippodromus was a match for the classical orators (*VS* 619). Aristides received similar acclaim in his dreams.[95] This identity was experienced in a depoliticised context in which prestige resulting from literary and cultural activities was at least equivalent to, and could even substitute for the prestige that arose from a political career.[96] The *Anabasis Alexandri* represented 'fatherland, family and public office' for Arrian, and he equated his literary reputation with the military fame of Alexander the Great;[97] Herodes Atticus attached more value to a reputation as sophist than to his consular status and origin.[98] Greek aristocrats could experience their identity and acquire prestige in a field that was more or less independent of political reality, while at the same time remaining loyal to Roman rule. On the one hand, they cherished autonomy in that field in which they felt themselves to be superior; on the other hand, apart from a few exceptions like Chrestus of Byzantium, they were constantly eager for recognition from the politically powerful: a recognition that the great sophists apparently experienced as a confirmation of the value of their art and of the prestige to which it gave rise. The same paradox is characteristic of the way in which the author of the *VS* deals with the relation between *paideia* and political power.

Notes

1. The lexicographer also mentions μελέται and διαλέξεις, which were characteristic of the sophist, among the literary products of Philostratus II.

2. Bowersock (1969) 12-15; Anderson (1986) 8-10; and see now Brunt (1994) 26-33. Brunt's article came to my attention too late to be taken fully into account.

3. On this undertaking see Brancacci (1986) 89. Brancacci (1986) is a slightly abbreviated and revised version of the sections of Brancacci (1985) dealing with Philostratus, Eunapius and Synesius.

4. See Russell (1988) 237: "The most impressive parts of the book are the excellent accounts of Philostratus and Synesius."

5. Brancacci (1985) 86-92; the citation is on p. 91. Cf. Brancacci (1986) 89-100.

6. Brancacci (1986) 91f. and esp. 96: ". . . le plan ontologique continue d'être présupposé par Philostrate."

7. *VS* 480: . . . ὁ παλαιὸς σοφιστὴς ὡς εἰδὼς λέγει. (. . .) ἡ δὲ τοιαύτη ἰδέα τῶν προοιμίων εὐγένειάν τε προηχεῖ τῶν λόγων καὶ φρόνημα καὶ κατάληψιν σαφῆ τοῦ ὄντος. Cf. Cassin (1986) 19: "la 'claire saisie de l'étant' à laquelle ils (the sophists, jjf) parviennent n'est jamais, et très explicitement, qu'un effet de style." For criticism of Brancacci's interpretation see *ibid.* n. 24.

8. See esp. Brancacci (1986) 94.

9. Brancacci (1986) 94f.

10. See Hahn (1989) 46-53, with Flinterman (1991) 505f.

11. *VS* 484-492; cf. Penella (1979a) 166; Anderson (1986) 9; Brunt (1994) 40f.

12. In assessing the content of this letter, my emphasis is slightly different from that of Penella (1979a) 165, who claims: "In making Plato emulate Gorgias, Philostratus is advocating the compatibility of philosophy and rhetoric/sophistry." This formulation does not adequately bring out the importance of style as an artistic category in the Philostratean concept of *paideia*.

13. Gell. 1.9.9f.; cf. Hahn (1989) 86f.

14. See Reardon (1971) 185-198, esp. 186, 190 and 198 for a similar assessment of Philostratus.

15. Cf. Penella (1979a) 165; Anderson (1986) 276.

16. Aristid., *or.* 2.465 (Lenz/Behr): τὸν τῶν ῥητόρων πατέρα καὶ διδάσκαλον. On Plato among representatives of the Second Sophistic cf. De Lacy (1974).

17. Aristid., *or.* 2.205-211 and 394-399 (Lenz/Behr); cf. Isoc., *Nicocles* 5-9.

18. Aristid., *or.* 3.509f. (Lenz/Behr): διαλεκτική forms a part of ῥητορική.

19. *Contra* Penella (1979a) 165: "If confronted with the Platonic denunciations, Philostratus might have responded with arguments like those employed by Aelius Aristides . . ."

20. Anderson (1986) 12.

21. Goudriaan (1989) 49-64.

22. Goudriaan (1989) 52-55; cf. Anderson (1989) 84-87 and (1993) 17-21; Brunt (1994) 30 and 47.

23. Anderson (1986) 82-85.

24. See Bowie (1982) 30 and 54f. Doubts on the correctness of the impression conveyed by the author of the *VS* in Anderson (1989) 148f.

25. Cf. Anderson (1986) 79f.

26. *VS* 511: οὗτος γὰρ ὁ Νικήτης παραλαβὼν τὴν ἐπιστήμην ἐς στενὸν ἀπειλημμένην ἔδωκεν αὐτῇ παρόδους πολλῷ λαμπροτέρας ὧν αὐτὸς τῇ σμύρνῃ ἐδείματο, συνάψας τὴν πόλιν ταῖς ἐπὶ τὴν Ἔφεσον πύλαις καὶ διὰ μέγεθος ἀντεξάρας λόγοις ἔργα. Cf. Anderson (1986) 36 and 70 for the significance of the metaphor, which refers to public works commissioned and funded by the sophist; Veyne (1976) 287-289 and Sartre (1991) 150f. for the financing of public works as a form of 'évergétisme'.

27. Goudriaan (1989) 56 and 59f. Further research would reveal whether this also applies to coins. According to Münsterberg (1915) 119, the title 'sophist' is only found on coins from Smyrna dating from the reign of Hadrian up to and including that of Septimius Severus. Brunt (1994) 33-37 explains Philostratus' chronology from a hypothetical blossoming of sophistic oratory from the second half of the first century A.D. onwards. This efflorescence was, in his view, a corollary of the gradual curtailment of the autonomy of Greek cities which resulted in a more and more exclusive concentration on 'mere epideictic' at the expense of deliberative and forensic oratory. This explanation seems to supplement rather than to contradict the one given here. Note, however, Brunt's cautionary notice on the relevance of the appearance of the title 'sophist' in inscriptions, *ibid.*, 35 n. 41.

28. Bowersock (1969) 58.

29. Bowie (1982) passim; cf. Brunt (1994) 34-36.

30. On this point cf. Goudriaan (1989) 30-38.

31. It should be borne in mind that Philostratus did not regard Dio as a sophist *pur sang,* but as a philosopher with the reputation of a sophist. Dio himself seems to have regarded bringing about concord in a city as a part of his philosophical activity, see e.g. *or.* 48.14 and cf. Hahn (1989) 171. Philostratus makes no mention of Aristides' speeches on concord before the cities of Asia (*or.* 23 Keil) and the citizens of Rhodes (*or.* 24 Keil).

32. Philostratus makes no mention of Antiochus' epigraphically attested role as an envoy of Aegae to Argos. On this mission see Robert (1977a) 119-129. I owe this reference to Professor H. W. Pleket.

33. On this question cf. Anderson (1986) 79.

34. See Anderson (1986) 31f.

35. In considering the numerous mentions of the holding of public office by sophists in the *VS,* it should be borne in mind that the distinction between magistracies and civic contributions no longer existed in this period, see Veyne (1976) 272-276 and 354 n. 252, where he refers to the use of language by the author of the *VS* in this connection; cf. Sartre (1991) 139-141. I still consider it useful to distinguish direct political activity, for example in the form of taking part in meetings of the council or the assembly, from *euergesia.*

36. See *VS* 494: demanding a μισθός is a πρᾶγμα οὐ μεμπτόν, ἃ γὰρ σὺν δαπάνῃ σπουδάζομεν, μᾶλλον ἀσπαζόμεθα τῶν προῖκα.

37. *VS* 605: . . . εἰπὼν πολλῷ ἥδιον ἐς τοιαῦτα δαπανᾶν παιδικὰ ἢ ἐς καλούς τε καὶ καλάς.

38. See e.g. *VS* 519 (Scopelian) and 606 (Damianus). Aristid., *or.* 32.16 (Keil) attributes precisely the attitude toward μισθός of which Philostratus approves to the grammarian Alexander of Cotiaeum: Μυρία δὲ εὐεργετήσας μυρίους οὐδένα πώποτε τῆς εὐεργεσίας μισθὸν ᾔτεσεν, τῆς μέντοι τέχνης οὐκ ἠσχύνετο λαμβάνων, ἐδόκει γὰρ αὐτῷ λυσιτελεῖν τοῖς νέοις μαθημάτων εἴνεκα τολμᾶν προίεσθαι, καὶ ταῦτα ὅστις δυνατός· ἐπεὶ τοὺς γε ἀδυνάτους οὐκ ἠνώχλει ἀλλὰ καὶ παρ' αὐτοῦ προστιθέντα αὐτὸν ἴσμεν.

39. *VS* 614; on the distinction cf. *VS* 567 (Theodotus) and 600 (Apollonius), with Rothe (1988) 60f.

40. *VS* 606; cf. *VS* 519 (Scopelian).

41. *VS* 524f.; Polemo's arrogance: *VS* 535.

42. The full material on delegations in Bowie (1982) 55f. Only a few cases will be mentioned here.

43. *VS* 520; cf. Suet., *Dom.* 7.2.

44. *VS* 582f.; cf. Aristid., *or.* 18-20 (Keil).

45. Bowie (1982) 33, who refers in particular to *VS* 570f. (Alexander of Seleucia before Antoninus Pius) and 622f. (Philiscus before Caracalla).

46. *VS* 561: . . . οὐδὲ σχηματίσας τὸν λόγον.

47. *VS* 560f. Cf. Philostratus' remarks on the case of Polemo and Antoninus Pius, *VS* 534f. When the future emperor was proconsul of Asia, he stayed temporarily in the sophist's house in Smyrna during a visit to the city. Polemo was not at home at the time, but when he returned at night, he made a scene and threw the proconsul out of doors. After becoming emperor, Antoninus made jokes about this incident, but he did not bear the sophist a grudge. Philostratus sees this as an illustration of exceptional mildness (πραότης). See also *VS* 489 (Hadrian and Favorinus).

48. *VS* 500: . . . μὴ ἐκκαλεῖσθαι τὰς τυραννίδας, μηδὲ ἐς ὀργὴν ἄγειν ἤθη ὠμά.

49. *VS* 607: ὑφ' ὧν παροξυνθῆναι τὸν βασιλέα μὴ ἀπιστῶμεν, καὶ γὰρ ἂν καὶ ἰδιώτην ταῦτα παρώξυνε βουλόμενόν γε τὸ δοκεῖν ἐπιβεβουλεῦσθαι μὴ ἀπιστεῖεθαι. See also the comments on the (unhistorical) execution of the sophist Antiphon by Dionysius of Syracuse (*VS* 499): Ἀπέθανε μὲν οὖν περὶ σικελίαν ὑπὸ Διονυσίου τοῦ τυράννου, τὰς δ' αἰτίας, ἐφ' αἷς ἀπέθανεν, Ἀντιφῶντι μᾶλλον ἢ Διονυσίῳ προσγράφομεν. For this version of the death of Antiphon, which is the result of confusion with the tragic poet of the same name (see Arist. *Rh.* 1385a9-13), cf. [Plu.], *Vita Antiphontis, Mor.* 833b-c. On *VS* 607 and 499 cf. Anderson (1986) 53 and 34. Incidentally, nowhere in the *VS* does Philostratus call Caracalla or any other emperor a tyrant. He does not make any disparaging remarks about Caracalla. The positive verdict on Nero's treatment of Nicetes in connection with the latter's conflict with Verginius Rufus is also remarkable, see *VS* 512 and cf. Fant (1981) 242: ". . . a Solomonic figure far removed from the Nero of the senatorial historians." See Fant (1981) 240f. n. 4 for arguments in favour of reading Νέρωνα (Wright) instead of Νερούα (Kayser).

50. On the παρρησία that philosophers are expected to display in the face of autocrats see Murray (1970) 306f.; Hahn (1989) 189f.; Rawson (1989) 253. In *VS* 625 Philostratus relates how his younger namesake levelled the accusation of

cowardice against Aelian, who had written a tirade against Elagabalus shortly after his fall, for not daring to voice his complaints until after the death of the tyrant. At first sight this appears to be in conflict with the present outline of the mentality of the author of the *VS.* However, there is no need to assume that Philostratus must have been in complete agreement with his namesake's criticisms of Aelian in order to appreciate his remark as a *bon mot,* see also Anderson (1986) 48. If *ep.* 72 (to 'Antoninus') is addressed to Caracalla and contains a veiled reference to the killing of Geta—which is by no means certain, see Münscher (1907) 535 and Solmsen (1941) 165—we may be certain that the emperor never read this letter, cf. Anderson (1986) 6.

51. Cf. Anderson (1986) 6.

52. On Marcus' attitude toward the Second Sophistic see Rutherford (1989) 80-89. As a colleague of Polemo (Polemo was so arrogant that he did not regard monarchs as his superiors, see *VS* 535) and as someone who saw himself as the equal of Alexander the Great in his own field (*or.* 50.49 Keil), Aristides' behaviour is less unaccountable than is supposed by Gascó (1989). Gascó's explanation of this behaviour—that the sophist was afraid to appear before the emperor because he was a friend of the father of Avidius Cassius, who had made an attempt to usurp the throne—is therefore unnecessary and far-fetched. On this episode see also Quet (1992) 383f.

53. On the importance of a congenial setting for a sophist's performance before an emperor cf. *VS* 614 (Philostratus' explanation of Heraclides' failure in a declamation before Septimius Severus).

54. SHA, *Hadr.* 15.12: *non recte suadetis, familiares, qui non patimini me illum doctiorem omnibus credere qui habet triginta legiones.* Cf. Baldwin (1982) 69f. and, for a similar anecdote on Tiberius and Ateius Capito, D.C. 57.17.1-3. On Favorinus' conflict with Hadrian see Swain (1989).

55. On this aspect cf. Millar (1977) 491-506.

56. *VS* 621 (καὶ γὰρ δὴ καὶ ἀπεσχεδίαζεν (sc. ὁ Κυρῖνος) προσφυέστερος δὲ ταῖς κατηγορίαις δοκῶν ἐπιστεύθη ἐκ βασιλέως τὴν τοῦ ταμιείου γλῶτταν) and *VS* 626 (Caracalla appointed Heliodorus *advocatus fisci* ὡς ἐπιτηδειότερον δικαστηρίοις καὶ δίκαις).

57. Philostratus refers to Alexander of Seleucia under Marcus Aurelius (*VS* 571), Hadrian of Tyre under Commodus (*VS* 590), Antipater of Hierapolis under Septimius Severus (*VS* 607), and Aspasius of Ravenna under Caracalla or Severus Alexander (*VS* 628).

58. *VS* 524; cf. Bowie (1982) 40 and Anderson (1986) 65.

59. *VS* 607; cf. Anderson (1986) 65. Philostratus singles out for praise the way in which Antipater empathised with the role of the emperor. Aspasius of Ravenna, on the other hand, remained too much of a sophist in his post as *ab epistulis,* with negative effects on the clarity of his correspondence, while lucidity was a stylistic priority for an emperor (*VS* 628). The criticisms of Aspasius in the *VS* echo the Lemnian's pamphlet against the *ab epistulis* (*Dial.* 1). However, while the Lemnian regards σαφήνεια as the top priority of letter-writing in general, the author of the *VS* appears to regard this quality as a necessary characteristic of *imperial* letter-writing. P. M. M. Leunissen pointed out to me that if Aspasius was *ab epistulis* under Severus Alexander and was responsible as such for formulating the emperor's edict on the *aurum coronarium* (*P. Fay.* 20; on the communis opinion that this is an edict of Severus Alexander see Oliver [1978] 479), the verdict of the Philostrati is not far off the mark.

60. See *VS* 524 for the incorporation of Dionysius of Miletus in the equestrian order and his appointment as 'satrap' (i.e. procurator, cf. Bowersock [1969] 52 with n. 3) of an unspecified province; *VS* 567 for the consular rank of Aristocles of Pergamum; *VS* 607 for Antipater's *adlectio inter consulares* and appointment as legatus of Pontus and Bithynia. The consulate of Herodes and his position as corrector of the free cities of Asia are only mentioned in passing in the *VS,* see *VS* 548, 554 and 536.

61. Bowie (1982) 46-50.

62. Bowie (1982) 50.

63. *VS* 536: ἦρα μὲν γὰρ τοῦ αὐτοσχεδιάζειν ὁ Ἡρώδης μᾶλλον ἢ τοῦ ὕπατός τε καὶ ἐξ ὑπάτων δοκεῖν.

64. *VS* 591f. On the priority of a reputation as a sophist above the consular status of a family or the holding of prestigious positions cf. *VS* 597 (Rufus of Perinth) and 612f. (Heraclides of Lycia). On this theme see also Anderson (1986) 81.

65. *VS* 524 (Dionysius) and 532f. (Polemo).

66. *VS* 588f.: ἀγασθεὶς δὲ αὐτὸν ὁ αὐτοκράτωρ επὶ μέγα ἦρε δωρεαῖς τε καὶ δώροις.

67. *VS* 582. Of course, Aristides himself calls Marcus and Commodus οἰκισταὶ τῆς πόλεως, but does not fail to mention his own influence on the emperors, *or.* 19.4 and 7 (Keil). In these cases, Polemo and Aristides acted as 'brokers in distributing *beneficia*'; on this phenomenon see Saller (1982) 74-78.

68. *VS* 530: ἐπιτηδειότατος τῶν πάλαι βασιλέων γενόμενος ἀρετὰς αὐξῆσαι.

69. See Hahn (1989) 185-191; Rawson (1989) 233-235.

70. The term σοφιστής has heavily pejorative connotations in a number of passages in the speeches of Aristides, see e.g. *or.* 28.128 and 131 (Keil); *or.* 33.29 (Keil); *or.* 34.47 (Keil) and *or.* 50.95 (Keil), and cf. Behr (1968) 106. Even Stanton (1973) 355, who differs from Behr in claiming that σοφιστής is not always a term of deprecation in Aristides, has to concede "that there remains a residue of passages where *sophistes* is a term which Aristides would not wish to have applied to himself." It is at any rate clear that Aristides wanted to distinguish himself from the sophists of his own day, whom he accused of greed and cheap sensationalism in their attempts to curry the favours of the audience; on his disapproval of *improvised* declamations cf. *VS* 583. All the same, there are insufficient grounds for excluding Aristides and his oeuvre of speeches, a large proportion of which are historical declamations, from the Second Sophistic; he is exceptional in certain respects, but he is not an outsider.

71. Aristid., *or.* 47.46 (Keil): Ἐνάτη ἐπὶ δέκα ἐδόκουν ἐν τοῖς βασιλείοις διατρίβειν, τὴν δ'ἐπιμέλειαν καὶ τιμὴν τῶν αὐτοκρατόρων εἰς ἐμὲ θαυμαστὴν καὶ ἀνυπέρβλητον εἶναι διὰ πάντων ἑξῆς ὧν ἔπραττον· μόνῳ γὰρ ἅπαντα γίγνεσθαι ὧν οὐδὲ μικρὸν ἄλλῳ τῳ.

72. *VS* 616: . . . τὴν τέχνην φίλαυτόν τε καὶ ἀλαζόνα . . .

73. On the rivalry between the two cities cf. D.Chr. *or.* 34.48.

74. As rightly pointed out by Bowersock (1969) 90.

75. D. Chr., *or.* 38; Aristid., *or.* 23 (Keil). On this subject cf. Robert (1977b) passim; C. P. Jones (1978) 83-94; Sheppard (1984-6) 231-237.

76. D.Chr., *or.* 34.48; cf. Aristid., *or.* 23.62f. (Keil).

77. C. P. Jones (1978) 85.

78. Hdn. 3.2.7-9.

79. Hdn. 3.2.2; D.C. 74.6.3; 74.10.1-14.6.

80. *VS* 616: . . . ὡς μὴ δοκοίη δι' ἑνὸς ἀνδρὸς κηρύττεσθαι πόλις ὅπλα ἐπὶ Ῥωμαίους ἠρμένη. Cf. the remark by Robert (1967) 26f., who points out that the incident "montre avec force comment la proclamation du vainqueur et celle de sa patrie sont étroitement liées."

81. *VS* 591: οὐχ αἱ μύριαι τὸν ἄνδρα. Dionysius of Miletus expressed the same idea to Hadrian's *ab*

epistulis Avidius Heliodorus (D.C. 69.3.5): Καῖσαρ χρήματα μέν σοι καὶ τιμὴν δοῦναι δύναται, ῥήτορα δέ σε ποιῆσαι οὐ δύναται.

82. Plu., *Mor.* 814a-c; cf. C. P. Jones (1972) 113f. and, for the dating, 136; Millar (1969) 13f.; Sheppard (1984-6) 238.

83. D. Chr., *or.* 50.2; cf. *or.* 43.3; Aristid., *or.* 24.23 (Keil) uses the significant term μειρακιῶδες, 'schoolboyish'.

84. . . . On this passage see also De Lacy (1974) 9.

85. The evidence has been collected by Kennedy (1974) 19. Of the approximate 45 ὑποθέσεις mentioned by Philostratus, 31 are of a historical nature. Five refer to Xerxes, three to Darius, and seven to Demosthenes. It may be added to the data presented by Kennedy that seven ὑποθέσεις refer to situations connected with the Peloponnesian war. See also Bowie (1970) 7: no themes postdating 326 B.C.

86. Russell (1983) 107: of the roughly 350 known historical ὑποθέσεις, 43 refer to the Persian wars, 90 to the Peloponnesian war and 125 to the period of Demonsthenes.

87. This is an example of an ἐσχηματισμένος λόγος: the speaker's aim was to convince the Athenians to do the opposite, viz. to take a stand and put up a fight. On this term see Russell (1983) 138.

88. Bowie (1970) passim; conclusions on pp. 35-41; the citation is from p. 41.

89. Bowie (1970) 6; cf. Bowie (1982) 44f.

90. C. P. Jones (1972) 126 with n. 23.

91. See e.g. Bowie (1970) 28: "To a certain extent the archaistic tendencies must be taken as a flight from the present. With the autonomy of Greek cities only nominal those Greeks who felt that in a different age they might have wielded political power in a Greek context must needs be dissatisfied with the present and attempt to convert it to the past where their ideal world lay."

92. So Meijer (1985) 62. On this subject see also Lane Fox (1986) 49; Reardon (1989) 274f. Anderson (1989) 142f. contests Bowie's 'political' interpretation of the archaism mainly by pointing out that archaism was no new phenomenon. However, it is difficult to find clear parallels from earlier periods for the dedication with which members of the social elite in the eastern half of the empire practised show rhetoric from the second half of the first century, and for the prestige that they derived from this cultural activity; see now also Anderson (1993) 101-132; Brunt (1994) 36.

93. On the *Panhellēnion* see Spawforth/Walker (1985) and (1986), esp. (1986) 104f. (conclusion); cf. Sheppard (1984-1986) 238f.

94. See Aalders (1981) 12 with n. 46, where he refers to *VS* 571, 587f., 613 and 617; Follet (1991) 206. Cf. Aristid., *or.* 33.24 (Keil) and *or* 50.87 (Keil) for terms (applied to himself) like τῶν Ἑλλήνων ἄκρος and πρῶτος Ἑλλήνων.

95. Aristid., *or.* 50.62 (Keil); *or.* 51.57f. (Keil); cf. Lucian, *Rh.Pr.* 21: τὶ γὰρ ὁ Παιανευς προς ἐμέ;

96. Cf. Aalders (1976) 8f.

97. Ar., *An.* 1.12.5 . . . On this passage cf. Moles (1985) passim. Arist. *or.* 50.49 (Keil) offers an interesting parallel. The orator dreams that he is to be buried with Alexander because Philip's son has achieved the peak of military achievement and he himself has attained the summit of eloquence.

98. *VS* 536.

ABBREVIATIONS

The abbreviations used in referring to the names of Greek authors and their works are those used in: H. G. Liddell, R. Scott, H. Stuart Jones, R. MacKenzie, *A Greek-English Lexicon* (Oxford 1940[9]; supplement 1968). For incidental references to this lexicon the standard abbreviation *LSJ* is used. The abbreviations *VA* (*Vita Apollonii*), *Epp. Apoll.* (*Epistulae Apollonii*), *VS* (*Vitae Sophistarum*) and *VP* (*De Vita Pythagorica* or *Vita Pythagorae*) are used in the main body of the text as well as in the references. Names of Christian Greek authors and their works not included in the list of abbreviations in *LSJ* are generally abbreviated in accordance with G. W. H. Lampe, *A Patristic Greek Lexicon* (Oxford 1961). The names of Latin authors and their works are abbreviated in accordance with the system of P. G. W. Glare (ed.), *Oxford Latin Dictionary* (Oxford 1982). In the few cases in which I have departed from the abbreviations used in these lexicons, I have generally given the full names of authors and/or works; otherwise, I hope that my abbreviations will not give the reader any problems. Titles of periodicals and series are abbreviated in the bibliography (see below) as in *L'Année Philologique*. Where reference is made in a note to an introduction or extended commentary in an edition of an ancient author, the edition in question is generally included under the name of the writer of the introduction or commentary in the bibliography. Collections of inscriptions and documentary papyri are referred to in accordance with the abbreviations used in the *Supplementum Epigraphicum Graecum* and the *Berichtigungsliste der griechischen Papyrusurkunden aus Ägypten* respectively.

Bibliography

AALDERS, G. J. D. (1976), 'Grieks zelfbewustzijn in de Romeinse keizertijd', in: *Handelingen van het vierendertigste Nederlands Filologencongres* (Amsterdam) 1-13

AALDERS, G. J. D. (1981), *Echt-Grieks.*Afscheidscollege gegeven bij zijn aftreden als hoogleraar in de Oude Geschiedenis en de Griekse en Romeinse staatsinstellingen aan de faculteit der Letteren van de Vrije Universiteit te Amsterdam op 17 oktober 1981 (Amsterdam)

ANDERSON, G. (1986), *Philostratus. Biography and belles lettres in the third century A.D.* (London etc.)

ANDERSON, G. (1993), *The Second Sophistic. A cultural phenomenon in the Roman Empire* (London/New York)

BALDWIN, B. (1982), 'Literature and society in the Later Roman Empire', in: B.K. Gold (ed.), *Literary and artistic patronage in ancient Rome* (Austin) 67-83

BEHR, C. A. (1968), *Aelius Aristides and the Sacred Tales* (Amsterdam)

BETZ, H. D. (1983), 'Gottmensch II', in: *Reallexikon für Antike und Christentum* 12: 234-312

BOWERSOCK, G. W. (1969), *Greek sophists in the Roman empire* (Oxford)

BOWIE, E. L. (1970), 'Greeks and their past in the second sophistic', in: *P & P* [*Past and Present*] 46: 3-41 [reprinted in: M.I. Finley (ed.), *Studies in Ancient Society* (London/Boston 1974) 166-209]

BOWIE, E. L. (1978), 'Apollonius of Tyana: tradition and reality', in: *ANRW* [*Aufstieg und Niedergang der Römischen Welt*] 2.16.2: 1652-1699

BOWIE, E. L. (1982), 'The importance of sophists', *YCIS* [*Yale Classical Studies*] 27: 29-59

BRADLEY, K. R. (1989), *Slavery and rebellion in the Roman world 140-70 B.C.* (Bloomington, Indiana/London)

BRANCACCI, A. (1985), *Rhetorike philosophousa. Dione Crisostomo nella cultura antica e bizantina* (Napoli)

BRANCACCI, A. (1986), 'Seconde sophistique, historiographie et philosophie (Philostrate, Eunape, Synésios)', in: B. Cassin (ed.), *Le plaisir de parler. Études de sophistique comparée* (Paris) 87-110

BRUNT, P. A. (1994), 'The bubble of the Second Sophistic', *BICS* [*Bulletin. Institute of Classical Studies*] 39 (1994), 25-52

BURKERT, W. (1961), 'Hellenistische Pseudopythagorica', *Philologus* 105: 16-43 and 226-246

BURKERT, W. (1972b), *Lore and science in Ancient Pythagoreanism* (Cambridge, Massachusetts)

CASSIN, B. (1986), 'Du faux ou du mensonge à la fiction (de *pseudos à plasma*)', in: B. Cassin (ed.), *Le plaisir de parler. Études de sophistique comparée* (Paris_ 3-29.

CHADWICK, H. (1953), *Origen. Contra Celsum.* Translated with an introduction and notes by H. Chadwick (Cambridge)

CORRINGTON, G. P. (1986), *The 'Divine Man'. His origin and functions in Hellenistic popular religion* (New York)

FANT, J. C. (1981), 'The choleric Roman official of Philostratus *Vitae Sophistarum* p. 512: L. Verginius Rufus', *Historia* 30: 240-243

FLINTERMAN, J. J. (1991), review of Hahn (1989), *Mnemosyne* 44: 504-507

FOLLET, S. (1991), 'Divers aspects de l'hellénisme chez Philostrate', in: S. Said (ed.), 'ΕΛΛΗΝΙσΜΟσ. *Quelques jalons pour une histoire de l'identité grecque.* Actes du Colloque de Strasbourg, 25-27 octobre 1989 (Leiden) 205-215

GALLAGHER, E. V. (1982), *Divine Man or Magician? Celsus and Origen on Jesus* (Chicago)

GASCÓ, F. (1989), 'The meeting between Aelius Aristides and Marcus Aurelius in Smyrna', *AJPh [American Journal of Philology]* 110: 471-478

GOUDRIAAN, K. (1989), *Over classicisme. Dionysius van Halicarnassus en zijn program van welsprekendheid, cultuur en politiek* (Amsterdam)

GOULET, R. (1981), 'Les vies de philosophes dans l'antiquité tardive et leur portée mystérique', in: *Les Actes apocryphes des apôtres. Christianisme et monde païen.* Publications de la Faculté de Théologie de l'Université de Genève 4 (Genève) 161-208

HAHN, J. (1989), *Der Philosoph und die Gesellschaft. Selbstverständnis, öffentliches Auftreten und populäre Erwartungen in der hohen Kaiserzeit* (Stuttgart)

HOPFNER, T. (1928), 'Mageia', in: *RE [Real-Encyclopädie der Klassischen Altertumswissenshaft]* 14.1: 301-393

JONES, C. P. (1972), *Plutarch and Rome* (Oxford²)

JONES, C. P. (1978), *The Roman world of Dio Chrysostom* (Cambridge, Massachusetts/London)

KENNEDY, G. (1974), 'The sophists as declaimers', in: G.W. Bowersock (ed.), *Approaches to the Second Sophistic* (University Park, Pennsylvania) 17-22

KOSKENNIEMI, E. (1986), 'Die religiösen Tendenzen des Philostratos in der Vita Apollonii Tyanesis', in: H. Koskenniemi, S. Jäkel, V. Pyykkö (Hrsgb.), *Literatur und Philosophie in der Antike* (Turku) 107-117

KOSKENNIEMI, E. (1991), *Der philostrateische Apollonios* (Helsinki)

KOSKENNIEMI, E. (1994), *Apollonios von Tyana in der neutestamentlichen Exegese* (Tübingen)

DE LACY, P. (1974), 'Plato and the intellectual life of the second century A.D.', in: G.W. Bowersock (ed.), *Approaches to the Second Sophistic* (University Park, Pennsylvania) 4-10

LANE FOX, R. (1986), *Pagans and Christians in the Mediterranean world from the second century A.D. to the conversion of Constantine* (London/Harmondsworth)

MACMULLEN, R. (1966), *Enemies of the Roman order. Treason, unrest and alienation in the Empire* (Cambridge, Massachusetts)

MEIJER, F. J. (1985), 'Vrijheid in onderworpenheid: de Grieken in het Imperium Romanum', *Lampas* 18: 53-65

MILLAR, F. (1969), 'P. Herennius Dexippus: the Greek world and the third century invasions', *JRS [Journal of Roman Studies]* 59: 12-29

MILLAR, F. (1977), *The emperor in the Roman world* (London)

MOLES, J. L. (1985), 'The interpretation of the "Second Preface" in Arrian's *Anabasis*', *JHS [Journal of Hellenic Studies]* 105: 162-168

MÜNSCHER, K. (1907), *Die Philostrate.* Philologus Supplementband 10: 467-558

MÜNSTERBERG, R. (1915), 'Die Münzen der Sophisten', *NZ [Neuphilologische Zeitschrift]* 48: 119-124

MURRAY, O. (1970), Περὶ βασιλείας. *Studies in the justification of monarchic power in the hellenistic world* (diss. Oxford)

OLIVER, J. H. (1978), 'On the edict of Severus Alexander (P. Fayum 20)', *AJPh* 99: 474-485

PALM, J. (1976), *Om Filostratus och hans Apolloniosbiografi* (Upsala)

PENELLA, R. J. (1979a), 'Philostratus' letter to Julia Domna', *Hermes* 107: 161-168

PENELLA, R. J. (1979b), *The Letters of Apollonius of Tyana. A critical text with prolegomena, translation and a commentary by R.J. Penella* (Leiden)

PHILLIPS, C. R. (1986), 'The sociology of religious knowledge in the Roman Empire to A.D. 284', in: *ANRW* 2.16.3: 2677-2773

POUPON, G. (1981), 'L'accusation de magie dans les actes apocryphes', in: *Les actes apocryphes des apôtres. Christianisme et mnde païen.* Publications de la Faculté de Théologie de Genève 4 (Genève) 71-85

QUET, M.-H., (1992), 'L'inscription de Vérone en l'honneur d'Aelius Aristide et le rayonnement de la Seconde Sophistique chez les "Grecs d'Égypte"', *REA [Revue des études anciennes]* 94: 379-401

RAWSON, E. (1989), 'Roman ruler and the philosophic adviser', in: M. Griffin/J. Barnes (eds), *Philosophia Togata. Essays on philosophy and Roman society* (Oxford) 233-257

REARDON, B. P. (1971), *Courants littéraires grecs des IIe et IIIe siècles après J.-C.* (Paris)

REARDON, B. P. (1989), review of C. P. Jones (1986), *CPh* [*Classical Philology*] 84: 271-275

REMUS, H. (1983), *Pagan-christian conflict over miracle in the second century* (Cambridge, Massachusetts)

ROBERT, L. (1977a), 'Documents d'Asie Mineure', *BCH* [*Bulletin de correspondance hellénique*] 101: 43-132

ROBERT, L. (1977b), 'La titulature de Nicée et de Nicomédie: la gloire et la haine', *HSCP* [*Harvard Studies in Classical Philology*] 81: 1-39 [= *Opera Minora Selecta* 6 (1989) 211-249]

RUSSELL, D. A. (1983), *Greek declamation* (Cambridge)

RUSSELL, D. A. (1988), review of Brancacci (1985), *JHS* 108: 237f.

RUTHERFORD, R. B. (1989), *The Meditations of Marcus Aurelius. A study* (Oxford)

SALLER, R. P. (1982), *Personal patronage under the Early Empire* (Cambridge etc.)

SARTRE, M. (1991), *L'Orient romain. Provinces et sociétés provinciales en Méditerranée orientale d'Auguste aux Sévères (31 avant J.-C.-235 après J.-C.)* (Paris)

SHEPPARD, A. R. R. (1984-6), '*Homonoia* in the Greek cities of the Roman Empire', *Anc Soc* [*Ancient Society*] 15-17: 229-252

SMITH, J. Z. (1978), *Map is not territory. Studies in the history of religions* (Leiden)

SMITH, M. (1973), *Clement of Alexandria and a secret gospel of Mark* (Cambridge, Massachusetts)

SOLMSEN, F. (1940), 'Some works of Philostratus the Elder', *TAPhA* [*Transactions and Proceedings. American Philological Association*] 71: 556-572 [= *Kleine Schriften* 2 (1968) 75-91]

SOLMSEN, F. (1941), 'Philostratus (9)-(12)', in:*RE* [*Real-Encyclopädie der Klassischen Altertumswissenshaft*] 20.1: 124-177 [= *Kleine Schriften* 2 (1968) 91-118]

SPAWFORTH, A. J./WALKER, S. (1985), 'The world of the Panhellenion. I. Athens and Eleusis', *JRS* 75: 78-104

STANTON, G. R. (1973), 'Sophists and philosophers: problems of classification', *AJPh* 94: 350-364

SWAIN, S. (1989), 'Favorinus and Hadrian', *ZPE* [*Zeitschrift für Papyrologie und Epigraphik*] 79: 150-158

TALBERT, C. H. (1978), 'Biographies of philosophers and rulers as instruments of religious propaganda in Mediterranean Antiguity', in:*ANRW* 2.16.2: 1619-1651

VERSNEL, H. S. (1991), 'Some reflections on the relationship magic-religion', *Numen* 38: 177-197

VEYNE, P. (1976), *Le pain et le cirque. Sociologie historique d'un pluralisme politique* (Paris)

Jaap-Jan Flinterman (essay date 1995)

SOURCE: Flinterman, Jaap-Jan. "The Main Character." In *Power, Paideia & Pythagoreanism: Greek Identity, Conceptions of the Relationship between Philosophers and Monarchs and Political Ideas in Philostratus's* Life of Apollonius, pp. 60-66. Amsterdam, Netherlands: J. C. Gieben, 1995.

[*In the following excerpt, Flinterman discusses Apollonius of Tyana, examining the ontological status of the main character, and expounding on Philostratus's attitude toward magic and his hero.*]

At numerous points in his work Philostratus explicitly states his intention of offering his readers a view of Apollonius which deviates from current opinion; in fact, it is at odds with it. Philostratus' view can be summarised as follows: Apollonius was a Pythagorean philosopher whose exceptional wisdom earned him the reputation of being a supernatural, divine being.[1] Philostratus provides an explicit statement of this objective in the programmatic chapters which introduce the book. *VA (Life of Apollonius of Tyana)* 1.1 deals with Pythagoreanism, and is directly followed by an outline of the main features of Philostratus' image of Apollonius (1.2). The succeeding chapters, on Apollonius' youth, focus on his choice of Pythagoreanism and the consequences it entails for his life-style: he abstains from meat and wine, adopts celibacy, and observes a strict rule of silence for five years (1.7f. and 13f.). Philostratus opposes this view of the sage of Tyana to the notion that Apollonius was a magician (*magos*) who engaged in *goēteia,* dishonest magic.[2] This view was connected with prophecies and miracles attributed to the sage of Tyana. Philostratus does not deny the supernatural capacities of his hero, but he repudiates the idea that Apollonius had anything at all do with *goēteia* or that he deserved the title *magos.* The miraculous stories in the *VA* are related to the hero's supernatural knowledge and wisdom; Philostratus presents Apollonius' prophecies and miracles as a corollary of his divine nature or as the result of his asceticism and his divine inspiration and assistance (7.38f.; 5.12; 8.7.9).

Contradictory views of a miracle-worker like those found in the *VA* play a crucial role in Celsus' attacks on Christianity and its founder and in Origen's reaction to them. The work of the pagan polemicist dates from the 170s; Origen's defence was written in the 240s.[3] The period of their debate thus corresponds exactly to the lifespan of the author of the *VA*. The terms of the debate come remarkably close to those used by Philostratus in his defence of Apollonius. Celsus claims time and again that the miracles performed by Jesus prove that he was a *goēs;* Origen is equally insistent that Jesus performed miracles by means of divine power.[4] It is plausible to suppose that such controversies were based on some tangible social phenomenon: the activities of charismatic wise men and miracle-workers, who operated more or less independently of the institutionalised cults, and who claimed a special relationship with the divine which was expressed in their supernatural powers.[5] Their activities provoked a wide range of reactions, ranging from devotion to disapproval. Either the supernatural powers of the sage and miracle-worker were attributed to a special relationship with the divine or divinity; or the supernatural acts were simply treated as instances of magic or *goēteia*. *Magos* and *goēs* were regarded as more or less synonymous in these debates; both terms were used in a pejorative sense.[6]

In general, for the inhabitants of the Greco-Roman world in the first centuries A.D. the term 'magic' meant the manipulation of supernatural forces by means of spells and rituals which were believed to bring about the desired effect automatically. At the same time, words like *magos* and *goēs* were used to stigmatise socially deviant, and therefore undesirable, views and behaviour.[7] The question of what people had to do to be accused of 'magic' cannot be answered with a simple reference to their alleged machinations; as we have seen, supernatural acts could be interpreted in very different ways, either as signs of divine assistance or as the result of dabbling in the supernatural. In inquiring into the background to an accusation of 'magic', we therefore have to begin by explaining in what respects the views and behaviour of the person accused of 'magic' deviated from the norms of the individuals or groups who wielded enough social influence to initiate the process of making allegations.[8]

In the case of charismatic sages and miracle-workers like Apollonius, one can point to the tension between such figures and the institutionalised cults. Sages and miracle-workers probably made regular attempts to use existing shrines as their seat of operations,[9] and they were sometimes successful; at the same time, their claim to a special relationship with the divine could be regarded as a threat to the position of institutionalised cults. Even if they were not inevitable, conflicts were certainly on the cards. The *VA* contains various indications to support the assumption that the existence of a tension between the sage of Tyana and the priests of the institutionalised cults was a recurrent theme in the Apol-

lonius tradition. Although Philostratus mentions that his hero lived for a time in the temple of Asclepius in Aegae (1.7-12), and records positive reactions to his activities from the oracles of Colophon and Didyma and the temple of Asclepius in Pergamum (4.1), he cannot gloss over the fact that, according to various local traditions, the first reaction when the sage of Tyana wanted to visit a shrine was to bar his entry as a *goēs* (witness his reception in Eleusis (4.18), the oracle of Trophonius in Lebadea (8.19), and the temple of Dictynna on Crete (8.30)).[10] The priests of these shrines were understandably averse to pretentious rivals; moreover, Apollonius' disapproval of sacrifices—a recurrent theme in various parts of the Apollonius tradition[11]—may help to explain their attitude. Sacrifices were the ideal opportunity for members of the urban elites to display their civic qualities by paying for the ceremonies and regaling their fellow citizens with wine and meat. They thereby demonstrated their indispensability in two ways: the community was dependent on them not only for its immediate material prosperity, but also for the maintenance of a harmonious relation with the gods by holding religious festivals with the appropriate ostentation.[12] To condemn sacrifices was thus more than an expression of religious non-conformism: it was an attack on a practice which played a key role in the legitimation of the social and political order.

As mentioned above, Philostratus sometimes explains Apollonius' prophecies and miracles in terms of divine revelation and assistance. The predominant view in the *VA* as a whole, however, is that the sage of Tyana is himself in possession of a supernatural, divine nature. Philostratus primarily conveys this impression to his readers through the reactions of people who are confronted by Apollonius and recognise him as a holy man (*theios anēr*) (2.17; 2.40; 8.15) or *daimōn* (1.19; 4.44).[13] There is a crucial episode in this respect in Book 7. After being thrown into irons in prison on the orders of Domitian, Apollonius frees his leg of the fetters in the presence of Damis. Damis now realises fully for the first time that his master is endowed with a 'divine and superhuman nature'.[14] The *VA* does not provide any unambiguous indication that Apollonius is in fact a god. However, although Philostratus' Apollonius declines divine honours (4.31) and seems to regard those who believe that he is a god as the victims of a delusion (in the speech written for his defence before Domitian, 8.7.7), the reader is given the impression that the author is motivated by a desire to avoid giving offence rather than by the need to refute incorrect views.[15]

The claim that Apollonius was endowed with a superhuman nature is stressed in the *VA* by stories about the omens connected with his birth (1.5), according to which he was an incarnation of Proteus (1.4) and a son of Zeus (1.6), and by the traditions on his miraculous departure from this life (8.29f.). Philostratus provides different versions of how Apollonius' life on earth ended. His own preference is for the tradition that the sage of Tyana ascended into heaven; he attempts to substantiate this tradition with the remark that, during his travels over virtually the entire globe, he has never come across a grave of Apollonius.[16] According to the *VA,* Apollonius derived the belief that good people are gods from the Indian sages (3.18; cf. 8.5). As he takes his leave of the sages, their leader Iarchas tells Apollonius that he will be revered by the people as a god not only after his death, but during his life as well (3.50). In the speech written in his defence before Domitian, Apollonius elaborates on this idea of the wise men of India to produce a portrait of the man who creates order in the souls of his fellow men and who is referred to as 'a god sent down by wisdom'.[17] There is no reason to doubt that the hero's words at this point are intended to refer to himself,[18] although the *VA* does not contain any unambiguous statements regarding Apollonius' ontological status. Philostratus resorts to suggestions and the opinions of other without tying himself down. The closest that he comes to voicing his own opinion is when he interprets a sign at the birth of Apollonius as a divine indication that he should 'transcend all things upon earth and approach the gods';[19] but here too he refuses to commit himself unequivocally.[20]

What is the reason for this ambiguity? We cannot rule out the possibility that some degree of reticence on the part of the author of the *VA* is involved; as we shall see, there are occasional signs in the *VA* that the writer felt certain reservations towards his theme, despite the openly professed apologetic intention of the work. More important, however, is the fact that, in so far as the pre-Philostratean tradition on Apollonius presented a positive image of the sage of Tyana, it was very likely marked by a similar ambivalence: the superhuman nature of Apollonius and his special relationship with the divine were affirmed without being defined more precisely. The same ambiguity was a typical feature of the tradition on the superhuman nature of Pythagoras himself.[21] According to Aristotle, an esoteric doctrine of the Pythagoreans was that there are three sorts of rational beings: gods, men, and those like Pythagoras.[22] After the revival of Pythagoreanism as a religious and philosophical current in the first century B.C., this doctrine of a third ontological category characterised by a special relationship with the divine or by divinity provided a context within which the activities of charismatic sages and miracle-workers could be set and legitimated.[23]

. . . Philostratus attempts to clear Apollonius of the charge of *goēteia* and to establish a connection between his supernatural powers and his superhuman knowledge and wisdom. It is evident that this endeavour sometimes creates problems for the writer.[24] For instance, while it is impossible to see the miraculous freeing in prison (7.38) as an expression of superior knowledge, nor is there any question of divine assistance, it is this very episode which forces Damis to recognise the superhuman nature of his master. Philostratus is at pains to stress that this is not an instance of *goēteia,* but he does not actually offer any alternative interpretation of this miracle (7.39). It is not enough to note the author's perplexity when faced with such material without inquiring into the background to this phenomenon. This entails an examination of the interaction between the norms and values of Philostratus, on the one hand, and the traditions on Apollonius on which he relied in the writing of the *VA,* on the other. Discussion of the form and content of these traditions will be postponed to the following section; for the time being it is sufficient to note that the Apollonius tradition on which the author of the *VA* drew contains numerous elements which are hard to reconcile with an attempt to clear the sage of Tyana of the charge of magic. I shall confine my remarks here to Philostratus' attitude to magic/*goēteia.*

Philostratus responds to accusations of magic against sophists on two occasions in the *VS* (523 and 590). In both cases he rejects the allegations by arguing that anyone whose reputation as an educated person (*pepaideumenos*) is at stake will keep *goēteia* at arm's length. The same distinction between magic/*goēteia,* on the one hand, and *paideia,* on the other, is postulated by Celsus, who claims that magic can only gain a grip on the intellectually undeveloped and corrupt, not on philosophers (Origen, *Cels.* 6.41). In this way, magic is equated with socio-cultural and moral deprivation, a common enough attitude among Greek intellectuals of the imperial age. Naturally enough, it was very closely connected with the use of the terms 'magic' and 'magician' to stigmatise socially deviant views and behaviour.[25] This rejection of magic/*goēteia* was not always accompanied by a denial of the possible effectiveness of magical practices. The view that identifies magic with simple trickery is mainly found among those who were connected in some way with Epicureanism. It was an Epicurean, a certain Celsus (not to be confused with Origen's pagan opponent), to whom Lucian addressed his satire on Alexander of Abonutichus;[26] Lucian refers to a text written by this Celsus against magicians in which the author apparently endeavoured to reveal magical practices as conjuring tricks.[27] It is interesting to note that Philostratus comes surprisingly close to this point of view in a passage in the *VA.* This is the tirade against *goēteia* (7.39) which follows the account of how Apollonius freed his leg from the fetters in prison (7.38), though it is independent of the content of the previous chapter.[28] Philostratus here claims that simple-minded people, such as athletes, traders and especially those in love, attribute such acts to wizardry.

They believe that any successes they score are the result of such practices (instead of resulting from chance, their own efforts or other purely human factors), and assume that any failure to achieve results is due to negligence in carrying out the recommendations of the magicians. The writer refers to the writings of those who make fun of magic/*goēteia* and reveal how magicians perform all kinds of 'miracles'; he is presumably referring to texts like the one written by the addressee of Lucian's *Alexander*. However, he adds a warning to young people not even to meddle in matters of this kind in this manner, and concludes his digression with the remark that magic/*goēteia* is equally condemned by nature and by law.[29]

The vehement denial of the effectiveness of magical practices and the emphasis on the decisive influence of chance and purely human factors on the results of human actions are highly reminiscent of Lucian's attitude.[30] All the same, it would be an exaggeration to credit Philostratus with a coherent system of views on nature and the supernatural on the basis of these passages from the *VS* and the *VA*. Undeterred by any need to be consistent, in another passage he defends Apollonius against the charge of *goēteia* in connection with his prophetic abilities by claiming that the sage of Tyana could only see into what was predestined thanks to divine inspiration, but that he did not attempt to bring about any changes in that future by means of magic (5.12; cf. 8.7.16). The only consistent feature in the attitude toward *goēteia* of the author of the *VA* and the *VS* is the combination of disdain and repugnance. It is hardly surprising that a writer with such an attitude runs up against difficulties once he undertakes to write a laudatory biography of a man of whom it was said that he could understand the language of birds (1.20; cf. 4.3), that he averted an epidemic by revealing the plague demon and having him stoned (4.10), and that he ordered another demon who had possessed a young man to leave his victim and to demonstrate the effectiveness of the exorcism by overturning a statue (4.20). The question which arises is why a writer who held an attitude of this kind felt inclined to write an apologetic *vie romancée* of Apollonius of Tyana.

It is customary in this connection to refer to the fact that Philostratus began work on the *VA* on the orders of Julia Domna, and to connect the explicit apologetic intention of the writer with the views of Apollonius that were current in her circle.[31] There is no reason to doubt Philostratus' statement that he started work on the life of Apollonius on the instructions of the empress. . . . [T]he literary and philosophical coterie of Julia Domna consisted of a variegated assortment, probably including Platonic and Pythagorean philosophers. It seems reasonable to suppose that both these philosophers and the empress attached importance to a positive image of

the sage of Tyana. However, we are not therefore entitled to assume that Philostratus' portrait of Apollonius met their expectations in every way. The *VA* was not completed until after the death of the empress, suggesting that Philostratus' interest in Apollonius was not just a reflection of the devotion shown Apollonius by the empress and her son.[32] In view of the author's distaste and scorn for anything which might seem to bear the taint of magic/*goēteia*, it is most likely that he was primarily interested in the sage of Tyana because the Apollonius tradition offered him attractive material for literary adaptation.[33] At the same time, his choice of theme reflected the growing interest in and acceptance of figures like Apollonius in educated circles. The controversial character of the protagonist made it virtually impossible for the author not to adopt a particular view of Apollonius; the nature of the material forced him to give vent to the reservations which he entertained with regard to certain aspects of the Apollonius tradition.

Notes

1. See esp. *VA* 1.2: . . . ἔψαυσε τοῦ δαιμόνιός τε καὶ θεῖος νομισθῆναι.

2. Unlike μάγος and μαγεία, γόης and γοητεία are completely pejorative terms, at least since the classical period, see Burkert (1962) 50; Poupon (1981) 71. The term γόης has various connotations, which can be summed up as 'meddler in the supernatural': a γόης is a dishonest magician, a charlatan and a cheat, see MacMullen (1966) 322 n. 20. Philostratus does not distinguish clearly between μάγος and γόης.

3. See Chadwick (1953) xxvi-xxviii and xiv-xv.

4. See e.g. Origen, *Cels.* 1.6, 38 and 68; 2.48-51. For conflicting views of sages and miracle-workers in the imperial age see Gallagher (1982) 41-150 (a full-length discussion of the *Contra Celsum*) and 157-165 (on the *VA*).

5. See e.g. D.S. 34/5.2.5-9, with Bradley (1989) 55-57 (Eunus, the leader of the first Sicilian slave revolt); Origen, *Cels.* 7.9, with Chadwick (1953) 402f. n. 6; *Act. Ap.* 8.9-24 (Simon Magus).

6. See M. Smith (1973) 227-229.

7. I am here following Aune (1980) 1510-1516, esp. 1515, whose definition of magic takes into account both the explicit criteria for the application of the term by Greco-roman users and its social function: "magic is defined as that form of religious deviance whereby individual and social goals are sought by means alternate to those normally sanctioned by the dominant religious institution. (. . .) Religious activities which fit

this first and primary criterion must also fit a second criterion: goals sought within the context of religious deviance are magical when attained through the management of supernatural powers in such a way that results are virtually guaranteed." For the debate on the term 'magic' and the validity of the distinction between 'magic' and 'religion' see Phillips (1986) 2711-2732; Versnel (1991).

8. See e.g. Remus (1983) 62.

9. Cf. the significant καὶ ἐν ἱεροῖς καὶ ἔξω ἱερῶν in Origen, *Cels.* 7.9.

10. Lane Fox (1986) 253 denies the existence of any tension between institutionalised religion and such figures as Apollonius. This is clearly incorrect. Lane Fox is probably right in arguing that there was no absolute distinction between the 'temple' and the 'magician' (p. 686 n. 34, *contra* J. Z. Smith, 'The Temple and the Magician', in J. Jervell and W. A. Meeks [eds], *God's Christ and His People. Studies . . . N. A. Dahl* [1977] 233ff., at 238 = J. Z. Smith [1978] 187f.), but such a claim ignores passages like *VA* 4.18, 8.19 and 8.30.

11. See esp. *Epp. Apoll.* 26 and 27; the complete material in Penella (1979b) 105.

12. See Gordon (1990) 224-231.

13. For the terms θεῖος ἀνήρ and δαίμων see Betz (1983) 235-238. Both θεῖοι ἄνδρες and δαίμονες belong to the domain between gods and humans; the difference between them is that θεῖος ἀνήρ emphasises the divine presence in a human being of flesh and blood, while δαίμονες are semi-divine beings. See, however, Betz (1983) 237: "Eine klare Trennung haben die Griechen nicht für notwendig gehalten." Gallagher (1982) 1-26, Corrington (1986) 1-43, Phillips (1986) 2752-2764, and Koskenniemi (1994) 64-100 provide surveys of the modern debate on the θεῖος ἀνήρ. Lane Fox (1986) 686 n. 34 dismisses the whole issue of the 'ubiquitous divine man' with the remark that the phenomenon requires more precise definition-hardly a fruitful approach. Of course, it is wrong to suppose that the term θεῖος ἀνήρ refers to an empirically observable phenomenon that can be defined in an unambiguous way. The ancient sources do bear witness, however, to a conflict between opposite assessments of sages and miracle-workers: one of the terms which can be used as a positive qualification for such figures is θεῖος ἀνήρ.

14. *VA* 7.38: . . . φύσις θεία τε καὶ κρείττων ἀνθρώπου. Cf. *VA* 8.13.

15. For the offensive character of claims to divinity cf. *Epp. Apoll.* 48.3.

16. Talbert (1978) 1638f. refers in this connection to 'a merger (. . .) of two originally distinct views of divinity'; at the end of his life, the θεῖος ἀνήρ is incorporated among the immortals.

17. *VA* 8.7.7.: . . . θεὸς ὑπὸ σοφίας ἥκων. On this passage see also below, p. 187.

18. Kee (1973) 407 denies this, but ignores the connection between this passage and the views which Apollonius is supposed to have derived from the Indian sages.

19. *VA* 1.5: . . . τὸ ἀγχοῦ θεῶν.

20. Cf. Gallagher (1982) 161f.; Cox (1983) 39.

21. See Burkert (1972b) 136-147; cf. J. Z. Smith, 'Good News is No News: Aretology and Gospel', in: J. Neusner (ed.), *Christianity, Judaism and other Greco-Roman Cults: Studies for Morton Smith at Sixty. Part One: New Testament* (Leiden 1975) 21-38 = J. Z. Smith (1978) 190-207, esp. 194-204.

22. Arist., fr. 192 Rose (= Iamb., *VP* 31): τοῦ λογικοῦ ζῴου τὸ μέν ἐστι θεός, τὸ δὲ ἄνθρωπος, τὸ δὲ οἷον Πυθαγόρας.

23. Goulet (1981) 175f.; Burkert (1972b) 146. On the revival of Pythagoreanism and the problem of continuity cf. Burkert (1961) 226-246. Of course, not everyone was convinced by such legitimation: Artemidorus (2.69) classifies the *Pythagoristai* among the false prophets who pull wool over the eyes of their audience with *goēteia*.

I cannot accept the contention of Koskenniemi (1994) 218, "dass die heidnischen Wundertäter, wie wir sie in den antiken Quellen finden, vor allem Teil der heidnischen Welt der ausgehenden 2. Jahrhunderts [A.D.] sind." Koskenniemi bases his claim on the scarcity of references to pagan miracle workers in the surviving sources from the Hellenistic period up to and including the first century A.D. In my opinion, the Finnish scholar does not sufficiently reckon with the rather poor state of preservation of pagan Greek prose literature of the Hellenistic and Julio-Claudian periods and with the possibility that the growth of our evidence reflects an increase in the respectability and social standing of miracle workers rather than an increase in their numbers. Besides, Eunus (above, p. 60 n. 11) is a fine example of a pagan miracle worker from the Hellenistic period.

24. Cf. Anderson (1986) 139: ". . . Philostratus was caught between two stools: he had to prove that Apollonius was not a γόης, consistent with being no ordinary mortal; he had therefore to invest his sage with 'rational' miracles."

25. Cf. Chadwick (1953) 356 n. 1; Aune (1980) 1521. See also M. Ant. 1.6, where Marcus Aurelius refers to Diognetus, one of his tutors during his youth, not just as the first to introduce him to philosophy, but also as the one who taught him τὸ ἀπιστητικὸν τοῖς ὑπὸ τῶν τερατευομένων καὶ γοήτων περὶ ἐπῳδῶν καὶ περὶ δαιμόνων ἀποπομπῆς καὶ τῶν τοιούτων λεγομένοις. On this passage cf. Rutherford (1989) 181-188.

26. Lucian, *Alex.* 1; cf. Chadwick (1953) xxiv-xxvi.

27. Lucian, *Alex.* 21. A similar text must have served as the basis for the chapters on magic by the Christian apologist Hippolytus (*Haer.* 4.28-42). Cf. C. P. Jones (1986) 137 and 139.

28. Philostratus himself speaks of an ἐκτροπὴ τοῦ λόγου (7.39).

29. On anti-magic legislation see Hopfner (1928) 384-387; MacMullen (1966) 124-126.

30. See e.g. *Alex.* 36, where Lucian makes fun of an oracle by Alexander's snake-god Glycon that was hung above the doors of numerous houses during the outbreak of the plague in the reign of Marcus Aurelius. According to Lucian, it was the residents in these houses that were often the hardest hit, either by chance or because they had a blind confidence in the power of the amulet and neglected to take other preventive measures.

31. See e.g. Solmsen (1941) 143; Esser (1969) 95 and 98.

32. On this question see the remarks by Palm (1976) 17-24.

33. Thus e.g. Bowie (1978) 1666: ". . . his aim was most plausibly that of a professional writer, to produce a well-rounded and entertaining piece of literature, rather than to further a propagandist interpretation of Apollonius as a Pythagorean sage." Cf. Reardon (1971) 266; Anderson (1986) 133f.; Koskenniemi (1986) passim and (1991) 70-79.

ABBREVIATIONS

The abbreviations used in referring to the names of Greek authors and their works are those used in: H. G. Liddell, R. Scott, H. Stuart Jones, R. MacKenzie, *A Greek-English Lexicon* (Oxford 1940^9; supplement 1968). For incidental references to this lexicon the standard abbreviation *LSJ* is used. The abbreviations *VA* (*Vita Apollonii*), *Epp. Apoll.* (*Epistulae Apollonii*), *VS* (*Vitae Sophistarum*) and *VP* (*De Vita Pythagorica* or *Vita Pythagorae*) are used in the main body of the text as well as in the references. Names of Christian Greek authors and their works not included in the list of ab-breviations in *LSJ* are generally abbreviated in accordance with G. W. H. Lampe, *A Patristic Greek Lexicon* (Oxford 1961). The names of Latin authors and their works are abbreviated in accordance with the system of P. G. W. Glare (ed.), *Oxford Latin Dictionary* (Oxford 1982). In the few cases in which I have departed from the abbreviations used in these lexicons, I have generally given the full names of authors and/or works; otherwise, I hope that my abbreviations will not give the reader any problems. Titles of periodicals and series are abbreviated in the bibliography (see below) as in *L'Année Philologique*. Where reference is made in a note to an introduction or extended commentary in an edition of an ancient author, the edition in question is generally included under the name of the writer of the introduction or commentary in the bibliography. Collections of inscriptions and documentary papyri are referred to in accordance with the abbreviations used in the *Supplementum Epigraphicum Graecum* and the *Berichtigungsliste der griechischen Papyrusurkunden aus Ägypten* respectively.

BIBLIOGRAPHY

AALDERS, G. J. D. (1976), 'Grieks zelfbewustzijn in de Romeinse keizertijd', in: *Handelingen van het vierendertigste Nederlands Filologencongres* (Amsterdam) 1-13

AALDERS, G. J. D. (1981), *Echt-Grieks.* Afscheidscollege gegeven bij zijn aftreden als hoogleraar in de Oude Geschiedenis en de Griekse en Romeinse staatsinstellingen aan de faculteit der Letteren van de Vrije Universiteit te Amsterdam op 17 oktober 1981 (Amsterdam)

ANDERSON, G. (1986), *Philostratus. Biography and belles lettres in the third century A.D.* (London etc.)

ANDERSON, G. (1993), *The Second Sophistic. A cultural phenomenon in the Roman Empire* (London/New York)

AUNE, D. E. (1980), 'Magic in early Christianity', in: *ANRW* 2.23.2: 1507-1557

BALDWIN, B. (1982), 'Literature and society in the Later Roman Empire', in: B. K. Gold (ed.), *Literary and artistic patronage in ancient Rome* (Austin) 67-83

BEHR, C. A. (1968), *Aelius Aristides and the Sacred Tales* (Amsterdam)

BETZ, H. D. (1983), 'Gottmensch II', in: *Reallexikon für Antike und Christentum* 12: 234-312

BOWERSOCK, G. W. (1969), *Greek sophists in the Roman empire* (Oxford)

BOWIE, E. L. (1970), 'Greeks and their past in the second sophistic', in: *P & P* 46: 3-41 [reprinted in: M. I. Finley (ed.), *Studies in Ancient Society* (London/Boston 1974) 166-209]

BOWIE, E. L. (1978), 'Apollonius of Tyana: tradition and reality', in: *ANRW* 2.16.2: 1652-1699

BOWIE, E. L. (1982), 'The importance of sophists', *YCLS* [*Yale Classical Studies*] 27: 29-59

BRADLEY, K. R. (1989), *Slavery and rebellion in the Roman world 140-70 B.C.* (Bloomington, Indiana/London)

BRANCACCI, A. (1985), *Rhetorike philosophousa. Dione Crisostomo nella cultura antica e bizantina* (Napoli)

BRANCACCI, A. (1986), 'Seconde sophistique, historiographie et philosophie (Philostrate, Eunape, Synésios)', in: B. Cassin (ed.), *Le plaisir de parler. Études de sophistique comparée* (Paris) 87-110

BRUNT, P. A. (1994), 'The bubble of the Second Sophistic', *BICS* [*Bulletin. Institute of Classical Studies*] 39 (1994), 25-52

BURKERT, W. (1961), 'Hellenistische Pseudopythagorica', *Philologus* 105: 16-43 and 226-246

BURKERT, W. (1962), ΓΟΗΣ. Zum griechischen "Schamanismus"', *RhM* [*Rheinisches Museum fuer Philologie*] 105: 36-55

BURKERT, W. (1972b), *Lore and science in Ancient Pythagoreanism* (Cambridge, Massachusetts)

CHADWICK, H. (1953), *Origen. Contra Celsum.* Translated with an introduction and notes by H. Chadwick (Cambridge)

CORRINGTON, G. P. (1986), *The 'Divine Man'. His origin and functions in Hellenistic popular religion* (New York)

COX, P. (1983), *Biography in Late Antiquity. A quest for the holy man* (Berkeley)

FANT, J. C. (1981), 'The choleric Roman official of Philostratus *Vitae Sophistarum* p. 512: L. Verginius Rufus', *Historia* 30: 240-243

FLINTERMAN, J. J. (1991), review of Hahn (1989), *Mnemosyne* 44: 504-507

ESSER, C. (1969), Formgeschichtliche Studien zur hellenistischen und frühchristlichen Literatur unter besonderer Berücksichtigung der Vita Apollonii des Philostrat und der Evangelien (Bonn)

FOLLET, S. (1991), 'Divers aspects de l'hellénisme chez Philostrate', in: S. Said (ed.), ΕΛΛΗΝΙσΜΟσ. *Quelques jalons pour une histoire de l'identité grecque.* Actes du Colloque de Strasbourg, 25-27 octobre 1989 (Leiden) 205-215

GALLAGHER, E. V. (1982), *Divine Man or Magician? Celsus and Origen on Jesus* (Chicago)

GASCÓ, F. (1989), 'The meeting between Aelius Aristides and Marcus Aurelius in Smyrna', *AJPh* [*American Journal of Philology*] 110: 471-478

GORDON, R. (1990), 'The Veil of Power: emperors, sacrificers and benefactors', in: M. Beard & J. North (eds), *Pagan priests. Religion and power in the ancient world* (London) 199-231

GOUDRIAAN, K. (1989), *Over classicisme. Dionysius van Halicarnassus en zijn program van welsprekendheid, cultuur en politiek* (Amsterdam)

GOULET, R. (1981), 'Les vies de philosophes dans l'antiquité tardive et leur portée mystérique', in: *Les Actes apocryphes des apôtres. Christianisme et monde païen.* Publications de la Faculté de Théologie de l'Université de Genève 4 (Genève) 161-208

HAHN, J. (1989), *Der Philosoph und die Gesellschaft. Selbstverständnis, öffentliches Auftreten und populäre Erwartungen in der hohen Kaiserzeit* (Stuttgart)

HOPFNER, T. (1928), 'Mageia', in: *RE* [*Real-Encyclopädie der Klassischen Altertumswissenshaft*] 14.1: 301-393

JONES, C. P. (1972), *Plutarch and Rome* (Oxford[2])

JONES, C. P. (1978), *The Roman world of Dio Chrysostom* (Cambridge, Massachusetts/London)

JONES, C. P. (1986), *Culture and society in Lucian* (Cambridge, Massachusetts/London)

KEE, H. C. (1973), 'Aretology and Gospel', *JBL* [*Journal of Biblical Literature*] 92: 202-22

KENNEDY, G. (1974), 'The sophists as declaimers', in: G. W. Bowersock (ed.), *Approaches to the Second Sophistic* (University Park, Pennsylvania) 17-22

KOSKENNIEMI, E. (1986), 'Die religiösen Tendenzen des Philostratos in der Vita Apollonii Tyanensis', in: H. Koskenniemi, S. Jäkel, V. Pyykkö (Hrsgb.), *Literatur und Philosophie in der Antike* (Turku) 107-117

KOSKENNIEMI, E. (1991), *Der philostrateische Apollonios* (Helsinki)

KOSKENNIEMI, E. (1994), *Apollonios von Tyana in der neutestamentlichen Exegese* (Tübingen)

DE LACY, P. (1974), 'Plato and the intellectual life of the second century A.D.', in: G. W. Bowersock (ed.), *Approaches to the Second Sophistic* (University Park, Pennsylvania) 4-10

LANE FOX, R. (1986), *Pagans and Christians in the Mediterranean world from the second century A.D. to the conversion of Constantine* (London/Harmondsworth)

MACMULLEN, R. (1966), *Enemies of the Roman order. Treason, unrest and alienation in the Empire* (Cambridge, Massachusetts)

MEIJER, F. J. (1985), 'Vrijheid in onderworpenheid: de Grieken in het Imperium Romanum', *Lampas* 18: 53-65

MILLAR, F. (1969), 'P. Herennius Dexippus: the Greek world and the third century invasions', *JRS* [*Journal of Roman Studies*] 59: 12-29

MILLAR, F. (1977), *The emperor in the Roman world* (London)

MOLES, J. L. (1985), 'The interpretation of the "Second Preface" in Arrian's *Anabasis*', *JHS* [*Journal of Hellenic Studies*] 105: 162-168

MÜNSCHER, K. (1907), *Die Philostrate.* Philologus Supplementband 10: 467-558

MÜNSTERBERG, R. (1915), 'Die Münzen der Sophisten', *NZ* [*Neuphilologische Zeitschrift*] 48: 119-124

MURRAY, O. (1970), Περὶ βασιλείας. *Studies in the justification of monarchic power in the hellenistic world* (diss. Oxford)

OLIVER, J. H. (1978), 'On the edict of Severus Alexander (P. Fayum 20)', *AJPH* 99: 474-485

PENELLA, R. J. (1979a), 'Philostratus' letter to Julia Domna', *Hermes* 107: 161-168

PENELLA, R. J. (1979b), *The Letters of Apollonius of Tyana.* A critical text with prolegomena, translation and a commentary by R. J. Penella (Leiden)

PHILLIPS, C. R. (1986), 'The sociology of religious knowledge in the Roman Empire to A.D. 284', in: *ANRW* 2.16.3: 2677-2773

QUET, M.-H., (1992), 'L'inscription de Vérone en l'honneur d'Aelius Aristide et le rayonnement de la Seconde Sophistique chez les "Grecs d'Égypte"', *REA* [*Revue des études anciennes*] 94: 379-401

RAWSON, E. (1989), 'Roman ruler and the philosophic adviser', in: M. Griffin/J. Barnes (eds), *Philosophia Togata. Essays on philosophy and Roman society* (Oxford) 233-257

REARDON, B. P. (1971), *Courants littéraires grecs des IIe et IIIe siècles après J.-C.* (Paris)

REARDON, B. P. (1989), review of C. P. Jones (1986), *CPh* [*Classical Philology*] 84: 271-275

REMUS, H. (1983), *Pagan-christian conflict over miracle in the second century* (Cambridge, Massachusetts)

ROBERT, L. (1977a), 'Documents d'Asie Mineure', *BCH* [*Bulletin de correspondance hellénique*] 101: 43-132

ROBERT, L. (1977b), 'La titulature de Nicée et de Nicomédie: la gloire et la haine', *HSCP* [*Harvard Studies in Classical Philology*] 81: 1-39 [= *Opera Minora Selecta* 6 (1989) 211-249]

RUSSELL, D. A. (1983), *Greek declamation* (Cambridge)

RUSSELL, D. A. (1988), review of Brancacci (1985), *JHS* 108: 237f.

RUTHERFORD, R. B. (1989), *The* Meditations *of Marcus Aurelius. A study* (Oxford)

SALLER, R. P. (1982), *Personal patronage under the Early Empire* (Cambridge etc.)

SARTRE, M. (1991), *L'Orient romain. Provinces et sociétés provinciales en Méditerranée orientale d'Auguste aux Sévères (31 avant J.-C-235 après J.-C.)* (Paris)

SHEPPARD, A. R. R. (1984-6), '*Homonoia* in the Greek cities of the Roman Empire', *Anc Soc* [*Ancient Society*] 15-17: 229-252

SMITH, J. Z. (1978), *Map is not territory. Studies in the history of religions* (Leiden)

SMITH, M. (1973), *Clement of Alexandria and a secret gospel of Mark* (Cambridge, Massachusetts)

SOLMSEN, F. (1940), 'Some works of Philostratus the Elder', *TAPhA* [*Transactions and Proceedings. American Philological Association*] 71: 556-572 [= *Kleine Schriften* 2 (1968) 75-91]

SPAWFORTH, A. J./WALKER, S. (1985), 'The world of the Panhellenion. I. Athens and Eleusis', *JRS* 75: 78-104

STANTON, G. R. (1973), 'Sophists and philosophers: problems of classification', *AJPh* 94: 350-364

SWAIN, S. (1989), 'Favorinus and Hadrian', *ZPE* [*Zeitschrift für Papyrologie und Epigraphik*] 79: 150-158

VERSNEL, H. S. (1991), 'Some reflections on the relationship magic-relgion', *Numen* 38: 177-197

VEYNE, P. (1976), *Le pain et le cirque. Sociologie historique d'un pluralisme politique* (Paris)

James A. Francis (essay date 1998)

SOURCE: Francis, James A. "Truthful Fiction: New Questions to Old Answers on Philostratus's *Life of Apollonius*." *American Journal of Philology* 19, no. 3 (1998): 419-41.

[*In the following essay, Francis critiques the assumptions and methods of scholarship often applied to* Apollonius of Tyana, *theorizing that new ideas about the nature of history and ancient fiction have opened up unexplored avenues for research into the text.*]

Within the past twenty years four extensive works have appeared treating Philostratus' **Life of Apollonius of Tyana** (**VA**) from various literary, historical, and cultural perspectives. These include E. L. Bowie's "Apollonius of Tyana: Tradition and Reality," Maria Dzielska's *Apollonius of Tyana in Legend and History*, Graham

Anderson's *Philostratus: Biography and Belles Lettres in the Third Century A.D.*, and my own lengthy chapter in *Subversive Virtue: Asceticism and Authority in the Second-Century Pagan World.*[1] The popularity of what has often been considered an "offbeat" text is striking—and largely explicable given concurrent interest in such subjects as the Second Sophistic, the novel, holy men, and asceticism. At this juncture it is thus appropriate to ask: how far have these studies advanced our appreciation and understanding of this text? In answer to this question, I propose first to critique the assumptions and methods of this body of work on *VA* and, second, to suggest that new insights into the nature of ancient fiction would provide both a resolution to old scholarly impasses and a more fruitful agenda for research.

Little is known about the historical Apollonius. He must have been born early in the first century C.E. in Tyana in Cappadocia and died sometime during or after the reign of Nerva (96-98). So little remains of sources prior to *VA* that the most that can be said further both with certainty and without fear of "contamination" from posthumous representations is that Apollonius appears to have been a wandering ascetic/philosopher/wonderworker of a type common to the eastern part of the early empire.[2] Philostratus' work, which appeared a century after the death of its hero, is usually thought to have been published sometime after the death of the empress Julia Domna in 217.[3] For a biography *VA* is extraordinarily long, eight books requiring two Loeb volumes. The work begins with a description of the birth of a "greater than Pythagoras" (1.2) and one who would "approach the gods" (1.5), then follows Apollonius' prodigious youth through his devotion to piety and learning, especially in regard to the god Asclepius. With his early training perfected, Apollonius sets out to discover the source of piety and wisdom among the Brahmans of India, which allows Philostratus to provide his reader with two and one-half books full of travel, adventure, and esoteric philosophy.[4] It is at the very beginning of this journey, while in Nineveh (1.19), that Apollonius first meets his lifelong companion and disciple Damis. Philostratus asserts that Damis kept a record of Apollonius' ideas, discourses, and prophecies and that a descendant of Damis' family presented these to Julia Domna (1.3). The empress, in turn, gave these "tablets" (*deltoi*) to Philostratus with the command that he recast them in more appropriate literary style.[5] It is these memoirs which, according to Philostratus, form the authoritative basis of his own work.

Upon his return from India, Apollonius is acclaimed by the Greek cultural world and becomes actively involved in the affairs of the cities of Asia Minor and Greece (4.2-33), even journeying to Rome to confront Nero (4.35-47), in an episode which presages Apollonius' climactic confrontation with Domitian. He journeys throughout the Mediterranean world, discoursing on true philosophy and religion, preaching Greek cultural ideals, prophesying, and performing the occasional miracle. He visits the gymnosophists of Egypt, and reaches the height of his reputation when Vespasian summons him to Alexandria to solicit his advice and blessing upon accession to imperial dignity (5.27-41). In the final two books, Apollonius is arrested and imprisoned by the unworthy son of Vespasian. Brought before Domitian, he refutes the accusations made against him and, as proof of both his innocence and his superior philosophical nature, simply vanishes from sight and materializes at the coast, where the faithful Damis has booked passage back to Greece. The episode allows Philostratus to deliver a reprise of the entire work and a virtual *apologia* in the form of a formal defense speech which Apollonius prepared but never delivered to the emperor, and which occupies more than half of book 8 (8.7.1-16). *VA* concludes in short order with a description of various legends concerning Apollonius' death, none of which Philostratus considers definitive; the very last chapter relates a miraculous appearance made by Apollonius after his death, for the express purpose of teaching that the soul is immortal (8.31).

Even from this brief synopsis, it is clear that elements of invention and reality are not only juxtaposed in *VA* but shaded one into the other so as to blur the distinctions between them. Modern scholars, however, have consistently approached *VA* with the view that fiction and history are mutually exclusive and antithetical categories. The first and fundamental task here is thus to expose the flaws of this overly schematic view and show how it has caused any element of *VA* deemed "novelistic" to be dismissed as mere sophistic invention, compounding misunderstanding of Philostratus and misinterpretation of his text. Next we must consider that this overly rigid conceptual distinction between fiction and history will have been quite alien to ancient readers who could, more readily than moderns, believe something to be truthful though not factual. Indeed, ensuing discussion will demonstrate that it was ancient historiography itself which first employed this complex dynamic of truthful fiction (as opposed to the merely plausible fiction of the modern historical novel), sharing modes of invention and presentation with other rhetorical and literary productions. There was, in fact, an entire repertoire of literary strategies shared by both fiction and history available to Philostratus in constructing his work. This, then, draws us to a reinterpretation of the "novelistic" elements of *VA* as means to facilitate belief and communicate truth.

Turning to the scholarship on *VA*, it appears at first glance to be steeped in controversy. Bowie and Anderson in particular stake out opposite and antithetical positions which link the literary form of *VA* to questions of its historical credibility—focusing on issues of anachronism, literary imitation, and whether the ever-devoted Damis really existed. Beneath these disagreements, however, lies a deeper and less articulated issue. Bowie presents *VA* as "novelistic" or "fictional" and thereby concludes that Philostratus intended this work to be merely an entertaining piece of sophistic literature, not meant to be taken seriously, and certainly not to be taken as history.[6] Dzielska largely follows Bowie on these points.[7] Anderson, in turn, goes to extremes to argue in favor of historicity—even to the point of identifying Damis from later Arabic sources—ultimately to show that *VA* should not be relegated purely to the realm of fantasy.[8] This rigid dichotomy between fiction and history, entertainment and seriousness, though called into question by B. P. Reardon seven years prior to Bowie's work,[9] has nevertheless dominated the discussion.[10]

In an earlier work on *VA* I sought to obviate this dichotomy first by simply redefining the historicity of the text, arguing that its historical value pertains to Philostratus' own time of the early third century and urging that the "Quest of the Historical Apollonius" of the first century be abandoned.[11] The point concerning historical value remains important, but at the same time it entailed skirting any literary discussion of *VA,* lest such a discussion, per Bowie's arguments, discredit the social-historical value of the text. Though seeking to undermine the wall that had been constructed between fiction and history—or literary study and social history—I ultimately only reinforced its rigidity. Perhaps because *VA* is such a long and complex text, those who study it have consistently been pushing into prominence only parts and aspects of the text, and applying often erudite and exquisite methodologies to the wrong questions.

This contention can be further illustrated with some arguments taken from this body of scholarship that have specific reference to the issue of fiction and history. From the very beginning of his article, Bowie makes his assumptions clear:

> Investigators of Apollonius must try to determine how much belongs to the first-century character and how much is attributable to elaborations in the second century and to Philostratus himself, while a student of Philostratus will wish to concentrate on the latter part of the enquiry and add the question how far and with what intent Philostratus was perpetrating a work of fiction.[12]

A valid agenda this, but one which skews towards an anticipated result by viewing history and fiction as black and white, mutually exclusive and antithetical categories, and by asserting that an analysis which then sorts

the text into either one or the other category will be the primary desideratum of the scholar. In this, Bowie claims to offer no more than a refinement and correction in detail of the position Eduard Meyer initially presented in 1917.[13] Following Meyer, Bowie moves within the space of one short paragraph to the essential thesis: "Damis is an invention of Philostratus, who will not have expected his readers to take him seriously."[14]

To prove Damis a fiction, and *VA* therefore fiction*al,* Bowie proceeds to reveal four crucial anachronisms in the text, arguing on the basis of a careful command of Neronian and Flavian chronology.[15] Having demonstrated that a contemporary, much less eyewitness, source would not have made such fundamental errors of time and fact, Bowie poses the question which serves to advance the distinction between fiction and history to an extreme: "If Damis was not what Philostratus asserts, what was he?"[16] The answer, paradoxically, is that he is a literary device meant to tell Philostratus' reader precisely that *VA* is *not* to be taken seriously! He concludes: "The foregoing arguments are offered to support the view that 'Damis' was most probably an invention of Philostratus himself, and, in that his readers would be expected to recognize the novelistic topos, the connection with Julia Domma cannot be used to warrant his authenticity."[17]

Calling attention to *VA* 1.3, where Philostratus speaks of "tablets" (*deltoi*) containing the so-called memoirs being brought to Julia Domna by a relative of Damis, Bowie draws an analogy to the wooden tablets of both Dictys of Crete and *The Wonders beyond Thule* and speaks of Philostratus' "conscious evocation of a novelistic tone and setting."[18] Drawing further parallels with the Philostratean *Heroicus,* the *Historia Apollonii Regis Tyrii,* Iamblichus' *Babyloniaca,* the Historia Alexandri Magni, and other novelistic productions, Bowie quotes with approval Reardon's description of *VA* as "presque un roman."[19] Concluding his argument, Bowie suggests that Philostratus' aim in *VA* was most plausibly that of any professional writer, "to produce a well-rounded and entertaining piece of literature."[20] In the end he must admit how little can actually be determined with certainty regarding the "Ur-Apollonius."[21] The problem is that along the way, he has left us with a text that, by the same token, is largely devoid of any serious meaning whatever.

The great paradox of *VA* scholarship, however, is that the defenders of a "serious" and "historical" text confront the document with the same predispositions regarding fiction and history as their opponents. Compare, for example, Anderson's stated approach to that of Bowie quoted above.

> The problem posed by the *Life* is where and how to draw the line between stylistic presentation, rhetorical exaggeration, and just plain falsehood. The solution

may not always lie in detecting deception by Philostratus as often as possible, but rather in recognizing how often it is inseparable from artistic license, sophistic reflex and bona fide historical reconstruction from treacherous sources.[22]

Frankly, I do not think it advances the inquiry much to hold that if and when Philostratus is lying, he might not have been able to help it or, put differently, that Philostratus' intention was to write "real history," and that on those occasions where he is clearly in error, he merely lost control of his sources. Such an approach leaves the student of *VA* with the same task as that prescribed by Bowie: to sift and sort the text into lists of the true and the false. We are left to think of Philostratus' work as either a failed novel or a bad history.

The view of literal, factual history as opposite to and exclusive of novelistic fiction produces a further irony by focusing both positions on excruciatingly narrow questions on which conclusions regarding the entire work, and even Philostratus himself, are perilously built. Nowhere is this more obvious than on the issue of the historical reality of Damis. Bowie's position has been outlined above, and again Anderson follows the same premises, believing that the existence of Damis "must have important consequences for our view of the integrity of Philostratus in other fields."[23] Indeed, it is odd to hear a staunch defender of the historicity of *VA* and the reputation of Philostratus state that with proof of a historical Damis "the whole balance of evidence will have to change, and with it our notion of how bad Philostratus' excesses really are."[24]

What then can be said of this controversy, not only in reference to *VA* but also in terms of the relationship between fiction and history? Glen Bowersock is perhaps more assertive than necessary, but fundamentally correct, when he states:

> With works of imaginative literature there is nothing more ruinous for historical understanding than genre theory or a mindless search for antecedents, origins, and distant parallels.[25]

Or again, and more kindly:

> The invocation of sources and antecedents never provides an explanation of an innovation: they can only reveal, inadequately at best, some of the building blocks that were used to construct it.[26]

The old answers regarding *VA* equate "truth" with "historical reliability," as if the only truth were that of the demonstrable fact, and relegate the historical value of the work to a matter of arguing mere plausibility. The old answers equate the "fictional" with the "novelistic," as if the two were synonymous terms—which they are clearly not. The old answers set "fic-

tion" and "history" as opposite poles, and one only has to consider how the Homeric poems were regarded in antiquity to realize what a false dichotomy this is to impose on the classical world.

Having assessed the shortcomings of previous scholarship regarding the schematized view of fiction and history, and the repercussions this has had on the estimation not only of *VA* itself but also of Philostratus' talent, we may now proceed to examine other, more flexible conceptions. Happily, recent studies in ancient fiction have taken their inspiration from both ancient theory, insofar as this was articulated, and even more so from a fresh, synoptic examination of ancient fictional and historical texts. Here we can integrate ancient practice and recent insights in a way that both obviates the old dichotomies and poses new questions that progress beyond the old answers offered regarding *VA*. For convenience, these new perspectives can be discussed under the broad rubrics of fiction and historiography and of fiction and the novel.[27]

J. R. Morgan has argued that the first condition of fiction is that both writer and reader recognize it for what it is, that there exists a "contract of fictional complicity" between author and audience and, of greater significance, that this contract was first extended to narrative prose precisely in historiography.[28] The first illustrative example that comes to mind is also the most potent and obvious: to what extent are Herodotus and Thucydides fictional? In answering this question, we would all eventually agree that both are fictional, but in different ways, and both are historical, but in different ways.[29] The link between fiction and history is so obvious to us all that it is indeed puzzling that we forget it so easily when we begin to discuss Greek literature at the beginning of the Common Era. Bowersock remarks:

> For any coherent and persuasive interpretation of the Roman empire it becomes obvious that fiction must be viewed as part of its history. We have long grown accustomed to hearing of late that history itself is a fiction, or rhetoric, or whatever. The ancients would not have found that a particularly surprising doctrine, inasmuch as they drew only a faint line between myth and history and, as Cicero put it, considered the writing of history an *opus oratorium*—a rhetorical work.[30]

The phenomenon is already well-developed at the very beginnings of history. Are Thucydides' speeches "rhetorical" or "historical"? Does it even make sense to force a choice between the two?

Further examples can be easily elaborated. As Morgan again suggests, what would we have ended up with, had Lucceius provided Cicero with the literarily elaborated and emotionally charged history of his consulship he requested in *Ad Familiares* (5.12)?[31] Plutarch gives lessons on writing biography at the beginning of his life of Alexander which should give us all pause:

I am not writing histories, but lives. Nor is there always in the most shining deeds a clear manifestation of virtue or wickedness, but rather a little thing or some word or quip often makes a greater revelation of character than great slaughtering battles, vast armies, or besieged cities. Therefore, just as painters get the likenesses of their portraits from the face and the expression of the eyes, in which character is revealed, but could care less about the other parts of their subjects, in the same way I must be permitted to concentrate rather on the marks of the soul and through them to portray the life of each, leaving the great feats to others.

(Alex. 1.2-3)

Indeed, as Bowersock further notes, Sextus Empiricus placed history proper, fiction, and myth all in "the historical part" (τὸ ἱστορικὸν μέρος) of γραμματική. History proper is the presentation (ἔκθεσις) of truths and what actually happened, whereas πλάσμα is the representation of things that did not happen but resemble things that have happened, and myth the representation of things that did not happen and are false (ψευδῆ).[32]

Surely, though, we are on firmer ground when it comes to chronology—the very stuff of history. Fiction and history must be distinguished here, and Bowie's arguments concerning *VA* which are based on anachronisms must hold. Here too Plutarch brings us up short in his comment on the meeting of Solon and Croesus:[33]

As for his meeting with Croesus, some scholars think to refute it by chronology as made up. But for my part, when a story is so famous and has so many witnesses and—what is a greater consideration—is so appropriate to Solon's character and so worthy of his greatness of soul and wisdom, I do not think it right to sacrifice it to any so-called chronological canons, which so many scholars are to this day trying to correct, without being able to bring their contradictions to any agreed result.

(Solon 27.1)

In light of these views, both ancient and modern, it is possible in fact to agree with Bowie that Damis is a pure fiction, invented by Philostratus, even that Philostratus intended his readers to recognize him as such, and argue nevertheless that, if anything, this is evidence that Philostratus intends to tell an important truth in *VA* and not simply contrive some artsy fabrication.

"Historical texts and fictional texts" says Andrew Laird, "have a great deal in common—both kinds of text seek to be believed. To achieve this end, they share many strategies."[34] It is in regard to these strategies shared by both history and fiction that discussion of the novel rightly enters into this inquiry.[35] Rather than remain in the realm of the theoretical, let us examine the application of this insight to some of the most contentious controversies surrounding *VA*.

Among the elements of the Damis controversy is that this source, or narrator, or character (and he is *all three,* an important point to be discussed below), as he appears in *VA,* does not behave or report in a manner consistent with what we would expect from an actual first-century observer: he knows either too much or too little, and on the wrong occasions. The reaches of Persia and India are described in detail, whereas Apollonius presents Demetrius the Cynic to Titus as his adviser in the same year the emperor banished that philosopher from Rome.[36] Bowie states succinctly:

"Damis" presents a historical background too sophisticated for his station while the palpable inexactitudes come precisely where he ought to be best informed, at Apollonius' entrances on stage.[37]

Anderson's rejoinder is, at this point, predictable:

On present evidence he [Philostratus] may have been as much at the mercy of his sources as of his rhetorical talents. The briefer and more enigmatic such sources were, the more scope he had for error as well as rhetorical expansion (*auxesis*). In spite of the discrepancies, it is still perfectly possible that he did set out to harmonise a rather jejune main account with letters and local tradition. The slimmer such an account [i.e., the original "Damis source"] and the vaguer its geographical and historical frame of reference, the easier it would have been to make false connections in good faith. If Philostratus was really setting out to forge, could he not have done better than the *Life* as it stands?[38]

Once again, we are left to choose between failed literature or bad history, between Philostratus the deliberate liar and Philostratus the unintending purveyor of deceit.

Until now, comparisons to the novel have only been adduced to advance the former position, that the novelistic equals the fictional equals the unserious: but recent studies have introduced a new application. Morgan notes that the combination of geographic realism with temporal ambiguity is characteristic of the ancient novel:

The entire geography of the novel's world—distances, directions, sailing-times—approximates so closely to reality that there seems nothing odd when the recent Budé Chariton includes a map tracing the fictitious movements of fictitious characters. . . . Temporal settings are less precise than geographical, and more variably sustained. Chariton's novel takes over characters and historical background from Thucydides' history. . . . The reader is given the sense that the story is somehow located in the gaps in real history. Not everything is tied up; in the novel Hermocrates is alive later than he should be, so that his lifetime overlaps with the reign of the Persian king Artaxerxes. In the later stages of the novel, the hero Chaereas leads an Egyptian revolt from Persia, which looks rather like the actual revolt of 360 B.C., with Chaereas playing the part of Chabrias.[39]

This characteristic of the novel parallels the lavish detail of *VA*'s travelogues and its chronological ambiguities. I quote these arguments at length to bring the differences in approach into sharp relief and to focus on how a different view of the novelistic character of *VA* can advance our understanding of the text.

If, then, constructing this sort of parallel with the novel is valid, we can follow Morgan into consideration of the broader and more important issue at stake here. If the purpose of, for example, geographic realism is to facilitate acceptance of and/or belief in the story, the question becomes not *if* the story is to be believed but *how* it is to be believed.[40] This question has, for all intents and purposes, never been asked of *VA*. To prove *VA* fictional only, in effect, to dismiss fiction as mere entertainment is to ignore the contract of fictional complicity[41] and the implications and power of fictive belief, which "is obviously something quite different from believing a lie,"[42] and "has its own truth, which carrie[s] conviction within its context."[43] In a somewhat different vein, but with the same import, Bowersock adduces the example of the Jewish interlocutor in Celsus' *True Doctrine* as an example of a novelistic fiction, clearly constructed and recognized as such, designed precisely to tell a truth.

> It cannot escape the reader's notice that Celsus has launched his attack on Christianity by creating a fictional setting of his own. In other words, Celsus has created a fiction in order to expose other people's fiction. Of course he is not claiming that his Jewish interlocutor is a real person. His is the kind of fiction that we clearly know to be fiction. But he saw in the Gospel stories another order of fabrication in which there was a claim to historical truth. The truth of Celsus' discourse obviously does not lie in his scenario but in what is said in the scenario. The alleged truth is embedded in the fiction, and Origen understood this perfectly well.[44]

Fictive belief and this dynamic of a truth embedded in fiction for the purpose of telling a greater truth constitute fundamental examples of the strategies shared by historical and fictional texts. In terms of both strategy and function within the broader text, Celsus' interlocutor and the Thucydidean speech have much in common.

Other more sophisticated shared strategies that emerge from an examination of the novel can be applied to specific issues concerning *VA*. This brings us back to the issue of Damis' *deltoi*. Bowie's arguments regarding parallels to such works as Dictys of Crete and *The Wonders beyond Thule* have been noted above, and again more recent discussions of this "recovered record" motif pave the way to a new and better understanding.[45] Rather than seek some elaborate "in" joke, designed to flag literati that they were not to believe Philostratus'

text, it is both more reasonable and more consistent to hold that Damis' *deltoi* perform the same function in *VA* that lost sources play in the novels. There they are grounds for fictive belief, "authorizing" the text by establishing its source and citing that source's provenance.[46] Once again, we can accept Bowie's analysis, but draw from it the opposite conclusion: the motif of the *deltoi* is an invitation to a complex and highly literary form of belief, one worthy of the sophistic talent all critics ascribe to Philostratus.

In the same way, it is just as important to note that the traditional opposing argument for historicity is equally a misunderstanding and misinterpretation of the intricate construction of *VA;* attempts to identify Damis or reconstruct his memoirs[47] are misguided. Rather than remain in the coarse, unrefined dichotomies of true/false, fiction/history, Bowersock, Morgan, and, I would argue, Philostratus himself demand a subtler, more sophisticated approach which, ironically, has been described precisely in reference to *The Wonders beyond Thule:*

> Doubtless many of the marvels were fabricated, but their value as entertainment would be negated if the reader acknowledged it. So to proclaim incredibility was to claim truthfulness. By setting a romantic fiction within this paradoxographical framework, Antonius produced a novel whose plausibility as fiction rested directly on its implausibility as fact. This was reinforced by a convoluted apparatus of authorization, detailing how an autobiographical document had been buried in the protagonist's grave, later discovered, and was now being published for the first time.[48]

The facile comparison of *VA* with the novel is no longer facile, either on the side of *VA* or that of the ancient novel.

Damis is, however, not only the adduced author of a source; he is a narrator within the text itself. It is not only the alleged memoirs of Damis that lend *VA* the authority of an account contemporary with the life of Philostratus' hero,[49] it is also the voice of Damis himself as both a narrator and a character within the narrative. *VA* possesses a complicated double, perhaps even triple, narration.[50] Damis as narrator and as character in the text serves to validate Damis as source. The *deltoi* come "alive" in the narration with the effect that any misapprehension, doubt, or disbelief the reader might have is deflected from the memoirs themselves and vested instead in Damis the character. In reading Philostratus' text, the reader might wonder: Did Damis really do this? In asking this question, however, the reader has already precluded doubting the source; that is, the reader will not ask the question "Did Damis really *say* he did this?" Damis the narrator and character validates Damis the source, and Damis the source lends credibility to both his narration and his character. Moving then to the level of the embracing narratological dynamic, Philostratus becomes more authoritative in having Damis as a source, while Damis becomes more authoritative by being accepted by Philostratus.[51] This raises the technique that John Winkler has termed "evidential accountability" to a new level of complexity.[52] We are now so far from Damis' flagging a patent and, therefore, unbelievable fiction[53] that, as T. G. Knoles has observed in his own quite different analysis, Damis the source would operate in the same way and produce the same effects regardless of whether the *deltoi* were a legitimate document, forged, or simply a literary device.[54] Philostratus has so constructed *VA* that the contract of fictional complicity operates on several levels simultaneously; there can be no question that he intends his reader to take his work "seriously."

It must also be remembered just how seriously readers took not only *VA,* but also the novels themselves. Laird points to the distressing fact that Dictys and similarly Dares the Phrygian, translated into Latin, were regarded in some circles for some time as authentic.[55] Likewise *VA,* read as a factual biography, was used as a bulwark of pagan religion and culture by Sossianus Hierocles, who in his *Philalethes* set up Apollonius as a rival and superior to Jesus.[56] In one of his most trenchant observations, Bowersock states: "Rewriting the past—the intrusion of fiction into what was taken to be history—becomes from this period of Lucillius and Martial an increasingly conspicuous feature of the Graeco-Roman world."[57] To confuse still further our tidy modern categories and distinctions between fiction and history, the credible and the incredible, Bowersock pointedly quotes Origen's reaction to all this "fictional revisionism":

> We are embarrassed by the fictitious stories which for some unknown reasons are bound up with the opinion, which everyone believes, that there really was a war in Troy between the Greeks and the Trojans.[58]
>
> (*C. Cels.* 1.42)

We may, indeed, take comfort that there was someone in antiquity who was able to distinguish—as clearly as we can today—Second Sophistic fictions and fabrications from the historical truth uttered by Homer!

Having begun with a critique of the too rigid distinction between fiction and history, we have returned to yet another example of this nebulous boundary as it exists in both ancient literature and in our own understanding. Ultimately this investigation resolves itself into an exploration of the various historical and fictional modes and strategies of telling a truth. The issue becomes even more complex when it concerns a retelling through historical revisionism. It is thus appropriate to conclude

this discussion of *VA* by suggesting what sort of truth Philostratus sought to convey by representing (or perhaps re-presenting) Apollonius in the way he did.

VA is itself part of a much larger phenomenon of the "rewriting of the past" Bowersock describes.[59] The obsession with historicity and the existence of Damis has overshadowed the fact that, leaving Damis aside, a number of various well-developed traditions about Apollonius clearly existed before *VA,* and that scholars of all opinions have always agreed that Philostratus reworked these source materials.[60] Thus *VA* is a work of fictional revisionism; what Bowersock says of fiction writing in the empire is seen to apply, as has so much of current thinking about ancient fiction, with particular force to *VA.*

> The overt creation of fiction as a means of rewriting or even inventing the past was a serious business for many of the ancients, and for us the enormous increase in fictional production of all kinds during the Roman empire poses major questions of historical interpretation. There was as much truth or falsehood in fiction as in history itself. Fiction must necessarily include not only overt works of the imagination, such as the novels and Lucian's *True Stories,* but also the rewriting of the mythic and legendary past as part of the creation of a new and miraculous present.[61]

Herein lies "the truth about Apollonius" which Philostratus sought to convey. It is something far more than mere biography; it is the invention of tradition.[62] As such, it clothes its truth with the fictional realism of Apollonius' life. I contend that Philostratus even gives some hint of this at the beginning of *VA:*

> δοκεῖ οὖν μοι μὴ περιιδεῖν τὴν τῶν πολλῶν ἄγνοιαν, ἀλλ' ἐξακριβῶσαι τὸν ἄνδρα τοῖς τε χρόνοις, καθ' οὓς εἶπέ τι ἢ ἔπραξε, τοῖς τε τῆς σοφίας τρόποις, ὑπ' ὧν ἔψαυσε τοῦ δαιμόνιός τε καὶ θεῖος νομισθῆναι.[63]
>
> (*VA* 1.2)

This is a claim to truth, indeed a truth superior to the ignorance of the many (τὴν τῶν πολλῶν ἄγνοιαν) and based on precision regarding the details of Apollonius' life (ἐξακριβῶσαι τὸν ἄνδρα). Philostratus has in this way already cleverly constructed and offered his contract to the reader, for it is precisely in the biographical precision that the fiction lies. Yet this is not deception. Rather, it is a strategy for telling the greater and ultimate truth about Apollonius: how he came to be *considered* a divine man (δαιμόνιός τε καὶ θεῖος νομισθῆναι).

This interpretation is further substantiated as Philostratus ends 1.2 about to tell his reader how he acquired his most precise or detailed information (ἀκριβέστερα). He then begins 1.3 with what by now should be seen as the awesome statement "There was a man Damis . . . ," and proceeds to relate the story of the *deltoi*. Directly thereafter, Philostratus warns his reader against Moiragenes' work, describing the author as ignorant about many things concerning (details about the life of) Apollonius (πολλὰ δὲ τῶν περὶ τὸν ἄνδρα ἀγνοήσαντι). By the very words he chooses, Philostratus allies himself and Damis in the cause of truth and exactitude (ἀκρίβεια); likewise he equates common opinion (and Moiragenes, apparently his major literary competitor) with ignorance (ἄγνοια). Philostratus claims to recover a lost truth. Is he, in the words of Origen quoted above, creating a new batch of "fictitious stories" contravening accepted truth or, as Philostratus himself announces, dispelling old ignorance? In antiquity as in our own day, that answer lies with the individual reader, for it depends on the perception of the sort of truth Philostratus intends to communicate by means of his fiction. "Men do not find the truth; they create it, as they create their history."[64]

So where does this leave the scholarship on *VA,* the ostensible question posed at the beginning of this inquiry? Largely in a state of paradoxical agreement. Bowie's erudite researches into first-century C.E. chronology and into literary form and history remain valuable: *VA* is "fictional," indeed it is "novelistic." But the meaning of these terms has changed since Bowie's treatment and their significance has become larger. Good methods led to wrong conclusions, fostered by incorrect assumptions. To call *VA* "fictional" or "novelistic" is not to deny the work serious meaning, but to invite the new questions: How was this work to be believed? What is the truth that is being told in it? To answer these questions we need not, indeed we must not, insist on literal "historicity" and fabricate ever more elaborate theories as to how *VA* can represent first-century fact. Anderson, in turn, has the right conclusions but the wrong methods. The "truth" of *VA* lies in the area of "fictional representation," an area only now being explored.[65] The old answers have proved both right and wrong, and have led to an impasse based on their mutual assumption that fiction and history are opposite and exclusive.

"Whereas all novels are fiction, not all fictions are novels."[66] This distinction is vital and can account for many of the peculiar difficulties of *VA.* If the first condition of fiction is that both sides recognize it for what it is,[67] we can ask whether by the complexities of his narration, representation, and fictional revisionism, Philostratus has actually violated his side of the contract of complicity.[68] Has *VA* ultimately "in trying to make the reader believe, succeeded only too well and ended up forfeiting its status as fiction"?[69] For modern scholars, it may sound very odd indeed to say that the problem with *VA* is that it is too believable, but there is every

reason to see that readers in antiquity found it so, especially in an age verging on "the new and miraculous present" that was to characterize late antiquity.[70]

Notes

1. Bowie 1978, Dzielska 1986, Anderson 1986, Francis 1995.

2. These prior sources include the first surviving (and highly uncomplimentary) reference, in Lucian (*Alex.* 5), a collection of purported letters, a so-called testament of Apollonius, a book by Maximus of Aegeae concerning Apollonius' activities in that city, and a biography by one Moiragenes, which Philostratus explicitly warns his readers against in *VA* 1.3-4, 1.19. See Bowie 1978, 1663-85; Speyer 1974; and Francis 1995, 85-89.

3. Since the work was commissioned by the empress (*VA* 1.3) but not dedicated to her-meager but plausible evidence, as is the case with so much concerning *VA*. That *VA* predates Philostratus' *Lives of the Sophists* (*VS*) is established by a reference to the former work at *VS* 570.

4. Though not immediately relevant to discussion here, a recent and intriguing argument against the historicity of Apollonius' Indian journey has been offered by Simon Swain (1995).

5. In 1.3 Philostratus states that these memoirs were written on "tablets" (*deltoi*). As will be seen below, the translation of *deltoi* here is crucial to one argument regarding the novelistic character of *VA*. The passage is worth citing in the original: οὗτος τῷ Ἀπολλωνίῳ προσφιλοσοφήσας ἀποδημίας τε αὐτοῦ ἀναγέγραφεν, ὧν κοινωνῆσαι καὶ αὐτός φησι, καὶ γνώμας καὶ λόγους καὶ ὁπόσα ἐς πρόγνωσιν εἶπε. καὶ προσήκων τις τῷ Δάμιδι τὰς δέλτους τῶν ὑπομνημάτων τούτων οὔπω γιγνωσκωμένας ἐς γνῶσιν ἤγαγεν Ἰουλίᾳ τῷ βασιλίδι. It is important to note that this passage allows for a number of subtle but significant variants in interpretation and would benefit from a complete, dedicated philological study of Philostratus-a task that remains to be done.

6. Reardon had reached similar conclusions, through different channels: "Il crée une oeuvre variée, dont l'élément commun est qu'elle est surtout le produit d'un artiste en littérature, et non d'un homme convaincu de quoi que ce soit" (1971, 190). And "En somme, il a 'remanié' Apollonios pour servir ses propres fins littéraires: il veut simplement captiver l'intérêt du lecteur, sans trop chercher la vérité. . . . Il cherche l'intéressant, au point éventuellement d'écarter le vrai" (1971, 266).

7. The area of Dzielska's original contribution, the nature and dissemination of Apollonius' post- and non-Philostratean legends, lies outside the scope of this essay. Her work is cited here only as it is relevant to issues under discussion, but it is certainly a worthy piece of scholarship in its own right and valuable for its collection of diverse evidence and testimony on Apollonius. Dzielska's argument (1986, 27-35) that Apollonius was not born until ca. 40 C.E. must, however, be rejected; see Bowie 1989.

8. Anderson 1986, 155-73. For refutation of the identification of Damis see Edwards 1991.

9. Reardon 1971, 410-11.

10. Both Bowie and Anderson inherit a wealth of scholarship with regard to their positions, as they themselves acknowledge. The highlights of the history of scholarship can be summarized as follows. E. Meyer (1917) first called the historicity of Damis and *VA* into question as a correction to R. Reitzenstein (1906). This view, with some exceptions, dominated until F. Grosso (1954) endeavored to rehabilitate *VA* as a historical source. Bowie (1978) refuted Grosso's arguments as having no formal validity and reasserted Meyer's position. This, in turn, prompted Anderson (1986) to argue against Bowie and assume a position generally similar to that of Grosso. More extensive histories can be found in Bowie 1978, 1652-55 (in fullest detail); Anderson 1986, 131 n. 2; and Francis 1995, 86-89.

11. Francis 1995, 85, 89, 128-29, 184-86.

12. Bowie 1978, 1652-53.

13. See above, note 10.

14. Bowie 1978, 1653.

15. Bowie 1978, 1655-62. The anachronisms in question concern the regnal dates of the Parthian king Vardanes, Apollonius' relation to Musonius Rufus, the depiction of Demetrius the Cynic, and Apollonius' meeting with Vespasian at Alexandria. This, I would hold, is an excellent example of erudite knowledge and method applied to the wrong question. For the opposing response to these arguments see Anderson 1986, 175-97.

16. Bowie 1978, 1662.

17. Bowie 1978, 1665-66.

18. Actually, as Bowie points out (1978, 1663 n. 34), questions about the *"deltoi"* have been with us since J. Göttsching (1889), and the connection to Dictys was made by Speyer (1974). Bowie was, however, the first to draw out the full implications and connections regarding this as a "novelistic" feature. On Dictys see Merkle 1994.

19. Bowie 1978, 1663-67. It must be noted, however, that Reardon's original comment stresses the "presque." Directly after coining this *bon mot* (1971, 189), Reardon points out that many of the most crucial elements in his definition of the ancient novel are, in fact, missing from *VA;* see also Reardon 1971, 265. Bowie (1994) has given further consideration to these novelistic elements, but in that brief chapter offers no substantive revision or retraction of his earlier position in the *ANRW* [*Aufstieg und Niedergang der Römischen Welt*] article (1978).

20. Bowie 1978, 1666.

21. Bowie 1978, 1686.

22. Anderson 1986, 123.

23. Anderson 1986, 166.

24. Anderson 1986, 285.

25. Bowersock 1994, 14-15, in reference to the generation of critics coming after Rohde. In fairness, it should be noted that Anderson makes a similar observation: "It is futile in the end to try to 'explain' *Apollonius* in terms of any single genre. Sophistic encomia were much less rigid than the stereotyped textbook headings would have us believe; and sophists frequently exercised their talents in exploring new combinations of classical authors and classical genres. Here in effect we have the encomium in the form of a biography: the author's apparent expansions are in Platonic dialogue rather than set speeches; while the nature of the subject, and the indications in his undoubtedly extant sources, keep Philostratus on the borderline between novel and hagiography. The label 'sophistic biography' takes account of the compromises Philostratus has made" (1986, 235). As is clear, Anderson does not follow the implications of his first sentence here into the broader and more radical context of Bowersock, and ultimately remains confined in the same sort of genre arguments as Bowie-another example, along with the Damis question, of the narrow focus of *VA* scholarship. The various literary taxonomies suggested for *VA* have been thoroughly and conveniently summarized in Dzielska 1986, 12, and in less detail in Anderson 1986, 236 nn. 1-2; see also Talbert 1978.

26. Bowersock 1994, 124-25.

27. It is important to emphasize here that the present essay does not attempt to deliver an overview or specific treatment of the ancient novel itself, but

only to discuss selected salient points of contact between the novel and *VA* and the broader topic of fiction and history. Work on the ancient novel is frighteningly voluminous; see, e.g., Bowie and Harrison 1993. A workable, recently revised bibliography may be found in Holzberg 1995, 109-26 (this English translation updates Holzberg's original German edition of 1986). Morgan and Stoneman 1994 also provides useful bibliographies at the end of each chapter. Tatum 1994 contains some of the more significant papers presented at the 1989 Dartmouth-NEH conference "The Ancient Novel: Classical Paradigms and Modern Perspectives"; now see also the review essay by Morgan (1996).

28. Morgan 1993, 186-87, 193. See also Reardon 1991, 46-76, for another excellent discussion of fiction in antiquity.

29. On this very question, in connection with the matter at hand, see Moles 1993.

30. Bowersock 1994, 12.

31. Morgan 1993, 191.

32. *Adversus Math.* 1.263-69, discussed in Bowersock 1994, 10-11 and n. 18. See also Morgan 1993, 187-93, for a similar discussion adducing other ancient sources.

33. See discussions in Pelling 1990, 19-21; Moles 1993, 120-21.

34. Laird 1993, 153.

35. Bowersock 1994, 13: "The richness and importance of fiction for the historian of the Roman empire has been little investigated or appreciated. This neglect seems largely to have been the result of the way philologists and literary critics handled it. For one thing the novels have tended to be studied independently of other fictional forms."

36. *VA* 6.31-33; see Bowie 1978, 1659.

37. Bowie 1978, 1662.

38. Anderson 1986, 191.

39. Morgan 1993, 198-201-though, for completeness, it should be mentioned that Philostratus apparently despised Chariton. See Philostr. *Ep.* 66, discussed briefly in Anderson 1989, 116-18.

40. Morgan 1993, 103.

41. See above, note 28.

42. Morgan 1993, 225. He continues: "What do we mean when we talk of fiction being believable? I have argued that readers believe; but it is hardly

sensible to ask whether something you believe is believable. Equally, I have argued that fiction also entails an awareness of its untruth; and again it seems inappropriate to ask if something you know for certain to be untrue is believable. The idea of 'believable fiction,' then, does not make sense from either of the reader's two perspectives in isolation. Rather, it is what mediates between and unites his two worlds. In monitoring a novel's believability, the reader is in a continual process of moving backwards and forwards between the world of fiction and the world of reality, checking that the correlation is sufficient to allow the game to go on. There is a chain of relativities: fictional pleasure requires belief, belief implies believability, but believability requires the evaluative distance of objective disbelief" (226).

43. Bowersock 1994, 118.

44. Bowersock 1994, 3-4. On Celsus see also Francis 1995, 131-79.

45. On this motif in general see Speyer 1970. It is no accident that Speyer has also produced a significant work on *VA* (1974), in which he holds the traditional fictional position regarding the controversial issues.

46. Morgan 1993, 208-10. On these novels see also Bowersock 1994, 9-13, 23, 35-44.

47. Anderson 1986, 165.

48. Morgan 1993, 196.

49. Knoles 1981, 42; Laird 1993, 154-55. Knoles's unfortunately unpublished and sadly often overlooked dissertation remains the only extensive study of the internal literary dynamics and structure of *VA*. A new published study incorporating both new insights into fiction and, just as important, a narratological analysis, is very much needed.

50. Depending on who is construed as the subject of *phasi* at various points in the text; see Knoles 1981, 53-57; Anderson 1986, 157-61. Knoles, reflecting the traditional historical approach to *VA,* suggests that the cumbersome narration is the result of Philostratus dealing with a difficult and fragmentary source document.

51. See Knoles 1981, 45. It may even be possible to distinguish further between Damis the narrator and Damis the character. By the standards established by Morgan (1993, 224-29), the sort of fictive belief evoked by *VA* is different from that of the novel, which lies more in the reader's participation in the "plot" or identification with the characters. *VA* does not elicit either of these

regarding Apollonius, even if the travelogues and drama serve to draw in the reader's emotional attention. Given this, it may be possible to view Damis the character as "sitting in" for the reader, providing a vicarious audience reaction to both his own situations and those of his beloved master. If this is so, this would constitute another level of interaction in which source, narrator, and character each serve to validate and reinforce the other, diffusing even farther the "evaluative distance of objective disbelief" (see above, note 42). This diminution of disbelief would then have important consequences. First is that the text would simply be taken as literal truth, which is discussed below. The second is that the contract of fictional complicity would not be recognized by the reader: that is, the reader believes the author is endeavoring to "pass off" his story as literal truth. Morgan notes (1993, 196-97) that Photius read *The Wonders beyond Thule* in exactly this way. He then goes on: "Perhaps this is an inevitable hazard of the game of fiction. There are plenty of modern instances of people forgetting the fictionality of fiction. Many people believe Sherlock Holmes to be a real person, partly through the sheer charisma of the character, but largely, I suspect, because of Dr. Watson's function as authenticating apparatus. Radio and television serials are notoriously taken as reality. There the medium authenticates itself" (197 n. 31). Does Damis then function as Watson to Apollonius' Holmes? Does *VA* itself serve as the self-authenticating medium of the *deltoi*?

52. Winkler 1985, 66-67; also discussed by Laird (1993, 173), in the context of his own conclusions regarding fictional and historical narratives.

53. Bowie 1978, 1663.

54. Knoles 1981, 44.

55. Laird 1993, 155, citing Clarke 1981.

56. Parts of Hierocles' work are preserved in Eusebius' *Contra Hieroclem;* see the important article by T. Hägg (1992). A succinct discussion with bibliographical references can be found in Francis 1995, 83 n. 1.

57. Bowersock 1994, 9.

58. Translation by H. Chadwick (1965, 39), quoted and discussed by Bowersock (1994, 9). This entire section in Origen's work is worth reading for the further complications Christianity added to the issue of fiction and history.

59. Bowersock 1994, 124: "It is, furthermore, a plain fact of chronology that the distinctive fictional forms of the Roman empire begin, on the present evidence, no earlier than the reign of Nero and proliferate conspicuously soon thereafter. To be sure, antecedents of this fiction, such as the Homeric tales, Ctesias's Persian fantasies, Xenophon's *Cyropaideia,* Hellenistic travel literature, and the lost lubricities of the short Milesian tales, serve to identify some of the scattered elements that the imperial writers assimilated, brought together, and transformed in order to create what, on any accounting, was a wholly new phenomenon in Graeco-Roman literature." See also 21-27.

60. See above, note 2. On the ultimate aim and significance of this rehabilitation of Apollonius see Francis 1995, esp. 125-29, 182-89.

61. Bowersock 1994, 13.

62. Though it concerns the historiography of a much later period, Hobsbawm and Ranger 1983 has offered valuable new methodological contributions which parallel the developments regarding fiction discussed here.

63. The Loeb translation by F.C. Conybeare (1912) reads: "It seems to be that I ought not to condone or acquiesce in the general ignorance, but write a true account of the man, detailing the exact times at which he said or did this or that, as also the habits and temper of wisdom by means of which he succeeded in being considered a supernatural and divine being."

64. Veyne 1988, xii; quoted with approval in Bowersock 1994, 11. On one level at least, the choice concerning Apollonius was that described by Jerome (*Ep.* 53 Hilberg): *sive ille magus ut vulgus loquitur, sive philosophus ut Pythagorici tradunt.* Though Philostratus explicitly wrote *VA* to combat the former reputation, it nevertheless persisted, despite Hierocles' further lionization of Apollonius, in forms encompassing both "white" and "black" magic; on this particular topic see Dzielska 1986.

65. Compare this to the conclusions reached by the traditional historical approach to *VA* when, for example, it has to deal with Philostratus' description of Apollonius' Indian and Ethiopian travels: "But in the end truth, error, and falsehood look remarkably alike; one of the functions of a sophist was to impose a facile consistency on all three" (Anderson 1986, 220).

66. Morgan 1993, 176; endorsed and quoted in Bowersock 1994, 9 n. 17.

67. See above, note 28.

68. "Strategies of realism (make believe) extend to the textual act of representation. Manner of narration, as well as content, is engineered to produce belief" (Morgan 1993, 205).

69. As Morgan (1993, 197) says of *The Wonders beyond Thule.*

70. "But this is merely to say that the implied view of the verisimilar differs from generally held modern ones. This is worth stressing, because it is here, rather than on the fundamental questions of what fiction is and what it is for, that the Greek novels are foreign to us" (Morgan 1993, 227). Yet the phenomenon itself is not foreign to us. Some seven hundred people a year write to Sherlock Holmes at Baker Street, as if he were not only real but actually still alive (Morgan 1993, 225). Less gullible tourists in London merely inquire as to the whereabouts of Holmes's grave (Knoles 1981, 153-64).

Bibliography

Anderson, Graham. 1986. *Philostratus: Biography and Belles Lettres in the Third Century A.D.* London: Croom Helm.

———. 1989. "The *Pepaideumenos* in Action: Sophists and Their Outlook in the Early Roman Empire." *ANRW* II.33.1 116-18.

Bowersock, Glen W. 1994. *Fiction as History: Nero to Julian.* Berkeley and Los Angeles: University of California Press.

Bowie, E. L. 1978. "Apollonius of Tyana: Tradition and Reality." *ANRW* II.16.2 1652-99.

———. 1989. Review of Dzielska 1986. *JRS* [*Journal of Roman Studies*] 79:252.

———. 1994. "Philostratus: Writer of Fiction." In *Greek Fiction: The Greek Novel in Context,* edited by J. R. Morgan and R. Stoneman, 187-96. London: Routledge.

Bowie, E. L., and S. J. Harrison. 1993. "The Romance of the Novel." *JRS* 83: 159-78.

Chadwick, Henry. 1965. *Origen: Contra Celsum.* Cambridge: Cambridge University Press.

Clarke, Howard W. 1981. *Homer's Readers: A Historical Introduction to the Iliad and the Odyssey.* Newark: University of Delaware Press.

Dzielska, Maria. 1986. *Apollonius of Tyana in Legend and History.* Translated by P. Pienkowski. Problemi e Ricerche di Storia Antica 10. Rome: L'"Erma" di Bretschneider. (Translation of *Appoloniusz z Tiany: legenda i rzeczywistosc.* Rozprawy habilitacyjne Uniwersytet Jagiellonski 78. Cracow: Nak. Uniwersytetu Jagiellonski, 1983.)

Edwards, M. J. 1991. "Damis the Epicurean." *CQ,* [*Classical Quarterly*] n.s. 41:563-66.

Francis, James A. 1995. *Subversive Virtue: Asceticism and Authority in the Second-Century Pagan World.* University Park: Pennsylvania State University Press.

Göttsching, Johannes. 1889. *Apollonius von Tyana.* Leipzig: M. Hoffman.

Grosso, F. 1954. "La 'Vita di Apollonio di Tiana' come fonte storica." *Acme* 7:333-52.

Hägg, Tomas. 1992. "Hierocles the Lover of Truth and Eusebius the Sophist." *Symbolae Osloenses* 67:138-50.

Hobsbawm, E. J., and T. O. Ranger, eds. 1983. *The Invention of Tradition.* Cambridge: Cambridge University Press.

Holzberg, Niklas. 1995. *The Ancient Novel: An Introduction.* Translated by C. Jackson-Holzberg. London: Routledge.

Knoles, T. G. 1981. *Literary Techniques and Theme in Philostratus' Life of Apollonius of Tyana.* Diss. Rutgers University.

Laird, Andrew. 1993. "Fiction, Bewitchment, and Story Worlds: The Implications of Claims to Truth in Apuleius." In *Lies and Fiction in the Ancient World,* edited by Christopher Gill and T. P. Wiseman, 147-74. Austin: University of Texas Press.

Merkle, Stefan. 1994. "Telling the True Story of the Trojan War: The Eyewitness Account of Dictys of Crete." In *The Search for the Ancient Novel,* edited by James Tatum, 183-96. Baltimore: The Johns Hopkins University Press.

Meyer, Eduard. 1917. "Apollonius von Tyana und die Biographie des Philostratos." *Hermes* 52:371-424. (= *Kleine Schriften* II 131-91. Halle: M. Niemeyer, 1924.)

Moles, J. L. 1993. "Truth and Untruth in Herodotus and Thucydides." In *Lies and Fiction in the Ancient World,* edited by Christopher Gill and T. P. Wiseman, 88-121. Austin: University of Texas Press.

Morgan, J. R. 1993. "Make-Believe and Make Believe: The Fictionality of the Greek Novels." In *Lies and Fiction in the Ancient World,* edited by Christopher Gill and T. P. Wiseman, 175-229. Austin: University of Texas Press.

———. 1996. "The Ancient Novel at the End of the Century: Scholarship since the Dartmouth Conference." *CP* [*Classical Philology*] 91:63-73.

Morgan, J. R., and Richard Stoneman, eds. 1994. *Greek Fiction: The Greek Novel in Context.* London: Routledge.

Pelling, C. B. R. 1990. "Truth and Fiction in Plutarch's Lives." In *Antonine Literature,* edited by D. A. Russell, 19-51. Oxford: Oxford University Press.

Reardon, B. P. 1971. *Courants littéraires grecs des IIe et IIIe siècles après J.-C.* Annales littéraires de l'Université de Nantes 3. Paris: Les Belles Lettres.

———. 1991. *The Form of Greek Romance.* Princeton: Princeton University Press.

Reitzenstein, Richard. 1906. *Hellenistische Wunder-erzählungen.* Leipzig: B. G. Teubner.

Speyer, Wolfgang. 1970. *Bücherfunde in der Glaubenswerbung der Antike.* Göttingen: Vandenhoeck & Ruprecht.

———. 1974. "Zum Bild des Apollonius von Tyana bei Heiden und Christen." *JbAC* [*Jahrbuch für Antike und Cristentum*] 17:47-63.

Swain, Simon. 1995. "Apollonius in Wonderland." In *Ethics and Rhetoric: Classical Essays for Donald Russell on His Seventy-Fifth Birthday,* edited by Doreen Innes, Harry Hine, and Christopher Pelling, 251-54. Oxford: Clarendon Press.

Talbert, C. H. 1978. "Biographies of Philosophers and Rulers as Instruments of Religious Propaganda in Mediterranean Antiquity." *ANRW* II.16.2 1619-51.

Tatum, James, ed. 1994. *The Search for the Ancient Novel.* Baltimore: The Johns Hopkins University Press.

Veyne, Paul. 1988. *Did the Greeks Believe in Their Myths?* Translated by P. Wissing. Chicago: University of Chicago Press.

Winkler, John J. 1985. *Auctor and Actor: A Narratological Reading of Apuleius's The Golden Ass.* Berkeley and Los Angeles: University of California Press.

Christopher Jones (essay date October 2000)

SOURCE: Jones, Christopher. "The Emperor and the Giant." *Classical Philology* 95, no. 4 (October 2000): 476-81.

[*In the following essay, Jones argues that a passage from Philostratus's* Heroikos *can help identify an emperor mentioned in a treatise by Pausanias; the critic claims that the man described is in fact Lucius Verus.*]

A passage of the periegete Pausanias mentions an "emperor (βασιλεύς) of the Romans" who discovered, or caused to be discovered, the bones of a giant in the bed of the river Orontes. Though the identification of the emperor has been discussed inconclusively for well over a century, it involves the history and topography of Antioch, one of the great cities of antiquity, and is therefore more than a mere puzzle. The present study argues that a passage of Philostratus' **Heroicus,** noticed in this connection but not read with sufficient care, may help to solve the problem.[1]

Pausanias' testimony can be translated as follows (8.29.3-4):

> The Syrian river Orontes does not flow to the sea over a level course throughout, but is borne towards a precipitous cliff and downwards from it. The emperor of the Romans wanted ships to sail up [the river] from the sea to the city of Antioch. So he had a canal suitable for navigation up-stream dug with labor and expense of money, and diverted the river into it. But when the previous bed had dried up, there was found in it an earthenware coffin of more than eleven cubits length, and the body [in it] was of a size commensurate with the coffin and human throughout its body. When the Syrians came to the oracle of the god at Claros, he declared that the body was [that of] Orontes, and that he was of the race of the Indians.

The passage raises some immediate problems. The expression "the emperor of the Romans" is used by Pausanias elsewhere in reference to Augustus and Hadrian, and the one meant here cannot be later than the latest emperor whom he mentions by name, "the second Antoninus" or Marcus Aurelius.[2] The word translated "canal," ἔλυτρον, is rare, and seems to be part of his consciously Herodotean vocabulary. Though Liddell and Scott translate it as "reservoir," in this passage it must mean "channel" or "canal," and perhaps in its other occurrences in this author.[3] A more concrete problem is that the geography of the Orontes between Antioch and the sea does not seem to allow for the diversion of the river into a new bed, even allowing for the changes in the terrain caused by seismic activity, and it may be that Pausanias has misunderstood the operation.[4]

Several emperors have been suggested for the one in this passage, and they may be taken in chronological order. A tradition found in Malalas and later writers reports that the Orontes had been called the "Drakon" until its name was changed in the reign of Tiberius. Accordingly, an old view favored Tiberius, or possibly his nephew Germanicus, as the ruler meant here. Though this view still finds adherents, it has little to recommend it, since the name "Orontes" occurs long before, and Malalas' work is a notorious farrago of true and false information.[5]

By contrast with Tiberius, accumulating evidence attests to the activity of Vespasian both in Syria generally and in connection with the Orontes in the region of Antioch and its port, Seleuceia Pieria, and he is the emperor now usually identified with the one in Pausanias.[6] A milestone found eleven kilometers upstream from Antioch shows that his legate M. Ulpius Traianus, father of the emperor, built or repaired a waterway three miles long; the purpose was probably to channel the Orontes where it meets a tributary coming from the lake of Antioch. Two stelai in Greek, also dating from the tenure of Traianus, record a canal that was dug with local labor between the river and the foothills of Mount Amanus, though its precise location is unknown. Downstream from the city, the late Denis van Berchem found evidence that blocks of stone had been placed into the riverbed at a point where it passes through a narrow defile, and he was inclined on the basis of Pausanias to think Vespasian responsible. At the same time, he noted that the river must have required constant maintenance, and he cited a constitution of Valentinian and Valens that showed troops from the *classis Seleucena* being employed *ad auxilium purgandi Orontis*. At Seleuceia itself, Vespasian began, and perhaps completed, a tunnel designed to divert runoff from the mountain overlooking the harbor; here too, however, it is certain that further work was necessary in the next century.[7]

A suggestion by an excellent scholar, Walther Ruge, has not drawn much attention. Arguing that Pausanias' words, "wanting ships to sail up [the river] from the sea to the city of Antioch," imply the emperor's presence in person, Ruge held that he was in Antioch on his way to an eastern campaign ("ein Kaiser, der persönlich von Antiocheia aus ins Feld zog"). Ruge therefore proposed Trajan, who is known to have visited the city on the way both to and from his Parthian campaign.[8] There seems no other evidence, however, for engineering works conducted under his auspices.

A hint in Pausanias might orient towards a later emperor: the mention of Claros. This oracle, dependent on the city of Colophon, had existed from archaic times, and early in the imperial period received a visit from Germanicus, memorably described by Tacitus (*Ann.* 2.54). Nevertheless, the oracle reached the summit of its fame only in the second century, after the completion of the god's temple by Hadrian. It was presumably for this reason that R. Merkelbach and J. Stauber, assembling the known oracles of Claros, suggested Lucius Verus as the emperor in Pausanias, apparently in all innocence of the debate whose course has been described here.[9]

Lucius made Antioch his base almost continuously from his arrival at the war front in 162 or 163 until his departure in 165 or 166. Modern accounts of his conduct of the war are influenced by the *Historia Augusta,* which in its characteristic way focuses on his easy living and on his love of entertainments, banquets, and women. Yet Fronto's *Principia Historiae,* though certainly biased in the other direction, and Lucian's similar treatise on the writing of history give the impres-

sion of an active and effective general, though Fronto is careful to insert a defense of Lucius' liking for stage players. (Malalas, who might have been useful on this point, confuses Lucius with Commodus, and so provides almost nothing.)[10] Within the last hundred years or so, however, archaeological and other discoveries have tipped the balance in Lucius' favor. A Fayum papyrus first published in 1895 contains a contract dated to 166 and drawn up in Seleuceia Pieria. The parties are an *optio* in the trireme *Tigris* of the Misene fleet and a soldier of the same ship selling him a slave of Mesopotamian origin, clearly booty from the recent campaign.[11] Henri Seyrig in 1939 studied two military cemeteries of Seleuceia, and observing that all the tombstones could be dated between 129 and 212 pointed to Lucius' Parthian War as the chief explanation: "Le mouvement de troupes qu'entraînèrent ces évènements, le plus grand qu'ait vu l'Orient au 2e siècle, expliquerait mieux que tout autre la présence d'une base navale importante à Seleucie."[12]

It is here that the passage of Philostratus referred to at the beginning of this paper may be of help. It occurs in his *Heroicus,* a dialogue between a rustic vine-dresser and a Phoenician merchant (for the present purpose, it does not greatly matter whether the author is the well-known Philostratus or his contemporary, Philostratus of Lemnos). The dramatic date must be approximately in the author's own time, as emerges above all from a discussion of the Phoenician athlete Aurelius Helix, who had his greatest successes in the reign of Elagabalus (147.15-28 K., 16.26-17.5 L.).[13] Near the beginning of the conversation, the rustic tries to break down the merchant's skepticism by mentioning a number of instances of men of superhuman size, whether heroes or giants. He begins with an account of the bones of Salaminian Ajax, revealed by the action of waves on the shore of Troy and reburied with proper care by the emperor Hadrian; the reburial took place in the lifetime of the rustic's grandfather, and it so happens that, in one of several coincidences between the two authors, Pausanias appears to mention the same event as narrated to him by an informant from Mysia (Philostr. *Her.* 137.15-23 K., 8.16-21 L.; Paus. 1.35.4-5). When the merchant proves incredulous, the rustic promises to bypass events from myth, and instead to give instances "in our time" (ἐφ ἡμῶν, 138.6 K., 9.4 L.). The first of these is said to have occurred "not long ago" (οὐ πάλαι, 138.8 K., 9.6 L.), a phrase that by contrast with the mythological era need only mean "in no very distant past."[14] The second occurred "not yet fifty years ago" (138.10 K., 9.7 L.), the next four years ago (139.2 K., 9.25 L.), the next "the other day" (πέρυσιν, 139.14 K., 10.5 L.), and the last is still true at the time of the dialogue (139.28 K., 10.16 L.).

The first incident, therefore, should have occurred in the lifetime of the speakers, and if it too belongs in order it should have fallen some fifty or sixty years before: assuming a dramatic date about 220-25, this would produce a range roughly from 160 to 175. Philostratus' words are: "Aryades, who some said was Ethiopian, others said Indian, thirty cubits long, lying in the land of the Assyrians, was revealed not long ago when the bank of the river Orontes was cut" (ἡ τοῦ Ὀρόντου ὄχθη σχισθεῖσα, 138.6-9 K., 9.5-7 L.). As several commentators have noticed, this appears to represent another version of the story told by Pausanias, though with some differences. Pausanias does not give the name "Aryades" or mention an Ethiopian origin, and he reports the giant's height as eleven cubits, not thirty. But both authors talk of excavation in the Orontes, of a gigantic body that was found in the riverbed, and of this body as belonging to an Indian eponym of the river.

If Philostratus does indeed refer to the same incident as Pausanias, then his text implies that it occurred not earlier than the mid-second century. It cannot be much later, since in this same book (8.43.6), Pausanias mentions Marcus' victory over the Germans in the mid-170s, the last dated event in his work. In sum, the identification of Lucius Verus as Pausanias' "emperor of the Romans" would satisfy Ruge's supposition that the emperor was present in person, and involved in an eastern campaign; it would suit the mention of Claros; and it would also fit the chronology both of Pausanias and of Philostratus. Why Pausanias does not name an emperor who had died only a few years before seems impossible to tell. In a somewhat similar way, he talks of Antoninus (that is, Pius) "leaving a son of the same name" as his successor, and of Marcus' defense of the empire, without any mention of Lucius (ibid.).

Another author, about two centuries later than Philostratus, appears to give a version of the same story. The seventeenth book of Nonnus' *Dionysiaca* includes the *aristeia* of Orontes, a giant allied to the Indian king Deriades, who is also his father-in-law.[15] Humiliated by Dionysus in battle, Orontes commits suicide, and falls into the river that thereafter is to bear his name. His body is carried downstream "until the river-banks vomited the lifeless corpse" (ἄπνουν ἠρεύγοντο νέκυν ποταμηίδες ὄχθαι, 17.309). The Nymphs bury it "beside the trunk of a golden laurel" (χρυσέης παρὰ πυθμένα δάφνης, 311) and write an epitaph over it: "Here lies Indian Orontes, leader of the army, who insulted Bacchus, slain with self-destroying hand" (Βάκχον ἀτιμήσας στρατίης πρόμος ἐνθάδε κεῖται / αὐτοφόνῳ παλάμῃ δεδαιγμένος Ἰδὸς Ὀρόντης, 313-14). The reference to a "golden laurel" points to the famous sanctuary of Daphne above Antioch, though that was not near the Orontes, and the whole story seems to be a variation on some local legend of the city. It seems impossible to determine whether the legend started from the discovery of the giant's body and the oracle of Claros, or whether the oracle made use of an already existing tradition about the origin of the name "Orontes." It may be relevant, however, that a historian of Lucius' Parthian War alleged that Roman forces had crossed the River Indus.[16] That is, the priesthood of Claros might have turned the discovery of the supposed giant's bones into a portent of imperial victory.[17]

Notes

1. All references to Philostratus are to C. L. Kayser's 1870-71 *editio maior* (the *Heroicus* is in 2:128-219) and to L. de Lannoy's 1977 edition of the *Heroicus*.

2. Unnamed emperors: Augustus, 5.23.3, 10.38.4; Hadrian, 8.16.5; "The second Antoninus": 8.43.6. Cf. Habicht 1985, 9-10, suggesting a completion date between 175 and 180 for the whole work.

3. LSJ[9], s.v. ἔλυτρον 5; cf. Paus. 2.27.7, 7.27.4 (in both cases with κρήνης), 8.14.3 (with Hitzig's transposition).

4. On the Orontes between Antioch and the sea, van Berchem 1985, 68: "Le relief accusé de la vallée exclut le creusement d'un canal qui eût permis au fleuve de s'écouler par un autre chemin."

5. For this view see Frazer 1898, 4:316 (tentative); Blümner and Hitzig 1896-1910, 3.1:216 ("der Kaiser wird wohl Tiberius sein"); Arafat 1996, 82 ("very uncertain"); Casevitz 1998, 228 (expressing no doubt).

6. For a general treatment of Syria under Vespasian, Bowersock 1973 (= Bowersock 1994b, 85-92). In favor of this identification, van Berchem 1985, 68; Bowersock 1994a, 426-27.

7. Latin inscription: van Berchem 1983 (*Ann Epigr* [*Annee Epigraphique*] 1983, 927); revised readings and interpretation, van Berchem 1985, 85-87. See also Feissel 1985, 85-86; Bowersock 1994b, 425-27. Greek inscriptions: Feissel 1985, 77-84 (*SEG* [*Supplementum Epigraphicum Graecum*] 35.1483; *AnnEpigr* 1986, 694). Work downstream: van Berchem 1985, 68, citing *Cod. Theod.* 10.23.1 = *Cod. Iust.* 11.13.1. Van Berchem however takes Pausanias to say that the river passed through a "gorge escarpée," when in fact he talks of it being carried over a precipitous cliff (ἐπὶ κρημνὸν ἀπορρῶγα . . . φερόμενον). Tunnel: van Berchem 1985, 53-59.

8. Ruge 1931, 1191.

9. Apogee of Claros: Robert 1954, 20 (= Robert 1969-90, 6:540): "Le IIe siècle de notre ère est la grande époque de Claros"; J. and L. Robert, *Bulletin épigraphique* 1976, 539 no. 610: "C'est aussi sous le règne de Trajan que Claros prend un nouveau départ, mais un peu plus tard, et c'est Hadrien qui montrera sa faveur à Claros en faisant achever le temple et le dédiant." Merkelbach and Stauber 1996, 40 no. 23: "wohl unter Kaiser Verus."

10. In general, Stein 1899, 1842: "Mit der Ankunft des Verus, wenn auch nicht durch sein Verdienst, begann der Feldzug mit grösserer Energie und besserem Erfolg geführt zu werden." Fronto: van den Hout 1954, 191-200. Lucian: MacLeod, 1972-87, 3:287-319.

11. Cavenaile, 1958, p. 232, no. 120.

12. Seyrig 1939, 1:458-59 (= Seyrig 1985, 1:365-66); Roxan 1978, nos. 44, 74; van Berchem 1985, 62.3.

13. *PIR*² A 1520; Cass. Dio, 80.10.2-3 (9:458-61 Cary); Jones 1998, 295.

14. Thus, correctly, Chuvin 1991, 173, "voici peu (ce qui s'entend par rapport à des temps beaucoup plus anciens) . . ." Cf. Philostr. *Vit. Soph.* 42.10 K., Hadrian counted among οἱ πάλαι βασιλεῖς as distinct from subsequent ones.

15. See in particular Chuvin 1991, 170-73. A reader for *CP* [*Classical Philology*] suggests that *Deriades* and *Aryades* are the same name, the initial D being the Aramaic prepositional particle meaning "of."

16. Lucian, *Hist. conscr.* 31.

17. I am grateful to the readers for *CP* for their comments.

Literature Cited

Arafat, K. W. 1996. *Pausanias' Greece: Ancient Artists and Roman Rulers.* Cambridge.

Berchem, D. van. 1983. Une inscription flavienne du Musée d'Antioche. *MH* [*Museum Helveticum*] 40:185-96.

———. 1985. Le Port de Séleucie de Piérie et l'infrastructure logistique des guerres parthiques. *Bonner Jahrbücher* 185:47-87.

Blümner, H., and H. Hitzig. 1896-1910. *Pausaniae "Graeciae Descriptio."* 3 vols. in 6. Berlin.

Bowersock, G. W. 1973. Syria under Vespasian. *JRS* [*Journal of Roman Studies*] 63:133-40.

———. 1994a. The Search for Antioch: Karl Otfried Müller's *Antiquitates Antiochenae*. In Bowersock 1994b:411-27.

———. 1994b. *Studies on the Eastern Roman Empire.* Goldbach.

Casevitz, M., ed. 1998. *Pausanias, "Description de la Grèce," Livre VIII.* Paris.

Cavenaile, R. 1958. *Corpus Papyrorum Latinarum.* Wiesbaden.

Chuvin, P. 1991. *Mythologie et géographie dionysiaques: Recherches sur l'oeuvre de Nonnos de Panopolis.* Clermont-Ferrand.

Dussaud, R. 1939. *Mélanges syriens offerts à Monsieur René Dussaud.* 2 vols. Paris.

Feissel, D. 1985. Deux Listes de quartiers d'Antioche. *Syria* 62:77-103.

Frazer, J. G. 1898. *Pausanias's "Description of Greece."* 6 vols. London.

Habicht, C. 1985. *Pausanias' "Guide to Ancient Greece."* Berkeley and Los Angeles.

Hout, M. P. J. van den, ed. 1954. *M. Cornelii Frontonis Epistulae.* Leiden.

Jones, C. P. 1998. The Pancratiasts Helix and Alexander on an Ostian Mosaic. *JRA* [*Journal of Roman Archeology*] 11:293-98.

Kayser, C. L., ed. 1870-71. *Flavii Philostrati Opera.* 2 vols. Leipzig.

Lannoy, L. de, ed. 1977. *Flavius Philostratus, "Heroicus."* Leipzig.

MacLeod, M. D., ed. 1972-87. *Luciani Opera.* 4 vols. Oxford.

Merkelbach, R., and J. Stauber. 1996. Die Orakel des Apollon von Klaros. *EA* 27:1-53.

Robert, L. 1954. *Les Fouilles de Claros.* Limoges.

———. 1969-90. *Opera Minora Selecta.* 7 vols. Amsterdam.

Roxan, M. M. 1978. *Roman Military Diplomas 1954-1977.* London.

Ruge, W. 1931. Seleukeia (Pieria). *RE* [*Real-Encyclopädie der Klassischen Altertumswissenshaft*] 2B.1:1184-1200.

Seyrig, H. 1939. Le Cimetière des marins de Piérie. In Dussaud 1939, 1:451-59.

———. 1985. *Scripta Varia: Mélanges d'archéologie et d'histoire.* 2 vols. Paris.

Stein, A. 1899. L. Ceionius Commodus. *RE* 3.2:1832-57.

D. Thomas Benediktson (essay date 2000)

SOURCE: Benediktson, D. Thomas. "Phantasia: Plato and Aristotle, Cicero and Other Romans, Dio Chrsysostom, and Philostratus." In *Power, Literature and Visual Arts in Ancient Greece and Rome*, pp. 185-88. Norman, Okla.: University of Oklahoma Press, 2000.

[*In the following excerpt, Benediktson explores Philostratus's ideas on the relationship between literature and the visual arts as they are expressed in* Apollonius of Tyana.]

The traditions of Plato, Cicero and Dio come together in Philostratus, the author of the *Life of Apollonius of Tyana.* . . . Along with his relative of the same name, who wrote the *Imagines*, Philostratus has received a great deal of study by art critics. The *Life* is a biography of a priestly man; the *Imagines*, . . . is a series of *ekphrases* or descriptions of paintings in a museum-guide format. Both treatises are written in Greek for a highly educated and sophisticated reader. A modern critic has tried to ground modern "reader reception" theory in the *Life of Apollonius* 2.20-41.[1]

In his *Life of Apollonius of Tyana,* Philostratus has Apollonius raise the same objection to the non-Greek gods that Dio had raised: the Egyptians deify animals (6.19; Butcher in fact cites Dio and Philostratus as exceptions to "how little notice the Greeks took of symbolical art"). Apollonius' interlocutor, Thespesion, asks about Greek portrayals (ἀγάλματα). Apollonius responds that the Greek gods are the most beautiful and appropriate (κάλλιστόν τε καὶ θεοφιλέστατον). Thespesion then brings up the theory we have seen, in varying degrees, in Cicero, Dio, and Plotinus: "'Your artists, then, like Ph[e]idias,' said the other, 'and like Praxiteles, went up, I suppose, to heaven and took a copy of the forms of the gods, and then reproduced these by their art, or was there any other influence which presided over and greeted their moulding?'" (*VA* 6.19) At this point, Philostratus at least attempts to free art and literature from the mimetic limits that had been imposed by Plato and Aristotle but that were beginning to show strain in Plutarch and Dio (*VA* 6.19):

> "There was," said Apollonius, "and an influence pregnant with wisdom and genius." "What was that?" said the other, "for I do not think you can adduce any except imitation (μιμήσεως)." "Imagination [*phantasia*]," said Apollonius, "wrought these works, a wiser and subtler artist by far than imitation; for imitation can only create as its handiwork what it has seen, but imagination equally what it has not seen; for it will conceive of its ideal with reference to the reality (τοῦ ὄντος), and imitation is often baffled by terror, but imagination by nothing; for it marches undismayed to the goal which it has itself laid down."[2]

The artist must create an internal and appropriate image, just as Pheidias did. Thespesion suggests, like Dio, that Egyptian animals are "symbols" (ξύμβολα), but Apollonius replies that surely these images are not effective: "for the mind can more or less delineate and figure them to itself better than can any artist; but you have denied to the gods the privilege of beauty both of the outer eye and of inner suggestion (καὶ τὸ ὁρᾶσθαι καλῶς καὶ τὸ ὑπονοείσθαι)" (*VA* 6.19). As Watson comments, "We have, then, in this passage a movement from the praise of art which is based on mental vision to the exaltation of the mental vision itself, even if, or especially when, it does not issue in art." We might say that for the first time in antiquity the "inner eye" and "inner ear" have been freed from the tyranny of the "outer eye" and the "outer ear." The creative intelligence is free to contemplate "reality" (τὸ ἄν) without reference to the perception of reality by the senses (τὸ ὁρᾶσθαι καλῶς). Interestingly, here the doctrine of political and forensic styles is alluded to one final time. Imitation is linked to the forensic style, to be examined on the level of accuracy to detail, while the imagination is linked to the more oral, political style, which attains greatness or Longinian sublime and is to be examined at a distance. Thus, the traditions of the sublime and *phantasia* do ultimately intertwine, and one of the doctrines linking literature and the visual arts throughout antiquity is ultimately used to dominate the doctrine of mimēsis.[3]

The centrality of the comparison between literature and the visual arts to Philostratus' *phantasia* can be seen better in chapter 4.7 of the *Life,* where Apollonius argues that people make greater fame for their cities than monuments, because they are more mobile:

> [H]e encouraged them and increased their zeal, and urged them to take pride rather in themselves than in the beauty of their city; for although they had the most beautiful of cities under the sun, and although they had a friendly sea at their doors, which held the springs of the zephyr, nevertheless, it was more pleasing for the city to be crowned with men than with porticos and pictures, or even with gold in excess of what they needed. For, he said, public edifices remain where they are, and are nowhere seen except in that particular part of the earth where they exist, but good men are conspicuous everywhere, and everywhere talked about.[4]

Philostratus continues with the familiar analogy to Pheidias' Zeus, bound in space to Olympia.

Cocking comments that Philostratus has not completely separated phantasia from mimēsis in an Aristotelian sense; but we cannot ignore the fact that an important step has been taken. Watson correctly states that here literature is greater than visual art because it is "less earthbound," and also rightly places the passage in the tradition of Cicero, Longinus, Quintilian, and Dio discussed here. Watson finds the source of this tradition in a blend of Stoicism and Neoplatonism, and indeed these schools may have been the proximate source. But the ultimate source of the ideas is to be traced back to Pindar, the lyric poets, and the Sophists, who understood the mobility and temporality of the word to be superior to the spatiality of the visual image before the issue was confused by the mimeticism of Plato and Aristotle. That the tradition extends back to the lyric poets is clear from the reference, noted by Watson in both Dio (*Or.* 12.79) and Quintilian (6.1.35), to the visual arts as "speechless."[5]

With Philostratus, literature is at least potentially freed from the spatial limitations of visual art, and visual art is at least potentially freed from the temporal limitations of literature. That these issues continue to dominate literary and artistic theory in the Renaissance and Enlightenment, and in fact are at the core of many issues in the Modernist movement, continues to be the subject of other studies.

Notes

1. Don Fowler, "Even Better," 58-62, 287-88.

2. Butcher, *Aristotle's Theory,* 393, n. 1; cf. Atkins (*Literary Criticism,* 2.344-45), who sees Philostratus in a line from Longinus and Dio to Plotinus and ultimately to Coleridge ("the truth"). For a comparison of Philostratus here and Dio 12.59, see Birmelin, "Die Kunsthistorischen Gedanken," 394. Translation in F. B. Conybeare, *Philostratus,* 2.77, 2.77-79.

3. Translation in Conybeare, *Philostratus,* 2.81. Watson, "Concept," 4767. On the political style, see Trimpi, "Meaning," 23, n. 31; on the sublime and phantasia see Rouveret, *Histoire,* 412-23.

4. Translation in Conybeare, *Philostratus,* 1.357-59.

5. Cocking, *Imagination,* 43-47. Watson, "Concept," especially 4769, 4775, and 4779. On phantasia in relation to sculpture, see Stewart, *Greek Sculpture,* 20, 45, 83, 220, 258, 262; and Pollitt, *Art of Ancient Greece,* 5-8, 223-24.

Bibliography

Butcher, S. H. *Aristotle's Theory of Poetry and Fine Art with a Critical Text and Translation of the Poetics: With a Prefatory Essay Aristotelian Literary Criticism by John Gassner.* 4th edition. New York: Dover, 1951.

Conybeare, F. C. *Philostratus: The Life of Apollonius of Tyana; The Epistles of Apollonius and the Treatise of Eusebius.* 2 volumes. Cambridge: Harvard University Press; London: Heinemann, 1912.

Cocking, J. M. *Imagination: A Study in the History of Ideas.* London and New York: Routledge, 1991.

Fowler, Don. "Even Better than the Real Thing: A Tale of Two Cities." In *Art and Text in Roman Culture,* edited by Jaś Elsner, 57-74 and 287-93. Cambridge: Cambridge University Press, 1996.

Pollitt, J. J. *The Ancient View of Greek Art: Criticism, History, and Terminology.* New Haven and London: Yale University Press, 1974.

———. *The Art of Ancient Greece: Sources and Documents.* Cambridge: Cambridge University Press, 1990.

Rouveret, Agnès. *Histoire et imaginaire de la peinture ancienne (Ve siècle av. J.-C.-Ier siècle ap. J.-C.).* Paris: École française de Rome, 1989.

Stewart, Andrew. *Greek Sculpture: An Exploration.* 2 volumes. New Haven and London: Yale University Press, 1990.

Trimpi, Wesley. "The Early Metaphorical Uses of σκιαγραφία and σκηνογραφία." *Traditio* 34 (1978): 403-13.

Watson, Gerard. "The Concept of 'Phantasia' from the Late Hellenistic Period to Early Platonism." *Aufstieg und Niedergang der römischen Welt* 36, no. 7 (1994): 4765-4810.

Christopher P. Jones (essay date 2001)

SOURCE: Jones, Christopher P. "Philostratus' *Heroikos* and Its Setting in Reality." *Journal of Hellenic Studies* 21 (2001): 141-49.

[*In the following essay, Jones examines the social and historical background of the events described in the* Heroikos, *first summarizing the work and then focusing on the date of composition, geographical setting, and the views expressed in it regarding heroes.*]

As recently as 1987, the dialogue **Heroikos** (**On the Heroes**), usually attributed to Philostratus 'the Athenian' or 'the Younger', was 'more often dismissed than discussed'. Since then the situation has changed. An Italian translation with short commentary and a German commentary have recently appeared, and further publications are expected.[1] Yet many aspects of the work continue to remain problematic. In the early twentieth century, some scholars held that it reflected the visit of Caracalla to Ilium in 214, and was essentially a piece of court literature written to celebrate the visit and to please the emperor. Others have held that it is merely a sophistic showpiece with only the barest connection to real life. Teresa Mantero, in what is still the best overall study of the work, did not contradict the political view, but also held that Philostratus intended to revive the cult of heroes. Robin Lane Fox has recently argued that the **Heroikos** has no relation to Caracalla; rather, it represents what educated readers were 'prepared to enjoy without altogether believing' about possible encounters between living persons and the Homeric heroes.[2]

In the present paper, I have not tried to solve all these problems. Rather, I wish to consider the **Heroikos'** relationship to reality, construing 'reality' broadly as the social and historical background against which a reader of Philostratus' time might have read it. For this purpose, I have first (1) briefly summarized the work, and thereafter I have divided the discussion into four sections, as follows: (2) the time of writing; (3) the dramatic date; (4) the geographical setting; (5) the work's relation to current beliefs about heroes. I have not entered into the question of its literary affinities or its place in literary history, except insofar as such questions impinge on those mentioned above.

I. SUMMARY

The speakers of the dialogue are a Phoenician merchant 'from the region of Tyre and Sidon' (1.1) and a vine-grower (*ampelourgos*) from Elaious in the Thracian Chersonese.[3] This man now makes his living in the country, though originally he was a well-educated townsman ruined by the dishonesty of his family's slaves (4.6-10). The merchant for his part is on a westward voyage from Egypt and Phoenicia. After putting in at Elaious, he had a dream in which he was reading Homer's 'catalogue of the Achaeans' in the second book of the *Iliad,* and then found himself inviting all these heroes aboard his ship. Now, therefore, fearing that the dream portended ill, and also seeking a favourable sign for the continuation of his voyage, he has come ashore and had a chance encounter with the vine-grower (6.3-6). He in turn claims to be the man to satisfy the other's doubts, since he has frequent meetings with the hero Protesilaos in person. The Phoenician is incredulous, and the dialogue begins with a preliminary conversation about the reality of heroes and giants. After that, the vine-grower relates what he has heard from Protesilaos. This narrative, a kind of gallery of the Achaean and Trojan warriors, is the main part of the work. It includes some not mentioned by Homer, such as Palamedes, but ends with the central figure of the *Iliad,* Achilles. The vine-grower not only describes that hero's appearance, but also expounds how he still lives and receives cult on an island in the Black Sea; this section thus forms a pendant to the description of Elaious, the cult-site of Protesilaos (54-7). At the end of the dialogue, as night begins to fall, the Phoenician declares himself convinced, and the vine-grower urges

him either to set sail on the next day, or to return and hear more. The Phoenician opts to do the latter, and the dialogue ends.

II. THE TIME OF WRITING

The essential evidence comes in a discussion of athletes seeking the advice of Protesilaos (14.4-15.10). The last to be named is a boxer and pancratiast called Helix, who is known from several sources other than the **Heroikos.**[4] When he asked the hero how many times he was fated to win at the Olympics, he received the answer, 'Twice, unless you wish to do so thrice.' The Phoenician, well informed about a champion from his own region, correctly interprets this 'oracle':

> (Helix) already had one victory, when he won at wrestling in the men's category after advancing from the boys' [literally, 'a man from among the boys', ἀνὴρ ἐκ παιδῶν].[5] He stripped for the subsequent Olympiad in both wrestling and the pancration. The Eleians became indignant at this, and wanted to shut him out of both events by inventing Olympian charges against him, but reluctantly crowned him for the pancration.

Cassius Dio tells virtually the same story in the context of a portent received by the emperor Elagabalus in Rome, probably in 219, the year of his arrival there (80.10.2). At the Capitolia, the great athletic festival held every four years, Helix won in both wrestling and the pancration; on the usual cycle this should have fallen in 218, but may have been delayed because of the emperor's absence.[6] Dio asserts that the Eleians denied Helix a double victory at his second Olympiad out of fear that he might win the prestigious title of 'eighth after Heracles'. This was given to those few athletes who had won in wrestling and the pancration at a single Olympic contest.[7]

Unlike Dio, Philostratus says nothing of Helix' success in Rome, and Karl Münscher inferred that he must have written before it had occurred. Convinced that the work was connected with Caracalla's visit to Ilium in 214, Münscher also placed Helix' first Olympic victory in 209, the second in 213. Julius Jüthner replied that Philostratus was not obliged to mention Helix' success at Rome, and that a 'heavy' athlete was unlikely to have enjoyed a long career. His two Olympic victories, therefore, fell more probably in 213 and 217, and 217 will be the *terminus post quem* of the **Heroikos.**[8]

A slightly later *terminus post* might be suggested by a passage near the end of the work.[9] This involves some illegality that the Thessalians had committed in connection with the production of purple; in consequence, they were now reduced to extreme poverty, even selling the tombs of their ancestors (53.22-3). Georges Radet brought this passage into connection with one in the

Historia Augusta which credits Alexander Severus (222-235) with an interest in purple-production; in addition, an inscription of Corinth, dated to the same reign, mentions a 'procurator of the purple-account' for Thessaly.[10] Further evidence may one day turn up to explain Philostratus' reference, but at present it seems too obscure to be of help. Nonetheless, a date under Alexander would fit what is known of the chronology of the best known of the Philostrati, the author of the *Life of Apollonius* and the *Lives of the Sophists.* The *Life of Apollonius* has a *terminus post* of 217, the year of Julia Domna's death, and it is earlier than the *Lives of the Sophists,* which was probably written in the 230s.[11]

III. THE 'DRAMATIC' DATE

If the Younger Philostratus did write the *Heroikos,* then the dramatic date must be roughly 'the present'; that is, he does not differentiate that date from the time of composition and of first publication. That might seem surprising, not simply because of the air of fantasy that seems to permeate the work, but also because of its interlocutors. The Phoenician sailor might seem to have wandered from the world of archaic Greece, and the virtuous rustic from romances such as Dio Chrysostom's *Euboean (Or. 7)* or Longus' *Daphnis and Chloe.* Nonetheless, the cities of the Phoenician coast maintained extensive trade in the Mediterranean in the imperial period; an inscription from Puteoli dated to 176 CE shows that the principal Phoenician city, Tyre, still had a *statio* or trading-post both there and in Rome, and grave-inscriptions from the city show a strong and diversified economy in the later Roman Empire.[12]

Philostratus' concern to anchor the dramatic date in current time is suggested by two passages, in both of which a series of references advances from past time to the present. One of these series concerns the discovery of heroic bones. The first set of bones to be mentioned belonged to Telamonian Ajax, and were uncovered in the reign of Hadrian, when the action of the sea broke open Ajax' tomb in the Troad. The vine-grower learned of this event from his grandfather (8.1). This is one of several points of contact between the *Heroikos* and Pausanias' *Description of Greece,* probably completed in the 170s. One of the Periegete's informants had entered this same tomb when it was broken open by the sea, and saw the corpse within (1.35.4-5).[13]

The Phoenician, however, is unimpressed by a report at second hand and so far in the past, so that the vine-grower makes only brief mention of cases known from early Greek history, and proceeds to some 'from our time' (ἐφ' ἡμῶν, 8.4). The first of these involves a certain 'Aryades, whom some called Ethiopian and others Indian'; his gigantic skeleton was exposed 'not long ago' in Syria when the bank of the river Orontes was

'split' (οὐ πάλαι . . . σχισθεῖσα, 8.5). This may be another point of contact with Pausanias, since he mentions a Roman emperor who diverted the river Orontes into a newly dug canal; when the old bed had gone dry, it revealed a body which Apollo of Claros identified as an Indian called Orontes, the eponym of the river (Paus. 8.29.3-4).[14] Of the vine-grower's next discoveries of gigantic bones, the first occurred not yet fifty years ago, while the last occurred shortly before the time of the dialogue (8.6-12), but none of these seems to be attested elsewhere.

The other series of references concerns athletes who had consulted Protesilaos. The vine-grower mentions the first of these only by his nickname, a Cilician pancratiast in the time of 'our fathers' (14.4).[15] The next three are boxers, a certain Ploutarchos and his opponent, the Egyptian Hermeias, and another Egyptian called Eudaemon (15.4-7). These four are unknown, though the vine-grower speaks of Eudaemon as still active. The last is Helix of Phoenicia, who (as we have seen) was also active at the dramatic date.

IV. THE GEOGRAPHICAL SETTING

The dialogue is clearly enough located at the city of Elaious in the Thracian Chersonese, or more precisely on its territory, and in the immediate proximity of several monuments of Protesilaos. Elaious is attested in many literary sources, from Herodotus to Procopius, and these show that it had been founded in the sixth century BCE, and still existed in the reign of Justinian. Its site is generally agreed to be at the village of Eski Hissarlik, where there is now a Turkish memorial to the fallen of the First World War. The ancient city stood on an acropolis that dominates the Bay of Morto, just within the entrance to the Dardanelles.[16] The first mention of Protesilaos as a local hero goes back to Herodotus' account of the Persian Artayktes (9.116-20). He mentions a tomb (*taphos*) of the hero within a sacred enclosure (*temenos*), and rich offerings of money, clothing, and the like in the same place. These must have been in some secure, roofed building, and this is probably the *adyton* that Herodotus mentions just below. This was used by the Persian Artayktes, who had gained possession of the sanctuary, when he 'sowed and harvested the enclosure . . . and lay with women in the *adyton*' (9.116.3). After the King's defeat, Artayktes met a condign fate at the hands of the Athenians.[17]

Philostratus' account of the cult-place involves several elements. He mentions first the hero's grave, 'this great mound on the left' (κολωνὸς μέγας οὑτοσί ὁ ἐν ἀριστέραι, 9.1). Also nearby is the sanctuary (*hieron*), barely visible after its despoliation by 'the Mede' (9.5); this seems to imply that all architectural elements on the site had disappeared, *temenos*-walls and *adyton* alike. There was still, however, a cult-image (*agalma*): 'The image here stands on a ship, for the base is in the shape of a ship's prow, and he is portrayed as the ship's captain. But the corrosion of time and, for that matter, the effect of people anointing it or attaching their vows to it have altered its appearance' (9.6). Philostratus is corroborated by coin-types of Elaious that appear only in the reign of Commodus (180-192). These show Protesilaos' image standing on its curious prow-shaped altar.[18]

Even without Philostratus' testimony, it is clear that the sanctuary lay on the territory of Elaious, and not in the city itself. Thucydides refers to an Athenian ship which beached, or ran aground, 'opposite the sanctuary of Protesilaos' (κατὰ τὸ ἱερὸν τοῦ Πρωτεσιλάου, 8.102.3). Similarly, the Elder Pliny enumerates in order 'the promontory of Chersonesus, Mastousia, opposite Sigeum . . . the shrine (*delubrum*) of Protesilaos, and at the extreme tip of Chersonesus the town of Elaious, which is called Aeolian' (*NH* 4.11.49).[19] Though Philostratus is the only author to refer to a mound, his evidence has customarily been accepted, and the mound has been identified with one some five hundred metres from the present shore of Morto Bay. This attracted the attention of Schliemann, and was excavated by French soldiers after the First World War.[20] Schliemann accompanies his account with a vivid and romantic engraving, and moreover describes the surroundings in words that graphically illustrate Philostratus' text.[21]

> The tumulus of Protesilaus lies near the further end of the small but beautiful valley of exuberant fertility, which extends between Seddul Bahr and Elaeus [sic]. This sepulchre . . . is not less than 126 metres in diameter. It is now only 10 m[etres] high, but as it is under cultivation, and has probably been tilled for thousands of years, it must originally have been much higher. In order to facilitate its cultivation, its west, south, and east sides have been transformed into three terraces, sustained by masonry, and planted with vines, almond-trees, and pomegranate-trees. The top and the northern slope are sown with barley, and also planted with vines, olive-trees, pomegranate-trees, and some beautiful elms, which last vividly called to my recollection the dialogue in Philostratus between an ἀμπελουργός (vine-dresser) and a Phoenician captain, in which the former speaks of the elm-trees planted round the tomb of Protesilaus by the Nymphs, of which he says that the branches turned towards Troy blossomed earlier, but that they also shed their leaves quickly and withered before the time [sic] . . . This tumulus is now called 'Kara Agatch Tepeh', which means, 'hill planted with black trees'.

Philostratus seems more vague when he describes the island of Achilles near the end of the *Heroikos.* By his account, its name is *Leuke,* 'White', and it is a favourite mooring-place for sailors 'sailing out of the Pontus' (54.6, *cf.* 56.4); at the same time it is 'towards the

inhospitable side' and 'towards Maiotis', or the Sea of Azov (54.2-3). Arrian in his *Circumnavigation of the Black Sea,* apparently describing the same island, also names it *Leuke,* and asserts that it contained a temple of Achilles. His account, naturally more precise than Philostratus', allows it to be identified with the modern 'Snake-Island' (*Phidonisi, Serpilor*). This 'lies 45 km NE of the Danube delta out in the Black Sea, [and is] that sea's only non-off-shore island'. In recent years, Ukrainian archaeologists have rediscovered the remains of the temple of Achilles there, and have found anchor-stocks as late as the third century CE, the century of Philostratus. It has also been argued that the Portland Vase shows the marriage of Achilles and Helen on this island, just as it is described by Philostratus. However, he appears to be wrong in placing it 'towards Maeotis', and he has greatly exaggerated its size.[22]

The choice of Protesilaos' sanctuary as the setting for his dialogue is clearly connected with his subject-matter, and may be compared with Plutarch's use of Delphi for certain of his dialogues such as *On the E at Delphi.* Even closer is another work of Plutarch, the dialogue *On Love* (*Amatorius*), which takes place at Thespiae in Boeotia, or more precisely at the sanctuary of the Muses on Thespian territory.[23] The central topic of the dialogue being married love, the setting is closely tied to the subject, as it is in Philostratus.

V. The Setting of Belief

Those who have written about the **Heroikos** have often been concerned to measure it against contemporary belief, in particular against belief in the existence of heroes and their posthumous activity. Though 'belief' is a potentially misleading term, being more appropriate to Christianity than to paganism, it may still serve to bring out those aspects of the work that interest modern readers most.

Philostratus' **Life of Apollonius of Tyana** can provide a preliminary *comparandum.* Apollonius certainly received cult from Caracalla, who founded a sanctuary (*hieron*) in his honour at Tyana, and there is ample evidence in literature and inscriptions for the belief in his posthumous existence and power.[24] Philostratus' account of him seems to the modern eye closer to fiction than fact; particular suspicion has fastened on the 'Assyrian' Damis, the follower of the sage whose papers, containing a hitherto unknown fund of information, came providentially into the author's hands. In the early fourth century, the historicity of Apollonius became an issue between Christians and their opponents. An anti-Christian official under Diocletian, Sossianus Hierocles, wrote a tract to show that pagans had not accepted Apollonius as more than a 'divine man', despite his wondrous deeds, while Eusebius of

Caesarea replied with a double set of arguments, both of which served his purpose: Philostratus freely invented many of Apollonius' miracles, and those which he had not invented proved his hero to be a magician in league with demons. While Hierocles' work is now known only from hostile quotations, he seems to have accepted Philostratus' account in its entirety, and even Eusebius evinces no doubt about the authenticity of Philostratus' sources, not even Damis.[25]

In the rest of this paper I will examine the *Heroikos* in the light of contemporary belief about heroes. Though we think of the archaic and classical periods of Greece as the heyday of heroes, in fact they continued to attract interest, and often to receive cult, down to late antiquity.[26] Heroes are notoriously difficult to classify, but for our purposes we may observe two categories: those celebrated in classical Greek literature, above all Homer, and ones newly created out of the recently dead. Brasidas at Amphipolis is in instance of the latter kind (Thuc. 5.11), and by imperial times such civic heroization had become widespread. Thus Athens and Sparta honour the young Statilius Lamprias of Epidaurus as a hero; Sosia Polla, who had probably died during her husband's year as proconsul of Asia, is a 'heroine'. In 242, the citizens of Arcesine on Amorgos honoured a certain Aurelius Octavius as a hero, 'the fairest crown of his family, a holy and decent man (*hieros kai euprepês anêr*)'. This decree, perhaps the last extant one known from a Greek city, is only slightly later in date than the *Heroikos*.[27]

The thinking behind such heroization is rarely easy for us to reconstruct, since we usually depend on literary works operating within a special frame of reference (though a work may be literary, and yet correspond to 'ordinary' belief).[28] Yet Aelius Aristides' funerary oration for his young pupil Eteoneus, though highly traditional, would have defeated its purpose of consoling Eteoneus' family and citizens if it had borne no relation to what they actually believed. 'Neither Cocytus nor Acheron have taken him, nor will a tomb receive and hide him, but renowned and ageless he now roams for ever as a hero' (31.15 Keil). So also 'Menander' when giving advice for composing a funeral oration, suggests the following: 'I feel convinced that he who has gone dwells in the Elysian fields, where dwell Rhadamanthus and Menelaus, and the son of Peleus and Thetis, and Memnon . . . Let us therefore sing his praises as a hero' (414.16-26, trans. Russell-Wilson).

Families had honoured their deceased members with sacrifice from early times, though it is not until the early Hellenistic period that they call such persons 'heroes' or 'heroines'.[29] A notable example of about 200 BCE is the funerary foundation of Epicteta of Thera, a city which seems to have had a particular tendency to treat its dead in this way.[30] In the imperial period,

especially in Asia Minor, the dead are often called 'heroes' and their tombs 'heroa'. Occasionally, the real feeling that lies behind such usages emerges from the chance discovery of documents. When Epicrates of Nacrason sets aside property for the tomb of his son and other family members, he does so 'not only in accord with affectionate feeling towards my child, but because the hero often visited me in dreams, signs and visions'.[31]

Though many authors mention Protesilaos' tomb at Elaious, the first evidence for him as a source of oracles comes from the third quarter or so of the second century, just when coins of the city show him on his peculiar altar.[32] Pausanias mentions him together with Amphiaraos at Oropos and Trophonios at Lebadeia as 'persons who were once men, but have the honours of gods among the Greeks, and have whole cities dedicated to them' (1.34.2); since Amphiaraos and Trophonios were famous for their oracles, the same may be inferred of Protesilaos. Similarly, when Lucian gives a list of impostors usurping the oracular role of Apollo, it ends with 'Hector in Ilium and Protesilaos in the Chersonese' (*Deor. Conc.* 12).

Philostratus credits his hero with several kinds of superhuman knowledge. His knowledge of the heroes of the Trojan War of course comes from his earthly lifetime, though he has supplemented it by conversing with them in the after-life. He also knows the past history of visitors to his sanctuary, and drives away the impious. Thus on one occasion a married man visited the shrine in the company of his unfaithful wife and her seducer. The husband went to sleep there at midday, and the hero 'stood over him' (*ephistatai*, a frequent term for dream-visitations)[33] and warned him that the two were plotting against his life (16.3-4). But his chief activity was to advise his suppliants in matters of their profession or of everyday life. Hence his advice to the vine-grower to change his way of life and take up viticulture (4.9) and his 'oracles' issued to athletes (15.3, 10); but he also gave medical advice over minor illnesses such as quartan fever (malaria), and over affairs of the heart (16.1-2). Since Philostratus talks of the sanctuary as ruined, and makes no mention of priests or prophets, the hero presumably gave his advice in the way he did to the cuckolded husband, in dreams.[34]

In most cases, suppliants probably came to venerate the hero's statue, told him their needs in prayer, and then received his answer either on the site itself or in Elaious; if their prayers were answered, they would later give thanks by plastering the statue with votives. A Hellenistic historian, Nymphodorus of Syracuse, mentions a similar procedure on Chios. Here the citizens set up a *herôon* on their territory for a certain Drimakos, in his lifetime the leader of a band of runaway slaves. 'They say', continues the historian, 'that he appears to many of the Chiotes in their dreams and warns them when their slaves are plotting; and those who receive his visitations sacrifice to him, coming to the place where his *herôon* is'.[35]

Such commonplace questions as Protesilaos' consultants put to him had by now become the common business even of the major oracles, as Plutarch complains (*de Pyth. orac.* 408 b-c). Nonetheless, the second century is an especially fertile period both for the revival of older oracles, such as those of Claros and Didyma, and for the creation of new ones. The most notorious example is Alexander of Abonuteichus and his oracle of the new snake-god, Glycon, which came into existence approximately in the reign of Antoninus Pius. About the same time, the millionaire Opramoas of Rhodiapolis helped to revive the ancient shrine of Apollo of Patara. Writing in the late 170s, the Christian Athenagoras mentions two recently deceased pagans as issuing oracles, the Cynic Peregrinus in Parium and a certain Neryllinus in Alexandria Troas.[36] The clustering of these cults in the region of the Homeric Troy (Alexandria Troas, Parium, Elaious, Thasos) is probably not accidental. This appears to have constituted a zone of Iliadic piety, in which local rivalries combined with the reverence accorded to Homer in fostering this creation of new oracles.

Thus it may be argued that even a sophisticated reader of Philostratus might have been ready to believe, not merely that Protesilaos issued oracles, but that he appeared to especially faithful devotees, and gave them privileged information from beyond the grave. A loving father like Epicrates of Nacrason obeyed his son when 'the hero' appeared to him and urged him to set aside property in his memory. Shortly before his immolation, Peregrinus Proteus sent 'angels of death' (*necrangeloi*) to numerous cities, which no doubt included his native Parium (Luc. *Peregr.* 41); within some ten years of his death, as Athenagoras shows, he was already effecting cures from beyond the grave. We need not suppose that Philostratus wrote with the motive of supplanting the Homeric account of the Trojan War: but he may well have hoped to promote belief in the powers of Protesilaos.

Notes

I am very grateful to Glen Bowersock for his comments, to audiences in Cambridge (England), Harvard and Pisa, and to the anonymous referees for *JHS* [*Journal of Hellenic Studies*]. I am also grateful to the Académie des Inscriptions et Belles Lettres, Paris, for permission to reproduce the map shown as PLATE 1a. (All references to the *Heroikos* will be to the edition of L. de Lannoy (1977), reprinted in Rossi (1997)).

1. The phrase cited is from Lane Fox (1987) 144. Italian translation: Rossi (1997). German commentary: Beschorner (1999). Peter Grossardt (Fribourg) is preparing a new translation and commentary in German, and a conference on the *Heroikos* was held in May, 2001 in Cambridge, Massachusetts.

2. Court literature: Huhn and Bethe (1917). Showpiece: Nilsson (1967-74) 2.563-4. Revival of hero-cult: Mantero (1966). Lane Fox: (1987) 144-8.

3. Not in Troy, as assumed by Lane Fox (1987) 144-8; *cf.* Bowie (1970) 30, 'a vintner on the Trojan plain is interviewed by the narrator [!] from the city'.

4. On Helix, *PIR*[2] [*Prosopographia Imperii Romani*, second edition] A 1520; Jones (1998) 295-6.

5. On athletes who passed from one age-category to another in the course of a single contest such as the Olympia, Robert (1940-65) 7.112-13. Note especially Julius Africanus *apud* Euseb. *Chron.* (ed. Schoene (1875) 200) on an athlete at Olympia who was 'excluded from the boys' boxing . . . , advanced to the men's [category], and defeated all in turn'; *cf.* Moretti (1957) 68-9, no.88.

6. There is a good discussion of the Capitolia in Friedländer (1921-3) 2.150-1, 4.276-80. The year 219 is favoured by Münscher (1907) 497, and many others; Moretti (1957) 171 no.915, followed by Jones (1998) 295, argued for 218.

7. On this kind of computation, Robert (1980) 428; for an athlete similarly cheated in 153 BCE: Schoene (1875) 218; Moretti (1957) 164-5 nos. 861-2.

8. Münscher (1907) 497-8, 505-8; against, Jüthner (1909) 87-8; so also Lane Fox (1987) 144, 'almost certainly after 217 and perhaps many years after'. It remains odd that Protesilaos promised Helix a third victory at the Olympia 'if he wished', if in fact he was deprived of it by trickery.

9. For the following argument, see Radet (1925).

10. Radet (1925), citing Hist. Aug. *Alex. Sev.* 40.6, *ILS* [*Inscriptiones Latinae Selectae*] 1575.

11. The *Vita Ap.* after Julia's death: *Vita Ap.* 1.3. Before the *Sophists*: *Vit. Soph.* 77.6 K. The *Sophists* probably between 231 and 238: de Lannoy (1997) 2387-8.

12. *OGIS* [*OGIS Orientis Graeci Inscriptiones Selectae*] 595, on which see now Sosin (1999). Grave-inscriptions: Rey-Coquais (1977), especially 154-60. On Phoenicians in the Greek world, see also Vattioni (1987-8).

13. On the chronology of the *Periegesis,* Habicht (1985) 9-11, and now Knoepfler (1999). On the site of the tomb of Ajax at in Tepe in the Troad, Cook (1973) 88-9.

14. I have argued elsewhere (Jones (2000)), following Merkelbach and Stauber (1996) 40 no.23, that this emperor is Lucius Verus.

15. Jüthner (1909) 259 suggests an identification with the Cilician wrestler Maron mentioned by Philostratus at *Gymn.* 36; Peter Grossardt will discuss this person elsewhere.

16. Map in Demangel (1926) facing p.2, whence Waiblinger (1978) 844 (here PLATE 1b). Excellent discussion in Isaac (1976) 192-4; Waiblinger (1978); see further Loukopoulou (1989) 35, 68.

17. On this episode and its function in Herodotus' narrative, Boedeker (1988). The term *adyton* implies that access was limited to cult personnel, not that it was totally inaccessible: Stengel, *RE* [*Real-Encyclopädie der Klassischen Altertumswissenshaft*] 1.441.

18. These are enumerated by Robert (1951) 75, observing that Schliemann found an example at Ilium; to his references add Babelon (1951) Pl. I no.9; *LIMC* [*Lexicon Iconographicum Mythologiae Classicae*] 7.2 (1994) 430 no.11.

19. However, Pliny's reference to a shrine suggests either that his information was out of date, or that a cult building had vanished between the time of his source and of Philostratus.

20. Schliemann (1884) 254-62, with fine engraving, 255 (here PLATE 2); Demangel (1926).

21. Schliemann (1884) 256-7.

22. Arrian: *Peripl.* 21-3, with the commentary of Silberman (1995) 59-62. Inscriptions: Latyschev (1916) nos.325-6. Recent excavations: Hind (1993) 91, whence the quotation in the text; Treister (1994) 9-11. Portland Vase: Hind (1995). A reader for *JHS* suggests that Philostratus thinks of the island as 'towards Maiotis' from the point of view of sailors coasting the Danube delta.

23. *Mor.* 748e-771e. On the site of the Mouseion, Roux (1954).

24. Caracalla and Apollonius: Cass. Dio 77.8.14. There is a large literature on this cult: Jones (1980) 193-4; Dzielska (1986) 51-84.

25. Accessible text in Conybeare (1912) 484-605. On Eusebius' riposte, Barnes (1981) 164-7.

26. Julian, *Ep.* 79 Bidez-Cumont, on a furtive cult of Hector at Ilium *c.* 355; note also the fourth- or fifth-century inscription from Megara concerning the heroes of the Persian Wars: *IG* [*Inscriptiones Graecae*]vii.53 = Page, *FGE* 'Simonides' xvi.

27. Lamprias: *IG* iv².82, 85. Polla: *IGR* [*IGR Inscriptiones Graecae ad Res Romanas Pertinentes*] iv.779-80 (Apamea); J. and L. Robert (1977) 418 no.489. Octavius: *IG* xii.7, 53 = *Syll.*³ 889.

28. Observe Parker (1996) 136: 'We must reject as an explanation any "two-tier" hypothesis, whereby the authors of the Funeral Speeches, resolutely intellectual, ignore the more religious emotions of their simpler auditors.'

29. The earliest case seems to be Antigonus of Cnidus (Blümel (1992) no.301) about 275.

30. Foundation of Epicteta: *IG* xii.3.330; Ritti (1981) no.31; *cf.* F. Deneken in Roscher, *Lex.* 2.2530-2, and now Wittenburg (1990). On 'heroization' in Thera, Deneken 2548; Robert (1944) 40-4 = (1969-90) 3.1406-10.

31. Herrmann and Polatkan (1969) 10, lines 33-5; *cf.* J. and L. Robert (1970) 440.

32. Above, n.18.

33. Bibliography in Robert (1940-65) 11/12, 544 n.5.

34. On prophetic and advisory dreams in antiquity, the literature is enormous: there is much useful material in Frenschskowski (1998). On dedications made *kat' onar,* van Straten (1976).

35. Athen. 6.265c-266e = Jacoby, *FGrHist* [*Fragmente der Griechischen Historiker*] 572 F4.

36. On oracular activity in this period, Robert (1980) 402-5, especially 402 n.38 on Opramoas; Lane Fox (1987) 200-61; on Peregrinus and Neryllinus, Athenag. *Leg.* 26.3-4, on which Jones (1985).

Bibliography

Babelon, J. (1951) 'Protésilas à Scioné', *Rev.Num.,* [*Revue Numismatique*] 5th ser. 13, 1-13

Barnes, T. D. (1981) *Eusebius and Constantine* (Cambridge, MA and London)

Beschorner, A. (1999) *Helden und Heroen, Homer und Caracalla: Übersetzung, Kommentar und Interpretationen zum Heroikos des Flavios Philostratos* (Bari)

Blümel, W. (1992) *Die Inschriften von Knidos* I (*Inschriften griechischer Städte aus Kleinasien 41,* Bonn)

Boedeker, D. (1988) 'Protesilaos and the End of Herodotos' *Histories*', *Class. Ant.* 7, 30-48

Bowie, E. L. (1970) 'Greeks and their past in the Second Sophistic', *Past & Present* 46, 3-41

Conybeare, F. C. (ed.) (1912) *Philostratus: The Life of Apollonius of Tyana* (Cambridge, MA and London)

Cook, J. M. (1973) *The Troad: An Archaeological and Topographical Study* (Oxford)

Demangel, R. (1926) *Le tumulus dit de Protésilas* (Paris)

Dzielska, M. (1986) *Apollonius of Tyana in Legend and History* (Rome)

Frenschskowski, M. (1998) 'Traum und Traumdeutung im Matthäusevangelium', _Jahrb. Ant. Christ._ 41, 5-47

Friedländer, L. (1921-3) _Darstellungen aus der Sittengeschichte Roms_ (9th and 10th edns, Leipzig)

Habicht, C. (1985) _Pausanias'_ Guide to Ancient Greece (Sather Classical Lectures 50, Berkeley, Los Angeles, London)

Herrmann, P. and K. Z. Polatkan (1969) _Das Testament des Epikrates und andere neue Inschriften aus dem Museum von Manisa_ (Sitz. Akad. Wiss. Wien 265.I, Vienna)

Hind, J. G. F. (1993) 'Archaeology of the Greek and barbarian peoples around the Black Sea 1983-1992', _Arch. Rep._ 39, 82-112

————(1995) 'The Portland Vase: new clues towards old solutions', _JHS_ 115, 153-5

Huhn, F. and E. Bethe (1917) 'Philostrats Heroikos und Diktys', _Hermes_ 53, 613-24

Isaac, B. (1976) _The Greek Settlements in Thrace until the Macedonian Conquest_ (Leiden)

Jones, C. P. (1980) 'An epigram on Apollonius of Tyana', _JHS_ 100, 190-4

————(1985) 'Neryllinus', _CP_ [_Classical Philology_] 80, 40-5

————(1998) 'The pancratiasts Helix and Alexander on an Ostian mosaic', _Journ. Rom. Arch._ 11, 293-8

————(2000) 'The emperor and the giant', _CP_ 95, 476-81

Jüthner, J. (1909) _Philostratus über Gymnastik_ (Leipzig and Berlin)

Knoepfler, D. (1999) 'Pausanias à Rome en l'an 148?', _REG_ [_Revue de études grecques_] 112, 485-509

Lane Fox, R. (1987) _Pagans and Christians_ (New York)

Lannoy, L. de (1977) _Flavius Philostratus: Heroicus_ (Leipzig)

————(1997) 'Le problème des Philostrate (état de la question)', _Aufstieg und Niedergang_ ii 34.3 (Berlin and New York) 2362-449

Latyschev, B. (1916) _Inscriptiones antiquae Orae septentrionalis Ponti Euxini_ 1 (2nd edn, St. Petersburg)

Loukopoulou, L. D. (1966) _Contribution à l'Histoire de la Thrace propontique durant la Période archaïque_ (Athens)

Mantero, T. (1966) _Ricerche sull'_ Heroikos _di Filostrato_ (Genoa)

Merkelbach, R. and J. Stauber (1996) 'Die Orakel des Apollon von Klaros', _Epigraphica Anatolica_ 27, 1-53

Moretti, L. (1957) _Olympionikai: I Vincitori negli antichi agoni olimpici_ (Atti Accad. Lincei, Memorie, Serie 8, vol. 8.2, Rome)

Münscher, K. (1907) 'Die Philostrate', _Philologus_ Suppl. 10.4 (Leipzig)

Nilsson, M. P. (1967-74) _Geschichte der griechischen Religion_ (3rd edn, Munich)

Parker, R. (1996) _Athenian Religion: A History_ (Oxford)

Radet, G. (1925) 'Notes sur l'Histoire d'Alexandre II: Les théores thessaliens au tombeau d'Achille', _REA_ [_REA Revue des études anciennes_] 27, 81-93

Rey-Coquais, J.-P. (1977) _Inscriptions grecques et latines découvertes dans les Fouilles de Tyr_ I: _Inscriptions de la Nécropole_ (Bull. Mus. Beyrouth 29, Paris)

Ritti, T. (1981) _Iscrizioni e rilievi greci nel Museo Maffeiano di Verona_ (Rome)

Robert, J. and L. (1970) 'Bulletin épigraphique', _REG_ 83, 362-488

————(1977) 'Bulletin épigraphique', _REG_ 90, 314-448

Robert, L. (1940-65) _Hellenica: Recueil d'epigraphie, de numismatique et d'antiquités grecques_ (Paris)

————(1944) 'Hellenica', _Rev. Phil._ [_Revue de Philologie_] 18 (1944) 5-56 = Robert (1969-90) 3.1371-422

————(1951) _Études de numismatique grecque_ (Paris)

————(1966) 'Inscriptions d'Aphrodisias: première partie', _Ant. Class._ 35, 377-432 = Robert (1969-90) 6.1-56

————(1969-90) _Opera Minora Selecta_ (Amsterdam)

————(1980) _A travers l'Asie Mineure_ (Bibl. Éc. fr. d'Athènes et de Rome 139, Paris)

Rossi, V. (1997) _Filostrato: Eroico_ (Venice)

Roux, G. (1954) 'Le Val des Muses et les Musées chez les auteurs anciens', _BCH_ [_Bulletin de correspondance hellénique_] 78, 22-48

Schliemann, H. (1884) _Troja: Results of the Latest Researches and Discoveries_ (London)

Schoene, A. (ed.) (1875) _Eusebi Chronicorum Liber Prior_ (Berlin)

Silberman, A. (1995) _Arrien: Périple du Pont-Euxin_ (Paris)

Sosin, J. (1999) 'Tyrian _stationarii_ at Puteoli', _Tyche_ 14, 275-84

Straten, F. T. van (1976) 'Daikrates' dream: a votive relief from Kos, and some other kat'onar dedications', _Babesch_ 51, 1-38

Treister, M. Y. (1994) 'Archaeological news from the northern Pontic region', _Ancient Civilizations from Scythia to Siberia_ 1.3-39

Vattioni, Fr. (1987-8) 'Fenici, Siri e Arabi emigrati in area greca', *Ann. Ist. Univ. Or. Napoli (AION)* 9-10, 91-124

Waiblinger, A. (1978) 'La ville grecque d'Éléonte en Chersonèse de Thrace et sa nécropole', *CRAI* [*Comptes Rendus. Academie des Inscriptions et Belles Lettres*], 843-57

Wittenburg, A. (1990) *Il Testamento di Epikteta* (Trieste)

FURTHER READING

Criticism

Francis, James A. Apollonius of Tyana: The Rehabilitated Ascetic. In *Power, Subversive Virtue: Asceticism and Authority in the Second-Century Pagan World,* pp. 83-189. University Park: Pennsylvania University Press, 1995.

Claims that with his biography of Apollonius of Tyana, Philostratus rehabilitates the ascetic Pythagorian philosopher into a model of classical ideals and social order, thereby admitting him into the literature and society of the cultured classes.

Raynor, D. H. "Moeragenes and Philostratus: Two Views of Apollonius of Tyana." *The Classical Quarterly* 34, 1 (1984): 222-26.

Considers why Philostratus disapproves of and dismisses the four books by the historian Moeragenes on Apollonius of Tyana despite certain similarities in their accounts.

Pliny the Younger
c. 61-112

(Full name Gaius Plinius Caecilius Secundus) Roman letter writer and orator.

INTRODUCTION

Pliny the Younger, nephew of the great naturalist Pliny the Elder, was a Roman orator and administrator who is now chiefly remembered for his *Epistulae* [1915; *Letters*], which offer a close look into public and private life during the height of the Roman Empire. Published between 100 and 109, the letters are preserved in ten volumes and include personal correspondence as well as Pliny's official communication with the Emperor Trajan from Bithinia. Also extant is Pliny's *Panegyricus Trajani* (100) [*Panegyric to Trajan*], a speech praising the Emperor Trajan. While the latter work has often been faulted for its stilted, bombastic language, Pliny's letters have been admired by scholars for their diverse style and vast variety of subjects covered. Although some commentators have found Pliny a somewhat uninteresting figure because of his moderate character and focus on administrative and personal affairs, others have appreciated his unusually sympathetic portrayal of women, his generosity, and his moral principles as revealed in his letters. The epistles are also highly regarded because they were the first of their kind—a new genre of the letter, written for publication. Because of their literary and rhetorical qualities, the works have also prompted discussion about Pliny's veracity regarding certain matters. Pliny also composed a significant body of poetry, but almost all of it has been lost. His reputation today rests almost entirely on his 318 letters, which are viewed as a unique record of Roman political history and social life in the first century.

BIOGRAPHICAL INFORMATION

Pliny was born in Como, Italy, around the year 61, to a rich landowning family. Tutored by Virginius Rufus, a general in the Roman army, after his father's death, Pliny was adopted by his uncle, Pliny the Elder, who brought him to Rome. There he studied under the Roman rhetorician Quintilian and the Greek rhetorician Nices Sacerdos. He began writing at the age of fourteen, mostly tragedies and poetry. After his uncle died in 79,

Pliny began his legal career and entered the Senate soon thereafter. He advanced rapidly through the imperial civil and military service, largely due to his reputation as an honest and moderate man. He held the positions of priest in the cult of the Emperor, civil judge, military tribune in Syria, commander of a cavalry squadron, and urban *quaestor* while in his twenties. In his thirties he was named a *tribunus plebis,* then *praetor, praefectus* of the military treasury, and consul. In 103 he became a member of the college of Augurs before assuming the post of director for the Tiber River, and finally, imperial governor in Bithinia. Pliny was highly regarded as a civil servant—he held most major Roman public offices during his career—and found favor with the emperors of the time, particularly Domitian and Trajan. He was also financially successful and owned several villas in Italy. He had three wives, although only his last wife, Calpurnia, is mentioned in detail in his letters. He died in 112 while serving in Bithinia.

MAJOR WORKS

Pliny's chief surviving work is his ten-volume *Epistulae* (*Letters*). The 247 personal letters contained in the first nine volumes were written beginning in 97, when Pliny was a Roman official. They continue until shortly before he took his post as governor of Bithinia. The letters cover a variety of subjects, with each epistle focusing on a single topic, using a distinct style—historical, poetical, or oratorical—suited to its theme. Examples include letters to young men whose careers Pliny wished to further; one to the historian Tacitus describing the eruption of Mount Vesuvius and the death of his uncle, Pliny the Elder; a letter to his wife's aunt describing the qualities of his new bride, and so on. Other famous letters, such as the first one in the collection, are directed to Septicius Clarus and serve as an introduction to the letters that follow, including some about his villas; one about Martial's death; and one that contains a fascinating ghost story and considers questions about the supernatural. The letters are unique because, while they are authentic pieces of correspondence to specific people, they are not spontaneous; each piece is carefully composed. Indeed the letters of the first nine books were carefully selected, rewritten, and arranged by Pliny for publication, and they appeared at various intervals between 100 and 109. The letters of the tenth volume, published posthumously, are very different from the others. This volume contains Pliny's correspondence with Trajan (71 letters from Pliny and 51 replies from the Emperor) between 109 and 111 and focuses largely on administrative business in the governance of Bithinia. The most famous exchange of letters in the tenth book is concerned with policies about how to deal with the Christian communities. While the letters in this last volume lack the color and grace of Pliny's more personal correspondence, they offer a close view of Roman administrative methods, providing specific insights into the regime of Trajan.

Pliny's only surviving oratory, the *Panegyricus,* also sheds light on Trajan's reign. Although the speech, which praises the Emperor, has been faulted for being badly constructed and overly verbose, it is the only surviving specimen of Latin oratory from the century-and-half after the death of Cicero. Pliny's poetry has not survived except in his letters, but it is clear that he took great pride in it, even though he considered it largely a diversion from the more serious business of state.

CRITICAL RECEPTION

While Pliny enjoyed a distinguished career as a Roman civil servant, he was not known for his literary achievements during his lifetime. In the centuries after his death, Pliny's reputation as an orator far surpassed his renown as a letter-writer, although some writers were clearly aware of the letters and used them as historical sources. Pliny's letters were likely preserved near the end of the fifth century, but because there was no commercial reproduction of the works, they were not widely read. There seemed to be little demand for the letters until the Renaissance, at which point there was an effort to publish an authoritative edition of the letters using extant manuscripts. It was not until the late-nineteenth century that such an edition of the work became available for study. Since then, there has been a small resurgence in scholarship on Pliny, focusing on the letters. Critics have paid attention to the manuscript history of the letters, discussed the portrait they provide of first-century Rome, remarked on Pliny's relatively enlightened view of women, and used them to highlight the portrait of a complex man. His letters reveal Pliny as magnanimous, stoical, efficient, and loyal; in some ways different from other Romans of his day, but at the same time representative of the type of official who made the vast administrative machinery of the Roman Empire workable. And while his poetry and surviving oratory are usually discussed only in passing or in relation to the correspondence, Pliny's letters are regarded by most classicists today as the best source available for information about the political and social climate of Rome in the early years of the first century.

PRINCIPAL WORKS

Panegyricus Trajani [*Panegyric to Trajan*] (oratory) 100
Epistulae [*Letters*]. 9 vols. (letters) 100-09
Epistulae [*Letters*]. 10 vols. (letters) date unknown

Principal English Translations

Select Letters of Pliny the Younger [translator iunknown] 1835
Letters: Pliny the Younger (translated by William Melmoth) 1915
Epistulae: A Critical Edition (translated by Selatie Edgar Stout) 1962
The Letters of the Younger Pliny (translated by Betty Radice) 1963
Letters and Panegyricus of Pliny (translated by Betty Radice) 1969

CRITICISM

Elmer Truesdell Merrill (essay date January-October 1915)

SOURCE: Merrill, Elmer Truesdell. "The Tradition of Pliny's *Letters*." *Classical Philology* 10 (January-October 1915): 8-25.

[*In the following essay, Merrill traces the manuscript history of and critical commentary on Pliny's* Letters *from Pliny's own day to the early twentieth century.*]

It is my purpose to attempt in these pages a mere outline sketch, therefore without much argument, of the tradition of Pliny's *Letters* i-ix from the time of their first appearance down to the era of the early printed editions. Where I could I have avoided the duplication of discussion by referring to articles already published.

Jean Masson in 1709 was apparently the first scholar to undertake seriously and in detail an investigation of the chronology of Pliny's life and writings. His conclusions, faulty as they were, held sway until Theodor Mommsen established more scientific ground by an examination of the dates of the individual books and letters. Mommsen's (not always justifiable) determinations have served as the text for later discussion by Stobbe, Gemoll, C. Peter, Asbach, Schultz, H. Peter, as well as, in single points, by other critics. All of these writings can be conveniently found from the bibliographical references in Bursian's *Jahresbericht* and Klussmann's supplement to Engelmann-Preuss, and in the third edition of Schanz's *Geschichte d. röm. Litteratur,* and need not be here cited more specifically. In general it seems to me likely that the individual books did not each contain letters exclusively of a certain year or years, any more than that strict chronological order was observed within each book. All that it appears safe to say is that the nine books of miscellaneous letters, brought into literary form and perhaps purged of all matter of merely temporary interest, were finally issued by Pliny, not singly, but in three or four groups (perhaps i-ii, iii-vi, vii-ix) at successive intervals between the years 97 or 98 and 108 or 109. Thus the whole *corpus* was completed and published before Pliny set out on his journey to Bithynia.

On the date and history of the unique book of correspondence with Trajan I will not speak specifically, though I must make a few necessary remarks farther on; here I will merely refer to my brief articles elsewhere printed ("Zur frühen Überlieferungsgeschichte des Briefwechsels zwischen Plinius und Trajan," *Wiener Studien,* XXXI [1909], 250 ff.; "On the Early Printed Editions of Pliny's Correspondence with Trajan," *Classical Philology,* V [1910], 451 ff.).

His own letters assure us that, while Pliny was yet living, these pleasant and graceful literary exercises of his were widely disseminated and read in the Roman world; nor is it doubtful that after his death they still found admirers. Nothing would appear more natural than that especially the letter-writers of the following centuries should be influenced by them. But despite the hopefulness of modern students of these matters, it appears impossible to substantiate the existence of such influence by citing imitation, except in the case of one man, Apollinaris Sidonius. Fronto, for example, shows no indication of acquaintance with the works of Pliny, and it is idle to imagine that the publication of his letters must in itself be accounted evidence of the influence of the earlier writer. Symmachus has been repeatedly cited in recent days as an imitator of Pliny. But the influence is not to be detected in the context of the letters of Symmachus or certified to by any quotation from Pliny. It consists, if at all, in the alleged fact that the letters of Symmachus were finally edited in nine books. But even this is not surely the case. The arrangement into books seems to be due to his son, and not to himself, which would, to be sure, merely remove the trace of possible influence one generation farther on. But the principle of arrangement within the books is quite different from that followed by Pliny, while an imitator in editing, as the younger Symmachus is claimed to be, would surely be likely to carry his imitation farther than the mere number of the books. And finally, even though recent editors have seen fit to assign the concluding letters of the long series to the ninth book, there is MS authority for counting them as a tenth book, possibly truncated by the loss of some letters at the end. Yet another bit of confirmatory evidence may be drawn from the attitude of Apollinaris Sidonius, who professedly adopts Symmachus and Pliny as his models of style (*Epist.* i. 1. 1). His quotations and imitations of both are very numerous; his admiration appears to be equally divided between them; but, when he wants a precedent for issuing a ninth book of letters to supplement the preceding eight (*Epist.* ix. 1. 1), he finds it in the example of Pliny alone, who thus completed his collection (Sidonius surely had no knowledge of the existence of any Trajan correspondence). It is very unlikely that if he could have quoted the equal authority of his other model, Symmachus, he would have failed to do so. I am therefore led to believe that no trace of acquaintance with or influence from Pliny is legitimately to be found in Symmachus.

Macrobius, to be sure (v. 1. 7), represents his character Eusebius as mentioning Pliny and Symmachus in the same breath as examples of the *genus dicendi pingue et floridum;* but Macrobius very evidently has in mind, not the **Letters** at all, but the **Panegyric,** which is also plainly referred to a century later by Cassiodorius (*Var.* 8. 13), in a passage which has even been understood to concern the correspondence with Trajan!

Sidonius, whom I have just had occasion to mention as a striking imitator of Pliny, speaks as if the nine books of the *Letters* were well known in his time and region. In Pliny's own day, indeed, copies had been sold in Lyons, the birthplace of Sidonius (Plin. *Ep.* ix. 11), and Gaul was in this later century the rallying-point of culture. Pliny may well have been known there by his *Letters* when he was not so known to Symmachus.

But the example of Sidonius does not seem to have had any effect upon the letter-writers of the centuries that follow, whose works have come down to us. To be sure, there has been great solicitude on the part of the moderns to discover such indications of reading and imitation. Salvianus, who in the middle of the fifth century wrote some theological treatises and appended nine letters to them, has been fondly imagined to have cherished therein some reminiscence of Pliny's nine books. Still more has been done for Ennodius, whose 297 letters, given in a single series in the MSS, were divided into nine books (of course after Pliny's model) by Sirmond, their Parisian editor, in 1611. Neither Salvianus nor Ennodius, any more than any of the rest of the epistolographers except Sidonius, betrays any knowledge of Pliny's *Letters.*

Of other references during the early Middle Ages there are just two classes: (1) mention of the persecution of Christians in Bithynia (Plin. *Trai.* 96, 97), and (2) brief biographical reference under the professed date of his death in various *chronica*. All the former are directly borrowed from Eusebius, who in turn copied from Tertullian (*Apol.* 2), who surely never saw the *Letters* himself; all the latter are copied from the Eusebian chronicles, or from Jerome's version, and so date back possibly to Suetonius. None are due to any contemporary knowledge of the *Letters.* Between the date of Sidonius (*ca.* 430-80) and that of Ratherius (890-974) no direct or indirect mention of Pliny's *Letters* occurs in any published works. For the basis of reconstruction of their history during the intermediate period we must turn to the extant MSS of the *Letters* themselves, and draw from them such inferences as appear reasonable.

The obviously rhetorical character of the *Letters,* written with an artifice that was at any rate much more sympathetic to the tastes of a revived scholasticism than was the style of Cicero's correspondence, or even that of the letter-essays of Seneca, admirably adapted them to the study of the rhetoricians of the fourth to the sixth centuries. To this period, when the revision and editing of earlier popular authors revived certain of the traditions of Alexandrian days, must probably be assigned the origin of such a sophisticated text of Pliny's *Letters* as is represented by one family of MSS (MV, etc., the "nine-book family"; cf. A. Otto, "Die Überlieferung der Briefe des jüngeren Plinius," *Hermes,* XXI [1886], 287 ff.). It is possible that this was the work of a single scholar; but no subscription attests it, such as MSS of certain other authors still retain. It is possible that the process of emendation extended over a considerable period of years, and was carried out by a succession of hands. At all events, when allowance has been made for such incidental and isolated error and emendation as any MS of any reasonably late age is likely to show, the remaining mass of relevant variants is of such a uniformity of characteristic as to suggest that it was due to persons of a single school, as it may be called, if not to a single person.

The "nine-book family" of MSS is of course judged to be in its present condition the result of a studious and reasonably consistent course of emendation, from a comparison of its readings with those of a second family (PBF, etc., the "ten-book family"). This ten-book family also offers, along with numerous enough copyists' blunders of the usual sort, some examples of evident emendation. It is conceivable that a competent scholar might judge, somewhat as Keil did (and Keil's merits are indisputable), that the nine-book family presents in general a sincere text, and the ten-book family a scholastically emended text—at any rate a less correct text. So much, however, ought at any rate to appear certain, that the families differ so frequently, and in such a manner, that if one family is sincere, the other is definitely sophisticated. The differences can hardly be rationally accounted for by the postulation in both cases of only the usual amount and character of textual error in copying and incidental emendation in after-study. Keil does not appear to have faced the problem at all in this way. He knew, indeed, in 1870 far less about the tradition of the "ten-book family" than is known today; and he appears merely to have judged in general that the excellently reading text supported by well-executed ninth-century MSS was far superior on the whole to the text supported by a single tenth-century (as he wrongly judged it) MS (F, S. Marci) and a few readings from a lost MS of uncertain age and relationship to the other, along with the doubtful testimony of Aldus. The state of the "ten-book" text is now better known by the rediscovery of the older lost codex (B, Beluacensis, uel Riccardianus) and the more extended knowledge of still another lost MS of the same family (P, Parisinus), which both Budaeus and Aldus used. The decision of the dilemma cannot be made to rest on any demonstrative evidence; it cannot depend upon the comparison of a few variants between the two families, such as could be quoted here; it must be settled by weighing the mass and character of the variants on either side. Further discussion of details must be omitted in this outline sketch. Decision will be helped by a consideration of the long list of examples selected by Otto in the article cited above; it will be more facilitated by a careful examination of all the variants in such an *apparatus criticus* as my forthcoming edition of Books i-ix will furnish. But full examination will hardly fail to convince the unprejudiced observer (as Otto was convinced) that the nine-book family, and not the ten-book, gives the scholastically emended form of the text.

As I take it, then, one or more MSS of the **Letters** fortunately escaped the hands of the studious emendators of the early Middle-Age revival of learning, and carried forward to later centuries a substantially unrevised text, which is represented for us by the ten-book family (PBF, etc.). It will be noted that I am quite unable to agree with the theory of Kukula (see the preface to his edition of the **Letters** in the *Bibliotheca Teubneriana*) that both the nine- and the ten-book families show the result of scholastic revision, but in different ways, the nine-book family substituting in very numerous cases other words for those of Pliny's choice, but scrupulously retaining the order of the words within the phrase, while the ten-book family adheres with accuracy to the Plinian vocabulary, but has not hesitated to change at will the order of the words. This sort of a *via media* appears to me quite delusive. It furnishes, to be sure, for the following of critics in the constitution of the text an easily worked practical rule, which amiably appears to avoid the difficulty of a direct and general verdict in favor of either family against the other, while yet it includes both under condemnation. But that, I concede, is not the important point. The important point is this: granted that a text is to be submitted in, say, the fifth century to a formal rhetorical revision, what scholars of that time would be likely to venture a tolerably bold alteration of words, and yet fear to touch the order of the words? Or what other school of revision would assail the order of words, but leave the words themselves chivalrously unharmed? What proved precedent is there that should justify us in postulating such a pair of similarly limited but substantially diverse critical tendencies? No precedent, surely, is to be found in the known history of text-tradition, and most certainly none in human nature. A scholastic reviser of that period, sitting down to improve a rhetorical text according to the rules of his art, would surely meddle with more than one class of things. Not words only, but the order of words, the turn of phrases, clausulae, and the like, would come within the scope of his emendation. Not two families, in diverse and yet strictly limited ways, but one family only must be judged to show the effects (if either does) of a formal revision in the interests of a scholastic rhetoric, and this family must be judged to show it in more than one class of

instances. I have before remarked that the comparison of readings appears to free the ten-book family from the charge of extended wilful emendation.

But yet a third family of MSS (the "eight-book family," Dmoux, etc.) has left descendants to our day which exhibit traces of a true ancient tradition. Its readings not infrequently disagree with those of the other two families, and appear on their intrinsic merits to be sometimes right as against each of the others. But in many instances the eight-book family agrees with the nine-book family against the ten-book. On the whole, where there is agreement with one or the other, it agrees more frequently with the nine-book than with the ten-book tradition. This might evidently be explained on various theories. One is that both the nine- and eight-book traditions, in cases of agreement, probably have preserved the true reading independently from an early date, and certify its antiquity, while the ten-book family has corrupted it, by accident or otherwise. But the fact is that in too many instances the agreement of the nine- and eight-book families is on readings that appear, in the light of comparison with those of the ten-book family, to fall under suspicion of being the result of the aforesaid rhetorical revision. Therefore it seems more simple and probable, on the theory that the nine-book tradition *has* been rhetorically revised, to suppose that the eight-book stock branched off from the nine-book during the fifth or sixth century, when the process of revision was under way, but had not yet reached its maximum; or else that at a later period the eight-book text, being in origin antecedent to the nine-book revision, was somewhat interpolated from it.

Either of these last-mentioned alternatives may represent the truth. The former of them is the more probable on account of the common presence in the nine- and eight-book traditions of a considerable number of small lacunae, which could hardly have been introduced by imitation from one into the other. Of course the larger lacunae in the nine-book text alone must have originated after the division of the two stocks; for there is no trace of any interpolation from the ten-book tradition into the eight-book till after the rediscovery of the latter in the fifteenth century. The eight-book text appears to have reached substantially its shape as recognized at present by the ninth century, that is, before Ratherius used the eight-book MS at Verona. For further discussion I must refer to an article already printed in this journal ("On the Eight-Book Tradition of Pliny's **Letters** in Verona," *Classical Philology,* V, 175 ff.), and to another that I hope to print soon on codices D and m.

To a MS of the most uncontaminated of the three families was appended as a tenth book, perhaps in the seventh or eighth century, the correspondence of Pliny with Trajan. This unique collection had heretofore led an independent existence. It was probably not published in Pliny's lifetime, and all extant literary references to it throughout the whole course of time down to its rediscovery at the opening of the sixteenth century are eventually copied from the single reference in Tertullian (*Apol.* 2), who was himself apparently not acquainted at first hand with the correspondence, but quoted his somewhat inaccurate statements from a source now unknown (cf. my article in *Wiener Studien* cited above. A reference in the *Chronicon* of Prosper of Aquitaine, which a correspondent has kindly called to my attention as a possibly overlooked *testimonium,* is taken bodily by Prosper from Eusebius-Jerome, who in turn got it from Tertullian). Before the time the Trajan-book was appended to a MS of what from this circumstance I have called the ten-book family, it appears to have acquired a special title for the book as a whole, and a lemma for each of the letters in it; for these indubitably were read in the now lost codex Parisinus, and they would not have been invented and affixed after the book of Trajan letters had been united with the rest, which had no such labels.

Thus we reach the ninth century with three well-marked families of Plinian MSS in existence, but none represented by more than a few codices at best, so far as we can judge from the indications of later as well as of earlier history. Also there is an almost total lack of literary reference, allusion, quotation, or imitation, except for the single valiant instance of Apollinaris Sidonius. Of each of these three families I wish to speak briefly, taking them up in the order in which they came to the knowledge of Renaissance scholars.

I. THE TEN-BOOK FAMILY

Of this branch of the tradition three MSS only can clearly be discerned (BFP), of which two (BF) are still in existence in the Laurentian Library at Florence, but the third (P) disappeared early in the sixteenth century. Codices B and F are derived from a common archetype which may probably be referred to the eighth or ninth century, but was already seriously mutilated at the end, or perhaps never completely copied (see F. E. Robbins, "The Relation between Codices B and F of Pliny's *Letters,*" *Classical Philology,* V, 467 ff.). For each codex extends no farther than the sixth letter of the fifth book, and this was doubtless the condition of their immediate common archetype. Yet it had still kept the heading, C. PLINII. SECVNDI. EPISTVLARVM. LIBRI. DECEM, and also indexes to the addresses and first words of the individual letters, compiled from a codex of yet earlier date. The heading and the indexes (through Book v) were faithfully copied, though with some difficulty, by the scribe of B, while the scribe of F, writing at a later date by a century or two, omitted them. On these indexes and certain genealogical questions connected

with and suggested by them, see F. E. Robbins, *Classical Philology,* V, 476 ff. The fact that, on account of the omission of iv. 26, BF contain just one hundred letters is surely without special significance.

Where codex B (saec. X) was written, I am unable to state. The question needs decision by a competent paleographer, which I am not. But it certainly existed in the thirteenth century, and probably earlier, in the chapter-library of St. Peter's at Beauvais. The inscription "S. Petri Beluacensis," though erased, can still be read at the bottom of the recto of the first folio, and is apparently of the twelfth century. This is almost without doubt the actual MS that Vincent of Beauvais (†1264) ran across there, and used—to no very good advantage (cf. his *Spec. Hist.* XI. 67). It was appended to a MS by the same scribe, or scribes, of the *Natural History;* and though Vincent read and excerpted the hundred letters with avidity (and doubtless iii. 5 among them), he could still account the two works to be by one and the same Pliny. At what time and in what manner the MS came to Florence into the Riccardian Library I have been unable to discover. There is no indication that it attracted the attention of scholars until 1729, when Kortte was preparing his edition of the **Letters** (published in 1734). At the request of Jacques Philippe d'Orville, Antonio Francesco Gori collated the MS for Kortte's use, and noted the fact of the collation upon the parchment binding of the book. A copy of Gori's collation, if not the original, I have observed in the Bodleian Library (*Summary Catalogue,* 16894). Kortte mentioned a number of Gori's readings in his edition, and the MS thereafter rested in peace till about 1830. The binding was in bad shape. A single attached leaf (as it seems) containing the last part of Plin. *Ep.* [*Epistualae*] v. 6 had disappeared even before Gori's time, consequent (if we may judge from the unusually worn and soiled appearance of fol. 18ᵛ, which was left as the last page) upon the loss of the back cover. The Riccardian Library was poorly cared for. So Libri, that infamous thief of so many MS treasures, found little difficulty in ripping the **Letters** off from the end of the *Natural History,* and carrying them away to sell with other codices to the English Lord Ashburnham. When his heir, many years afterward, parted with his wonderful collection, Italy bought this back among other purchases, and L. Havet identified it (cf. Havet, *Revue critique,* XV, 251 ff., and Stangl, *Philologus,* XLV, 220 ff. and 642 ff.).

Meanwhile Keil had tried to find the MS in the Riccardian and failed; so that the best he could do even in 1870 was to reprint the scanty and often erroneous readings that Kortte had seen fit to excerpt from Gori's collation.

The early history of codex F (saec. XI-XII) is equally unknown. At the time of the revival of learning it was in the library of S. Marco at Florence. Keil imagined (preface to edition of 1870, p. xi) that it came thither from Lorsch, and was the *liber epistolarum Gaii Plinii* mentioned in a tenth-century catalogue of Lorsch MSS. But Keil was surely mistaken in supposing F could have been written as early as the tenth century; and I can find no trace of the existence of MSS of this family in Rhenish lands at anything like this early period. But whatever its source, for three centuries almost all Italian scholars drew their entire knowledge of Pliny's *Letters* from this one codex. It was repeatedly copied and recopied. Even after Guarino had made known (in 1419) a MS containing eight books instead of less than five, many justly preferred the old text, so far as it went, to the new; whence it happens that numerous fifteenth-century MSS of the *Letters* are now extant which faithfully reproduce the text of F through v. 6, but from that point on the (always conjecturally emended) eight-book text; in others the eight-book text serves as a basis, but has been more or less freely emended through v. 6 from the F-tradition. Many or all of this last group of MSS (of which oux are examples) are due to the labors of Guarino and his contemporaries.

Codex F itself was somewhat emended in the fifteenth century. Especially the Greek words and phrases in it were not infrequently carefully erased, and rewritten in neat and correct minuscules. But a direct copy of F (H, Bernensis 136), made in the thirteenth century (not saec. XI-XII, as Hagen's catalogue of the Berne MSS has it), is useful for its preservation of these readings in their original form.

Of codex Parisinus (P), apparently the single MS that preserved the ten books entire till the sixteenth century, and its progeny I may forbear to speak further in this place, since it has been sufficiently treated by Dr. Robbins in the articles cited above, and by myself in articles "On a Bodleian Copy of Pliny's *Letters*" (*Classical Philology*, II, 130 ff.), and "On the Early Printed Editions of Pliny's Correspondence with Trajan" (*ibid.*, V, 451 ff.). I will merely add here that the Bodleian volume, with its MS supplements and its hundreds of individual readings taken from P by Budaeus, was lent by its later possessor, Thomas Hearne, to Jean Masson, who mentions the fact, and speaks of the book with some accuracy in his *Plinii Vita* (p. 165). Mr. E. G. Hardy, who called renewed attention to the volume in 1889, was apparently not aware of this earlier mention by Masson. Aldus came into possession of P by the kindness of the Venetian ambassador to the court at Paris, and used it enthusiastically but not too rigidly in the preparation of his edition of 1508. What he did with it then, no one knows. It vanished from sight.

That Aldus described the Paris MS as written "adeo diuersis a nostris characteribus, ut nisi quis diu assueuerit, non queat legere," and "ita antiquum, ut putem scrip-

tum Plinii temporibus," will astonish no one who is acquainted with the vague notions of Renaissance scholars about paleography. If the MS was written, for example, in Beneventan script, or in that which prevailed in northern Italy before the Carolingian reform acquired a footing there, or even in uncials, it would have looked different enough from the current fifteenth-century style to appear to Aldus very ancient and very difficult.

II. The Eight-Book Family

As early as the time of Ratherius (890-974) a MS of Pliny's *Letters* apparently lay in the chapter-library at Verona, that store-house of so much that was precious. But for four hundred years nothing further is heard of it. Yet it cannot be doubted that the MS of the *Letters* used by Johannes de Matociis in the second decade of the fourteenth century, and by the anonymous compiler of the Veronese *Flores moralium auctoritatum* in 1329 was precisely this same MS, and that this and no other was the MS acquired and exploited by Guarino Guarini in 1419 (see my article in *Classical Philology*, V, 175 ff.). Guarino was delighted with his new find. He praises it for its extreme and yet vigorous age, the correctness of its text, the number of the letters it included—eight books, when only four and a fraction had been thus far known to the Italians—the neatness of its page arrangement in three columns. From this last detail L. Traube judged that the MS must have been written in Spain and in uncial characters. I can only add here, with deference to Traube's supreme authority, that I have not discovered in the purer copies of the MS any traces of such an origin suggested by the actual readings; indeed, some textual errors appear to look in another direction.

Guarino in his first enthusiasm praised the text of the codex as excellent ("emendatissimae mihi uisae sunt [*sc.* epistulae] et, quod non laetitiae solum sed etiam admirationi fuit, in tanta uetustate et aetate iam decrepita nusquam delirare uidentur"). But his transports somewhat abated on further examination. The MS, wonderful though it was for its content, yet evidently did need emendation, and Guarino set about his editorial task of copying and correcting with great zeal and devotion. He will let his friends see the work when he has completed his operations on it; and although, in the correspondence published by Sabbadini, Guarino repeatedly writes of lending the book to others, I do not feel at all sure that he does not usually mean his emended copy and not the original. That disappeared, and has not since been rediscovered. I have sometimes been tempted to think that Guarino, knowing that it had been purloined from the Verona library, destroyed it to prevent discovery of the theft. But perhaps it is enough to suppose that, as scholars of his age and a long time thereafter set no particular store upon old MSS as such, but preferred a supposedly more accurate text, even though it had been secured by modern editing, Guarino cast his old MS carelessly aside, when once he had in possession improved copies of it.

From the activity of Guarino and his contemporaries over the new text, numerous copies were spread abroad throughout Italy. Some scholars, as I have before remarked, preferred the F-text through v. 6, and merely supplemented it from there on by the text of the eight-book version; others took the new text as their basis, but substituted through v. 6 more or less readings of the F-tradition (as in oux). Some person of the century even started to add to F itself the letters from v. 7 on according to the new text, but fortunately desisted before getting fairly under way. Almost all of these fifteenth-century copies display in addition a large and varying number and quality of purely conjectural emendations, due, doubtless, primarily to the initiative of Guarino, and produced yet further in accordance with the notions of the age. But two MSS appear to have been copied from the eight-book Veronensis without being substantially emended. One of these is the elegant piece of penmanship, codex Dresdensis D 166 (D, saec. XV). It gives the complete text that stood in Veronensis, viz., eight books (the eighth being omitted, and the ninth numbered as the eighth) with certain other incidental omissions (i. 8, 12, 23, 24; ix. 16) and dislocations of order within Books v and ix. These peculiarities it shares in general with all the other eight-book MSS that have not copied as far as it went the F-text, and doubtless drew from Veronensis. That the order in D is perturbed, and not original, may be inferred with certainty from the concurrent testimony of the two other MS families; for the later discovered codex Mediceus (M) of the nine-book class agrees in the fifth book with the index in B, and in the arrangement and numbering of, and order within, the eighth and ninth books, as well as in the fifth book, with Aldus, who certainly knew nothing of either B or M, and must have taken his order from P. That the text of D has not suffered a fifteenth-century course of emendation is inferred from a comparison of the general mass of variants between it and the other eight-book MSS—just such a process (and even more convincing) as leads to the verdict concerning the earlier emendation of the nine-book family.

The second example of an unemended copy of Veronensis is not an elegant book, but a mere little scratchy notebook of miscellaneous brief copies, such as many that are still extant, which fifteenth-century scholars who were not calligraphers made more or less hastily for their own use. It is a Venetian codex (m, Marcianus Lat. class. XI. 37, saec. XV), and contains among other matter the best text known to me of the "Breuis Adnotatio de duobus Pliniis" which it doubtless took directly

from the autograph of Johannes de Matociis prefixed to the Veronese codex, followed by the first book of Pliny's **Letters** in a text closely agreeing with that of D, but plainly (as may be seen, among other evidence, by examination of lacunae in D as compared with m) copied not from D but from D's archetype—that is, from Veronensis. Of m, as of D, I intend to speak on another occasion. There are traces of yet other MSS with readings like D, but they may be passed over for the present.

The first printed edition of the **Letters** (1471) was an eight-book text of the type of the Guarinian recension. Whether this printed book itself, or merely such MSS as it followed (they were plenty enough before the end of the century), was the basis of several later printed editions before 1500, can hardly be determined. At all events only the Roman edition of Schurener (1474) and that of Pomponius Laetus (1490) used other materials than the F and Guarino texts. Beroaldus in 1498 practically reproduced the text of Laetus with some emendations of his own. Catanaeus followed Laetus and Beroaldus in 1506.

III. The Nine-Book Family

The scholastically revised text that dates from the fifth or sixth century apparently migrated bodily in early days to Germany, where it played a prominent part, as F did in Italy. Traces of the text appear in several places, though it is not likely that it was often reproduced; for mediaeval library catalogues here and there mention the **Letters,** but, except for a few excerpts and two codices, one incomplete toward the end of the ninth book (M) and the other containing only Books i-iv (V), no one of those active Italian travelers of the fourteenth and fifteenth centuries who searched the country to secure Latin MSS was able to find any copy of the **Letters.**

But in the course of the fifteenth century there was also a current setting northward from Italy, and MSS of the eight-book text, into which had already been incorporated readings from the F-tradition, crossed the Alps, and were there further corrected by readings from the nine-book text there prevalent, and especially were supplemented by the text of the eighth book, which was still unknown in Italy. This eighth book was naturally appended to the eight-book MSS and numbered as the ninth. It was a MS of this mixed order, imported into Italy, that Schurener, a printer from Boppard on the Rhine, substantially reproduced in his edition printed at Rome in 1474 (r). Unfortunately this MS, or rather its archetype, had lost some sheets in the most valued part of the book (containing viii. 8. 3-18. 11). Schurener's MS copy, as usual, vanished; and no codices of the sort had been noticed by scholars till my pupil, Miss Dora Johnson, whose sudden death shortly thereafter ended a promising career, discovered three, Taurinensis 297 (t), Chigianus H. V. 154 (c, which formerly belonged to Francesco Piccolomini—Pope Pius III, †1503), and Oratorianus 34 (n, Neapolitanus; see Miss Johnson's classified list of MSS of the *Letters* in *Classical Philology,* VII, 66 ff.). All of these MSS exhibit the same great lacuna in the eighth book as the Roman edition (r). Of the three codices, t appears most interesting as having preserved more readings of the German tradition than c. Both contain some of the readings which attracted the attention of Keil in 1870 in the edition of Laetus, and led him to the accurate remark (preface to his edition, p. xx) that Laetus must have had before him a MS of the same class as that used by Schurener in 1474, but a better one. Codex c is more closely related to the immediate archetype of r than is t, but is not so much like it as to lead to the conclusion that one was copied from the other. I have seen neither codex n nor a photograph of it; but the few notes about it that Miss Johnson left appear to indicate so close a connection with the 1498 edition of Beroaldus that I am inclined to the provisional opinion that it is mainly or entirely a copy of that printed text.

While the course of the text was passing through this history in Germany, another MS of the same nine-book tradition (saec. IX-X) was lying unnoticed in the Vatican Library (V, Vaticanus lat. 38. 64). Pomponius Laetus finally discovered it, and noted many of its readings in the margins of his own copy of the edition of the *Letters* that had been issued at Treviso in 1483. This particular book from the collection of Laetus, with its numerous marginalia from V and from a MS of the ctr-class, I hold in possession, having bought it in 1899 from a bookseller in Rome. Laetus had apparently equipped the volume provisionally as copy for the printer of his own edition, which appeared in 1490. It may be not without interest to remark that I also own a copy of the edition of Laetus which bears the indubitable autograph of Lorenzo de'Medici at the top of its first page of the text, and was (I imagine) carried off when the Medici palace at Florence was plundered in 1494.

The earlier provenience of the Vatican codex is yet undetermined, though I suspect it to have been brought down from Germany. Its contents are (in this order) Caesar *B.G.* i-viii, a fragment of Ethicus, Pliny's *Letters* i-iv, speeches and letters attributed to Sallust. Professor B. L. Ullman has recently made to me the interesting suggestion that the archetype of V, if not the MS itself, may possibly be mentioned in the catalogue (*ca.* 1200) of the Korvey collection printed by Becker in his *Catalogi bibliothecarum antiqui,* p. 282 (136. Corbeia), where there is recorded, "191. historia Gaii Caesaris belli Gallici.—192. cronica eiusdem cum quibusdam epistolis.—193. Philippicarum." It should be noted that in V no general title is prefixed to the four books of *Letters* ascribing them to Pliny.

No other MS akin to V was known to the Italians up to the end of the fifteenth century. But quite certainly from Korvey came about 1508 that unique MS that has preserved to us, originally within the same covers, not merely the nine books of Pliny's *Letters* (M, saec. IX), but also the first six books of the *Annals* of Tacitus. Unfortunately the copyist had become weary in face of the difficulties offered by the voluminous Greek quotations in ix. 26, and brought his work to a precipitate end in the eighth section of that letter. The MS was acquired by Pope Leo X (Medici), and later transferred to Florence along with other MSS, and deposited in the re-established Medici Library, where it still is. At some unknown date, however, the *Letters* were separated from the *Annals.* The character and history of the MS have been so frequently described and discussed (latest by H. Rostagno, the Laurentian prefect, in his preface to the Leyden facsimile of the *Annals*—cod. Mediceus 68. I, as well as in the text accompanying the Chatelain and Vitelli-Paoli facsimiles) that I need not here treat of it at length. Philippus Beroaldus, who first edited the accompanying part of the *Annals,* called the attention of Catanaeus to it, and he used it in the preparation of his second edition (published in 1518; see his prefatory epistle). The two codices M and V exhibit (so far as V extends) the same considerable lacunae, but that V is not a copy of M (Keil erred in thinking that it might possibly be older than M), but is rather of a common descent, may be readily seen by the comparison of even a brief selection of readings: e.g., in i. 7. 1 the Homeric quotation; i. 12. 1 facilis M fatalis (corrected by first hand from *falis,* which was apparently the archetypal reading) V; i. 12. 12 doleo M doleo doleo (rightly)V; ii. 11. 1 per *om.* M, *add.* V; ii. 14. 8 potui *om.* M, *add.* V; iii. 7. 12 Piso pater *om.* M, *add.* V; iii. 16. 3 pari *om.* M, *add.* V; iii. 5. 16 inquid horas non impenderetur (this last word corrected by second hand from *impederetur;* a later hand added the sign of an omission, and in the margin wrote *desunt*) M inquid non perdereperireenim arbitrabatur quiaquid studiis non impenderetur V.

Two other extant MSS bear testimony to the existence of the nine-book text in the same geographical region; Monacensis (olim Ratisbonensis Emmeramus) 14641 (saec. IX), which, among other miscellany, contains *Ep.* i. 6 and vi. 10, and Leidensis Vossianus Lat. 98 (saec. X), in which a copyist has written out i. 1-2. 6, partly in Tironian notes.

But a more unhappy fate overtook the nine-book tradition in German lands. Some of the letters were lost, the rest confused in order and in arrangement by books, the text depraved. Of this class are codices Pragensis XIV. A. 12 and Harleianus 2497 (*olim Cusanus*). Titze waxed delirious over the virtues of the Prague MS in the preface to his edition printed in 1820 (not 1823, as the date stands in Keil), claiming it to be a copy of a Visigothic MS of the fifth century, which was itself transcribed from a codex of Pliny's own time. Therefore he believed the disordered selections of the Prague MS to represent the first, quasi-autographic, edition of the *Letters* as issued by Pliny himself! The Harleian codex was secured by Robert Harley from the curators of the Hospital foundation of Nicolas Cusanus at Cues on the Moselle, doubtless as one item in that beautiful operation of exchange which a modern collector might well envy, whereby Harley gave the curators for their library certain fine, spick-and-span, Basel-printed folios, and took as an equivalent some of their old, worn-out, illegibly handwritten affairs! I ran across the Harleian codex in the British Museum in 1906. Both the Prague and the London MSS have the same lacunae as MV, but in the former they have been partly filled out afterward from some different source. In Harleianus they are left untouched, and that is accordingly the better representative of its worthless class.

Selatie Edgar Stout (essay date 1954)

SOURCE: Stout, Selatie Edgar. Introduction to *Scribe and Critic at Work in Pliny's Letters: Notes on the History and Present Status of the Text*, pp. 1-10. Bloomington: Indiana University Press, 1954.

[*In the following essay, Stout offers a publication history of Pliny's* Letters *and notes that textual criticism on the work from the 1800s sheds important light on the authoritativeness of the source of the manuscripts used by scholars.*]

For about 375 years after the death of Pliny the Younger, which probably occurred A.D. 113, his *Epistulae* were circulated in two corpuses, one containing the nine books of the *Letters to His Friends* and the other containing in a single book the correspondence between him and the Emperor Trajan.

In a prefatory letter introducing Book i of the *Letters to His Friends* Pliny says that he has put together for publication some of his letters that had been written with especial care, and that if this venture meets with favor from the public he will look up some that have been omitted and publish them along with others that he may write from time to time. This introduction leads us to think it probable that the first publication of his epistles contained only a part of the nine books of these *Letters* and that other portions of the collection, as we

now have it, followed at intervals. This inference receives some support from his statement in ix.19 that his correspondent Ruso had seen the letter that is published as vi.10 and wished to discuss a statement made in it. When these *Letters* first come to our knowledge, however, the nine books are together in one corpus.

Since this collection contains no letters that were written after 108 or 109, and since Pliny was not burdened with administrative duties in the years 108-110 and was awaiting assignment as governor of a province, it seems not unreasonable to assume that if these letters had been published in units of one or more books at a time, he may have brought them together and published them as a collection about 109 or 110. Since he did not include in this corpus any of the first fourteen letters of Book x, in spite of the fact that Trajan's name and evident personal friendship for him would have added luster to the collection, we may perhaps also infer that at the time of this publication Pliny already had in mind the idea of publishing his correspondence with the emperor as a separate work and was reserving these letters for inclusion in it.

Pliny was governor of Bithynia and Pontus probably in A.D. 111-113, somewhat less than three years.[1] In the 52nd letter and again in the 102nd letter of the correspondence with the emperor, Pliny informs Trajan that the soldiers and civilians in the province had joined him in offering thanks to the gods on the anniversary of the emperor's accession to the headship of the state and had prayed for his preservation and continued success. These religious observances were on the *dies imperi* of Trajan, January 27, 112 and 113. It may be regarded as certain that similar *sollemnia* would have been observed on this anniversary in 114 and reported in another letter if Pliny had remained as governor until that date. There are no letters of governor or emperor in the collection that have in view the termination of Pliny's unusually personal representation of the emperor in the province or the arrival of a successor. This, combined with the fact that no trace of Pliny is found anywhere after this time, makes it highly probable that he died in service in the province before January 27, 114, and leads to the further conclusion that his correspondence with Trajan was published by someone else after Pliny's death. The manuscript may have been found among his papers, ready for publication up to the point where it breaks off, but awaiting additions that were never made because death cut short his administration and the correspondence. Pliny can hardly have planned to have the collection close as we have it at present.

These two works, the nine-book collection of the *Letters to His Friends* and the one-book volume of the correspondence with the emperor, were preserved separately until near the end of the fifth century. We have no evidence that anyone ever saw the nine-book corpus in that interval, and during the same period the only person that gives any evidence of having seen the other is Tertullian, about A.D. 200. Directly or indirectly, he knew the contents of x.96 and 97, in which the problem presented by the presence of the Christians in Pliny's province is discussed. It is probable on the whole, therefore, that the letters of Pliny were not much read in the late second, the third, and the fourth centuries, and that the making of manuscripts of them was infrequent or that it ceased entirely in these centuries.

In the fifth century we find Apollinaris Sidonius (c. 430-480), toward the end of his life an enthusiastic admirer and imitator of Pliny, intimately acquainted with the *Panegyric* and the nine books of the *Letters to His Friends,* but without any knowledge of the correspondence with Trajan.

Sidonius was thoroughly trained in his youth in the schools of southern Gaul, in which a wide range of literature was studied, chiefly from the rhetorical standpoint. His family belonged to the nobility, both his grandfather and his father having been prefects of Gaul. In his early manhood he gave himself to the writing of poetry but did not give up entirely an ambition for political power. His father-in-law, Avitus, was emperor at Rome for a brief time (455-456). Sidonius gained great reputation by the poetic panegyric which he delivered when Avitus assumed the consulship at Rome, January 1, 456.

After the defeat of Avitus, Sidonius continued in favor at times with others who reached the principate and welcomed the support of his pen. He delivered a poetic panegyric when Maiorianus assumed the consulship, January 1, 458. Again, on January 1, 468, he honored Anthemius by a similar tribute, winning such favor that he was at once appointed *Praefectus Urbi* at Rome for that year. At the end of his year as *Praefectus Urbi,* apparently discouraged by the rough state of turmoil of the time, he renounced political life for service in the church. His great reputation and his connections gained him a bishopric at once, in spite of his total lack of training for that office. It may be noted that Avitus also was made a bishop at once when he gave up the throne, thirteen years before this. Sidonius was assigned to the see of Clermont, whose territory included his home of many years at Auvergne. From 469 until his death in about 480 he did excellent and courageous service for his people here as the pressure of the Goths in that portion of the empire continually increased.

At the beginning of his bishopric he gave up the writing of poetry. His poetry had been steeped in pagan mythology rather than in Christian lore and imagery.

Induced evidently by his enthusiasm for Pliny's *Letters,* he began in 469 to collect and revise his own letters for publication. These *Letters* constituted his main contribution to literature from that time until his death. He repeatedly lets it be known that he is modeling his work on that of Pliny. As in Pliny, each of his letters as published is practically confined to one subject. In vocabulary and phrasing, these letters of Sidonius show many reminiscences of Pliny. Many of these Plinian touches may have been added as the letters were reworked for publication. Geisler's list of parallels in Sidonius to earlier writers[2] notes 337 echoes of Plinian diction and ideas, drawn almost evenly from each of the nine books of the *Letters to His Friends,* but the list contains not one such parallel with the language of the correspondence with Trajan, which Sidonius clearly did not know. Geisler lists ten possible reminiscences of Pliny in the *carmina* of Sidonius. This is a very small number, and in none of them is the parallelism close. In most of them Sidonius seems to be echoing Horace or Ovid or Persius or Statius, all of whom influenced him at this period of his life, rather than to be borrowing from Pliny. This suggests that Sidonius may have picked up his nine-book manuscript of Pliny's *Letters* in Italy late in his life and that he did not know them in his earlier years in Gaul. His late enthusiasm for them and his high standing in literary, political, and ecclesiastical circles were certain to stimulate interest in Pliny as his own *Letters* were published.

The commercial reproduction of the *Epistulae* of Pliny was almost certainly given up early in the second century, not to be revived until many centuries later. There is no evidence that they were ever again in demand in the market before the Renaissance. Even in Pliny's lifetime they did not rank with his orations in the book mart nor in the author's esteem. Pliny nowhere seems to think of his *Epistulae* as literary productions, or to look to them for recognition as an author during his lifetime or for fame in the future. His hope for this was in his orations, although he was tempted at times, without however seriously yielding to the temptation, to venture into poetry or history. *Epp.* [*Epistualae*] ix.11 has been thought by some to show that his *Epistulae* were on sale in Lugdunum about 108 or 109, but *libellos* in this passage, as again in iv.26, has no reference to *Epistulae.* In vii.2 Pliny himself sets up a contrast between *epistulae* and his *scripta,* for which his correspondent Iustus had asked.

Most of the existing copies would gradually disappear after commercial publication of the *Epistulae* ceased. Their preservation to the later world depended on the chance preservation of a copy or a few copies that might rest undisturbed in libraries until some Sidonius stumbled upon one of them, found it interesting, and brought it to the attention of others. This would lead to the making of copies that would get distributed more or less widely, and they would thus once more enter the stream of current intellectual life. How many precious works of antiquity failed to come to the notice of an understanding and appreciative discoverer before the loss of the last copy that had been thus laid away!

Of the nine-book corpus of the **Letters to His Friends,** each of two copies, both apparently in Italy, left a descendant before suffering destruction. From these two copies are derived all the manuscripts of the first nine books of the *Letters* which either now exist or have left traces of their past existence in descendants known to us. One of these two, which I shall refer to as W, became the immediate or the remote mother of what we now call the eight-book and the nine-book families of the manuscripts of the **Letters to His Friends;** the other became the immediate or the remote mother of the nine-book manuscript of these *Letters* which was incorporated with a manuscript of the correspondence with Trajan by a late fifth-century editor, probably in Italy, to form the mother manuscript, Z, of the ten-book family of the manuscripts of the *Letters.*

The studies of Keil on the sources available for the constitution of the text of the *Letters* are fundamental. These were published in 1853, 1865, 1866, and 1870. Good scholars, some of them keen critics, had worked at the problem of the text at times for centuries before he began its study. Especially in Italy, in the fifteenth century and the early years of the sixteenth, these critical efforts engaged the interest of many excellent scholars. But their results, although valuable in some respects, serve on the whole to make the problem more complex and difficult for the modern critic. The effort to perfect the text of the *Letters* continued to interest at intervals some of the best scholars between 1518 and 1853, but they brought the problem no nearer solution. The best text developed through these unscientific efforts before the editions of Keil is found in the edition of Cortius and Longolius in Amsterdam in 1734. This is due to the fact that these editors had at hand the largest collection of manuscripts and collations ever brought together before the editions of Keil and Merrill. It included readings from M and B, important manuscripts that had not been carefully studied before. All the critics and editors before Keil were baffled by insufficient command of the manuscript evidence, and even more by their inability to evaluate scientifically the sources which they had.

The methods of text criticism had been reduced to a rudimentary science by Keil's time, and this enabled him to bring order into the study of the text of the *Letters.* He was the first to discover that all the manuscripts that have been preserved to our time descend from three originals and therefore fall into three families. This is

the greatest contribution ever made to the study of the text. These families he called the nine-book, the eight-book, and the ten-book families, names which still serve well enough in spite of some inaccuracy in the name of the second family.

Since Keil's day several other manuscripts of portions of the *Letters* have been found and identified, and their places in Keil's three families determined by Merrill, Miss Johnson, and Rand. Merrill has also made available in his edition of 1922 the readings of most of the important manuscripts. His contribution to the study of the problems of the text are of prime importance, second only to that of Keil. The discovery of what is now called the *Morgan Fragment* and the searching study of it by Lowe and Rand in 1922 have helped to clarify the course of development of the modern text. The student of the text of the *Letters* today has at his service more and better fundamental information and expert guidance than was ever available before.

In an article in *TAPA* [*Transactions of the American Philological Association*], 55 (1924), 62-72, the present writer made the claim that the nine-book and the eight-book families of Keil derive from a common parent. This statement presents the fundamental thesis of the present study, in which the evidence of the manuscripts in many disputed readings is newly evaluated under rules of interpretation that necessarily follow if a common origin for the nine-book and the eight-book families is accepted.

One of the best evidences of a common ancestor for two manuscripts is the omission in both of them of identical portions of the text. The omission of iv.26 and of all the text after v.6 in both B and F shows them to have descended from a common ancestor in which these losses had already occurred. The omission of epistles 8, 12, 23, and 24 of Book i in any manuscript identifies it at once as descending from the common ancestor of the eight-book manuscripts. Frequent instances of the omission of an identical word or group of words of the correct text is sufficient to prove a common ancestor for the manuscripts in which the identical omissions occur. The following five identical omissions in one book of the *Letters* first suggested to me that X and Y had a common ancestor:

> iv.5.4 (94.18)[3] quo sit excusatius quod ipsum librum non tamen ultra causae amplitudinem extendimus Z *om.* XY
>
> iv.7.7 (96.2) risum magis possit exprimere quam gemitum Z *om.* XY
>
> iv.10.3 (100.11) neque enim minus apud nos honestas quam apud alios necessitas valet Z *om.* XY
>
> iv.12.5 (103.9) ut ego statim feci Z *om.* XY

iv.15.11 (107.27) quia votis suis amor plerumque prae-currit Z *om.* XY.

All modern editors[4] accept from the Z tradition the added part of the text in the first four of the above readings. The identical omission of exactly the same words in X and Y in each of these four cases, without similar words or endings to induce the omissions and to limit their extent, can not be plausibly explained except on the assumption that X and Y are from the same ancestor, in which these omissions had already been made. The added text in the fifth reading cited above is accepted by all modern editors except Keil. For critics who accept as original the words omitted in both X and Y in this reading, they are added proof that X and Y are from the same parent manuscript, in which the omission had already been made.

As stated above, my first conviction that X and Y are merely two branches of a single tradition was based on their identical omissions in these five cases. Further study of the character of the Z tradition, however, has convinced me that the added words in each of these five readings are editorial additions in the ten-book tradition and do not belong in the original text of the *Letters*.[5] If I am right in this, these common omissions are not omissions at all; they illustrate the reliability of the united testimony of X and Y to the text and fit in perfectly with the assumption of a common origin for X and Y, but do not prove it. That can be proved only by errors and peculiarities that are traceable to a common ancestor. To establish the common origin of the X and Y families it will now be necessary to examine other readings in which X and Y have an identical incorrect reading.

The three following apparent omissions deserve consideration:

ii.17.17 (57.3) cryptoporticum *xystus violis odoratus; teporem solis infusi repercussu cryptoporticus* Z *om.* XY

ii.19.5. (60.18) cum labore etiam *cum labore* Z *om.* XY

iv.12.3 (103.4) quaestio *sed tamen quaestio* Z *om.* XY

The words omitted by X and Y clearly belong in the text. The fact that all three omissions are due to jumps made from a word to the same word further along makes the error in each case an easy one. In any one case the assumption that the jump was independently made by two different scribes need not be felt to be inherently impossible, but that such an identical jump should be made in three different cases by two scribes copying the same text independently is highly improbable. No such list could be made of identical jumps by scribes of X and Z or of Y and Z. I doubt whether a parallel could be found in the work of independent

scribes in any author in an equal amount of text. It seems necessary to assume that the three omissions go back to a common ancestor in the history of the X and the Y traditions in which the loss had already occurred.

The omission of single words, especially of short ones, occurs occasionally in the work of scribes, but if two scribes agree frequently in the omission of identical words at the same point in the text, the omission must be assumed to go back to a common ancestor which did not have the omitted words.

The X and the Y families agree in omitting many single words that are found in the Z sources, but in practically all these cases the consensus of critics has been gradually recognizing that these words do not belong in the original text but have been contributed by editors in the Z tradition. For example, in the ten-book manuscripts an editor has frequently completed the construction for Pliny by adding connectives such as *et* or *-que* or *ut*, pronominal forms such as *hic* or *suus* or *meus*, prepositions such as *a* or *ex*, and various forms of *sum*. The fact that X and Y agree in not having these words that Pliny did not place in the text but which have been supplied editorially in the ten-book manuscripts furnishes evidence of the high percentage of validity for readings which are attested by both X and Y, and is consistent with, but does not prove, the assumption that X and Y are from a common source. For editors who accept many of these "improvements" into the text, however, they do prove that X and Y have a common source. This is also true of the following three readings:

v.6.40 (130.23) fistulis *om.* XY *add.* Z

iv.7.2 (95.12) librum *om.* XY *add.* Z

iv.11.9 (101.18) cubiculum *om.* XY *add.* Z

The first of these is accepted into the text by all modern editors, the second and third by all except Keil and Schuster. For those who accept them, their omission in both X and Y practically proves a common origin for X and Y; but I think that all three words were supplied editorially in the ten-book tradition, probably by the original editor of the first manuscript of the tradition. If I am right in this, their omission in X and Y is but another proof of the faithful witness to the text found in W, their original source.

Another suggestion of the common source of X and Y is found in the form of the names of the addresses in the *Letters*.[6] The parent manuscript, Z, of the ten-book family evidently gave both the nomen and the cognomen of the persons addressed in the *Letters* where the editor had been able to determine them. The nine-book and the eight-book manuscripts regularly give one name only, sometimes the nomen, sometimes the cognomen;

but whichever is used, they uniformly have the same. Their practice in this represents the usage which we should expect of Pliny himself in the original correspondence and in his own publication of the **Letters.** In the 212 letters in which we have readings of both the X and the Y traditions, the only exception to the broad general statement as to the agreement of X and Y in the superscriptions that can not readily be seen to be the result of scribal error is in the superscription of v.10, where Y preserves the reading of W in using *Tranquillus,* while some scribe of the X tradition has consciously or unconsciously substituted the nomen *Suetonius* of this well-known correspondent. In all the other letters addressed to Suetonius both X and Y have only the superscription *Tranquillus.*

The final and crucial test of the hypothesis that X and Y are derived from the same text, W, of the **Letters** comes when the evaluation of the manuscript evidence which this hypothesis makes necessary is applied to the variant readings throughout the **Letters.** If the application of this necessary rule for evaluating the manuscript evidence gives correct readings, conviction that it is correct must grow as we proceed, and the hypothesis must be accepted. . . .

If X and Y are independent derivatives from W, and Z is independent of both X and Y, (1) where X and Z agree and Y differs from them, X must be assumed to have preserved the text of W, and there is thus no real manuscript evidence for the reading of Y; the reading preserved in both X and Z carries the only ultimate manuscript authority for the text; and (2) likewise, where Y and Z agree and X differs from them, the concurrent reading of Y and Z carries the only ultimate manuscript authority for the text.

The first of these two rules for evaluating the manuscript readings at any point has been observed from the time of Keil's studies in 1865, 1866, and 1870, resulting in great improvement of the text of the **Letters.** The second has never been applied in the determination of the text, although it has generally been recognized that the agreement of Y and Z against X brought the reading of X into some doubt and required careful consideration. (*See* Keil, 1870, *Praefatio* XXVII.) The full acceptance of the rule is decisive for the text in hundreds of places.

Since the publication of Keil's text, additional manuscript evidence has been made available, but a faulty interpretation of this evidence, based upon Otto's unscientific article[7] in *Hermes* (1886), carried the editors Müller (1903), Kukula (1908), and Merrill (1922) progressively farther astray, introducing about 400 unjustified changes into the text of Keil. Throughout this period good scholars have published careful studies of a total of hundreds of readings of the **Letters.** By the

methods of logical criticism, applied with constantly improved tests for checking their results, such as a knowledge of Pliny's *clausulae* and new studies of idiosyncrasies of his style, many of the errors of the editors already mentioned have been convincingly corrected. So many of these now generally accepted corrections are verified by the application of our rule 2 as to give strong proof of its correctness. This in turn gives support to, amounting practically to proof of, the hypothesis upon which the rule is founded, namely that X and Y are merely two branches of one tradition, W. . . .

Notes

1. His administration covered almost three years. From *Epp.* x.42, 61, 62, and 77 it is known that Calpurnius Macer was governor of Moesia Inferior during Pliny's first and second years in Bithynia. From *CIL* III 777 Macer is known to have been in Moesia in 112, and from *CIL* III 12470 that he had a successor in Moesia by 116. See Stout, *The Governors of Moesia,* Princeton, 1910, pp. 62-63. The dates assumed for Pliny's governorship in Bithynia, 111-113, may not be entirely accurate, but they are not far wrong.

2. Geisler's list is published at the end of Luitjohn's edition of the poems and letters of Sidonius in *Monumenta Germaniae Historica* VIII 351 ff.

3. References in parentheses are by page and line to the text of Merrill's *editio maior* of the *Letters,* 1922.

4. "All modern editors": In the last eighty-one years six critical editions of the complete correspondence of Pliny have been published in which reexamination of the text has been a prime purpose of the editor. They are the four Teubner editions by Keil, 1870, Müller, 1903, Kukula, 1908, Schuster, 1933, and the editions of Merrill, 1922, and Mlle Guillemin, 1927. Throughout this study the expression "all modern editors" is to be interpreted as referring to these six critical editions. Reference will occasionally be made to other editions, complete or partial, published in this same period, in which a careful restudy of the problems of the text seems to have been only a secondary interest of the editor.

5. The discussion of the genuineness of these readings is deferred until further preparation for it has been made by some study of the history of the text. All the readings referred to in this introductory statement will be discussed in detail later.

6. An interesting detailed study of the names of the addresses in the manuscripts is given in Barwick, "Zwei antike Ausgaben der Pliniusbriefe?" *Philol.*

91 (1937) 423-448, and in an earlier article by Robbins, "Tables of Contents in the MSS of Pliny's *Letters*," CP [*Classical Philology*] 5 (1910) 476-480. My own study of the matter discussed in this paragraph was made in 1926.

7. For a discussion of the methods and conclusions of Otto see Stout 1926.5-31.

Bibliographical References

Barwick, Karl. "Zwei antike Ausgaben der Plinius Briefe?" *Philol.*, 91 (1936), 443-448.

Guillemin, Anne-Marie. "Quelques remarques sur la critique du texte de Pline le Jeune," *Rev. de Philol.*, 49 (1925), 93-100.

Keil, H. *C. Plini Caecili Epistularum libri Novem, Epistularum ad Traianum liber, Panegyricus,* editio minor, Leipzig, 1853; and editio maior, Leipzig, 1870.

Merrill, E. T. *C. Plini Caecili Secundi Epistularum Libri Decem.* Leipzig, 1922.

Schuster, M. *Studien zur Textkritik des jüngeren Plinius.* Vienna, 1919.

———. "The Mind of the Scribe," *CJ* [*Classical Journal*] 22 (1926-1927), 405-417.

A. N. Sherwin-White (essay date 1966)

SOURCE: Sherwin-White, A. N. "General Introduction to the Private Letters." In *The Letters of Pliny: A Historical and Social Commentary*, pp. ix-xli. Oxford: Clarendon Press, 1966.

[*In the following essay, Sherwin-White praises the formal, yet simple language used by Pliny to illustrate the major themes and subjects in his* Letters,*, discusses their chronology and composition, and evaluates their authenticity as correspondence.*]

I. The Origins and Characteristics of the Letters

Satura nostra tota est, was the Roman claim. They might have added *epistula quoque,* with justice so far as the surviving literature is concerned.[1] There is a chapter on the theory of letter-writing in a late Greek treatise, Demetrius, *De Interpretatione* 223-39, and the late rhetoricians have left behind two summaries of types of letters, the *formae epistolicae* and the *characteres epistolici,* with short examples of each type. The numbering of types is twenty-one and forty-one respectively (p. 42). But the surviving Greek letters are mostly addresses and long essays meant for publication, in the style of Isocrates, *Ad Nicoclem.* The Greek theorist recognized the letter as a by-form of literature akin to the dialogue, with a similar though simpler style (Demetrius, 223). But the Roman letter, as it emerges full-grown in the correspondence of Cicero and his friends, is the private letter of genuine intercourse, whether concerned with *res domesticae* or *res publicae.* Cicero in a passage of the Philippics brings out the characteristics of his own letters: 'quam multa ioca solent esse in epistulis quae prolatae si sint inepta videantur, quam multa seria neque tamen ullo modo divolganda' (2. 7). In several passages he finds the mark of private letters in the *iocus* and *iocatio,* and in the use of *sermo cotidianus* (*Ad Fam.* 2. 4. 1, 9. 21. 1; *Ad Att.* 7. 5. 5, 10. 11. 5) which seem to be the equivalent of τὸ λαλεῖν in the treatise *De Interpretatione.* But for serious matters the tone might be *severum et grave* (*Ad Fam.* 2. 4. 1). Cicero knows something of the theoretical types of letter catalogued by the later rhetoricians, and mentions three categories, the *promissio auxili*—characteristically unknown to the Greek lists—the *consolatio doloris,* and *litterae commendaticiae.* But apart from Book 12 of the *Ad Familiares,* which is a collection of the latter, his own letters to or from his friends would be hard to classify under any detailed scheme, except for a few, such as the well-known consolation of Sulpicius to Cicero on the death of Tullia.

It is a great jump from the letters of Cicero to those of Pliny. The gap is not bridged by the metrical Epistles of Horace or by the letters in prose of Seneca to Lucilius. One or two of Horace's themes recur in Pliny's Letters, notably the 'invitation to a feast', and the 'enquiry to a man of letters overseas' (**Ep.** [**Epistulae**] I. 3 and 5). These are not so remote from the manner and treatment of Pliny, not least in their brevity. But the rest are mostly letters of philosophic admonition with a gossipy social setting in which description plays a minor role, written in a rambling style very different from the concentrated method of Pliny. Peter, in his history of the Roman letter, omits Seneca altogether, and even Guillemin, who ransacks Latin literature in the search for predecessors, invokes Seneca seldom.[2] Seneca writes in a different tradition, continuing the vein of the Greek letter of admonition, the προτρεπτικός, and his letters make no claim to be considered as private correspondence. They belong with those defined by Artemon as 'half dialogue' (Demetrius, 223). Seneca claims that they are in the language of conversation, and rejects with disgust the notion of *accuratas . . . epistulas.*[3] Pliny's letters are not Senecan, though he adapts the letter of admonition to his own purposes (p. 42). But neither are they Ciceronian, though he claims a conditional comparison with Cicero (III. 20. 10 'veteribus', IX. 2. 2-3). Peter suggested that the true origin of Pliny's letter-type lies in the oratorical *egressus,* or formal digression, and that the immediate model was provided by the *Silvae* of Statius, a collection of occasional pieces in verse. Quintilian (*Inst.* 4. 3. 12), Pliny's master, characterized the *egressus* as concerned with: 'laus hominum locorum-que, expositio rerum gestarum . . . etiam fabulosarum, descriptio regionum'. Statius first detached the *egressus* from oratory and gave it a life of its own in verse. This is true of many of the themes of Statius—the praises of Rutilius Gallicus and other notables, the description of the villa of Pollius, or of the Via Domitiana and the events of Domitian's seventeenth consulship (*Silvae* I. 4, 2. 2, 4. 1, 3). Such themes recur in Pliny (p. 43-44). It may be added that conversely Statius borrowed an epistolary theme for his numerous Consolations, and once adopted the epistolary *iocatio* in his *hendecasyl-labi iocosi* to Plotius Grypus. But apart from the metrical form there is a marked difference between Pliny's Letters and Statius' *Silvae* in length. The letters of a length comparable to many of the *Silvae* are exceptional (p. 4).

Martial comes to mind as an alternative influence. Guillemin rightly calls him the 'true master' of Pliny.[4] His influence may be seen not only in the style and language, where it is pervasive,[5] but in the greater variety of topics, and in the comparative brevity of most of the pieces. All three writers were experimenting in a new form of literature, which may be better described as occasional pieces than as essays in verse or prose. Martial was Pliny's protégé (III. 21), while Statius, as Peter noted, is never mentioned by Pliny, although echoes can be detected at least in the first villa-description (II. 17 pref.).[6] This is hardly out of jealousy or dislike, since Pliny has much to say about his forensic rival and enemy Aquilius Regulus. Statius, unlike Martial, did not survive to balance his flatteries of Domitian by flattering his successors. Hence he was out of fashion and favour in the literary coteries of the period of the letters. Pliny's direct copying of Martial is apparent in his books of verse, described in IV. 14, VIII. 21, which have taken over from the letter its *iocatio*, which plays a very subsidiary role in Pliny (p. 43).

Pliny defines his type of letter variously (I. 1. 1, VII. 9. 8, IX. 2. 3, 28. 5), as *epistulae curatius* or *curiosius* or *diligentius scriptae,* and distinguishes them from the Senecan essay in epistolary form, *scholasticas litteras.*[7] He and his friends were in the habit of exchanging such letters (I. 16. 6, II. 13. 7, IX. 2. 1-3, 28. 5). Once a friend proposes a subject for a letter of this type, and Pliny promises to compose it (IX. 11. 1 n.). Certain principles of composition can be inferred from Pliny. Each letter is normally confined to a single theme.[8] There are few exceptions to this rule. Only three or four times in the whole collection does Pliny introduce an alien topic or notably change the subject. In II. 20. 9 he quotes the *lex scholastica* that a theme should be illustrated by three examples. This defends the unity of several letters where three different anecdotes illustrate

a common theme: II. 20, the captations of Regulus; III. 16, the courage of Arria; VII. 27, the ghost letter, and perhaps the first part of VI. 31, the trials at Centum Cellae. In two groups of letters he is at pains to contrive a connexion where possible between alien topics. The first group is concerned with travels. In V. 14. 1-6 the account of Cornutus' career and that of Pliny's vacation are linked by a reference to Pliny's official leave of absence from his own post. In IV. 13. 1-2 mention of the movements and occupations of Tacitus and Pliny leads on to the subject of the schoolmaster of Comum, ibid. 3-11. So too in IV. 1 the account of Pliny's journey to Comum is intertwined with that of the dedication of his temple at Tifernum. These hardly count as exceptions to the rule of unity. The reference to travel is a regular form of opening and ending a letter, managed more briefly in, for example, I. 22. 1, V. 6. 1, VIII. 1. 1, 2. 1.

The second group is more miscellaneous. Twice there is a brief and unexpected postscript acknowledging the receipt of a gift. In I. 7 it stands unrelated to the rest of the letter, but in VII. 21. 4 the intrusion is connected with the subject of the letter, Pliny's eyesight. Much more notable changes of subject occur in VI. 19, 31, VII. 6, VIII. 14, IX. 11, 28. In the first an account of Trajan's measures to check bribery is linked with that of a rise in the price of land, but the link is that of a genuine cause and effect (ibid. n.). The second describes three trials before the cabinet of Trajan, the hospitality of the emperor, and the building of the harbour at Centum Cellae. The three topics are linked only by the unity of the occasion, Pliny's visit to Trajan. In VII. 6 the report of a phase in the prosecution of Varenus is interrupted by the story of another criminal trial which bears only a strained similarity to that of Varenus. Pliny makes a formal apology for the change of subject (s. 6): 'quid enim prohibet, quamquam alia ratio scribendae epistulae fuerit, de studiis disputare?' In VIII. 14 a diatribe against the *servitus priorum temporum* is ingeniously linked to a technical discussion of the rules of division in senatorial debates, with which it has no genuine connexion. In IX. 11 the request of Geminus for a literary letter and the sale of Pliny's books at Lugdunum lack vital connexion. In XI. 28 three diverse topics—the vintage, a friend's visit, and an account of a speech of Pliny—are formally connected as the contents of three letters of which Pliny acknowledges receipt; possibly the *lex scholastica* may be invoked here.

With these limited exceptions Pliny sticks to the rule of the single theme. In II. 1. 12 he neatly makes a virtue out of this necessity: 'volui tibi multa alia scribere, sed totus animus in hac una contemplatione defixus est'.

A second rule forbids excessive length. In V. 6. 42-44 he insists that length should be appropriate to the subject, and in general he deprecates the long letter. In all but one of the few letters of exceptional length there is some apology for this, expressly in III. 9. 27, 37, V. 6. 41-45, IX. 13. 26, and indirectly in I. 20. 25, II. 11. 25, 17. 29. The exception is VIII. 14, a letter noted above for its lack of unity. The length of these letters does not fall below some five or six pages of text, and rises to about eight in V. 6. In an intermediate group of eleven letters of about three to four pages in length there is a touch of apology only twice, in III. 5. 20, IV. 11. 16, but none in 1. 5. 8, IV. 9, VI. 16, 20, 31, VII. 27, VIII, 6, IX. 26. Yet surprisingly in VII. 9. 16 he apologizes for undue length after a somewhat repetitive exposition in less than three pages of a theme from which he does not seriously digresss.

The third rule concerns style—the colour and pattern of language and the tone of feeling. Pliny develops this beyond the doctrine of his master Quintilian, who remarked briefly that *oratio soluta* was suitable to letters unless they were concerned with philosophy or public affairs, and that letters should avoid hiatus and cultivate rhythm (*Inst.* 9. 4. 19). Pliny states in VII. 9. 8: 'volo epistulam diligentius scribas. nam saepe in oratione quoque non historica modo sed prope poetica descriptionum necessitas incidit, et pressus sermo purusque ex epistulis petitur'. In I. 16. 6 he commends the letters of Pompeius Saturninus for their Plautian or Terentian simplicity of vocabulary. Peter (op. cit. 113) noted the connexion between the statements of Pliny and Quintilian about the poetic style appropriate in digressions (*Ep.* II. 5. 5; *Inst.* 2. 4. 3). Evidently Pliny intended a mixture of poetic vocabulary and simple language. How far he achieved it is not the subject of an historical commentary.[9] More pervasive than either aim is undoubtedly his ingrained technique as an orator, from which he could not hope to divest himself. In certain, but not many, letters, notably in descriptions of natural scenery, some poetical colour is obvious enough (VI. 20, VII. 27, VIII. 8, 17). The use of Vergilian language in the account of the building operations at Centum Cellae is merely the clearest instance (VI. 31. 15-17 nn.). The oratorical devices of the Panegyric dominate the account of the Vestal trial and the long letter about Pallas (IV. 11, VIII. 6), though Pliny there apologizes for the use of unsuitable language (VIII. 6. 17). More unexpected perhaps is the style of the argument on senatorial procedure in VIII. 14, which sounds more suitable to the Centumviral court of civil law, where Pliny spent a good deal of his professional career.

How far the use of *pressus purusque sermo* goes beyond the choice of plain words in factual narrative and quiet passages generally is questionable. Pliny's simplicity is decidedly studied. Passages may be taken, especially from the opening of letters, which at first sight promise simplicity, but artifice is soon apparent in the construction, if not in the vocabulary. A random sample, the opening of VII. 16, is characteristic. 'Calestrium Tironem familiarissime diligo, et privatis mihi et publicis necessitatibus implicitum. simul militavimus simul quaestores Caesaris fuimus. ille me in tribunatu liberorum iure praecessit, ego illum in praetura sum consecutus.' The commonest of nouns, only the most essential of adverbs and adjectives are used. But the cunning of the artist's hand appears in the order and arrangement. The letters to Trajan provide a fair comparison. The recommendation of Rosianus Geminus (X. 26) is very close to VII. 16. Or another random sample, from an official report (X. 31. 3), gives the same mixture of plain vocabulary and complex construction: 'nam et reddere poenae post longum tempus plerosque iam senes et quantum adfirmatur frugaliter modesteque viventes nimis severum arbitrabar, et in publicis officiis retinere damnatos non satis honestum putabam'. Pliny is perhaps plain when there is no special reason to be otherwise, even in the literary letters, but he cannot be simple even in his official correspondence. It has been noted that in the more colourful passages he has a fondness for diminutives, and even invents some when they were not ready to hand, e.g. *columbulus, cumbula, metula, prominulus* in V. 6. 15 and 35, VIII. 20. 7, IX. 25. 3.[10]

Pliny carries Quintilian's advice about the use of prose rhythm in letters to its logical conclusion. Both the private and the public letters follow the rules of oratorical prose for the *clausula*.[11]

This discussion of style demonstrates the extent to which the letters are literary compositions. Their formality is shown also by the frequent use of somewhat standardized opening phrases which affirm the subject of the letter. In the following list the types and their variants have been catalogued. Surprisingly little attention has been paid to this stylistic device hitherto. Guillemin (*VL*, 145) noted only the first two types.

VI. 18 rogas ut agam Firmanorum . . . causam.

VI. 27 rogas ut cogitem quid designatus consul . . . censeas.

I. 14 petis ut fratris tui filiae prospiciam maritum. . . .

III. 15 petis ut libellos tuos . . . legam. . . .

IV. 26 petis ut libellos . . . emendandos . . . curem.

VI. 16 petis ut tibi avunculi mei exitum scribam. . . .

V. 13 et tu rogas et ego promisi . . . scripturum . . . quem habuisset eventum postulatio Nepotis. . . .

VII. 14 tu quidem honestissime, quod tam impense et rogas et exigis ut accipi iubeam. . . .

VII. 9 quaeris quemadmodum . . . putem te studere oportere.

IX. 36 quaeris quemadmodum in Tuscis diem . . . disponam.

VII. 15 requiris quid agam. quae nosti. distringor officio. . . .

I. 23 consulis an existimem te in tribunatu. . . .

VII. 18 deliberas mecum quemadmodum pecunia . . . salva sit. . . .

I. 1 frequenter hortatus es ut epistulas . . . publicarem. . . .

II. 19 hortaris ut orationem . . . recitem. . . .

II. 16 tu quidem pro . . . reverentia admones me codicillos. . . .

IV. 17 et admones et rogas ut suscipiam causam Corelliae. . . .

IX. 1 saepe te monui ut libros . . . emitteres. . . .

V. 8 suades ut historiam scribam. . . .

IV. 13 salvum in urbem venisse gaudeo. . . .

IV. 16 gaude meo gaude tuo . . . nomine: adhuc studiis honor durat.

VI. 26 gaudeo et gratulor quod . . . filiam . . . destinasti. . . .

VII. 23 gaudeo quidem esse te tam fortem. . . .

IV. 8 gratularis mihi quod auguratum acceperim. . . .

II. 11 solet esse gaudio tibi si quid acti est in senatu. . . .

VII. 32 delector iucundum tibi fuisse Tironis mei adventum. . . .

II. 17 miraris cur me Laurentinum . . . delectet. . . .

VII. 11 miraris quod Hermes . . . agros . . . addixerit. . . .

I. 9 mirum est quam singulis diebus in urbe ratio . . . constet. . . .

VII. 22 minus miraberis me . . . petisse ut . . . conferres tribunatum. . . .

VII. 30 torqueor quod discipulum . . . amisisti. . . .

VII. 19 angit me Fanniae valetudo. . . .

VII. 1 terret me haec tua . . . valetudo. . . .

IX. 22 magna me sollicitudine adfecit . . . valetudo. . . .

II. 9 anxium me . . . habet petitio Sexti. . . .

III. 8 facis pro cetera reverentia . . . quod petis ut tribunatum. . . .

VIII. 4 optime facis quod bellum Dacicum . . . scribere paras. . . .

VI. 34 recte fecisti quod gladiatorium munus. . . .

IX. 5 egregie facis . . . quod iustitiam . . . provincialibus . . . commendas. . . .

IX. 2 facis iucunde quod . . . epistulas . . . flagitas. . . .

IX. 24 bene fecisti quod libertum. . . .

VIII. 13 probo quod libellos . . . legisti. . . .

IX. 9 unice probo quod Pompei . . . morte . . . adficeris. . . .

VII. 6 rara et notabilis res Vareno contigit. . . .

VI. 22 magna res acta est omnium qui sunt provinciis praefuturi. . . .

VI. 15 mirificae rei non interfuisti. . . .

V. 4 res parva sed initium non parvae: vir praetorius. . . .

III. 14 rem atrocem . . . Macedo . . . passus est. . . .

I. 16 amabam Pompeium. . . .

IV. 12 amas Egnatium. . . .

VI. 8 Atilium Crescentem et nosti et amas. . . .

VII. 31 Claudius Pollio amari a te cupit. . . .

IV. 4 Varisidium Nepotem valdissime diligo. . . .

VII. 16 Calestrium Tironem familiarissime diligo. . . .

IV. 15 si quid omnino hoc certe iudicio facio quod Asinium singulariter amo.

IV. 1 cupis . . . neptem . . . videre. . . .

VIII. 10 quo magis cupis . . . pronepotes videre. . . .

IX. 10 cupio praeceptis tuis parere. . . .

VI. 6 si quando nunc praecipue cuperem esse te Romae. . . .

III. 21 audio Valerium Martialem decessisse. . . .

IV. 11 audistine Valerium Licinianum in Sicilia profiteri?

III. 7 modo nuntiatus est Silius . . . finisse vitam. . . .

V. 5 nuntiatur mihi C. Fannium decessisse. . . .

V. 14 secesseram in municipium cum mihi nuntiatum est Cornutum. . . .

I. 5 vidistine quemquam M. Regulo timidiorem . . . ?

I. 7 vide in quo me fastigio collocaris cum. . . .

V. 19 video quam molliter tuos habeas. . . .

VI. 13 umquamne vidisti quemquam tam laboriosum . . . ?

VIII. 8 vidistine aliquando Clitumnum fontem . . . ?

V. 17 scio quantopere bonis artibus faveas. . . .

VI. 19 scis tu accessisse pretium agris . . . ?

VI. 28 scio quae tibi causa fuerit impedimento quominus. . . .

IV. 5 Aeschinen aiunt petentibus . . . legisse. . . .

VI. 20 ais te . . . cupere cognoscere quos ego Miseni relictus. . . .

VII. 4 ais legisse te hendecasyllabos meos. . . .

VII. 28 ais quosdam apud te reprehendisse. . . .

IV. 7 saepe tibi dico inesse vim Regulo. . . .

IX. 26 dixi de quodam oratore saeculi nostri. . . .

IX. 19 significas legisse te . . . iussisse Verginium. . . .

I. 18 scribis te perterritum somnio. . . .

IV. 10 scribis mihi Sabinam, quae nos reliquit heredes. . . .

IV. 25 scripseram tibi verendum esse ne ex . . . suffragiis. . . .

V. 16 tristissimus haec tibi scribo Fundani nostri filia. . . .

VI. 5 scripseram tenuisse Varenum. . . .

VI. 7 scribis te absentia mea . . . adfici. . . .

VI. 25 scribis Robustum . . . iter peregisse. . . .

IX. 7 aedificare te scribis. . . .

IX. 40 scribis pergratas . . . fuisse litteras meas quibus. . . .

IV. 23 magnam cepi voluptatem cum . . . cognovi te . . . disponere otium. . . .

VI. 31 evocatus in consilium a Caesare . . . maximam cepi voluptatem. . . .

IX. 16 summam te voluptatem percepisse ex isto . . . genere venandi. . . .

These sixteen sets of stylized phrases, with minor variations, reveal a formalization of the terms that naturally suggest themselves to a writer when he introduces the principal subject of his letter. It is remarkable that the most obvious letter-opening, a direct reference to the receipt or dispatch of a letter or a book, of which there are twenty instances, shows much less stylization.

I. 2 quia . . . adventum . . . prospicio, librum quem . . . promiseram exhibeo. . . .

II. 5 actionem . . . promissam exhibui. . . .

III. 13 librum quo . . . gratias egi misi. . . .

VII. 12 libellum formatum . . . quo . . . amicus . . . uteretur misi. . . .

VII. 20 librum tuum legi et . . . adnotavi. . . .

VIII. 3 librum quem novissime tibi misi . . . significas.

IX. 35 librum quem misisti recepi. . . .

I. 8 peropportune mihi redditae sunt litterae tuae quibus. . . .

I. 11 olim mihi nullas epistulas mittis. . . .

V. 11 recepi litteras tuas ex quibus cognovi. . . .

V. 21 varie me adfecerunt litterae tuae. . . .

VII. 13 eadem epistula . . . significat. . . .

VIII. 6 cognovisse iam ex epistula . . . debes. . . .

IX. 11 epistulam tuam iucundissimam accepi. . . .

IX. 17 recepi litteras tuas quibus. . . .

IX. 18 qua intentione . . . legeris libellos meos, epistula tua ostendit. . . .

IX. 20 tua vero epistula . . . iucundior fuit. . . .

IX. 28 post longum tempus epistulas tuas, sed tres pariter, recepi.

Of these eighteen instances only three from either group employ a closely similar form—III. 13, VIII. 3, IX. 35 from the first, and V. 11, IX. 11, 17 from the second. These six formal openings may be added to the preceding list.

Altogether in the two sections there are some ninety-eight letters out of the whole collection of 248 which use stylized openings. The first three books account for only fourteen, or a seventh, of these openings, in sixty-six letters or rather more than a quarter of the whole collection. The middle four books, IV-VII, use them much more freely: out of 118 letters precisely half use stylized openings. In Book VIII they become rarer, with five formal openings out of twenty-four, in much the same proportion as in I-III. Then Book IX, with its miscellaneous forty letters, returns to a higher rate with some fifteen stylized openings, according to the present lists. The figures, if not statistical, are of some interest. They may suggest that the middle books hold the highest proportion of letters consciously written for publication, or that Pliny revised and wrote more according to formula in these than in I-III and VIII.

When Pliny does not employ stylized openings and their variants, he usually plunges straight into his theme with a specific statement, e.g.

I. 13 magnum proventum poetarum annus hic attulit.

III. 18 officium consulatus iniunxit mihi ut reipublicae nomine. . . .

VII. 24 Ummidia Quadratilla paulo minus octogensimo aetatis anno decessit. . . .

VIII. 5 grave vulnus Macrinus noster accepit. . . .

But in certain letters he employs a less direct approach, beginning with a general statement or proverbial remark, from which he proceeds to the particular. These openings are decidedly rare in the early books. The earliest seems to be III. 16: 'adnotasse videor facta dictaque virorum feminarumque alia clariora esse alia maiora'. Possibly I. 17 also comes under the definition: 'est adhuc curae hominibus fides et officium . . .'. There are only four other examples of this type in III-VI: III. 20, VI. 21 and 24, and V. 17 which combines a stylized opening with it. Then in VII and VIII there comes a spate of them, nine in all. Surprisingly these are not distributed evenly through the two books, but they come bunched together. Book IX adds four others, better distributed.

VII. 25 quantum eruditorum aut modestia ipsorum aut quies operit ac subtrahit famae. . . .

VII. 26 nuper me cuiusdam amici languor admonuit optimos esse nos dum infirmi sumus. . . .

VII. 27 et mihi discendi et tibi docendi facultatem otium praebet. igitur perquam velim scire, . . .

VIII. 2 alii in praedia sua proficiscuntur ut locupletiores revertantur, ego ut pauperior.

VIII. 18 falsum est nimirum quod creditur vulgo, testamenta hominum speculum esse morum, cum Domitius Tullus, . . .

VIII. 19 et gaudium mihi et solacium in litteris, nihilque tam laetum quod his laetius tam triste quod non per has minus triste. itaque et infirmitate uxoris, . . .

VIII. 20 ad quae noscenda iter ingredi, transmittere mare solemus, ea sub oculis posita neglegimus, . . .

VIII. 21 ut in vita sic in studiis pulcherrimum et humanissimum existimo severitatem comitatemque miscere . . . qua ratione ductus, . . .

VIII. 22 nostine hos qui omnium libidinum servi sic aliorum vitiis irascuntur quasi invideant, . . . ?

IX. 3 alius aliud; ego beatissimum existimo qui bonae . . . famae praesumptione perfruitur, . . .

IX. 23 frequenter agenti mihi evenit ut centumviri laudarent . . . frequenter e senatu famam . . . rettuli . . . numquam tamen maiorem cepi voluptatem quam nuper, . . .

IX. 27 quanta potestas quanta dignitas quanta maiestas . . . sit historiae, cum frequenter alias tum proxime sensi. recitaverat quidam. . . .

IX. 29 ut satius unum aliquid insigniter facere quam plurima mediocriter, ita plurima mediocriter si non possis unum aliquid insigniter. quod intuens ego, . . .

Pliny seems to be deliberately developing a new style in the last three books. In VIII. 20 the general thought is expounded for eleven lines before he comes to the specific subject. In VIII. 22 the generalization is developed for the same length, and the specific instance is cut off short and left unspoken: 'quaeris fortasse quo commotus haec scribam. nuper quidam,—sed melius coram'. In IX. 3 the generalization continues for twelve lines, in somewhat similar fashion, and is briefly applied to the addressee.

II. The Authenticity of the Letters as Correspondence

The study of the letter openings gives some notion of the meaning of the term *epistulae curatius scriptae,* and some hints of the development of Pliny's technique. It also gives some tentative support to the argument, based on less subjective criteria, that on the whole the letters were composed in a chronological series approximating to the present order of books. It also leads naturally to the question of the authenticity of the letters as letters. Pliny presents the letters as part of a genuine literary correspondence. Modern scholars have taken no very coherent line about this. Some regard the letters as entirely fictitious, written for the books in which they appear. Peter saw little organic connexion between the contents of the letters and the persons to whom they are addressed. Others speak of the letters being written up for publication from simpler originals. These opinions emerged from the various discussions of the chronology of the letters. Mommsen held that the letters belonged in their composition to specific, successive periods (pp. 20 f.). His critics implied that the letters were being composed at widely varying dates and were later collected into books. Such a view has been taken again, in recent years, by Monti and Hanslik in studies of particular letters (cf. IV. 1, 11, V. 1, 3 nn.).

The more personal letters of advice on social, political, and literary problems, which Peter admitted were appropriate to their addressees—such as the letters to young protégés, Pedanius Fuscus, Ummidius Quadratus, and Rosianus Geminus (VII. 9, IX. 36, 40, VI. 29, VII. 1, VIII. 22) and earlier to Pompeius Falco and Iunius Avitus (I. 23, II. 6)—form a special group. They are highly polished specimens. Yet it is unlikely that their topics and occasions were entirely fictitious. It is certain that a praetorian senator called Maximus was sent on a special mission to Achaea, as in VIII. 24. The serious illness of young Geminus and the absence of the young advocate Fuscus from Rome on a long holiday need be no less genuine (VII. 9). So too the appropriate advice that each received. Anything is possible, no doubt, in the field of the imagination. But it would require an extraordinary ingenuity to invent so many convincing minor details for the setting of so miscellaneous a subject-matter as that of these letters. It must be reckoned at least a probability that Pliny was in the habit of advising or consoling his friends on occasion with appropriate *litterae curiosius scriptae,* and that these formed one basis of the collection.

A second group offers a firmer grip to the investigator. The letters dealing with Pliny's business affairs and domestic arrangements are full of precise and particular details that can hardly have been invented. They read as literary revisions of practical letters which have been polished in language and style and simplified by omission of the most technical and transient details. The instructions to an architect in IX. 39 to prepare a plan and buy materials for a small shrine lack the precise measurements necessary for the task, but otherwise give a clear account of the type of building required and the peculiarities of the site. So too the short letter of instructions to Pliny's agent at Comum to set up a Corinthian bronze with a dedicatory inscription (III. 6). Here the elaborate description of the bronze is an obvious expansion. The discussion of the prospective purchase of an estate, with a clear account of its condition, values, and previous mismanagement, and certain details about its necessary equipment, is hardly an invention (III. 19). So too the long description of Pliny's method of dealing with his vintage merchants with mathematical details, has the authentic ring (VIII. 2). There is a similarly convincing letter about an innovation in his system of agricultural leases (IX. 37).

These letters are close to the realities of correspondence. So too are the letters of recommendation for promotion written for equestrian friends and young senators in the public service, containing summary accounts of their careers, standing, and qualities. Both groups can be checked by comparison with certain of the letters to Trajan, which like the rest of Book X show no sign of literary revision, and have never been regarded as other than genuine letters. The account of Pliny's agricultural leases in X. 8 is put forward very much as in IX. 37, as the explanation of a necessary absence from Rome, and the agrictural situation is akin. The recommendation of Rosianus Geminus for senatorial preferment and of Suetonius Tranquillus for the *ius trium liberorum* (X. 26, 94) are generally similar in content to the recommendations of Arrianus Maturus and Cornelius Minicianus (III. 2, VII. 22), not least in their rather generalized descriptions of character and the absence of precise details about the men's careers. Equally comparable are the longer letters recommending Voconius Romanus to a consular legate for equestrian promotion, and to Trajan for senatorial status (II. 13, X. 4), which were writ-

ten within a year of each other. The private and literary letter has in fact more to say about the candidate than the letter to the emperor. A noteworthy feature of these letters of recommendation is the stress laid on *studia,* the forensic and literary activity of the candidates. This though stronger in the letter to personal friends is equally present in the recommendations to the unliterary Trajan (X. 4. 4, 94. 1). Contrarily, the uncompromising brevity of X. 13, commending Accius Sura to Trajan for a praetorship, may be compared to that of IV. 4, commending Varisidius Nepos to Sosius Senecio for an equestrian commission. The latter has been thought cool and evasive; more likely, it is merely very close to its original form.

The numerous brief notes, covering the receipt and dispatch of letters and books, with a brief comment, or giving information about the movements or occupations of the writer, seem to carry the signs of authenticity. Though regularly distributed through the first six books in threes or fours, they are a great deal commoner in the last three, and form a quarter of the items in Book IX. One would hardly sit down to invent this kind of thing—often described by scholars as 'fillers'—in excessive numbers, even if they may be considered with Guillemin epigrams in prose.[12] It is notable that in this type of note the introductory sentences or phrases are less stereotyped than in the longer letters (p. 9). The following list excludes notes of more than ten or eleven lines, except for the bracketed items, which are notes of twelve to thirteen lines—while IV. 10 and VII. 10, though very short, are excluded because of their special subject-matter—: I. 1, 11, 21; II. 2, 8, 15; III. (12), 17; IV. 16, 18, 20, (26), 29; V. 2 (10), (12), 15, 18; VI. 3, 9, 14, 28; VII. 2, 5, 7, 8, 13, 14, 15, (21), 23, 28, 32; VIII. 1, 3, 7, 9, 13, 15, (19); IX. 4, 8, 11, 14, 15, 16, 18, 20, 24, 32, 38. This list supports the evidence on other grounds that in Books VII-IX Pliny was becoming short, not of letters as such, but of *curiosius scriptae* to make up his volumes.

There are a number of somewhat longer notes, akin to those just discussed, which may represent worked-up versions of shorter originals, developing a notion more fully, e.g. VII. 3, VIII. 22, IX. 2. Others seem so tightly packed that they may be close to their original form. Thus in V. 11 Pliny says a good deal in a short space to his grandfather-in-law about municipal benefactions. Again IX. 28, discussing the miscellaneous contents of three letters from Voconius Romanus, touches on topics as diverse as the harvest, a commission to the emperor's wife, an invitation for a holiday, and literary criticism. It seems unlikely that such a letter is a literary fiction.

These four groups—letters of advice, business letters, personal recommendations, and notes of receipt and dispatch—establish a claim to be considered as originating in genuine correspondence. What then of the letters of substance for which they form the setting, the *litterae curiosius scriptae* in the strictest sense, the long descriptions of character, of political and social events, of natural phenomena, and the rest? Were they written at the apparent date of composition, so far as this is determinable by their contents, or are they of later compilation? It is probably impossible to prove whether the long formal letters were written for separate circulation among literary friends or for collective publication. But there is no reason why Pliny should not have written long descriptions of his famous trials, for example, to his educated friends at Comum and elsewhere, who otherwise would depend for public news solely on what appeared in the *acta diurna* (V. 13. 8 n.), the contents of which can hardly have been on the scale or contained the personal bias of Pliny's versions. The private exchange of news, in plain or in literary form, is an obvious result of the broad distribution of the administrative class of the empire, and of its international origins and connexions.

The composition of the longer letters is so careful that most do not disclose their secret to the subtlest investigation. This in itself suggests that they were mostly written in their present form, and not as a recension of earlier compositions. But a few offer some clues to the investigator, notably three long political letters, I. 5, VIII. 14, IX. 13, and the shorter VII. 6.

The first describes the political situation in January 97, and an incident of the first day of that January. Pliny is considering the initiation of a charge against Aquilius Regulus, a prop of the former régime, but he remarks that he will wait for the return of Junius Mauricus from exile and take his advice. The whole letter is written in terms of the present moment. The verbal tenses are carefully managed to give the impression of a letter written soon after the incident of the first of January, and before the return of Mauricus. 'Exspecto Mauricum', Pliny writes twice, and also 'dum Mauricum venit'. But to the first phrase he adds a note (s. 10) 'nondum ab exsilio venerat'. This seems to indicate, as is commonly assumed, that the letter was revised later than its date of composition, when Book I was being put together for publication. Either the note was unnecessary for the recipient Romanus, who was in Italy, or the perfect tense should have been used. Pliny added a similar note in the similar context of IX. 13. 5 (below), but there it is appropriate because the story is being retold a decade later for the benefit of the addressee.

VIII. 14, addressed to the jurisprudent Titius Aristo, has already been mentioned for its peculiarities. It is one of the very few letters that extensively violate the rule of unity of subject. A technical discussion, filling three O.C.T. pages, of a single point in the rules governing senatorial debates, is preceded by an explanation in two pages of the reasons for Pliny's uncertainty. Pliny is elaborating with historical details his opening statement: 'priorum temporum servitus ut aliarum optimarum artium sic etiam iuris senatorii oblivionem quandam et ignorantiam induxit'. The section is an *egressus* in the rhetorical tradition, and appears absurd in a letter addressed to Titius Aristo, who was in a position to know all about the matter. Pliny's other historical and political narratives are addressed to persons to whom the information was new, as is several times emphasized: II. 11. 1, III. 4. 1, 9. 1, IV. 11. 1, 15, VI. 16. 1, 20. 1, IX. 13. 1. The first part of VIII. 14 seems to be a clear example of the elaborate expansion of a much shorter original. The elaboration can easily be detected in its limits and pruned down without harming the sense of the rest (cf. Commentary, ad loc.). This discovery is the more interesting because VIII. 14 is the most certain instance in Books VII and VIII of a letter earlier than the apparent date of the book. It deals with an event of mid-105, the murder of a consul suffect, which should be some two years earlier than the general compilation date of VIII. No other letter betrays so elaborate a revision except VII. 6.

The digression in VII. 6 has already been mentioned (p. 4). Pliny adds a lengthy anecdote, about a different trial, taking twenty-two lines out of a total of fifty-six, to his account of a phase of the action against Varenus, with a formal apology to the reader. The digression seriously interrupts the narrative, which is resumed after its end, and it can be totally removed without leaving any jagged edges. The narrative closes neatly around the gap, and presents what may well be the original shape of the letter.[13]

In IX. 13 Pliny recounts for the benefit of the young Ummidius Quadratus the circumstances of his attempted prosecution of Publicius Certus in mid-97. It could be argued that the bulk of the letter belongs to 97, and that it was not published in I or II out of political caution—since Certus was a man of some political influence (s. 11)—or because Pliny was satisfied with the publication of his speech against Certus. This is more probable, because Certus died apparently in 97 (IX. 13. 24), just after this publication. The reviser's hand may appear in the references to the death of Pliny's wife in ss. 4 and 13: 'quamquam tum maxime tristis amissa nuper uxore'. 'Bittius Proculus . . . uxoris . . . meae quam amiseram vitricus'. These notes were necessary for Quadratus in 107 because the wife lost in 97 had been succeeded by Calpurnia, whom Pliny had not yet married in 97. So too in s. 5 'nuntia Arriae et Fanniae (ab exsilio redierant) consule te consule illas'—the parenthesis interrupting the flow of the speech suggests the hand of revision. But otherwise IX. 13 is a coherent whole. An attempt to prove similarly that V. 1 was written a decade earlier and subsequently revised, breaks down, and need not here be considered (Commentary, ad loc.). These are the only letters among the major pieces in which the touch of revision is so obvious, though III. 9 may be added to the list (below, p. 19) of possible revisions. Less certain indications of revision are noted in the Commentary on II. 15. 1, IV. 10. 4, 11. 5, V. 7. 3, VII. 9. 16.

LITERARY IMITATION

Another aspect of the historicity of the letters needs some attention. Pliny certainly writes under strong literary influences, both in the language and the content of the letters. Reminiscences of Vergil and of various subsequent writers of the imperial period are common enough. Themes from the letters of Cicero, the *Silvae* of Statius, and the lyrics of Martial recur. These influences are not generally the subject of this commentary. But Guillemin, in *Pline et la vie littéraire,* ch. iii, musters them for an attack on the truth and accuracy of the letters. Because Pliny writes in the language of his predecessors on themes of Statius or Martial, the whole thing is taken to be a fiction. This seems a rather crude approach to the understanding of classical literature, though not without its parallel in the study of Tacitus, for example, in recent years. The influences are to be expected, but their purpose and effect is another matter. The extreme example is the criticism of Pliny's account of the building of the new harbour at Centum Cellae in VI. 31. 15-17. This is discussed in detail in the Commentary, where it is argued that Pliny simply uses Vergilian language to describe what he saw with his own eyes. The notion that the description is a literary commonplace applicable to any harbour is easily shown to be false from the narrative itself and from external evidence. So too the description of Pliny's two villas cannot be dismissed as literary reproduction of a stock theme, as with Guillemin (*VL,* 141 f.). This might be said of the brief sketch of Caninius' villa in I. 3. But the accounts of the Laurentine and the Tuscan villas in II. 17 and V. 6 are altogether different in scale of detail and length from the limited and very selective snapshots in Seneca, Statius, and Martial, of certain aspects or features of the parks and palaces of their friends (see II. 17, pref.).

The account of the Tiber floods in VIII. 17 is similarly reduced to a literary pattern derived from Horace and used again by Tacitus (*VL,* 120). But as usual the individuality of Pliny's picture is more striking than the literary echoes (nn.), and comparison with the other scenic letters is reassuring. Against the accounts of Vesuvius, the spring of Clitumnus, and the islets of Vadimon (VI. 16, 20, VIII. 8, 20), no more can be alleged than echoes of occasional phrases in earlier writers. The only letters which closely resemble a type well established in previous literature are the two 'invitations to dinner', which exploit the stock comparison of the plain and the extravagant meal (I. 15, III. 12 nn.; *VL,* 135 ff.). Other attempts to establish the stylization of themes break down. Of the letters to his wife (VI. 4, 7, VII. 5) it is admitted that Pliny himself is creating the type out of various passages of Cicero and Ovid (*VL,* 138 f.). Others might prefer to say that Pliny used the obvious literary language to discuss the natural topics of Calpurnia's absence and illness. Very curiously Pliny's accurate summary of the main features of Trajan's second Dacian war (VIII. 4. 2 nn.) is regarded as stock treatment of the 'triumphal theme' (*VL,* 143 f.). But for the vast majority of the letters the establishment of stock themes is not even attempted.

A somewhat similar criticism was made by another scholar, rather paradoxically, of Pliny's report to Trajan about the Christians in Book X, where echoes of Livy are alleged (X. 96 nn.). The echoes turn out to be genuine but faint and dim, and in no way affect the historicity of the narrative. The question is much more subtle than such critics conceive. To a man immersed by long education and continued reading in his *native* literature, the appropriate language arose from memory's store at the prompting of the theme. It is doubtful whether this is a wholly conscious process. The notion that Pliny, like a modern student writing a Latin prose, looked up suitable parallel passages in Latin literature before attempting a particular composition, does not correspond to the advice which he gave to Pedanius Fuscus on the formation of style in VII. 9. He there recommends the practice of translation from the Greek classics as a preparatory technique, not for particular occasions but for the total linguistic culture of the writer, because (s. 2) 'imitatione optimorum similia *inveniendi facultas* paratur'. He speaks of 'copying and following' Demosthenes' speech against Meidias when he wrote his *De Helvidi Ultione* but with limitations: 'quantum aut diversitas ingeniorum . . . aut causae dissimilitudo pateretur' (VII. 30. 5) and *dumtaxat figuris orationis* (I. 2. 2). He claimed also to have copied Cicero's 'paintpots' in his colourful digressions (I. 2. 4). Yet though here and in I. 5. 11-12 he claimed Cicero among his masters, and refused to be content with *eloquentia saeculi nostri,* the Panegyric exists to show how far he is from being Ciceronian. The style of this eschews the use of Ciceronian periods, and has as one of its marked characteristics the emphatic use of a verb or verbal phrase at the opening of a sentence. The limitations of 'imitation' may be seen by considering the great difference, noted in the Commentary on II. 17, between Pliny's two 'descriptions of a villa' and that of Statius, despite an occasional verbal echo. The existence of literary influences detracts no more—nor less—from the historicity of the letters than from that of any other of the consciously erudite writers of the Empire.

The Elaboration of the Extortion Letters

Something may be gleaned from a comparison of the form of the letters about extortion trials, which are the largest group of letters with a common subject, a trial before the senatorial court. Despite the similarities imposed by the subject, there are notable differences of treatment. Both the trial of Marius Priscus and that of the associates of Caecilius Classicus are presented in two letters each, one lengthy and one short (II. 11-12, III. 4, 9). Letter II. 11 describes the accusation and double trial of Priscus in a single letter, while II. 12 adds as a postscript an account of the trial of his legate. But in Book III the shorter letter is concerned with the preliminaries to the main trial, which in the Priscus case are given in the long letter. The punishments are a great feature of each description. But whereas in II. 11-12 they are given formally with the names of the consulars or consuls designate who proposed them, in III. 9. 17-18, 22 only the substance of the sentence is given without the names of the movers. This is true also of the subsidiary trial for *praevaricatio* of Norbanus in III. 9, the leader of the original accusation, although Pliny names the consulars who gave evidence against him (ibid. ss. 29-34). This deliberate variation of method, characteristic of the Letters as a whole, is hardly accidental. In both accounts the narrative is clear and historical, but in the second the arrangement is less straightforward than in the former. Apart from the absence of names of the movers of motions, the order of events is altered so as to keep the trial of Norbanus until the end of the letter, though it took place between two parts of the main trial (nn. ad loc.).

In IV. 9, the trial of Bassus, Pliny combines the methods of II. 11 and III. 9. A single letter contains the whole story of the accusation, the trial, and an ineffective counter-accusation against the prosecutors, as in III. 9, while the sentences are given as in II. 11 with the names of the proposers.

The following conclusion may be hazarded. The Pricus letters may well be reports written shortly after the occasion, though it would be more natural for Pliny to have reported by itself the first part of the Priscus trial, which was separated by many months from his main trial. The second letter, about the subsidiary trial of Firminus, reports separately the events of a session of the Senate later than the condemnation of Priscus himself. Possibly II. 11 is an amalgamation of two news-letters about the different phases of Priscus' own trial. The main Classicus letter, III. 9, is so complex that it must be the product of leisured composition and written in deliberate contrast to II. 11.[14] But this consideration tends to guarantee the character of III. 4 as a genuine letter, especially as its contents are summarized at the beginning of III. 9, so that it is not neces-

sary for the understanding of III. 9. Some details in III. 4 of Pliny's invitation to lead the case against Classicus closely echo a statement about his circumstances at this time in a letter to Trajan (X. 8): both refer to a visit to Tifernum, on official leave, to organize the building of a temple at his own expense. Also Pliny inserts in III. 4 a rather clumsy reminder of the title of his public office, unnecessary for his correspondent but essential in a publication: 'cum . . . in Tuscos excucurrissem, accepto *ut praefectus aerari commeatu*'. Contrarily, he obscurely refers to the present brief as 'munere hoc iam tertio' (s. 8 n.), although in this letter he has only mentioned one other of his two previous extortion cases. The statement would be clear to his friend and correspondent, but is obscure to the general reader. III. 4 then has all the signs of a genuine letter revised for publication.

The Varenus case is treated quite differently from the rest (V. 20, VI. 13, VII. 6, 10). Each phase of the prosecution is described in a separate letter of short or medium length. Since the case never came on for formal trial there was no occasion for a report like II. 11 or III. 9. The phases described in each letter were short procedural operations in the Senate or before the Princeps. The best parallel to V. 20 and VI. 13, which describe the manœuvres of the accuser and the accused in the opening phase, is the pair of letters V. 4 and 13 about the charge of *destitutio* against the advocate Tuscilius, handled in two sessions of the Senate. It cannot be maintained that Pliny was deliberately avoiding the use of long letters in these books: contrast the great length of the villa letter and the Vesuvius pair (V. 6, VI. 16, 20). Hence V. 20 and VI. 13 cannot be dismissed as fictitious epistles on that ground. It is noteworthy that the third Varenus letter (VII. 6) contains an unusual and deliberate digression (above, p. 15). This is an anecdote about an earlier criminal trial in which Pliny appeared, unconnected with Varenus. It is possible that since the Varenus case did not allow Pliny to present himself in the Ciceronian role that he assumes for himself in the trials of II-IV, he has expanded this letter to make the most of his achievements. So too in VII. 33 he resurrects the story of his advocacy against Baebius Massa in the year 93, and in IX. 13 he resurrects the attempted prosecution of Certus in 97. In Book VIII, lacking a trial altogether, he produced Ep. 14, the long procedural argument from the debate of 105, as a substitute.

This group of letters reveals the development of the technique of managing a complicated subject in an *epistula curatius scripta*. These letters have developed from genuine letters, and within limits Pliny is faithful to the principle of authenticity. When there are no long trials there are no long letters, and when there are no trials at all he harks back to reporting events of an earlier period.

But these latter reports are dressed up in a possibly genuine contemporary disguise, one as a submission of raw material to Tacitus for a volume of his Histories, and another as a letter of explanation to a recent pupil.

III. CHRONOLOGY OF THE LETTERS

NATURE OF THE PROBLEM

Pliny, in the letter which forms a preface to Book I, states that the order of the Letters is not chronological, 'non servato temporis ordine', but that he took them as he found them: 'ut quaeque in manus venerat'. Some of the early commentators, notably Masson, assumed that this applied to all nine books, and that there was no chronological order either in individual books or in the series as a whole. Mommsen in his study of Pliny's life rudely reversed this doctrine, holding that the nine books are in chronological order, and that each book contains the letters of a specific period, in order likewise. Pliny's remark was taken as a literary gesture intended to give an air of artificial carelessness to the first volume. Mommsen had two main arguments. First, it is easy to discern series of chronologically arranged letters about particular topics both within separate books and divided between consecutive books. Second, in each book, letters of which the content can be exactly dated fall within narrow limits, and the dates that can be established thus for the nine books are in chronological order. From these arguments Mommsen constructed the theory of 'book-dates'—that the letters in each book all belong to the period of the datable letters, none earlier, none later. On the general chronology thus established Mommsen based his account of Pliny's life. It was because of certain difficulties that then arose over the dating of some events in Pliny's career—and particularly the indictments of Classicus and Bassus— that two generations of scholars criticized or rejected the rigidity of Mommsen's scheme, and raised fresh difficulties over the dating of a number of other letters. The more moderate, notably Schultz, held that though Mommsen's framework was generally correct individual letters in any book might be earlier than the date of the bulk of the letters of the book. Others, such as Asbach, suggested that the books were published in groups a good deal later than the apparent dates of composition, and hence that the spread of letters in each group—and book—was much wider than Mommsen's system allowed. The most radical, including C. Peter and Otto, abandoned the chronology of Mommsen, and returned to the position of Masson. For historical purposes, it may be observed, the more moderate criticism is as disturbing as the more radical, since no letter which is not internally datable need belong to the 'book-date'.

Two remarks may be made about the reaction to Mommsen. First, it was piecemeal and was concerned with particular letters. None of Mommsen's critics started from an analysis of the collection as a whole, and none seems to have had anything like Mommsen's knowledge of the letters. Second, as Merrill observed, the critics frequently contradicted one another in their arguments about particular letters. Fresh evidence from inscriptions and papyri that has accrued in the last twenty years, particularly in the calendars of Ostia and Potentia, has given the years of several consuls and suffect consuls mentioned in the Letters but hitherto undated, and the advance of prosopographical study has clarified the careers of many other officials who occur in them. The new evidence has tended to confirm the general scheme of Mommsen against his critics, and to overthrow some of their principal strictures. But it is still true that there are letters in the first three and the last two books that do not conform to the rigidity of Mommsen's chronology.

The remark in I. 1 on the lack of chronological order in the Letters, which had much weight with the critics of Mommsen, only counts against his type of chronological scheme if it can be proved that all nine books were published together. But this has not been maintained, still less proved, by any of the principal studies of the Letters. On the usual, and equally non-proven, theory of publication by triads (pp. 52 f.), the remark can only apply to the first three books. But the conjoint publication of I-III is decidedly uncertain, whatever may be held about the conjoint publication of the later books (p. 52). The most reasonable interpretation of I. 1 is that this remark refers only to the internal order of the letters in that book—and possibly in subsequent books—and not to the chronology of the successive books as wholes. The weakest point in Mommsen's system is the insistence that the internal order of letters in each book is chronological, although serial letters on the same topic are naturally given in serial order. Pliny may intend to warn his reader that unlike the editors of Cicero's Letters, which he allusively claims as his model, he has made variety of topic rather than chronology the guiding principle of the internal arrangement, so far as this was possible within groups of letters belonging to limited periods (pp. 46 f.).

The stream of criticism continued unchecked after Otto's article on the life of Pliny, through von Premerstein's discussion of the career of Julius Bassus— relevant to the dates of letters in Books IV-VII—down to more recent discussions by Hanslik, who alone showed a slight hesitancy in the face of the latest evidence, and Monti, who has attempted the positive re-dating of certain letters on internal evidence. Recently the school of Otto was challenged by Syme, who in an appendix of his *Tacitus* boldly and briefly reaffirmed the chronology of Mommsen, with minor reservations. But this discussion, though cogent, was not based on an exhaustive examination of the Letters as a whole.

Historians have generally paid little attention to the interrelationship of the letters that have no special historical significance. The miscellaneous character of the collection has discouraged the study of it as a whole. But in the course of such a study as the present a remarkable number of obscure links and connexions emerge, concerning the journeys and holidays, and the literary development of Pliny, which put the question of serial order and chronology in a new light. When this material is combined with the newer epigraphical information, the chronology can be established book by book on a sounder foundation. This is a lengthy task involving a large number of particular points. For clarity the following procedure has been adopted. The conclusions reached in the Commentary about the date and connexions of each letter are here summarized book by book; the detailed argument is to be found in the Commentary. The analysis seeks to show what can be reasonably established by an impartial critic about the compilation and publication dates of each book, without trying to defend or attack a particular thesis.

In this analysis the term 'book-date' means the period covered by the datable contemporary events described in the component letters of each book. This is not necessarily the same as the date of the compilation of the book in its present form, and still less of its publication. When such book-dates can be established, the question arises next whether letters in each book that lack not only dates but any sort of link with dated letters belong to the same period. Some light is cast on this question, and on the allied question of publication, by a systematic inquiry, hitherto attempted incompletely and only by H. Peter, into the distribution of the letters by categories of subject-matter throughout the nine books. This second inquiry also helps to illuminate the literary method and purpose of Pliny in making this collection. A special section is devoted to the dates of the extortion trials, and the letters about them, which were the starting-point of the controversy about chronology, and which have been the object of extensive and contradictory discussion.

Notes

1. The basic discussion is H. Peter, *Der Brief in der römischem Litteratur* (Abh. Philol.-hist. Kl. d. Kgl.-Sächs. Ges. der Wiss. XX (1903)): ch. v is devoted to Pliny.

2. Chiefly for the villa theme, *VL,* 142 ff.

3. Sen. *Ep.* 75. 1: 'quis enim accurate loquitur nisi qui vult putide loqui?'

4. *VL,* 147 ff. Cf. R. Syme, *Tacitus,* 97.

5. Cf. Guillemin, *VL,* ch. iii, for a detailed study: the parallels with Martial are always the most convincing. For an extreme instance cf. IX. 7. 4 n.

6. Cf. ibid. 125 ff.

7. See I. 1. 1 n.

8. Cf. Guillemin, *VL,* 128, 130, 146-7, who, however, did not seriously consider the exceptions, which are significant for the genuine character of the letters.

9. See Guillemin, *VL,* ch. iii, for an analysis of extensive poetical influences in Pliny's letters. But some of the parallels seem rather forced.

10. In general see J. Niemirska-Pliszczyńska, *De elocutione Pliniana,* Lublin, 1955, the latest of a long series of studies on this theme, with bibliography p. 163. For the diminutives, ibid. 10, 14. Also, d'Agostino, *I diminutivi in Plinio il Giovane,* Turin, 1931. O.C.T. disallows *prominulam,* V. 6. 15 n.

11. C. Hofacker, *De clausulis C. Caecili Plini Secundi,* diss. Bonn., 1903. Or, Th. Zieliński, 'Das Ausleben des Clauselgesetzes in der röm. Kunstprosa', *Philologus Suppl.* X (1907), 431 f.

12. *VL,* 150; cf. II. 15. 1 n.

13. Commentary, ad loc. The end of s. 6, 'multum me intra silentium tenui' could have been followed immediately by s. 14, 'consules, ut Polyaenus postulabat, omnia integra principi servaverunt'.

14. The reviser's hand is revealed in s. 16: '*solet dicere Claudius Restitutus qui mihi respondit . . . nunquam sibi tantum caliginis offusum, . . .*', which was hardly written immediately after the event.

Bibliography

Th. Mommsen, *Gesammelte Schriften* (Berlin, 1907), iv 366: *Hermes,* iii (1869), 31 ff.

H. F. Stobbe, 'Plinius' Briefe', *Philologus,* xxx (1870), 347 ff.

C. Peter, 'Plinius der Jüngere', *Philologus* xxxii (1872), 698 ff.

I. Asbach, 'Zur Chronologie der Briefe des j. Plinius', *Rhein. Mus.* xxxvi (1881), 38 ff.

M. Schultz, *De Plinii Epistulis Quaestiones Chronologicae* (Diss. Inaug.), Berlin, 1899.

H. Peter, 'Der Brief in d. röm. Litt.', *Abh. Sächs. Akad. Wiss. Phil.-hist. Kl.* xx (1903), ch. v. 101 ff.

W. Otto, 'Zur Lebensgeschichte des j. Plinius', *Sb. Bayer. Akad. Wiss. Phil.-hist. Kl.* 1919, 17 ff.

A. von Premerstein, 'C. Iulius Quadratus Bassus', ibid. 1934, 3, 72 ff.

R. HANSLIK, 'Der Prozess des Varenus Rufus', *Wiener Studien*, 1 (1932), 195 ff.; 'Zu Plinius' Ep. V. 1', ibid. lii (1934), 156 ff.; 'Die neuen Fragmente von Ostia, etc.', ibid. lxiii (1948), 133 ff.

S. PRETE, 'Saggi Pliniani', *Studi di filologia classica,* i (Bologna 1948), 84 ff.

S. MONTI, 'Pliniana', *Rend. Acc. Arch. Litt. Bell. Art. Napoli,* xxvii (1952), 161 ff.; xxviii (1953), 311 ff.; xxxii (1957), 90 ff.; *Ann. Fac. Litt. Napoli,* 1956, 69 ff.

R. SYME, *Tacitus* (Oxford, 1958), ii, Appendix xxi, 660 ff.

J. ZARANKA, *De Plinii Epistularum Novem Libris Quaestiones Chronologicae.* This doctoral dissertation from Louvain 1949 has not been published except in dactylographic form, and is otherwise known only in a brief summary of cardinal points in *Lustrum,* vi (1961), 285 f.

ABBREVIATIONS

The following abbreviations are frequently used throughout the Commentary.

Acta Ap.: Acts of the Apostles.

Act. Arv.: Acta Fratrum Arvalium in *CIL* vi.

AE: L'Année épigraphique, Paris.

A-J: F. W. Abbot, A. C. Johnson, *Municipal Administration in the Roman Empire,* Princeton, 1926.

Am. J.: Phil. American Journal of Philology, Baltimore.

Ap. Ty.: Philostratus, *De Apollonio Tyanensi.*

Asbach: I. Asbach, 'Zur Chronologie der Briefe des jüngeren Plinius', *Rhein. Mus.* xxxvi (1881), 38 ff.

Ashby, *Top. Dict.:* T. Ashby, S. B. Platner, *A Topographical Dictionary of Ancient Rome,* Oxford, 1929.

Bardon: H. Bardon, *La Littérature latine inconnue,* Paris, 1952-6.

B.C.: Appian, *Bella Civilia Romanorum.*

B.G.: Caesar, *Bellum Gallicum.*

C. Bosch: *Die kleinasiatischen Münzen der römischen Kaiserzeit* ii. 1, Stuttgart, 1935.

U. Brasiell: o *La Repressione penale in diritto romano,* Napoli, 1937.

Bruns: C. G. Bruns, *Fontes iuris Romani antiqui,* Tübingen, 1919.

BSA: Annual of the British School at Athens, London.

BSR: Papers of the British School at Rome, London.

CAH: Cambridge Ancient History, vols. x and xi, Cambridge, 1934-6.

Carcopino: J. Carcopino, *Daily Life in Ancient Rome,* London, 1941.

CERP: A. H. M. Jones, *Cities of the Eastern Roman Provinces,* Oxford, 1937.

Charlesworth, *Documents*: M. P. Charlesworth, *Documents illustrating the reigns of Claudius and Nero,* Cambridge 1939.

Chilver, *Cisalpine Gaul*: G. E. F. Chilver, *Cisalpine Gaul, Social and Economic History,* Oxford, 1941.

Chrestomathie: L. Mitteis, U. Wilcken, *Grundzüge und Chrestomathie der Papyruskunde,* i-ii, Leipzig-Berlin, 1912.

Chron. Min.: Chronica Minora, ed. C. Frich, Leipzig, 1892.

CIG: Corpus Inscriptionum Graecarum, i-iv, Berlin, 1828-77.

CIL: Corpus Inscriptionum Latinarum, i-xvi, Berlin, 1863-1936.

Cl. Phil.: Classical Philology, Chicago.

Cl. Q.: The Classical Quarterly, London.

Cl. Rev.: The Classical Review, Oxford.

Cod. Iust.: Codex Iustinianus in *Corpus Iuris Civilis.*

D. or *Dig.: Digesta Iuris Romani* in *Corpus Iuris Civilis.*

Dio, *Or.:* Dio Chrysostomus, *Orationes.*

Ditt. *Syll.* or *D.S.:* W. Dittenberger, *Sylloge Inscriptionum Graecarum,* i-iv, Leipzig, 1915-24.

Diz. Epigr.: E. de Ruggiero, *Dizionario epigrafico di Antichità Romane,* Rome, 1886-.

Domaszewski, *Rangordnung*: A. von Domaszewski, *Die Rangordnung des römischen Heeres,* Bonn, 1908.

D. Pen. R.: Th. Mommsen, *Droit pénal romain,* Paris, 1903.

Dörner, *Inschiften*: F. K. Dörner, *Inschriften und Denkmäler aus Bithynien* (Istanbule Forschungen 14), Berlin, 1941.

Dörner, *Reise*: idem, *Bericht über eine Reise in Bithynien* (Öst. Ak. Wiss. ph.-hist. Kl. D. 75, 1), Wien, 1952.

DPR: Th. Mommsen, *Droit public romain* i-vi, Paris, 1889-93.

D-S Ch.: Daremberg, E. Saglio, *Dictionnaire des antiquités grecques et romaines,* Paris, 1877-1919.

Ec. Survey: T. Frank, *An Economic Survey of Ancient Rome,* vols. i-v, Baltimore, 1933-40.

E-J: V. Ehrenberg, A. H. M. Jones, *Documents Illustrating the Reigns of Augustus and Tiberius*[2], Oxford, 1955.

Ep. de Caes.: Anonymous, *Epitome de Caesaribus,* printed in texts of Aurelius Victor.

Fast. Pot. or *F. Pot. : Fasti Potentiae,* in *AE* 1949, n. 23.

FIR: C. G. Bruns, O. Gradenvitz, *Fontes Iuris Romani,* Tübingen, 1909.

FIRA: S. Riccobono, *Fontes Iuris Romani Anteiustiniani,* i-iii, Florence, 1941-3.

FO: Fasti Ostienses in *Inscriptiones Italiae,* XIII. i, ed. A. Degrassi, Rome, 1947. See below pp. 734-6.

Fr. Vat.: Fragmenta Vaticana in *FIRA.*

Garzetti, C., Inc.: A. Garzetti, *Nerva,* Rome, 1950; numbers in the list of senators, certainly and uncertainly attributed.

GC: A. H. M. Jones, *The Greek City,* Oxford, 1940.

Gnomon Id.: Forma Idiologi, in *FIRA* i.

GS: Th. Mommsen, *Gesammelte Schriften,* i-viii, Berlin, 1905-13.

Guillemin, ad loc.: A.-M. Guillemin, *Pline le Jeune, Lettres,* Paris, 1927-47.

Hartleben: See L-H.

HE: Eusebius, *Historia Ecclesiae.*

IGRR: Inscriptiones Graecae ad res Romanas pertinentes, Paris, 1911-27, ed. R. Cagnat etc.

ILA: Insciptions Latines d'Afrique, ed. R. Cagnat, A. Merlin, Paris, 1923.

I.L.Al.: Inscriptions Latines de l'Algérie, i-ii, ed. S. Gsell, H.-G. Pflaum, Paris, 1922, 1957.

ILS: H. Dessau, *Inscriptiones latinae selectae,* Berlin, 1892-1916.

Index Verborum: Printed in Longolius, below, but now replaced by X. Jacques, J. von Oosteghem, *Index de Pline le Jeune,* Brussels, 1965.

Ital. agr.: V. A. Sirago, *L'Italia agraria sotto Traiano,* Louvain, 1958.

JB: Bursians Jahresberichte.

Jones, *Cities*: See *C.E.R.P.*

Jones, *Greek City*: See *G.C.*

JRS: The Journal of Roman Studies, London.

Lambrechts: P. Lambrechts, *La Composition du Sénat Romain,* Antwerp, 1936.

Lex Mal.: Lex municipii Malacitani in *FIRA.*

L-H: K. Lehman-Hartleben, *Plinio il Giovane, Lettere Scelte,* Florence, 1936.

Liebenam: W. Liebenam, *Städteverwaltung im römischen Kaiserreiche,* Leipzig, 1900.

Longolius: *Caii Plinii Secundi Epistolarum libros decem cum notis selectis.* G. Cortius, P. D. Longolius, Amsterdam, 1734.

Magie, *Romans*: D. Magie, *Roman rule in Asia Minor to the end of the third century after Christ,* i-ii, Princeton, 1950.

Marquardt, *Manuel*: J. Marquardt, *La Vie privée des romains,* Paris, 1892-3.

Merrill: E. T. Merrill, *Pliny, Select Letters,* London, 1903.

Monti, *Pliniana*: See p. 23.

O.C.T.: Plinius Minor, *Epistulae,* Oxford, 1963.

OGIS: W. Dittenberger, *Orientis Graeci Inscriptiones Selectae* i-ii, Leipzig, 1903-5.

Otto: W. Otto, 'Zur Lebensgeschichte des jüngeren Plinius', *S. B. Bayer. Ak. Wiss.* Phil.-hist. Kl. 1919, 1, ff.

Peter: C. Peter, 'Plinius der Jüngere', *Philologus,* xxxiii (1873), 698 f.

Pflaum, *Proc. Eq.*: H. G. Pflaum, *Les Procurateurs équestres sous le Haut-empire Romain,* Paris, 1950.

Pflaum.: n. idem, *Les Carrières procuratoriennes équestres sous le Haut-empire romain,* Paris, 1960-1.

Philol.: Philologus, Zeitschift für klassisches Altertum, Leipzig.

PIR: Prosopographia Imperii Romani, ed. 1, Berlin, 1897-8, ed. 2, 1933-.

P. Ox.: The Oxyrhyncus Papyri, London, 1898-.

Prete: S. Prete, 'Saggi Pliniani', *Studi di Fil. Class. I,* Bologna, 1948.

Rangordnung: A. von Domaszweski, *Die Rangordnung des römischen Heeres,* Bonn, 1908.

RC: A.N. Sherwin-White, *The Roman Citizenship,* Oxford, 1939.

RE: Paulys Real-enzyclopädie der klassischen Altertumswissenschaft,[2] Stuttgart, 1894-.

RG: Res Gestae Divi Augusti in E-J.

Rev. Int. Dr. Ant.: Revue internationale des droits de l'antiquité, Brussels, 1948-.

RIC: H. Mattingly, E. A. Sydenham, *The Roman Imperial Coinage*, ii, London, 1926.

Rev. Hist. Dr. Fr.: *Revue historique de droit français et étranger*, Paris, 1922-.

Schultz: M. Schultz, *De Plinii epistulis quaestiones chronologicae*, Berlin, 1899.

SEG: *Supplementum Epigraphicum Graecum*, Leyden, 1923-.

SEHRE: M. Rostovtzeff, *The Social and Economic History of the Roman Empire*[2], i-ii, Oxford, 1957, revised by P. M. Fraser.

Sent.: *Pauli Sententiae receptae Paulo tributae* in *FIRA* ii.

SG: (Eng. Tr.) L. Friedländer, *Roman Life and manners under the early Empire* (translated by L. A. Magnus), i-iv, London, 1908-13.

SHA: Scriptores Historiae Augustae.

Stout: S. E. Stout, *Scribe and Critic at work in Pliny's Letters*, Indiana University publications, Bloomington, 1954.

Strack: P. L. Strack, *Untersuchungen zur römischen Reichsprägung des zweiten Jahrhunderts*, i, Stuttgart, 1931.

Studi Paoli: *Studi in onore di Ugo Enrico Paoli*, Firenze, 1955.

Syme, *Tac.*: R. Syme, *Tacitus*, Oxford, 1958.

Tab. Her.: *Tabula Heracleensis* in *FIRA* i.

T. A. Ph. A.: *Transactions and Proceedings of the American Philological Association*, Philadelphia.

Thes. L. L.: *Thesaurus Linguae Latinae*.

Tit. Ulp.: *Tituli ex corpore Ulpiani* in *FIRA* ii.

Vidman, *Étude*: L. Vidman, *Étude sur la correspondance de Pline le jeune avec Trajan* (Rozpravy Československé Ak. Věd. 70), Praha, 1960.

VL: A.-M. Guillemin, *Pline et la vie littéraire de son temps*, Paris, 1929.

von Arnim: H. von Arnim, *Leben und Werke des Dio von Prusa*, Berlin, 1898.

VS: Philostratus, *Vitae Sophistarum*.

Waddington, *Receuil* W. H. Waddington, *Receuil général des monnaies grecques d'Asie mineure*, Paris, 1904-9. Second ed. Paris, 1925.

Weber, *Festgabe*: W. Weber, *Festgabe von Fachgenossen v. K. Müller*, Tübingen, 1922.

W-C: M. McCrum, A. G. Woodhead, *Select Documents of the Principates of the Flavian Emperors*, Cambridge, 1961.

WS: *Wiener Studien*, Zeitschrift für klassische Philologie, Wien.

Zaranka: J. Zaranka, *De Plinii epistularum . . . quaestiones chronologicae.* Dissertation, Louvain, 1949. See p. 23.

ZS: *Zeitschrift des Savigny-Stiftung für Rechtsgeschichte* (Romanistische Abt.).

Bibliographical Summaries

Items appear annually in *Année Philologique* under the heading *Plinius Minor*. The following contain periodic summaries of writings in the twentieth century.

Bursians Jahresbericht: cliii (1911), 1 ff. (K. Burkhard).
ccxxi (1929), 1 ff. (M. Schuster).
ccxlii (1934), 9 ff. (M. Schuster).
cclxxxii (1943), 38 ff. (R. Hanslik).

Also R. Hanslik, *Anzeiger für die Altertumswissenschaft*, 1955, 8. 1 ff. J. Beaujeu, *Lustrum*, vi (1961) 272 ff.

Note that in the commentary letter references to other letters in the same book are given in the form 'Ep. 23', while references to letters in other books are given by plain numbers, e.g. 'I. 23. 2', with Roman numerals indicating the book-number.

A. N. Sherwin-White (essay date April 1969)

SOURCE: Sherwin-White, A. N. "Pliny, the Man and His Letters." *Greece and Rome* 16, no. 1 (April 1969): 76-90.

[*In the following essay, Sherwin-White examines Pliny's letters and notes that they reveal much about the writer's own personality, including his humanity, generosity, boldness, his weaknesses, and his pleasant nature.*]

Pliny lived in the heyday of the Roman empire, being born in A.D. 62 in the middle of the reign of Nero, at Comum by Lake Como in north Italy, and he lived until about A.D. 112. His family were not of the old Roman nobility but belonged to the second grade of the Roman upper classes, the so-called Knights or *equites Romani*. Pliny trained to become an advocate in the courts of civil law, and partly by his talents and partly through the influence of family friends in the senatorial class he gained promotion to the senior grade of the Roman administration. He became a Roman senator when he was about twenty-eight years old, and eventually climbed to the top rung of the Roman public service. So he was in Roman terms a self-made man, the first senator of his family. But he was also a highly educated man; as a young man he attended the schools of the most famous professors of literature at Rome, and especially that of the great Quintilian, whose book on the art of rhetoric survives to show the sort of education that Pliny received.[1]

We know Pliny from a collection of his private letters which he published in a series of nine short volumes when he was about forty to forty-five years old. The letters start in the year A.D. 97, when Pliny was 35 years old and in mid-career as a Roman official, and they continue till 108, after which Pliny left Rome to take up the governorship of the province of Bithynia in northwestern Turkey. The letters cover a tremendous variety of topics—themes of public life and politics, anecdotes about high society, family life, business affairs, the literary circles of Rome, descriptions of natural scenery, and portents such as ghosts, floods, and volcanoes. But there is a caution to be made. There are letters and letters. In any age the really revealing letter is the one written white-hot and with no thought of publication, scribbled down on the spot for immediate action, report, or advice. Most of Cicero's letters are like that, and take you straight into the mind and heart of the man without screens and defences. Pliny's letters are different. Though like all good letters they are about affairs of the moment, particular occasions of pleasure and trouble, crisis or success, in the form in which Pliny published them they are not exactly spontaneous.[2]

Pliny belonged to a society that was wealthy, leisured, and overeducated on the literary side. He and his friends despite their public duties had a great deal of spare time, and they spent much of it in literary exercises of various sorts—writing verses, reciting and polishing their speeches as specimens of oratory, and listening to public readings of other people's efforts. One of their exercises was, very much as in Victorian England, the composition of private letters in a refined and polished style, and the circulation of these letters amongst themselves. Many of Pliny's friends lived not at Rome but scattered through the provincial cities of Italy where they administered their estates, which were the main source of their wealth. So like the rustic Victorians they had a great appetite for letters as a means of getting news, but they expected to have their letters written in the best Latin prose. Such letters were called 'letters written in style'—*litterae curiosius scriptae*. Pliny was the first Latin writer to have the idea of developing this kind of letter into an art form, written with great concentration and according to a set of rules apparently invented by himself. Pliny had a flair for this kind of writing and succeeded in producing a series of miniature masterpieces, perhaps of craftsmanship rather than art.

He succeeds because the basic framework, the hard core, was a genuine news-letter, and because the really was a master of language so long as he worked in a small compass.

Pliny was a professional advocate, a pleader in the courts, trained in all the artifices of Roman rhetoric. We have a long speech of his, a formal address to the emperor Trajan, describing and praising the first two years of his reign. The speech is terrible—because Pliny took all the space he could, elaborated everything, repeated everything. But in his letters he proceeded on the opposite principle, that of compression. The basic rule was that each letter deal only with a single subject or event, and that it must be short. Most of the letters are from a third of a page of twenty-eight lines to two or three such pages long. Greater length is allowed only when the subject is genuinely big, like the eruption of Vesuvius, or a court trial. Such subjects get only six or seven pages at most, and the matter is squeezed into what for them is a short space. So Pliny practised compression, but at the same time used the sharp, emotive, powerful, or colourful language of the Roman rhetorical schools, according to the needs of each topic, as in this account of the murder of a Roman magnate.[3] 'Something terrible has happened to the senator Larcius Macedo. His slaves did it. He was a proud and cruel master—he never could forget that his own father had been a slave. Macedo was taking his bath, when his slaves poured round him. They hit him in the throat, in the face, chest and belly too. When they thought he was done for they threw him on top of the furnace casing, to see if he was still alive. He either did not feel it or pretended not to, and shammed dead. Then they carried him out, as if finished off by the heat. Some loyal slaves took him over, and the palace women came howling and shrieking round him. The noise and the cool air revived him, his eyes flickered, and he stirred. Realizing that he was safe, he admitted that he was alive. The other slaves all fled, but most of them were caught, and the rest are being hunted down. So Macedo survived long enough to see his own murder punished.'[4]

That is a good piece of reporting. Just the right details are briefly picked out, and just the right amount of explanatory comment is provided. We see it happening and understand why. The man was a brute to his servants, and had it coming to him. It is Pliny's narrative style at its best. The particular effect depends on the side comments, which here are mildly satirical.

Max Beerbohm once said that Pliny's letters were the only writings of antiquity that could be enjoyed without knowing anything about the ancient world. But Beerbohm himself lived in a society of polished ease, wealth, and literary sophistication that was not so very different in its setting from the sort of society in which Pliny lived. It is often more difficult for us than for Max. It is no good reading Pliny if you are looking for modern attitudes of mind. You must allow for the standards and values of his own day. Many people are put off liking Pliny by the tone of a certain letter written about his wife Calpurnia. A year after his marriage he wrote to his wife's aunt like this: 'As you are devoted to your niece you will, I am sure, be delighted to hear that Calpurnia is turning out to be a regular chip of the old block. She is very quick-witted and not at all extravagant. She is really devoted to me, which shows that she is not a flirt, and out of her liking for me she has taken to literature. She reads my speeches, and even learns them by heart. When I am going to plead in court she arranges for messengers to report how I have done, and how much applause I have received. Altogether she behaves just as I should expect from a girl brought up in your household.'[5]

Not at all the sort of letter a newly-wed is likely to write or to want written about his or her partner in this year of grace. But when you remember that this was a normal Roman marriage between a man of forty-two—who had already buried two wives—and a girl of fifteen or sixteen at most, the tone becomes less surprising. Roman marriages never began as love-affairs between young folk, but were family matches of convenience.[6] Yet Pliny is much more modern than he sounds at first. He wants to share his chief interests with his young wife, and he looks forward to a genuine life partnership. He adds: 'I have great hopes that we will build up a growing and enduring bond of unity.' That was not the normal expectation in Roman society, in which divorce was easy and frequent. But Pliny often refers to long-lasting marriages with warm respect. Thus: 'My dear Macrinus has had a heavy blow. He has lost a wife who would have been exceptional even in the old days. They lived together for thirty-nine years without any quarrels or bad feeling. It must be a great consolation to Macrinus that he had so fine a wife for so long, but I shall be worried about him until I hear that the wound is healing.'[7] Pliny writes to his young wife directly in terms of strong affection when she is away from Rome. 'We are not used to being parted. At night I wake up and think about you, and in the daytime my feet draw me to the boudoir where I used to see you. I turn back at the door of the empty room sick and sad, like a rejected lover. I am only free from these *tortures* when I am busy in the law-courts.'[8] That may sound to our ears affected and stilted, or quite ordinary—any nineteenth-century husband to any wife. But in fact it was something new. Pliny was not writing in the conventional language of a Roman marriage, but for the first time in the ancient world a writer was applying the language of lovers to the relationship of marriage. In Ovid and Propertius this kind of talk is reserved for semi-romantic grand passions of a very different sort.

Pliny is the first man known to have written a love-letter to his own wife. But you would never have understood that unless you knew something about the social habits of the Roman world.

Pliny could be malicious on occasion. He particularly detested his great rival, the successful lawyer Regulus, who had once been a prosecutor in political trials on the side of the government and had ruined certain friends of Pliny. There are five substantial letters about Regulus, all hostile.[10] No one else receives this treatment in Pliny's letters. Pliny starts by exulting over the great shock that Regulus had when his patron the emperor Domitian died:[6] 'Have you seen anyone more frightened and repressed than Regulus since the death of Domitian? The memory of his crimes is troubling him, and he is visiting all my friends with abject pleas to manage a reconciliation between us.' Pliny was planning a prosecution of Regulus to avenge his friends. But he remarked at the end of a long letter: 'I won't do anything until I have asked my friend Mauricus for his advice. I know Regulus will be hard to attack. He is rich, and has many political friends, and plenty of people are afraid of him—which is more effective than liking.'[11] In the end the cautious Pliny dropped his prosecution and took his revenge in words. Regulus was an old man with a young son. The boy died, and Pliny wrote an unpleasant letter about them: 'Regulus is mourning his son like a madman. The boy had a number of pets—ponies, dogs, and cage-birds. Regulus had them all slain round the boy's grave. That was not an act of mourning but a kind of showing-off. He is now confining himself to his country-house outside Rome, which has great porticoes filled with statues of himself. He says that he wants to marry again—behaving with his usual bad taste. You will soon hear of the marriage of an old man who is still in formal mourning. Not that Regulus has said as much—but he is bound to do whatever is unbecoming.'[12]

That is Pliny in his most malicious mood. Elsewhere his touch is usually lighter, and combines well with his gift for catching the essence of the social scene. Consider this account of a well-born lady, who had long outlived the days of her glory at the imperial court: 'Ummidia Quadratilla has died at the age of nearly eighty. She was a lively old lady until her last illness, and much more powerfully built than is normal with our society beauties. She had rather naughty tastes for an old woman. She kept a troupe of opera singers, and was much too lavish with them for a lady of her station. But she would not let her young grandson Quadratus watch them, either at home or in the public theatre. I have heard her say when she was questioning me about her grandson's education, that it was her habit as a woman of unfettered leisure to relax by playing dice and watching her actors, but when she was going to do this she always told Quadratus to go away and study.' This letter is the more interesting when you realize that Ummidia was a relict of the gay, pleasure-loving court of the emperor Nero. It was now fifty years later, social attitudes were becoming stricter, and Ummidia, though she does not change her own ways, yet brings her grandson up according to the new conventions.[13]

Pliny preferred the sober young Quadratus to the gay old grandmother. He was one of several young men whose training for the career of advocate was supervised by Pliny, who was a great encourager of young talent. He writes with enthusiasm about their first successes in court: 'What a happy day for me! I sat on the bench of the metropolitan magistrate and heard two brilliant young men speaking on opposite sides in a case, Salinator and Quadratus. They will be a glory to our times and to Latin literature itself. They have all the good qualities wanted in orators—and they regard me as their tutor: all the people knew that they were my pupils and following in my footsteps.' There is a certain mixture of simplicity and conceit in this.[14] Pliny was a man well pleased with himself and with his successful career. Many moderns don't like this, but his self-satisfaction is ever redeemed by a touch of naiveté. Once he wrote a short letter about an unusual incident in the courts. 'Rejoice on my account,' he said. 'Rejoice for the common cause. There is still respect for the art of oratory. Yesterday when I was going to speak in the inheritance court, the hall was so crowded that I could only get in through the judges' dais. What is more, a well-dressed young fellow lost his tunic in the struggle for a place, and stood wearing only his toga for seven hours while listening to me speaking. What a glorious tribute! There really is an audience for good oratory.' It is hardly possible not to like a man who could be as simple as that, even if one quails at the thought of his seven-hour speech.[15]

This simplicity appears in Pliny's friendly and generous attitude towards his slaves and freedmen. This was far from the rule in Roman society, which was normally harsh and utilitarian in dealing with servile workers. Once Pliny was worried by the sickness of his favourite trained reader, the freedman Zosimus. The professional reader was the ancient equivalent of TV, cinema, and radiogram. Pliny explains: 'Zosimus is a trained comedy actor. He has a first-class voice and recites with intelligence and taste. But he is equally good at reading oratory, history, and poetry. You can see how many of my interests he caters for. Besides, I am fond of the man, and his dangerous condition makes me fonder. A few years ago after an exhausting performance he showed symptoms of tuberculosis. So I sent him on a voyage to Egypt from which he returned much better. Recently when he was giving a long series of recitations the cough came back again. So, my dear Paulinus, I should like to send him to your country-house in Provence. I have often heard you say the climate and the local milk are very good for these cases. Please write to your steward to prepare a room for Zosimus, and to look after him in every way.'[16]

This letter shows the kindliness in Pliny, but it also shows the compressed and crystalline self-explanatory style of a first-rate letter-writer. It is the sort of thing Beerbohm admired in Pliny. Never a word too many, though all the necessary information about Pliny's feelings and the state of the patient is given. There is no unnecessary repetition, no rhetorical expansion. This is the general quality of the letters. The insistence on brevity saved Pliny from the fearful faults of his grand rhetorical style as revealed in his *Panegyric of Trajan,* where every fact and point, every adjective and adverb, is swollen and multiplied in a series of turgid restatements. Only twice did Pliny write a letter in that style, and each time the result was a disastrously bad letter.[17] In each he was pleading a case to which he was personally committed, and wrote a speech instead of a letter of description. They were both about the status of freedmen, and in one he pours out his indignation at the insolent behaviour of a notorious imperial secretary who was too big for his boots. These two were among the longest of Pliny's letters. 'I set aside the fact that the honour of a Roman magistrate was being offered to the servile personage of Pallas. I set aside the fact that the Roman senate proposed that the creature Pallas should be induced, nay compelled, to wear the official trappings of a Roman senator. These were transient monstrosities. The worst of it was that the Roman senate humbly thanked the emperor in the name of Pallas—in the name of Pallas if you please—and no ceremony of purification was thought necessary.' That is the kind of thing. Good ranting perhaps—but not delicate writing.[18]

Pliny in fact uses many devices of Roman rhetoric throughout the letters, but so economically that one is hardly conscious of them. The piling up of adjectives, for example, does not offend our ears because each one is saying something different. The freedman Zosimus is described as 'homo probus officiosus litteratus'—personally honest, scrupulous in his professional duties, and a man of wide reading. The three words are packed with meaning—a complete testimonial in thirteen syllables. Colourful and poetic language was another characteristic of the Panegyric. But in the letters it is reserved for the right subject at the right moment—scenes of terror or of beauty in life and nature, such as the famous description of the eruption of Vesuvius, and the destruction of the surrounding district.[19] 'Ashes were falling, and a thick fog poured over us like a river. It was utterly dark, not like a moonless or cloudy night, but as if we were caught in a shuttered room with all lights extinguished. You could hear women shrieking, children crying, and men shouting. In their extreme fear some prayed for death, many raised their hands in supplication to the gods, and many others cried out that the gods were gone and that this was the final and unending night of the world's destruction.' That is powerful writing, but the rhetorician's skill can be detected in the crescendo describing the different cries of the human sufferers: 'ululatus feminarum infantum quiritatus, clamores virorum.'[20] These verbal plays, especially in word order, do not I think, bother us much, and incidentally for good or ill they mostly disappear in translation, so that Pliny translated appears a simpler writer than he really is. Play with word order is going on all the time.[21] Pliny is very fond of inverting the word order in parallel phrases. Speaking of a prisoner under trial who had already been sentenced on another count, he says, 'It was difficult to speak against one who was crushed by the appalling nature of the charge, but protected by pity for his previous sentence.' Do you notice the arrangement? In Latin it comes out much more clearly. 'Erat ergo perquam onerosum accusare damnatum, quem ut premebat atrocitas criminis, ita quasi peractae damnationis miseratio tuebatur.'[22]

What does bother the English reader is Pliny's habit of introducing little critical asides, usually in the form of a brief moral epigram. In the Zosimus letter Pliny adds a rather chilling comment to his warm outpouring of feeling: 'Nature has so fashioned us that nothing stirs up our affection for a person so much as the fear of losing him.' In the account of the Vesuvius eruption he curiously notes: 'it was a great comfort against the threat of death that I was perishing with the universe and the universe with me.'[23] Comments of this sort, known as *sententiae,* were one of the great devices of prose style in Pliny's day, successfully managed by the historian Tacitus. They were the height of fashion, and Pliny also felt bound to introduce them.[24] But his weak epigrams are apt to deflate his effects and to check the rapidity of his narrative.

His use of them gives a somewhat misleading expression of Pliny's character. When Pliny ends an account of a criminal trial with the remark that: 'the pleasure of securing revenge is not so great as the misery of being swindled', one is bound to feel for a moment that the man is a sententious ass.[25] Now careful analysis of the Letters shows that many of them were revised and rewritten for publication from an earlier and simpler version.[26] It is at this revision stage that the *sententia* was added. Pliny himself explains his own passion for rewriting everything that he composed, often with the help of an audience of literary friends.[27] He does not say that he followed this system in composing his letters, but he certainly rewrote them, not always to their advantage. The adverse impression they sometimes

convey about Pliny himself would be much less strong if he could have brought himself to omit those unnecessary epigrams. Anyone who writes moral epigrams that don't come off is bound to appear a prig.

This somewhat accidental appearance of priggishness ties up most unfortunately with the undoubted fact that Pliny was a cautious and conservative person, who politically was an undeviating supporter of the imperial government, and took care never to criticize a reigning emperor until he was dead. His early promotion as a senator was due to the unpleasant and despotic emperor Domitian. Instead of admitting this fact, as others did, as something unavoidable, Pliny tries to give the impression, in certain political anecdotes, that he had been a secret sympathizer with the few brave men who had criticized Domitian during his lifetime, and who paid the penalty. He hints darkly that an accusation had been laid against himself which was stopped only by the emperor's death.[28] All this is unadmirable. Pliny was no hero, but perhaps he is rather likeable or forgiveable just because he was uneasy or ashamed of his cosy time under Domitian. Some of Pliny's circle had been among the victims of Domitian, and Pliny felt that he had let them down. To make some atonement Pliny published a letter describing the heroic behaviour of the lady Fannia at her trial for treason. She was sent into exile, while Pliny watched, and all he could do was to look after her interests at Rome. But he admits 'non feci paria'—'I did not pay my score'. It is a *cri de cœur.*[29]

Pliny was a political trimmer—no doubt of that—but so were nearly all his contemporaries. Let us observe him trimming on rather a grand scale. One of the most famous events at Rome under Domitian was a great scandal involving the Vestal Virgins—the sacred order of six dedicated ladies responsible for maintaining the holy fire on which the domestic health of the Roman state was, in ancient belief, thought to depend. Four of these ladies, including the very Abbess of the order, the Vestalis Maxima, were proved to have been no better than they ought to have been. This was a very serious matter. There was no alternative but punishment with death—properly it should have been in the horrid traditional form of inhumation. Domitian in fact applied this only to the Vestalis Maxima. Now this affair has been described by another contemporary—the biographer Suetonius. Though Suetonius was generally critical of Domitian he approved the punishment of the Vestals, as did every other writer who referred to it.[30] But Pliny turns all his skill as an advocate to the job of representing the now dead emperor as a bestial tyrant sentencing an innocent lady to horrible punishment for his own satisfaction: 'Domitian, who thought such examples glorified his reign, *wanted* to have the lady Vestal buried alive. He pretended to act as high priest of the Roman state, but really it was the unbridled licence of a despotic tyrant. As she walked off, the Vestal stretched out her hands to the gods and exclaimed "Does he think *me* guilty though I presided over the divine ceremonies when he marched in triumph through the streets of Rome after his victories?" Whether this was flattery or mockery due to her confidence or her contempt I cannot tell. But she maintained her plea until she was led to execution.' Then Pliny adds the revealing comment 'she went to her death, perhaps not an innocent woman, but as if she were'. Pliny knew perfectly well that the Vestal was guilty, but for his own purpose he works the story up so that all our sympathy is on the prisoner's side, and we boil with hatred of Domitian—but Pliny pulls back just at the end and avoids committing himself in a published letter to what everyone knew was a falsehood. That is what we mean when we speak of the rhetorical element and an advocate's skill in Pliny's letters.

Let us now look at Pliny as a man of business. His wealth was in land, and he frequently writes in his letters about the management of his estates. On one occasion he shows the land-hunger of a true capitalist. 'My dear Calvisius, I need your private advice. There is an estate for sale next to my estate in Tuscany. The lands interlock, and I am keen to buy, but there is a disturbing factor. Yet I am urged on by the beauty of adding to my lands. Besides, it would be economical as well as pleasant to manage two estates with the same office staff, though it is a bit unwise to invest a great sum at the same risks in the same district. It is safer to scatter one's holdings. Yet this estate is rich, fertile, and well watered. The farming is mixed—cornland, vineyards, and productive woodlands. But the working peasantry who form the tenant farmers are a poor lot. The previous owner undermined their economic position by selling up their working equipment to secure the payment of overdue rents, but they are still in arrears. I shall have to re-equip the farms with tools. What is the price, you will ask? Three millions—a reduction of two millions on its former price, which has been cut because of the bad times and the bad state of the peasants.' Pliny reveals a nice mixture of shrewdness, and financial caution, tempered by the passion of acquisition and the belief that he was on to a good thing.[31]

This shrewdness comes out again when Pliny set up a system of children's allowances for needy families at Comum. The usual way of establishing a foundation of this sort was by the gift of land or of a lump sum, since there were no stocks and shares in antiquity. Pliny first thought of handing over a group of farms to the city, which would use the rents to pay for the allowances. But then he had doubts. 'If a sum of money is paid over to the city, it will be frittered away. Give them land and they will neglect it because it is common property. So I invented a new device.' This was a complicated legal dodge. Pliny kept the farms as private property, but saddled them with a fixed charge well below the market rental value, and payable to the city. He reckoned the land would always find a tenant, and the tenant would always be able to pay, so that the children would always get their money.[32]

Pliny had a certain instinct for ingenious financial devices. Like all the landlords of his day in Italy he was faced by a drop in farming prosperity. After ten years during which he was perpetually reducing rents without any improvement in the general situation he suddenly produced a brand-new solution to the problem. He writes: 'I must make new arrangements for the letting of my farms. For the past five years despite my reductions of rent the tenants have been piling up arrears. They now quite despair of paying off their debts, and are carrying off the crops, eating everything, and storing nothing. They won't save just to benefit the owner. The only cure is to change the rental system from a fixed rent in cash to a rent in kind based on a percentage of the harvest. I shall have to form a staff of collectors and storekeepers, but there is no fairer charge than one based on the yield of each season determined by weather and soil conditions.'[33]

Pliny evidently had sharp insight and long vision in matters of business. These qualities are reflected in his career as an imperial official: three successive emperors—Domitian, Nerva, and Trajan—regarded him as an expert in financial and practical administration. As a young man, when he served as an officer in the Roman army, his commander gave him the job of checking the accounts of the provincial regiments. Back at Rome in the nineties A.D. he was appointed head of the two principal Roman treasuries in turn—the Army Bank and the Bank of Rome. Later he is found administering the drainage and sewerage system of the capital. Finally the Emperor Trajan picked him about A.D. 109 for a special mission.[34]

The prosperous Greek cities of Bithynia-with-Pontus, in north-west Turkey, had been indulging in an orgy of extravagant expenditure which threatened to ruin the economy of the province. Pliny was commissioned to examine the situation, and to set things to rights.[35] The task suited his talents, and as a literary man he would be sympathetic to the civilized but touchy Greek inhabitants. We have the record of his work in a collection of his reports to the Emperor Trajan, the only complete dossier of the activity of a Roman governor that survives. Pliny referred problems back to Rome when the solution which he preferred was contrary to the original instructions that he had been given, or when his solution conflicted with normal provincial usage.[36] One problem concerned the treatment of certain convicts. He wrote: 'In many cities convicts who were sentenced years ago to hard labour in the mines are actually serving their sentences as municipal clerks in the local civic offices, and are even receiving a regular salary. I am not at all sure what to do about this. It seems very harsh to restore to their proper sentences a pack of old men who are living quiet and useful lives, and yet it is not right to treat convicts as public servants. It would be very silly to maintain them at the cities' expense if they do no work, but perhaps dangerous not to allow them subsistence.' Pliny reveals what we would call a 'social conscience'. He does not react sharply as a disciplinarian to a somewhat scandalous situation, and he consults the emperor because he did not want to carry out the strict letter of the law. But the emperor was less kindly, and instructed Pliny to send back to the mines all convicts of less than ten years' standing.[37]

In this letter Pliny is applying the same principles and values as we find in his private letters about servants and tenants. It is not that he is a *soft* man. He had no hesitation, as he reveals in his famous letter about the Christians of Pontus, in chopping off the heads of the first batch of adult Christians hauled before him. But he is both a merciful and a practical man. When he found that the Christians were a large community, and that women and children were involved, he wrote to Rome for fresh instructions. He did not want to alter the official policy towards Christians, but he was keen to apply age differentiations in his punishments, and to follow a line that would encourage the Christians to abandon their illegal activities by releasing those who could prove that they had ceased to practise actively as Christians. Once again he was more open-minded than the emperor, who agreed to the acquittal of the lapsed Christians, but insisted on the execution of all the rest without respect for age or sex.[38]

The practicality of Pliny is seen in the affair of the fire-brigades. There had been devastating fires in the great cities of Nicaea and Nicomedia. Pliny discovered that there were no fire-brigades and no fire-fighting equipment. So he proposed that a brigade should be formed in each city on the model with which he was familiar in Italy, where it was the custom to license the guilds of city craftsmen to form an amateur brigade or fire-fighting club as a regular social service. But the emperor turned down this request flat, on the surprising ground that such arrangements were politically dangerous in the eastern provinces: the fire-brigades would become subversive associations. This was a fixed principle with the central government, which regarded the popular masses in the east with considerable suspicion. Pliny noted in his report that the proletarian crowds stood and watched the palaces of the rich burning, without lifting a finger to help.[39]

The precise observation is characteristic of Pliny. There is a group of private letters in which this gift of observa-

tion is applied to natural objects and physical phenomena in the manner of a nineteenth-century naturalist, and is combined with another modern quality—logical speculation about the causes of physical phenomena. I have touched on the letters about the eruption of Vesuvius for their colourful and dramatic effect. But Pliny's description was not vague and romantic in *method*. It is even quoted by modern volcanologists as a first-rate account of what they call a Vesuvianic type of eruption. Here is his description of the great cloud of dust-laden vapour blown out of the volcano. 'A cloud of dust had risen from a hill which was afterwards identified as Vesuvius. Its shape most resembled that of a flat-headed pine-tree. The cloud reached up into the sky as a lofty trunk which then spread out into broad horizontal branches. The mass glowed with a white sheen stained with dark blotches where it was laden with soil and ash. It rose in this shape, I believe, because it was carried up by a strong blast of air, and as this lost its force and as the weight of the component particles took effect the cloud spread out sideways.' You can observe the natural scientist at work, since Pliny gives all this as his own explanation.[40]

Pliny was fascinated by the physical presence of water. In his country villa in Tuscany, described at great length in a very detailed letter, there was water everywhere, in cunningly contrived channels and fountains.[41] Two others of his letters are devoted to descriptions of two springs of unusual character. These letters differ in an interesting manner. One of the springs is the famous fountain of Clitumnus, on the Flaminian Way near Spoleto, which is still a favourite beauty spot for its stretch of water in a parched summer landscape. 'From under a low hill, mantled by a shady forest of ancient cypress, there issue a number of streams of varying size, which join and spread into a broad pool, clear and glassy. Driven by its sheer volume, the water rolls on as a river of some size, which can now take boats.' Pliny goes on to describe the merry scene at festivals, when the stream is thronged with boating parties rowing or poling hard upstream and then drifting back at leisure. He mentions the little country shrine and the local oracle that existed, with its scripts on view, like a small Italian Delphi.[42]

This is Pliny at his pleasantest, at once poetical and precise, but there are here no scientific explanations. The second letter concerns a spring near Pliny's northern home at Como in the Alpine foothills. 'My dear Sura, here is a problem worth the attention of a learned man. There is a spring in the hills round Comum which has a very strange feature. Three times a day it ebbs and flows with regular alterations in its water level. At specific intervals the water ebbs, sinks down, and floods up. If you put a ring or some other object on the dry edge it is quickly washed over and finally covered, and then in turn uncovered and left high and dry. If you stay long enough you can see this happen three times a day.' So far the facts. Then Pliny tries to explain them. He offers four different explanations, each being a speculation in terms of physical forces, though they are not all easy to understand. He imagines a current of air hidden in the earth's internal passages, which exerts pressure to open or close what he calls the throat and mouth of the spring—the narrow passage within the earth through which the water is issuing. He compares the behaviour of water in a wide bottle with a long narrow neck, bubbling and struggling against the air pressure to get out. Not a bad effort of thinking. Then Pliny uses the analogy of the tides moved by a regular recurrent force, though he seems unaware of the influence of the moon. Next he draws on the parallel of rivers checked at their mouth by strong winds from flowing out to sea. Finally he applies a difficult analogy from the water works of the Roman aqueducts, which he may have learned from his duties as Commissioner of the Roman sewers at this time. He asks: 'Is there a sort of natural water-gauge that measures a fixed quantity of water and reduces the volume of the stream, while it is collecting up the amount to make good what it has already let out? or is there some mechanism of levels, hidden inside the earth, which empties and drives out the water and checks its flow when the level is itself empty?' Pliny seems to be on the verge of inventing the idea of ball-cocks when he gives up the inquiry.[43]

Pliny was neither a scientist nor a philosopher, but as a man superficially educated in the philosophical disciplines of his own day he was a rationalist, and his rationalism is not perverted or obscured by his devotion as a writer to the cult of style. It is in the balance of these two qualities that his particular excellence lies. He was not a great writer any more than he was a great man, but he did little things well.

There you have him—a Roman of the empire whom we know better than any other Roman of that time, and he is the less admired because of it. We see his weaknesses as a man, and some of his weaknesses are the unpopular ones. He was a conventional man, and a government man—the terrible vice nowadays when it is safe to be 'agin the government'. But he was a very humane person, and he genuinely admired the few who had stood against the government. There were less courageous men at Rome than Pliny. When it seemed safe to do so he launched an accusation against the great enemy of his dead friends. But even then there were those who drew him to one side and whispered: 'Be careful what you are up to. No one knows who will succeed to the throne. You are attacking a man with

many political friends. The next emperor may be watching you.'[44] In such a Rome it was not easy to do more or to write more boldly than Pliny did. And few wrote as pleasantly.

Notes

1. For the historical background of Pliny's life and times see Sir R. Syme, *Tacitus* (Oxford, 1958), chs. iii, vii, viii; for his local setting, G. E. F. Chilver, *Cisalpine Gaul, Social and Economic History* (Oxford, 1941), ch. vi, 2; and for the details of his career my *Letters of Pliny* (Oxford, 1966), 72 ff. (cited as *Letters*). For a shorter account, A. N. Sherwin-White, *Fifty Letters of Pliny* (Oxford, 1966), ix-xv. The best account of the literary life of his circle is A.-M. Guillemin, *Pline et la vie littéraire de son temps* (Paris, 1929). The *Letters* and the *Panegyricus* are now available in O.C.T., and a modern translation in the 'Penguin' series by Mrs. Radice, who is shortly producing a new edition in the Loeb collection.

2. The character of the Letters is discussed at length in *Letters*, pp. 1-18.

3. My versions of Pliny's letters are throughout compressed and abbreviated translations and paraphrases, intended to reveal the character and flavour of the originals, to those for whom his qualities are still obscured by the formalities of his prose.

4. Pliny, *Epp.* iii. 14. For brief commentary see my *Fifty Letters*, no. 14, cited henceforth as *FL*.

5. *Epp.* iv. 19 (*FL*, no. 19).

6. See the account of a Roman engagement in *Epp.* i. 14. 8.

7. *Epp.* viii. 5.

8. *Epp.* vii. 5.

9. *Epp.* i. 5; ii. 20; iv. 2; vi. 2.

10. Domitian died October 96. He had persecuted senators who criticized his dictatorial methods.

11. From *Epp.* i. 5. 1, 8, 15.

12. *Epp.* iv. 7. 1-3.

13. *Epp.* vii. 24 (*FL*, no. 29).

14. *Epp.* vi. 11.

15. *Epp.* iv. 16.

16. *Epp.* v. 19 (*FL*, no. 24). For slaves and freedmen see J. Carcopino, *Daily Life in Ancient Rome*, 56 ff.

17. *Epp.* vii. 6 and 14.

18. *Epp.* viii. 6. Pallas held the financial secretariat (*a rationibus*) under the emperor Claudius A.D. 41-54. Tacitus recounts this affair in *Ann.* xii. 53.

19. There are two letters, *Epp.* vi. 16 and 20. Vesuvius erupted 24 August 79.

20. *Epp.* vi. 20. 13-15.

21. For a brief discussion see *FL* xvii.

22. *Epp.* ii. 11. 13 (*FL*, no. 10).

23. *Epp.* v. 19. 5; vi. 20. 17.

24. Quintilian discusses *sententiae* in *Inst.* viii. 5.

25. *Epp.* vi. 22. 8.

26. See *Letters,* pp. 14-16.

27. *Epp.* vii. 17 (*FL*, no. 27); vii. 21 (*FL*, no. 34).

28. *Epp.* vii. 27. 14 (*FL*, no. 30).

29. *Epp.* vii. 19.

30. *Epp.* iv. 11. See *Letters* ad loc. Cf. Suetonius, *Dom.* 8, 4. The trial took place between A.D. 89 and 91.

31. *Epp.* iii. 19 (*FL*, no. 16).

32. *Epp.* vii. 18. Similar foundations were established throughout Italy by Trajan and his successors.

33. *Epp.* ix. 37.

34. Cf. *FL* x-xi.

35. *FL* xiii-xv.

36. *Epp.* x, *Epistulae ad Traianum,* contains some forty major consultations and Trajan's replies, in addition to some minor and formal exchanges. The relative responsibility of Trajan, Pliny, and the Roman secretariat in the formulation of policy has been much discussed. See *Letters,* 526 ff., and F. Millar, 'Emperors at Work', *JRS* [*Journal of Roman Studies*] (1967), 9 ff.

37. *Epp.* x. 31-2 (*FL*, no. 41-2).

38. *Epp.* x. 96-7 (*FL*, no. 47-8).

39. *Epp.* x. 33-4 (*FL*, no. 43-4).

40. *Epp.* vi. 16. 5-6 (*FL*, no. 25).

41. *Epp.* v. 6, 20, 23, 36, 37, 40.

42. *Epp.* viii. 8 (*FL*, no. 37).

43. *Epp.* iv. 30 (*FL*, no. 21).

44. *Epp.* ix. 13. 10.

Elizabeth Spalding Dobson (essay date April 1982)

SOURCE: Spalding Dobson, Elizabeth. "Pliny the Younger's Depiction of Women." *The Classical Bulletin* 58, no. 6 (April 1982): 81-85.

[*In the following essay, Spalding Dobson examines Pliny's letters, focusing specifically on his portraits of intelligent, virtuous, and heroic upper-class Roman women, noting the uniqueness of these characterizations in comparison with female characterizations by Pliny's contemporaries.*]

A study of Pliny the Younger's letters to and about women provides some interesting cultural insights into the position of the aristocratic woman of Rome and its environs in the early second century A.D. At the same time, the reader gains insight into Pliny's own attitude toward these women. In view of the generally optimistic tone of Pliny's correspondence, it is not very surprising to find that the letters present a flattering and quite sympathetic view of women as his spiritual and moral equals.

Too frequently, portraits of the upper-class Roman woman of the first and second centuries A.D. emphasize the notorious and sensational. The lascivious Messalinda and the ruthless Agrippina have been immortalized in Tacitus's *Annals.* Juvenal's *Satire 6* is a diatribe against the women of his time, from the merely irritating to the truly repulsive. The intellectual and the adulteress suffer equal condemnation. As to marriage, Juvenal advises: "If you are simply devoted to one alone, bend your neck, / Bow to the yoke; no lover finds mercy in any woman."[1]

In contrast to his misogynistic contemporaries, Pliny offers a gallery of virtuous women. Discussion of the women in Pliny has usually been confined to the heroic Arria and his own dutiful wife, Calpurnia. Yet at least 57 of the 368 letters contain some reference to women.[2] Of these, only three (2.4, 6.31, 8.10) could be deemed uncomplimentary. It would not be possible to present all these letters in a short study; therefore, discussion will be confined to only some illustrative letters.

Ingrained social attitudes such as the equation of the virtuous woman with the married woman and acceptance of the inferior legal status of women were tempered in Pliny by his respect for the doctrines of Stoicism, particularly the teachings of Gaius Musonius Rufus for whom Pliny openly expresses his admiration. Although Stoics generally regarded passion as a disease, Musonius Rufus praised the marriage which brings with it love and sympathy, the complete unselfish union of interests.[3] He championed the spiritual, moral and intellectual equality of men and women. Education, especially in philosophy, will enable women to act with "excellence of disposition and nobility of character; for philosophy is the practice of nobility, and nothing else but that."[4] These are the qualities which Pliny, too, praises in women. The influence of Stoicism is also apparent in Pliny's use of the morally uplifting lesson, or *exemplum:* "Not only is it always a pleasure to hear something new, but also through examples we study the art of living" (8.18.12). Heroic women are the subjects of several such *exempla.*

Thanks to Pliny's philosophical inclinations and in spite of his conventional outlook, memorable women appear throughout his correspondence: women of outstanding virtue, heroic women, and ordinary matrons struggling with the everyday problems of existence.

The virtuous woman is the married woman. Most frequently, Pliny praises her *pietas*. For the Roman matron, *pietas* is devotion to husband and family. Pliny's own wife, Calpurnia, embodies this quality. Pliny writes to her aunt Calpurnia Hispulla (who herself earns the epithet *pietatis exemplum* from him), informing her of his satisfaction with his young bride. Calpurnia shows her devotion by her interest in his work and his pastimes, and even by setting his verses to music. Pliny concludes: "All this gives me the highest reason to hope that our mutual happiness will last forever and go on increasing day by day" (4.19). Nor did Calpurnia's *pietas* encompass only her husband. In Pliny's last letter to Trajan, we hear of Calpurnia traveling home alone to Comum from Bithynia after receiving news of her grandfather's death (10.120).

In a letter to Rosianus Geminus, Pliny mourns the death of the devoted wife of Macrinus: "Our friend Macrinus has had a terrible blow; he has lost his wife, one who would have been exemplary even in former times, after they had lived together for thirty-nine years without quarrel or misunderstanding. She always treated her husband with the greatest respect, while deserving the highest regard herself" (8.5.1). In fact, Pliny is extremely worried about his grieving friend, which supports the impression that this unnamed matron was not merely a demeaned slave, but a beloved companion.

Another devoted wife receiving praise is the spouse of Domitius Tullus, who married despite the censure of family and friends. "Crippled and deformed in every limb," Tullus is cared for by his wife whom Pliny calls "uxor optima et patientissima." In fact, Tullus lived as long as he did chiefly because of his wife's devotion, as Pliny reminds us: "Yet he went on living and kept his will to live helped chiefly by his wife, whose devoted care turned the former criticism of her marriage into a tribute of admiration" (8.18).

Even Ummidia Quadratilla, in spite of her decadent lifestyle, merits Pliny's respect. Although she did not lead a particularly virtuous life—she had a penchant for gambling and the theater—she insisted that her grandson avoid frivolous pastimes. When she died at age seventy-eight, Pliny acknowledged: "It is a joy to witness the family affection shown by the deceased and the honor done to an excellent young man" (7.24).

Another quality in women Pliny frequently praises is intelligence. Certainly, some of the Roman ladies of this era achieved more than functional literacy. Juvenal's tirade against women who ventured to discuss poetry, philosophy, or the fine points of grammar gives evidence to this (*Sat.* 6.434-56). Pliny, however, proudly writes of Calpurnia's *acumen* or "sharpness," praising her interest in literature, and especially his own: "She keeps copies of my works to read again and again and even learn by heart" (4.19). During their separations, Calpurnia is a conscientious correspondent, and her letters must have been of some literary merit, for Pliny, the critic, takes pleasure in reading them over and over: "I, too, am always reading your letters, and returning to them again and again as if they were new to me" (6.7).

Pliny praises the accomplishments of the wife of Pompeius Saturnius, although he hesitates to admit that she actually excelled at his own pet genre: "He recently read me some letters which he said were written by his wife, but sounded to me like Plautus or Terence read in prose. Whether they are all really his wife's as he says, or his own (which he denies), one can only admire him either for what he writes or for the way he has cultivated and refined the taste of the girl he married" (1.16.6).

On the tragic death of Minicia Marcella, Pliny laments the termination of a blossoming intellect: "She loved her nurses, her attendants, and her teachers, each one for the service given to her; she applied herself intelligently to her books and was moderate and restrained in her play" (5.16.3). Her education, brief as it was, perhaps contributed to the "sheer force of will" which "neither the length of her illness nor fear of death could break . . ." (5.16.4). Apparently, this adolescent girl achieved that strength of character through education of which Musonius Rufus spoke.

Elsewhere, Pliny responds kindly to women who seek his advice about educating their children (3.3, 7.24.5). At least one of the women Pliny describes had sufficient intellectual energy to gather evidence for a court inquiry into her son's death (8.6.8). Such examples show that not only were some women in Pliny's day well-educated, but that there were men who appreciated their intellectual accomplishments.

Although devotion and intelligence are the qualities which Pliny most frequently mentions, there are others he praises. One is trustworthiness. This virtue was particularly important to the Roman of senatorial class, for women were apparently considered to be inclined toward extortion.[5] Pliny himself relates the proceedings of one such extortion trial (3.9). Thus, when he describes the final illness of the senator Corellius Rufus, he notes that Corellius's wife is "omnis secreti capacissima" (1.12.7).

Other qualities that Pliny finds laudable in women are *frugalitas* (thrift), *castitas* (chastity), *suavitas* (sweetness), and *gravitas* (dignity).[6] We may suppose that the women he calls virtuous exhibit some of all of these qualities. (See, for example, 3.1.5, 4.17, 4.21, 5.21.4).

Some of Pliny's women emerge as heroines, exemplifying virtue at the risk of their lives. Pliny gives us detailed accounts of three such women, among them Arria, whose devotion to her husband Paetus is astounding. She courageously conceals the death of their son from her ailing husband, choosing to grieve alone rather than hinder his convalescence. When Paetus was being returned to Rome on a prison ship for his role in a revolt against Claudius, Arria asked to be allowed to accompany him as his slave. Her request refused, she followed the galley across the Adriatic in a tiny, hired fishing smack. Determined to die with her husband once he had been sentenced, she proved her resolve by dashing her head against the wall so violently that she lost consciousness. Pliny bemoans the fact that these courageous deeds are less well known than her suicide which immortalized her remark: "Paete, non dolet" (3.16). In Arria, *pietas* extended to the sacrifice of her own life.

Fannia, the granddaughter of Arria, displayed heroism in more than one respect. Because of her devotion to her husband, she suffered exile three times. She risked further punishment by smuggling his diaries into exile with her. In addition to her courage, she possesses that sweetness of disposition that Pliny so admires. Thus, Pliny mourns her lingering death: "Will there be anyone now whom we can hold up as a model to our wives, from whose courage our own sex can also take example and whom we can admire as much as the heroines of history while she is still in our midst?" (7.19).

Pliny was no stranger to heroic women. His own mother displayed both her quiet courage and her devotion to her family during the eruption of Mount Vesuvius. She refused to abandon her brother, the elder Pliny, who had gone to the aid of some friends. Finally, she begs her son to save himself: "Then my mother implored, entreated and commanded me to escape as best I could—a young man might escape whereas she was old and slow and could die in peace as long as she had not been the cause of my death too" (6.20.12).

Pliny's letters to his wife, Calpurnia, are loving expression of his affection for her. According to Andrew Sherwin-White, commentator on the letters, Pliny was the first Roman writer to apply the language of lovers to the marital relationship.[7] André Maniet likewise believes that, although Pliny may have had his moments of insincerity, he had no ulterior motives for writing so lovingly to his wife. His purpose was to express his affection for her.[8] Since Pliny is known to have admired the teachings of Musonius Rufus, it is not unlikely that he actually found and cultivated that ideal state of love and sympathy in marriage that the philosopher describes. Pliny's word choices clearly express his feelings: love—*corpusculum, ardentissime, diligo, desiderium, accendor, me delectet, amor*; pain at their separation—*torqueat, desiderio tui tenear, aeger et maestus, tormentis, in miseria curisque solacium*; concern for Calpurnia's health—"Indeed I should worry when you are away even if you were well, for there are always anxious moments without news of anyone one loves dearly" (6.4.3). Pliny lets us know that the pain of separation was mutual: "You say that you are feeling my absence very much, and your only comfort when I am not there is to hold my writings in your hand and often put them in my place by your side" (6.7.1). Such evidence as this makes it difficult to accept the judgment of some writers that the Roman man never admitted that the aim of marriage was personal happiness or common moral development.[9] These are the very aims of which Pliny speaks in his letters to and about Calpurnia.

Several letters make it clear that Pliny had female friends whose company he must have enjoyed. Although only one letter is actually addressed to her, Pliny seems to have valued the friendship of Pompeia Celerina, the mother of his former wife, now deceased (1.4, 1.18.3, 6.10.1). Unfortunately, he also expresses an affectionate interest in her estates. In another letter, Pliny declares his affection for Corellia, the sister of Corellius Rufus, and sells her land at a very reasonable price (8.14). In naming his friends who suffered under Domitian, Pliny includes Gratilla, Arria the Younger, and Fannia (3.11.3). These examples help to prove that Pliny, for one, considered women worthy and capable of sustaining a relationship, not necessarily sexual or servile, with men.

In the courtroom, Pliny shows a sympathetic attitude toward women in case after case. He retells the sensational trial of the chief Vestal Virgin Cornelia, accused of breaking her vows. Although she was generally condemned, Pliny, at least, gives her the benefit of the doubt in writing, "Whether she was innocent or not, she certainly appeared to be so" (4.11.9).[10] He takes the part of the disinherited daughter Attia Viriola in a highly publicized court case (6.33). During the extortion trial of Classicus, Pliny refrains from prosecuting his wife, whom he believed to be innocent, commenting: "I felt that the only just course was to refrain from pressing a charge against an innocent person; and I said so openly in many ways" (3.9.20). Various other letters show Pliny handling kindly the numerous legal problems of women (4.10, 5.1, 10.4).

Finally, Pliny generously gives his time and money to assist women with domestic problems, contributing a substantial sum to a young girl's dowry (6.32), promising a friend he will find a husband for her daughter (1.14), and donating a small farm as a pension to his nurse (6.3).

After examining so many letters favorable to the female, one may begin to wonder whether Pliny ever had an unkind word for her. Three letters especially show that Pliny's view of the opposite sex was not entirely uncritical. Actually, these three letters may be seen as additional proof of Pliny's sincerity as a correspondent. If his letters were uniformly cheery, one might begin to suspect a lack of honesty.

First Pliny writes to Cornelianus of Galitta's adultery trial which he attended. The punishment for adultery was severe. Under the "Lex Iulia de Adulteriis," a convicted woman forfeited half her dowry, one-third of her property, and was banished to an island. If her husband refused to prosecute, he was liable for punishment as a procurer. Yet even though Galitta's own husband is reluctant to prosecute her, Pliny feels no sympathy for the woman and thus comments that "it was essential that the woman would be convicted, however unwilling her accusor. She was duly found guilty and sentenced under the Julian law" (6.31.6). Apparently only virtuous women merited Pliny's compassion.

In a letter to Calvinia, Pliny abandons his usual tact and bluntly reminds the woman of her indebtedness to him (2.4). This lack of delicacy may be attributed to the fact that Calvinia, too, has behaved in a dishonorable manner—by not repaying a loan. There remains to be explained the uncharacteristically cold letter addressed to Calpurnius Fabatus concerning his granddaughter Calpurnia's miscarriage (8.10). First, one must consider the recipient. Calpurnius Fabatus must have been a fairly old man, a retired equestrian politician.[11] With such a background, one might imagine him a rather conservative gentleman. If so, he might not be inclined to view women as sympathetically as the men of Pliny's generation. And so Pliny explains away his personal tragedy as the result of a young girl's foolishness in saying that "She has had a severe lesson and paid for her mistake by seriously endangering her life" (8.10.1,2). Perhaps this explanation was a true reflection of Pliny's initial disappointment, but after some reflection, he produced the more tender letter to his wife's aunt. This letter directly follows the one to Fabatus, and expresses much greater compassion for Calpurnia: "The danger was indeed grave—I hope I may safely say so now—through no fault of her own, but perhaps of her youth. Hence her miscarriage, a sad proof of unsuspected pregnancy" (8.11.2).

In summary, if we accept Pliny's reliability as a reporter and his sincerity as a writer, then his letters form a pleasant picture of the upper class Roman woman of this era. The letters provide a valuable contrast to the unflattering portraits drawn by such contemporaries as Juvenal and Tacitus. The women Pliny writes of are devoted wives and family members. He depicts them as morally and intellectually equal to men and capable of the same heroism. Pliny's letters show that there was indeed warmth and love, not only in the Roman marriage, but in friendships between men and women.

It is tempting, but rash, to accuse Roman men of oppressing women. Pliny's letters illustrate the impossibility of a fair comparison between women's rights in the second and twentieth centuries. Pliny is no opinionated bigot who presumes to dictate the proper role and attitude for the female, as did Cato, for example. Nor is he a feminist who advocates equal rights and responsibilities for both sexes. In Rome under Trajan's rule, he is a humane gentleman who perceives no inferiority of character or intellect in women. His letters treat people as people, and he does not question the social or economic distinctions which exist between them. The virtuous woman in Pliny would probably not be displeased to lie beneath this well-known epitaph of a much earlier era:

> . . . she loved her husband in her heart. She bore two sons, one of whom she left on earth, the other beneath it. She was pleasant to talk with and she walked with grace. She kept the house and worked in wool. That is all. You may go.[12]

Notes

1. Juvenal, *Satires,* tr. Rolfe Humphries (Bloomington 1958) 71.

2. All references to Pliny's *Letters* are based on the following text and will hereafter be cited in the text by book, number, and section where appropriate. G. Caecilius Secundus Plinius, *Letters and Panegyricus,* tr. Betty Radice, Loeb Library (Cambridge 1969). E. S. Stout's critical edition *Epistulae* (Bloomington 1962) was also consulted. A complete listing of letters referring to women follows: Book 1: 4, 8, 10, 12, 14, 16; Book 2: 4, 20; Book 3: 1, 3, 9, 10, 11, 16; Book 4: 2, 10, 11, 17, 19, 21; Book 5: 1, 16, 21; Book 6: 3, 4, 7, 10, 12, 16, 20, 24, 26, 31, 32, 33, 34; Book 9: 13, 36; Book 10: 4, 5, 6, 11, 51, 96, 120. See also *Panegyricus* 83 and 34.

3. Martin P. Charlesworth, *Five Men: Character Studies from the Roman Empire* (Cambridge 1936) 40-41.

4. *Ibid.* 44.

5. Andrew Sherwin-White, *Letters of Pliny* (Oxford 1966) 234-35.

6. 4.19.2. For a detailed discussion of these and other qualities Pliny praises in women, see André Maniet, "Pline le Jeuane et Calpurnie" *L'Antiquité Classique* 35(1966) 149-85.

7. Andrew Sherwin-White, "Pliny: The Man and His Letters" *Greece and Rome* 16 (1969) 79.

8. Maniet, *op. cit.* 174-84.

9. See for example Gugliemo Ferrero, *The Women of the Caesars* (New York 1911) 11. Or M. I. Finley, "The Silent Women of Rome" *Horizon* 7 (1965) 60-64.

10. For a different opinion of her guilt, see Suetonius, *Domitian* 8.4.

11. Sherwin-White, *Letters,* 742.

12. Mary K. Lekkowitz and Maureen Fant, *Women in Greece and Rome* (Toronto 1977) 104.

Albert A. Bell (essay date 1990)

SOURCE: Bell, Albert A. "Pliny the Younger: The Kinder, Gentler Roman." *Classical Bulletin* 66, no. 1-2 (1990): 37-41.

[*In the following essay, Bell argues that Pliny's gentle nature and reputation as a good husband, generous employer, fair master, tender man, and principled public servant—evidence of which is culled from his letters—suggest a kinder side to Roman life than depicted by other, more satiric classical authors.*]

If one were to play word association, the mention of "Roman" almost certainly would not evoke responses such as "kind" or "gentle." Orgies, slaughter in the amphitheatre, exposure of newborn children, brutal treatment of slaves, general indifference to human suffering—these are the associations one might more typically expect. Unfortunately, much of the extant Roman literature and art support that interpretation.

To pick only a handful of the most appalling examples of Roman callousness and inhumanity: Catullus laughs at a man who is so starved he can scarcely defecate (23); several characters in the *Satyricon* peep through a crack in a door to watch two prepubescent youngsters on their "wedding night" (25, 26); Martial boasts about the tortures inflicted on victims in the amphitheatre (*De Spectaculis* 5, 7, and 8). Though they had easy access to classical Greek tragedy and comedy, the Romans preferred coarse farces based on "traditional crudity of jest and language"[1] or indecent mimes in which actresses appeared nude.[2] The combined effect of their entertainment and the harshness of their daily lives

could hardly have been other than "demoralizing in the extreme, encouraging a cowardly delight in the sufferings of others and fostering every base passion."[3]

And yet one Roman, whom we know best from his correspondence, does not fit this mold at all. Even allowing for some self-serving exaggeration on his part, Pliny the Younger emerges from the pages of his letters as "a man one would like to have known—an affectionate husband, loyal friend, considerate master, and conscientious public servant."[4] I will examine this kinder, gentler facet of Pliny's personality and suggest that there was a more admirable side to Roman life than that depicted by Petronius, Martial, Juvenal, and other cynical, satiric Silver Age authors.

This is not to claim that Pliny is more typical of his age than the people of Martial's epigrams. He sees himself as somehow different. He does not enjoy loud, boisterous dinner parties (9.17), though he admits that most of his contemporaries would find his calm, "Socratic" dinners boring. He has no interest in gladiatorial games or chariot races, nor any respect for people who do (4.22, 9.6). He disdains the lower classes, and there is something of the air of a country gentleman about him.[5] His letters were, in fact, more highly regarded in the eighteenth and nineteenth centuries when his audience was composed of people more like himself.[6] He intimates that his friends[7] shared his tastes, but we cannot assume that this circle is representative of the society as a whole. It is, however, a side of the society we cannot ignore if we want to have an accurate picture of the whole.

What is significant is that in Pliny we see a person who operates by a set of values that differ rather markedly from those of his society, as it is depicted by contemporary writers. How he came to believe in those values we may not be able to determine,[8] but it can be enlightening just to see what they were and how they influenced his daily life.

In the first place, Pliny is a generous man. This is all the more remarkable in a society noted for its stinginess.[9] Polybius summed up the Roman attitude toward charity: "No Roman willingly gives anything to anyone" (31.25, 9-10). Only in Trajan's reign did the government institute a program (the *alimenta*) to provide support for destitute children.[10] An example of the era's new spirit of generosity may be the charitable society referred to in Pliny's correspondence with Trajan (10.92, 93). A more traditional sort of gift-giving was common in imperial Rome, but the gifts always had "hooks" in them, as Martial says (5.18, 5.59). Gifts, favors and praise of the giver were expected in return (Martial 4.88, 5.52).

Pliny, however, takes a different view. In 9.30 he admits that he is reluctant to praise the alleged generosity of a man who gives only to "certain people." The truly generous man, he thinks, is one who gives "to his country, neighbors, relatives, and friends, but by them I mean his friends without means; unlike the people who bestow their gifts on those best able to make a return . . . so few instances are there even of partial generosity."[11] While this theme occurs in other Latin moralists, "Pliny's own example is more impressive, even if well advertised, because it was realized in hard cash."[12]

Pliny did give away large sums of money. He built or rebuilt temples for townspeople who lived near his estates (3.4, 4.1, 9.39, 10.8). He established a library for his hometown of Comum (1.8) and paid part of the salary of a teacher so that local children would not have to travel to Milan (4.13). He arranged for income from one of his properties to be used to support Comum's needy children (7.18). In his will he funded public baths and provided money to support a hundred of his freedmen and to give an annual dinner for the city's populace.[13] The bequest amounted to some two million sesterces, after he had already donated approximately that much to the town during his life.[14]

His generosity extended to individuals as well. Martial and Juvenal both lament the stinginess of their patrons,[15] but Pliny seems to have been extremely generous by the standards of his, or any, day. He gave Martial money to travel back to Spain. In 2.4 he writes off an apparently large debt which a woman had inherited from her father. He mentions that he had also contributed 100,000 sesterces toward her dowry. Admittedly the tone of the letter is pretentious, but in that Pliny is simply a creature of his age. Other examples of his generosity to individuals are found in 1.19, 5.1, and 6.32. We know of no largess to the mass of the poor and needy of Rome, but to expect such would be to require Pliny to conform to our eleemosynary standards.[16] As M. I. Finley suggests, Pliny's benefactions were "probably unsurpassed in Italy or the western empire."[17]

Another trait that becomes evident from even a casual reading of the letters is the essential humaneness of the man. As already noted, he is repulsed by the gladiatorial games and other amusements of the arena and the circus. His treatment of his slaves provides the best evidence of his humaneness. His kindness toward his reader Zosimus (5.19) may be dismissed as enlightened self-interest, but his refusal to work his slaves in chains (3.19) and his anxiety over the illness of a single slave (8.1) or a group of them (8.16) evidence his genuine concern for these people.[18] He is no radical reformer out to abolish slavery, but not even the early Christian church took that step.[19] As a man of his times Pliny sees no alternative to the institution; he simply tries to make

it as tolerable as possible for those whose fate places them in servitude. He is a kind man who condemns harshness in a master (3.14). Such sentiments are not unique in circles imbued with Stoic thought on the subject, but Pliny puts his ideals into practice. He allows his slaves to make wills like free men (8.16), and we do not find him jovially whipping his cook after a poor dinner, as Martial (8.23) pictures himself doing.

Fairness is another of Pliny's appealing traits. This characteristic comes out in his eagerness to observe the spirit of the law rather than the letter. The charge that he is a niggling bureaucrat becomes absurd in the face of a letter like 4.10. A certain Sabina had left a legacy to one of her slaves, using the formula "to Modestus whom I have ordered to be set free." But there was no specific clause in her will granting Modestus his freedom. Legal experts whom Pliny had consulted felt the man should receive neither his freedom nor his legacy. To Pliny, however, "it seems obvious that it was a mistake on Sabina's part, and I think we ought to act as if she had set out in writing what she believed she had written." In 5.7 he bends the law again to carry out the intentions of another friend's will, although it costs him 400,000 sesterces to do so. (Remember that that sum of money qualified one for membership in the order of the knights; Pliny is voluntarily forfeiting a small fortune.) In 2.16 he mentions that it is his own private practice to be bound by the wishes of the deceased, even though they might not have been expressed in the best legal form.

This basic fairness comes out in his resolution of an economic problem on one of his estates. The grape harvest had been poor, and people who had contracted to buy at certain prices stood to lose money. Instead of just expecting them to absorb the whole loss, Pliny refunded to each one an eighth of what he had spent (an idea that is hardly likely to gain favor in our own commodity futures markets). Those who had laid out more than 10,000 sesterces were given an additional ten percent of anything above that sum (8.2). It would have been simpler to give everyone the same rebate, "but hardly fair, and I hold the view that one of the most important things in life is to practice justice in private as in public life, in small matters as in great, and apply it to one's own affairs no less than to other people's."

We see him applying this principle at a dinner party where the guests have been served differing fare depending on their social status.[20] Another guest asks Pliny if he approves of the practice. Pliny replies that there are no distinctions at his table: "I serve the same to everyone, for when I invite guests it is for a meal, not to make class distinctions." It is not overly expensive, he explains, for he serves the same modest fare at all the tables instead of costly meals to some guests and budget-saving scraps to others (2.6).

Pliny is a man of principle in all things. He refuses to accept gifts for his conduct of court cases (5.13.9). He believes that "one ought to make personal and temporary interests give place to public and permanent advantages" (7.18.3), and his own career is an illustration of his credo. He had no need of public office and often found it burdensome (3.1, 4.23, 7.3, 8.9), but he remained in public service out of a sense of duty, inspired by the example of his uncle and by his reading of Cicero.[21]

Tenderness in a man might not have been a desideratum to the Romans, but Pliny thinks it should be: "A true man is affected by grief and has feelings, though he may fight them" (8.16). His own tenderness shows through in a number of his letters. Even here, though, modern scholars have been slow to admit the obvious. Jerome Carcopino claimed that Pliny's letters about his wife's miscarriage show how aloof and cold he is toward her.[22] But those letters (8.10, 11), on a very difficult subject, were written to her grandfather and aunt who raised her. There is a difference in tone between them, the first—to the grandfather—being more formal and restrained, probably because that was the nature of the person to whom he was writing.[23]

But these letters are not the place to look for clues to Pliny's relationship with Calpurnia. When he writes directly to her, we see him missing her so much that he rereads her letters (6.4 and 7) and meanders into her room when he should be working (7.5). It is closer to the mark to say that Pliny is "the first man known to have written a love letter to his own wife."[24]

There is one element of this picture that might seem at first to argue against my interpretation of Pliny as a man kinder and gentler than his times. In 10.96 he describes to Trajan the steps he has taken to suppress the Christian *superstitio* in Bithynia. People who were accused and refused to recant he had ordered to be led away to execution, "for, whatever the nature of their admission, I am convinced that their stubbornness and unshakeable obstinacy ought not to go unpunished." He also ordered two female slaves, members of the group with the title *ministrae,* to be tortured in order to gain further information.

That bit of bureaucratic brutality does not accord well with the essential humaneness and fairness that Pliny has demonstrated throughout the rest of his letters. Is this the real man and the rest just a literary pose? I think not. As governor, Pliny had the power of *coercitio,* the power to enforce his will—however arbitrary and unjust—on the populace of his province.[25] Under a cruel governor the provincials lived in dread of this prerogative, as Pliny notes in a letter describing a suit against a governor (3.9). The provincials bringing the suit claimed that "as provincials they were terrorized into carrying out any order of the governor."

We cannot know with what degree of enthusiasm or reluctance Pliny ordered these executions. He had been sent to Bithynia to restore order to a province plagued by maladministration and civil unrest for several years. The primary responsibility of provincial officials was to ensure stability and calm.[26] This was why Pilate acceded to Jewish demands to crucify Jesus (Mark 15.15) and why the tribune Claudius Lysias brought in troops to rescue Paul from a mob in Jerusalem (Acts 21.31-36). The magistrate's personal feelings seem to have had little to do with his actions when faced with a threat to social order. The Christians appeared to Pliny a major part of the problem and seemed to require harsh repressive measures.

In other cases, however, he suggests a lenient course of action which Trajan vetoes. In 10.31 he has discovered that some men sentenced years before to work in the mines had evaded their punishment and now, in old age, "by all accounts are quietly leading honest lives." It seems "too hard" to him to send them back to the mines. But Trajan (10.32) takes the more typically Roman approach. Men who have avoided punishment within the past ten years must be returned to the mines. Older men can be put to work cleaning public baths or repairing roads.[27]

In 10.33 Pliny suggests to the emperor that a volunteer fire brigade be authorized for Nicomedia, to prevent a repetition of a disastrous fire which had recently struck the town. Its size will be strictly controlled, he promises, and it will not be allowed to diverge from its purpose. Trajan vetoes the idea in no uncertain terms (10.34). Such groups tend to become political clubs. Just provide the equipment, he decrees, and let property owners get help from the crowds who gather to watch a fire.

For too long Pliny has been dismissed as a stuffy, self-important dabbler in literature, "a colorless prig lacking the full Roman charm and the saving sense of humor."[28] Martial and Juvenal may be more colorful, but does that also mean that they embody "the full Roman charm"? Reliance on their work as sources for the study of the social history of imperial Rome has created an impression of Roman society that may overemphasize the shocking, degraded side of life which every civilization produces. Today's readers of tabloid newspapers and viewers of more sensational types of television shows could conclude that our society is not much healthier than the Rome of Martial and Juvenal. (Even serious scholars can compare the women of that era to modern women of less than exemplary virtue.[29]

Pliny embodies the "kinder, gentler" side of Roman life. More sympathetic study of his letters would restore a balance to our picture of Rome at the height of its power.

Notes

1. W. Beare, *The Roman Stage. A Short History of Latin Drama in the Time of the Republic,* 3rd ed. (London: Methuen, 1964) 142.

2. Ibid., 151. Mimes remained a scandalous form of entertainment in Pliny's day (9.17).

3. H. Mattingly, *Roman Imperial Civilisation* (New York: Doubleday, 1959) 195. Cf. R. Auguet, *Cruelty and Civilization. The Roman Games* (London: Allen and Unwin, 1972).

4. B. Radice, "Introduction," *Pliny: Letters and Panegyricus* (London: Heinemann, 1969) Vol. I, xvii.

5. F. S. Dunham, "The Younger Pliny—Gentleman and Citizen," *CJ* [*Classical Journal*] 40 (1944-45) 417-426.

6. M. Johnston, "John Adams and Pliny the Younger," *CW* [*Classical World*] 27 (1933) 46.

7. R. Syme, "People in Pliny," *JRS* [*Journal of Roman Studies*] 58 (1968) 135-151, and "Pliny's Less Successful Friends," *Historia* 9 (1960) 362-379.

8. One unmistakable influence is the Stoic philosopher Musonius Rufus, whom Pliny "greatly admired" and "loved" (3.11). Musonius' thought had close parallels to early Christian teaching at certain points; cf. P. W. van der Horst, "Musonius Rufus and the New Testament: A Contribution to the Corpus Hellenisticum," *NT* [*New Testament*] 16 (1974) 306-315.

9. J. B. Skemp, "Service to the Needy in the Graeco-Roman World," in *Parresia. Karl Barth zum 80. Geburtstag am 10. Mai 1966,* ed. E. Busch et al. (Zurich: EVZ-Verlag, 1966) 17-26. A.R. Hands, *Charities and Social Aid in Greece and Rome* (London: Thames and Hudson, 1968).

10. F. C. Bourne, "The Roman Alimentary Program and Italian Agriculture," *TAPhA* [*Transactions of the American Philological Association*] 91 (1960) 47-75; R.P. Duncan-Jones, "The Purpose and Organization of the Alimenta," *PBSR* [*Papers, British School at Rome*] 32 (1964) 123-146; P. Garnsey, "Trajan's *Alimenta.* Some Problems," *Historia* 17 (1968) 367-381.

11. This and all subsequent quotations from Pliny are from B. Radice's translation, published in two forms: in the Loeb Library edition (cf. above, n. 4) and in *The Letters of the Younger Pliny* (Baltimore: Penguin Books, 1963).

12. A.N. Sherwin-White, *The Letters of Pliny: A Historical and Social Commentary* (Oxford: Clarendon Press, 1966) 513.

13. J. Nichols, "Pliny and the Patronage of Communities," *Hermes* 108 (1980) 365-385.

14. Radice (above, n. 4) 24.

15. Martial 1.59, 1.108, 2.5, 2.43, 2.46, 3.14, 3.36, 3.60, 5.19; Juvenal 5.107-113, 7.36-97.

16. Pliny was in fact an unabashed snob, declaring in 9.6,3 that the plebs were worth no more than a dirty tunic. Such an attitude was unexceptional among his peers.

17. *The Ancient Economy* (Berkeley: Univ. of California Press, 1973) 39.

18. Slaves on country estates routinely suffered brutal treatment and were often worked in chain gangs. Cf. Columella, *De re rustica* 1.3; Pliny, *Hist. nat.* 18.35, and R.H. Barrow, *Slavery in the Roman Empire* (London: Methuen, 1928) 65-97.

19. Ephesians 6.5 and Titus 2.9 both urge slaves to be obedient to their masters. Whether these letters were actually written by Paul is immaterial; they certainly represent Christian attitudes in Pliny's lifetime.

20. Evidently a common practice; cf. Martial 1.20, 3.60, 4.68, 6.11.

21. W. C. Korfmacher, "Pliny and the Gentleman of Cicero's *Offices,*" *CW* 40 (1946) 50-53.

22. *Daily Life in Ancient Rome* (New Haven: Yale Univ. Press, 1940) 89-90.

23. E. S. Dobson, "Pliny the Younger's Depiction of Women," *CB* [*Classical Bulletin*] 58 (1982) 84-85.

24. A. N. Sherwin-White, "Pliny, the Man and His Letters," *G&R* [*Greece & Rome*] 16 (1969) 79.

25. A. N. Sherwin-White, *Roman Society and Roman Law in the New Testament* (Oxford: Clarendon Press, 1963) 1-23; P. Garnsey, "The Criminal Jurisdiction of Governors," *JRS* 58 (1968) 51-59; D. Liebs, "Das *ius gladii* der römischen Provinzgouverneure in der Kaiserzeit," *ZPE* [*Zeitschrift fuer Papyrologie und Epigraphik*] 43 (1981) 217-223.

26. G. Downey, "'Un-Roman Activities': The Ruling Race and the Minorities," *Anglican Theological Rev.* 58 (1976) 432-443.

27. F. Millar, "Condemnation to Hard Labour in the Roman Empire, from the Julio-Claudians to Constantine," *PBSR* 52 (1984) 124-147.

28. Korfmacher, (above, n. 21) 53.

29. S. Treggiari, "Libertine Ladies," *CW* 64 (1971) 196-198; J. P. Sullivan, "Lady Chatterly in Rome," *Pacific Coast Philology* 15 (1980) 53-62.

Frederick Jones (essay date 1991)

SOURCE: Jones, Frederick. "Naming in Pliny's *Letters*." *Symbolae Osleonses* 66 (1991): 147-70.

[*In the following essay, Jones studies Pliny's* Letters *as a means of gaining insight into the social conditions and protocols under which Latin name forms were used.*]

Language inevitably makes and enacts presuppositions about the social conditions under which communication takes place. Thus Cicero distinguished private and various kinds of public discourse (*ad Famm.* 9.21; 15.21), Quintilian distinguished persuasive functions (12.10.59), and writing and speaking (12.10.49f), and stressed the importance of gauging the audience and the circumstances (4.1.52; cf. also [Quint.] *Decl. Min.* 316.2 with Winterbottom *ad loc.*), attributing an intelligent formulation to Cicero: *eius (= iudicis) vultus saepe ipse rector est dicentis* (12.10.56). Vocabulary, syntax, thematic material, stylistic ornamentation provide some of the *differentia* involved; another way of looking at the differences is to consider utterances in the light of their interactive value, interactive, that is, between speaker and hearer.[1] One aspect of this is name-usage. Nomenclature has been widely used for prosopographical purposes, and to some extent for textual purposes, and there is considerable literature on the development of the *tria nomina*. However, study of the sociolinguistic protocols applying to the use of personal names in Greek and Latin as a matter of interest and importance in itself is less advanced. Conspicuous are the articles of Adams and Vidman on Cicero and Pliny respectively.[2] Adams provided considerable detail about the social conditions under which particular name forms (single or double; the various possible combinations of the three parts of the *tria nomina*) were used. Within narrower limits Vidman performed the same service for Pliny, but since the two studies were independent of each other an opportunity was missed for attempting to identify more general linguistic characteristics. I intend here to consider Pliny's practice against the Ciceronian background (on which I hope to publish further material myself) and thereby identify a paradigm of Latin name-usage in the phenomenon of the introduction.

When we come to Pliny's letters two features of great value in assessing Cicero's usage are either lacking or unreliable. Any original distinctions made in letter headings to the various addressees are thoroughly distorted and overlaid, and (apart from the letters from Trajan or his secretariat in Book 10) there are no letters to Pliny from his correspondents. Moreover, Books 1-9 are avowedly (*Ep.* [*Epistulae*] 1.1) tidied up for publication and selected with a literary self-consciousness. Nevertheless the epistolary format is the same so that legitimate comparisons may be made, and it will be seen that there is a great deal of consistency.

The fundamental tendency to denominate with greater fullness (chiefly by using more than one name) for a character's first mention in a letter and thereafter to use single names as anaphorics, clearly visible throughout Cicero's letters, is also present very clearly in Pliny. In Cicero the main variations to this pattern are: (i) the stratification according to the status or distance of the addressee whereby letters to intimates contain a higher proportion of single-naming than letters to superiors or persons with whom Cicero was not on good terms; (ii) the tendency to decrease formality of reference as regards the initial mention in a letter of persons who have been introduced into the correspondence in earlier letters between the same writer and addressee; (iii) the special treatment (in varying degree) accorded to the names of the relatives of writer or addressee, and of women; (iv) the avoidance or replacement of the names of those disliked by, or at friction with, the writer, or whose mention could offend or embarass the addressee, and the avoidance of names for other reasons of discretion. To different degrees there are traces of all these variations in Pliny's letters. In addition, as with Cicero, some special comment on direct and indirect address and self-naming is required.

Of the first of these variations there is little sign in Books 1-9. Single names are scattered through the collection in various functions, but there are no perceptible accumulations in letters to any specific individuals. On the other hand the collocation of 7.7 to Saturninus about *Priscus noster* and 7.8 to Priscus about *Saturninus noster* is clearly meant to represent or exemplify a certain level of informality. Furthermore, certain individuals in certain letters receive only a single name apparently because they were well known to writer and addressee.[3] The general absence of overall informality in letters to particular friends is a direct result, presumably, of the nature of Pliny's collection: selection, polishing, editing and re-writing with an eye to the public readership conspire to raise the level of literary self-awareness shown, and tend to produce a more even level of formality.

However, this does not mean that such variation is absent from Pliny's correspondence, for there is a noticeable difference between the first nine books and the tenth. In the latter initial references to Roman citizens almost universally use double-naming. The one exception is Virdius Gemellinus introduced into the correspondence by Pliny (10.27) as *Gemellino, optimo viro,* to which Trajan replies with *Virdio Gemellino, procuratore meo* (10.28; see too 10.84). Perhaps this may be explained as the result of Trajan's prior reference to the man indicated in Pliny's letter by *iussisti.*[4] Not only is double-naming the staple,[5] but very frequent also are appositional phrases (like those found exceptionally often in Cicero's very formal letters to Appius

Claudius in *ad Famm.* 3); see 10.2.1.; 5.2; 6.1; 10.1; 11.1; 21.1; 25; 27; 28; 29.1; 51.1; 56.2; 56.4; 57.1; 58.3; 60.1; 60.2; 61.5; 63; 65.3; 67.1; 74.1; 75.1; 77.1; 81.1; 84; 85; 86a; 87.1; 87.3; 94.1; 106; 107; 112. Furthermore, while references to any particular individual in the first nine books may, after an initial double-naming, be by single-name, especially within the same letter (where this tendency is very regular), the position in Book 10 is somewhat different. Usually here a reference to a character in a letter later than that in which he first appeared retains the double-name (or triple, where relevant) as at 10.10, 22 and 86a, 30, 57, 61 and 62 and 77, 66, 76, 82, 95, 105, 107. Double-naming is replaced by single-naming only by Trajan (10.60, Paulus and Archippus; 10.71, Claudius) and in one of these cases Pliny retains the double-name after Trajan has moved to single-naming (10.81, Flavius Archippus).[6] Similarly, Pliny is more likely to retain appositives than Trajan (cf. 10.22, 30, 62, 66, 95 where Trajan omits an appositive; 10.61.5 (cf. 42); 77.1 (cf. 62); 86a (cf. 22.1) for cases where Pliny uses an appositive where Trajan had not).[7] It is very clear that Trajan is allowed more flexibility and initiative than Pliny, a clear status differentiation, and that the whole correspondence is more formal than that of Books 1-9 where the distance between writer and addressee is consistently smaller.

Comparison between the use of address in Books 1-9 and Book 10, and within Book 10, confirms this picture. Excluding quotations there are only two vocative addresses in Books 1-9, *Spurinna* at 3.10.1 (in a letter whose heading includes two addressees, one of whom is here singled out) and *collega carissime* at 7.21.1 (to Cornutus; *collega* has some rhetorical point). Sherwin-White (n. at 7.21.1) implies that the rarity of the vocative in Books 1-9 is connected with the intention or process of publication. That the incidence of the vocative in these books is unnaturally low might be supposed on grounds of comparison with Cicero, a somewhat suspect argument; of more secure significance is the comparative frequency of name vocatives in quotations in these letters, which argues a certain normal level of address by name (in spoken language) between peers and approximate peers. The reciprocal arrangement at 9.19.5 is particularly relevant.

On this basis it is possible to add weight to an already more substantial contrast between Pliny's mode of addressing Trajan, and the latter's way of addressing Pliny in Book 10. Pliny addresses Trajan with a vocative *imperator* + adjective twice in 10.1 (because of his recent salutation), "in *Ep.* 14 for his military victories, and in *Ep.* 4.1 for no clear reason" (Sherwin-White at 10.1.1). Otherwise he uses *domine* (sometimes twice) in every letter except 10.41. 59, 64, 86b (where the text is insecure), 102 and 116. On the other hand Trajan uses

mi Secunde carissime in fourteen letters, *Secunde carissime* in five, and *mi Secunde* in one (10.97): there is no address in thirty-one letters. Sherwin-White observes the omission in the three private rescripts (10.3b; 10.7; 10.9), but this may be insignificant (n. at 10.16). He also suggests that the omission of the address "in several rescripts of substance is probably due to the compilers of the collection" (p. 546). A very clear pattern is visible. Whereas Pliny is, apparently, almost bound to use address (and it is very tempting to regard the six omissions as the results of someone's carelessness), Trajan may or may not (and only does so in about two fifths of the cases). Furthermore, whereas Pliny does not use a name, Trajan when he uses address at all uses the name, and with the familiar *mi* in sixteen out of twenty-one cases at that. Pliny's usage here bears comparison with his references to Emperors in general (details below), for he tends to use a title only for the current Emperor, but a title + name for favoured dead Emperors. It is clear that with regard to the Emperor Pliny is at the lower end of a non-reciprocal system both for address and for name-use; this system parallels the distinction already observed, that the initiative for reducing formality in third person reference rests mainly with Trajan in Book 10. Although the various non-reciprocal address systems in Cicero are not as nakedly differentiated as *mi* + name vs *domine,* there is a definite parallel, and *domine* had been a common form of upward address between individuals of different status in a broad range of social levels, including from children to parents (see Sherwin-White at 10.2.1). It follows that the situation in Book 10 is simply a more extreme version of the normal linguistic differentiations which depend on and support social inequalities and that the use of someone's name is a privilege, confirmation of which is dependent upon such inequalities.[8]

It should be noted that this argument and the preceding material do not depend on Trajan's personal authorship of the rescripts, for Pliny consistently writes as though he were dealing directly with the Emperor, whether this is a mere formality or not (see Sherwin-White, p. 541), and the rescripts are consistently written in the *persona* of the Emperor, however much a secretary may have had to do with the drafting (see Sherwin-White, pp. 536-546, with 545-6 on the formula *mi Secunde carissime*).

We can, then, see a general system which distinguishes both Pliny's approach to Trajan and the reverse, and Pliny's approach to Trajan and his approach to his other addressees, in terms of name-usage between the correspondents and in third person references to others. Within Books 1-9 such distinctions are negligible (especially in comparison with the variegations of Cicero's usage), a fact which should be attributed to the effects connected with publication.

Of the second variation of the underlying system in Cicero mentioned at the outset, that characters introduced into a sequence of letters between two individuals may in later letters be referred to with less formality, there are signs in Pliny. We have already observed something of such a tendency in Book 10, where the initiative tends to lie with Trajan, and there is more evidence in the other books.

There is a clear tendency for the objects of recommendation to be introduced with considerable formality, particularly with the *tria nomina,* in Cicero. The position in Pliny is less clear, but worth observing. In the specific case of petitions for citizen rights in letters to Trajan Pliny uses the *tria nomina* which he does not do elsewhere (see Vidman, p. 586); in other recommendations to Trajan he uses two names (see 10.4, 94). In recommendations or introductions to others Pliny again uses two names (usually with introductory paraphernalia, such as relatives, qualitities, biographical detail etc.), as at 2.13, 4.15, 7.16, 7.31 (cf. 9.28.2); sometimes the combination *praenomen* + *nomen* (as 1.14.6; 2.9.1; 4.4.1.; 4.17.1) is used for the object and/or one of his relatives, which certainly suggests formality (see Vidman, pp. 585, 594); although sometimes this combination distinguishes otherwise homonymous fathers and sons (Sherwin-White at 2.9.1),[9] this necessity could perhaps be satisfied by using the recommendee's name and, for his father, *pater.* When the double-name does not include the *praenomen* a degree of formality is still present, but one must presume that this arises from the specific character of these letters on rather thin grounds: the nature of the collection has already raised the level of formality in general, so that double-naming is not necessarily distinctive in itself, nevertheless the absence of single-names in initial references in these letters (but note 1.24.1) and the presence of introductory formulae suggest that double-naming was an original requirement. A sequence of letters later than the original introduction (which is not recorded in the letters) is given at 7.7, 7.8 and 7.15 and in these the single-name is used, just as in Cicero letters subsequent to a recommendation may show less formality.

Sequences of letters provide further interest. Vidman (p. 586) has noted the tendency in Pliny for two names to be used for a new character, thereafter one, *vor allem in demselben Brief* (see too p. 591 and cf. Sherwin-White, p. 113), implicitly treating the collection as a single unit as arranged for publication, irrespective of the various addressees.

There are two clear cases of diminishing formality within a particular correspondence in Pliny. The first concerns an introduction and its sequel. In 7.16 Pliny writes to Calpurnius Fabatus, his wife's grandfather, introducing Calestrius Tiro with two names (and

biographical details) and promising his assistance to Fabatus. In 7.23 and 7.32 he writes to Fabatus in later stages of the same business, now referring to Tiro with one name only (we might recall here the informality of reference of 7.7, 7.8 and 7.15 referred to above). Somewhat similarly, in 2.11 he writes to Maturus Arrianus about the Priscus trail: at 2.11.23 he mentions a minor matter still hanging over, involving one Hostilius Firminus, and at 2.12.1, to the same addressee, he picks this minor matter up, but now using one name for Firminus. Two other cases show a certain complication. Four letters to Cornelius Ursus and four other letters are involved. In the description of the trial of Julius Bassus Pliny refers to the role of Titius (but the text is not certain) Homullus (4.9.15). In the description of the trial of Varenus Rufus, a sort of follow-on, Homullus receives one name (but Julius Bassus still receives two), at 5.20.6. In the same letter Varenus receives two names (5.20.1), but in two sequels only one (6.5.1; 6.13.1 where Acilius Rufus receives two names for a second time: 5.20.6; 6.13.5). The complication is that after their appearance in letters to Ursus both Homullus and Varenus still receive single-names in letters to other addressees, Homullus at 6.19.3 to Nepos, and Varenus at 6.29.11 to Quadratus, and 7.6.1 and 7.10.1 to Macrinus, more sequels.

This complication becomes rather more troublesome when we see that certain characters appear with two names in a letter to one addressee, and subsequently with one in letters to *other* addressees. In 1.14 Pliny writes a letter introducing Minicius Acilianus to Junius Mauricius (Acilianus has two names at 1.14.3). Later Acilianus has one name in a letter to Annius (2.16.1). We might discount this on the grounds that the earlier formality is required by its introductory nature. But this will not apply to Fonteius Magnus who receives two names at his first appearance (5.20.4) to Ursus (*unus ex Bithynis* explains who he is) and one at 7.6.2 (with *ille*) and 7.10.1, both to Macrinus. Since these three letters concern stages of the same affair (and the same goes for Homullus and Varenus), and Pliny makes a point of the continuum at 7.10.1, it may begin to look as though the difference in addressees becomes a secondary consideration (in which case *ille* at 7.6.2 might refer to the man's role in 5.20), and that we are seeing the normal tendency to reduce the number of names after the first mention in the same work. Certainly Pliny was aware of the audience beyond the addressee, and in a letter to Cremutius Ruso (9.19) he notes that Cremutius has read something *in quadam epistula mea.* Since this refers to a letter in an earlier book (as of course it would have to), 6.10 to Lucceius Albinus, we may see that there is no difficulty in the fact that the sequences we are considering extend over more than one book. And there are more examples. M. Regulus receives two names on his first appearance in the whole collection (1.5.1, to Voconius Romanus) and subsequently only Regulus (1.20.14, to Tacitus; 2.11.22, to Arrianus; 2.20.2, to Calvisius; 4.2.1, to Attius Clemens; 4.7.1, to Catius Lepidus) until 6.2.1 where, in a letter to Arrianus (again) he receives two: but this is an obituary notice and we shall see below that this is a sufficient explanation for the return to formality.[10] Ummidius Quadratus provides another example: two names at 6.11.1 (to Maximus), one at 7.28.6 (to Geminus). So too Julius Frontinus: see 4.8.3; 5.1.5; 9.19.1; all to different addressees, two names only in the first reference. Similarly Julius Servianus is given two names at 7.6.8 to Macrinus and one a 8.23.5 to Marcellinus (the double-name at 10.2.1 is justified by the context of Book 10). Similarly Arulenus Rusticus (two names at 1.5.2 and 1.14.2, one at 3.11.3 and 5.1.8; all to different addressees) and Mettius Carus (two names at 1.5.3 and 7.19.5 (well separated) and one at 7.27.14, all to different addressees).

There are some more puzzling cases. Atilius Crescens receives one name at 1.9.8 (to Fundanus) and 2.14.2 (to Maximus), and two at 6.8.1 (to Priscus). Since in the first two cases the name is accompanied by *noster* and the last is a letter of commendation we may have a trace of the introductory paradigm so clear in Cicero. Spurinna receives one name at 1.5.8, 3.1.1 and 4.27.5 (all different addressees), and two at 2.7.1 (to a fourth), possibly because of the formal subject matter. Fronto Catius receives two names at 2.11.3 (to Arrianus) and one at 4.9.15 (to Ursus), but then in another letter to Ursus (6.13.2) he is back to two names. This case appears to be a genuine anomaly, but not a serious impediment to the other patterns. Perhaps Fronto was simply not memorable enough to continue to survive on one name (unless the formal context is at work). The double-name references to Licinius Nepos at 6.5.1 (contrast 5.4.2; 5.9.3; 5.13.1; Licinius had been introduced with two names at 4.29.2) and to Corellius Rufus at 7.11.3 (introduced with two names at 1.12.1, but then see 4.17.2; 5.1.5; 7.31.4; 9.13.6) are also hard to explain, but in both cases we should observe the basic pattern of introduction by two names followed by letters to other addresses using single-names which is only slightly disturbed by the anomalous references noted here.

There are, then, traces of progressive decreases in formality in name-usage between correspondents, but they are heavily overlaid with a pattern of decreasing formality irrespective of addressee. To a large extent this justifies Vidman's implication that the collection is in some degree a single literary work (p. 586, cited above). This suggests literary self-awareness and editorial planning and activity. Furthermore, this allows us to see that, in a sense, the reader replaces the various addressees with the result that the new pattern of name-usage may be regarded as a good parallel to the Cicero-

nian (and thus provides evidence which suggests that in Pliny's original correspondence he followed the same principles).[11]

It would follow from the tenor of this discussion that the use of a single-name for the first appearance of a character should be distinctive, as indeed it proves to be. But since this raises the question of the hierarchy of name-forms, discussion had better take place in that context. Adams produced the following schema for Cicero (p. 164):—

a) highly formal	three name reference
b) formal	two names
c) informal	one name
d) intimate	*mi* + one name (voc.) *praenomen* with or without *mi*

Adams further observed the greater aristocratic exclusivity of *praenomen* + *cognomen* as against *nomen* + *cognomen* and (even more) *praenomen* + *nomen*. Arguably, Pliny preserves the high formality of the triple name reference in the pleas for citizen rights in letters to Trajan. We have certainly seen evidence that the distinction between (b) and (c) still obtains, and *mi* + one name (voc.) is characteristic of Trajan's rescripts to Pliny: not intimacy, but the familiarity which the great allow themselves. The *praenomen* is exceptional in Pliny and needs treatment below. As to the distinct strata of name forms in (b), Pliny shows a considerable difference. The *praenomen* + *cognomen* (aristocratic for Cicero) is characteristic of references to historical characters (Sherwin-White, p. 113; Vidman, pp. 593ff); the *praenomen* + *nomen* is formal, but not associated with a particular social level; rather it is used for introductions, recommendations and other formal contexts (Sherwin-White, p. 113; Vidman, pp. 594ff). The usual form of reference is *nomen* + *cognomen,* but senatorials may be treated to two *cognomina* instead (Vidman, pp. 588f). This may be seen as a result of the shift in the values of the *nomen* and the *cognomen* at the expense of the former which becomes visible after Cicero's time. Vidman's study shows Cornutus Tertullus whose official name, as it were, was C. Iulius Cornutus (p. 588), but also Arulenus Rusticus (two *cognomina*) cited in the *Fasti Ostienses* and *Potentini* as Q. Arulenus Rusticus. Vidman provides further examples (p. 589) showing that the *cognomen* (or rather the first *cognomen*) has achieved something of the status of the *nomen*. Moreover, whereas in Cicero the single *nomen* is used for men of lower status than the single *cognomen*, in Pliny the *cognomen* is the usual name for single-name references. Although that distinction has virtually disappeared in Pliny (see Vidman, p. 593 for single *nomina*), it may still be the case that the difference between *nomen* + *cognomen* and *cognomen* +

cognomen was felt and that the Ciceronian social distinction has shifted rather than disappeared.

As to the single-name there are distinct occasions for its use, some well known. Non-citizens (Vidman, p. 587), Greeks, even some with citizenship (Vidman, p. 589f), and, less markedly and with other peculiarities, women tend to be designated by single-name (women need further discussion below). Otherwise very well known contemporaries, especially senatorials (Vidman, p. 590), or those well known to Pliny and his addressee (Vidman, p. 591f), are so designated as well, the latter with *meus* or *noster*. Both usages are reflections of the introductory paradigm where formality is greatest when the person referred to is not known to the addressee/ reader or not well known to the writer.

A noticeable sub-category of the very well known is that of certain poets. The Editor of *Liverpool Classical Monthly* cited in one editorial (*LCM* 13.10 (1988), 130-131) "Macniece's *Eclogue for Christmas* (death and eminence have earned the author the right to drop the forename)." Clearly dead people do not necessarily achieve single-names, even famous ones, as we may see from Vidman's list of historical characters who are designated by *praenomen* + *cognomen* (p. 594). Indeed the recently dead receive in their obituary notices two names (even if they have been referred to by either double- or single-name already in the collection, and even if other characters are single-named in the obituary letters), unless they are women (4.21; 5.16; 8.5; none named; but even here see 7.24, Ummidia Quadratilla). The only exceptions are more apparent than real, a pupil of the addressee in a *consolatio* to Julius Genitor (7.30) and a history of the Elder Pliny's death for Tacitus (6.16): neither are named. See in this regard: 1.12; 3.7; 3.21; 5.5; 6.2; 7.24; 8.18; 8.23; cf. also 9.9. Turning to dead poets we see that almost invariably they do receive a single name (I omit Greek poets who have only one name anyway). Thus Ennius and Accius at 5.3.6; Catullus at 1.16.5, 4.14.5 and 4.27.4; Horace at 9.22.2; Lucretius at 4.18.1; Nonianus (apparently) at 1.13.3; Plautus and Terence at 1.16.6 (cf. 6.21.4): Propertius at 6.15.1 and 9.22.1. Calvus is single-named as a poet at 1.16.5 and 4.27.4, but also as an orator at 1.2.2 (with *meum*), and at 5.3.5 he is double-named as an orator (who also wrote light verse) in a list of orators and public figures. Virgil is anonymously quoted at 5.8.3, 6.20.1, 6.33.1 and 7.20.4. But at 3.7.8 and 5.6.43 he is single-named as a poet. Oddly he is treated to two names (*praenomen* + *nomen*) at 5.3.6. The anomaly is curious and one notices the proximity of *Ennius Acciusque;* but also of *Cornelius Nepos* and a long list of orators and public figures (5.3.5) double-named. Both Senecas only use the *nomen* for Virgil, but Quintilian uses the *nomen* some 45 times and once the same combination as Pliny, *P. Vergilius,* at

8.3.24. This may have something to do with Virgil's exceptional status and we shall see a similar curiosity in Pliny's treatment of Cicero. Silius Italicus (3.7) and Valerius Martialis (3.21) are double-named, but this is a case of obituary formality (perhaps the same may be said of Valerius Flaccus and Caesius Bassus at Quint. 10.1.90 and 10.1.96). Pomponius Secundus is double-named at 3.5.3 in the title of the Elder Pliny's biography and in a slightly curious way at 7.17.11 (*Pomponius Secundus* (*hic scriptor tragoediarum*) . . .). An element of quality judgement could perhaps be present in that Pomponius was an amateur whose plays and poems were unpopular. Quintilian too uses the double-name in his review of literature (10.1.98), perhaps *somewhat* unusually in the poets' section). At any rate, Pliny also double-names Seneca in a list of public figures at 5.3.5, while writers as such are separately listed at 5.3.6. Living poets (see 1.16; 6.15; 6.21; 9.22) have double names, but in these cases we are clearly dealing with contemporary figures whose writing is only a part of their life, or whose status as poet is unconfirmed. When a person who writes poem dies, he may become a poet, a historical figure who also wrote, or a non-entity: until then he is, as it were, *sub judice,* only such a person as his status and character make him, and subject to the normal etiquette of naming. A poet, on the other is distinctive, everybody's property: he may be treated as informally as friends or possessions.

Other kinds of writer seem to be differentiated. Dead orators (apart from Cicero) may be double-named (a list at 5.3.5 including Calvus) or single-named (Calvus at 1.2.2); dead historians are double-named (Cornelius Nepos at 5.3.6; Titus Livius at 2.3.8 and 6.20.5). In Quintillian's review of literature we find Sallustius and Cremutius, but Titus Livius, Servilius Nonianus and Bassus Aufidius (10.1.101-104): under orators (excluding Cicero) we find 7 double-named and 4 single-named. Under poets the proportions are more or less reversed: 8 double-named (a number of these may be explained as obituary or as distinguishing homonymous poets) and 16 different single-named poets. Arguably orators and historians are more likely to retain double-names postumously than certified poets, possibly in part because they tended to be more engaged in public life. Cicero deserves special mention. Quintilian calls him *M. Tullius* and *Cicero* (10.1.105f) and Pliny calls him *M. Tullius* (1.20.4; 3.15.1; 4.8.4; 5.3.5; 9.2.2; 9.26.8), *Cicero* (1.5.11; 7.4.3, 6), *M. Cicero* (7.17.13) and *Marcus noster* (1.2.4., one of the only two single-name *praenomina* in the collection). The extreme variation is a sign of a special relationship Pliny seems to have felt existed between himself and his model.

Death, eminence and the single-name are found combined also in the case of some dead Emperors. Generally in Books 1-9 dead Emperors are designated by single-name or by name + title (*imperator, Caesar, princeps* or *divus*) whereas the current Emperor is designated by title alone (usually *imperator, princeps* or *Caesar,* with or without epithets). The only significant difference appearing in Book 10 is that Nerva too is not designated by name, but as Trajan's (adoptive) father (10.1; 10.4; 10.8; 10.58). As to the selection of single-name or name + title for dead Emperors, a pattern emerges, albeit with slightly indeterminate edges: disfavoured Emperors are unlikely to receive the title. Thus Domitian is referred to in thirteen letters by name alone (including two, to and from Trajan), but the title is only used as 4.11.7 (*Caesar* in a contemporary quotation), 4.11.8 (*princeps,* where the office is at point)[12] and 10.60 (a letter by Trajan where *princeps* is used as an anaphoric after the single-name). Conspicuously the name alone is used in 10.65 (by Pliny) in company with Augustus, Vespasian and Titus, each of whom has *divus* attached to the name. (At 1.12 we find *isti latroni* in a contemporary quote.) Similarly, Nero is designated by name alone in six letters (1.5; 3.5; 3.7; 5.3; 5.5; 6.31 in a quote), in one of which we find *divum Iulium, divum Augustum, divum Nervam, Tiberium Caesarem* followed by *Neronem enim transeo* (5.3.5-6). Galba (2.20) and Vitellius (3.7) are referred to once each and only the single name is used (the context is neutral), but since such a clearly favoured Emperor as Nerva is designated by single name at 4.9.2 (and anaphorically at 4.22.4) against Pliny's usual practice for him, Galba and Vitellius must remain in a shadowy interstice. By contrast, Augustus is always designate by name + *divus*[13] (5.3; 8.8; 10.65; 10.79; 10.80; 10.84; the last from Trajan); Vespasian by name + *divus* (1.14; 10.65) or *imperator* (3.5) except in a letter which begins with a dense collocation of dead Emperors designated by name alone (4.9: Nerva, Domitian, Vespasian Titus); Nerva has name + *divus* three times (4.11.14; 5.3; 7.33), name + *imperator* three times (4.17; 4.22; 7.31, name alone in the letter (4.9) just mentioned. Nerva is also designated by *Caesar* alone (with aspectual point) at 9.13.22, by *princeps* alone in a quotation (9.13.23) and by name alone as an anaphoric after name + *imperator* at 4.22 (similarly *ipse imperator* in the same letter). Titus is designated by name + *divus* (10.65); otherwise only at 1.18.3 (unless this is Domitian; see Sherwin-White *ad loc.*) as part of the set phrase *Caesaris amici. Caesar* is attached to Tiberius at 5.3.5-6 (in company with Julius, Augustus and Nerva, all with *divus,* and Nero designated by name alone), and to Claudius at 1.13.3 and 10.70. *Caesar* and *princeps* are both used on their own for Claudius in 8.6 where the intention may be to highlight Pallas' outrageous behaviour by concentrating attention on the office. Only at 10.71 is the name alone used, and that by Trajan in a rescript to a letter of Pliny which used *Claudius Caesar* (10.70).

To sum up: the current Emperor is not to be named (either in direct address or in third person reference), but is designated by title, usually *princeps* or *Caesar.* Dead Emperors' names are available (and may have been needed for identification sometimes), but only single-names are used (sometimes with a title too), partly through the public accessibility of fame, partly through complications with *praenomina* and imperial *cognomina.* Domitian and Nero are conspicuously designated almost always by name alone, Augustus, Vespasian and Nerva almost always by name + title, except that Nerva becomes Trajan's *pater* in letters to Trajan. Like poets, Emperors belong to everybody, as it were (unless they are also someone's relative, like Nerva) and therefore are treated with something resembling informality.

A special use of single names deserves mention. Whereas there is a high proportion of double-naming in Books 1-9 (even higher in Book 10), out of some 40 persons (excluding Emperors and Greeks and direct address) designated by name in quotations only four are designated by double-name (Satrius Rufus and Mettius Modestus in 1.5; Domitius Afer in 2.14.10; Publicius Certus in 9.13.17). This seems to suggest a difference between spoken language and written language of a certain level of formality. Somewhat similarly, vocatives are almost lacking in Books 1-9 and in Book 10 name-vocatives are addressed down the social scale not up it: but name-vocatives are comparatively frequent in quotations in Books 1-9 and always use the single-name (*Secunde,* 1.5.5; *Paete,* 3.16.6, 13; *Curiane,* 5.1.6; *Suberane,* 7.6.11; *Secunde,* 9.13.8; *vir clarissime Veiento,* 9.13.19; *Vergini,* 9.19.5; *Cluvi,* 9.19.5) even in formal contexts.

That fame, or certain kinds of fame, enable a name to become public property is to some extent tangential to the decreasing formality of reference under investigation. Nevertheless it leads conveniently to the third deviation from the basic system visible in Cicero, viz. a certain reticence about the name of (some) relatives and (some) women, for which it may be regarded as a corollary.

Pliny refers to a number of his relatives in letters within and without his family circle, including letters to Trajan. About his mother he writes to Calpurnius Fabatus (7.11.3), but also to Tacitus (6.16.4, 21; 6.20.4, 5, 12) and Romatius Firmus (1.19.1). About his second wife only to Quadratus (9.13.4). About his second wife's mother only to non-relatives (1.18.3; 3.19.8; 6.10.1; 10.51.1). About his uncle similarly (1.19.1, to Romatius, 3.5.1, 12; 5.8.5; 6.16.1, 12; 6.20.1, 2 to Tacitus). Calpurnius Fabatus is referred to in letters to his daughter, Hispulla (4.19.1; 8.11.3), and to outsiders (5.14.8; 8.20.3; 10.120.2). Calpurnia's father to his father, Calpurnia's grandfather, Fabatus (5.11.2; 6.12.3; 6.30.4), and to his sister, Hispulla (4.19.1; 8.11.1), but not to outsiders (he was dead and hardly news). Calpurnia is referred to in letters to her grandfather and her aunt, but also Pontius (as was her grandfather), Maximus and (official) Trajan. The aunt is referred to in letters to her father, Calpurnia's grandfather, but also Pontius (again) and (official) Trajan. In all of these cases kin-terms are used, never names. On the other hand, Pliny refers to a relative by marriage of his ex-mother-in-law by name (*adfinem eius, Caelium Clementem*) in a plea to Trajan (10.51.1), and his ex-wife's step-father also by name at 9.13.13 (*Bittius Proculus . . . uxoris meae, quem amiseram, vitricus*) in a letter to Quadratus.

The two exceptions are remote and both need to be named in the context. Apart from them there is complete consistency. Pliny's side of the family is never mentioned to members of his wife's, except his mother at 7.11.3, but this is clearly not a policy of exclusion (no letters to members of his own side were published) and Pliny does not seem to have particularly restricted mention of his family to others (naturally *mutual* relatives will turn up fairly often in correspondence). That his father is never mentioned is not to do with him being a relative, but probably because Pliny lived with his mother, and his father died while Pliny was young. Similar reasons explain the restriction on references to Calpurnia's father. In Pliny's letters, then, we meet a much more specific *name*-avoidance than is shown in the partial restrictions visible in Cicero, but it is not possible to tell whether this stems from a respect for his relatives in general (as addressees and as subjects), or for his *elder* relatives (Calpurnia excepted, but other factors enter here), nor can we, therefore, be confident about assessing the importance of the intent to publish as a factor in the final state of the use of kin-terms in the published letters. Nevertheless, the name-avoidance is significant irrespective of this question, for the reading public can be seen as an extension of the class of non-family to which of Pliny's addressees belong.

The relatives of Pliny's addressees, other than the shared relatives already discussed, are treated in very much the same way. Relatives of the following are referred to by kin-terms: Romatius Firmus (who appeared as an addressee in the preceding paragraph as well) at 1.19.1; Calvina at 2.4; Corellia Hispulla at 3.3; Spurinna and Cottia at 3.10.1; Calpurnius Macer at 5.18.1; Servianus at 6.26.1; Quintilian (not the rhetorician) at 6.32.1; Maximus at 6.34.1; Praesens 7.3.1; Genialis at 8.13.1. There are, perhaps, four special cases. Pliny consistently refers to Junius Mauricius' nephews and niece by kin-terms in 1.14 and 2.18. Junius' brother is called *frater* four times in those letters. However, at 1.14.2 he explains that it is an honour

to choose a husband (for Junius' niece) *ex quo nasci nepotes Aruleno Rustico deceat*. It may be relevant that the name is in an oblique case, but it is certainly of the greatest moment that the use of the name is pregnant, suggesting that the name and all it means must be continued properly (cf. *nomina* at 3.3.7 and 8.10.3 and cf. Cic. *ad Famm.* 2.16.5). It is also significant that Pliny usually refers to Avienus as Junius' *frater* in these two letters. A similar case appears at 6.32.1 to Quintilian: *quamvis et ipse sis continentissimus et filiam tuam ita institueris, ut decebat tuam filiam, Tutili neptem . . .* (at 6.32.2 Pliny calls the girl *puellae nostrae* as a gesture of warmth). At 3.8.1 to Suetonius, Pliny refers to *Caesennium Silvanum, propinquum tuum* in a response to a letter of recommendation. The name would have been necessary in Suetonius' letter, perhaps here too, and the closeness of the relationship is not great. Finally, in a letter to Statius Sabinus Pliny writes, *scribis mihi Sabinam, quae nos reliquit heredes, Modestum servum suum, nusquam liberum esse iussisse* (4.10.1; the name, Sabina, recurs at 4.10.2). Such is the pattern developed so far, that despite the homonymity and the fact that Statius was one of Sabina's heirs, one must suppose that if the two were related, they were not closely related. In general we can see in the matter of relatives a much greater strictness about names in Pliny than in Cicero, but, or rather therefore, one misses the distinction that allows Cicero some degree of greater freedom over his own relatives' names than over his addressees' relatives' names. One may also see the virtual disappearance of the *praenomen* used on its own (or with a kin-term). In Pliny it occurs only at 1.2.4 (*Marci nostri* = Cicero) and 2.9.2 as an anaphoric, picking up *Sexti Eruci mei* (2.9.1) where it distinguishes an otherwise homonymous son from his father (see Vidman, p. 595). Neither of these, be it noted, is a relative (note also the *cognomen* used in address by Thrasea Paetus' wife at 3.16.6, 13).

Only the slightest distinction between male and female relatives can be discerned in the preceding material (because of the almost total ban on names), and that only in the idea that men have a name to pass on and be lived up to. In other references to women there is a distinction, however. The bulk of references to women does not use names. Most often they are denominated *uxor, filia* or *mater* and defined in terms of a male relative. Sometimes the genitive of a man's name is attached (3.9.17; 3.16.9; 6.32.1; 9.13.16), most often it is easily supplied from the context. A few are defined in terms of a female relative or patron (4.11.11; 7.19.9; 7.24.2), and *municeps nostra* (in a quotation at 6.24.2) and *amiculam quandam* (3.9.13) are quite exceptional. About a third of the references to women in Books 1-9 use names, and of these, references to 8 locate them in relationships to men (1.5.5; 1.12.9; 1.14.6; 2.20.2; 3.9.29; 6.16.8 (on Tascus see Syme, *JRS* [*Journal of*

Roman Studies] 58 (1968), 140); 9.13.3; 9.13.4), two define them as Vestals (4.11.6; 7.19.1), and two place them in relationships to the remarkable Arria (3.16.1-2; 9.13.3). Eleven individual women are referred to in their own right by name: Aurelia, a distinguished lady signing her will, at 2.20.10; Gratilla, Arria and Fannia, notable exiles, at 3.11.3; Gratilla again at 5.1.8, Arria at 6.24.5 and Fannia at 7.19.1; Sabina, a lady whose will is discussed, 4.10.1, 2; Corellia at 4.17.1 and 7.11.1 (in both letters she is later located in relationships, chiefly to her father); Pomponia Galla, who disinherited her son, at 5.1.1; Gallita, on a charge of adultery, 6.31.4; Attia Viriola, disinherited and taking matters into her own hands, 6.33.2; Ummidia Quadratilla, subject of an obituary character piece (including testamentary details), 7.24.1; Plotina, Trajan's wife (but this is not mentioned), 9.28.1.

The women referred to by name alone and those referred to by name with an indication of their relationship to a male relative form overlapping groups: Corellia, Fannia, Arria are in both. Although there are differences of degree they are all independent, heroic or (Gallita, 6.31.4; Casta, 3.9.29) outrageous. The role of most women would be that of someone's female relative and we have seen that Pliny uses almost only kinterms for all relatives of his own or of his addressees, whether male or female. In other cases it seems to be presupposed that the woman is an adjunct of her male relative, and to use the name would suggest something unusual or notable about her. Since this could well be ambiguous one may presume that name-avoidance was practised (if one knew the name in the first place). It is certainly striking that in letters of commendation Pliny may fill in the family background of his candidate and may mention a mother or grandmother, but only once does Pliny use the woman's name (1.14.6) and he stresses here probity anyway. In Book 10 the proportion of names increases because Pliny's pleas for his clients need the specification, but the location in relationship to a man remains constant. Only *Antonia Maximilla, ornatissima femina* (10.5.2) and Furia Prima, Flavius Archippus' accuser (10.60) stand out. As with relatives, so with women, Pliny is in some respects stricter than Cicero. Although prominent women like Arria, Fannia and Quadratilla can be named without any slur and with a freedom not visible in Cicero (Clodia is quite differently treated), the restriction on the names of the bulk of women seems greater and may indicate a polarization at least partly due to conspicuous examples of emancipation.

The fourth variation programmed at the beginning of this section concerned name-avoidance. Quite often Cicero seems ill at ease with using a particular name, either through uncertainty about the social dynamics (see Adams, pp. 163ff) or through distaste for the person (e.g. Clodia, Antony and, at times, Dolabella, Terentia and Pompey) or to avoid giving offense to his addressee (as with Dolabella's name in the letters to Appius Claudius: Dolabella's engagement to Tullia was embarrassing). This last category seems to be absent in Pliny, possibly because sensitive letters of this kind were weeded out before publication. As to the first two types, there is hardly a sign. *Isti latroni* for Domitian (1.12.8) against Pliny's usual practice for that person is a clear case, but is a quotation of an utterance of Corellius Rufus. Perhaps Regulus' *Stoicorum simiam* (of Rusticus Arulenus) is another case, but again quoted (1.5.2). The avoidance of Publicius Certus' name until 9.13.13 is in Pliny's own words, but is an imitation in the letter of a rhetorical ploy used by Pliny at the time of the events described. Apart from these insignificant cases Pliny criticizes dead people by name (see Sherwin-White, pp. 54-55), but in these cases the lapse of time since the events is a complicating factor. A letter written at the time might later be considerably clarified by the insertion of names (if, of course, any had been omitted in the first place); a letter written later would be less subject to the emotions that cause avoidance (and would again be the clearer for using names). There is, however, a certain amount of anonymous criticism in Pliny (2.6, *quendam;* 3.11.2, *quibusdam;* 6.8.3, *cuiusdam . . .* ; 6.17, *duo aut tres;* 8.22, *quidam* (8.22.4); 9.12 *quidam;* 9.27, *amici cuiusdam;* cf. 9.26.1, *quodam oratore . . . parum grandi et ornato*). In some cases it might look as though a name could have been (rather than definitely was) suppressed for publication as a measure of discretion, and this seems possible also in non-critical cases (see 1.24.1, *amicus tuus;* or was this just a name that would mean nothing to the wider audience? 3.9.25, *reo gratiosissimo;* 3.11.2; 4.17.2, *isto;* 6.17.1, *cuiusdam amici;* 7.31.1, *discipulum;* 8.3.1, *cuiusdam eruditissumi;* 9.27.1, *cuiusdam*). Sometimes a moral exemplum for good or ill is constructed and the individual is not terribly important (2.6; 7.26; 8.22; 9.12), but an overlapping category is the anecdotal usage where the characters do not require names, or where names would obtrude too much detail or individuality (1.20.1, *quodam docto;* 2.3.8, *Gaditanum quendam;* 2.6.3, *qui mihi proximus recumbebat;* 3.5.12, *quendam ex amicis;* 4.9.9; 4.12)—or where the name was simply forgotten. In general, then, Pliny's non-naming (except for slaves and official titles, such as *consul* etc.) does not suggest the variety or directness of Ciceronian emotions, but rather an eye on the wider audience.

The most consistently comparable feature in the two name-systems is that a character tends to be named more formally on his first appearance in a letter than later in the same letter. At the outset of this discussion I called this a fundamental tendency, and did so on the grounds that it is so common (it is widespread throughout Latin literature). But in fact it is itself only one aspect of a more general tendency, unevenly reflected in literature, that an introduction requires a formal transfer of information which need not be repeated, or fully repeated, thereafter. Material obviously relevant to this tendency was designated as a variation (the second) at the beginning of this discussion simply because of its spasmodic appearance in literature: in Cicero it requires a good sequence of letters between the same correspondents, and in Pliny the blurring of the boundaries between different addressees further reduces detail. Nevertheless, it can still be seen that the introduction provides a paradigm of name-usage: the use of a name is the assumption of a privilege which, once granted, may be continued with less formality. Status, gender and family relationships have clear effects on the degree of restriction there is on the privilege (thus variations (i) and (iii) too fall into the area covered by the paradigm). We may see supporting evidence or parallels for this analysis in the description of an "introduction" in Horace (*Sat.* 1.6.54ff), in greetings scenes in Roman Comedy and in the role of the *nomenclator* as intermediary. It may now be suggested that the use of a name is felt to be a privilege because of its special bonding with its bearer. A vast amount of evidence is available in Greek and Latin for this idea, but it is intractible in a confined space. In this context we may at least recall certain pregnant uses of names in Cicero, for example *ad Famm.* 2.4.1, *quid est quod possit graviter a Cicerone scribi ad Curionem, nisi de Republica?* (in a letter to Curio); *ad Famm.* 4.5.5, *noli te oblivisci Ciceronem esse;* and *ad Famm.* 9.26.2, *in eo, inquis, convivio Cicero ille!* Such pregnant uses are found in Pliny and two have already been observed (1.14.2, *Aruleno Rustico;* 6.32.1, *Tutili*) and parallels might be added (4.17.2, *Corelli,* and probably 7.11.3, *Corelli Rufi*). For such a use in self-reference there is *ego Plinius ille quem nosti* (1.6.1). Finally, we might consider the anecdote at 9.23.2-3. Some intelligent, so the story goes, bystander asked Tacitus '*Tacitus es an Plinius?*' The question may help to suggest an aspect of names which has some role in establishing the bond between name and name-bearer, for the speaker is not asking if his neighbour is called Tacitus or Pliny, but if he "is" Tacitus or Pliny. Although this use of *esse* is hardly unusual, we might, however, look also at the pleonastic use of εἶναι e.g. Hdts 4.33.[14]

Notes

1. See e.g. N. E. Collinge, "Thoughts on the pragmatics of Ancient Greek" *PCPhS* [*Proceedings, Cambridge Philological Society*] 34 (1988), 1ff.

2. J. N. Adams, *CQ* 28 (1978), 145f; L. Vidman, *Klio* 63 (1981), 585f. Cf. also D. Schaps, *CQ* [*Classical Quarterly*] 27 (1977), 323ff on women in Greek oratory; A. H. Sommerstein, *Quaderni di Storia* 11 (1980), 393ff on women in Greek and Roman Comedy. Hereafter Adams and Vidman are cited by name only.

3. See Vidman, p. 590, 591-2.

4. See Sherwin-White, p. 534 on *iussisti;* see Vidman, p. 587 on the question of the single name.

5. This is also true for persons such as Pompeius Planta, Suetonius Tranquillus and Voconius Romanus, single-named in Books 1-9.

6. Only Pliny replaces a double name with other forms of reference (10.6, for Antonia Maximilla), but this is one of his friends, and the earlier letter was his own, not Trajan's.

7. In three places Trajan or his secretariat uses fuller nomenclature than Pliny's earlier letter: 10.28, responding to Pliny's unique Gemellinus (10.27): Trajan uses the double-name again at 10.84. For this case see Vidman, p. 587. Perhaps there is something still to be said for supplmenting the text. Secondly, 10.57 for which see Vidman, p. 586; thirdly, 10.60.2 (cf. 10.59) where Pliny's appendix must have supplied the name.

8. Pliny's letters to Trajan commonly use such phrases as *tua pietas* (10.1.1), *bonitas tua* (10.2.3) etc., which have not yet reached the status of third person substitutes for direct address (*ex hypothesi* an extremely unpresuming and humble mode in terms of address and of name use), but are related. On this matter see J. Svennung, *Anredeformen* (Lund, 1958).

9. *Praenomen + cognomen* is generally used for historical characters: see below.

10. Formal context in an obvious sense explains the later formality at 10.94-95 (cf. 1.24) and 10.2.1 (cf. 8.23.5); but see also 9.13.13 (cf. 4.22.4) and perhaps 4.22.3 (cf. earlier references to Iunius Mauricus at 1.5.10f; 3.11.3; all three letters are to different persons).

11. Certain persons are always, or virtually always, referred to by double-name: Cornutus Tertullus is always so named for his first appearance in a letter except in a quote in 4.17.9; see too Verginius Rufus and Marius Priscus. Herennius Senecio is double-named at 1.5.3 and 4.11.12, but single named in a list of single-named persons at 3.11.3.

12. If 1.18.3 (Caesar) refers to Domitian (see Sherwin-White, *ad loc.,* arguing for Titus) the same may be said, for *Caesaris amici* is practically a technical term.

13. Julius Caesar is also designated by single-name (Iulius) + *divus:* 5.3; 8.6.

14. A final observation: there is a very high degree of consistency between the system observed in Pliny's letters and that shown in Tacitus' *Dialogus*.

Mark P. O. Morford (essay date 1992)

SOURCE: Morford, Mark P. O. "*Iubes Esse Liberos:* Pliny's *Panegyricus* and Liberty." *American Journal of Philology* 113 (1992): 575-93.

[*In the following essay, Morford defends Pliny's* Panegyricus *from the harsh criticism it has received, arguing that the work should be viewed within the conventions of ceremonial rhetoric.*]

Pliny's **Panegyricus** has been harshly treated in recent decades. The opinion of Frank Goodyear is typical: "It has fallen, not undeservedly, into almost universal contempt."[1] Sir Ronald Syme is hardly more subtle: "The **Panegyricus** survives as the solitary specimen of Latin eloquence from the century and a half that had elapsed since the death of Cicero. It has done no good to the reputation of the author or the taste of the age."[2] Such opinions from eminent scholars show how far removed our age of scholarship is from an understanding of the *genos epideiktikon,* and they express impatience with the conventions of ceremonial rhetoric, an important category of rhetoric under a monarchy.[3] I propose to show that within these conventions Pliny was offering to Trajan and to his fellow senators a serious statement on the relationship between the princeps and his colleagues after the autocracy of Domitian. Central to this statement is the attempt to define *libertas* under a monarchy, and it will be shown that Pliny's definition displayed the vice of *adulatio* principally insofar as it was required by convention. The necessary attributes of *libertas* for him, as for his friend Tacitus, were *obsequium* and *modestia,* which could be displayed without falling into the extremes of *adulatio* or *ferocia.*[4] I will further show that the choice of an appropriate style for the political content of the speech was important to Pliny and his hearers.[5]

The occasion for the speech was the *gratiarum actio* delivered by the incoming *consules suffecti* on 1 September 100 C.E.[6] The published version may be as much as three times the length of the version delivered in the Curia.[7] Three of Pliny's letters (3.13, 3.18, 6.27) give important information about the rhetorical and political problems involved in composing and revising the speech. In 3.18.4 he records how he recited the revised version to his *amici* over a period of three days, extended, at the request of the audience, from the two days originally planned. He probably read the whole speech in these sessions (rather than just the "lengthy extracts" that Sherwin-White suggests). Attending a recitation was generally a burdensome duty (as Pliny observes in 3.18.4), and busy men would not have given up three days to the recitation if all he had to offer was flattery of Trajan.

In Pliny's view (*Ep.* [*Epistulae*] 3.18.5) the expanded speech was an example of *studia quae prope exstincta refoventur.* He wished it to mark the revival of political oratory whose content might make a difference in the political decisions of the princeps. Syme has correctly observed that "the speech is not merely an encomium of Trajan—it is a kind of senatorial manifesto in favour of constitutional monarchy."[8] Pliny's views are like those of Tacitus in the introduction to the *Agricola.* Neither Tacitus nor Pliny for a moment would have welcomed a return to the oratory of the Republic, which Tacitus in the *Dialogus* explicitly describes as a recipe for anarchy.[9] But Pliny believed that his speech represented a break with its predecessors in the genre, in style, content, and significance.[10]

Pliny emphasizes that both the style and the *materia* of the speech led his friends to give up so much time to his recitation:

> at cui materiae hanc sedulitatem praestiterunt? nempe quam in senatu quoque, ubi perpeti necesse erat, gravari tamen vel puncto temporis solebamus, eandem nunc et qui recitare et qui audire triduo velint inveniuntur, non quia eloquentius quam prius, sed quia liberius ideoque etiam libentius scribitur. accedet ergo hoc quoque laudibus principis nostri, quod res antea tam invisa quam falsa, nunc ut vera ita amabilis facta est.
>
> (*Ep.* 3.18.6-7)

Pliny thus claims that he has transformed the conventional *gratiarum actio* into a statement welcome to the princeps and deserving of the thoughtful attention of his fellow senators. The ultimate audience for the expanded speech, moreover, was not restricted to the group of *amici* who heard the recitation but included all who would read the published version: *memini quidem, me non multis recitasse quod omnibus scripsi* (3.18.9).

The **Panegyricus** represented a new type of oratory at Rome. It was the first time that a living princeps had been eulogized in his presence by means of a speech that was designed to persuade rather than to flatter.[11] Cicero's *Pro Marcello* at first sight appears to be a model for Pliny, for there are many similarities in style and vocabulary.[12] Nevertheless, it is not a valid analogy. Unlike Pliny, Cicero was in an ambiguous situation, and there were grave political uncertainties in a Republic that to many people, including Cicero, still appeared capable of revival in some form. Caesar's position, moreover, was very different from that of Trajan in 100

C.E. He had defeated his enemies in a civil war, and the sign of his power was the exercise of *clementia,* a cause of resentment to the survivors among his enemies and of ambiguous rhetoric to politicians like Cicero. Thus what was outwardly a *gratiarum actio* was also a vehicle for scarcely concealed satire and, as has recently been suggested, possibly even for a call for the removal of Caesar.[13] In two letters written shortly after the original *Pro Marcello* was delivered in the Senate, Cicero revealed more of his intentions. To Servius Sulpicius, writing in the early autumn of 46, he says:

> itaque pluribus verbis egi Caesari gratias . . . sed tamen, quoniam effugi eius offensionem, qui fortasse arbitraretur me hanc rem publicam non putare, si perpetuo tacerem, modice hoc faciam aut etiam intra modum, ut et illius voluntati et meis studiis serviam.
>
> (*Ad Fam.* 4.4.4)

Writing to Papirius Paetus during the summer of 46 he says:

> ergo in officio boni civis non sum reprehendendus. reliquum est, ne quid stulte, ne quid temere dicam aut faciam contra potentes.
>
> (*Ad Fam.* 9.16.5)

The *Pro Marcello,* therefore, is not a true forerunner of the **Panegyricus,** except insofar as Cicero's cautious attitude towards the *potentes* is similar to that of Pliny, or of any politician who seeks to discharge the *officium boni civis* under an autocracy.

A truer model is to be found in the *Evagoras* of Isocrates, where the author points out the difficulty of eulogizing a living person in prose. The poets, he says, are free to use language, imagery, and associative techniques that are denied to the political orator, whose use of language must be precise and factual.[14] Pliny set out to solve the same problems as those defined by Isocrates. He had first to develop an appropriate style as the vehicle for his message, and, second, he had to speak *in honorem principis* without flattery or excessive frankness, that is, without falling into the extremes of *adulatio* or *contumacia.* His language had to be precise and based upon fact. These were Pliny's goals, we must emphasize: how successful he was in achieving them is not our primary concern here.

Sometime before the recitation described in **Epistles** 3.18 Pliny sent a copy of the *Panegyricus* to his friend Voconius Romanus.[15] In the covering letter he emphasizes the difficulty of dealing with a subject on which there was little to be said that was new: *in hac* [*materia*] *nota vulgata dicta sunt omnia.* The choice of an appropriate style, however, was especially difficult. Even philistines, he said, can manage *inventio* and *enuntiatio,* but it takes careful research to be successful in arrangement and ornamentation: *nam invenire praeclare, enuntiare magnifice interdum etiam barbari solent, disponere apte, figurare varie nisi eruditis negatum est* (**Ep.** 3.13.3).[16]

He chose the intermediate style, that is, between the *genus subtile* and the *genus grande atque robustum* as defined by Quintilian.[17] This style allowed for variety and flexibility in figures of speech:

> medius hic modus et translationibus crebrior et figuris erit iucundior, egressionibus amoenus, compositione aptus, sententiis dulcis, lenior tamen ut amnis et lucidus quidem set virentibus utrimque silvis inumbratus.
>
> (Quint. *Inst.* 12.10.60)[18]

The metaphor of light and shade refers to Quintilian's analogy of painting and rhetoric explained earlier in *Inst.* 12.10. Just as Zeuxis had discovered the system of using light and shade—*luminum umbrarumque invenisse rationem . . . traditur*—so the orators of the intermediate style used light and shade in their figures.[19] This also was Pliny's principle in the *Panegyricus: nec vero adfectanda sunt semper elata et excelsa. nam ut in pictura lumen non alia res magis quam umbra commendat, ita orationem tam summittere quam attollere decet* (**Ep.** 3.13.4).

Pliny's careful attention to the intermediate style has been overlooked by those critics who are offended by his "woolly repetitiveness" (Goodyear) and "exuberant redundance" (Syme).[20] The evidence clearly indicates that he chose the varied style because it best would combine the rhetorical functions of pleasure and persuasion, exactly as Quintilian had defined its purpose: *tertium illud . . . delectandi sive, ut alii dicunt, conciliandi praestare videatur officium* (*Inst.* 12.10.59).[21] The intermediate style was distinguished by variety and figures. The importance of figured speech in situations where tact and indirection are necessary has been shown by Ahl and Dyer.[22] Its appropriateness to Pliny's situation is well expressed by the words of Demetrius: "To flatter is disgraceful, to censure is dangerous. Best is the intermediate style, that is, the figured style (*to eschēmatizomenon*)."[23]

The idea of the mean goes back to Aristotle and is expressed by Cicero, for example, in the *Orator:*[24]

> itaque neque humilem et abiectam orationem nec nimis altam et exaggeratam probat [sc., Aristoteles], plenam tamen eam vult esse gravitatis, ut eos qui audient ad maiorem admirationem possit traducere.
>
> (*Or.* 192)

Cicero discusses the intermediate style in *Orator* 91-96, and a few quotations will illustrate the close connection between his doctrine and the style chosen by Pliny:

(91) uberius est aliud aliquantoque robustius quam hoc humile de quo dictum est, summissius autem quam illud de quo iam dicetur amplissimum. hoc in genere nervorum vel minimum, suavitatis autem est vel plurimum . . . (92) huic omnia dicendi ornamenta conveniunt plurimumque est in hac orationis forma suavitatis . . . (95) in idem genus orationis—loquor enim de illa modica ac temperata—verborum cadunt lumina omnia, multa etiam sententiarum . . . (96) est enim quoddam etiam insigne et florens orationis pictum et expolitum genus, in quo omnes verborum, omnes sententiarum inligantur lepores.

The student of the **Panegyricus** cannot consider its political purpose without understanding the significance of Pliny's choice of style. Style and purpose are inseparable, as Pliny shows in his description of the reworking of the speech in *Ep.* 3.18. The intermediate style, with its *figurae*, was the only choice for the orator who wished to make policy suggestions that might also imply criticism of the princeps. Cicero is quite clear about the modest expectations (and therefore modest risks for the orator) of this style:[25]

> medius ille [sc., orator] autem, quem modicum et temperatum voco . . . non extimescet ancipites dicendi incertosque casus; etiam si quando minus succedet, ut saepe fit, magnum tamen periculum non adibit: alte enim cadere non potest.

> (*Or.* 98)

It is true that Cicero is here concerned primarily with style, but he also is considering its effect on the audience. In Pliny's case the effect on the audience (that is, primarily Trajan) was his principal concern, and the choice of style was therefore as much a political as an aesthetic decision.

Finally, the choice of style was influenced by the importance of knowing what was appropriate, *to prepon* in Greek, in Latin, *decorum*.[26] Quintilian points out that Thersites' criticism of Agamemnon aroused contempt: put the words in Diomedes' mouth and everyone will find *magnum animum* in them.[27] He recognizes the dangers faced by the orator: *nec tamen quis et pro quo, sed etiam apud quem dicas interest: facit enim fortuna discrimen et potestas, nec eadem apud principem . . . ratio est (Inst.* 11.1.43). Pliny's style, therefore, is a part of his political message. Those (and this includes nearly all modern critics) who are quick to dismiss the **Panegyricus** as mere flattery ignore an essential part of Pliny's technique and purpose.

Once he had chosen the appropriate style, Pliny was faced by a greater problem, that is, how to praise the princeps in his presence with moderation and credibility. Quintilian again is a guide for understanding Pliny's approach. In giving rules for praising human beings he focuses upon the moral qualities of the recipient of praise: *animi semper vera laus,* he says, *sed non una per hoc opus* [sc. *laudationem*] *via ducitur.*[28] Quintilian was following Cicero, who gives the primary position to *laudes virtutis.*[29]

Cicero also had distinguished between the *naturae et fortunae bona,* which Quintilian specifies as the education of the recipient, the early evidence of his good character, and his mature virtues, as shown by his *facta et dicta.*[30] Quintilian adds that the chance of praising the living is unusual: *rara haec occasio est (Inst.* 3.10.17). This point, in fact, is further evidence for the originality of Pliny's speech. Indeed, Cicero introduces his discussion of *laudationes* by pointing out that they are a Greek genre, developed more to give pleasure to the audience and to compliment the recipient of praise.[31] Roman *laudationes,* however, are most often funeral eulogies marked by brevity and simplicity.[32] Cicero does admit that *laudationes* in the Greek fashion are sometimes necessary, but rarely. They do not seem to have become any more frequent in the 150 years after the writing of the *De Oratore,* so that Pliny's originality can confidently be assumed.[33]

While Pliny observes the rules laid down by Cicero and Quintilian, they do not address his particular dilemma. A professor writing a textbook does not have to be as circumspect as a consul addressing the princeps. Pliny analyzes the problem in connection with a speech earlier than the **Panegyricus:**[34]

> omni hac, etsi non adulatione, specie tamen adulationis abstinui, non tamquam liber et constans, sed tamquam intellegens principis nostri, cuius videbam hanc esse praecipuam laudem, si nihil quasi ex necessitate decernerem.

> (*Ep.* 6.27.2)

He counsels matching the words to the occasion, but does not provide an adequate answer to the charge of indulging in flattery. Both in this letter, however, and in the exordium to the **Panegyricus,** he claims to have avoided even the appearance of flattery.[35] In other words, his praise of the princeps (so he would have us believe) is based on facts and on the circumstances of the speech, and is not therefore just a repetition of empty formulae. Secondly, he maintains that his views are given voluntarily, which supports his claim to be speaking with *fides* and *veritas.* For a tyrant demands praise, which is freely given to a princeps whose character welcomes freedom of speech. Such praise, spoken in the Senate, may attempt also to define *libertas* restored.

The central political theme of the **Panegyricus** is the relationship between the princeps and the Senate, which defines *libertas.* We have seen that Pliny sought to avoid the appearance of *adulatio,* and he says very clearly in the letter to Severus that he equally avoided *contumacia:* he spoke, he says, *non tamquam liber et constans* (***Ep.*** 6.27.2). The attributes of *libertas* (in speech) and *constantia* are those of the Stoic opponents of principes, Thrasea or the younger Helvidius Priscus, whose execution seven years earlier was still a vivid memory.[36] Pliny, like Tacitus, did not choose the noble but politically ineffectual path of *contumacia* leading to martyrdom.[37]

Serious attempts to define *libertas* under the Principate began with Seneca. His hopes for a workable relationship between the princeps and his senatorial colleagues were expressed in the *De Clementia* and in the policy speech at the beginning of Nero's reign.[38] Central to Seneca's definition were the separation of the *domus* of the princeps from the public business of the state and the collegial assumption of responsibilities by Senate and princeps in their separate spheres. But Seneca's vision was impractical and gave way to a personal concern with *otium* and withdrawal from political activity.[39] A more flexible definition of *libertas* emerged after the executions of Stoics and other critics of the regime under Nero and the Flavians. This is the definition of Tacitus and Pliny: by it a good man could obtain high office and perform significant service to the *res publica* even under a bad princeps like Domitian. This is expressed in the *Agricola,* when Tacitus contrasts those who pursued their view of liberty even to death with men like Agricola:

> Domitiani vero natura . . . moderatione tamen prudentiaque Agricolae leniebatur, quia non contumacia neque inani iactatione libertatis famam fatumque provocabat. sciant, quibus moris est inlicita mirari, posse etiam sub malis principibus magnos viros esse, obsequiumque ac modestiam, si industria ac vigor adsint, eo laudis excedere, quo plerique per abrupta sed in nullum rei publicae usum ambitiosa morte inclaruerunt.

> (*Agr.* 42.3-4)

Under Trajan, *optimo principe, libertas* was still defined by inequalities of power. No one (least of all Pliny) could deny that the autocratic power of Domitian was still wielded by Trajan.[40] Therefore the practical mode of displaying *libertas* was that of *obsequium* and *moderatio,* as opposed to *adulatio* or *contumacia.* This is precisely the formula developed by Tacitus in his estimate of the public career of Agricola.

The *Panegyricus,* therefore, for all its ceremonial rhetoric, was a serious attempt to define a working relationship between Senate and princeps. Pliny was trying to show *obsequium* with dignity towards a ruler who held overwhelming power, since the *Lex de Imperio Vespasiani* had already defined the constitutional limits of senatorial *libertas.*[41] His purpose in speaking

was explicitly to outline a course of action for the princeps: *ut consulis voce sub titulo gratiarum agendarum boni principes quae facerent recognoscerent, mali quae facere deberent (Pan.* 4.1).[42] Fundamental to this policy was the subordination of the princeps to the laws, whose supremacy had been affirmed by the *Lex de Imperio Vespasiani:*

> utique quaecunque ex usu reipublicae maiestate divinarum humanarum publicarum privatarumque rerum esse censebit, ei agere ius potestasque sit, ita ut divo Aug. Tiberioque Iulio Caesari Aug. Tiberioque Claudio Caesari Aug. Germanico fuit.

> (*ILS* 244, 17-21)

The princeps had the same power to act *legibus solutus* as his predecessors:[43]

> utique quibus legibus plebeive scitis scriptum fuit, ne divus Aug. [etc.] tenerentur, iis legibus plebisque scitis imp. Caesar Vespasianus solutus sit.

> (*ILS* 244, 23-25)

This power was exercised so insensitively by Domitian that he aroused the bitter resentment of many moderate senators, including those, like Tacitus and Pliny, whose political careers had been advanced under him. Trajan was less blunt, even though the inequalities of power between princeps and Senate were the same. To gain the cooperation of the Senate, which he must have seen as necessary to the stability of his regime, he needed to clothe his legal authority to act *legibus solutus* in the appearance of acting as if he were *legibus subiectus.* In the end the power of the princeps was the same, since by law (that is, the *Lex de Imperio Vespasiani*) he had as much power as he needed to pursue whatever policy he wished to implement. His power would not have been diminished if he were (as Pliny suggests) subject to the law, since the law did not limit his power. Yet the appearance of subjection to the law showed *moderatio* on the part of the princeps, and the act of taking the oath to obey the laws guaranteed the favor of the gods. Therefore Pliny could meaningfully say: *non est princeps super leges sed leges super principem, idemque Caesari consuli quod ceteris non licet. iurat in leges attendentibus dis (**Pan.** [Panegyricus] 65.1).*

The position of Trajan vis-à-vis the laws is central to Pliny's effort to define *libertas.* As the ***Pan.*** 65.1 shows, Trajan's consulship was the political context in which the issue of senatorial liberty was most delicate. When the ***Panegyricus*** was delivered in the Senate, Trajan had been consul three times. Pliny passes over his first consulship in silence (except for a passing mention at 64.4); he devotes one chapter (56) to his second consulship, and thirty-four (57-80) to his third. The imbalance reflects the relative importance of each consulship to

Pliny's design. He ignores the first, because it was held (in 91) under Domitian, and to acknowledge Trajan's adherence to the Flavians would have been embarrassing in a speech which repeatedly criticized Domitian.[44] The second consulship was held in 98. It began on 1 January, when Trajan was already in Germany as *legatus Augusti*. After the death of Nerva on 27 January, Trajan, who was at Cologne at the time, stayed in Germany, and he did not return to Rome until October 99. He spent the whole of his second consulship (which he held until the end of April) campaigning and inspecting the armies on the Rhine and Danube.[45] Pliny, therefore, praises this consulship briefly, since Trajan's *acta* did not directly concern the topics upon which the speech is primarily focused, that is, liberty and the relationship of Senate and princeps.

Trajan returned to Rome in October 99 and held his third consulship during the first two months of 100, the year of Pliny's suffect consulship, the trial of Marius Priscus, and the delivery of the **Panegyricus**.[46] It was a specially important year for Pliny, and therefore he devotes one-third of the speech to Trajan's third consulship, which he makes the context for his most significant remarks about senatorial liberty. Chapters 60-77 deal directly with the consulship: three preliminary chapters (57-59) lead up to Trajan's acceptance of the third consulship, and three concluding chapters (78-80) anticipate a fourth consulship (actually held in January 101) and end with a comparison of Trajan to Jupiter himself:

> talia esse crediderim, quae ille mundi parens temperat nutu, si quando oculos demisit in terras, et fata mortalium inter divina opera numerare dignatus est; qua nunc parte liber solutusque tantum caelo vacat, postquam te dedit, qui erga hominum genus vice sua fungereris. fungeris enim sufficisque mandanti, cum tibi dies omnis summa cum utilitate nostra, summa cum tua laude condatur.
>
> (80.4-5)

This statement should be considered in the context of Jupiter's importance in imperial ideology.[47] It finds its visual expression in the attic of the Trajanic arch at Beneventum.[48] Although it appears to be one of the most extreme examples of flattery in the speech, its placement, as the concluding flourish to chapters 57-80, is an indication of the importance which Pliny attached to the third consulship.[49]

The central part of the review of the consulship occupies chapters 63-77, beginning with *praevertor iam ad consulatum tuum*.[50] Its unity is marked by the two *renuntiationes,* respectively for the ordinary and suffect consulships of 100.[51] Pliny's rhetorical *color* focuses upon the collegiality of the princeps. Thus at the first *renuntiatio* Trajan's *civilitas* was shown in his personal attendance, an example for his successors and a contrast with his predecessors, notably Domitian (63.1). By attending he acted as an ordinary candidate of senatorial rank, *unus ex nobis* (63.2). His predecessors' absence from their *renuntiatio* was an indication of their contempt for the forms of the political process in the *res publica* (63.4-6), whereas Trajan's attendance displayed his *moderatio* and *sanctitas* (63.8).

In the next chapter (64.1-3) Pliny recalls how Trajan stood before the seated consul and took the oath to perform the duties of office faithfully:

> peracta erant sollemnia comitiorum, si principem cogitares, iamque se omnis turba commoverat, cum tu mirantibus cunctis accedis ad consulis sellam, adigendum te praebes in verba principibus ignota, nisi cum iurare cogerent alios. . . . Imperator ergo et Caesar et Augustus <et> pontifex maximus stetit ante gremium consulis, seditque consul principe ante se stante . . . quin etiam sedens stanti praeiit ius iurandum, et ille iuravit, expressit explanavitque verba quibus caput suum domum suam, si scienter fefellisset, deorum irae consecraret.

The *renuntiatio* of 99 is especially significant for Pliny's definition of senatorial *libertas*. He does not conceal that the ritual of *renuntiatio* was mostly symbolic: the spoken formulae were *longum illud carmen comitiorum* (63.2), and the procedure was but the *liberae civitatis simulatio* (63.5).[52] What was important was that the princeps had publicly shown himself as a senator among senators, a citizen among citizens. His power was superior to all, but he still shared the rank and duties of his colleagues. Thus the antithesis between *dominus* and *princeps* is significant (63.6): *haec persuasio [sc. abstinendi comitiis] superbissimis dominis erat, ut sibi viderentur principes esse desinere, si quid facerent tamquam senatores.* A *dominus* orders the *renuntiatio* of his election (63.5, *renuntiareque te consulem iussisse contentus*), but a constitutional princeps orders his fellow senators to act as free citizens (66.4, *iubes esse liberos*). Finally, the sincerity of Trajan's words and actions was proved by the symbolism of his standing to take the oath administered by the seated consul.

The virtues of such a princeps are *moderatio* and *sanctitas* (63.8), the former being the counterpart of the *obsequium* shown by his fellow citizens. In 64.4 Trajan acts as a citizen subject to the laws, even though he has the power to act as a *dominus: idem tertio consulem fecisse quod primo, idem principem quod privatum, idem imperatorem quod sub imperatore.* Pliny then shows Trajan's display of the same *moderatio* on taking office on 1 January 100. This was the occasion for showing to the *populus* that he would observe the laws: *ipse te legibus subiecisti* (65.1). As has been shown above, the laws in fact gave Trajan all the power he needed: nevertheless, to show publicly that he was subject to them was to display *moderatio* and *sanctitas*. Thus the Roman republican tradition of the supremacy of law and the establishment of the *pax deorum* continued under Trajan. Pliny shows in chapters 63-65 how the essential legal, moral, and religious foundations of the *res publica* were maintained by the new princeps.

With this lengthy preparation, Pliny is now in a position to approach the heart of his discussion of the relationship of the princeps to the Senate. He describes Trajan's attendance in the Senate on 1 January 100:

> inluxerat primus consulatus tui dies, quo tu curiam ingressus nunc singulos, nunc universos adhortatus es resumere libertatem, capessere quasi communis imperii curas, invigilare publicis utilitatibus et insurgere . . .[53] iubes esse liberos: erimus; iubes quae sentimus promere in medium: proferemus.

> (66.2-4)

These words, which on a superficial reading might seem to be ironic or ridiculous, attempt to express a definition of *libertas* within the confines of the unequal relationship of princeps and Senate. Pliny has elaborately shown how the princeps observes the laws. His *moderatio* is reciprocated by senatorial *obsequium*, which is a virtue if joined to *vigor et industria* and exercised *ex usu rei publicae*. Thus Pliny treads the narrow path between flattery and independence. He recalls (no doubt with some exaggeration, given his own successful career) that under Domitian senators had been reluctant to cooperate with the princeps.[54] By respecting the laws and the dignity of the Senate, Pliny suggests, Trajan will be sure of the energetic (*insurgere*) cooperation of the Senate in administering the state. It is notable that this chapter (66) is the only one (other than 80) in the whole passage dealing with the third consulship, in which Pliny makes prominent use of tropes.[55] The metaphors of the sea, shipwreck, and storm serve several purposes. They allow Pliny to veil a delicate topic in allegorical language, for both he and Trajan had been among those who had successfully navigated the political seas of cooperation with Domitian. They recall well-known passages in Seneca and Lucretius, where the same metaphors had been used for the tranquil *otium* of the virtuous man who avoids or retires from political activity.[56] They illuminate a comparatively unfigured section of the speech so as to contrast light and shade at a point where stylistic *variatio* can be most effective.[57] Finally, they draw attention to the most significant statements in the speech, where Pliny seeks to define senatorial liberty. Thus Pliny chooses stylistic *variatio* exactly where he needs it.

After dealing with Trajan's activities in connection with the *comitia* (67-75), Pliny turns to an example of cooperation between Trajan and the Senate during Tra-

jan's third consulship (76). The trial of Marius Priscus is delayed until the end of the review of the consulship so as to appear in an especially prominent place.[58] Since Pliny himself took a leading part in the trial, he does not need to draw particular attention to his own part.[59] Instead he focuses upon the princeps.[60] Trajan attends the Senate in person on three successive days: he presides as consul, and asks senators to express their opinions openly. Thus Pliny shows how the Senate responded to the command of 66.4 (*iubes esse liberos*), and he does not need to remind his hearers that he had taken the leading part in speaking as a senator before the princeps in his role as consul:[61]

> iam quam antiquum, quam consulare quod triduum totum senatus sub exemplo patientiae tuae sedit, cum interea nihil praeter consulem ageres! interrogatus censuit quisque quod placuit; <licuit> dissentire discedere, et copiam iudicii sui rei publicae facere; consulti omnes atque etiam dinumerati sumus, vicitque sententia non prima sed melior.

> (*Pan.* 76.1-2)

The chapter on the trial of Marius exhibits senatorial *libertas* in action. It shows the *moderatio* of the princeps, and it displays Senate and consul acting according to the ancient traditions of the Roman Republic. Its purpose is to show that senatorial *libertas* can still be practiced. Limited as such liberty is, it is nevertheless meaningful in a context where the lesser partner in an unequal relationship of power still has significant administrative responsibilities. In this context senators were still motivated by a tradition of public service and personal dignity. These are significant attributes of liberty under a constitutional monarch, for under a tyrant (which is the *color* repeatedly used by Pliny for Domitian, not least in this very chapter) even their limited display was suppressed.[62]

It is hard in modern and democratic societies to understand, much less sympathize with, such political role-playing. Nevertheless, it is irresponsible to dismiss the **Panegyricus** without an effort to understand how the political circumstances of Rome in 100 C.E. compelled Pliny to choose the style and material displayed in the speech. Perhaps some understanding can be gained from an episode during the Renaissance. In November 1599 the archdukes Albert and Isabella, governors of the Spanish Netherlands, visited the University of Leuven. Its leading professor, Lipsius, addressed them on a passage from Seneca's *De Clementia*.[63] Later he dedicated his commentary on the **Panegyricus** to them. remarking in the preface that he had not been interested in *schemata & ornatus illos floridae orationis*. These he found to be trivial and pedantic.[64] What concerned him, and should concern us, was the substance of the speech, which focuses upon the political relationship between the ruler and those whose cooperation is necessary for the effective government of the state.[65]

Notes

1. F. R. D. Goodyear in *Cambridge History of Classical Literature* II (Cambridge 1982) 660 (paperback ed., II.4 164). For a survey of scholarship on the *Panegyricus* see P. Fedeli, "Il 'Panegirico' di Plinio nella critica moderna," *ANRW* [*Aufstieg und Niedergang der Roemischen Welt*] II.33.1, 387-514. For the structure and purpose of the *Panegyricus* see D. Feurstein, *Aufbau und Argumentation im Plinianischen Panegyricus* (Innsbruck 1979). I have used the text of W. Kühn, *Plinius der Jüngere Panegyrikus* (Darmstadt 1985), and the commentary of M. Durry, *Pline le Jeune, Panégyrique de Trajan* (Paris 1938). Useful also are M. Durry, *Pline le Jeune, IV: Lettres, Livre X, et Panégyrique de Trajan* (Paris 1947), and B. Radice, *Pliny, Letters and Panegyric* II (London and Cambridge, Mass., 1969).

2. R. Syme, *Tacitus* (Oxford 1958) 114; cf. also 94-95. For a more balanced assessment see R. Syme, review of Durry's *Pline le Jeune, Panégyrique* in *JRS* [*Journal of Roman Studies*] 28 (1938) 217-24.

3. For epideictic oratory see George Kennedy, *The Art of Persuasion in Greece* (Princeton 1963) 152-54; idem, *The Art of Rhetoric in the Roman World* (Princeton 1972) 21-23, 428-30, 510, 634-37. Quintilian (*Inst.* 3.7) does not deal with the type represented by Pliny's *gratiarum actio*. The two essays on epideictic attributed to Menander, while much later than Pliny's speech, usefully summarize the rules for epideictic: see L. Spengler, *Rhetores Graeci* (Leipzig 1856) III 329-67, 368-446. In the second essay only § 229 (pp. 376.31-377.9 Sp.) is at all close to Pliny's speech: the topic is comparison of the recipient of praise with his predecessor. In the chapters on the *Technē peri tōn Panegyrikōn* attributed to Dionysius of Halicarnassus (*Opuscula* 2 [*Opera* VI], ed. H. Usener and L. Radermacher [Stuttgart 1965] 255-60), only § 8 (on *boulēsis*) is relevant to Pliny. See also S. McCormack, "Latin Prose Panegyrics," in *Empire and Aftermath*, ed. T. A. Dorey (London 1975) 143-205.

4. For these components of *libertas* see M. Vielberg, *Pflichten, Werte, Ideale*, Hermes, Einzelschriften 52 (Stuttgart 1987). Cf. Fedeli (note 1 above) 497: "il senato si accontentava del rispetto della sua *dignitas* e . . . della . . . *securitas;* anche se si trattava di una *securitas* garantita dall'*obsequium.*" For relations between Senate and princeps see

further M. Morford, "How Tacitus Defined Liberty," *ANRW* II.33.4, 3420-49. esp. 3440-42; D. C. A. Shotter, "Tacitus' View of Emperors and the Principate," *ANRW* II.33.4, 3263-3361, esp. 3314-27; P. Soverini, "Impero e imperatori nell'opera di Plinio il Giovane," *ANRW* II.33.1, 515-54.

5. For the connection between rhetorical style and political content see F. M. Ahl. "The Art of Safe Criticism in Greece and Rome," *AJP* 105 (1984) 174-208; Ahl does not discuss Pliny's *Panegyricus*. For discussion of the relationship between rhetoric and politics in Pliny see G. Picone, *L'eloquenza di Plinio* (Palermo 1978) esp. 159-90 (173ff. for *Pan.*). See also Kennedy 1972 (note 3 above) 543-46, who concludes (548) that "it was possible . . . to use the art of persuasion in a speech to the emperor." Further references for style and language appear in Fedeli (note 1 above) 417-21.

6. See R. J. A. Talbert, *The Senate of Imperial Rome* (Princeton 1984) 227-28, for the *gratiarum actio* as part of senatorial procedure. Cf. B. Radice, "Pliny and the *Panegyricus*," *G&R* [*Greece & Rome*] 15 (1968) 166-72, who emphasizes Pliny's originality in using the *gratiarum actio* for substantive political discussion.

7. A. N. Sherwin-White, *The Letters of Pliny* (Oxford 1967) 251-52 (on *Pan.* 4) estimates three sessions of one and one-half hours each; cf. Durry 1938 and 1947 (note 1 above) 87. Syme 1958 (note 2 above) 94 estimates about three to four times the length (one hour) of the original. Both estimates are dismissed by Fedeli (note 1 above) 405 as "semplici ipotesi." Pliny could speak for even longer: see *Ep.* 2.11.14 (five hours) and 4.16.3 (seven hours). For the relationship between the *Panegyricus* and *Ep.* 3.18 see Fedeli (note 1 above) 405-11. Still useful is J. Mesk, "Die Überarbeitung des Plinianischen Panegyricus auf Trajan," *WS* [*Wiener Studien*] 32 (1910) 239-60.

8. Syme 1938 (note 2 above) 223: cf. Fedeli (note 1 above) 492-97.

9. *Dial.* 38.2. Although Maternus is the speaker, the views are those of Tacitus. *Ep.* 9.13 appears to show that Pliny spoke more freely than Tacitus, but that letter refers to a debate that took place before Trajan's accession (indeed, probably before his adoption). In a speech given in the presence of the princeps Pliny was as circumspect as Tacitus. For the relationship of the *Panegyricus* to Tacitus in matters of style see R. T. Bruère, "Tacitus and Pliny's *Panegyricus*," *CP* [*Classical Philology*] 49 (1954) 161-79.

10. For a negative view of Pliny's optimism see Syme 1938 (note 2 above) 224.

11. Cf. Durry 1947 (note 1 above) 88-89: "Pline créait un genre. . . . [P]our la première fois l'éloge d'un empereur vivant faisait le sujet d'un livre entier." For details of Pliny's style see F. Gamberini, *Stylistic Theory and Practice in the Younger Pliny* (Hildesheim 1983) 377-448 (for the *Panegyricus*), 393-99 ("Devices of Eulogy," for the use of rhetorical figures in praising Trajan). For the limitations of Gamberini's approach see R. Pitkäranta in *Gnomon* 59 (1987) 357-59.

12. See G. Suster, "De Plinio Ciceronis imitatore," *RFIC* [*Rivista di Filologia e di Istruzione Classica*] 18 (1890) 74-86.

13. See R. R. Dyer, "Rhetoric and Intention in Cicero's *Pro Marcello*," *JRS* 80 (1990) 17-30: "it issues, under the veil of figures, a clear summons to tyrannicide" (30). For an example of Cicero's satire see *Pro Mar.* 5, with its fulsome hyperbole and extravagant figures.

14. Isoc. *Ev.* 8-10. Xenophon imitated Isocrates in his *Agesilaos*. See J. Mesk, "Zur Quellenanalyse des Plinianischen Panegyricus," *WS* 33 (1911) 71-100, esp. 78-79 (for *Ev.*) and 80 (for *Ages.*). Mesk (note 7 above) 82-84 overvalues *Pro Marcello* as a model for the *Panegyricus*.

15. *Ep.* 3.13. Sherwin-White (note 7 above) 245 suggests that the letter was written "a good while after his delivery of the *Panegyricus* . . . and before his recitation of the final version."

16. For the antithesis of *eruditi* and *barbari* cf. Velleius 2.73.1, of Sextus Pompeius: *hic adulescens erat studiis rudis, sermone barbarus.*

17. Quint. *Inst.* 12.10.58.

18. R. G. Austin, *Quintiliani Institutionis Oratoriae Liber XII* (Oxford 1972) 201 suggests that Quintilian is combining two passages from Cicero, *Or.* 21 and 96. The latter passage, especially, with its metaphors of flowers and color is a likely model.

19. Quint. *Inst.* 12.10.1-9. For perceptive commentary see Austin (note 18 above) 135-52. Zeuxis' system is referred to in 12.10.4. The analogy of the visual arts and oratory is used by Cicero (*Br.* 70 and, most explicitly, *De Or.* 3.26).

20. See notes 1 and 2 above for references. Gamberini (note 11 above) 402-3, 496. more accurately points out the lack of variety in the "long continuum of figures."

21. The function of *conciliandi* is a prerequisite for persuasion and is achieved by the modesty of the speaker (see *Inst.* 11.3.161) as well as by the attractiveness of his style.

22. Ahl (note 5 above) 185-97; Dyer (note 13 above) 26-30.

23. *On Style* 294, quoted by Dyer (note 13 above) 27. Demetrius is specifically discussing figured speech in a democracy, but the passage is part of a general discussion of indirect criticism beginning (289) with criticism of "a tyrant or any other violent person." The precise translation of *schēma, to schēmatizomenon,* etc., is harder to achieve in English than in Latin, where *oratio figurata* better indicates the connotations of art and indirection than Grube's "innuendo" and Roberts's "covert hint" (quoted by Dyer [note 13 above] n. 57). For the Peripatetic origins of the doctrines of Demetrius see F. Solmsen, "Demetrius *peri hermeneias* und sein Peripatetisches Quellenmaterial," *Hermes* 66 (1931) 241-67.

24. Cf. Arist. *Rh.* 1404b3-4. In *Ad Fam.* 1.9.23 (Dec. 54) Cicero acknowledges his debt to Aristotle in the *De Oratore*. For the relationship between Roman rhetoric and the Peripatetic tradition see F. Solmsen, "The Aristotelian Tradition in Ancient Rhetoric," *AJP* 62 (1941) 35-50, 169-90. For the Aristotelian *mesotēs* see G. L. Hendrickson, "The Peripatetic Mean of Style and the Three Stylistic Characters," *AJP* 25 (1904) 125-46. See also Solmsen 1931 (note 23 above); Kennedy 1963 (note 3 above) 272-84.

25. Cf. Quint. *Inst.* 9.2.67-69.

26. Discussed by Cicero at *Or.* 69-74.

27. *Inst.* 11.1.37.

28. Quint. *Inst.* 3.7.10-18: § 15 is quoted. The fullest exposition of the rules for *laudationes* is that of Cic. *De Or.* 2.341-49.

29. *De Or.* 2.343. Cicero divides the *virtutes* into several categories in 2.343-45.

30. Cic. *De Or.* 2.342, 346-47; Quint. *Inst.* 3.7.15.

31. Cic. *De Or.* 2.341-49 (341 quoted).

32. *De Or.* 2.341.

33. *Encomium* was a regular part of the *progymnasmata* in the schools; see Quint. *Inst.* 2.4.20. Cf. S. F. Bonner, *Education in Ancient Rome* (Berkeley 1977) 264-66; Kennedy 1972 (note 3 above) 636-37; and see note 3 above for the *basilikoi logoi* of Menander. Fedeli (note 1 above) 411-16 denies the independence of Pliny and concludes (416): "Plinio dipende strettamente dallo schema del *basilikos logos*."

34. Sherwin-White (note 7 above) 387 suggests that Pliny is referring to the session of the Senate described in *Pan.* 78, at which senators urged Tra-

jan to take a fourth consulship. He was *Cos. IV* in Jan. 101, so that this session would have taken place not long before Pliny's *gratiarum actio*. The words *omni hac . . . abstinui* are appropriately translated by Guillemin "j'ai renoncé à cet usage qui, sans être une flatterie, ressemble à une flatterie."

35. *Pan.* 1.6, [he prays] *utque omnibus quae dicentur a me, libertas fides veritas constet, tantumque a specie adulationis absit gratiarum actio mea quantum abest a necessitate.*

36. Tac. *Agr.* 45.1, *mox nostrae duxere Helvidium in carcerem manus.* For senatorial feeling in the aftermath of the execution of Helvidius see Pliny *Ep.* 9.13 (cf. note 9 above).

37. Tac. *Agr.* 42.4.

38. Tac. *Ann.* 13.4.2, *discretam domum et rem publicam. teneret antiqua munia senatus.*

39. As expressed, for example, in *De Otio, De Tranquillitate* 3-5, *Ep.* 19.

40. See K. H. Waters, "Traianus Domitiani Continuator," *AJP* 90 (1969) 385-404: "the two emperors were in fact committed to an almost identical policy. That policy was one of increasing autocracy." Waters does refer to Pliny's letter about Helvidius (391, where 9.13 should be read for 9.3), but he does not have time for the style and purpose of the *Panegyricus* (398, "arrant compost of wishful thinking," etc.).

41. *ILS* [*Inscriptiones Latinae Selectae*] 244; M. McCrum and A. G. Woodhead, *Select Documents of the Principates of the Flavian Emperors, A.D. 68-96* (Cambridge, 1966) 1. Discussion by P. A. Brunt, "Lex de Imperio Vespasiani," *JRS* 67 (1977) 95-116.

42. Cf. Sen. *De Clem.* 1.1, *scribere de clementia, Nero Caesar, institui, ut quodam modo speculi vice fungerer et te tibi ostenderem.* The function of being "a mirror for princes" is closely related to that of giving advice.

43. As Brunt (note 41 above) 109 has pointed out, this chapter is superfluous, since the previous one (*ILS* 244, 17-21) has already given the same legal power to the princeps.

44. See Syme 1958 (note 2 above) 33-35; R. Hanslik, in *RE* [*Revue de Esthetique*] Supp. 10, 1037.

45. *Pan.* 56.4, *gestum non in hoc urbis otio et intimo sinu pacis, sed iuxta barbaras gentes.* Earlier allusions to the campaigns of 97-99 were made at *Pan.* 9.5, 10.3, 12.3-4, 16.2. Cf. Tac. *Germ.* 37.2;

Syme 1958 (note 2 above) 16-18, 46-49, 642-43, 648; Hanslik (note 44 above) 1044-49. See also R. Syme, "Consulates in Absence," *JRS* 48 (1958) 1-9.

46. Cf. *Pan.* 92.2, *quid, quod eundem in annum consulatum nostrum <in quem tuum> contulisti?* See Hanslik (note 44 above) 1053; Syme 1958 (note 2 above) 18; Durry 1938 (note 1 above) 237-38, who prefers the end of April for the term of Trajan's consulship, relying on *Pan.* 61.6.

47. R. Fears, "The Cult of Jupiter and Roman Imperial Ideology," *ANRW* II.17.1, 3-141 (80-85 for Trajan).

48. See Fears (note 47 above) 83-85, with plate XI, nos. 70a and b (bibl. on 83). Cf. D. E. Strong, *Roman Art* (Harmondsworth 1976) 87-88 and plates 90-91. There are verbal echoes in Pliny of Lucan *BC* 1.56-59 (part of the *laudes Neronis*, 1.33-66); other references are noted by Durry 1938 (note 1 above) 204-5.

49. Trajan is likened to Hercules at *Pan.* 14.5 and 82.7; see Syme 1958 (note 2 above) 57; Hanslik (note 44 above) 1055; Durry 1938 (note 1 above) 108.

50. For *praevertor* cf. *Ep.* 5.14.7 and Durry 1938 (note 1 above) 181, where 7 should be read for 17.

51. The *renuntiatio* of chapter 63 must have taken place after Trajan's return to Rome in October 99, that of chapter 77 probably before the trial of Priscus in the Senate, perhaps on 12 January 100. See Talbert (note 6 above) 204-5; Durry 1938 (note 1 above) 244-45. For elections in the early Empire see Talbert, 341-45, with bibl. on 341, n. 1; Durry, 241-42; B. M. Levick, "Imperial Control of the Elections in the Early Principate," *Historia* 16 (1967) 207-30; and further references in Fedeli (note 1 above) 435-38. For a description of electoral procedure in the Senate see Pliny *Ep.* 3.20 (cf. Talbert, 205, 343).

52. The truth is also revealed at *Pan.* 72.1 (*uni tibi in quo et res publica et nos sumus*), *Ep.* 3.20.12 (*sunt quidem cuncta sub unius arbitrio*), and 4.25.5. For difficulties in interpreting Pliny's evidence for Trajan's role in the elections see Levick (note 51 above) 219-28, and cf. *Pan.* 92.3.

53. The words *invigilare* and *insurgere* express the same ideas as Tacitus' phrase (*Agr.* 42.4) *si industria ac vigor adsint.*

54. *Pan.* 62.3-5; cf. 66.3.

55. For the limited use of tropes in *Pan.* 61-80 see Gamberini (note 11 above) 444. 'Trope' is defined by Quintilian (*Inst.* 8.6.1) as *verbi vel sermonis a*

propria significatione in aliam cum virtute muta-tio. The special *virtus* of the metaphors of the storm and shipwreck at 66.3 is that they allow Pliny to speak *decentius* (see *Inst.* 8.6.6) on a delicate topic. Cf. Pliny's choice of the word *decet* at *Ep.* 3.13.4.

56. Seneca *De Otio* 8.4; *Ep.* 19.2; Lucretius 2.1-13.

57. See Pliny *Ep.* 3.13.4, and cf. note 19 above and related remarks in the text.

58. See Sherwin-White (note 7 above) 166 ("the trial is placed out of order in *Pan.* 76"), 168, and (for the chronology of the trial) 56-62.

59. He does this fully in *Ep.* 2.11, esp. 2.11.4-6, where he is careful to note Trajan's special concern for his well-being.

60. See Talbert (note 6 above) 183; and Durry 1938 (note 1 above) 198-99, for the presence of principes in the Senate.

61. Cf. *Ep.* 2.11.10, *Princeps praesidebat (erat enim consul); 2.11.11, imaginare quae sollicitudo nobis, qui metus, quibus super tanta re in illo coetu praesente Caesare dicendum erat.*

62. *Pan.* 76.3, *at quis antea loqui, quis hiscere audebat praeter miseros illos qui primi interrogabantur?* The usual view of modern scholars is expressed by L. Wickert. *RE* 22 (1954) 1998-2296, s.v. *princeps*, that *libertas* in Pliny's time was but "die zahme Behaglichkeit des Untertanen" (col. 2098). Cf. C. Wirszubski, *Libertas as a Political Idea at Rome during the Late Republic and Early Principate* (Cambridge 1950) 167, defining it as "merely the courage to keep one's *dignitas* alive." But see Morford (note 4 above) 3440-42.

63. *De Clem.* 1.3.3, from *illius demum magnitudo stabilis fundataque est* to *se opponunt.* The passage expresses the necessity of harmony between ruler and subjects for the stability of the state. The same passage is quoted by Mesk 1911 (note 14 above), without mention of Lipsius, as a model for *Pan.* 48. Lipsius' extemporaneous address was published together with his commentary on the *Panegyricus: Iusti Lipsi Dissertatiuncula Apud Principes: Item C. Plini Panegyricus Liber Traiano Dictus, Cum Eiusdem Lipsi perpetuo Commentario* (Antwerp 1600).

64. Lipsius, *Ad Lectorem Panegyrici: quid quod nec schemata & ornatus illos floridae orationis tango? nam visum mihi pertenuia haec & scholastica esse, quae didicisse oporteat magis quam discere, aut alio certe doctore discere. neque "Aquila," ut in proverbio est, "captat muscas."*

65. I am grateful to the editor and an anonymous reader for many helpful suggestions.

Gunhild Vidén (essay date 1993)

SOURCE: Vidén, Gunhild. "Women in the Works of Pliny the Younger." In *Women in Roman Literature: Attitudes of Authors under the Early Empire*, pp. 91-107. Goteborg, Sweden: Acta Universitatis Gothoburgensis, 1993.

[*In the following essay, Vidén discusses Pliny's* Letters *to and about Roman women, illustrating that Pliny included a number of women among his friends and that his traditional Roman view of marriage and family reflected his idea of the exemplary woman.*]

It is hard to think of any author who differs more in tone from Tacitus than his contemporary and friend Pliny the younger. Where Tacitus gives proof of severity and harsh judgement Pliny's work abounds in amiability and benevolence, and if we were only to judge from his letters we would be tempted to say that Rome was never more full of noble men and virtuous women than during his lifetime. Another difference lies in the setting that is described in their works: while Tacitus relates Roman history and society at large, Pliny introduces his private world, with day-to-day glimpses of individuals within the upper classes, in contexts concerning health, economy, career, and other facts of human life. We cannot go to Pliny for a third opinion on the females of the Julio-Claudian house, since that is not his theme, nor can we check his text for references to bad women in general, or to what was considered bad behaviour in a woman in his day, since Pliny is far more concerned with 'nice people' than with their opposites. What we do get are certain glimpses of the lives of Roman upper class women: legal and economic state, as well as their position in the Roman family.

Another thing we get is information about what was considered good female behaviour in Pliny's days; if he is reluctant to offer more hostile portraits than he deems absolutely necessary,[1] he is on the other hand happy to devote his time to portraits of good human beings and bring them forward as *exempla* for others. We have thus a number of letters that deal with exemplary behaviour in men and women, from which we can collect evidence about what was deemed praiseworthy in Pliny's circles.

The glimpses into the world of upper class women that we are allowed through Pliny's letters show us a society where these women were in some respects on an equal footing with men: we find women who sue their opponents, buy property, make wills and manumit their slaves.[2] Pliny seems to take all this as a matter of course, and not worthy of comment, and we can safely assume that his letters are a true reflection of society in this respect: many women enjoyed a considerable degree of economic independence and knew how to use it. This is in no way synonymous with 'equal rights'; all we can deduce is that by this time certain women were economically their own mistresses and that contemporary society had accepted this fact.

The comparatively independent state of the women in Pliny's circle emerges clearly from his own relations to them, as mirrored by his letters. Although the great majority of his letters are addressed to men, there is also a handful addressed to women. The number is not very high,[3] but the interesting point is that Pliny does actually include women in his edition for publication. He seems to have made a representative choice of correspondents for each book, and this choice is, it appears, to include a lady.[4] It seems therefore that women were part of Pliny's circle in their own right, and the matters he deals with in his letters to them are not different from matters discussed with male friends—financial matters, advice, consolation.

FRIENDSHIP WITH WOMEN

Pliny expressly includes women among his friends and in such a way that it is obvious that he is referring to the same kind of friendship towards both men and women. The best example is 3.11.3: 'I lent money to our friend Artemidorus, at a point of time when seven of my friends had been killed or exiled—Senecio, Rusticus and Helvidius were killed and Mauricus, Gratilla, Arria and Fannia were exiled—and a similar fate seemed to be looming over me.'[5] This was a time when friendship, in the specific sense of what is implied in the Latin word *amicitia*,[6] could be dangerous, and the people enumerated by Pliny belonged to a circle of opponents to Domitian, the women just as much as the men.

Another example, probably referring to the same group of people, is found in 5.14.4: 'Cornutus Tertullus and I have both always esteemed highly all those men and women who are examples to the rest of us these days; and such common ties of friendship have joined us very closely together.'[7] Tertullus and Pliny both belong to this group and claim *amicitia* with both the men and the women in the group.

Pliny's *amicitia* with the same women is brought forward once again in 9.13, where it is referred to as one of the reasons why Pliny undertook to write the books on the avenging of Helvidius: 'I was Helvidius' friend, as much as it was possible to be the friend of someone who in fear of the prevalent political situation retired from public life, thereby suppressing his great name and his equally great virtues; I was also the friend of Arria and Fannia, one of whom was Helvidius' stepmother, the other the stepmother's mother'.[8] Friendship with Helvidius obliged Pliny to work in Helvidius'

interests, and this obligation was strengthened by his friendship with other members of Helvidius' family, even female ones.[9]

Another case of *amicitia* with a woman is found in 7.11, a letter where Pliny gives his reasons for selling land cheaply to Corellia. He ends the letter with the wish: 'I hope my co-heirs will accept without protest that I have sold separately what I need not have sold at all. They do not have to follow my example since they are not tied to Corellia by the same obligations as I am. They can look to their own interests; I looked to my friendship with Corellia instead.'[10] This example shows clearly that *amicitia* with a woman was of the same kind as *amicitia* with a man: a tie between two people that included certain reciprocal obligations of a more or less formalized character.[11] This interpretation of *amicitia* is underlined by Pliny's use of the word *iura* to characterize his relationship with Corellia; *iura* could, amongst other things, mean 'the obligations, bonds, or claims arising out of a given relationship.'[12]

The general impression one gets from how Pliny describes his contacts with women is that men and women could meet on more or less equal terms. A woman was not only interesting in traditional roles like those of a lover or protégée; she could conduct business transactions and legal activities and give help and financial support to male friends as well as receive them, and a man could be obliged to a woman through *amicitia* just as much as to another man.[13] Pliny belonged to a group that was bound together by the ties of *amicitia,* and the women that belonged to that group were probably included at the outset because of their connexions with the men in it—as daughters, sisters, and wives. From the examples above it is clear, though, that the bonds of friendship came to be applied to them as individuals, not as mere appendages to certain men. There could be various reasons for that—fathers and husbands died or were exiled, the women came into possession of considerable wealth, or their personal conduct might just as well be such as to gain them a position of their own. That was probably the case with Arria and Fannia. Whatever the reasons, the lasting result was that they counted in their own right in the group.

MARRIED LIFE

The fact that Pliny's contacts with women seem to be contacts between people of equal standing and that there exist terms of friendship between them is no proof of his having liberal ideas on women's position in society. On the contrary, he is a strong adherent of traditional standards and is on all counts a firm supporter of the Augustan marriage legislation.[14] He praises married life in different ways, and most of his family portraits show loyalty and affection between husband and wife, between parents and children.

Mothers could be useful to their children in many ways. The role played by mothers in passing the glory of noble birth to their sons is evident in some letters of recommendation, e. g. 2.13, a recommendation for Voconius Romanus, who is said to be the son of a father who was distinguished in the equestrian order, a stepfather who was even more distinguished and a mother who came from one of the best families.[15] Not only did mothers play this rather passive part of contributing to their sons' nobility; the good mother also took an active interest in her son's activities and successes. Such a mother appears in 5.17 where Pliny praises Calpurnius Piso's recital performance, adding that he congratulated both the mother and the brother of Piso on his success. It seems that they were both present during the recital, although it is the brother who is most highly praised for his display of *pietas* towards his brother during the performance.[16] *Pietas* is the loyalty, dutiful respect and affection that members of a family owed to each other, and as such it was an important virtue for both men and women. Pliny brings up several examples of *pietas* in women, as we will see later on.

Affection and loyalty are common features in Pliny's description of the relations between husbands and wives. The best known case is that of Arria; I will return to her at a later point in the discussion. There are, however, some less obvious cases, where the wives are only mentioned in passing, but in such a way as to give evidence of wifely care and affection. One is 1.12, about Corellius Rufus' death, where the wife Hispulla sends word for Pliny to come and try to talk Corellius out of his decision to starve himself to death; she and her daughter have done everything they can to persuade him to abstain from his decision, but in vain.[17] A similar example is 1.22. Titius Aristo is ill and wants to know whether it is incurable or not: if it is not, he owes it to his wife's prayers, to his daughter's tears and to his friends not to seek a premature death by his own hands.[18]

These two glimpses of worried women show us a world where the wife cares for her husband and where her affection for him is her motive for encouraging him to continue his life. The affection between father and daughter is also evident, and the picture we get is one of a close unity, secured by mutual bonds: the wife and daughter are in a position to urge the husband and father to listen to their claims upon his loyalty towards family members, and by doing so they prove their own loyalty and affection for him. Corellius Rufus is so determined that not even the demands of his closest kin can make him change his decision, but Titius Aristo is at least ready to avoid offending these obligations if at all possible. It seems that his obligations to wife and daughter

have priority over his obligations to his friends; the Latin phrase for the latter is *dandum etiam nobis amicis,* where I take *etiam* as a signal that the claim of his friends did not have quite the same force as that of his wife and daughter.

Another touching description of a loyal and affectionate wife is found in 8.18: Tullus, a decidedly disagreeable character in life, had died and quite unexpectedly left his money to his adopted daughter. He also left a considerable bequest to his wife, who was once heavily reproached for marrying a rich, old and sickly man, but who now turned reproach into praise through her blameless conduct as his wife. We are not spared the sordid details of his crippled state, 'that would have been a burden even to a wife he had married while still young and vigorous';[19] but he carried on living and wanted to live because of the support of his wife who thus changed the reproach she had encountered at the beginning of her marriage into praise for her steadfastness.[20]

Not content with describing marriage in terms of happiness and affection, Pliny also counts it among the blessings of life. This is apparent from several passages, e. g. 1.12 (already mentioned) where Pliny laments the voluntary death of his friend Corellius Rufus. Corellius chose to take his life after long suffering; it was done with due consideration, as befits a wise man, 'and yet he had so many reasons to continue his life: a good conscience, an excellent reputation, great influence, besides a daughter, a wife, a grandchild, sisters, and in addition to all those dear to him also true friends.'[21] Another example is a letter to Calpurnius Macer: 'I am happy that you have a good time; you have your wife and son with you, and you are enjoying the beautiful surroundings of your villa'.[22] Calpurnius is relaxing on one of his estates, and to Pliny the fact that he has his family with him ought to increase his sense of well-being.

A third example is found in 8.23, again a lamentation for a deceased friend. The young Iunius Avitus is dead, and Pliny laments: 'I am grief-stricken because of his youth, because of the blow to his family. He had an aged mother, he had a wife whom he married only a year ago when she was still a virgin, he had a newly-born daughter. What hope, what happiness was not turned into its opposite in one day! He had just become aedile designate, husband and father when he left the magistracy untouched, his mother childless, his wife a widow, his daughter an orphan who will never know her father.'[23]

Another letter suggests that a wife can add to her husband's glory by her good manners or literary achievements, since they are proof of his successful education of her. Letter 1.16 is a letter of praise for

Pompeius Saturninus' literary accomplishments. He has read some letters to Pliny, claiming that they were written by his wife. 'It does not matter whether they are composed by his wife, as he claims, or by himself, which he denies; it is equally glorious to have composed such letters or to have educated his wife, whom he married while she was still a young maiden, to such learning and refinement'.[24] A similar notion emerges from his description of his own young wife Calpurnia.[25] Most of her good qualities are claimed to be the result of the good upbringing her aunt gave her (not surprisingly, since the aunt is the addressee of the letter), but her literary interests are the result of her marriage to Pliny. With becoming modesty, Pliny refrains from claiming that he educated her: her studies are, rather, the result of her love for him.[26] But the image is similar to that of Pompeius Saturninus' marriage: the young girl is a *tabula rasa* at the point of marriage, but due to the good influence of her husband she can develop her intellectual abilities. This description is probably more due to the fact that Pliny wants to enhance the qualities of Pompeius Saturninus than to any true image of female education. It appears from 5.16, the eulogy over the young Minicia Marcella, that intellectual training was part of a young girl's education before marriage.

EXEMPLA

The most interesting aspect of Pliny's descriptions of women are his portraits of women as exemplary. These texts are good indications of what were considered desirable qualities in a woman, or at least what qualities Pliny found it important to bring forward. We cannot expect a full representation of good female qualities since, after all, we are dealing with portraits of certain individuals, and even if Pliny idealized there is no reason to believe that he did not give a basically accurate picture of the person in question. The qualities he does bring forward ought, however, to give us an idea of what was commendable in a woman.

Pliny composed some famous and unforgettable portraits of women, e. g. the heroic Fannia, the robust Ummidia Quadratilla, or his own young wife Calpurnia. Several of the women portrayed by him are exemplary in the true sense: Pliny regards them as models for others, and often declares in what respect they are exemplary.[27] When Pliny recommends Minicius Acilianus as a suitable son-in-law to one of his friends he includes the merits of Minicius' relatives in the catalogue of the man's values, and among other things he can boast of being the grandson of Serrana Procula from Patavium. 'You know the morals of that place; Serrana however is an example of gravity even to the Patavians'.[28] Letter 3.1 describes the dignified life of the aged Spurinna, whose wife is said to be 'a wife of most exemplary character'.[29] Another model to other women appears in

8.5: Macrinus has lost his wife, 'a wife of most exemplary character, even by ancient standards'.[30] Calpurnia Hispulla, the aunt of Pliny's wife, is called 'a model of sisterly affection and loyalty' in the letter directed to her.[31] So, in two of these cases, the woman is 'a wife of most exemplary character,' in Latin *uxor singularis exempli,* without any precise indication of what the exemplary quality consists of, while in two cases we get the precise indication: gravity and *pietas,* this word that must be explained rather than translated and which concerns here the obligations between people who belong to the same family.

Pliny's admiration for Arria, her daughter of the same name and her granddaughter Fannia recurs in several letters. One letter is devoted to the elder Arria and one to Fannia. The main theme of the letter about Arria is that the most famous deeds of men and women are not always the greatest.[32] To illustrate this theme Pliny describes the courage of Arria in episodes that are not as well-known as her famous suicide:[33] concealing from her sick husband the fact that their son was dead; following the large ship that took him to Rome in a small vessel when her request to accompany him as his servant on board the same ship was denied; showing her determination to commit suicide with her husband by trying to kill herself in a very brutal way when she perceived that her family was trying to prevent it.

Pliny tells these stories with comments on what a great thing it is to perform such acts, where there is no promise of glory and perpetual fame, much more so than the suicide itself, which Arria knew would lead to eternal glory.[34] Arria, as she is depicted here, provides clear examples of *pietas,* but Pliny does not attribute that term to her acts, nor does he comment on her conduct except in the above-mentioned context of how much greater it is to perform those things that remain in obscurity. Hence he does not praise explicitly her *pietas, constantia, fides* or the other wifely virtues that are exemplified by Arria's behaviour: they are simply not at issue here.

The case of Fannia is different. She is portrayed in letter 7.19; she is gravely ill and Pliny fears for her life. The whole letter is a kind of proleptic obituary, which praises Fannia in all respects. 'I lament that such a great woman is going to be torn away from the eyes of the state, and I doubt that they will ever see the like of her. What chastity she has, what integrity, what gravity, what constancy!'[35]

Here we find a catalogue of desirable qualities in a woman: *castitas, sanctitas, gravitas, constantia.* *Castitas* need not be further explained, whereas the other nouns are less strictly defined.[36] *Sanctitas* signifies moral purity and integrity and is a quality that is praiseworthy in men and women alike. It is noteworthy that the only time Plotina, the wife of Trajan, is mentioned in the letters, it is with the epithet *sanctissima femina*.[37] This gives us an idea of how commendable *sanctitas* was in a woman: Pliny can hardly be suspected of having used anything but the highest praise about Trajan's wife. This is written at a time when superlatives and abstract nouns began to be used as epithets of magistrates and emperors.[38] The epithets that gradually came to be used of the emperors are those that express qualities desirable in a ruler, such as *pietas, clementia* etc. *Sanctissimus* or *sanctitas* never became stock epithets, but when Pliny uses *sanctissima* of the emperor's wife we can be certain that *sanctitas* was an virtue appropriate in a woman.

Gravitas and *constantia* are words that are quite close to each other in significance: gravity, seriousness, steadfastness in character and behaviour. They are combined with each other on occasion, especially by Cicero.[39] In the present instance Pliny wanted a parallelism, as is evident from his use of *quae . . . quae, quanta . . . quanta*. The story that follows immediately on this exclamation is an illustration of Fannia's *constantia*: she accompanied her husband into exile twice and was exiled because of him once, the reason being that she had asked Senecio to write a book on his life. The latter was brought to trial because of the books and put the blame on Fannia, who was interrogated and eventually exiled. Her bearing during the trial gives proof of *constantia*: she made no attempts at denying the accusations, she answered straightforwardly and did not moderate her answers to evade the danger. She even carried the books that were the cause of her exile with her in that same exile.[40]

Later on she is described as charming, affable, lovable, but also venerable.[41] With these words Pliny gives a new touch to the portrait. The first impression is that of a rather stern lady, a Roman *matrona* of the old kind, full of gravity and constancy; now it turns out that she is also a very agreeable and pleasant person. Pliny's way of arranging her various characteristics here is antithetically: after his description of her courageous behaviour in the trial and exile he goes on to state that she is also charming, with an emphasis on 'also';[42] however, the period is rounded off with *veneranda*. The combination of being both lovable and venerable is unusual, Pliny says, but he does not suggest that it is a contradiction to be both at once. Certainly, the words are contrasted, and we may assume that there is a careful stylistic consideration behind the combination: Pliny wanted his readers to open their eyes a little. Yet there is nothing wrong if even an exemplary lady is the one, as long as she is also the other.

In the next phrase Pliny states that she is an *exemplum*, and of a very special kind: she is a model to both men and women. 'Will we ever again have someone whom we can display as an example to our wives? Will we ever again have a woman who serves as a model even to us men? Whom we see and hear in our presence but admire as much as the women we can only read of?'[43] These rhetorical questions match the preceding characterization: *gravitas* and *constantia* are attributes of a moral bearing worthy of a man, whereas *iucunda, comis* and *amabilis* suggest more traditional female traits. This is not to say that one characteristic is exclusively male and another exclusively female, since all of them could be used of both women and men. Her *constantia* drives her to actions that would be deemed praiseworthy even in a man, e. g. the courage she displays in following her husband into exile and defending his memory, but she is not the only woman to be described as *constans,* and when Pliny recommends her as an example to his own and to other men's wives, it seems fair to assume that it is both her *gravitas* and her affability that are worthy of imitation. She is both the righteous, morally outstanding person that would serve as a model to any Roman man[44] and the charming, affable lady that the same man would happily present as a model to his wife.

Another example of a loyal wife is found in 6.24, where Pliny hears a story about an anonymous woman who finds out that her husband is incurably ill. Not only does she encourage him to seek death but she accompanies him in death, tying herself to him and throwing herself with him into the lake, 'a comrade, nay, even guide and model and coercion in death'.[45] This was a deed, Pliny comments, that was not worth less than the famous act of Arria; if it is less known, it is because the woman was of lower rank than Arria. High reputation and status is not all, a woman can show her dignity through her deeds even if she comes from humble origins.

Letter 5.16 is an obituary. Minicius Fundanus' younger daughter is dead, a young girl of 13, but of an old woman's wisdom.[46] Pliny almost exceeds himself in finding words of praise for her, and we find a whole catalogue of good qualities. She was joyous, lovable and worthy of not only a longer life but almost of immortality.[47] She combined an old woman's wisdom and the gravity of a *matrona* with the sweetness and modesty of a young girl.[48] She was caring, she was intelligent and devoted to her studies, and when she spent time on play it was only with great moderation.[49] She endured her final illness with admirable patience and self-control.[50] More bitter than her death in itself was the moment at which it occurred: she was engaged to be married to an excellent young man, the day was appointed and the guests invited; now her father had to use the money he had intended for the wedding to buy the materials for the funeral.[51]

We find in this portrait a combination of characteristics that resemble those of the portrait of Fannia. The young Minicia is *gravis* and *constans,* like Fannia, but she is also *suavis,* just as Fannia was *iucunda.*[52] Her youth and her maidenhood are underlined, and while Fannia had the *comitas,* graciousness, of the adult woman, Minicia had the *verecundia,* modesty, of the young virgin. The two portraits differ from each other in that Pliny includes a reference to Minicia's intellectual interests, a point which he does not touch upon in the other portrait.

A quite different portrait is the obituary of the almost octogenarian Ummidia Quadratilla, 7.24. It is not an obituary in the same sense as the letter on Minicia, since it does not deal in such detail with the character of the deceased. The description is such as to make us suspect that this is a realistic portrait. Minicia was barely a teenager and yet had already aquired the prudence of an old woman and the gravity of a *matrona;* Ummidia Quadratilla was almost 80 years old, enjoyed good health until her last illness, and 'was even more physically robust than is common in a *matrona*'.[53] In one letter, praise of the mental qualities that exceed what could be expected from the girl's age, in the other the statement of a physical quality that exceeds the norm, too, but not to the woman's advantage. His Minicia is intended to raise admiration and respect, his Quadratilla is a description of the worthy lady's actual appearance.

Later on, Quadratilla is described as *delicata,* 'luxurious,' but in such a way as to turn it into praise of her. Her grandson was educated in her house, and although she lived a luxurious life herself, he was brought up most rigidly, quite in accordance with her wishes.[54] She indulged in dice and in watching her own troupe of mime actors, whom she 'cherished more than is becoming in a lady of high social standing',[55] Pliny says with a slight frown, but whenever she did indulge in such pleasures she sent the boy away to his studies.[56] Pliny has nothing but praise for the way she treated her grandson, and he characterizes it as *pietas,* something which brings him joy.[57]

While his Minicia was idealistic, the realistic nature of his Quadratilla appears from certain unflattering details: the information about Quadratilla's physical appearance, the disclosure of the old lady's unconventional pastimes, which Pliny finds faintly shocking. The point he stresses in her favour is that she had the sound judgement to keep these pastimes for herself and set stricter rules for her young grandson. It was possible to show forbearance with the liberties of an old lady so long as she did not seduce the youth, and this lady showed great sense of responsibility in the education of her grandson. She is not an example to others, but her *pietas* is laudable and hence mentioned by Pliny.

An excellent source for what was considered good behaviour in a woman is found in the letter where Pliny describes his wife, 4.19. There is no reason to doubt Pliny's sincerity in expressing his affection for his young wife;[58] on the other hand it is reasonable to expect that he will describe her in idealized terms when addressing her aunt and teacher: 'nothing else (i. e. than the way she conducts herself) would have been appropriate for a girl who was educated by you.'[59] So, what are his points of praise for this well-bred girl?

To begin with, she has turned out in a way that is worthy of her family, not only of the aunt who educated her but also of her distinguished forefathers.[60] She is intelligent, she is economical, and she is chaste.[61] *Frugalitas,* an economical cast of mind, is the opposite of *luxuria,*[62] which the Romans saw as a most objectionable quality.[63] The praise of *frugalitas* is therefore important, since it underlines the young wife's simple and uncorrupted mind.[64] She loves Pliny, which is a guarantee of chastity. Love was not a self-evident ingredient in upper-class marriages, which were marriages of convenience;[65] the girl had not much to say in the choice of husband, and so it is worth noting when a young bride does feel affection for the man she has not chosen for herself. Again, love is a protection against sexual corruption: a young girl, married to a much older man, could easily fall in love with a younger and more handsome man and be easily seduced, but Calpurnia loves Pliny and is not likely to be corrupted by any seducer.[66]

Her love for Pliny instigates a literary interest, albeit an interest that is only concerned with Pliny's own works. Here we are not dealing with the intellectual lady so much despised by e. g. Juvenal.[67] The young Calpurnia studies, not for her own sake, but because of her interest in her husband's activities. She never exceeds the boundary of becoming modesty,[68] and her unaffected manners are pointed out: 'she even sings my poems, playing tunes on the cithara; no artist has given her instruction except love, the best of teachers.'[69]

'For these reasons,' Pliny continues, 'I am assured that we will go on to live in ever-increasing harmony'.[70] *Concordia,* marital harmony, stands out as a key-word for Pliny's view of his marriage: it is what he hopes for and what he finds good reason to expect from his wife's attitude towards him. He goes on to give the reason why he believes that this harmony will be everlasting: 'for she does not love me because of my age or my physical appearance, things which gradually wither and grow old, no, it is my glory that she loves'.[71]

The portrait of Calpurnia has roused much indignation among readers of later times for its alleged display of Pliny's male egocentricity; we must, however, not forget the structure of the society of which both Pliny and Calpurnia were part. The good wife should take interest in her husband's glory, because that glory belonged to and promoted the whole family, not only the individual. Had Calpurnia loved only her husband's 'age and body,' i. e. had she chosen a handsome lover her own age, she would have proved herself an egoist without any consideration for the demands of the Roman family structure. By her love for her husband's *gloria* she shows that she is a worthy Roman *matrona,* aware of the *dignitas* for the family as a whole.[72] The family she emerges from is a solid Roman one, and through her conduct she shows herself worthy of it.[73] Pliny's high esteem of family values and family loyalty has already been pointed out, and it is in this light we ought to see his praise of his young wife: she is loyal to her husband and cares for the family dignity in a manner worthy of old times and values. Her aunt is to be praised for that in that she set such a good example to her: 'she never saw anything in your household that was not virtuous and respectable.'[74] Virtuous, artless, unaffected by luxury and good looks, and loyal to all demands on a wife and member of a traditional Roman family, that is how Calpurnia emerges from Pliny's letter.[75]

SUMMARY

With the portrait of Calpurnia it is time to sum up Pliny's view on women. The information we can extract from his works is above all on how the Romans expected a 'good' woman to behave. His benevolent attitude to the various people he deals with in his letters results in several portraits of morally outstanding women (and, naturally, men) from which we can draw conclusions about what was considered morally superior in society. Many women are described as *exempla* to others—examples of *severitas, fides, pietas,* or sometimes *exempla* in a general, unspecified sense. The most loyal wife is the one who shares her husband's fate in all situations, even in death, and who is morally capable of setting him an example in that moment. It is most laudable to do such things not in order to gain personal glory but away from the limelight of the world. But women could be examples even without such heroic deeds: examples to wards, to other men's wives, even to men.

Pliny values marriage very highly, and his pictures of married life are generally characterized by loyalty and affection between husband and wife. His view of what marriage ought to include is evident not least from his portrait of his own wife Calpurnia. The reason for his esteem of marriage does not appear from the letters in themselves, but it seems reasonable to associate it with his general views on philosophy and his inclinations to Stoicism.[76] Besides, Pliny was by all accounts a law-abiding person, and it is no surprise to find that he adheres to the imperial ideology on the need for lawful marriage and legitimate children.[77]

When he praises women for their moral conduct we can observe that he includes both elements that could be used in praise of both sexes, as well as more specifically female traits. The women he praises most, Fannia and the young Minicia, are both described as grave, strict, steadfast and dignified; yet at the same time they are sweet, affectionate and caring. Loyalty (sometimes specified by the word *fides,* sometimes just described in its effect) and steadfastness (*constantia*) are recurring elements of morally virtuous behaviour. So is chastity: the unmarried girl's modesty, the young bride's lack of interest for anybody but her husband, the mature woman's spotless fame. Thus the image of the ideal woman emerges: strict, steadfast, grave and chaste, yet not boring but on the contrary sweet, affable, gentle and charming; intellectually well educated but using that education only in her husband's interest; loyal even in death.

It is interesting to compare these words of praise with what Pliny has to say about Plotina in the ***Panegyricus.*** If there is any place where we could expect him to bring forward all possible womanly virtues it is here; there is no limit to his praise for Trajan, and praise for Plotina is a way of praising Trajan. Pliny even introduces his passages on Plotina with words to that end: an unworthy wife has encumbered the reputation of many illustrious men, and someone who is inferior in his domestic affairs cannot be considered a great man in public life. Plotina, however, is no obstacle to Trajan's fame; on the contrary.[78] She is pure, she has all the old virtues;[79] she is *constans* and she shows *frugalitas.*[80] Another of her virtues is *verecundia,* modesty. In the letters she is only mentioned once, with the epithet *sanctissima femina.*[81] *Sanctus* signifies 'morally blameless, virtuous', and is used of both men and women. We have seen examples of *sanctitas* as a female trait in Tacitus' Annals, where it is used of Livia[82] and of Octavia,[83] but it is in no way an exclusively female trait. *Sanctissima* in 9.28, used of the empress, looks like the use of adjectives in the superlative as honorary titles for the emperors and certain magistrates, but there is no indication that *sanctus, sancta* ever became a formula.[84] It seems to have been a praiseworthy trait for any human being, but did not express a specific female virtue. When Plotina is called *sanctissima femina* Pliny is just attaching a general epithet of praise to her name, but her true female virtues are those described in the ***Panegyricus.***

Plotina can thus be said to be a summary of Pliny's view on the ideal Roman woman, incorporating what was seen as desirable in a Roman wife. Examples of less desirable conduct is hard to find in Pliny's letters, but that need not bother us; such examples are abundant elsewhere among his contemporaries.

Notes

1. Cf. the Regulus letters, e. g. 1.5, or the Pallas letter 8.6 for examples of a spiteful Pliny.

2. E. g. 4.10, 6.33, 7.11, 10.5.

3. One letter in each of books 1, 2, 4 and 8, none in books 5 and 9, two in book 3 if we include 3.10 that is directed to Spurinna and Cottia as a couple, two each in books 6 and 7; of these last four letters three are directed to his wife Calpurnia.

4. Cf. Sherwin-White (1966) 65-69 for a discussion on Pliny's choice of addresses.

5. 3.11.3 *atque haec feci cum septem amicis meis aut occisis aut relegatis, occisis Senecione, Rustico, Helvidio, relegatis Maurico, Gratilla, Arria, Fannia, tot circa me iactis fulminibus quasi ambustus mihi quoque impendere idem exitium certis quibusdam notis augurarer.*

6. Wistrand (1979) 20-22.

7. 5.14.4 *una diligimus, una dileximus omnes fere, quos aetas nostra in utroque sexu aemulandos tulit; quae societas amicitiarum artissima nos familiaritate coniunxit.*

8. 9.13 *fuerat alioqui mihi cum Helvidio amicitia, quanta potuerat esse cum eo, qui metu temporum nomen ingens paresque virtutes secessu tegebat, fuerat cum Arria et Fannia, quarum altera Helvidi noverca, altera mater novercae.*

9. There is not a trace here of suggestions about 'the wicked step-mother,' discussed in chapter 2 above. The exemplary Arria and Fannia will be discussed further below.

10. 7.11 *superest ut coheredes aequo animo ferant separatim me vendidisse, quod mihi licuit omnino non vendere. nec vero coguntur imitari meum exemplum; non enim illis eadem cum Corellia iura. possunt ergo intueri utilitatem suam, pro qua mihi fuit amicitia.*

11. Cf. Wistrand (1979) 20-22.

12. Cf. *OLD* s. v. *ius* 9.

13. For support from a woman to a man, cf. Pliny's helpful mother-in-law 3.19.8.

14. Cf. 4.15.3 *sunt ei* (sc. *Asinio Rufo*) *liberi plures. nam in hoc quoque functus est optimi civis officio, quod fecunditate uxoris large frui voluit eo saeculo, quo plerisque etiam singulos filios orbitatis praemia graves faciunt.*

15. 2.13.4 *pater ei in equestri gradu clarus, clarior vitricus, . . . mater e primis.*

16. 5.17.5 *gratulatus sum optimae matri, gratulatus et fratri, qui ex auditorio illo non minorem pietatis gloriam quam ille alter eloquentiae tulit: tam notabiliter pro fratre recitante primum metus eius, mox gaudium eminuit.*

17. 1.12 *destinasse Corellium mori nec aut suis aut filiae precibus inflecti.*

18. 1.22 *dandum enim precibus uxoris, dandum filiae lacrimis, dandum etiam nobis amicis, ne spes nostras, si modo non essent inanes, voluntaria morte desereret.*

19. 8.18.8 *divitis senis ita perditi morbo ut esse taedio posset uxori, quam iuvenis sanusque duxisset.*

20. 8.18 *vivebat tamen et vivere volebat, sustentante maxime uxore, quae culpam incohati matrimonii in gloriam perseverantia verterat.*

21. 1.12 *quamquam plurimas vivendi causas habentem, optimam conscientiam, optimam famam, maximam auctoritatem, praeterea filiam, uxorem, nepotem, sorores interque tot pignora veros amicos.*

22. 5.18 *Bene est mihi, quia tibi bene est. habes uxorem tecum, habes filium; frueris mari, fontibus, viridibus, agro, villa amoenissima.*

23. 8.23 *Adficior adulescentia ipsius, adficior necessitudinum casu. erat illi grandis natu parens, erat uxor, quam ante annum virginem acceperat, erat filia, quam paulo ante sustulerat. tot spes, tot gaudia dies unus in adversa convertit. modo designatus aedilis, recens maritus, recens pater intactum honorem, orbam matrem, viduam uxorem, filiam pupillam ignaramque patris reliquit.*

24. 1.16.6 *quae sive uxoris sunt, ut adfirmat, sive ipsius, ut negat, pari gloria dignus, qui aut illa componat aut uxorem, quam virginem accepit, tam doctam politamque reddiderit.*

25. 4.19.

26. 4.19.2 *accedit his studium litterarum, quod ex mei caritate concepit.*

27. Dobson (1982) 82 attributes Pliny's use of *exempla* to Stoic influence.

28. 1.14.6 *habet aviam maternam Serranam Proculam e municipio Patavio. nosti loci mores: Serrana tamen Patavinis quoque severitatis exemplum est.*

29. 3.1.5 *adsumit uxorem singularis exempli.*

30. 8.5.1 *amisit uxorem singularis exempli, etiam si olim fuisset.*

31. 4.19 *pietatis exemplum.* This expression cannot be translated verbally; her *pietas* is her dutiful respect and care for her relatives, in this case brother and niece.

32. Letter 3.16.

33. When her husband Caecina Paetus hesitated on the brink of committing suicide she took his weapon, thrust it into her own breast, pulled it out again and gave it to her husband with the words 'Paete, non dolet.'

34. 3.16.6 *sed tamen ista facienti, ista dicenti gloria et aeternitas ante oculos erant; quo maius est sine praemio aeternitatis, sine praemio gloriae abdere lacrimas, operire luctum amissoque filio matrem adhuc agere.*

35. 7.19.4 *doleo enim feminam maximam eripi oculis civitatis nescio an aliquid simile visuris. Quae castitas illi, quae sanctitas, quanta gravitas, quanta constantia!*

36. Maniet (1966) 151-152 has discussed Pliny's use of *castitas.*

37. 9.28.1.

38. Hirschfeld (1913); Svennung (1958).

39. E. g. *tusc.* 1.2; 4.60; *Deiot.* 37; *Sest.* 88.

40. *Ep.* 7.19.5 *quaerente minaciter Mettio Caro an rogasset respondit: 'rogavi'; an commentarios scripturo dedisset: 'dedi'; an sciente matre: 'nesciente'; postremo nullam vocem cedentem periculo emisit. quin etiam illos ipsos libros, quamquam ex necessitate et metu temporum abolitos senatus consulto, publicatis bonis servavit, habuit tulitque in exsilium exsilii causam.*

41. 7.19.7 *eadem quam iucunda, quam comis, quam denique, quod paucis datum est, non minus amabilis quam veneranda!*

42. 7.19.7 *eadem quam iucunda.*

43. 7.19.7 *eritne quam postea uxoribus nostris ostentare possimus? erit a qua viri quoque fortitudinis exempla sumamus, quam sic cernentes audientesque miremur ut illas quae leguntur?*

44. Not least, perhaps, to Pliny himself; cf. 7.19.10 *non feci tamen paria,* and Sherwin-White's commentary *ad loc.*

45. 6.24.4 *comesque ipsa mortis, dux immo et exemplum et necessitas fuit.*

46. 5.16.2 *anilis prudentia.* The manuscripts give her age as 'not yet 14'; her epitaph, *CIL* VI 16631, states her age as 12 years, 11 months and 7 days.

47. 5.16.1 *qua puella nihil umquam festivius, amabilius nec modo longiore vita, sed prope immortalitate dignius vidi.*

48. 5.16.2 *iam illi anilis prudentia, matronalis gravitas erat et tamen suavitas puellaris cum virginali verecundia.*

49. 5.16.3 *ut nutrices, ut paedagogos, ut praeceptores pro suo quemque officio diligebat! quam studiose, quam intellegenter lectitabat! ut parce custoditeque ludebat!* Sherwin-White (1966) interprets *ludebat* as 'witty conversation,' an interpretation that I do not find convincing. Pliny describes a young girl on her way out of childhood, mixing *matronalis gravitas* with *puellaris suavitas;* she is a diligent schoolgirl and when she is tempted to devote time to more lax business, it seems more consistent with her age to play than to engage in 'witty conversation.'

50. 5.16.3 *qua illa temperantia, qua patientia, qua etiam constantia novissimam valetudinem tulit!*

51. 5.16.6-7 *iam destinata erat egregio iuveni, iam electus nuptiarum dies, iam nos vocati. quod gaudium quo maerore mutatum est! non possum exprimere verbis, quantum animo vulnus acceperim, cum audivi Fundanum ipsum, ut multa luctuosa dolor invenit, praecipientem, quod in vestes margarita gemmas fuerat erogaturus hoc in tus et unguenta et odores impenderetur.*

52. *Suavitas* is discussed by Maniet (1966) 157-161.

53. 7.24.1 *atque etiam ultra matronalem modum compacto corpore et robusto.*

54. 7.24.3 *vixit in contubernio aviae delicatae severissime et tamen obsequentissime.*

55. 7.24.4 *habebat illa pantomimos fovebatque effusius, quam principi feminae convenit.*

56. 7.24.5 *audivi ipsam cum mihi commendaret nepotis sui studia solere se, ut feminam in illo otio sexus, laxare animum lusu calculorum, solere spectare pantomimos suos; sed cum factura esset alterutrum semper se nepoti suo praecepisse abiret studeretque.*

57. 7.24.8 *iucundum est mihi quod ceperam gaudium scribendo retractare. gaudeo enim pietate defunctae . . .*

58. Cf. Dobson (1982) 83-84.

59. 4.19.6 *nec aliud decet tuis manibus educatam, tuis praeceptis institutam.*

60. 4.19.1 *dignam patre, dignam te, dignam avo evadere.*

61. 4.19.2 *summum est acumen summa frugalitas; amat me, quod castitatis indicium est.*

62. Cf. *paneg.* 3.4.

63. Cf. *Rhet. Her.* 2.21.34.

64. Cf. the discussion in Maniet (1966) 150-151. I think it deserves to be underlined that Calpurnia's *frugalitas* contains a notion of her being incorruptible: she is not tempted by luxury and hence cannot be corrupted.

65. Cf. e. g. Griffin (1985) 118-119.

66. Cf. 1.14, where Pliny recommends a suitable husband for a young girl, and states that good looks are a fair reward for the girl's chastity, 1.14.8 *est illi facies liberalis multo sanguine, multo rubore suffusa, est ingenua totius corporis pulchritudo et quidam senatorius decor. quae ego nequaquam arbitror neglegenda; debet enim hoc castitati puellarum quasi praemium dari.* The good-looking husbands ought to be given to the young girls as the reward for their chastity, or, to turn it the other way round: good looks in the husband remove the motive for unchastity.

67. Iuv. 6.434-456.

68. 4.19.3 *si quando recito in proximo discreta velo sedet.*

69. 4.19.4 *versus quidem meos cantat etiam formatque cithara, non artifice aliquo docente, sed amore, qui magister est optimus.*

70. 4.19.5 *his ex causis in spem certissimam adducor, perpetuam nobis maioremque in dies futuram esse concordiam.*

71. 4.19.5 *non enim aetatem meam aut corpus, quae paulatim occidunt ac senescunt, sed gloriam diligit.* I disagree with Maniet (1966) 176, who interprets *quae paulatim* etc. as referring to Pliny's actual state of growing older ('lesquels sont en train de se flétrir insensiblement'). Pliny does not say 'I have been young and handsome, but it is not these qualities, that are vanishing anyhow, that she loves in me.' What he says is 'What she loves in me is not youth or physical beauty, i. e. I am not a young handsome lover. It is just as well, since these are things that disappear. What she loves in me is much better, since it is something that will last and even increase.'

72. Cf. Maniet's (1966) definition of *gloria,* p. 154: 'un idéal éthique et souvent patriotique, intimement lié aux intérêts de la *gens* et de la *res publica.*'

73. 4.19.1 *dignam patre, dignam te, dignam avo.*

74. 4.19.6 *quae nihil in contubernio tuo viderit nisi sanctum honestumque.*

75. I have not included Pliny's letters to Calpurnia in my discussion, since they are not actual descriptions of her. Cf. Maniet (1966) for a thorough discussion on them.

76. Cf. Dobson (1982) 81-82.

77. It seems that he took some care not to offend the emperor and managed to stay out of the turmoil that led to punishment and exile for many of his friends, cf. 3.11. Cf. also 7.19.10, where he seems to admit that he was not as courageous as his friends.

78. *Paneg.* 83.4 *multis illustribus dedecori fuit aut inconsultius uxor adsumpta aut retenta patientius: ita foris claros domestica destruebat infamia, et, ne maximi cives haberentur, hoc efficiebatur, quod mariti minores erant. tibi uxor in decus et gloriam cedit.*

79. Such is my translation of *antiquius* in 83.5 *quid enim illa sanctius, quid antiquius?*

80. *constanter* in 83.6; 83.7 is an enumeration of her modest behaviour, which I see as examples of *frugalitas.*

81. 9.28.1.

82. *Ann.* 5.1.3. This is almost the only virtue with which Tacitus credits Livia; cf. chapter 2 above.

83. *Ann.* 14.60.

84. In the *leges novellae ad Theodosianum pertinentes* senators are addressed as *sanctissimi patres* twice, Valent. 1.3 and Maior. 1, and Theodosius addresses Valentinian as *domine sancte fili Auguste venerabilis* in Theod. 2.

Bibliography

Dobson, Elizabeth Spalding. 1982. "Pliny the Younger's Depiction of Women." *Classical Bulletin* 58: 81–85.

Griffin, Jasper. 1985. *Latin Poets and Roman Life.* London.

Hirschfeld, Otto. 1913. 'Die Rangtitel der römischen Kaiserzeit." In *Kleine Schriften,* 646–81. Berlin.

Maniet, Andrée. 1966. 'Pline le jeune et Calpurnia." *L'antiquité classique* 35: 149–85.

Sherwin-White, A. N. 1966. *The Letters of Pliny: A Historical and Social Commentary.* Oxford.

Wistrand, Erik. 1979. *Caesar and Contemporary Roman Society.* Göteborg.

John Bodel (essay date fall 1995)

SOURCE: Bodel, John. "Minicia Marcella: Taken before Her Time." *American Journal of Philology* 116, no. 3 (fall 1995): 453-60.

[*In the following essay, Bodel discusses discrepancies in an obituary composed by Pliny, theorizing that Pliny's account is not so concerned with factual details regarding the death as it is about the rhetorical, literary, and philosophical implications of the young woman's passing.*]

Writing to his friend Aefulanus Marcellinus sometime in A.D. 105 or 106, the younger Pliny lamented the untimely death of the daughter of a mutual friend, Minicius Fundanus: destined for an advantageous marriage, the girl had been deprived of her appointed wedding day and cut down in the bloom of youth, before she had completed her fourteenth year: *nondum annos quattuordecim impleverat.*[1] Until 1881 Pliny's tribute provided all that was known about the unfortunate girl, but in that year the unearthing of a familial tomb on Monte Mario just outside Rome disclosed a pair of funerary altars of late Flavian or Trajanic date, evidently carved by the same hand and bearing the names of a woman, Statoria M. f. Marcella, and a girl, Minicia Marcella Fundani f(ilia). After briefly considering other possibilities of identification, the first editor of the two inscriptions plausibly concluded that Minicia must be the daughter of Pliny's friend and the Statoria named in the neighboring epitaph: having predeceased her like-named daughter, the mother naturally found no place in Pliny's condolences.[2] Dates, names, and circumstances fit.[3] Only one difficulty stood in the way: the girl's epitaph gives a summary statement of her age at death, precise and unequivocal and seemingly contradictory to Pliny's account: *v(ixit) a(nnis) XII, m(ensibus) XI, d(iebus) VII.* When manuscripts and inscriptions disagree on numbers, the possible sources of error are many and various, and in this instance modern opinion has shown little consistency in sorting them out.

Sherwin-White in the standard commentary on Pliny's letters (347 ad loc.) declared it "better to accept the discrepancy than to correct the manuscripts" but declined to pass judgment on the accuracy of either Pliny or the anonymous stonecutter. Stout, who was similarly disinclined to correct manuscripts, conceded that Pliny may have been mistaken but preferred to lay blame for the error at the stonecutter's door, and others have simply accepted the transmitted text without attempting to vindicate its authority.[4] No one, it seems, has directly impugned Pliny's accuracy, but the precise figure cannot have mattered much to him personally, and the possibility that he was merely guessing or somehow miscalculated cannot be ruled out: his correspondent, Aefulanus Marcellinus, seems to have been a connoisseur of Pliny's obituary notices (the only other letter apparently addressed to him, 8.23, also falls into this category) and was no doubt more concerned with rhetorical coloring than the unvarnished truth.[5] Some editors tacitly correct the manuscripts to agree with the stone, a solution for which Goold has offered an attractive defense.[6] Following Dressel (16), Goold (144) proposes that the discrepancy arose from a scribal slip, the letters *xiiiimpleverat* written in minuscule in a common ancestor of the eight- and nine-book families of manuscripts having been miscopied into *xiiiiinpleverat* (that is, *m* was transcribed as *in*). The emendation is simple, the resolution gratifying; and the genesis of the supposed error is easily paralleled.[7] In this case, however, the presumed path of transmission is twisted and forked, and it does not appear to lead to the original text.

Whereas the chief representative of the nine-book family (*M*, saec. IX) and several Renaissance witnesses to the eight-book tradition are said to exhibit Roman numerals at this point, elsewhere in the manuscripts of all three families of Pliny's **Letters** numbers indicating ages were evidently transcribed verbally, whereas numerals were reserved for dates and monetary amounts.[8] The head of the ten-book tradition and our oldest surviving witness (Π, saec. V ex.), now reduced to just six leaves preserving the text only of **Letters** 2.20.13-3.5.4, shows both cardinal and ordinal numbers written out, and contemporary inscriptional evidence to be adduced below indicates that in Pliny's day ages represented by the formula *nondum compleverat annos tot* were normally spelled out in words.[9] It therefore seems probable that in describing Minicia's age at death, Pliny wrote out the figure verbally. The question that needs to be asked, then, unless we suppose that the same scribal error (*xiiiiin* for *xiiiim*) arose independently and late in separate branches of the tradition, is how the common ancestor of the eight- and nine-book families of manuscripts came to preserve a Roman numeral here, when elsewhere it apparently represented ages with words. Surely it is more plausible to suppose that it did not and that the translation from a verbal to a numerical representation of Minicia's age occurred after the two branches of the family had split, in which case the likelihood of an identical error underlying the reading *XIIII* transmitted in both traditions becomes more remote. Certainty in these matters cannot be expected, but unless we are prepared to posit an unusually deep corruption—*tredecim* copied to *xiii,* misread as *xiiii,* and converted back to *quattuordecim*—in the early stages of transmission in antiquity, prior to the creation of the parent of the eight- and nine-book families, we must conclude that in substance, at least, if not in form, the manuscripts correctly report the number that Pliny wrote: *quattuordecim.* How, then, to resolve the discrepancy? Consideration of the diverse contexts from which our information derives suggests that emendation may be unnecessary.

Tombstones purporting to indicate the age at death of the deceased tend, naturally, toward a spurious precision. The same cannot be said of a consular orator revising his more carefully written correspondence (*epistulae curatius scriptae,* 1.1.1) for publication as a literary opus. Here in particular the theme called for discriminating treatment. The special pathos of the maiden snatched away just before marriage, enshrined already in Sophocles' *Antigone,* had by Pliny's day grown into a well-worn topos demanding, among other things, a nuanced appreciation of the poignancy of the loss.[10] That Pliny was prepared to comply with conventional expectations in exploiting the motif may be seen from his novel adaptation of a standard device designed to convey the desiderated tragic irony: a catalogue of ambivalent images drawn from the marriage and funeral rites, arranged in pairs, and represented as a series of dismal exchanges. Where traditional treatments focused on the bride and the central paraphernalia of the two ceremonies (funeral torches for wedding tapers, a dirge for a marriage hymn, a bier for a bridal bed, and so on), Pliny alludes instead—and self-consciously, as his parenthetical aside shows—to the father's ancillary role in procuring the requisite accessories: . . . *audivi Fundanum ipsum, ut multa luctuosa dolor invenit, praecipientem, quod in vestes margarita gemmas fuerat erogaturus, hoc in tus et unguenta et odores impenderetur* (5.16.6).[11] Where literary modeling of this sort is so patently contrived, biometrical precision in the matter of the girl's age at death is hardly to be expected. Nor is it found.

In searching for a delicate way to suggest the premature termination of youth, Pliny invoked an age that conveyed to contemporary readers the incipient advance of puberty, an age agreed upon by medical and popular opinion alike as marking the boundary between childhood and adolescence. Lawyers fixed the minimum age for many rights and responsibilities at fourteen for boys and twelve for girls, but conventional wisdom—based, as always, on empirical observation—tended to regard fourteen as the age of sexual maturity in girls as well as in boys, and a popular system of measuring life in hebdomads, grounded in numerical symbolism and credited by followers of Hippocrates to Solon, naturally saw the end of the fourteenth year as marking the transition from childhood to youth in both sexes.[12] In alluding to this watershed, Pliny does not in fact pretend to say precisely at what age Minicia died; he merely observes that she had not yet completed a certain stage of life. Not yet, but nearly so, for she bore the virginal charms of youth with a wisdom and dignity beyond her years: *nondum annos quattuordecim impleverat, et iam illi*

anilis prudentia, matronalis gravitas erat et tamen suavitas puellaris cum virginali verecundia (5.16.2). In painting this picture of youth hovering at the threshold of maturity, Pliny embellishes the portrait with a motif drawn from a palette comprising the full array of feminine virtues, among which diversity of virtue ranked as a virtue itself.[13] What mattered in this rhetorical setting, more than chronological precision, were thematic concinnity and unobtrusiveness. Elsewhere, when it was length of years that counted and verisimilitude was sought, Pliny could be clinically exact.[14] The present context demanded subtlety and a lighter touch.

So, here, as elsewhere in eulogizing the dead, Pliny slips comfortably and unobtrusively into the language of epitaph.[15] The dactylic phrase *nondum tot compleverat annos* and its variants occur so frequently in Latin inscriptions of the early imperial period (always, it seems, with the number written out verbally) that we may assume a popular association of the formula with funerary commemoration.[16] At the same time, the verbs *implere* and *complere* in Pliny's day had come to apply in temporal contexts not only to the duration of a specific period of time (years, months, and days) but also, more generally, to the completion or fulfillment of a recognized stage of life (infancy, youth, old age, etc.).[17] When the two usages overlapped, any original distinction in meaning tended to become blurred. Compare, for example, a tombstone set up at Beneventum by a bereaved father for a young daughter whose "youth had already twice filled out six years and was holding out the promise of marriage" (*bis mihi iam senos aetas impleverat annos / spemque dabat thalami*).[18] We do not know how old the girl was when she died, but it would be rash to assume she had not completed her thirteenth year, since the collocation of references to a twelfth birthday and the prospect of matrimony, though it may incidentally point to her actual age, was probably intended in the first place to indicate her eligibility for a formal marriage under Roman law.[19]

Lawyers set the minimum limit, but attention to a prospective bride's physical development, as well as to her age in years, no doubt normally played a part in considerations of her readiness for married life.[20] That some Romans regarded thirteen as the right age for a girl to marry is shown by a metrical epitaph discovered near Pozzuoli, which combines a popular element from the "death of a bride" motif (the marriage torch turned to the funeral) with a clear statement that the deceased, who died at thirteen, had reached the age for the bridal bed: *quae thalamis aetas fuerat iam nubilis apta / destituit sponsum flebilis et soceros.*[21] At Rome, it seems, many girls did indeed marry young, between the ages of eleven and thirteen (Morizot, "L'âge au mariage"); elsewhere in Italy and the western provinces a first marriage came more normally, perhaps, in the late teens (Shaw, "Age of Roman Girls at Marriage"). What is more to the point, the emperor Hadrian evidently regarded girls as having attained full puberty at fourteen; beyond that age alimentary support was felt to be no longer necessary.[22] Such was the enlightened social thinking of Pliny's day, and it is with its norms that his own attitudes generally conformed.

When the young daughter of his friend Minicius Fundanus died shortly before her wedding day, the unfortunate but happy coincidence of social circumstance and literary convention made Pliny's artistic path clear. The epitaph inscribed on her monument duly recorded for posterity the total sum of her days of life; it fell to Pliny, writing too for posterity but in a different medium and with a different purpose, to lament the loss of a girl on the cusp of womanhood, ripe for the marriage of which she was now cruelly deprived. Both texts purport to represent her age at death. Neither is demonstrably accurate, and yet each, within its rhetorical and cultural context, is perfectly correct.

Notes

1. *Ep.* 5.16.2; cf. § 6, *iam destinata erat egregio iuveni, iam electus nuptiarum dies, iam nos vocati.* For the father, C. Minicius Fundanus, suffect consul in 107, see Syme, *Roman Papers* VII 603-19.

2. Dressel, "Camera sepolcrale" 14-16, remarking Pliny's silence about the mother at 5.16.4, *sororem patrem* [sc. *puella*] *adhortabatur.* The inscriptions, along with a third found in the same tomb, are reproduced at *CIL* VI 16630-32, that of Minicia (16631) also at *ILS* 1030. Both monuments are preserved in the Gabinetto delle Maschere of the Vatican Museums; see Boschung, *Antike Grabaltäre* 16-17 (stylistic dating), 81 no. 97, 85 no. 245.

3. If the speaker, Fundanus, at Plut. *De Coh. Ira* 6 (*Mor.* 455 F) is identical with Pliny's friend, his reference to a wife and "little daughters" (θυγάτρια—but the diminutive is perhaps merely affective) confirms the configuration of Minicius' immediate family and furthermore helps to date the dialogue: see Jones, "Chronology" 61-62. The mother's *gentilicium* suggests a Transpadane origin, as befits the wife of a native of Ticinum: see Syme, *Roman Papers* VII 608-9; cf. Raepsaet-Charlier, *Prosopographie des femmes* 582 no. 733 (456 no. 552 for Minicia Marcella).

4. Stout, *Scribe and Critic* 209. Others: e.g., Mynors; Syme *Roman Papers* VII 608 and n. 33.

5. Gamberini (*Stylistic Theory* 290-94) remarks and briefly analyzes the rhetorical elaboration of the two letters to Marcellinus, who is otherwise unknown.

6. So Kukula, Merrill, and Guillemin ad loc.; cf. *PIR*[2] M 631. See Goold's review of Stout's edition.

7. Cf. Nipperdey at Tac. *Ann.* 14.64.1, *puella vicesimo aetatis anno* (Octavia in A.D. 62): "Wahrscheinlich . . . Tac. schrieb *duoetvicesimo,* was *IIetvicesimo* geschrieben seinen Anfang wegen der Ähnlichkeit der drei letzten Buchstaben von *puella* verlor."

8. Ages are written out at *Ep.* 1.12.4, 11 (see below, note 14), 3.1.10, 7.4.2, 10.79.2 (10.80); cf. 8.5.1 (below, note 15). Jacques and van Ooteghem (*Index* 965) register the passages where Roman numerals are preserved. For the various branches of the manuscript tradition of Pliny's *Letters* see briefly Reynolds, "The Younger Pliny."

9. See Lowe and Rand, *Sixth-Century Fragment* (Pierpont Morgan Library M.462) at 2.20.13, 3.1.4, 3.1.7-8, 3.1.10, 3.2.3.

10. A staple of the Hellenistic epigrammatists (e.g., *Anth. Pal.* 7.182, 186, 188, 711, 712) and the authors of funerary poems (e.g., Peek, *Grab-Epigramme* nos. 683, 988, 1238), the motif was popular also with the novelists (Apul. *Met.* 4.33.4; Ach. Tat. 1.13.5-6; Xen. Eph. 3.7.2; Heliod. 2.29.3-4, 10.16.10) and in Pliny's day was sometimes found even in more elevated forms (e.g., Sil. *Pun.* 13.547): see further Seaford, "Tragic Wedding" 106-10, and Rehm, *Marriage to Death,* on Soph. *Ant.* 810-13 and related examples in tragedy; Szepessy, "The Girl Who Died"; and, more generally on the "death of a maiden" motif in epitaphs, Lattimore, *Themes in Epitaphs* 192-94.

11. Sen. *Contr.* 6.6, *versae sunt in exsequias nuptiae mutatusque genialis lectus in funebrem, subiectae rogo felices faces,* illustrates the banality of the conceit in less skilled hands.

12. Legal barriers: *CIL* I[2] 594 = *FIRA* [*Fontes Iuris Romani Antiqui*] I[2] 21 (*lex col. Gen. Iul.*) ch. 98; *Dig.* 28.1.5, 28.6.2.pr. (Ulpian); Macr. *Sat.* 7.7.6; and below, note 19. Medical opinion: Soran. *Gynaec.* 1.20, setting the age of menarche "generally around the fourteenth year"; Galen 17 (2) 6.37.8-9, 792.12-13 K.; cf. Macr. *Somn.* 1.6.71, *post annos autem bis septem ipsae aetatis necessitate pubescit. tunc enim moveri incipit vis generationis in masculis et purgatio feminarum.* Hebdomancy: e.g., Philo *Op. Mundi* 103-5; Censor. 7.2; Hieron.

Epist. 32.9, *Amos* 6. See further Eyben, "View of Puberty" 695-96.

13. Compare Pliny's enthusiasm for the elderly spouse of Macrinus: *quot quantasque virtutes, ex diversis aetatibus sumptas, collegit et miscuit!* (*Ep.* 8.5.1).

14. Cf. *Ep.* 1.12.4, 11, on the suicide of Corellius Rufus after a long struggle with gout, *tertio et tricensimo anno, ut ipsum audiebam, pedum dolore correptus est . . . implevit quidem annum septimum et sexagensimum;* and see note 15 below.

15. Cf. *Ep.* 8.5.1, on the marriage of Macrinus, upon the death of his wife, *vixit cum hac viginti novem annis sine iurgio sine offensa,* with, e.g., *CIL* IX 1530, *sine iurg(io) sine querella;* VI 8438, *sine ulla offensa;* further, Lattimore, *Themes in Epitaphs* 279-80, citing scores of examples with numerous slight variations.

16. E.g., *CIL* III 9418 (*CLE* 1141), VI 21151 (*CLE* 398), 23010 (*CLE* 503), 25617 (*CLE* 965, of A.D. 10), 37412 (*CLE* 2125); *ICUR* III 8234 (*CLE* 735); *CIL* XIV 2737 (*CLE* 1297).

17. Cf. Ov. *Met.* 3.312, *maternaque tempora complet* ("bring a pregnancy to term"; cf. 11.311); Tac. *Ann.* 4.58.3, *extremam senectam compleverit;* and, somewhat later, *Dig.* 28.6.41.7 (Papinian), *puberem aetatem complevit* (probably "finish adolescence"—cf. *Dig.* 4.4.1.2 [Ulpian]; below, note 22—rather than "reach puberty"); 36.1.11.2 (Ulpian), *cum nubilem aetatem complesset.* The sense of "arriving at" a definite point in life probably grew out of legal usage: cf. *Dig.* 33.1.21.2 (Scaevola) and 36.1.48 (Javolenus), both concerning a designated age of inheritance, and see further *TLL* s.v. *compleo* III 2095.63-69, s.v. *impleo,* VII 634.71-635.15.

18. *CIL* IX 1817 (*CLE* 1055).

19. Cf. *Cod. Iust.* 5.4.24, *post duodecimum annum;* Cass. Dio 54.16.7; *Dig.* 23.1.9 (Ulpian). Some girls of course did in fact marry during their thirteenth year: e.g., *CIL* VI 3604, 10867, 29324.

20. The jurist Labeo is typically direct: *non potest videri nupta quae virum pati non potest* (*Dig.* 36.2.30); cf. Fest. p. 250 M., *femina a duodecim* (sc. *annis*) *viri potens, sive patiens;* Servius at *Aen.* 7.53, "*iam matura viro, iam plenis nubilis annis*"; *CIL* XII 743 (*CLE* 454), of a girl dead at seventeen, . . . *pervixit virgo; ubi iam matura placebat, nuptias indixit;* further, Gardner, *Women* 38-41, and Treggiari, *Roman Marriage* 39-42.

21. *AE* 1974, 260, dated by the editor (D'Arms, "Inscriptions from Puteoli" 165) to the early second century A.D.

22. *Dig.* 34.1.14.1 (Ulpian). For the concept of *plena pubertas* see *Dig.* 1.7.40.1 (Modestinus); *Inst.* 1.11.4; Censor. 7.3 (setting it at seventeen).

Bibliography

Boschung, Dietrich. *Antike Grabaltäre aus den Nekropolen Roms.* Acta Bernensia 10. Bern: Stämpfli, 1987.

D'Arms, J. H. "Eighteen Unedited Latin Inscriptions from Puteoli and Vicinity." *AJA* [*American Journal of Archaeology*] 77 (1973) 151-67.

Dressel, Heinrich. "Camera sepolcrale sul monte Mario." *Bollettino dell'Istituto di Corrispondenza Archeologica* (1881) 12-17.

Eyben, Emiel. "Antiquity's View of Puberty." *Latomus* 31 (1972) 677-97.

Gamberini, Federico. *Stylistic Theory and Practice in the Younger Pliny.* Altertumswissenschaftliche Texte und Studien 11. Hildesheim: Olms-Weidmann, 1983.

Gardner, J. F. *Women in Roman Law and Society.* London: Croom Helm, 1986.

Goold, G. P. Review of *Plinius, Epistulae: A Critical Edition,* by S. E. Stout. *Phoenix* 17 (1963) 141-47.

Guillemin, A.-M. *Pline le Jeune: Lettres.* Paris: Les Belles Lettres, 1927-28.

Jacques, Xavier, and J. van Ooteghem. *Index de Pline le Jeune.* Académie Royal de Belgique, Classe des Lettres et des Sciences Morales et Politiques, Mémoires, ser. 2, 58.3. Brussels: Palais des Académies, 1965.

Jones, C. P. "Towards a Chronology of Plutarch's Works." *JRS* [*Journal of Roman Studies*] 56 (1966) 61-74.

Kukula, R. C. *C. Plini Caecili Secundi Epistularum Libri Novem, Epistularum ad Traianum Liber, Panegyricus.* 2d ed. Leipzig: Teubner, 1912.

Lattimore, Richmond. *Themes in Greek and Latin Epitaphs.* Illinois Studies in Language and Literature 28.1-2. Urbana: University of Illinois Press, 1942.

Lowe, E. A., and E. K. Rand. *A Sixth-Century Fragment of the Letters of Pliny the Younger.* Washington: The Carnegie Institution, 1922.

Merrill, E. T. *C. Plini Caecili Secundi Epistularum Libri Decem.* Leipzig: Teubner, 1922.

Morizot, Pierre. "L'âge au mariage des jeunes romaines à Rome et en Afrique." *CRAI* [*Comptes Rendus, Academie de Inscriptions et Belles Lettres*] (1989) 656-68.

Mynors, R. A. B. *C. Plinii Caecili Secundi Epistularum Libri Decem.* Oxford: Oxford University Press, 1963.

Peek, Werner. *Griechische Vers-Inschriften.* Vol. I, *Grab-Epigramme.* Berlin: Akademie-Verlag, 1955.

Raepsaet-Charlier, M.-T. *Prosopographie des femmes de l'ordre sénatorial (Ier-IIe siècles).* Louvain: Peeters, 1987.

Rehm, Rush. *Marriage to Death: The Conflation of Wedding and Funeral Rituals in Greek Tragedy.* Princeton: Princeton University Press, 1994.

Reynolds, L. D. "The Younger Pliny." In *Texts and Transmission: A Survey of the Latin Classics,* edited by L. D. Reynolds, 316-22. Oxford: Oxford University Press, 1983.

Seaford, Richard. "The Tragic Wedding." *JHS* 107 (1987) 106-30.

Shaw, B. D. "The Age of Roman Girls at Marriage: Some Reconsiderations." *JRS* 77 (1987) 30-46.

Sherwin-White, A. N. *The Letters of Pliny: A Historical and Social Commentary.* Oxford: Oxford University Press, 1966.

Stout, S. E. *Scribe and Critic at Work in Pliny's Letters.* Bloomington: Indiana University Press, 1954.

Syme, Ronald. *Roman Papers.* Vol. VII. Edited by A. R. Birley. Oxford: Oxford University Press, 1991.

Szepessy, T. "The Story of the Girl Who Died on the Day of Her Wedding." *AAntHung* [*Acta Archaeologica. Academiae Scientiarum Hungaricae*] 20 (1972) 341-57.

Treggiari, Susan. *Roman Marriage: Iusti Coniuges from the Time of Cicero to the Time of Ulpian.* Oxford: Oxford University Press, 1991.

Debra Hershkowitz (essay date 1995)

SOURCE: Hershkowitz, Debra. "Pliny the Poet." *Greece and Rome* 42, no. 2 (1995): 168-81.

[*In the following essay, Hershkowitz notes that although Pliny considered his poetry an interest that was secondary to his oratory, it was a significant part of his literary activity, often aiding him greatly in his work as a statesman and an orator.*]

In letter 4.14, Pliny the Younger remarks that he doesn't worry too much about criticism of his poetry since he's not planning to give up the day job (§10):

> nam si hoc opusculum nostrum aut potissimum esset aut solum, fortasse posset durum uideri dicere 'quaere quod agas': molle et humanum est 'habes quod agas'.

> For if this little work were my chief or sole effort it might possibly seem unkind to tell me to 'find something else to do': but there is nothing unkind in the gentle reminder that I '*have* something else to do'.[1]

This well sums up Pliny's basic outlook on his poetic composition, as a hobby rather than a full-fledged occupation. His comments on his poetry throughout his letters demonstrate that the writing of poems as a literary activity is, for Pliny, secondary to the 'real' work of oratory. Nevertheless, Pliny still managed to compose two, or possibly three, books of poetry.[2] Not only did he circulate this poetry among his friends (often the letters accompany his verses (e.g., 9.16), or are responses to friends' comments on his most recent offerings (e.g., 5.3 or 9.25)), but his work was also published more widely; Pliny also recited his poetry to select gatherings of friends (8.21; cf. 5.3.1 and 9.34).

Rather than taking up time which could be devoted to his oratorical work, Pliny wrote poetry only in his spare moments: at 4.14.2 he describes how he composes hendecasyllables 'in uehiculo, in balineo, inter cenam' ('in my carriage, my bath, or at dinner').[3] By filling his free time with poetic composition, however, Pliny displays the same workaholic industry and zeal that he regularly shows with respect to his oratory. His time for *otium,* like his time for *negotium,* is consumed by activity. Gamberini is especially interested in the distinction between *otium* and *negotium,* and also in the different kinds of *otium,* which, he points out, can be divided as 'brief spaces of time' and 'the period of retirement from the *cursus honorum* and official duties in old age', as well as longer, but still fairly brief, breaks from public life, such as a summer vacation.[4] Gamberini goes on to say that while Pliny seems to support the view that poetry is, for some, 'capable of featuring as a *negotium* in [the] scale of values', Pliny himself always keeps the composition of poetry reserved for the short periods of *otium* that arise in his busy schedule.[5] Nevertheless, Pliny's poetic endeavours were not wholly divorced from his oratorical work; rather, writing poetry was seen to have *utilitas* as an aid to speech-writing. In 7.9.12, Pliny notes that the great orators of the past both amused and trained themselves with verse composition. The main utility of such training lies, from Pliny's point of view, in the fact that writing prose is easier than writing poetry (7.9.14): 'quod, metri necessitate deuincti, soluta oratione laetamur et quod facilius esse conparatio ostendit libentius scribimus' ('when we have been bound by the restrictions of metre, we delight in the freedom of prose and gladly return to what comparison has shown to be the easier style').

When Pliny gives advice to Pedanius Fuscus Salinator in 7.9 about what sorts of literary exercises would be helpful in his oratorical training, he recommends, among other activities, the composition of original poetry. He does not advise Fuscus to embark on a large poetic undertaking, however: 'carmine . . . non dico continuo et longo', he says in section 9, 'sed hoc arguto et breui' ('not a long continuous poem . . . but one of those short, polished sets of verses'). The reason he gives for this recommendation is that while the composition of long poems, which cannot be completed quickly, is not suited to *otium,* at least that sort of limited *otium* enjoyed by busy men in their prime, writing short poems gives one just the right break from other responsibilities. An additional reason which might be seen behind Pliny's advice is of a more stylistic nature, what I would call 'expedient Callimacheanism', a depoliticized poetics filtered through Catullus and the neoterics and through the Augustan Age's peculiarly Roman appropriation and internalization of Callimachean poetics.[6] A *carmen* which is *continuum* and *longum* recalls ἕν ἄεισμα διηνεκές which the Telchines criticized Callimachus for not writing (*Aetia* fr. 1.3 Pf.), or Ovid's *perpetuum carmen* (*Met.* 1.4) which, in good Callimachean fashion, he asks the gods to *deducere*.[7] The continuous and long poem also fits into the Hellenistically influenced *poema/poesis* distinction which was often made by literary theoreticians, taking the side of lengthy, epic *poesis* (cf. especially Varro, *Men.* 398: 'poema est lexis enrythmos, id est, uerba plura modice in quandam coniecta formam; itaque etiam distichon epigrammation uocant poema. poesis est perpetuum argumentum e rhythmis, ut Ilias Homeri et Annalis Enni' ['"Poema" is rhythmical language, that is, many words, according to a rule, placed in a certain form; thus even a two-line epigram is called a "poema". "Poesis" is continuous narrative in accordance with rhythm, like the *Iliad* of Homer and the *Annals* of Ennius']).[8] Instead of this kind of poem, Pliny, conforming to the Alexandrian-cum-neoteric aesthetic of his age, suggests writing poetry which is *argutum* and *breue,* the *poema* in Varro's opposition. Pliny's use of *argutus* may especially point in this direction. Cicero applies the word to poetry at *In Pisonem* 70, when he describes a poet writing a poem so elegant, 'nihil ut fieri possit argutius' ('that nothing would be able to be more clever'). Vergil uses the word as a Callimachean signpost at *Eclogue* 9.35-6, when Lycidas says that though others call him a poet, he does not believe it, 'nam neque adhuc Vario uideor nec dicere Cinna / digna, sed argutos inter strepere anser olores' ('for I do not yet seem to speak things worthy of Varius or Cinna, but am a goose among tuneful swans'). Compare also Vergil's Callimachean Circe at *Aeneid* 7.14, who 'arguto tenuis percurrens pectine telas' ('weaving slender threads with an acute comb'). Pliny, when he is complimenting himself on one of his orations in 6.33, says that it has 'copia rerum et arguta diuisione' (a 'lively arrangement of the abundant material') (§8). Pliny uses *argutus* in an explicitly Callimachean context at 4.3.3-4 when he is complimenting Arrius Antoninus on his Greek epigrams:

> quantum ibi humanitatis uenustatis, quam dulcia illa, quam amantia, quam arguta, quam recta! Callimachum me uel Heroden uel si quid his melius tenere credebam.

> Their sensitivity and grace, their charm and warmth of feeling, their wit which never wants propriety, made me imagine I held Callimachus or Herodas in my hands, or even some greater poet.

Not only are Callimachus and the Hellenistic poets referred to directly in this way, but also their early exponents in Rome: when Pliny mentions the poetry of Pompeius Saturninus at 1.16.5 he enthuses

> facit uersus, quales Catullus aut Caluus. quantum illis leporis, dulcedinis, amaritudinis, amoris! inserit sane, sed data opera, mollibus leuibusque duriusculos quosdam, et hoc quasi Catullus aut Caluus.

> He also writes verses in the style of Catullus and Calvus which might indeed be theirs, for these are full of wit and charm, bitterness and passion; and, though he sometimes strikes a harsher note in the even flow of his measures, it is done deliberately and in imitation of his models.[9]

All this skirting around issues of poetics begs the question of Pliny's own stylistic views on poetry. Certainly his approach to poetry is made to fit conveniently around the far more pressing concerns of oratory and 'real' work, but, in spite of Gamberini's claim that Pliny, who is so concerned with the stylistic theory of oratory, lacks any interest in the stylistic theory of poetry,[10] I think Pliny's various remarks can be regarded cumulatively as expressing a view, if only a by-this-point conventional, post-Augustan-Callimachean view, defused of its polemical content, about poetic style, but without adherence to the poetic *life*style which was part and parcel of a 'genuine' Callimachean aesthetics. If anything, Pliny might be aligned not so much with Catullus and the neoterics as with the pre-neoterics like Lutatius Catulus (mentioned by Pliny in his list of past orator/poets at 5.3.5) who were strongly influenced by Hellenistic poetics and wrote short, careful, varied *nugae*. As Conte explains, these poems were 'the product of *otium,* of time withdrawn from civil duties and devoted instead to reading and intelligent conversation', but nonetheless, 'for a Catulus poetry was marginal, an occasional diversion from a life still centred on the duties of the citizen—it is not a coincidence that the same Catulus is also a writer of historical works'.[11] The similarities with Pliny and his attitude towards his poetic composition are obvious. But it is not necessary to go back quite so far to find a model for Pliny's literary activity: Calvus, mentioned in the same breath as Catullus by Pliny, was not only a well-known and influential neoteric poet, but also a prominent orator, a rival to Cicero (he is classified by Pliny as an orator at 1.2.2, 5.3.5 and as a poet, with Callimachus, at 1.16.5, 4.27.4).

To say that Pliny held a Romanized-Callimachean viewpoint, then, is not to say that he shunned the epic genre, any more than Vergil or Ovid, though steeped in Callimachean poetics, shunned it. While Pliny chose not to pursue the composition of epic in his limited spare time, he still appreciated it, as his frequent quotations of Homer and Vergil demonstrate.[12] Moreover, he holds up epic poetry as a model for literary sublimity. It was a commonly held idea in antiquity that a general familiarity with poetry is beneficial for the orator, since he can then include quotations in his speeches, as well as use the sublimity of poetry to elevate his own work. Quintilian discusses the value of including poetic quotations in speeches at *Institutio Oratoria* 1.8.10-12; at *Inst.* 10.1.27 Quintilian sums up poetry's overall contribution in oratory:

> plurimum dicit oratori conferre Theophrastus lectionem poetarum multique eius iudicium sequuntur, neque immerito. namque ab his in rebus spiritus et in uerbis sublimitas et in adfectibus motus omnis et in personis decor petitur, praecipueque uelut attrita cotidiano actu forensi ingenia optime rerum talium blanditia reparantur . . .

> Theophrastus says that much is contributed to an orator's training by reading poetry, and many follow this lead, reasonably enough: for the poets are a source of inspiration in subject, sublimity in language, range of emotion, appropriateness in depiction of character. In particular, minds deadened by the daily round of legal activity find especial refreshment in the attractions of poetry.[13]

'Longinus', discussing the value of imitating the style of great men in *On the Sublime*, recommends asking 'How would Homer have said such-and-such?', when something needs to be expressed in an elevated and grand way (14.1). A slightly more cynical view of the influence of poetry on oratory appears in Tacitus' *Dialogus de oratoribus*, in which the orator Aper is trying to convince Maternus to abandon poetry and to devote himself whole-heartedly to oratory; Aper remarks at 20.4 that young men are especially impressed 'siue sensus aliquis arguta et breui sententia efflusit, siue locus exquisito et poetico cultu enituit?' ('by some short, sharp, brilliant epigram, or a passage resplendent with out-of-the-way poetic colouring'[14]), and he continues (§5-6):

> exigitur enim iam ab oratore etiam poeticus decor, non Accii aut Pacuuii ueterno inquinatus, sed ex Horatii et Vergilii et Lucani sacrario prolatus. horum igitur auribus et iudiciis obtemperans nostrorum oratorum aetas pulchrior et ornatior exstitit.

> Yes, an orator now has to provide poetic beauty as well, not the Accius or Pacuvius variety, mildewed with age, but drawn from the shrines of Horace, Vergil, and Lucan. These are the ears and these the judgements that contemporary orators have to pander to—and it is for this reason that they have become more pretty and more ornate in style.

Pliny allows for the possibility and suitability of epic sublimity in oratory, for example in 7.9.8, where he says that the subject matter of a speech may call for such elevation, and in 2.5.5 where he notes that in a particular oration it was proper for him to treat the descriptions of places 'non historice tantum sed prope poetice' ('[with] a touch of poetry [in] plain prose'). In his consideration of the topic in 9.26, because he is not discussing his own work, Pliny expresses the most admiration for poetic diction in orations, although not without ambivalence. Unlike Tacitus' Aper, who thinks poetic flights of fancy inappropriate in proper oratory, Pliny supports the view that getting carried away in one's style can contribute to the impressiveness of one's oration,[15] although he himself does not write in such a manner (§7):

> nec nunc ego me his [i.e. certain Homeric verses] similia aut dixisse aut posse dicere puto. non ita insanio; sed hoc intellegi uolo, laxandos esse eloquentiae frenos nec angustissimo gyro ingeniorum impetus refrigendos.

> Not that I think that these are the times and I am the person to have written words like these, nor that I have the ability to do so: I am not so foolish. But I want to make the point that eloquence should be given its head, and the pace of genius should not be confined within too narrow a ring.

He then goes on to discuss the idea 'at enim alia conditio oratorum, alia poetarum' ('you may say that orators are different from poets') (§8), and, using Demosthenes as his example, illustrates that in fact orators frequently can reach epic heights. At times, moreover, Pliny himself aims at epic sublimity in his letter writing: for example, at 5.6.43 he defends the length of his description of his Tuscan villa on the grounds that Homer and Vergil devoted many verses to the descriptions of Achilles' and Aeneas' shields.[16]

Not only was Pliny versed in epic and other 'higher' poetic genres, but he also enjoyed less elevated, more popular genres: at 5.3.2 he mentions his familiarity with comedy, mime, lyric poetry, and notoriously obscene Sotadic verse. This catholic taste was not limited to what Pliny read; Pliny also wrote poetry in a number of genres. In 7.4 he provides a brief account of his poetic career in which he tells how he wrote a Greek tragedy (or at least something which bore a figured relationship to a Greek tragedy) at the age of 14 (§2), and also mentions that as a young man he dabbled in elegy and epic (§3). He then explains that he was inspired to his new poetic work in hendecasyllables after hearing some epigrams of Cicero (§3); this experience resulted, for Pliny, in a restless afternoon siesta—which neatly echoes Catullus' restless night in poem 50 after he spends a *dies otiosus* writing poetry with Licinius[17]–and in Pliny's composition of a poem about his new inspiration to write (reproduced in §6)—which also neatly echoes the self-reflexive outcome of Catullus 50, namely, poem 50 itself. Pliny then describes how he tried his hand at other metres, including elegiacs (§7), and settled on producing the volume of hendecasyllables (§8) (once more following in Catullan footsteps), which Pontius, the letter's addressee, has just read.

Pliny's poetry concerned various topics. Of his three extant poems, one deals with his renewed desire to compose verse, and specifically love poetry (at 7.4.6), one praises the virtue of flexibility (at 7.9.11), and one, the authenticity of which is questionable,[18] is a drinking song in elegiacs (which can be found at *Anth. Lat.* 710R). At 7.9.13 Pliny says that poetry can deal with 'amores, odia, iras, misericordiam, urbanitatem, omnia denique quae in uita atque etiam in foro causisque uersantur' ('our loves and hatreds, our indignation, compassion and wit, in fact every phase of life and every detail of our public and professional activities'), and at 4.14.3 he tells how in his own hendecasyllables 'iocamur, ludimus, amamus, dolemus, querimur, irascimur' ('here are my jokes and witticisms, my loves, sorrows, complaints and vexations'); all of this suggests that Pliny's poetry covered a wide variety of subject matter. Furthermore, Pliny handled these different topics in a number of ways: 'describimus aliquid modo pressius modo elatius' ('now my style is simple, now more elevated') (§3), which may imply that the poetry was in a variety of genres, although Pliny at 4.14.9 explains (in a comment which reflects the uncertainty, prevalent in both ancient and modern literary criticism, over whether or not genres should be assigned to poems according to their metre or subject matter) that he himself prefers to classify the work simply by its metre:

> proinde siue epigrammata siue idyllia siue eclogas siue, ut multi, poematia seu quod aliud uocare malueris licebit uoces, ego tantum hendecasyllabos praesto.
>
> You call them what you like—epigrams, idylls, eclogues, or simply 'short poems', which is the popular name, but I shall stick to my 'hendecasyllables'.

It is worth noting that, in spite of Pliny's remark that many people use the name *poematia,* it is a rare word, the Latin version of the equally rare Greek word ποιημάτιον, and appears twice in Pliny's letters (also 4.27.1) but nowhere else. The use of *poematia* may again signal the Romanized Hellenistic aesthetic which finds its way into Pliny's poetic outlook; compare 'Longinus' 33.5, where the *Erigone* of Callimachus' follower Eratosthenes is called an ἀμώμητον ποιημάτιον (a 'flawless little poem'). Elsewhere Pliny talks about a book of poetry he has composed which is 'opusculis uarius et metris' ('consist[ing] of short pieces in different metres') (8.21.3); he gives as a reason for this variety his fear of boring his audience (§4),

although this fear appears ever so slightly disingenuous since it did not prevent him from detaining his audience for two days while he recited the book in its entirety, and no doubt a desire to display his technical mastery of poetic form is not completely absent from his motivation as well. But his main concern, that of satisfying his audience, appears again: Pliny remarks in 4.14.3 that he covers a variety of subjects in a variety of styles because he wishes to provide the proverbial something for everyone: 'ipsa uarietate temptamus efficere ut alia aliis, quaedam fortasse omnibus placeant' ('I try through variety to appeal to different tastes and produce a few things to please everyone'). This idea of *uariatio,* then, is an important aspect of Pliny's own poetic work and outlook, and is one which he recommends to and praises in the poetry of others.[19] The *poematia* of Sentius Augurinus, for example, are especially pleasing to Pliny because of their stylistic diversity (4.27.1): 'multa tenuiter, multa sublimiter, multa uenuste, multa tenere, multa dulciter, multa cum bile' ('many are simple, many in a grand style: many are full of delicate charm and express either tender feelings or indignation'); compare also the *uariatio* of Pompeius Saturninus' poetry highlighted by Pliny at 1.16.5 (quoted above), or the praise of Calpurnius Piso's poetic style (5.17.2): 'apte enim et uarie nunc attollebatur nunc residebat: excelsa depressis, exilia plenis, seueris iucunda mutabat, omnia ingenio pari' ('he showed an appropriate versatility in raising or lowering his tone, and the same talent whether he descended from the heights to a lower level, rose to complexity from simplicity or moved between a lighter and more serious approach to his subject'). The concept of *uariatio* is also noteworthy as it is an important—and initially controversial—element of Callimachean poetics: the Diegesis on *Iambus* 13 explains that the poem was an answer to critics who complained about the πολυείδεια of Callimachus' poetry.

In spite of its carefully considered *uariatio,* how successful Pliny's poetry actually was at pleasing everyone is another matter. On several occasions Pliny must defend his choice of subjects and their presentation from charges that they are not serious enough and that they are even somewhat offensive. In 5.3 he argues in favour of writing 'non numquam uersiculos seueros parum' ('verse which is far from serious') (§2) on the grounds that many great and learned men—orators, senators, even emperors—have written such verses. Justifying his own 'non nulla . . . paulo petulantiora' ('rather indelicate') poems at 4.14.4, Pliny says that in the past serious men have 'non modo lasciuia rerum sed ne uerbis quidem nudis abstinuisse' ('neither avoided lascivious subjects nor refrained from expressing them in plain language'). At the same time he quotes Catullus' defence of poetic free speech, based on the separation of author and text, 'nam castum esse decet pium poetam / ipsum, uersiculos nihil necesse est' ('the true poet should be chaste himself, though his poetry need not be') (Catul. 16.5); but notably Pliny leaves unsaid that poem's truly licentious refrain, 'pedicabo ego uos et irrumabo'.

Pliny is not alarmed by his public's occasional objections to his poetry. He is pleased by the debate his poetry has prompted in Titius Aristo's household (5.3.1):

> cum plurima officia tua mihi grata et iucunda sunt, tum uel maxime quod me celandum non putastis fuisse apud te de uersiculis meis multum copiosumque sermonem, eumque diuersitate iudiciorum longius processisse . . .

> I have many welcome acts of kindness to thank you for, but you do me a real service by thinking I ought to know that my verses have been the subject of much discussion at your house, a discussion which was prolonged because of difference of opinion.

On the whole, however, the response to Pliny's poetry, as this is presented by Pliny, is highly positive. Pomponius Mamilianus has been complaining about his duties, Pliny writes at 9.25.1, but 'lusus et ineptias nostras legis, amas, flagitas, meque ad similia condenda non mediocriter incitas' ('you can read my bits of nonsense as if you had all the leisure in the world—you even enjoy them, clamour for them, and are insistent that I produce more like them'). Augurinus, whose poetic work Pliny so admires, is so taken with Pliny's poetry that he devotes a poem to it (reproduced in 4.27); here is Radice's translation:

> My verse is light and tender, as Catullus long ago,
> But what care I for poets past, when I my Pliny know?
> Outside the courts in mutual love and song he makes his name;
> You lovers and you statesmen, to Pliny yield your fame!

Radice notes 'the free translation reflects the banality of the original'. Not surprisingly, Pliny finds Augurinus' poem about Pliny the poet altogether delightful: 'uides quam acuta omnia, quam apta, quam expressa' ('this will give you an idea of the wit and polished perfection of his style') (§5); on such grounds are mutual admiration societies formed. Nor is this positive reception limited to his friends: Pliny reports that his poems are met with wide approbation and acclaim, so much so that Greeks are learning Latin just to be able to read and sing them (7.4.9); at home, his wife's appreciation of his poems leads her to set them to music (4.19.4).

Pliny's own attitude towards his poetry is somewhat different from that of his adoring public. The self-deprecating stance he takes on his own poems, even if we take the view that it is just false modesty (but we do not have to take this view), is still notable. He refers to his poetry as *lusus* (4.14.1, 9.25.1), *ineptiae* (4.14.8, 9.25.1), *nugae* (4.14.8, 7.2.2), and *uersiculi* (5.3.1) which are belittling, sometimes derogatory terms, but also are descriptive of the very type of poetry which Pliny extols and which was practised by, among others, Catullus (writing his *libellum* of *nugae* [Catul. 1.1.4]) and Callimachus. A statesman first and a poet second, Pliny is always quick to supplement his reports of poetic success with modest disclaimers: so, for example, at 7.4.10, after relating his contribution to the Latin education of Greeks, he hastens to add:

> sed quid ego tam gloriose? quamquam poetis furere concessum est: et tamen non de meo sed de aliorum iudicio loquor.

> But I must not boast (though poets can talk wildly!) even if it is not my own opinion I am quoting but other people's.

But Pliny seems to take his poetry a bit more seriously than his modest remarks at first indicate: certainly his defence of his poetry in 4.14 and 5.3 suggests that he was serious enough about it not to dismiss criticism of it,[20] as does the fact that he devoted two days to reading a book of poetry to his friends in order to revise it in the light of their comments (8.21), and also that he requests comments from those to whom he sends his work: in this way Pliny treats his poetry with the same perfectionist intensity with which he treats his orations. At times Pliny hints at the larger possibilities offered by poetic composition, which can rival those offered by oratory: great poetry, like great oratory, can win glory for its author.[21] At 9.25.2, Pliny tells Mamilianus, who has praised his poetry,

> incipio enim ex hoc genere studiorum non solum oblectationem uerum etiam gloriam petere post iudicium tuum, uiri grauissimi, eruditissimi, ac super ista uerissimi.

> I am in fact beginning to think that I can look for more than mere amusement from this kind of writing, and now that I have the opinion of one who is both learned and serious, and above all sincere, I may even think of fame.

While Pliny is, of course, being ironic here, as is further made clear by his subsequent promise to send his 'little sparrows and doves' to Mamilianus, who can either allow them to go among his eagles or can put them in a cage or nest (§3), nevertheless there is a sense that something genuine underlies the remark. During his discussion of the benefits of poetic composition in 7.9, Pliny mentions in a more straightforward way the potential for glory from writing poetry (§10): 'lusus uocantur: sed hi lusus non minorem interdum gloriam quam seria consequuntur' ('this is called light verse, but it sometimes brings its authors as much fame as serious work').

As an aside, the idea, closely related to that of gaining glory from writing poetry, of gaining glory from being the subject of poetry comes up several times in Pliny's letters (e.g., 1.17.3, 2.1.2),[22] most explicitly, and most relevantly from Pliny's perspective, in 3.21, which concerns the death of Martial. In the letter Pliny repeats part of Martial's flattering poem about him (Mart. 10.20) and then comments (§6)

> dedit enim mihi quantum maximum potuit, daturus amplius, si potuisset. tametsi quid homini potest dari maius quam gloria et laus et aeternitas?

> He gave me of his best, and would have given more had he been able, though surely nothing more can be given to a man than a tribute which will bring him fame and immortality?

before delivering his famous verdict of the epigrammatist's work, that it would probably not last forever, even though Martial intended that it should (Pliny, anyway, was doing his bit to make sure that the poem about him *would* last by including it in his [published] letter).[23]

It might be useful to compare Pliny's gently ironic approach to his poetry and to the possibilities offered by poetry to the more intense approach of Cicero.[24] In addition to translating Greek poetry into Latin (including Aratus and passages from Homer and the tragedians), Cicero also wrote his own poetry, including the infamous 'o fortunatam natam me consule Romam', mocked by Juvenal in his tenth satire. In his youth, Cicero, influenced by the Hellenistic poetics which he would later criticize, wrote in various metres and genres, and in his maturity he composed, or contemplated composing, a number of epic poems: the *Marius,* at least one epic concerning Caesar, and two epics devoted to himself—the *De consulatu* and the unfinished *De temporibus suis.* These last two he had to write himself since no one else would do it for him; but he did so without too many qualms, since as he remarks on his choice of subject matter, 'si est enim apud homines quicquam quod potius laudetur, nos uituperemur, qui non potius alia laudemus' ('if there is any more fitting subject for eulogy, then I am willing to be blamed for not choosing some other subject') (*Att.* 1.19.10).[25] Cicero, like Pliny, valued *gloria* highly,[26] and saw the potential of poetry to deliver it: in the *Pro Archia* he explains that his desire to have his consulship recorded in verse arises from 'amore gloriae nimis acri fortasse, uerum tamen honesto' ('a passion for fame over-keen perhaps, but assuredly honourable') (11.28); the poet Archias was to have composed such a poem and had even begun it (*Arch.* 11.28), but then prudently changed his mind (*Att.* 1.16.15).

Unlike Pliny, who, while eager to have his poetry accepted, was not overwrought at the prospect of either its positive or negative reception, Cicero was very anxious about the public response to his poetry, or at least of one member of the public: he writes to Quintus (*Q. fr.* 2.16.5):

> sed heus tu, celari uideor a te. quomodonam, mi frater, de nostris uersibus Caesar? nam primum librum se legisse scripsit ad me ante, et prima sic, ut neget, se ne Graeca quidem meliora legisse. reliqua ad quemdam locum ῥᾳθυμότερα. hoc enim utitur uerbo. dic mihi uerum, num aut res eum, aut χαρακτήρ non delectat?

> But look here you, it seems to me that you are keeping something back from me. What oh what, my dear brother, did Caesar think of my verses? He wrote to me some time ago that he had read my first book; and of the first part he declared that he had never read anything better, even in Greek; the rest of it, as far as a certain passage, was rather 'happy-go-lucky'– that is the term he uses. Tell me the truth—is it the subject or the style that does not please him?

It is hard to imagine Pliny worrying so much over his poetry's reception, nor was there any real need for him to do so. It was Cicero's politically expedient desire to ingratiate himself with Caesar that prompted him to undertake the composition of an epic about Caesar's expedition to Britain; he informs Quintus of his decision to write it in *Q. fr.* 2.14.2, but later he produces a number of excuses for why he cannot continue with the task, including lack of time, lack of energy, lack of inspiration, and no lack of anxiety for concerns weightier than poetry (*Q. fr.* 3.4.4). One wonders whether Caesar was disappointed or relieved.

Cicero, however, was not an unimportant poet. He made significant contributions to the development of the Latin hexameter, and allusions to his poetry can be found in such poets as Horace and Vergil.[27] In his day, as Plutarch notes in his *Life of Cicero* (2), Cicero was renowned for his poetic ability:

> ἔδοξεν οὐ μόνον ῥήτωρ, ἀλλὰ καὶ ποιητὴς ἄριστος εἶναι Ῥωμαίων. ἡ μὲν οὖν ἐπὶ τῇ ῥητορικῇ δόξα μέχρι νῦν διαμένει, καίπερ οὐ μικρᾶς γεγενημένης περὶ τοὺς λόγους καινοτομίας, τὴν δὲ ποιητικὴν αὐτοῦ, πολλῶν εὐφυῶν ἐπιγενομένων, παντάπασιν ἀκλεῆ καὶ ἄτιμον ἔρρειν συμβέβηκεν.

> Cicero got the name of being not only the best orator, but also the best poet among the Romans. His fame for oratory abides to this day, although there have been great innovations in style; but his poetry, since many gifted poets have followed him, has altogether fallen into neglect and disrepute.

As the Plutarch passage hints, Cicero the poet is most famous for engendering critical ill-will. Juvenal was by no means his only critic in antiquity, although he was one of the more mocking. The Elder Seneca states 'Ciceronem eloquentia sua in carminibus destituit' ('Cicero's eloquence left him in poetry') (*Contr.* 3, *praef.* 8). Aper in the *Dialogus,* discussing other Republican orators, remarks 'fecerunt enim et carmina . . . non melius quam Cicero, sed felicius, quia illos fecisse pauciores sciunt' ('they did write poetry . . . they were no greater than Cicero, but they had more luck— fewer know about it') (21.6). Although he claims that Cicero did not over-praise himself in his orations, Quintilian finds fault with his boastfulness in his poetry: 'in carminibus utinam pepercisset' ('would that he had been more sparing in poetry') (*Inst.* 11.1.23). Pliny himself, far from mocking or even criticizing Cicero the poet, pays him the great compliment of saying that it was Cicero's poetry which inspired him to take up his stylus once again (7.4.3, 6). But it is notable that Pliny's inspiration came from what must be one of Cicero's early 'Hellenistic' poems, a *lasciuum lusum.* No doubt he was also inspired by the Republican orator's additional fame as a poet, and names Cicero first and without apologies in his list of great figures of the past who wrote praiseworthy light poetry (5.3.5). Pliny politely ignores Cicero's later, embarrassing epics.

Pliny's poetry, far from serving overtly political aims, functions rather as a depoliticized leisure activity, a temporary diversion fom the pressures of public life. When he suggests the possibility of attaining glory from his poetry—one of Cicero's main purposes in composing his self-serving epics—it is only in an off-handed way, and this glory would be reflected on him from the success of his verses rather than from having enshrined himself within them (there were others who might do that for him). Cicero the poet had the double pressure of a self-aware talent and of the need to use it to its— and his—best advantage. Pliny the poet was under no such pressures. While his modesty may appear disingenuous at times, Pliny never made any serious pretensions to poetic greatness. If, then, he never achieved poetic greatness, it is not a source of posthumous embarrassment; at least he gained the satisfaction of a certain amount of popular success in his own day. As a poet, he did not reach Cicero's heights, and consequently did not have Cicero's great fall (and not only in poetry, but also, of course, in politics). Besides, he always trusted not in his vacation verse composition but in his day job to win him enduring glory, and, as literary history has shown, this trust was not wholly misplaced.

Notes

1. All translations of Pliny are from B. Radice's Penguin edition.

2. See F. Gamberini, *Stylistic Theory and Practice in the Younger Pliny* (Hildesheim, 1983), pp. 90-91 on the possible third book.

3. Pliny also mentions writing while travelling in 9.10.2, although it is not clear if the 'non nulla leuiora' are the languishing *poemata* referred to two sentences later.

4. Gamberini (n. 2), p. 103; on *otium* and *negotium,* pp. 103-9.

5. Gamberini (n. 2), p. 109.

6. Cf. Gamberini's qualification of the notion of Pliny as a 'neoteric' at pp. 92, 111.

7. Ovid's blending of Callimachean and non-Callimachean practices in the *Metamorphoses* is a striking illustration of the complicated, sometimes politicized, sometimes depoliticized approach to Callimacheanism which developed in Roman poetry, a full consideration of which is beyond the scope of this paper; on Ovid's Callimacheanism see, e.g., H. Hofmann, 'Ovid's *Metamorphoses: carmen perpetuum, carmen deductum*', *PLLS* 5 (1985), 223-41, B. Harries, 'The spinner and the poet: Arachne in Ovid's *Metamorphoses*', *PCPhS* [*Proceedings, Cambridge Philological Society*] n.s. 36 (1990), 64-82, J. Wills, 'Callimachean Models for Ovid's "Apollo-Daphne"', *MD* 24 (1990), 143-56; on Callimacheanism in Roman poetry in general, see, e.g., W. Wimmel, *Kallimachos in Rom, Hermes* Einzelschriften 16 (Wiesbaden, 1960), W. Clausen, 'Callimachus and Latin Poetry', *GRBS* [*Greek, Roman, and Byzantine Studies*] 5 (1964), 181-96, G. A. Kennedy (ed.), *The Cambridge History of Literary Criticism. Volume I: Classical Criticism* (Cambridge, 1989), pp. 246-54.

8. On this distinction see, e.g., H. Dahlmann, 'Varros Schrift "de poematis" und die hellenistischrömische Poetik', *Abh. Mainz* 3 (1953), N. A. Greenberg, 'The Use of *Poiema* and *Poiesis*', *HSCPh* [*Harvard Studies in Classical Philology*] 65 (1961), 263-89, R. Häussler, 'Poiema und Poiesis', in W. Wimmel (ed.), *Forschungen zur römischen Literatur* (Wiesbaden, 1970), pp. 125-37.

9. Cf. the beginning of Sentius Augurinus' poem, recorded and praised by Pliny in 4.27, which also displays this type of retro-neoteric aesthetic: 'canto carmina uersibus minutis, / his olim quibus et meus Catullus / et Caluus ueteresque.'

10. Gamberini (n. 2), p. 111.

11. G. B. Conte (J. B. Solodow, trs.) *Latin Literature: A History* (Baltimore, 1994), p. 137.

12. See Gamberini (n. 2), pp. 92, 111-12.

13. All translations of Quintilian by M. Winterbottom, from D. A. Russell and M. Winterbottom (edd.), *Ancient Literary Criticism* (Oxford, 1972).

14. Translations of the *Dialogus* by M. Winterbottom, from Russell and Winterbottom (n. 13).

15. Relevant here, perhaps, is the on-going conflict between the exuberant Asianic and the more restrained Attic styles of oratory; on this (frequently deconstructible) opposition see in general, e.g., Cicero, *Orat.* 22-32, *Brut.* 325, *Opt. Gen.* 7-13, Dionysius of Halicarnassus *Orat. Vett., praef.,* Quintilian *Inst.* 12.10.10-26 with R. G. Austin (ed.), *Quintilian Book XII* (Oxford, 1948), and §10.16; U. v. Wilamowitz, 'Asianismus und Atticismus', *Hermes* 35 (1900), 1-52, R. Syme, *The Roman Revolution* (Oxford, 1939), pp. 245-6, A. D. Leeman, *Orationis Ratio: The Stylistic Theories and Practice of the Roman Orators, Historians and Philosophers* (Amsterdam, 1963), pp. 140-67, 219-42.

16. Often it was deemed necessary in antiquity for an overt distinction to be made between poetry and oratory: see Leeman (n. 15), pp. 311-14, who cites as examples Cicero, *Orat.* 68 and Quintilian, *Inst.* 10.1.28; cf. Tacitus' *Dialogus,* which takes as its starting point the separate merits of poetry and oratory. The distinction between the two fields became increasingly elided; see, for example, the question of whether or not Vergil was an orator, e.g., in Florus' lost dialogue *Vergilius orator an poeta,* or in Macrobius' *Saturnalia* (esp. 5.1.1ff.); for the debate over Vergil see G. Highet, *The Speeches in Vergil's* Aeneid (Princeton, 1972), pp. 3-8, 277-90. At all times the two literary fields are closely related, although the exact nature of the relationship is highly variable: see, in general, D. A. Russell, *Criticism in Antiquity* (London, 1981), pp. 15-16.

17. The siesta-time setting of Pliny's scene (§4: '. . . cum meridie [erat enim aestas] . . .') also recalls the setting of Ovid's afternoon love-making session with Corinna (*Am.* 1.5.1: 'aestus erat'), lending Pliny's scene an erotic undertone which will be reflected in his announced turn to amorous poetry.

18. See E. Courtney (ed.), *The Fragmentary Latin Poets* (Oxford, 1993), pp. 369-70.

19. Gamberini (n. 2), pp. 113-14.

20. Gamberini (n. 2), p. 98.

21. Cf. Vergil *Geo.* 4.6-7: 'in tenui labor; at tenuis non gloria, si quem / numina laeua sinunt auditque uocatus Apollo' ('the work is on a small scale, but the glory will not be slight, if unpropitious divinities grant it [to the poet], and Apollo, being spoken to, hears'); note that the poet's *gloria* is a result of his Callimachean poetry (see R. F. Thomas [ed.], *Virgil, Georgics III-IV* [Cambridge, 1988] ad loc.). *Gloria* was, of course, a major concern not only to Pliny, who refers to it repeatedly, but to Romans in general, for whom it was an important, non-negligible motivator (see, e.g., Caesar, *Gal.* 7.50.4, Vergil, *Aen.* 4.232-72, *Aen.* 5.394, Valerius Flaccus 1.76-7 ('tu sola animos mentesque peruris, / Gloria . . .' ('you alone, Glory, fire spirits and minds')), but also with the potential for harm if pursued too zealously (see, e.g., Horace, *Odes* 1.18.15, Vergil, *Aen.* 11.708); on *gloria* see, e.g., U. Knoche, 'Der römische Ruhmesgedanke', in H. Oppermann (ed.), *Römische Wertbegriffe* (Darmstadt, 1967), pp. 420-45, J. Hellegouarc'h, *Le Vocabulaire latin des relations et des partis politiques sous la république* (Paris, 1972), pp. 369-83.

22. This is another common *topos:* cf., e.g., Cicero, *Arch.* 19-22, esp. 23, Ovid, *Pont.* 3.2.35-6 ('uos etiam seri laudabunt saepe nepotes, / claraque erit scriptis gloria uestra meis' ['often late-born descendants will praise you, and your glory will be bright because of my writings']).

23. This is not the only time Pliny expresses his opinion of a contemporary (and still extant) poet: see 3.7.5, where he gives his cautious judgement of Silius Italicus: 'scribebat carmina maiore cura quam ingenio' ('he took great pains over his verses, though they cannot be called inspired'). He is more complimentary of the poets in his immediate social circle: see, e.g., 1.16.5 (Pompeius Saturninus), 4.27 (Sentius Augurinus), 5.17.2 (Calpurnius Piso), 4.3.3-5, 4.18, and 5.15 (Arrius Antoninus); cf. 1.13.1 ('magnum prouentum poetarum annus hic attulit' ['this year has raised a fine crop of poets']).

24. For a study of Cicero's poetry, as well as a commentary on the fragments, see W. W. Ewbank, *The Poems of Cicero* (London, 1933); see also Conte (n. 11), pp. 200-2.

25. All Cicero translations are from the Loebs.

26. Cicero even wrote a treatise on the subject; the *testamonia* and fragments are in Garbarino's editions of Cicero's *fragmenta* (Turin, 1984).

27. On Cicero's hexameters: Ewbank (n. 24), pp. 40-71, Conte (n. 11), pp. 201-2; on later poets' allusions to Cicero's poetry: Ewbank (n. 24), p. 16.

Andrew M. Riggsby (essay date winter 1998)

SOURCE: Riggsby, Andrew M. "Self and Community in Pliny the Younger." *Arethusa* 31, no. 1 (winter 1998): 75-97.

[*In the following essay, Riggsby shows how a comparison between Pliny's letters and those of other Roman authors who concerned themselves with the role of the orator reveals him as an extremely conservative intellectual in terms of his thinking on the relationship between the individual and community.*]

Pliny the Younger described himself as an imitation, if a somewhat pale one, of Cicero (4.8.4-5, 9.2.2-3). In a recent paper examining this connection, I argued that its value for Pliny lay in the identification of both men as orators and the further identification of the orator as an "engaged public figure."[1] In this paper, I want to nuance that claim by giving further consideration to the connection between "engaged" and "public." Examination of this notion involves consideration of the interaction of individuals with a community and the way this interaction is framed in ethical terms. This, in turn, leads to the question of the precise nature of the individual/community distinction. A reading of Pliny's letters against the texts of some of his near contemporaries reveals significant differences in their respective theories of the self and its interaction with the world. In particular, Pliny can be shown (contrary to some recent accounts) to employ for the most part a remarkably conservative notion of the relationship between individual and community.

In letter 5.3, Pliny defends his production of light verse not only with exempla of senators and emperors (including Cicero) who did the same (5.3.5), but also of Vergil, Nepos, Accius, and Ennius, who are included on the strength of their *sanctitas morum* (5.3.6).[2] The Roman elite had always conflated their social standing and political authority with moral superiority to some degree. It would be but a short step for Pliny to construct, if only locally, a hierarchy of authority based purely on moral grounds; he makes only a token apology for the possible innovation. Compare Pliny's teacher Quintilian, who enthusiastically adopts Cato's definition of the orator as a *uir bonus dicendi peritus,* "a good man, skilled in speaking" (1.pr.9; 2.15.33-34, 16.11, 17.31; 12.1.1, 3). This definition and Quintilian's entire discussion of the perfect orator (12.1) focus on an ethical interpretation of the role of the orator, quite likely in response to the role of *delatores* in unpopular prosecutions.[3] To Pliny's *priuata exempla* we might also compare the entire collection of Valerius Maximus. Bloomer 1992. 19, 147-229 notes a procedure of "dehistoricization" that goes on in the composition of his exempla. The details of Republican power politics are elided so as to better fit the stories to the moral categories that structure Valerius' work. We ask, then, whether Pliny's view of the orator has taken part in this moralization. If so, does that make the orator's significance more "private" or is Pliny merely extending the traditional tendency to conflate moral and social order?

Pliny's most extensive discussion of the function of the orator is 6.29. He starts (§§1-2) by accepting the three reasons advanced by one Thrasea for accepting legal cases:[4] friendship, charity to those without other options, and the importance of precedent-setting (*ad exemplum pertinentes*) cases. He then adds a fourth category of his own: glorious and notable cases (§3). Friendship is certainly an ethical issue; charity could be considered under this head, though Pliny also recommends it because it will improve the orator's reputation (§2). Similarly, famous cases will improve the orator's visibility. But why the cases *ad exemplum pertinentes*? Because their outcome actually matters (§2): *quia plurimum referret, bonum an malum induceretur,* "because it matters much whether good or ill results." At the end of the letter, Pliny lists several cases he has undertaken under this head (§§8-11). They are all criminal prosecutions and defenses (mostly *repetundae*), public cases the likes of which had made Cicero's reputation. Thus the orator not only may, but must, take action which is "public" in the strongest sense: it is not only visible, but consequential for the community. In some sense, this too may be regarded as a demand on the orator's character, but the orator is nonetheless judged ultimately by concrete effects he will have on those around him.

This last distinction is crucial for understanding the place of the orator in Pliny's scheme. Even when he discusses taking these political cases, Pliny uses the same ethical language that he used of less obviously public activity like writing poetry (*deceat*, 6.29.11; cf. 5.3.5). We may well accept that Pliny represents the roles of orator and senator as, in general, ethical roles. Yet his persistent references to the engagement and effectiveness of the orator should remind us to be careful about what this might have meant in a Roman context. It does not imply a focus on an "inner" self that it might for a modern American (or even for someone like Seneca the Younger).[5] Pliny also had available a more conservative view in which virtue is constructed under (perhaps even by) the gaze of the community.[6]

Before proceeding further with the analysis of Pliny, I would like to introduce a theoretical distinction proposed by Michael Carrithers. Carrithers (drawing his terminology from Marcel Mauss) distinguishes "*personne*-theories" and "*moi*-theories" of the individual.[7] A *personne*-theory is socially oriented; it is a "conception of the individual human being as a member of a (1) significant and (2) ordered collectivity" (Carrithers 1985.235). By contrast, *moi*-theories are both more and less individualizing; they offer a "conception of (1) the physical and mental individuality of human beings within (2) a natural or spiritual cosmos, and (3) interacting with each other as moral agents" (Carrithers 1985.236). The second clause produces a universalizing tendency, while the last gives *moi*-theories a certain individualistic flavor. That is, on the one hand, "natural" and other universal standards are conducive to understanding individuals serially and separately. On the other, a social standard requires considering communities holistically. For expository purposes, Carrithers restricts himself to the description of explicit, well-articulated theories rather than "folk" theories or pervasive metaphorical structures, but there is no need to so limit ourselves here. Furthermore, I am not interested in discussing such questions as whether all societies exhibit both (or even either) types of theory or whether all theories of the individual can usefully be described in one or the other set of terms.[8] I suggest only that the distinction will be useful in characterizing Pliny's understanding of the "public" and bringing out his differences with a number of contemporary thinkers. Finally, it is important to point out that it is possible (perhaps even normal) for a single person to hold theories of both sorts. The question in what follows will be how Pliny and others made different use of the available theories at roughly the same time.

In the terms just introduced, Roman traditions of evaluation (which we will see Pliny tends to follow) constitute a normative theory of the *personne*: these traditions emphasize evaluation of individuals by the community and in terms of their effects on that community.[9] Obligations are both based on the social role of the individual and defined in terms of the interaction of that role with other roles and with the society as a whole. Traditional aristocratic thinking may well have included some sort of *moi*-idea, but it was the *personne* around which their values were organized. As the epitaph of L. Cornelius Scipio (cos. 259) says (*CIL* I[1].9.1-2, 5-6):

> Honc oino ploirume consentiont R[omai]
> Duonoro optumo fuise uiro . . .
> Hec cepit Corsica Aleriaque urbe.
> Dedet Tempestatebus aide mereto[d].[10]

> Most at Rome agree that this one
> Was the best man of all the good . . .
> He took Corsica and the city of Aleria.
> He rightly gave a temple to the Storms.

This inscription illustrates both the standard of community evaluation and a concomitant emphasis on public achievement. The aristocrat's duty is not so much to be good, as to do good.[11] Nor was this mode of evaluation restricted to certain spheres; the Romans did not in this sense distinguish the domestic from the public. Dionysius remarked with surprise that the censors' gaze at Rome did not (at least in principle) stop at the door of a man's house, as would be expected of state surveillance in Greece (*AR* [*Archaeological Review*] 20.13.3).[12] The language of political invective had always been intensely domestic: descent, sexual perversions, luxury, personal appearance.[13] Though not logically entailed by the principle that moral value is assigned by collective

judgment, this situation illustrates the reach of that principle. If domestic life is to be afforded any moral value at all, it inevitably becomes a public matter. Conventional Roman moralizing takes place under a socially-oriented theory, a *personne*-oriented one.

To demonstrate Pliny's employment of the same kind of social standards outside of oratory we may look to two of Pliny's letters that deal with his poetry (4.14, 5.3). These letters will show that even "private" (in the sense of domestic) actions are given value by their public reception. *Ep.* 4.14 is a cover letter for a collection of light verse; 5.3 discusses rumored reactions to this or similar verse. In both letters, Pliny spends most of his time defending the propriety of writing such poetry. This move has understandably been described as "a fervent defense of his private lyrical self," but it is a defense based on public, collectivist grounds. At 4.14.10 Pliny asks for his correspondent's honest judgment in a curious way: *a simplicitate tua peto, quod de libello meo dicturus es alii, mihi dicas,* "I call on your frankness in asking that you tell me what you are going to tell another about my book." He wants to know the evaluations of himself that will be in circulation. Note also that the indicative *es* shows that he assumes that this circulation will naturally take place.[14] We may compare this to the opening of the other letter (5.3.1): *Cum plurima officia tua mihi grata et iucunda sunt, tum uel maxime quod me celandum non putasti, fuisse apud te de uersiculis meis multum copiosumque sermonem* . . . [reported criticism follows]. "Your many services to me are pleasing and obliging, and especially the fact that you thought that it ought not be hid from me that there was much discussion about my verses at your house." In the following section, Pliny defiantly asserts his indulgence in this and other forms of light entertainment, finally concluding: *aliquando praeterea rideo, iocor, ludo, utque omnia innoxiae remissionis genera breuiter amplectar, homo sum,* "Sometimes I laugh, I jest, I play, and, to briefly encompass all forms of harmless relaxation, I am human." This appears to appeal to a different standard: a *moi*-theory under which, apparently, an individual may consult a generalized "human nature" on his own behalf rather than deferring to a community audience.

But in the immediately following words, he returns to a socially oriented standard (5.3.3): *Nec uero moleste fero hanc esse de moribus mei existimationem, ut qui nesciunt talia doctissimos grauissimos sanctissimos homines scriptitasse, me scribere mirentur,* "Nor do I take this judgment of my character hard; consequently those who do not know that the gravest, most solemn, and most learned men have written such things, wonder that I write them."[15] On this follows the long list of poet/statesman exempla cited above, including Cicero, Calvus, Pollio, Seneca, Augustus, and Nerva (5.3.5). Now,

Habinek MS.42-48 has pointed out that the Roman use of exempla can be conceived of as retrojection of the process of *existimatio* into the (ideologically privileged) past; exempla are understood to show what the ancestors (*maiores*) approved or disapproved of.[16] This is precisely what is happening in this passage. Pliny, in defense against the negative evaluation (§3: *existimationem*) of his contemporaries, does not for long reject their authority in favor of a completely different kind of authority (i.e., essential human nature). Rather he appeals to a more weighty (*doctissimos, grauissimos, sanctissimos*) evaluating audience in the form of Cicero, Calvus, Asinius Pollio, et al.

After reviewing his various classes of exempla (republican senators, emperors, and virtuous poets), Pliny admits that he does not know whether they gave public recitations (5.3.7). That he himself does so is, he says, a sign of his greater modesty (§7): *sed illi iudicio suo poterant esse contenti, mihi modestior constantia est quam ut satis absolutum putem, quod a me probetur,* "They could be content with their own judgment; I am not so rash as to think that what I approve of is polished enough." He expands on this theme for the rest of the letter, finally concluding (§11): *Atque haec ita disputo quasi populum in auditorium, non in cubiculum amicos aduocarim,* "I discuss these things as if I have called the people into an auditorium, not friends into my chamber."[17] Thus Pliny claims ultimately to submit his "private" poetry to the same general public scrutiny as his oratory. This last remark of Pliny's may also suggest an interpretation of the fact that letter 4.14 asks for the recipient's judgment of the enclosed poems (§§6-8, 10). On the one hand, the friend could be like Seneca's Lucilius—a practical check on one's skill and honesty in approaching some absolute goal.[18] On the other hand, a friend might be asked to serve as a representative of the judgment of the community at large. That Pliny asks his addressee to give him the same evaluation he gives others (4.14.10, quoted above) supports the latter interpretation. Pliny's later (5.3.11) deescription of his recital audience as *quasi populum in auditori[o]* confirms this view.

These letters have a direct bearing on issues already raised in this paper and in Riggsby 1995, but they are also of interest because of the somewhat different use to which Eleanor Leach has put them in her innovative discussion of "public" and "private" in Pliny's letters and in contemporary portrait sculpture. In this article (1990.20, 32, 38), Leach observes that the topic may profitably be studied with reference to Foucault's comments on the "individualism" or "turn inward" or "turn to the self" that is often taken to characterize the early centuries A.D. Foucault 1986.42-43 points out that several, quite distinct, phenomena could be understood to fall under these rubrics: (1) the valorization and

autonomy of the individual vis-à-vis the group, (2) the valorization of domestic life, and (3) an increase in "the intensity of the relations to self, that is, of the forms in which one is called upon to take oneself as an object of knowledge and a field of action, so as to transform, correct, and purify oneself, and find salvation . . . a 'cultivation of the self,' wherein the relations of oneself to oneself were intensified and valorized." In short, Leach and Foucault locate in Pliny and his contemporaries a new ethics which, in the terms adopted here, constitutes a *moi*-theory. It emphasizes individuals interacting as such with each other and with themselves. Furthermore, the background for most of these theories is an organized (whether by reason or nature or both) cosmos.

Pliny clearly gives short shrift to the considerations of the first sort, the valorization and autonomy of the individual vis-à-vis the group. As we have already discussed, the individual (for Pliny) is to act for the benefit of the community, and his correctness is defined by the collective opinion of that community. We might also note in this connection the frequent qualifications Pliny makes to expressions of rejoicing, e.g., *nec priuatim magis quam publice,* "no more myself than as a member of the community" (5.14.6; cf. 2.7.6, 4.16.1, 5.11.2, 6.11.3, 10.1.2, 10.86b.1). Pliny appears anxious about expressing joy purely on his own behalf or on his own judgment (or perhaps either). Having isolated Pliny from this aspect of the "turn to the self," we might reasonably ask whether he allows himself to be guided by a *moi*-oriented theory in other respects.

It seems to me that Pliny does not participate in a significant, new valorization of the private or domestic. Leach 1990.31-35 discusses a number of cases in Pliny's letters where he seems to privilege private life (both his own and that of others), particularly as a check on the evaluation of more public behavior. This conception of the private is said to derive from the frequent, coerced discrepancy between public and private actions under Domitian, and to have led to Pliny's aggressive presentation of his private self under the more congenial reign of Trajan. But, as noted above, the domestic had for the Romans never been "private" in the modern sense. Pliny's stated views in this respect were not exceptional. To take one of Leach's proposed examples, a novice poet whose blushes proved his "real" (private) modesty, we see that Pliny says not once, but twice (5.17.1, 4), that the youth has met the standards of his ancestors, and so (§4) he will then form part of the standard for his descendants.[19] Pliny's final hope is (5.17.6): *mireque cupio ne nobiles nostri nihil in domibus suis pulchrum nisi imagines habeant,* "I have a wondrous desire for the nobles of our age to have something fine in their homes besides the *imagines.*" The *imagines,* the masks of the ancestors, are the concrete symbol of *existimatio* by the ultimate collective audience—Roman tradition (Habinek MS.27-28; Polybius 6.52-54). The youth's "private" self is subjected to public scrutiny in an utterly conventional way. Pliny does attach significance to the private, domestic self, but not in a way that indicates any local fluctuation in historical context.

What, then, about the "cultivation of the self" proper? One manifestation of this phenomenon is the pervasive use of regimens and tests to control the self: dietetics, regularly scheduled self-interrogations, self-imposed denials and temptations (Foucault 1986.50-64). Both Stoic and, to a lesser extent, Epicurean practice follow this mode.[20] A less frequently discussed example is Pliny's teacher Quintilian. The first and most important thing to note about Quintilian's work is described by its title: the *Institutio Oratoria* is focused not on the [*tehne*] of speaking (as Aristotle's *Rhetoric*, the *Rhetorica ad Herennium,* or Cicero's *de Inuentione*) or even on the final character of the orator (as Cicero's *de Oratore*). Rather, it is concerned with the formation of the orator.[21] It provides a graded set of exercises (both written and spoken), discusses physical aspects of creating an orator (1.3.14-18, 10.25-26, 11.15-19), and even gives the occasional rule of thumb for self-testing (e.g., 10.1.112: *ille se profecisse sciat cui Cicero ualde placebit,* "You will know you have made a good start if you find Cicero very pleasing"). Nor does this shaping end completely when the young orator leaves the rhetor's school. Quintilian's detailed reading list (10.1.46-131) is intended for the benefit of those whose schooling is over (10.1.4), and he recommends that the orator return for renewed formal education after he has had some actual experience (12.6.6-7).[22] It is true that Quintilian takes pains to explain that the aspiring orator can learn during his youth the many things expected of him (12.11.9-30), but this is largely a question of learning the facts and precepts. The exercise of these precepts is a matter of continual effort (12.1.31): *Quare, iuuentus, immo omnis aetas . . . totis mentibus huc tendamus, in haec elaboremus: forsan et consummare contingat,* "Wherefore in youth, nay every age . . . we strive in this direction, we work towards this: perhaps it will even be possible to achieve it."[23] This continual striving is only to be expected since the station of the perfect orator, like that of the Stoic *sapiens,* is so lofty that it has yet to be attained (12.1.14-20). We should also recall here that the goal of Quintilian's teaching is the *uir bonus.* These exercises are not just extensive (i.e., spread over time and method), but also intensive (they affect his whole character).[24] Thus Quintilian's program in rhetoric begins to exemplify the same cultivation of the self Foucault located in scientific and philosophical discourses.

Does Pliny exemplify either the intensity or the targeting of this new cultivation of the self? We can certainly find traces. Of his time in a Laurentine villa, Pliny says (4.6.2): *ipsum me studiis excolo,* "I cultivate myself in my studies." In this letter and in 1.9.4-7 he describes his regimen of reading, writing, exercise, and self-reflection (1.9.5: *mecum tantum et cum libellis loquor,* "I speak only with myself and my books"). The object of this effort is the cultivation of mind and body in harmony (1.9.4): *aut lego aliquid aut scribo aut etiam corpori uaco, cuius fulturis animus sustinetur,* "I read or write or even make time for my body, on which the mind is supported." This sense of *uacatio* is precisely that which Foucault (1986.46) notes in Seneca, and the self-reflexivity and mind/body harmony bear a striking resemblance to his Stoic teachings (Seneca *EM* 106, *de Ira* 3.13.1-2). But, as we have said, 4.6 sets this exercise in a rural villa,[25] and the whole point of 1.9.1-3, 8 is that these practices are in fact only possible in such a setting.[26] This spatial localization is part of a general pattern in Pliny: use of a formal regimen is consistently connected with some category (here, the rural) which is marginalized in Roman thought. Spurinna is praised for his daily regimen (3.1.4-9), as is Pomponius Bassus (4.23.1). But both are *senes* (3.1.10, 4.23.2). Pliny himself, however, cannot yet take up this regimen (3.1.11): *Hanc ego uitam uoto et cogitatione praesumo, ingressurus auidissime, ut primum ratio aetatis receptui canere permiserit. Interim mille laboribus conteror . . . ,*" I take up this life in my hopes and imagination, and I am eager to enter it for real as soon as my age permits me to take a retreat. In the meantime, I am worn down by a thousand labors . . ." In the later letter, Pliny is more specific (4.23.3): *Nam et prima uitae tempora et media patriae, extrema nobis impertire debemus,* "For we owe both the first and middle portions of our lives to our country, the last to ourselves." Another person praised for his regimen and self-restraint is Artemidorus (3.11.6), who appears to be an alien.[27] The reason that these regimens are connected to the marginal term of each significant opposition (urban/rural, adult/old, Roman/alien) has already been suggested by some of the above quotations: they are, for Pliny, in conflict with the *officia* that structure the life expected of an adult male citizen.[28] This is made most explicit in a passage in which Pliny explains why he cannot match his famous uncle's literary production (3.5.19): *Ego autem tantum, quem partim publica partim amicorum officia distringunt?* "But can I do so much, whom duties to friends and fatherland distract?"

Even given this marginalization of formal regimens, one could reasonably imagine recourse to less systematic practices that would still produce a life-style grounded in one's relationship to oneself (Leach 1990.20, 32-33). Again, there are traces of these phenomena in Pliny; at 9.3.3 he tells his correspondent that he worries daily about the criteria by which he should measure his own actions (*haec . . . quae cotidie mecum*, "These things which I ponder daily with myself").[29] And Pliny locates his (and his friends') obligation to erect Verginius Rufus' epitaph in a debt to themselves (6.10.5): *ipsi nobis debeamus etiam conditoria exstruere*, "We owe it to ourselves to erect the tomb as well."[30] But, as with the use of formal regimens, a broadly self-directed mode of life is given only marginal status in Pliny's letters.

In fact, Pliny seems to devote less energy to controlling himself and more to controlling what others think about him. For instance, in letter 2.5 Pliny expresses anxiety over circulating a speech. Normally, he says, this would subject his *diligentia* and *fides* to popular *existimatio,* but in this case his *pietas* is also being judged (2.5.3). Not only his skill and effort are subject to public evaluation, but also his motivation. Later, he expresses a desire that posterity maintain positive contemporary judgments of his poetry whether they are right or wrong (7.4.10): *qui siue iudicant siue errant, me delectant. Vnum precor: ut posteri quoque aut errent similiter aut iudicent*, "They please me whether they judge correctly or err. I pray only one thing: that posterity either err or judge similarly."[31] The most striking thing about this strategy, however, is that Pliny announces it publicly. Apparently he can legitimately take the position that community approval is sufficient in itself, regardless of the character of the underlying actions that are notionally being judged.

The extreme examples of this community-oriented mode of life are cases where Pliny does not adjust his own life-style in general to suit individual others, but attempts to shape the popular estimation of third parties to make himself look good by comparison. In two letters recommending candidates for election, Pliny expresses anxiety over the consequences for himself should his candidate lose (2.9.1, 6.6.9). As he says in the former passage: *mea existimatio, mea dignitas in discrimen adducitur,* "It is my standing and my worth which are brought into question." The election of these recommendees, insofar as it bears on Pliny at all, is a test of his reputation completely divorced from how that reputation came to be. Furthermore, Pliny demands his friends' support on these very grounds (2.9.5-6, 6.6.8); he is not merely interested in the election as a test of standing, he wants to influence it as a way of constructing that standing.

We also have a pair of slightly different examples of a similar strategy of praising. In 4.17.3, Pliny considers aiding the consul-designate in a legal matter in order to increase the prestige of an office he himself once held (the consulship). Eventually, he decides to take the other side to improve his personal reputation for loyalty to friends (4.17.10), but this is not a rejection of the

principle of the first strategy; it has merely been superseded by the particulars of this case. Similarly, at 6.17.4, Pliny gives the rule that one should praise authors whose talent is less than or equal to one's own. Why? *Quia pertinet ad tuam gloriam quam maxime uideri quem praecidis uel exaequas,* "Because it is relevant to your own glory that he whom you surpass or equal seem as great as possible." Again the strategy is to artificially inflate the reputation of others to whom one stands in some fixed relation. Pliny attempts to adjust his standing within the community without regard for any concrete standard of behavior. Incidentally, we may note here that Pliny expects the same kinds of rules of judgment to apply in what we might distinguish as moral and literary spheres. This seems to be a general principle for Pliny, but it is particularly important for his oratory, which could readily be judged in either sphere in any case (cf. above on 2.5.3 and 5.3).

In both of the electioneering examples, the possible defense of the ex-consul, and the praise of lesser authors, we see again that Pliny does not merely take steps to improve his reputation, but also openly advertises that fact. Moreover, as with the letter in which he expressed hope that posterity would retain a positive judgment of his poetry (even if it is in some sense "wrong"), this concern with reputation is divorced from indications that the underlying actions or motivations have any inherent value. Pliny displays no anxieties over this approach in which the object of moral evaluation is neither a physical nor a mental self, but a set of social facts. This is a good example of a *personne*-theory. Examples like these also suggest a way to read other passages in which Pliny interests himself in the politics of reputation. He is not being shallow; he is merely operating in a world in which the most legitimate measure of his worth is whether he fills an appropriate place in the order of the community.[32] In this connection, we should recall that it is not only the construction of Pliny's own reputation which is the subject of his concern. We have also seen that Pliny prefers to evaluate (or claim to evaluate) not from his personal point of view, but as a representative of a collective social judgment (2.7.6, 4.16.1, 5.11.2, 5.14.6, 6.9.2, 10.1.2, 10.86b.1; 2.6.3-4).

In general, Pliny's moral judgments do not depend on the confrontation of individual moral agents with themselves or with some universal, "natural" standard, but on the role of the individual as a representative of one or more social categories.[33] One might include here Pliny's comments on the role of *senes* (3.1.4, 12; 4.23.3 quoted above), though it could be objected that the reduced responsibilities of the *senex* are an individual (if predictable) response to the reduction of one's physical capacities through old age.[34] Clearer is the importance Pliny accords to membership in the senate.[35] He begins letter 2.11 with the words *solet esse gaudio tibi, si quid acti est in senatu dignum ordine illo,* "You always rejoice if anything is done in the senate worthy of that order." *Dignum ordine illo* suggests that senators *qua* senators are subject to standards different from merely exercising general or individual faculties in the taking of senatorial decisions. In the following letter, Pliny argues that a senator would be more harshly (*durior tristiorque*) punished by being excluded from a pro-magistracy than by being removed from the senate entirely (2.12.2-3).[36] The accused's interests as a member of the senatorial class are assumed to be more important (to himself and to others) than his individual interests. Finally, we should recall the passage (5.3.6) in which Pliny implies that greater *sanctitas* is expected of senators than poets. In a related way, letter 4.17 treats consulars as an ethical class. In a somewhat different vein, Pliny sometimes uses geographical origin as a means of praise (1.14.4, 6; 2.13.4). Moral judgment is made not on the individual, but on the class.[37]

Contrast this to contemporary trends in philosophy. What all of the exercise and testing is directed at is the unique individual agent; rather than seeing each person as an example of a class or occupation or other ephemeral category, the goal is the improvement of his (or, more rarely, her) natural self. This results in appeals to general notions of humanity, rationality, or virtue depending on one's precise notion of "natural." This is the explicit goal of Stoicism: the improvement of the rational governing faculty . . . and its control over impulses and perceptions in accordance with nature.[38] The individual may have to fulfil the role of an . . . exercise responsibility with respect to, e.g., kin or fellow citizens, but these actions are not conceived of as specific to the relevant office/descent/citizenship, but as the exercise of more general faculties in response to the particular situation in which one finds oneself (Foucault 1986.88-92). Similarly, Epicureanism urges a renouncement of worldly things to ensure that one does not depend on anything outside himself for happiness.[39]

We can see that Quintilian begins to bring these standards too into the sphere of rhetoric. Again, the key is his interpretation of the *uir bonus* definition of the perfect orator.[40] To the extent that he is male (*uir*), he conforms to conventional, strongly-gendered expectations. Quintilian also suggests that he will be a Roman (12.2.7). However, given Quintilian's respect for Demosthenes (e.g., 10.1.105-06, 12.1.14), the latter restriction may be more an acknowledgment of political reality than a claim about national identity. At least in principle, Quintilian's potential audience is quite general.[41] Furthermore, the virtues which bring success to the "good" man are not specific to oratory. Rather, they are quite general characteristics which could find their exercise in virtually any activity: the *uir malus* is *ipso*

facto foolish and therefore will be an inferior pleader (12.1.4); only the *uir bonus* has a clear enough conscience to argue well (12.1.4-7); only he can attend properly to the labors that are involved in the orator's self-fashioning (12.1.8); virtuous action is itself one of the key topics of oratory and is best discussed by someone who practices it (12.1.8, 12.2.15-17); the virtuous man will never want for words because he can simply speak the honest truth (12.1.29-30). Quintilian, of course, asserts the need for technical learning (12.2.1), but it is largely through the exercise of generalizable personal virtue that one fulfils the functions of the orator.

So far, I have been concerned primarily with more-or-less explicit theories expressed in Pliny's letters. It will also be useful to say a few words about the practice of letter writing itself. For Seneca, the writing of the *Epistulae Morales* could itself constitute part of the cultivation of the self. It provided an opportunity both for review of past actions (in light of which necessary corrections could be made) and for anticipation of the future (both to make rational decisions and to prepare oneself to bear their consequences appropriately). There seems to be no trace of any of these functions in most of Pliny's letters. What is notable is the care taken in preparing the letters that were destined for publication (*paulo accuratius scripsissem*, 1.1.1).[42] In fact, anxiety over just what to publish is something of a topos for Pliny (cf. 1.8, 2.19, 3.5, 5.12). And in 2.10 he goes to some length to tell Octavius how important it is that the latter release his works to the public. The writing of the letters (or other works) is not sufficient in itself, as it might be for Stoic self-development; it is their publication that gives them their primary value. Thus Pliny's practice of writing and publishing his letters reflects the same community-oriented ethic that those very letters describe.

Foucault and Leach are right to say that there is no necessary contradiction between, on the one hand, a society in which the individual has strong obligations to the community or in which most actions are subject to public inspection and, on the other, one in which ethical rules are conceived of in terms of one's proper relation to oneself. It is even possible that a society which places a high value on community evaluation could use this standard as part of a "turn to the self." This is particularly true in a case where (as at Rome) tradition (*mos maiorum*) or collective opinion (e.g., *consensus bonorum*) were often figured as consistent and unchanging. Thus either (or both) could serve the same kind of role as right reason in Stoic thought or the will of God in early Christianity: the guide according to which the self is shaped. But Pliny does not cultivate his character so much as his standing. It is not clear that, on his own account, he even *has* a character distinct from his public standing. This is true in two important senses. First, he does not try to shape himself into a person who will characteristically perform right actions (however they may be defined), but each action is submitted *ad hoc* for the approval of the community. To use a modern economic metaphor, we may think of the individual as the producer of his own actions. Pliny invests his efforts solely in individual products, while Seneca and Quintilian claim to invest heavily in the means of production. Hence Pliny proposes little anticipatory study or emulation of Cicero (or anyone else) in the letters, as opposed to after-the-fact use of him as a self-justificatory rhetorical figure.[43] Second, popular opinion is valued not as a check or standard by which one judges one's progress, which might nonetheless be taken to exist independently, but as an end unto itself.[44] This is shown most clearly by Pliny's willingness to improve his reputation by distorting the mechanisms of praise and blame.

Also, Pliny accepts an identity based on rank (senator, *consularis*), profession (orator), and (in other cases) origin, rather than on a more individualized sense of self. The exposure of his "private" life, meaningful as a response to the late first-century crisis of representation, should not be mistaken for a cultivation of, or increased sense of, responsibility, to some kind of burgeoning modern "inner self."[45] Pliny was perhaps something of a reactionary even in his own time, committed (in practice, if not in theory) to a series of external judgments and categories. In a way, Cicero, a figure from the now distant republican past, really is a peculiarly appropriate symbol for Pliny's mode of self-fashioning.

But what about those few passages where Pliny does seem to allot value to some sort of *moi* (e.g., 1.9.4, 5.3.2, 6.10.5). Are these simply fragments of *Zeitgeist* which have "rubbed off" on Pliny? Perhaps, but I would suggest that the situation is a little more complicated than that. Pliny is engaging in a deliberate display. The new technologies of the self require, in practice if not always by their own description, considerable time and resources to acquire. The theory presumes a philosophical, if not actually a Greek, education. The practices themselves require, as Pliny suggests, an investment of leisure time. Pliny is displaying an aristocratic indulgence, much as he might display a work of art.

There is, I think, an illustrative parallel to this kind of display in contemporary American society. The anthropologist George Marcus has made a study of "eccentricity" as a characteristic of possessors of great hereditary wealth in this country (largely third to fifth generation descendants of nineteenth-century industrialists). They share with Roman aristocrats inherited wealth and status

and the lack of a profession by which they might define themselves.[46] In this study Marcus remarks (1995.49):

> [E]ccentricity . . . becomes associated by a larger public with a certain aggressive superiority that the rich and powerful as eccentrics are able to impose and that stands for a presumed entitlement to bend the environments over which they have control toward indulging their nonconformist excesses. The eccentric rich, thus, have the capacity to normalize the institutions and personnel they control in line with what others judge as their peculiarities.

Among other things, these eccentrics show "inversions of common sense habits, gender identifications, and dress" (Marcus 1995.50). It may seem counter-intuitive to compare Pliny, who has rightly been described as the consummate conformist, to these eccentrics. The paradox, however, lies in the norms to which Pliny was conforming. Roman aristocratic culture was highly competitive and involved its members in a constant search for distinction. The double sense of "distinction" is important here—distinction as prestige requires distinction as difference, at least within limits.

American society places considerable value on a *moi*, in the form of the "personality," under any circumstances. In such a context effective display requires a dramatically different personality. Hence, the eccentric's characteristic inversions of ordinary behavior. In the Roman context, individuality is not ordinarily a virtue. Hence, more subtle calibration of the *moi* will be salient. Those small investments in a *moi* can pay dividends for a Roman aristocrat; larger investments may not be proportionally more profitable and may even be counterproductive. Aristocrats allowed themselves such indulgences, while the ethical canons to which they subscribed required that they restrain them. Or rather, the display value of the indulgences is at some point overmatched by the display value of certain virtues, such as *moderatio* and devotion to *officia*. Displays of self-fashioning thus earn two kinds of profit. In themselves, they are a classic example of conspicuous consumption. Properly calculated, they also set the more traditional virtues in higher relief by showing how easily the aristocrat can meet his societal obligations. Pliny performs the required restraint by marginalization (as described above) and by the simple fact of recording them in his letters. In a precisely parallel fashion, Cicero displays cultural capital like his knowledge of Greek language and art in his letters in a way unthinkable in the more egalitarian context of a speech.[47] For a Seneca, cultivation of the unique individual self was claimed to be a way of life; for Pliny it was decoration on an individual already constituted as an element of a larger community.

Notes

1. Riggsby 1995.133.

2. Roller MS gives a detailed analysis of the argument of this letter in light of Pliny's other comments on poetic composition.

3. Pliny's ethical criticism of *delatores* does not imply that his targets have failed *qua* orators in his eyes, *pace* Picone 1977.155. For a contrasting contemporary view, see Winterbottom 1964 on Quintilian and the *delatores*. Quintilian makes it clear that the moral qualities are necessary not just to be a *good* orator (as he understands the notion), but to be an orator at all: *Neque enim tantum id dico, eum qui sit orator uirum bonum esse oportere, sed ne futurum quidem oratorem nisi uirum bonum,* "For I claim not only this, that a person who happens to be an orator ought to be a good man, but that he will not even be an orator unless he is a good man" (12.1.3, cf. 1.pr.9), *orator, id est uir bonus,* "an orator, i.e., a good man" (2.17.3).

4. Nothing militates against the common identification with P. Clodius Thrasea Paetus (cos. suff. 56), more clearly implied at 3.16.10.

5. Seneca (*EM* 102.12-13) rejects the apparently common view that true *gloria* requires the *consensum multorum* (for which view cf. Cic. *TD* 3.3, *Phil.* 1.29). Rather, for Seneca, truth can be arrived at rationally and so does not require ratification. Later in this paper we will see other conflicts between Seneca's inner-directed Stoicism and a more traditional Roman collectivism. For Cicero, *gloria* is granted oligarchically, not democratically (Earl 1967.30 and citations above), but for the present purposes this still makes him a representative of (apparently) received tradition.

6. Picone 1977.151-53 traces this view in Pliny and notes that he may be even more conservative in some respects than his model Cicero. Picone takes the differences in stance (between Cicero and Pliny) to be symptomatic of a more general difference in attitudes towards "theory." I suggest that the causality (if any) may flow in the other direction. The public aspects of the role of the orator are not, of course, completely neglected by Quintilian (e.g., 12.1.26, 7.2).

7. Carrithers deliberately and, I think, rightly retains Mauss' French terms to avoid the distracting baggage that any roughly equivalent English words would bring.

8. An obvious problem case for this typology would be the Stoic persona theory of Cic. *Off.* 1.107-25. I would claim that, as we have it, this theory brings together a *personne*-theory and a *moi*-theory while doing little or nothing to reconcile or even relate them; cf. DeLacy 1977.163-65, 170-72. Gill 1988 examines Cicero's presentation (especially the examples) and argues persuasively that for Cicero and Panaetius "it begins to look as though, in practice, the advice to maintain the universal human persona (and to maintain one's own specific persona) [i.e., the *moi* aspect] may amount to little more than . . . sharing the competitive ethos of Greco-Roman society" [i.e., the *personne* aspect] (p. 185). . . .

9. Earl 1967.20-26, 33-36, Minyard 1985.7-12, and Habinek MS. Cf. *CIL* I^2.15.5-6 (epitaph of Cn. Cornelius Scipio Hispanus, praet. 139): *Maiorum optenui laudem, ut sibei me esse creatum / Laetentur; CIL* I^2.2274 (L. Sulpicius): *Ille probatis iudicieis multeis cognatis atque propinqueis;* and the epitaph of Atilius Calatinus (Cic. *Sen.* 61). The fact that these inscriptions also mention external, evaluating audiences confirms the role of the audience in the inscription quoted below in constructing, not merely noting, virtue. See also Feldherr 1991 on the interpretation of spectacle in Livy.

10. R[omai Sirmond, R[omane Grotefend. In more classical Latin: *Hunc unum plurimi consentiunt Romae / Bonorum optimum fuisse uirum . . . / Hic cepit Corsicam Aleriamque urbem. / Dedit Tempestatibus aedem merito.* I have omitted a list of offices held *a[pud vos]* in lines 3-4 (the reconstruction is guaranteed by comparison with his father's epitaph). On the elogia of the Scipios see Van Sickle 1987 including bibliography on both the texts and archeological context.

11. Leach 1990.29n36 offers as an example of separation of public and private Cic. *Clu.* 138-42, in which Cicero claims the right as an advocate to offer different interpretations of history (in this case the *iudicium Iunianum*) in different speeches. From this it is inferred that, at least in an oratorical situation, one's inner self is not held responsible for one's public actions. However, even leaving aside the embarrassing context of Cicero's theoretical claim, we can cite two facts of oratorical practice that belie it. First, in this very passage Cicero also cites M. Antonius' refusal to publish his speeches lest he be so caught out (*Clu.* 140); the audience would not allow the separation that Cicero appears to call for. Second, as May 1988.7-10 points out, one of the major differences between Greek and Roman forensic oratory is the deep interdependence in the latter of ethos with the extrinsic facts of social life (i.e., the *auctoritas* and *dignitas* generated in other practices, discur-

sive and otherwise). Rhetorical arguments from character (*ingenium, natura, persona*) might in principle make better evidence for a public/private distinction, but in fact this kind of character is so closely equated with the set of a person's (public) deeds as to make this argument very difficult.

12. Cf. Dionysius 4.24.8, 19.16.5; specific examples are recorded at, e.g., Gellius *NA* 1.6, 4.20; Suet. *Aug.* 89; Dionysius 2.25.

13. On invective topoi see Nisbet 1961.192-97.

14. An example of a slightly different kind of collective judgment, though not one delivered from a broadly significant social position, is found at 2.6.3-4 where Pliny does not merely criticize a host's hospitality on his own authority, but reports a conversation he had with another guest to the same effect.

15. Cf. 4.14.4: *erit eruditionis tuae cogitare summos illos et grauissimos uiros qui talia scripserunt non modo lasciuia rerum, sed ne uerbis quidem nudis abstinuisse.*

16. The same connection is perhaps implied by the organization into a single chapter of "*auctoritas* und *exemplum*" by Bütler 1970, especially pp. 91-92.

17. Earlier in the letter Pliny had also used the metaphor of the *consilium,* the informal collective judging body at the familial level (and now also the emperor's "cabinet"): *quasi ex consilii sententia* (§8).

18. On the role of the *amicus* in Senecan Stoicism see Foucault 1986.52-54. The topic will be considered much more extensively in Livia Tenzer's forthcoming Stanford dissertation.

19. On these chains of copies becoming exemplars see Riggsby 1995.132n18.

20. Epicureans: Epicurus *Ep. Men.* 129-31, Porphyry *Abst.* 1.51.6-52.1. Stoics: Seneca *EM* 16.2-3, 20.3-4. This paper is not primarily a study of Roman use of Hellenistic philosophy; the references here and in the following notes should be taken as exemplary rather than exhaustive.

21. On the title and its implications see Kennedy 1969.31, 143.

22. This apparently applies to many of the readings and exercises described in book 10 such as the writing recommended on Cicero's authority (10.3.1), or Demosthenes' practice in isolation (10.3.25) or at the seashore (10.3.30), or the translation exercises practiced by a variety of authorities (10.5.1-3). Quintilian mentions *iuuenes* several times throughout the book, but the exemplars are all adults, as the chapter opening suggests. Another example is the constant exercise of memory needed not only to establish, but to maintain that faculty (11.2.41).

23. Cf. 12.11.16-17: *Discendi ratio talis ut non multos <poscat> annos . . . Reliqua est <exercitatio>, quae vires cito facit, cum fecit tuetur. Rerum cognitio cotidie crecscit,* "Such is the nature of the learning that it does not demand many years . . . The rest is exercise which swiftly lends strength and guards it once established. The understanding of affairs grows daily."

24. *IO* 12.2.1 makes it explicit that the *disciplina* of the orator is directed at shaping moral character as well as imparting technical knowledge: *Mores ante omnia oratori studiis erunt excolendi . . . ,* "Above all, the orator must tend to his character in his studies . . ." Roller 1992 shows that a technique of oratorical *inventio* advocated by Pliny is also at work in other types of composition. This type of "cognitive seepage" shows that even formally rhetorical exercises can shape the orator in more general ways. Note also Quintilian's extensive discussion of gesture (11.3.65-144) which requires the orator's constant monitoring and control over his physical self (on which see Gleason 1990.395, 403).

25. Exercise of the self is also set in the country at 5.6.46, 7.9, 7.10, 9.40; in an urban setting (where the difficulties are pointed out): 7.30.4. The extent to which the villas of the rich were all, in fact, places of leisured retreat may be questioned (D'Arms 1981.78-87), but that is certainly their symbolic value in most of Roman literature, as quite clearly in this letter (though contrast 9.15).

26. Cicero employs a more extreme strategy of marginalization in *de Re Publica.* He sets the dialogue nearer the city, but in *horti* outside the pomerium (*Rep.* 1.14; Zetzel 1995.111). The text also frequently reminds the reader that a holiday (the *feriae Latinae*) provided the opportunity for the recorded discussion (*Rep.* 1.14.1, 14.2, 20.1, 33.3). Finally, the discussion is justified at length on the grounds that it is more practical and Roman than theoretical and Greek (*Rep.* 1.33-37). This triple justification indicates that Cicero is working with a conception of aristocratic duty which is even more hostile to intellectual work than the one with which Pliny attempts to compromise. Other Ciceronian dialogues are also set during holidays (*ND* 1.15, *de Or.* 1.24), or more general periods of *otium* (*Fin.* 1.14, *ND* 2.3, *Leg.* 1.13), and/or in

rural villas (*Div.* 1.8, *Fin.* 1.14, *Acad.* 1.1, 2.9, *de Or.* 1.24, *Leg.* 1.1).

27. Pliny met Artemidorus in Syria (3.11.5); this and his name suggest that he was not a Roman. Sherwin-White 1966.244 points out that Pliny's habit was to give naturalized citizens their full names. That Artemidorus was son-in-law of C. Musonius Rufus (§§5,7) might be taken to argue to the contrary.

28. Bütler 1970.51-55 notes this age difference and usefully compares 7.3 where Pliny criticizes a friend (Praesens) who seems to have retired too early. Foucault 1986.51 records the deferral until old age of the aggressive "possession of the self" in several authors (including Pliny), but makes nothing of it.

29. On the other hand, the two criteria proposed (§§1-2) depend on reputation.

30. The specific principle seems to be roughly "do unto others as you would have them do unto you."

31. Cf. 7.17.8-9 where Pliny says he is more nervous over a large audience than over a single person *quamlibet doctus.*

32. In a similar vein, Gill 1988. 194 shows that in Cicero's discussion of decorum in *Off.* there is a tendency to teach avoidance of showing one's *uitia,* rather than the correction of those *uitia.*

33. Bütler 1970.66-70 discusses the importance of "Rollenkonformismus" to Pliny's ethics. His discussion is useful, but he is too ready to attribute the full sophistication of Ciceronian/Panaetian *persona*-theory to Pliny. In nearly all his examples, the role is a public, collective one (e.g., Iavolenus Priscus in 6.15.3 is a jurisconsult and participant in *consilia,* Severus in 6.27 is a consul designate). The question in most of these cases is not the choice between the demands of conflicting *personae,* but the duties incumbent on the occupier of a single role in a variety of circumstances, a lower-level question. It is this difference of circumstance which provides the *facultatem noua, magna, uera censendi* (6.27.5), rather than a more complex question of individual roles. The latter is perhaps only clearly illustrated in 1.23.

34. This individualizing interpretation would require that we take Pliny's comments about the three stages of life (4.23.3) fairly loosely.

35. Bütler 1970.69 is good on this point; on the other end of the spectrum, 8.16.2 grudgingly recognizes the "virtual" community (*res publica quaedam et quasi ciuitas*) of slaves.

36. Pliny preferred the imposition of the other sentence (2.12.4), but the reasoning about the strictness of the one imposed is presented as his own.

37. Contrast Quintilian for whom the same virtues make someone a good speaker, a good counselor, a good citizen, and a good man (12.11.1): *His dicendi uirtutibus usus orator in iudiciis consiliis contionibus senatu, in omni denique officio boni ciuis, Þnem quoque dignum et optimo uiro et opere sanctissimo faciet.*

38. Long 1986.173-209; Diogenes 7.89, Plutarch *Virt. Mor.* 440e-41d, Seneca *EM* 124.13-14.

39. Long 1986.66-67, 69-71; Epicurus *Ep. Men.* 130, *SV* 58, 81; Seneca *EM* 9.3.

40. A referee raises the interesting question of the relationship between Cato's *uir bonus* and Quintilian's, given my claim that Quintilian represents an innovative view of personhood while Cato is presumably more traditional. I see two possibilities here. (1) The *uir bonus* definition is quite epigrammatic and therefore readily subject to different interpretations. For Cato, *bonus* may have presupposed more about the class and status of a subject than it seems to have for Quintilian. Compare Cicero's use of *boni* to refer to a small political group. (2) While Cato was used (by himself as well as later authors) as a figure of traditional virtue, we should not forget that he was, in fact, a *novus homo.* Defining the orator as a (potentially self-made) *uir bonus,* rather than as the incumbent of a certain social position would have been very much to his advantage. I incline towards the second possibility.

41. The leisure and formal education required to produce the orator also seem to assume a fair degree of wealth, but this is never made explicit. In fact, the detailed rhetorics of the first century might seem designed as a way of redefining the Roman elite to take in a variety of new families from new areas (Bloomer 1992.12-13, 259). In this respect Quintilian's *IO* represents a leveling force.

42. This is true whether the letters were heavily revised for publication or, as Shelton 1987.137n48 and Bell 1989.462, 464-65 plausibly suggest, most letters in Pliny's circle were written in polished literary style to begin with.

43. Exceptions are, perhaps, passages which depict others' attempts to influence Pliny towards certain courses of action by use of the Ciceronian model. Yet this preemptive self-fashioning is possible only if it is preceded by a preemptive external evaluation.

44. Contrast the physiognomic texts analyzed by Gleason 1990. Personal appearance and grooming are not merely signifiers of character, but, through a kind of *sympatheia,* can sometimes affect it (pp. 400-01, 402-03).

45. Bartsch 1994.214-15.

46. There are, of course, significant differences as well. Most significantly here, American eccentrics are often reacting against their own perceptions that other aspects of their selves, e.g., financial and legal personae, are not under their own control but under that of lawyers, accountants, and other experts (Marcus 1995.43-44).

47. Art: cf. the coy posturing of *Verr.* 2.4 to *Fam.* 5.12. Language (and literature): see Steele 1900 and Boyance 1956.116-20, 124-28. In particular, contrast the free citation of Greek literature in a letter like *Fam.* 13.15 to the exclusive use of Latin in even an already literary speech like *pro Caelio.* For the class-based restriction of learning see Brunt 1988.302. Habinek 1994 traces Cicero's program of reinforcing Roman aristocratic authority with Greek cultural capital.

Bibliography

Bartsch, Shadi. 1994. *Actors in the Audience: Theatricality and Doublespeak from Nero to Hadrian.* Cambridge.

Bell, Albert. 1989. "A Note on Revision and Authenticity in Pliny's Letters," *AJP* [*American Journal of Philology*] 110.460-66.

Bloomer, W. Martin. 1992. *Valerius Maximus and the Rhetoric of the New Nobility.* Chapel Hill.

Boyance, Pierre. 1956. "La connaissance du grec à Rome," *RÉL* [*Revue de Études Latines*] 34.111-31.

Brunt, Peter. 1988. *The Fall of the Roman Republic and Related Essays.* Oxford.

Bütler, Hans-Peter. 1970. *Die geistige Welt des jüngern Plinius: Studien zur Thematike seiner Briefe* (Bibliothek der Klassischen Altertumswissenschaften NF, 2R, Band 38). Heidelberg.

Carrithers, Michael. 1985. "An Alternative Social History of the Self," in M. Carrithers, S. Collins, and S. Lukes, eds., *The Category of the Person: Anthropology, Philosophy, History.* Cambridge. 234-56

D'Arms, John. 1981. *Commerce and Social Standing in Ancient Rome.* Cambridge.

DeLacy, Philip. 1977. "The Four Stoic Personae," *ICS* [*Illinois Classical Studies*] 2.163-72.

Earl, Donald. 1967. *The Moral and Political Tradition of Rome.* Ithaca.

Feldherr, Andrew. 1991. *Spectacle and Society in Livy's History.* diss. UC Berkeley.

Foucault, Michel. 1986. *The Care of the Self (The History of Sexuality,* volume 3) (trans. R. Hurley). New York.

Gamberini, Federico. 1983. *Stylistic Theory and Practice in the Younger Pliny.* Hildesheim.

Gill, Christopher. 1988. "Personhood and Personality: The Four-Personae Theory in Cicero, *de Officiis I,*" *Oxford Studies in Ancient Philosophy* 6.169-99.

Gleason, Maud. 1990. "The Semiotics of Gender: Physiognomy and Self-Fashioning in the Second Century c.e.," in David Halperin et al., eds., *Before Sexuality.* Princeton. 389-415.

Habinek, Thomas. 1994. "Ideology for an Empire in the Prefaces to Cicero's Dialogues," *Ramus* 23.55-67.

———. MS. "Why Was Latin Literature Invented?" in T. Habinek, *The Politics of Latin Literature* (forthcoming).

Kennedy, George. 1969. *Quintilian.* New York.

Leach, Eleanor. 1990. "The Politics of Self-Presentation: Pliny's Letters and Roman Portrait Sculpture," *CA* [*Classical Antiquity*] 9.14-39 and unpaginated plates following.

Long, Anthony. 1986. *Hellenistic Philosophy: Stoics, Epicureans, Sceptics*[2]. London.

Marcus, George. 1995. "On Eccentricity," in Debbora Battaglia, ed., *Rhetorics of Self-Making.* Berkeley. 43-58.

May, James. 1988. *Trials of Character: The Eloquence of Ciceronian Ethos.* Chapel Hill.

Minyard, Douglas. 1985. *Lucretius and the Late Republic* (Mnemosyne Supplement 90). Leiden.

Nisbet, Robin (ed.) 1961. *Cicero: in L. Calpurnium Pisonem Oratio.* Oxford.

Picone, Giusto. 1977. *L'eloquenza di Plinio: Teoria e prassi.* Palermo.

Riggsby, Andrew. 1995. "Pliny on Cicero and Oratory: Self-Fashioning in the Public Eye," *AJP* 116.123-35.

Roller, Matthew. 1992. "Plinian Reminiscences of Catullus and Literary Inventio," *AAPA* 124.47.

———. MS. "The Politics of Literary Appropriation."

Shelton, Jo-Ann. 1987. "Pliny's Letter 3.11: Rhetoric and Autobiography," *C&M* [*Classical et Mediaevalia*] 38.121-39.

Sherwin-White, Adrian. 1966. *The Letters of Pliny.* Oxford.

Steele, R. B. 1900. "On the Greek in Cicero's Epistles," *TAPA* [*Transactions of the American Philological Society*] 31.xvi-xvii.

Van Sickle, John. 1987. "The Elogia of the Cornelii Scipiones and the Origin of the Epigram at Rome," *AJP* 108.41-55.

Winterbottom, Michael. 1964. "Quintilian and the Vir Bonus," *JRS* 54.90-97.

Zetzel, James (ed.) 1995. *Cicero: de Re Publica, Selections.* Cambridge.

FURTHER READING

Criticism

Griffin, Miriam. "Review of *The Anxieties of Pliny the Younger,* by S. E. Hoffer." *Journal of Roman Studies* 91 (2001): 253-54.
> Brief, positive review of S. E. Hoffer's analysis of Pliny's Letters, Book I.

Hoffer, Stanley E. Introduction to *The Anxieties of Pliny the Younger,* pp. 1–14. Atlanta: Scholars Press, 1999.
> Argues that Pliny's confident and reassured tone in his letters belies many underlying tensions in Roman society and in his own personal life.

Rand, Edward Kennard. "A New Approach to the Text of Pliny's *Letters,* Article I." *Harvard Studies in Classical Philology* 32 (1923): 79-191.
> First in a series of three highly technical articles that discuss the manuscript history of Pliny's *Letters.*

———. "A New Approach to the Text of Pliny's *Letters,* Article II." *Harvard Studies in Classical Philology* 35 (1924): 137–69.
> Second in a series of three highly technical articles that discuss the manuscript history of Pliny's *Letters.*

———. "A New Approach to the Text of Pliny's *Letters,* Article III." *Harvard Studies in Classical Philology* 36 (1925): 1–41.
> Third in a series of three highly technical articles that discuss the manuscript history of Pliny's *Letters.*

Ronnick, Michelle Valerie. "Benjamin Franklin's Almanac of 1738 and Pliny the Younger's Letter 6.16.3 to Tacitus." *English Language Notes* 32, no. 4 (June 1995): 48-50.
> Suggests that the source of a quotation in Benjamin Franklin's *Poor Richard's Almanac* of 1738 is one of Pliny's letters.

Stout, S. E. "The Mind of a Scribe." *Classical Journal* 22, no. 6 (March 1927): 405-17.
> Uses illustrations from Pliny's *Letters* to discuss the attitudes, interests, and approach of the ancient scribe.

Additional coverage of Pliny the Younger's life and career is contained in the following sources published by the Gale Group: *Ancient Writers,* **Vol. 2;** *Dictionary of Literary Biography,* **Vol. 211.**

How to Use This Index

The main references

> **Calvino, Italo**
>   1923-1985 .... **CLC 5, 8, 11, 22, 33, 39,**
>   **73; SSC 3, 48**

list all author entries in the following Gale Literary Criticism series:

AAL = *Asian American Literature*
BG = *The Beat Generation: A Gale Critical Companion*
BLC = *Black Literature Criticism*
BLCS = *Black Literature Criticism Supplement*
CLC = *Contemporary Literary Criticism*
CLR = *Children's Literature Review*
CMLC = *Classical and Medieval Literature Criticism*
DC = *Drama Criticism*
HLC = *Hispanic Literature Criticism*
HLCS = *Hispanic Literature Criticism Supplement*
HR = *Harlem Renaissance: A Gale Critical Companion*
LC = *Literature Criticism from 1400 to 1800*
NCLC = *Nineteenth-Century Literature Criticism*
NNAL = *Native North American Literature*
PC = *Poetry Criticism*
SSC = *Short Story Criticism*
TCLC = *Twentieth-Century Literary Criticism*
WLC = *World Literature Criticism, 1500 to the Present*
WLCS = *World Literature Criticism Supplement*

The cross-references

> See also CA 85-88, 116; CANR 23, 61;
> DAM NOV; DLB 196; EW 13; MTCW 1, 2;
> RGSF 2; RGWL 2; SFW 4; SSFS 12

list all author entries in the following Gale biographical and literary sources:

AAYA = *Authors & Artists for Young Adults*
AFAW = *African American Writers*
AFW = *African Writers*
AITN = *Authors in the News*
AMW = *American Writers*
AMWR = *American Writers Retrospective Supplement*
AMWS = *American Writers Supplement*
ANW = *American Nature Writers*
AW = *Ancient Writers*
BEST = *Bestsellers*
BPFB = *Beacham's Encyclopedia of Popular Fiction: Biography and Resources*
BRW = *British Writers*
BRWS = *British Writers Supplement*
BW = *Black Writers*
BYA = *Beacham's Guide to Literature for Young Adults*
CA = *Contemporary Authors*
CAAS = *Contemporary Authors Autobiography Series*
CABS = *Contemporary Authors Bibliographical Series*
CAD = *Contemporary American Dramatists*
CANR = *Contemporary Authors New Revision Series*
CAP = *Contemporary Authors Permanent Series*
CBD = *Contemporary British Dramatists*
CCA = *Contemporary Canadian Authors*
CD = *Contemporary Dramatists*
CDALB = *Concise Dictionary of American Literary Biography*
CDALBS = *Concise Dictionary of American Literary Biography Supplement*
CDBLB = *Concise Dictionary of British Literary Biography*

CMW = *St. James Guide to Crime & Mystery Writers*
CN = *Contemporary Novelists*
CP = *Contemporary Poets*
CPW = *Contemporary Popular Writers*
CSW = *Contemporary Southern Writers*
CWD = *Contemporary Women Dramatists*
CWP = *Contemporary Women Poets*
CWRI = *St. James Guide to Children's Writers*
CWW = *Contemporary World Writers*
DA = *DISCovering Authors*
DA3 = *DISCovering Authors 3.0*
DAB = *DISCovering Authors: British Edition*
DAC = *DISCovering Authors: Canadian Edition*
DAM = *DISCovering Authors: Modules*
   DRAM: *Dramatists Module;* **MST:** *Most-studied Authors Module;*
   MULT: *Multicultural Authors Module;* **NOV:** *Novelists Module;*
   POET: *Poets Module;* **POP:** *Popular Fiction and Genre Authors Module*
DFS = *Drama for Students*
DLB = *Dictionary of Literary Biography*
DLBD = *Dictionary of Literary Biography Documentary Series*
DLBY = *Dictionary of Literary Biography Yearbook*
DNFS = *Literature of Developing Nations for Students*
EFS = *Epics for Students*
EXPN = *Exploring Novels*
EXPP = *Exploring Poetry*
EXPS = *Exploring Short Stories*
EW = *European Writers*
FANT = *St. James Guide to Fantasy Writers*
FW = *Feminist Writers*
GFL = *Guide to French Literature,* Beginnings to 1789, 1798 to the Present
GLL = *Gay and Lesbian Literature*
HGG = *St. James Guide to Horror, Ghost & Gothic Writers*
HW = *Hispanic Writers*
IDFW = *International Dictionary of Films and Filmmakers: Writers and Production Artists*
IDTP = *International Dictionary of Theatre: Playwrights*
LAIT = *Literature and Its Times*
LAW = *Latin American Writers*
JRDA = *Junior DISCovering Authors*
MAICYA = *Major Authors and Illustrators for Children and Young Adults*
MAICYAS = *Major Authors and Illustrators for Children and Young Adults Supplement*
MAWW = *Modern American Women Writers*
MJW = *Modern Japanese Writers*
MTCW = *Major 20th-Century Writers*
NCFS = *Nonfiction Classics for Students*
NFS = *Novels for Students*
PAB = *Poets: American and British*
PFS = *Poetry for Students*
RGAL = *Reference Guide to American Literature*
RGEL = *Reference Guide to English Literature*
RGSF = *Reference Guide to Short Fiction*
RGWL = *Reference Guide to World Literature*
RHW = *Twentieth-Century Romance and Historical Writers*
SAAS = *Something about the Author Autobiography Series*
SATA = *Something about the Author*
SFW = *St. James Guide to Science Fiction Writers*
SSFS = *Short Stories for Students*
TCWW = *Twentieth-Century Western Writers*
WLIT = *World Literature and Its Times*
WP = *World Poets*
YABC = *Yesterday's Authors of Books for Children*
YAW = *St. James Guide to Young Adult Writers*

Literary Criticism Series
Cumulative Author Index

Allen, Sarah A.
See Hopkins, Pauline Elizabeth
Allen, Sidney H.
See Hartmann, Sadakichi
Allen, Woody 1935- .... **CLC 16, 52**
See also AAYA 10, 51; CA 33-36R; CANR
27, 38, 63; DAM POP; DLB 44; MTCW
1
Allende, Isabel 1942- ... **CLC 39, 57, 97, 170;**
HLC 1; WLCS
See also AAYA 18; CA 125; 130; CANR
51, 74; CDWLB 3; CWW 2; DA3; DAM
MULT, NOV; DLB 145; DNFS 1; EWL
3; FW; HW 1, 2; INT CA-130; LAIT 5;
LAWS 1; LMFS 2; MTCW 1, 2; NCFS 1;
NFS 6, 18; RGSF 2; RGWL 3; SSFS 11,
16; WLIT 1
Alleyn, Ellen
See Rossetti, Christina (Georgina)
Alleyne, Carla D. .... **CLC 65**
Allingham, Margery (Louise)
1904-1966 .... **CLC 19**
See also CA 5-8R; 25-28R; CANR 4, 58;
CMW 4; DLB 77; MSW; MTCW 1, 2
Allingham, William 1824-1889 ...... **NCLC 25**
See also DLB 35; RGEL 2
Allison, Dorothy E. 1949- .... **CLC 78, 153**
See also AAYA 53; CA 140; CANR 66, 107;
CSW; DA3; FW; MTCW 1; NFS 11;
RGAL 4
Alloula, Malek .... **CLC 65**
Allston, Washington 1779-1843 .... **NCLC 2**
See also DLB 1, 235
Almedingen, E. M. .... **CLC 12**
See Almedingen, Martha Edith von
See also SATA 3
Almedingen, Martha Edith von 1898-1971
See Almedingen, E. M.
See also CA 1-4R; CANR 1
Almodovar, Pedro 1949(?)- .... **CLC 114;**
HLCS 1
See also CA 133; CANR 72; HW 2
Almqvist, Carl Jonas Love
1793-1866 .... **NCLC 42**
Alonso, Damaso 1898-1990 .... **CLC 14**
See also CA 110; 131; 130; CANR 72; DLB
108; EWL 3; HW 1, 2
Alov
See Gogol, Nikolai (Vasilyevich)
Al Siddik
See Rolfe, Frederick (William Serafino
Austin Lewis Mary)
See also GLL 1; RGEL 2
Alta 1942- .... **CLC 19**
See also CA 57-60
Alter, Robert B(ernard) 1935- .... **CLC 34**
See also CA 49-52; CANR 1, 47, 100
Alther, Lisa 1944- .... **CLC 7, 41**
See also BPFB 1; CA 65-68; CAAS 30;
CANR 12, 30, 51; CN 7; CSW; GLL 2;
MTCW 1
Althusser, L.
See Althusser, Louis
Althusser, Louis 1918-1990 .... **CLC 106**
See also CA 131; 132; CANR 102; DLB
242
Altman, Robert 1925- .... **CLC 16, 116**
See also CA 73-76; CANR 43
Alurista .... **HLCS 1**
See Urista, Alberto H.
See also DLB 82
Alvarez, A(lfred) 1929- .... **CLC 5, 13**
See also CA 1-4R; CANR 3, 33, 63, 101;
CN 7; CP 7; DLB 14, 40
Alvarez, Alejandro Rodriguez 1903-1965
See Casona, Alejandro
See also CA 131; 93-96; HW 1

Alvarez, Julia 1950- .... **CLC 93; HLCS 1**
See also AAYA 25; AMWS 7; CA 147;
CANR 69, 101; DA3; DLB 282; LATS 1;
MTCW 1; NFS 5, 9; SATA 129; WLIT 1
Alvaro, Corrado 1896-1956 .... **TCLC 60**
See also CA 163; DLB 264; EWL 3
Amado, Jorge 1912-2001 ... **CLC 13, 40, 106;**
HLC 1
See also CA 77-80; 201; CANR 35, 74;
DAM MULT, NOV; DLB 113; EWL 3;
HW 2; LAW; LAWS 1; MTCW 1, 2;
RGWL 2, 3; TWA; WLIT 1
Ambler, Eric 1909-1998 .... **CLC 4, 6, 9**
See also BRWS 4; CA 9-12R; 171; CANR
7, 38, 74; CMW 4; CN 7; DLB 77; MSW;
MTCW 1, 2; TEA
Ambrose, Stephen E(dward)
1936-2002 .... **CLC 145**
See also AAYA 44; CA 1-4R; 209; CANR
3, 43, 57, 83, 105; NCFS 2; SATA 40,
138
Amichai, Yehuda 1924-2000 .. **CLC 9, 22, 57,**
116; PC 38
See also CA 85-88; 189; CANR 46, 60, 99;
CWW 2; EWL 3; MTCW 1
Amichai, Yehudah
See Amichai, Yehuda
Amiel, Henri Frederic 1821-1881 .... **NCLC 4**
See also DLB 217
Amis, Kingsley (William)
1922-1995 ...... **CLC 1, 2, 3, 5, 8, 13, 40,**
44, 129
See also AITN 2; BPFB 1; BRWS 2; CA
9-12R; 150; CANR 8, 28, 54; CDBLB
1945-1960; CN 7; CP 7; DA; DA3; DAB;
DAC; DAM MST, NOV; DLB 15, 27,
100, 139; DLBY 1996; EWL 3; HGG;
INT CANR-8; MTCW 1, 2; RGEL 2;
RGSF 2; SFW 4
Amis, Martin (Louis) 1949- .... **CLC 4, 9, 38,**
62, 101
See also BEST 90:3; BRWS 4; CA 65-68;
CANR 8, 27, 54, 73, 95; CN 7; DA3;
DLB 14, 194; EWL 3; INT CANR-27;
MTCW 1
Ammianus Marcellinus c. 330-c.
395 .... **CMLC 60**
See also AW 2; DLB 211
Ammons, A(rchie) R(andolph)
1926-2001 ...... **CLC 2, 3, 5, 8, 9, 25, 57,**
108; PC 16
See also AITN 1; AMWS 7; CA 9-12R;
193; CANR 6, 36, 51, 73, 107; CP 7;
CSW; DAM POET; DLB 5, 165; EWL 3;
MTCW 1, 2; RGAL 4
Amo, Tauraatua i
See Adams, Henry (Brooks)
Amory, Thomas 1691(?)-1788 .... **LC 48**
See also DLB 39
Anand, Mulk Raj 1905- .... **CLC 23, 93**
See also CA 65-68; CANR 32, 64; CN 7;
DAM NOV; EWL 3; MTCW 1, 2; RGSF
2
Anatol
See Schnitzler, Arthur
Anaximander c. 611B.C.-c.
546B.C. .... **CMLC 22**
Anaya, Rudolfo A(lfonso) 1937- ...... **CLC 23,**
148; HLC 1
See also AAYA 20; BYA 13; CA 45-48;
CAAS 4; CANR 1, 32, 51; CN 7; DAM
MULT, NOV; DLB 82, 206, 278; HW 1;
LAIT 4; MTCW 1, 2; NFS 12; RGAL 4;
RGSF 2; WLIT 1
Andersen, Hans Christian
1805-1875 .... **NCLC 7, 79; SSC 6, 56;**
WLC
See also CLR 6; DA; DA3; DAB; DAC;
DAM MST, POP; EW 6; MAICYA 1, 2;
RGSF 2; RGWL 2, 3; SATA 100; TWA;
WCH; YABC 1

Anderson, C. Farley
See Mencken, H(enry) L(ouis); Nathan,
George Jean
Anderson, Jessica (Margaret) Queale
1916- .... **CLC 37**
See also CA 9-12R; CANR 4, 62; CN 7
Anderson, Jon (Victor) 1940- .... **CLC 9**
See also CA 25-28R; CANR 20; DAM
POET
Anderson, Lindsay (Gordon)
1923-1994 .... **CLC 20**
See also CA 125; 128; 146; CANR 77
Anderson, Maxwell 1888-1959 .... **TCLC 2**
See also CA 105; 152; DAM DRAM; DFS
16; DLB 7, 228; MTCW 2; RGAL 4
Anderson, Poul (William)
1926-2001 .... **CLC 15**
See also AAYA 5, 34; BPFB 1; BYA 6, 8,
9; CA 1-4R; 181; 199; CAAE 181; CAAS
2; CANR 2, 15, 34, 64, 110; CLR 58;
DLB 8; FANT; INT CANR-15; MTCW 1,
2; SATA 90; SATA-Brief 39; SATA-Essay
106; SCFW 2; SFW 4; SUFW 1, 2
Anderson, Robert (Woodruff)
1917- .... **CLC 23**
See also AITN 1; CA 21-24R; CANR 32;
DAM DRAM; DLB 7; LAIT 5
Anderson, Roberta Joan
See Mitchell, Joni
Anderson, Sherwood 1876-1941 .. **SSC 1, 46;**
TCLC 1, 10, 24, 123; WLC
See also AAYA 30; AMW; BPFB 1; CA
104; 121; CANR 61; CDALB 1917-1929;
DA; DA3; DAB; DAC; DAM MST, NOV;
DLB 4, 9, 86; DLBD 1; EWL 3; EXPS;
GLL 1; MTCW 1, 2; NFS 4; RGAL 4;
RGSF 2; SSFS 4, 10, 11; TUS
Andier, Pierre
See Desnos, Robert
Andouard
See Giraudoux, Jean(-Hippolyte)
Andrade, Carlos Drummond de ..... **CLC 18**
See Drummond de Andrade, Carlos
See also EWL 3; RGWL 2, 3
Andrade, Mario de .... **TCLC 43**
See de Andrade, Mario
See also EWL 3; LAW; RGWL 2, 3; WLIT
1
Andreae, Johann V(alentin)
1586-1654 .... **LC 32**
See also DLB 164
Andreas Capellanus fl. c. 1185- .... **CMLC 45**
See also DLB 208
Andreas-Salome, Lou 1861-1937 ... **TCLC 56**
See also CA 178; DLB 66
Andreev, Leonid
See Andreyev, Leonid (Nikolaevich)
See also EWL 3
Andress, Lesley
See Sanders, Lawrence
Andrewes, Lancelot 1555-1626 .... **LC 5**
See also DLB 151, 172
Andrews, Cicily Fairfield
See West, Rebecca
Andrews, Elton V.
See Pohl, Frederik
Andreyev, Leonid (Nikolaevich)
1871-1919 .... **TCLC 3**
See Andreev, Leonid
See also CA 104; 185
Andric, Ivo 1892-1975 .... **CLC 8; SSC 36;**
TCLC 135
See also CA 81-84; 57-60; CANR 43, 60;
CDWLB 4; DLB 147; EW 11; EWL 3;
MTCW 1; RGSF 2; RGWL 2, 3
Androvar
See Prado (Calvo), Pedro
Angelique, Pierre
See Bataille, Georges

Arrick, Fran .... CLC 30
See Gaberman, Judie Angell
See also BYA 6

Arriey, Richmond
See Delany, Samuel R(ay), Jr.

Artaud, Antonin (Marie Joseph)
1896-1948 .... DC 14; TCLC 3, 36
See also CA 104; 149; DA3; DAM DRAM;
DLB 258; EW 11; EWL 3; GFL 1789 to
the Present; MTCW 1; RGWL 2, 3

Arthur, Ruth M(abel) 1905-1979 ..... CLC 12
See also CA 9-12R; 85-88; CANR 4; CWRI
5; SATA 7, 26

Artsybashev, Mikhail (Petrovich)
1878-1927 .... TCLC 31
See also CA 170

Arundel, Honor (Morfydd)
1919-1973 .... CLC 17
See also CA 21-22; 41-44R; CAP 2; CLR
35; CWRI 5; SATA 4; SATA-Obit 24

Arzner, Dorothy 1900-1979 .... CLC 98

Asch, Sholem 1880-1957 .... TCLC 3
See also CA 105; EWL 3; GLL 2

Ash, Shalom
See Asch, Sholem

Ashbery, John (Lawrence) 1927- .. CLC 2, 3,
4, 6, 9, 13, 15, 25, 41, 77, 125; PC 26
See Berry, Jonas
See also AMWS 3; CA 5-8R; CANR 9, 37,
66, 102; CP 7; DA3; DAM POET; DLB
5, 165; DLBY 1981; EWL 3; INT
CANR-9; MTCW 1, 2; PAB; PFS 11;
RGAL 4; WP

Ashdown, Clifford
See Freeman, R(ichard) Austin

Ashe, Gordon
See Creasey, John

Ashton-Warner, Sylvia (Constance)
1908-1984 .... CLC 19
See also CA 69-72; 112; CANR 29; MTCW
1, 2

Asimov, Isaac 1920-1992 ..... CLC 1, 3, 9, 19,
26, 76, 92
See also AAYA 13; BEST 90:2; BPFB 1;
BYA 4, 6, 7, 9; CA 1-4R; 137; CANR 2,
19, 36, 60; CLR 12, 79; CMW 4; CPW;
DA3; DAM POP; DLB 8; DLBY 1992;
INT CANR-19; JRDA; LAIT 5; LMFS 2;
MAICYA 1, 2; MTCW 1, 2; RGAL 4;
SATA 1, 26, 74; SCFW 2; SFW 4; SSFS
17; TUS; YAW

Askew, Anne 1521(?)-1546 .... LC 81
See also DLB 136

Assis, Joaquim Maria Machado de
See Machado de Assis, Joaquim Maria

Astell, Mary 1666-1731 .... LC 68
See also DLB 252; FW

Astley, Thea (Beatrice May) 1925- .. CLC 41
See also CA 65-68; CANR 11, 43, 78; CN
7; EWL 3

Astley, William 1855-1911
See Warung, Price

Aston, James
See White, T(erence) H(anbury)

Asturias, Miguel Angel 1899-1974 .... CLC 3,
8, 13; HLC 1
See also CA 25-28; 49-52; CANR 32; CAP
2; CDWLB 3; DA3; DAM MULT, NOV;
DLB 113; EWL 3; HW 1; LAW; LMFS
2; MTCW 1, 2; RGWL 2, 3; WLIT 1

Atares, Carlos Saura
See Saura (Atares), Carlos

Athanasius c. 295-c. 373 .... CMLC 48

Atheling, William
See Pound, Ezra (Weston Loomis)

Atheling, William, Jr.
See Blish, James (Benjamin)

Atherton, Gertrude (Franklin Horn)
1857-1948 .... TCLC 2
See also CA 104; 155; DLB 9, 78, 186;
HGG; RGAL 4; SUFW 1; TCWW 2

Atherton, Lucius
See Masters, Edgar Lee

Atkins, Jack
See Harris, Mark

Atkinson, Kate 1951- .... CLC 99
See also CA 166; CANR 101; DLB 267

Attaway, William (Alexander)
1911-1986 .... BLC 1; CLC 92
See also BW 2, 3; CA 143; CANR 82;
DAM MULT; DLB 76

Atticus
See Fleming, Ian (Lancaster); Wilson,
(Thomas) Woodrow

Atwood, Margaret (Eleanor) 1939- ... CLC 2,
3, 4, 8, 13, 15, 25, 44, 84, 135; PC 8;
SSC 2, 46; WLC
See also AAYA 12, 47; AMWS 13; BEST
89:2; BPFB 1; CA 49-52; CANR 3, 24,
33, 59, 95; CN 7; CP 7; CPW; CWP; DA;
DA3; DAB; DAC; DAM MST, NOV,
POET; DLB 53, 251; EWL 3; EXPN; FW;
INT CANR-24; LAIT 5; MTCW 1, 2;
NFS 4, 12, 13, 14; PFS 7; RGSF 2; SATA
50; SSFS 3, 13; TWA; YAW

Aubigny, Pierre d'
See Mencken, H(enry) L(ouis)

Aubin, Penelope 1685-1731(?) .... LC 9
See also DLB 39

Auchincloss, Louis (Stanton) 1917- .. CLC 4,
6, 9, 18, 45; SSC 22
See also AMWS 4; CA 1-4R; CANR 6, 29,
55, 87; CN 7; DAM NOV; DLB 2, 244;
DLBY 1980; EWL 3; INT CANR-29;
MTCW 1; RGAL 4

Auden, W(ystan) H(ugh) 1907-1973 . CLC 1,
2, 3, 4, 6, 9, 11, 14, 43, 123; PC 1;
WLC
See also AAYA 18; AMWS 2; BRW 7;
BRWR 1; CA 9-12R; 45-48; CANR 5, 61,
105; CDBLB 1914-1945; DA; DA3;
DAB; DAC; DAM DRAM, MST, POET;
DLB 10, 20; EWL 3; EXPP; MTCW 1, 2;
PAB; PFS 1, 3, 4, 10; TUS; WP

Audiberti, Jacques 1900-1965 .... CLC 38
See also CA 25-28R; DAM DRAM; EWL 3

Audubon, John James 1785-1851 . NCLC 47
See also ANW; DLB 248

Auel, Jean M(arie) 1936- .... CLC 31, 107
See also AAYA 7, 51; BEST 90:4; BPFB 1;
CA 103; CANR 21, 64, 115; CPW; DA3;
DAM POP; INT CANR-21; NFS 11;
RHW; SATA 91

Auerbach, Erich 1892-1957 .... TCLC 43
See also CA 118; 155; EWL 3

Augier, Emile 1820-1889 .... NCLC 31
See also DLB 192; GFL 1789 to the Present

August, John
See De Voto, Bernard (Augustine)

Augustine, St. 354-430 .... CMLC 6; WLCS
See also DA; DA3; DAB; DAC; DAM
MST; DLB 115; EW 1; RGWL 2, 3

Aunt Belinda
See Braddon, Mary Elizabeth

Aunt Weedy
See Alcott, Louisa May

Aurelius
See Bourne, Randolph S(illiman)

Aurelius, Marcus 121-180 .... CMLC 45
See Marcus Aurelius
See also RGWL 2, 3

Aurobindo, Sri
See Ghose, Aurabinda

Aurobindo Ghose
See Ghose, Aurabinda

Austen, Jane 1775-1817 ...... NCLC 1, 13, 19,
33, 51, 81, 95, 119; WLC
See also AAYA 19; BRW 4; BRWC 1;
BRWR 2; BYA 3; CDBLB 1789-1832;
DA; DA3; DAB; DAC; DAM MST, NOV;
DLB 116; EXPN; LAIT 2; LATS 1; LMFS
1; NFS 1, 14, 18; TEA; WLIT 3; WYAS
1

Auster, Paul 1947- .... CLC 47, 131
See also AMWS 12; CA 69-72; CANR 23,
52, 75; CMW 4; CN 7; DA3; DLB 227;
MTCW 1; SUFW 2

Austin, Frank
See Faust, Frederick (Schiller)
See also TCWW 2

Austin, Mary (Hunter) 1868-1934 . TCLC 25
See Stairs, Gordon
See also ANW; CA 109; 178; DLB 9, 78,
206, 221, 275; FW; TCWW 2

Averroes 1126-1198 .... CMLC 7
See also DLB 115

Avicenna 980-1037 .... CMLC 16
See also DLB 115

Avison, Margaret 1918- .... CLC 2, 4, 97
See also CA 17-20R; CP 7; DAC; DAM
POET; DLB 53; MTCW 1

Axton, David
See Koontz, Dean R(ay)

Ayckbourn, Alan 1939- ...... CLC 5, 8, 18, 33,
74; DC 13
See also BRWS 5; CA 21-24R; CANR 31,
59, 118; CBD; CD 5; DAB; DAM DRAM;
DFS 7; DLB 13, 245; EWL 3; MTCW 1,
2

Aydy, Catherine
See Tennant, Emma (Christina)

Ayme, Marcel (Andre) 1902-1967 ... CLC 11;
SSC 41
See also CA 89-92; CANR 67; CLR 25;
DLB 72; EW 12; EWL 3; GFL 1789 to
the Present; RGSF 2; RGWL 2, 3; SATA
91

Ayrton, Michael 1921-1975 .... CLC 7
See also CA 5-8R; 61-64; CANR 9, 21

Aytmatov, Chingiz
See Aitmatov, Chingiz (Torekulovich)
See also EWL 3

Azorin .... CLC 11
See Martinez Ruiz, Jose
See also EW 9; EWL 3

Azuela, Mariano 1873-1952 .. HLC 1; TCLC
3
See also CA 104; 131; CANR 81; DAM
MULT; EWL 3; HW 1, 2; LAW; MTCW
1, 2

Ba, Mariama 1929-1981 .... BLCS
See also AFW; BW 2; CA 141; CANR 87;
DNFS 2; WLIT 2

Baastad, Babbis Friis
See Friis-Baastad, Babbis Ellinor

Bab
See Gilbert, W(illiam) S(chwenck)

Babbis, Eleanor
See Friis-Baastad, Babbis Ellinor

Babel, Isaac
See Babel, Isaak (Emmanuilovich)
See also EW 11; SSFS 10

Babel, Isaak (Emmanuilovich)
1894-1941(?) .... SSC 16; TCLC 2, 13
See Babel, Isaac
See also CA 104; 155; CANR 113; DLB
272; EWL 3; MTCW 1; RGSF 2; RGWL
2, 3; TWA

Babits, Mihaly 1883-1941 .... TCLC 14
See also CA 114; CDWLB 4; DLB 215;
EWL 3

Babur 1483-1530 .... LC 18

Babylas 1898-1962
See Ghelderode, Michel de

Barnes, Djuna 1892-1982 .... **CLC 3, 4, 8, 11, 29, 127; SSC 3**
See Steptoe, Lydia
See also AMWS 3; CA 9-12R; 107; CAD; CANR 16, 55; CWD; DLB 4, 9, 45; EWL 3; GLL 1; MTCW 1, 2; RGAL 4; TUS

Barnes, Jim 1933- .... **NNAL**
See also CA 108, 175; CAAE 175; CAAS 28; DLB 175

Barnes, Julian (Patrick) 1946- . **CLC 42, 141**
See also BRWS 4; CA 102; CANR 19, 54, 115; CN 7; DAB; DLB 194; DLBY 1993; EWL 3; MTCW 1

Barnes, Peter 1931- .... **CLC 5, 56**
See also CA 65-68; CAAS 12; CANR 33, 34, 64, 113; CBD; CD 5; DFS 6; DLB 13, 233; MTCW 1

Barnes, William 1801-1886 .... **NCLC 75**
See also DLB 32

Baroja (y Nessi), Pio 1872-1956 .... **HLC 1; TCLC 8**
See also CA 104; EW 9

Baron, David
See Pinter, Harold

Baron Corvo
See Rolfe, Frederick (William Serafino Austin Lewis Mary)

Barondess, Sue K(aufman) 1926-1977 .... **CLC 8**
See Kaufman, Sue
See also CA 1-4R; 69-72; CANR 1

Baron de Teive
See Pessoa, Fernando (Antonio Nogueira)

Baroness Von S.
See Zangwill, Israel

Barres, (Auguste-)Maurice 1862-1923 .... **TCLC 47**
See also CA 164; DLB 123; GFL 1789 to the Present

Barreto, Afonso Henrique de Lima
See Lima Barreto, Afonso Henrique de

Barrett, Andrea 1954- .... **CLC 150**
See also CA 156; CANR 92

Barrett, Michele .... **CLC 65**

Barrett, (Roger) Syd 1946- .... **CLC 35**

Barrett, William (Christopher) 1913-1992 .... **CLC 27**
See also CA 13-16R; 139; CANR 11, 67; INT CANR-11

Barrie, J(ames) M(atthew) 1860-1937 .... **TCLC 2**
See also BRWS 3; BYA 4, 5; CA 104; 136; CANR 77; CDBLB 1890-1914; CLR 16; CWRI 5; DA3; DAB; DAM DRAM; DFS 7; DLB 10, 141, 156; EWL 3; FANT; MAICYA 1, 2; MTCW 1; SATA 100; SUFW; WCH; WLIT 4; YABC 1

Barrington, Michael
See Moorcock, Michael (John)

Barrol, Grady
See Bograd, Larry

Barry, Mike
See Malzberg, Barry N(athaniel)

Barry, Philip 1896-1949 .... **TCLC 11**
See also CA 109; 199; DFS 9; DLB 7, 228; RGAL 4

Bart, Andre Schwarz
See Schwarz-Bart, Andre

Barth, John (Simmons) 1930- ... **CLC 1, 2, 3, 5, 7, 9, 10, 14, 27, 51, 89; SSC 10**
See also AITN 1, 2; AMW; BPFB 1; CA 1-4R; CABS 1; CANR 5, 23, 49, 64, 113; CN 7; DAM NOV; DLB 2, 227; EWL 3; FANT; MTCW 1; RGAL 4; RGSF 2; RHW; SSFS 6; TUS

Barthelme, Donald 1931-1989 ... **CLC 1, 2, 3, 5, 6, 8, 13, 23, 46, 59, 115; SSC 2, 55**
See also AMWS 4; BPFB 1; CA 21-24R; 129; CANR 20, 58; DA3; DAM NOV; DLB 2, 234; DLBY 1980, 1989; EWL 3; FANT; LMFS 2; MTCW 1, 2; RGAL 4; RGSF 2; SATA 7; SATA-Obit 62; SSFS 17

Barthelme, Frederick 1943- ...... **CLC 36, 117**
See also AMWS 11; CA 114; 122; CANR 77; CN 7; CSW; DLB 244; DLBY 1985; EWL 3; INT CA-122

Barthes, Roland (Gerard) 1915-1980 .... **CLC 24, 83; TCLC 135**
See also CA 130; 97-100; CANR 66; EW 13; EWL 3; GFL 1789 to the Present; MTCW 1, 2; TWA

Barzun, Jacques (Martin) 1907- ..... **CLC 51, 145**
See also CA 61-64; CANR 22, 95

Bashevis, Isaac
See Singer, Isaac Bashevis

Bashkirtseff, Marie 1859-1884 .... **NCLC 27**

Basho, Matsuo
See Matsuo Basho
See also PFS 18; RGWL 2, 3; WP

Basil of Caesaria c. 330-379 .... **CMLC 35**

Bass, Kingsley B., Jr.
See Bullins, Ed

Bass, Rick 1958- .... **CLC 79, 143; SSC 60**
See also ANW; CA 126; CANR 53, 93; CSW; DLB 212, 275

Bassani, Giorgio 1916-2000 .... **CLC 9**
See also CA 65-68; 190; CANR 33; CWW 2; DLB 128, 177; EWL 3; MTCW 1; RGWL 2, 3

Bastian, Ann .... **CLC 70**

Bastos, Augusto (Antonio) Roa
See Roa Bastos, Augusto (Antonio)

Bataille, Georges 1897-1962 .... **CLC 29**
See also CA 101; 89-92; EWL 3

Bates, H(erbert) E(rnest) 1905-1974 .... **CLC 46; SSC 10**
See also CA 93-96; 45-48; CANR 34; DA3; DAB; DAM POP; DLB 162, 191; EWL 3; EXPS; MTCW 1, 2; RGSF 2; SSFS 7

Bauchart
See Camus, Albert

Baudelaire, Charles 1821-1867 . **NCLC 6, 29, 55; PC 1; SSC 18; WLC**
See also DA; DA3; DAB; DAC; DAM MST, POET; DLB 217; EW 7; GFL 1789 to the Present; LMFS 2; RGWL 2, 3; TWA

Baudouin, Marcel
See Peguy, Charles (Pierre)

Baudouin, Pierre
See Peguy, Charles (Pierre)

Baudrillard, Jean 1929- .... **CLC 60**

Baum, L(yman) Frank 1856-1919 .. **TCLC 7, 132**
See also AAYA 46; CA 108; 133; CLR 15; CWRI 5; DLB 22; FANT; JRDA; MAICYA 1, 2; MTCW 1, 2; NFS 13; RGAL 4; SATA 18, 100; WCH

Baum, Louis F.
See Baum, L(yman) Frank

Baumbach, Jonathan 1933- .... **CLC 6, 23**
See also CA 13-16R; CAAS 5; CANR 12, 66; CN 7; DLBY 1980; INT CANR-12; MTCW 1

Bausch, Richard (Carl) 1945- .... **CLC 51**
See also AMWS 7; CA 101; CAAS 14; CANR 43, 61, 87; CSW; DLB 130

Baxter, Charles (Morley) 1947- . **CLC 45, 78**
See also CA 57-60; CANR 40, 64, 104; CPW; DAM POP; DLB 130; MTCW 2

Baxter, George Owen
See Faust, Frederick (Schiller)

Baxter, James K(eir) 1926-1972 .... **CLC 14**
See also CA 77-80; EWL 3

Baxter, John
See Hunt, E(verette) Howard, (Jr.)

Bayer, Sylvia
See Glassco, John

Baynton, Barbara 1857-1929 .... **TCLC 57**
See also DLB 230; RGSF 2

Beagle, Peter S(oyer) 1939- .... **CLC 7, 104**
See also AAYA 47; BPFB 1; BYA 9, 10; CA 9-12R; CANR 4, 51, 73, 110; DA3; DLBY 1980; FANT; INT CANR-4; MTCW 1; SATA 60, 130; SUFW 1, 2; YAW

Bean, Normal
See Burroughs, Edgar Rice

Beard, Charles A(ustin) 1874-1948 .... **TCLC 15**
See also CA 115; 189; DLB 17; SATA 18

Beardsley, Aubrey 1872-1898 .... **NCLC 6**

Beattie, Ann 1947- ..... **CLC 8, 13, 18, 40, 63, 146; SSC 11**
See also AMWS 5; BEST 90:2; BPFB 1; CA 81-84; CANR 53, 73; CN 7; CPW; DA3; DAM NOV, POP; DLB 218, 278; DLBY 1982; EWL 3; MTCW 1, 2; RGAL 4; RGSF 2; SSFS 9; TUS

Beattie, James 1735-1803 .... **NCLC 25**
See also DLB 109

Beauchamp, Kathleen Mansfield 1888-1923
See Mansfield, Katherine
See also CA 104; 134; DA; DA3; DAC; DAM MST; MTCW 2; TEA

Beaumarchais, Pierre-Augustin Caron de 1732-1799 .... **DC 4; LC 61**
See also DAM DRAM; DFS 14, 16; EW 4; GFL Beginnings to 1789; RGWL 2, 3

Beaumont, Francis 1584(?)-1616 .. **DC 6; LC 33**
See also BRW 2; CDBLB Before 1660; DLB 58; TEA

Beauvoir, Simone (Lucie Ernestine Marie Bertrand) de 1908-1986 .... **CLC 1, 2, 4, 8, 14, 31, 44, 50, 71, 124; SSC 35; WLC**
See also BPFB 1; CA 9-12R; 118; CANR 28, 61; DA; DA3; DAB; DAC; DAM MST, NOV; DLB 72; DLBY 1986; EW 12; EWL 3; FW; GFL 1789 to the Present; LMFS 2; MTCW 1, 2; RGSF 2; RGWL 2, 3; TWA

Becker, Carl (Lotus) 1873-1945 ..... **TCLC 63**
See also CA 157; DLB 17

Becker, Jurek 1937-1997 .... **CLC 7, 19**
See also CA 85-88; 157; CANR 60, 117; CWW 2; DLB 75; EWL 3

Becker, Walter 1950- .... **CLC 26**

Beckett, Samuel (Barclay) 1906-1989 .. **CLC 1, 2, 3, 4, 6, 9, 10, 11, 14, 18, 29, 57, 59, 83; SSC 16; WLC**
See also BRWR 1; BRWS 1; CA 5-8R; 130; CANR 33, 61; CBD; CDBLB 1945-1960; DA; DA3; DAB; DAC; DAM DRAM, MST, NOV; DFS 2, 7, 18; DLB 13, 15, 233; DLBY 1990; EWL 3; GFL 1789 to the Present; LATS 1; LMFS 2; MTCW 1, 2; RGSF 2; RGWL 2, 3; SSFS 15; TEA; WLIT 4

Beckford, William 1760-1844 .... **NCLC 16**
See also BRW 3; DLB 39, 213; HGG; LMFS 1; SUFW

Beckham, Barry (Earl) 1944- .... **BLC 1**
See also BW 1; CA 29-32R; CANR 26, 62; CN 7; DAM MULT; DLB 33

Beckman, Gunnel 1910- .... **CLC 26**
See also CA 33-36R; CANR 15, 114; CLR 25; MAICYA 1, 2; SAAS 9; SATA 6

Becque, Henri 1837-1899 .... **DC 21; NCLC 3**
See also DLB 192; GFL 1789 to the Present

Becquer, Gustavo Adolfo
1836-1870 .... **HLCS 1; NCLC 106**
See also DAM MULT

Beddoes, Thomas Lovell 1803-1849 .. **DC 15;
NCLC 3**
See also DLB 96

Bede c. 673-735 .... **CMLC 20**
See also DLB 146; TEA

Bedford, Denton R. 1907-(?) .... **NNAL**

Bedford, Donald F.
See Fearing, Kenneth (Flexner)

Beecher, Catharine Esther
1800-1878 .... **NCLC 30**
See also DLB 1, 243

Beecher, John 1904-1980 .... **CLC 6**
See also AITN 1; CA 5-8R; 105; CANR 8

Beer, Johann 1655-1700 .... **LC 5**
See also DLB 168

Beer, Patricia 1924- .... **CLC 58**
See also CA 61-64; 183; CANR 13, 46; CP
7; CWP; DLB 40; FW

Beerbohm, Max
See Beerbohm, (Henry) Max(imilian)

Beerbohm, (Henry) Max(imilian)
1872-1956 .... **TCLC 1, 24**
See also BRWS 2; CA 104; 154; CANR 79;
DLB 34, 100; FANT

Beer-Hofmann, Richard
1866-1945 .... **TCLC 60**
See also CA 160; DLB 81

Beg, Shemus
See Stephens, James

Begiebing, Robert J(ohn) 1946- .... **CLC 70**
See also CA 122; CANR 40, 88

Behan, Brendan (Francis)
1923-1964 .... **CLC 1, 8, 11, 15, 79**
See also BRWS 2; CA 73-76; CANR 33,
121; CBD; CDBLB 1945-1960; DAM
DRAM; DFS 7; DLB 13, 233; EWL 3;
MTCW 1, 2

Behn, Aphra 1640(?)-1689 .. **DC 4; LC 1, 30,
42; PC 13; WLC**
See also BRWS 3; DA; DA3; DAB; DAC;
DAM DRAM, MST, NOV, POET; DFS
16; DLB 39, 80, 131; FW; TEA; WLIT 3

Behrman, S(amuel) N(athaniel)
1893-1973 .... **CLC 40**
See also CA 13-16; 45-48; CAD; CAP 1;
DLB 7, 44; IDFW 3; RGAL 4

Belasco, David 1853-1931 .... **TCLC 3**
See also CA 104; 168; DLB 7; RGAL 4

Belcheva, Elisaveta Lyubomirova
1893-1991 .... **CLC 10**
See Bagryana, Elisaveta

Beldone, Phil "Cheech"
See Ellison, Harlan (Jay)

Beleno
See Azuela, Mariano

Belinski, Vissarion Grigoryevich
1811-1848 .... **NCLC 5**
See also DLB 198

Belitt, Ben 1911- .... **CLC 22**
See also CA 13-16R; CAAS 4; CANR 7,
77; CP 7; DLB 5

Bell, Gertrude (Margaret Lowthian)
1868-1926 .... **TCLC 67**
See also CA 167; CANR 110; DLB 174

Bell, J. Freeman
See Zangwill, Israel

Bell, James Madison 1826-1902 .... **BLC 1;
TCLC 43**
See also BW 1; CA 122; 124; DAM MULT;
DLB 50

Bell, Madison Smartt 1957- ...... **CLC 41, 102**
See also AMWS 10; BPFB 1; CA 111; 183;
CAAE 183; CANR 28, 54, 73; CN 7;
CSW; DLB 218, 278; MTCW 1

Bell, Marvin (Hartley) 1937- .... **CLC 8, 31**
See also CA 21-24R; CAAS 14; CANR 59,
102; CP 7; DAM POET; DLB 5; MTCW
1

Bell, W. L. D.
See Mencken, H(enry) L(ouis)

Bellamy, Atwood C.
See Mencken, H(enry) L(ouis)

Bellamy, Edward 1850-1898 ...... **NCLC 4, 86**
See also DLB 12; NFS 15; RGAL 4; SFW
4

Belli, Gioconda 1949- .... **HLCS 1**
See also CA 152; CWW 2; EWL 3; RGWL
3

Bellin, Edward J.
See Kuttner, Henry

Belloc, (Joseph) Hilaire (Pierre Sebastien
Rene Swanton) 1870-1953 .... **PC 24;
TCLC 7, 18**
See also CA 106; 152; CWRI 5; DAM
POET; DLB 19, 100, 141, 174; EWL 3;
MTCW 1; SATA 112; WCH; YABC 1

Belloc, Joseph Peter Rene Hilaire
See Belloc, (Joseph) Hilaire (Pierre Sebastien Rene Swanton)

Belloc, Joseph Pierre Hilaire
See Belloc, (Joseph) Hilaire (Pierre Sebastien Rene Swanton)

Belloc, M. A.
See Lowndes, Marie Adelaide (Belloc)

Belloc-Lowndes, Mrs.
See Lowndes, Marie Adelaide (Belloc)

Bellow, Saul 1915- . **CLC 1, 2, 3, 6, 8, 10, 13,
15, 25, 33, 34, 63, 79; SSC 14; WLC**
See also AITN 2; AMW; AMWR 2; BEST
89:3; BPFB 1; CA 5-8R; CABS 1; CANR
29, 53, 95; CDALB 1941-1968; CN 7;
DA; DA3; DAB; DAC; DAM MST, NOV,
POP; DLB 2, 28; DLBD 3; DLBY 1982;
EWL 3; MTCW 1, 2; NFS 4, 14; RGAL
4; RGSF 2; SSFS 12; TUS

Belser, Reimond Karel Maria de 1929-
See Ruyslinck, Ward
See also CA 152

Bely, Andrey .... **PC 11; TCLC 7**
See Bugayev, Boris Nikolayevich
See also EW 9; EWL 3; MTCW 1

Belyi, Andrei
See Bugayev, Boris Nikolayevich
See also RGWL 2, 3

Bembo, Pietro 1470-1547 .... **LC 79**
See also RGWL 2, 3

Benary, Margot
See Benary-Isbert, Margot

Benary-Isbert, Margot 1889-1979 .... **CLC 12**
See also CA 5-8R; 89-92; CANR 4, 72;
CLR 12; MAICYA 1, 2; SATA 2; SATA-
Obit 21

Benavente (y Martinez), Jacinto
1866-1954 .... **HLCS 1; TCLC 3**
See also CA 106; 131; CANR 81; DAM
DRAM, MULT; EWL 3; GLL 2; HW 1,
2; MTCW 1, 2

Benchley, Peter (Bradford) 1940- .. **CLC 4, 8**
See also AAYA 14; AITN 2; BPFB 1; CA
17-20R; CANR 12, 35, 66, 115; CPW;
DAM NOV, POP; HGG; MTCW 1, 2;
SATA 3, 89

Benchley, Robert (Charles)
1889-1945 .... **TCLC 1, 55**
See also CA 105; 153; DLB 11; RGAL 4

Benda, Julien 1867-1956 .... **TCLC 60**
See also CA 120; 154; GFL 1789 to the
Present

Benedict, Ruth (Fulton)
1887-1948 .... **TCLC 60**
See also CA 158; DLB 246

Benedikt, Michael 1935- .... **CLC 4, 14**
See also CA 13-16R; CANR 7; CP 7; DLB
5

Benet, Juan 1927-1993 .... **CLC 28**
See also CA 143; EWL 3

Benet, Stephen Vincent 1898-1943 ... **SSC 10;
TCLC 7**
See also AMWS 11; CA 104; 152; DA3;
DAM POET; DLB 4, 48, 102, 249, 284;
DLBY 1997; EWL 3; HGG; MTCW 1;
RGAL 4; RGSF 2; SUFW; WP; YABC 1

Benet, William Rose 1886-1950 ..... **TCLC 28**
See also CA 118; 152; DAM POET; DLB
45; RGAL 4

Benford, Gregory (Albert) 1941- .... **CLC 52**
See also BPFB 1; CA 69-72; 175; CAAE
175; CAAS 27; CANR 12, 24, 49, 95;
CSW; DLBY 1982; SCFW 2; SFW 4

Bengtsson, Frans (Gunnar)
1894-1954 .... **TCLC 48**
See also CA 170; EWL 3

Benjamin, David
See Slavitt, David R(ytman)

Benjamin, Lois
See Gould, Lois

Benjamin, Walter 1892-1940 .... **TCLC 39**
See also CA 164; DLB 242; EW 11; EWL
3

Benn, Gottfried 1886-1956 .. **PC 35; TCLC 3**
See also CA 106; 153; DLB 56; EWL 3;
RGWL 2, 3

Bennett, Alan 1934- .... **CLC 45, 77**
See also BRWS 8; CA 103; CANR 35, 55,
106; CBD; CD 5; DAB; DAM MST;
MTCW 1, 2

Bennett, (Enoch) Arnold
1867-1931 .... **TCLC 5, 20**
See also BRW 6; CA 106; 155; CDBLB
1890-1914; DLB 10, 34, 98, 135; EWL 3;
MTCW 2

Bennett, Elizabeth
See Mitchell, Margaret (Munnerlyn)

Bennett, George Harold 1930-
See Bennett, Hal
See also BW 1; CA 97-100; CANR 87

Bennett, Gwendolyn B. 1902-1981 .... **HR 2**
See also BW 1; CA 125; DLB 51; WP

Bennett, Hal .... **CLC 5**
See Bennett, George Harold
See also DLB 33

Bennett, Jay 1912- .... **CLC 35**
See also AAYA 10; CA 69-72; CANR 11,
42, 79; JRDA; SAAS 4; SATA 41, 87;
SATA-Brief 27; WYA; YAW

Bennett, Louise (Simone) 1919- .... **BLC 1;
CLC 28**
See also BW 2, 3; CA 151; CDWLB 3; CP
7; DAM MULT; DLB 117; EWL 3

Benson, A. C. 1862-1925 .... **TCLC 123**
See also DLB 98

Benson, E(dward) F(rederic)
1867-1940 .... **TCLC 27**
See also CA 114; 157; DLB 135, 153;
HGG; SUFW 1

Benson, Jackson J. 1930- .... **CLC 34**
See also CA 25-28R; DLB 111

Benson, Sally 1900-1972 .... **CLC 17**
See also CA 19-20; 37-40R; CAP 1; SATA
1, 35; SATA-Obit 27

Benson, Stella 1892-1933 .... **TCLC 17**
See also CA 117; 154, 155; DLB 36, 162;
FANT; TEA

Bentham, Jeremy 1748-1832 .... **NCLC 38**
See also DLB 107, 158, 252

Bentley, E(dmund) C(lerihew)
1875-1956 .... **TCLC 12**
See also CA 108; DLB 70; MSW

Bentley, Eric (Russell) 1916- .... **CLC 24**
See also CA 5-8R; CAD; CANR 6, 67;
CBD; CD 5; INT CANR-6

ben Uzair, Salem
See Horne, Richard Henry Hengist

Beranger, Pierre Jean de
1780-1857 .... **NCLC 34**

Berdyaev, Nicolas
See Berdyaev, Nikolai (Aleksandrovich)

Berdyaev, Nikolai (Aleksandrovich)
1874-1948 .... **TCLC 67**
See also CA 120; 157

Berdyayev, Nikolai (Aleksandrovich)
See Berdyaev, Nikolai (Aleksandrovich)

Berendt, John (Lawrence) 1939- ...... **CLC 86**
See also CA 146; CANR 75, 93; DA3;
MTCW 1

Beresford, J(ohn) D(avys)
1873-1947 .... **TCLC 81**
See also CA 112; 155; DLB 162, 178, 197;
SFW 4; SUFW 1

Bergelson, David 1884-1952 .... **TCLC 81**
See Bergelson, Dovid

Bergelson, Dovid
See Bergelson, David
See also EWL 3

Berger, Colonel
See Malraux, (Georges-)Andre

Berger, John (Peter) 1926- .... **CLC 2, 19**
See also BRWS 4; CA 81-84; CANR 51,
78, 117; CN 7; DLB 14, 207

Berger, Melvin H. 1927- .... **CLC 12**
See also CA 5-8R; CANR 4; CLR 32;
SAAS 2; SATA 5, 88; SATA-Essay 124

Berger, Thomas (Louis) 1924- .. **CLC 3, 5, 8,
11, 18, 38**
See also BPFB 1; CA 1-4R; CANR 5, 28,
51; CN 7; DAM NOV; DLB 2; DLBY
1980; EWL 3; FANT; INT CANR-28;
MTCW 1, 2; RHW; TCWW 2

Bergman, (Ernst) Ingmar 1918- ...... **CLC 16,
72**
See also CA 81-84; CANR 33, 70; DLB
257; MTCW 2

Bergson, Henri(-Louis) 1859-1941 . **TCLC 32**
See also CA 164; EW 8; EWL 3; GFL 1789
to the Present

Bergstein, Eleanor 1938- .... **CLC 4**
See also CA 53-56; CANR 5

Berkeley, George 1685-1753 .... **LC 65**
See also DLB 31, 101, 252

Berkoff, Steven 1937- .... **CLC 56**
See also CA 104; CANR 72; CBD; CD 5

Berlin, Isaiah 1909-1997 .... **TCLC 105**
See also CA 85-88; 162

Bermant, Chaim (Icyk) 1929-1998 ... **CLC 40**
See also CA 57-60; CANR 6, 31, 57, 105;
CN 7

Bern, Victoria
See Fisher, M(ary) F(rances) K(ennedy)

Bernanos, (Paul Louis) Georges
1888-1948 .... **TCLC 3**
See also CA 104; 130; CANR 94; DLB 72;
EWL 3; GFL 1789 to the Present; RGWL
2, 3

Bernard, April 1956- .... **CLC 59**
See also CA 131

Berne, Victoria
See Fisher, M(ary) F(rances) K(ennedy)

Bernhard, Thomas 1931-1989 ..... **CLC 3, 32,
61; DC 14**
See also CA 85-88; 127; CANR 32, 57; CD-
WLB 2; DLB 85, 124; EWL 3; MTCW 1;
RGWL 2, 3

Bernhardt, Sarah (Henriette Rosine)
1844-1923 .... **TCLC 75**
See also CA 157

Bernstein, Charles 1950- .... **CLC 142,**
See also CA 129; CAAS 24; CANR 90; CP
7; DLB 169

Berriault, Gina 1926-1999 .... **CLC 54, 109;
SSC 30**
See also CA 116; 129; 185; CANR 66; DLB
130; SSFS 7,11

Berrigan, Daniel 1921- .... **CLC 4**
See also CA 33-36R; CAAE 187; CAAS 1;
CANR 11, 43, 78; CP 7; DLB 5

Berrigan, Edmund Joseph Michael, Jr.
1934-1983
See Berrigan, Ted
See also CA 61-64; 110; CANR 14, 102

Berrigan, Ted .... **CLC 37**
See Berrigan, Edmund Joseph Michael, Jr.
See also DLB 5, 169; WP

Berry, Charles Edward Anderson 1931-
See Berry, Chuck
See also CA 115

Berry, Chuck .... **CLC 17**
See Berry, Charles Edward Anderson

Berry, Jonas
See Ashbery, John (Lawrence)
See also GLL 1

Berry, Wendell (Erdman) 1934- ... **CLC 4, 6,
8, 27, 46; PC 28**
See also AITN 1; AMWS 10; ANW; CA
73-76; CANR 50, 73, 101; CP 7; CSW;
DAM POET; DLB 5, 6, 234, 275; MTCW
1

Berryman, John 1914-1972 ... **CLC 1, 2, 3, 4,
6, 8, 10, 13, 25, 62**
See also AMW; CA 13-16; 33-36R; CABS
2; CANR 35; CAP 1; CDALB 1941-1968;
DAM POET; DLB 48; EWL 3; MTCW 1,
2; PAB; RGAL 4; WP

Bertolucci, Bernardo 1940- ...... **CLC 16, 157**
See also CA 106

Berton, Pierre (Francis Demarigny)
1920- .... **CLC 104**
See also CA 1-4R; CANR 2, 56; CPW;
DLB 68; SATA 99

Bertrand, Aloysius 1807-1841 .... **NCLC 31**
See Bertrand, Louis oAloysiusc

Bertrand, Louis oAloysiusc
See Bertrand, Aloysius
See also DLB 217

Bertran de Born c. 1140-1215 .... **CMLC 5**

Besant, Annie (Wood) 1847-1933 ..... **TCLC 9**
See also CA 105; 185

Bessie, Alvah 1904-1985 .... **CLC 23**
See also CA 5-8R; 116; CANR 2, 80; DLB
26

Bethlen, T. D.
See Silverberg, Robert

Beti, Mongo .... **BLC 1; CLC 27**
See Biyidi, Alexandre
See also AFW; CANR 79; DAM MULT;
EWL 3; WLIT 2

Betjeman, John 1906-1984 ...... **CLC 2, 6, 10,
34, 43**
See also BRW 7; CA 9-12R; 112; CANR
33, 56; CDBLB 1945-1960; DA3; DAB;
DAM MST, POET; DLB 20; DLBY 1984;
EWL 3; MTCW 1, 2

Bettelheim, Bruno 1903-1990 .... **CLC 79**
See also CA 81-84; 131; CANR 23, 61;
DA3; MTCW 1, 2

Betti, Ugo 1892-1953 .... **TCLC 5**
See also CA 104; 155; EWL 3; RGWL 2, 3

Betts, Doris (Waugh) 1932- ..... **CLC 3, 6, 28;
SSC 45**
See also CA 13-16R; CANR 9, 66, 77; CN
7; CSW; DLB 218; DLBY 1982; INT
CANR-9; RGAL 4

Bevan, Alistair
See Roberts, Keith (John Kingston)

Bey, Pilaff
See Douglas, (George) Norman

Bialik, Chaim Nachman
1873-1934 .... **TCLC 25**
See also CA 170; EWL 3

Bickerstaff, Isaac
See Swift, Jonathan

Bidart, Frank 1939- .... **CLC 33**
See also CA 140; CANR 106; CP 7

Bienek, Horst 1930- .... **CLC 7, 11**
See also CA 73-76; DLB 75

Bierce, Ambrose (Gwinett)
1842-1914(?) ..... **SSC 9; TCLC 1, 7, 44;
WLC**
See also AMW; BYA 11; CA 104; 139;
CANR 78; CDALB 1865-1917; DA;
DA3; DAC; DAM MST; DLB 11, 12, 23,
71, 74, 186; EWL 3; EXPS; HGG; LAIT
2; RGAL 4; RGSF 2; SSFS 9; SUFW 1

Biggers, Earl Derr 1884-1933 .... **TCLC 65**
See also CA 108; 153

Billiken, Bud
See Motley, Willard (Francis)

Billings, Josh
See Shaw, Henry Wheeler

Billington, (Lady) Rachel (Mary)
1942- .... **CLC 43**
See also AITN 2; CA 33-36R; CANR 44;
CN 7

Binchy, Maeve 1940- .... **CLC 153**
See also BEST 90:1; BPFB 1; CA 127; 134;
CANR 50, 96; CN 7; CPW; DAM
POP; INT CA-134; MTCW 1; RHW

Binyon, T(imothy) J(ohn) 1936- .... **CLC 34**
See also CA 111; CANR 28

Bion 335B.C.-245B.C. .... **CMLC 39**

Bioy Casares, Adolfo 1914-1999 ... **CLC 4, 8,
13, 88; HLC 1; SSC 17**
See Casares, Adolfo Bioy; Miranda, Javier;
Sacastru, Martin
See also CA 29-32R; 177; CANR 19, 43,
66; DAM MULT; DLB 113; EWL 3; HW
1, 2; LAW; MTCW 1, 2

Birch, Allison .... **CLC 65**

Bird, Cordwainer
See Ellison, Harlan (Jay)

Bird, Robert Montgomery
1806-1854 .... **NCLC 1**
See also DLB 202; RGAL 4

Birkerts, Sven 1951- .... **CLC 116**
See also CA 128; 133, 176; CAAE 176;
CAAS 29; INT 133

Birney, (Alfred) Earle 1904-1995 .. **CLC 1, 4,
6, 11**
See also CA 1-4R; CANR 5, 20; CP 7;
DAC; DAM MST, POET; DLB 88;
MTCW 1; PFS 8; RGEL 2

Biruni, al 973-1048(?) .... **CMLC 28**

Bishop, Elizabeth 1911-1979 ..... **CLC 1, 4, 9,
13, 15, 32; PC 3, 34; TCLC 121**
See also AMWR 2; AMWS 1; CA 5-8R;
89-92; CABS 2; CANR 26, 61, 108;
CDALB 1968-1988; DA; DA3; DAC;
DAM MST, POET; DLB 5, 169; EWL 3;
GLL 2; MAWW; MTCW 1, 2; PAB; PFS
6, 12; RGAL 4; SATA-Obit 24; TUS; WP

Bishop, John 1935- .... **CLC 10**
See also CA 105

Bishop, John Peale 1892-1944 ..... **TCLC 103**
See also CA 107; 155; DLB 4, 9, 45; RGAL
4

Bissett, Bill 1939- .... **CLC 18; PC 14**
See also CA 69-72; CAAS 19; CANR 15;
CCA 1; CP 7; DLB 53; MTCW 1

Bissoondath, Neil (Devindra)
1955- .... **CLC 120**
See also CA 136; CN 7; DAC

Bitov, Andrei (Georgievich) 1937- ... **CLC 57**
See also CA 142

Biyidi, Alexandre 1932-
See Beti, Mongo
See also BW 1, 3; CA 114; 124; CANR 81;
DA3; MTCW 1, 2

Bjarme, Brynjolf
See Ibsen, Henrik (Johan)

Bjoernson, Bjoernstjerne (Martinius)
1832-1910 .... TCLC 7, 37
See also CA 104

Black, Robert
See Holdstock, Robert P.

Blackburn, Paul 1926-1971 .... CLC 9, 43
See also BG 2; CA 81-84; 33-36R; CANR
34; DLB 16; DLBY 1981

Black Elk 1863-1950 .... NNAL; TCLC 33
See also CA 144; DAM MULT; MTCW 1;
WP

Black Hawk 1767-1838 .... NNAL

Black Hobart
See Sanders, (James) Ed(ward)

Blacklin, Malcolm
See Chambers, Aidan

Blackmore, R(ichard) D(oddridge)
1825-1900 .... TCLC 27
See also CA 120; DLB 18; RGEL 2

Blackmur, R(ichard) P(almer)
1904-1965 .... CLC 2, 24
See also AMWS 2; CA 11-12; 25-28R;
CANR 71; CAP 1; DLB 63; EWL 3

Black Tarantula
See Acker, Kathy

Blackwood, Algernon (Henry)
1869-1951 .... TCLC 5
See also CA 105; 150; DLB 153, 156, 178;
HGG; SUFW 1

Blackwood, Caroline 1931-1996 .... CLC 6, 9,
100
See also CA 85-88; 151; CANR 32, 61, 65;
CN 7; DLB 14, 207; HGG; MTCW 1

Blade, Alexander
See Hamilton, Edmond; Silverberg, Robert

Blaga, Lucian 1895-1961 .... CLC 75
See also CA 157; DLB 220; EWL 3

Blair, Eric (Arthur) 1903-1950 .... TCLC 123
See Orwell, George
See also CA 104; 132; DA; DA3; DAB;
DAC; DAM MST, NOV; MTCW 1, 2;
SATA 29

Blair, Hugh 1718-1800 .... NCLC 75

Blais, Marie-Claire 1939- .... CLC 2, 4, 6, 13,
22
See also CA 21-24R; CAAS 4; CANR 38,
75, 93; DAC; DAM MST; DLB 53; EWL
3; FW; MTCW 1, 2; TWA

Blaise, Clark 1940- .... CLC 29
See also AITN 2; CA 53-56; CAAS 3;
CANR 5, 66, 106; CN 7; DLB 53; RGSF
2

Blake, Fairley
See De Voto, Bernard (Augustine)

Blake, Nicholas
See Day Lewis, C(ecil)
See also DLB 77; MSW

Blake, Sterling
See Benford, Gregory (Albert)

Blake, William 1757-1827 . NCLC 13, 37, 57,
127; PC 12; WLC
See also AAYA 47; BRW 3; BRWR 1; CD-
BLB 1789-1832; CLR 52; DA; DA3;
DAB; DAC; DAM MST, POET; DLB 93,
163; EXPP; LATS 1; LMFS 1; MAICYA
1, 2; PAB; PFS 2, 12; SATA 30; TEA;
WCH; WLIT 3; WP

Blanchot, Maurice 1907-2003 .... CLC 135
See also CA 117; 144; 213; DLB 72; EWL
3

Blasco Ibanez, Vicente 1867-1928 . TCLC 12
See also BPFB 1; CA 110; 131; CANR 81;
DA3; DAM NOV; EW 8; EWL 3; HW 1,
2; MTCW 1

Blatty, William Peter 1928- .... CLC 2
See also CA 5-8R; CANR 9; DAM POP;
HGG

Bleeck, Oliver
See Thomas, Ross (Elmore)

Blessing, Lee 1949- .... CLC 54
See also CAD; CD 5

Blight, Rose
See Greer, Germaine

Blish, James (Benjamin) 1921-1975 . CLC 14
See also BPFB 1; CA 1-4R; 57-60; CANR
3; DLB 8; MTCW 1; SATA 66; SCFW 2;
SFW 4

Bliss, Reginald
See Wells, H(erbert) G(eorge)

Blixen, Karen (Christentze Dinesen)
1885-1962
See Dinesen, Isak
See also CA 25-28; CANR 22, 50; CAP 2;
DA3; DLB 214; LMFS 1; MTCW 1, 2;
SATA 44

Bloch, Robert (Albert) 1917-1994 .... CLC 33
See also AAYA 29; CA 5-8R, 179; 146;
CAAE 179; CAAS 20; CANR 5, 78;
DA3; DLB 44; HGG; INT CANR-5;
MTCW 1; SATA 12; SATA-Obit 82; SFW
4; SUFW 1, 2

Blok, Alexander (Alexandrovich)
1880-1921 .... PC 21; TCLC 5
See also CA 104; 183; EW 9; EWL 3;
LMFS 2; RGWL 2, 3

Blom, Jan
See Breytenbach, Breyten

Bloom, Harold 1930- .... CLC 24, 103
See also CA 13-16R; CANR 39, 75, 92;
DLB 67; EWL 3; MTCW 1; RGAL 4

Bloomfield, Aurelius
See Bourne, Randolph S(illiman)

Blount, Roy (Alton), Jr. 1941- .... CLC 38
See also CA 53-56; CANR 10, 28, 61;
CSW; INT CANR-28; MTCW 1, 2

Blowsnake, Sam 1875-(?) .... NNAL

Bloy, Leon 1846-1917 .... TCLC 22
See also CA 121; 183; DLB 123; GFL 1789
to the Present

Blue Cloud, Peter (Aroniawenrate)
1933- .... NNAL
See also CA 117; CANR 40; DAM MULT

Bluggage, Oranthy
See Alcott, Louisa May

Blume, Judy (Sussman) 1938- .... CLC 12, 30
See also AAYA 3, 26; BYA 1, 8, 12; CA 29-
32R; CANR 13, 37, 66; CLR 2, 15, 69;
CPW; DA3; DAM NOV, POP; DLB 52;
JRDA; MAICYA 1, 2; MAICYAS 1;
MTCW 1, 2; SATA 2, 31, 79, 142; WYA;
YAW

Blunden, Edmund (Charles)
1896-1974 .... CLC 2, 56
See also BRW 6; CA 17-18; 45-48; CANR
54; CAP 2; DLB 20, 100, 155; MTCW 1;
PAB

Bly, Robert (Elwood) 1926- .... CLC 1, 2, 5,
10, 15, 38, 128; PC 39
See also AMWS 4; CA 5-8R; CANR 41,
73; CP 7; DA3; DAM POET; DLB 5;
EWL 3; MTCW 1, 2; PFS 6, 17; RGAL 4

Boas, Franz 1858-1942 .... TCLC 56
See also CA 115; 181

Bobette
See Simenon, Georges (Jacques Christian)

Boccaccio, Giovanni 1313-1375 ... CMLC 13,
57; SSC 10
See also EW 2; RGSF 2; RGWL 2, 3; TWA

Bochco, Steven 1943- .... CLC 35
See also AAYA 11; CA 124; 138

Bode, Sigmund
See O'Doherty, Brian

Bodel, Jean 1167(?)-1210 .... CMLC 28

Bodenheim, Maxwell 1892-1954 .... TCLC 44
See also CA 110; 187; DLB 9, 45; RGAL 4

Bodenheimer, Maxwell
See Bodenheim, Maxwell

Bodker, Cecil 1927-
See Bodker, Cecil

Bodker, Cecil 1927- .... CLC 21
See also CA 73-76; CANR 13, 44, 111;
CLR 23; MAICYA 1, 2; SATA 14, 133

Boell, Heinrich (Theodor)
1917-1985 ..... CLC 2, 3, 6, 9, 11, 15, 27,
32, 72; SSC 23; WLC
See Boll, Heinrich
See also CA 21-24R; 116; CANR 24; DA;
DA3; DAB; DAC; DAM MST, NOV;
DLB 69; DLBY 1985; MTCW 1, 2; TWA

Boerne, Alfred
See Doeblin, Alfred

Boethius c. 480-c. 524 .... CMLC 15
See also DLB 115; RGWL 2, 3

Boff, Leonardo (Genezio Darci)
1938- .... CLC 70; HLC 1
See also CA 150; DAM MULT; HW 2

Bogan, Louise 1897-1970 .... CLC 4, 39, 46,
93; PC 12
See also AMWS 3; CA 73-76; 25-28R;
CANR 33, 82; DAM POET; DLB 45, 169;
EWL 3; MAWW; MTCW 1, 2; RGAL 4

Bogarde, Dirk
See Van Den Bogarde, Derek Jules Gaspard
Ulric Niven
See also DLB 14

Bogosian, Eric 1953- .... CLC 45, 141
See also CA 138; CAD; CANR 102; CD 5

Bograd, Larry 1953- .... CLC 35
See also CA 93-96; CANR 57; SAAS 21;
SATA 33, 89; WYA

Boiardo, Matteo Maria 1441-1494 .... LC 6

Boileau-Despreaux, Nicolas 1636-1711 . LC 3
See also DLB 268; EW 3; GFL Beginnings
to 1789; RGWL 2, 3

Boissard, Maurice
See Leautaud, Paul

Bojer, Johan 1872-1959 .... TCLC 64
See also CA 189; EWL 3

Bok, Edward W. 1863-1930 .... TCLC 101
See also DLB 91; DLBD 16

Boker, George Henry 1823-1890 . NCLC 125
See also RGAL 4

Boland, Eavan (Aisling) 1944- .. CLC 40, 67,
113
See also BRWS 5; CA 143; CAAE 207;
CANR 61; CP 7; CWP; DAM POET;
DLB 40; FW; MTCW 2; PFS 12

Boll, Heinrich
See Boell, Heinrich (Theodor)
See also BPFB 1; CDWLB 2; EW 13; EWL
3; RGSF 2; RGWL 2, 3

Bolt, Lee
See Faust, Frederick (Schiller)

Bolt, Robert (Oxton) 1924-1995 .... CLC 14
See also CA 17-20R; 147; CANR 35, 67;
CBD; DAM DRAM; DFS 2; DLB 13,
233; EWL 3; LAIT 1; MTCW 1

Bombal, Maria Luisa 1910-1980 .... HLCS 1;
SSC 37
See also CA 127; CANR 72; EWL 3; HW
1; LAW; RGSF 2

Bombet, Louis-Alexandre-Cesar
See Stendhal

Bomkauf
See Kaufman, Bob (Garnell)

Bonaventura .... NCLC 35
See also DLB 90

Calasso, Roberto 1941- .... **CLC 81**
 See also CA 143; CANR 89

Calderon de la Barca, Pedro
 1600-1681 .... **DC 3; HLCS 1; LC 23**
 See also EW 2; RGWL 2, 3; TWA

Caldwell, Erskine (Preston)
 1903-1987 .... **CLC 1, 8, 14, 50, 60; SSC
 19; TCLC 117**
 See also AITN 1; AMW; BPFB 1; CA 1-4R;
 121; CAAS 1; CANR 2, 33; DA3; DAM
 NOV; DLB 9, 86; EWL 3; MTCW 1, 2;
 RGAL 4; RGSF 2; TUS

Caldwell, (Janet Miriam) Taylor (Holland)
 1900-1985 .... **CLC 2, 28, 39**
 See also BPFB 1; CA 5-8R; 116; CANR 5;
 DA3; DAM NOV, POP; DLBD 17; RHW

Calhoun, John Caldwell
 1782-1850 .... **NCLC 15**
 See also DLB 3, 248

Calisher, Hortense 1911- ..... **CLC 2, 4, 8, 38,
 134; SSC 15**
 See also CA 1-4R; CANR 1, 22, 117; CN
 7; DA3; DAM NOV; DLB 2, 218; INT
 CANR-22; MTCW 1, 2; RGAL 4; RGSF
 2

Callaghan, Morley Edward
 1903-1990 .... **CLC 3, 14, 41, 65**
 See also CA 9-12R; 132; CANR 33, 73;
 DAC; DAM MST; DLB 68; EWL 3;
 MTCW 1, 2; RGEL 2; RGSF 2

Callimachus c. 305B.C.-c.
 240B.C. .... **CMLC 18**
 See also AW 1; DLB 176; RGWL 2, 3

Calvin, Jean
 See Calvin, John
 See also GFL Beginnings to 1789

Calvin, John 1509-1564 .... **LC 37**
 See Calvin, Jean

Calvino, Italo 1923-1985 .... **CLC 5, 8, 11, 22,
 33, 39, 73; SSC 3, 48**
 See also CA 85-88; 116; CANR 23, 61;
 DAM NOV; DLB 196; EW 13; EWL 3;
 MTCW 1, 2; RGSF 2; RGWL 2, 3; SFW
 4; SSFS 12

Camara Laye
 See Laye, Camara
 See also EWL 3

Camden, William 1551-1623 .... **LC 77**
 See also DLB 172

Cameron, Carey 1952- .... **CLC 59**
 See also CA 135

Cameron, Peter 1959- .... **CLC 44**
 See also AMWS 12; CA 125; CANR 50,
 117; DLB 234; GLL 2

Camoens, Luis Vaz de 1524(?)-1580
 See Camoes, Luis de
 See also EW 2

Camoes, Luis de 1524(?)-1580 . **HLCS 1; LC
 62; PC 31**
 See Camoens, Luis Vaz de
 See also DLB 287; RGWL 2, 3

Campana, Dino 1885-1932 .... **TCLC 20**
 See also CA 117; DLB 114; EWL 3

Campanella, Tommaso 1568-1639 .... **LC 32**
 See also RGWL 2, 3

Campbell, John W(ood, Jr.)
 1910-1971 .... **CLC 32**
 See also CA 21-22; 29-32R; CANR 34;
 CAP 2; DLB 8; MTCW 1; SCFW; SFW 4

Campbell, Joseph 1904-1987 .... **CLC 69;
 TCLC 140**
 See also AAYA 3; BEST 89:2; CA 1-4R;
 124; CANR 3, 28, 61, 107; DA3; MTCW
 1, 2

Campbell, Maria 1940- .... **CLC 85; NNAL**
 See also CA 102; CANR 54; CCA 1; DAC

Campbell, (John) Ramsey 1946- ..... **CLC 42;
 SSC 19**
 See also AAYA 51; CA 57-60; CANR 7,
 102; DLB 261; HGG; INT CANR-7;
 SUFW 1, 2

Campbell, (Ignatius) Roy (Dunnachie)
 1901-1957 .... **TCLC 5**
 See also AFW; CA 104; 155; DLB 20, 225;
 EWL 3; MTCW 2; RGEL 2

Campbell, Thomas 1777-1844 .... **NCLC 19**
 See also DLB 93, 144; RGEL 2

Campbell, Wilfred .... **TCLC 9**
 See Campbell, William

Campbell, William 1858(?)-1918
 See Campbell, Wilfred
 See also CA 106; DLB 92

Campion, Jane 1954- .... **CLC 95**
 See also AAYA 33; CA 138; CANR 87

Campion, Thomas 1567-1620 .... **LC 78**
 See also CDBLB Before 1660; DAM POET;
 DLB 58, 172; RGEL 2

Camus, Albert 1913-1960 ...... **CLC 1, 2, 4, 9,
 11, 14, 32, 63, 69, 124; DC 2; SSC 9;
 WLC**
 See also AAYA 36; AFW; BPFB 1; CA 89-
 92; DA; DA3; DAB; DAC; DAM DRAM,
 MST, NOV; DLB 72; EW 13; EWL 3;
 EXPN; EXPS; GFL 1789 to the Present;
 LATS 1; LMFS 2; MTCW 1, 2; NFS 6,
 16; RGSF 2; RGWL 2, 3; SSFS 4; TWA

Canby, Vincent 1924-2000 .... **CLC 13**
 See also CA 81-84; 191

Cancale
 See Desnos, Robert

Canetti, Elias 1905-1994 .. **CLC 3, 14, 25, 75,
 86**
 See also CA 21-24R; 146; CANR 23, 61,
 79; CDWLB 2; CWW 2; DA3; DLB 85,
 124; EW 12; EWL 3; MTCW 1, 2; RGWL
 2, 3; TWA

Canfield, Dorothea F.
 See Fisher, Dorothy (Frances) Canfield

Canfield, Dorothea Frances
 See Fisher, Dorothy (Frances) Canfield

Canfield, Dorothy
 See Fisher, Dorothy (Frances) Canfield

Canin, Ethan 1960- .... **CLC 55**
 See also CA 131; 135

Cankar, Ivan 1876-1918 .... **TCLC 105**
 See also CDWLB 4; DLB 147; EWL 3

Cannon, Curt
 See Hunter, Evan

Cao, Lan 1961- .... **CLC 109**
 See also CA 165

Cape, Judith
 See Page, P(atricia) K(athleen)
 See also CCA 1

Capek, Karel 1890-1938 .... **DC 1; SSC 36;
 TCLC 6, 37; WLC**
 See also CA 104; 140; CDWLB 4; DA;
 DA3; DAB; DAC; DAM DRAM, MST,
 NOV; DFS 7, 11; DLB 215; EW 10; EWL
 3; MTCW 1; RGSF 2; RGWL 2, 3; SCFW
 2; SFW 4

Capote, Truman 1924-1984 . **CLC 1, 3, 8, 13,
 19, 34, 38, 58; SSC 2, 47; WLC**
 See also AMWS 3; BPFB 1; CA 5-8R; 113;
 CANR 18, 62; CDALB 1941-1968; CPW;
 DA; DA3; DAB; DAC; DAM MST, NOV,
 POP; DLB 2, 185, 227; DLBY 1980,
 1984; EWL 3; EXPS; GLL 1; LAIT 3;
 MTCW 1, 2; NCFS 2; RGAL 4; RGSF 2;
 SATA 91; SSFS 2; TUS

Capra, Frank 1897-1991 .... **CLC 16**
 See also AAYA 52; CA 61-64; 135

Caputo, Philip 1941- .... **CLC 32**
 See also CA 73-76; CANR 40; YAW

Caragiale, Ion Luca 1852-1912 .... **TCLC 76**
 See also CA 157

Card, Orson Scott 1951- .... **CLC 44, 47, 50**
 See also AAYA 11, 42; BPFB 1; BYA 5, 8;
 CA 102; CANR 27, 47, 73, 102, 106;
 CPW; DA3; DAM POP; FANT; INT
 CANR-27; MTCW 1, 2; NFS 5; SATA
 83, 127; SCFW 2; SFW 4; SUFW 2; YAW

Cardenal, Ernesto 1925- .... **CLC 31, 161;
 HLC 1; PC 22**
 See also CA 49-52; CANR 2, 32, 66; CWW
 2; DAM MULT, POET; EWL 3; HW 1, 2;
 LAWS 1; MTCW 1, 2; RGWL 2, 3

Cardozo, Benjamin N(athan)
 1870-1938 .... **TCLC 65**
 See also CA 117; 164

Carducci, Giosue (Alessandro Giuseppe)
 1835-1907 .... **PC 46; TCLC 32**
 See also CA 163; EW 7; RGWL 2, 3

Carew, Thomas 1595(?)-1640 . **LC 13; PC 29**
 See also BRW 2; DLB 126; PAB; RGEL 2

Carey, Ernestine Gilbreth 1908- ...... **CLC 17**
 See also CA 5-8R; CANR 71; SATA 2

Carey, Peter 1943- .... **CLC 40, 55, 96**
 See also CA 123; 127; CANR 53, 76, 117;
 CN 7; EWL 3; INT CA-127; MTCW 1, 2;
 RGSF 2; SATA 94

Carleton, William 1794-1869 .... **NCLC 3**
 See also DLB 159; RGEL 2; RGSF 2

Carlisle, Henry (Coffin) 1926- .... **CLC 33**
 See also CA 13-16R; CANR 15, 85

Carlsen, Chris
 See Holdstock, Robert P.

Carlson, Ron(ald F.) 1947- .... **CLC 54**
 See also CA 105; CAAE 189; CANR 27;
 DLB 244

Carlyle, Thomas 1795-1881 ..... **NCLC 22, 70**
 See also BRW 4; CDBLB 1789-1832; DA;
 DAB; DAC; DAM MST; DLB 55, 144,
 254; RGEL 2; TEA

Carman, (William) Bliss 1861-1929 ... **PC 34;
 TCLC 7**
 See also CA 104; 152; DAC; DLB 92;
 RGEL 2

Carnegie, Dale 1888-1955 .... **TCLC 53**

Carossa, Hans 1878-1956 .... **TCLC 48**
 See also CA 170; DLB 66; EWL 3

Carpenter, Don(ald Richard)
 1931-1995 .... **CLC 41**
 See also CA 45-48; 149; CANR 1, 71

Carpenter, Edward 1844-1929 .... **TCLC 88**
 See also CA 163; GLL 1

Carpenter, John (Howard) 1948- ... **CLC 161**
 See also AAYA 2; CA 134; SATA 58

Carpenter, Johnny
 See Carpenter, John (Howard)

Carpentier (y Valmont), Alejo
 1904-1980 . **CLC 8, 11, 38, 110; HLC 1;
 SSC 35**
 See also CA 65-68; 97-100; CANR 11, 70;
 CDWLB 3; DAM MULT; DLB 113; EWL
 3; HW 1, 2; LAW; LMFS 2; RGSF 2;
 RGWL 2, 3; WLIT 1

Carr, Caleb 1955(?)- .... **CLC 86**
 See also CA 147; CANR 73; DA3

Carr, Emily 1871-1945 .... **TCLC 32**
 See also CA 159; DLB 68; FW; GLL 2

Carr, John Dickson 1906-1977 .... **CLC 3**
 See Fairbairn, Roger
 See also CA 49-52; 69-72; CANR 3, 33,
 60; CMW 4; MSW; MTCW 1, 2

Carr, Philippa
 See Hibbert, Eleanor Alice Burford

Carr, Virginia Spencer 1929- .... **CLC 34**
 See also CA 61-64; DLB 111

Carrere, Emmanuel 1957- .... **CLC 89**
 See also CA 200

Carrier, Roch 1937- .... **CLC 13, 78**
 See also CA 130; CANR 61; CCA 1; DAC;
 DAM MST; DLB 53; SATA 105

Chabon, Michael 1963- ... **CLC 55, 149; SSC 59**
See also AAYA 45; AMWS 11; CA 139; CANR 57, 96; DLB 278

Chabrol, Claude 1930- .... **CLC 16**
See also CA 110

Chairil Anwar
See Anwar, Chairil
See also EWL 3

Challans, Mary 1905-1983
See Renault, Mary
See also CA 81-84; 111; CANR 74; DA3; MTCW 2; SATA 23; SATA-Obit 36; TEA

Challis, George
See Faust, Frederick (Schiller)
See also TCWW 2

Chambers, Aidan 1934- .... **CLC 35**
See also AAYA 27; CA 25-28R; CANR 12, 31, 58, 116; JRDA; MAICYA 1, 2; SAAS 12; SATA 1, 69, 108; WYA; YAW

Chambers, James 1948-
See Cliff, Jimmy
See also CA 124

Chambers, Jessie
See Lawrence, D(avid) H(erbert Richards)
See also GLL 1

Chambers, Robert W(illiam)
1865-1933 .... **TCLC 41**
See also CA 165; DLB 202; HGG; SATA 107; SUFW 1

Chambers, (David) Whittaker
1901-1961 .... **TCLC 129**
See also CA 89-92

Chamisso, Adelbert von
1781-1838 .... **NCLC 82**
See also DLB 90; RGWL 2, 3; SUFW 1

Chance, James T.
See Carpenter, John (Howard)

Chance, John T.
See Carpenter, John (Howard)

Chandler, Raymond (Thornton)
1888-1959 .... **SSC 23; TCLC 1, 7**
See also AAYA 25; AMWS 4; BPFB 1; CA 104; 129; CANR 60, 107; CDALB 1929-1941; CMW 4; DA3; DLB 226, 253; DLBD 6; EWL 3; MSW; MTCW 1, 2; NFS 17; RGAL 4; TUS

Chang, Diana 1934- .... **AAL**
See also CWP; EXPP

Chang, Eileen 1921-1995 .... **AAL; SSC 28**
See Chang Ai-Ling
See also CA 166; CWW 2

Chang, Jung 1952- .... **CLC 71**
See also CA 142

Chang Ai-Ling
See Chang, Eileen
See also EWL 3

Channing, William Ellery
1780-1842 .... **NCLC 17**
See also DLB 1, 59, 235; RGAL 4

Chao, Patricia 1955- .... **CLC 119**
See also CA 163

Chaplin, Charles Spencer
1889-1977 .... **CLC 16**
See Chaplin, Charlie
See also CA 81-84; 73-76

Chaplin, Charlie
See Chaplin, Charles Spencer
See also DLB 44

Chapman, George 1559(?)-1634 . **DC 19; LC 22**
See also BRW 1; DAM DRAM; DLB 62, 121; LMFS 1; RGEL 2

Chapman, Graham 1941-1989 .... **CLC 21**
See Monty Python
See also CA 116; 129; CANR 35, 95

Chapman, John Jay 1862-1933 .... **TCLC 7**
See also CA 104; 191

Chapman, Lee
See Bradley, Marion Zimmer
See also GLL 1

Chapman, Walker
See Silverberg, Robert

Chappell, Fred (Davis) 1936- .... **CLC 40, 78, 162**
See also CA 5-8R; CAAE 198; CAAS 4; CANR 8, 33, 67, 110; CN 7; CP 7; CSW; DLB 6, 105; HGG

Char, Rene(-Emile) 1907-1988 .... **CLC 9, 11, 14, 55**
See also CA 13-16R; 124; CANR 32; DAM POET; DLB 258; EWL 3; GFL 1789 to the Present; MTCW 1, 2; RGWL 2, 3

Charby, Jay
See Ellison, Harlan (Jay)

Chardin, Pierre Teilhard de
See Teilhard de Chardin, (Marie Joseph) Pierre

Chariton fl. 1st cent. (?)- .... **CMLC 49**

Charlemagne 742-814 .... **CMLC 37**

Charles I 1600-1649 .... **LC 13**

Charriere, Isabelle de 1740-1805 .. **NCLC 66**

Chartier, Emile-Auguste
See Alain

Charyn, Jerome 1937- .... **CLC 5, 8, 18**
See also CA 5-8R; CAAS 1; CANR 7, 61, 101; CMW 4; CN 7; DLBY 1983; MTCW 1

Chase, Adam
See Marlowe, Stephen

Chase, Mary (Coyle) 1907-1981 .... **DC 1**
See also CA 77-80; 105; CAD; CWD; DFS 11; DLB 228; SATA 17; SATA-Obit 29

Chase, Mary Ellen 1887-1973 .... **CLC 2; TCLC 124**
See also CA 13-16; 41-44R; CAP 1; SATA 10

Chase, Nicholas
See Hyde, Anthony
See also CCA 1

Chateaubriand, Francois Rene de
1768-1848 .... **NCLC 3**
See also DLB 119; EW 5; GFL 1789 to the Present; RGWL 2, 3; TWA

Chatterje, Sarat Chandra 1876-1936(?)
See Chatterji, Saratchandra
See also CA 109

Chatterji, Bankim Chandra
1838-1894 .... **NCLC 19**

Chatterji, Saratchandra .... **TCLC 13**
See Chatterje, Sarat Chandra
See also CA 186; EWL 3

Chatterton, Thomas 1752-1770 .... **LC 3, 54**
See also DAM POET; DLB 109; RGEL 2

Chatwin, (Charles) Bruce
1940-1989 .... **CLC 28, 57, 59**
See also AAYA 4; BEST 90:1; BRWS 4; CA 85-88; 127; CPW; DAM POP; DLB 194, 204; EWL 3

Chaucer, Daniel
See Ford, Ford Madox
See also RHW

Chaucer, Geoffrey 1340(?)-1400 .. **LC 17, 56; PC 19; WLCS**
See also BRW 1; BRWC 1; BRWR 2; CD-BLB Before 1660; DA; DA3; DAB; DAC; DAM MST, POET; DLB 146; LAIT 1; PAB; PFS 14; RGEL 2; TEA; WLIT 3; WP

Chavez, Denise (Elia) 1948- .... **HLC 1**
See also CA 131; CANR 56, 81; DAM MULT; DLB 122; FW; HW 1, 2; MTCW 2

Chaviaras, Strates 1935-
See Haviaras, Stratis
See also CA 105

Chayefsky, Paddy .... **CLC 23**
See Chayefsky, Sidney
See also CAD; DLB 7, 44; DLBY 1981; RGAL 4

Chayefsky, Sidney 1923-1981
See Chayefsky, Paddy
See also CA 9-12R; 104; CANR 18; DAM DRAM

Chedid, Andree 1920- .... **CLC 47**
See also CA 145; CANR 95; EWL 3

Cheever, John 1912-1982 ..... **CLC 3, 7, 8, 11, 15, 25, 64; SSC 1, 38, 57; WLC**
See also AMWS 1; BPFB 1; CA 5-8R; 106; CABS 1; CANR 5, 27, 76; CDALB 1941-1968; CPW; DA; DA3; DAB; DAC; DAM MST, NOV, POP; DLB 2, 102, 227; DLBY 1980, 1982; EWL 3; EXPS; INT CANR-5; MTCW 1, 2; RGAL 4; RGSF 2; SSFS 2, 14; TUS

Cheever, Susan 1943- .... **CLC 18, 48**
See also CA 103; CANR 27, 51, 92; DLBY 1982; INT CANR-27

Chekhonte, Antosha
See Chekhov, Anton (Pavlovich)

Chekhov, Anton (Pavlovich)
1860-1904 ...... **DC 9; SSC 2, 28, 41, 51; TCLC 3, 10, 31, 55, 96; WLC**
See also BYA 14; CA 104; 124; DA; DA3; DAB; DAC; DAM DRAM, MST; DFS 1, 5, 10, 12; DLB 277; EW 7; EWL 3; EXPS; LAIT 3; LATS 1; RGSF 2; RGWL 2, 3; SATA 90; SSFS 5, 13, 14; TWA

Cheney, Lynne V. 1941- .... **CLC 70**
See also CA 89-92; CANR 58, 117

Chernyshevsky, Nikolai Gavrilovich
See Chernyshevsky, Nikolay Gavrilovich
See also DLB 238

Chernyshevsky, Nikolay Gavrilovich
1828-1889 .... **NCLC 1**
See Chernyshevsky, Nikolai Gavrilovich

Cherry, Carolyn Janice 1942-
See Cherryh, C. J.
See also CA 65-68; CANR 10

Cherryh, C. J. .... **CLC 35**
See Cherry, Carolyn Janice
See also AAYA 24; BPFB 1; DLBY 1980; FANT; SATA 93; SCFW 2; SFW 4; YAW

Chesnutt, Charles W(addell)
1858-1932 .... **BLC 1; SSC 7, 54; TCLC 5, 39**
See also AFAW 1, 2; BW 1, 3; CA 106; 125; CANR 76; DAM MULT; DLB 12, 50, 78; EWL 3; MTCW 1, 2; RGAL 4; RGSF 2; SSFS 11

Chester, Alfred 1929(?)-1971 .... **CLC 49**
See also CA 196; 33-36R; DLB 130

Chesterton, G(ilbert) K(eith)
1874-1936 . **PC 28; SSC 1, 46; TCLC 1, 6, 64**
See also BRW 6; CA 104; 132; CANR 73; CDBLB 1914-1945; CMW 4; DAM NOV, POET; DLB 10, 19, 34, 70, 98, 149, 178; EWL 3; FANT; MSW; MTCW 1, 2; RGEL 2; RGSF 2; SATA 27; SUFW 1

Chiang, Pin-chin 1904-1986
See Ding Ling
See also CA 118

Chief Joseph 1840-1904 .... **NNAL**
See also CA 152; DA3; DAM MULT

Chief Seattle 1786(?)-1866 .... **NNAL**
See also DA3; DAM MULT

Ch'ien, Chung-shu 1910-1998 .... **CLC 22**
See also CA 130; CANR 73; MTCW 1, 2

Chikamatsu Monzaemon 1653-1724 ... **LC 66**
See also RGWL 2, 3

Child, L. Maria
See Child, Lydia Maria

Cozzens, James Gould 1903-1978 . **CLC 1, 4, 11, 92**
See also AMW; BPFB 1; CA 9-12R; 81-84; CANR 19; CDALB 1941-1968; DLB 9; DLBD 2; DLBY 1984, 1997; EWL 3; MTCW 1, 2; RGAL 4

Crabbe, George 1754-1832 .... **NCLC 26, 121**
See also BRW 3; DLB 93; RGEL 2

Crace, Jim 1946- .... **CLC 157; SSC 61**
See also CA 128; 135; CANR 55, 70; CN 7; DLB 231; INT CA-135

Craddock, Charles Egbert
See Murfree, Mary Noailles

Craig, A. A.
See Anderson, Poul (William)

Craik, Mrs.
See Craik, Dinah Maria (Mulock)
See also RGEL 2

Craik, Dinah Maria (Mulock)
1826-1887 .... **NCLC 38**
See Craik, Mrs.; Mulock, Dinah Maria
See also DLB 35, 163; MAICYA 1, 2; SATA 34

Cram, Ralph Adams 1863-1942 ..... **TCLC 45**
See also CA 160

Cranch, Christopher Pearse
1813-1892 .... **NCLC 115**
See also DLB 1, 42, 243

Crane, (Harold) Hart 1899-1932 .... **PC 3; TCLC 2, 5, 80; WLC**
See also AMW; AMWR 2; CA 104; 127; CDALB 1917-1929; DA; DA3; DAB; DAC; DAM MST, POET; DLB 4, 48; EWL 3; MTCW 1, 2; RGAL 4; TUS

Crane, R(onald) S(almon)
1886-1967 .... **CLC 27**
See also CA 85-88; DLB 63

Crane, Stephen (Townley)
1871-1900 ...... **SSC 7, 56; TCLC 11, 17, 32; WLC**
See also AAYA 21; AMW; AMWC 1; BPFB 1; BYA 3; CA 109; 140; CANR 84; CDALB 1865-1917; DA; DA3; DAB; DAC; DAM MST, NOV, POET; DLB 12, 54, 78; EXPN; EXPS; LAIT 2; LMFS 2; NFS 4; PFS 9; RGAL 4; RGSF 2; SSFS 4; TUS; WYA; YABC 2

Cranshaw, Stanley
See Fisher, Dorothy (Frances) Canfield

Crase, Douglas 1944- .... **CLC 58**
See also CA 106

Crashaw, Richard 1612(?)-1649 .... **LC 24**
See also BRW 2; DLB 126; PAB; RGEL 2

Cratinus c. 519B.C.-c. 422B.C. ..... **CMLC 54**
See also LMFS 1

Craven, Margaret 1901-1980 .... **CLC 17**
See also BYA 2; CA 103; CCA 1; DAC; LAIT 5

Crawford, F(rancis) Marion
1854-1909 .... **TCLC 10**
See also CA 107; 168; DLB 71; HGG; RGAL 4; SUFW 1

Crawford, Isabella Valancy
1850-1887 .... **NCLC 12, 127**
See also DLB 92; RGEL 2

Crayon, Geoffrey
See Irving, Washington

Creasey, John 1908-1973 .... **CLC 11**
See Marric, J. J.
See also CA 5-8R; 41-44R; CANR 8, 59; CMW 4; DLB 77; MTCW 1

Crebillon, Claude Prosper Jolyot de (fils)
1707-1777 .... **LC 1, 28**
See also GFL Beginnings to 1789

Credo
See Creasey, John

Credo, Alvaro J. de
See Prado (Calvo), Pedro

Creeley, Robert (White) 1926- .. **CLC 1, 2, 4, 8, 11, 15, 36, 78**
See also AMWS 4; CA 1-4R; CAAS 10; CANR 23, 43, 89; CP 7; DA3; DAM POET; DLB 5, 16, 169; DLBD 17; EWL 3; MTCW 1, 2; RGAL 4; WP

Crevecoeur, Hector St. John de
See Crevecoeur, Michel Guillaume Jean de
See also ANW

Crevecoeur, Michel Guillaume Jean de
1735-1813 .... **NCLC 105**
See Crevecoeur, Hector St. John de
See also AMWS 1; DLB 37

Crevel, Rene 1900-1935 .... **TCLC 112**
See also GLL 2

Crews, Harry (Eugene) 1935- ..... **CLC 6, 23, 49**
See also AITN 1; AMWS 11; BPFB 1; CA 25-28R; CANR 20, 57; CN 7; CSW; DA3; DLB 6, 143, 185; MTCW 1, 2; RGAL 4

Crichton, (John) Michael 1942- .... **CLC 2, 6, 54, 90**
See also AAYA 10, 49; AITN 2; BPFB 1; CA 25-28R; CANR 13, 40, 54, 76; CMW 4; CN 7; CPW; DA3; DAM NOV, POP; DLBY 1981; INT CANR-13; JRDA; MTCW 1, 2; SATA 9, 88; SFW 4; YAW

Crispin, Edmund .... **CLC 22**
See Montgomery, (Robert) Bruce
See also DLB 87; MSW

Cristofer, Michael 1945(?)- .... **CLC 28**
See also CA 110; 152; CAD; CD 5; DAM DRAM; DFS 15; DLB 7

Criton
See Alain

Croce, Benedetto 1866-1952 .... **TCLC 37**
See also CA 120; 155; EW 8; EWL 3

Crockett, David 1786-1836 .... **NCLC 8**
See also DLB 3, 11, 183, 248

Crockett, Davy
See Crockett, David

Crofts, Freeman Wills 1879-1957 .. **TCLC 55**
See also CA 115; 195; CMW 4; DLB 77; MSW

Croker, John Wilson 1780-1857 .... **NCLC 10**
See also DLB 110

Crommelynck, Fernand 1885-1970 .. **CLC 75**
See also CA 189; 89-92; EWL 3

Cromwell, Oliver 1599-1658 .... **LC 43**

Cronenberg, David 1943- .... **CLC 143**
See also CA 138; CCA 1

Cronin, A(rchibald) J(oseph)
1896-1981 .... **CLC 32**
See also BPFB 1; CA 1-4R; 102; CANR 5; DLB 191; SATA 47; SATA-Obit 25

Cross, Amanda
See Heilbrun, Carolyn G(old)
See also BPFB 1; CMW; CPW; MSW

Crothers, Rachel 1878-1958 .... **TCLC 19**
See also CA 113; 194; CAD; CWD; DLB 7, 266; RGAL 4

Croves, Hal
See Traven, B.

Crow Dog, Mary (Ellen) (?)- .... **CLC 93**
See Brave Bird, Mary
See also CA 154

Crowfield, Christopher
See Stowe, Harriet (Elizabeth) Beecher

Crowley, Aleister .... **TCLC 7**
See Crowley, Edward Alexander
See also GLL 1

Crowley, Edward Alexander 1875-1947
See Crowley, Aleister
See also CA 104; HGG

Crowley, John 1942- .... **CLC 57**
See also BPFB 1; CA 61-64; CANR 43, 98; DLBY 1982; SATA 65, 140; SFW 4; SUFW 2

Crud
See Crumb, R(obert)

Crumarums
See Crumb, R(obert)

Crumb, R(obert) 1943- .... **CLC 17**
See also CA 106; CANR 107

Crumbum
See Crumb, R(obert)

Crumski
See Crumb, R(obert)

Crum the Bum
See Crumb, R(obert)

Crunk
See Crumb, R(obert)

Crustt
See Crumb, R(obert)

Crutchfield, Les
See Trumbo, Dalton

Cruz, Victor Hernandez 1949- ... **HLC 1; PC 37**
See also BW 2; CA 65-68; CAAS 17; CANR 14, 32, 74; CP 7; DAM MULT, POET; DLB 41; DNFS 1; EXPP; HW 1, 2; MTCW 1; PFS 16; WP

Cryer, Gretchen (Kiger) 1935- .... **CLC 21**
See also CA 114; 123

Csath, Geza 1887-1919 .... **TCLC 13**
See also CA 111

Cudlip, David R(ockwell) 1933- .... **CLC 34**
See also CA 177

Cullen, Countee 1903-1946 .... **BLC 1; HR 2; PC 20; TCLC 4, 37; WLCS**
See also AFAW 2; AMWS 4; BW 1; CA 108; 124; CDALB 1917-1929; DA; DA3; DAC; DAM MST, MULT, POET; DLB 4, 48, 51; EWL 3; EXPP; LMFS 2; MTCW 1, 2; PFS 3; RGAL 4; SATA 18; WP

Culleton, Beatrice 1949- .... **NNAL**
See also CA 120; CANR 83; DAC

Cum, R.
See Crumb, R(obert)

Cummings, Bruce F(rederick) 1889-1919
See Barbellion, W. N. P.
See also CA 123

Cummings, E(dward) E(stlin)
1894-1962 .. **CLC 1, 3, 8, 12, 15, 68; PC 5; TCLC 137; WLC**
See also AAYA 41; AMW; CA 73-76; CANR 31; CDALB 1929-1941; DA; DA3; DAB; DAC; DAM MST, POET; DLB 4, 48; EWL 3; EXPP; MTCW 1, 2; PAB; PFS 1, 3, 12, 13; RGAL 4; TUS; WP

Cunha, Euclides (Rodrigues Pimenta) da
1866-1909 .... **TCLC 24**
See also CA 123; LAW; WLIT 1

Cunningham, E. V.
See Fast, Howard (Melvin)

Cunningham, J(ames) V(incent)
1911-1985 .... **CLC 3, 31**
See also CA 1-4R; 115; CANR 1, 72; DLB 5

Cunningham, Julia (Woolfolk)
1916- .... **CLC 12**
See also CA 9-12R; CANR 4, 19, 36; CWRI 5; JRDA; MAICYA 1, 2; SAAS 2; SATA 1, 26, 132

Cunningham, Michael 1952- .... **CLC 34**
See also CA 136; CANR 96; GLL 2

Cunninghame Graham, R. B.
See Cunninghame Graham, Robert (Gallnigad) Bontine

Cunninghame Graham, Robert (Gallnigad) Bontine 1852-1936 .... **TCLC 19**
See Graham, R(obert) B(ontine) Cunninghame
See also CA 119; 184

Author Index

Dodson, Owen (Vincent) 1914-1983 .. **BLC 1; CLC 79**
See also BW 1; CA 65-68; 110; CANR 24; DAM MULT; DLB 76

Doeblin, Alfred 1878-1957 .... **TCLC 13**
See Doblin, Alfred
See also CA 110; 141; DLB 66

Doerr, Harriet 1910-2002 .... **CLC 34**
See also CA 117; 122; 213; CANR 47; INT CA-122; LATS 1

Domecq, H(onorio Bustos)
See Bioy Casares, Adolfo

Domecq, H(onorio) Bustos
See Bioy Casares, Adolfo; Borges, Jorge Luis

Domini, Rey
See Lorde, Audre (Geraldine)
See also GLL 1

Dominique
See Proust, (Valentin-Louis-George-Eugene) Marcel

Don, A
See Stephen, Sir Leslie

Donaldson, Stephen R(eeder)
1947- .... **CLC 46, 138**
See also AAYA 36; BPFB 1; CA 89-92; CANR 13, 55, 99; CPW; DAM POP; FANT; INT CANR-13; SATA 121; SFW 4; SUFW 1, 2

Donleavy, J(ames) P(atrick) 1926- .... **CLC 1, 4, 6, 10, 45**
See also AITN 2; BPFB 1; CA 9-12R; CANR 24, 49, 62, 80; CBD; CD 5; CN 7; DLB 6, 173; INT CANR-24; MTCW 1, 2; RGAL 4

Donnadieu, Marguerite
See Duras, Marguerite
See also CWW 2

Donne, John 1572-1631 ... **LC 10, 24, 91; PC 1, 43; WLC**
See also BRW 1; BRWC 1; BRWR 2; CD-BLB Before 1660; DA; DAB; DAC; DAM MST, POET; DLB 121, 151; EXPP; PAB; PFS 2, 11; RGEL 2; TEA; WLIT 3; WP

Donnell, David 1939(?)- .... **CLC 34**
See also CA 197

Donoghue, P. S.
See Hunt, E(verette) Howard, (Jr.)

Donoso (Yanez), Jose 1924-1996 ... **CLC 4, 8, 11, 32, 99; HLC 1; SSC 34; TCLC 133**
See also CA 81-84; 155; CANR 32, 73; CD-WLB 3; DAM MULT; DLB 113; EWL 3; HW 1, 2; LAW; LAWS 1; MTCW 1, 2; RGSF 2; WLIT 1

Donovan, John 1928-1992 .... **CLC 35**
See also AAYA 20; CA 97-100; 137; CLR 3; MAICYA 1, 2; SATA 72; SATA-Brief 29; YAW

Don Roberto
See Cunninghame Graham, Robert (Gallnigad) Bontine

Doolittle, Hilda 1886-1961 . **CLC 3, 8, 14, 31, 34, 73; PC 5; WLC**
See H. D.
See also AMWS 1; CA 97-100; CANR 35; DA; DAC; DAM MST, POET; DLB 4, 45; EWL 3; FW; GLL 1; LMFS 2; MAWW; MTCW 1, 2; PFS 6; RGAL 4

Doppo, Kunikida .... **TCLC 99**
See Kunikida Doppo

Dorfman, Ariel 1942- .... **CLC 48, 77; HLC 1**
See also CA 124; 130; CANR 67, 70; CWW 2; DAM MULT; DFS 4; EWL 3; HW 1, 2; INT CA-130; WLIT 1

Dorn, Edward (Merton)
1929-1999 .... **CLC 10, 18**
See also CA 93-96; 187; CANR 42, 79; CP 7; DLB 5; INT 93-96; WP

Dor-Ner, Zvi .... **CLC 70**

Dorris, Michael (Anthony)
1945-1997 .... **CLC 109; NNAL**
See also AAYA 20; BEST 90:1; BYA 12; CA 102; 157; CANR 19, 46, 75; CLR 58; DA3; DAM MULT, NOV; DLB 175; LAIT 5; MTCW 2; NFS 3; RGAL 4; SATA 75; SATA-Obit 94; TCWW 2; YAW

Dorris, Michael A.
See Dorris, Michael (Anthony)

Dorsan, Luc
See Simenon, Georges (Jacques Christian)

Dorsange, Jean
See Simenon, Georges (Jacques Christian)

Dos Passos, John (Roderigo)
1896-1970 ... **CLC 1, 4, 8, 11, 15, 25, 34, 82; WLC**
See also AMW; BPFB 1; CA 1-4R; 29-32R; CANR 3; CDALB 1929-1941; DA; DA3; DAB; DAC; DAM MST, NOV; DLB 4, 9; DLBD 1, 15, 274; DLBY 1996; EWL 3; MTCW 1, 2; NFS 14; RGAL 4; TUS

Dossage, Jean
See Simenon, Georges (Jacques Christian)

Dostoevsky, Fedor Mikhailovich
1821-1881 .. **NCLC 2, 7, 21, 33, 43, 119; SSC 2, 33, 44; WLC**
See Dostoevsky, Fyodor
See also AAYA 40; DA; DA3; DAB; DAC; DAM MST, NOV; EW 7; EXPN; NFS 3, 8; RGSF 2; RGWL 2, 3; SSFS 8; TWA

Dostoevsky, Fyodor
See Dostoevsky, Fedor Mikhailovich
See also DLB 238; LATS 1; LMFS 1, 2

Doty, M. R.
See Doty, Mark (Alan)

Doty, Mark
See Doty, Mark (Alan)

Doty, Mark (Alan) 1953(?)- .... **CLC 176**
See also AMWS 11; CA 161, 183; CAAE 183; CANR 110

Doty, Mark A.
See Doty, Mark (Alan)

Doughty, Charles M(ontagu)
1843-1926 .... **TCLC 27**
See also CA 115; 178; DLB 19, 57, 174

Douglas, Ellen .... **CLC 73**
See Haxton, Josephine Ayres; Williamson, Ellen Douglas
See also CN 7; CSW

Douglas, Gavin 1475(?)-1522 .... **LC 20**
See also DLB 132; RGEL 2

Douglas, George
See Brown, George Douglas
See also RGEL 2

Douglas, Keith (Castellain)
1920-1944 .... **TCLC 40**
See also BRW 7; CA 160; DLB 27; EWL 3; PAB; RGEL 2

Douglas, Leonard
See Bradbury, Ray (Douglas)

Douglas, Michael
See Crichton, (John) Michael

Douglas, (George) Norman
1868-1952 .... **TCLC 68**
See also BRW 6; CA 119; 157; DLB 34, 195; RGEL 2

Douglas, William
See Brown, George Douglas

Douglass, Frederick 1817(?)-1895 ..... **BLC 1; NCLC 7, 55; WLC**
See also AAYA 48; AFAW 1, 2; AMWC 1; AMWS 3; CDALB 1640-1865; DA; DA3; DAC; DAM MST, MULT; DLB 1, 43, 50, 79, 243; FW; LAIT 2; NCFS 2; RGAL 4; SATA 29

Dourado, (Waldomiro Freitas) Autran
1926- .... **CLC 23, 60**
See also CA 25-28R, 179; CANR 34, 81; DLB 145; HW 2

Dourado, Waldomiro Autran
See Dourado, (Waldomiro Freitas) Autran
See also CA 179

Dove, Rita (Frances) 1952- . **BLCS; CLC 50, 81; PC 6**
See also AAYA 46; AMWS 4; BW 2; CA 109; CAAS 19; CANR 27, 42, 68, 76, 97; CDALBS; CP 7; CSW; CWP; DA3; DAM MULT, POET; DLB 120; EWL 3; EXPP; MTCW 1; PFS 1, 15; RGAL 4

Doveglion
See Villa, Jose Garcia

Dowell, Coleman 1925-1985 .... **CLC 60**
See also CA 25-28R; 117; CANR 10; DLB 130; GLL 2

Dowson, Ernest (Christopher)
1867-1900 .... **TCLC 4**
See also CA 105; 150; DLB 19, 135; RGEL 2

Doyle, A. Conan
See Doyle, Sir Arthur Conan

Doyle, Sir Arthur Conan
1859-1930 .... **SSC 12; TCLC 7; WLC**
See Conan Doyle, Arthur
See also AAYA 14; BRWS 2; CA 104; 122; CDBLB 1890-1914; CMW 4; DA; DA3; DAB; DAC; DAM MST, NOV; DLB 18, 70, 156, 178; EXPS; HGG; LAIT 2; MSW; MTCW 1, 2; RGEL 2; RGSF 2; RHW; SATA 24; SCFW 2; SFW 4; SSFS 2; TEA; WCH; WLIT 4; WYA; YAW

Doyle, Conan
See Doyle, Sir Arthur Conan

Doyle, John
See Graves, Robert (von Ranke)

Doyle, Roddy 1958(?)- .... **CLC 81, 178**
See also AAYA 14; BRWS 5; CA 143; CANR 73; CN 7; DA3; DLB 194

Doyle, Sir A. Conan
See Doyle, Sir Arthur Conan

Dr. A
See Asimov, Isaac; Silverstein, Alvin; Silverstein, Virginia B(arbara Opshelor)

Drabble, Margaret 1939- ...... **CLC 2, 3, 5, 8, 10, 22, 53, 129**
See also BRWS 4; CA 13-16R; CANR 18, 35, 63, 112; CDBLB 1960 to Present; CN 7; CPW; DA3; DAB; DAC; DAM MST, NOV, POP; DLB 14, 155, 231; EWL 3; FW; MTCW 1, 2; RGEL 2; SATA 48; TEA

Drakulic, Slavenka 1949- .... **CLC 173**
See also CA 144; CANR 92

Drakulic-Ilic, Slavenka
See Drakulic, Slavenka

Drapier, M. B.
See Swift, Jonathan

Drayham, James
See Mencken, H(enry) L(ouis)

Drayton, Michael 1563-1631 .... **LC 8**
See also DAM POET; DLB 121; RGEL 2

Dreadstone, Carl
See Campbell, (John) Ramsey

Dreiser, Theodore (Herman Albert)
1871-1945 .... **SSC 30; TCLC 10, 18, 35, 83; WLC**
See also AMW; AMWR 2; CA 106; 132; CDALB 1865-1917; DA; DA3; DAC; DAM MST, NOV; DLB 9, 12, 102, 137; DLBD 1; EWL 3; LAIT 2; LMFS 2; MTCW 1, 2; NFS 17; RGAL 4; TUS

Drexler, Rosalyn 1926- .... **CLC 2, 6**
See also CA 81-84; CAD; CANR 68; CD 5; CWD

Dyer, George 1755-1841 .... **NCLC 129**
   See also DLB 93

Dylan, Bob 1941- .... **CLC 3, 4, 6, 12, 77; PC 37**
   See also CA 41-44R; CANR 108; CP 7; DLB 16

Dyson, John 1943- .... **CLC 70**
   See also CA 144

Dzyubin, Eduard Georgievich 1895-1934
   See Bagritsky, Eduard
   See also CA 170

E. V. L.
   See Lucas, E(dward) V(errall)

Eagleton, Terence (Francis) 1943- .. **CLC 63, 132**
   See also CA 57-60; CANR 7, 23, 68, 115; DLB 242; LMFS 2; MTCW 1, 2

Eagleton, Terry
   See Eagleton, Terence (Francis)

Early, Jack
   See Scoppettone, Sandra
   See also GLL 1

East, Michael
   See West, Morris L(anglo)

Eastaway, Edward
   See Thomas, (Philip) Edward

Eastlake, William (Derry)
   1917-1997 .... **CLC 8**
   See also CA 5-8R; 158; CAAS 1; CANR 5, 63; CN 7; DLB 6, 206; INT CANR-5; TCWW 2

Eastman, Charles A(lexander)
   1858-1939 .... **NNAL; TCLC 55**
   See also CA 179; CANR 91; DAM MULT; DLB 175; YABC 1

Eaton, Edith Maude 1865-1914 .... **AAL**
   See Far, Sui Sin
   See also CA 154; DLB 221; FW

Eaton, Winnifred 1875-1954 .... **AAL**
   See also DLB 221; RGAL 4

Eberhart, Richard (Ghormley)
   1904- .... **CLC 3, 11, 19, 56**
   See also AMW; CA 1-4R; CANR 2; CDALB 1941-1968; CP 7; DAM POET; DLB 48; MTCW 1; RGAL 4

Eberstadt, Fernanda 1960- .... **CLC 39**
   See also CA 136; CANR 69

Echegaray (y Eizaguirre), Jose (Maria Waldo) 1832-1916 .... **HLCS 1; TCLC 4**
   See also CA 104; CANR 32; EWL 3; HW 1; MTCW 1

Echeverria, (Jose) Esteban (Antonino)
   1805-1851 .... **NCLC 18**
   See also LAW

Echo
   See Proust, (Valentin-Louis-George-Eugene) Marcel

Eckert, Allan W. 1931- .... **CLC 17**
   See also AAYA 18; BYA 2; CA 13-16R; CANR 14, 45; INT CANR-14; MAICYA 2; MAICYAS 1; SAAS 21; SATA 29, 91; SATA-Brief 27

Eckhart, Meister 1260(?)-1327(?) ... **CMLC 9**
   See also DLB 115; LMFS 1

Eckmar, F. R.
   See de Hartog, Jan

Eco, Umberto 1932- .... **CLC 28, 60, 142**
   See also BEST 90:1; BPFB 1; CA 77-80; CANR 12, 33, 55, 110; CPW; CWW 2; DA3; DAM NOV, POP; DLB 196, 242; EWL 3; MSW; MTCW 1, 2; RGWL 3

Eddison, E(ric) R(ucker)
   1882-1945 .... **TCLC 15**
   See also CA 109; 156; DLB 255; FANT; SFW 4; SUFW 1

Eddy, Mary (Ann Morse) Baker
   1821-1910 .... **TCLC 71**
   See also CA 113; 174

Edel, (Joseph) Leon 1907-1997 .. **CLC 29, 34**
   See also CA 1-4R; 161; CANR 1, 22, 112; DLB 103; INT CANR-22

Eden, Emily 1797-1869 .... **NCLC 10**

Edgar, David 1948- .... **CLC 42**
   See also CA 57-60; CANR 12, 61, 112; CBD; CD 5; DAM DRAM; DFS 15; DLB 13, 233; MTCW 1

Edgerton, Clyde (Carlyle) 1944- ...... **CLC 39**
   See also AAYA 17; CA 118; 134; CANR 64; CSW; DLB 278; INT 134; YAW

Edgeworth, Maria 1768-1849 .... **NCLC 1, 51**
   See also BRWS 3; DLB 116, 159, 163; FW; RGEL 2; SATA 21; TEA; WLIT 3

Edmonds, Paul
   See Kuttner, Henry

Edmonds, Walter D(umaux)
   1903-1998 .... **CLC 35**
   See also BYA 2; CA 5-8R; CANR 2; CWRI 5; DLB 9; LAIT 1; MAICYA 1, 2; RHW; SAAS 4; SATA 1, 27; SATA-Obit 99

Edmondson, Wallace
   See Ellison, Harlan (Jay)

Edson, Russell 1935- .... **CLC 13**
   See also CA 33-36R; CANR 115; DLB 244; WP

Edwards, Bronwen Elizabeth
   See Rose, Wendy

Edwards, G(erald) B(asil)
   1899-1976 .... **CLC 25**
   See also CA 201; 110

Edwards, Gus 1939- .... **CLC 43**
   See also CA 108; INT 108

Edwards, Jonathan 1703-1758 .... **LC 7, 54**
   See also AMW; DA; DAC; DAM MST; DLB 24, 270; RGAL 4; TUS

Edwards, Sarah Pierpont 1710-1758 .. **LC 87**
   See also DLB 200

Efron, Marina Ivanovna Tsvetaeva
   See Tsvetaeva (Efron), Marina (Ivanovna)

Egoyan, Atom 1960- .... **CLC 151**
   See also CA 157

Ehle, John (Marsden, Jr.) 1925- ...... **CLC 27**
   See also CA 9-12R; CSW

Ehrenbourg, Ilya (Grigoryevich)
   See Ehrenburg, Ilya (Grigoryevich)

Ehrenburg, Ilya (Grigoryevich)
   1891-1967 .... **CLC 18, 34, 62**
   See Erenburg, Il'ia Grigor'evich
   See also CA 102; 25-28R; EWL 3

Ehrenburg, Ilyo (Grigoryevich)
   See Ehrenburg, Ilya (Grigoryevich)

Ehrenreich, Barbara 1941- .... **CLC 110**
   See also BEST 90:4; CA 73-76; CANR 16, 37, 62, 117; DLB 246; FW; MTCW 1, 2

Eich, Gunter
   See Eich, Gunter
   See also RGWL 2, 3

Eich, Gunter 1907-1972 .... **CLC 15**
   See Eich, Gunter
   See also CA 111; 93-96; DLB 69, 124; EWL 3

Eichendorff, Joseph 1788-1857 .... **NCLC 8**
   See also DLB 90; RGWL 2, 3

Eigner, Larry .... **CLC 9**
   See Eigner, Laurence (Joel)
   See also CAAS 23; DLB 5; WP

Eigner, Laurence (Joel) 1927-1996
   See Eigner, Larry
   See also CA 9-12R; 151; CANR 6, 84; CP 7; DLB 193

Einhard c. 770-840 .... **CMLC 50**
   See also DLB 148

Einstein, Albert 1879-1955 .... **TCLC 65**
   See also CA 121; 133; MTCW 1, 2

Eiseley, Loren
   See Eiseley, Loren Corey
   See also DLB 275

Eiseley, Loren Corey 1907-1977 .... **CLC 7**
   See Eiseley, Loren
   See also AAYA 5; ANW; CA 1-4R; 73-76; CANR 6; DLBD 17

Eisenstadt, Jill 1963- .... **CLC 50**
   See also CA 140

Eisenstein, Sergei (Mikhailovich)
   1898-1948 .... **TCLC 57**
   See also CA 114; 149

Eisner, Simon
   See Kornbluth, C(yril) M.

Ekeloef, (Bengt) Gunnar
   1907-1968 .... **CLC 27; PC 23**
   See Ekelof, (Bengt) Gunnar
   See also CA 123; 25-28R; DAM POET

Ekelof, (Bengt) Gunnar 1907-1968
   See Ekeloef, (Bengt) Gunnar
   See also DLB 259; EW 12; EWL 3

Ekelund, Vilhelm 1880-1949 .... **TCLC 75**
   See also CA 189; EWL 3

Ekwensi, C. O. D.
   See Ekwensi, Cyprian (Odiatu Duaka)

Ekwensi, Cyprian (Odiatu Duaka)
   1921- .... **BLC 1; CLC 4**
   See also AFW; BW 2, 3; CA 29-32R; CANR 18, 42, 74; CDWLB 3; CN 7; CWRI 5; DAM MULT; DLB 117; EWL 3; MTCW 1, 2; RGEL 2; SATA 66; WLIT 2

Elaine .... **TCLC 18**
   See Leverson, Ada Esther

El Crummo
   See Crumb, R(obert)

Elder, Lonne III 1931-1996 ..... **BLC 1; DC 8**
   See also BW 1, 3; CA 81-84; 152; CAD; CANR 25; DAM MULT; DLB 7, 38, 44

Eleanor of Aquitaine 1122-1204 ... **CMLC 39**

Elia
   See Lamb, Charles

Eliade, Mircea 1907-1986 .... **CLC 19**
   See also CA 65-68; 119; CANR 30, 62; CD-WLB 4; DLB 220; EWL 3; MTCW 1; RGWL 3; SFW 4

Eliot, A. D.
   See Jewett, (Theodora) Sarah Orne

Eliot, Alice
   See Jewett, (Theodora) Sarah Orne

Eliot, Dan
   See Silverberg, Robert

Eliot, George 1819-1880 ...... **NCLC 4, 13, 23, 41, 49, 89, 118; PC 20; WLC**
   See also BRW 5; BRWC 1; BRWR 2; CD-BLB 1832-1890; CN 7; CPW; DA; DA3; DAB; DAC; DAM MST, NOV; DLB 21, 35, 55; LATS 1; LMFS 1; NFS 17; RGEL 2; RGSF 2; SSFS 8; TEA; WLIT 3

Eliot, John 1604-1690 .... **LC 5**
   See also DLB 24

Eliot, T(homas) S(tearns)
   1888-1965 ...... **CLC 1, 2, 3, 6, 9, 10, 13, 15, 24, 34, 41, 55, 57, 113; PC 5, 31; WLC**
   See also AAYA 28; AMW; AMWC 1; AMWR 1; BRW 7; BRWR 2; CA 5-8R; 25-28R; CANR 41; CDALB 1929-1941; DA; DA3; DAB; DAC; DAM DRAM, MST, POET; DFS 4, 13; DLB 7, 10, 45, 63, 245; DLBY 1988; EWL 3; EXPP; LAIT 3; LATS 1; LMFS 2; MTCW 1, 2; NCFS 5; PAB; PFS 1, 7; RGAL 4; RGEL 2; TUS; WLIT 4; WP

Elizabeth 1866-1941 .... **TCLC 41**

Elkin, Stanley L(awrence)
   1930-1995 .. **CLC 4, 6, 9, 14, 27, 51, 91; SSC 12**
   See also AMWS 6; BPFB 1; CA 9-12R; 148; CANR 8, 46; CN 7; CPW; DAM NOV, POP; DLB 2, 28, 218, 278; DLBY 1980; EWL 3; INT CANR-8; MTCW 1, 2; RGAL 4

Evans, Evan
See Faust, Frederick (Schiller)
See also TCWW 2
Evans, Marian
See Eliot, George
Evans, Mary Ann
See Eliot, George
Evarts, Esther
See Benson, Sally
Everett, Percival
See Everett, Percival L.
See also CSW
Everett, Percival L. 1956- .... CLC 57
See Everett, Percival
See also BW 2; CA 129; CANR 94
Everson, R(onald) G(ilmour)
1903-1992 .... **CLC 27**
See also CA 17-20R; DLB 88
Everson, William (Oliver)
1912-1994 .... **CLC 1, 5, 14**
See also BG 2; CA 9-12R; 145; CANR 20;
DLB 5, 16, 212; MTCW 1
Evtushenko, Evgenii Aleksandrovich
See Yevtushenko, Yevgeny (Alexandrovich)
See also RGWL 2, 3
Ewart, Gavin (Buchanan)
1916-1995 .... **CLC 13, 46**
See also BRWS 7; CA 89-92; 150; CANR
17, 46; CP 7; DLB 40; MTCW 1
Ewers, Hanns Heinz 1871-1943 ..... **TCLC 12**
See also CA 109; 149
Ewing, Frederick R.
See Sturgeon, Theodore (Hamilton)
Exley, Frederick (Earl) 1929-1992 .... **CLC 6,
11**
See also AITN 2; BPFB 1; CA 81-84; 138;
CANR 117; DLB 143; DLBY 1981
Eynhardt, Guillermo
See Quiroga, Horacio (Sylvestre)
Ezekiel, Nissim 1924- .... **CLC 61**
See also CA 61-64; CP 7; EWL 3
Ezekiel, Tish O'Dowd 1943- .... **CLC 34**
See also CA 129
Fadeev, Aleksandr Aleksandrovich
See Bulgya, Alexander Alexandrovich
See also DLB 272
Fadeev, Alexandr Alexandrovich
See Bulgya, Alexander Alexandrovich
See also EWL 3
Fadeyev, A.
See Bulgya, Alexander Alexandrovich
Fadeyev, Alexander .... **TCLC 53**
See Bulgya, Alexander Alexandrovich
Fagen, Donald 1948- .... **CLC 26**
Fainzilberg, Ilya Arnoldovich 1897-1937
See Ilf, Ilya
See also CA 120; 165
Fair, Ronald L. 1932- .... **CLC 18**
See also BW 1; CA 69-72; CANR 25; DLB
33
Fairbairn, Roger
See Carr, John Dickson
Fairbairns, Zoe (Ann) 1948- .... **CLC 32**
See also CA 103; CANR 21, 85; CN 7
Fairfield, Flora
See Alcott, Louisa May
Fairman, Paul W. 1916-1977
See Queen, Ellery
See also CA 114; SFW 4
Falco, Gian
See Papini, Giovanni
Falconer, James
See Kirkup, James
Falconer, Kenneth
See Kornbluth, C(yril) M.
Falkland, Samuel
See Heijermans, Herman

Fallaci, Oriana 1930- .... **CLC 11, 110**
See also CA 77-80; CANR 15, 58; FW;
MTCW 1
Faludi, Susan 1959- .... **CLC 140**
See also CA 138; FW; MTCW 1; NCFS 3
Faludy, George 1913- .... **CLC 42**
See also CA 21-24R
Faludy, Gyoergy
See Faludy, George
Fanon, Frantz 1925-1961 .... **BLC 2; CLC 74**
See also BW 1; CA 116; 89-92; DAM
MULT; LMFS 2; WLIT 2
Fanshawe, Ann 1625-1680 .... **LC 11**
Fante, John (Thomas) 1911-1983 ..... **CLC 60**
See also AMWS 11; CA 69-72; 109; CANR
23, 104; DLB 130; DLBY 1983
Far, Sui Sin .... **SSC 62**
See Eaton, Edith Maude
See also SSFS 4
Farah, Nuruddin 1945- ...... **BLC 2; CLC 53,
137**
See also AFW; BW 2, 3; CA 106; CANR
81; CDWLB 3; CN 7; DAM MULT; DLB
125; EWL 3; WLIT 2
Fargue, Leon-Paul 1876(?)-1947 .... **TCLC 11**
See also CA 109; CANR 107; DLB 258;
EWL 3
Farigoule, Louis
See Romains, Jules
Farina, Richard 1936(?)-1966 .... **CLC 9**
See also CA 81-84; 25-28R
Farley, Walter (Lorimer)
1915-1989 .... **CLC 17**
See also BYA 14; CA 17-20R; CANR 8,
29, 84; DLB 22; JRDA; MAICYA 1, 2;
SATA 2, 43, 132; YAW
Farmer, Philip Jose 1918- .... **CLC 1, 19**
See also AAYA 28; BPFB 1; CA 1-4R;
CANR 4, 35, 111; DLB 8; MTCW 1;
SATA 93; SCFW 2; SFW 4
Farquhar, George 1677-1707 .... **LC 21**
See also BRW 2; DAM DRAM; DLB 84;
RGEL 2
Farrell, J(ames) G(ordon)
1935-1979 .... **CLC 6**
See also CA 73-76; 89-92; CANR 36; DLB
14, 271; MTCW 1; RGEL 2; RHW; WLIT
4
Farrell, James T(homas) 1904-1979 . **CLC 1,
4, 8, 11, 66; SSC 28**
See also AMW; BPFB 1; CA 5-8R; 89-92;
CANR 9, 61; DLB 4, 9, 86; DLBD 2;
EWL 3; MTCW 1, 2; RGAL 4
Farrell, Warren (Thomas) 1943- ...... **CLC 70**
See also CA 146; CANR 120
Farren, Richard J.
See Betjeman, John
Farren, Richard M.
See Betjeman, John
Fassbinder, Rainer Werner
1946-1982 .... **CLC 20**
See also CA 93-96; 106; CANR 31
Fast, Howard (Melvin) 1914-2003 .. **CLC 23,
131**
See also AAYA 16; BPFB 1; CA 1-4R, 181;
214; CAAE 181; CAAS 18; CANR 1, 33,
54, 75, 98; CMW 4; CN 7; CPW; DAM
NOV; DLB 9; INT CANR-33; LATS 1;
MTCW 1; RHW; SATA 7; SATA-Essay
107; TCWW 2; YAW
Faulcon, Robert
See Holdstock, Robert P.
Faulkner, William (Cuthbert)
1897-1962 .... **CLC 1, 3, 6, 8, 9, 11, 14,
18, 28, 52, 68; SSC 1, 35, 42; TCLC
141; WLC**
See also AAYA 7; AMW; AMWR 1; BPFB
1; BYA 5; CA 81-84; CANR 33; CDALB
1929-1941; DA; DA3; DAB; DAC; DAM

MST, NOV; DLB 9, 11, 44, 102; DLBD
2; DLBY 1986, 1997; EWL 3; EXPN;
EXPS; LAIT 2; LATS 1; LMFS 2; MTCW
1, 2; NFS 4, 8, 13; RGAL 4; RGSF 2;
SSFS 2, 5, 6, 12; TUS
Fauset, Jessie Redmon
1882(?)-1961 .. **BLC 2; CLC 19, 54; HR
2**
See also AFAW 2; BW 1; CA 109; CANR
83; DAM MULT; DLB 51; FW; LMFS 2;
MAWW
Faust, Frederick (Schiller)
1892-1944(?) .... **TCLC 49**
See Austin, Frank; Brand, Max; Challis,
George; Dawson, Peter; Dexter, Martin;
Evans, Evan; Frederick, John; Frost, Fred-
erick; Manning, David; Silver, Nicholas
See also CA 108; 152; DAM POP; DLB
256; TUS
Faust, Irvin 1924- .... **CLC 8**
See also CA 33-36R; CANR 28, 67; CN 7;
DLB 2, 28, 218, 278; DLBY 1980
Faustino, Domingo 1811-1888 ...... **NCLC 123**
Fawkes, Guy
See Benchley, Robert (Charles)
Fearing, Kenneth (Flexner)
1902-1961 .... **CLC 51**
See also CA 93-96; CANR 59; CMW 4;
DLB 9; RGAL 4
Fecamps, Elise
See Creasey, John
Federman, Raymond 1928- .... **CLC 6, 47**
See also CA 17-20R; CAAE 208; CAAS 8;
CANR 10, 43, 83, 108; CN 7; DLBY
1980
Federspiel, J(uerg) F. 1931- .... **CLC 42**
See also CA 146
Feiffer, Jules (Ralph) 1929- ...... **CLC 2, 8, 64**
See also AAYA 3; CA 17-20R; CAD; CANR
30, 59; CD 5; DAM DRAM; DLB 7, 44;
INT CANR-30; MTCW 1; SATA 8, 61,
111
Feige, Hermann Albert Otto Maximilian
See Traven, B.
Feinberg, David B. 1956-1994 .... **CLC 59**
See also CA 135; 147
Feinstein, Elaine 1930- .... **CLC 36**
See also CA 69-72; CAAS 1; CANR 31,
68, 121; CN 7; CP 7; CWP; DLB 14, 40;
MTCW 1
Feke, Gilbert David .... **CLC 65**
Feldman, Irving (Mordecai) 1928- ..... **CLC 7**
See also CA 1-4R; CANR 1; CP 7; DLB
169
Felix-Tchicaya, Gerald
See Tchicaya, Gerald Felix
Fellini, Federico 1920-1993 .... **CLC 16, 85**
See also CA 65-68; 143; CANR 33
Felltham, Owen 1602(?)-1668 .... **LC 92**
See also DLB 126, 151
Felsen, Henry Gregor 1916-1995 ..... **CLC 17**
See also CA 1-4R; 180; CANR 1; SAAS 2;
SATA 1
Felski, Rita .... **CLC 65**
Fenno, Jack
See Calisher, Hortense
Fenollosa, Ernest (Francisco)
1853-1908 .... **TCLC 91**
Fenton, James Martin 1949- .... **CLC 32**
See also CA 102; CANR 108; CP 7; DLB
40; PFS 11
Ferber, Edna 1887-1968 .... **CLC 18, 93**
See also AITN 1; CA 5-8R; 25-28R; CANR
68, 105; DLB 9, 28, 86, 266; MTCW 1,
2; RGAL 4; RHW; SATA 7; TCWW 2
Ferdowsi, Abu'l Qasem 940-1020 . **CMLC 43**
See also RGWL 2, 3
Ferguson, Helen
See Kavan, Anna

Foote, Horton 1916- .... **CLC 51, 91**
See also CA 73-76; CAD; CANR 34, 51, 110; CD 5; CSW; DA3; DAM DRAM; DLB 26, 266; EWL 3; INT CANR-34

Foote, Mary Hallock 1847-1938 .. **TCLC 108**
See also DLB 186, 188, 202, 221

Foote, Shelby 1916- .... **CLC 75**
See also AAYA 40; CA 5-8R; CANR 3, 45, 74; CN 7; CPW; CSW; DA3; DAM NOV, POP; DLB 2, 17; MTCW 2; RHW

Forbes, Cosmo
See Lewton, Val

Forbes, Esther 1891-1967 .... **CLC 12**
See also AAYA 17; BYA 2; CA 13-14; 25-28R; CAP 1; CLR 27; DLB 22; JRDA; MAICYA 1, 2; RHW; SATA 2, 100; YAW

Forche, Carolyn (Louise) 1950- .... **CLC 25, 83, 86; PC 10**
See also CA 109; 117; CANR 50, 74; CP 7; CWP; DA3; DAM POET; DLB 5, 193; INT CA-117; MTCW 1; PFS 18; RGAL 4

Ford, Elbur
See Hibbert, Eleanor Alice Burford

Ford, Ford Madox 1873-1939 ... **TCLC 1, 15, 39, 57**
See Chaucer, Daniel
See also BRW 6; CA 104; 132; CANR 74; CDBLB 1914-1945; DA3; DAM NOV; DLB 34, 98, 162; EWL 3; MTCW 1, 2; RGEL 2; TEA

Ford, Henry 1863-1947 .... **TCLC 73**
See also CA 115; 148

Ford, Jack
See Ford, John

Ford, John 1586-1639 .... **DC 8; LC 68**
See also BRW 2; CDBLB Before 1660; DA3; DAM DRAM; DFS 7; DLB 58; IDTP; RGEL 2

Ford, John 1895-1973 .... **CLC 16**
See also CA 187; 45-48

Ford, Richard 1944- .... **CLC 46, 99**
See also AMWS 5; CA 69-72; CANR 11, 47, 86; CN 7; CSW; DLB 227; EWL 3; MTCW 1; RGAL 4; RGSF 2

Ford, Webster
See Masters, Edgar Lee

Foreman, Richard 1937- .... **CLC 50**
See also CA 65-68; CAD; CANR 32, 63; CD 5

Forester, C(ecil) S(cott) 1899-1966 ... **CLC 35**
See also CA 73-76; 25-28R; CANR 83; DLB 191; RGEL 2; RHW; SATA 13

Forez
See Mauriac, Francois (Charles)

Forman, James
See Forman, James D(ouglas)

Forman, James D(ouglas) 1932- .... **CLC 21**
See also AAYA 17; CA 9-12R; CANR 4, 19, 42; JRDA; MAICYA 1, 2; SATA 8, 70; YAW

Forman, Milos 1932- .... **CLC 164**
See also CA 109

Fornes, Maria Irene 1930- . **CLC 39, 61; DC 10; HLCS 1**
See also CA 25-28R; CAD; CANR 28, 81; CD 5; CWD; DLB 7; HW 1, 2; INT CANR-28; MTCW 1; RGAL 4

Forrest, Leon (Richard) 1937-1997 .... **BLCS; CLC 4**
See also AFAW 2; BW 2; CA 89-92; 162; CAAS 7; CANR 25, 52, 87; CN 7; DLB 33

Forster, E(dward) M(organ) 1879-1970 ...... **CLC 1, 2, 3, 4, 9, 10, 13, 15, 22, 45, 77; SSC 27; TCLC 125; WLC**
See also AAYA 2, 37; BRW 6; BRWR 2; CA 13-14; 25-28R; CANR 45; CAP 1; CDBLB 1914-1945; DA; DA3; DAB; DAC; DAM MST, NOV; DLB 34, 98, 162, 178, 195; DLBD 10; EWL 3; EXPN; LAIT 3; LMFS 1; MTCW 1, 2; NCFS 1; NFS 3, 10, 11; RGEL 2; RGSF 2; SATA 57; SUFW 1; TEA; WLIT 4

Forster, John 1812-1876 .... **NCLC 11**
See also DLB 144, 184

Forster, Margaret 1938- .... **CLC 149**
See also CA 133; CANR 62, 115; CN 7; DLB 155, 271

Forsyth, Frederick 1938- .... **CLC 2, 5, 36**
See also BEST 89:4; CA 85-88; CANR 38, 62, 115; CMW 4; CN 7; CPW; DAM NOV, POP; DLB 87; MTCW 1, 2

Forten, Charlotte L. 1837-1914 .... **BLC 2; TCLC 16**
See Grimke, Charlotte L(ottie) Forten
See also DLB 50, 239

Fortinbras
See Grieg, (Johan) Nordahl (Brun)

Foscolo, Ugo 1778-1827 .... **NCLC 8, 97**
See also EW 5

Fosse, Bob .... **CLC 20**
See Fosse, Robert Louis

Fosse, Robert Louis 1927-1987
See Fosse, Bob
See also CA 110; 123

Foster, Hannah Webster
1758-1840 .... **NCLC 99**
See also DLB 37, 200; RGAL 4

Foster, Stephen Collins
1826-1864 .... **NCLC 26**
See also RGAL 4

Foucault, Michel 1926-1984 . **CLC 31, 34, 69**
See also CA 105; 113; CANR 34; DLB 242; EW 13; EWL 3; GFL 1789 to the Present; GLL 1; LMFS 2; MTCW 1, 2; TWA

Fouque, Friedrich (Heinrich Karl) de la Motte 1777-1843 .... **NCLC 2**
See also DLB 90; RGWL 2, 3; SUFW 1

Fourier, Charles 1772-1837 .... **NCLC 51**

Fournier, Henri-Alban 1886-1914
See Alain-Fournier
See also CA 104; 179

Fournier, Pierre 1916- .... **CLC 11**
See Gascar, Pierre
See also CA 89-92; CANR 16, 40

Fowles, John (Robert) 1926- . **CLC 1, 2, 3, 4, 6, 9, 10, 15, 33, 87; SSC 33**
See also BPFB 1; BRWS 1; CA 5-8R; CANR 25, 71, 103; CDBLB 1960 to Present; CN 7; DA3; DAB; DAC; DAM MST; DLB 14, 139, 207; EWL 3; HGG; MTCW 1, 2; RGEL 2; RHW; SATA 22; TEA; WLIT 4

Fox, Paula 1923- .... **CLC 2, 8, 121**
See also AAYA 3, 37; BYA 3, 8; CA 73-76; CANR 20, 36, 62, 105; CLR 1, 44; DLB 52; JRDA; MAICYA 1, 2; MTCW 1; NFS 12; SATA 17, 60, 120; WYA; YAW

Fox, William Price (Jr.) 1926- .... **CLC 22**
See also CA 17-20R; CAAS 19; CANR 11; CSW; DLB 2; DLBY 1981

Foxe, John 1517(?)-1587 .... **LC 14**
See also DLB 132

Frame, Janet .. **CLC 2, 3, 6, 22, 66, 96; SSC 29**
See Clutha, Janet Paterson Frame
See also CN 7; CWP; EWL 3; RGEL 2; RGSF 2; TWA

France, Anatole .... **TCLC 9**
See Thibault, Jacques Anatole Francois
See also DLB 123; EWL 3; GFL 1789 to the Present; MTCW 1; RGWL 2, 3; SUFW 1

Francis, Claude .... **CLC 50**
See also CA 192

Francis, Dick 1920- .... **CLC 2, 22, 42, 102**
See also AAYA 5, 21; BEST 89:3; BPFB 1; CA 5-8R; CANR 9, 42, 68, 100; CDBLB 1960 to Present; CMW 4; CN 7; DA3; DAM POP; DLB 87; INT CANR-9; MSW; MTCW 1, 2

Francis, Robert (Churchill)
1901-1987 .... **CLC 15; PC 34**
See also AMWS 9; CA 1-4R; 123; CANR 1; EXPP; PFS 12

Francis, Lord Jeffrey
See Jeffrey, Francis
See also DLB 107

Frank, Anne(lies Marie)
1929-1945 .... **TCLC 17; WLC**
See also AAYA 12; BYA 1; CA 113; 133; CANR 68; DA; DA3; DAB; DAC; DAM MST; LAIT 4; MAICYA 2; MAICYAS 1; MTCW 1, 2; NCFS 2; SATA 87; SATA-Brief 42; WYA; YAW

Frank, Bruno 1887-1945 .... **TCLC 81**
See also CA 189; DLB 118; EWL 3

Frank, Elizabeth 1945- .... **CLC 39**
See also CA 121; 126; CANR 78; INT 126

Frankl, Viktor E(mil) 1905-1997 ...... **CLC 93**
See also CA 65-68; 161

Franklin, Benjamin
See Hasek, Jaroslav (Matej Frantisek)

Franklin, Benjamin 1706-1790 .... **LC 25; WLCS**
See also AMW; CDALB 1640-1865; DA; DA3; DAB; DAC; DAM MST; DLB 24, 43, 73, 183; LAIT 1; RGAL 4; TUS

Franklin, (Stella Maria Sarah) Miles (Lampe) 1879-1954 .... **TCLC 7**
See also CA 104; 164; DLB 230; FW; MTCW 2; RGEL 2; TWA

Fraser, Antonia (Pakenham) 1932- . **CLC 32, 107**
See also CA 85-88; CANR 44, 65, 119; CMW; DLB 276; MTCW 1, 2; SATA-Brief 32

Fraser, George MacDonald 1925- ...... **CLC 7**
See also AAYA 48; CA 45-48, 180; CAAE 180; CANR 2, 48, 74; MTCW 1; RHW

Fraser, Sylvia 1935- .... **CLC 64**
See also CA 45-48; CANR 1, 16, 60; CCA 1

Frayn, Michael 1933- . **CLC 3, 7, 31, 47, 176**
See also BRWS 7; CA 5-8R; CANR 30, 69, 114; CBD; CD 5; CN 7; DAM DRAM, NOV; DLB 13, 14, 194, 245; FANT; MTCW 1, 2; SFW 4

Fraze, Candida (Merrill) 1945- .... **CLC 50**
See also CA 126

Frazer, Andrew
See Marlowe, Stephen

Frazer, J(ames) G(eorge)
1854-1941 .... **TCLC 32**
See also BRWS 3; CA 118; NCFS 5

Frazer, Robert Caine
See Creasey, John

Frazer, Sir James George
See Frazer, J(ames) G(eorge)

Frazier, Charles 1950- .... **CLC 109**
See also AAYA 34; CA 161; CSW

Frazier, Ian 1951- .... **CLC 46**
See also CA 130; CANR 54, 93

Frederic, Harold 1856-1898 .... **NCLC 10**
See also AMW; DLB 12, 23; DLBD 13; RGAL 4

Frederick, John
See Faust, Frederick (Schiller)
See also TCWW 2

Frederick the Great 1712-1786 .... **LC 14**

Fredro, Aleksander 1793-1876 .... **NCLC 8**

Freeling, Nicolas 1927- .... **CLC 38**
See also CA 49-52; CAAS 12; CANR 1, 17, 50, 84; CMW 4; CN 7; DLB 87

Gerhardie, William Alexander
1895-1977 .... **CLC 5**
See also CA 25-28R; 73-76; CANR 18;
DLB 36; RGEL 2
Gerson, Jean 1363-1429 .... **LC 77**
See also DLB 208
Gersonides 1288-1344 .... **CMLC 49**
See also DLB 115
Gerstler, Amy 1956- .... **CLC 70**
See also CA 146; CANR 99
Gertler, T. .... **CLC 34**
See also CA 116; 121
Gertsen, Aleksandr Ivanovich
See Herzen, Aleksandr Ivanovich
Ghalib .... **NCLC 39, 78**
See Ghalib, Asadullah Khan
Ghalib, Asadullah Khan 1797-1869
See Ghalib
See also DAM POET; RGWL 2, 3
Ghelderode, Michel de 1898-1962 ..... **CLC 6, 11; DC 15**
See also CA 85-88; CANR 40, 77; DAM
DRAM; EW 11; EWL 3; TWA
Ghiselin, Brewster 1903-2001 .... **CLC 23**
See also CA 13-16R; CAAS 10; CANR 13;
CP 7
Ghose, Aurabinda 1872-1950 .... **TCLC 63**
See Ghose, Aurobindo
See also CA 163
Ghose, Aurobindo
See Ghose, Aurabinda
See also EWL 3
Ghose, Zulfikar 1935- .... **CLC 42**
See also CA 65-68; CANR 67; CN 7; CP 7;
EWL 3
Ghosh, Amitav 1956- .... **CLC 44, 153**
See also CA 147; CANR 80; CN 7
Giacosa, Giuseppe 1847-1906 .... **TCLC 7**
See also CA 104
Gibb, Lee
See Waterhouse, Keith (Spencer)
Gibbon, Lewis Grassic .... **TCLC 4**
See Mitchell, James Leslie
See also RGEL 2
Gibbons, Kaye 1960- .... **CLC 50, 88, 145**
See also AAYA 34; AMWS 10; CA 151;
CANR 75; CSW; DA3; DAM POP;
MTCW 1; NFS 3; RGAL 4; SATA 117
Gibran, Kahlil 1883-1931 . **PC 9; TCLC 1, 9**
See also CA 104; 150; DA3; DAM POET,
POP; EWL 3; MTCW 2
Gibran, Khalil
See Gibran, Kahlil
Gibson, William 1914- .... **CLC 23**
See also CA 9-12R; CAD 2; CANR 9, 42,
75; CD 5; DA; DAB; DAC; DAM
DRAM, MST; DFS 2; DLB 7; LAIT 2;
MTCW 2; SATA 66; YAW
Gibson, William (Ford) 1948- ... **CLC 39, 63; SSC 52**
See also AAYA 12; BPFB 2; CA 126; 133;
CANR 52, 90, 106; CN 7; CPW; DA3;
DAM POP; DLB 251; MTCW 2; SCFW
2; SFW 4
Gide, Andre (Paul Guillaume)
1869-1951 ..... **SSC 13; TCLC 5, 12, 36; WLC**
See also CA 104; 124; DA; DA3; DAB;
DAC; DAM MST, NOV; DLB 65; EW 8;
EWL 3; GFL 1789 to the Present; MTCW
1, 2; RGSF 2; RGWL 2, 3; TWA
Gifford, Barry (Colby) 1946- .... **CLC 34**
See also CA 65-68; CANR 9, 30, 40, 90
Gilbert, Frank
See De Voto, Bernard (Augustine)
Gilbert, W(illiam) S(chwenck)
1836-1911 .... **TCLC 3**
See also CA 104; 173; DAM DRAM, POET;
RGEL 2; SATA 36

Gilbreth, Frank B(unker), Jr.
1911-2001 .... **CLC 17**
See also CA 9-12R; SATA 2
Gilchrist, Ellen (Louise) 1935- .. **CLC 34, 48, 143; SSC 14, 63**
See also BPFB 2; CA 113; 116; CANR 41,
61, 104; CN 7; CPW; CSW; DAM POP;
DLB 130; EWL 3; EXPS; MTCW 1, 2;
RGAL 4; RGSF 2; SSFS 9
Giles, Molly 1942- .... **CLC 39**
See also CA 126; CANR 98
Gill, Eric 1882-1940 .... **TCLC 85**
See Gill, (Arthur) Eric (Rowton Peter
Joseph)
Gill, (Arthur) Eric (Rowton Peter Joseph)
1882-1940
See Gill, Eric
See also CA 120; DLB 98
Gill, Patrick
See Creasey, John
Gillette, Douglas .... **CLC 70**
Gilliam, Terry (Vance) 1940- .... **CLC 21, 141**
See Monty Python
See also AAYA 19; CA 108; 113; CANR
35; INT 113
Gillian, Jerry
See Gilliam, Terry (Vance)
Gilliatt, Penelope (Ann Douglass)
1932-1993 .... **CLC 2, 10, 13, 53**
See also AITN 2; CA 13-16R; 141; CANR
49; DLB 14
Gilman, Charlotte (Anna) Perkins (Stetson)
1860-1935 ...... **SSC 13, 62; TCLC 9, 37, 117**
See also AMWS 11; BYA 11; CA 106; 150;
DLB 221; EXPS; FW; HGG; LAIT 2;
MAWW; MTCW 1; RGAL 4; RGSF 2;
SFW 4; SSFS 1, 18
Gilmour, David 1946- .... **CLC 35**
Gilpin, William 1724-1804 .... **NCLC 30**
Gilray, J. D.
See Mencken, H(enry) L(ouis)
Gilroy, Frank D(aniel) 1925- .... **CLC 2**
See also CA 81-84; CAD; CANR 32, 64,
86; CD 5; DFS 17; DLB 7
Gilstrap, John 1957(?)- .... **CLC 99**
See also CA 160; CANR 101
Ginsberg, Allen 1926-1997 .... **CLC 1, 2, 3, 4, 6, 13, 36, 69, 109; PC 4, 47; TCLC 120; WLC**
See also AAYA 33; AITN 1; AMWC 1;
AMWS 2; BG 2; CA 1-4R; 157; CANR
2, 41, 63, 95; CDALB 1941-1968; CP 7;
DA; DA3; DAB; DAC; DAM MST,
POET; DLB 5, 16, 169, 237; EWL 3; GLL
1; LMFS 2; MTCW 1, 2; PAB; PFS 5;
RGAL 4; TUS; WP
Ginzburg, Eugenia .... **CLC 59**
Ginzburg, Natalia 1916-1991 .... **CLC 5, 11, 54, 70**
See also CA 85-88; 135; CANR 33; DFS
14; DLB 177; EW 13; EWL 3; MTCW 1,
2; RGWL 2, 3
Giono, Jean 1895-1970 .... **CLC 4, 11; TCLC 124**
See also CA 45-48; 29-32R; CANR 2, 35;
DLB 72; EWL 3; GFL 1789 to the
Present; MTCW 1; RGWL 2, 3
Giovanni, Nikki 1943- ...... **BLC 2; CLC 2, 4, 19, 64, 117; PC 19; WLCS**
See also AAYA 22; AITN 1; BW 2, 3; CA
29-32R; CAAS 6; CANR 18, 41, 60, 91;
CDALBS; CLR 6, 73; CP 7; CSW; CWP;
CWRI 5; DA; DA3; DAB; DAC; DAM
MST, MULT, POET; DLB 5, 41; EWL 3;
EXPP; INT CANR-18; MAICYA 1, 2;
MTCW 1, 2; PFS 17; RGAL 4; SATA 24,
107; TUS; YAW

Giovene, Andrea 1904-1998 .... **CLC 7**
See also CA 85-88
Gippius, Zinaida (Nikolaevna) 1869-1945
See Hippius, Zinaida
See also CA 106; 212
Giraudoux, Jean(-Hippolyte)
1882-1944 .... **TCLC 2, 7**
See also CA 104; 196; DAM DRAM; DLB
65; EW 9; EWL 3; GFL 1789 to the
Present; RGWL 2, 3; TWA
Gironella, Jose Maria (Pous)
1917-2003 .... **CLC 11**
See also CA 101; 212; EWL 3; RGWL 2, 3
Gissing, George (Robert)
1857-1903 .... **SSC 37; TCLC 3, 24, 47**
See also BRW 5; CA 105; 167; DLB 18,
135, 184; RGEL 2; TEA
Giurlani, Aldo
See Palazzeschi, Aldo
Gladkov, Fedor Vasil'evich
See Gladkov, Fyodor (Vasilyevich)
See also DLB 272
Gladkov, Fyodor (Vasilyevich)
1883-1958 .... **TCLC 27**
See Gladkov, Fedor Vasil'evich
See also CA 170; EWL 3
Glancy, Diane 1941- .... **NNAL**
See also CA 136; CAAS 24; CANR 87;
DLB 175
Glanville, Brian (Lester) 1931- .... **CLC 6**
See also CA 5-8R; CAAS 9; CANR 3, 70;
CN 7; DLB 15, 139; SATA 42
Glasgow, Ellen (Anderson Gholson)
1873-1945 .... **SSC 34; TCLC 2, 7**
See also AMW; CA 104; 164; DLB 9, 12;
MAWW; MTCW 2; RGAL 4; RHW;
SSFS 9; TUS
Glaspell, Susan 1882(?)-1948 ..... **DC 10; SSC 41; TCLC 55**
See also AMWS 3; CA 110; 154; DFS 8,
18; DLB 7, 9, 78, 228; MAWW; RGAL
4; SSFS 3; TCWW 2; TUS; YABC 2
Glassco, John 1909-1981 .... **CLC 9**
See also CA 13-16R; 102; CANR 15; DLB
68
Glasscock, Amnesia
See Steinbeck, John (Ernst)
Glasser, Ronald J. 1940(?)- .... **CLC 37**
See also CA 209
Glassman, Joyce
See Johnson, Joyce
Gleick, James (W.) 1954- .... **CLC 147**
See also CA 131; 137; CANR 97; INT CA-
137
Glendinning, Victoria 1937- .... **CLC 50**
See also CA 120; 127; CANR 59, 89; DLB
155
Glissant, Edouard (Mathieu)
1928- .... **CLC 10, 68**
See also CA 153; CANR 111; CWW 2;
DAM MULT; EWL 3; RGWL 3
Gloag, Julian 1930- .... **CLC 40**
See also AITN 1; CA 65-68; CANR 10, 70;
CN 7
Glowacki, Aleksander
See Prus, Boleslaw
Gluck, Louise (Elisabeth) 1943- .. **CLC 7, 22, 44, 81, 160; PC 16**
See also AMWS 5; CA 33-36R; CANR 40,
69, 108; CP 7; CWP; DA3; DAM POET;
DLB 5; MTCW 2; PFS 5, 15; RGAL 4
Glyn, Elinor 1864-1943 .... **TCLC 72**
See also DLB 153; RHW
Gobineau, Joseph-Arthur
1816-1882 .... **NCLC 17**
See also DLB 123; GFL 1789 to the Present
Godard, Jean-Luc 1930- .... **CLC 20**
See also CA 93-96

Godden, (Margaret) Rumer
1907-1998 .... **CLC 53**
See also AAYA 6; BPFB 2; BYA 2, 5; CA
5-8R; 172; CANR 4, 27, 36, 55, 80; CLR
20; CN 7; CWRI 5; DLB 161; MAICYA
1, 2; RHW; SAAS 12; SATA 3, 36; SATA-
Obit 109; TEA

Godoy Alcayaga, Lucila 1899-1957 .. **HLC 2;
PC 32; TCLC 2**
See Mistral, Gabriela
See also BW 2; CA 104; 131; CANR 81;
DAM MULT; DNFS; HW 1, 2; MTCW 1,
2

Godwin, Gail (Kathleen) 1937- ..... **CLC 5, 8,
22, 31, 69, 125**
See also BPFB 2; CA 29-32R; CANR 15,
43, 69; CN 7; CPW; CSW; DA3; DAM
POP; DLB 6, 234; INT CANR-15;
MTCW 1, 2

Godwin, William 1756-1836 .... **NCLC 14**
See also CDBLB 1789-1832; CMW 4; DLB
39, 104, 142, 158, 163, 262; HGG; RGEL
2

Goebbels, Josef
See Goebbels, (Paul) Joseph

Goebbels, (Paul) Joseph
1897-1945 .... **TCLC 68**
See also CA 115; 148

Goebbels, Joseph Paul
See Goebbels, (Paul) Joseph

Goethe, Johann Wolfgang von
1749-1832 .... **DC 20; NCLC 4, 22, 34,
90; PC 5; SSC 38; WLC**
See also CDWLB 2; DA; DA3; DAB;
DAC; DAM DRAM, MST, POET; DLB
94; EW 5; LATS 1; LMFS 1; RGWL 2,
3; TWA

Gogarty, Oliver St. John
1878-1957 .... **TCLC 15**
See also CA 109; 150; DLB 15, 19; RGEL
2

Gogol, Nikolai (Vasilyevich)
1809-1852 .... **DC 1; NCLC 5, 15, 31;
SSC 4, 29, 52; WLC**
See also DA; DAB; DAC; DAM DRAM,
MST; DFS 12; DLB 198; EW 6; EXPS;
RGSF 2; RGWL 2, 3; SSFS 7; TWA

Goines, Donald 1937(?)-1974 ... **BLC 2; CLC
80**
See also AITN 1; BW 1, 3; CA 124; 114;
CANR 82; CMW 4; DA3; DAM MULT;
POP; DLB 33

Gold, Herbert 1924- ... **CLC 4, 7, 14, 42, 152**
See also CA 9-12R; CANR 17, 45; CN 7;
DLB 2; DLBY 1981

Goldbarth, Albert 1948- .... **CLC 5, 38**
See also AMWS 12; CA 53-56; CANR 6,
40; CP 7; DLB 120

Goldberg, Anatol 1910-1982 .... **CLC 34**
See also CA 131; 117

Goldemberg, Isaac 1945- .... **CLC 52**
See also CA 69-72; CAAS 12; CANR 11,
32; EWL 3; WLIT 1

Golding, William (Gerald)
1911-1993 ..... **CLC 1, 2, 3, 8, 10, 17, 27,
58, 81; WLC**
See also AAYA 5, 44; BPFB 2; BRWR 1;
BRWS 1; BYA 2; CA 5-8R; 141; CANR
13, 33, 54; CDBLB 1945-1960; DA;
DA3; DAB; DAC; DAM MST, NOV;
DLB 15, 100, 255; EWL 3; EXPN; HGG;
LAIT 4; MTCW 1, 2; NFS 2; RGEL 2;
RHW; SFW 4; TEA; WLIT 4; YAW

Goldman, Emma 1869-1940 .... **TCLC 13**
See also CA 110; 150; DLB 221; FW;
RGAL 4; TUS

Goldman, Francisco 1954- .... **CLC 76**
See also CA 162

Goldman, William (W.) 1931- ...... **CLC 1, 48**
See also BPFB 2; CA 9-12R; CANR 29,
69, 106; CN 7; DLB 44; FANT; IDFW 3,
4

Goldmann, Lucien 1913-1970 .... **CLC 24**
See also CA 25-28; CAP 2

Goldoni, Carlo 1707-1793 .... **LC 4**
See also DAM DRAM; EW 4; RGWL 2, 3

Goldsberry, Steven 1949- .... **CLC 34**
See also CA 131

Goldsmith, Oliver 1730-1774 .... **DC 8; LC 2,
48; WLC**
See also BRW 3; CDBLB 1660-1789; DA;
DAB; DAC; DAM DRAM, MST, NOV,
POET; DFS 1; DLB 39, 89, 104, 109, 142;
IDTP; RGEL 2; SATA 26; TEA; WLIT 3

Goldsmith, Peter
See Priestley, J(ohn) B(oynton)

Gombrowicz, Witold 1904-1969 .... **CLC 4, 7,
11, 49**
See also CA 19-20; 25-28R; CANR 105;
CAP 2; CDWLB 4; DAM DRAM; DLB
215; EW 12; EWL 3; RGWL 2, 3; TWA

Gomez de Avellaneda, Gertrudis
1814-1873 .... **NCLC 111**
See also LAW

Gomez de la Serna, Ramon
1888-1963 .... **CLC 9**
See also CA 153; 116; CANR 79; EWL 3;
HW 1, 2

Goncharov, Ivan Alexandrovich
1812-1891 .... **NCLC 1, 63**
See also DLB 238; EW 6; RGWL 2, 3

Goncourt, Edmond (Louis Antoine Huot) de
1822-1896 .... **NCLC 7**
See also DLB 123; EW 7; GFL 1789 to the
Present; RGWL 2, 3

Goncourt, Jules (Alfred Huot) de
1830-1870 .... **NCLC 7**
See also DLB 123; EW 7; GFL 1789 to the
Present; RGWL 2, 3

Gongora (y Argote), Luis de
1561-1627 .... **LC 72**
See also RGWL 2, 3

Gontier, Fernande 19(?)- .... **CLC 50**

Gonzalez Martinez, Enrique
1871-1952 .... **TCLC 72**
See also CA 166; CANR 81; EWL 3; HW
1, 2

Goodison, Lorna 1947- .... **PC 36**
See also CA 142; CANR 88; CP 7; CWP;
DLB 157; EWL 3

Goodman, Paul 1911-1972 ..... **CLC 1, 2, 4, 7**
See also CA 19-20; 37-40R; CAD; CANR
34; CAP 2; DLB 130, 246; MTCW 1;
RGAL 4

Gordimer, Nadine 1923- ...... **CLC 3, 5, 7, 10,
18, 33, 51, 70, 123, 160, 161; SSC 17;
WLCS**
See also AAYA 39; AFW; BRWS 2; CA
5-8R; CANR 3, 28, 56, 88; CN 7; DA;
DA3; DAB; DAC; DAM MST, NOV;
DLB 225; EWL 3; EXPS; INT CANR-28;
LATS 1; MTCW 1, 2; NFS 4; RGEL 2;
RGSF 2; SSFS 2, 14; TWA; WLIT 2;
YAW

Gordon, Adam Lindsay
1833-1870 .... **NCLC 21**
See also DLB 230

Gordon, Caroline 1895-1981 . **CLC 6, 13, 29,
83; SSC 15**
See also AMW; CA 11-12; 103; CANR 36;
CAP 1; DLB 4, 9, 102; DLBD 17; DLBY
1981; EWL 3; MTCW 1, 2; RGAL 4;
RGSF 2

Gordon, Charles William 1860-1937
See Connor, Ralph
See also CA 109

Gordon, Mary (Catherine) 1949- .... **CLC 13,
22, 128; SSC 59**
See also AMWS 4; BPFB 2; CA 102;
CANR 44, 92; CN 7; DLB 6; DLBY
1981; FW; INT CA-102; MTCW 1

Gordon, N. J.
See Bosman, Herman Charles

Gordon, Sol 1923- .... **CLC 26**
See also CA 53-56; CANR 4; SATA 11

Gordone, Charles 1925-1995 .. **CLC 1, 4; DC
8**
See also BW 1, 3; CA 93-96, 180; 150;
CAAE 180; CAD; CANR 55; DAM
DRAM; DLB 7; INT 93-96; MTCW 1

Gore, Catherine 1800-1861 .... **NCLC 65**
See also DLB 116; RGEL 2

Gorenko, Anna Andreevna
See Akhmatova, Anna

Gorky, Maxim .... **SSC 28; TCLC 8; WLC**
See Peshkov, Alexei Maximovich
See also DAB; DFS 9; EW 8; EWL 3;
MTCW 2; TWA

Goryan, Sirak
See Saroyan, William

Gosse, Edmund (William)
1849-1928 .... **TCLC 28**
See also CA 117; DLB 57, 144, 184; RGEL
2

Gotlieb, Phyllis Fay (Bloom) 1926- .. **CLC 18**
See also CA 13-16R; CANR 7; DLB 88,
251; SFW 4

Gottesman, S. D.
See Kornbluth, C(yril) M.; Pohl, Frederik

Gottfried von Strassburg fl. c.
1170-1215 .... **CMLC 10**
See also CDWLB 2; DLB 138; EW 1;
RGWL 2, 3

Gotthelf, Jeremias 1797-1854 .... **NCLC 117**
See also DLB 133; RGWL 2, 3

Gottschalk, Laura Riding
See Jackson, Laura (Riding)

Gould, Lois 1932(?)-2002 .... **CLC 4, 10**
See also CA 77-80; 208; CANR 29; MTCW
1

Gould, Stephen Jay 1941-2002 .... **CLC 163**
See also AAYA 26; BEST 90:2; CA 77-80;
205; CANR 10, 27, 56, 75; CPW; INT
CANR-27; MTCW 1, 2

Gourmont, Remy(-Marie-Charles) de
1858-1915 .... **TCLC 17**
See also CA 109; 150; GFL 1789 to the
Present; MTCW 2

Govier, Katherine 1948- .... **CLC 51**
See also CA 101; CANR 18, 40; CCA 1

Gower, John c. 1330-1408 .... **LC 76**
See also BRW 1; DLB 146; RGEL 2

Goyen, (Charles) William
1915-1983 .... **CLC 5, 8, 14, 40**
See also AITN 2; CA 5-8R; 110; CANR 6,
71; DLB 2, 218; DLBY 1983; EWL 3;
INT CANR-6

Goytisolo, Juan 1931- .... **CLC 5, 10, 23, 133;
HLC 1**
See also CA 85-88; CANR 32, 61; CWW
2; DAM MULT; EWL 3; GLL 2; HW 1,
2; MTCW 1, 2

Gozzano, Guido 1883-1916 .... **PC 10**
See also CA 154; DLB 114; EWL 3

Gozzi, (Conte) Carlo 1720-1806 .... **NCLC 23**

Grabbe, Christian Dietrich
1801-1836 .... **NCLC 2**
See also DLB 133; RGWL 2, 3

Grace, Patricia Frances 1937- .... **CLC 56**
See also CA 176; CANR 118; CN 7; EWL
3; RGSF 2

Griffin, Gerald 1803-1840 .... **NCLC 7**
See also DLB 159; RGEL 2
Griffin, John Howard 1920-1980 ..... **CLC 68**
See also AITN 1; CA 1-4R; 101; CANR 2
Griffin, Peter 1942- .... **CLC 39**
See also CA 136
Griffith, D(avid Lewelyn) W(ark)
1875(?)-1948 .... **TCLC 68**
See also CA 119; 150; CANR 80
Griffith, Lawrence
See Griffith, D(avid Lewelyn) W(ark)
Griffiths, Trevor 1935- .... **CLC 13, 52**
See also CA 97-100; CANR 45; CBD; CD
5; DLB 13, 245
Griggs, Sutton (Elbert)
1872-1930 .... **TCLC 77**
See also CA 123; 186; DLB 50
Grigson, Geoffrey (Edward Harvey)
1905-1985 .... **CLC 7, 39**
See also CA 25-28R; 118; CANR 20, 33;
DLB 27; MTCW 1, 2
Grile, Dod
See Bierce, Ambrose (Gwinett)
Grillparzer, Franz 1791-1872 .... **DC 14;**
NCLC 1, 102; SSC 37
See also CDWLB 2; DLB 133; EW 5;
RGWL 2, 3; TWA
Grimble, Reverend Charles James
See Eliot, T(homas) S(tearns)
Grimke, Angelina (Emily) Weld
1880-1958 .... **HR 2**
See Weld, Angelina (Emily) Grimke
See also BW 1; CA 124; DAM POET; DLB
50, 54
Grimke, Charlotte L(ottie) Forten
1837(?)-1914
See Forten, Charlotte L.
See also BW 1; CA 117; 124; DAM MULT,
POET
Grimm, Jacob Ludwig Karl
1785-1863 .... **NCLC 3, 77; SSC 36**
See also DLB 90; MAICYA 1, 2; RGSF 2;
RGWL 2, 3; SATA 22; WCH
Grimm, Wilhelm Karl 1786-1859 .. **NCLC 3,**
77; SSC 36
See also CDWLB 2; DLB 90; MAICYA 1,
2; RGSF 2; RGWL 2, 3; SATA 22; WCH
Grimmelshausen, Hans Jakob Christoffel
von
See Grimmelshausen, Johann Jakob Christ-
offel von
See also RGWL 2, 3
Grimmelshausen, Johann Jakob Christoffel
von 1621-1676 .... **LC 6**
See Grimmelshausen, Hans Jakob Christof-
fel von
See also CDWLB 2; DLB 168
Grindel, Eugene 1895-1952
See Eluard, Paul
See also CA 104; 193; LMFS 2
Grisham, John 1955- .... **CLC 84**
See also AAYA 14, 47; BPFB 2; CA 138;
CANR 47, 69, 114; CMW 7; CPW;
CSW; DA3; DAM POP; MSW; MTCW 2
Grosseteste, Robert 1175(?)-1253 . **CMLC 62**
See also DLB 115
Grossman, David 1954- .... **CLC 67**
See also CA 138; CANR 114; CWW 2;
EWL 3
Grossman, Vasilii Semenovich
See Grossman, Vasily (Semenovich)
See also DLB 272
Grossman, Vasily (Semenovich)
1905-1964 .... **CLC 41**
See Grossman, Vasilii Semenovich
See also CA 124; 130; MTCW 1
Grove, Frederick Philip .... **TCLC 4**
See Greve, Felix Paul (Berthold Friedrich)
See also DLB 92; RGEL 2

Grubb
See Crumb, R(obert)
Grumbach, Doris (Isaac) 1918- . **CLC 13, 22,**
64
See also CA 5-8R; CAAS 2; CANR 9, 42,
70; CN 7; INT CANR-9; MTCW 2
Grundtvig, Nicolai Frederik Severin
1783-1872 .... **NCLC 1**
Grunge
See Crumb, R(obert)
Grunwald, Lisa 1959- .... **CLC 44**
See also CA 120
Gryphius, Andreas 1616-1664 .... **LC 89**
See also CDWLB 2; DLB 164; RGWL 2, 3
Guare, John 1938- .... **CLC 8, 14, 29, 67; DC**
20
See also CA 73-76; CAD; CANR 21, 69,
118; CD 5; DAM DRAM; DFS 8, 13;
DLB 7, 249; EWL 3; MTCW 1, 2; RGAL
4
Gubar, Susan (David) 1944- .... **CLC 145**
See also CA 108; CANR 45, 70; FW;
MTCW 1; RGAL 4
Gudjonsson, Halldor Kiljan 1902-1998
See Laxness, Halldor
See also CA 103; 164; CWW 2
Guenter, Erich
See Eich, Gunter
Guest, Barbara 1920- .... **CLC 34**
See also BG 2; CA 25-28R; CANR 11, 44,
84; CP 7; CWP; DLB 5, 193
Guest, Edgar A(lbert) 1881-1959 ... **TCLC 95**
See also CA 112; 168
Guest, Judith (Ann) 1936- .... **CLC 8, 30**
See also AAYA 7; CA 77-80; CANR 15,
75; DA3; DAM NOV, POP; EXPN; INT
CANR-15; LAIT 5; MTCW 1, 2; NFS 1
Guevara, Che .... **CLC 87; HLC 1**
See Guevara (Serna), Ernesto
Guevara (Serna), Ernesto
1928-1967 .... **CLC 87; HLC 1**
See Guevara, Che
See also CA 127; 111; CANR 56; DAM
MULT; HW 1
Guicciardini, Francesco 1483-1540 ..... **LC 49**
Guild, Nicholas M. 1944- .... **CLC 33**
See also CA 93-96
Guillemin, Jacques
See Sartre, Jean-Paul
Guillen, Jorge 1893-1984 . **CLC 11; HLCS 1;**
PC 35
See also CA 89-92; 112; DAM MULT,
POET; DLB 108; EWL 3; HW 1; RGWL
2, 3
Guillen, Nicolas (Cristobal)
1902-1989 .... **BLC 2; CLC 48, 79; HLC**
1; PC 23
See also BW 2; CA 116; 125; 129; CANR
84; DAM MST, MULT, POET; DLB 283;
EWL 3; HW 1; LAW; RGWL 2, 3; WP
Guillen y Alvarez, Jorge
See Guillen, Jorge
Guillevic, (Eugene) 1907-1997 .... **CLC 33**
See also CA 93-96; CWW 2
Guillois
See Desnos, Robert
Guillois, Valentin
See Desnos, Robert
Guimaraes Rosa, Joao 1908-1967 .... **HLCS 2**
See also CA 175; LAW; RGSF 2; RGWL 2,
3
Guiney, Louise Imogen
1861-1920 .... **TCLC 41**
See also CA 160; DLB 54; RGAL 4
Guinizelli, Guido c. 1230-1276 ...... **CMLC 49**
Guiraldes, Ricardo (Guillermo)
1886-1927 .... **TCLC 39**
See also CA 131; EWL 3; HW 1; LAW;
MTCW 1

Gumilev, Nikolai (Stepanovich)
1886-1921 .... **TCLC 60**
See Gumilyov, Nikolay Stepanovich
See also CA 165
Gumilyov, Nikolay Stepanovich
See Gumilev, Nikolai (Stepanovich)
See also EWL 3
Gunesekera, Romesh 1954- .... **CLC 91**
See also CA 159; CN 7; DLB 267
Gunn, Bill .... **CLC 5**
See Gunn, William Harrison
See also DLB 38
Gunn, Thom(son William) 1929- .. **CLC 3, 6,**
18, 32, 81; PC 26
See also BRWS 4; CA 17-20R; CANR 9,
33, 116; CDBLB 1960 to Present; CP 7;
DAM POET; DLB 27; INT CANR-33;
MTCW 1; PFS 9; RGEL 2
Gunn, William Harrison 1934(?)-1989
See Gunn, Bill
See also AITN 1; BW 1, 3; CA 13-16R;
128; CANR 12, 25, 76
Gunn Allen, Paula
See Allen, Paula Gunn
Gunnars, Kristjana 1948- .... **CLC 69**
See also CA 113; CCA 1; CP 7; CWP; DLB
60
Gunter, Erich
See Eich, Gunter
Gurdjieff, G(eorgei) I(vanovich)
1877(?)-1949 .... **TCLC 71**
See also CA 157
Gurganus, Allan 1947- .... **CLC 70**
See also BEST 90:1; CA 135; CANR 114;
CN 7; CPW; CSW; DAM POP; GLL 1
Gurney, A. R.
See Gurney, A(lbert) R(amsdell), Jr.
See also DLB 266
Gurney, A(lbert) R(amsdell), Jr.
1930- .... **CLC 32, 50, 54**
See Gurney, A. R.
See also AMWS 5; CA 77-80; CAD; CANR
32, 64, 121; CD 5; DAM DRAM; EWL 3
Gurney, Ivor (Bertie) 1890-1937 ... **TCLC 33**
See also BRW 6; CA 167; DLBY 2002;
PAB; RGEL 2
Gurney, Peter
See Gurney, A(lbert) R(amsdell), Jr.
Guro, Elena 1877-1913 .... **TCLC 56**
Gustafson, James M(oody) 1925- ... **CLC 100**
See also CA 25-28R; CANR 37
Gustafson, Ralph (Barker)
1909-1995 .... **CLC 36**
See also CA 21-24R; CANR 8, 45, 84; CP
7; DLB 88; RGEL 2
Gut, Gom
See Simenon, Georges (Jacques Christian)
Guterson, David 1956- .... **CLC 91**
See also CA 132; CANR 73; MTCW 2;
NFS 13
Guthrie, A(lfred) B(ertram), Jr.
1901-1991 .... **CLC 23**
See also CA 57-60; 134; CANR 24; DLB 6,
212; SATA 62; SATA-Obit 67
Guthrie, Isobel
See Grieve, C(hristopher) M(urray)
Guthrie, Woodrow Wilson 1912-1967
See Guthrie, Woody
See also CA 113; 93-96
Guthrie, Woody .... **CLC 35**
See Guthrie, Woodrow Wilson
See also LAIT 3
Gutierrez Najera, Manuel
1859-1895 .... **HLCS 2**
See also LAW

Harford, Henry
See Hudson, W(illiam) H(enry)

Hargrave, Leonie
See Disch, Thomas M(ichael)

Harjo, Joy 1951- ..... **CLC 83; NNAL; PC 27**
See also AMWS 12; CA 114; CANR 35, 67, 91; CP 7; CWP; DAM MULT; DLB 120, 175; EWL 3; MTCW 2; PFS 15; RGAL 4

Harlan, Louis R(udolph) 1922- .... **CLC 34**
See also CA 21-24R; CANR 25, 55, 80

Harling, Robert 1951(?)- .... **CLC 53**
See also CA 147

Harmon, William (Ruth) 1938- .... **CLC 38**
See also CA 33-36R; CANR 14, 32, 35; SATA 65

Harper, F. E. W.
See Harper, Frances Ellen Watkins

Harper, Frances E. W.
See Harper, Frances Ellen Watkins

Harper, Frances E. Watkins
See Harper, Frances Ellen Watkins

Harper, Frances Ellen
See Harper, Frances Ellen Watkins

Harper, Frances Ellen Watkins
1825-1911 ..... **BLC 2; PC 21; TCLC 14**
See also AFAW 1, 2; BW 1, 3; CA 111; 125; CANR 79; DAM MULT, POET; DLB 50, 221; MAWW; RGAL 4

Harper, Michael S(teven) 1938- ... **CLC 7, 22**
See also AFAW 2; BW 1; CA 33-36R; CANR 24, 108; CP 7; DLB 41; RGAL 4

Harper, Mrs. F. E. W.
See Harper, Frances Ellen Watkins

Harpur, Charles 1813-1868 .... **NCLC 114**
See also DLB 230; RGEL 2

Harris, Christie 1907-
See Harris, Christie (Lucy) Irwin

Harris, Christie (Lucy) Irwin
1907-2002 .... **CLC 12**
See also CA 5-8R; CANR 6, 83; CLR 47; DLB 88; JRDA; MAICYA 1, 2; SAAS 10; SATA 6, 74; SATA-Essay 116

Harris, Frank 1856-1931 .... **TCLC 24**
See also CA 109; 150; CANR 80; DLB 156, 197; RGEL 2

Harris, George Washington
1814-1869 .... **NCLC 23**
See also DLB 3, 11, 248; RGAL 4

Harris, Joel Chandler 1848-1908 ..... **SSC 19; TCLC 2**
See also CA 104; 137; CANR 80; CLR 49; DLB 11, 23, 42, 78, 91; LAIT 2; MAICYA 1, 2; RGSF 2; SATA 100; WCH; YABC 1

Harris, John (Wyndham Parkes Lucas) Beynon 1903-1969
See Wyndham, John
See also CA 102; 89-92; CANR 84; SATA 118; SFW 4

Harris, MacDonald .... **CLC 9**
See Heiney, Donald (William)

Harris, Mark 1922- .... **CLC 19**
See also CA 5-8R; CAAS 3; CANR 2, 55, 83; CN 7; DLB 2; DLBY 1980

Harris, Norman .... **CLC 65**

Harris, (Theodore) Wilson 1921- .... **CLC 25, 159**
See also BRWS 5; BW 2, 3; CA 65-68; CAAS 16; CANR 11, 27, 69, 114; CDWLB 3; CN 7; CP 7; DLB 117; EWL 3; MTCW 1; RGEL 2

Harrison, Barbara Grizzuti
1934-2002 .... **CLC 144**
See also CA 77-80; 205; CANR 15, 48; INT CANR-15

Harrison, Elizabeth (Allen) Cavanna
1909-2001
See Cavanna, Betty
See also CA 9-12R; 200; CANR 6, 27, 85, 104, 121; MAICYA 2; YAW

Harrison, Harry (Max) 1925- .... **CLC 42**
See also CA 1-4R; CANR 5, 21, 84; DLB 8; SATA 4; SCFW 2; SFW 4

Harrison, James (Thomas) 1937- ...... **CLC 6, 14, 33, 66, 143; SSC 19**
See Harrison, Jim
See also CA 13-16R; CANR 8, 51, 79; CN 7; CP 7; DLBY 1982; INT CANR-8

Harrison, Jim
See Harrison, James (Thomas)
See also AMWS 8; RGAL 4; TCWW 2; TUS

Harrison, Kathryn 1961- .... **CLC 70, 151**
See also CA 144; CANR 68, 122

Harrison, Tony 1937- .... **CLC 43, 129**
See also BRWS 5; CA 65-68; CANR 44, 98; CBD; CD 5; CP 7; DLB 40, 245; MTCW 1; RGEL 2

Harriss, Will(ard Irvin) 1922- .... **CLC 34**
See also CA 111

Hart, Ellis
See Ellison, Harlan (Jay)

Hart, Josephine 1942(?)- .... **CLC 70**
See also CA 138; CANR 70; CPW; DAM POP

Hart, Moss 1904-1961 .... **CLC 66**
See also CA 109; 89-92; CANR 84; DAM DRAM; DFS 1; DLB 7, 266; RGAL 4

Harte, (Francis) Bret(t)
1836(?)-1902 ... **SSC 8, 59; TCLC 1, 25; WLC**
See also AMWS 2; CA 104; 140; CANR 80; CDALB 1865-1917; DA; DA3; DAC; DAM MST; DLB 12, 64, 74, 79, 186; EXPS; LAIT 2; RGAL 4; RGSF 2; SATA 26; SSFS 3; TUS

Hartley, L(eslie) P(oles) 1895-1972 ... **CLC 2, 22**
See also BRWS 7; CA 45-48; 37-40R; CANR 33; DLB 15, 139; EWL 3; HGG; MTCW 1, 2; RGEL 2; RGSF 2; SUFW 1

Hartman, Geoffrey H. 1929- .... **CLC 27**
See also CA 117; 125; CANR 79; DLB 67

Hartmann, Sadakichi 1869-1944 ... **TCLC 73**
See also CA 157; DLB 54

Hartmann von Aue c. 1170-c.
1210 .... **CMLC 15**
See also CDWLB 2; DLB 138; RGWL 2, 3

Hartog, Jan de
See de Hartog, Jan

Haruf, Kent 1943- .... **CLC 34**
See also AAYA 44; CA 149; CANR 91

Harvey, Gabriel 1550(?)-1631 .... **LC 88**
See also DLB 167, 213, 281

Harwood, Ronald 1934- .... **CLC 32**
See also CA 1-4R; CANR 4, 55; CBD; CD 5; DAM DRAM, MST; DLB 13

Hasegawa Tatsunosuke
See Futabatei, Shimei

Hasek, Jaroslav (Matej Frantisek)
1883-1923 .... **TCLC 4**
See also CA 104; 129; CDWLB 4; DLB 215; EW 9; EWL 3; MTCW 1, 2; RGSF 2; RGWL 2, 3

Hass, Robert 1941- ... **CLC 18, 39, 99; PC 16**
See also AMWS 6; CA 111; CANR 30, 50, 71; CP 7; DLB 105, 206; EWL 3; RGAL 4; SATA 94

Hastings, Hudson
See Kuttner, Henry

Hastings, Selina .... **CLC 44**

Hathorne, John 1641-1717 .... **LC 38**

Hatteras, Amelia
See Mencken, H(enry) L(ouis)

Hatteras, Owen .... **TCLC 18**
See Mencken, H(enry) L(ouis); Nathan, George Jean

Hauptmann, Gerhart (Johann Robert)
1862-1946 .... **SSC 37; TCLC 4**
See also CA 104; 153; CDWLB 2; DAM DRAM; DLB 66, 118; EW 8; EWL 3; RGSF 2; RGWL 2, 3; TWA

Havel, Vaclav 1936- ..... **CLC 25, 58, 65, 123; DC 6**
See also CA 104; CANR 36, 63; CDWLB 4; CWW 2; DA3; DAM DRAM; DFS 10; DLB 232; EWL 3; LMFS 2; MTCW 1, 2; RGWL 3

Haviaras, Stratis .... **CLC 33**
See Chaviaras, Strates

Hawes, Stephen 1475(?)-1529(?) .... **LC 17**
See also DLB 132; RGEL 2

Hawkes, John (Clendennin Burne, Jr.)
1925-1998 .. **CLC 1, 2, 3, 4, 7, 9, 14, 15, 27, 49**
See also BPFB 2; CA 1-4R; 167; CANR 2, 47, 64; CN 7; DLB 2, 7, 227; DLBY 1980, 1998; EWL 3; MTCW 1, 2; RGAL 4

Hawking, S. W.
See Hawking, Stephen W(illiam)

Hawking, Stephen W(illiam) 1942- . **CLC 63, 105**
See also AAYA 13; BEST 89:1; CA 126; 129; CANR 48, 115; CPW; DA3; MTCW 2

Hawkins, Anthony Hope
See Hope, Anthony

Hawthorne, Julian 1846-1934 .... **TCLC 25**
See also CA 165; HGG

Hawthorne, Nathaniel 1804-1864 ... **NCLC 2, 10, 17, 23, 39, 79, 95; SSC 3, 29, 39; WLC**
See also AAYA 18; AMW; AMWC 1; AMWR 1; BPFB 2; BYA 3; CDALB 1640-1865; DA; DA3; DAB; DAC; DAM MST, NOV; DLB 1, 74, 183, 223, 269; EXPN; EXPS; HGG; LAIT 1; NFS 1; RGAL 4; RGSF 2; SSFS 1, 7, 11, 15; SUFW 1; TUS; WCH; YABC 2

Haxton, Josephine Ayres 1921-
See Douglas, Ellen
See also CA 115; CANR 41, 83

Hayaseca y Eizaguirre, Jorge
See Echegaray (y Eizaguirre), Jose (Maria Waldo)

Hayashi, Fumiko 1904-1951 .... **TCLC 27**
See Hayashi Fumiko
See also CA 161

Hayashi Fumiko
See Hayashi, Fumiko
See also DLB 180; EWL 3

Haycraft, Anna (Margaret) 1932-
See Ellis, Alice Thomas
See also CA 122; CANR 85, 90; MTCW 2

Hayden, Robert E(arl) 1913-1980 ..... **BLC 2; CLC 5, 9, 14, 37; PC 6**
See also AFAW 1, 2; AMWS 2; BW 1, 3; CA 69-72; 97-100; CABS 2; CANR 24, 75, 82; CDALB 1941-1968; DA; DAC; DAM MST, MULT, POET; DLB 5, 76; EWL 3; EXPP; MTCW 1, 2; PFS 1; RGAL 4; SATA 19; SATA-Obit 26; WP

Hayek, F(riedrich) A(ugust von)
1899-1992 .... **TCLC 109**
See also CA 93-96; 137; CANR 20; MTCW 1, 2

Hayford, J(oseph) E(phraim) Casely
See Casely-Hayford, J(oseph) E(phraim)

Hayman, Ronald 1932- .... **CLC 44**
See also CA 25-28R; CANR 18, 50, 88; CD 5; DLB 155

Hayne, Paul Hamilton 1830-1886 . **NCLC 94**
See also DLB 3, 64, 79, 248; RGAL 4

Herrick, Robert 1591-1674 .... **LC 13; PC 9**
See also BRW 2; DA; DAB; DAC; DAM
MST, POP; DLB 126; EXPP; PFS 13;
RGAL 4; RGEL 2; TEA; WP

Herring, Guilles
See Somerville, Edith Oenone

Herriot, James 1916-1995 .... **CLC 12**
See Wight, James Alfred
See also AAYA 1; BPFB 2; CA 148; CANR
40; CLR 80; CPW; DAM POP; LAIT 3;
MAICYA 2; MAICYAS 1; MTCW 2;
SATA 86, 135; TEA; YAW

Herris, Violet
See Hunt, Violet

Herrmann, Dorothy 1941- .... **CLC 44**
See also CA 107

Herrmann, Taffy
See Herrmann, Dorothy

Hersey, John (Richard) 1914-1993 .... **CLC 1,
2, 7, 9, 40, 81, 97**
See also AAYA 29; BPFB 2; CA 17-20R;
140; CANR 33; CDALBS; CPW; DAM
POP; DLB 6, 185, 278; MTCW 1, 2;
SATA 25; SATA-Obit 76; TUS

Herzen, Aleksandr Ivanovich
1812-1870 .... **NCLC 10, 61**
See Herzen, Alexander

Herzen, Alexander
See Herzen, Aleksandr Ivanovich
See also DLB 277

Herzl, Theodor 1860-1904 .... **TCLC 36**
See also CA 168

Herzog, Werner 1942- .... **CLC 16**
See also CA 89-92

Hesiod c. 8th cent. B.C.- .... **CMLC 5**
See also AW 1; DLB 176; RGWL 2, 3

Hesse, Hermann 1877-1962 ... **CLC 1, 2, 3, 6,
11, 17, 25, 69; SSC 9, 49; WLC**
See also AAYA 43; BPFB 2; CA 17-18;
CAP 2; CDWLB 2; DA; DA3; DAB;
DAC; DAM MST, NOV; DLB 66; EW 9;
EWL 3; EXPN; LAIT 1; MTCW 1, 2;
NFS 6, 15; RGWL 2, 3; SATA 50; TWA

Hewes, Cady
See De Voto, Bernard (Augustine)

Heyen, William 1940- .... **CLC 13, 18**
See also CA 33-36R; CAAS 9; CANR 98;
CP 7; DLB 5

Heyerdahl, Thor 1914-2002 .... **CLC 26**
See also CA 5-8R; 207; CANR 5, 22, 66,
73; LAIT 4; MTCW 1, 2; SATA 2, 52

Heym, Georg (Theodor Franz Arthur)
1887-1912 .... **TCLC 9**
See also CA 106; 181

Heym, Stefan 1913-2001 .... **CLC 41**
See also CA 9-12R; 203; CANR 4; CWW
2; DLB 69; EWL 3

Heyse, Paul (Johann Ludwig von)
1830-1914 .... **TCLC 8**
See also CA 104; 209; DLB 129

Heyward, (Edwin) DuBose
1885-1940 .... **HR 2; TCLC 59**
See also CA 108; 157; DLB 7, 9, 45, 249;
SATA 21

Heywood, John 1497(?)-1580(?) .... **LC 65**
See also DLB 136; RGEL 2

Hibbert, Eleanor Alice Burford
1906-1993 .... **CLC 7**
See Holt, Victoria
See also BEST 90:4; CA 17-20R; 140;
CANR 9, 28, 59; CMW 4; CPW; DAM
POP; MTCW 2; RHW; SATA 2; SATA-
Obit 74

Hichens, Robert (Smythe)
1864-1950 .... **TCLC 64**
See also CA 162; DLB 153; HGG; RHW;
SUFW

Higgins, George V(incent)
1939-1999 .... **CLC 4, 7, 10, 18**
See also BPFB 2; CA 77-80; 186; CAAS 5;
CANR 17, 51, 89, 96; CMW 4; CN 7;
DLB 2; DLBY 1981, 1998; INT CANR-
17; MSW; MTCW 1

Higginson, Thomas Wentworth
1823-1911 .... **TCLC 36**
See also CA 162; DLB 1, 64, 243

Higgonet, Margaret ed. .... **CLC 65**

Highet, Helen
See MacInnes, Helen (Clark)

Highsmith, (Mary) Patricia
1921-1995 .... **CLC 2, 4, 14, 42, 102**
See Morgan, Claire
See also AAYA 48; BRWS 5; CA 1-4R; 147;
CANR 1, 20, 48, 62, 108; CMW 4; CPW;
DA3; DAM NOV, POP; MSW; MTCW 1,
2

Highwater, Jamake (Mamake)
1942(?)-2001 .... **CLC 12**
See also AAYA 7; BPFB 2; BYA 4; CA 65-
68; 199; CAAS 7; CANR 10, 34, 84; CLR
17; CWRI 5; DLB 52; DLBY 1985;
JRDA; MAICYA 1, 2; SATA 32, 69;
SATA-Brief 30

Highway, Tomson 1951- ...... **CLC 92; NNAL**
See also CA 151; CANR 75; CCA 1; CD 5;
DAC; DAM MULT; DFS 2; MTCW 2

Hijuelos, Oscar 1951- .... **CLC 65; HLC 1**
See also AAYA 25; AMWS 8; BEST 90:1;
CA 123; CANR 50, 75; CPW; DA3; DAM
MULT, POP; DLB 145; HW 1, 2; MTCW
2; NFS 17; RGAL 4; WLIT 1

Hikmet, Nazim 1902(?)-1963 .... **CLC 40**
See also CA 141; 93-96; EWL 3

Hildegard von Bingen 1098-1179 . **CMLC 20**
See also DLB 148

Hildesheimer, Wolfgang 1916-1991 .. **CLC 49**
See also CA 101; 135; DLB 69, 124; EWL
3

Hill, Geoffrey (William) 1932- ...... **CLC 5, 8,
18, 45**
See also BRWS 5; CA 81-84; CANR 21,
89; CDBLB 1960 to Present; CP 7; DAM
POET; DLB 40; EWL 3; MTCW 1; RGEL
2

Hill, George Roy 1921-2002 .... **CLC 26**
See also CA 110; 122; 213

Hill, John
See Koontz, Dean R(ay)

Hill, Susan (Elizabeth) 1942- ...... **CLC 4, 113**
See also CA 33-36R; CANR 29, 69; CN 7;
DAB; DAM MST, NOV; DLB 14, 139;
HGG; MTCW 1; RHW

Hillard, Asa G. III .... **CLC 70**

Hillerman, Tony 1925- .... **CLC 62, 170**
See also AAYA 40; BEST 89:1; BPFB 2;
CA 29-32R; CANR 21, 42, 65, 97; CMW
4; CPW; DA3; DAM POP; DLB 206;
MSW; RGAL 4; SATA 6; TCWW 2; YAW

Hillesum, Etty 1914-1943 .... **TCLC 49**
See also CA 137

Hilliard, Noel (Harvey) 1929-1996 ... **CLC 15**
See also CA 9-12R; CANR 7, 69; CN 7

Hillis, Rick 1956- .... **CLC 66**
See also CA 134

Hilton, James 1900-1954 .... **TCLC 21**
See also CA 108; 169; DLB 34, 77; FANT;
SATA 34

Hilton, Walter (?)-1396 .... **CMLC 58**
See also DLB 146; RGEL 2

Himes, Chester (Bomar) 1909-1984 .. **BLC 2;
CLC 2, 4, 7, 18, 58, 108; TCLC 139**
See also AFAW 2; BPFB 2; BW 2; CA 25-
28R; 114; CANR 22, 89; CMW 4; DAM
MULT; DLB 2, 76, 143, 226; EWL 3;
MSW; MTCW 1, 2; RGAL 4

Hinde, Thomas .... **CLC 6, 11**
See Chitty, Thomas Willes
See also EWL 3

Hine, (William) Daryl 1936- .... **CLC 15**
See also CA 1-4R; CAAS 15; CANR 1, 20;
CP 7; DLB 60

Hinkson, Katharine Tynan
See Tynan, Katharine

Hinojosa(-Smith), Rolando (R.)
1929- .... **HLC 1**
See Hinojosa-Smith, Rolando
See also CA 131; CAAS 16; CANR 62;
DAM MULT; DLB 82; HW 1, 2; MTCW
2; RGAL 4

Hinton, S(usan) E(loise) 1950- .. **CLC 30, 111**
See also AAYA 2, 33; BPFB 2; BYA 2, 3;
CA 81-84; CANR 32, 62, 92; CDALBS;
CLR 3, 23; CPW; DA; DA3; DAB; DAC;
DAM MST, NOV; JRDA; LAIT 5; MAI-
CYA 1, 2; MTCW 1, 2; NFS 5, 9, 15, 16;
SATA 19, 58, 115; WYA; YAW

Hippius, Zinaida .... **TCLC 9**
See Gippius, Zinaida (Nikolaevna)
See also EWL 3

Hiraoka, Kimitake 1925-1970
See Mishima, Yukio
See also CA 97-100; 29-32R; DA3; DAM
DRAM; GLL 1; MTCW 1, 2

Hirsch, E(ric) D(onald), Jr. 1928- .... **CLC 79**
See also CA 25-28R; CANR 27, 51; DLB
67; INT CANR-27; MTCW 1

Hirsch, Edward 1950- .... **CLC 31, 50**
See also CA 104; CANR 20, 42, 102; CP 7;
DLB 120

Hitchcock, Alfred (Joseph)
1899-1980 .... **CLC 16**
See also AAYA 22; CA 159; 97-100; SATA
27; SATA-Obit 24

Hitchens, Christopher (Eric)
1949- .... **CLC 157**
See also CA 152; CANR 89

Hitler, Adolf 1889-1945 .... **TCLC 53**
See also CA 117; 147

Hoagland, Edward 1932- .... **CLC 28**
See also ANW; CA 1-4R; CANR 2, 31, 57,
107; CN 7; DLB 6; SATA 51; TCWW 2

Hoban, Russell (Conwell) 1925- ... **CLC 7, 25**
See also BPFB 2; CA 5-8R; CANR 23, 37,
66, 114; CLR 3, 69; CN 7; CWRI 5; DAM
NOV; DLB 52; FANT; MAICYA 1, 2;
MTCW 1, 2; SATA 1, 40, 78, 136; SFW
4; SUFW 2

Hobbes, Thomas 1588-1679 .... **LC 36**
See also DLB 151, 252, 281; RGEL 2

Hobbs, Perry
See Blackmur, R(ichard) P(almer)

Hobson, Laura Z(ametkin)
1900-1986 .... **CLC 7, 25**
See Field, Peter
See also BPFB 2; CA 17-20R; 118; CANR
55; DLB 28; SATA 52

Hoccleve, Thomas c. 1368-c. 1437 ...... **LC 75**
See also DLB 146; RGEL 2

Hoch, Edward D(entinger) 1930-
See Queen, Ellery
See also CA 29-32R; CANR 11, 27, 51, 97;
CMW 4; SFW 4

Hochhuth, Rolf 1931- .... **CLC 4, 11, 18**
See also CA 5-8R; CANR 33, 75; CWW 2;
DAM DRAM; DLB 124; EWL 3; MTCW
1, 2

Hochman, Sandra 1936- .... **CLC 3, 8**
See also CA 5-8R; DLB 5

Hochwaelder, Fritz 1911-1986 .... **CLC 36**
See Hochwalder, Fritz
See also CA 29-32R; 120; CANR 42; DAM
DRAM; MTCW 1; RGWL 3

Hochwalder, Fritz
See Hochwaelder, Fritz
See also EWL 3; RGWL 2

Hocking, Mary (Eunice) 1921- .... **CLC 13**
See also CA 101; CANR 18, 40

Hodgins, Jack 1938- .... **CLC 23**
See also CA 93-96; CN 7; DLB 60

Hodgson, William Hope
1877(?)-1918 .... **TCLC 13**
See also CA 111; 164; CMW 4; DLB 70,
153, 156, 178; HGG; MTCW 2; SFW 4;
SUFW 1

Hoeg, Peter 1957- .... **CLC 95, 156**
See also CA 151; CANR 75; CMW 4; DA3;
DLB 214; EWL 3; MTCW 2; NFS 17;
RGWL 3; SSFS 18

Hoffman, Alice 1952- .... **CLC 51**
See also AAYA 37; AMWS 10; CA 77-80;
CANR 34, 66, 100; CN 7; CPW; DAM
NOV; MTCW 1, 2

Hoffman, Daniel (Gerard) 1923- . **CLC 6, 13, 23**
See also CA 1-4R; CANR 4; CP 7; DLB 5

Hoffman, Stanley 1944- .... **CLC 5**
See also CA 77-80

Hoffman, William 1925- .... **CLC 141**
See also CA 21-24R; CANR 9, 103; CSW;
DLB 234

Hoffman, William M(oses) 1939- ..... **CLC 40**
See Hoffman, William M.
See also CA 57-60; CANR 11, 71

Hoffmann, E(rnst) T(heodor) A(madeus)
1776-1822 .... **NCLC 2; SSC 13**
See also CDWLB 2; DLB 90; EW 5; RGSF
2; RGWL 2, 3; SATA 27; SUFW 1; WCH

Hofmann, Gert 1931- .... **CLC 54**
See also CA 128; EWL 3

Hofmannsthal, Hugo von 1874-1929 ... **DC 4;
TCLC 11**
See also CA 106; 153; CDWLB 2; DAM
DRAM; DFS 17; DLB 81, 118; EW 9;
EWL 3; RGWL 2, 3

Hogan, Linda 1947- ..... **CLC 73; NNAL; PC
35**
See also AMWS 4; ANW; BYA 12; CA 120;
CANR 45, 73; CWP; DAM MULT; DLB
175; SATA 132; TCWW 2

Hogarth, Charles
See Creasey, John

Hogarth, Emmett
See Polonsky, Abraham (Lincoln)

Hogg, James 1770-1835 .... **NCLC 4, 109**
See also DLB 93, 116, 159; HGG; RGEL 2;
SUFW 1

Holbach, Paul Henri Thiry Baron
1723-1789 .... **LC 14**

Holberg, Ludvig 1684-1754 .... **LC 6**
See also RGWL 2, 3

Holcroft, Thomas 1745-1809 .... **NCLC 85**
See also DLB 39, 89, 158; RGEL 2

Holden, Ursula 1921- .... **CLC 18**
See also CA 101; CAAS 8; CANR 22

Holderlin, (Johann Christian) Friedrich
1770-1843 .... **NCLC 16; PC 4**
See also CDWLB 2; DLB 90; EW 5; RGWL
2, 3

Holdstock, Robert
See Holdstock, Robert P.

Holdstock, Robert P. 1948- .... **CLC 39**
See also CA 131; CANR 81; DLB 261;
FANT; HGG; SFW 4; SUFW 2

Holinshed, Raphael fl. 1580- .... **LC 69**
See also DLB 167; RGEL 2

Holland, Isabelle (Christian)
1920-2002 .... **CLC 21**
See also AAYA 11; CA 21-24R; 181; 205;
CAAE 181; CANR 10, 25, 47; CLR 57;
CWRI 5; JRDA; LAIT 4; MAICYA 1, 2;
SATA 8, 70; SATA-Essay 103; SATA-Obit
132; WYA

Holland, Marcus
See Caldwell, (Janet Miriam) Taylor
(Holland)

Hollander, John 1929- .... **CLC 2, 5, 8, 14**
See also CA 1-4R; CANR 1, 52; CP 7; DLB
5; SATA 13

Hollander, Paul
See Silverberg, Robert

Holleran, Andrew 1943(?)- .... **CLC 38**
See Garber, Eric
See also CA 144; GLL 1

Holley, Marietta 1836(?)-1926 .... **TCLC 99**
See also CA 118; DLB 11

Hollinghurst, Alan 1954- .... **CLC 55, 91**
See also CA 114; CN 7; DLB 207; GLL 1

Hollis, Jim
See Summers, Hollis (Spurgeon, Jr.)

Holly, Buddy 1936-1959 .... **TCLC 65**
See also CA 213

Holmes, Gordon
See Shiel, M(atthew) P(hipps)

Holmes, John
See Souster, (Holmes) Raymond

Holmes, John Clellon 1926-1988 ...... **CLC 56**
See also BG 2; CA 9-12R; 125; CANR 4;
DLB 16, 237

Holmes, Oliver Wendell, Jr.
1841-1935 .... **TCLC 77**
See also CA 114; 186

Holmes, Oliver Wendell
1809-1894 .... **NCLC 14, 81**
See also AMWS 1; CDALB 1640-1865;
DLB 1, 189, 235; EXPP; RGAL 4; SATA
34

Holmes, Raymond
See Souster, (Holmes) Raymond

Holt, Victoria
See Hibbert, Eleanor Alice Burford
See also BPFB 2

Holub, Miroslav 1923-1998 .... **CLC 4**
See also CA 21-24R; 169; CANR 10; CD-
WLB 4; CWW 2; DLB 232; EWL 3;
RGWL 3

Holz, Detlev
See Benjamin, Walter

Homer c. 8th cent. B.C.- .... **CMLC 1, 16, 61;
PC 23; WLCS**
See also AW 1; CDWLB 1; DA; DA3;
DAB; DAC; DAM MST, POET; DLB
176; EFS 1; LAIT 1; LMFS 1; RGWL 2,
3; TWA; WP

Hongo, Garrett Kaoru 1951- .... **PC 23**
See also CA 133; CAAS 22; CP 7; DLB
120; EWL 3; EXPP; RGAL 4

Honig, Edwin 1919- .... **CLC 33**
See also CA 5-8R; CAAS 8; CANR 4, 45;
CP 7; DLB 5

Hood, Hugh (John Blagdon) 1928- . **CLC 15,
28; SSC 42**
See also CA 49-52; CAAS 17; CANR 1,
33, 87; CN 7; DLB 53; RGSF 2

Hood, Thomas 1799-1845 .... **NCLC 16**
See also BRW 4; DLB 96; RGEL 2

Hooker, (Peter) Jeremy 1941- .... **CLC 43**
See also CA 77-80; CANR 22; CP 7; DLB
40

hooks, bell
See Watkins, Gloria Jean

Hope, A(lec) D(erwent) 1907-2000 .... **CLC 3,
51**
See also BRWS 7; CA 21-24R; 188; CANR
33, 74; EWL 3; MTCW 1, 2; PFS 8;
RGEL 2

Hope, Anthony 1863-1933 .... **TCLC 83**
See also CA 157; DLB 153, 156; RGEL 2;
RHW

Hope, Brian
See Creasey, John

Hope, Christopher (David Tully)
1944- .... **CLC 52**
See also AFW; CA 106; CANR 47, 101;
CN 7; DLB 225; SATA 62

Hopkins, Gerard Manley
1844-1889 .... **NCLC 17; PC 15; WLC**
See also BRW 5; BRWR 2; CDBLB 1890-
1914; DA; DA3; DAB; DAC; DAM MST,
POET; DLB 35, 57; EXPP; PAB; RGEL
2; TEA; WP

Hopkins, John (Richard) 1931-1998 .. **CLC 4**
See also CA 85-88; 169; CBD; CD 5

Hopkins, Pauline Elizabeth
1859-1930 .... **BLC 2; TCLC 28**
See also AFAW 2; BW 2, 3; CA 141; CANR
82; DAM MULT; DLB 50

Hopkinson, Francis 1737-1791 .... **LC 25**
See also DLB 31; RGAL 4

Hopley-Woolrich, Cornell George 1903-1968
See Woolrich, Cornell
See also CA 13-14; CANR 58; CAP 1;
CMW 4; DLB 226; MTCW 2

Horace 65B.C.-8B.C. .... **CMLC 39; PC 46**
See also AW 2; CDWLB 1; DLB 211;
RGWL 2, 3

Horatio
See Proust, (Valentin-Louis-George-Eugene)
Marcel

**Horgan, Paul (George Vincent
O'Shaughnessy)** 1903-1995 .. **CLC 9, 53**
See also BPFB 2; CA 13-16R; 147; CANR
9, 35; DAM NOV; DLB 102, 212; DLBY
1985; INT CANR-9; MTCW 1, 2; SATA
13; SATA-Obit 84; TCWW 2

Horkheimer, Max 1895-1973 .... **TCLC 132**
See also CA 41-44R

Horn, Peter
See Kuttner, Henry

Horne, Frank (Smith) 1899-1974 .... **HR 2**
See also BW 1; CA 125; 53-56; DLB 51;
WP

Horne, Richard Henry Hengist
1802(?)-1884 .... **NCLC 127**
See also DLB 32; SATA 29

Hornem, Horace Esq.
See Byron, George Gordon (Noel)

**Horney, Karen (Clementine Theodore
Danielsen)** 1885-1952 .... **TCLC 71**
See also CA 114; 165; DLB 246; FW

Hornung, E(rnest) W(illiam)
1866-1921 .... **TCLC 59**
See also CA 108; 160; CMW 4; DLB 70

Horovitz, Israel (Arthur) 1939- .... **CLC 56**
See also CA 33-36R; CAD; CANR 46, 59;
CD 5; DAM DRAM; DLB 7

Horton, George Moses
1797(?)-1883(?) .... **NCLC 87**
See also DLB 50

Horvath, odon von 1901-1938
See von Horvath, Odon
See also EWL 3

Horvath, Oedoen von -1938
See von Horvath, Odon

Horwitz, Julius 1920-1986 .... **CLC 14**
See also CA 9-12R; 119; CANR 12

Hospital, Janette Turner 1942- .... **CLC 42,
145**
See also CA 108; CANR 48; CN 7; DLBY
2002; RGSF 2

Hostos, E. M. de
See Hostos (y Bonilla), Eugenio Maria de

Hostos, Eugenio M. de
See Hostos (y Bonilla), Eugenio Maria de

Hostos, Eugenio Maria
See Hostos (y Bonilla), Eugenio Maria de

Hostos (y Bonilla), Eugenio Maria de
1839-1903 .... **TCLC 24**
See also CA 123; 131; HW 1

Jacobs, W(illiam) W(ymark)
1863-1943 .... **TCLC 22**
See also CA 121; 167; DLB 135; EXPS;
HGG; RGEL 2; RGSF 2; SSFS 2; SUFW
1

Jacobsen, Jens Peter 1847-1885 .... **NCLC 34**

Jacobsen, Josephine 1908- .... **CLC 48, 102**
See also CA 33-36R; CAAS 18; CANR 23,
48; CCA 1; CP 7; DLB 244

Jacobson, Dan 1929- .... **CLC 4, 14**
See also AFW; CA 1-4R; CANR 2, 25, 66;
CN 7; DLB 14, 207, 225; EWL 3; MTCW
1; RGSF 2

Jacqueline
See Carpentier (y Valmont), Alejo

Jagger, Mick 1944- .... **CLC 17**

Jahiz, al- c. 780-c. 869 .... **CMLC 25**

Jakes, John (William) 1932- .... **CLC 29**
See also AAYA 32; BEST 89:4; BPFB 2;
CA 57-60; CAAE 214; CANR 10, 43, 66,
111; CPW; CSW; DA3; DAM NOV, POP;
DLB 278; DLBY 1983; FANT; INT
CANR-10; MTCW 1, 2; RHW; SATA 62;
SFW 4; TCWW 2

James I 1394-1437 .... **LC 20**
See also RGEL 2

James, Andrew
See Kirkup, James

James, C(yril) L(ionel) R(obert)
1901-1989 .... **BLCS; CLC 33**
See also BW 2; CA 117; 125; 128; CANR
62; DLB 125; MTCW 1

James, Daniel (Lewis) 1911-1988
See Santiago, Danny
See also CA 174; 125

James, Dynely
See Mayne, William (James Carter)

James, Henry Sr. 1811-1882 .... **NCLC 53**

James, Henry 1843-1916 .... **SSC 8, 32, 47;**
TCLC 2, 11, 24, 40, 47, 64; WLC
See also AMW; AMWC 1; AMWR 1; BPFB
2; BRW 6; CA 104; 132; CDALB 1865-
1917; DA; DA3; DAB; DAC; DAM MST,
NOV; DLB 12, 71, 74, 189; DLBD 13;
EWL 3; EXPS; HGG; LAIT 2; MTCW 1,
2; NFS 12, 16; RGAL 4; RGEL 2; RGSF
2; SSFS 9; SUFW 1; TUS

James, M. R.
See James, Montague (Rhodes)
See also DLB 156, 201

James, Montague (Rhodes)
1862-1936 .... **SSC 16; TCLC 6**
See James, M. R.
See also CA 104; 203; HGG; RGEL 2;
RGSF 2; SUFW 1

James, P. D. .... **CLC 18, 46, 122**
See White, Phyllis Dorothy James
See also BEST 90:2; BPFB 2; BRWS 4;
CDBLB 1960 to Present; DLB 87, 276;
DLBD 17; MSW

James, Philip
See Moorcock, Michael (John)

James, Samuel
See Stephens, James

James, Seumas
See Stephens, James

James, Stephen
See Stephens, James

James, William 1842-1910 .... **TCLC 15, 32**
See also AMW; CA 109; 193; DLB 270,
284; NCFS 5; RGAL 4

Jameson, Anna 1794-1860 .... **NCLC 43**
See also DLB 99, 166

Jameson, Fredric (R.) 1934- .... **CLC 142**
See also CA 196; DLB 67; LMFS 2

Jami, Nur al-Din 'Abd al-Rahman
1414-1492 .... **LC 9**

Jammes, Francis 1868-1938 .... **TCLC 75**
See also CA 198; EWL 3; GFL 1789 to the
Present

Jandl, Ernst 1925-2000 .... **CLC 34**
See also CA 200; EWL 3

Janowitz, Tama 1957- .... **CLC 43, 145**
See also CA 106; CANR 52, 89; CN 7;
CPW; DAM POP

Japrisot, Sebastien 1931- .... **CLC 90**
See Rossi, Jean-Baptiste
See also CMW 4; NFS 18

Jarrell, Randall 1914-1965 .... **CLC 1, 2, 6, 9,**
13, 49; PC 41
See also AMW; BYA 5; CA 5-8R; 25-28R;
CABS 2; CANR 6, 34; CDALB 1941-
1968; CLR 6; CWRI 5; DAM POET;
DLB 48, 52; EWL 3; EXPP; MAICYA 1,
2; MTCW 1, 2; PAB; PFS 2; RGAL 4;
SATA 7

Jarry, Alfred 1873-1907 .... **SSC 20; TCLC 2,**
14
See also CA 104; 153; DA3; DAM DRAM;
DFS 8; DLB 192, 258; EW 9; EWL 3;
GFL 1789 to the Present; RGWL 2, 3;
TWA

Jarvis, E. K.
See Ellison, Harlan (Jay)

Jawien, Andrzej
See John Paul II, Pope

Jaynes, Roderick
See Coen, Ethan

Jeake, Samuel, Jr.
See Aiken, Conrad (Potter)

Jean Paul 1763-1825 .... **NCLC 7**

Jefferies, (John) Richard
1848-1887 .... **NCLC 47**
See also DLB 98, 141; RGEL 2; SATA 16;
SFW 4

Jeffers, (John) Robinson 1887-1962 .. **CLC 2,**
3, 11, 15, 54; PC 17; WLC
See also AMWS 2; CA 85-88; CANR 35;
CDALB 1917-1929; DA; DAC; DAM
MST, POET; DLB 45, 212; EWL 3;
MTCW 1, 2; PAB; PFS 3, 4; RGAL 4

Jefferson, Janet
See Mencken, H(enry) L(ouis)

Jefferson, Thomas 1743-1826 . **NCLC 11, 103**
See also ANW; CDALB 1640-1865; DA3;
DLB 31, 183; LAIT 1; RGAL 4

Jeffrey, Francis 1773-1850 .... **NCLC 33**
See Francis, Lord Jeffrey

Jelakowitch, Ivan
See Heijermans, Herman

Jelinek, Elfriede 1946- .... **CLC 169**
See also CA 154; DLB 85; FW

Jellicoe, (Patricia) Ann 1927- .... **CLC 27**
See also CA 85-88; CBD; CD 5; CWD;
CWRI 5; DLB 13, 233; FW

Jemyma
See Holley, Marietta

Jen, Gish .... **CLC 70**
See Jen, Lillian

Jen, Lillian 1956(?)-
See Jen, Gish
See also CA 135; CANR 89

Jenkins, (John) Robin 1912- .... **CLC 52**
See also CA 1-4R; CANR 1; CN 7; DLB
14, 271

Jennings, Elizabeth (Joan)
1926-2001 .... **CLC 5, 14, 131**
See also BRWS 5; CA 61-64; 200; CAAS
5; CANR 8, 39, 66; CP 7; CWP; DLB 27;
EWL 3; MTCW 1; SATA 66

Jennings, Waylon 1937- .... **CLC 21**

Jensen, Johannes V(ilhelm)
1873-1950 .... **TCLC 41**
See also CA 170; DLB 214; EWL 3; RGWL
3

Jensen, Laura (Linnea) 1948- .... **CLC 37**
See also CA 103

Jerome, Saint 345-420 .... **CMLC 30**
See also RGWL 3

Jerome, Jerome K(lapka)
1859-1927 .... **TCLC 23**
See also CA 119; 177; DLB 10, 34, 135;
RGEL 2

Jerrold, Douglas William
1803-1857 .... **NCLC 2**
See also DLB 158, 159; RGEL 2

Jewett, (Theodora) Sarah Orne
1849-1909 .... **SSC 6, 44; TCLC 1, 22**
See also AMW; AMWR 2; CA 108; 127;
CANR 71; DLB 12, 74, 221; EXPS; FW;
MAWW; NFS 15; RGAL 4; RGSF 2;
SATA 15; SSFS 4

Jewsbury, Geraldine (Endsor)
1812-1880 .... **NCLC 22**
See also DLB 21

Jhabvala, Ruth Prawer 1927- . **CLC 4, 8, 29,**
94, 138
See also BRWS 5; CA 1-4R; CANR 2, 29,
51, 74, 91; CN 7; DAB; DAM NOV; DLB
139, 194; EWL 3; IDFW 3, 4; INT CANR-
29; MTCW 1, 2; RGSF 2; RGWL 2;
RHW; TEA

Jibran, Kahlil
See Gibran, Kahlil

Jibran, Khalil
See Gibran, Kahlil

Jiles, Paulette 1943- .... **CLC 13, 58**
See also CA 101; CANR 70; CWP

Jimenez (Mantecon), Juan Ramon
1881-1958 .... **HLC 1; PC 7; TCLC 4**
See also CA 104; 131; CANR 74; DAM
MULT, POET; DLB 134; EW 9; EWL 3;
HW 1; MTCW 1, 2; RGWL 2, 3

Jimenez, Ramon
See Jimenez (Mantecon), Juan Ramon

Jimenez Mantecon, Juan
See Jimenez (Mantecon), Juan Ramon

Jin, Ha .... **CLC 109**
See Jin, Xuefei
See also CA 152; DLB 244; SSFS 17

Jin, Xuefei 1956-
See Jin, Ha
See also CANR 91

Joel, Billy .... **CLC 26**
See Joel, William Martin

Joel, William Martin 1949-
See Joel, Billy
See also CA 108

John, Saint 107th cent. -100 .... **CMLC 27**

John of the Cross, St. 1542-1591 .... **LC 18**
See also RGWL 2, 3

John Paul II, Pope 1920- .... **CLC 128**
See also CA 106; 133

Johnson, B(ryan) S(tanley William)
1933-1973 .... **CLC 6, 9**
See also CA 9-12R; 53-56; CANR 9; DLB
14, 40; EWL 3; RGEL 2

Johnson, Benjamin F., of Boone
See Riley, James Whitcomb

Johnson, Charles (Richard) 1948- .... **BLC 2;**
CLC 7, 51, 65, 163
See also AFAW 2; AMWS 6; BW 2, 3; CA
116; CAAS 18; CANR 42, 66, 82; CN 7;
DAM MULT; DLB 33, 278; MTCW 2;
RGAL 4; SSFS 16

Johnson, Charles S(purgeon)
1893-1956 .... **HR 3**
See also BW 1, 3; CA 125; CANR 82; DLB
51, 91

Just, Ward (Swift) 1935- .... **CLC 4, 27**
    See also CA 25-28R; CANR 32, 87; CN 7;
    INT CANR-32
Justice, Donald (Rodney) 1925- .. **CLC 6, 19,
    102**
    See also AMWS 7; CA 5-8R; CANR 26,
    54, 74, 121, 122; CP 7; CSW; DAM
    POET; DLBY 1983; EWL 3; INT CANR-
    26; MTCW 2; PFS 14
Juvenal c. 60-c. 130 .... **CMLC 8**
    See also AW 2; CDWLB 1; DLB 211;
    RGWL 2, 3
Juvenis
    See Bourne, Randolph S(illiman)
K., Alice
    See Knapp, Caroline
Kabakov, Sasha .... **CLC 59**
Kacew, Romain 1914-1980
    See Gary, Romain
    See also CA 108; 102
Kadare, Ismail 1936- .... **CLC 52**
    See also CA 161; EWL 3; RGWL 3
Kadohata, Cynthia .... **CLC 59, 122**
    See also CA 140
Kafka, Franz 1883-1924 ... **SSC 5, 29, 35, 60;
    TCLC 2, 6, 13, 29, 47, 53, 112; WLC**
    See also AAYA 31; BPFB 2; CA 105; 126;
    CDWLB 2; DA; DA3; DAB; DAC; DAM
    MST, NOV; DLB 81; EW 9; EWL 3;
    EXPS; LATS 1; LMFS 2; MTCW 1, 2;
    NFS 7; RGSF 2; RGWL 2, 3; SFW 4;
    SSFS 3, 7, 12; TWA
Kahanovitsch, Pinkhes
    See Der Nister
Kahn, Roger 1927- .... **CLC 30**
    See also CA 25-28R; CANR 44, 69; DLB
    171; SATA 37
Kain, Saul
    See Sassoon, Siegfried (Lorraine)
Kaiser, Georg 1878-1945 .... **TCLC 9**
    See also CA 106; 190; CDWLB 2; DLB
    124; EWL 3; LMFS 2; RGWL 2, 3
Kaledin, Sergei .... **CLC 59**
Kaletski, Alexander 1946- .... **CLC 39**
    See also CA 118; 143
Kalidasa fl. c. 400-455 .... **CMLC 9; PC 22**
    See also RGWL 2, 3
Kallman, Chester (Simon)
    1921-1975 .... **CLC 2**
    See also CA 45-48; 53-56; CANR 3
Kaminsky, Melvin 1926-
    See Brooks, Mel
    See also CA 65-68; CANR 16
Kaminsky, Stuart M(elvin) 1934- ..... **CLC 59**
    See also CA 73-76; CANR 29, 53, 89;
    CMW 4
Kandinsky, Wassily 1866-1944 .... **TCLC 92**
    See also CA 118; 155
Kane, Francis
    See Robbins, Harold
Kane, Henry 1918-
    See Queen, Ellery
    See also CA 156; CMW 4
Kane, Paul
    See Simon, Paul (Frederick)
Kanin, Garson 1912-1999 .... **CLC 22**
    See also AITN 1; CA 5-8R; 177; CAD;
    CANR 7, 78; DLB 7; IDFW 3, 4
Kaniuk, Yoram 1930- .... **CLC 19**
    See also CA 134
Kant, Immanuel 1724-1804 ..... **NCLC 27, 67**
    See also DLB 94
Kantor, MacKinlay 1904-1977 .... **CLC 7**
    See also CA 61-64; 73-76; CANR 60, 63;
    DLB 9, 102; MTCW 2; RHW; TCWW 2
Kanze Motokiyo
    See Zeami

Kaplan, David Michael 1946- .... **CLC 50**
    See also CA 187
Kaplan, James 1951- .... **CLC 59**
    See also CA 135; CANR 121
Karadzic, Vuk Stefanovic
    1787-1864 .... **NCLC 115**
    See also CDWLB 4; DLB 147
Karageorge, Michael
    See Anderson, Poul (William)
Karamzin, Nikolai Mikhailovich
    1766-1826 .... **NCLC 3**
    See also DLB 150; RGSF 2
Karapanou, Margarita 1946- .... **CLC 13**
    See also CA 101
Karinthy, Frigyes 1887-1938 .... **TCLC 47**
    See also CA 170; DLB 215; EWL 3
Karl, Frederick R(obert) 1927- .... **CLC 34**
    See also CA 5-8R; CANR 3, 44
Kastel, Warren
    See Silverberg, Robert
Kataev, Evgeny Petrovich 1903-1942
    See Petrov, Evgeny
    See also CA 120
Kataphusin
    See Ruskin, John
Katz, Steve 1935- .... **CLC 47**
    See also CA 25-28R; CAAS 14, 64; CANR
    12; CN 7; DLBY 1983
Kauffman, Janet 1945- .... **CLC 42**
    See also CA 117; CANR 43, 84; DLB 218;
    DLBY 1986
Kaufman, Bob (Garnell) 1925-1986 . **CLC 49**
    See also BG 3; BW 1; CA 41-44R; 118;
    CANR 22; DLB 16, 41
Kaufman, George S. 1889-1961 ...... **CLC 38;
    DC 17**
    See also CA 108; 93-96; DAM DRAM;
    DFS 1, 10; DLB 7; INT CA-108; MTCW
    2; RGAL 4; TUS
Kaufman, Sue .... **CLC 3, 8**
    See Barondess, Sue K(aufman)
Kavafis, Konstantinos Petrou 1863-1933
    See Cavafy, C(onstantine) P(eter)
    See also CA 104
Kavan, Anna 1901-1968 .... **CLC 5, 13, 82**
    See also BRWS 7; CA 5-8R; CANR 6, 57;
    DLB 255; MTCW 1; RGEL 2; SFW 4
Kavanagh, Dan
    See Barnes, Julian (Patrick)
Kavanagh, Julie 1952- .... **CLC 119**
    See also CA 163
Kavanagh, Patrick (Joseph)
    1904-1967 .... **CLC 22; PC 33**
    See also BRWS 7; CA 123; 25-28R; DLB
    15, 20; EWL 3; MTCW 1; RGEL 2
Kawabata, Yasunari 1899-1972 ..... **CLC 2, 5,
    9, 18, 107; SSC 17**
    See Kawabata Yasunari
    See also CA 93-96; 33-36R; CANR 88;
    DAM MULT; MJW; MTCW 2; RGSF 2;
    RGWL 2, 3
Kawabata Yasunari
    See Kawabata, Yasunari
    See also DLB 180; EWL 3
Kaye, M(ary) M(argaret) 1909- .... **CLC 28**
    See also CA 89-92; CANR 24, 60, 102;
    MTCW 1, 2; RHW; SATA 62
Kaye, Mollie
    See Kaye, M(ary) M(argaret)
Kaye-Smith, Sheila 1887-1956 .... **TCLC 20**
    See also CA 118; 203; DLB 36
Kaymor, Patrice Maguilene
    See Senghor, Leopold Sedar
Kazakov, Yuri Pavlovich 1927-1982 . **SSC 43**
    See Kazakov, Yury
    See also CA 5-8R; CANR 36; MTCW 1;
    RGSF 2

Kazakov, Yury
    See Kazakov, Yuri Pavlovich
    See also EWL 3
Kazan, Elia 1909- .... **CLC 6, 16, 63**
    See also CA 21-24R; CANR 32, 78
Kazantzakis, Nikos 1883(?)-1957 .... **TCLC 2,
    5, 33**
    See also BPFB 2; CA 105; 132; DA3; EW
    9; EWL 3; MTCW 1, 2; RGWL 2, 3
Kazin, Alfred 1915-1998 ..... **CLC 34, 38, 119**
    See also AMWS 8; CA 1-4R; CAAS 7;
    CANR 1, 45, 79; DLB 67; EWL 3
Keane, Mary Nesta (Skrine) 1904-1996
    See Keane, Molly
    See also CA 108; 114; 151; CN 7; RHW
Keane, Molly .... **CLC 31**
    See Keane, Mary Nesta (Skrine)
    See also INT 114
Keates, Jonathan 1946(?)- .... **CLC 34**
    See also CA 163
Keaton, Buster 1895-1966 .... **CLC 20**
    See also CA 194
Keats, John 1795-1821 ...... **NCLC 8, 73, 121;
    PC 1; WLC**
    See also BRW 4; BRWR 1; CDBLB 1789-
    1832; DA; DA3; DAB; DAC; DAM MST,
    POET; DLB 96, 110; EXPP; LMFS 1;
    PAB; PFS 1, 2, 3, 9, 16; RGEL 2; TEA;
    WLIT 3; WP
Keble, John 1792-1866 .... **NCLC 87**
    See also DLB 32, 55; RGEL 2
Keene, Donald 1922- .... **CLC 34**
    See also CA 1-4R; CANR 5, 119
Keillor, Garrison .... **CLC 40, 115**
    See Keillor, Gary (Edward)
    See also AAYA 2; BEST 89:3; BPFB 2;
    DLBY 1987; EWL 3; SATA 58; TUS
Keillor, Gary (Edward) 1942-
    See Keillor, Garrison
    See also CA 111; 117; CANR 36, 59; CPW;
    DA3; DAM POP; MTCW 1, 2
Keith, Carlos
    See Lewton, Val
Keith, Michael
    See Hubbard, L(afayette) Ron(ald)
Keller, Gottfried 1819-1890 .... **NCLC 2; SSC
    26**
    See also CDWLB 2; DLB 129; EW; RGSF
    2; RGWL 2, 3
Keller, Nora Okja 1965- .... **CLC 109**
    See also CA 187
Kellerman, Jonathan 1949- .... **CLC 44**
    See also AAYA 35; BEST 90:1; CA 106;
    CANR 29, 51; CMW 4; CPW; DA3;
    DAM POP; INT CANR-29
Kelley, William Melvin 1937- .... **CLC 22**
    See also BW 1; CA 77-80; CANR 27, 83;
    CN 7; DLB 33; EWL 3
Kellogg, Marjorie 1922- .... **CLC 2**
    See also CA 81-84
Kellow, Kathleen
    See Hibbert, Eleanor Alice Burford
Kelly, M(ilton) T(errence) 1947- ...... **CLC 55**
    See also CA 97-100; CAAS 22; CANR 19,
    43, 84; CN 7
Kelly, Robert 1935- .... **SSC 50**
    See also CA 17-20R; CAAS 19; CANR 47;
    CP 7; DLB 5, 130, 165
Kelman, James 1946- .... **CLC 58, 86**
    See also BRWS 5; CA 148; CANR 85; CN
    7; DLB 194; RGSF 2; WLIT 4
Kemal, Yashar 1923- .... **CLC 14, 29**
    See also CA 89-92; CANR 44; CWW 2
Kemble, Fanny 1809-1893 .... **NCLC 18**
    See also DLB 32
Kemelman, Harry 1908-1996 .... **CLC 2**
    See also AITN 1; BPFB 2; CA 9-12R; 155;
    CANR 6, 71; CMW 4; DLB 28

Kinsey, Alfred C(harles)
1894-1956 .... **TCLC 91**
See also CA 115; 170; MTCW 2

Kipling, (Joseph) Rudyard 1865-1936 . **PC 3;
SSC 5, 54; TCLC 8, 17; WLC**
See also AAYA 32; BRW 6; BRWC 1; BYA
4; CA 105; 120; CANR 33; CDBLB
1890-1914; CLR 39, 65; CWRI 5; DA;
DA3; DAB; DAC; DAM MST, POET;
DLB 19, 34, 141, 156; EWL 3; EXPS;
FANT; LAIT 3; LMFS 1; MAICYA 1, 2;
MTCW 1, 2; RGEL 2; RGSF 2; SATA
100; SFW 4; SSFS 8; SUFW 1; TEA;
WCH; WLIT 4; YABC 2

Kirk, Russell (Amos) 1918-1994 .. **TCLC 119**
See also AITN 1; CA 1-4R; 145; CAAS 9;
CANR 1, 20, 60; HGG; INT CANR-20;
MTCW 1, 2

Kirkland, Caroline M. 1801-1864 . **NCLC 85**
See also DLB 3, 73, 74, 250, 254; DLBD
13

Kirkup, James 1918- .... **CLC 1**
See also CA 1-4R; CAAS 4; CANR 2; CP
7; DLB 27; SATA 12

Kirkwood, James 1930(?)-1989 .... **CLC 9**
See also AITN 2; CA 1-4R; 128; CANR 6,
40; GLL 2

Kirsch, Sarah 1935- .... **CLC 176**
See also CA 178; CWW 2; DLB 75; EWL
3

Kirshner, Sidney
See Kingsley, Sidney

Kis, Danilo 1935-1989 .... **CLC 57**
See also CA 109; 118; 129; CANR 61; CD-
WLB 4; DLB 181; EWL 3; MTCW 1;
RGSF 2; RGWL 2, 3

Kissinger, Henry A(lfred) 1923- ..... **CLC 137**
See also CA 1-4R; CANR 2, 33, 66, 109;
MTCW 1

Kivi, Aleksis 1834-1872 .... **NCLC 30**

Kizer, Carolyn (Ashley) 1925- ... **CLC 15, 39,
80**
See also CA 65-68; CAAS 5; CANR 24,
70; CP 7; CWP; DAM POET; DLB 5,
169; EWL 3; MTCW 2; PFS 18

Klabund 1890-1928 .... **TCLC 44**
See also CA 162; DLB 66

Klappert, Peter 1942- .... **CLC 57**
See also CA 33-36R; CSW; DLB 5

Klein, A(braham) M(oses)
1909-1972 .... **CLC 19**
See also CA 101; 37-40R; DAB; DAC;
DAM MST; DLB 68; EWL 3; RGEL 2

Klein, Joe
See Klein, Joseph

Klein, Joseph 1946- .... **CLC 154**
See also CA 85-88; CANR 55

Klein, Norma 1938-1989 .... **CLC 30**
See also AAYA 2, 35; BPFB 2; BYA 6, 7,
8; CA 41-44R; 128; CANR 15, 37; CLR
2, 19; INT CANR-15; JRDA; MAICYA
1, 2; SAAS 1; SATA 7, 57; WYA; YAW

Klein, T(heodore) E(ibon) D(onald)
1947- .... **CLC 34**
See also CA 119; CANR 44, 75; HGG

Kleist, Heinrich von 1777-1811 ...... **NCLC 2,
37; SSC 22**
See also CDWLB 2; DAM DRAM; DLB
90; EW 5; RGSF 2; RGWL 2, 3

Klima, Ivan 1931- .... **CLC 56, 172**
See also CA 25-28R; CANR 17, 50, 91;
CDWLB 4; CWW 2; DAM NOV; DLB
232; EWL 3; RGWL 3

Klimentev, Andrei Platonovich
See Klimentov, Andrei Platonovich

Klimentov, Andrei Platonovich
1899-1951 .... **SSC 42; TCLC 14**
See also Platonov, Andrei Platonovich; Platonov,
Andrey Platonovich
See also CA 108

Klinger, Friedrich Maximilian von
1752-1831 .... **NCLC 1**
See also DLB 94

Klingsor the Magician
See Hartmann, Sadakichi

Klopstock, Friedrich Gottlieb
1724-1803 .... **NCLC 11**
See also DLB 97; EW 4; RGWL 2, 3

Kluge, Alexander 1932- .... **SSC 61**
See also CA 81-84; DLB 75

Knapp, Caroline 1959-2002 .... **CLC 99**
See also CA 154; 207

Knebel, Fletcher 1911-1993 .... **CLC 14**
See also AITN 1; CA 1-4R; 140; CAAS 3;
CANR 1, 36; SATA 36; SATA-Obit 75

Knickerbocker, Diedrich
See Irving, Washington

Knight, Etheridge 1931-1991 ... **BLC 2; CLC
40; PC 14**
See also BW 1, 3; CA 21-24R; 133; CANR
23, 82; DAM POET; DLB 41; MTCW 2;
RGAL 4

Knight, Sarah Kemble 1666-1727 .... **LC 7**
See also DLB 24, 200

Knister, Raymond 1899-1932 .... **TCLC 56**
See also CA 186; DLB 68; RGEL 2

Knowles, John 1926-2001 ... **CLC 1, 4, 10, 26**
See also AAYA 10; AMWS 12; BPFB 2;
BYA 3; CA 17-20R; 203; CANR 40, 74,
76; CDALB 1968-1988; CN 7; DA; DAC;
DAM MST, NOV; DLB 6; EXPN; MTCW
1, 2; NFS 2; RGAL 4; SATA 8, 89; SATA-
Obit 134; YAW

Knox, Calvin M.
See Silverberg, Robert

Knox, John c. 1505-1572 .... **LC 37**
See also DLB 132

Knye, Cassandra
See Disch, Thomas M(ichael)

Koch, C(hristopher) J(ohn) 1932- .... **CLC 42**
See also CA 127; CANR 84; CN 7

Koch, Christopher
See Koch, C(hristopher) J(ohn)

Koch, Kenneth (Jay) 1925-2002 .... **CLC 5, 8,
44**
See also CA 1-4R; 207; CAD; CANR 6,
36, 57, 97; CD 5; CP 7; DAM POET;
DLB 5; INT CANR-36; MTCW 2; SATA
65; WP

Kochanowski, Jan 1530-1584 .... **LC 10**
See also RGWL 2, 3

Kock, Charles Paul de 1794-1871 . **NCLC 16**

Koda Rohan
See Koda Shigeyuki

Koda Rohan
See Koda Shigeyuki
See also DLB 180

Koda Shigeyuki 1867-1947 .... **TCLC 22**
See Koda Rohan
See also CA 121; 183

Koestler, Arthur 1905-1983 ... **CLC 1, 3, 6, 8,
15, 33**
See also BRWS 1; CA 1-4R; 109; CANR 1,
33; CDBLB 1945-1960; DLBY 1983;
EWL 3; MTCW 1, 2; RGEL 2

Kogawa, Joy Nozomi 1935- ...... **CLC 78, 129**
See also AAYA 47; CA 101; CANR 19, 62;
CN 7; CWP; DAC; DAM MST, MULT;
FW; MTCW 2; NFS 3; SATA 99

Kohout, Pavel 1928- .... **CLC 13**
See also CA 45-48; CANR 3

Koizumi, Yakumo
See Hearn, (Patricio) Lafcadio (Tessima
Carlos)

Kolmar, Gertrud 1894-1943 .... **TCLC 40**
See also CA 167; EWL 3

Komunyakaa, Yusef 1947- .. **BLCS; CLC 86,
94**
See also AFAW 2; AMWS 13; CA 147;
CANR 83; CP 7; CSW; DLB 120; EWL
3; PFS 5; RGAL 4

Konrad, George
See Konrad, Gyorgy
See also CWW 2

Konrad, Gyorgy 1933- .... **CLC 4, 10, 73**
See Konrad, George
See also CA 85-88; CANR 97; CDWLB 4;
CWW 2; DLB 232; EWL 3

Konwicki, Tadeusz 1926- .... **CLC 8, 28, 54,
117**
See also CA 101; CAAS 9; CANR 39, 59;
CWW 2; DLB 232; EWL 3; IDFW 3;
MTCW 1

Koontz, Dean R(ay) 1945- .... **CLC 78**
See also AAYA 9, 31; BEST 89:3, 90:2; CA
108; CANR 19, 36, 52, 95; CMW 4;
CPW; DA3; DAM NOV, POP; HGG;
MTCW 1; SATA 92; SFW 4; SUFW 2;
YAW

Kopernik, Mikolaj
See Copernicus, Nicolaus

Kopit, Arthur (Lee) 1937- ...... **CLC 1, 18, 33**
See also AITN 1; CA 81-84; CABS 3; CD
5; DAM DRAM; DFS 7, 14; DLB 7;
MTCW 1; RGAL 4

Kopitar, Jernej (Bartholomaus)
1780-1844 .... **NCLC 117**

Kops, Bernard 1926- .... **CLC 4**
See also CA 5-8R; CANR 84; CBD; CN 7;
CP 7; DLB 13

Kornbluth, C(yril) M. 1923-1958 .... **TCLC 8**
See also CA 105; 160; DLB 8; SFW 4

Korolenko, V. G.
See Korolenko, Vladimir Galaktionovich

Korolenko, Vladimir
See Korolenko, Vladimir Galaktionovich

Korolenko, Vladimir G.
See Korolenko, Vladimir Galaktionovich

Korolenko, Vladimir Galaktionovich
1853-1921 .... **TCLC 22**
See also CA 121; DLB 277

Korzybski, Alfred (Habdank Skarbek)
1879-1950 .... **TCLC 61**
See also CA 123; 160

Kosinski, Jerzy (Nikodem)
1933-1991 .... **CLC 1, 2, 3, 6, 10, 15, 53,
70**
See also AMWS 7; BPFB 2; CA 17-20R;
134; CANR 9, 46; DA3; DAM NOV;
DLB 2; DLBY 1982; EWL 3; HGG;
MTCW 1, 2; NFS 12; RGAL 4; TUS

Kostelanetz, Richard (Cory) 1940- .. **CLC 28**
See also CA 13-16R; CAAS 8; CANR 38,
77; CN 7; CP 7

Kostrowitzki, Wilhelm Apollinaris de
1880-1918
See Apollinaire, Guillaume
See also CA 104

Kotlowitz, Robert 1924- .... **CLC 4**
See also CA 33-36R; CANR 36

Kotzebue, August (Friedrich Ferdinand) von
1761-1819 .... **NCLC 25**
See also DLB 94

Kotzwinkle, William 1938- ..... **CLC 5, 14, 35**
See also BPFB 2; CA 45-48; CANR 3, 44,
84; CLR 6; DLB 173; FANT; MAICYA
1, 2; SATA 24, 70; SFW 4; SUFW 2;
YAW

Kowna, Stancy
See Szymborska, Wislawa

Kozol, Jonathan 1936- .... **CLC 17**
See also AAYA 46; CA 61-64; CANR 16,
45, 96

Lowell, James Russell 1819-1891 ... **NCLC 2, 90**
See also AMWS 1; CDALB 1640-1865; DLB 1, 11, 64, 79, 189, 235; RGAL 4

Lowell, Robert (Traill Spence, Jr.)
1917-1977 .... **CLC 1, 2, 3, 4, 5, 8, 9, 11, 15, 37, 124; PC 3; WLC**
See also AMW; AMWR 2; CA 9-12R; 73-76; CABS 2; CANR 26, 60; CDALBS; DA; DA3; DAB; DAC; DAM MST, NOV, DLB 5, 169; EWL 3; MTCW 1, 2; PAB; PFS 6, 7; RGAL 4; WP

Lowenthal, Michael (Francis)
1969- .... **CLC 119**
See also CA 150; CANR 115

Lowndes, Marie Adelaide (Belloc)
1868-1947 .... **TCLC 12**
See also CA 107; CMW 4; DLB 70; RHW

Lowry, (Clarence) Malcolm
1909-1957 .... **SSC 31; TCLC 6, 40**
See also BPFB 2; BRWS 3; CA 105; 131; CANR 62, 105; CDBLB 1945-1960; DLB 15; EWL 3; MTCW 1, 2; RGEL 2

Lowry, Mina Gertrude 1882-1966
See Loy, Mina
See also CA 113

Loxsmith, John
See Brunner, John (Kilian Houston)

Loy, Mina .... **CLC 28; PC 16**
See Lowry, Mina Gertrude
See also DAM POET; DLB 4, 54

Loyson-Bridet
See Schwob, Marcel (Mayer Andre)

Lucan 39-65 .... **CMLC 33**
See also AW 2; DLB 211; EFS 2; RGWL 2, 3

Lucas, Craig 1951- .... **CLC 64**
See also CA 137; CAD; CANR 71, 109; CD 5; GLL 2

Lucas, E(dward) V(errall)
1868-1938 .... **TCLC 73**
See also CA 176; DLB 98, 149, 153; SATA 20

Lucas, George 1944- .... **CLC 16**
See also AAYA 1, 23; CA 77-80; CANR 30; SATA 56

Lucas, Hans
See Godard, Jean-Luc

Lucas, Victoria
See Plath, Sylvia

Lucian c. 125-c. 180 .... **CMLC 32**
See also AW 2; DLB 176; RGWL 2, 3

Lucretius c. 94B.C.-c. 49B.C. .... **CMLC 48**
See also AW 2; CDWLB 1; DLB 211; EFS 2; RGWL 2, 3

Ludlam, Charles 1943-1987 .... **CLC 46, 50**
See also CA 85-88; 122; CAD; CANR 72, 86; DLB 266

Ludlum, Robert 1927-2001 .... **CLC 22, 43**
See also AAYA 10; BEST 89:1, 90:3; BPFB 2; CA 33-36R; 195; CANR 25, 41, 68, 105; CMW 4; CPW; DA3; DAM NOV, POP; DLBY 1982; MSW; MTCW 1, 2

Ludwig, Ken .... **CLC 60**
See also CA 195; CAD

Ludwig, Otto 1813-1865 .... **NCLC 4**
See also DLB 129

Lugones, Leopoldo 1874-1938 .... **HLCS 2; TCLC 15**
See also CA 116; 131; CANR 104; DLB 283; EWL 3; HW 1; LAW

Lu Hsun .... **SSC 20; TCLC 3**
See Shu-Jen, Chou
See also EWL 3

Lukacs, George .... **CLC 24**
See Lukacs, Gyorgy (Szegeny von)

Lukacs, Gyorgy (Szegeny von) 1885-1971
See Lukacs, George
See also CA 101; 29-32R; CANR 62; CD-WLB 4; DLB 215, 242; EW 10; EWL 3; MTCW 2

Luke, Peter (Ambrose Cyprian)
1919-1995 .... **CLC 38**
See also CA 81-84; 147; CANR 72; CBD; CD 5; DLB 13

Lunar, Dennis
See Mungo, Raymond

Lurie, Alison 1926- ..... **CLC 4, 5, 18, 39, 175**
See also BPFB 2; CA 1-4R; CANR 2, 17, 50, 88; CN 7; DLB 2; MTCW 1; SATA 46, 112

Lustig, Arnost 1926- .... **CLC 56**
See also AAYA 3; CA 69-72; CANR 47, 102; CWW 2; DLB 232; EWL 3; SATA 56

Luther, Martin 1483-1546 .... **LC 9, 37**
See also CDWLB 2; DLB 179; EW 2; RGWL 2, 3

Luxemburg, Rosa 1870(?)-1919 ..... **TCLC 63**
See also CA 118

Luzi, Mario 1914- .... **CLC 13**
See also CA 61-64; CANR 9, 70; CWW 2; DLB 128; EWL 3

L'vov, Arkady .... **CLC 59**

Lydgate, John c. 1370-1450(?) .... **LC 81**
See also BRW 1; DLB 146; RGEL 2

Lyly, John 1554(?)-1606 .... **DC 7; LC 41**
See also BRW 1; DAM DRAM; DLB 62, 167; RGEL 2

L'Ymagier
See Gourmont, Remy(-Marie-Charles) de

Lynch, B. Suarez
See Borges, Jorge Luis

Lynch, David (Keith) 1946- ...... **CLC 66, 162**
See also CA 124; 129; CANR 111

Lynch, James
See Andreyev, Leonid (Nikolaevich)

Lyndsay, Sir David 1485-1555 .... **LC 20**
See also RGEL 2

Lynn, Kenneth S(chuyler)
1923-2001 .... **CLC 50**
See also CA 1-4R; 196; CANR 3, 27, 65

Lynx
See West, Rebecca

Lyons, Marcus
See Blish, James (Benjamin)

Lyotard, Jean-Francois
1924-1998 .... **TCLC 103**
See also DLB 242; EWL 3

Lyre, Pinchbeck
See Sassoon, Siegfried (Lorraine)

Lytle, Andrew (Nelson) 1902-1995 ... **CLC 22**
See also CA 9-12R; 150; CANR 70; CN 7; CSW; DLB 6; DLBY 1995; RGAL 4; RHW

Lyttelton, George 1709-1773 .... **LC 10**
See also RGEL 2

Lytton of Knebworth, Baron
See Bulwer-Lytton, Edward (George Earle Lytton)

Maas, Peter 1929-2001 .... **CLC 29**
See also CA 93-96; 201; INT CA-93-96; MTCW 2

Macaulay, Catherine 1731-1791 .... **LC 64**
See also DLB 104

Macaulay, (Emilie) Rose
1881(?)-1958 .... **TCLC 7, 44**
See also CA 104; DLB 36; EWL 3; RGEL 2; RHW

Macaulay, Thomas Babington
1800-1859 .... **NCLC 42**
See also BRW 4; CDBLB 1832-1890; DLB 32, 55; RGEL 2

MacBeth, George (Mann)
1932-1992 .... **CLC 2, 5, 9**
See also CA 25-28R; CANR 61, 66; DLB 40; MTCW 1; PFS 8; SATA 4; SATA-Obit 70

MacCaig, Norman (Alexander)
1910-1996 .... **CLC 36**
See also BRWS 6; CA 9-12R; CANR 3, 34; CP 7; DAB; DAM POET; DLB 27; EWL 3; RGEL 2

MacCarthy, Sir (Charles Otto) Desmond
1877-1952 .... **TCLC 36**
See also CA 167

MacDiarmid, Hugh .... **CLC 2, 4, 11, 19, 63; PC 9**
See Grieve, C(hristopher) M(urray)
See also CDBLB 1945-1960; DLB 20; EWL 3; RGEL 2

MacDonald, Anson
See Heinlein, Robert A(nson)

Macdonald, Cynthia 1928- .... **CLC 13, 19**
See also CA 49-52; CANR 4, 44; DLB 105

MacDonald, George 1824-1905 .... **TCLC 9, 113**
See also BYA 5; CA 106; 137; CANR 80; CLR 67; DLB 18, 163, 178; FANT; MAI-CYA 1, 2; RGEL 2; SATA 33, 100; SFW 4; SUFW; WCH

Macdonald, John
See Millar, Kenneth

MacDonald, John D(ann)
1916-1986 .... **CLC 3, 27, 44**
See also BPFB 2; CA 1-4R; 121; CANR 1, 19, 60; CMW 4; CPW; DAM NOV, POP; DLB 8; DLBY 1986; MSW; MTCW 1, 2; SFW 4

Macdonald, John Ross
See Millar, Kenneth

Macdonald, Ross ..... **CLC 1, 2, 3, 14, 34, 41**
See Millar, Kenneth
See also AMWS 4; BPFB 2; DLBD 6; MSW; RGAL 4

MacDougal, John
See Blish, James (Benjamin)

MacDougal, John
See Blish, James (Benjamin)

MacDowell, John
See Parks, Tim(othy Harold)

MacEwen, Gwendolyn (Margaret)
1941-1987 .... **CLC 13, 55**
See also CA 9-12R; 124; CANR 7, 22; DLB 53, 251; SATA 50; SATA-Obit 55

Macha, Karel Hynek 1810-1846 .... **NCLC 46**

Machado (y Ruiz), Antonio
1875-1939 .... **TCLC 3**
See also CA 104; 174; DLB 108; EW 9; EWL 3; HW 2; RGWL 2, 3

Machado de Assis, Joaquim Maria
1839-1908 .... **BLC 2; HLCS 2; SSC 24; TCLC 10**
See also CA 107; 153; CANR 91; LAW; RGSF 2; RGWL 2, 3; TWA; WLIT 1

Machen, Arthur .... **SSC 20; TCLC 4**
See Jones, Arthur Llewellyn
See also CA 179; DLB 156, 178; RGEL 2; SUFW 1

Machiavelli, Niccolo 1469-1527 ... **DC 16; LC 8, 36; WLCS**
See also DA; DAB; DAC; DAM MST; EW 2; LAIT 1; LMFS 1; NFS 9; RGWL 2, 3; TWA

MacInnes, Colin 1914-1976 .... **CLC 4, 23**
See also CA 69-72; 65-68; CANR 21; DLB 14; MTCW 1, 2; RGEL 2; RHW

MacInnes, Helen (Clark)
1907-1985 .... **CLC 27, 39**
See also BPFB 2; CA 1-4R; 117; CANR 1, 28, 58; CMW 4; CPW; DAM POP; DLB 87; MSW; MTCW 1, 2; SATA 22; SATA-Obit 44

Martineau, Harriet 1802-1876 .... **NCLC 26**
See also DLB 21, 55, 159, 163, 166, 190;
FW; RGEL 2; YABC 2
Martines, Julia
See O'Faolain, Julia
Martinez, Enrique Gonzalez
See Gonzalez Martinez, Enrique
Martinez, Jacinto Benavente y
See Benavente (y Martinez), Jacinto
Martinez de la Rosa, Francisco de Paula
1787-1862 .... **NCLC 102**
See also TWA
Martinez Ruiz, Jose 1873-1967
See Azorin; Ruiz, Jose Martinez
See also CA 93-96; HW 1
Martinez Sierra, Gregorio
1881-1947 .... **TCLC 6**
See also CA 115; EWL 3
Martinez Sierra, Maria (de la O'LeJarraga)
1874-1974 .... **TCLC 6**
See also CA 115; EWL 3
Martinsen, Martin
See Follett, Ken(neth Martin)
Martinson, Harry (Edmund)
1904-1978 .... **CLC 14**
See also CA 77-80; CANR 34; DLB 259;
EWL 3
Martyn, Edward 1859-1923 .... **TCLC 131**
See also CA 179; DLB 10; RGEL 2
Marut, Ret
See Traven, B.
Marut, Robert
See Traven, B.
Marvell, Andrew 1621-1678 .... **LC 4, 43; PC
10; WLC**
See also BRW 2; BRWR 2; CDBLB 1660-
1789; DA; DAB; DAC; DAM MST,
POET; DLB 131; EXPP; PFS 5; RGEL 2;
TEA; WP
Marx, Karl (Heinrich)
1818-1883 .... **NCLC 17, 114**
See also DLB 129; LATS 1; TWA
Masaoka, Shiki -1902 .... **TCLC 18**
See Masaoka, Tsunenori
See also RGWL 3
Masaoka, Tsunenori 1867-1902
See Masaoka, Shiki
See also CA 117; 191; TWA
Masefield, John (Edward)
1878-1967 .... **CLC 11, 47**
See also CA 19-20; 25-28R; CANR 33;
CAP 2; CDBLB 1890-1914; DAM POET;
DLB 10, 19, 153, 160; EWL 3; EXPP;
FANT; MTCW 1, 2; PFS 5; RGEL 2;
SATA 19
Maso, Carole 19(?)- .... **CLC 44**
See also CA 170; GLL 2; RGAL 4
Mason, Bobbie Ann 1940- ... **CLC 28, 43, 82,
154; SSC 4**
See also AAYA 5, 42; AMWS 8; BPFB 2;
CA 53-56; CANR 11, 31, 58, 83;
CDALBS; CN 7; CSW; DA3; DLB 173;
DLBY 1987; EWL 3; EXPS; INT CANR-
31; MTCW 1, 2; NFS 4; RGAL 4; RGSF
2; SSFS 3,8; YAW
Mason, Ernst
See Pohl, Frederik
Mason, Hunni B.
See Sternheim, (William Adolf) Carl
Mason, Lee W.
See Malzberg, Barry N(athaniel)
Mason, Nick 1945- .... **CLC 35**
Mason, Tally
See Derleth, August (William)
Mass, Anna .... **CLC 59**
Mass, William
See Gibson, William
Massinger, Philip 1583-1640 .... **LC 70**
See also DLB 58; RGEL 2

Master Lao
See Lao Tzu
Masters, Edgar Lee 1868-1950 ...... **PC 1, 36;
TCLC 2, 25; WLCS**
See also AMWS 1; CA 104; 133; CDALB
1865-1917; DA; DAC; DAM MST,
POET; DLB 54; EWL 3; EXPP; MTCW
1, 2; RGAL 4; TUS; WP
Masters, Hilary 1928- .... **CLC 48**
See also CA 25-28R; CANR 13, 47, 97; CN
7; DLB 244
Mastrosimone, William 19(?)- .... **CLC 36**
See also CA 186; CAD; CD 5
Mathe, Albert
See Camus, Albert
Mather, Cotton 1663-1728 .... **LC 38**
See also AMWS 2; CDALB 1640-1865;
DLB 24, 30, 140; RGAL 4; TUS
Mather, Increase 1639-1723 .... **LC 38**
See also DLB 24
Matheson, Richard (Burton) 1926- .. **CLC 37**
See also AAYA 31; CA 97-100; CANR 88,
99; DLB 8, 44; HGG; INT 97-100; SCFW
2; SFW 4; SUFW 2
Mathews, Harry 1930- .... **CLC 6, 52**
See also CA 21-24R; CAAS 6; CANR 18,
40, 98; CN 7
Mathews, John Joseph 1894-1979 .. **CLC 84;
NNAL**
See also CA 19-20; 142; CANR 45; CAP 2;
DAM MULT; DLB 175
Mathias, Roland (Glyn) 1915- .... **CLC 45**
See also CA 97-100; CANR 19, 41; CP 7;
DLB 27
Matsuo Basho 1644-1694 .... **LC 62; PC 3**
See Basho, Matsuo
See also DAM POET; PFS 2, 7
Mattheson, Rodney
See Creasey, John
Matthews, (James) Brander
1852-1929 .... **TCLC 95**
See also DLB 71, 78; DLBD 13
Matthews, Greg 1949- .... **CLC 45**
See also CA 135
Matthews, William (Procter III)
1942-1997 .... **CLC 40**
See also AMWS 9; CA 29-32R; 162; CAAS
18; CANR 12, 57; CP 7; DLB 5
Matthias, John (Edward) 1941- .... **CLC 9**
See also CA 33-36R; CANR 56; CP 7
Matthiessen, F(rancis) O(tto)
1902-1950 .... **TCLC 100**
See also CA 185; DLB 63
Matthiessen, Peter 1927- ... **CLC 5, 7, 11, 32,
64**
See also AAYA 6, 40; AMWS 5; ANW;
BEST 90:4; BPFB 2; CA 9-12R; CANR
21, 50, 73, 100; CN 7; DA3; DAM NOV;
DLB 6, 173, 275; MTCW 1, 2; SATA 27
Maturin, Charles Robert
1780(?)-1824 .... **NCLC 6**
See also BRWS 8; DLB 178; HGG; LMFS
1; RGEL 2; SUFW
Matute (Ausejo), Ana Maria 1925- .. **CLC 11**
See also CA 89-92; EWL 3; MTCW 1;
RGSF 2
Maugham, W. S.
See Maugham, W(illiam) Somerset
Maugham, W(illiam) Somerset
1874-1965 .. **CLC 1, 11, 15, 67, 93; SSC
8; WLC**
See also BPFB 2; BRW 6; CA 5-8R; 25-
28R; CANR 40; CDBLB 1914-1945;
CMW 4; DA; DA3; DAB; DAC; DAM
DRAM, MST, NOV; DLB 10, 36, 77, 100,
162, 195; EWL 3; LAIT 3; MTCW 1, 2;
RGEL 2; RGSF 2; SATA 54; SSFS 17
Maugham, William Somerset
See Maugham, W(illiam) Somerset

Maupassant, (Henri Rene Albert) Guy de
1850-1893 . **NCLC 1, 42, 83; SSC 1, 64;
WLC**
See also BYA 14; DA; DA3; DAB; DAC;
DAM MST; DLB 123; EW 7; EXPS; GFL
1789 to the Present; LAIT 2; LMFS 1;
RGSF 2; RGWL 2, 3; SSFS 4; SUFW;
TWA
Maupin, Armistead (Jones, Jr.)
1944- .... **CLC 95**
See also CA 125; 130; CANR 58, 101;
CPW; DA3; DAM POP; DLB 278; GLL
1; INT 130; MTCW 2
Maurhut, Richard
See Traven, B.
Mauriac, Claude 1914-1996 .... **CLC 9**
See also CA 89-92; 152; CWW 2; DLB 83;
EWL 3; GFL 1789 to the Present
Mauriac, Francois (Charles)
1885-1970 .... **CLC 4, 9, 56; SSC 24**
See also CA 25-28; CAP 2; DLB 65; EW
10; EWL 3; GFL 1789 to the Present;
MTCW 1, 2; RGWL 2, 3; TWA
Mavor, Osborne Henry 1888-1951
See Bridie, James
See also CA 104
Maxwell, William (Keepers, Jr.)
1908-2000 .... **CLC 19**
See also AMWS 8; CA 93-96; 189; CANR
54, 95; CN 7; DLB 218, 278; DLBY
1980; INT CA-93-96; SATA-Obit 128
May, Elaine 1932- .... **CLC 16**
See also CA 124; 142; CAD; CWD; DLB
44
Mayakovski, Vladimir (Vladimirovich)
1893-1930 .... **TCLC 4, 18**
See Maiakovskii, Vladimir; Mayakovsky,
Vladimir
See also CA 104; 158; EWL 3; MTCW 2;
SFW 4; TWA
Mayakovsky, Vladimir
See Mayakovski, Vladimir (Vladimirovich)
See also EW 11; WP
Mayhew, Henry 1812-1887 .... **NCLC 31**
See also DLB 18, 55, 190
Mayle, Peter 1939(?)- .... **CLC 89**
See also CA 139; CANR 64, 109
Maynard, Joyce 1953- .... **CLC 23**
See also CA 111; 129; CANR 64
Mayne, William (James Carter)
1928- .... **CLC 12**
See also AAYA 20; CA 9-12R; CANR 37,
80, 100; CLR 25; FANT; JRDA; MAI-
CYA 1, 2; MAICYAS 1; SAAS 11; SATA
6, 68, 122; SUFW 2; YAW
Mayo, Jim
See L'Amour, Louis (Dearborn)
See also TCWW 2
Maysles, Albert 1926- .... **CLC 16**
See also CA 29-32R
Maysles, David 1932-1987 .... **CLC 16**
See also CA 191
Mazer, Norma Fox 1931- .... **CLC 26**
See also AAYA 5, 36; BYA 1, 8; CA 69-72;
CANR 12, 32, 66; CLR 23; JRDA; MAI-
CYA 1, 2; SAAS 1; SATA 24, 67, 105;
WYA; YAW
Mazzini, Guiseppe 1805-1872 .... **NCLC 34**
McAlmon, Robert (Menzies)
1895-1956 .... **TCLC 97**
See also CA 107; 168; DLB 4, 45; DLBD
15; GLL 1
McAuley, James Phillip 1917-1976 .. **CLC 45**
See also CA 97-100; DLB 260; RGEL 2
McBain, Ed
See Hunter, Evan
See also MSW

Megged, Aharon 1920- .... **CLC 9**
See also CA 49-52; CAAS 13; CANR 1;
EWL 3
Mehta, Gita 1943- .... **CLC 179**
See also DNFS 2
Mehta, Ved (Parkash) 1934- .... **CLC 37**
See also CA 1-4R; CAAE 212; CANR 2,
23, 69; MTCW 1
Melanchthon, Philipp 1497-1560 .... **LC 90**
See also DLB 179
Melanter
See Blackmore, R(ichard) D(oddridge)
Meleager c. 140B.C.-c. 70B.C. ...... **CMLC 53**
Melies, Georges 1861-1938 .... **TCLC 81**
Melikow, Loris
See Hofmannsthal, Hugo von
Melmoth, Sebastian
See Wilde, Oscar (Fingal O'Flahertie Wills)
Melo Neto, Joao Cabral de
See Cabral de Melo Neto, Joao
See also EWL 3
Meltzer, Milton 1915- .... **CLC 26**
See also AAYA 8, 45; BYA 2, 6; CA 13-
16R; CANR 38, 92, 107; CLR 13; DLB
61; JRDA; MAICYA 1, 2; SAAS 1; SATA
1, 50, 80, 128; SATA-Essay 124; WYA;
YAW
Melville, Herman 1819-1891 ..... **NCLC 3, 12,**
29, 45, 49, 91, 93, 123; SSC 1, 17, 46;
WLC
See also AAYA 25; AMW; AMWR 1;
CDALB 1640-1865; DA; DA3; DAB;
DAC; DAM MST, NOV; DLB 3, 74, 250,
254; EXPN; EXPS; LAIT 1, 2; NFS 7, 9;
RGAL 4; RGSF 2; SATA 59; SSFS 3;
TUS
Members, Mark
See Powell, Anthony (Dymoke)
Membreno, Alejandro .... **CLC 59**
Menander c. 342B.C.-c. 293B.C. .... **CMLC 9,**
51; DC 3
See also AW 1; CDWLB 1; DAM DRAM;
DLB 176; LMFS 1; RGWL 2, 3
Menchu, Rigoberta 1959- .. **CLC 160; HLCS**
2
See also CA 175; DNFS 1; WLIT 1
Mencken, H(enry) L(ouis)
1880-1956 .... **TCLC 13**
See also AMW; CA 105; 125; CDALB
1917-1929; DLB 11, 29, 63, 137, 222;
EWL 3; MTCW 1, 2; NCFS 4; RGAL 4;
TUS
Mendelsohn, Jane 1965- .... **CLC 99**
See also CA 154; CANR 94
Menton, Francisco de
See Chin, Frank (Chew, Jr.)
Mercer, David 1928-1980 .... **CLC 5**
See also CA 9-12R; 102; CANR 23; CBD;
DAM DRAM; DLB 13; MTCW 1; RGEL
2
Merchant, Paul
See Ellison, Harlan (Jay)
Meredith, George 1828-1909 ... **TCLC 17, 43**
See also CA 117; 153; CANR 80; CDBLB
1832-1890; DAM POET; DLB 18, 35, 57,
159; RGEL 2; TEA
Meredith, William (Morris) 1919- .... **CLC 4,**
13, 22, 55; PC 28
See also CA 9-12R; CAAS 14; CANR 6,
40; CP 7; DAM POET; DLB 5
Merezhkovsky, Dmitry Sergeevich
See Merezhkovsky, Dmitry Sergeyevich
See also EWL 3
Merezhkovsky, Dmitry Sergeyevich
1865-1941 .... **TCLC 29**
See Merezhkovsky, Dmitry Sergeevich
See also CA 169

Merimee, Prosper 1803-1870 ... **NCLC 6, 65;**
SSC 7
See also DLB 119, 192; EW 6; EXPS; GFL
1789 to the Present; RGSF 2; RGWL 2,
3; SSFS 8; SUFW
Merkin, Daphne 1954- .... **CLC 44**
See also CA 123
Merlin, Arthur
See Blish, James (Benjamin)
Mernissi, Fatima 1940- .... **CLC 171**
See also CA 152; FW
Merrill, James (Ingram) 1926-1995 .. **CLC 2,**
3, 6, 8, 13, 18, 34, 91; PC 28
See also AMWS 3; CA 13-16R; 147; CANR
10, 49, 63, 108; DA3; DAM POET; DLB
5, 165; DLBY 1985; EWL 3; INT CANR-
10; MTCW 1, 2; PAB; RGAL 4
Merriman, Alex
See Silverberg, Robert
Merriman, Brian 1747-1805 .... **NCLC 70**
Merritt, E. B.
See Waddington, Miriam
Merton, Thomas (James)
1915-1968 . **CLC 1, 3, 11, 34, 83; PC 10**
See also AMWS 8; CA 5-8R; 25-28R;
CANR 22, 53, 111; DA3; DLB 48; DLBY
1981; MTCW 1, 2
Merwin, W(illiam) S(tanley) 1927- ... **CLC 1,**
2, 3, 5, 8, 13, 18, 45, 88; PC 45
See also AMWS 3; CA 13-16R; CANR 15,
51, 112; CP 7; DA3; DAM POET; DLB
5, 169; EWL 3; INT CANR-15; MTCW
1, 2; PAB; PFS 5, 15; RGAL 4
Metcalf, John 1938- .... **CLC 37; SSC 43**
See also CA 113; CN 7; DLB 60; RGSF 2;
TWA
Metcalf, Suzanne
See Baum, L(yman) Frank
Mew, Charlotte (Mary) 1870-1928 .. **TCLC 8**
See also CA 105; 189; DLB 19, 135; RGEL
2
Mewshaw, Michael 1943- .... **CLC 9**
See also CA 53-56; CANR 7, 47; DLBY
1980
Meyer, Conrad Ferdinand
1825-1898 .... **NCLC 81**
See also DLB 129; EW; RGWL 2, 3
Meyer, Gustav 1868-1932
See Meyrink, Gustav
See also CA 117; 190
Meyer, June
See Jordan, June (Meyer)
Meyer, Lynn
See Slavitt, David R(ytman)
Meyers, Jeffrey 1939- .... **CLC 39**
See also CA 73-76; CAAE 186; CANR 54,
102; DLB 111
Meynell, Alice (Christina Gertrude
Thompson) 1847-1922 .... **TCLC 6**
See also CA 104; 177; DLB 19, 98; RGEL
2
Meyrink, Gustav .... **TCLC 21**
See Meyer, Gustav
See also DLB 81; EWL 3
Michaels, Leonard 1933- .... **CLC 6, 25; SSC**
16
See also CA 61-64; CANR 21, 62, 119; CN
7; DLB 130; MTCW 1
Michaux, Henri 1899-1984 .... **CLC 8, 19**
See also CA 85-88; 114; DLB 258; EWL 3;
GFL 1789 to the Present; RGWL 2, 3
Micheaux, Oscar (Devereaux)
1884-1951 .... **TCLC 76**
See also BW 3; CA 174; DLB 50; TCWW
2
Michelangelo 1475-1564 .... **LC 12**
See also AAYA 43
Michelet, Jules 1798-1874 .... **NCLC 31**
See also EW 5; GFL 1789 to the Present

Michels, Robert 1876-1936 .... **TCLC 88**
See also CA 212
Michener, James A(lbert)
1907(?)-1997 .. **CLC 1, 5, 11, 29, 60, 109**
See also AAYA 27; AITN 1; BEST 90:1;
BPFB 2; CA 5-8R; 161; CANR 21, 45,
68; CN 7; CPW; DA3; DAM NOV, POP;
DLB 6; MTCW 1, 2; RHW
Mickiewicz, Adam 1798-1855 . **NCLC 3, 101;**
PC 38
See also EW 5; RGWL 2, 3
Middleton, (John) Christopher
1926- .... **CLC 13**
See also CA 13-16R; CANR 29, 54, 117;
CP 7; DLB 40
Middleton, Richard (Barham)
1882-1911 .... **TCLC 56**
See also CA 187; DLB 156; HGG
Middleton, Stanley 1919- .... **CLC 7, 38**
See also CA 25-28R; CAAS 23; CANR 21,
46, 81; CN 7; DLB 14
Middleton, Thomas 1580-1627 ...... **DC 5; LC**
33
See also BRW 2; DAM DRAM, MST; DFS
18; DLB 58; RGEL 2
Migueis, Jose Rodrigues 1901-1980 . **CLC 10**
See also DLB 287
Mikszath, Kalman 1847-1910 .... **TCLC 31**
See also CA 170
Miles, Jack .... **CLC 100**
See also CA 200
Miles, John Russiano
See Miles, Jack
Miles, Josephine (Louise)
1911-1985 .... **CLC 1, 2, 14, 34, 39**
See also CA 1-4R; 116; CANR 2, 55; DAM
POET; DLB 48
Militant
See Sandburg, Carl (August)
Mill, Harriet (Hardy) Taylor
1807-1858 .... **NCLC 102**
See also FW
Mill, John Stuart 1806-1873 .... **NCLC 11, 58**
See also CDBLB 1832-1890; DLB 55, 190,
262; FW 1; RGEL 2; TEA
Millar, Kenneth 1915-1983 .... **CLC 14**
See Macdonald, Ross
See also CA 9-12R; 110; CANR 16, 63,
107; CMW 4; CPW; DA3; DAM POP;
DLB 2, 226; DLBD 6; DLBY 1983;
MTCW 1, 2
Millay, E. Vincent
See Millay, Edna St. Vincent
Millay, Edna St. Vincent 1892-1950 .... **PC 6;**
TCLC 4, 49; WLCS
See Boyd, Nancy
See also AMW; CA 104; 130; CDALB
1917-1929; DA; DA3; DAB; DAC; DAM
MST, POET; DLB 45, 249; EWL 3;
EXPP; MAWW; MTCW 1, 2; PAB; PFS
3, 17; RGAL 4; TUS; WP
Miller, Arthur 1915- ...... **CLC 1, 2, 6, 10, 15,**
26, 47, 78, 179; DC 1; WLC
See also AAYA 15; AITN 1; AMW; AMWC
1; CA 1-4R; CABS 3; CAD; CANR 2,
30, 54, 76; CD 5; CDALB 1941-1968;
DA; DA3; DAB; DAC; DAM DRAM,
MST; DFS 1, 3, 8; DLB 7, 266; EWL 3;
LAIT 1, 4; LATS 1; MTCW 1, 2; RGAL
4; TUS; WYAS 1
Miller, Henry (Valentine)
1891-1980 .... **CLC 1, 2, 4, 9, 14, 43, 84;**
WLC
See also AMW; BPFB 2; CA 9-12R; 97-
100; CANR 33, 64; CDALB 1929-1941;
DA; DA3; DAB; DAC; DAM MST, NOV;
DLB 4, 9; DLBY 1980; EWL 3; MTCW
1, 2; RGAL 4; TUS

Miller, Jason 1939(?)-2001 .... **CLC 2**
See also AITN 1; CA 73-76; 197; CAD;
DFS 12; DLB 7

Miller, Sue 1943- .... **CLC 44**
See also AMWS 12; BEST 90:3; CA 139;
CANR 59, 91; DA3; DAM POP; DLB
143

Miller, Walter M(ichael, Jr.)
1923-1996 .... **CLC 4, 30**
See also BPFB 2; CA 85-88; CANR 108;
DLB 8; SCFW; SFW 4

Millett, Kate 1934- .... **CLC 67**
See also AITN 1; CA 73-76; CANR 32, 53,
76, 110; DA3; DLB 246; FW; GLL 1;
MTCW 1, 2

Millhauser, Steven (Lewis) 1943- .... **CLC 21,
54, 109; SSC 57**
See also CA 110; 111; CANR 63, 114; CN
7; DA3; DLB 2; FANT; INT CA-111;
MTCW 2

Millin, Sarah Gertrude 1889-1968 ... **CLC 49**
See also CA 102; 93-96; DLB 225; EWL 3

Milne, A(lan) A(lexander)
1882-1956 .... **TCLC 6, 88**
See also BRWS 5; CA 104; 133; CLR 1,
26; CMW 4; CWRI 5; DA3; DAB; DAC;
DAM MST; DLB 10, 77, 100, 160; FANT;
MAICYA 1, 2; MTCW 1, 2; RGEL 2;
SATA 100; WCH; YABC 1

Milner, Ron(ald) 1938- .... **BLC 3; CLC 56**
See also AITN 1; BW 1; CA 73-76; CAD;
CANR 24, 81; CD 5; DAM MULT; DLB
38; MTCW 1

Milnes, Richard Monckton
1809-1885 .... **NCLC 61**
See also DLB 32, 184

Milosz, Czeslaw 1911- ...... **CLC 5, 11, 22, 31,
56, 82; PC 8; WLCS**
See also CA 81-84; CANR 23, 51, 91; CD-
WLB 4; CWW 2; DA3; DAM MST,
POET; DLB 215; EW 13; EWL 3; MTCW
1, 2; PFS 16; RGWL 2, 3

Milton, John 1608-1674 ..... **LC 9, 43, 92; PC
19, 29; WLC**
See also BRW 2; BRWR 2; CDBLB 1660-
1789; DA; DA3; DAB; DAC; DAM MST,
POET; DLB 131, 151, 281; EFS 1; EXPP;
LAIT 1; PAB; PFS 3, 17; RGEL 2; TEA;
WLIT 3; WP

Min, Anchee 1957- .... **CLC 86**
See also CA 146; CANR 94

Minehaha, Cornelius
See Wedekind, (Benjamin) Frank(lin)

Miner, Valerie 1947- .... **CLC 40**
See also CA 97-100; CANR 59; FW; GLL
2

Minimo, Duca
See D'Annunzio, Gabriele

Minot, Susan 1956- .... **CLC 44, 159**
See also AMWS 6; CA 134; CANR 118;
CN 7

Minus, Ed 1938- .... **CLC 39**
See also CA 185

Mirabai 1498(?)-1550(?) .... **PC 48**

Miranda, Javier
See Bioy Casares, Adolfo
See also CWW 2

Mirbeau, Octave 1848-1917 .... **TCLC 55**
See also DLB 123, 192; GFL 1789 to the
Present

Mirikitani, Janice 1942- .... **AAL**
See also CA 211; RGAL 4

Miro (Ferrer), Gabriel (Francisco Victor)
1879-1930 .... **TCLC 5**
See also CA 104; 185; EWL 3

Misharin, Alexandr .... **CLC 59**

Mishima, Yukio ... **CLC 2, 4, 6, 9, 27; DC 1;
SSC 4**
See Hiraoka, Kimitake
See also AAYA 50; BPFB 2; GLL 1; MJW;
MTCW 2; RGSF 2; RGWL 2, 3; SSFS 5,
12

Mistral, Frederic 1830-1914 .... **TCLC 51**
See also CA 122; 213; GFL 1789 to the
Present

Mistral, Gabriela
See Godoy Alcayaga, Lucila
See also DLB 283; DNFS 1; EWL 3; LAW;
RGWL 2, 3; WP

Mistry, Rohinton 1952- .... **CLC 71**
See also CA 141; CANR 86, 114; CCA 1;
CN 7; DAC; SSFS 6

Mitchell, Clyde
See Ellison, Harlan (Jay)

Mitchell, Emerson Blackhorse Barney
1945- .... **NNAL**
See also CA 45-48

Mitchell, James Leslie 1901-1935
See Gibbon, Lewis Grassic
See also CA 104; 188; DLB 15

Mitchell, Joni 1943- .... **CLC 12**
See also CA 112; CCA 1

Mitchell, Joseph (Quincy)
1908-1996 .... **CLC 98**
See also CA 77-80; 152; CANR 69; CN 7;
CSW; DLB 185; DLBY 1996

Mitchell, Margaret (Munnerlyn)
1900-1949 .... **TCLC 11**
See also AAYA 23; BPFB 2; BYA 1; CA
109; 125; CANR 55, 94; CDALBS; DA3;
DAM NOV, POP; DLB 9; LAIT 2;
MTCW 1, 2; NFS 9; RGAL 4; RHW;
TUS; WYAS 1; YAW

Mitchell, Peggy
See Mitchell, Margaret (Munnerlyn)

Mitchell, S(ilas) Weir 1829-1914 .... **TCLC 36**
See also CA 165; DLB 202; RGAL 4

Mitchell, W(illiam) O(rmond)
1914-1998 .... **CLC 25**
See also CA 77-80; 165; CANR 15, 43; CN
7; DAC; DAM MST; DLB 88

Mitchell, William (Lendrum)
1879-1936 .... **TCLC 81**
See also CA 213

Mitford, Mary Russell 1787-1855 ... **NCLC 4**
See also DLB 110, 116; RGEL 2

Mitford, Nancy 1904-1973 .... **CLC 44**
See also CA 9-12R; DLB 191; RGEL 2

Miyamoto, (Chujo) Yuriko
1899-1951 .... **TCLC 37**
See Miyamoto Yuriko
See also CA 170, 174

Miyamoto Yuriko
See Miyamoto, (Chujo) Yuriko
See also DLB 180

Miyazawa, Kenji 1896-1933 .... **TCLC 76**
See Miyazawa Kenji
See also CA 157; RGWL 3

Miyazawa Kenji
See Miyazawa, Kenji
See also EWL 3

Mizoguchi, Kenji 1898-1956 .... **TCLC 72**
See also CA 167

Mo, Timothy (Peter) 1950(?)- ... **CLC 46, 134**
See also CA 117; CN 7; DLB 194; MTCW
1; WLIT 4

Modarressi, Taghi (M.) 1931-1997 ... **CLC 44**
See also CA 121; 134; INT 134

Modiano, Patrick (Jean) 1945- .... **CLC 18**
See also CA 85-88; CANR 17, 40, 115;
CWW 2; DLB 83; EWL 3

Mofolo, Thomas (Mokopu)
1875(?)-1948 .... **BLC 3; TCLC 22**
See also AFW; CA 121; 153; CANR 83;
DAM MULT; DLB 225; EWL 3; MTCW
2; WLIT 2

Mohr, Nicholasa 1938- .... **CLC 12; HLC 2**
See also AAYA 8, 46; CA 49-52; CANR 1,
32, 64; CLR 22; DAM MULT; DLB 145;
HW 1, 2; JRDA; LAIT 5; MAICYA 2;
MAICYAS 1; RGAL 4; SAAS 8; SATA
8, 97; SATA-Essay 113; WYA; YAW

Moi, Toril 1953- .... **CLC 172**
See also CA 154; CANR 102; FW

Mojtabai, A(nn) G(race) 1938- ..... **CLC 5, 9,
15, 29**
See also CA 85-88; CANR 88

Moliere 1622-1673 ..... **DC 13; LC 10, 28, 64;
WLC**
See also DA; DA3; DAB; DAC; DAM
DRAM, MST; DFS 13, 18; DLB 268; EW
3; GFL Beginnings to 1789; LATS 1;
RGWL 2, 3; TWA

Molin, Charles
See Mayne, William (James Carter)

Molnar, Ferenc 1878-1952 .... **TCLC 20**
See also CA 109; 153; CANR 83; CDWLB
4; DAM DRAM; DLB 215; EWL 3;
RGWL 2, 3

Momaday, N(avarre) Scott 1934- ...... **CLC 2,
19, 85, 95, 160; NNAL; PC 25; WLCS**
See also AAYA 11; AMWS 4; ANW; BPFB
2; CA 25-28R; CANR 14, 34, 68;
CDALBS; CN 7; CPW; DA; DA3; DAB;
DAC; DAM MST, MULT, NOV, POP;
DLB 143, 175, 256; EWL 3; EXPP; INT
CANR-14; LAIT 4; LATS 1; MTCW 1,
2; NFS 10; PFS 2, 11; RGAL 4; SATA
48; SATA-Brief 30; WP; YAW

Monette, Paul 1945-1995 .... **CLC 82**
See also AMWS 10; CA 139; 147; CN 7;
GLL 1

Monroe, Harriet 1860-1936 .... **TCLC 12**
See also CA 109; 204; DLB 54, 91

Monroe, Lyle
See Heinlein, Robert A(nson)

Montagu, Elizabeth 1720-1800 .... **NCLC 7,
117**
See also FW

Montagu, Mary (Pierrepont) Wortley
1689-1762 .... **LC 9, 57; PC 16**
See also DLB 95, 101; RGEL 2

Montagu, W. H.
See Coleridge, Samuel Taylor

Montague, John (Patrick) 1929- ..... **CLC 13,
46**
See also CA 9-12R; CANR 9, 69, 121; CP
7; DLB 40; EWL 3; MTCW 1; PFS 12;
RGEL 2

Montaigne, Michel (Eyquem) de
1533-1592 .... **LC 8; WLC**
See also DA; DAB; DAC; DAM MST; EW
2; GFL Beginnings to 1789; LMFS 1;
RGWL 2, 3; TWA

Montale, Eugenio 1896-1981 ... **CLC 7, 9, 18;
PC 13**
See also CA 17-20R; 104; CANR 30; DLB
114; EW 11; EWL 3; MTCW 1; RGWL
2, 3; TWA

Montesquieu, Charles-Louis de Secondat
1689-1755 .... **LC 7, 69**
See also EW 3; GFL Beginnings to 1789;
TWA

Montessori, Maria 1870-1952 ...... **TCLC 103**
See also CA 115; 147

Montgomery, (Robert) Bruce 1921(?)-1978
See Crispin, Edmund
See also CA 179; 104; CMW 4

Montgomery, L(ucy) M(aud)
1874-1942 .... **TCLC 51, 140**
See also AAYA 12; BYA 1; CA 108; 137;
CLR 8, 91; DA3; DAC; DAM MST; DLB
92; DLBD 14; JRDA; MAICYA 1, 2;
MTCW 2; RGEL 2; SATA 100; TWA;
WCH; WYA; YABC 1

Montgomery, Marion H., Jr. 1925- .... **CLC 7**
See also AITN 1; CA 1-4R; CANR 3, 48;
CSW; DLB 6

Montgomery, Max
See Davenport, Guy (Mattison, Jr.)

Montherlant, Henry (Milon) de
1896-1972 .... **CLC 8, 19**
See also CA 85-88; 37-40R; DAM DRAM;
DLB 72; EW 11; EWL 3; GFL 1789 to
the Present; MTCW 1

Monty Python
See Chapman, Graham; Cleese, John
(Marwood); Gilliam, Terry (Vance); Idle,
Eric; Jones, Terence Graham Parry; Palin,
Michael (Edward)
See also AAYA 7

Moodie, Susanna (Strickland)
1803-1885 .... **NCLC 14, 113**
See also DLB 99

Moody, Hiram (F. III) 1961-
See Moody, Rick
See also CA 138; CANR 64, 112

Moody, Minerva
See Alcott, Louisa May

Moody, Rick .... **CLC 147**
See Moody, Hiram (F. III)

Moody, William Vaughan
1869-1910 .... **TCLC 105**
See also CA 110; 178; DLB 7, 54; RGAL 4

Mooney, Edward 1951-
See Mooney, Ted
See also CA 130

Mooney, Ted .... **CLC 25**
See Mooney, Edward

Moorcock, Michael (John) 1939- ...... **CLC 5,
27, 58**
See Bradbury, Edward P.
See also AAYA 26; CA 45-48; CAAS 5;
CANR 2, 17, 38, 64, 122; CN 7; DLB 14,
231, 261; FANT; MTCW 1, 2; SATA 93;
SCFW 2; SFW 4; SUFW 1, 2

Moore, Brian 1921-1999 ... **CLC 1, 3, 5, 7, 8,
19, 32, 90**
See Bryan, Michael
See also CA 1-4R; 174; CANR 1, 25, 42,
63; CCA 1; CN 7; DAB; DAC; DAM
MST; DLB 251; EWL 3; FANT; MTCW
1, 2; RGEL 2

Moore, Edward
See Muir, Edwin
See also RGEL 2

Moore, G. E. 1873-1958 .... **TCLC 89**
See also DLB 262

Moore, George Augustus
1852-1933 .... **SSC 19; TCLC 7**
See also BRW 6; CA 104; 177; DLB 10,
18, 57, 135; EWL 3; RGEL 2; RGSF 2

Moore, Lorrie .... **CLC 39, 45, 68**
See Moore, Marie Lorena
See also AMWS 10; DLB 234

Moore, Marianne (Craig)
1887-1972 .... **CLC 1, 2, 4, 8, 10, 13, 19,
47; PC 4, 49; WLCS**
See also AMW; CA 1-4R; 33-36R; CANR
3, 61; CDALB 1929-1941; DA; DA3;
DAB; DAC; DAM MST, POET; DLB 45;
DLBD 7; EWL 3; EXPP; MAWW;
MTCW 1, 2; PAB; PFS 14, 17; RGAL 4;
SATA 20; TUS; WP

Moore, Marie Lorena 1957- .... **CLC 165**
See Moore, Lorrie
See also CA 116; CANR 39, 83; CN 7; DLB
234

Moore, Thomas 1779-1852 .... **NCLC 6, 110**
See also DLB 96, 144; RGEL 2

Moorhouse, Frank 1938- .... **SSC 40**
See also CA 118; CANR 92; CN 7; RGSF
2

Mora, Pat(ricia) 1942- .... **HLC 2**
See also AMWS 13; CA 129; CANR 57,
81, 112; CLR 58; DAM MULT; DLB 209;
HW 1, 2; MAICYA 2; SATA 92, 134

Moraga, Cherrie 1952- .... **CLC 126**
See also CA 131; CANR 66; DAM MULT;
DLB 82, 249; FW; GLL 1; HW 1, 2

Morand, Paul 1888-1976 .... **CLC 41; SSC 22**
See also CA 184; 69-72; DLB 65; EWL 3

Morante, Elsa 1918-1985 .... **CLC 8, 47**
See also CA 85-88; 117; CANR 35; DLB
177; EWL 3; MTCW 1, 2; RGWL 2, 3

Moravia, Alberto .... **CLC 2, 7, 11, 27, 46;
SSC 26**
See Pincherle, Alberto
See also DLB 177; EW 12; EWL 3; MTCW
2; RGSF 2; RGWL 2, 3

More, Hannah 1745-1833 .... **NCLC 27**
See also DLB 107, 109, 116, 158; RGEL 2

More, Henry 1614-1687 .... **LC 9**
See also DLB 126, 252

More, Sir Thomas 1478(?)-1535 .... **LC 10, 32**
See also BRWC 1; BRWS 7; DLB 136, 281;
LMFS 1; RGEL 2; TEA

Moreas, Jean .... **TCLC 18**
See Papadiamantopoulos, Johannes
See also GFL 1789 to the Present

Moreton, Andrew Esq.
See Defoe, Daniel

Morgan, Berry 1919-2002 .... **CLC 6**
See also CA 49-52; 208; DLB 6

Morgan, Claire
See Highsmith, (Mary) Patricia
See also GLL 1

Morgan, Edwin (George) 1920- .... **CLC 31**
See also CA 5-8R; CANR 3, 43, 90; CP 7;
DLB 27

Morgan, (George) Frederick 1922- .. **CLC 23**
See also CA 17-20R; CANR 21; CP 7

Morgan, Harriet
See Mencken, H(enry) L(ouis)

Morgan, Jane
See Cooper, James Fenimore

Morgan, Janet 1945- .... **CLC 39**
See also CA 65-68

Morgan, Lady 1776(?)-1859 .... **NCLC 29**
See also DLB 116, 158; RGEL 2

Morgan, Robin (Evonne) 1941- .... **CLC 2**
See also CA 69-72; CANR 29, 68; FW;
GLL 2; MTCW 1; SATA 80

Morgan, Scott
See Kuttner, Henry

Morgan, Seth 1949(?)-1990 .... **CLC 65**
See also CA 185; 132

**Morgenstern, Christian (Otto Josef
Wolfgang)** 1871-1914 .... **TCLC 8**
See also CA 105; 191; EWL 3

Morgenstern, S.
See Goldman, William (W.)

Mori, Rintaro
See Mori Ogai
See also CA 110

Moricz, Zsigmond 1879-1942 .... **TCLC 33**
See also CA 165; DLB 215; EWL 3

Morike, Eduard (Friedrich)
1804-1875 .... **NCLC 10**
See also DLB 133; RGWL 2, 3

Mori Ogai 1862-1922 .... **TCLC 14**
See Ogai
See also CA 164; DLB 180; EWL 3; RGWL
3; TWA

Moritz, Karl Philipp 1756-1793 .... **LC 2**
See also DLB 94

Morland, Peter Henry
See Faust, Frederick (Schiller)

Morley, Christopher (Darlington)
1890-1957 .... **TCLC 87**
See also CA 112; DLB 9; RGAL 4

Morren, Theophil
See Hofmannsthal, Hugo von

Morris, Bill 1952- .... **CLC 76**

Morris, Julian
See West, Morris L(anglo)

Morris, Steveland Judkins 1950(?)-
See Wonder, Stevie
See also CA 111

Morris, William 1834-1896 .... **NCLC 4**
See also BRW 5; CDBLB 1832-1890; DLB
18, 35, 57, 156, 178, 184; FANT; RGEL
2; SFW 4; SUFW

Morris, Wright 1910-1998 .. **CLC 1, 3, 7, 18,
37; TCLC 107**
See also AMW; CA 9-12R; 167; CANR 21,
81; CN 7; DLB 2, 206, 218; DLBY 1981;
EWL 3; MTCW 1, 2; RGAL 4; TCWW 2

Morrison, Arthur 1863-1945 .... **SSC 40;
TCLC 72**
See also CA 120; 157; CMW 4; DLB 70,
135, 197; RGEL 2

Morrison, James Douglas 1943-1971
See Morrison, Jim
See also CA 73-76; CANR 40

Morrison, Jim .... **CLC 17**
See Morrison, James Douglas

Morrison, Toni 1931- ..... **BLC 3; CLC 4, 10,
22, 55, 81, 87, 173**
See also AAYA 1, 22; AFAW 1, 2; AMWC
1; AMWS 3; BPFB 2; BW 2, 3; CA 29-
32R; CANR 27, 42, 67, 113; CDALB
1968-1988; CN 7; CPW; DA; DA3; DAB;
DAC; DAM MST, MULT, NOV, POP;
DLB 6, 33, 143; DLBY 1981; EWL 3;
EXPN; FW; LAIT 2, 4; LATS 1; LMFS
2; MAWW; MTCW 1, 2; NFS 1, 6, 8, 14;
RGAL 4; RHW; SATA 57; SSFS 5; TUS;
YAW

Morrison, Van 1945- .... **CLC 21**
See also CA 116; 168

Morrissy, Mary 1957- .... **CLC 99**
See also CA 205; DLB 267

Mortimer, John (Clifford) 1923- ..... **CLC 28,
43**
See also CA 13-16R; CANR 21, 69, 109;
CD 5; CDBLB 1960 to Present; CMW 4;
CN 7; CPW; DA3; DAM DRAM, POP;
DLB 13, 245, 271; INT CANR-21; MSW;
MTCW 1, 2; RGEL 2

Mortimer, Penelope (Ruth)
1918-1999 .... **CLC 5**
See also CA 57-60; 187; CANR 45, 88; CN
7

Mortimer, Sir John
See Mortimer, John (Clifford)

Morton, Anthony
See Creasey, John

Morton, Thomas 1579(?)-1647(?) .... **LC 72**
See also DLB 24; RGEL 2

Mosca, Gaetano 1858-1941 .... **TCLC 75**

Moses, Daniel David 1952- .... **NNAL**
See also CA 186

Mosher, Howard Frank 1943- .... **CLC 62**
See also CA 139; CANR 65, 115

Mosley, Nicholas 1923- .... **CLC 43, 70**
See also CA 69-72; CANR 41, 60, 108; CN
7; DLB 14, 207

Mosley, Walter 1952- .... **BLCS; CLC 97**
See also AAYA 17; AMWS 13; BPFB 2;
BW 2; CA 142; CANR 57, 92; CMW 4;
CPW; DA3; DAM MULT, POP; MSW;
MTCW 2

Moss, Howard 1922-1987 . **CLC 7, 14, 45, 50**
See also CA 1-4R; 123; CANR 1, 44; DAM
POET; DLB 5

Mossgiel, Rab
See Burns, Robert

Motion, Andrew (Peter) 1952- .... **CLC 47**
See also BRWS 7; CA 146; CANR 90; CP
7; DLB 40

Motley, Willard (Francis)
1909-1965 .... **CLC 18**
See also BW 1; CA 117; 106; CANR 88;
DLB 76, 143

Motoori, Norinaga 1730-1801 .... **NCLC 45**

Mott, Michael (Charles Alston)
1930- .... **CLC 15, 34**
See also CA 5-8R; CAAS 7; CANR 7, 29

Mountain Wolf Woman 1884-1960 . **CLC 92;
NNAL**
See also CA 144; CANR 90

Moure, Erin 1955- .... **CLC 88**
See also CA 113; CP 7; CWP; DLB 60

Mourning Dove 1885(?)-1936 .... **NNAL**
See also CA 144; CANR 90; DAM MULT;
DLB 175, 221

Mowat, Farley (McGill) 1921- .... **CLC 26**
See also AAYA 1, 50; BYA 2; CA 1-4R;
CANR 4, 24, 42, 68, 108; CPW;
DAC; DAM MST; DLB 68; INT CANR-
24; JRDA; MAICYA 1, 2; MTCW 1, 2;
SATA 3, 55; YAW

Mowatt, Anna Cora 1819-1870 ..... **NCLC 74**
See also RGAL 4

Moyers, Bill 1934- .... **CLC 74**
See also AITN 2; CA 61-64; CANR 31, 52

Mphahlele, Es'kia
See Mphahlele, Ezekiel
See also AFW; CDWLB 3; DLB 125, 225;
RGSF 2; SSFS 11

Mphahlele, Ezekiel 1919- ... **BLC 3; CLC 25,
133**
See Mphahlele, Es'kia
See also BW 2, 3; CA 81-84; CANR 26,
76; CN 7; DA3; DAM MULT; EWL 3;
MTCW 2; SATA 119

Mqhayi, S(amuel) E(dward) K(rune Loliwe)
1875-1945 .... **BLC 3; TCLC 25**
See also CA 153; CANR 87; DAM MULT

Mrozek, Slawomir 1930- .... **CLC 3, 13**
See also CA 13-16R; CAAS 10; CANR 29;
CDWLB 4; CWW 2; DLB 232; EWL 3;
MTCW 1

Mrs. Belloc-Lowndes
See Lowndes, Marie Adelaide (Belloc)

Mrs. Fairstar
See Horne, Richard Henry Hengist

M'Taggart, John M'Taggart Ellis
See McTaggart, John McTaggart Ellis

Mtwa, Percy (?)- .... **CLC 47**

Mueller, Lisel 1924- .... **CLC 13, 51; PC 33**
See also CA 93-96; CP 7; DLB 105; PFS 9,
13

Muggeridge, Malcolm (Thomas)
1903-1990 .... **TCLC 120**
See also AITN 1; CA 101; CANR 33, 63;
MTCW 1, 2

Muhammad 570-632 .... **WLCS**
See also DA; DAB; DAC; DAM MST

Muir, Edwin 1887-1959 . **PC 49; TCLC 2, 87**
See Moore, Edward
See also BRWS 6; CA 104; 193; DLB 20,
100, 191; EWL 3; RGEL 2

Muir, John 1838-1914 .... **TCLC 28**
See also AMWS 9; ANW; CA 165; DLB
186, 275

Mujica Lainez, Manuel 1910-1984 ... **CLC 31**
See Lainez, Manuel Mujica
See also CA 81-84; 112; CANR 32; EWL
3; HW 1

Mukherjee, Bharati 1940- ..... **AAL; CLC 53,
115; SSC 38**
See also AAYA 46; BEST 89:2; CA 107;
CANR 45, 72; CN 7; DAM NOV; DLB
60, 218; DNFS 1, 2; EWL 3; FW; MTCW
1, 2; RGAL 4; RGSF 2; SSFS 7; TUS

Muldoon, Paul 1951- .... **CLC 32, 72, 166**
See also BRWS 4; CA 113; 129; CANR 52,
91; CP 7; DAM POET; DLB 40; INT 129;
PFS 7

Mulisch, Harry 1927- .... **CLC 42**
See also CA 9-12R; CANR 6, 26, 56, 110;
EWL 3

Mull, Martin 1943- .... **CLC 17**
See also CA 105

Muller, Wilhelm .... **NCLC 73**

Mulock, Dinah Maria
See Craik, Dinah Maria (Mulock)
See also RGEL 2

Munday, Anthony 1560-1633 .... **LC 87**
See also DLB 62, 172; RGEL 2

Munford, Robert 1737(?)-1783 .... **LC 5**
See also DLB 31

Mungo, Raymond 1946- .... **CLC 72**
See also CA 49-52; CANR 2

Munro, Alice 1931- .... **CLC 6, 10, 19, 50, 95;
SSC 3; WLCS**
See also AITN 2; BPFB 2; CA 33-36R;
CANR 33, 53, 75, 114; CCA 1; CN 7;
DA3; DAC; DAM MST, NOV; DLB 53;
EWL 3; MTCW 1, 2; RGEL 2; RGSF 2;
SATA 29; SSFS 5, 13

Munro, H(ector) H(ugh) 1870-1916 .... **WLC**
See Saki
See also CA 104; 130; CANR 104; CDBLB
1890-1914; DA; DA3; DAB; DAC; DAM
MST, NOV; DLB 34, 162; EXPS; MTCW
1, 2; RGEL 2; SSFS 15

Murakami, Haruki 1949- .... **CLC 150**
See Murakami Haruki
See also CA 165; CANR 102; MJW; RGWL
3; SFW 4

Murakami Haruki
See Murakami, Haruki
See also DLB 182; EWL 3

Murasaki, Lady
See Murasaki Shikibu

Murasaki Shikibu 978(?)-1026(?) ... **CMLC 1**
See also EFS 2; LATS 1; RGWL 2, 3

Murdoch, (Jean) Iris 1919-1999 ... **CLC 1, 2,
3, 4, 6, 8, 11, 15, 22, 31, 51**
See also BRWS 1; CA 13-16R; 179; CANR
8, 43, 68, 103; CDBLB 1960 to Present;
CN 7; CWD; DA3; DAB; DAC; DAM
MST, NOV; DLB 14, 194, 233; EWL 3;
INT CANR-8; MTCW 1, 2; NFS 18;
RGEL 2; TEA; WLIT 4

Murfree, Mary Noailles 1850-1922 .. **SSC 22;
TCLC 135**
See also CA 122; 176; DLB 12, 74; RGAL
4

Murnau, Friedrich Wilhelm
See Plumpe, Friedrich Wilhelm

Murphy, Richard 1927- .... **CLC 41**
See also BRWS 5; CA 29-32R; CP 7; DLB
40; EWL 3

Murphy, Sylvia 1937- .... **CLC 34**
See also CA 121

Murphy, Thomas (Bernard) 1935- ... **CLC 51**
See also CA 101

Murray, Albert L. 1916- .... **CLC 73**
See also BW 2; CA 49-52; CANR 26, 52,
78; CSW; DLB 38

Murray, James Augustus Henry
1837-1915 .... **TCLC 117**

Murray, Judith Sargent
1751-1820 .... **NCLC 63**
See also DLB 37, 200

Murray, Les(lie Allan) 1938- .... **CLC 40**
See also BRWS 7; CA 21-24R; CANR 11,
27, 56, 103; CP 7; DAM POET; DLBY
2001; EWL 3; RGEL 2

Murry, J. Middleton
See Murry, John Middleton

Murry, John Middleton
1889-1957 .... **TCLC 16**
See also CA 118; DLB 149

Musgrave, Susan 1951- .... **CLC 13, 54**
See also CA 69-72; CANR 45, 84; CCA 1;
CP 7; CWP

Musil, Robert (Edler von)
1880-1942 .... **SSC 18; TCLC 12, 68**
See also CA 109; CANR 55, 84; CDWLB
2; DLB 81, 124; EW 9; EWL 3; MTCW
2; RGSF 2; RGWL 2, 3

Muske, Carol .... **CLC 90**
See Muske-Dukes, Carol (Anne)

Muske-Dukes, Carol (Anne) 1945-
See Muske, Carol
See also CA 65-68; CAAE 203; CANR 32,
70; CWP

Musset, (Louis Charles) Alfred de
1810-1857 .... **NCLC 7**
See also DLB 192, 217; EW 6; GFL 1789
to the Present; RGWL 2, 3; TWA

Mussolini, Benito (Amilcare Andrea)
1883-1945 .... **TCLC 96**
See also CA 116

My Brother's Brother
See Chekhov, Anton (Pavlovich)

Myers, L(eopold) H(amilton)
1881-1944 .... **TCLC 59**
See also CA 157; DLB 15; EWL 3; RGEL
2

Myers, Walter Dean 1937- .. **BLC 3; CLC 35**
See also AAYA 4, 23; BW 2; BYA 6, 8, 11;
CA 33-36R; CANR 20, 42, 67, 108; CLR
4, 16, 35; DAM MULT, NOV; DLB 33;
INT CANR-20; JRDA; LAIT 5; MAICYA
1, 2; MAICYAS 1; MTCW 2; SAAS 2;
SATA 41, 71, 109; SATA-Brief 27; WYA;
YAW

Myers, Walter M.
See Myers, Walter Dean

Myles, Symon
See Follett, Ken(neth Martin)

Nabokov, Vladimir (Vladimirovich)
1899-1977 .... **CLC 1, 2, 3, 6, 8, 11, 15,
23, 44, 46, 64; SSC 11; TCLC 108;
WLC**
See also AAYA 45; AMW; AMWC 1;
AMWR 1; BPFB 2; CA 5-8R; 69-72;
CANR 20, 102; CDALB 1941-1968; DA;
DA3; DAB; DAC; DAM MST, NOV;
DLB 2, 244, 278; DLBD 3; DLBY 1980,
1991; EWL 3; EXPS; LATS 1; MTCW 1,
2; NCFS 4; NFS 9; RGAL 4; RGSF 2;
SSFS 6, 15; TUS

Naevius c. 265B.C.-201B.C. .... **CMLC 37**
See also DLB 211

Nagai, Kafu .... **TCLC 51**
See Nagai, Sokichi
See also DLB 180

Nagai, Sokichi 1879-1959
See Nagai, Kafu
See also CA 117

Nagy, Laszlo 1925-1978 .... **CLC 7**
See also CA 129; 112

Naidu, Sarojini 1879-1949 .... **TCLC 80**
See also EWL 3; RGEL 2

Naipaul, Shiva(dhar Srinivasa)
1945-1985 .... **CLC 32, 39**
See also CA 110; 112; 116; CANR 33;
DA3; DAM NOV; DLB 157; DLBY 1985;
EWL 3; MTCW 1, 2

Nixon, Agnes Eckhardt 1927- .... **CLC 21**
   See also CA 110
Nizan, Paul 1905-1940 .... **TCLC 40**
   See also CA 161; DLB 72; EWL 3; GFL
   1789 to the Present
Nkosi, Lewis 1936- .... **BLC 3; CLC 45**
   See also BW 1, 3; CA 65-68; CANR 27,
   81; CBD; CD 5; DAM MULT; DLB 157,
   225
Nodier, (Jean) Charles (Emmanuel)
   1780-1844 .... **NCLC 19**
   See also DLB 119; GFL 1789 to the Present
Noguchi, Yone 1875-1947 .... **TCLC 80**
Nolan, Christopher 1965- .... **CLC 58**
   See also CA 111; CANR 88
Noon, Jeff 1957- .... **CLC 91**
   See also CA 148; CANR 83; DLB 267;
   SFW 4
Norden, Charles
   See Durrell, Lawrence (George)
Nordhoff, Charles Bernard
   1887-1947 .... **TCLC 23**
   See also CA 108; 211; DLB 9; LAIT 1;
   RHW 1; SATA 23
Norfolk, Lawrence 1963- .... **CLC 76**
   See also CA 144; CANR 85; CN 7; DLB
   267
Norman, Marsha 1947- .... **CLC 28; DC 8**
   See also CA 105; CABS 3; CAD; CANR
   41; CD 5; CSW; CWD; DAM DRAM;
   DFS 2; DLB 266; DLBY 1984; FW
Normyx
   See Douglas, (George) Norman
Norris, (Benjamin) Frank(lin, Jr.)
   1870-1902 .... **SSC 28; TCLC 24**
   See also AMW; BPFB 2; CA 110; 160;
   CDALB 1865-1917; DLB 12, 71, 186;
   LMFS 2; NFS 12; RGAL 4; TCWW 2;
   TUS
Norris, Leslie 1921- .... **CLC 14**
   See also CA 11-12; CANR 14, 117; CAP 1;
   CP 7; DLB 27, 256
North, Andrew
   See Norton, Andre
North, Anthony
   See Koontz, Dean R(ay)
North, Captain George
   See Stevenson, Robert Louis (Balfour)
North, Captain George
   See Stevenson, Robert Louis (Balfour)
North, Milou
   See Erdrich, Louise
Northrup, B. A.
   See Hubbard, L(afayette) Ron(ald)
North Staffs
   See Hulme, T(homas) E(rnest)
Northup, Solomon 1808-1863 ...... **NCLC 105**
Norton, Alice Mary
   See Norton, Andre
   See also MAICYA 1; SATA 1, 43
Norton, Andre 1912- .... **CLC 12**
   See Norton, Alice Mary
   See also AAYA 14; BPFB 2; BYA 4, 10,
   12; CA 1-4R; CANR 68; CLR 50; DLB
   8, 52; JRDA; MAICYA 2; MTCW 1;
   SATA 91; SUFW 1, 2; YAW
Norton, Caroline 1808-1877 .... **NCLC 47**
   See also DLB 21, 159, 199
Norway, Nevil Shute 1899-1960
   See Shute, Nevil
   See also CA 102; 93-96; CANR 85; MTCW
   2
Norwid, Cyprian Kamil
   1821-1883 .... **NCLC 17**
   See also RGWL 3
Nosille, Nabrah
   See Ellison, Harlan (Jay)
Nossack, Hans Erich 1901-1978 .... **CLC 6**
   See also CA 93-96; 85-88; DLB 69; EWL 3

Nostradamus 1503-1566 .... **LC 27**
Nosu, Chuji
   See Ozu, Yasujiro
Notenburg, Eleanora (Genrikhovna) von
   See Guro, Elena
Nova, Craig 1945- .... **CLC 7, 31**
   See also CA 45-48; CANR 2, 53
Novak, Joseph
   See Kosinski, Jerzy (Nikodem)
Novalis 1772-1801 .... **NCLC 13**
   See also CDWLB 2; DLB 90; EW 5; RGWL
   2, 3
Novick, Peter 1934- .... **CLC 164**
   See also CA 188
Novis, Emile
   See Weil, Simone (Adolphine)
Nowlan, Alden (Albert) 1933-1983 ... **CLC 15**
   See also CA 9-12R; CANR 5; DAC; DAM
   MST; DLB 53; PFS 12
Noyes, Alfred 1880-1958 ...... **PC 27; TCLC 7**
   See also CA 104; 188; DLB 20; EXPP;
   FANT; PFS 4; RGEL 2
Nugent, Richard Bruce 1906(?)-1987 ... **HR 3**
   See also BW 1; CA 125; DLB 51; GLL 2
Nunn, Kem .... **CLC 34**
   See also CA 159
Nwapa, Flora (Nwanzuruaha)
   1931-1993 .... **BLCS; CLC 133**
   See also BW 2; CA 143; CANR 83; CD-
   WLB 3; CWRI 5; DLB 125; EWL 3;
   WLIT 2
Nye, Robert 1939- .... **CLC 13, 42**
   See also CA 33-36R; CANR 29, 67, 107;
   CN 7; CP 7; CWRI 5; DAM NOV; DLB
   14, 271; FANT; HGG; MTCW 1; RHW;
   SATA 6
Nyro, Laura 1947-1997 .... **CLC 17**
   See also CA 194
Oates, Joyce Carol 1938- .. **CLC 1, 2, 3, 6, 9,
   11, 15, 19, 33, 52, 108, 134; SSC 6;
   WLC**
   See also AAYA 15, 52; AITN 1; AMWS 2;
   BEST 89:2; BPFB 2; BYA 11; CA 5-8R;
   CANR 25, 45, 74, 113, 113; CDALB
   1968-1988; CN 7; CP 7; CPW; DA;
   DA3; DAB; DAC; DAM MST, NOV,
   POP; DLB 2, 5, 130; DLBY 1981; EWL
   3; EXPS; FW; HGG; INT CANR-25;
   LAIT 4; MAWW; MTCW 1, 2; NFS 8;
   RGAL 4; RGSF 2; SSFS 17; SUFW 2;
   TUS
O'Brian, E. G.
   See Clarke, Arthur C(harles)
O'Brian, Patrick 1914-2000 .... **CLC 152**
   See also CA 144; 187; CANR 74; CPW;
   MTCW 2; RHW
O'Brien, Darcy 1939-1998 .... **CLC 11**
   See also CA 21-24R; 167; CANR 8, 59
O'Brien, Edna 1936- ..... **CLC 3, 5, 8, 13, 36,
   65, 116; SSC 10**
   See also BRWS 5; CA 1-4R; CANR 6, 41,
   65, 102; CDBLB 1960 to Present; CN 7;
   DA3; DAM NOV; DLB 14, 231; EWL 3;
   FW; MTCW 1, 2; RGSF 2; WLIT 4
O'Brien, Fitz-James 1828-1862 .... **NCLC 21**
   See also DLB 74; RGAL 4; SUFW
O'Brien, Flann .... **CLC 1, 4, 5, 7, 10, 47**
   See O Nuallain, Brian
   See also BRWS 2; DLB 231; EWL 3;
   RGEL 2
O'Brien, Richard 1942- .... **CLC 17**
   See also CA 124
O'Brien, (William) Tim(othy) 1946- . **CLC 7,
   19, 40, 103**
   See also AAYA 16; AMWS 5; CA 85-88;
   CANR 40, 58; CDALBS; CN 7; CPW;
   DA3; DAM POP; DLB 152; DLBD 9;
   DLBY 1980; MTCW 2; RGAL 4; SSFS
   5, 15

Obstfelder, Sigbjoern 1866-1900 .... **TCLC 23**
   See also CA 123
O'Casey, Sean 1880-1964 .... **CLC 1, 5, 9, 11,
   15, 88; DC 12; WLCS**
   See also BRW 7; CA 89-92; CANR 62;
   CBD; CDBLB 1914-1945; DA3; DAB;
   DAC; DAM DRAM, MST; DLB 10;
   EWL 3; MTCW 1, 2; RGEL 2; TEA;
   WLIT 4
O'Cathasaigh, Sean
   See O'Casey, Sean
Occom, Samson 1723-1792 .... **LC 60; NNAL**
   See also DLB 175
Ochs, Phil(ip David) 1940-1976 .... **CLC 17**
   See also CA 185; 65-68
O'Connor, Edwin (Greene)
   1918-1968 .... **CLC 14**
   See also CA 93-96; 25-28R
O'Connor, (Mary) Flannery
   1925-1964 .... **CLC 1, 2, 3, 6, 10, 13, 15,
   21, 66, 104; SSC 1, 23, 61; TCLC 132;
   WLC**
   See also AAYA 7; AMW; AMWR 2; BPFB
   3; CA 1-4R; CANR 3, 41; CDALB 1941-
   1968; DA; DA3; DAB; DAC; DAM MST,
   NOV; DLB 2, 152; DLBD 12; DLBY
   1980; EWL 3; EXPS; LAIT 5; MAWW;
   MTCW 1, 2; NFS 3; RGAL 4; RGSF 2;
   SSFS 2, 7, 10; TUS
O'Connor, Frank .... **CLC 23; SSC 5**
   See O'Donovan, Michael Francis
   See also DLB 162; EWL 3; RGSF 2; SSFS
   5
O'Dell, Scott 1898-1989 .... **CLC 30**
   See also AAYA 3, 44; BPFB 3; BYA 1, 2,
   3, 5; CA 61-64; 129; CANR 12, 30, 112;
   CLR 1, 16; DLB 52; JRDA; MAICYA 1,
   2; SATA 12, 60, 134; WYA; YAW
Odets, Clifford 1906-1963 ..... **CLC 2, 28, 98;
   DC 6**
   See also AMWS 2; CA 85-88; CAD; CANR
   62; DAM DRAM; DFS 17; DLB 7, 26;
   EWL 3; MTCW 1, 2; RGAL 4; TUS
O'Doherty, Brian 1928- .... **CLC 76**
   See also CA 105; CANR 108
O'Donnell, K. M.
   See Malzberg, Barry N(athaniel)
O'Donnell, Lawrence
   See Kuttner, Henry
O'Donovan, Michael Francis
   1903-1966 .... **CLC 14**
   See O'Connor, Frank
   See also CA 93-96; CANR 84
Oe, Kenzaburo 1935- .. **CLC 10, 36, 86; SSC
   20**
   See Oe Kenzaburo
   See also CA 97-100; CANR 36, 50, 74;
   CWW 2; DA3; DAM NOV; DLB 182;
   DLBY 1994; EWL 3; LATS 1; MJW;
   MTCW 1, 2; RGSF 2; RGWL 2, 3
Oe Kenzaburo
   See Oe, Kenzaburo
   See also EWL 3
O'Faolain, Julia 1932- .... **CLC 6, 19, 47, 108**
   See also CA 81-84; CAAS 2; CANR 12,
   61; CN 7; DLB 14, 231; FW; MTCW 1;
   RHW
O'Faolain, Sean 1900-1991 ...... **CLC 1, 7, 14,
   32, 70; SSC 13**
   See also CA 61-64; 134; CANR 12, 66;
   DLB 15, 162; MTCW 1, 2; RGEL 2;
   RGSF 2
O'Flaherty, Liam 1896-1984 .... **CLC 5, 34;
   SSC 6**
   See also CA 101; 113; CANR 35; DLB 36,
   162; DLBY 1984; MTCW 1, 2; RGEL 2;
   RGSF 2; SSFS 5
Ogai
   See Mori Ogai
   See also MJW

Owens, Louis (Dean) 1948-2002 .... **NNAL**
See also CA 137, 179; 207; CAAE 179;
CAAS 24; CANR 71

Owens, Rochelle 1936- .... **CLC 8**
See also CA 17-20R; CAAS 2; CAD;
CANR 39; CD 5; CP 7; CWD; CWP

Oz, Amos 1939- .... **CLC 5, 8, 11, 27, 33, 54**
See also CA 53-56; CANR 27, 47, 65, 113;
CWW 2; DAM NOV; EWL 3; MTCW 1,
2; RGSF 2; RGWL 3

Ozick, Cynthia 1928- .... **CLC 3, 7, 28, 62,**
155; SSC 15, 60
See also AMWS 5; BEST 90:1; CA 17-20R;
CANR 23, 58, 116; CN 7; CPW; DA3;
DAM NOV, POP; DLB 28, 152; DLBY
1982; EWL 3; EXPS; INT CANR-23;
MTCW 1, 2; RGAL 4; RGSF 2; SSFS 3,
12

Ozu, Yasujiro 1903-1963 .... **CLC 16**
See also CA 112

Pabst, G. W. 1885-1967 .... **TCLC 127**

Pacheco, C.
See Pessoa, Fernando (Antonio Nogueira)

Pacheco, Jose Emilio 1939- .... **HLC 2**
See also CA 111; 131; CANR 65; DAM
MULT; EWL 3; HW 1, 2; RGSF 2

Pa Chin .... **CLC 18**
See Li Fei-kan
See also EWL 3

Pack, Robert 1929- .... **CLC 13**
See also CA 1-4R; CANR 3, 44, 82; CP 7;
DLB 5; SATA 118

Padgett, Lewis
See Kuttner, Henry

Padilla (Lorenzo), Heberto
1932-2000 .... **CLC 38**
See also AITN 1; CA 123; 131; 189; EWL
3; HW 1

Page, James Patrick 1944-
See Page, Jimmy
See also CA 204

Page, Jimmy 1944- .... **CLC 12**
See Page, James Patrick

Page, Louise 1955- .... **CLC 40**
See also CA 140; CANR 76; CBD; CD 5;
CWD; DLB 233

Page, P(atricia) K(athleen) 1916- ...... **CLC 7,**
18; PC 12
See Cape, Judith
See also CA 53-56; CANR 4, 22, 65; CP 7;
DAC; DAM MST; DLB 68; MTCW 1;
RGEL 2

Page, Stanton
See Fuller, Henry Blake

Page, Stanton
See Fuller, Henry Blake

Page, Thomas Nelson 1853-1922 .... **SSC 23**
See also CA 118; 177; DLB 12, 78; DLBD
13; RGAL 4

Pagels, Elaine Hiesey 1943- .... **CLC 104**
See also CA 45-48; CANR 2, 24, 51; FW;
NCFS 4

Paget, Violet 1856-1935
See Lee, Vernon
See also CA 104; 166; GLL 1; HGG

Paget-Lowe, Henry
See Lovecraft, H(oward) P(hillips)

Paglia, Camille (Anna) 1947- .... **CLC 68**
See also CA 140; CANR 72; CPW; FW;
GLL 2; MTCW 2

Paige, Richard
See Koontz, Dean R(ay)

Paine, Thomas 1737-1809 .... **NCLC 62**
See also AMWS 1; CDALB 1640-1865;
DLB 31, 43, 73, 158; LAIT 1; RGAL 4;
RGEL 2; TUS

Pakenham, Antonia
See Fraser, Antonia (Pakenham)

Palamas, Costis
See Palamas, Kostes

Palamas, Kostes 1859-1943 .... **TCLC 5**
See Palamas, Kostis
See also CA 105; 190; RGWL 2, 3

Palamas, Kostis
See Palamas, Kostes
See also EWL 3

Palazzeschi, Aldo 1885-1974 .... **CLC 11**
See also CA 89-92; 53-56; DLB 114, 264;
EWL 3

Pales Matos, Luis 1898-1959 .... **HLCS 2**
See Pales Matos, Luis
See also HW 1; LAW

Paley, Grace 1922- .. **CLC 4, 6, 37, 140; SSC**
8
See also AMWS 6; CA 25-28R; CANR 13,
46, 74, 118; CN 7; CPW; DA3; DAM
POP; DLB 28, 218; EWL 3; EXPS; FW;
INT CANR-13; MAWW; MTCW 1, 2;
RGAL 4; RGSF 2; SSFS 3

Palin, Michael (Edward) 1943- .... **CLC 21**
See Monty Python
See also CA 107; CANR 35, 109; SATA 67

Palliser, Charles 1947- .... **CLC 65**
See also CA 136; CANR 76; CN 7

Palma, Ricardo 1833-1919 .... **TCLC 29**
See also CA 168; LAW

Pancake, Breece Dexter 1952-1979
See Pancake, Breece D'J
See also CA 123; 109

Pancake, Breece D'J .... **CLC 29; SSC 61**
See Pancake, Breece Dexter
See also DLB 130

Panchenko, Nikolai .... **CLC 59**

Pankhurst, Emmeline (Goulden)
1858-1928 .... **TCLC 100**
See also CA 116; FW

Panko, Rudy
See Gogol, Nikolai (Vasilyevich)

Papadiamantis, Alexandros
1851-1911 .... **TCLC 29**
See also CA 168; EWL 3

Papadiamantopoulos, Johannes 1856-1910
See Moreas, Jean
See also CA 117

Papini, Giovanni 1881-1956 .... **TCLC 22**
See also CA 121; 180; DLB 264

Paracelsus 1493-1541 .... **LC 14**
See also DLB 179

Parasol, Peter
See Stevens, Wallace

Pardo Bazan, Emilia 1851-1921 .... **SSC 30**
See also EWL 3; FW; RGSF 2; RGWL 2, 3

Pareto, Vilfredo 1848-1923 .... **TCLC 69**
See also CA 175

Paretsky, Sara 1947- .... **CLC 135**
See also AAYA 30; BEST 90:3; CA 125;
129; CANR 59, 95; CMW 4; CPW; DA3;
DAM POP; INT CA-129; MSW; RGAL 4

Parfenie, Maria
See Codrescu, Andrei

Parini, Jay (Lee) 1948- .... **CLC 54, 133**
See also CA 97-100; CAAS 16; CANR 32,
87

Park, Jordan
See Kornbluth, C(yril) M.; Pohl, Frederik

Park, Robert E(zra) 1864-1944 ..... **TCLC 73**
See also CA 122; 165

Parker, Bert
See Ellison, Harlan (Jay)

Parker, Dorothy (Rothschild)
1893-1967 .. **CLC 15, 68; PC 28; SSC 2**
See also AMWS 9; CA 19-20; 25-28R; CAP
2; DA3; DAM POET; DLB 11, 45, 86;
EXPP; FW; MAWW; MTCW 1, 2; PFS
18; RGAL 4; RGSF 2; TUS

Parker, Robert B(rown) 1932- .... **CLC 27**
See also AAYA 28; BEST 89:4; BPFB 3;
CA 49-52; CANR 1, 26, 52, 89; CMW 4;
CPW; DAM NOV, POP; INT CANR-26;
MSW; MTCW 1

Parkin, Frank 1940- .... **CLC 43**
See also CA 147

Parkman, Francis, Jr. 1823-1893 .. **NCLC 12**
See also AMWS 2; DLB 1, 30, 183, 186,
235; RGAL 4

Parks, Gordon (Alexander Buchanan)
1912- .... **BLC 3; CLC 1, 16**
See also AAYA 36; AITN 2; BW 2, 3; CA
41-44R; CANR 26, 66; DA3; DAM
MULT; DLB 33; MTCW 2; SATA 8, 108

Parks, Tim(othy Harold) 1954- ...... **CLC 147**
See also CA 126; 131; CANR 77; DLB 231;
INT CA-131

Parmenides c. 515B.C.-c.
450B.C. .... **CMLC 22**
See also DLB 176

Parnell, Thomas 1679-1718 .... **LC 3**
See also DLB 95; RGEL 2

Parr, Catherine c. 1513(?)-1548 .... **LC 86**
See also DLB 136

Parra, Nicanor 1914- ... **CLC 2, 102; HLC 2;**
PC 39
See also CA 85-88; CANR 32; CWW 2;
DAM MULT; DLB 283; EWL 3; HW 1;
LAW; MTCW 1

Parra Sanojo, Ana Teresa de la
1890-1936 .... **HLCS 2**
See de la Parra, (Ana) Teresa (Sonojo)
See also LAW

Parrish, Mary Frances
See Fisher, M(ary) F(rances) K(ennedy)

Parshchikov, Aleksei 1954- .... **CLC 59**
See Parshchikov, Aleksei Maksimovich

Parshchikov, Aleksei Maksimovich
See Parshchikov, Aleksei
See also DLB 285

Parson, Professor
See Coleridge, Samuel Taylor

Parson Lot
See Kingsley, Charles

Parton, Sara Payson Willis
1811-1872 .... **NCLC 86**
See also DLB 43, 74, 239

Partridge, Anthony
See Oppenheim, E(dward) Phillips

Pascal, Blaise 1623-1662 .... **LC 35**
See also DLB 268; EW 3; GFL Beginnings
to 1789; RGWL 2, 3; TWA

Pascoli, Giovanni 1855-1912 .... **TCLC 45**
See also CA 170; EW 7; EWL 3

Pasolini, Pier Paolo 1922-1975 .. **CLC 20, 37,**
106; PC 17
See also CA 93-96; 61-64; CANR 63; DLB
128, 177; EWL 3; MTCW 1; RGWL 2, 3

Pasquini
See Silone, Ignazio

Pastan, Linda (Olenik) 1932- .... **CLC 27**
See also CA 61-64; CANR 18, 40, 61, 113;
CP 7; CSW; CWP; DAM POET; DLB 5;
PFS 8

Pasternak, Boris (Leonidovich)
1890-1960 ...... **CLC 7, 10, 18, 63; PC 6;**
SSC 31; WLC
See also BPFB 3; CA 127; 116; DA; DA3;
DAB; DAC; DAM MST, NOV, POET;
EW 11; MTCW 1, 2; RGSF 2; RGWL 2,
3; TWA; WP

Patchen, Kenneth 1911-1972 .... **CLC 1, 2, 18**
See also BG 3; CA 1-4R; 33-36R; CANR
3, 35; DAM POET; DLB 16, 48; EWL 3;
MTCW 1; RGAL 4

Price, (Edward) Reynolds 1933- ... **CLC 3, 6, 13, 43, 50, 63; SSC 22**
See also AMWS 6; CA 1-4R; CANR 1, 37, 57, 87; CN 7; CSW; DAM NOV; DLB 2, 218, 278; EWL 3; INT CANR-37; NFS 18

Price, Richard 1949- .... **CLC 6, 12**
See also CA 49-52; CANR 3; DLBY 1981

Prichard, Katharine Susannah
1883-1969 .... **CLC 46**
See also CA 11-12; CANR 33; CAP 1; DLB 260; MTCW 1; RGEL 2; RGSF 2; SATA 66

Priestley, J(ohn) B(oynton)
1894-1984 .... **CLC 2, 5, 9, 34**
See also BRW 7; CA 9-12R; 113; CANR 33; CDBLB 1914-1945; DA3; DAM DRAM, NOV; DLB 10, 34, 77, 100, 139; DLBY 1984; EWL 3; MTCW 1, 2; RGEL 2; SFW 4

Prince 1958- .... **CLC 35**
See also CA 213

Prince, F(rank) T(empleton) 1912- .. **CLC 22**
See also CA 101; CANR 43, 79; CP 7; DLB 20

Prince Kropotkin
See Kropotkin, Peter (Alekseievich)

Prior, Matthew 1664-1721 .... **LC 4**
See also DLB 95; RGEL 2

Prishvin, Mikhail 1873-1954 .... **TCLC 75**
See Prishvin, Mikhail Mikhailovich

Prishvin, Mikhail Mikhailovich
See Prishvin, Mikhail
See also DLB 272; EWL 3

Pritchard, William H(arrison)
1932- .... **CLC 34**
See also CA 65-68; CANR 23, 95; DLB 111

Pritchett, V(ictor) S(awdon)
1900-1997 ... **CLC 5, 13, 15, 41; SSC 14**
See also BPFB 3; BRWS 3; CA 61-64; 157; CANR 31, 63; CN 7; DA3; DAM NOV; DLB 15, 139; EWL 3; MTCW 1, 2; RGEL 2; RGSF 2; TEA

Private 19022
See Manning, Frederic

Probst, Mark 1925- .... **CLC 59**
See also CA 130

Prokosch, Frederic 1908-1989 ...... **CLC 4, 48**
See also CA 73-76; 128; CANR 82; DLB 48; MTCW 2

Propertius, Sextus c. 50B.C.-c. 16B.C. .... **CMLC 32**
See also AW 2; CDWLB 1; DLB 211; RGWL 2, 3

Prophet, The
See Dreiser, Theodore (Herman Albert)

Prose, Francine 1947- .... **CLC 45**
See also CA 109; 112; CANR 46, 95; DLB 234; SATA 101

Proudhon
See Cunha, Euclides (Rodrigues Pimenta) da

Proulx, Annie
See Proulx, E(dna) Annie

Proulx, E(dna) Annie 1935- ...... **CLC 81, 158**
See also AMWS 7; BPFB 3; CA 145; CANR 65, 110; CN 7; CPW 1; DA3; DAM POP; MTCW 2; SSFS 18

Proust, (Valentin-Louis-George-Eugene)
Marcel 1871-1922 .... **TCLC 7, 13, 33; WLC**
See also BPFB 3; CA 104; 120; CANR 110; DA; DA3; DAB; DAC; DAM MST, NOV; DLB 65; EW 8; EWL 3; GFL 1789 to the Present; MTCW 1, 2; RGWL 2, 3; TWA

Prowler, Harley
See Masters, Edgar Lee

Prus, Boleslaw 1845-1912 .... **TCLC 48**
See also RGWL 2, 3

Pryor, Richard (Franklin Lenox Thomas)
1940- .... **CLC 26**
See also CA 122; 152

Przybyszewski, Stanislaw
1868-1927 .... **TCLC 36**
See also CA 160; DLB 66; EWL 3

Pteleon
See Grieve, C(hristopher) M(urray)
See also DAM POET

Puckett, Lute
See Masters, Edgar Lee

Puig, Manuel 1932-1990 .... **CLC 3, 5, 10, 28, 65, 133; HLC 2**
See also BPFB 3; CA 45-48; CANR 2, 32, 63; CDWLB 3; DA3; DAM MULT; DLB 113; DNFS 1; EWL 3; GLL 1; HW 1, 2; LAW; MTCW 1, 2; RGWL 2, 3; TWA; WLIT 1

Pulitzer, Joseph 1847-1911 .... **TCLC 76**
See also CA 114; DLB 23

Purchas, Samuel 1577(?)-1626 .... **LC 70**
See also DLB 151

Purdy, A(lfred) W(ellington)
1918-2000 .... **CLC 3, 6, 14, 50**
See also CA 81-84; 189; CAAS 17; CANR 42, 66; CP 7; DAC; DAM MST, POET; DLB 88; PFS 5; RGEL 2

Purdy, James (Amos) 1923- .... **CLC 2, 4, 10, 28, 52**
See also AMWS 7; CA 33-36R; CAAS 1; CANR 19, 51; CN 7; DLB 2, 218; EWL 3; INT CANR-19; MTCW 1; RGAL 4

Pure, Simon
See Swinnerton, Frank Arthur

Pushkin, Aleksandr Sergeevich
See Pushkin, Alexander (Sergeyevich)
See also DLB 205

Pushkin, Alexander (Sergeyevich)
1799-1837 .... **NCLC 3, 27, 83; PC 10; SSC 27, 55; WLC**
See Pushkin, Aleksandr Sergeevich
See also DA; DA3; DAB; DAC; DAM DRAM, MST, POET; EW 5; EXPS; RGSF 2; RGWL 2, 3; SATA 61; SSFS 9; TWA

P'u Sung-ling 1640-1715 .... **LC 49; SSC 31**

Putnam, Arthur Lee
See Alger, Horatio, Jr.

Puzo, Mario 1920-1999 .... **CLC 1, 2, 6, 36, 107**
See also BPFB 3; CA 65-68; 185; CANR 4, 42, 65, 99; CN 7; CPW; DA3; DAM NOV, POP; DLB 6; MTCW 1, 2; NFS 16; RGAL 4

Pygge, Edward
See Barnes, Julian (Patrick)

Pyle, Ernest Taylor 1900-1945
See Pyle, Ernie
See also CA 115; 160

Pyle, Ernie .... **TCLC 75**
See Pyle, Ernest Taylor
See also DLB 29; MTCW 2

Pyle, Howard 1853-1911 .... **TCLC 81**
See also BYA 2, 4; CA 109; 137; CLR 22; DLB 42, 188; DLBD 13; LAIT 1; MAI-CYA 1, 2; SATA 16, 100; WCH; YAW

Pym, Barbara (Mary Crampton)
1913-1980 .... **CLC 13, 19, 37, 111**
See also BPFB 3; BRWS 3; CA 13-14; 97-100; CANR 13, 34; CAP 1; DLB 14, 207; DLBY 1987; EWL 3; MTCW 1, 2; RGEL 2; TEA

Pynchon, Thomas (Ruggles, Jr.)
1937- ...... **CLC 2, 3, 6, 9, 11, 18, 33, 62, 72, 123; SSC 14; WLC**
See also AMWS 2; BEST 90:2; BPFB 3; CA 17-20R; CANR 22, 46, 73; CN 7; CPW 1; DA; DA3; DAB; DAC; DAM MST, NOV, POP; DLB 2, 173; EWL 3; MTCW 1, 2; RGAL 4; SFW 4; TUS

Pythagoras c. 582B.C.-c. 507B.C. . **CMLC 22**
See also DLB 176

Q
See Quiller-Couch, Sir Arthur (Thomas)

Qian, Chongzhu
See Ch'ien, Chung-shu

Qian Zhongshu
See Ch'ien, Chung-shu

Qroll
See Dagerman, Stig (Halvard)

Quarrington, Paul (Lewis) 1953- ..... **CLC 65**
See also CA 129; CANR 62, 95

Quasimodo, Salvatore 1901-1968 .... **CLC 10; PC 47**
See also CA 13-16; 25-28R; CAP 1; DLB 114; EW 12; EWL 3; MTCW 1; RGWL 2, 3

Quatermass, Martin
See Carpenter, John (Howard)

Quay, Stephen 1947- .... **CLC 95**
See also CA 189

Quay, Timothy 1947- .... **CLC 95**
See also CA 189

Queen, Ellery .... **CLC 3, 11**
See Dannay, Frederic; Davidson, Avram (James); Deming, Richard; Fairman, Paul W.; Flora, Fletcher; Hoch, Edward D(entinger); Kane, Henry; Lee, Manfred B(ennington); Marlowe, Stephen; Powell, (Oval) Talmage; Sheldon, Walter J(ames); Sturgeon, Theodore (Hamilton); Tracy, Don(ald Fiske); Vance, John Holbrook
See also BPFB 3; CMW 4; MSW; RGAL 4

Queen, Ellery, Jr.
See Dannay, Frederic; Lee, Manfred B(ennington)

Queneau, Raymond 1903-1976 ..... **CLC 2, 5, 10, 42**
See also CA 77-80; 69-72; CANR 32; DLB 72, 258; EW 12; EWL 3; GFL 1789 to the Present; MTCW 1, 2; RGWL 2, 3

Quevedo, Francisco de 1580-1645 .... **LC 23**

Quiller-Couch, Sir Arthur (Thomas)
1863-1944 .... **TCLC 53**
See also CA 118; 166; DLB 135, 153, 190; HGG; RGEL 2; SUFW 1

Quin, Ann (Marie) 1936-1973 .... **CLC 6**
See also CA 9-12R; 45-48; DLB 14, 231

Quincey, Thomas de
See De Quincey, Thomas

Quinn, Martin
See Smith, Martin Cruz

Quinn, Peter 1947- .... **CLC 91**
See also CA 197

Quinn, Simon
See Smith, Martin Cruz

Quintana, Leroy V. 1944- ...... **HLC 2; PC 36**
See also CA 131; CANR 65; DAM MULT; DLB 82; HW 1, 2

Quiroga, Horacio (Sylvestre)
1878-1937 .... **HLC 2; TCLC 20**
See also CA 117; 131; DAM MULT; EWL 3; HW 1; LAW; MTCW 1; RGSF 2; WLIT 1

Quoirez, Francoise 1935- .... **CLC 9**
See Sagan, Francoise
See also CA 49-52; CANR 6, 39, 73; CWW 2; MTCW 1, 2; TWA

Raabe, Wilhelm (Karl) 1831-1910 . **TCLC 45**
See also CA 167; DLB 129

Rabe, David (William) 1940- .. **CLC 4, 8, 33; DC 16**
See also CA 85-88; CABS 3; CAD; CANR 59; CD 5; DAM DRAM; DFS 3, 8, 13; DLB 7, 228; EWL 3

Rosenblatt, Joseph 1933-
See Rosenblatt, Joe
See also CA 89-92; CP 7; INT 89-92
Rosenfeld, Samuel
See Tzara, Tristan
Rosenstock, Sami
See Tzara, Tristan
Rosenstock, Samuel
See Tzara, Tristan
Rosenthal, M(acha) L(ouis)
1917-1996 .... **CLC 28**
See also CA 1-4R; 152; CAAS 6; CANR 4,
51; CP 7; DLB 5; SATA 59
Ross, Barnaby
See Dannay, Frederic
Ross, Bernard L.
See Follett, Ken(neth Martin)
Ross, J. H.
See Lawrence, T(homas) E(dward)
Ross, John Hume
See Lawrence, T(homas) E(dward)
Ross, Martin 1862-1915
See Martin, Violet Florence
See also DLB 135; GLL 2; RGEL 2; RGSF
2
Ross, (James) Sinclair 1908-1996 ... **CLC 13;
SSC 24**
See also CA 73-76; CANR 81; CN 7; DAC;
DAM MST; DLB 88; RGEL 2; RGSF 2;
TCWW 2
Rossetti, Christina (Georgina)
1830-1894 .... **NCLC 2, 50, 66; PC 7;
WLC**
See also AAYA 51; BRW 5; BYA 4; DA;
DA3; DAB; DAC; DAM MST, POET;
DLB 35, 163, 240; EXPP; LATS 1; MAI-
CYA 1, 2; PFS 10, 14; RGEL 2; SATA
20; TEA; WCH
Rossetti, Dante Gabriel 1828-1882 . **NCLC 4,
77; PC 44; WLC**
See also AAYA 51; BRW 5; CDBLB 1832-
1890; DA; DAB; DAC; DAM MST,
POET; DLB 35; EXPP; RGEL 2; TEA
Rossi, Cristina Peri
See Peri Rossi, Cristina
Rossi, Jean-Baptiste 1931-2003
See Japrisot, Sebastien
See also CA 201; 215
Rossner, Judith (Perelman) 1935- . **CLC 6, 9,
29**
See also AITN 2; BEST 90:3; BPFB 3; CA
17-20R; CANR 18, 51, 73; CN 7; DLB 6;
INT CANR-18; MTCW 1, 2
Rostand, Edmond (Eugene Alexis)
1868-1918 .... **DC 10; TCLC 6, 37**
See also CA 104; 126; DA; DA3; DAB;
DAC; DAM DRAM, MST; DFS 1; DLB
192; LAIT 1; MTCW 1; RGWL 2, 3;
TWA
Roth, Henry 1906-1995 ..... **CLC 2, 6, 11, 104**
See also AMWS 9; CA 11-12; 149; CANR
38, 63; CAP 1; CN 7; DA3; DLB 28;
EWL 3; MTCW 1, 2; RGAL 4
Roth, (Moses) Joseph 1894-1939 ... **TCLC 33**
See also CA 160; DLB 85; EWL 3; RGWL
2, 3
Roth, Philip (Milton) 1933- ... **CLC 1, 2, 3, 4,
6, 9, 15, 22, 31, 47, 66, 86, 119; SSC
26; WLC**
See also AMWR 2; AMWS 3; BEST 90:3;
BPFB 3; CA 1-4R; CANR 1, 22, 36, 55,
89; CDALB 1968-1988; CN 7; CPW 1;
DA; DA3; DAB; DAC; DAM MST, NOV,
POP; DLB 2, 28, 173; DLBY 1982; EWL
3; MTCW 1, 2; RGAL 4; RGSF 2; SSFS
12, 18; TUS
Rothenberg, Jerome 1931- .... **CLC 6, 57**
See also CA 45-48; CANR 1, 106; CP 7;
DLB 5, 193

Rotter, Pat ed. .... **CLC 65**
Roumain, Jacques (Jean Baptiste)
1907-1944 .... **BLC 3; TCLC 19**
See also BW 1; CA 117; 125; DAM MULT;
EWL 3
Rourke, Constance Mayfield
1885-1941 .... **TCLC 12**
See also CA 107; 200; YABC 1
Rousseau, Jean-Baptiste 1671-1741 ...... **LC 9**
Rousseau, Jean-Jacques 1712-1778 .... **LC 14,
36; WLC**
See also DA; DA3; DAB; DAC; DAM
MST; EW 4; GFL Beginnings to 1789;
LMFS 1; RGWL 2, 3; TWA
Roussel, Raymond 1877-1933 .... **TCLC 20**
See also CA 117; 201; EWL 3; GFL 1789
to the Present
Rovit, Earl (Herbert) 1927- .... **CLC 7**
See also CA 5-8R; CANR 12
Rowe, Elizabeth Singer 1674-1737 ..... **LC 44**
See also DLB 39, 95
Rowe, Nicholas 1674-1718 .... **LC 8**
See also DLB 84; RGEL 2
Rowlandson, Mary 1637(?)-1678 .... **LC 66**
See also DLB 24, 200; RGAL 4
Rowley, Ames Dorrance
See Lovecraft, H(oward) P(hillips)
Rowling, J(oanne) K(athleen)
1965- .... **CLC 137**
See also AAYA 34; BYA 13, 14; CA 173;
CLR 66, 80; MAICYA 2; SATA 109;
SUFW 2
Rowson, Susanna Haswell
1762(?)-1824 .... **NCLC 5, 69**
See also DLB 37, 200; RGAL 4
Roy, Arundhati 1960(?)- .... **CLC 109**
See also CA 163; CANR 90; DLBY 1997;
EWL 3; LATS 1
Roy, Gabrielle 1909-1983 .... **CLC 10, 14**
See also CA 53-56; 110; CANR 5, 61; CCA
1; DAB; DAC; DAM MST; DLB 68;
EWL 3; MTCW 1; RGWL 2, 3; SATA 104
Royko, Mike 1932-1997 .... **CLC 109**
See also CA 89-92; 157; CANR 26, 111;
CPW
Rozanov, Vasily Vasilyevich
See Rozanov, Vassili
See also EWL 3
Rozanov, Vassili 1856-1919 .... **TCLC 104**
See Rozanov, Vasily Vasilyevich
Rozewicz, Tadeusz 1921- ...... **CLC 9, 23, 139**
See also CA 108; CANR 36, 66; CWW 2;
DA3; DAM POET; DLB 232; EWL 3;
MTCW 1, 2; RGWL 3
Ruark, Gibbons 1941- .... **CLC 3**
See also CA 33-36R; CAAS 23; CANR 14,
31, 57; DLB 120
Rubens, Bernice (Ruth) 1923- .... **CLC 19, 31**
See also CA 25-28R; CANR 33, 65; CN 7;
DLB 14, 207; MTCW 1
Rubin, Harold
See Robbins, Harold
Rudkin, (James) David 1936- .... **CLC 14**
See also CA 89-92; CBD; CD 5; DLB 13
Rudnik, Raphael 1933- .... **CLC 7**
See also CA 29-32R
Ruffian, M.
See Hasek, Jaroslav (Matej Frantisek)
Ruiz, Jose Martinez .... **CLC 11**
See Martinez Ruiz, Jose
Rukeyser, Muriel 1913-1980 . **CLC 6, 10, 15,
27; PC 12**
See also AMWS 6; CA 5-8R; 93-96; CANR
26, 60; DA3; DAM POET; DLB 48; EWL
3; FW; GLL 2; MTCW 1, 2; PFS 10;
RGAL 4; SATA-Obit 22
Rule, Jane (Vance) 1931- .... **CLC 27**
See also CA 25-28R; CAAS 18; CANR 12,
87; CN 7; DLB 60; FW

Rulfo, Juan 1918-1986 .. **CLC 8, 80; HLC 2;
SSC 25**
See also CA 85-88; 118; CANR 26; CD-
WLB 3; DAM MULT; DLB 113; EWL 3;
HW 1, 2; LAW; MTCW 1, 2; RGSF 2;
RGWL 2, 3; WLIT 1
Rumi, Jalal al-Din 1207-1273 ...... **CMLC 20;
PC 45**
See also RGWL 2, 3; WP
Runeberg, Johan 1804-1877 .... **NCLC 41**
Runyon, (Alfred) Damon
1884(?)-1946 .... **TCLC 10**
See also CA 107; 165; DLB 11, 86, 171;
MTCW 2; RGAL 4
Rush, Norman 1933- .... **CLC 44**
See also CA 121; 126; INT 126
Rushdie, (Ahmed) Salman 1947- .... **CLC 23,
31, 55, 100; WLCS**
See also BEST 89:3; BPFB 3; BRWS 4;
CA 108; 111; CANR 33, 56, 108; CN 7;
CPW 1; DA3; DAB; DAC; DAM MST,
NOV, POP; DLB 194; EWL 3; FANT;
INT CA-111; LATS 1; LMFS 2; MTCW
1, 2; RGEL 2; RGSF 2; TEA; WLIT 4
Rushforth, Peter (Scott) 1945- .... **CLC 19**
See also CA 101
Ruskin, John 1819-1900 .... **TCLC 63**
See also BRW 5; BYA 5; CA 114; 129; CD-
BLB 1832-1890; DLB 55, 163, 190;
RGEL 2; SATA 24; TEA; WCH
Russ, Joanna 1937- .... **CLC 15**
See also BPFB 3; CA 5-28R; CANR 11,
31, 65; CN 7; DLB 8; FW; GLL 1;
MTCW 1; SCFW 2; SFW 4
Russ, Richard Patrick
See O'Brian, Patrick
Russell, George William 1867-1935
See A.E.; Baker, Jean H.
See also BRWS 8; CA 104; 153; CDBLB
1890-1914; DAM POET; EWL 3; RGEL
2
Russell, Jeffrey Burton 1934- .... **CLC 70**
See also CA 25-28R; CANR 11, 28, 52
Russell, (Henry) Ken(neth Alfred)
1927- .... **CLC 16**
See also CA 105
Russell, William Martin 1947-
See Russell, Willy
See also CA 164; CANR 107
Russell, Willy .... **CLC 60**
See Russell, William Martin
See also CBD; CD 5; DLB 233
Rutherford, Mark .... **TCLC 25**
See White, William Hale
See also DLB 18; RGEL 2
Ruyslinck, Ward .... **CLC 14**
See Belser, Reimond Karel Maria de
Ryan, Cornelius (John) 1920-1974 ..... **CLC 7**
See also CA 69-72; 53-56; CANR 38
Ryan, Michael 1946- .... **CLC 65**
See also CA 49-52; CANR 109; DLBY
1982
Ryan, Tim
See Dent, Lester
Rybakov, Anatoli (Naumovich)
1911-1998 .... **CLC 23, 53**
See also CA 126; 135; 172; SATA 79;
SATA-Obit 108
Ryder, Jonathan
See Ludlum, Robert
Ryga, George 1932-1987 .... **CLC 14**
See also CA 101; 124; CANR 43, 90; CCA
1; DAC; DAM MST; DLB 60
S. H.
See Hartmann, Sadakichi
S. S.
See Sassoon, Siegfried (Lorraine)

Saramago, Jose 1922- ..... **CLC 119; HLCS 1**
See also CA 153; CANR 96; DLB 287;
EWL 3; LATS 1

Sarduy, Severo 1937-1993 .... **CLC 6, 97;
HLCS 2**
See also CA 89-92; 142; CANR 58, 81;
CWW 2; DLB 113; EWL 3; HW 1, 2;
LAW

Sargeson, Frank 1903-1982 .... **CLC 31**
See also CA 25-28R; 106; CANR 38, 79;
EWL 3; GLL 2; RGEL 2; RGSF 2

Sarmiento, Domingo Faustino
1811-1888 .... **HLCS 2**
See also LAW; WLIT 1

Sarmiento, Felix Ruben Garcia
See Dario, Ruben

Saro-Wiwa, Ken(ule Beeson)
1941-1995 .... **CLC 114**
See also BW 2; CA 142; 150; CANR 60;
DLB 157

Saroyan, William 1908-1981 ... **CLC 1, 8, 10,
29, 34, 56; SSC 21; TCLC 137; WLC**
See also CA 5-8R; 103; CAD; CANR 30;
CDALBS; DA; DA3; DAB; DAC; DAM
DRAM, MST, NOV; DFS 17; DLB 7, 9,
86; DLBY 1981; EWL 3; LAIT 4; MTCW
1, 2; RGAL 4; RGSF 2; SATA 23; SATA-
Obit 24; SSFS 14; TUS

Sarraute, Nathalie 1900-1999 .... **CLC 1, 2, 4,
8, 10, 31, 80**
See also BPFB 3; CA 9-12R; 187; CANR
23, 66; CWW 2; DLB 83; EW 12; EWL
3; GFL 1789 to the Present; MTCW 1, 2;
RGWL 2, 3

Sarton, (Eleanor) May 1912-1995 ..... **CLC 4,
14, 49, 91; PC 39; TCLC 120**
See also AMWS 8; CA 1-4R; 149; CANR
1, 34, 55, 116; CN 7; CP 7; DAM POET;
DLB 48; DLBY 1981; EWL 3; FW; INT
CANR-34; MTCW 1, 2; RGAL 4; SATA
36; SATA-Obit 86; TUS

Sartre, Jean-Paul 1905-1980 . **CLC 1, 4, 7, 9,
13, 18, 24, 44, 50, 52; DC 3; SSC 32;
WLC**
See also CA 9-12R; 97-100; CANR 21; DA;
DA3; DAB; DAC; DAM DRAM, MST,
NOV; DFS 5; DLB 72; EW 12; EWL 3;
GFL 1789 to the Present; LMFS 2;
MTCW 1, 2; RGSF 2; RGWL 2, 3; SSFS
9; TWA

Sassoon, Siegfried (Lorraine)
1886-1967 .... **CLC 36, 130; PC 12**
See also BRW 6; CA 104; 25-28R; CANR
36; DAB; DAM MST, NOV, POET; DLB
20, 191; DLBD 18; EWL 3; MTCW 1, 2;
PAB; RGEL 2; TEA

Satterfield, Charles
See Pohl, Frederik

Satyremont
See Peret, Benjamin

Saul, John (W. III) 1942- .... **CLC 46**
See also AAYA 10; BEST 90:4; CA 81-84;
CANR 16, 40, 81; CPW; DAM NOV,
POP; HGG; SATA 98

Saunders, Caleb
See Heinlein, Robert A(nson)

Saura (Atares), Carlos 1932-1998 .... **CLC 20**
See also CA 114; 131; CANR 79; HW 1

Sauser, Frederic Louis
See Sauser-Hall, Frederic

Sauser-Hall, Frederic 1887-1961 ...... **CLC 18**
See Cendrars, Blaise
See also CA 102; 93-96; CANR 36, 62;
MTCW 1

Saussure, Ferdinand de
1857-1913 .... **TCLC 49**
See also DLB 242

Savage, Catharine
See Brosman, Catharine Savage

Savage, Thomas 1915- .... **CLC 40**
See also CA 126; 132; CAAS 15; CN 7;
INT 132; TCWW 2

Savan, Glenn (?)- .... **CLC 50**

Sax, Robert
See Johnson, Robert

Saxo Grammaticus c. 1150-c.
1222 .... **CMLC 58**

Saxton, Robert
See Johnson, Robert

Sayers, Dorothy L(eigh)
1893-1957 .... **TCLC 2, 15**
See also BPFB 3; BRWS 3; CA 104; 119;
CANR 60; CDBLB 1914-1945; CMW 4;
DAM POP; DLB 10, 36, 77, 100; MSW;
MTCW 1, 2; RGEL 2; SSFS 12; TEA

Sayers, Valerie 1952- .... **CLC 50, 122**
See also CA 134; CANR 61; CSW

Sayles, John (Thomas) 1950- . **CLC 7, 10, 14**
See also CA 57-60; CANR 41, 84; DLB 44

Scammell, Michael 1935- .... **CLC 34**
See also CA 156

Scannell, Vernon 1922- .... **CLC 49**
See also CA 5-8R; CANR 8, 24, 57; CP 7;
CWRI 5; DLB 27; SATA 59

Scarlett, Susan
See Streatfeild, (Mary) Noel

Scarron 1847-1910
See Mikszath, Kalman

Schaeffer, Susan Fromberg 1941- ..... **CLC 6,
11, 22**
See also CA 49-52; CANR 18, 65; CN 7;
DLB 28; MTCW 1, 2; SATA 22

Schama, Simon (Michael) 1945- ..... **CLC 150**
See also BEST 89:4; CA 105; CANR 39,
91

Schary, Jill
See Robinson, Jill

Schell, Jonathan 1943- .... **CLC 35**
See also CA 73-76; CANR 12, 117

Schelling, Friedrich Wilhelm Joseph von
1775-1854 .... **NCLC 30**
See also DLB 90

Scherer, Jean-Marie Maurice 1920-
See Rohmer, Eric
See also CA 110

Schevill, James (Erwin) 1920- .... **CLC 7**
See also CA 5-8R; CAAS 12; CAD; CD 5

Schiller, Friedrich von 1759-1805 ...... **DC 12;
NCLC 39, 69**
See also CDWLB 2; DAM DRAM; DLB
94; EW 5; RGWL 2, 3; TWA

Schisgal, Murray (Joseph) 1926- .... **CLC 6**
See also CA 21-24R; CAD; CANR 48, 86;
CD 5

Schlee, Ann 1934- .... **CLC 35**
See also CA 101; CANR 29, 88; SATA 44;
SATA-Brief 36

Schlegel, August Wilhelm von
1767-1845 .... **NCLC 15**
See also DLB 94; RGWL 2, 3

Schlegel, Friedrich 1772-1829 .... **NCLC 45**
See also DLB 90; EW 5; RGWL 2, 3; TWA

Schlegel, Johann Elias (von)
1719(?)-1749 .... **LC 5**

Schleiermacher, Friedrich
1768-1834 .... **NCLC 107**
See also DLB 90

Schlesinger, Arthur M(eier), Jr.
1917- .... **CLC 84**
See also AITN 1; CA 1-4R; CANR 1, 28,
58, 105; DLB 17; INT CANR-28; MTCW
1, 2; SATA 61

Schlink, Bernhard 1944- .... **CLC 174**
See also CA 163; CANR 116

Schmidt, Arno (Otto) 1914-1979 ...... **CLC 56**
See also CA 128; 109; DLB 69; EWL 3

Schmitz, Aron Hector 1861-1928
See Svevo, Italo
See also CA 104; 122; MTCW 1

Schnackenberg, Gjertrud (Cecelia)
1953- .... **CLC 40; PC 45**
See also CA 116; CANR 100; CP 7; CWP;
DLB 120, 282; PFS 13

Schneider, Leonard Alfred 1925-1966
See Bruce, Lenny
See also CA 89-92

Schnitzler, Arthur 1862-1931 ..... **DC 17; SSC
15, 61; TCLC 4**
See also CA 104; CDWLB 2; DLB 81, 118;
EW 8; EWL 3; RGSF 2; RGWL 2, 3

Schoenberg, Arnold Franz Walter
1874-1951 .... **TCLC 75**
See also CA 109; 188

Schonberg, Arnold
See Schoenberg, Arnold Franz Walter

Schopenhauer, Arthur 1788-1860 .. **NCLC 51**
See also DLB 90; EW 5

Schor, Sandra (M.) 1932(?)-1990 ..... **CLC 65**
See also CA 132

Schorer, Mark 1908-1977 .... **CLC 9**
See also CA 5-8R; 73-76; CANR 7; DLB
103

Schrader, Paul (Joseph) 1946- .... **CLC 26**
See also CA 37-40R; CANR 41; DLB 44

Schreber, Daniel 1842-1911 .... **TCLC 123**

Schreiner, Olive (Emilie Albertina)
1855-1920 .... **TCLC 9**
See also AFW; BRWS 2; CA 105; 154;
DLB 18, 156, 190, 225; EWL 3; FW;
RGEL 2; TWA; WLIT 2

Schulberg, Budd (Wilson) 1914- .. **CLC 7, 48**
See also BPFB 3; CA 25-28R; CANR 19,
87; CN 7; DLB 6, 26, 28; DLBY 1981,
2001

Schulman, Arnold
See Trumbo, Dalton

Schulz, Bruno 1892-1942 .. **SSC 13; TCLC 5,
51**
See also CA 115; 123; CANR 86; CDWLB
4; DLB 215; EWL 3; MTCW 2; RGSF 2;
RGWL 2, 3

Schulz, Charles M(onroe)
1922-2000 .... **CLC 12**
See also AAYA 39; CA 9-12R; 187; CANR
6; INT CANR-6; SATA 10; SATA-Obit
118

Schumacher, E(rnst) F(riedrich)
1911-1977 .... **CLC 80**
See also CA 81-84; 73-76; CANR 34, 85

Schuyler, George Samuel 1895-1977 .... **HR 3**
See also BW 2; CA 81-84; 73-76; CANR
42; DLB 29, 51

Schuyler, James Marcus 1923-1991 .. **CLC 5,
23**
See also CA 101; 134; DAM POET; DLB
5, 169; EWL 3; INT 101; WP

Schwartz, Delmore (David)
1913-1966 ... **CLC 2, 4, 10, 45, 87; PC 8**
See also AMWS 2; CA 17-18; 25-28R;
CANR 35; CAP 2; DLB 28, 48; EWL 3;
MTCW 1, 2; PAB; RGAL 4; TUS

Schwartz, Ernst
See Ozu, Yasujiro

Schwartz, John Burnham 1965- .... **CLC 59**
See also CA 132; CANR 116

Schwartz, Lynne Sharon 1939- .... **CLC 31**
See also CA 103; CANR 44, 89; DLB 218;
MTCW 2

Schwartz, Muriel A.
See Eliot, T(homas) S(tearns)

Schwarz-Bart, Andre 1928- .... **CLC 2, 4**
See also CA 89-92; CANR 109

Schwarz-Bart, Simone 1938- . **BLCS; CLC 7**
See also BW 2; CA 97-100; CANR 117;
EWL 3

Shalamov, Varlam (Tikhonovich)
1907(?)-1982 .... **CLC 18**
See also CA 129; 105; RGSF 2
Shamlu, Ahmad 1925-2000 .... **CLC 10**
See also CWW 2
Shammas, Anton 1951- .... **CLC 55**
See also CA 199
Shandling, Arline
See Berriault, Gina
Shange, Ntozake 1948- ... **BLC 3; CLC 8, 25, 38, 74, 126; DC 3**
See also AAYA 9; AFAW 1, 2; BW 2; CA 85-88; CABS 3; CAD; CANR 27, 48, 74; CD 5; CP 7; CWD; CWP; DA3; DAM DRAM, MULT; DFS 2, 11; DLB 38, 249; FW; LAIT 5; MTCW 1, 2; NFS 11; RGAL 4; YAW
Shanley, John Patrick 1950- .... **CLC 75**
See also CA 128; 133; CAD; CANR 83; CD 5
Shapcott, Thomas W(illiam) 1935- .. **CLC 38**
See also CA 69-72; CANR 49, 83, 103; CP 7
Shapiro, Jane 1942- .... **CLC 76**
See also CA 196
Shapiro, Karl (Jay) 1913-2000 ...... **CLC 4, 8, 15, 53; PC 25**
See also AMWS 2; CA 1-4R; 188; CAAS 6; CANR 1, 36, 66; CP 7; DLB 48; EWL 3; EXPP; MTCW 1, 2; PFS 3; RGAL 4
Sharp, William 1855-1905 .... **TCLC 39**
See Macleod, Fiona
See also CA 160; DLB 156; RGEL 2
Sharpe, Thomas Ridley 1928-
See Sharpe, Tom
See also CA 114; 122; CANR 85; INT CA-122
Sharpe, Tom .... **CLC 36**
See Sharpe, Thomas Ridley
See also CN 7; DLB 14, 231
Shatrov, Mikhail .... **CLC 59**
Shaw, Bernard
See Shaw, George Bernard
See also DLB 190
Shaw, G. Bernard
See Shaw, George Bernard
Shaw, George Bernard 1856-1950 .. **TCLC 3, 9, 21, 45; WLC**
See Shaw, Bernard
See also BRW 6; BRWC 1; BRWR 2; CA 104; 128; CDBLB 1914-1945; DA; DA3; DAB; DAC; DAM DRAM, MST; DFS 1, 3, 6, 11; DLB 10, 57; EWL 3; LAIT 3; LATS 1; MTCW 1, 2; RGEL 2; TEA; WLIT 4
Shaw, Henry Wheeler 1818-1885 .. **NCLC 15**
See also DLB 11; RGAL 4
Shaw, Irwin 1913-1984 .... **CLC 7, 23, 34**
See also AITN 1; BPFB 3; CA 13-16R; 112; CANR 21; CDALB 1941-1968; CPW; DAM DRAM, POP; DLB 6, 102; DLBY 1984; MTCW 1, 21
Shaw, Robert 1927-1978 .... **CLC 5**
See also AITN 1; CA 1-4R; 81-84; CANR 4; DLB 13, 14
Shaw, T. E.
See Lawrence, T(homas) E(dward)
Shawn, Wallace 1943- .... **CLC 41**
See also CA 112; CAD; CD 5; DLB 266
Shchedrin, N.
See Saltykov, Mikhail Evgrafovich
Shea, Lisa 1953- .... **CLC 86**
See also CA 147
Sheed, Wilfrid (John Joseph) 1930- . **CLC 2, 4, 10, 53**
See also CA 65-68; CANR 30, 66; CN 7; DLB 6; MTCW 1, 2

Sheehy, Gail 1937- .... **CLC 171**
See also CA 49-52; CANR 1, 33, 55, 92; CPW; MTCW 1
Sheldon, Alice Hastings Bradley
1915(?)-1987
See Tiptree, James, Jr.
See also CA 108; 122; CANR 34; INT 108; MTCW 1
Sheldon, John
See Bloch, Robert (Albert)
Sheldon, Walter J(ames) 1917-1996
See Queen, Ellery
See also AITN 1; CA 25-28R; CANR 10
Shelley, Mary Wollstonecraft (Godwin)
1797-1851 ...... **NCLC 14, 59, 103; WLC**
See also AAYA 20; BPFB 3; BRW 3; BRWS 3; BYA 5; CDBLB 1789-1832; DA; DA3; DAB; DAC; DAM MST, NOV; DLB 110, 116, 159, 178; EXPN; HGG; LAIT 1; LMFS 1, 2; NFS 1; RGEL 2; SATA 29; SCFW; SFW 4; TEA; WLIT 3
Shelley, Percy Bysshe 1792-1822 .. **NCLC 18, 93; PC 14; WLC**
See also BRW 4; BRWR 1; CDBLB 1789-1832; DA; DA3; DAB; DAC; DAM MST, POET; DLB 96, 110, 158; EXPP; LMFS 1; PAB; PFS 2; RGEL 2; TEA; WLIT 3; WP
Shepard, Jim 1956- .... **CLC 36**
See also CA 137; CANR 59, 104; SATA 90
Shepard, Lucius 1947- .... **CLC 34**
See also CA 128; 141; CANR 81; HGG; SCFW 2; SFW 4; SUFW 2
Shepard, Sam 1943- .... **CLC 4, 6, 17, 34, 41, 44, 169; DC 5**
See also AAYA 1; AMWS 3; CA 69-72; CABS 3; CAD; CANR 22, 120; CD 5; DA3; DAM DRAM; DFS 3, 6, 7, 14; DLB 7, 212; EWL 3; IDFW 3, 4; MTCW 1, 2; RGAL 4
Shepherd, Michael
See Ludlum, Robert
Sherburne, Zoa (Lillian Morin)
1912-1995 .... **CLC 30**
See also AAYA 13; CA 1-4R; 176; CANR 3, 37; MAICYA 1, 2; SAAS 18; SATA 3; YAW
Sheridan, Frances 1724-1766 .... **LC 7**
See also DLB 39, 84
Sheridan, Richard Brinsley
1751-1816 .... **DC 1; NCLC 5, 91; WLC**
See also BRW 3; CDBLB 1660-1789; DA; DAB; DAC; DAM DRAM, MST; DFS 15; DLB 89; WLIT 3
Sherman, Jonathan Marc .... **CLC 55**
Sherman, Martin 1941(?)- .... **CLC 19**
See also CA 116; 123; CAD; CANR 86; CD 5; DLB 228; GLL 1; IDTP
Sherwin, Judith Johnson
See Johnson, Judith (Emlyn)
See also CANR 85; CP 7; CWP
Sherwood, Frances 1940- .... **CLC 81**
See also CA 146
Sherwood, Robert E(mmet)
1896-1955 .... **TCLC 3**
See also CA 104; 153; CANR 86; DAM DRAM; DFS 11, 15, 17; DLB 7, 26, 249; IDFW 3, 4; RGAL 4
Shestov, Lev 1866-1938 .... **TCLC 56**
Shevchenko, Taras 1814-1861 .... **NCLC 54**
Shiel, M(atthew) P(hipps)
1865-1947 .... **TCLC 8**
See Holmes, Gordon
See also CA 106; 160; DLB 153; HGG; MTCW 2; SFW 4; SUFW
Shields, Carol 1935-2003 .... **CLC 91, 113**
See also AMWS 7; CA 81-84; CANR 51, 74, 98; CCA 1; CN 7; CPW; DA3; DAC; MTCW 2

Shields, David 1956- .... **CLC 97**
See also CA 124; CANR 48, 99, 112
Shiga, Naoya 1883-1971 ..... **CLC 33; SSC 23**
See Shiga Naoya
See also CA 101; 33-36R; MJW; RGWL 3
Shiga Naoya
See Shiga, Naoya
See also DLB 180; EWL 3; RGWL 3
Shilts, Randy 1951-1994 .... **CLC 85**
See also AAYA 19; CA 115; 127; 144; CANR 45; DA3; GLL 1; INT 127; MTCW 2
Shimazaki, Haruki 1872-1943
See Shimazaki Toson
See also CA 105; 134; CANR 84; RGWL 3
Shimazaki Toson .... **TCLC 5**
See Shimazaki, Haruki
See also DLB 180; EWL 3
Sholokhov, Mikhail (Aleksandrovich)
1905-1984 .... **CLC 7, 15**
See also CA 101; 112; DLB 272; EWL 3; MTCW 1, 2; RGWL 2, 3; SATA-Obit 36
Shone, Patric
See Hanley, James
Showalter, Elaine 1941- .... **CLC 169**
See also CA 57-60; CANR 58, 106; DLB 67; FW; GLL 2
Shreve, Susan Richards 1939- .... **CLC 23**
See also CA 49-52; CAAS 5; CANR 5, 38, 69, 100; MAICYA 1, 2; SATA 46, 95; SATA-Brief 41
Shue, Larry 1946-1985 .... **CLC 52**
See also CA 145; 117; DAM DRAM; DFS 7
Shu-Jen, Chou 1881-1936
See Lu Hsun
See also CA 104
Shulman, Alix Kates 1932- .... **CLC 2, 10**
See also CA 29-32R; CANR 43; FW; SATA 7
Shusaku, Endo
See Endo, Shusaku
Shuster, Joe 1914-1992 .... **CLC 21**
See also AAYA 50
Shute, Nevil .... **CLC 30**
See Norway, Nevil Shute
See also BPFB 3; DLB 255; NFS 9; RHW; SFW 4
Shuttle, Penelope (Diane) 1947- .... **CLC 7**
See also CA 93-96; CANR 39, 84, 92, 108; CP 7; CWP; DLB 14, 40
Shvarts, Elena 1948- .... **PC 50**
See also CA 147
Sidhwa, Bapsy (N.) 1938- .... **CLC 168**
See also CA 108; CANR 25, 57; CN 7; FW
Sidney, Mary 1561-1621 .... **LC 19, 39**
See Sidney Herbert, Mary
Sidney, Sir Philip 1554-1586 . **LC 19, 39; PC 32**
See also BRW 1; BRWR 2; CDBLB Before 1660; DA; DA3; DAB; DAC; DAM MST, POET; DLB 167; EXPP; PAB; RGEL 2; TEA; WP
Sidney Herbert, Mary
See Sidney, Mary
See also DLB 167
Siegel, Jerome 1914-1996 .... **CLC 21**
See Siegel, Jerry
See also CA 116; 169; 151
Siegel, Jerry
See Siegel, Jerome
See also AAYA 50
Sienkiewicz, Henryk (Adam Alexander Pius)
1846-1916 .... **TCLC 3**
See also CA 104; 134; CANR 84; EWL 3; RGSF 2; RGWL 2, 3
Sierra, Gregorio Martinez
See Martinez Sierra, Gregorio

Sierra, Maria (de la O'LeJarraga) Martinez
See Martinez Sierra, Maria (de la O'LeJarraga)

Sigal, Clancy 1926- .... **CLC 7**
See also CA 1-4R; CANR 85; CN 7

Sigourney, Lydia H.
See Sigourney, Lydia Howard (Huntley)
See also DLB 73, 183

Sigourney, Lydia Howard (Huntley)
1791-1865 .... **NCLC 21, 87**
See Sigourney, Lydia H.; Sigourney, Lydia Huntley
See also DLB 1

Sigourney, Lydia Huntley
See Sigourney, Lydia Howard (Huntley)
See also DLB 42, 239, 243

Siguenza y Gongora, Carlos de
1645-1700 .... **HLCS 2; LC 8**
See also LAW

Sigurjonsson, Johann 1880-1919 ... **TCLC 27**
See also CA 170; EWL 3

Sikelianos, Angelos 1884-1951 .... **PC 29; TCLC 39**
See also EWL 3; RGWL 2, 3

Silkin, Jon 1930-1997 .... **CLC 2, 6, 43**
See also CA 5-8R; CAAS 5; CANR 89; CP 7; DLB 27

Silko, Leslie (Marmon) 1948- .... **CLC 23, 74, 114; NNAL; SSC 37; WLCS**
See also AAYA 14; AMWS 4; ANW; BYA 12; CA 115; 122; CANR 45, 65, 118; CN 7; CP 7; CPW 1; CWP; DA; DA3; DAC; DAM MST, MULT, POP; DLB 143, 175, 256, 275; EWL 3; EXPP; EXPS; LAIT 4; MTCW 2; NFS 4; PFS 9, 16; RGAL 4; RGSF 2; SSFS 4, 8, 10, 11

Sillanpaa, Frans Eemil 1888-1964 ... **CLC 19**
See also CA 129; 93-96; EWL 3; MTCW 1

Sillitoe, Alan 1928- .. **CLC 1, 3, 6, 10, 19, 57, 148**
See also AITN 1; BRWS 5; CA 9-12R; CAAE 191; CAAS 2; CANR 8, 26, 55; CDBLB 1960 to Present; CN 7; DLB 14, 139; EWL 3; MTCW 1, 2; RGEL 2; RGSF 2; SATA 61

Silone, Ignazio 1900-1978 .... **CLC 4**
See also CA 25-28; 81-84; CANR 34; CAP 2; DLB 264; EW 12; EWL 3; MTCW 1; RGSF 2; RGWL 2, 3

Silone, Ignazione
See Silone, Ignazio

Silver, Joan Micklin 1935- .... **CLC 20**
See also CA 114; 121; INT 121

Silver, Nicholas
See Faust, Frederick (Schiller)
See also TCWW 2

Silverberg, Robert 1935- .... **CLC 7, 140**
See also AAYA 24; BPFB 3; BYA 7, 9; CA 1-4R, 186; CAAE 186; CAAS 3; CANR 1, 20, 36, 85; CLR 59; CN 7; CPW; DAM POP; DLB 8; INT CANR-20; MAICYA 1, 2; MTCW 1, 2; SATA 13, 91; SATA-Essay 104; SCFW 2; SFW 4; SUFW 2

Silverstein, Alvin 1933- .... **CLC 17**
See also CA 49-52; CANR 2; CLR 25; JRDA; MAICYA 1, 2; SATA 8, 69, 124

Silverstein, Shel(don Allan)
1932-1999 .... **PC 49**
See also AAYA 40; BW 3; CA 107; 179; CANR 47, 74, 81; CLR 5; CWRI 5; JRDA; MAICYA 1, 2; MTCW 2; SATA 33, 92; SATA-Brief 27; SATA-Obit 116

Silverstein, Virginia B(arbara Opshelor)
1937- .... **CLC 17**
See also CA 49-52; CANR 2; CLR 25; JRDA; MAICYA 1, 2; SATA 8, 69, 124

Sim, Georges
See Simenon, Georges (Jacques Christian)

Simak, Clifford D(onald) 1904-1988 . **CLC 1, 55**
See also CA 1-4R; 125; CANR 1, 35; DLB 8; MTCW 1; SATA-Obit 56; SFW 4

Simenon, Georges (Jacques Christian)
1903-1989 .... **CLC 1, 2, 3, 8, 18, 47**
See also BPFB 3; CA 85-88; 129; CANR 35; CMW 4; DA3; DAM POP; DLB 72; DLBY 1989; EW 12; EWL 3; GFL 1789 to the Present; MSW; MTCW 1, 2; RGWL 2, 3

Simic, Charles 1938- .... **CLC 6, 9, 22, 49, 68, 130**
See also AMWS 8; CA 29-32R; CAAS 4; CANR 12, 33, 52, 61, 96; CP 7; DA3; DAM POET; DLB 105; MTCW 2; PFS 7; RGAL 4; WP

Simmel, Georg 1858-1918 .... **TCLC 64**
See also CA 157

Simmons, Charles (Paul) 1924- .... **CLC 57**
See also CA 89-92; INT 89-92

Simmons, Dan 1948- .... **CLC 44**
See also AAYA 16; CA 138; CANR 53, 81; CPW; DAM POP; HGG; SUFW 2

Simmons, James (Stewart Alexander)
1933- .... **CLC 43**
See also CA 105; CAAS 21; CP 7; DLB 40

Simms, William Gilmore
1806-1870 .... **NCLC 3**
See also DLB 3, 30, 59, 73, 248, 254; RGAL 4

Simon, Carly 1945- .... **CLC 26**
See also CA 105

Simon, Claude (Henri Eugene)
1913-1984 .... **CLC 4, 9, 15, 39**
See also CA 89-92; CANR 33, 117; DAM NOV; DLB 83; EW 13; EWL 3; GFL 1789 to the Present; MTCW 1

Simon, Myles
See Follett, Ken(neth Martin)

Simon, (Marvin) Neil 1927- ... **CLC 6, 11, 31, 39, 70; DC 14**
See also AAYA 32; AITN 1; AMWS 4; CA 21-24R; CANR 26, 54, 87; CD 5; DA3; DAM DRAM; DFS 2, 6, 12, 18; DLB 7, 266; LAIT 4; MTCW 1, 2; RGAL 4; TUS

Simon, Paul (Frederick) 1941(?)- ..... **CLC 17**
See also CA 116; 153

Simonon, Paul 1956(?)- .... **CLC 30**

Simonson, Rick ed. .... **CLC 70**

Simpson, Harriette
See Arnow, Harriette (Louisa) Simpson

Simpson, Louis (Aston Marantz)
1923- .... **CLC 4, 7, 9, 32, 149**
See also AMWS 9; CA 1-4R; CAAS 4; CANR 1, 61; CP 7; DAM POET; DLB 5; MTCW 1, 2; PFS 7, 11, 14; RGAL 4

Simpson, Mona (Elizabeth) 1957- ... **CLC 44, 146**
See also CA 122; 135; CANR 68, 103; CN 7; EWL 3

Simpson, N(orman) F(rederick)
1919- .... **CLC 29**
See also CA 13-16R; CBD; DLB 13; RGEL 2

Sinclair, Andrew (Annandale) 1935- . **CLC 2, 14**
See also CA 9-12R; CAAS 5; CANR 14, 38, 91; CN 7; DLB 14; FANT; MTCW 1

Sinclair, Emil
See Hesse, Hermann

Sinclair, Iain 1943- .... **CLC 76**
See also CA 132; CANR 81; CP 7; HGG

Sinclair, Iain MacGregor
See Sinclair, Iain

Sinclair, Irene
See Griffith, D(avid Lewelyn) W(ark)

Sinclair, Mary Amelia St. Clair 1865(?)-1946
See Sinclair, May
See also CA 104; HGG; RHW

Sinclair, May .... **TCLC 3, 11**
See Sinclair, Mary Amelia St. Clair
See also CA 166; DLB 36, 135; EWL 3; RGEL 2; SUFW

Sinclair, Roy
See Griffith, D(avid Lewelyn) W(ark)

Sinclair, Upton (Beall) 1878-1968 ..... **CLC 1, 11, 15, 63; WLC**
See also AMWS 5; BPFB 3; BYA 2; CA 5-8R; 25-28R; CANR 7; CDALB 1929-1941; DA; DA3; DAB; DAC; DAM MST, NOV; DLB 9; EWL 3; INT CANR-7; LAIT 3; MTCW 1, 2; NFS 6; RGAL 4; SATA 9; TUS; YAW

Singe, (Edmund) J(ohn) M(illington)
1871-1909 .... **WLC**

Singer, Isaac
See Singer, Isaac Bashevis

Singer, Isaac Bashevis 1904-1991 .. **CLC 1, 3, 6, 9, 11, 15, 23, 38, 69, 111; SSC 3, 53; WLC**
See also AAYA 32; AITN 1, 2; AMW; AMWR 2; BPFB 3; BYA 1, 4; CA 1-4R; 134; CANR 1, 39, 106; CDALB 1941-1968; CLR 1; CWRI 5; DA; DA3; DAB; DAC; DAM MST, NOV; DLB 6, 28, 52, 278; DLBY 1991; EWL 3; EXPS; HGG; JRDA; LAIT 3; MAICYA 1, 2; MTCW 1, 2; RGAL 4; RGSF 2; SATA 3, 27; SATA-Obit 68; SSFS 2, 12, 16; TUS; TWA

Singer, Israel Joshua 1893-1944 .... **TCLC 33**
See also CA 169; EWL 3

Singh, Khushwant 1915- .... **CLC 11**
See also CA 9-12R; CAAS 9; CANR 6, 84; CN 7; EWL 3; RGEL 2

Singleton, Ann
See Benedict, Ruth (Fulton)

Singleton, John 1968(?)- .... **CLC 156**
See also AAYA 50; BW 2, 3; CA 138; CANR 67, 82; DAM MULT

Sinjohn, John
See Galsworthy, John

Sinyavsky, Andrei (Donatevich)
1925-1997 .... **CLC 8**
See Sinyavsky, Andrey Donatovich; Tertz, Abram
See also CA 85-88; 159

Sinyavsky, Andrey Donatovich
See Sinyavsky, Andrei (Donatevich)
See also EWL 3

Sirin, V.
See Nabokov, Vladimir (Vladimirovich)

Sissman, L(ouis) E(dward)
1928-1976 .... **CLC 9, 18**
See also CA 21-24R; 65-68; CANR 13; DLB 5

Sisson, C(harles) H(ubert)
1914-2003 .... **CLC 8**
See also CA 1-4R; CAAS 3; CANR 3, 48, 84; CP 7; DLB 27

Sitting Bull 1831(?)-1890 .... **NNAL**
See also DA3; DAM MULT

Sitwell, Dame Edith 1887-1964 ..... **CLC 2, 9, 67; PC 3**
See also BRW 7; CA 9-12R; CANR 35; CDBLB 1945-1960; DAM POET; DLB 20; EWL 3; MTCW 1, 2; RGEL 2; TEA

Siwaarmill, H. P.
See Sharp, William

Sjoewall, Maj 1935- .... **CLC 7**
See Sjowall, Maj
See also CA 65-68; CANR 73

Sjowall, Maj
See Sjoewall, Maj
See also BPFB 3; CMW 4; MSW

Skelton, John 1460(?)-1529 ..... **LC 71; PC 25**
  See also BRW 1; DLB 136; RGEL 2
Skelton, Robin 1925-1997 .... **CLC 13**
  See Zuk, Georges
  See also AITN 2; CA 5-8R; 160; CAAS 5;
    CANR 28, 89; CCA 1; CP 7; DLB 27, 53
Skolimowski, Jerzy 1938- .... **CLC 20**
  See also CA 128
Skram, Amalie (Bertha)
    1847-1905 .... **TCLC 25**
  See also CA 165
Skvorecky, Josef (Vaclav) 1924- ...... **CLC 15,
    39, 69, 152**
  See also CA 61-64; CAAS 1; CANR 10,
    34, 63, 108; CDWLB 4; DA3; DAC;
    DAM NOV; DLB 232; EWL 3; MTCW
    1, 2
Slade, Bernard .... **CLC 11, 46**
  See Newbound, Bernard Slade
  See also CAAS 9; CCA 1; DLB 53
Slaughter, Carolyn 1946- .... **CLC 56**
  See also CA 85-88; CANR 85; CN 7
Slaughter, Frank G(ill) 1908-2001 ... **CLC 29**
  See also AITN 2; CA 5-8R; 197; CANR 5,
    85; INT CANR-5; RHW
Slavitt, David R(ytman) 1935- ..... **CLC 5, 14**
  See also CA 21-24R; CAAS 3; CANR 41,
    83; CP 7; DLB 5, 6
Slesinger, Tess 1905-1945 .... **TCLC 10**
  See also CA 107; 199; DLB 102
Slessor, Kenneth 1901-1971 .... **CLC 14**
  See also CA 102; 89-92; DLB 260; RGEL
    2
Slowacki, Juliusz 1809-1849 .... **NCLC 15**
  See also RGWL 3
Smart, Christopher 1722-1771 . **LC 3; PC 13**
  See also DAM POET; DLB 109; RGEL 2
Smart, Elizabeth 1913-1986 .... **CLC 54**
  See also CA 81-84; 118; DLB 88
Smiley, Jane (Graves) 1949- ...... **CLC 53, 76,
    144**
  See also AMWS 6; BPFB 3; CA 104;
    CANR 30, 50, 74, 96; CN 7; CPW 1;
    DA3; DAM POP; DLB 227, 234; EWL 3;
    INT CANR-30
Smith, A(rthur) J(ames) M(arshall)
    1902-1980 .... **CLC 15**
  See also CA 1-4R; 102; CANR 4; DAC;
    DLB 88; RGEL 2
Smith, Adam 1723(?)-1790 .... **LC 36**
  See also DLB 104, 252; RGEL 2
Smith, Alexander 1829-1867 .... **NCLC 59**
  See also DLB 32, 55
Smith, Anna Deavere 1950- .... **CLC 86**
  See also CA 133; CANR 103; CD 5; DFS 2
Smith, Betty (Wehner) 1904-1972 .... **CLC 19**
  See also BPFB 3; BYA 3; CA 5-8R; 33-
    36R; DLBY 1982; LAIT 3; RGAL 4;
    SATA 6
Smith, Charlotte (Turner)
    1749-1806 .... **NCLC 23, 115**
  See also DLB 39, 109; RGEL 2; TEA
Smith, Clark Ashton 1893-1961 .... **CLC 43**
  See also CA 143; CANR 81; FANT; HGG;
    MTCW 2; SCFW 2; SFW 4; SUFW
Smith, Dave .... **CLC 22, 42**
  See Smith, David (Jeddie)
  See also CAAS 7; DLB 5
Smith, David (Jeddie) 1942-
  See Smith, Dave
  See also CA 49-52; CANR 1, 59, 120; CP
    7; CSW; DAM POET
Smith, Florence Margaret 1902-1971
  See Smith, Stevie
  See also CA 17-18; 29-32R; CANR 35;
    CAP 2; DAM POET; MTCW 1, 2; TEA
Smith, Iain Crichton 1928-1998 .... **CLC 64**
  See also CA 21-24R; 171; CN 7; CP 7; DLB
    40, 139; RGSF 2

Smith, John 1580(?)-1631 .... **LC 9**
  See also DLB 24, 30; TUS
Smith, Johnston
  See Crane, Stephen (Townley)
Smith, Joseph, Jr. 1805-1844 .... **NCLC 53**
Smith, Lee 1944- .... **CLC 25, 73**
  See also CA 114; 119; CANR 46, 118;
    CSW; DLB 143; DLBY 1983; EWL 3;
    INT CA-119; RGAL 4
Smith, Martin
  See Smith, Martin Cruz
Smith, Martin Cruz 1942- .. **CLC 25; NNAL**
  See also BEST 89:4; BPFB 3; CA 85-88;
    CANR 6, 23, 43, 65, 119; CMW 4; CPW;
    DAM MULT, POP; HGG; INT CANR-
    23; MTCW 2; RGAL 4
Smith, Patti 1946- .... **CLC 12**
  See also CA 93-96; CANR 63
Smith, Pauline (Urmson)
    1882-1959 .... **TCLC 25**
  See also DLB 225; EWL 3
Smith, Rosamond
  See Oates, Joyce Carol
Smith, Sheila Kaye
  See Kaye-Smith, Sheila
Smith, Stevie .... **CLC 3, 8, 25, 44; PC 12**
  See Smith, Florence Margaret
  See also BRWS 2; DLB 20; EWL 3; MTCW
    2; PAB; PFS 3; RGEL 2
Smith, Wilbur (Addison) 1933- .... **CLC 33**
  See also CA 13-16R; CANR 7, 46, 66;
    CPW; MTCW 1, 2
Smith, William Jay 1918- .... **CLC 6**
  See also AMWS 13; CA 5-8R; CANR 44,
    106; CP 7; CSW; CWRI 5; DLB 5; MAI-
    CYA 1, 2; SAAS 22; SATA 2, 68
Smith, Woodrow Wilson
  See Kuttner, Henry
Smith, Zadie 1976- .... **CLC 158**
  See also AAYA 50; CA 193
Smolenskin, Peretz 1842-1885 .... **NCLC 30**
Smollett, Tobias (George) 1721-1771 ... **LC 2,
    46**
  See also BRW 3; CDBLB 1660-1789; DLB
    39, 104; RGEL 2; TEA
Snodgrass, W(illiam) D(e Witt)
    1926- .... **CLC 2, 6, 10, 18, 68**
  See also AMWS 6; CA 1-4R; CANR 6, 36,
    65, 85; CP 7; DAM POET; DLB 5;
    MTCW 1, 2; RGAL 4
Snorri Sturluson 1179-1241 .... **CMLC 56**
  See also RGWL 2, 3
Snow, C(harles) P(ercy) 1905-1980 ... **CLC 1,
    4, 6, 9, 13, 19**
  See also BRW 7; CA 5-8R; 101; CANR 28;
    CDBLB 1945-1960; DAM NOV; DLB 15,
    77; DLBD 17; EWL 3; MTCW 1, 2;
    RGEL 2; TEA
Snow, Frances Compton
  See Adams, Henry (Brooks)
Snyder, Gary (Sherman) 1930- . **CLC 1, 2, 5,
    9, 32, 120; PC 21**
  See also AMWS 8; ANW; BG 3; CA 17-
    20R; CANR 30, 60; CP 7; DA3; DAM
    POET; DLB 5, 16, 165, 212, 237, 275;
    EWL 3; MTCW 2; PFS 9; RGAL 4; WP
Snyder, Zilpha Keatley 1927- .... **CLC 17**
  See also AAYA 15; BYA 1; CA 9-12R;
    CANR 38; CLR 31; JRDA; MAICYA 1,
    2; SAAS 2; SATA 1, 28, 75, 110; SATA-
    Essay 112; YAW
Soares, Bernardo
  See Pessoa, Fernando (Antonio Nogueira)
Sobh, A.
  See Shamlu, Ahmad
Sobol, Joshua 1939- .... **CLC 60**
  See Sobol, Yehoshua
  See also CA 200; CWW 2

Sobol, Yehoshua 1939-
  See Sobol, Joshua
  See also CWW 2
Socrates 470B.C.-399B.C. .... **CMLC 27**
Soderberg, Hjalmar 1869-1941 ...... **TCLC 39**
  See also DLB 259; EWL 3; RGSF 2
Soderbergh, Steven 1963- .... **CLC 154**
  See also AAYA 43
Sodergran, Edith (Irene) 1892-1923
  See Soedergran, Edith (Irene)
  See also CA 202; DLB 259; EW 11; EWL
    3; RGWL 2, 3
Soedergran, Edith (Irene)
    1892-1923 .... **TCLC 31**
  See Sodergran, Edith (Irene)
Softly, Edgar
  See Lovecraft, H(oward) P(hillips)
Softly, Edward
  See Lovecraft, H(oward) P(hillips)
Sokolov, Alexander V(sevolodovich) 1943-
  See Sokolov, Sasha
  See also CA 73-76
Sokolov, Raymond 1941- .... **CLC 7**
  See also CA 85-88
Sokolov, Sasha .... **CLC 59**
  See Sokolov, Alexander V(sevolodovich)
  See also CWW 2; DLB 285; EWL 3; RGWL
    2, 3
Sokolov, Sasha .... **CLC 59**
Solo, Jay
  See Ellison, Harlan (Jay)
Sologub, Fyodor .... **TCLC 9**
  See Teternikov, Fyodor Kuzmich
  See also EWL 3
Solomons, Ikey Esquir
  See Thackeray, William Makepeace
Solomos, Dionysios 1798-1857 .... **NCLC 15**
Solwoska, Mara
  See French, Marilyn
Solzhenitsyn, Aleksandr I(sayevich)
    1918- .. **CLC 1, 2, 4, 7, 9, 10, 18, 26, 34,
    78, 134; SSC 32; WLC**
  See Solzhenitsyn, Aleksandr Isaevich
  See also AAYA 49; AITN 1; BPFB 3; CA
    69-72; CANR 40, 65, 116; DA; DA3;
    DAB; DAC; DAM MST, NOV; EW 13;
    EXPS; LAIT 4; MTCW 1, 2; NFS 6;
    RGSF 2; RGWL 2, 3; SSFS 9; TWA
Solzhenitsyn, Aleksandr Isaevich
  See Solzhenitsyn, Aleksandr I(sayevich)
  See also EWL 3
Somers, Jane
  See Lessing, Doris (May)
Somerville, Edith Oenone
    1858-1949 .... **SSC 56; TCLC 51**
  See also CA 196; DLB 135; RGEL 2; RGSF
    2
Somerville & Ross
  See Martin, Violet Florence; Somerville,
    Edith Oenone
Sommer, Scott 1951- .... **CLC 25**
  See also CA 106
Sondheim, Stephen (Joshua) 1930- . **CLC 30,
    39, 147**
  See also AAYA 11; CA 103; CANR 47, 67;
    DAM DRAM; LAIT 4
Sone, Monica 1919- .... **AAL**
Song, Cathy 1955- .... **AAL; PC 21**
  See also CA 154; CANR 118; CWP; DLB
    169; EXPP; FW; PFS 5
Sontag, Susan 1933- .... **CLC 1, 2, 10, 13, 31,
    105**
  See also AMWS 3; CA 17-20R; CANR 25,
    51, 74, 97; CN 7; CPW; DA3; DAM POP;
    DLB 2, 67; EWL 3; MAWW; MTCW 1,
    2; RGAL 4; RHW; SSFS 10

Stegner, Wallace (Earle) 1909-1993 .. **CLC 9, 49, 81; SSC 27**
    See also AITN 1; AMWS 4; ANW; BEST 90:3; BPFB 3; CA 1-4R; 141; CAAS 9; CANR 1, 21, 46; DAM NOV; DLB 9, 206, 275; DLBY 1993; EWL 3; MTCW 1, 2; RGAL 4; TCWW 2; TUS

Stein, Gertrude 1874-1946 .... **DC 19; PC 18; SSC 42; TCLC 1, 6, 28, 48; WLC**
    See also AMW; CA 104; 132; CANR 108; CDALB 1917-1929; DA; DA3; DAB; DAC; DAM MST, NOV, POET; DLB 4, 54, 86, 228; DLBD 15; EWL 3; EXPS; GLL 1; MAWW; MTCW 1, 2; NCFS 4; RGAL 4; RGSF 2; SSFS 5; TUS; WP

Steinbeck, John (Ernst) 1902-1968 ... **CLC 1, 5, 9, 13, 21, 34, 45, 75, 124; SSC 11, 37; TCLC 135; WLC**
    See also AAYA 12; AMW; BPFB 3; BYA 2, 3, 13; CA 1-4R; 25-28R; CANR 1, 35; CDALB 1929-1941; DA; DA3; DAB; DAC; DAM DRAM, MST, NOV; DLB 7, 9, 212, 275; DLBD 2; EWL 3; EXPS; LAIT 3; MTCW 1, 2; NFS 17; RGAL 4; RGSF 2; RHW; SATA 9; SSFS 3, 6; TCWW 2; TUS; WYA; YAW

Steinem, Gloria 1934- .... **CLC 63**
    See also CA 53-56; CANR 28, 51; DLB 246; FW; MTCW 1, 2

Steiner, George 1929- .... **CLC 24**
    See also CA 73-76; CANR 31, 67, 108; DAM NOV; DLB 67; EWL 3; MTCW 1, 2; SATA 62

Steiner, K. Leslie
    See Delany, Samuel R(ay), Jr.

Steiner, Rudolf 1861-1925 .... **TCLC 13**
    See also CA 107

Stendhal 1783-1842 .. **NCLC 23, 46; SSC 27; WLC**
    See also DA; DA3; DAB; DAC; DAM MST, NOV; DLB 119; EW 5; GFL 1789 to the Present; RGWL 2, 3; TWA

Stephen, Adeline Virginia
    See Woolf, (Adeline) Virginia

Stephen, Sir Leslie 1832-1904 .... **TCLC 23**
    See also BRW 5; CA 123; DLB 57, 144, 190

Stephen, Sir Leslie
    See Stephen, Sir Leslie

Stephen, Virginia
    See Woolf, (Adeline) Virginia

Stephens, James 1882(?)-1950 .... **SSC 50; TCLC 4**
    See also CA 104; 192; DLB 19, 153, 162; EWL 3; FANT; RGEL 2; SUFW

Stephens, Reed
    See Donaldson, Stephen R(eeder)

Steptoe, Lydia
    See Barnes, Djuna
    See also GLL 1

Sterchi, Beat 1949- .... **CLC 65**
    See also CA 203

Sterling, Brett
    See Bradbury, Ray (Douglas); Hamilton, Edmond

Sterling, Bruce 1954- .... **CLC 72**
    See also CA 119; CANR 44; SCFW 2; SFW 4

Sterling, George 1869-1926 .... **TCLC 20**
    See also CA 117; 165; DLB 54

Stern, Gerald 1925- .... **CLC 40, 100**
    See also AMWS 9; CA 81-84; CANR 28, 94; CP 7; DLB 105; RGAL 4

Stern, Richard (Gustave) 1928- ... **CLC 4, 39**
    See also CA 1-4R; CANR 1, 25, 52, 120; CN 7; DLB 218; DLBY 1987; INT CANR-25

Sternberg, Josef von 1894-1969 .... **CLC 20**
    See also CA 81-84

Sterne, Laurence 1713-1768 .... **LC 2, 48; WLC**
    See also BRW 3; BRWC 1; CDBLB 1660-1789; DA; DAB; DAC; DAM MST, NOV; DLB 39; RGEL 2; TEA

Sternheim, (William Adolf) Carl 1878-1942 .... **TCLC 8**
    See also CA 105; 193; DLB 56, 118; EWL 3; RGWL 2, 3

Stevens, Mark 1951- .... **CLC 34**
    See also CA 122

Stevens, Wallace 1879-1955 . **PC 6; TCLC 3, 12, 45; WLC**
    See also AMW; AMWR 1; CA 104; 124; CDALB 1929-1941; DA; DA3; DAB; DAC; DAM MST, POET; DLB 54; EWL 3; EXPP; MTCW 1, 2; PAB; PFS 13, 16; RGAL 4; TUS; WP

Stevenson, Anne (Katharine) 1933- .. **CLC 7, 33**
    See also BRWS 6; CA 17-20R; CAAS 9; CANR 9, 33; CP 7; CWP; DLB 40; MTCW 1; RHW

Stevenson, Robert Louis (Balfour) 1850-1894 ...... **NCLC 5, 14, 63; SSC 11, 51; WLC**
    See also AAYA 24; BPFB 3; BRW 5; BRWC 1; BRWR 1; BYA 1, 2, 4, 13; CDBLB 1890-1914; CLR 10, 11; DA; DA3; DAB; DAC; DAM MST, NOV; DLB 18, 57, 141, 156, 174; DLBD 13; HGG; JRDA; LAIT 1, 3; MAICYA 1, 2; NFS 11; RGEL 2; RGSF 2; SATA 100; SUFW; TEA; WCH; WLIT 4; WYA; YABC 2; YAW

Stewart, J(ohn) I(nnes) M(ackintosh) 1906-1994 .... **CLC 7, 14, 32**
    See Innes, Michael
    See also CA 85-88; 147; CAAS 3; CANR 47; CMW 4; MTCW 1, 2

Stewart, Mary (Florence Elinor) 1916- .... **CLC 7, 35, 117**
    See also AAYA 29; BPFB 3; CA 1-4R; CANR 1, 59; CMW 4; CPW; DAB; FANT; RHW; SATA 12; YAW

Stewart, Mary Rainbow
    See Stewart, Mary (Florence Elinor)

Stifle, June
    See Campbell, Maria

Stifter, Adalbert 1805-1868 .. **NCLC 41; SSC 28**
    See also CDWLB 2; DLB 133; RGSF 2; RGWL 2, 3

Still, James 1906-2001 .... **CLC 49**
    See also CA 65-68; 195; CAAS 17; CANR 10, 26; CSW; DLB 9; DLBY 01; SATA 29; SATA-Obit 127

Sting 1951-
    See Sumner, Gordon Matthew
    See also CA 167

Stirling, Arthur
    See Sinclair, Upton (Beall)

Stitt, Milan 1941- .... **CLC 29**
    See also CA 69-72

Stockton, Francis Richard 1834-1902
    See Stockton, Frank R.
    See also CA 108; 137; MAICYA 1, 2; SATA 44; SFW 4

Stockton, Frank R. .... **TCLC 47**
    See Stockton, Francis Richard
    See also BYA 4, 13; DLB 42, 74; DLBD 13; EXPS; SATA-Brief 32; SSFS 3; SUFW; WCH

Stoddard, Charles
    See Kuttner, Henry

Stoker, Abraham 1847-1912
    See Stoker, Bram
    See also CA 105; 150; DA; DA3; DAC; DAM MST, NOV; HGG; SATA 29

Stoker, Bram .... **SSC 62; TCLC 8; WLC**
    See Stoker, Abraham
    See also AAYA 23; BPFB 3; BRWS 3; BYA 5; CDBLB 1890-1914; DAB; DLB 36, 70, 178; LATS 1; NFS 18; RGEL 2; SUFW; TEA; WLIT 4

Stolz, Mary (Slattery) 1920- .... **CLC 12**
    See also AAYA 8; AITN 1; CA 5-8R; CANR 13, 41, 112; JRDA; MAICYA 1, 2; SAAS 3; SATA 10, 71, 133; YAW

Stone, Irving 1903-1989 .... **CLC 7**
    See also AITN 1; BPFB 3; CA 1-4R; 129; CAAS 3; CANR 1, 23; CPW; DA3; DAM POP; INT CANR-23; MTCW 1, 2; RHW; SATA 3; SATA-Obit 64

Stone, Oliver (William) 1946- .... **CLC 73**
    See also AAYA 15; CA 110; CANR 55

Stone, Robert (Anthony) 1937- ... **CLC 5, 23, 42, 175**
    See also AMWS 5; BPFB 3; CA 85-88; CANR 23, 66, 95; CN 7; DLB 152; EWL 3; INT CANR-23; MTCW 1

Stone, Zachary
    See Follett, Ken(neth Martin)

Stoppard, Tom 1937- ... **CLC 1, 3, 4, 5, 8, 15, 29, 34, 63, 91; DC 6; WLC**
    See also BRWC 1; BRWR 2; BRWS 1; CA 81-84; CANR 39, 67; CBD; CD 5; CDBLB 1960 to Present; DA; DA3; DAB; DAC; DAM DRAM, MST; DFS 2, 5, 8, 11, 13, 16; DLB 13, 233; DLBY 1985; EWL 3; LATS 1; MTCW 1, 2; RGEL 2; TEA; WLIT 4

Storey, David (Malcolm) 1933- . **CLC 2, 4, 5, 8**
    See also BRWS 1; CA 81-84; CANR 36; CBD; CD 5; CN 7; DAM DRAM; DLB 13, 14, 207, 245; EWL 3; MTCW 1; RGEL 2

Storm, Hyemeyohsts 1935- ... **CLC 3; NNAL**
    See also CA 81-84; CANR 45; DAM MULT

Storm, (Hans) Theodor (Woldsen) 1817-1888 .... **NCLC 1; SSC 27**
    See also CDWLB 2; DLB 129; EW; RGSF 2; RGWL 2, 3

Storni, Alfonsina 1892-1938 . **HLC 2; PC 33; TCLC 5**
    See also CA 104; 131; DAM MULT; DLB 283; HW 1; LAW

Stoughton, William 1631-1701 .... **LC 38**
    See also DLB 24

Stout, Rex (Todhunter) 1886-1975 ..... **CLC 3**
    See also AITN 2; BPFB 3; CA 61-64; CANR 71; CMW 4; MSW; RGAL 4

Stow, (Julian) Randolph 1935- ... **CLC 23, 48**
    See also CA 13-16R; CANR 33; CN 7; DLB 260; MTCW 1; RGEL 2

Stowe, Harriet (Elizabeth) Beecher 1811-1896 .... **NCLC 3, 50; WLC**
    See also AAYA 53; AMWS 1; CDALB 1865-1917; DA; DA3; DAB; DAC; DAM MST, NOV; DLB 1, 12, 42, 74, 189, 239, 243; EXPN; JRDA; LAIT 2; MAICYA 1, 2; NFS 6; RGAL 4; TUS; YABC 1

Strabo c. 64B.C.-c. 25 .... **CMLC 37**
    See also DLB 176

Strachey, (Giles) Lytton 1880-1932 .... **TCLC 12**
    See also BRWS 2; CA 110; 178; DLB 149; DLBD 10; EWL 3; MTCW 2; NCFS 4

Stramm, August 1874-1915 .... **PC 50**
    See also CA 195; EWL 3

Strand, Mark 1934- .... **CLC 6, 18, 41, 71**
    See also AMWS 4; CA 21-24R; CANR 40, 65, 100; CP 7; DAM POET; DLB 5; EWL 3; PAB; PFS 9, 18; RGAL 4; SATA 41

Stratton-Porter, Gene(va Grace) 1863-1924
    See Porter, Gene(va Grace) Stratton
    See also ANW; CA 137; CLR 87; DLB 221; DLBD 14; MAICYA 1, 2; SATA 15

Szymborska, Wislawa 1923- ..... **CLC 99; PC 44**
See also CA 154; CANR 91; CDWLB 4; CWP; CWW 2; DA3; DLB 232; DLBY 1996; EWL 3; MTCW 2; PFS 15; RGWL 3

T. O., Nik
See Annensky, Innokenty (Fyodorovich)

Tabori, George 1914- .... **CLC 19**
See also CA 49-52; CANR 4, 69; CBD; CD 5; DLB 245

Tacitus c. 55-c. 117 .... **CMLC 56**
See also AW 2; CDWLB 1; DLB 211; RGWL 2, 3

Tagore, Rabindranath 1861-1941 .... **PC 8; SSC 48; TCLC 3, 53**
See also CA 104; 120; DA3; DAM DRAM, POET; EWL 3; MTCW 1, 2; PFS 18; RGEL 2; RGSF 2; RGWL 2, 3; TWA

Taine, Hippolyte Adolphe
1828-1893 .... **NCLC 15**
See also EW 7; GFL 1789 to the Present

Talayesva, Don C. 1890-(?) .... **NNAL**

Talese, Gay 1932- .... **CLC 37**
See also AITN 1; CA 1-4R; CANR 9, 58; DLB 185; INT CANR-9; MTCW 1, 2

Tallent, Elizabeth (Ann) 1954- .... **CLC 45**
See also CA 117; CANR 72; DLB 130

Tallmountain, Mary 1918-1997 .... **NNAL**
See also CA 146; 161; DLB 193

Tally, Ted 1952- .... **CLC 42**
See also CA 120; 124; CAD; CD 5; INT 124

Talvik, Heiti 1904-1947 .... **TCLC 87**
See also EWL 3

Tamayo y Baus, Manuel
1829-1898 .... **NCLC 1**

Tammsaare, A(nton) H(ansen)
1878-1940 .... **TCLC 27**
See also CA 164; CDWLB 4; DLB 220; EWL 3

Tam'si, Tchicaya U
See Tchicaya, Gerald Felix

Tan, Amy (Ruth) 1952- . **AAL; CLC 59, 120, 151**
See also AAYA 9, 48; AMWS 10; BEST 89:3; BPFB 3; CA 136; CANR 54, 105; CDALBS; CN 7; CPW 1; DA3; DAM MULT, NOV, POP; DLB 173; EXPN; FW; LAIT 3, 5; MTCW 2; NFS 1, 13, 16; RGAL 4; SATA 75; SSFS 9; YAW

Tandem, Felix
See Spitteler, Carl (Friedrich Georg)

Tanizaki, Jun'ichiro 1886-1965 ... **CLC 8, 14, 28; SSC 21**
See Tanizaki Jun'ichiro
See also CA 93-96; 25-28R; MJW; MTCW 2; RGSF 2; RGWL 2

Tanizaki Jun'ichiro
See Tanizaki, Jun'ichiro
See also DLB 180; EWL 3

Tanner, William
See Amis, Kingsley (William)

Tao Lao
See Storni, Alfonsina

Tapahonso, Luci 1953- .... **NNAL**
See also CA 145; CANR 72; DLB 175

Tarantino, Quentin (Jerome)
1963- .... **CLC 125**
See also CA 171

Tarassoff, Lev
See Troyat, Henri

Tarbell, Ida M(inerva) 1857-1944 . **TCLC 40**
See also CA 122; 181; DLB 47

Tarkington, (Newton) Booth
1869-1946 .... **TCLC 9**
See also BPFB 3; BYA 3; CA 110; 143; CWRI 5; DLB 9, 102; MTCW 2; RGAL 4; SATA 17

Tarkovskii, Andrei Arsen'evich
See Tarkovsky, Andrei (Arsenyevich)

Tarkovsky, Andrei (Arsenyevich)
1932-1986 .... **CLC 75**
See also CA 127

Tartt, Donna 1964(?)- .... **CLC 76**
See also CA 142

Tasso, Torquato 1544-1595 .... **LC 5**
See also EFS 2; EW 2; RGWL 2, 3

Tate, (John Orley) Allen 1899-1979 .. **CLC 2, 4, 6, 9, 11, 14, 24; PC 50**
See also AMW; CA 5-8R; 85-88; CANR 32, 108; DLB 4, 45, 63; DLBD 17; EWL 3; MTCW 1, 2; RGAL 4; RHW

Tate, Ellalice
See Hibbert, Eleanor Alice Burford

Tate, James (Vincent) 1943- ..... **CLC 2, 6, 25**
See also CA 21-24R; CANR 29, 57, 114; CP 7; DLB 5, 169; EWL 3; PFS 10, 15; RGAL 4; WP

Tauler, Johannes c. 1300-1361 ...... **CMLC 37**
See also DLB 179; LMFS 1

Tavel, Ronald 1940- .... **CLC 6**
See also CA 21-24R; CAD; CANR 33; CD 5

Taviani, Paolo 1931- .... **CLC 70**
See also CA 153

Taylor, Bayard 1825-1878 .... **NCLC 89**
See also DLB 3, 189, 250, 254; RGAL 4

Taylor, C(ecil) P(hilip) 1929-1981 .... **CLC 27**
See also CA 25-28R; 105; CANR 47; CBD

Taylor, Edward 1642(?)-1729 .... **LC 11**
See also AMW; DA; DAB; DAC; DAM MST, POET; DLB 24; EXPP; RGAL 4; TUS

Taylor, Eleanor Ross 1920- .... **CLC 5**
See also CA 81-84; CANR 70

Taylor, Elizabeth 1932-1975 ..... **CLC 2, 4, 29**
See also CA 13-16R; CANR 9, 70; DLB 139; MTCW 1; RGEL 2; SATA 13

Taylor, Frederick Winslow
1856-1915 .... **TCLC 76**
See also CA 188

Taylor, Henry (Splawn) 1942- .... **CLC 44**
See also CA 33-36R; CAAS 7; CANR 31; CP 7; DLB 5; PFS 10

Taylor, Kamala (Purnaiya) 1924-
See Markandaya, Kamala
See also CA 77-80; NFS 13

Taylor, Mildred D(elois) 1943- .... **CLC 21**
See also AAYA 10, 47; BW 1; BYA 3, 8; CA 85-88; CANR 25, 115; CLR 9, 59, 90; CSW; DLB 52; JRDA; LAIT 3; MAICYA 1, 2; SAAS 5; SATA 135; WYA; YAW

Taylor, Peter (Hillsman) 1917-1994 .. **CLC 1, 4, 18, 37, 44, 50, 71; SSC 10**
See also AMWS 5; BPFB 3; CA 13-16R; 147; CANR 9, 50; CSW; DLB 218, 278; DLBY 1981, 1994; EWL 3; EXPS; INT CANR-9; MTCW 1, 2; RGSF 2; SSFS 9; TUS

Taylor, Robert Lewis 1912-1998 .... **CLC 14**
See also CA 1-4R; 170; CANR 3, 64; SATA 10

Tchekhov, Anton
See Chekhov, Anton (Pavlovich)

Tchicaya, Gerald Felix 1931-1988 .. **CLC 101**
See Tchicaya U Tam'si
See also CA 129; 125; CANR 81

Tchicaya U Tam'si
See Tchicaya, Gerald Felix
See also EWL 3

Teasdale, Sara 1884-1933 .... **PC 31; TCLC 4**
See also CA 104; 163; DLB 45; GLL 1; PFS 14; RGAL 4; SATA 32; TUS

Tecumseh 1768-1813 .... **NNAL**
See also DAM MULT

Tegner, Esaias 1782-1846 .... **NCLC 2**

Teilhard de Chardin, (Marie Joseph) Pierre
1881-1955 .... **TCLC 9**
See also CA 105; 210; GFL 1789 to the Present

Temple, Ann
See Mortimer, Penelope (Ruth)

Tennant, Emma (Christina) 1937- .. **CLC 13, 52**
See also CA 65-68; CAAS 9; CANR 10, 38, 59, 88; CN 7; DLB 14; EWL 3; SFW 4

Tenneshaw, S. M.
See Silverberg, Robert

Tenney, Tabitha Gilman
1762-1837 .... **NCLC 122**
See also DLB 37, 200

Tennyson, Alfred 1809-1892 ... **NCLC 30, 65, 115; PC 6; WLC**
See also AAYA 50; BRW 4; CDBLB 1832-1890; DA; DA3; DAB; DAC; DAM MST, POET; DLB 32; EXPP; PAB; PFS 1, 2, 4, 11, 15; RGEL 2; TEA; WLIT 4; WP

Teran, Lisa St. Aubin de .... **CLC 36**
See St. Aubin de Teran, Lisa

Terence c. 184B.C.-c. 159B.C. ...... **CMLC 14; DC 7**
See also AW 1; CDWLB 1; DLB 211; RGWL 2, 3; TWA

Teresa de Jesus, St. 1515-1582 .... **LC 18**

Terkel, Louis 1912-
See Terkel, Studs
See also CA 57-60; CANR 18, 45, 67; DA3; MTCW 1, 2

Terkel, Studs .... **CLC 38**
See Terkel, Louis
See also AAYA 32; AITN 1; MTCW 2; TUS

Terry, C. V.
See Slaughter, Frank G(ill)

Terry, Megan 1932- .... **CLC 19; DC 13**
See also CA 77-80; CABS 3; CAD; CANR 43; CD 5; CWD; DFS 18; DLB 7, 249; GLL 2

Tertullian c. 155-c. 245 .... **CMLC 29**

Tertz, Abram
See Sinyavsky, Andrei (Donatevich)
See also CWW 2; RGSF 2

Tesich, Steve 1943(?)-1996 .... **CLC 40, 69**
See also CA 105; 152; CAD; DLBY 1983

Tesla, Nikola 1856-1943 .... **TCLC 88**

Teternikov, Fyodor Kuzmich 1863-1927
See Sologub, Fyodor
See also CA 104

Tevis, Walter 1928-1984 .... **CLC 42**
See also CA 113; SFW 4

Tey, Josephine .... **TCLC 14**
See Mackintosh, Elizabeth
See also DLB 77; MSW

Thackeray, William Makepeace
1811-1863 .... **NCLC 5, 14, 22, 43; WLC**
See also BRW 5; CDBLB 1832-1890; DA; DA3; DAB; DAC; DAM MST, NOV; DLB 21, 55, 159, 163; NFS 13; RGEL 2; SATA 23; TEA; WLIT 3

Thakura, Ravindranatha
See Tagore, Rabindranath

Thames, C. H.
See Marlowe, Stephen

Tharoor, Shashi 1956- .... **CLC 70**
See also CA 141; CANR 91; CN 7

Thelwell, Michael Miles 1939- .... **CLC 22**
See also BW 2; CA 101

Theobald, Lewis, Jr.
See Lovecraft, H(oward) P(hillips)

Theocritus c. 310B.C.- .... **CMLC 45**
See also AW 1; DLB 176; RGWL 2, 3

Theodorescu, Ion N. 1880-1967
See Arghezi, Tudor
See also CA 116

Van Dine, S. S. .... **TCLC 23**
See Wright, Willard Huntington
See also MSW
Van Doren, Carl (Clinton)
1885-1950 .... **TCLC 18**
See also CA 111; 168
Van Doren, Mark 1894-1972 .... **CLC 6, 10**
See also CA 1-4R; 37-40R; CANR 3; DLB
45, 284; MTCW 1, 2; RGAL 4
Van Druten, John (William)
1901-1957 .... **TCLC 2**
See also CA 104; 161; DLB 10; RGAL 4
Van Duyn, Mona (Jane) 1921- ...... **CLC 3, 7,**
63, 116
See also CA 9-12R; CANR 7, 38, 60, 116;
CP 7; CWP; DAM POET; DLB 5
Van Dyne, Edith
See Baum, L(yman) Frank
van Itallie, Jean-Claude 1936- .... **CLC 3**
See also CA 45-48; CAAS 2; CAD; CANR
1, 48; CD 5; DLB 7
Van Loot, Cornelius Obenchain
See Roberts, Kenneth (Lewis)
van Ostaijen, Paul 1896-1928 .... **TCLC 33**
See also CA 163
Van Peebles, Melvin 1932- .... **CLC 2, 20**
See also BW 2, 3; CA 85-88; CANR 27,
67, 82; DAM MULT
van Schendel, Arthur(-Francois-Emile)
1874-1946 .... **TCLC 56**
See also EWL 3
Vansittart, Peter 1920- .... **CLC 42**
See also CA 1-4R; CANR 3, 49, 90; CN 7;
RHW
Van Vechten, Carl 1880-1964 ... **CLC 33; HR**
3
See also AMWS 2; CA 183; 89-92; DLB 4,
9, 51; RGAL 4
van Vogt, A(lfred) E(lton) 1912-2000 . **CLC 1**
See also BPFB 3; BYA 13, 14; CA 21-24R;
190; CANR 28; DLB 8, 251; SATA 14;
SATA-Obit 124; SCFW; SFW 4
Vara, Madeleine
See Jackson, Laura (Riding)
Varda, Agnes 1928- .... **CLC 16**
See also CA 116; 122
Vargas Llosa, (Jorge) Mario (Pedro)
1939- .... **CLC 3, 6, 9, 10, 15, 31, 42, 85;**
HLC 2
See Llosa, (Jorge) Mario (Pedro) Vargas
See also BPFB 3; CA 73-76; CANR 18, 32,
42, 67, 116; CDWLB 3; DA; DA3; DAB;
DAC; DAM MST, MULT, NOV; DLB
145; DNFS 2; EWL 3; HW 1, 2; LAIT 5;
LATS 1; LAW; LAWS 1; MTCW 1, 2;
RGWL 2; SSFS 14; TWA; WLIT 1
Vasiliu, George
See Bacovia, George
Vasiliu, Gheorghe
See Bacovia, George
See also CA 123; 189
Vassa, Gustavus
See Equiano, Olaudah
Vassilikos, Vassilis 1933- .... **CLC 4, 8**
See also CA 81-84; CANR 75; EWL 3
Vaughan, Henry 1621-1695 .... **LC 27**
See also BRW 2; DLB 131; PAB; RGEL 2
Vaughn, Stephanie .... **CLC 62**
Vazov, Ivan (Minchov) 1850-1921 . **TCLC 25**
See also CA 121; 167; CDWLB 4; DLB
147
Veblen, Thorstein B(unde)
1857-1929 .... **TCLC 31**
See also AMWS 1; CA 115; 165; DLB 246
Vega, Lope de 1562-1635 .... **HLCS 2; LC 23**
See also EW 2; RGWL 2, 3
Vendler, Helen (Hennessy) 1933- ... **CLC 138**
See also CA 41-44R; CANR 25, 72; MTCW
1, 2

Venison, Alfred
See Pound, Ezra (Weston Loomis)
Verdi, Marie de
See Mencken, H(enry) L(ouis)
Verdu, Matilde
See Cela, Camilo Jose
Verga, Giovanni (Carmelo)
1840-1922 .... **SSC 21; TCLC 3**
See also CA 104; 123; CANR 101; EW 7;
EWL 3; RGSF 2; RGWL 2, 3
Vergil 70B.C.-19B.C. ... **CMLC 9, 40; PC 12;**
WLCS
See Virgil
See also AW 2; DA; DA3; DAB; DAC;
DAM MST, POET; EFS 1; LMFS 1
Verhaeren, Emile (Adolphe Gustave)
1855-1916 .... **TCLC 12**
See also CA 109; EWL 3; GFL 1789 to the
Present
Verlaine, Paul (Marie) 1844-1896 .. **NCLC 2,**
51; PC 2, 32
See also DAM POET; DLB 217; EW 7;
GFL 1789 to the Present; LMFS 2; RGWL
2, 3; TWA
Verne, Jules (Gabriel) 1828-1905 ... **TCLC 6,**
52
See also AAYA 16; BYA 4; CA 110; 131;
CLR 88; DA3; DLB 123; GFL 1789 to
the Present; JRDA; LAIT 2; LMFS 2;
MAICYA 1, 2; RGWL 2, 3; SATA 21;
SCFW; SFW 4; TWA; WCH
Verus, Marcus Annius
See Aurelius, Marcus
Very, Jones 1813-1880 .... **NCLC 9**
See also DLB 1, 243; RGAL 4
Vesaas, Tarjei 1897-1970 .... **CLC 48**
See also CA 190; 29-32R; EW 11; EWL 3;
RGWL 3
Vialis, Gaston
See Simenon, Georges (Jacques Christian)
Vian, Boris 1920-1959(?) .... **TCLC 9**
See also CA 106; 164; CANR 111; DLB
72; EWL 3; GFL 1789 to the Present;
MTCW 2; RGWL 2, 3
Viaud, (Louis Marie) Julien 1850-1923
See Loti, Pierre
See also CA 107
Vicar, Henry
See Felsen, Henry Gregor
Vicker, Angus
See Felsen, Henry Gregor
Vidal, Gore 1925- ...... **CLC 2, 4, 6, 8, 10, 22,**
33, 72, 142
See Box, Edgar
See also AITN 1; AMWS 4; BEST 90:2;
BPFB 3; CA 5-8R; CAD; CANR 13, 45,
65, 100; CD 5; CDALBS; CN 7; CPW;
DA3; DAM NOV, POP; DFS 2; DLB 6,
152; EWL 3; INT CANR-13; MTCW 1,
2; RGAL 4; RHW; TUS
Viereck, Peter (Robert Edwin)
1916- .... **CLC 4; PC 27**
See also CA 1-4R; CANR 1, 47; CP 7; DLB
5; PFS 9, 14
Vigny, Alfred (Victor) de
1797-1863 .... **NCLC 7, 102; PC 26**
See also DAM POET; DLB 119, 192, 217;
EW 5; GFL 1789 to the Present; RGWL
2, 3
Vilakazi, Benedict Wallet
1906-1947 .... **TCLC 37**
See also CA 168
Villa, Jose Garcia 1914-1997
See Villa, Jose Garcia
Villa, Jose Garcia 1914-1997 .... **AAL; PC 22**
See also CA 25-28R; CANR 12, 118; EWL
3; EXPP

Villarreal, Jose Antonio 1924- .... **HLC 2**
See also CA 133; CANR 93; DAM MULT;
DLB 82; HW 1; LAIT 4; RGAL 4
Villaurrutia, Xavier 1903-1950 ...... **TCLC 80**
See also CA 192; EWL 3; HW 1; LAW
Villaverde, Cirilo 1812-1894 .... **NCLC 121**
See also LAW
Villehardouin, Geoffroi de
1150(?)-1218(?) .... **CMLC 38**
Villiers de l'Isle Adam, Jean Marie Mathias
Philippe Auguste 1838-1889 ... **NCLC 3;**
SSC 14
See also DLB 123, 192; GFL 1789 to the
Present; RGSF 2
Villon, Francois 1431-1463(?) . **LC 62; PC 13**
See also DLB 208; EW 2; RGWL 2, 3;
TWA
Vine, Barbara .... **CLC 50**
See Rendell, Ruth (Barbara)
See also BEST 90:4
Vinge, Joan (Carol) D(ennison)
1948- .... **CLC 30; SSC 24**
See also AAYA 32; BPFB 3; CA 93-96;
CANR 72; SATA 36, 113; SFW 4; YAW
Viola, Herman J(oseph) 1938- .... **CLC 70**
See also CA 61-64; CANR 8, 23, 48, 91;
SATA 126
Violis, G.
See Simenon, Georges (Jacques Christian)
Viramontes, Helena Maria 1954- .... **HLCS 2**
See also CA 159; DLB 122; HW 2
Virgil
See Vergil
See also CDWLB 1; DLB 211; LAIT 1;
RGWL 2, 3; WP
Visconti, Luchino 1906-1976 .... **CLC 16**
See also CA 81-84; 65-68; CANR 39
Vittorini, Elio 1908-1966 .... **CLC 6, 9, 14**
See also CA 133; 25-28R; DLB 264; EW
12; EWL 3; RGWL 2, 3
Vivekananda, Swami 1863-1902 .... **TCLC 88**
Vizenor, Gerald Robert 1934- .... **CLC 103;**
NNAL
See also CA 13-16R; CAAE 205; CAAS
22; CANR 5, 21, 44, 67; DAM MULT;
DLB 175, 227; MTCW 2; TCWW 2
Vizinczey, Stephen 1933- .... **CLC 40**
See also CA 128; CCA 1; INT 128
Vliet, R(ussell) G(ordon)
1929-1984 .... **CLC 22**
See also CA 37-40R; 112; CANR 18
Vogau, Boris Andreyevich 1894-1937(?)
See Pilnyak, Boris
See also CA 123
Vogel, Paula A(nne) 1951- ... **CLC 76; DC 19**
See also CA 108; CAD; CANR 119; CD 5;
CWD; DFS 14; RGAL 4
Voigt, Cynthia 1942- .... **CLC 30**
See also AAYA 3, 30; BYA 1, 3, 6, 7, 8;
CA 106; CANR 18, 37, 40, 94; CLR 13,
48; INT CANR-18; JRDA; LAIT 5; MAI-
CYA 1, 2; MAICYAS 1; SATA 48, 79,
116; SATA-Brief 33; WYA; YAW
Voigt, Ellen Bryant 1943- .... **CLC 54**
See also CA 69-72; CANR 11, 29, 55, 115;
CP 7; CSW; CWP; DLB 120
Voinovich, Vladimir (Nikolaevich)
1932- .... **CLC 10, 49, 147**
See also CA 81-84; CAAS 12; CANR 33,
67; MTCW 1
Vollmann, William T. 1959- .... **CLC 89**
See also CA 134; CANR 67, 116; CPW;
DA3; DAM NOV, POP; MTCW 2
Voloshinov, V. N.
See Bakhtin, Mikhail Mikhailovich

Ward, Douglas Turner 1930- .... **CLC 19**
See also BW 1; CA 81-84; CAD; CANR 27; CD 5; DLB 7, 38

Ward, E. D.
See Lucas, E(dward) V(errall)

Ward, Mrs. Humphry 1851-1920
See Ward, Mary Augusta
See also RGEL 2

Ward, Mary Augusta 1851-1920 ... **TCLC 55**
See Ward, Mrs. Humphry
See also DLB 18

Ward, Peter
See Faust, Frederick (Schiller)

Warhol, Andy 1928(?)-1987 .... **CLC 20**
See also AAYA 12; BEST 89:4; CA 89-92; 121; CANR 34

Warner, Francis (Robert le Plastrier)
1937- .... **CLC 14**
See also CA 53-56; CANR 11

Warner, Marina 1946- .... **CLC 59**
See also CA 65-68; CANR 21, 55, 118; CN 7; DLB 194

Warner, Rex (Ernest) 1905-1986 ...... **CLC 45**
See also CA 89-92; 119; DLB 15; RGEL 2; RHW

Warner, Susan (Bogert)
1819-1885 .... **NCLC 31**
See also DLB 3, 42, 239, 250, 254

Warner, Sylvia (Constance) Ashton
See Ashton-Warner, Sylvia (Constance)

Warner, Sylvia Townsend
1893-1978 .. **CLC 7, 19; SSC 23; TCLC 131**
See also BRWS 7; CA 61-64; 77-80; CANR 16, 60, 104; DLB 34, 139; EWL 3; FANT; FW; MTCW 1, 2; RGEL 2; RGSF 2; RHW

Warren, Mercy Otis 1728-1814 ..... **NCLC 13**
See also DLB 31, 200; RGAL 4; TUS

Warren, Robert Penn 1905-1989 .. **CLC 1, 4, 6, 8, 10, 13, 18, 39, 53, 59; PC 37; SSC 4, 58; WLC**
See also AITN 1; AMW; BPFB 3; BYA 1; CA 13-16R; 129; CANR 10, 47; CDALB 1968-1988; DA; DA3; DAB; DAC; DAM MST, NOV, POET; DLB 2, 48, 152; DLBY 1980, 1989; EWL 3; INT CANR-10; MTCW 1, 2; NFS 13; RGAL 4; RGSF 2; RHW; SATA 46; SATA-Obit 63; SSFS 8; TUS

Warrigal, Jack
See Furphy, Joseph

Warshofsky, Isaac
See Singer, Isaac Bashevis

Warton, Joseph 1722-1800 .... **NCLC 118**
See also DLB 104, 109; RGEL 2

Warton, Thomas 1728-1790 .... **LC 15, 82**
See also DAM POET; DLB 104, 109; RGEL 2

Waruk, Kona
See Harris, (Theodore) Wilson

Warung, Price .... **TCLC 45**
See Astley, William
See also DLB 230; RGEL 2

Warwick, Jarvis
See Garner, Hugh
See also CCA 1

Washington, Alex
See Harris, Mark

Washington, Booker T(aliaferro)
1856-1915 .... **BLC 3; TCLC 10**
See also BW 1; CA 114; 125; DA3; DAM MULT; LAIT 2; RGAL 4; SATA 28

Washington, George 1732-1799 .... **LC 25**
See also DLB 31

Wassermann, (Karl) Jakob
1873-1934 .... **TCLC 6**
See also CA 104; 163; DLB 66; EWL 3

Wasserstein, Wendy 1950- .. **CLC 32, 59, 90; DC 4**
See also CA 121; 129; CABS 3; CAD; CANR 53, 75; CD 5; CWD; DA3; DAM DRAM; DFS 17; DLB 228; EWL 3; FW; INT CA-129; MTCW 2; SATA 94

Waterhouse, Keith (Spencer) 1929- . **CLC 47**
See also CA 5-8R; CANR 38, 67, 109; CBD; CN 7; DLB 13, 15; MTCW 1, 2

Waters, Frank (Joseph) 1902-1995 .. **CLC 88**
See also CA 5-8R; 149; CAAS 13; CANR 3, 18, 63, 121; DLB 212; DLBY 1986; RGAL 4; TCWW 2

Waters, Mary C. .... **CLC 70**

Waters, Roger 1944- .... **CLC 35**

Watkins, Frances Ellen
See Harper, Frances Ellen Watkins

Watkins, Gerrold
See Malzberg, Barry N(athaniel)

Watkins, Gloria Jean 1952(?)- .... **CLC 94**
See also BW 2; CA 143; CANR 87; DLB 246; MTCW 2; SATA 115

Watkins, Paul 1964- .... **CLC 55**
See also CA 132; CANR 62, 98

Watkins, Vernon Phillips
1906-1967 .... **CLC 43**
See also CA 9-10; 25-28R; CAP 1; DLB 20; EWL 3; RGEL 2

Watson, Irving S.
See Mencken, H(enry) L(ouis)

Watson, John H.
See Farmer, Philip Jose

Watson, Richard F.
See Silverberg, Robert

Watts, Ephraim
See Horne, Richard Henry Hengist

Waugh, Auberon (Alexander)
1939-2001 .... **CLC 7**
See also CA 45-48; 192; CANR 6, 22, 92; DLB 14, 194

Waugh, Evelyn (Arthur St. John)
1903-1966 .. **CLC 1, 3, 8, 13, 19, 27, 44, 107; SSC 41; WLC**
See also BPFB 3; BRW 7; CA 85-88; 25-28R; CANR 22; CDBLB 1914-1945; DA; DA3; DAB; DAC; DAM MST, NOV, POP; DLB 15, 162, 195; EWL 3; MTCW 1, 2; NFS 17; RGEL 2; RGSF 2; TEA; WLIT 4

Waugh, Harriet 1944- .... **CLC 6**
See also CA 85-88; CANR 22

Ways, C. R.
See Blount, Roy (Alton), Jr.

Waystaff, Simon
See Swift, Jonathan

Webb, Beatrice (Martha Potter)
1858-1943 .... **TCLC 22**
See also CA 117; 162; DLB 190; FW

Webb, Charles (Richard) 1939- .... **CLC 7**
See also CA 25-28R; CANR 114

Webb, James H(enry), Jr. 1946- ...... **CLC 22**
See also CA 81-84

Webb, Mary Gladys (Meredith)
1881-1927 .... **TCLC 24**
See also CA 182; 123; DLB 34; FW

Webb, Mrs. Sidney
See Webb, Beatrice (Martha Potter)

Webb, Phyllis 1927- .... **CLC 18**
See also CA 104; CANR 23; CCA 1; CP 7; CWP; DLB 53

Webb, Sidney (James) 1859-1947 .. **TCLC 22**
See also CA 117; 163; DLB 190

Webber, Andrew Lloyd .... **CLC 21**
See Lloyd Webber, Andrew
See also DFS 7

Weber, Lenora Mattingly
1895-1971 .... **CLC 12**
See also CA 19-20; 29-32R; CAP 1; SATA 2; SATA-Obit 26

Weber, Max 1864-1920 .... **TCLC 69**
See also CA 109; 189

Webster, John 1580(?)-1634(?) ...... **DC 2; LC 33, 84; WLC**
See also BRW 2; CDBLB Before 1660; DA; DAB; DAC; DAM DRAM, MST; DFS 17; DLB 58; IDTP; RGEL 2; WLIT 3

Webster, Noah 1758-1843 .... **NCLC 30**
See also DLB 1, 37, 42, 43, 73, 243

Wedekind, (Benjamin) Frank(lin)
1864-1918 .... **TCLC 7**
See also CA 104; 153; CANR 121, 122; CDWLB 2; DAM DRAM; DLB 118; EW 8; EWL 3; LMFS 2; RGWL 2, 3

Wehr, Demaris .... **CLC 65**

Weidman, Jerome 1913-1998 .... **CLC 7**
See also AITN 2; CA 1-4R; 171; CAD; CANR 1; DLB 28

Weil, Simone (Adolphine)
1909-1943 .... **TCLC 23**
See also CA 117; 159; EW 12; EWL 3; FW; GFL 1789 to the Present; MTCW 2

Weininger, Otto 1880-1903 .... **TCLC 84**

Weinstein, Nathan
See West, Nathanael

Weinstein, Nathan von Wallenstein
See West, Nathanael

Weir, Peter (Lindsay) 1944- .... **CLC 20**
See also CA 113; 123

Weiss, Peter (Ulrich) 1916-1982 .. **CLC 3, 15, 51**
See also CA 45-48; 106; CANR 3; DAM DRAM; DFS 3; DLB 69, 124; EWL 3; RGWL 2, 3

Weiss, Theodore (Russell) 1916- ... **CLC 3, 8, 14**
See also CA 9-12R; CAAE 189; CAAS 2; CANR 46, 94; CP 7; DLB 5

Welch, (Maurice) Denton
1915-1948 .... **TCLC 22**
See also BRWS 8; CA 121; 148; RGEL 2

Welch, James 1940- ... **CLC 6, 14, 52; NNAL**
See also CA 85-88; CANR 42, 66, 107; CN 7; CP 7; CPW; DAM MULT, POP; DLB 175, 256; LATS 1; RGAL 4; TCWW 2

Weldon, Fay 1931- . **CLC 6, 9, 11, 19, 36, 59, 122**
See also BRWS 4; CA 21-24R; CANR 16, 46, 63, 97; CDBLB 1960 to Present; CN 7; CPW; DAM POP; DLB 14, 194; EWL 3; FW; HGG; INT CANR-16; MTCW 1, 2; RGEL 2; RGSF 2

Wellek, Rene 1903-1995 .... **CLC 28**
See also CA 5-8R; 150; CAAS 7; CANR 8; DLB 63; EWL 3; INT CANR-8

Weller, Michael 1942- .... **CLC 10, 53**
See also CA 85-88; CAD; CD 5

Weller, Paul 1958- .... **CLC 26**

Wellershoff, Dieter 1925- .... **CLC 46**
See also CA 89-92; CANR 16, 37

Welles, (George) Orson 1915-1985 .. **CLC 20, 80**
See also AAYA 40; CA 93-96; 117

Wellman, John McDowell 1945-
See Wellman, Mac
See also CA 166; CD 5

Wellman, Mac .... **CLC 65**
See Wellman, John McDowell; Wellman, John McDowell
See also CAD; RGAL 4

Wellman, Manly Wade 1903-1986 ... **CLC 49**
See also CA 1-4R; 118; CANR 6, 16, 44; FANT; SATA 6; SATA-Obit 47; SFW 4; SUFW

Wells, Carolyn 1869(?)-1942 .... **TCLC 35**
See also CA 113; 185; CMW 4; DLB 11

Whittemore, (Edward) Reed, Jr.
1919- .... CLC 4
See also CA 9-12R; CAAS 8; CANR 4,
119; CP 7; DLB 5

Whittier, John Greenleaf
1807-1892 .... NCLC 8, 59
See also AMWS 1; DLB 1, 243; RGAL 4

Whittlebot, Hernia
See Coward, Noel (Peirce)

Wicker, Thomas Grey 1926-
See Wicker, Tom
See also CA 65-68; CANR 21, 46

Wicker, Tom .... CLC 7
See Wicker, Thomas Grey

Wideman, John Edgar 1941- ... BLC 3; CLC
5, 34, 36, 67, 122; SSC 62
See also AFAW 1, 2; AMWS 10; BPFB 4;
BW 2, 3; CA 85-88; CANR 14, 42, 67,
109; CN 7; DAM MULT; DLB 33, 143;
MTCW 2; RGAL 4; RGSF 2; SSFS 6, 12

Wiebe, Rudy (Henry) 1934- .. CLC 6, 11, 14,
138
See also CA 37-40R; CANR 42, 67; CN 7;
DAC; DAM MST; DLB 60; RHW

Wieland, Christoph Martin
1733-1813 .... NCLC 17
See also DLB 97; EW 4; LMFS 1; RGWL
2, 3

Wiene, Robert 1881-1938 .... TCLC 56

Wieners, John 1934- .... CLC 7
See also BG 3; CA 13-16R; CP 7; DLB 16;
WP

Wiesel, Elie(zer) 1928- .... CLC 3, 5, 11, 37,
165; WLCS
See also AAYA 7; AITN 1; CA 5-8R; CAAS
4; CANR 8, 40, 65; CDALBS; DA; DA3;
DAB; DAC; DAM MST, NOV; DLB 83;
DLBY 1987; EWL 3; INT CANR-8;
LAIT 4; MTCW 1, 2; NCFS 4; NFS 4;
RGWL 3; SATA 56; YAW

Wiggins, Marianne 1947- .... CLC 57
See also BEST 89:3; CA 130; CANR 60

Wiggs, Susan .... CLC 70
See also CA 201

Wight, James Alfred 1916-1995
See Herriot, James
See also CA 77-80; SATA 55; SATA-Brief
44

Wilbur, Richard (Purdy) 1921- ..... CLC 3, 6,
9, 14, 53, 110
See also AMWS 3; CA 1-4R; CABS 2;
CANR 2, 29, 76, 93; CDALBS; CP 7;
DA; DAB; DAC; DAM MST, POET;
DLB 5, 169; EWL 3; EXPP; INT CANR-
29; MTCW 1, 2; PAB; PFS 11, 12, 16;
RGAL 4; SATA 9, 108; WP

Wild, Peter 1940- .... CLC 14
See also CA 37-40R; CP 7; DLB 5

Wilde, Oscar (Fingal O'Flahertie Wills)
1854(?)-1900 ..... DC 17; SSC 11; TCLC
1, 8, 23, 41; WLC
See also AAYA 49; BRW 5; BRWC 1;
BRWR 2; CA 104; 119; CANR 112; CD-
BLB 1890-1914; DA; DA3; DAB; DAC;
DAM DRAM, NOV; DFS 4, 8, 9;
DLB 10, 19, 34, 57, 141, 156, 190; EXPS;
FANT; LATS 1; RGEL 2; RGSF 2; SATA
24; SSFS 7; SUFW; TEA; WCH; WLIT 4

Wilder, Billy .... CLC 20
See Wilder, Samuel
See also DLB 26

Wilder, Samuel 1906-2002
See Wilder, Billy
See also CA 89-92; 205

Wilder, Stephen
See Marlowe, Stephen

Wilder, Thornton (Niven)
1897-1975 .. CLC 1, 5, 6, 10, 15, 35, 82;
DC 1; WLC
See also AAYA 29; AITN 2; AMW; CA 13-
16R; 61-64; CAD; CANR 40; CDALBS;
DA; DA3; DAB; DAC; DAM DRAM,
MST, NOV; DFS 1, 4, 16; DLB 4, 7, 9,
228; DLBY 1997; EWL 3; LAIT 3;
MTCW 1, 2; RGAL 4; RHW; WYAS 1

Wilding, Michael 1942- ...... CLC 73; SSC 50
See also CA 104; CANR 24, 49, 106; CN
7; RGSF 2

Wiley, Richard 1944- .... CLC 44
See also CA 121; 129; CANR 71

Wilhelm, Kate .... CLC 7
See Wilhelm, Katie (Gertrude)
See also CAAS 5; DLB 8; INT
CANR-17; SCFW 2

Wilhelm, Katie (Gertrude) 1928-
See Wilhelm, Kate
See also CA 37-40R; CANR 17, 36, 60, 94;
MTCW 1; SFW 4

Wilkins, Mary
See Freeman, Mary E(leanor) Wilkins

Willard, Nancy 1936- .... CLC 7, 37
See also BYA 5; CA 89-92; CANR 10, 39,
68, 107; CLR 5; CWP; CWRI 5; DLB 5,
52; FANT; MAICYA 1, 2; MTCW 1;
SATA 37, 71, 127; SATA-Brief 30; SUFW
2

William of Malmesbury c. 1090B.C.-c.
1140B.C. .... CMLC 57

William of Ockham 1290-1349 ..... CMLC 32

Williams, Ben Ames 1889-1953 ..... TCLC 89
See also CA 183; DLB 102

Williams, C(harles) K(enneth)
1936- .... CLC 33, 56, 148
See also CA 37-40R; CAAS 26; CANR 57,
106; CP 7; DAM POET; DLB 5

Williams, Charles
See Collier, James Lincoln

Williams, Charles (Walter Stansby)
1886-1945 .... TCLC 1, 11
See also CA 104; 163; DLB 100, 153, 255;
FANT; RGEL 2; SUFW 1

Williams, Ella Gwendolen Rees
See Rhys, Jean

Williams, (George) Emlyn
1905-1987 .... CLC 15
See also CA 104; 123; CANR 36; DAM
DRAM; DLB 10, 77; IDTP; MTCW 1

Williams, Hank 1923-1953 .... TCLC 81
See Williams, Hiram King

Williams, Hiram Hank
See Williams, Hank

Williams, Hiram King
See Williams, Hank
See also CA 188

Williams, Hugo (Mordaunt) 1942- ... CLC 42
See also CA 17-20R; CANR 45, 119; CP 7;
DLB 40

Williams, J. Walker
See Wodehouse, P(elham) G(renville)

Williams, John A(lfred) 1925- . BLC 3; CLC
5, 13
See also AFAW 2; BW 2, 3; CA 53-56;
CAAE 195; CAAS 3; CANR 6, 26, 51,
118; CN 7; CSW; DAM MULT; DLB 2,
33; EWL 3; INT CANR-6; RGAL 4; SFW
4

Williams, Jonathan (Chamberlain)
1929- .... CLC 13
See also CA 9-12R; CAAS 12; CANR 8,
108; CP 7; DLB 5

Williams, Joy 1944- .... CLC 31
See also CA 41-44R; CANR 22, 48, 97

Williams, Norman 1952- .... CLC 39
See also CA 118

Williams, Sherley Anne 1944-1999 ... BLC 3;
CLC 89
See also AFAW 2; BW 2, 3; CA 73-76; 185;
CANR 25, 82; DAM MULT, POET; DLB
41; INT CANR-25; SATA 78; SATA-Obit
116

Williams, Shirley
See Williams, Sherley Anne

Williams, Tennessee 1911-1983 . CLC 1, 2, 5,
**7, 8, 11, 15, 19, 30, 39, 45, 71, 111; DC
4; WLC**
See also AAYA 31; AITN 1, 2; AMW;
AMWC 1; CA 5-8R; 108; CABS 3; CAD;
CANR 31; CDALB 1941-1968; DA;
DA3; DAB; DAC; DAM DRAM, MST;
DFS 17; DLB 7; DLBD 4; DLBY 1983;
EWL 3; GLL 1; LAIT 4; LATS 1; MTCW
1, 2; RGAL 4; TUS

Williams, Thomas (Alonzo)
1926-1990 .... CLC 14
See also CA 1-4R; 132; CANR 2

Williams, William C.
See Williams, William Carlos

Williams, William Carlos
1883-1963 .... CLC 1, 2, 5, 9, 13, 22, 42,
67; PC 7; SSC 31
See also AAYA 46; AMW; AMWR 1; CA
89-92; CANR 34; CDALB 1917-1929;
DA; DA3; DAB; DAC; DAM MST,
POET; DLB 4, 16, 54, 86; EWL 3; EXPP;
MTCW 1, 2; NCFS 4; PAB; PFS 1, 6, 11;
RGAL 4; RGSF 2; TUS; WP

Williamson, David (Keith) 1942- ..... CLC 56
See also CA 103; CANR 41; CD 5

Williamson, Ellen Douglas 1905-1984
See Douglas, Ellen
See also CA 17-20R; 114; CANR 39

Williamson, Jack .... CLC 29
See Williamson, John Stewart
See also CAAS 8; DLB 8; SCFW 2

Williamson, John Stewart 1908-
See Williamson, Jack
See also CA 17-20R; CANR 23, 70; SFW 4

Willie, Frederick
See Lovecraft, H(oward) P(hillips)

Willingham, Calder (Baynard, Jr.)
1922-1995 .... CLC 5, 51
See also CA 5-8R; 147; CANR 3; CSW;
DLB 2, 44; IDFW 3, 4; MTCW 1

Willis, Charles
See Clarke, Arthur C(harles)

Willy
See Colette, (Sidonie-Gabrielle)

Willy, Colette
See Colette, (Sidonie-Gabrielle)
See also GLL 1

Wilmot, John 1647-1680 .... LC 75
See Rochester
See also BRW 2; DLB 131; PAB

Wilson, A(ndrew) N(orman) 1950- .. CLC 33
See also BRWS 6; CA 112; 122; CN 7;
DLB 14, 155, 194; MTCW 2

Wilson, Angus (Frank Johnstone)
1913-1991 . CLC 2, 3, 5, 25, 34; SSC 21
See also BRWS 1; CA 5-8R; 134; CANR
21; DLB 15, 139, 155; EWL 3; MTCW 1,
2; RGEL 2; RGSF 2

Wilson, August 1945- ... BLC 3; CLC 39, 50,
63, 118; DC 2; WLCS
See also AAYA 16; AFAW 2; AMWS 8; BW
2, 3; CA 115; 122; CAD; CANR 42, 54,
76; CD 5; DA; DA3; DAB; DAC; DAM
DRAM, MST, MULT; DFS 3, 7, 15, 17;
DLB 228; EWL 3; LAIT 4; LATS 1;
MTCW 1, 2; RGAL 4

Wilson, Brian 1942- .... CLC 12

Wilson, Colin 1931- .... CLC 3, 14
See also CA 1-4R; CAAS 5; CANR 1, 22,
33, 77; CMW 4; CN 7; DLB 14, 194;
HGG; MTCW 1; SFW 4

Wright, Frank Lloyd 1867-1959 .... **TCLC 95**
See also AAYA 33; CA 174
Wright, Jack R.
See Harris, Mark
Wright, James (Arlington)
1927-1980 .... **CLC 3, 5, 10, 28; PC 36**
See also AITN 2; AMWS 3; CA 49-52; 97-
100; CANR 4, 34, 64; CDALBS; DAM
POET; DLB 5, 169; EWL 3; EXPP;
MTCW 1, 2; PFS 7, 8; RGAL 4; TUS;
WP
Wright, Judith (Arundell)
1915-2000 .... **CLC 11, 53; PC 14**
See also CA 13-16R; 188; CANR 31, 76,
93; CP 7; CWP; DLB 260; EWL 3;
MTCW 1, 2; PFS 8; RGEL 2; SATA 14;
SATA-Obit 121
Wright, L(aurali) R. 1939- .... **CLC 44**
See also CA 138; CMW 4
Wright, Richard (Nathaniel)
1908-1960 ... **BLC 3; CLC 1, 3, 4, 9, 14,
21, 48, 74; SSC 2; TCLC 136; WLC**
See also AAYA 5, 42; AFAW 1, 2; AMW;
BPFB 3; BW 1; BYA 2; CA 108; CANR
64; CDALB 1929-1941; DA; DA3; DAB;
DAC; DAM MST, MULT, NOV; DLB 76,
102; DLBD 2; EWL 3; EXPN; LAIT 3,
4; MTCW 1, 2; NCFS 1; NFS 1, 7; RGAL
4; RGSF 2; SSFS 3, 9, 15; TUS; YAW
Wright, Richard B(ruce) 1937- .... **CLC 6**
See also CA 85-88; CANR 120; DLB 53
Wright, Rick 1945- .... **CLC 35**
Wright, Rowland
See Wells, Carolyn
Wright, Stephen 1946- .... **CLC 33**
Wright, Willard Huntington 1888-1939
See Van Dine, S. S.
See also CA 115; 189; CMW 4; DLBD 16
Wright, William 1930- .... **CLC 44**
See also CA 53-56; CANR 7, 23
Wroth, Lady Mary 1587-1653(?) .... **LC 30;
PC 38**
See also DLB 121
Wu Ch'eng-en 1500(?)-1582(?) .... **LC 7**
Wu Ching-tzu 1701-1754 .... **LC 2**
Wulfstan c. 10th cent. -1023 .... **CMLC 59**
Wurlitzer, Rudolph 1938(?)- ...... **CLC 2, 4, 15**
See also CA 85-88; CN 7; DLB 173
Wyatt, Sir Thomas c. 1503-1542 . **LC 70; PC
27**
See also BRW 1; DLB 132; EXPP; RGEL
2; TEA
Wycherley, William 1640-1716 .... **LC 8, 21**
See also BRW 2; CDBLB 1660-1789; DAM
DRAM; DLB 80; RGEL 2
Wylie, Elinor (Morton Hoyt)
1885-1928 .... **PC 23; TCLC 8**
See also AMWS 1; CA 105; 162; DLB 9,
45; EXPP; RGAL 4
Wylie, Philip (Gordon) 1902-1971 ... **CLC 43**
See also CA 21-22; 33-36R; CAP 2; DLB
9; SFW 4
Wyndham, John .... **CLC 19**
See Harris, John (Wyndham Parkes Lucas)
Beynon
See also DLB 255; SCFW 2
Wyss, Johann David Von
1743-1818 .... **NCLC 10**
See also CLR 92; JRDA; MAICYA 1, 2;
SATA 29; SATA-Brief 27
Xenophon c. 430B.C.-c. 354B.C. ... **CMLC 17**
See also AW 1; DLB 176; RGWL 2, 3
Xingjian, Gao 1940-
See Gao Xingjian
See also CA 193; RGWL 3
Yakamochi 718-785 .... **CMLC 45; PC 48**
Yakumo Koizumi
See Hearn, (Patricio) Lafcadio (Tessima
Carlos)

Yamada, Mitsuye (May) 1923- .... **PC 44**
See also CA 77-80
Yamamoto, Hisaye 1921- .... **AAL; SSC 34**
See also CA 214; DAM MULT; LAIT 4;
SSFS 14
Yamauchi, Wakako 1924- .... **AAL**
See also CA 214
Yanez, Jose Donoso
See Donoso (Yanez), Jose
Yanovsky, Basile S.
See Yanovsky, V(assily) S(emenovich)
Yanovsky, V(assily) S(emenovich)
1906-1989 .... **CLC 2, 18**
See also CA 97-100; 129
Yates, Richard 1926-1992 .... **CLC 7, 8, 23**
See also AMWS 11; CA 5-8R; 139; CANR
10, 43; DLB 2, 234; DLBY 1981, 1992;
INT CANR-10
Yeats, W. B.
See Yeats, William Butler
Yeats, William Butler 1865-1939 .... **PC 20;
TCLC 1, 11, 18, 31, 93, 116; WLC**
See also AAYA 48; BRW 6; BRWR 1; CA
104; 127; CANR 45; CDBLB 1890-1914;
DA; DA3; DAB; DAC; DAM DRAM,
MST, POET; DLB 10, 19, 98, 156; EWL
3; EXPP; MTCW 1, 2; NCFS 3; PAB;
PFS 1, 2, 5, 7, 13, 15; RGEL 2; TEA;
WLIT 4; WP
Yehoshua, A(braham) B. 1936- .. **CLC 13, 31**
See also CA 33-36R; CANR 43, 90; EWL
3; RGSF 2; RGWL 3
Yellow Bird
See Ridge, John Rollin
Yep, Laurence Michael 1948- .... **CLC 35**
See also AAYA 5, 31; BYA 7; CA 49-52;
CANR 1, 46, 92; CLR 3, 17, 54; DLB 52;
FANT; JRDA; MAICYA 1, 2; MAICYAS
1; SATA 7, 69, 123; WYA; YAW
Yerby, Frank G(arvin) 1916-1991 ..... **BLC 3;
CLC 1, 7, 22**
See also BPFB 3; BW 1, 3; CA 9-12R; 136;
CANR 16, 52; DAM MULT; DLB 76;
INT CANR-16; MTCW 1; RGAL 4; RHW
Yesenin, Sergei Alexandrovich
See Esenin, Sergei (Alexandrovich)
Yesenin, Sergey
See Esenin, Sergei (Alexandrovich)
See also EWL 3
Yevtushenko, Yevgeny (Alexandrovich)
1933- ...... **CLC 1, 3, 13, 26, 51, 126; PC
40**
See Evtushenko, Evgenii Aleksandrovich
See also CA 81-84; CANR 33, 54; CWW
2; DAM POET; EWL 3; MTCW 1
Yezierska, Anzia 1885(?)-1970 .... **CLC 46**
See also CA 126; 89-92; DLB 28, 221; FW;
MTCW 1; RGAL 4; SSFS 15
Yglesias, Helen 1915- .... **CLC 7, 22**
See also CA 37-40R; CAAS 20; CANR 15,
65, 95; CN 7; INT CANR-15; MTCW 1
Yokomitsu, Riichi 1898-1947 .... **TCLC 47**
See also CA 170; EWL 3
Yonge, Charlotte (Mary)
1823-1901 .... **TCLC 48**
See also CA 109; 163; DLB 18, 163; RGEL
2; SATA 17; WCH
York, Jeremy
See Creasey, John
York, Simon
See Heinlein, Robert A(nson)
Yorke, Henry Vincent 1905-1974 ..... **CLC 13**
See Green, Henry
See also CA 85-88; 49-52
Yosano Akiko 1878-1942 .... **PC 11; TCLC 59**
See also CA 161; EWL 3; RGWL 3
Yoshimoto, Banana .... **CLC 84**
See Yoshimoto, Mahoko
See also AAYA 50; NFS 7

Yoshimoto, Mahoko 1964-
See Yoshimoto, Banana
See also CA 144; CANR 98; SSFS 16
Young, Al(bert James) 1939- ... **BLC 3; CLC
19**
See also BW 2, 3; CA 29-32R; CANR 26,
65, 109; CN 7; CP 7; DAM MULT; DLB
33
Young, Andrew (John) 1885-1971 ...... **CLC 5**
See also CA 5-8R; CANR 7, 29; RGEL 2
Young, Collier
See Bloch, Robert (Albert)
Young, Edward 1683-1765 .... **LC 3, 40**
See also DLB 95; RGEL 2
Young, Marguerite (Vivian)
1909-1995 .... **CLC 82**
See also CA 13-16; 150; CAP 1; CN 7
Young, Neil 1945- .... **CLC 17**
See also CA 110; CCA 1
Young Bear, Ray A. 1950- ... **CLC 94; NNAL**
See also CA 146; DAM MULT; DLB 175
Yourcenar, Marguerite 1903-1987 ... **CLC 19,
38, 50, 87**
See also BPFB 3; CA 69-72; CANR 23, 60,
93; DAM NOV; DLB 72; DLBY 1988;
EW 12; EWL 3; GFL 1789 to the Present;
GLL 1; MTCW 1, 2; RGWL 2, 3
Yuan, Chu 340(?)B.C.-278(?)B.C. . **CMLC 36**
Yurick, Sol 1925- .... **CLC 6**
See also CA 13-16R; CANR 25; CN 7
Zabolotsky, Nikolai Alekseevich
1903-1958 .... **TCLC 52**
See Zabolotsky, Nikolay Alekseevich
See also CA 116; 164
Zabolotsky, Nikolay Alekseevich
See Zabolotsky, Nikolai Alekseevich
See also EWL 3
Zagajewski, Adam 1945- .... **PC 27**
See also CA 186; DLB 232; EWL 3
Zalygin, Sergei -2000 .... **CLC 59**
Zamiatin, Evgenii
See Zamyatin, Evgeny Ivanovich
See also RGSF 2; RGWL 2, 3
Zamiatin, Evgenii Ivanovich
See Zamyatin, Evgeny Ivanovich
See also DLB 272
Zamiatin, Yevgenii
See Zamyatin, Evgeny Ivanovich
Zamora, Bernice (B. Ortiz) 1938- .. **CLC 89;
HLC 2**
See also CA 151; CANR 80; DAM MULT;
DLB 82; HW 1, 2
Zamyatin, Evgeny Ivanovich
1884-1937 .... **TCLC 8, 37**
See Zamiatin, Evgenii; Zamiatin, Evgenii
Ivanovich; Zamiatin, Yevgeny Ivanovich
See also CA 105; 166; EW 10; SFW 4
Zamyatin, Yevgeny Ivanovich
See Zamyatin, Evgeny Ivanovich
See also EWL 3
Zangwill, Israel 1864-1926 ... **SSC 44; TCLC
16**
See also CA 109; 167; CMW 4; DLB 10,
135, 197; RGEL 2
Zappa, Francis Vincent, Jr. 1940-1993
See Zappa, Frank
See also CA 108; 143; CANR 57
Zappa, Frank .... **CLC 17**
See Zappa, Francis Vincent, Jr.
Zaturenska, Marya 1902-1982 ..... **CLC 6, 11**
See also CA 13-16R; 105; CANR 22
Zeami 1363-1443 .... **DC 7; LC 86**
See also DLB 203; RGWL 2, 3
Zelazny, Roger (Joseph) 1937-1995 . **CLC 21**
See also AAYA 7; BPFB 3; CA 21-24R;
148; CANR 26, 60; CN 7; DLB 8; FANT;
MTCW 1, 2; SATA 57; SATA-Brief 39;
SCFW; SFW 4; SUFW 1, 2

Literary Criticism Series
Cumulative Topic Index

This index lists all topic entries in Gale's *Classical and Medieval Literature Criticism* (CMLC), *Contemporary Literary Criticism* (CLC), *Drama Criticism* (DC), *Literature Criticism from 1400 to 1800* (LC), *Nineteenth-Century Literature Criticism* (NCLC), *Short Story Criticism* (SSC), and *Twentieth-Century Literary Criticism* (TCLC). The index also lists topic entries in the Gale Critical Companion Collection, which includes the following publications: *The Beat Generation* (BG), and *Harlem Renaissance* (HR).

CMLC Cumulative Nationality Index

CMLC Cumulative Title Index

Title Index

Title Index

ISBN 0-7876-6765-X

90000